PUBLIC PAPE

UNI

PUBLIC PAPERS OF THE PRESIDENTS
OF THE
UNITED STATES

George W. Bush

2008–2009

(IN TWO BOOKS)

BOOK I—JANUARY 1 TO JUNE 30, 2008

UNITED STATES GOVERNMENT PRINTING OFFICE
WASHINGTON : 2012

Published by the
Office of the Federal Register
National Archives and Records Administration

For sale by the Superintendent of Documents, U.S. Government Printing Office
• Internet: bookstore.gpo.gov • Phone: (202) 512–1800 • Fax: (202) 512–2104
• Mail: Stop IDCC, Washington, DC 20401

Foreword

This volume collects my speeches and papers from the first half of 2008, the last year of my Presidency.

As the year began, I appeared before Congress to deliver my final State of the Union message. I said, "Seven years have passed since I first stood before you at this rostrum. In that time, our country has been tested in ways none of us could have imagined. We faced hard decisions about peace and war, rising competition in the world economy, and the health and welfare of our citizens. These issues call for vigorous debate, and I think it's fair to say we've answered the call. Yet history will record that amid our differences, we acted with purpose. And together, we showed the world the power and resilience of American self-government."

This resilience was tested in the early days of 2008, when the Nation's 52 consecutive months of job creation—the longest such period on record—came to an end. As our economy began to slow, my Administration took action to ease the burden on the American people. We implemented a bipartisan stimulus plan that provided tax rebates for nearly 120 million American households. We continued to push for Congressional approval of free trade agreements with Colombia, Panama, and South Korea—agreements that would open up new opportunities for American workers, business owners, farmers, and ranchers. And we worked to keep more Americans in their homes during a time of increasing foreclosures.

This was also an important period in the war on terror. On the domestic front, I urged Congress to modernize the Foreign Intelligence Surveillance Act to address the dangers of the 21st century. Internationally, we saw important gains in Iraq. In April, General David Petraeus and Ambassador Ryan Crocker reported to Congress on the dramatic reductions in violence that had occurred in the wake of the troop surge that began in 2007. Because of the effectiveness of this strategy, the five brigades that had been added to our forces in Iraq began returning home on success— and the Iraqi people grew increasingly confident in their democracy.

These months also saw some of the most intensive international travel of my Presidency. In January, I toured the Middle East, visiting Israel, the West Bank, Kuwait, Bahrain, the United Arab Emirates, Saudi Arabia, and Egypt. In February, Laura and I took a moving trip to Africa, where we saw firsthand the gratitude of those who had been helped by America's efforts to fight disease and support development and social justice on that continent. During the course of a week, we traveled to Benin, Tanzania, Rwanda, Ghana, and Liberia. In April, I was in Romania to attend the 2008 NATO summit, a trip that also included stops in Ukraine, Croatia, and Russia. In May, I traveled to the Middle East once more, commemorating the 60th anniversary of the state of Israel with a speech in Jerusalem and visiting Egypt and

Saudi Arabia. And In June, I made my final trip to Europe as President, with stops in Slovenia, Germany, Italy, the Holy See, France, and the United Kingdom.

Notwithstanding the extensive travel schedule Laura and I were keeping, two of the most meaningful events of this period took place here at home. In April, Pope Benedict XVI visited the White House. The arrival ceremony, which took place on the Pope's 81st birthday, drew more than 13,000 well-wishers to the South Lawn. And in May, Laura and I made an emotional trip to Texas for the wedding of our daughter Jenna and Henry Hager. The couple had a beautiful ceremony at our ranch in Crawford. And I was proud to give my daughter away on what was one of the most important days of her life.

Finally, this period saw two new cabinet secretaries join my Administration. In February, Ed Schafer was sworn in as the Secretary of Agriculture, and in June, Steve Preston took the oath of office as Secretary of Housing and Urban Development.

In the days to follow, the election season would hit full stride and the end of my term would draw near. I pledged to serve out my time in office with as much energy as I had brought to my earliest days in the White House. And in the coming months, my Administration would make good on this promise to sprint to the finish.

Preface

This book contains the papers and speeches of the 43d President of the United States that were issued by the Office of the Press Secretary during the period January 1–June 30, 2008. The material has been compiled and published by the Office of the Federal Register, National Archives and Records Administration.

The material is presented in chronological order, and the dates shown in the headings are the dates of the documents or events. In instances when the release date differs from the date of the document itself, that fact is shown in the textnote. Every effort has been made to ensure accuracy: Remarks are checked against a tape recording, and signed documents are checked against the original. Textnotes and cross references have been provided by the editors for purposes of identification or clarity. At the request of the Office of the Press Secretary, the Bush property known as Prairie Chapel Ranch in Crawford, Texas, is referred to simply as the Bush Ranch. Speeches were delivered in Washington, DC, unless indicated. The times noted are local times. All materials that are printed full-text in the book have been indexed in the subject and name indexes, and listed in the document categories list.

The Public Papers of the Presidents series was begun in 1957 in response to a recommendation of the National Historical Publications Commission. An extensive compilation of messages and papers of the Presidents covering the period 1789 to 1897 was assembled by James D. Richardson and published under congressional authority between 1896 and 1899. Since then, various private compilations have been issued, but there was no uniform publication comparable to the Congressional Record or the United States Supreme Court Reports. Many Presidential papers could be found only in the form of mimeographed White House releases or as reported in the press. The Commission therefore recommended the establishment of an official series in which Presidential writings, addresses, and remarks of a public nature could be made available.

The Commission's recommendation was incorporated in regulations of the Administrative Committee of the Federal Register, issued under section 6 of the Federal Register Act (44 U.S.C. 1506), which may be found in title 1, part 10, of the Code of Federal Regulations.

A companion publication to the Public Papers series, the Weekly Compilation of Presidential Documents, was begun in 1965 to provide a broader range of Presidential materials on a more timely basis to meet the needs of the contemporary reader. Beginning with the administration of Jimmy Carter, the Public Papers series expanded its coverage to include additional material as printed in the Weekly Compilation. That coverage provides a listing of the President's daily schedule and meetings, when announced, and other items of general interest issued by the Office of the Press Secretary. Also included are lists of the President's nominations submitted to the Senate, materials released by the Office of the Press Secretary that are not printed full-text in the book, and proclamations, Executive orders, and other Presidential documents released by the Office of the Press Secretary and published in the *Federal Register*. This information appears in the appendixes at the end of the book.

Volumes covering the administrations of Presidents Herbert Hoover, Harry S. Truman, Dwight D. Eisenhower, John F. Kennedy, Lyndon B. Johnson, Richard Nixon, Gerald R. Ford, Jimmy Carter, Ronald Reagan, George Bush, and William J. Clinton are also included in the Public Papers series.

The Public Papers of the Presidents publication program is under the direction of Michael L. White, Managing Editor, Office of the Federal Register. The series is produced by the Presidential and Legislative Publications Unit. The Chief Editor of this book was Stacey A. Mulligan, assisted by Lois Davis, Michael J. Forcina, Joseph G. Frankovic, Diane Hiltabidle, Alfred Jones, Joshua H. Liberatore, Heather N. McDaniel, Amelia E. Otovo, D. Gregory Perrin, Matthew R. Regan, and Joseph K. Vetter.

The frontispiece and photographs used in the portfolio were supplied by the White House Photo Office. The typography and design of the book were developed by the Government Printing Office under the direction of Davita Vance-Cooks, Acting Public Printer.

Michael L. White
Acting Director of the Federal Register

David S. Ferriero
Archivist of the United States

Contents

Cabinet

Secretary of State .... Condoleezza Rice

Secretary of the Treasury .... Henry M. Paulson, Jr.

Secretary of Defense .... Robert M. Gates

Attorney General .... Michael B. Mukasey

Secretary of the Interior .... Dirk Kempthorne

Secretary of Agriculture .... Edward T. Schafer
(appointed 1/28)

Secretary of Commerce .... Carlos M. Gutierrez

Secretary of Labor .... Elaine L. Chao

Secretary of Health and Human
Services .... Michael O. Leavitt

Secretary of Housing and Urban
Development .... Alphonso R. Jackson
(resigned 4/18)
Steven C. Preston
(appointed 6/5)

Secretary of Transportation .... Mary E. Peters

Secretary of Energy .... Samuel W. Bodman

Secretary of Education .... Margaret Spellings

Secretary of Veterans Affairs .... James B. Peake

Secretary of Homeland Security .... Michael Chertoff

Chief of Staff .... Joshua B. Bolten

Administrator of the Environmental
Protection Agency .... Stephen L. Johnson

United States Trade Representative .... Susan C. Schwab

Director of the Office of Management
and Budget .... James A. Nussle

Director of National Drug Control
Policy .... John P. Walters

Administration of George W. Bush

2008–2009

Remarks on Departure From Waco, Texas
January 1, 2008

The President. Laura and I wish our fellow Americans a happy and healthy 2008. I particularly want to say something to our troops and their families: This country respects you, we admire you, and we wish you a great 2008 as well.

We've just come off the ranch; had a good rest and good New Year's with some friends. And I'm looking forward to getting back to Washington to work on policies to keep this country safe and to keep this country prosperous.

I just wanted to stop by and wish everybody a happy 2008. Thank you.

The First Lady. Happy New Year, everybody.

NOTE: The President spoke at 10:35 a.m. at Texas State Technical College. A tape was not available for verification of the content of these remarks.

Interview With Nahum Barnea and Shimon Shiffer of Yedioth Ahronoth
January 2, 2008

President's Upcoming Visit to Israel/Former Prime Minister Ariel Sharon of Israel

Q. First of all, we would like to thank you very much for your readiness to see us and to have this interview for us. We can assure you that in Israel, you can be elected for the third term—[*laughter*]—with one exception: The day after the first day in office, the media will kill you. [*Laughter*] This is Israel. But you have so many, really, admirers in Israel.

The President. Well, thank you. I'm really looking forward to going again. As you know, this is my first trip as the President. I had the honor——

Q. I saw you. I had the opportunity to shake your hand in the Knesset.

The President. I was thrilled to go in 1998. One of the great ironies of my first trip to Israel was that, as well documented, I was given a tour of the West Bank by Ariel Sharon. Little did we both realize then that we would be sitting together in the hopes of constructing peace, that we knew we'd be—we didn't know that we'd be President and Prime Minister at the time.

Q. And yet he was the leader of the opposition at the time.

The President. Well, he was in the Cabinet. He was a settlements man. And we were flying, and it was a very interesting moment. And I can remember so well Prime Minister Sharon pointing to a hill, and he said, "This is where I engaged as a young tank officer, my first battle, and see how far it is to our capital and our civilization." In other words, it was—his purpose was to make it clear to me the strategic issues facing Israel. And then we flew over the West Bank, and it was a fascinating moment.

And it was—history works in odd ways, and sometimes you're never sure about the twists and turns that life will bring. And so I'm looking forward to meeting with the

Sharon family and express my admiration for a man with whom I was able to——

Q. Two years from today he had his stroke.

The President. Yes, 2 years to this day.

Q. Today, today.

The President. Anyway, it will be an interesting moment for me, to express my sympathies to his family. He was an interesting man, and anyway, I'm looking forward to going to see the current leadership in Israel as well as the Palestinians and the Arab region.

President's Upcoming Visit to Israel

Q. Could we ask—could we start asking questions?

The President. Please, yes.

Q. Your visit to Israel, what is the vision you would like to convey to the Israeli public?

The President. The vision is, one, that I fully understand that the world is confronting extremists—the world must confront extremists who want to impose their ideology on peaceful people by the use of terror; and that we're engaged in an ideological struggle that requires resolve and vision; and that the best way to defeat the ideology of hate is with an ideology of hope, and that is manifested in a society based upon liberty; that the two-state solution is in Israel's long-term security interests, and that there's hard work to be done by the leaders of the Palestinians and the Israelis.

I will also assure Israel that there is no way that a Israeli democracy can accept a terrorist state on her border; that there is a way—and I'm optimistic that there are enough Palestinians committed to a state based upon liberty—that we can achieve—that they can achieve, with U.S. help, the vision of two states side by side in peace.

Iran

Q. Mr. President, the Israeli people are worried, first and foremost, because of the danger that Iran will acquire nuclear weap-

ons. Can you, Mr. President, assure the Israelis that such a danger will never occur under your watch?

The President. Well, I can assure the people of Israel and others in the Middle East that an Iran with a nuclear weapon would be a danger to world peace. I have said so very explicitly. I believe that the— and I believe we have put in place a system that encourages pressure on the Iranians to come up with—to either have a choice between isolation and financial difficulty or a rational approach to what they claim is their sovereign right, which is the ability to have nuclear power.

Now, they have been untrustworthy; they have been unwilling to be transparent and open. And so our demands are to the Iranians, not only with our voice, but the voice of the international community thus far, is, you must be transparent; you must be open; and you—because of your failure to report programs, that you cannot be trusted with the ability to learn how to enrich. And so my message to the Israeli people is, I fully understand the threat, that we spend a lot of time on this issue, and that we will continue to exert maximum pressure through the international community to peacefully resolve this issue.

Q. I'm sure you've heard the report by the American intelligence——

The President. Yes, I have. *[Laughter]*

Q. Unfortunately for us, we followed it too. How it affected the chances to stop Iran from becoming a danger?

The President. Actually, if you study the report carefully, it basically said—not basically—it said that Iran had a secret program——

Q. In the year 2003.

The President. Right. But my message to the American people was—is that a nontransparent society that had a program could easily have another program. And therefore, the intensity of the effort must not decline, but must stay strong—and the intensity of the effort being to prevent them from developing the know-how.

Secondly, there are three stages to the development of a nuclear weapon: one, materials out of which to make a weapon—that's why we've got to stop them from enriching, and that's where our focus is; two, the ability to take materials and to make it into a warhead or a bomb—and we don't know their capacities at this point in time, but it's fairly general knowledge on how to produce a weapon out of materials; and three, rockets. Well, two of the three continue to exist. And therefore, to say a weapons program does not exist is not the complete truth. And so our focus is to prevent the one thing over which we believe the international community can have influence, which is to stop the capacity to enrich.

Thirdly, the report did say that as a result of pressures, the Iranians suspended their military program. Well, if pressures worked in the past, my hope is that pressures will work in the future. Part of the reason I'm going to the Middle East is to make it abundantly clear to nations in that part of the world that we view Iran as a threat, and that the NIE in no way lessens that threat, but in fact, clarifies the threat.

Middle East Peace Process/Iran

Q. If Israel comes with a smoking gun during the year 2008, are you going to back an Israeli operation—military operation?

The President. My message to all in the region is, I believe we can solve this diplomatically and that pressure must work. I have said, of course, that the United States keeps all options on the table. That's the United States policy. And that—but I believe the best solution is going to be one that encourages Iranian isolation through international pressures that will cause the Iranians to have to make a strategic choice. Now, people say: "Well, what do you mean by that? What kind of pressures?" Well, there are financial pressures that we have exerted and will continue to work with others to exert.

Now, look, I readily recognize that one of the real challenges is to convince people that peace is more important than market share, that achieving long-term peace in the Middle East is more important than someone's companies having a share of equipment——

Q. American or——

The President. Well, I'm saying any company. Of course, American companies are not involved with the exportation of goods and services to Iran. Therefore, in this case, I mean, the logic would say that extends to not only European countries but countries from around the world. Same with financial institutions, that we expect there to be significant pressure placed upon Iranian financial institutions, particularly those that are known to be involved in proliferation.

And so the strategy is more than just words; it is an action-oriented strategy, aimed at convincing people inside of Iran that there's a better way forward. If you look at my speeches or listen to my speeches, you'll notice that I constantly speak to the Iranian people and make it clear to them that the isolation that they're now suffering and the economic deprivation that is occurring as a result of isolation is a result of their Government's decisions. Our beef is not with the Iranian people, our beef is with a Government that has hidden the program.

And by the way, back to the NIE very quickly. The international response ought to be that, okay, whether or not you agree with the NIE or not, at least recognize that they had a program at one point in time, and demand that Iran explain it. We shouldn't be trying to explain why we know what we know. We ought to be focusing on the Iranians to say, you tell us why you had a program; you tell us about the—if you want to be an international player, it's up to you to explain.

U.S. Foreign Policy

Q. Mr. President, I'll try to put the question another way. If the Israeli Prime Minister will present you with a smoking gun and will tell you, look, we can't live with such a threat, and we'll destroy the Iranian nuclear sites, you will support Israel? You will give Israel—you will let Israel to do so?

The President. The policy of the United States is to solve this diplomatically.

Prime Minister Ehud Olmert of Israel/ Middle East Peace Process/President's Upcoming Visit to Israel

Q. You know, Israel is—Israeli people are confused regarding our own Government. There is now a big discussion in Israel regarding the blunders of the second Lebanon war. And at the same time, you are familiar with the September 6th—whatever happens there, we don't know; I'm sure you know. Can you tell us what is your impression of the, I would say, of the way the Israeli Government is handling our own military?

The President. I can only tell you about my personal relationship with Prime Minister Olmert. That's the person with whom I have spent the most time. I, of course, see the Foreign Minister or the Defense Minister at meetings, but my time is spent with Prime Minister Olmert. I trust him, I like him, and I think he's a man of strength.

Prime Minister Olmert, first of all, one thing I look for is, I look for vision. Can somebody see a hopeful future? A lot of times in the—this complicated world in which we live, we stay so focused on the moment that it's hard to see a vision that reaches beyond the immediate. And so when I talk to Prime Minister Olmert, I listen very carefully about his vision for the future because what we're talking about at Annapolis is vision, is giving people something to be for, something to hope for.

The whole purpose of our discussions at Annapolis has been to advance what a state would look like. The state is subject to the roadmap, the obligations of both sides before the state can come into being; it's subject to the roadmap. But there's got to be a vision because a vision is inspirational, a vision is hopeful. There's got to be something that the Palestinians can say, if— "Here's what we're for. Therefore, let us renounce our desire to destroy Israel; let us recognize that it must exist as a neighbor. So support us." I believe there's enough people in the Palestinian Territories who are sick of the failures of the past, sick of broken promise. And yet they have yet to have something specifically defined around which they can rally. That's the purpose.

And so when I talk to Prime Minister Olmert, I listen very carefully to whether or not he's able to think beyond the moment. And I've come to the conclusion that, yes, he is a man of vision. He understands the significance of defining a hopeful state. And it's hopeful not just for the Palestinians, but it's hopeful for Israel as well. After all, he ran on a platform that said—now, this is a major shift in Israeli policy; it started with Ariel Sharon, as you know— which is two states, based upon the premise that liberty will bring peace. Now, of course, his concern is that the imposition of a state before certain conditions have been met—that's why I say, "subject to the roadmap." And the United States, as I said early, recognizes that there cannot be a state that harbors the desire to destroy its neighbor. No government can accept that, and I understand that.

And so I trust Olmert. His——

Q. Do you?

The President. I do trust him.

Q. You trust Olmert, period?

The President. I trust him. I hope— hopefully, he'll say the same about me. Hopefully—you see, one of the things in politics that happens often is, people sometimes won't tell you really what's on their mind. It happens here in America. For example, you'll have politicians walk in the

Oval Office and say, "Hey, President, I'm with you." And then all of a sudden, the heat gets on—[*laughter*]—and it turns out, they're not with you.

Q. You feel it at your back.

The President. Yes. Well, I feel—and I've had enough conversations, heart-to-heart conversations with the Prime Minister. I understand Israeli politics is very complicated. It's tough. It is full-contact karate. [*Laughter*] And——

Q. Not unlike American——

The President. Not really. Not really. Because the President is—even though we've got our politics and even though I've got tough relations at times with Congress, the President sets foreign policy. He is constantly worried about a coalition. And I understand that. I understand the difficulty he faces. But in spite of those difficulties, I'm interested in strategic visions based upon peace. And I firmly believe he has that vision. And obviously, he's going to have to work his way through the Israeli politics, and he's going to have to be mindful of what's happening elsewhere.

And the United States, by the way, can help both parties. That's why I'm going, to help boost the confidence of both parties to reach out for a vision. And by the way, the trip is more than just going to Israel and the Palestinian Territories. I'm also going to the Arab world for two reasons. One is to convince the Arab nations that Israel is a partner—should be a partner in peace; that this vision is in the interests not only of Israel and Palestinians, but it's in the interests of the Arab world.

Q. You expect to achieve something tangible?

The President. Well, we achieved something very tangible. Look, you got to understand that in a matter as complicated as this issue, that it requires a lot of diligence and a lot of time and a lot of effort. There was a major breakthrough at Annapolis when the Israeli Prime Minister and the Palestinian President addressed a roomful of diplomats, high-ranking officials from the Middle East, as well as the rest of the world. And so now we must follow up on that success. In other words, they were in the room listening very carefully to the visions of both nations. And the American President can help move the process forward by reminding friends and allies in the Middle East about the importance of the two-state solution and what they can do to help.

And the third thing, of course, is to spend time talking about the strategic implications of a U.S. presence in a way that bolsters governments and, at the same time, helps serve as a bulwark against aggressive regimes such as Iran. And so it's a multifaceted agenda that I'm really looking forward to carrying on there in the Middle East.

Middle East Peace Process

Q. But still, Mr. President, do you see a chance to sign a comprehensive peace agreement between Israel and the——

The President. Yes, I do, before I leave.

Q. Before you leave?

The President. Yes, I do. I do. I'm an optimistic guy.

Q. ——by initials or by full execution?

The President. Well, first of all—no. First of all, the—I envision Israel and Palestine sitting down at a table, signing—this is what a state would look like, subject to the roadmap. There's work to be done.

Q. And concluding an agreement?

The President. On what the state would look like, absolutely. Yes, I do. I think it can happen. And I believe both parties want it to happen. Now, they got work to do, and one of the reasons I'm going is to remind them of the work they got to do. See, people say to me, "All you got to do is go over there and say—impose the solution." No, we want the solution to last. This has got to be negotiated in good faith, and it's hard work. Both leaders have got constituencies they've got to deal with, skeptical publics. And I believe the U.S.

President can help keep the process moving, and that's what my trip is all about.

Israeli Settlements/Middle East Peace Process

Q. Unauthorized settlement, it is something which—an issue which is between the United States and Israel for a long time.

The President. Yes, we expect them to honor their commitments. The Israeli Government has said that they're going to get rid of unauthorized settlements, and that's what we expect. That's what we've been told.

Q. Not before you come, you know.

The President. Well, that will be on the—that will, of course, be an agenda item. But Prime Minister—both Prime Ministers with whom I have worked understand our position. Both have agreed, by the way, of unauthorized settlements.

Q. They agree?

The President. Both understand, as well, that I said conditions on the ground, the realities of the situation will help determine what a—the borders look like. And so I have made some—at least from what the U.S. perspective looks like—some statements that will help move the process forward. But the unauthorized settlements, which is different from authorized settlements, is an issue we've been very clear on. But I've also made statements on the settlements as well.

As I said, realities on the ground will help define the border—the eventual border of what the Palestinian state will look like. And the state will come into being subject to the conditions set out in the roadmap, which means we've got a lot of work to do. One of the things I'll be doing is visiting with Tony Blair there in order to make—to catch up on what he is doing to help the Palestinians. Look, developing a state out of—is difficult. There's got to be institutions that provide stability, and it's hard to do.

That's what happening in Iraq. It's hard to go from dictatorship, like they had in Iraq, to one in which there is solid institutions that will enable a democracy to survive. I have come to the conclusion that it's absolutely necessary work for the sake of peace because if we're in an ideological struggle, the only way to defeat the ideology that preys upon fear and hate is through the development of societies that respond to the will of the people. And democracies—it turns out, democracies throughout our history tend not to fight each other because democracies respond to the will of the people, and most people do not want war and bloodshed and violence. Most people just want to live a normal, peaceful life.

I tell the American people all the time that Iraqi mothers want the same thing for their children that American mothers want for theirs, a place for their child to grow up and get a good education and be able to realize dreams. Same thing for the Palestinian mothers and the Israeli mothers. There's a commonality there, and yet, unfortunately, in the world in which we live today, there are people who simply do not like the idea of societies based upon the will of the people and will use violence to stop the advance of freedom. And it's not just in the Palestinian Territories that you find the violence, you find it in Lebanon, you find it in Iraq, you find it in Afghanistan, you find it in Pakistan.

Q. You find it in Gaza.

The President. Yes. You find people who will kill innocent life to stop the advance of freedom, which should call the world to—should cause the world to rally. If killers want to stop liberty, it should be a clear signal to all of us that we must do everything we can to advance liberty. And one of the things I find very hopeful about a Palestinian state is that many in the world want to help the Palestinians develop institutions and stability. And I—President Abbas and Prime Minister Fayyad are committed to the development of a state. They need a lot of help. And one of the things we can provide help for—besides some practical help on organizing their security forces and obviously to encourage investment—is to—there's got to be a vision, see. People have got to be for something. And that's where we're trying to take the process over the next year.

Iraq/U.S. Foreign Policy/President's Decisionmaking

Q. Mr. President, you just mentioned Iraq. Can you clarify to us whether there was any Israeli involvement in your decision to invade Iraq?

The President. No, not at all, none whatsoever. My decision was based upon U.S. intelligence, based upon the desire to provide security for our peoples and others. It was based upon my willingness to work with the international community on this issue. Remember, if you look back at the history, there was a unanimous vote in the Security Council: disclose, disarm, or face serious consequences. And when he defied, when he refused to allow the inspectors in, when he made a statement by his actions that he didn't really care what the international community said, that I decided to make sure words meant something.

And so I acted based upon our own security interests. And—but it also fit into this notion of—and remember, Zarqawi—there was some terrorist connections, not with the 9/11 attacks, but terrorist connections. Abu Nidal, he had been using—he'd been funding families of suicide bombers. In other words, as far as we were concerned, he had weapons of mass destruction, which could have been used in a deadly way. It turns out, he didn't have the weapons, but he had the know-how on how to make weapons, which could easily have been reconstituted. The sanctions regime turns out to have been corrupt and wasn't working. In other words, there's a variety of aspects to my decision, all of which were aimed at making sure that U.S. security, first and foremost, was enhanced.

National Security Council Press Secretary Gordon Johndroe. One last question.

2008 Presidential Election

Q. You follow the primaries now, in America.

The President. Yes. [*Laughter*]

Q. We wonder if there is a moment when you tell yourself, wow, why can't I join the fray?

The President. That's interesting.

Q. I can do it better. [*Laughter*]

The President. No, no, I appreciate that question. It's a very interesting question. I believe strongly that democracies are enhanced by change—by the peaceful change of government. And as much as I'll miss being President—and there will be a lot of aspects I'll miss about it—it is in our Nation's interests that there be a healthy debate and that the process move on. And so I'm realistic about what's going to happen this year.

You know, I loved campaigning. We were reminiscing at the ranch this weekend—Laura and I and some friends were—about how exciting Presidential campaigns can be. And I also understand how grueling they can be. This is a time of high anxiety for campaigns and candidates as they come in the final day of the Iowa caucuses. I can remember distinctly what it felt like campaigning in these States——

Q. In the snow.

The President. ——in the snow—on the last day. And so there's a lot of excitement to it. But I'm very comfortable about this year. We've got a lot to do. We've got a lot to do domestically and a lot to do internationally. I fully understand there's going to be a lot of focus on the Presidential primaries and the Presidential general election, which is good. There ought to be a healthy debate. In the meantime, however, I am not going to allow domestic politics to get in the way of implementing a vision, of doing—laying that foundation for peace, one of the things history will look back on.

President's Legacy

Q. When you are talking about vision, Mr. President—and this will be our last question—how do you wish to be remembered in world history?

The President. Well, first of all, I'll be dead before the true history of the Bush administration is written. Here in the Oval Office, there are portraits of two Presidents, George Washington and Abraham Lincoln. In the past couple of years, I have read extensive analyses of both of those men's Presidencies. My attitude is that it's going to take a while for objective historians to realize the contributions that this administration has made to peace.

Q. Like Harry Truman's legacy, which developed.

The President. Well, each President has his own set of circumstances with which to deal. I would hope that people, when they look back at this administration, would say that President Bush and his administration worked diligently to protect the American people from harm; that he recognized the threats of the 21st century; that he acted in a—when he needed to be tough, he acted strong, and when he needed to have vision, he understood the power of freedom to be transformative.

Our foreign policy is more than just confronting terrorists. Our foreign policy is to confront the conditions that enable these ideologues to recruit, such as HIV/AIDS on the continent of Africa or feeding the hungry or dealing with malaria. Our foreign policy is based upon our great trust in the capacity of the common person to dictate a peaceful course for government. But just so you know, I fully understand I'll be long gone before the accurate history of this administration is reflected in the history books.

Q. In our country, you won't have to wait so long.

The President. Well, I don't worry about it, sir. I just really don't. It's such an honor to be the President. You betray the office if you get so caught up in your own personal—your personal standing. I remind people that the President should—must understand, like in the Middle East, that the conditions must be ripe for people to go for peace and that you cannot force peace based upon a President's calendar. You can use the calendar by saying to the parties, you know this guy, you know his vision; now is the time for you to come to conclusion. But a President must never try to force others to accept something that they themselves don't want to accept because there will be—it won't last.

Now, we can work hard, and I believe the time is ripe; that's what I'm trying to say to you. We've got leaders who have made commitments to a vision. They have both told me and told each other, we are committed. And these men know me. And so I believe—to answer your question—yes, there will be a comprehensive peace signed by the end of this year, because if they're committed, like they say they are—and I believe they are, and I believe their people, the majority of the people want there to be peace—now is the time to move.

Anyway.

Mr. Johndroe. Thanks, guys.

NOTE: The interview was taped at 9:55 a.m. in the Oval Office at the White House. In his remarks, the President referred to Deputy Prime Minister and Minister of Foreign Affairs Tzipora "Tzipi" Livni and Minister of Defense Ehud Barak of Israel; President Mahmoud Abbas and Prime Minister Salam Fayyad of the Palestinian Authority; and former Prime Minister Tony Blair of the United Kingdom, Quartet Representative in the Middle East. The transcript was released by the Office of the Press Secretary on January 4. A tape was not available for verification of the content of this interview.

Interview With Foreign Print Media
January 4, 2008

The President. How are you doing? Welcome. Pleasure to be with you all. Thank you.

What are the ground rules here, Dana, in terms of the American press?

White House Press Secretary Dana Perino. It's all on the record, but can't be used until after these fine folks are able to publish.

The President. Yes, so delay your stories, will you? [*Laughter*]

Q. It's very hospitable of you, Mr. President.

The President. A couple of things—one, I'm excited about going on the trip. I have never been to Saudi Arabia. I have never been to Bahrain. I have never been to Kuwait. I have been to Egypt. I have not been to the Palestinian Territories or Israel as a sitting President.

So this is a really good opportunity to travel and be with friends and have frank discussions about particularly three items: one, the United States commitment to the peace process; that what happened in Annapolis is the beginning of serious discussions, a serious attempt by the United States to encourage the Israelis and the Palestinians to develop a vision of what a Palestinian state will look like.

And I am very optimistic that such a vision will come into being by the time I leave office. And the reason I am is because I know the two leaders well, and I believe both are committed to a two-state solution, and both understand that in order for that state to come into being, subject to the roadmap, that there has to be more than just words; there has to be clarity in what a Palestinian state will look like.

Secondly, I'm looking forward to sitting down with friends and allies to assure them of my commitment to Middle Eastern peace and to work with them to make sure they're committed to Middle Eastern peace; that I will remind them that we've got a three-track strategy: one is the vision; two is the implementation of the road-map—in other words, the United States chairs a committee with the Palestinians and the Israelis to deal with roadmap issues; and three, a commitment by the United States and others to build the institutions necessary for a Palestinian democracy to thrive.

In other words, there's got to be a recognition that we need institution-building; there needs to be work. For example, the United States is very much involved in helping modernize their security forces and create a chain of command, so that when good men like President Abbas and Prime Minister Fayyad see a security situation needs to be taken care of, they can give a command and something happens, for the good of the Palestinian people. In other words, a state, in order to be credible and viable, must be able to provide security for its people.

The EU is very much involved with institution building and basically enhancing the entrepreneurial spirit of the Palestinian people, which is very strong. So I'll be visiting with Tony Blair, for example, when I'm there to see the progress he's making. My only point is, is that it's going to be very important for the nations that I visit to be active participants in not only helping the Palestinians, but recognizing that a two-state solution recognizes Israel's right to exist.

Thirdly, I will be also talking to our friends and allies about our strong commitment to regional security, that the United States is engaged and will remain engaged in the security of the region.

And so this is a trip that will be—it's going to be interesting, it will be stimulating, and it's going to be substantive. And

9

as I say, I'm looking forward to it, I really am.

We'll start—Joyce, why don't you crank her up here? We'll go a couple of rounds.

Lebanon

Q. Thank you again, Mr. President, for having us. Happy New Year.

The President. Thank you. It is going to be a happy New Year.

Q. Hopefully, more peace in the region.

The President. It will be a joyous New Year. [*Laughter*] Isn't that right, guys? Very skeptical—[*laughter*]. Don't be.

Q. If I can open up by asking you about Lebanon. The country is entering the second month, and the Presidency is still void over there. Who do you think is responsible for creating this situation and maintaining it? And what is your administration and maybe the French—Mr. Sarkozy, good friend of yours—doing to end this stalemate?

The President. Thank you. First of all, the United States is strongly committed to Lebanese democracy. We believe that a Lebanon that is democratic and peaceful is in the interests of world peace.

I have been very impressed by Prime Minister Siniora, by the way, as a man who's committed to the well-being of all the Lebanese people. Secondly, I am disappointed that the Presidency has not been selected and believe very much that Syrian influence is preventing the selection. Thirdly, part of my trip is to remind our friends and allies how important it is for Lebanon to succeed and how important it is for all of us to work to free that Government from foreign interference.

My position has been that the March 14th coalition, if it had mustered a majority plus one, 50 percent plus one, should be allowed to go forward with the selection of the President. We are working with not only our friends in the region who share the commitment for Lebanon to be free of foreign interference, but also the European countries.

And so there needs to be a clear message to the Syrians from all us that you will continue to be isolated, you will continue to be viewed as a nation that is thwarting the will of the Lebanese people. There needs to be a focused voice, and so our efforts diplomatically are to convince others that they must continue to pressure Syria so that the Lebanese process can go forward.

Sa'ad.

Iran

Q. Yes, again, Mr. President, I'd like to reiterate the remark of Joyce of thanking you for giving us this——

The President. Yes, thrilled to do it.

Q. ——historic opportunity. You talked about the regional security. And back in the Gulf States, the number-one issue nowadays, in terms of security of the region, is the Iranian nuclear profile and issue. And we'd like to know your position on that now, the development of that. The region is nervously—nervous about having another war, confrontation, on the one hand; yet they are also very nervous about the Iranians possessing the nuclear weapons. And I'd like to follow up on that.

The President. Well, thank you. First of all, the NIE, the National Intelligence Estimate, ought to be viewed as a clear signal that Iran is a threat to peace, that—the NIE said the following things: One, the Iranians had a covert military nuclear weapons program, and that international pressure caused them to suspend the program.

There are three elements to a nuclear weapons program: one, the ability to enrich uranium that can be converted into the basis of a bomb; secondly, the know-how to be able to assemble that enriched material into a bomb; and third, the capacity to deliver the weapon through rocketry. As far as we know, two of those programs still are ongoing. One is the rocketry program; two, there is a civilian enrichment program. And the danger of a civilian enrichment program is, once that knowledge is gained, that it could be easily transferred back to a covert military program. And therefore, the NIE should be a clear signal to all of us that Iran is a threat to peace. And they're a threat to peace because they have been nontransparent. They have not lived up to their obligations under the IAEA. They have not been truthful about their program.

And so one of my messages is that I, too, take the Iranian issue seriously, and that we have a plan to deal with it in a diplomatic way. It's important for the people in the region to know that while all options remain on the table, that I believe we can solve this problem diplomatically. And the way to do that is to continue to isolate Iran in the international community.

My message to the Iranian people is that there's a better way forward for you, that your Government has made decisions that have caused you to be isolated from the world, have caused there to be economic deprivation, because they refuse to be transparent and open about their enrichment programs.

And so I understand this is an issue, and it's going to be an agenda item on my travel. It's not going to be the only item, of course. The Middle Eastern peace process is something that will be on the leaders' minds. The commitment of the United States to remain active in the region will be on their minds. I'm sure that these leaders fear that the United States may become isolationist and basically throw up its hands and say, who cares what happens. I will remind them that what happens in parts of the world matters to the security of the United States of America, and that we look forward to being a constructive force and working with allies like allies should do.

And so I'm sure the subject will come up, and I'm looking forward to clarifying once again our position.

Jasim.

Bahrain

Q. Thank you, Mr. President, for this opportunity. It is a dream comes true.

The President. Thank you, sir. The American press feels the same way when they talk to me. It's a dream come true. [*Laughter*] You might want to clarify that. [*Laughter*] Some of them are very serious this morning. They're very grim, serious.

Q. It's cold outside, sir.

The President. It is cold outside.

Q. King Hamad of Bahrain has launched democratic reforms that included a new Constitution, and Bahrain now has an elected Parliament. How do you assess this experiment, especially in light of your drive to spread democracy in the region?

The President. I have complimented His Majesty on recognizing that Bahraini-style democracy, a democracy that reflects the traditions, customs of Bahrain, is a important part of dealing with real threats that we face in the world, which is extremism based upon hopelessness; and that there is a true threat to peace, and that is radicals who prey upon frustrations of people in order to convince them to become suicide bombers and to kill in the name of an ideology. And the best antidote to that is democracy.

And I applaud his efforts. And we are very active in helping nations, if they so choose to receive our help, in moving forward through the MEPI program, for example. And it is a way to help people build the institutions necessary for a—I repeat— a democracy that reflects their traditions and history of the respective countries.

And people go at different paces. And I don't expect Jeffersonian democracy to break out instantly, nor do I expect the forms of government to reflect that which we have in the United States. But I do hope that people recognize that popular sovereignty, that listening to people and responding to people, is how to build a stable and peaceful world.

And so I applaud His Majesty. I'm looking forward to bringing up the subject with the Amir of Kuwait as well. You know, women are now very active in the Kuwaiti Parliament. And I think—I feel these are constructive engagements. My friend King Abdallah of Saudi Arabia doesn't get enough credit for beginning to reform his society.

And again, I want to repeat: It is important for the American President not to insist that countries do it our way. I believe it is incumbent upon the American President to listen very carefully to the concerns of other leaders and to recognize obstacles and problems, but also remind them of this ideological struggle in which we're involved, all of us are involved; and that—I'll repeat it: Extremists prey upon hopelessness, and forms of government can create hopeless people, people who are frustrated, people who don't feel like the government is responsive to their needs.

The people that we—that kill the innocent have no positive vision. The only thing they can do is prey upon frustration—and that a way to deal with this ideological conflict is to defeat the ideology of hate with one of hope. And that's what's happening in the Middle East. It's—there's an awareness. And I'm looking forward to discussing that with the various leaders.

Yes, sir, Talat.

Saudi Arabia

Q. Yes, sir. Thank you for giving me this opportunity—and others. Sir, you're talking about the Middle East peace. I just would like to see, how do you see the role of King Abdallah in promoting the peace process and stability in the Middle East? And also, how do you evaluate the Saudi-American—comparing the terror in the region?

The President. Well, thank you. First of all, I admire King Abdallah. I admire him because he is a man who commands a lot of respect from me personally and a lot of respect in the region. When he speaks,

people listen. It's not to say that other people don't listen as well, but Saudi Arabia is geographically important, is the guardian of holy sites, and he's a well-respected man.

And so in terms of the Middle Eastern peace process, the fact that he sent his Foreign Minister to Annapolis sent a very strong message that Middle Eastern peace is going to require the participation of more than just the United States and Israel and the Palestinians, that a true peace is going to require a commitment in the neighborhood of supporting two states living side by side in peace—two democratic states living side by side in peace. So he has laid out his own initiative in the past. It commanded great respect. It is a commitment to a process. And so I value him as—I view him as invaluable in the process.

Secondly, the Kingdom of Saudi Arabia recognized that murderers threaten not only other parts of the world, but threaten the Kingdom's own security. And the security forces there have done a magnificent job of using intelligence to find the few that would murder the many. I have been impressed—and any objective observer would be impressed—by Saudi Arabia's commitment to finding those people that use murder as a weapon.

And so I—to answer your question, I am satisfied with our cooperation. I'm appreciative of the efforts that the intelligence community inside Saudi has been making to deal with these extremists, some of whom conduct murder in—within the Kingdom, some of whom leave the Kingdom to conduct murder. And the King is fully aware that this is a—such a presence is a threat to his own internal securities, as well as recognizing an obligation to prevent those from going outside the country to murder.

Talha.

President's Upcoming Visit to the Middle East

Q. Thank you. Thank you again, Mr. President. Mr. President, I wanted to ask you, your visit to the region will not include the Maghreb Arab.

The President. Will not include——

Q. The Maghreb Arab——

The President. Yes, that's right.

Q. ——Morocco, Algeria, and Tunisia. Those countries actually played a very important role in the peace process in the past, and I think that they are willing to do it again. And my question, Mr. President, if there is any reason for excluding the Maghreb Arab from your visit?

The President. Only because I ran out of time. It's certainly not as a result of any lack of respect or understanding that the contribution of those—of that area would be a significant contribution to achieving peace. And I appreciate very much the leadership in the King of Morocco as well as President Bouteflika. I'd like to go some time. I just—I don't want to make excuses, but I will. I've got to prepare the State of the Union Address. [*Laughter*] And so I'm leaving for a lengthy period of time and need to get back home.

And having said that, one of my great trips as a civilian—I guess you'd call me a civilian—non-President, nonpolitical figure—was when I went to Morocco. I had the great pleasure of going to Marrakesh, for example. And I'll never forget drinking crushed almond milk, and enjoyed the wonders of the desert and then was able to see snow-capped mountains shortly in the distance—in the short distance. And so it's—I threw snowballs in Morocco one time in the Atlas mountain range. So I had a wonderful experience there. Not to be kind of nostalgic, looking back, but—you know, it's interesting—for example, there are a lot of Moroccan Jews in Israel.

Q. And in Morocco also.

The President. What?

Q. And in Morocco.

The President. Yes, and in Morocco, which provides the King an interesting opportunity to be a healer and a unifier. And I believe he's committed to that. So I view these three countries as important, and I am—wish I could have gone, but I was unable to do so.

Middle East Peace Process

Q. I want to ask you about the peace process. You voiced confidence that there might be a deal before the end of your second term. However, previous attempts to broker such a peace between Palestinians and Israelis have not succeeded. President Clinton, when he tried with Camp David, the intifada broke. And today, with the situation on the ground, with Syria and Iran not being fully engaged in the process, what makes you more confident that this might really go through?

The President. First of all, the Annapolis meeting was able to happen because of a lot of work we had done prior to the meeting with the parties. Step one is for there to be a recognition that the two-state solution was necessary for the security of both peoples. There had to be a philosophical change of attitude. People had to recognize that two states was the vision necessary for Israel to feel secure and for the Palestinians to feel hopeful.

Secondly, leadership had to emerge on both sides that was committed to the two-state solution and leadership that was committed to recognizing that extremists are trying to undermine that solution and must be dealt with, particularly the Palestinian leadership. President Abbas understands that there are people, sometimes inspired by foreign government, that will do everything in their power to stop the advance of a democracy. He is committed to dealing with that. Sometimes you've got to make sure, though, that the commitment is coupled with the capacity to deal with it, and that's one of the concerns that we're helping them deal with.

Thirdly, in order for there to be lasting peace, there has to be a regional commitment. In other words, the Palestinian leadership as well as the Israeli leadership has to know that when they negotiate a vision, it will be supported by people in the region. One of the failures of the past is that people attempted to lay out a state—lay out the vision of a state, and yet there wasn't regional support, which made the political—the politics on the ground much more difficult for the leadership. And so I—those three issues have been addressed in the runup to Annapolis.

Finally, this really is a leadership issue that we're talking about. There has to be a firm commitment by the leaders involved to do—to make hard decisions. The United States can help, and I will help, and the State Department under Condi Rice's leadership will help, and the National Security under Hadley's leadership will help. We will help them make hard decisions. But these decisions must be made by the leadership in order for there to be lasting peace. And when those decisions are made, they must be supported by the region. And so I think those ingredients are now in place, and I'm optimistic that it will get done by the time I leave office, and more importantly, so is President Abbas and Prime Minister Olmert.

Now, what's going to happen is, is that there will be moments—there will be issues over settlements or Katyusha rocket attacks. These are going to be opportunities for those who don't want the vision to go forward to keep the process mired. We have a way to deal with that, and that is through a trilateral—the roadmap group to deal with these issues. My job is to remind people that laying out a substantive, real vision around which people of good faith can rally is instrumental to peace.

Now, keep in mind, when we define the state, it will be implemented subject to the roadmap. That's why the roadmap—the trilateral committee on the roadmap is important. And so there's going to be a lot of work to be done. And it's being done now. Institution-building is being done; security force modernization and reform is being done. The entrepreneurial spirit, which is strong amongst the Palestinians, can be tapped into. It's hard to get capital to invest, however, unless there is certainty—or more certainty about security and a vision.

And so we're working a three-pronged strategy, and I believe all three of those prongs have come together in such a way as to give me confidence this deal can be done by the time I leave office.

Guantanamo Bay Detainees/Iran

Q. Mr. President, allow me to communicate to you a Kuwaiti sort of question or hope or plea. Needless to say that Kuwait is a true ally of the United States. There is so much gratitude for the role the United States played in the liberation of Kuwait back in 1991. Kuwait was the only launching pad for Operation Iraqi Freedom. When push came to shove, we were true allies.

Now, back in Kuwait, as your visit is approaching, the Kuwaitis are actually wondering if there will be an end to the four Kuwaiti detainees in Guantanamo. There are four of them. To the best of our knowledge, all paperwork has been done; all security assurances have been——

The President. To be transferred back to——

Q. To Kuwait.

The President. ——from Guantanamo to Kuwait. We'll look at it. Our strategy, by the way, is to transfer as many Guantanamo detainees back to their countries of origin as possible, subject to the no torture agreement.

Q. The security assurances and the paperwork——

The President. Security assurances, right, as well as the assurances that the people will be treated humanely. I just will have to look into this.

Q. That will be great news, Mr. President, actually.

The President. Okay, we'll look into it.

Q. If this is broken, that—the paperwork is done——

The President. I understand. Well, some of the detainees are going to need to be tried in our court system. The crimes were such that we believe they ought to be brought to justice in a U.S. court system, which is—it's having a little trouble getting started because we've had a few court challenges for our court system. The whole purpose of the exercise was to send people home and try those who remain. And I just have to check on the four.

Q. That's very kind of you. If I may follow up on that earlier question——

The President. Please.

Q. ——which is, also—I'm here actually to reflect on some sort of a conspiratorial thinking back in the region. You know that's a region——

The President. Has that ever happened? [*Laughter*]

Q. ——whose middle name is actually "conspiracy"—that everything seems to be going for the mullahs' regimes in Iran, over the past 20 years of the United States strategy. The United States had eliminated the northern ideological enemy of Iran, U.S.S.R.; the eastern sectarian enemy of Iran, Taliban regime; the old-time foe, Saddam Hussein, in the west, without having—for the Iranians to resume the 8-long war—8-year-long war—and everything seems to be going their way. And yet, at the same time, here we are. As true allies, we want to have sort of a clear strategy of what exactly are we to adopt with our main ally, the United States of America——

The President. I appreciate that.

Q. ——in terms of the confrontation of the threat for peace that is coming from Iran.

The President. What you've just described is one way to look at it. I look—let me look at it a different way, that now on the Iranian borderst exists a democracy, with a Constitution that is the most modern Constitution written in the Middle East; a democracy that is beginning to grow in confidence; a democracy that will recognize the rights of all citizens within its border; a democracy that will be responsive to the people, which stands in stark contrast to the system of government in Tehran that's not a democracy; it is in many ways a theocracy.

Secondly, there is a—within Iran, there is—I mean, Iraq, there's a different attitude of the Shi'a. There's a quietus school; there's a school that says religion definitely has a part in society, but religion isn't going to run government, which is a—it's just an interesting way to view the neighborhood. Secondly, Afghanistan is now a democracy, a functioning democracy. Are these easy situations? No, they're difficult situations. Democracy takes a while to grow and flourish. But nevertheless, there is a competing form of government in Afghanistan, a different kind of form of government in Afghanistan.

Thirdly, Russia is very much engaged in the region. Russia has been helpful with Iran. Russia has supported the U.N. Security Council resolutions. Russia put forth an interesting proposal, which I've supported, that said, if you want to have a civilian nuclear program, you say your program is civilian in nature, there's no need for you to enrich because we'll provide the fuel for you. In other words, Russia has basically taken that argument away from the Iranians that said, we are—have the sovereign right to have a civilian nuclear program, and they said, fine.

This, by the way, I have said publicly. Of course they have a sovereign right to have a civilian nuclear program. The problem is, because this nation did not level with the IAEA, they are to be not trusted with the capacity to enrich, because once you learn to enrich, you could easily transfer that to a covert military program.

And so I view the situation differently, and I will be—I'm looking forward to talking to the Amir about it. What he'll want to know is whether or not we take the Iranian threat seriously. That's what he's going to want to know. And as my first answer to the question was, it should be clear to you, I do. And secondly, he's going to want to know, do we have a strategy to deal with it? And I'll be glad to lay out again the strategy to deal with it. And thirdly, he'll want to know whether or not the United States is going to remain active in the region, will we be working with friends and allies on developing a security plan? And the answer to that question is, absolutely, we will be. That's one of the main purposes of the trip, to talk about U.S. commitment to the region.

Jasim.

Bahrain-U.S. Relations

Q. Bahrain and the United States are now benefiting from the free trade agreement——

The President. Yes.

Q. ——they signed in 2004. Are there any new initiatives to reinforce economic and military cooperation? And how true are the reports which are saying that the United States will abandon its base in Bahrain?

The President. Well, I can handle that one right now: They're not true. You're right about the conspiracy theory. [*Laughter*] He's asking whether we're going to pull the 5th Fleet out of Bahrain, and the answer is no. And if that's a concern of His Majesty, it won't take long for me to allay his concerns. As a matter of fact, I'm looking forward to not only dealing with the Bahraini officials and His Majesty, of course, but to talk to our troops there in Bahrain. I'm looking forward to thanking them for their service to the country, which ought to be a very powerful signal that the answer is no.

Bahrain is a very hospitable place for our Navy and other Armed Forces, and that in itself is a—should be a signal to people that we view Bahrain as a stable, strong country, which is all part of tracking investment. You asked about how do you enhance trade. Well, one way you enhance trade is to make sure that capital is—capital looks for secure places. Capital doesn't like

to invest and have a high-risk component based upon instability. So that in itself ought to—that signal in itself ought to facilitate division of a free trade agreement.

Talat.

Energy

Q. Yes, sir. Sir, you're talking about civilian nuclear, and you don't have any objection for that if it's going to be under the supervision of the international arena. DCC recently approached to have a civilian nuclear facility for water desalinization for power. What is your stand on that?

The President. It's a—very interesting, Talat. First of all, desalinization requires an enormous amount of power. And the best power source for desalinization, to make it more economical, is nuclear power.

Secondly, I believe if the world is serious about dealing with global warming, emissions, then the best way to deal with it is for us to power up through nuclear power. And so therefore, I'm a advocate for nuclear power, with proper safeguards to make sure that untrustworthy nations, nations that will not subject themselves to IAEA scrutiny, are called to account. So I would support nuclear power for the sake of desalinization.

People say: "Well, you're awash with oil. Why do you need nuclear power?" Well, nuclear power is environmentally sound, and nuclear power is really the best way to deal with issues such as desalinization. If I were in the Middle East and worried about water, which is a valuable resource, I too would be looking for economic ways to desalinize the water. I think it's a smart policy.

Q. Thank you, sir.

The President. Final question. It's been an interesting session.

Q. Thank you.

The President. You're trying to—one more question, Joyce. Quick. If I give you, then I have to go around again. [*Laughter*]

Situation in Darfur

Q. Thank you, Mr. President. You will visit Egypt, sir, which has recently deployed troops in Darfur——

The President. Yes.

Q. ——part of the hybrid force. You also signed a bill against Sudan, which it seems from my point of view again to affect the people—the Sudanese people, but not the Government. My question, Mr. President: If Darfur would be part of your agenda when you meet with President Mubarak?

The President. Absolutely. First, I'll thank him for sending troops. Secondly, I'm going to correct you on the sanctions. The sanctions were aimed at individuals within the Sudanese regime, people that were obstructing the peace process—including a rebel leader. They were aimed at the elite and companies owned by the elite, as opposed to the Sudanese people.

In order for there to be the peace that we all want—now, this is dealing with Darfur—and as you know, the situation is very complicated because we're not only dealing with Darfur, we're dealing with the north-south agreement as well—in order to—well, let me do north-south very quickly. We have been working with the southern leaders to get them to participate in the Government of Khartoum, so long as the Government of Khartoum is forthcoming with their agreements, such as the sharing of oil revenues.

Secondly, we have insisted that both parties not be provocative when it comes to military incursions upon an ill-defined border.

Thirdly, we're providing aid to the people of southern Sudan. And it's interesting; one of the really interesting things about America is, total strangers are going to help total strangers all the time. And there's a lot of church and faith-based groups involved in southern Sudan trying to improve the lot of people living there—in other words, the great humanitarian outreach that takes place.

Darfur—in order for there to be the peace that we all want in Darfur, there has to be, one, a united rebel group willing to sit down at the table with Khartoum in good faith. And one of the reasons I put the sanctions on individuals in Sudan—we did have sanctions prior to that, general sanctions, but these ones you're referring to are targeted at folks—is because there was a lack of effort by the Government on truly trying to promote the peace process. I recognize, however, that there has to be a more united effort by the rebel groups. In other words, the rebel groups cannot take advantage of—continue to take advantage of this notion that they can do what they want without being serious about the peace. And so the United States is sending a dual message: one, to the Government of Khartoum; and two, to the rebels.

When we first got going in the process, by the way, there was three major rebel groups, which made it easier to convince people to come to the table. Now there are 20; the groups are beginning to split. And so we support the U.N. process, coupled with the AU: one, to get troops in there as quickly as possible to be able to help the folks who are living in these dispersed camps have a normal life. And the United States, by the way, when you talk about direct humanitarian aid, has provided more direct humanitarian aid than any country in the world by far because we care about the human condition, we care about people's lives.

Secondly, that we support the U.N. efforts to get the rebels to the table. There was one attempt in Libya, as you know, recently, and our efforts are to support Jan Eliasson—he was the former Ambassador for Sweden here—as he works to bring cohesion so that there's a cohesive unit of rebels to negotiate with the Government.

And so I'm—I have been frustrated, frankly, with the pace of the United Nations and the AU to get troops in there because, as I say, my concern is about the individual that's out in the remote regions of Darfur, maybe going hungry, definitely worried about violence. But I would repeat to you that in order to solve this problem, there has to be cohesion amongst the rebels and a genuine, real peace process where people sit down seriously—to seriously discuss a better way forward. And the United States will participate. We have participated by sanctioning, to send the signal that we expect the Government to participate seriously. And we're also—by the way, as I told you, we sanctioned a rebel leader—trying to send the same message. It's a terrible situation and one that we hope can be resolved as quickly as possible.

With that, I want to thank you all. Looking forward to seeing you again.

Q. Thank you, same here.

The President. Enjoyed it.

NOTE: The interview was taped at 10:25 a.m. in the Roosevelt Room at the White House. In his remarks, the President referred to Prime Minister Ehud Olmert of Israel; President Mahmoud Abbas and Prime Minister Salam Fayyad of the Palestinian Authority; former Prime Minister Tony Blair of the United Kingdom, Quartet Representative in the Middle East; Prime Minister Fuad Siniora of Lebanon; King Hamad bin Isa al-Khalifa of Bahrain; Amir Sabah al-Ahmad al-Jabir al-Sabah of Kuwait; Minister of Foreign Affairs Saud al-Faysal bin Abd al-Aziz Al Saud of Saudi Arabia; King Mohamed VI of Morocco; President Abdelaziz Bouteflika of Algeria; President Mohamed Hosni Mubarak of Egypt; and United Nations Secretary-General's Special Envoy for Darfur Jan Eliasson. A reporter referred to President Nicolas Sarkozy of France. A tape was not available for verification of the content of this interview.

Remarks Following a Meeting With the President's Working Group on Financial Markets
January 4, 2008

I just had a fascinating and productive meeting with the President's Working Group on Financial Markets, chaired by Secretary Paulson. I want to thank the members for working diligently to monitor our capital market system, our financial system. And while there is some uncertainty, the report is, is that the financial markets are strong and solid. And I want to thank you for being diligent.

This economy of ours is on a solid foundation, but we can't take economic growth for granted. And there are signs that will cause us to be ever more diligent and to make sure that good policies come out of Washington. For example, we've had 52 straight months of job creation, but job growth slowed last month. The core inflation is low, but U.S. consumers are paying more for gasoline and for food. The consumer spending is strong, yet the values on many of the homes in America are beginning to decline and—which leads me to say to the American people: For those of you who are paying more and are worried about your home, we understand that. That's why we have an aggressive policy to help creditworthy people stay in their homes.

The Congress and the President have got to work together when they come back to, one, make sure taxes remain low. If there are—if the foundation is strong yet indicators are mixed, the worst thing that Congress could do is raise taxes on the American people and on American businesses. Secondly, we have got to understand that if we are worried about gasoline prices, we ought to expand refineries here in the United States, and we ought to explore for oil and gas in environmentally friendly ways in the United States. As I mentioned, the Secretary and Secretary Jackson are leading an initiative on housing called HOPE NOW, but there's legislation that can be passed to make it easier for people to refinance their homes.

And so when Congress comes back, I look forward to working with them to deal with the economic realities of the moment and to assure the American people that we will do everything we can to make sure we remain a prosperous country.

Thank you very much.

NOTE: The President spoke at 1:47 p.m. in the Roosevelt Room at the White House.

The President's Radio Address
January 5, 2008

Good morning. On Tuesday, I will board Air Force One and depart for a trip to the Middle East. This is a region of great strategic importance to the United States, and I'm looking forward to my visit.

My first stops will be in the Holy Land, where I'll meet with Israeli Prime Minister Olmert and Palestinian President Abbas. I will encourage both leaders to move forward with the peace negotiations they began last November in Annapolis. This is difficult work. It will require tough decisions on complex questions, but I am optimistic about the prospects. And I will make clear that America is deeply committed to helping both parties realize the historic vision we share: two democratic states, Israel and Palestine, living side by side in peace and security.

During the second part of my trip, I will visit five of America's key allies in the Arab world: Kuwait, Bahrain, the United Arab Emirates, Saudi Arabia, and Egypt. I will thank the leaders of these countries for their friendship. I will urge them to strongly support negotiations between the Israelis and Palestinians. I will discuss the importance of countering the aggressive ambitions of Iran. And I will assure them that America's commitment to the security of our friends in the region is strong and enduring.

I know it is not always obvious why events in the nations of the Middle East should matter to the American people. But in the 21st century, developments there have a direct impact on our lives here. As we saw on September the 11th, 2001, dangers that arise on the other side of the world can bring death and destruction to our own streets. Since then, extremists have assassinated democratic leaders from Afghanistan to Lebanon to Pakistan. They have murdered innocent people from Saudi Arabia to Jordan and Iraq. They are seeking new weapons and new operatives so they can attack America again, overthrow governments in the Middle East, and impose their hateful vision on millions.

On my trip, I will consult closely with our partners in the war against these extremists. I will reaffirm our pledge to use every necessary tool of intelligence, law enforcement, diplomacy, finance, and military power to bring our common enemies to justice. The terrorists and extremists will not let down their guard, and we must not let down ours.

At its core, the battle unfolding in the Middle East is more than a clash of arms, it is an ideological struggle. On one side are the forces of terror and death; on the other are tens of millions of ordinary people who want a free and peaceful life for

19

their children. The future of the Middle East depends on the outcome of this struggle, and so does the security of the United States. We know that societies growing in tolerance and hope are less likely to become sources of radicalism and violence. So America will stay engaged in the region. We will support democrats and reformers from Beirut and Baghdad to Damascus and Tehran. We will stand with all those working to build a future of liberty and justice and peace.

Prevailing in this struggle will not be easy, but we know from history that it can be done. After World War II, many said that advancing freedom in Europe and East Asia would be impossible. Yet America invested the time and resources to help nations make the transition from dictatorship to democracy. There were trying moments along the way, and progress did not arrive overnight. But with patience and resolve, we have seen an extraordinary return on

our investment: vital regions of the world that live in stability and prosperity and peace with America.

I believe a similar transformation can take place in the Middle East. At this decisive moment in their history, the people of the Middle East can have confidence in the power of liberty to overcome tyranny and terror. And all who step forward in freedom's cause can count on a friend in the United States. I look forward to sharing this message in the region.

Thank you for listening.

NOTE: The address was recorded at 7:45 a.m. on January 4 in the Roosevelt Room at the White House for broadcast at 10:06 a.m. on January 5. The transcript was made available by the Office of the Press Secretary on January 4, but was embargoed for release until the broadcast. The Office of the Press Secretary also released a Spanish language transcript of this address.

Interview With Yonit Levi of Channel 2 News of Isreal
January 4, 2008

Middle East Peace Process

Ms. Levi. Mr. President, firstly, thank you so much for taking the time to talk to us.

The President. Welcome to Washington.

Ms. Levi. Thank you very much. You're just about to come to the Middle East. And in Annapolis, you said that the parties will make every effort to reach an agreement, until the end of 2008. And I—you know, I don't want to sound skeptic, but I'm an Israeli, and it's in our nature.

The President. Right. [*Laughter*]

Ms. Levi. Why do you believe that you can reach peace in 12 months, when it hasn't been attainable in the 7 years of your Presidency and long before that?

The President. Yes. I think we can reach a vision of what a Palestinian state would

look like. But I have made it abundantly clear that the existence of a state will be subject to the obligations in the roadmap. And so the goal is to have the—a—something other than just verbs, words. In other words, that the state—here's what a state will look like. And what's important for that is that the Palestinians need to have something to hope for, something to be for. There needs—Abbas, who has agreed that Israel has the right to exist, must be able to say to his people: "Be for me, support me, and this is what can happen. If you follow the way of the terrorists and the killers, this will never happen."

And so I'm optimistic that we can have the outlines of a state defined. And in other words, negotiations on borders and right of return and these different issues can be settled. I'm optimistic because I believe Prime Minister Olmert and President Abbas want to achieve that objective. I know I'm willing to help. But I believe we can get that done, and I think it's in Israel's interest to get it done.

One reason why it was impossible to get a two-state solution moving forward previous to this is, one, when we first came into office, there was an intifada. Secondly, a lot of people didn't necessarily agree with the two-state solution as being in Israel's interest. Ariel Sharon changed that point of view. Prime Minister Olmert campaigned on that. And so we have a good chance.

I do want to emphasize, however, that the state won't come into being just because we defined a state. It will come into being subject to the roadmap, and that's important for the Israeli people to understand.

Ms. Levi. So there won't necessarily be a complete, ratified, signed agreement by the end of 2008.

The President. There will be an agreement on what a state would look like, in my judgment. I think it'll happen. I also believe that the leaders know me, and I know them, and that there's a—you know, they say, "Well, are you going to have a timetable?" One timetable is the departure of President George W. Bush from the White House—not that—that I'm any great, heroic figure, but they know me, and they're comfortable with me, and I am a known quantity. And therefore, the question is, will they decide to make the efforts necessary to get the deal done while I'm President, as opposed to maybe the next person won't agree with a two-state, or maybe the next person will take a while to get moving?

And so there's a—I am not going to try to force the issue because of my own timetable. On the other hand, I do believe Prime Minister Olmert and President Abbas want to see this done. And therefore, I'm optimistic it will get done by 2008.

Iran

Ms. Levi. So I am moving on to Iran, and I think the question on every Israeli's mind—and you're the best man to answer it—is, is Iran an immediate threat to the existence of Israel?

The President. Yes. First of all, if I were an Israeli, I would take the words of the Iranian President seriously. And as President of the United States, I take him seriously. And I've spoken very bluntly about what that would mean, what an attack on Israel would mean if Iran were to do that.

Ms. Levi. You said world war III, if I——

The President. Well, I did. And I said that we will defend our ally, no ands, ifs, or buts. And so—now, I am—one of the concerns, I'm sure, amongst the Israeli population is whether this intelligence estimate that came out—what does it mean? It means to me that Iran was a threat, and Iran is a threat. In other words, just because they had a weapons—a military covert program that it suspended doesn't mean, one, they could restart it, and two, doesn't mean that their capacity to enrich couldn't—in a so-called civilian program—couldn't be transferred to a military. So I see it as a threat.

Whether there's an imminent attack coming—I don't think so. The Iranians, I'm confident, know that there would be a significant retaliation. The key, however, is to make sure that they don't end up with a weapon. And one of the things I will talk to the Prime Minister about again is our strategy to solve this issue diplomatically.

U.S. Foreign Policy

Ms. Levi. You say "diplomatically," but is a military strike still an option until the end of your Presidency?

The President. Well, the U.S. always maintained a military option. I have told the American people that I believe we can solve this issue diplomatically. Diplomacy works best when all options are on the table. And we're making some progress.

The Russians and the Chinese as well as the other members of the U.N. Security Council supported two Security Council resolutions, which, some might say, aren't very effective. I think they are.

I think they're effective in the sense that it creates a sense of isolation amongst the Iranians. And I constantly speak to the Iranian people when I say, you can do better than a Government which is causing you to be isolated; your economy can do better than it's doing. Because of your Government's decision not to be honest with the world, not to be transparent, not to listen to the IAEA, there will be continued economic sanctions, some of them unilaterally, some of them bilaterally. The sanctions on their financial institutions, for example, can be very effective.

And so the United States—we've spent a lot of time on this issue, keeping the pressure on the Iranians.

2008 Presidential Election

Ms. Levi. So we're—let's move to something a lot nicer, namely, the upcoming U.S. elections. And I seem to recall you liked to be on the campaign trail. You were there twice, and you won. Are you a little bit, you know, envious of the candidates?

The President. It's an interesting question. I know exactly what they're going through. Laura and I—well, Laura and I were talking about what it was like the day before, like, the Iowa caucuses. You know, I've been through three Iowa caucuses: one, when my dad beat Ronald Reagan in 1980 and then lost; two, that when my dad came in third in Iowa in 1988 and won; and of course, our own caucus, which then—you know, we win Iowa, go immediately to New Hampshire, lose, and eventually win.

And so there's a—it's just the beginning of a long process. And it's an important process for an American politician because it does two things: one, it lets the electorate see how people handle stress; and equally importantly, it lets the candidate, the run-ning—person running determine whether or not they have the inner fortitude necessary to be the President of the United States. Because if things were okay and everything is, you know, smooth, it's—the job is kind of—it's interesting. And it's always interesting—don't get me wrong—but it's—when times are tough is when you're really tested, when you have to make the tough decisions of war and peace. And you—it requires an inner fortitude that I think that you begin to develop when you're out there in those primaries.

So this is the beginning of a fairly long process, although it's been—to answer your question, I don't wish for things that are impossible to wish for. And so I'm an observer, but with a pretty intimate knowledge of the sentiments that these candidates are going through.

President's Legacy

Ms. Levi. I imagine so. You are, you know, reaching the end of your Presidency in a year, and it's sort of the season to summarize. Can you tell me what your—you consider as your biggest achievement, and what, if anything, do you regret?

The President. Yes. First of all, I'm going to get a lot done next year.

Ms. Levi. Of course.

The President. I really am. You know, there's this great myth about how the President—because there's an election or because it's the last year of his Presidency, not much is going to get done. Quite the contrary. We'll get a lot done.

I would think that—first of all, I don't believe there's such a thing as an accurate short-term history. I'm still—I read a lot of history these days. I like to read a lot about Abraham Lincoln, for example. And if they're still analyzing the 16th—the history of the 16th President, see, then I—the 43d guy just doesn't need to worry about it. I'll be long gone. But I do believe that——

Ms. Levi. Isn't that kind of sad, that you won't be appreciated enough until after you're gone?

The President. No, what really matters in life is, do you have a set of principles, and are you willing to live your life based upon those principles? That's what matters most to me. My priorities are really my faith and my family. And we're blessed with a lot of friends. And I just am not the kind of person that's—I don't spend a lot of time looking in the mirror, I guess is the best way to say it. But I do believe that—I can predict that the historians will say that George W. Bush recognized the threats of the 21st century, clearly defined them, and had great faith in the capacity of liberty to transform hopelessness to hope, and laid the foundation for peace by making some awfully difficult decisions.

President's Future

Ms. Levi. And finally, can I ask you, when you do leave the White House— you're still fairly young, you know—what's next for you after you're the leader of the free world?

The President. Yes, you know, I don't know. I do know where I'm going to live, and that's in Texas.

Ms. Levi. Texas.

The President. I tell my friends from Texas, I left the State with a set of principles, and I'm returning with the same set of principles. And I didn't compromise my beliefs in order to be the popular guy or the hip guy or the guy that every— you know, the cultural elite likes. But I don't know. I'm going to build a library with a freedom institute attached to it.

And it's not just freedom from tyranny, it's freedom from disease. One of the great initiatives of my administration has been the HIV/AIDS initiative on the continent of Africa. Laura and I are very much involved in an initiative to end malaria. And thanks to the taxpayers of our country, we've dedicated about $1.6 billion to help save babies' lives. It's the tyranny of hun-ger, the tyranny of ignorance. I mean, there's all kinds of ways that I think I can help others realize the great blessings of life.

But I haven't gotten there yet. I've got too much to do. I mean, I've been thinking about this trip to the Middle East today, and I'm excited to go, I really am. You know, my first trip to Israel—and only trip to Israel—was in 1998. And I remember being in a hotel room and opened the curtain over the Old City, and the sun was just coming up, and it just glowed. It was golden. And I told Laura, I said, "I can't believe what I'm looking at." And after she got her contacts on—*[laughter]*—she came and looked.

And you know, one of the great ironies of that trip was that I was on a helicopter tour of the West Bank with Ariel Sharon. You know, life works in funny ways. I had just finished a reelection campaign in Texas, and there was a lot of pressure and a lot of talk about me running for President. But I don't think either of us would have guessed that both of us would have been serving in our respective offices at a defining moment in history. And that defining moment is the willingness of free nations to confront the ideology of hate, those who use murder to achieve political objectives. And yet there we were.

I'm saddened by the fact that he's in the state he's in. But nevertheless, it was— the beginning of a relationship started in a helicopter flying over the West Bank in 1998, and I'm glad—I'm really glad to be coming back. And I'm looking forward to being with my friend Prime Minister Olmert and other leaders.

Ms. Levi. Mr. President, thank you so much——

The President. Thank you.

Ms. Levi. ——again for taking the time to talk to us. Thank you so much.

The President. You bet. Thank you.

Ms. Levi. And have a safe trip, and best of luck. We're all keeping our fingers crossed for you.

The President. We'll be fine.

Ms. Levi. Thank you.

NOTE: The interview was taped at 4:05 p.m. in the Map Room at the White House for later broadcast. In his remarks, the President referred to President Mahmoud Abbas of the Palestinian Authority; Prime Minister Ehud Olmert and former Prime Minister Ariel Sharon of Israel; and President Mahmud Ahmadi-nejad of Iran. The transcript was released by the Office of the Press Secretary on January 6. Portions of this interview could not be verified because the tape was incomplete.

Interview With Hisham Bourar of Alhurra Television
January 4, 2008

President's Upcoming Visit to the Middle East

Mr. Bourar. Thank you, Mr. President, for taking the time to do this interview on Alhurra TV. Big trip to the Middle East—what are your objectives, and why now?

The President. Now because I believe that it's possible to advance the Annapolis agenda; now because I believe this is going to be an—that it will be a chance to be effective on my trip. I am going to talk—advance three things: one, the vision of two states, Palestine and Israel, living side by side in peace; two, to convince our friends and allies in the region that it is in their interest to support the peace process; and three is to remind people that the United States is committed to helping secure the region, that we have a active presence in the Middle East, and that presence is not going to wane. It's a—that we're committed to helping people realize—deal with the threats and the problems of the 21st century.

President's Role in the Peace Process

Mr. Bourar. What can you do personally to press both sides, the Israelis and the Palestinians, to reach an agreement this year?

The President. Yes. Well, first of all, the agreement—they must decide they want to reach agreement. In other words—and so the first thing I can do is to make sure there's a sincere desire on the parts of President Abbas and Prime Minister Olmert to achieve an agreement. I believe that desire exists. The Annapolis conference was a success because they wanted it to be a success. And it's to give them confidence and to encourage them to come up with the—what a state will look like, the—define that state so that people there in the region can have hope that this kind of a long-time conflict will finally come to an end. And the first step is the definition of a state.

I can press when there needs to be pressed. I can hold hands when there needs to be—hold hands. And so I'm—I will go to encourage them to stay focused on the big picture. There's going to be all kinds of distractions, and people will be trying to throw up roadblocks, and people will be trying to cause these gentlemen to—not to—to lose sight of what's possible. And my job is to help them keep a vision on what is possible.

Palestinian State

Mr. Bourar. Do you still believe that the—your vision of a Palestinian state can be achieved before you leave office?

The President. I think the outlines, the definition of a state can be achieved. The implementation of a state will be subject to a roadmap. In other words, there's a lot of work that has to be done. Palestinian security forces have to be reformed—which we're helping with, by the way. The entrepreneurial class of people has to be encouraged with new capital. The institutions of government need to be strengthened.

And so the state will come into being, subject to—but the first step is to—here's what a state will look like. And I believe we can get that done by the time I leave office.

Middle East Peace Process

Mr. Bourar. Will you be asking Gulf countries, including Saudi Arabia, to normalize relations with Israel?

The President. I'll be reminding the Gulf countries, including Saudi Arabia, that in order for this to be successful, in order for this process to work, there has to be strong support for both the Palestinians and the Israelis in the neighborhood. And that's why the Annapolis conference—another reason it was an important conference, because in that room were the—my friend, the King of Saudi Arabia, kindly sent his Foreign Minister to that Annapolis meeting. I thought it was a strong signal. And so both sides are going to need to know that they'll have support from the neighborhood.

Iran

Mr. Bourar. Recently, there has been some rapprochement between Gulf countries and Iran. Do you feel that the last NIE report makes it difficult for you to convince these countries that Iran still poses a threat to national security?

The President. Yes. I'm sure this subject will come up, and I will remind them that the NIE said that, one, Iran had a military covert program. They suspended the program. I will also remind them that a regime that once had a program could easily start the program up again, and that the key ingredients to having a weapons program is, one, the capacity to enrich uranium; secondly, the ability to take that uranium and make a bomb; and thirdly, the ability to deliver the uranium—the bomb by rockets.

Well, the rocket program still exists. As you know, they say they had—only for civilian purposes, they're learning to enrich. Well, if you can learn to enrich for civilian purposes, you can easily transfer that knowledge for military purposes. And therefore, Iran is a threat. And so that will be my message.

And my other message will be, we've got a strategy to deal with it, and that is to prevent them from learning how to enrich. And I'll explain to them the different types of sanctions and international efforts we're making and how they can help as well.

Syria

Mr. Bourar. Recent visits to Damascus by U.S. lawmakers, like a recent one by Senator Arlen Specter, a Republican, and Senator Kennedy: Do they help or undermine your position toward Syria?

The President. That's an interesting question. I don't know. But President Asad must understand that if he wants better relations with the United States—and frankly better relations in the region—the first thing he's got to do is stop interfering in the Lebanese Presidential process. And I would hope that those representatives sent that message to President Asad.

I don't know how he interprets these meetings, but one thing he can't be mistaken about is the position of the U.S. Government, the White House. And our position is, is that you can have better relations, a better way forward with the United States, but you have got to get out of Lebanon, in terms of the Presidential elections, and stop harboring Hamas, stop letting suiciders go into Iraq. And you—there's a better way forward.

Lebanon

Mr. Bourar. Speaking of Lebanon, what could the United States do to break the current stalemate which left the country without a President?

The President. Yes. We're making it awfully clear to—publicly and privately—that the—Sleiman, who was selected by the—by a lot of the players there inside Lebanon, is the right choice; if that's what they want, that's who we support—and that the obstacle to that Presidency going forward is Syria.

So I'll be spending some time there in the Middle East discussing this very subject because a free Lebanon is in the interests of everybody in the region. And there's a lot of common ground with the U.S. position, and there—like the Saudis and other nations agree that we ought to have a free Lebanon, free of Syrian influence.

President's Legacy

Mr. Bourar. Last question, Mr. President. How do you think people in the Middle East will remember you?

The President. I hope they remember me as the guy who was willing to fight extremists who murdered the innocent to achieve political objectives and, at the same time, had great faith in the people, the average citizen of the Middle East, to self-govern; that the Middle East has got a fantastic future, and that I admire the great traditions of the Middle East and believe that the average man can succeed mightily; that societies are best served when they respond to the will of people, and that we must reject the extremists who have a different view of that, the people who only prey on hopelessness. That's what I would hope.

I would hope that they would say, President Bush respects my religion and has great love for the human being and believes in human dignity. I know my image can be different at times. I had to make some tough choices on war and peace. On the other hand, I hope people are now beginning to see the emergence of a free Iraq, based upon a modern Constitution, is part of my vision for achieving peace that we all want.

Mr. Bourar. Thank you, sir. Thank you very much.

The President. Yes, sir.

Mr. Bourar. Thank you.

The President. Happy New Year.

Mr. Bourar. Happy New Year to you.

The President. Thank you.

NOTE: The interview was taped at 4:22 p.m. in the Map Room at the White House for later broadcast. In his remarks, the President referred to President Mahmoud Abbas of the Palestinian Authority; Prime Minister Ehud Olmert of Israel; King Abdallah bin Abd al-Aziz Al Saud and Minister of Foreign Affairs Saud al-Faysal bin Abd al-Aziz Al Saud of Saudi Arabia; President Bashar al-Asad of Syria; and Gen. Michel Sleiman, commander, Lebanese Armed Forces. The transcript was released by the Office of the Press Secretary on January 6.

Interview With Nadia Bilbassy Charters of Al Arabiya Television
January 4, 2008

Middle East Peace Process

Ms. Bilbassy Charters. Mr. President, thank you very much for your time, as always, and thank you for the interview.

The President. Thank you.

Ms. Bilbassy Charters. The major obstacle to peace is the settlement activities. Would you request from Prime Minister Olmert a freeze on the settlements?

The President. I think the major obstacle to peace is going to be the politics of both Palestinians and Israelis trying to take advantage of the difficult work that these two leaders are going to have to do to define a state; that's what I think. I think that extremists, in some instances, will try to stop the peace. I believe there is a lot of forces at play in Israel that will try to stop these two men from defining what a state will look like. And my job is to help them stay on the big picture and have the confidence necessary to make tough decisions.

No question, the settlement activity is a problem. But there's a mechanism to deal with that, and that is the roadmap commission, for the best word—is the trilateral commission, which we head, to deal with these roadmap issues. Now, we can solve those—we can work through those problems, but the key is to define a state. Now is the time.

And I believe it's going to get done before my Presidency is over. And the reason I believe it is because these two men, with whom I've spent a fair amount of time, are committed. The state will come into being subject to a roadmap. But the first step is to define what is possible; here's what a state will look like. And that is very important for both the Palestinians and the Israelis.

Middle East Peace Process/President's Upcoming Visit to the Middle East

Ms. Bilbassy Charters. Well, in this case, what is exactly your strategy to implement your vision of a Palestinian state by 2008?

The President. Well, the key is for me to convince the two leaders to work through the hard issues. I'll help them, but in order for there to be lasting peace, they've got to come to the table; they have got to negotiate it. And what ends up happening in this process is that the leaders will commit, and then they'll get their committees to work, and it gets stuck. And that's when I'll have to work with Condi Rice to unstick it, just to keep it moving.

One thing is, is that they know that they've got a good partner in peace in me. They also know that I'm not going to be in office a year from now, so there's a certain urgency to get this state defined.

And my trip is going to be to just kind of keep momentum. The Annapolis conference was a successful conference for two reasons: One, it was a chance for the Palestinians and the Israelis to know that the United States is serious about helping them, and equally importantly, it gave the world a chance to come to the table. The rest of the Middle East was there, and that's an important movement. It's going to be important for both Israel and the Palestinians to know that an agreement they reach will be supported by the Middle East.

And so part of my—one of the goals of my trip is to remind our friends and allies in the Middle East that they have got to be supportive of the Middle East peace process as well. They're going to want to know whether or not I'm going to push. And I'm going to want to know— and I'm going to tell them, yes, I am, but we expect you to be constructive players too.

Ms. Bilbassy Charters. Exactly, but, I mean, can you elaborate a little bit about this? I mean, what more can you do? I mean, support is enough? I mean, one visit is enough? Will you be involved——

The President. But you see, to get it to this place—I mean, a visit is important, but I'm on the phone a lot, and Condi is on the phone a lot. There's a little—look, visits are important, obviously. And there's a reason why the timing of this visit is what it is. I mean, there was an intifada when I first came into office. Secondly, the— that there is a philosophical change about a two-state solution. I mean, I supported it as the first American President ever to support it. The Israelis, under Ariel Sharon, came to the conclusion that this is in their interests.

We're pushing a lot, let me put it to you that way. I repeat to you, though, that the notion that somehow America can impose its will on two parties, I don't think it works. I think the—America can facilitate. And so you just got to—I hope that as a result of this interview and my trip, the people come away with the notion that George Bush understands now is the time to move.

Freedom Agenda

Ms. Bilbassy Charters. I mean, people know that you are close friend of Israel. What would you want to do to win hearts and minds of the Palestinians, to assure them that the United States is a fair broker in the peace process?

The President. You know, I've heard that. I've heard that, "Well, George Bush is so pro-Israeli he doesn't—he can't possibly care about the plight of the Palestinian person." I would hope that my record, one of liberation and—liberation, by the way, not only from dictatorship, but from the disease around the world, like HIV/AIDS or malaria—is one that will say to people, he cares about the human condition, that he cares about each individual, that my religion teaches me to love your neighbor.

I have spoken clearly about my belief that—I believe—I pray to the same God as a Muslim prays—that the freedom agenda is really aimed at liberating people, and that the hope is, is that there will be an active, real Palestinian state so people can realize their dreams. But they're going to have to be—they're going to have to do some work. They're going to have to have security forces that protect the average person. They're going to have to have institutions that bring confidence for the Palestinians. They have to have the ability to attract investment. The Palestinians are great entrepreneurs, and if just given a chance, I'm confident the business community will flourish. And most importantly, though, they're going to have to reject the extremists who murder innocent people. And by the way, we're engaged in a great ideological struggle.

Middle East Peace Process

Ms. Bilbassy Charters. Absolutely. I mean, in retrospect, would you regret not being involved earlier in the peace process, 7 years ago?

The President. I think that you would find that I have been very much involved in the peace process when you look at the facts. I mean, attitudinal changes don't happen overnight. And the reason we've been able to have this successful conference in Annapolis is because people's attitudes lined up in—kind of in the same direction. There was common interests; common ground has been now recognized. The two-state solution wasn't accepted for the first——

Ms. Bilbassy Charters. So this is the right time, you say?

The President. ——for the couple of years of my administration. It took a while to convince people that the two-state solution was in the security interests of both parties. And plus, there was a couple of difficult—there was a difficult situation, the truth be known. One was the intifada, which made it awfully hard to discuss peace at that time. The other was the Iraq invasion. It just—it created the conditions that made it more difficult to get people's minds in the right place to begin the process. And so now I think we've got the stars lined up, and I think we got a shot, and I'm going for it.

Ms. Bilbassy Charters. Great. I know he's telling me——

The President. You're fine. Go ahead.

Iran/U.S. Foreign Policy

Ms. Bilbassy Charters. Thank you, sir. Part of the visit, as well, is Iran and the Gulf States. What exactly do you want from the Gulf States regarding Iran? And would you ask for their cooperation in case of a military strike?

The President. First of all, I will assure the Gulf States that I believe we can solve this problem diplomatically. Secondly, I will—they're going to want more from me than I'm going to want from them. They're going to want to know what this NIE was all about.

Ms. Bilbassy Charters. Exactly.

The President. And I'm going to remind them that at my press conference when I explained the NIE, I clearly said, Iran was, is, and will be a danger if they're allowed to enrich, because they can take the knowledge on how to enrich and convert it to a covert program. If they've had one—a program once, they can easily start a program.

And so I view the Iranian regime as a danger. I also believe that the Iranian people are not bad—they're good people—and that they can have a better way forward. We'll tell our—I'm sure the—our friends and allies will say: "Well, what are you going to do about it? It's one thing to define the problem, do you have a strategy? And if you say you can solve it diplomatically, what is your strategy?" And I'll explain the strategy of economic isolation, that—you know, it's sad; we really don't need to have to be in this position. If the Iranian Government would suspend their enrichment programs, like the international community has demanded, there's a better way forward for them.

But they say that they need this program. And my answer is, is that if you need it, then why haven't you been transparent and disclosed it and honest about it? And what were you doing with a military—secret military program in the first place?

And so I view Iran as a danger; I truly do. And I don't view the people as a danger, I view the Government as a danger.

Iran/President's Upcoming Visit to the Middle East

Ms. Bilbassy Charters. Of course. But will it be harder for you to try to convince the Gulf States what—the American position after the intelligence report?

The President. The fact that I'm having to explain it means it's harder after the report. But I believe I'll be able to convince them. What they want to know is whether or not I think they're a danger. They know Iran can be a danger. They want to know whether I think it's a danger and are we committed to helping people achieve security. And part of the trip is to tell people, yes, we've got—we are engaged to help you, if you want our help to enhance security.

Now, look, nobody wants to be dictated to, and I'm certainly not going to do that. I am there to reassure and to look people in the eye and say, I believe Iran is a threat, we have a strategy to deal with it, and we want to work with you.

U.S. Foreign Policy

Ms. Bilbassy Charters. Did you ever discuss a military option with the Gulf States?

The President. Will I ever do that?

Ms. Bilbassy Charters. Did you, or will you?

The President. No, I haven't, because I believe we can solve this diplomatically. On the other hand, as you've heard me say many times since you cover the White House, that all options must be on the table in order to make sure diplomacy is effective.

Ms. Bilbassy Charters. Absolutely. Secretary Gates told Al Arabiya in an interview recently that the diplomatic option is still 100 percent in focus. Does that mean that you're going to still pressure Iran on the diplomatic front? And how far can you go before your patience will run out?

The President. Yes, definitely. We'll continue to pressure them on the diplomatic front. And it's hard, because sometimes people are more interested in market share for their goods than they are for achieving peace. And so I've spent a lot of time with allies in Europe, for example, convincing them of the importance of working together to send a common message to the Iranian regime. So yes, the diplomatic option is on the table, and it's active, and we're working hard.

Syria/Lebanon's Presidential Election

Ms. Bilbassy Charters. On the Syria issue—I don't know if I'm allowed to ask one——

The President. Keep going.

Ms. Bilbassy Charters. I'm sorry.

The President. All you got to do is ask; I'll handle it. [*Laughter*]

Ms. Bilbassy Charters. Thank you, sir. Thank you. On the Syria issue, I mean, we already talked about—you actually told me that you—patience with Asad is running out. But we still have no Lebanese election.

The President. Yes.

Ms. Bilbassy Charters. What does it mean? What can you do? Is it negotiation? Is it a military strike? Is it sanction against Syria? What can you do?

The President. Well, what we can do is make sure that the world understands our position and try to convince them that we ought to work together to say to the Syrians, let Sleiman go forward. That's the President that the people want there in Beirut, and he ought to go forward. And that's going to be on my agenda when I talk to friends and allies in the Middle East, that—and we can collectively send the message to President Asad.

We've sanctioned Syria, and I'm looking at different ways to keep sending a tough message because, so far, he has shown no willingness to be constructive on Lebanon or in dealing with a militant Hamas or in stopping suiciders from heading into Iraq—in other words, some reasonable things that we would like to see done in order to improve relations which he has not done.

We're working very carefully—closely with the French, for example. I've had a conversation with President Sarkozy on the subject. I'll be talking to my friend King Abdallah of Saudi Arabia on the subject, who has got a very keen interest in seeing to it that the Lebanese democracy goes forward. And so we've got a very good chance to have a more focused, concerted, uni-versal message that President Asad, I hope, will listen to.

Ms. Bilbassy Charters. But some will say they might wait for another year until you leave office, and then——

The President. Well, he could try that. But in the meantime, there will be others around who he will have irritated as a result of his stubbornness. And so yes, I mean, he could try to wait me out, but there's other leaders in the world that are as equally concerned as I am about Syria not letting the Presidency go forward and really hurting this very important democracy in the Middle East.

Lebanon's survival as a democracy is, in my judgment, very important for the world. And Syria is—has been—when we passed the resolution out of the United Nations, it worked. President Chirac and I worked together, got our foreign ministries working together, and it worked. And yet as opposed to honoring the notion of staying out of the—and to stop obstructing politics—Syria has just not been helpful at all.

Ms. Bilbassy Charters. So will you impose sanction on Syria?

The President. We have already, and we're looking at different options, of course.

Ms. Bilbassy Charters. A tougher sanction.

The President. Well, we're always looking for ways to make sure that we're effective. It's—sanctions, individual sanctions are okay. They're much more effective when they're—other people join along.

President's Upcoming Visit to the Middle East/Lebanon

Ms. Bilbassy Charters. Absolutely. To show that you actually supporting Prime Minister Siniora, why not visiting Lebanon on this trip?

The President. Good question. You have to just—I've got only so much time. There's other countries I won't be going to either. We've had plenty of high-ranking officials go to support Prime Minister Siniora. I think about Condi, and I think about Admiral Fallon, who I sent over there to help analyze what the Lebanese forces need.

Listen, I was very impressed when Prime Minister Siniora made the decision to move Lebanese forces into the extremist stronghold and dealt with them. That's what you're supposed to do. And in order to have a safe and secure society, the state has got to show that it can provide security for the people and not tolerate pockets of extreme radicals who are murderous in their intentions, and he did. And right after that, I sent Admiral Fallon in to say, look, we need to help strengthen this man. He showed courage and leadership, and he needs to have a military that is able to function at the behest of a state to provide security. And so we're in the process of inventorying and analyzing and seeing how we can help from that perspective.

Lebanon's Presidential Election

Ms. Bilbassy Charters. But do you hope the election will go forward in Lebanon?

The President. Soon. I was hoping it would go forward last week. They keep delaying it, and I'm convinced a lot of it has to do with the fact that Syria is not helpful. And therefore, part of our strategy is to get others to send the same message that I've consistently been sending to President Asad: If you want to be isolated, if you want to be—or if you want—you have a choice: Do you want to be isolated, or a part of the world? You can make the choice. You can hang out with a limited number of friends, like Iran, or you can have better relations in the neighborhood and in the world. It's your choice to make.

Step one is to get out of the way of these Presidential elections. They've got a good candidate. A lot of people agree that this is the person, and now Syria needs to get out of the way.

Progress in Iraq

Ms. Bilbassy Charters. Sir, on the Iraq issue, the security has improved. Does that

mean you're going to withdraw troops by the end of the year?

The President. Our troops decisions will be made based upon the considered recommendations of our commanders. And success in Iraq is essential, and therefore, I'll make the decisions along with those recommendations based upon success. The surge has been successful. The economy is getting better, and the politics is getting better. There is still a lot of work to be done, however, and I am—you know what thrills me the most is that the average Iraqi's life is becoming more hopeful.

Here's what I tell people. I tell people here in America that an Iraqi mother wants the same thing for her children that an American mother wants: the chance for that child to grow up in peace and to realize dreams; a chance for the child to go outside and play and not fear harm. And it's beginning to happen. The average—you know, it's still tough. There's still too many suiciders, but the level of violence is declining. I didn't see this, but I was told that the celebrations at New Year's Eve in Baghdad were festive. And life is coming back, and it's—that's exciting to me.

Military Operations in Iraq

Ms. Bilbassy Charters. And just to follow up on that, the generals were saying that Iran and Syria actually has been playing a role in stopping the suiciders of coming to Iraq. Would you credit them for that at least?

The President. I'm not willing to credit the Iranians yet. I don't have enough evidence. One general said that, then he corrected his story. I think so long as we're finding sophisticated IEDs—that could only have been manufactured in Iran, that are killing innocent people inside Iraq—that's cause for concern. I'm willing to have dialogues with the Iranians about Iraq in Iraq, but our message will be, if we catch you providing arms and trained—training people, then we'll—we're going to hold them to account. You just got to understand that.

I would give—if, in fact, Syria is trying to stop suiciders, I will give them credit, of course. I hope that's the case. It's certainly one way to begin to earning better relations with the United States, is to stop the exportation of suiciders who go kill innocent people.

And I'm looking forward to the trip. I'm glad you're going.

President's Legacy

Ms. Bilbassy Charters. Me too. Finally, how do you want the people in the Middle East to remember you, sir?

The President. History is odd. I will be long gone before the true history of the Bush administration is written. I'm still reading analyses of Abraham Lincoln's Presidency. I would hope, at least, at the very minimum, people would say that George W. Bush respected my religion and has great concern for the human condition; that he hurts when he sees poverty and hopelessness; that he's a realistic guy, because he understands that the only way that these extremists who murder the innocent can recruit is when you find—when they find hopeless situations—they have no vision that's positive; and that he helped present an alternative, and that was one based upon liberty and the rights of men and women in a just and free society. That's how I hope you remember me.

Ms. Bilbassy Charters. Thank you very much, sir, for your time and for your generosity. Thank you very much.

NOTE: The interview was taped at 4:37 p.m. in the Map Room at the White House for later broadcast. In his remarks, the President referred to President Mahmoud Abbas of the Palestinian Authority; Prime Minister Ehud Olmert and former Prime Minister Ariel Sharon of Israel; Gen. Michel Sleiman, commander, Lebanese Armed Forces; President Bashar al-Asad of Syria; President Nicolas Sarkozy and former President Jacques Chirac of France; Prime Minister Fuad Siniora of Lebanon; Adm. William J. "Fox" Fallon, USN, commander, U.S. Central Command; and Gen. David H. Petraeus, USA, commanding general, Multi-National Force—Iraq. The transcript was released by the Office of the Press Secretary on January 6.

Remarks at Horace Greeley Elementary School in Chicago, Illinois
January 7, 2008

The President. Thank you all. Please be seated. Thank you very much for coming. I am so honored to be at Horace Greeley. People say, "Why would you want to come to Horace Greeley?" Because it's a center of excellence. It's a place for this country to realize what is possible when you have a good principal that's supported by the community, when you've got teachers who work hard and students willing to learn.

Coming with me today is the Secretary of Education, Margaret Spellings. Madam Secretary, I'm honored you're here. She's—she and I share the same philosophy. It starts with our refusal to accept school systems that do not teach every child how to read and write and add and subtract and our firm belief that local folks can figure out the best way to chart a path to excellence.

I'm proud that Congressman Rahm Emanuel is here. Mr. Congressman, thank you. As you know, we're from different political parties. [*Laughter*] But we share a common concern, and that is doing what's right for America. We—both of us understand that educational excellence is not a partisan issue; it is an issue that is important for the future of this country. So, Congressman, I'm proud you're here.

I'm also proud to be here with His Honor, Mayor Daley. I've come to know the mayor over 7 years of being your President. The first thing I learned about him: It's better to have him for you than against you when you run for office. [*Laughter*] He loves his city, and he's, in my judgment, one of our Nation's best mayors. He also has taken advantage of a reform that gave mayors the capability of setting the tone and the pace for education in our big cities. Some of the best reforms in America have taken place when the mayor has taken the lead, and, Mr. Mayor, you have certainly taken the lead.

And I'm proud of your passion. I can remember visiting with you earlier on—about education, before No Child Left Behind came into being. And the mayor had this strong sense and strong feeling that this country needed to do something differently if we wanted to make sure every child got a good education.

I'm proud to be here with Rufus Williams. He's a Chicago Board of Education man. I appreciate you being here, Rufus. And I also want to thank Arne Duncan. These two men are very much involved in making sure that if something is working, it is enhanced, and if something is not working, it is changed for the sake of our children. Every good school—every school that succeeds—by the way, it's a blue ribbon school. So I asked Margaret—like, I remember coming up; everybody was a blue ribbon school. I don't know if you remember those days. It was kind of a feel-good era. Just say, okay, you're a blue ribbon school, and everybody feels better about education.

There's less than 300 blue ribbon schools across America this year. I think—what did you say, 13——

Secretary of Education Margaret Spellings. Two hundred and thirty-nine public schools.

The President. Two thirty-nine public schools are blue ribbon schools and maybe a dozen here in the State of Illinois. This is one of the blue ribbon schools. It's a blue ribbon school because it's excelling; it's meeting standards. And one of the reasons is, it's got a fine principal in Carlos. I'm proud to be with you, Carlos. Carlos understands that we have got to set high standards for our children and work with the teachers to achieve those standards.

I was honored to go to some of the classes. It was—it's exciting to go back to the classroom. One of my messages is to the teachers: America can't thank you enough for teaching. It's truly important to—for our teachers to be thanked. It's also important for parents to be involved, and for those of you who are parents, thank you for being here today.

Tomorrow is the sixth anniversary of the day that I signed the No Child Left Behind Act into law. And since that day, we've come a long way. Fewer students are falling behind. People are beginning to get used to the notion that there's accountability in the public school system. Now, look, I recognize some people don't like accountability. In other words, accountability says, if you're failing, we're going to expose that and expect you to change. Accountability also says that when you're succeeding, you'll get plenty of praise.

I think it's—I know No Child Left Behind has worked. And I believe this country needs to build upon the successes. The philosophy behind No Child Left Behind was, in return for money, there ought to be results. It's pretty commonsensical, it seems like to me. That's what the mayor asks when he is running his city. That's what corporations ask: If we're going to spend money, are we going to get a return on the money? That's what our schools ought to be asking too.

In other words, in return—and I—you know, I was an old Governor of a State. I didn't particularly like it when the Federal Government got involved with my business. I felt Texas could pretty well handle it on her own. On the other hand, I recognize that if we're spending Federal money, that we ought to be held to account for that money. And there's some Federal money involved in education, and it makes sense for those of us in Washington to say, "Sure, we'll spend it, but we want to make sure that that money is being spent for a good reason." And there's no better reason than to teach every single child how to read, write, and add and subtract.

And so we have set standards, expectations. And by the way, I believe if you have low expectations, you're going to get lousy results. As a matter of fact, I know that's what's going to happen. But if you have high expectations, it's amazing what can happen.

This school, Horace Greeley, set high expectations. It's easy to set low expectations, you know. It's easy to consign a whole group of students to mediocrity. That's the easy way out. What No Child Left Behind says, is that we're going to take the hard way. We're going to set high standards, and then we're going to measure to determine whether or not those standards are being met. It's really important to measure. It's also important to disaggregate results, which is like a fancy word for, we want to know whether or not each student is learning. We want to make sure that no child is left behind.

Horace Greeley measures, and they measure for a reason. They want to know, first of all, whether or not the curriculum is working, whether or not the instruction is working. And they also want to know whether or not they can—they need to tailor specific programs to meet the needs of specific children. One reason this school is a blue ribbon school: It is not afraid of accountability. It views the accountability system as a tool to enhance excellence. And so do I.

Now, the other thing that's important is, is that the accountability system allows each school to know where it stands relative to another school. You know, from my time as Governor, I can remember parents saying: "Oh, my school is doing just fine. I like my school, Governor." And then all of a sudden, the test scores came out— sometimes a school wasn't doing just fine. Sometimes—not sometimes, all the time, accountability lays out the truth. There's nothing better, in my judgment, to making sure that we have a educated workforce and everybody has a hopeful future than to just lay out some simple truths.

And one of the simple truths is, can this child read at grade level at the appropriate time? That's a simple truth. Another one is, can the person add and subtract at the appropriate time? And if so, we'll say thank you. And if not, the system ought to say, we better change early, before it's too late.

I found too often that in some schools, like in my State, it was just easy to move them through, you know; let's just shuffle people through. That's why—I can remember somebody standing up and saying, "No Child Left Behind Act is really one of the civil rights—it's a civil rights piece of legislation," because this person was sick and tired of the day when people were just moved through the school system, without wondering whether or not the child could read and write and add and subtract.

Test results are all a part of making sure we achieve a great national goal, and that is, every child be at grade level by 2014. The other thing it does is, as you measure, it lets us know how we're doing as a nation. There's an achievement gap in America that's just not acceptable. That means Anglo students are more proficient at reading than Latinos or African American students. It's just not acceptable for our country. It's an indication to me that there is something wrong, and it needs to be addressed now.

And so—but we measure for that reason. We want to know whether or not this Nation is going to be competitive and whether or not it's going to be hopeful. And the achievement gap said, here's a problem. But the good news is, is that because of high standards and accountability throughout this country, the achievement gap is closing. We have what's called a National Report Card. One of Margaret's jobs is to herald the successes or failures of the National Report Card. Eighth graders set a record high for math scores last year. Our fourth graders are—more and more fourth graders are learning to read at grade level. Scores for minority and poorer students are reaching alltime highs in a number of areas, and the achievement gap is closing. If we didn't measure, we wouldn't know; we'd be just guessing, and it's not worthwhile to guess when a child's future is at stake.

The other thing that's interesting about measurement is that when you find a problem, there will be resources like afterschool tutoring to help a child address those problems. And it's important to do this early, rather than late. People who have been involved in education can tell you that a school system that doesn't test and doesn't measure oftentimes wakes up at the end of the process and says, we need remedial education as the child heads into high school or out of high school. That's just not acceptable anymore. The world is too competitive to have a lax system in place. And we don't now, with No Child Left Behind.

And so now is the time for Congress to reauthorize it. I'm sure a lot of people look around the country and say, it's impossible for Congress and the President to work together. I strongly disagree. We worked together to get the bill written in the first place, and I believe we can work together to get it reauthorized. If it's not reauthorized, then I've instructed our Secretary to move forward on some reforms or to analyze reforms that she can do through the administrative process. If Congress passes a bill that weakens the accountability system in the No Child Left Behind Act, I will strongly oppose it and veto it because the act will continue on. In other words, this act isn't expiring, it just needs to be reauthorized.

And what are some of the things we can do? Margaret has been listening to Members of Congress, but equally importantly, she's been listening to Governors and local school boards. We need to increase the flexibility for our States and districts. We don't want the No Child Left Behind Act to be viewed as something that hamstrings innovation. There ought to be flexibility in the system. We're going to provide help for struggling schools—extra help. We want to make sure that a high school degree means something. We don't want people getting out of high school and it's not meaning something.

She's been talking with Members of Congress to give schools credit for growth and achievement that individual students make from year to year—in other words, flexibility in the accountability system without undermining the core principle of accountability. We're going to implement a more accurate system for measuring high school dropout rate and make it easier for our students to enroll in the tutoring programs. There's things we can do, and must do, by working together.

I am optimistic about the country because I come to places like Horace Greeley Elementary School, a little center of excellence, a place where, you know, some might say, "Well, these kids can't possibly achieve such high standards." But, in fact, they are. This is a school that's got a significant number of Latinos whose families may not speak English as a first language. This is a school where there's some newly arrived to our country here. This is a school that is exceeding expectations because of high standards and using the accountability system as a tool to make sure that no child is left behind.

It is my honor to be with you. Thank you for letting me come and share our philosophy about how to achieve educational excellence for every student. God bless.

NOTE: The President spoke at 10:46 a.m. In his remarks, he referred to Carlos G.

Azcoitia, principal, Horace Greeley Elementary School; Mayor Richard M. Daley of Chicago, IL; Rufus Williams, president, Chicago Board of Education; and Arne Duncan, chief executive officer, Chicago Public Schools.

Remarks Following a Meeting With the Chicago 2016 Bid Committee and United States Olympic Committee Members in Chicago
January 7, 2008

I want to thank the members of the 2016 Chicago bid to get the Olympics. Listen, Mr. Mayor, you and your committee have put together a great plan. It's a plan that will make America proud.

They say that the Olympics will come to Chicago if we're fortunate enough to be selected, but really it's coming to America. And I can't think of a better city to represent the United States than Chicago.

This is a well-thought-out venue. There will be—the athletes will be taken care of. People who will be coming from around the world will find that this good city has got fantastic accommodations and great restaurants. It will be safe.

And so I—this country supports your bid strongly. And our hope is that the judges will take a good look at Chicago and select Chicago for the 2016 Olympics.

Thank you all.

NOTE: The President spoke at 11:35 a.m. at the Union League Club of Chicago. In his remarks, he referred to Mayor Richard M. Daley of Chicago, IL.

Remarks on the National Economy in Chicago
January 7, 2008

Thank you all. Thank you all very much. Thanks for coming. I'm glad to be here with the members of the Illinois Chamber. Mr. Mayor, thank you very much. You've given me a lot to do today. [*Laughter*]

First thing is, the mayor runs the school system. And I went by Horace Greeley Elementary, and the reason I did is because Horace Greeley is a blue ribbon school. I remember awhile back, everybody was a blue ribbon school. But that's not the way it is these days because we're judicious in who gets awarded a blue ribbon school. A blue ribbon school is one which sets high standards and measures and achieves results.

Mr. Mayor, you're a reformer when it comes to education because you understand when we find mediocrity, when we find schools that aren't teaching, we're going to have to do something about it if the United States wants to remain competitive in the 21st century.

Then the mayor had me briefed by the 2016 Olympic committee bid team, and you got a good bid. I'm absolutely convinced that Chicago will represent the entire country the right way if the Olympics are here in 2016. Mr. Mayor, you've put together an outstanding team, and I just want to— [*applause*]—I just want the judges to understand that the United States of America stands squarely behind Chicago's bid.

I am really pleased to be here at the Union League Club. I did a little research into the history, and it turns out, Winston

Churchill came here in 1932, right before I was born. [*Laughter*] When people think of Churchill, of course, they marvel at what he managed to do with the English language. When people think of me—[*laughter*]—never mind, Congressman Emanuel. [*Laughter*] I appreciate the Congressman for joining us. He'd been with me all day long.

You know, there's a lot of partisanship in our Nation's Capital. I bet both of us would say, too much. But it—I appreciate the fact that when the President of the United States came to his district, he showed up. It shows a lot about the man. I'm honored you're here. Thanks for coming.

I do want to talk about keeping our economy growing and creating jobs for our citizens. I had a New Year's resolution, and it was to make sure that Congress keeps the taxes low and to make sure that when we spend your money, we do it wisely or not at all. And it's a resolution I intend to keep.

Before I talk a little bit about the economy, I do want to thank Joe Dively, who's the chairman of the Illinois Chamber who's hosting this event. I want to thank the chamber members who are here. I'm honored that you'd take time out of your day to give me a chance to come and visit. I'm sure you know what I know, that many Americans are anxious about our economy. And this frankly is not unprecedented.

Over the last 7 years, over the span of my Presidency, we've had other challenges. There have been other times when people have been anxious about the economy. After all, we've been through a recession, terrorist attacks, corporate scandals, wars in Afghanistan and Iraq, as well as devastating natural disasters. It's 7 years we've had experience in dealing with anxiety. Every time, our economy absorbed those shocks; we dealt with them and managed to grow and prosper.

In other words, this is a resilient economy because we rely on the free enterprise system. Our economy is flexible; it is—motivates people to take risk. We are the most prosperous nation in the world. There's a sense where we can be optimistic. We have seen anxiety—dealt with anxiety before; this isn't the first time.

We have a strong foundation in our economy, but we cannot take economic growth for granted. That's what I want to share with you. I understand that while there is a foundation that would be the envy of a lot of other nations, we cannot take growth for granted. We confront economic challenges, from the downturn of the housing sector to high energy prices to painful adjustments in some of the financial markets.

Recent economic indicators have become increasingly mixed. Last Friday, we learned that our economy has now had 52 months of uninterrupted job growth. That's a record. That's the longest period of job creation on record. Our entrepreneurs are taking risks. Our small businesses are expanding. Yet we also learned that our jobs are growing at a slower pace and that the unemployment rate ticked up to 5 percent. So in other words, on the one hand, we're continuing to set a record; on the other hand, there's mixed news. Same when it comes to pricing. Core inflation is low—except when you're going to the gas pump, it doesn't seem that low, or when you're buying food, it doesn't seem that low. So core inflation is low, but energy and food prices are on the rise—have risen. Consumer spending is strong, yet housing values are declining. The mixed report only reinforces the need for sound policies in Washington, DC, policies which do not create more regulation and create more lawsuits.

Policies include opening new markets for U.S. goods and services. One of the interesting adjustments that has happened in our economic horizon has been that trade has been a significant part of growth. In other words, when you open up markets where our goods and services are treated fairly, we can compete with anybody, anytime.

It's in our interests that we open up markets. It's in our interests that we demand people treat us the way we treat them in the marketplace. And we got some trade votes that will be coming up this year: Colombia, Panama, and South Korea. It's in the interest of economic vitality and growth that we provide opportunities for businesses, large and small, to be able to sell goods and services.

Secondly, energy prices—there is no quick fix. As a matter of fact, I signed good legislation, passed by Republicans and Democrats, that enable us to begin to diversify away from oil and gas, and that's good. But the diversification isn't going to happen overnight. We ought to be exploring for more oil and gas in the United States of America, and I'm convinced we can do so in environmentally friendly ways. And the truth of the matter is, if we're deeply concerned about the environment and want to make sure we're wealthy enough to deal with environmental challenges, we ought to be using nuclear power.

We're working on policies to reform our mortgage markets. But most importantly, the smartest thing we can do is to keep taxes low. In a time of economic uncertainty, we don't need to be taking money out of your pocket. In a time of economic uncertainty, we ought to be sending a clear signal that taxes will remain low. Now, I've worked with Congress to cut taxes, and progrowth economic policies work. When you cut taxes, it means that people have more money to save, spend, or invest, more money in your pocket, more money where you can do—you can support your family, or if you're a small-business owner, you can reinvest to create more job opportunity in the community in which you live.

It turns out, tax cuts have helped our economy overcome uncertainties. Economic growth yielded more revenues for our Federal Treasury. And when you combine that

with spending discipline, then that deficit is beginning to shrink, particularly as a percentage of GDP. Our deficit percent of GDP is low relative to historic averages. It's possible to keep taxes low, grow your economy, and deal with your deficit, is what I'm trying to explain to you.

In times of uncertainty, it's very important to make sure that the people on the frontlines of job growth—that would be the entrepreneur—knows taxes are going to remain low. And so one of the first basic principles that I'll be talking to Congress about is, this administration will use its authorities to keep taxes low.

I don't think there are many folks who believe that Washington really needs more of your money; I certainly don't. Unfortunately, Americans could be facing higher taxes unless Congress takes action to stop it. You see, in less than 3 years, the tax cuts that we passed are set to expire. That creates uncertainty. If you're an entrepreneur thinking about investing, and all of a sudden, you're looking at a horizon where your taxes may be going up, it creates uncertainty. We don't need more uncertainty in an uncertain market. If Congress allows this to happen, we'll see an end to the measures that have helped our economy grow, including the 10 percent individual income tax bracket, the reductions in the marriage tax penalty, and reduced rates on regular income, capital gains, and dividends.

And one of the interesting things that happens if taxes go up—people say, "Well, we're just going to tax the rich." The problem is, many small businesses pay taxes at the individual income tax rate because they're subchapter S's or limited partnerships. And we don't need to be running up taxes on small-business owners. After all, 70 percent of new jobs are created by small businesses in America. Increasing the tax burden on small businesses will make it less likely people will be willing to create new jobs.

And so I will strongly urge that the Congress keep taxes low. One way to do it is to make sure that all the tax cuts we passed are made permanent. If you're interested in taking uncertainty—[*applause*]. One of the other taxes that's going to return will be the death tax, which is being phased out. And in 2011, it kicks back in, which means it's going to be hard on estate planning, let me put it to you that way. I hope a lot of people don't decide to move on just because of the tax cut. [*Laughter*] I'm absolutely convinced we can do a better job of having the estate tax put on the road to extinction and then let it pop back up. It makes no sense.

Listen, the estate tax is a lousy deal, particularly for farmers and small-business owners. I mean, you get taxed twice. You tax it when you build your business, and then they tax you when you die. And I'm absolutely convinced that there is a deal to be done in getting rid of the estate tax once and for all for the sake of economic vitality and growth and fairness.

I want to tell you what it means if these taxes go up. If you're a single mom with two children and 30,000 in earnings, her taxes will go up by 67 percent, or about $1,600. If the taxes aren't made permanent, this is going to affect a lot of Americans in very negative ways. If you're an elderly couple with $40,000 in income, they would see their taxes go up by about 155 percent, or $900. Now, that may not sound like a lot to some of us in Washington, where they throw around numbers in billions; it means a lot to an elderly couple making $40,000 a year.

Twenty-six million small-business owners would see their taxes go up by nearly 17 percent, or $4,000 on average. For somebody struggling with health care costs and 4,000 more dollars goes over to the Federal Government, it's going to make it harder for you to stay in business. It just doesn't make any sense, in times of uncertainty, to be sending uncertain messages about the Tax Code. And so I'm looking forward to working with the Congress to get these Tax Codes—cuts made permanent.

Secondly, the Federal Government can play a positive role. We can play a negative role if we get too aggressive. If we overregulate, it's a negative role. If we pass law that—and opens up businesses and firms and small businesses to lawsuits, that's a negative role. We got too many lawsuits in America to begin with, in my judgment. But there are some things we can do to help.

For example, the housing market—what's interesting about the housing market is that, you know, in the old days, you'd sit down with your lender and work out a deal. And then if you came on a hard time and you're still creditworthy, then he would help you refinance the loan. Well, those mortgages that have been made in recent times have been bundled up into financial instruments and sold. So it's hard to get the borrower and the lender face to face to help the borrower stay in the home. That's the challenge.

Now, Hank Paulson and Alphonso Jackson, that would be the Secretary of the Treasury and the Secretary of Housing and Urban Development, have come together with an innovative plan called HOPE NOW. It doesn't cost one dime of your money, but it's the use of Federal influence to bring investors and counselors and lenders and servicers of loans together to help find those who have creditworthy—to help them stay in their homes. In times of uncertainty in the housing market, it makes sense to help people refinance loans.

And Congress can help as well. By the way, they passed good law. You know, I don't know if you know this or not, but if you refinance your home, it's a tax liability for you. The value of the—the computed value of the difference between what was viewed as your value of your home and the new one after refinancing—new value after refinancing was a tax liability. It made no sense. Somebody is trying to stay in their home, and they get refinanced, and then there's an additional tax liability. It makes it harder to stay in the home. And we passed good law to make that easier.

But there's some other things we can do together. In other words, there's a constructive role for the Federal Government that I believe will help us during these times of uncertainty, and one of them is to expand the reach of the Federal Housing Administration. In other words, this is a program all aimed at helping creditworthy people refinance their home so they can stay in it during this times of uncertainty.

Now, look, there are some people that probably shouldn't have bought a home in the first place. There are speculators that don't deserve help, in my judgment. But there are good, solid, hard-working Americans that we can help stay in their home by providing a—by helping them on refinancing.

Another place where Congress and the administration can work together is dealing with tax-exempt bonds. Tax-exempt bonds, some of them for the housing purposes, can be used to help people buy a new house. I believe, in this time of uncertainty, we ought to have the authority for tax-exempt bonds to be used to help somebody stay in their current house. In other words, these are constructive ways to deal with the problem we face. Congress needs to pass a reform bill to strengthen the regulation of Fannie Mae and Freddie Mac so they can stay focused on their core mission, which is housing. And I'm looking forward to working with the Congress to help us through this period of correction in the housing market.

Now, secondly, we can help people deal with health care. There's a fundamental debate taking place in Washington. I'm on the side of, let's strengthen private medicine rather than weaken private medicine. I'm on the side that says, the more consumerism, the more choices people have in health care, the better off the health care system will be. I'm on the side of

saying to small businesses, health savings accounts are a smart way for you to be able to insure your people. I'm on the side of small businesses by saying, I believe businesses ought to pool—be allowed to pool risk across jurisdictional boundaries. That's fancy words for, if you're a restaurant in Chicago, you ought to be able to put your employees in the same risk pool as a restaurant in Texas so you can get discounts on your insurance, just like big companies can get discounts on their insurance.

And I'm for changing the Tax Code. The current Tax Code penalizes people who go shopping for health care in the individual market. If you're a small-business owner, you know what I'm talking about. It's hard to go find insurance in the individual market because the Tax Code, frankly, discriminates against the individual relative to the person who gets tax—health insurance through corporate America. And I think all families ought to get a $15,000 deduction for health care, or individuals a $7,500 deduction for health care, regardless of where they work.

And all of a sudden, the playing field gets level, and it's more likely an individual market begins to grow. And when you couple that with transparency of pricing and information technology, you can begin to see the emergence of a health care system that's patient reliant, that focuses more on the doctor-patient relationship and less on instruction from Washington, DC. And there's a fundamental debate, and I strongly believe the Government, by passing good policies, can help us deal—help small businesses deal with health care, is a key issue.

And so those are some of the things I'm looking forward to working with Congress about to deal with these times. As I say, we've been through this before. People said, "Are you optimistic?" I said, absolutely, absolutely optimistic. Do I recognize the reality of the situation? You bet I do. If during my 7 years as President have I seen the great American economy bounce back? I have. People say, "Why do you think?" I say, because our people are optimistic, hard-working, decent people. That's why. I mean, this economy rests in the hands of the American people, not in the halls of our Government.

Winston Churchill, when he came here, by the way—I dug out a quote that I'd like to read to you. He said: "Some . . . regard private enterprise as a predatory tiger to be shot, while others look at it as a cow that they can milk. Only a handful see it for what it really is: the strong and willing horse that pulls the whole cart along." I don't know if he said it right here in this very hall, but that's what he said. Government policy ought to recognize

who's pulling this economy, and that would be the entrepreneurs and workers of America.

So I want to thank you for giving me a chance to share some thoughts with you. Thank you for taking risk. Thank you for helping Chicago and the area around Chicago. You're one of the really great locations in the United States of America. Mr. Mayor, I'm honored to be with you again. Appreciate your time. God bless you. May God bless America.

NOTE: The President spoke at 1:18 p.m. at the Union League Club of Chicago. In his remarks, he referred to Mayor Richard M. Daley of Chicago, IL.

Statement on the Situation in Kenya
January 7, 2008

I welcome the visit of African Union Chairman John Kufuor to Nairobi to help facilitate a dialogue to resolve Kenya's political crisis. I condemn the use of violence as a political tool and appeal to both sides to engage in peaceful dialogue aimed at finding a lasting political solution. The Government of Kenya has acknowledged that voting irregularities have occurred, and the Orange Democratic Movement has pledged to refrain from further protests that could

detract from reconciliation efforts. I now urge both sides to enter this dialogue in good faith to earn back the trust of the Kenyan people, who deserve a political process that reflects their dedication to democracy. I remain heartened by the voices of peace that have emerged through Kenya's robust media and civil society. The United States supports their efforts to continue to hold their political leaders to account.

Remarks Following a Meeting With President Abdullah Gul of Turkey
January 8, 2008

President Bush. It's been my honor to welcome the President of Turkey here. Mr. President, I'm glad you're here. This is not his first trip to Washington. I can remember many a time you sitting in the Oval Office as the Foreign Minister, and now

you come representing the—representing a great strategic partner as its President.

Turkey is a strategic partner of the United States. Relations between the United States and Turkey are important for our country. And we have worked hard to make them strong, and I believe they are strong. We deal with common problems.

One such problem is our continuing fight against a common enemy, and that's terrorists and such a common enemy as the PKK. It's an enemy to Turkey, it's an enemy to Iraq, and it's an enemy to people who want to live in peace. The United States is— along with Turkey, are confronting these folks. And we will continue to confront them for the sake of peace.

I strongly believe that Europe will benefit with Turkey as a member of the European Union. I have held this position ever since I've been the President. I feel it as strongly today as when I first articulated it. I think Turkey sets a fantastic example for nations around the world to see where it's possible to have a democracy coexist with a great religion like Islam. And that's important. I view Turkey as a bridge between Europe and the Islamic world, a constructive bridge. And so I believe it's in the interests of peace that Turkey be admitted into the EU.

We talked about energy and the need for all of us to help secure more energy supplies. We talked about—I'm about to brief the President on my trip to the Middle East. I know he's deeply concerned about whether or not it's possible to achieve a two-state solution in the Middle East. I believe it is, and I'm looking forward to sharing the strategy.

All in all, we've had a very constructive conversation, and that's what you'd expect when you're—when two friends are in the room together.

So, Mr. President, thank you for coming, and welcome.

President Gul. Thank you, Mr. President. I would like to thank the President for his invitation here. Turkey and the United States are longstanding allies, and the relationship between our two continue—countries continue to be strengthened. We have a—we share a common vision, and we work together. And the relations between the two countries are such that they have an impact not only on the two countries but also on a regional and global scale.

Our relations are important, and we will continue to work together to ensure that peace, stability, and prosperity continue to grow around the world. And we are also working against our common enemy, the PKK, and we have once again underlined the importance of our cooperation in fighting against the PKK. And I would like to thank the President for his determination, as well, on this regard.

As the President has said, we have discussed some other important issues such as energy and the issues with respect to the Middle East. The President is engaged very much in efforts to ensure peace in the Middle East, and we believe that these are important efforts which can yield results.

We've also discussed Iraq, and we will continue to discuss issues such as Iraq, the Balkans, and other issues. And I would like to thank the President for this meeting very much.

President Bush. Thank you very much.

NOTE: The President spoke at 11:54 a.m. on the South Lawn at the White House. In his remarks, he referred to the Kurdistan Worker's Party (PKK). President Gul spoke in Turkish, and his remarks were translated by an interpreter.

Remarks Following a Video Teleconference With Iraq Provincial Reconstruction Team Leaders and Brigade Combat Commanders and an Exchange With Reporters
January 8, 2008

The President. Thank you very much. I had a series of good meetings today to discuss the situation in Iraq, including a video teleconference this morning with General Petraeus, Ambassador Crocker, and members of the national security team. I also spoke by video with Prime Minister Maliki to discuss the return of the Iraqi parliament that—it was clear from my discussions that there's great hope in Iraq, that the Iraqis are beginning to see political progress that is matching the dramatic security gains for the past year. There's still work to be done, but it was a very hopeful conversation.

Today I just had a good discussion with some of our bravest citizens, members of our Nation's Provincial Reconstruction Teams and their brigade commanders in Iraq, three of whom are with me today, along with the Secretary and Deputy Secretary. I thank you all for coming. And the others were by SVTS, by video from Baghdad. I first of all thanked them for the progress they've helped make possible during the past year and the important work that they're doing in the communities all across Iraq.

Provincial Reconstruction Teams are called PRTs, are a central part of the new strategy in Iraq that I announced a year ago. The strategy was built around three key elements: first was a surge of additional troops into Iraq, with a new mission to protect the Iraqi people from terrorists, insurgents, and illegal militias; second was a surge of operations that began in June once the troops were in place, with new offenses across the country to drive the terrorists and militias out of their strongholds; and third was a surge of Provincial Reconstruction Teams, was a civilian surge, which deployed across Iraq to ensure the military

progress was quickly followed up with real improvements in the daily lives of the Iraqi citizens.

Over the past year, we've doubled the number of PRTs in Iraq. There are now 24 of these teams serving in all 18 Iraqi Provinces. Many are embedded with military units and work closely with our troops to support their operations. Their mission is to help strengthen moderate leaders at the local, municipal, and Provincial level by providing assistance to help create jobs, deliver basic services, and build up local economies. The teams are helping Provincial governments spend their money more effectively. Across the country, these teams are helping to bring Iraqis together so that reconciliation can happen from the ground up.

The leaders I met today updated me on important work they're doing and the progress they have made. For example, our PRT leaders in Baghdad report they have now mentored district councils and public work departments in several neighborhoods, provided funding for generation—generators to help build up local markets, and support a microgrant program to help small businesses reopen across their district in the city.

Our PRT leaders in Kirkuk report that they helped broker a settlement that brought Sunnis back into the Provincial Council after a year-long boycott. They also helped the Provincial government successfully execute the budget, assisted local enterprises with small business loans, and helped establish a major crimes court in a Province—in the Province that is providing citizens with equal justice under the law.

Our PRT leaders in Najaf, which happens to be one of Shi'a Islam's holiest cities, report that they're working with Iraqis to build a modern airport that will allow Shi'a Muslims from around the world to travel to the city on pilgrimage. These PRT leaders briefed us on the changes they're seeing on the ground in Iraq. Because they live and work among the Iraqi people, they see the progress that is taking firsthand.

And here's what they tell me: Violence across the country continues to decrease. Tens of thousands of Iraqis have stepped forward to join Concerned Local Citizens groups that are fighting Al Qaida and other extremists. And as the security improves, life is returning to normal in communities across Iraq, with children back in school and shops reopening and markets bustling with commerce.

Improvements on the ground in Iraq are allowing some U.S. forces to return home. That's what we're—the strategy is called return on success. It has now begun. I don't think most Americans know this, but one Army brigade and one Marine expeditionary unit have come home and will not be replaced. And in the coming months, four additional brigades and two Marine battalions will follow suit.

As we withdraw these forces, we will continue to pursue Al Qaida and other extremists in Iraq. Our enemies in Iraq have suffered blows in recent months, but they're still dangerous. They're not yet defeated. As we saw yesterday, when terrorists killed the leader of a Concerned Local Citizens group, the enemy remains capable of horrific violence. We're not going to allow these terrorists to find respite anywhere in Iraq, and we're not going to allow them to regain the strongholds that they've lost.

The PRT leaders have gotten to know the Iraqi people. They understand the vast majority of Iraqis want to live in freedom and peace; that's what they know. You know why? Because the citizens tell them just that. They're helping give ordinary Iraqis confidence by rejecting the extrem-

ists and reconciling with one another so they can claim their place in a free Iraq and build a better life for their families.

The men and women of our PRTs are serving on the frontlines in the war on terror. These are courageous souls. They could be doing a lot of other things, but they chose to go to the frontline where they can make a difference in world peace. And I can't thank you enough for the vital work you've done and for helping 2007, particularly the end of 2007, become incredibly successful beyond anybody's expectations. And we believe 2008, you're going to see continued progress.

These people are helping improve the lives of citizens they've never met before, and in so doing, they're making this country more secure, and they're helping lay down a foundation for peace. And I want to thank them from the bottom of my heart, and I thank your families, as well, for the sacrifices they have made. We are so honored to have such courageous citizens such as yourself. And now I'll answer a couple of questions.

Knoller [Mark Knoller, CBS Radio].

Iran

Q. Mr. President, what do you make of the incident in the Strait of Hormuz with Iran on Sunday? Do you think they were trying to provoke a fight with the U.S.?

The President. Well, Mark, we viewed it as a provocative act. It is a dangerous situation, and they should not have done it, pure and simple.

Q. What do you think they were up to?

The President. I don't know what I think—what their thinking was, but I'm telling you what I think it was. I think it was a provocative act.

Q. What will your message be to the 5th Fleet then when you're there in Bahrain?

The President. My message is, thanks for serving the United States of America; we're proud of you. And my message today to the Iranians is, they shouldn't have done what they did.

Roger [Roger Runningen, Bloomberg News].

National Economy/Housing Market

Q. Yes, Mr. President. The index of people buying used homes fell more than expected in a report that came out today. And Secretary Paulson says that the housing really has not yet reached bottom. Does that nudge you further towards some sort of economic stimulus package?

The President. Well, you know, I'm optimistic about the economy. I'm optimistic because I've seen this economy go through periods of uncertainty. I mean, in the 7 years that I've been the President, we've had a recession, corporate scandals, the 9/11 attack, major national disasters, two wars in Afghanistan and Iraq. All that created was uncertainty, each one of those incidences, and we've been able to come through it because we've been resilient.

And as I said yesterday and a couple of days earlier than that, I am—I like the fundamentals; they look strong, but there are new signals that should cause concern. And one of the signals is the fact that the housing market is soft, and it's going to take a while to work through the downturn. The number you just reflected is an indication of softness.

And so what can you do about it? Well, one thing we can do about it is to help people who are creditworthy stay in their homes. And that's why Secretary Paulson and Secretary Jackson have put together what's called a HOPE NOW project, all aiming to get lenders and borrowers and investors and counselors together to help people find out how to renegotiate a loan and then get it done.

As I told the people yesterday in Chicago, in the old days, you'd walk in and borrow your—borrow the money to buy a home, and then if you got in a bind, you'd go back to the loan officer. Well, what happens in these days is, you'll borrow the money, and all of a sudden, that loan is sold somewhere else, and you're not sure who to negotiate with. And so it's a much more complex world for many homeowners, and we're helping them, as best as we possibly can, find out how to renegotiate the home so they can stay in.

Secondly, the Congress needs to pass the Federal Housing Administration reform act so that we can get more people better refinancing to stay in their home. There's some practical things that can be done. And so I'm—we're watching very carefully, and we're listening to different ideas about what may or may not need to happen. And it's—we'll work through this. We'll work through this period of time. And the entrepreneurial spirit is strong. And any rate—yes.

Taxes

Q. Thoughts about a tax cut?

The President. Pardon me?

Q. Thoughts about a tax cut?

The President. Well, I can tell you something about taxes. Congress doesn't need to raise taxes, for starters. I know a bunch of them up there would like to. They'd like to get a little more money out of the people's pocket. But in times of uncertainty, you don't need to be raising taxes.

Secondly, in times of uncertainty, it seems like Congress ought to be sending a message that we're not going to raise your taxes in the next 3 years by making the tax cuts permanent. And beyond that, we'll look at all different options.

Listen, thank you. I'm looking forward to going on the trip. I hope people are coming. Does any of you get to come with me? That's too bad. [*Laughter*]

Well, here's what we're going to do. We're going to go over and stress three themes. First theme is, is that it's important to lay out a vision in order for there to be a Palestinian state once roadmap obligations are met. What has to happen in order for there to be a peaceful settlement of a longstanding dispute is there to be a outlines of a state clearly defined so that at some point in time, the Palestinians who agree that Israel ought to be—exist and agree that a state ought to live side by side with Israel in peace have something to be for. They need to have a vision that's clearly defined that competes with the terrorists and the killers who murder the innocent people to stop the advance of democracy.

Secondly, I intend to work with our Arab friends and allies on this very issue, and remind them about, one, the strategy; and two, the obligations they have to help this vision become a reality; and thirdly, remind our friends and allies that the United States is committed to security in the region.

One of the problems we have is that the intelligence report on Iran sent a mixed signal. And I'm going to remind them what I said in that press conference when I sat there and answered some of your questions: Iran was a threat, Iran is a threat, and Iran will continue to be a threat if they are allowed to learn how to enrich uranium.

And so I'm looking forward to making it clear that the United States of America sees clearly the threats of this world, and we intend to work with our friends and allies to make the—that part of the world more secure.

Thank you all very much. See you when I get back.

NOTE: The President spoke at 2:12 p.m. in the Rose Garden at the White House. In his remarks, he referred to Gen. David H. Petraeus, USA, commanding general, Multi-National Force—Iraq; Prime Minister Nuri al-Maliki of Iraq; Kristin Hagerstrom, team leader, Ramadi Embedded Provincial Reconstruction Team; John Jones, team leader, Diyala Provincial Reconstruction Team; John Smith, team leader, Embedded Provincial Reconstruction Team, Baghdad 7; and Riyadh Samarrai, leader of the Adhamiya Awakening group, who was killed by a suicide bomber in Baghdad on January 8.

Statement on Peace Efforts in Sudan
January 8, 2008

Tomorrow marks the third anniversary of the signing of the comprehensive peace agreement in Sudan, which ended 21 years of civil war in that country. I am proud of the role the United States played in achieving that historic result. I remain committed to assisting both sides with the rigorous and complete implementation of all aspects of the agreement. While much progress has been made in forming a Government of National Unity, sharing wealth, and respecting a cessation of hostilities, many challenges remain to the agreement's full implementation. Every effort should be made to ensure that a nationwide census is immediately conducted to allow national elections to be held on time next year. The work of Sudan's border commission also

must be reinvigorated, along with efforts to redeploy troops away from disputed border areas to reduce the chances of a return to violence. The comprehensive peace agreement laid the groundwork for lasting peace and unity for all of Sudan, and its vigorous application will continue to underpin U.S. involvement across Sudan.

I have asked my new Special Envoy for Sudan, Ambassador Richard Williamson, to continue the United States strong involvement on north-south issues to help find solutions to these challenges. Ambassador Williamson is also charged with advancing efforts to end the violence in Darfur. I am deeply troubled that innocent civilians continue to fall victim to the scourge of Government and rebel-led attacks in

Darfur. I remain firmly committed to the rapid deployment of an effective peacekeeping force, coupled with serious political dialogue between the parties, to help end the crisis and the suffering of the innocent people of Darfur.

Remarks at a Welcoming Ceremony in Tel Aviv, Israel
January 9, 2008

President Peres and Prime Minister Olmert, I thank you for your warm welcome. You know, it's been nearly a decade since I've been in Israel, and I've really been looking forward to coming back. Truth of the matter is, when I was here last time, I really didn't think I'd be coming back as President of the United States. But I knew I'd come back because Israel is a special place. And it's a great honor to make my first visit as the President of the United States. Thank you all for coming out to welcome me.

My one regret is that my wife isn't traveling today. Laura is back home in Washington, but she sends her very best regards to both of you all and to the people of Israel.

The United States and Israel are strong allies. The source of that strength is a shared belief in the power of human freedom. Our people have built two great democracies under difficult circumstances. We built free economies to unleash the potential of our people. And the alliance between our two nations helps guarantee Israel's security as a Jewish state.

Each of our nations must guard against terror. We must firmly resist those who murder the innocent to achieve their political objectives. We must recognize that the great ideology based upon liberty is hopeful. In working the lines here, one of the religious leaders said, "Remember, Mr. President, justice and love." Justice and love is based upon a society that welcomes human rights and human dignity, a society which recognizes the universality of freedom. And that's what we stand for today. We will do more than defend ourselves. We seek lasting peace. We see a new opportunity for peace here in the Holy Land and for freedom across the region.

I look forward to my meetings with President Peres and Prime Minister Olmert. We will discuss our deep desire for security, for freedom, and for peace throughout the Middle East. I want to thank the people of Israel for their friendship and hospitality, and I appreciate the opportunity to visit your beautiful country once again. God bless.

NOTE: The President spoke at 12:23 p.m. at Ben Gurion International Airport.

Remarks Following a Meeting With President Shimon Peres of Israel in Jerusalem, Israel
January 9, 2008

President Peres. Mr. President, distinguished guests: As the President of the state, I am delighted to speak on behalf of our people. I want to tell you in simple language, you came to a land and a people that loves deeply the United States of America, and without any reservation.

And also, may I say that I have the highest respect for you——

President Bush. Thank you, sir.

President Peres. ——and the highest regard, because, speaking as a politician, you have introduced character in politics. It's a great contribution to politics—character, courage, vision. And I'm thinking about the last few years; you did really three things of importance: your address in 2002, which for the first time established the basis for a solution and the basis for a consensus in the Arab countries and the rest of— the two-state solution.

Then you and the Secretary worked very hard in Annapolis, in spite of all the skeptics around. Finally, Annapolis gave us one thing, at least: a year to work and make progress.

President Bush. Yes, sir.

President Peres. And time is so precious. Dare I say that, firstly, I believe it won't be the last year, but it may be the best year for peace. God knows what can happen later on; we'll have to take it extremely seriously.

And I also believe that the process may be slow, but the progress can be sweet. The process will be slow because negotiations by character calls for time between the opening positions and the fallback positions. You argue. You argue; you have to wait for them. But in the meantime, you can build a support for the negotiation that can make it realistic, tangible. I'm referring to economy; it can raise the standard of the life of the people. That will help immensely the Arabs, the Palestinians, Abu Mazen, nothing more than an economic— [*inaudible*]—advance, and also the security arrangements, which are also possible.

About the economy, may I say, it can be done very quickly because things are ready, and that will have the most profound impact upon all people around. And I would like to add also that while the political side is controversial in our country,

economic is a win-win situation. It is accepted by the whole Parliament; it is accepted by the Arabs; it is accepted by you and the Europeans. And you can really build a constructive coalition with the Europeans on that issue under your leadership.

We take your visit not as a ceremonial occasion—very powerful—but a third opening after the two states, after the year of Annapolis, and now the year to implement the highest and the greatest hopes we have. It is in this spirit that I welcome you so much.

President Bush. Thank you. Mr. President, thank you for your kind words about me. I'm just following your example. [*Laughter*]

President Peres. Be careful. [*Laughter*]

Q. Ten years to follow.

President Bush. I wouldn't say that. [*Laughter*]

You're well known in my country, and you're well respected. And so I bring the respect of America not only to you but to the people of Israel. Secondly, I come as an optimistic person and a realistic person—realistic in my understanding that it's vital for the world to fight terrorists, to confront those who would murder the innocent to achieve political objectives. We've been called to this task in the past. World War II was such a time, when the world was called to fight people who murdered the innocent to achieve a dark political vision.

Here in the 21st century, America knows firsthand, just like Israel knows firsthand, what it's like to confront those who would murder innocent men, women, and children in order to achieve a political objective. And this war, Mr. President, goes on not only in this part of the world, but it goes on in Iraq, in Afghanistan, in Lebanon; it goes on in capitals in Europe. And we must be steadfast in confronting it.

Secondly, the best way to defeat an ideology of hate is with an ideology of hope. And so I come to Israel as a man who believes strongly in liberty and the power of democracy and freedom to be transformative. And your country has shown that to the world. Israel is a thriving democracy, and its politics can be rough sometimes, just like the politics of America can be rough.

President Peres. [*Inaudible*]—the Israeli. [*Laughter*]

President Bush. Yes. Well, we share a common vision, though, of peace. I come with high hopes. And the role of the United States will be to foster a vision of peace. The role of the Israeli leadership and the Palestinian leadership is going to do the hard work necessary to define a vision. And so I thank you for your hospitality. I've really been looking forward to this trip, and it's such an honor to be in your presence, sir.

President Peres. Thank you very much. We met, actually, the first time in 1990——

President Bush. That's right.

President Peres. ——the young American President on his ship.

President Bush. That's exactly right.

President Peres. And since then, we are sailing.

NOTE: The President spoke at 3:12 p.m. at the President's Residence. President Peres referred to Secretary of State Condoleezza Rice; and President Mahmoud Abbas (Abu Mazen) of the Palestinian Authority. A portion of these remarks could not be verified because the tape was incomplete.

The President's News Conference With Prime Minister Ehud Olmert of Israel in Jerusalem
January 9, 2008

Prime Minister Olmert. Good evening. I am proud and delighted to welcome President Bush to the Prime Minister's home in Jerusalem. We spent more than 2½ hours talking privately and with the delegations, and this was a very interesting and, I think, very important meeting, Mr. President.

I think your visit is timely and is very important to encourage the process that you and Secretary Rice helped start in Annapolis a few weeks ago, and that we, both sides, I believe, are very seriously trying to move forward with now in order to realize the vision of a two-state solution, a Palestinian state for the Palestinian people and the State of Israel, the homeland of the Jewish people and the Jewish state.

I want to thank you—this opportunity—for the friendship and the support for the security of the State of Israel that you have manifested for a long period of time, throughout your tenure as President of the United States of America. This last year, you decided to increase the annual support for the State of Israel for an overall package of $30 billion, which is remarkable and important and is very helpful for the future of the State of Israel.

We discussed regional issues and the bilateral relations between Israel and America and naturally, of course, the progress that we envisage for the negotiations between Israel and the Palestinians. And I hope, Mr. President, that you felt through these talks that the Israeli team is absolutely committed to carry on these negotiations in a very serious manner, to deal with all the core issues that we need to deal in order to bring about an agreement that will have to be implemented, subject, of course, to the implementation of the roadmap, as we agreed with the Palestinians and as you have announced in Annapolis in the international meeting. That was a very important and encouraging meeting, with the participation of so many countries coming from the region and from all parts of the world.

We are dealing with serious security problems. Only today the terrorists were shooting many Qassam rockets on the southern part of Israel, and mortar shells and few of the rockets landed inside the city of Sderot. This is a serious problem. Israel does not tolerate and will not tolerate the continuation of these vicious attacks on uninvolved and innocent civilians living in our cities. And we made it clear to everyone that we'll take all the necessary measures in order to reach out for those who are responsible for these attacks, and we will not hesitate to take all the necessary measures in order to stop them.

There will be no peace unless terror is stopped, and terror will have to be stopped everywhere. We made it clear to the Palestinians; they know it, and they understand that Gaza must be a part of the package and that as long as there will be terror from Gaza, it will be very, very hard to reach any peaceful understanding between us and the Palestinians.

Mr. President, I want to thank you for your visit, for your efforts, for your friendship, for the power that you use for good causes for this region and for the world. Welcome.

President Bush. Mr. Prime Minister, thank you. I view this as an historic moment. It's a historic opportunity, Mr. Prime Minister, first of all, to work together to deal with the security of Israel and the Palestinian people—a matter of fact, the security of people who just simply want to live in peace.

We're in conflict with radicals and extremists who are willing to murder innocent people to achieve a dark vision. And this is an historic opportunity for the world to fight that—to fight those terrorists. It's an historic opportunity to spread freedom as a great alternative to their ideology, as a

society based upon human rights and human dignity, a society in which every man, woman, and child is free. And it's a historic opportunity to work for peace. And I want to thank you for being a partner in peace.

I believe that two democratic states, Israel and Palestine, living side by side in peace, is in the best interests of America and the world. I believe it's in the long-term security interests of Israel, and, I know, it'll provide a more hopeful society for the Palestinians. And that's why I articulated this vision early in my Presidency. And that's why I'm so pleased to have—to watch two leaders, you and President Abbas, work hard to achieve that vision.

It's in the interests of all of us that that vision come to be. I'm under no illusions; it's going to be hard work. I fully understand that there's going to be some painful political compromises. I fully understand that there's going to be some tough negotiations. And the role of the United States is to help in those negotiations.

It's essential that people understand America cannot dictate the terms of what a state will look like. The only way to have lasting peace, the only way for an agreement to mean anything, is for the two parties to come together and make the difficult choices. But we'll help, and we want to help. If it looks like there needs to be a little pressure, Mr. Prime Minister, you know me well enough to know I'll be more than willing to provide it. I will say the same thing to President Abbas tomorrow as well.

I come—you know, people in America say, well, do you really think these guys are serious? We've heard a lot of rhetoric in the past, a lot of grand proclamations. I wouldn't be standing here if I did not believe that you, Mr. Prime Minister, and President Abbas and your negotiators were serious. It is my considered judgment that people now understand the stakes and the opportunity. And our job, Mr. Prime Minister, is to help you seize that opportunity.

In the rest of my trip, I will be talking about the opportunity for Middle Eastern peace and remind people in the neighborhood that if they truly want to see two states living side by side in peace, they have an obligation—Arab leaders have an obligation to recognize Israel's important contribution to peace and stability in the Middle East and to encourage and support the Palestinians as they make tough choices. I'm an optimistic people—people say, do you think it's possible during your Presidency? And the answer is, I'm very hopeful and will work hard to that end.

We also talked about Iran. Iran is a threat to world peace. There was a recent intelligence report that came out that I think sent the signal to some that said, perhaps the United States does not view an Iran with a nuclear weapon as serious—as a serious problem. And I want to remind people, Mr. Prime Minister, what I said at the press conference when I discussed that National Intelligence Estimate. I said then that Iran was a threat, Iran is a threat, and Iran will be a threat if the international community does not come together and prevent that nation from the development of the know-how to build a nuclear weapon.

A country which once had a secret program can easily restart a secret program. A country which can enrich for civilian purposes can easily transfer that knowledge to a military program. A country which has made statements that it's made about the security of our friend Israel is a country that needs to be taken seriously. And the international community must understand with clarity the threat that Iran provides to world peace.

And we will continue to work with European countries and Russia and China, as well as nations in this neighborhood, to make it abundantly clear that—the threat that Iran poses for world peace.

So we've had a very constructive dialogue, and I'm not surprised. This isn't the first time we've had a chance to visit. Every time we've had, I've come away impressed by your steadfast desire to not only protect your people but to implement a vision that will lead to peace in the long term. Thanks for having me.

Prime Minister Olmert. Thank you.

Iran

Q. [*Inaudible*]—Israel's finding about Iran are completely different than the NIE report. Given the duration and the unpopularity of the war in Iraq, there is a fear, a concern in Israel that your administration will not take the necessary action against Iran.

[*At this point, the reporter asked a question in Hebrew, which was translated by an interpreter as follows.*]

And the question to Prime Minister Olmert: Did you perhaps present to Mr. Bush positions that run counter to those of the Americans, and perhaps you are concerned that what he said now actually indicates that his hands are tied when it comes to Iran?

President Bush. [*Inaudible*]—what the NIE actually said. It said that, as far as the intelligence community could tell, at one time, the Iranians had a military—covert military program that was suspended in 2003 because of international pressure. My attitude is that a nontransparent country, a country which has yet to disclose what it was up to, could easily restart a program. The fact that they suspended the program is heartening in that the international community's response had worked. The fact that they had one is discouraging because they could restart it.

Secondly, there are three aspects to a weapons program. One is the capacity to have—enrich so that you can have the materials necessary to make a bomb. They're claiming they're enriching for civilian purposes. I believe that knowledge gained for civilian purposes could be transferred for military purposes. Therefore, our efforts are to stop them from enriching.

Secondly, the knowledge of how to convert any materials into a bomb—we don't know whether they have that knowledge or not. However, for the sake of peace, we ought to assume they do and, therefore, rally the world to convince others that they're a threat. Third, they've got missiles in which they can use to deliver the bomb. So no matter how you might have interpreted the NIE, I interpreted it to mean you better take the Iranians' threat seriously.

Secondly, I have always told the American people that I believe it's incumbent upon the American Presidents to solve problems diplomatically. And that's exactly what we're in the process of doing. I believe that pressure—economic pressure, financial sanctions—will cause the people inside of Iran to have to make a considered judgment about whether or not it makes sense for them to continue to enrich or face world isolation. The country is paying an economic price for its intransigence and its unwillingness to tell the truth.

The Iranian people, we have no qualm with the Iranian people; I'm sure Israel doesn't either. It's people with a proud history and a great tradition. But they are being misled by their Government. The actions of their Government are causing there to be isolation and economic stagnation. People went into office saying, we promise you this, and we promise you this economic benefit, but they're simply not being delivered. And so we'll continue to keep the pressure on the Iranians, and I believe we can solve this problem diplomatically.

[Prime Minister Olmert spoke in Hebrew, which was translated by an interpreter as follows.]

Prime Minister Olmert. We had a very thorough discussion, which, of course, also covered the Iranian subject, as President Bush said. And we discussed all aspects of this issue, and of course, it goes without saying that we shared with one another what we know and what we—what the

Americans know when it comes to this topic. And without my sharing with you right now all of the details, of course, despite the natural curiosity, which I appreciate, I believe that what has just been said now by the President of the United States is particularly important. The President of the largest power in the world, the most important power in the world, is standing right here, and he has said in no uncertain terms that Iran was a threat and remains a threat.

And the fact that it has certain technological capacities is a fact. And through this, it is capable of realizing that potential and creating nuclear weapons. And considering the nature of the Government there and the type of threats that they are voicing, one cannot possibly disregard that power, and we must do everything possible to thwart them.

Of course, the United States will decide for itself just what steps to take. I can only say one thing, namely, my impression based on this conversation as well as previous talks that we had—and we talk quite frequently, apart from the face-to-face meetings—my impression is that we have here a leader who is exceptionally determined, exceptionally loyal to the principles in which he believes. He has proven this throughout his term in office in his preparedness to take exceptional measures in order to defend the principles in which he believes and in his deep commitment to the security of the State of Israel.

Inasmuch as I could sum up all of these impressions this evening, I would say that I certainly am encouraged and reinforced having heard the position of the United States under the leadership of George Bush, particularly on this subject.

White House Press Secretary Dana Perino. Anne Gearan of the Associated Press, please.

Middle East Peace Process

Q. Mr. President, are you disappointed that the Israelis and the Palestinians haven't made more specific progress since Annapolis? And is it maybe time for you to apply some of that direct pressure you referred to earlier?

And for the Prime Minister, did you offer any new assurances to the President—or do you plan to—that Israel will stop disputed settlement and construction activity?

President Bush. Step one of any complicated process that is going to require a lot of hard work and serious dialogue is whether the mindset is right. It's one thing for somebody to say to the President, sure, we're for a two state, just to make the President feel okay. That's not the case here. The fundamental questions that I was seeking at Annapolis and on my return trip is the understanding about the power of what a vision will do for peace.

You know, one of the concerns I had was that, whether it be the unprovoked rocket attacks or the issues of settlement, that the leaders would be so bogged down in the moment that they would lose sight of the potential for a historic agreement. And I've come away with the belief that while those issues are important and certainly create consternation amongst the respective constituencies, that both leaders are determined to make the hard choices necessary.

Now, implicit in your question is whether or not the President should butt in and actually dictate the end result of the agreement. In my judgment, that would cause there to be a nonlasting agreement. In my judgment, the only way for there to be a vision that means something is for the parties to seriously negotiate that vision. If you're asking me, am I nudging them forward, well, my trip was a pretty significant nudge, because yesterday they had a meeting.

And by the way, the atmosphere in America was, nothing is going to happen, see; that these issues are too big on the ground. Therefore, you two can't get together and come up with any agreements.

You just heard the man talk about their desire to deal with core issues, which, I guess for the uneducated on the issue, that means dealing with the issues like territory and right of return and Jerusalem. Those are tough issues—the issue of Israeli security. And they're going to sit down at the table and discuss those issues in seriousness.

And I've been briefed today from the Israeli perspective of those discussions. Tomorrow I'll be briefed by the Palestinians about their interpretation.

Now, there's three tracks going on, by the way, during this process. One is the vision track. Let me just make sure everybody understands—in our delegation—the goal. The goal is for there to be a clear vision of what a state would look like so that, for example, reasonable Palestinian leadership can say, here's your choice: You can have the vision of Hamas, which is dangerous and will lead to war and violence, or you can have the vision of a state, which should be hopeful.

The second track is to help both parties deal with roadmap issues. Settlements is a roadmap issue; security is a roadmap issue, in a certain limited sense. Third issue is to help the Palestinians, one, organize their security forces so that they can better assure their own people and, equally importantly, better assure Israel that they can deal with the extremists in their midst. That's what General Dayton is doing here, for example. Or an economic track—listen, the best way to make sure that the Palestinians realize there's a hopeful future in which it's in their interests to live at peace with Israel is for them to realize that they've got an economy in which they can make a living. And Tony Blair is helpful on that, and so is America.

And so you're watching three tracks parallel each other. And the one, of course, you're asking about is whether or not the leadership has got the willingness and the desire and the drive to design a state, compatible to both sides. And my answer is, yes, I think they will.

Prime Minister Olmert. I hope that I don't disappoint anyone—certainly not the President, because we talked at length—if I will say that the President didn't ask for me to make any commitments other than the ones that Israel made already with regard to the peace process and as I have spelled it out on many different occasions, including in Annapolis, which was a very, as I said, a very important event. The commitment of Israel is absolutely to carry on in this process in order to realize the vision of two states living side by side, as I said before.

Now, there are many issues. Settlement is one of the issues. We made clear our position. And I know that sometimes not everyone is happy with this position, but we are very sincere. And we were never trying to conceal any of these facts from anyone, starting with President Bush and Secretary Rice and, of course, our Palestinian partners.

They know that there is a moratorium on new settlements and the new expropriation of land in the Territories. But they also know, and we have made it clear, that Jerusalem, as far as we are concerned, is not in the same status. And they know that the population centers are not in the same status. And there might be things that will happen in the population centers or in Jerusalem which they may not be in love with, but we will discuss them, and we will not hide them. We are not going to build any new settlements or expropriate land in the Territories. We made it clear, and we will stand by our commitments. And we will fulfill all our commitments as part of the roadmap because this is an essential part for any progress that will have to take place in the future.

But there are some aspects only just realized which one can't ignore, and everyone knows that certain things in Jerusalem are not in the same tactical level as they are in other parts of the Territories which are outside the city of Jerusalem. And so it's true about some population centers. So there was nothing that happened that was not known in advance to all our partners in this process. We made clear our positions. We made clear exactly what we can do, what we can't do, what we want to do, and what we will not be able to do. And I think that they all know it, and they—at least even when sometimes they disagree with us, they at least respect our sincerity and openness about these issues.

Obligations of Middle East Peace Process Participants

Q. Mr. President, regarding the issues of rockets and settlements that you mentioned before, what should—what could Israel do regarding the ever-growing threat from Gaza? And regarding the settlements, did you get any new assurances from the Prime Minister regarding the removal of illegal outposts? Do you believe that this time it will be implemented? Do you care about it?

President Bush. Yes.

[*The reporter asked a question in Hebrew, which was translated by an interpreter as follows.*]

Q. Mr. Prime Minister, are you concerned that the core issues are going to be affected? Because as soon as Mr.—Member of Knesset, Mr. Lieberman, is going to withdraw from the coalition.

President Bush. As to the rockets, my first question is going to be to President Abbas: What do you intend to do about them? Because ultimately, in order for there to be the existence of a state, there has to be a firm commitment by a Palestinian Government to deal with extremists and terrorists who might be willing to use Palestinian Territory as a launching pad into Israel. So I'll be asking that question tomorrow. And what can we do to help you?

I believe that he knows it's not in his interests to have people launching rockets from a part of the Territory into Israel. A matter of fact, maybe the Prime Minister can comment on this in a while, in a second, but at least he's told me that he fully recognizes, in order for there to be a state, he cannot be a safe haven for terrorists that want to destroy Israel. You can't expect the Israelis—and I certainly don't—to accept a state on their border which would become a launching pad for terrorist activities. And that's why the vision of a democracy is an important vision.

How Israel deals with the rocket attacks, I would hope is done in a way that not only protects herself but worries about innocent life. And I'm convinced the Prime Minister does. He understands he has an obligation to protect Israel. He also understands that he's got to be circumspect and reasonable about how he does it so that innocent people don't suffer. He just gave you the answer on the settlements.

In terms of outposts, yes, they ought to go. Look, I mean, we've been talking about it for 4 years. The agreement was, get rid of outposts, illegal outposts, and they ought to go. And——

[Prime Minister Olmert spoke in Hebrew, and his remarks were translated by an interpreter as follows.]

Prime Minister Olmert. [*Inaudible*]—earlier, and I say once again—I think it's important to repeat this—Israel has commitments, and the Palestinians have commitments. We must abide by our commitments, and we shall do so. I do not want to use this as an excuse, as a pretext, and therefore, I say, we demand of the Palestinians that they uphold all of their commitments.

And some have not been upheld, not a single one, particularly the most important things that have to do with terrorism, that have to do with the security of the State of Israel—not only in Gaza. The fact that we, over the past year, have had fewer casualties from terrorism than in any year of the recent years previously is not because the Palestinians have made fewer attempts, but because we have been more successful, in a very sophisticated and courageous way, of our general security service and our IDF in preventing these terrorist acts.

I'm not using this as a pretext. I'm saying, we must uphold our commitment. I believe that the President has said this fairly and appropriately. We have made commitments; we should uphold them; and we shall. But let us present a balanced picture. By the same token, we will not refrain from demanding and insisting that the Palestinians abide by all of their commitments. And their commitments when it comes to terrorism are the central key, the pivot to bringing this negotiation process to a successful conclusion. And I hope it will happen this year, as all of us hope.

I very much sincerely hope that all of those in the coalition will remain in the coalition as full partners, and I would certainly not like to have a political crisis. I don't think that anyone who is responsible—has a responsibility such as I have would like to see any kind of an undermining of the stability of this Government. It is a stable Government, a Government that has been operating in many different directions, with very impressive achievements, which the party of Avigdor Lieberman, Yisrael Beiteinu, is part of this effort, part of these achievements; whether it's in the economic field or the political one or in—when it comes to security or the deterrence ability of the State of Israel.

And everyone knows that this Government has had some very impressive achievements on its record over the past year. And Lieberman's party was certainly a partner in this process, and I'd like them to stay part of the process. I think that the gap between us is smaller than it appears, and I will do everything within my power to ensure that the coalition remains stable. The State of Israel must be part of a serious peace process. We cannot forego this; we cannot obscure it; we must not delay it. It would be wrong to delay it.

Let me say something in Hebrew—since I know that the President does not speak Hebrew, I'll say it in Hebrew because, after all, you know, you're not supposed to praise people in their presence, so I'll say it in Hebrew. Well, then, what I'd like to say is, thank God I can conduct political negotiations with George Bush at my side as one of my partners. Thank God we can conduct political negotiations when the largest and most important power in the world, and the most important for us, is headed by such an important friend of Israel.

We have no interest in delaying matters. We don't want to procrastinate with the negotiations, lest changes for the worse take place on the Palestinian front. And we certainly don't want to delay the negotiation process when we have such political assistance, assistance in—with respect to our security too, when it comes to the most important power in the world, being led by a person who is so deeply committed to the security of the State of Israel and to realizing the vision of two states; a person who is fair, who does not hide his viewpoints, who speaks openly about his will to establish a Palestinian state alongside Israel, a state that will be secure not at the expense of the interests of the State of Israel.

I believe that any responsible political leader in the State of Israel will understand that this is a moment that must not be missed. This is an opportunity that must not be passed up. We must do everything we can. Okay, we can have occasional internal arguments. The President has said that some very difficult decisions must be made. He is right, but I am not afraid of difficult decisions. I am willing to contend with difficult decisions. I am willing to make decisions that will entail painful compromises, so long as they enable us to reach the goal that we have dreamt of for so long, to

secure ourselves—to ensure ourselves of security and to give the Palestinians the state of their own that will be vibrant, democratic, open, and living in peace alongside Israel.

At the head of our negotiating team is the Deputy Prime Minister and Foreign Minister. She bears a very heavy responsibility. We work in full cooperation, and I am convinced that she will wisely succeed, together with Abu Ala, head of the Palestinian team, in navigating through these negotiations in such a manner that the vital interests of the State of Israel are served well on the basis of a deep understanding.

President Bush. The interpreter got it right. [*Laughter*] Thank you.

Prime Minister Olmert. Thank you, Mr. President.

President Bush. Yes, Toby [Tabassum Zakaria, Reuters].

Strait of Hormuz Naval Incident

Q. Mr. President, what is the United States prepared—what action is the United States prepared to take if there is another confrontation with Iranian ships in the Strait of Hormuz? Your National Security Adviser this morning spoke about consequences if there was a repeat.

And, Mr. Prime Minister, why is there no three-way meeting scheduled on this trip?

President Bush. The National Security Adviser was making it abundantly clear that all options are on the table to protect our assets.

She's referring to, Mr. Prime Minister, the fact that our ships were moving along very peacefully off the Iranian border in territorial water—international waters, and Iranian boats came out and were very provocative. And it was a dangerous gesture on their part. We have made it clear publicly, and they know our position, and that is, there will be serious consequences if they attack our ships, pure and simple. And my advice to them is, don't do it.

United States-Israel-Palestinian Authority Meeting

Q. Why is there no three-way meeting on this trip?

Prime Minister Olmert. We had a three-way meeting in the United States just a month ago. We are starting now a serious process directly with the Palestinians. The President met with the Israeli delegation and with me today. He will meet tomorrow with the—with President Mahmoud Abbas, and I'm sure that all the necessary information will be provided and all the curiosity of the President will be satisfied. And ideally, this is a very good and comfortable—[*inaudible*].

I don't rule out, by the way, trilateral meetings. Maybe in the future we'll have trilateral meetings. We are not against it. We just found out at this time in life, considering what we have achieved already and what we are about to start now in a serious manner, that it was not essential in order to fulfill the desires that we all share, which is to move forward on this process between us and the Palestinians.

I can reassure you, and perhaps through you, many of your people in America, that we think, and I'm sure that the Palestinians think, that the visit of the President is very, very helpful to the process that we are engaged in and that it contributes—and it will contribute a lot to the stability and the very comfortable environment within which we will conduct our negotiations.

And therefore, I again want to take this opportunity, Mr. President—now you don't even get—[*laughter*]—to thank you very much, really, to thank you for your friendship and your support and the courage that you inspire in all of us to carry on with our obligations. It's not easy. You know, sometimes it's not easy, but when I look at you—and I know what you have to take upon your shoulders and how you do it, the manner in which you do it, the courage that you have, the determination that you have, and your loyalty to the principles that you believe in—it makes all of us feel that we can also—in trying to match you, which we can—we can move forward. Thank you very much.

President Bush. Thank you, sir.

NOTE: The President's news conference began at 6:36 p.m. at the Prime Minister's residence. In his remarks, he referred to President Mahmoud Abbas of the Palestinian Authority; Lt. Gen. Keith W. Dayton, USA, U.S. Security Coordinator to Israel and the Palestinian Authority; and former Prime Minister Tony Blair of the United Kingdom, Quartet Representative in the Middle East. Prime Minister Olmert referred to Knesset Member and Yisrael Beiteinu Party leader Avigdor Lieberman and Deputy Prime Minister and Minister of Foreign Affairs Tzipora "Tzipi" Livni of Israel; and former Prime Minister Ahmed Qurei (Abu Ala) of the Palestinian Authority.

The President's News Conference With President Mahmoud Abbas of the Palestinian Authority in Ramallah, Palestinian Territories
January 10, 2008

President Abbas. Your Excellency, President George Bush, President of the United States of America, I welcome you in Ramallah, as well as in Bethlehem, on the land of Palestine, that welcomes you today

as a great guest, that goes with him—commitment towards the peace process. It's a historic visit that gives our people great hope in the fact that your great nation is standing and supporting their dream and their yearning towards freedom and independence and living in peace in this area alongside their neighbors.

Our people will not forget, Your Excellency, your invitation and your commitment towards the establishment of an independent Palestinian state. You are the first American President that confirms and reiterates this right.

[*At this point, there was a problem with the translation earpiece.*]

President Bush. I haven't got it yet. You may have to start over. [*Laughter*] Not yet. You better stay awake. [*Laughter*]

President Abbas. Our people, Your Excellency——

President Bush. I agree completely. [*Laughter*]

President Abbas. Your commitment towards the establishment of the independent Palestinian state—you are the first American President to reiterate this right. The conferences of Annapolis and Paris were historic step from you and from the American people and the world as a whole to protect this commitment and push it forward.

Our Palestinian people, who committed to peace as a strategic option, want to see, through your support and your intervention, an end to its suffering and the suffering of its people and their families, and wants to move freely in their homeland and develop their life and their economy without any obstacles that hinder that progress; and without a separation wall that fragments the land; and without settlements that is governing its land and future. We want to see a different future, where prisons are not crowded with thousands of prisoners and where hospitals are not crowded with tens of innocent victims every day, without checkpoints and queues of ordinary people who suffer from humiliation and siege.

I would like to point out here that we instructed our Government to continue the work towards enhancing security and imposing public order and establishing good governance that is based on the rule of law and to consolidate the role of our democratic institutions and strengthen the work of the civil society, as well as work on consolidating development and administrative and financial reform and transparency so that we can lay the foundations for a modern and democratic state.

And the Government is taking intensive steps in that direction, and I would like to express our appreciation for the support of your administration in the economic sphere in order to develop the infrastructure and provide new job opportunities and improve the level of services and all other projects that contribute in improving the lives and the conditions of living for our people.

We and our Israeli neighbors, and under your direct sponsorship—bilateral negotiations that address all issues of final status are core issues—that we would like to end these negotiations during your term in office; and that we—it will be ending by the—ending of the occupation that started in 1967, and that establishment of an independent Palestinian state and its capital, Jerusalem, based on your vision and the international resolutions; and that we find a fair solution for the tragedy of refugees, according to the Arab initiative for peace and according to the U.N. resolutions.

And on this occasion, I would like to reiterate before you our full commitment to all our obligations that we agreed to. And we call upon Israel as well to fulfill its commitments according to the roadmap plan, because we firmly believe that peace is made by a will and a shared commitment among all parties.

Your historic visit today to the Palestinian Territories is highly appreciated by our people, and it's a new expression of your deep commitment towards establishing peace on the land of peace. We appreciate the complete seriousness that characterizes your visit and your efforts today to continue and build on, capitalize on this important opportunity that is available to us and to the Israelis.

We start with you a new year, hoping that this will be the year for the creation of peace. You will hear today in Bethlehem the call for prayers from the mosques and the heralding of bells at the Church of Nativity. That confirms our common message, the message of human tolerance and real peace that is deeply rooted in our conscience and in our heritage. Your presence today amongst us, Your Excellency, is a reiteration for the call for comprehensive and just peace that you called for and you committed yourself to. And the echo of this call reaches all the people and the countries in our region, because the voice that is now going out of Palestine is the closest and the deepest in reaching the hearts of all the people in the region.

Please, Your Excellency, trust that peace in the world starts from here, from the Holy Land. We welcome you again, our dear guest and our dear friend, here in Palestine.

President Bush. Mr. President, thank you for your hospitality. We have met a lot in the past, and I'm glad to finally have a chance to sit down in your office to discuss important issues.

[*There was another problem with the translation earpiece.*]

Is it working? [*Laughter*] Listen, they say I have enough problems speaking English as it is. [*Laughter*]

I have had numerous opportunities to visit with the President. And the fundamental question I have is whether or not he is committed to peace. It's the same question I had for the Prime Minister of Israel. And I've come to the conclusion that both men understand the importance of two democratic states living side by side in peace.

President Abbas was elected on a platform of peace. In other words, he just wasn't somebody who starts talking about it lately; he campaigned on it. He also said

that if you give me a chance, I'll work hard to improve the lives of the average Palestinians, and that's what he has done. It's certainly not easy work. The conditions on the ground are very difficult, and nevertheless, this man and his Government not only works for a vision but also works to improve the lives of the average citizens, which is essential for the emergence of a Palestinian democracy.

I talked today about how—what we can do to help, and as he mentioned, the United States has been an active financial giver. We helped at the Paris conference. I firmly believe that the Palestinians are entrepreneurial people who, if just given a chance, will be able to grow their businesses and provide jobs.

We talked about the need to fight off the extremists. The world in which we live is a dangerous world because there are people who murder innocent people to achieve political objectives, not just here in this immediate part of the world but around the world. That's what we're dealing with in Iraq and Afghanistan and Lebanon. And the fundamental question is, will nations stand up and help those who understand the ideological struggle we're in? And the President understands the ideological struggle. He knows that a handful of people want to dash the aspirations of the Palestinian people by creating chaos and violence.

And I appreciate that, Mr. President. And I appreciate your understanding that, ultimately, the way to achieve peace is to offer an alternative vision, and that's a vision based upon liberty.

Now, look, there are some in the world who don't believe in the universality of freedom. I understand that. They say, like, freedom is okay for some of us, but maybe not all of us. I understand it, but I reject it. I believe in the universality of freedom. I believe deep in the soul of every man, woman, and child on the face of this Earth is the desire to live in a free society. And I also believe free societies yield peace.

And therefore, this notion of two states living side by side in peace is based upon the universality of freedom, and if given a chance, the Palestinian people will work for freedom.

And that's a challenge ahead of us—is, is it possible for the Israelis and the Palestinians to work out their differences on core issues so that a vision can emerge? And my answer is, absolutely, it's possible. Not only is it possible, it's necessary. And I'm looking forward to helping.

You know, there's a great anticipation that all the American President has got to do is step in and just say, okay, this is the way it's going to be. That's not how the system works. In order for there to be lasting peace, President Abbas and Prime Minister Olmert have to come together and make tough choices. And I'm convinced they will. And I believe it's possible—not only possible; I believe it's going to happen—that there will be a signed peace treaty by the time I leave office. That's what I believe. And the reason I believe that is because I hear the urgency in the voice of both the Prime Minister of Israel and the President of the Palestinian Authority.

Is it going to be hard work? You bet. And we can help support these negotiations, and will. I was asked yesterday at a press conference, you know, what do you intend to do? If you're not going to write the agreement, what do you intend to do? I said, nudge the process forward. Like, pressure; be a pain if I need to be a pain, which in some people's mind isn't all that hard. And they said, well, like—yesterday somebody said, well, are you disappointed? I arrived, and it nudged the process forward. In other words, we can help influence the process, and will. But the only lasting peace will be achieved when the duly elected leaders of the respective peoples do the hard work.

And so I want to help. And I want to help in the region as well, Mr. President. The rest of my trip will be talking about,

obviously, security threats, but also the opportunity to achieve peace. And the Arab world has got an opportunity and obligation, in my judgment, to help both parties in these negotiations move the process forward.

I explained yesterday, and I just want to explain again today, there are three tracks to this process, as far as we're concerned. One is the negotiations to define a vision that will be subject to the roadmap.

Secondly, is to resolve—help resolve roadmap issues. And today I introduced the President to the general—three-star Air Force general who will be running this process. We have agreed to a trilateral process and want to help the Israelis and the Palestinians resolve their differences over roadmap issues.

And thirdly is to help the Palestinians develop the infrastructure necessary for a democracy, an economy, and security forces that are capable of doing what the President and the Prime Minister want to have done. And we're very much engaged. I'm looking forward to seeing Tony Blair tomorrow, who is the Quartet's representative, and to find out what he has been doing and what progress is being made.

I am confident that with proper help a— the state of Palestine will emerge. And I'm confident that when it emerges, it will be a major step toward peace. I am confident that the status quo is unacceptable, Mr. President, and we want to help you. And I appreciate your vision, and I appreciate your courage, and I appreciate your hospitality, and I appreciate you giving me a chance to talk to the press, of course. [*Laughter*]

A couple of questions, I understand.

Palestinian Authority-Israel Security Situation/Israeli Settlements

Q. Mr. President Abu Mazen, what are the results of your—this visit? Mr. President Bush, you said more than once that the Palestinian side must fulfill its obligations, and Mr. Fayyad has had a security plan to help. And—[*inaudible*]—went to Annapolis, and he commended that security plan, and then Israel destroyed all those efforts in Annapolis. How can the Palestinian Authority do security efforts that are successful while Israel destroys and undermines all their efforts in the occupied territories?

The other side of the question: Are you willing to give guarantees for the Palestinian side to declaring a freezing on settlements immediately? And thank you.

President Abbas. We are fully satisfied with the outcome that we reached through this visit of Mr. President George Bush. We spoke about all topics that might occur to your mind and that might not occur to your mind as well. All the issues are in agreement. We are agreed on all topics. All topics are clear.

In the near future, in the coming few days, we are going to bilateral negotiations with the Israelis in order to discuss the final status negotiations, final status issues. And as Mr. President said, there are three themes. The other theme is implementing the roadmap through the committee, the trilateral committee. And the third point is the economic and security conditions in Palestinian Territories. We have great hopes that during 2008 we will reach the final status and a peace treaty with Israel.

President Bush. Each side has got obligations under the roadmap. Settlements are clearly stated in the roadmap obligations for Israel. We have made our concerns about expansion of settlements known, and we expect both parties to honor their obligations under the roadmap.

Secondly, we're spending—General Dayton is spending a lot of time trying to help the President and the Prime Minister develop security forces that are effective. There's no question in my mind the commitment to provide security for the average citizen is strong. The question is the capabilities. And the truth of the matter is, there needs to be a fair amount of work done to make sure that the security forces

are modernized, well trained, and prepared with a proper chain of command to respond. And I will tell you, I firmly believe the security forces are improving.

I remember our visit in New York, and we discussed this during the U.N. General Assembly. And by any objective measurement, the Palestinian security forces in the West Bank are improving.

And so my message to the Israelis is that they ought to help, not hinder, the modernization of the Palestinian security force. It's in their interests that a government dedicated to peace and understanding the need for two states to live side by side in peace have a modern force.

It's got—very important for the Government to be able to assure people that if there is a need, there will be an effective force to provide security. That's just step one of having credibility with the people. And to the extent that Israeli actions have undermined the effectiveness of the Palestinian force or the authority of the state relative to the average citizen is something that we don't agree with and have made our position clear.

Myers [Steven Lee Myers, New York Times], she just called on you.

Palestinian Authority-Israel Security Situation/Palestinian State

Q. [*Inaudible*]

President Bush. No, that's the roadmap obligation I was talking about.

Q. Mr. President, thank you. I understand you drove in today, and so I assume you passed through the security barrier on the way in——

President Bush. Yes.

Q. ——and President Abbas talked about some of the obstacles that confront Palestinians in their daily life. And I wonder if you could reflect on your own impression.

President Bush. Yes. He's asking me about the checkpoints I drove through and what—my impression about what it was like to drive through checkpoints. I can understand why the Palestinians are frustrated driving through checkpoints. I can also understand that until confidence is gained on both sides, why the Israelis would want there to be a sense of security. In other words, they don't want a state on their border from which attacks would be launched. I can understand that. Any reasonable person can understand that. Why would you work to have a state on your border if you weren't confident they'd be a partner in peace?

And so checkpoints create frustrations for people. They create a sense of security for Israel; they create massive frustrations for the Palestinians. You'll be happy to hear that my motorcade of a mere 45 cars was able to make it through without being stopped. But—[*laughter*]—I'm not so exactly sure that's what happens to the average person. And so the whole object is to create a state that is capable of defending itself internally and giving confidence to its neighbor that checkpoints won't be needed.

Now, the vision of the Palestinian state is one of contiguous territory. In other words, as I said earlier in my administration, I said, Swiss cheese isn't going to work when it comes to the outline of a state. And I mean that. There is no way that this good man can assure the Palestinians of a hopeful future if there's not contiguous territory. And we—that position is abundantly clear to both sides. Therefore, the ultimate vision, of course, is there be no checkpoints throughout the Palestinian state-to-be.

And you know, this is the issue. We're working through how to gain enough confidence on both sides so that checkpoints won't be necessary and a state can emerge. My judgment is, I can understand frustrations. I mean, I hear it a lot. I heard it but—you know, the chief negotiator spent 2 hours at a checkpoint. All he was trying to do was go negotiate. And I can see that—I can see the frustrations. Look, I

also understand that people in Israel—and the truth of the matter is, in the Palestinian Territories, the average citizen wants to know whether or not there's going to be protection from the violent few who murder.

The security of a state is essential, particularly in a day and age when people simply disregard the value of human life and kill. And so these checkpoints reflect the reality, Myers. And what we're trying to do is alter the reality by laying out a vision that is much more hopeful than the status quo.

Question.

Middle East Peace Process/Israeli Settlements

Q. [*Inaudible*]—Mr. President George W. Bush, you lead the superpower in this world. You launched war against Iraq after the Iraqi leadership refused to implement the United Nations resolutions. My question now is, what the problem to ask Israel just to accept and to respect the United Nations resolutions relating to the Palestinian problem, which—[*inaudible*]—facilitating the achievement of ending the Israeli occupation to the Arab territories and—[*inaudible*]—facilitating also the solution between Palestinians and the Israelis?

And for Mahmoud Abbas, did you ask President George Bush to ask Israel to freeze settlements fully in order to enable negotiations from success?

President Bush. Yes, but tell me the part about the U.N. thing again? What were you—I couldn't understand you very well.

Q. I just asked, why you ask Israel to accept the United Nations resolutions related to the Palestinian problem just to facilitate the solution and to end the occupation?

President Bush. Yes, actually, I'm asking Israel to negotiate in good faith with an elected leader of the Palestinian Territory to come up with a permanent solution that—look, the U.N. deal didn't work in the past. And so now we're going to have an opportunity to redefine the future by having a state negotiated between an elected leader of the Palestinian people as well as the Prime Minister of Israel. This is an opportunity to move forward. And the only way for—the only way to defeat the terrorists in the long run is to offer an alternative vision that is more hopeful. And that's what we're attempting to do, sir.

We can stay stuck in the past, which will yield nothing good for the Palestinians, in my judgment. We can chart a hopeful future, and that's exactly what this process is intending to do: to redefine the future for the Palestinian citizens and the Israelis.

I am confident that two democratic states living side by side in peace is in the interests not only of the Palestinians and the Israelis but of the world. The question is whether or not the hard issues can be resolved and the vision emerges so that the choice is clear amongst the Palestinians, the choice being, do you want this state, or do you want the status quo? Do you want a future based upon a democratic state, or do you want the same old stuff? And that's a choice that I'm confident if the Palestinian people are given, they will choose peace.

And so that's what we're trying to do, sir.

President Abbas. The settlement for us is considered an obstacle for negotiations. And we have spoke more than once with the—Mr. Prime Minister Olmert very frankly. And we also spoke in this meeting with President George Bush, and consequently, the President understood this issue. And we have heard the statements given by the Secretary of State, Dr. Rice, and she had her point of view regarding settlements was very positive.

Gaza/Hamas

Q. Good morning. President Bush, Prime Minister Olmert said that peace is unlikely as long as Gaza militants continue their attacks on Israel. How do you see President Abbas getting control of Gaza?

And you, Mr. President Abbas, how do you intend, actually, to get control of Gaza, and do you think this is feasible by the end of the year and by—at the end of Mr. Bush Presidency?

President Bush. First of all, Gaza is a tough situation. I don't know whether you can solve it in a year or not. But I know this: It can't be solved unless the Prime Minister—the President has a vision that he can lay out to the people of Gaza that says, here's your choice: Do you want those who have created chaos to run your country, or do you want those of us who negotiated a settlement with the Israelis that will lead for lasting peace?

There is a competing vision taking place in Gaza. And in my judgment, Hamas, which I felt ran on a campaign of, we're going to improve your lives through better education and better health, have delivered nothing but misery. And I'm convinced his Government will yield a hopeful future. And the best way to make that abundantly clear is for there to be a vision that's understandable.

See, the past has just been empty words, you know. We've—actually, it hasn't been that much—I'm the only President that's really articulated a two-state solution so far. But saying two states really doesn't have much bearing until borders are defined, right of return issues resolved, there's—Jerusalem is understood, the security measures—the common security measures will be in place. That's what I'm talking about. I'm talking about a clear, defined state around which people can rally.

And there's going to be no—there will be no better difference, a clearer difference, than the vision of Hamas in Gaza and the vision of the President and the Prime Minister and his team based here in Ramallah. And to me, that's how you solve the issue in the long term. And the definition of long term, I don't know what it means. I'm not a timetable person. Actually, I am on a timetable; I've got 12 months. [*Laughter*] But it's—I'm impressed by the President's understanding about how a vision and a hopeful future is—will help clearly define the stakes amongst the Palestinian people.

President Abbas. Gaza is considered a coup by us; we consider it a coup d'etat, what happened in Gaza.

[*A call to prayer could be heard in the background.*]

President Abbas. Now with a call to prayer—we consider it a coup d'etat. [*Laughter*] And we deal with Gaza at two levels. The first is that we deal with the people as part of us, and we take full responsibility that is necessary towards our people. We spend in Gaza 58 percent of our budget. This is not to—it is our duty towards our people that we provide them with all they need.

As for the issue of Hamas, we said that this is a coup, and they have to retreat from this coup, and they have to recognize international legitimacy, all international legitimacy, and to recognize the Arab Peace Initiative as well. In this case, we can—we will have another talk.

President Bush. Thank you all.

NOTE: The President's news conference began at 11:12 a.m. at the Muqata. In his remarks, the President referred to Prime Minister Ehud Olmert of Israel; Lt. Gen. William M. Fraser III, USAF, U.S. monitor of the Israeli-Palestinian roadmap peace plan; Lt. Gen. Keith W. Dayton, USA, U.S. security coordinator to Israel and the Palestinian Authority; and former Prime Minister Tony Blair of the United Kingdom, Quartet Representative in the Middle East. A reporter referred to Prime Minister Salam Fayyad of the Palestinian Authority. President Abbas and some reporters spoke in Arabic, and their remarks were translated by an interpreter.

Remarks Following a Visit to the Church of the Nativity in Bethlehem, Palestinian Territories
January 10, 2008

Madam Minister, thank you very much for your hospitality. It's been a moving moment for me and the delegation to be here at the Church of the Nativity. For those of us who practice the Christian faith, there's really no more holy site than the place where our Savior was born.

And I want to thank the Government for arranging this trip. I also thank very much the three different churches for welcoming me here. It's a fascinating history in this church, and so not only was my soul uplifted, my knowledge of history was enriched.

I want to thank the people of Bethlehem for enduring a Presidential trip. I know it's been inconvenient for you. I very much appreciate your tolerating my entourage.

And someday, I hope that as a result of a formation of a Palestinian state, there won't be walls and checkpoints, that people will be able to move freely in a democratic state. That's the vision, greatly inspired by my belief that there is an Almighty and a gift of that Almighty to each man, woman, and child on the face of the Earth is freedom. And I felt it strongly here today.

Anyway, thank you very much.

NOTE: The President spoke at 2:46 p.m. In his remarks, he referred to Minister of Tourism and Antiquities Khouloud Daibes of the Palestinian Authority.

Remarks on the Middle East Peace Process in Jerusalem, Israel
January 10, 2008

Good afternoon. I'd like to first thank Prime Minister Olmert and President Abbas for their hospitality during my trip here to the Holy Land. We've had very good meetings, and now is the time to make difficult choices.

I underscored to both Prime Minister Olmert and President Abbas that progress needs to be made on four parallel tracks. First, both sides need to fulfill their commitments under the roadmap. Second, the Palestinians need to build their economy and their political and security institutions. And to do that, they need the help of Israel, the region, and the international community. Third, I reiterate my appreciation for the Arab League Peace Initiative, and I call upon the Arab countries to reach out to Israel, a step that is long overdue.

In addition to these three tracks, both sides are getting down to the business of negotiating. I called upon both leaders to make sure their teams negotiate seriously, starting right now. I strongly supported the decision of the two leaders to continue their regular summit meetings, because they are the ones who can and must and, I am convinced, will lead.

I share with these two leaders the vision of two democratic states, Israel and Palestine, living side by side in peace and security. Both of these leaders believe that the outcome is in the interest of their peoples and are determined to arrive at a negotiated solution to achieve it.

The point of departure for permanent status negotiations to realize this vision seems clear. There should be an end to the occupation that began in 1967. The agreement must establish Palestine as a homeland for the Palestinian people, just as Israel is a homeland for the Jewish people. These negotiations must ensure that Israel has secure, recognized, and defensible borders. And they must ensure that the state of Palestine is viable, contiguous, sovereign, and independent.

It is vital that each side understands that satisfying the other's fundamental objectives is key to a successful agreement. Security for Israel and viability for the Palestinian state are in the mutual interests of both parties.

Achieving an agreement will require painful political concessions by both sides. While territory is an issue for both parties to decide, I believe that any peace agreement between them will require mutually agreed adjustments to the armistice lines of 1949 to reflect current realities and to ensure that the Palestinian state is viable and contiguous. I believe we need to look to the establishment of a Palestinian state and new international mechanisms, including compensation, to resolve the refugee issue.

I reaffirm to each leader that implementation of any agreement is subject to implementation of the roadmap. Neither party should undertake any activity that contravenes roadmap obligations or prejudices the final status negotiations. On the Israeli side, that includes ending settlement expansion and removing unauthorized outposts. On the Palestinian side, that includes confronting terrorists and dismantling terrorist infrastructure.

I know Jerusalem is a tough issue. Both sides have deeply felt political and religious concerns. I fully understand that finding a solution to this issue will be one of the most difficult challenges on the road to peace, but that is the road we have chosen to walk.

Security is fundamental. No agreement and no Palestinian state will be born of terror. I reaffirm America's steadfast commitment to Israel's security.

The establishment of the state of Palestine is long overdue. The Palestinian people deserve it, and it will enhance the stability of the region, and it will contribute to the security of the people of Israel. The peace agreement should happen and can happen by the end of this year. I know each leader shares that important goal, and I am committed to doing all I can to achieve it.

Thank you.

NOTE: The President spoke at 5:27 p.m. at the King David Hotel. In his remarks, he referred to Prime Minister Ehud Olmert of Israel; and President Mahmoud Abbas of the Palestinian Authority.

Remarks During a Visit to Yad Vashem in Jerusalem
January 11, 2008

Mr. President and Mr. Prime Minister, thank you for your wonderful hospitality. I would hope as many people in the world would come to this place, it would be a sobering reminder that evil exists and a call that when we find evil, we must resist it. It also is a—I guess I came away with this impression, that I was most impressed that people, in the face of horror and evil, would not forsake their God, that in the face of unspeakable crimes against humanity, brave souls, young and old, stood strong for what they believe.

It's an honor to be here. It is a moving experience, and it is a living memory that is important. Thank you, sir.

NOTE: The President spoke at 9:43 a.m. In his remarks, he referred to President Shimon Peres and Prime Minister Ehud Olmert of Israel; and Avner Shalev, chairman, Yad Vashem Directorate.

Remarks Following a Meeting With Senior Administration Officials and an Exchange With Reporters at Camp Arifjan, Kuwait
January 12, 2008

Good morning. I just had a really good meeting with Ambassador Crocker, General Petraeus, Secretary Rice, and members of my national security team. We discussed the situation in Iraq. We discussed the progress that's being made, the challenges that lie ahead, and we discussed the fact that what happens in Iraq impacts everything else in this vital region.

I really appreciate you all coming over, but more importantly, I appreciate your service to the country.

One year ago, I addressed the American people to announce a new way forward in Iraq. At that time, Iraq was riven by sectarian violence. The violence had increased over the course of 2006, and it threatened the collapse of the political process. Economic activity was languishing. Al Qaida was strengthening its grip in critical parts of Iraq, including parts of the capital city of Baghdad. Shi'a extremist groups, some with the backing from Iran, were increasing their attacks on coalition and Iraqi forces.

Our strategy simply wasn't working, and the world was watching. Our friends and foes had the same question: Would we turn our back on our friends and allow Iraq to descend into chaos? Or would we change our approach and stand with the Iraqi people and help them take back their country from the terrorists and extremists?

We chose to support our Iraqi partners; we chose to help them protect the Iraqi people from the terrorists and radicals. The new way forward I announced 1 year ago changed our approach in fundamental ways. We sent more combat troops to Iraq. We refocused their mission to protecting the Iraqi people and to fighting the enemy in the strongholds and denying sanctuary anywhere in the country. We began a diplomatic surge to cut off the networks of foreign fighters that were flowing into Iraq from Syria and to cut the support of Shi'a extremists coming from Iran and to encourage the region to give more support to the Iraqi Government. We surged civilians into Iraq to support our military efforts, doubling the number of Provincial Reconstruction Teams and facilitating Iraqi political reconciliation from the bottom up.

I nominated General Petraeus and Ambassador Crocker to carry out this new strategy. This was a tough assignment for them. And they and all the good men and women they're privileged to lead are doing an outstanding job.

Iraq is now a different place from 1 year ago. Much hard work remains, but levels of violence are significantly reduced. Hope is returning to Baghdad, and hope is returning to towns and villages throughout the country. Iraqis who fled the violence are beginning to return and rebuild their lives.

Al Qaida remains dangerous, and it will continue to target the innocent with violence. But we've dealt Al Qaida in Iraq heavy blows, and it now faces a growing uprising of ordinary Iraqis who want to live peaceful lives. Extremist militias remain a concern, but they too have been disrupted, and moderates are turning on those who espouse violence. Iran's role in fomenting violence has been exposed. Iranian agents are in our custody, and we are learning more about how Iran has supported extremist groups with training and lethal aid.

Iraqis are gradually take control of their country. Over the past year, Iraqi forces conducted a surge of their own, generating well over 100,000 more Iraqi police and soldiers to sustain the security gains. Tens of thousands of concerned local citizens are protecting their communities and working with coalition and Iraqi forces to ensure Al Qaida cannot return. The Iraqi Government is distributing oil revenues across the country so that reconstruction can follow hard-won security gains. And from Kirkuk to Ramadi to Karbala to Baghdad, the people of Iraq—Sunni, Shi'a, and Kurd—are coming together at the grassroots to build a common future.

These improvements are allowing some U.S. forces to return home, a return on success that has now begun. One Army brigade and one Marine expeditionary unit have already come home, and they will not be replaced. In the coming months, four additional brigades and two Marine battalions will follow suit. Any additional reduction will be based on the recommendation of General Petraeus, and those recommendations will be based entirely on the conditions on the ground in Iraq.

The months ahead offer prospects for further progress. Iraq's local leaders need to continue to improve conditions from the bottom up. And Iraq's national leaders need to follow up on the successful adoption of pension reform by passing a revised de-Ba'athification law and a national budget. And the linkages between the local and national levels must be strengthened and expanded. Iraqi security forces need to continue to grow and improve and take the fight to Al Qaida and other extremist groups. Criminals need to be defeated in Iraqi neighborhoods. Syria needs to further reduce the flow of terrorists to the territory, especially suicide bombers. Iran must stop supporting the militia special groups that attack Iraqi and coalition forces and kidnap and kill Iraqi officials.

The international community must remain engaged, including through the third expanded ministerial meeting on Iraq, which will take place right here in Kuwait. I had the honor last night of telling His Highness how much we appreciated the fact that Kuwait has taken the lead in hosting these meetings.

We cannot take the achievements of 2007 for granted. We must do all we can to ensure that 2008 brings even greater progress for Iraq's young democracy.

America is going to do our part. Long-term success in Iraq is vital to our friends here in the region and to America's national security. And long-term success will require active U.S. engagement that outlasts my Presidency. So at the invitation of Iraqi leaders, we're now building an enduring relationship with Iraq. This relationship will have diplomatic, economic, and security components, similar to relationships we have with Kuwait and other nations in this region and around the world. Most important, in a place where Saddam Hussein once menaced the world, the new U.S.-Iraqi relationship will strengthen a democracy that serves its people, fights terrorists, and serves as a beacon of freedom for millions across the Middle East.

Ambassador Crocker and General Petraeus will continue to carry out our policy in Iraq. And they need to get back to Baghdad, so I better stop talking. I want to thank them for your service. I want you to thank your families for how much I appreciate your sacrifices. I also want to thank the soldiers, sailors, airmen, marines, and coastguardsmen, as well as the diplomats, intelligence officers, civilian employees, and contractors and all their families who are doing the work necessary to lay the foundation for peace.

Thank you all for being here, and God bless you.

I'll answer a couple of questions. I'm going to ask them to lay out for a second; hold on for a minute.

Yes.

U.S. Troop Levels in Iraq/U.S. Personnel Serving Overseas

Q. Mr. President, did you hear anything today that makes you think that you can accelerate the troop withdrawals that you already talked about?

The President. General Petraeus made it clear to me that, from his perspective, that conditions on the ground will be that which guides his recommendations. And I made it clear that's what I want. In other words, our general has got to understand that success in Iraq is critical. In other words, that ought to be the primary concern when it comes to determining troop levels. And no better person to ask as to—on how to achieve success in Iraq than the general in charge of Iraq.

So that's what we discussed about. He didn't talk about specific levels; he talked about continually assessing the situation on the ground and will report to Congress in March. I wanted to assure him that any decision he recommends needs to be based upon success. That's what happened the last time around. When we were failing, I said, what's it take to—what do you need to win, not lose? What is it we need to—what troop levels do we need to make sure that we can achieve this objective?

And a lot of people thought that I was going to recommend pulling out or pulling back. Quite the contrary; I recommended increasing the number of forces so they could get more in the fight, because I believe all along, if people are given a chance to live in a free society, they'll do the hard work necessary to live in a free society.

And I understand the fundamental conflict we're in. We're in a conflict between those who want to live in peace and those who murder the innocent to achieve a hateful vision. People say, "What are you talking about, hateful vision?" Well, I said, all you got to do is look at what life was like if you were a young girl under the Taliban in Afghanistan. These haters have no vision of hope. They want to impose their ideology on every man, woman, and child in the societies which they feel like they should dominate. Our vision is different, and the vision of most Iraqis is different. And that is, they want to be free; they want to be able to express themselves in a free society. And I believe, if given a chance, the ordinary citizen will sacrifice for that vision every time. But they needed the security; they needed the feeling of security in order to do so.

So it's that same principle that's going to guide my decision. And I made it clear to the general that I need to know his considered judgment about what it takes to make sure the security gains we have achieved remain in place. And that's what the discussion was about, besides me thanking him.

But we cannot take for granted our troops overseas and our diplomats overseas. These folks have been gone from their home for a long time, and they miss their families. And so one of the purposes of this trip is to make it abundantly clear to those serving our country that, one, they have earned the respect of the United States of America, and that as the President of a great country, I look forward to telling these great people how much we admire them and appreciate them.

Yes.

U.S. Troop Levels in Iraq

Q. It sounds like you feel like you're on track for a possible drawdown. Can you say that you feel you're on track from what you heard from General Petraeus?

The President. I think the only thing I can tell you we're on track for is to follow through on that which he recommended last September and that we'll be on track getting down to 15. And that's what we're on track for. My attitude is, if he didn't want to continue the drawdown, that's fine with me, in order to make sure we succeed, see. I said to the general, if you want to slow her down, fine; it's up to you. And so the only thing I can tell you we're on track for is, we're doing what we said was going to happen: One battalion is out; the Marines are out to the extent that we said they were going to come out; and then four more are coming down and be out by July, just like he recommended.

Progress in Iraq

Q. What about the political benchmarks? Do those no longer matter?

The President. Of course they matter. They matter to the Iraqis a lot. It's a sign of reconciliation. I just mentioned they passed a pension law, which, of course, got a huge yawn in our press. But that's—well, that's okay. [*Laughter*] But it was a—we can't pass our—we can't reform our own pension system, like Social Security, but they did. And is that the only answer? No. I mean, they got a lot more work to do, but they're passing law. And they're now in the process of a budget—getting their budget passed and a de-Ba'ath law. And we expect them to work hard on the federalism issue. And yes, that's absolutely important, benchmarks.

Q. Are they behind where you thought they would be, the significant benchmarks?

The President. Are they behind? I wouldn't say "significant." I think that's an exaggeration of what I think. I would say that I wish they had passed more law. Of course, in December, I was wishing our Legislature had passed more law at times too. But, no, they've got work to do, no question about it. There are two types of reconciliation: that which can be achieved by passage of national law; and the other kind is the bottom-up reconciliation, where people in neighborhoods are just—who are sick and tired of criminality and violence say, "Look, let's do something about it."

That's—one of the interesting things, Martha [Martha Raddatz, ABC News], and you follow this a lot closer than a lot of these other folks have—not to be blowing your horn or anything, but—is these concerned citizen groups, CLCs, people who have stepped forward and said, we've had enough of this; we're sick and tired of violence. Some 80,000 local citizens who are now helping provide local security so their children can have—grow up in a free society, and they can be peaceful; that's what you're seeing. And a part of the Iraqi surge was not only 100,000 additional troops and police, but local citizens coming forward and to—helping to provide security for their neighborhoods. And that's bottom-up reconciliation.

I'm not making excuses for a government, but to go from a tyranny to a democracy overnight is virtually impossible. And so when you say, am I pleased with the progress? What they have gone through and where they are today, I think, is good

progress. Have they done enough? No. Are we going to continue to work with them to do more? Absolutely. Absolutely. Our message is very clear: It's in your interest that you pass good law. And so I'm optimistic they'll get laws passed here pretty quick, and we'll continue to press to make it happen.

Listen, thank you very much. I'm going to speak to the troops, and I'm looking forward to it. Thank you.

NOTE: The President spoke at 10:05 a.m. In his remarks, he referred to Gen. David H. Petraeus, USA, commanding general, Multi-National Force—Iraq; and Amir Sabah al-Ahmad al-Jabir al-Sabah of Kuwait.

Remarks to Military Personnel at Camp Arifjan
January 12, 2008

The President. Hooah!

Audience members. Hooah!

The President. Yes, thanks for coming out. [*Laughter*] It's good to see you. Command Sergeant Major Harbin, thank—he's a silver-tongued fox. [*Laughter*] Thank you for the introduction, Command Sergeant. I'm honored to be introduced by one of our enlisted personnel. After all, our military is strong because of the sergeant corps of the military.

I'm also proud to be with our officers. I particularly want to thank General Lovelace for his leadership. I'm honored to be with the brave men and women of the 3d Army. I also offer greetings to the marines, sailors, airmen, coastguardsmen——

Audience member. Whoo! [*Laughter*]

The President. ——as well as all the Department of Army civilians——

Audience member. Hooray! [*Laughter*]

The President. I'm here to thank you for your service. I want you to know, the

American people are mighty proud of you, and so am I. Sorry my wife is not with me. She was here the other day, though. She sends her best. I'm traveling today with the Secretary of State, Condoleezza Rice. I just had a meeting with our Ambassador and our commander on the ground in Iraq. I'm proud to be here with Ambassador Ryan Crocker and General David Petraeus.

Since the 3d Army was established at the close of World War I, its soldiers have proven themselves true to their motto, "The Third . . . Always First." You're the first bunch I've been talking to here on my trip, first bunch of those wearing the uniform. People say, "You looking forward to the trip?" I said, one thing I'm really looking forward to is seeing the men and women who represent the United States in our military. The reason I am is—anxious to be here is because we can't thank you enough and we can't thank your families enough for doing the hard work necessary to protect the United States of America.

I appreciate what this 3d Army did in World War II. I hope you do too, as well. After all, you're members of Patton's own; played a vital role in the destruction of the Nazi war machine. They helped liberate about 12,000 towns; at least that's according to the history of the 3d Army. From their noble ranks came soldiers with some of our Nation's highest directors [decorations],[*] including 19 recipients of the Medal of Honor. You—a distinguished history, and you're making history yourselves. Sometimes it's hard to forecast what the history pages are going to see when you're right in the midst of it all. Sometimes it's hard to judge how the 3d Army will be talked about by future Presidents when you're in the midst of protecting the country, when you're in the midst of dealing in a dangerous region.

But I want to tell you what the history will say. The history will say, it was when you were called upon, you served, and the service you rendered was absolutely necessary to defeat an enemy overseas so we do not have to face them here at home. It will say loud and clear that this military, comprised of brave men and women who sacrificed on behalf of a noble cause called peace, the men and women of this military understood that we're in an ideological struggle, that we're facing coldblooded murderers who kill the innocent to achieve their hateful vision of a future.

And they understood—history will show that those who wore the uniform in the beginning of the 21st century understood a timeless truth: that the ideology of—

---

[*] White House correction.

based upon liberty is necessary for peace; that in this ideological struggle, on the short term, we will find and bring the enemies to justice. But in the long term, the best way to defeat the ideology of hate is, one, with an ideology of hope, and that's one with liberty at its fundamental core.

It's hard work that you're doing, but it's necessary work. It's hard to be away from your home, but that's a soldier's life. When you get to e-mailing your family, you tell them I checked in with you. [*Laughter*] And you're looking pretty good. It looks like you haven't missed a meal. [*Laughter*] But you also tell them that the message I brought was, they're in this fight as well. And the citizens of the United States of America respect our military, and we respect our military families. And this Government will make sure that our families have a good life, with good support, when you're deployed overseas.

And so I thank you for what you're doing. There is no doubt in my mind that we will succeed. There is no doubt in my mind, when history was written, the final page will say, victory was achieved by the United States of America for the good of the world; that by doing the hard work now, we can look back and say, the United States of America is more secure and generations of Americans will be able to live in peace.

God bless you, and God bless the United States.

NOTE: The President spoke at 10:38 a.m. In his remarks, he referred to CSM Don Harbin, USA, command sergeant major, Area Support Group—Kuwait; Lt. Gen. James L. Lovelace, USA, commanding general, 3d Army; and Gen. David H. Petraeus, USA, commanding general, Multi-National Force—Iraq.

Remarks Prior to a Discussion on Democracy and Development With Kuwaiti Women in Kuwait City, Kuwait
January 12, 2008

The President. I want to thank these ladies from Kuwait for joining me and the Charge. I'm really looking forward to the conversation. Laura had met with some before and came back very impressed by the spirit and desire of Kuwaiti women to be full participants in Kuwaiti society.

First, I'd like to thank His Highness for his hospitality. Secondly, last night in a conversation with His Highness, I said, "Any regrets about having women vote in elections and run for elections?" He said, "Absolutely not." He said, "Our society is enriched by the participation of our women." And he's right. All societies are enriched by the participation of women. I happen to believe very strongly in the freedom agenda, and I think an integral part of that agenda is making sure that all participants in society have got an equal voice.

And one of the interesting—I think when people look back at the history of the Middle East and history of the world, it's going to be women who helped lead the freedom agenda. And it's happening right here in Kuwait. We've had people here at the table who ran for Kuwaiti parliament. And Jenan ran; she said—I told her the first race I ever ran, I lost. [*Laughter*]. And she said, "Well, the first race I ever ran, I lost too." But she intends to win next time around.

And so I appreciate you all coming. I'm honored to be with you. We want to help. Part of our democracy agenda, of course, is the empowerment of women.

And so thank you for taking time. Doctor, would you like to have a few comments?

Former Minister of Health Maasouma Al-Mubarak of Kuwait. Of course. First of all, we'd like to welcome you, Mr. President. As you probably watched the—our media this morning, the media said that we are saying it from the deep of our hearts: Welcome, Mr. President.

The President. Thank you.

Ms. Al-Mubarak. Definitely, we Kuwaitis look with great appreciation to the role that the American people played in the liberation of Kuwait, and we remember with great appreciation your father role, Mr. Bush. And we call him here in Kuwait, Bu Abdullah. That means he's so close to us, and the role that he played, really still and forever, we remember it as Kuwaitis.

And looking to the domestic issues in Kuwait, and especially the freedom that we are enjoying, looking to this group of ladies that are gathered totally by the Embassy, this is something that you don't have as much in lots of the countries and rarely in the Middle Eastern countries. Our Government has nothing to do with the gathering and nothing to do with this election of the people. And that gives a great idea that we speak our minds; we speak our hearts. And we are so glad to be with you, Mr. President.

And regarding the issues, really, that we are having in mind, Mr. President, as women and as mothers, we're really asking you, as a person and as the leader of the great United States, for to put an end for the agony of mothers in Kuwait, for the people, and for our fellow citizens in Guantanamo. And we are sure that your human feelings so much with us in that, and we need really your role and your assistance in that regard.

And also, as citizens and people from this region, we deserve to live in peace. We are looking forward to live in peace. We are really—not only in Kuwait, but in the whole region, this region, the Gulf region, suffered for years and years from—suffering from the wars and the impact of the wars. And we need your assistance, your help, your good will to have peace in this part of the world. And as you've played lots of roles in having peace and security in lots of parts of the world—you, your father, and the other President.

Again, welcome, Mr. President.

The President. Thank you. Thanks.

NOTE: The President spoke at 12:03 p.m. at the U.S. Embassy. In his remarks, he referred to Deputy Chief of Mission and Charge d'Affaires Alan Misenheimer of the U.S. Embassy in Kuwait; Amir Sabah al-Ahmad al-Jabir al-Sabah of Kuwait; and Jenan Boushehri, former candidate for the Kuwait Municipal Council.

Remarks at a Welcoming Ceremony in Manama, Bahrain
January 12, 2008

Your Majesty, thank you very much for bestowing upon me the award. I'm most honored. I accept it on behalf of the people of the United States of America. I also thank you and the Crown Prince and the Prime Minister for your gracious hospitality. I am really honored to be the first U.S. sitting President to have visited your country. Perhaps I should say, it's about time.

The American people have a long friendship with the people of Bahrain. For decades, Bahrain has welcomed the United States Navy and is now home to our 5th Fleet. Two years ago, I was pleased to sign legislation that strengthened our friendship and our relationship. It was the free trade agreement with Bahrain; it's America's first such agreement with any nation in the Gulf. This agreement is helping to pave way to freer and fairer trade between our countries so we can create jobs and opportunity and hope in both our lands.

Our two nations share a common vision for the future of the Middle East. Through our alliance, we share the burdens and risks of maintaining security as well as defending freedom throughout the region. We also believe in the power of democratic reform. Your Majesty, I appreciate the fact that

you're on the forefront of providing hope for people through democracy. Your nation has held two free elections since 2000. And in 2006, your people elected a woman to your parliament. Bahrain's reforms are making your nation stronger. You're showing strong leadership, and you're showing the way forward for other nations.

Your Majesty, I look forward to our meetings later today. I look forward to discussing how we continue—can continue to advance peace in the Middle East. I look forward to sharing with you my experiences that I had in Israel and the Palestinian Territories. I look forward to talking about how we can continue to ensure security in the Gulf. Together, we will continue to strengthen our friendship and our cooperation, and I'm proud to be with you, sir.

NOTE: The President spoke at 3:55 p.m. at Sakhir Palace. In his remarks, he referred to King Hamad bin Isa al-Khalifa, Crown Prince Sheikh Salman bin Hamad bin Isa al-Khalifa, and Prime Minister Khalifa bin Salman al-Khalifa of Bahrain. He also referred to Lateefa al-Geood, who was the first woman elected to the Council of Representatives of the National Assembly of Bahrain in 2006.

The President's Radio Address
January 12, 2008

Good morning. I'm speaking to you from the Middle East, where I have been meeting with friends and allies. We're discussing how we can work together to confront the extremists who threaten our future. And I have encouraged them to take advantage of the historic opportunity we have before us to advance peace, freedom, and security in this vital part of the world.

My first stop was Israel and the Palestinian Territories. I had good meetings with Israeli Prime Minister Olmert and Palestinian President Abbas. Both these men are committed to peace in the Holy Land. Both these men have been elected by their people. And both share a vision of two democratic states, Israel and Palestine, living side by side in peace and security.

I came away encouraged by my meetings with Israeli and Palestinian leaders. Each side understands that the key to achieving its own goals is helping the other side achieve its goals. For the Israelis, their main goal is ensuring the safety of their people and the security of their nation. For the Palestinians, the goal is a state of their own, where they can enjoy the dignity that comes with sovereignty and self-government.

In plain language, the result must be the establishment of a free and democratic homeland for the Palestinian people, just as Israel is a free and democratic homeland for the Jewish people. For this to happen, the Israelis must have secure, recognized, and defensible borders, and the Palestinians must have a state that is viable, contiguous, sovereign, and independent. Achieving this vision will require tough decisions and painful concessions from both sides.

I believe that a peace agreement between Israelis and Palestinians that defines a Palestinian state is possible this year. Prime Minister Olmert made clear to me that he understands a democratic Palestinian state is in the long-term security interests of Israel. President Abbas is committed to achieving this Palestinian state through negotiation. The United States cannot impose an agreement on the Israelis and Palestinians; that is something they must work out themselves. But with hard work and good will on both sides, they can make it happen. And both men are getting down to the serious work of negotiation to make sure it does happen.

The United States will do all we can to encourage these negotiations and promote reconciliation between Israelis and Palestinians. But the international community has a responsibility to help as well. In particular, the Arab nations of the Gulf have a responsibility both to support President Abbas, Prime Minister Fayyad, and other Palestinian leaders as they work for peace and to work for a larger reconciliation between Israel and the Arab world. And in my meetings with Arab leaders over the next few days, I will urge them to do their part.

A democratic Palestinian state is in the interests of the Palestinians. It is in the long-term security interests of Israel. And it is in the interests of a world at war with terrorists and extremists trying to impose their brutal vision on the Middle East. By helping the Israeli and Palestinian people lay the foundation for lasting peace, we will help build a more hopeful future for the Holy Land and a safer world for the American people.

Thank you for listening.

NOTE: The address was recorded at 5:05 p.m. on January 11 at the Bayan Palace Guest House in Kuwait City, Kuwait, for broadcast at 10:06 a.m., e.d.t., on January 12. The transcript was made available by the Office of the Press Secretary on January 11, but was embargoed for release until the broadcast.

Due to the 8-hour time difference, the address was broadcast after the President's remarks in Kuwait and Bahrain. In his address, the President referred to Prime Minister Salam Fayyad of the Palestinian Authority. The Office of the Press Secretary also released a Spanish language transcript of this address.

Remarks in Abu Dhabi, United Arab Emirates
January 13, 2008

Dr. Aida, thank you very much for the kind introduction. Ministers, members of the diplomatic corps, and distinguished guests: I am honored by the opportunity to stand on Arab soil and speak to the people of this nation and this region.

Throughout the sweep of history, the lands that the Arab people call home have played a pivotal role in world affairs. These lands sit at the juncture of three great continents, Europe and Asia and Africa. These lands have given birth to three of the world's major religions. These lands have seen the rise and fall of great civilizations. And in the 21st century, these lands are once again playing a central role in the human story.

A great new era is unfolding before us. This new era is founded on the equality of all people before God. This new era is being built with the understanding that power is a trust that must be exercised with the consent of the governed and deliver equal justice under the law. And this new era offers hope for the millions across the Middle East who yearn for a future of peace and progress and opportunity.

Here in Abu Dhabi, we see clearly the outlines of this future. Beginning with the revered father of this country, Sheikh Zayed, you have succeeded in building a prosperous society out of the desert. You have opened your doors to the world economy. You have encouraged women to contribute to the development of your nation, and they have occupied some of your highest ministerial posts. You have held historic elections for the Federal National Council.

You have shown the world a model of a Muslim state that is tolerant toward people of other faiths. I'm proud to stand in a nation where the people have an opportunity to build a better future for themselves and their families. Thank you for your warm hospitality.

In my country, we speak of these developments as the advance of freedom. Others may call it the advance of justice. Yet whatever term we use, the ideal is the same. In a free and just society, every person is treated with dignity. In a free and just society, leaders are accountable to those they govern. And in a free and just society, individuals can rise as far as their talents and hard work will take them.

For decades, the people of this region saw their desire for liberty and justice denied at home and dismissed abroad in the name of stability. Today, your aspirations are threatened by violent extremists who murder the innocent in pursuit of power. These extremists have hijacked the noble religion of Islam and seek to impose their totalitarian ideology on millions. They hate freedom and they hate democracy because it fosters religious tolerance and allows people to chart their own future. They hate your government because it does not share their dark vision. They hate the United States because they know we stand with you in opposition to their brutal ambitions. And everywhere they go, they use murder and fear to foment instability to advance their aims.

One cause of instability is the extremists supported and embodied by the regime that sits in Tehran. Iran is today the world's leading state sponsor of terror. It sends hundreds of millions of dollars to extremists around the world, while its own people face repression and economic hardship at home. It undermines Lebanese hopes for peace by arming and aiding the terrorist group Hizballah. It subverts the hopes for peace in other parts of the region by funding terrorist groups like Hamas and the Palestine Islamic Jihad. It sends arms to the Taliban in Afghanistan and Shi'a militants in Iraq. It seeks to intimidate its neighbors with ballistic missiles and bellicose rhetoric. And finally, it defies the United Nations and destabilizes the region by refusing to be open and transparent about its nuclear programs and ambitions. Iran's actions threaten the security of nations everywhere. So the United States is strengthening our longstanding security commitments with our friends in the Gulf and rallying friends around the world to confront this danger, before it is too late.

The other major cause of instability is the extremists embodied by Al Qaida and its affiliates. On September 11th, 2001, Al Qaida murdered nearly 3,000 people on America's home soil. Some of the victims that day were innocent Muslims. And since then, Al Qaida and its allies have killed many more Muslims here in the Middle East, including women and children. In Afghanistan under the Taliban, on Iraq's Anbar Province, they ruled by intimidation and murder. Their goal is to impose that same dark rule across the Middle East. So they seek to topple your governments, acquire weapons of mass destruction, and drive a wedge between the people of the United States and the people of the Middle East. And they will fail. The United States joins you in your commitment to the freedom and security of this region, and we will not abandon you to terrorists or extremists.

The fight against the forces of extremism is the great ideological struggle of our time. And in this fight, our nations have a weapon more powerful than bombs or bullets. It is the desire for freedom and justice written into our hearts by Almighty God, and no terrorists or tyrant can take that away.

We see this desire in the 12 million Iraqis who dipped their fingers in purple ink as they voted in defiance of Al Qaida. We see the desire in the Palestinians who elected a President committed to peace and reconciliation. We see this desire in the thousands of Lebanese whose protests helped rid their country of a foreign occupier. And we see this desire in the brave dissidents and journalists who speak out against terror and oppression and injustice. We see this desire in the ordinary people across the Middle East who are sick of violence, who are sick of corruption, sick of empty promises, and who choose a free future whenever they are given a chance.

We also see leaders across this region beginning to respond to the desires of their people and take the steps that will help enhance the stability and prosperity of their nations. The recent elections to your Federal National Council represent the first part of a larger reform designed to make your government more modern and more representative. Algeria held its first competitive Presidential elections. Kuwait held elections in which women were allowed to vote and hold office for the first time. Citizens have voted in municipal elections in Saudi Arabia, in competitive parliamentary elections in Jordan and Morocco and Bahrain, and in a multiparty Presidential election in Yemen. Across the world, the majority of Muslim people live in a free and democratic society, and the people of the Middle East must continue to work for the day where that is also true of the lands that Islam first called home.

As freedom and justice advance in this part of the world, elections are important, but they're only a start. Free and just societies require strong civic institutions, such as houses of worship, universities, professional associations, local governments, and community groups. Free and just societies require habits of self-government that contribute to the rule of law. And free and just societies ultimately depend on the emergence of an engaged public whose citizens feel they have a real stake in their nation's future. All these developments contribute to the bond between government and the governed, between a people and their nation.

Free and just societies also create opportunities for their citizens. This opportunity begins with economic growth. In any society, the greatest resource is not the oil in the ground or the minerals beneath the soil; it is the skills and talents of the people, or as one Nobel-winning economist calls this, human capital. Across this region, you have an abundance of human capital in the men and women who are your citizens. By strengthening your education systems and opening your economies, you will unlock their potential, create vibrant and entrepreneurial societies, and usher in a new era where people have confidence that tomorrow will bring more opportunities than today.

In the last few years, the nations of this region have made some great progress. The World Bank reports that economic growth is strong, and it is rising. Saudi Arabia has joined the World Trade Organization. Jordan, Oman, Bahrain, and Morocco have signed free trade agreements with the United States. Your nations are attracting more foreign investment. Oil accounts for much of the economic growth here, but the nations of the Middle East are now investing in their people and building infrastructure and opening the door to foreign trade and investment.

America supports you in these efforts. We believe that trade and investment is the key to the future of hope and opportunity. We also believe that as we demand you open your markets, we should open ours as well. We're encouraged by the movement toward economic freedom that we're seeing across the Middle East.

Unfortunately, amid some steps forward in this region, we've also seen some setbacks. You cannot build trust when you hold an election where opposition candidates find themselves harassed or in prison. You cannot expect people to believe in the promise of a better future when they are jailed for peacefully petitioning their government. And you cannot stand up a modern and confident nation when you do not allow peace—people to voice their legitimate criticisms.

The United States appreciates that democratic progress requires tough choices. Our own history teaches us that the road to freedom is not always even, and democracy does not come overnight. Yet we also know that for all the difficulties, a society based on liberty is worth the sacrifice. We know that democracy is the only form of government that treats individuals with the dignity and equality that is their right. We know from experience that democracy is the only system of government that yields lasting peace and stability. In a democracy, leaders depend on their people, and most people do not want war and bloodshed and violence. Most people want lives of peace and opportunity. So it is the declared policy of the United States to support these peoples as they claim their freedom, as a matter of natural right and national interest.

I recognize that some people, including some in my own country, believe it is a mistake to support democratic freedom in the Middle East. They say that the Arab people are not ready for democracy. Of course, that is exactly what people said about the Japanese after World War II. Some said that having an emperor was incompatible with democracy. Some said that the Japanese religion was incompatible with democracy. Some said that advancing freedom in Japan and the Pacific was unwise because our interests lay in supporting pro-American leaders no matter how they ruled their people.

Fortunately, America rejected this advice, kept our faith in freedom, and stood with the people of Asia. The results are now in. Today, the people of Japan have both a working democracy and a hereditary emperor. They have preserved their traditional religious practices while tolerating the faiths of others. They are surrounded by many democracies that reflect the full diversity of the region. Some of these democracies have constitutional monarchies, some have parliaments, and some have presidents. Some of these democracies have Christian majorities, some have Muslim majorities, some have Hindu or Buddhist majorities. Yet for all the differences, the free nations of Asia all derive their authority from the consent of the governed, and all know the lasting stability that only freedom can bring.

This transformation would not have been possible without America's presence and perseverance over many decades. And just as our commitment to Asia helped people there secure their freedom and prosperity, our commitment to the Middle East will help you achieve yours. And you can know from our record in Asia that our commitment is real, it is strong, and it is lasting.

Today, America is using its influence to foster peace and reconciliation in the Holy Land. The Israelis have raised a thriving modern society out of rocky soil and want to live their lives in freedom and security at home and at peace with their neighbors. The Palestinian people aspire to build a nation of their own, where they can live in dignity and realize their dreams.

Today, Israelis and Palestinians each understand that the only way to realize their own goals is by helping one another. In other words, an independent, viable, democratic, and peaceful Palestinian state is more than the dream of the Palestinians; it's also the best guarantee for peace for all its neighbors. And the Israelis understand this. Leaders on both sides still have many tough decisions ahead, and they will need to back these decisions with real commitments. But the time has come for a Holy Land where Palestinian and Israeli live together in peace.

America will do our part. In Annapolis in November, the United States invited the Israelis and the Palestinians and other members of the international community to come to a conference. And I appreciate the fact that your country sent a delegate. It was a remarkable thing, to see a Palestinian President and an Israeli Prime Minister address a roomful of Arab leaders together. And the result was that the Palestinians and Israelis launched negotiations for the establishment of a Palestinian state and a broader peace.

The talks are just beginning, and our hopes are high. At the beginning of my trip, I met with both Israeli and Palestinian leaders. I was impressed by their commitment to move forward. And by supporting the legitimate aspirations of both sides, we will encourage reconciliation between the Israeli and Palestinian people, foster reconciliation between Israelis and Arabs, and build a foundation for lasting peace that will contribute to the security of every state in the Gulf.

And as you build a Middle East growing in peace and prosperity, the United States will be your partner. As we have done in places from Asia to Europe, we have forged new relationships with friends and allies, designed to help you protect your people and your borders. As we have done in places from Asia to Europe, we're helping you bring your economies into the global market. And as we have done in places from Asia to Europe, we have launched programs designed to help you promote economic reform and educational opportunity and political participation.

The United States has no desire for territory. We seek our shared security in your liberty. We believe that stability can only come through a free and just Middle East, where the extremists are marginalized by millions of moms and dads who want the same opportunities for their children that we have for ours. So today I would like to speak directly to the people of the Middle East.

To the Palestinian people: The dignity and sovereignty that is your right is within your reach. In President Abbas, you have a leader who understands that the path forward is through peaceful negotiations. Help him as he makes the tough decisions for peace. Oppose the extremists and terrorists who represent the greatest threat to a Palestinian state. The United States will help you build the institutions of democracy and prosperity and make your dreams of a state come true.

To the people of Israel: You know that peace and reconciliation with your neighbors is the best path to long-term security. We believe that peace is possible, though it requires tough decisions. The United States will always stand with Israel in the face of terrorism. And we will support you as you work to ensure that—the security of your people and bring peace and reconciliation to the Holy Land.

To the people of Iraq: You have made your choice for democracy, and you have stood firm in the face of terrible acts of murder. The terrorists and extremists cannot prevail. They are tormented by the sight of an old man voting or a young girl going to school, because they know a successful democracy is a mortal threat to their ambitions. The United States is fighting side by side with Sunni and Shi'a and Kurd to root out the terrorists and extremists. We have dealt them serious blows. The United States will continue to support you as you build the institutions of a free society. And together, we'll defeat our common enemies.

To the people of Iran: You are rich in culture and talent. You have a right to live under a government that listens to your wishes, respects your talents, and allows you to build better lives for your families. Unfortunately, your Government denies you these opportunities and threatens the peace and stability of your neighbors. So we call on the regime in Tehran to heed your will and to make itself accountable to you. The day will come when the people of Iran have a government that embraces liberty and justice and Iran joins the community of free nations. And when that good day comes, you will have no better friend than the United States of America.

To the leaders across the Middle East who are fighting the extremists: The United States will stand with you as you confront the terrorists and radicals. We urge you to join us in committing the resources to help the Palestinians build the institutions of a free society. Help the citizens of Lebanon preserve their Government and their sovereignty in the face of outside pressure from their neighbors. Show the Iraqis that you support them in their effort to build a more hopeful nation. And as you do these things, the best way to defeat the extremists in your midst is by opening your societies and trusting in your people and in giving them a voice in their nation.

And finally, to the people of the Middle East: We hear your cries for justice. We share your desire for a free and prosperous future. And as you struggle to find your voice and make your way in this world, the United States will stand with you.

For most of the world, there's no greater symbol of America than the Statue of Liberty. It was designed by a man who traveled wildly—widely in this part of the world and who had originally envisioned his woman bearing a torch as standing over the Suez Canal. Ultimately, of course, it was erected in New York Harbor, where it has been an inspiration to generations of immigrants. One of these immigrants was a poet-writer named Ameen Rihani. Gazing at her lamp held high, he wondered whether her sister might be erected in the lands of his Arab forefathers. Here is how he put it: "When will you turn your face toward the East, O Liberty?"

My friends, a future of liberty stands before you. It is your right, it is your dream, and it is your destiny.

God bless.

NOTE: The President spoke at 3:50 p.m. at the Emirates Palace Hotel. In his remarks, he referred to Aida Abdullah Al-Azdi, executive director, Emirates Center for Strategic Studies and Research; President Mahmoud Abbas of the Palestinian Authority; Nobel Prize winner and economist Gary S. Becker; and Prime Minister Ehud Olmert of Israel.

Remarks During a Tour of an Alternative Fuel Sources Exhibit in Abu Dhabi
January 14, 2008

It's amazing, isn't it? This country has gotten its wealth from the ground and is now reinvesting in alternative forms of energy, sometimes joint venturing with U.S. institutions, like MIT.

[*At this point, the tour continued, and no transcript was provided. The remarks continued as follows.*]

It's a modern society that is using its wealth not only to educate its people but to stay on the leading edge of technological change.

And, Your Highness, it's been an amazing experience for me. And I don't think most Americans understand the UAE. And I don't think most Americans understand that your education systems are modern and that you're thinking about the future in constructive ways. I appreciate the chance to learn about you.

[*The tour continued, and no transcript was provided. The remarks later concluded as follows.*]

My hope is my visit shines a spotlight on the Middle East, the opportunities to work constructively with our friends and allies, and shows people the truth about what life is like here in the UAE. This is a remarkable place. The architecture is beautiful, but the can-do spirit is amazing.

And we just heard a briefing about how they're going to construct a city based entirely upon renewable energy. It is—it will be an opportunity to see what works, what won't work, and an opportunity to share that technology with others.

And I appreciate the commitment to conservation and to the environment that the leadership has shown here. This has been a very interesting experience. I can't thank you enough for your hospitality.

NOTE: The President spoke at 9:37 a.m. at the Emirates Palace Hotel. In his remarks, he referred to Crown Prince Muhammad bin Zayid Al Nuhayyan of Abu Dhabi.

Remarks Prior to a Discussion With Young Arab Leaders in Dubai, United Arab Emirates
January 14, 2008

President Bush. Thank you, sir. I'm proud to be with you. Your Highness, thank you very much. I appreciate you picking this particular location, because it is a fantastic view of your—of Dubai.

First of all, just a couple of impressions: I'm most impressed with what I've seen here. The entrepreneurial spirit is strong and, equally importantly, the desire to make sure that all aspects of society are—

have hope and encouragement. And I appreciate your leadership, Your Highness.

And I want to thank you, sir, for having me. I'm looking forward to talking to the young leaders from around the region. I am going to answer your questions. And I also want you to understand something about America: that we respect you, we respect your religion, and we want to work together for the sake of freedom and peace.

And I thank—I'm particularly pleased to know that you have set up interchanges with some of the young in my country.

You'll find them to be compassionate, decent people who share the same goals and dreams. And so I want to thank you for coming.

Your Highness, I'm so honored by your hospitality.

Ruler of Dubai Sheikh Muhammad bin Rashid Al Maktum. Thank you, sir. It is our pleasure to have you.

President Bush. Thank you, sir.

NOTE: The President spoke at 1:22 p.m. at the Burj Al Arab Hotel.

Interview With Journalists in Riyadh, Saudi Arabia
January 15, 2008

White House Press Secretary Dana Perino. We'll start on the record, just some general comments and answer a couple of questions. And then if you feel like you want to go off the record, then we'll ask them to turn their tape recorders off.

The President. Okay, I'd like to go off the record. [*Laughter*]

Q. Give us a couple. [*Laughter*]

The President. We'll start with the older people first. [*Laughter*]

Secretary of State Condoleezza Rice/Iraq

Q. Well, one of the things that we were all interested in is Secretary Rice going to Iraq. When did you decide about that, and what's that all about?

The President. Decided when it looked like that there was serious momentum on the legislative front, that she could help push the momentum by her very presence. So I can't remember the exact moment; I would say it was maybe 10 days ago or something like that, when we were getting word that their budget moving, the de-Ba'ath law was on its—it had gone through two readings, I think, before the holidays. So it seemed to make sense that she go sit down with the—and the Presidency

Council happened to meet yesterday, which was good. So she's going to go and sit down with the leaders and encourage them to continue making progress.

Q. But not you, you decided it wasn't right for you to go.

The President. Yes. Yes, I decided it was best for Condi to go. I'm not going.

By the way, I talk to the Prime Minister quite frequently on secure SVTS, which is a real-time feed from our Embassy in Baghdad to the Situation Room in the White House. And we meet biweekly. I meet with Ryan Crocker and David—General Petraeus weekly, and it's like a meeting.

Q. So she's just in and out? This is real quick?

The President. Yes, she'll be back this evening; probably hold a press conference here this evening. The Saudis want to have a press conference with the Foreign Minister and Condi. Yes, it's just a quick trip.

White House Press Secretary Perino. Timing and location are still being worked out.

The President. Time and location because, you know, you don't want to set

81

the time and have her not be back for it. But her intention is to get back here for dinner at the King's ranch.

Q. What time——

The President. She left this morning at 6:40 a.m.—or left the facility here at 6:40 a.m. And I presume it's, like, on the news, right?

Q. Yes.

The President. I haven't seen the news.

Q. It's been reported.

Q. So is it basically to promote——

The President. It's to, first of all, be there. And secondly, is to—there's a momentum; there's a political process that has been working that is—with some of those laws coming to fruition. Her job is to be there, sitting down with them, explaining how much we appreciate what they've done, how they need to do more and keep moving the process.

Progress in Iraq

Q. You know, we've been talking about these benchmarks for so long. Do you really feel like maybe now it's starting to turn a corner a bit, or is that too early to say?

The President. First of all, I think—we've been talking about the benchmarks for how long? When you say "so long"——

Q. Almost a year now, isn't it?

The President. Yes, I think that's right; it has been almost a year. A political system evolves and grows. It grows when people have confidence. It grows when the grassroots begins to agitate for change. It grows when there's alternatives. There's competition emerging. Those are all the forces necessary to bring people together to get things done. And the leadership is more confident. The grassroots is more involved. There's been more reconciliation taking place at the local level. And the Government is beginning to respond.

This is—we assume that democracy is a natural phenomenon for people out there. These are people that lived under tyranny. They lived in a society that was divided by a dictator. And they're beginning to

form the habits of self-government, manifested in laws being passed. I'm not going to predict, Steven Lee [Steven Lee Myers, New York Times], about moving this forward. I can only assure you that we will continue to work the process as hard as we can.

I reminded everybody last year, you know, people did focus on the benchmarks, and so do I. But I also reminded everybody last year that one way to determine whether or not a government is functioning is to look at their budgeting process and how they distribute revenues from central Government out to the Provinces, which is a key component of a federalized-type system. And the definition of federalism, by the way, has yet to be clearly defined in Iraq, and that's part of the issues they're working through. But it's a proper role between the state government—central Government and the Provinces, and that's another piece of legislation that is part of the benchmark process.

But nevertheless, even though they haven't passed that, there is revenue sharing. In other words, there is a process. There's a way to allocate revenues. Do they have an oil law yet? No. Are they sharing oil revenues that would be inherent under an oil law? Yes, they are.

Organization of the Petroleum Exporting Countries (OPEC)

Q. Sir.

The President. Yes, Holly [Holly Rosenkrantz, Bloomberg News].

Q. Thank you.

The President. I knew you were anxious to ask because you're waving your hand. Look, this is not like the White House press conferences.

Q. I never know when you're going to be shuffled out before I get a chance. [*Laughter*] It's been a long day. [*Laughter*]

The President. Atta girl. Stand your ground, whatever you do. [*Laughter*]

Q. I just wanted to ask you if you could just clarify a little bit your statement this morning to OPEC. What specific action would you like them to take at their first meeting coming up February?

The President. I would like for them to realize that high energy prices affect the economies of consuming nations, and that if these economies weaken, those economies will eventually be buying fewer barrels of oil. And having said that, there is not a lot of excess capacity in the marketplace. What's happened is, is that demand for energy has outstripped new supply. And that's why there's high price. And I fully understand how it affects the U.S. consumer. And my point to His Majesty is going to be, when consumers have less purchasing power because of high prices of gasoline—in other words, when it affects their families—it could cause this economy to slow down. If the economy slows down, there will be less barrels of oil purchased.

Now in our case, just so the American people know, most of our oil comes from Canada and Mexico. But oil is a market; it's globalized; it's fungible. That's what I meant.

Q. ——brought it up with King Abdallah already?

The President. Excuse me?

Q. Did you bring it up already?

The President. No, I have not. I brought it up with members of his administration and will do so with him tonight on the farm.

President's Visit to Saudi Arabia/Iran

Q. Can you talk a little bit about your discussions with him so far and whether you've had a meeting of minds on any issues, whether it's Iran, Iraq——

The President. I appreciate that. He is most interested in two subjects, right off the bat: first, the Israeli-Palestinian peace process. I think what he really wanted to determine was how—when I said, "optimistic about a state being defined," why? So he's interested in the meetings, interested in the behind-the-scenes observations that I was able to share with him.

He is—part of my mission was to make it clear that one reason why the talks failed in the past is that there wasn't participation by the neighbors. And I thanked him, in front of the people assembled there, for sending his Foreign Minister to Annapolis, because the presence of Saudi at Annapolis inspired the Palestinians as well as sent a message to the Israelis—Israeli population, for example.

We did spend time on Iran. The interesting issue on Iran is the effect of the NIE. And I went over the NIE with him.

[*At this point, the interview continued, and no transcript was provided. The remarks later continued as follows.*]

The President. I assured him that our intelligence services came to an independent judgment. I reminded him of what I said at my press conference when we got involved with that story. They were a threat, they are a threat, and they will be a threat if we don't work together to stop their enrichment. So we spent a fair amount of time on Iran. I have spent a fair amount of time on Iran in every stop.

It is not the only subject. There's probably more interest in my discussions on the Middle Eastern peace. Many of the leaders in the region, many of the people I have spoken to, equate troubled times with no peace between the Palestinian and Israelis. It's the subject matter that, if you follow this subject, you know that this is on a lot of people's minds.

And so they were—they wanted to make sure that the efforts by the United States were real and how we conducted our policy wise. It's interesting; they weren't all that interested in, okay, give me the negotiating points, or where are you, or what are the talking points on both sides, or where are we in the negotiations. They're interested in commitment and vision.

I would like to share a universal concern I've heard on this trip, and that is, the United States will not welcome foreign capital or does not welcome foreign capital.

I heard it from entrepreneurs; I've heard it from government leaders. They are concerned about reinvestment of dollars back into the United States. There's a genuine concern about protectionism. And there's—our visa policy concerns the leaders because they know full well that the best way—these are pro-American leaders, and they know the best way to defeat some perceptions that may exist on the street is for their people to go see America firsthand, like colleges and business travel. And our visa policy is getting better in some fronts, but we've still got some work to do.

So I came away with the distinct impression about a concern by government and citizen alike that the United States says, "not welcome." And that troubles me because that's not the way our country is.

National Intelligence Estimate

Q. Just a couple quick follow-ups on Iran. On the NIE, did you—were you, in effect, distancing yourself from the conclusions of the NIE, and these guys——

The President. No, I was making it clear it was an independent judgment, because what they basically came to the conclusion of, is that he's trying—you know, this is a way to make sure that all options aren't on the table. So I defended our intelligence services, but made it clear that they're an independent agency, that they come to conclusions separate from what I may or may not want.

Iran

Q. And on the issue of Iran, did the question of a possible military strike either by the United States or Israel come up?

The President. I just made it clear that all options are on the table. But I'd like to solve this diplomatically—and think we can—and talked about making sure consistent messages emanated from all parts of the world to the Iranians.

Strait of Hormuz Naval Incident

Q. Related to that, this confrontation in the Straits with the Iranian gunboats, are the rules of engagement going to change on that? You've warned of serious consequences if they do it again.

The President. I did. I said, "If they destroy our ships," yes. If they destroy our ships, there will be serious consequences.

Q. Yes, but I'm saying, if they——

The President. I didn't say, "If they do it again." If they do it again, I don't know. What do you mean, "If they do it again"?

Q. Well, if they approach the ships and would there——

The President. Well, there is clear rules of engagement. Our captains—I was briefed by the admiral in Bahrain about the rules of engagement. But please don't confuse hitting our ships with explosives or attacking our ships and serious——

Q. Okay, I won't. But I just was wondering whether the next time something like that is attempted by one of these Iranian boats, they might be fired on.

The President. I don't know. It's going to be up to the captain to determine whether or not his vessel is in jeopardy. My only point is, they shouldn't be doing it. It was provocative in the first place, and our captain showed restraint. These are judgment calls, and there are clear rules of engagement. Our people operate under very strict rules in the Straits, and so should the Iranians. And they better be careful of—and not be provocative and, you know, get out there and cause an incident, because there's going to be serious consequences. And what I said in my statement was, if they hit one of our ships, there are going to be serious consequences, and I meant it.

Q. Do you have any sense of what they were up to? What motive——

The President. I don't know.

Q. Were they test——

The President. I don't know.

Q. Do you think they were playing some sort of game?

The President. I don't know. I don't know. I was briefed; I spent some time in Bahrain with—you know, when I went over there for the breakfast with the troops, command briefed us, our security team, on what are the rules of engagement, you know, and how do they work, how does it react. This is one of these moments where there's no time to be spending a lot time on the phone trying to figure out what to do. And there's—these are highly trained professionals who, I thought, dealt with it in a very professional way.

Q. Sir, are you sure of whether or not this was actually directed out of Tehran, the President's office, or whether it's some separate——

The President. It could be. IRGC or—versus the military, but you know something? It's not going to matter to me one way or the other if they hit our ships, and the Iranian Government has got to understand that. This is serious business. We lost lives when one of those boats loaded with explosives attacked us—called the USS *Cole.* In this case, it would be states—it would be the actions of a state. And so my message was clear to the Iranian Government: Whoever made the—is in control of these boats best be careful.

Q. You were suggesting that this could be—could have been directed by the Revolutionary Guard?

The President. No, I'm not. His question was, do we know the chain of command? There's several chains of command inside the—it was a very perceptive comment by the lad, and it was—there are separate military organizations, separate organizations inside Iran, and so we don't know.

Q. The IRGC, was that the——

The President. The IRGC could be—is a player inside Iran. I don't know. Do not write the story that I'm predicting who made this decision, because I'm telling you—I can't be any more plain about it—

I don't know. I do know it was a provocative incident.

And my other was, it's not going to matter who made the decision. If they hit our ships, we will hold Iran responsible.

Q. Okay. Can we ask you on——

The President. You can ask me anything you want. If I don't want to answer, I'll say, I don't want to answer it. [*Laughter*] I'm feeling quite feisty here, Steven Lee. [*Laughter*]

Q. You are? Are you in a good mood?

The President. Yes, a great mood.

Q. I do.

The President. Dates put you in a good mood, right? I'm in a great mood.

Q. Which kind of dates are you talking about? [*Laughter*]

The President. Not bad. Not bad. [*Laughter*] Pretty good. A wordsmith. [*Laughter*] All right, go ahead.

Iran

Q. In your discussions with King Abdallah and other Gulf Arab leaders, were they in any way urging restraint? There's been some concern——

The President. What?

Q. Were they in any way urging you restraint in your dealings with Iran?

The President. I told them that I want to solve this issue diplomatically. My position has not altered. I explained to them the diplomacy we're going through. They need to help. They need to make it clear to nations that do business with Iran that if we want to solve this diplomatically, there needs to be pressure on the regime so that some—the hope is, is that somebody shows up and says, "We're tired of being isolated, and we're tired of the economic deprivation that comes from our desire to enrich."

I also explained to them why I support the Russian position. And for those of you who follow the White House and have listened carefully to what I've been saying, know full well that's been my position for quite a while. Because I said early on that I supported the Iranian desire for—they said, every sovereign nation has the right for a civilian nuclear power. I said, you're right. I said, the problem with you is, you haven't honored the international agreements—"you" being the Iranians. And secondly—therefore, we can't trust you with enrichment.

But because I believe that you have a sovereign right for nuclear power, I support the Russian idea of providing you with enriched uranium and collecting the spent uranium, thereby undermining their position that they need to learn to enrich in order to have civilian nuclear power. And the danger with enrichment for civilian—so-called civilian purposes is, is that that technology can be transferred easily to another covert military program. Knowledge is transferable, and so what I've explained to our friends in the region is the best way to stop any potential weapons program is——

[*There was an interruption, and the remarks continued as follows.*]

The President. I'm not starting over. I'm not starting over. [*Laughter*]

Q. That's all right; you don't have to.

The President. Good, yes. Anyway—is to start a weapons program—to stop a weapons program is to stop their ability to enrich. I've also explained to them our position is, is that if they verifiably suspend their program, there is a way forward for dialogue through the P–3 process. What do you call—what do we call that? The group of five——

White House Press Secretary Perino. The P–5-plus-1.

The President. The P–5-plus-1 process.

Q. Mr. President——

The President. Are you hogging this?

Q. Yes. [*Laughter*]

The President. I'm teasing. Go ahead.

Israel/Iran

Q. Just one quick follow-up on Iran, just because it comes up, I mean, this issue of what Israel will do has been out there

ever since Vice President Cheney raised it with Don Imus in the very beginning of your second term, about the Israelis having a——

The President. I don't remember that. What did he say?

Q. Oh, he said there was concern about what the Israelis might do. And particularly in the weeks since the NIE, there has been murmuring in Israel—Israeli defense circles. One of your own former officials, Bruce Riedel, told me a few weeks ago——

The President. Who?

Q. Bruce Riedel—he used to work on the NSC—said that he came back from a visit to Iran——

[*The interview continued, and no transcript was provided. The remarks later continued as follows.*]

Press Secretary Perino. I would recommend—you have about 10 more minutes.

National Economy

Q. Can we ask you about—let's go back on the economy. You talked about the threat of the economy slowing down if consumers buy less oil, or can——

The President. The price of energy can have an effect on economic growth. I was talking about—they were asking me about what I'm going to say to King Abdallah. And I'm going to say, high energy prices can affect economic growth because it's painful for our consumers.

Q. My question is, you've talked about inheriting a recession when you came into office. You're a year away from leaving office. Do you think that your successor is going to wind up in the same boat?

The President. I've always said these are times of economic uncertainty, but I have confidence in the future—immediate future because the underpinnings of our economy are good. Inflation—core inflation—is low; we've still got some. And employment has been strong. We've still got some issues, obviously, and one of them is the housing market. That's one of the things the leaders have been interested in, is my views on the economy.

Q. But, sir, since——

Q. It's the "R" word.

The President. No, I'm optimistic, as I said. My position hasn't changed from 3 days ago, or whatever it was, when I commented on this.

Q. The fact that you're optimistic, that suggests—does that mean that you are not going to suggest any change in your tax policy or——

The President. Look, I'm going to watch very carefully. And we'll let you know if I decide one way or the other.

Middle East Peace Process

Q. Mr. President, I'm wondering if you can talk a little bit about what you're hearing from Arab leaders——

The President. Sorry, Mike [Mike Emanuel, FOX News], I've already answered that. Next. [*Laughter*] No, I'm teasing.

Q. I'm used to it.

The President. He actually was a Texas reporter.

Q. About the Palestinian-Israeli issue, what kind of feedback are you hearing?

Press Secretary Perino. We did cover that before you——

The President. I'll be glad to tell you again. The first question in their mind is, one, why do I sound optimistic? Two, are we going to spend the time and effort to help move the process? I made it clear to them that in order for this to work, they've got to be supportive of the Palestinians and make it clear that Israel is an important part of the future of the Middle East.

Q. Do the Arab States recognize Israel? I mean, do they want to—have they shown any sign that they want to improve relations with Israel?

The President. I think the fact that they sent major players in their administration to Annapolis was a sign. That answers your question. And they want to see a deal done,

and they want progress because the issue frustrates them. As I said earlier, Michael, this issue is kind of the touchstone in their mind for a lot of other problems in the Middle East; you solve this, then a lot of other problems go away. I hope they're right on that. But this is, no question, a very important issue, and it's one that— go ahead. I'll be glad to go off the record and tell you why now.

Q. Sir, if I could just follow on that point. I noted that the King of Bahrain mentioned the peace process in his statement when he welcomed you. We haven't heard similar statements. I understand that they sent their representatives. Do you think that many of the Arab leaders are still holding back a little bit; they want to see, perhaps, a little more progress towards a deal before they're willing to come out and start talking about things like recognition of Israel?

The President. That's an interesting question. First of all, after years of disappointment, those of us directly involved in the process have a lot of work to try to instill confidence in the people. And I think laying back is too strong a word, but I think wondering whether this can happen is the right way to put it, Steven Lee.

They definitely want it to happen. They're willing to send a—in the Saudis' case, their Foreign Minister to Annapolis. They are most interested—we spent a lot of time on this subject in each stop because they're most interested in getting my point of view about how I think the process is going to unfold, what are the problems, what can the U.S. do to help, and will we be actively involved. They have this great hope that the United States involvement will cause the process to be more likely to move forward.

Q. I want to apologize for our tardiness.

The President. It's my fault—roadblocks.

Q. If you covered this, I apologize for that too.

The President. Which reminds me of the question, did you get what I mouthed to you there?

Q. I did.

The President. It was—I thought it was a really interesting question.

President's Visit to Saudi Arabia/Oil Supply

Q. What do you hope to get out of the King, or what do you hope to accomplish with this talk about our economy and the impact of high prices?

The President. Well, first of all is a realization that high energy prices can damage consuming economies. It can hurt the economy. And it hasn't—it's been—it's affected our families. Don't get me wrong; paying more for gasoline hurts some of the American families. And I'll make that clear to him. But I also understand the dynamics behind the issue, and that is growing demand from U.S., but more particularly, China and India, relative to supply.

Oil is a commodity; it isn't something you just turn a tap. I mean, it requires investment, exploration, a lot of capital. I talked to His Majesty early on in my Presidency in the hopes that they would explore for new fields; they have. They've increased their capacity. But in the meantime, demand has gone up quite substantially.

Oil Prices

Q. Well, do you want him to open the spigot more? Do you want him to lower the prices?

The President. Well, that's the question: What does that mean? That's what—I hope that OPEC, if possible, understands that if they could put more supply on the market, it would be helpful. But a lot of these economies are going—a lot of these oil-producing countries are full out.

Press Secretary Perino. We have time for one more on-the-record question. And we will get the transcript to you, Peter [Peter Maer, CBS Radio] and Mike, as soon as possible.

The President. I hope I answered the second way the same way I did the first way.

Q. I'll just ask—[*laughter*].

Middle East Peace Process

Q. I would follow up on that—the security barrier—what I was trying to get out of my question was the notion that if——

The President. You didn't think of it until I said, "Nice question."

Q. No, no, no.

The President. You were coming with this?

Q. I wanted to ask, but the mike went down, remember. And so I didn't get a follow-up.

The President. I wasn't going to give you a follow-up in front of the cameras anyway.

Q. Fair enough. The question I had is, do you see a day someday when some President in the future will come and say to some Israeli leader and Palestinian leader that it's time for that wall to come down, not unlike Ronald Reagan's——

The President. You know, I don't think in the short term that day will come. I do think there will be a day—your question was not the wall; your question was checkpoints, which I guess is the wall.

Q. I meant barrier, is what I meant, the barrier you drove through——

The President. Well, barrier—this is not barriers.

Q. It's the same question, really.

The President. Well, no, it's not, in all due respect to the questioner. It was your question; of course, it's the same question. [*Laughter*]

Q. What I meant to say was—[*laughter*].

The President. Yes, exactly. [*Laughter*]

Look, first of all, the state comes into being subject to the roadmap, which requires security measures being in place so that the Israeli population is comfortable that it's not going to have a state that harbors people that want to destroy them. The reason why you articulate a vision is to give people inside the Palestinian Territories, who don't want violence and who don't want to destroy Israel, a chance to be for something. This is how I answered the question.

The wall is a—was necessary, in the Israelis' minds, to protect themselves. It is that sense of security which I hope will give them a chance—their politicians a chance to negotiate the deal. The deal becomes more security. In other words, it's a series of security measures that will eventually cause a state to come into being. And whether or not the wall comes down or not, I can't predict that to you, Steven Lee. I can tell you, though, there's no such thing as a state if it's going to be occupied. In other words, when I said contiguous, that means contiguous territory that does not—Swiss cheese, that it's—and I thought that's actually what you were referring to with those interior roadblocks.

Q. Thank you.

NOTE: The interview was taped at 1:16 p.m. at Nasiriyah Guest Palace. In his remarks, the President referred to Prime Minister Nuri al-Maliki of Iraq; Gen. David H. Petraeus, USA, commanding general, Multi-National Force—Iraq; Minister of Foreign Affairs Saud al-Faysal bin Abd al-Aziz Al Saud and King Abdallah bin Abd al-Aziz Al Saud of Saudi Arabia; Vice Adm. Kevin J. Cosgriff, USN, commander, U.S. Naval Forces Central Command, U.S. 5th Fleet, and Combined Maritime Forces; and Cmdr. Jeffrey James, USN, commanding officer, USS *Hopper*. A reporter referred to radio personality Don Imus; and King Hamad bin Isa al-Khalifa of Bahrain. A tape was not available for verification of the content of this interview.

Remarks Prior to a Discussion With Saudi Entrepreneurs in Riyadh
January 15, 2008

I'm George W. Bush, President of the United States. [*Laughter*] Thank you all for joining us. Ambassador, thanks for setting this up. It's important for the President to hear thoughts, hopes, dreams, aspirations, concerns from folks that are out making a living. And I really appreciate you taking time out of your day to come and visit with me. I'm looking forward to hearing your thoughts.

One thing is for certain: The United States benefits when people come to my country. And one of my concerns was, after September the 11th, that our visa policy, particularly for Saudis, was tightened to the point where we missed opportunity to show young and old alike what our country is really about. I love the fact that some of you were educated in America. I think you'll find you got a good education there, but more importantly, Americans get to see

you, and you get to see them. And the best way to achieve better understanding in the world is for folks just to get together and get to understand that we share the same God, we share the same aspirations for children and for our futures.

And so this is an important visit for me. I'm thrilled to be in the Kingdom. I have— I've got very close relations with His Majesty. We had a good visit last night on a variety of subjects. We talked about Palestinian peace; we talked about the security issues of the region. I talked to the Ambassador and will again talk to His Majesty tonight about the fact that oil prices are very high, which is tough on our economy, and that I would hope, as OPEC considers different production levels, that they understand that if their—one of their biggest consumer's economy suffers, it will mean less purchases, less oil and gas sold.

And so we've got a lot of things to talk about, but I want to assure you it's from the spirit of friendship. And the hospitality last night was warm, and the conversation was excellent, just like this one is going to be.

So I want to thank you for coming. I appreciate your time.

NOTE: The President spoke at 8:51 p.m. at the U.S. Embassy. In his remarks, he referred to U.S. Ambassador to Saudi Arabia Ford M. Fraker; and King Abdallah bin Abd al-Aziz Al Saud of Saudi Arabia.

Memorandum on Presidential Exemption from the Coastal Zone Management Act
January 15, 2008

Memorandum for the Secretary of Defense and the Secretary of Commerce
Subject: Presidential Exemption from the Coastal Zone Management Act

By the authority vested in me as President by the Constitution and the laws of the United States, including section 1456(c)(1)(B) of title 16, United States Code, and to ensure effective and timely training of the United States naval forces in anti-submarine warfare using mid-frequency active sonar:

I hereby exempt from compliance with the requirements of section 1456(c)(1)(A) of title 16 (section 307(c)(1)(A) of the Coastal Zone Management Act) those elements of the Department of the Navy's anti-submarine warfare training during Southern California Operating Area Composite Training Unit Exercises (COMPTUEX) and Joint Task Force Exercises (JTFEX) involving the use of mid-frequency active sonar. These exercises are more fully described in the Environmental Assessment/Overseas Environmental Assessment prepared for the Commander, United States Pacific Fleet, dated February 2007.

On January 3, 2008, as modified on January 10, 2008, the United States District Court for the Central District of California determined that the Navy's use of mid-frequency active sonar was not in compliance with section 1456(c)(1)(A), and issued an order that is appealable under section 1291 or 1292 of title 28, United States Code. On January 11, 2008, the Secretary of Commerce made a written request that the Navy be exempted from compliance with section 1456(c)(1)(A) in its use of mid-frequency active sonar during COMPTUEX and JTFEX. As part of that request, the Secretary of Commerce certified that mediation under section 1456(h) is not likely to result in the Navy's compliance with section 1456(c)(1)(A).

I hereby determine that the COMPTUEX and JTFEX, including the use of mid-frequency active sonar in these exercises, are in the paramount interest of the United States. Compliance with section 1456(c)(1)(A) would undermine the Navy's ability to conduct realistic training exercises that are necessary to ensure the combat effectiveness of carrier and expeditionary strike groups. This exemption will enable the Navy to train effectively and to certify carrier and expeditionary strike groups for deployment in support of world-wide operational and combat activities, which are essential to national security.

GEORGE W. BUSH

NOTE: This memorandum was released by the Office of the Press Secretary on January 16.

Remarks Following a Meeting With President Mohamed Hosni Mubarak of Egypt in Sharm el-Sheikh, Egypt
January 16, 2008

President Mubarak. I'd like to welcome President Bush here in Egypt and, particularly, in Sharm el-Sheikh City. It is the City of Peace.

We briefed Mr. Bush—he briefed us on the outcome of his visits in the region, and we held very important consultations, which dealt with the security situation now and bilateral and mutual efforts for the sake of peace, security, and stability in the Middle East.

I emphasized through our consultations the Egyptian situation, underscoring and supporting peace and our aspirations that Mr. Bush follows up the negotiations between both the Israeli and Palestinian sides, and I also said that I wish to reach a peace agreement before the end of his term. I emphasized that the Palestinian question, of course, is the core of problems and conflict in the Middle East, and it is the entry to contain the crises and tension in the region and the best means to face what's going on in the world and our region; I mean by that, the escalation of violence, extremism, and terrorism.

I also underscored the strategic importance we focus on here in Egypt: that the Gulf, its peoples—sisterly peoples and states—they are part and parcel of the national security of Egypt, the security of the Middle East, and the world. The Egyptian-American relations actually have been very important, and this importance has been getting more important. And this importance addressed the interests of both people in all the region and issues in the Middle East.

Our consultations today showed that we believe and understand the mutual interests of both sides in continuing our dialogue and consultations—and I mean by that, strategic consultations—for the sake of the peace, security, and stability of the Middle East and the development of its states and the prosperity of its people. I also emphasized that we need to—we are keen on supporting peace efforts; that we're ready, hand in hand with the United States of America and the Quartet and all other regional and international stakeholders and parties, for the sake of comprehensive and just peace, to put an end to this Israeli-Palestinian conflict and, finally, to open new horizons for the Middle East, for a more peaceful and security future, to have more justice and security in the region.

I reiterate our welcome words for Mr. Bush, and I hope that his efforts for the sake of peace would reach a success. And now I'll give you the floor, sir.

President Bush. Mr. President, thank you, sir. It's a pleasure to be back in Egypt. This is such a beautiful site, Mr. President. Thank you for hosting my visit here. As you mentioned, I've been on a long trip, and I can't think of a better place to end it than right here with you in this beautiful setting.

President Mubarak. But needs much more days.

President Bush. Yes. He wants me back, okay. [*Laughter*] He's extended an invitation, and thank you for that, sir.

It's an important stop for me because the United States has a longstanding friendship with Egypt. It's important for the people of Egypt to understand, our Nation respects you, respects your history, respects your traditions, and respects your culture. Our friendship is strong. It's a cornerstone of—one of the main cornerstones of our policy in this region, and it's based on our shared commitment to peace, security, and prosperity.

I appreciate the opportunity, Mr. President, to give you an update on my trip. And I appreciate the advice you've given me. You've seen a lot in your years as President. You've got a great deal of experience, and I appreciate your feeling comfortable in sharing that experience once again with me.

I really appreciate Egypt's support in the war on terror. I appreciate the fact that you've given peacekeepers for Sudan. I did brief you on my talks in Israel and with the Palestinians, and they were positive talks. And I said, I'm optimistic an agreement can be reached. And the reason I am, is because I believe the leadership in Israel and the leadership of the Palestinians is committed to a two-state solution. And I know nations in the neighborhood are willing to help, particularly yourself. And I appreciate your strong, constructive support for the process.

And I told the President, I'm going to stay—there's a wonder whether or not the American President, when he says something, whether he actually means it. When I say, "I'm coming back to stay engaged," I mean it. And when I say, "I'm optimistic we can get a deal done," I mean what I'm saying. And so I appreciate the chance to talk.

We also talked about Lebanon, and we agreed it's important for nations in this region to support Prime Minister Siniora. It's important to encourage the holding of immediate and unconditional Presidential elections according to the Lebanese Constitution and to make it clear to Syria, Iran, and their allies, they must end their interference and efforts to undermine the process.

We talked—and by the way, when it came to the Israeli-Palestinian peace talks, I want to thank you for your support of Annapolis. It was important that you were there. As a matter of fact, you didn't hesitate, because you knew that both those parties had to have supportive people in the region. And I thank you very much for that.

We spent time on Iraq. The President asked me how I thought things were going

there. The decision to send more troops is working. Violence is down. Secretary Rice came back from Iraq yesterday and briefed me that she was able to see life returning back to the streets, where moms are out with their children. Normal life is coming back, and political life is moving.

Mr. President, I'm sure you followed the fact that the Council of Representatives passed the de-Ba'athification law as part of an important reconciliation package. The Government isn't perfect, but nevertheless, progress is being made. And I assure to you, Mr. President—I want to share this with the press corps—that the United States will continue to help the Iraqi people secure their democracy.

I also talked about Egypt's role in the world. Egypt is an important nation that sends a clear signal. People watch Egypt. I appreciate very much the long and proud tradition that you've had for a vibrant civil society. I appreciate the fact that women play an important role in your society, Mr. President. I do so because not only am I'm a proud father of two young professional women, I also know how important it is for any vibrant society to have women involved in constructive and powerful ways. And I appreciate the example that your nation is setting.

Progress toward greater political openness is being led by the Egyptians themselves, by pioneering journalists—some of whom even may be here—bloggers or judges insisting on independence or other strong civic and religious leaders who love their country and are determined to build a democratic future.

Because of the predominate role you play and because I strongly believe that Egypt can play a role in the freedom and justice movement, you and I have discussed the issue. You have taken steps toward economic openness, and I discussed that with your Prime Minister—and democratic reform. And my hope is that the Egyptian Government will build on these important steps and give the people of this proud nation a greater voice in your future. I think it will lead to peace, and I think it will lead to justice.

Our friendship with Egypt is deep and broad. Egypt will continue to be a vital strategic partner of the United States. We will work together to build a safer and more peaceful world. And, Mr. President, I thank your leadership on the issue of peace and security.

I've had a great trip. I've been impressed by the warmth and the energy of the people I have met. This is a dynamic part of the world that is seeing significant changes. I wish my fellow citizens would be able to come and see firsthand the vibrancy and excitement in the Middle East. People here are working to embrace the opportunities of a modern global economy and, in doing so, are not abandoning their traditions or cultures or their faith.

This isn't easy work, as we head into the 21st century, and it's going to require social, economic, and political reform. And it takes time for people to resolve the challenges in their respective societies; same in my country. But I'm absolutely confident the people of the Middle East are working hard to build a society based upon justice. And I've assured them that as they make the journey, the United States will be a steady friend and partner.

Thank you for your time. God bless.

President Mubarak. Thank you.

NOTE: The President spoke at 1:46 p.m. in the Royal Suite Garden at the Four Seasons Resort. In his remarks, he referred to Prime Minister Fuad Siniora of Lebanon; and Prime Minister Ahmed Mohamed Nazif of Egypt. President Mubarak spoke partly in Arabic, and those portions of his remarks were translated by an interpreter.

Letter to Congressional Leaders on Review of Title III of the Cuban Liberty and Democratic Solidarity (LIBERTAD) Act of 1996
January 16, 2008

Dear _____ :

Consistent with section 306(c)(2) of the Cuban Liberty and Democratic Solidarity (LIBERTAD) Act of 1996 (Public Law 104–114)(the "Act"), I hereby determine and report to the Congress that suspension for 6 months beyond February 1, 2008, of the right to bring an action under title III of the Act is necessary to the national interests of the United States and will expedite a transition to democracy in Cuba.

Sincerely,

GEORGE W. BUSH

NOTE: Identical letters were sent to Joseph R. Biden, Jr., chairman, and Richard G. Lugar, ranking member, Senate Committee on Foreign Relations; Robert C. Byrd, chairman, and Thad Cochran, ranking member, Senate Committee on Appropriations; Tom Lantos, chairman, and Ileana Ros-Lehtinen, ranking member, House Committee on Foreign Affairs; and David R. Obey, chairman, and Jerry Lewis, ranking member, House Committee on Appropriations.

Remarks Following a Meeting With United States Special Envoy to Sudan Richard S. Williamson
January 17, 2008

The President. I've just had an extensive visit with Madam Secretary and members of my national security team, Rich Williamson, who is the Presidential Envoy—Special Envoy to Sudan.

We talked about our common commitment and the commitment of this Government to help the suffering of citizens in Sudan who, you know, suffers deprivation, rape. My administration called this a genocide. Once you label it genocide, you obviously have to do something about it.

Our discussion centered upon our mutual desire to develop a strategy that will help the United Nations become more effective. The United Nations is—considers the Darfur issue a central issue, and it's on its agenda. And we agree. The United States can help what has been a process, frankly, that has unfolded a little too slow for our liking. And we can help.

And secondly, we want to make sure that the peace agreement negotiated through this administration by Ambassador Danforth, between the north and south, holds. So Rich is going to report back to me quickly with, you know, a plan to accelerate our efforts.

You know, America is probably wondering why, why do you care? And one reason we care about the suffering in Sudan is because we care about the human condition all across the face of the Earth. And we fully understand that when people suffer, it is in our interest to help. And we also understand that when people suffer, it makes it more likely that some may turn to the ideology of those who use murder as a weapon. So it's in our national security interest and it's in our—in the interest of our conscience to confront this, what we have called a genocide. And I want to thank you for taking this on.

Ambassador Williamson. Thank you, Mr. President.

The President. It's a big deal; you've got my full support.

Ambassador Williamson. I appreciate it. Thank you, sir.

The President. Yes, sir.

NOTE: The President spoke at 10:56 a.m. in the Oval Office at the White House. In his remarks, he referred to former U.S. Ambassador to the United Nations John C. Danforth, in his capacity as former U.S. Special Envoy to Sudan.

Letter to the Speaker of the House of Representatives Transmitting a Request for Additional Funds for Veterans Resources
January 17, 2008

Dear Madam Speaker:

My Administration is committed to providing the resources needed to ensure that veterans, including those returning from current combat operations, receive the quality care and services they deserve.

In the FY 2008 Consolidated Appropriations Act, Public Law 110–161, $3,691,391,000 was designated by the Congress as an emergency requirement contingent upon a formal budget request by me that includes designation of the entire amount as an emergency requirement.

While I believe that these funds should have been considered as regular appropriations, the men and women who have sacrificed for our country should not be held hostage to budgetary wrangling in Washington. Therefore, to provide these funds in a timely manner I hereby request and designate as an emergency requirement the $3,691,391,000, consistent with Public Law 110–161.

Additional information on this action is set forth in the enclosed letter from the Director of the Office of Management and Budget.

Sincerely,

GEORGE W. BUSH

Remarks on the National Economy
January 18, 2008

Over the past several months, I've held a series of meetings with my economic team on the outlook of—for the U.S. economy. And before I left for the Middle East, I directed them to conduct a thorough assessment of our economic condition, consult with Members of Congress, and provide me with their recommendations about any actions we might need to take.

The economic team reports that our economy has a solid foundation, but that there are areas of real concern. Our economy is still creating jobs, though at a reduced pace. Consumer spending is still growing, but the housing market is declining. Business investment and exports are still rising, but the cost of imported oil has increased.

My administration has been watching our economy carefully. My advisers and many outside experts expect that our economy will continue to grow over the coming year, but at a slower rate than we have enjoyed for the past few years. And there is a risk of a downturn. Continued instability in the housing and financial markets could cause additional harm to our overall economy and put our growth and job creation in jeopardy.

In recent months, we've taken steps to shore up the housing market, including measures to help struggling homeowners avoid foreclosure and to keep their homes. I've also—have asked Congress to pass legislation to modernize the Federal Housing Administration and enable it to provide additional assistance to struggling homeowners. The House passed a bill, and the Senate passed a bill, and now they need to get together and get a bill to my desk as quickly as possible.

After careful consideration and after discussions with Members of the Congress, I have concluded that additional action is needed. To keep our economy growing and creating jobs, Congress and the administration need to work to enact an economic growth package as soon as possible.

As Congress considers such a plan, there are certain principles that must guide its deliberations. This growth package must be big enough to make a difference in an economy as large and dynamic as ours, which means it should be about 1 percent of GDP. This growth package must be built on broad-based tax relief that will directly affect economic growth and not the kind of spending projects that would have little immediate impact on our economy. This growth package must be temporary and take effect right away so we can get help to our economy when it needs it most. And this growth package must not include any tax increases.

Specifically, this growth package should bolster both business investment and consumer spending, which are critical to economic growth. And this would require two key provisions. To be effective, a growth package must include tax incentive for American businesses, including small businesses, to make major investments in their enterprises this year. Giving them an incentive to invest now will encourage businessowners to expand their operations, create new jobs, and inject new energy into our economy in the process.

To be effective, a growth package must also include direct and rapid income tax relief for the American people. Americans could use this money as they see fit: to help meet their monthly bills, cover higher costs at the gas pump, or pay for other basic necessities. Letting Americans keep more of their own money should increase consumer spending and lift our economy at a time when people otherwise might spend less.

Yesterday I spoke to members of the congressional leadership from both political parties. They shared with me their thoughts on the best way forward, and I was encouraged by those discussions. And I believe there is enough broad consensus that we can come up with a package that can be approved with bipartisan support. I've asked Treasury Secretary Hank Paulson to lead my administration's efforts to forge an agreement with Congress so that we can deliver this needed boost to our economy as quickly as possible.

Passing a new growth package is our most pressing economic priority. When that is done, Congress must turn to the most important economic priority for our country, and that's making sure the tax relief that is now in place is not taken away. A source of uncertainty in our economy is that this tax relief is set to expire at the end of 2010. Unless Congress acts, the American people will face massive tax increases in less than 3 years. The marriage penalty will make a comeback, the child tax credit will be cut in half, the death tax will come back to life, and tax rates will go up on regular income, capital gains, and dividends. This tax increase would put jobs and economic growth at risk, and Congress has a responsibility to keep that from happening. So it's critical that Congress make this tax relief permanent.

We're in the midst of a challenging period, and I know that Americans are concerned about their economic future. But our economy has seen challenging times before, and it is resilient.

In a vibrant economy, markets rise and decline. We cannot change that fundamental dynamic. As a matter of fact, eliminating risk altogether would also eliminate the innovation and productivity that drives the creations of jobs and wealth in America. Yet there are also times when swift and temporary actions can help ensure that inevitable market adjustments do not undermine the health of the broader economy. This is such a moment.

By passing an effective growth package quickly, we can provide a shot in the arm to keep a fundamentally strong economy healthy. And it will help keep economic sectors that are going through adjustments, such as the housing market, from adversely affecting other parts of our economy.

I'm optimistic about our economic future because Americans have shown time and again that they are the most industrious, creative, and enterprising people in the world. That is what has made our economy strong, and that is what will make it stronger in the challenging times ahead.

Thank you.

NOTE: The President spoke at 11:34 a.m. in the Roosevelt Room at the White House.

Remarks Following a Tour of Wright Manufacturing, Inc., in Frederick, Maryland
January 18, 2008

The President. Let me tell you why I'm here. This man started his own business. He is a manufacturer, he employs over a hundred people, and he represents the backbone of the American economy. And today I talked about our economy, and the fundamentals are strong, but there's uncertainty. And there's a opportunity to work with Congress to pass a progrowth package that'll deal with the uncertainty.

Any package has got to remember that jobs are created by small businesses. A good package will have incentives for investment in it. The package we passed early in my administration helped him. He bought some equipment, made his firm more productive, kept him in business. That's the same spirit that needs to be in this next growth package.

The other thing is, is that we've got to make sure that we benefit consumers. We want our consumers out there spending, and the best way to do that is through broad-based tax relief. Now, this plan ought to be broad-based, it ought to be simple, and it ought to be temporary.

I had a conversation with Congressmen, with the leadership on both sides of the aisle yesterday, and I was encouraged by what I heard. And I believe we can come together on a growth package very quickly. We're going to need to. We need to get this deal done and get it out and get money in the hands of our consumers and small-business owners to help this economy.

I'm optimistic, I truly am. One reason I'm optimistic is cause I understand we got all kinds of Americans just like this man

here, who is working hard to provide a living for folks and to make a product people want.

And so while there's some uncertainty right now, if we act quickly and in a smart way that helps growth, we're going to be just fine.

Anyway, thanks for letting me come by. I'm proud to be—I love the entrepreneurial class in America. I love people who have a dream and work hard to achieve the dream.

And so a fine-looking machine you got here.

William Wright. Thank you. It's a team effort. We're thanking you, thanking you for all your work too.

The President. Do you wonder where they got the name "Wright"? That's his name. And his wife is the cofounder of the company. And this is—it's really great to be with you.

And, Congressman, thank you for being here. I'm proud to be with your workers. You've got some fine workers.

Mr. Wright. We've got a great team here, don't we?

The President. Yes, you do. And if they get a little more money in their pocket as a result of the growth package, it'll help make sure this economy continues to grow.

Anyway, thank you all very much.

NOTE: The President spoke at 1:55 p.m. In his remarks, he referred to William Wright, president and chief executive officer, Wright Manufacturing, Inc., and his wife Margie; and Rep. Roscoe G. Bartlett.

Letter to Congressional Leaders on Continuation of the National Emergency With Respect to Terrorists Who Threaten To Disrupt the Middle East Peace Process
January 18, 2008

Dear Madam Speaker: (Dear Mr. President:)

Section 202(d) of the National Emergencies Act (50 U.S.C. 1622(d)) provides for the automatic termination of a national emergency unless, prior to the anniversary date of its declaration, the President publishes in the *Federal Register* and transmits to the Congress a notice stating that the emergency is to continue in effect beyond the anniversary date. In accordance with this provision, I have sent to the *Federal Register* for publication the enclosed notice, stating that the emergency declared with respect to foreign terrorists who threaten to disrupt the Middle East peace process is to continue in effect beyond January 23, 2008.

The crisis with respect to the grave acts of violence committed by foreign terrorists who threaten to disrupt the Middle East peace process that led to the declaration of a national emergency on January 23, 1995, as expanded on August 20, 1998, has not been resolved. Terrorist groups continue to engage in activities that have the purpose or effect of threatening the Middle East peace process and that are hostile to United States interests in the region. Such actions constitute an unusual and extraordinary threat to the national security, foreign policy, and economy of the United States. For these reasons, I have determined that it is necessary to continue the national emergency declared with respect to foreign terrorists who threaten to disrupt the Middle East peace process and to maintain in force the economic sanctions against them to respond to this threat.

Sincerely,

GEORGE W. BUSH

NOTE: Identical letters were sent to Nancy Pelosi, Speaker of the House of Representatives, and Richard B. Cheney, President of the Senate. The notice is listed in Appendix D at the end of this volume.

The President's Radio Address
January 19, 2008

Good morning. Yesterday I visited Wright Manufacturing, a business in Frederick, Maryland, that makes commercial lawnmowers. Businesses like Wright are the driving force behind our economic success. They create jobs and opportunities for millions of workers. And entrepreneurs like those at Wright Manufacturing keep our economy growing.

This is a challenging period for our economy, and I know many of you listening are concerned about the future. My advisers and many outside experts expect that our economy will continue to grow over the coming year, but at a slower rate than we have enjoyed for the past few years. And there's a risk of a downturn. Continued instability in the housing market, for example, could cause additional harm to the overall economy and put our growth and job creation in jeopardy.

In recent months, we have taken steps to shore up the housing sector, including measures to help struggling homeowners avoid foreclosure and keep their homes. I have also asked Congress to pass legislation to modernize the Federal Housing Administration and enable it to provide more assistance to struggling homeowners. Congress needs to send me a bill with these reforms right away.

After careful consideration and discussion with Members of Congress, I have concluded that additional action is needed to keep our economy growing and creating jobs. Congress and my administration need to work together to enact an economic growth package as soon as possible.

As Congress considers such a plan, there are certain principles that should guide their deliberations. This growth package must be big enough to make a difference in an economy as large and dynamic as ours, which means it should be about 1 percent of GDP. This growth package must be built on broad-based tax relief that will directly affect economic growth, not the kind of spending projects that would have little immediate impact on our economy. This growth package must be temporary and take effect right away so we can get help to our economy when it is needed most. And this growth package must not include any tax increases.

Specifically, this growth package should bolster both business investment and consumer spending, which are critical to economic growth. This requires two key provisions. To be effective, a growth package must include tax incentives for American businesses, including small businesses, to make investments in their enterprises this year. And it must also include direct and rapid income tax relief for Americans like you.

Passing a new growth package is our most pressing economic priority. And when that is done, Congress must turn to the most important economic priority for our country: making sure the tax relief now in place is not taken away from you. Unless Congress acts, the marriage penalty will make a comeback, the child tax credit will be cut in half, the death tax will come back to life, and tax rates will go up on regular income, capital gains, and dividends. This tax increase would put jobs and economic growth at risk. So it is critical that Congress make this tax relief permanent.

I am optimistic about our economy because people like you have shown time and again that Americans are the most industrious, creative, and enterprising people in the world. That is what has made our economy strong, and that is what will make it stronger in the challenging times ahead.

Thank you for listening.

NOTE: The address was recorded at 12:15 p.m. on January 18 in the Cabinet Room at the White House for broadcast at 10:06 a.m. on January 19. The transcript was made available by the Office of the Press Secretary on January 18, but was embargoed for release until the broadcast. The Office of the Press Secretary also released a Spanish language transcript of this address.

Remarks During a Visit to the Martin Luther King, Jr., Memorial Library
January 21, 2008

Thanks for having us. Listen, Laura and I are thrilled to be with you. We're honored to be with the Mayor and Councilman Jack Evans. We appreciate very much the—Serve DC, that is working to inspire volunteerism, and I want to thank this beautiful library for hosting us.

I just got a couple of comments I want to say. First of all, Martin Luther King Day is—means two things to me. One is the opportunity to renew our deep desire for America to be a hope—a land of promise for everybody, a land of justice, and a land of opportunity. It's also an opportunity to serve our fellow citizens. They say Martin Luther King Day is not a day off, it should be a day on. And so today Laura and I witnessed acts of compassion as citizens were here in the library volunteering their time, and that's what's happening all across America today.

But a day on should be not just one day, it really ought to be every day. And our fellow citizens have got to understand that by loving a neighbor like you'd like to be loved yourself, by reaching out to someone who hurts, by just simply living a life of kindness and compassion, you can make America a better place and fulfill the dream of Martin Luther King.

Martin Luther King is a towering figure in the history of our country. And it is fitting that we honor his service and his courage and his vision. And today we're witnessing people doing just that by volunteering their time.

So we're honored to be with you. We're proud to be with you on this important national holiday. Mr. Mayor, thank you for coming. Jack, glad you're here. Appreciate you all taking time out of your day to visit with us.

And thank you.

NOTE: The President spoke at 9:42 a.m. In his remarks, he referred to Mayor Adrian M. Fenty of Washington, DC; and Jack Evans, council member, Council of the District of Columbia.

Remarks to March for Life Participants
January 22, 2008

Nellie, good to be with you. We're fellow west Texans who care deeply about the value of human life. Other members of the board of directors for the March for Life, leaders of the pro-life community, and all those who are here with us for the march, it's good to have you here, and welcome to the White House.

As I look out at you, I'll see some folks who have been traveling all night to get here. [*Laughter*] You're slightly bleary eyed. [*Laughter*] I'll see others who are getting ready for a day out in the cold. But mostly I see faces that shine with a love for life.

I see people with a deep conviction that even the most vulnerable member of the human family is a child of God. You're here because you know that all life deserves to be protected. And as you begin your march, I'm proud to be standing with you.

Thirty-five years ago today, the United States Supreme Court declared and de-cided that under the law, an unborn child is not considered a person. But we know many things about the unborn. Biology confirms that from the start, each unborn child is a separate individual with his or her own genetic code. Babies can now survive outside the mother's womb at younger and younger ages. And the fingers and toes and beating hearts that we can see on an unborn child's ultrasound come with something that we cannot see, a soul.

Today we're heartened by the news that the number of abortions is declining. But the most recent data reports that more than one in five pregnancies end in an abortion. America is better than this, so we will continue to work for a culture of life where a woman with an unplanned pregnancy knows there are caring people who will support her, where a pregnant teen can carry her child and complete her education, where the dignity of both the mother and child is honored and cherished.

We aspire to build a society where each one of us is welcomed in life and protected in law. We haven't arrived, but we are making progress. Here in Washington, we passed good laws that promote adoption and extend legal protection to children who are born despite abortion attempts. We came together to ban the cruel practice of partial-birth abortion. And in the past year, we have prevented that landmark law from being rolled back.

We've seen the dramatic breakthroughs in stem cell research, that it is possible to advance medical science while respecting the sanctity of life. Building a culture of life requires more than law; it requires changing hearts. And as we reach out to others and find common ground, we can see the glimmerings of a new America on a far shore. This America is rooted in our belief that in a civilized society, the strong protect the weak. This America is nurtured by people like you, who speak up for the weak and the innocent. This America is the destiny of a people whose founding document speaks of the right to life that is a gift of our Creator, not a grant of the state.

My friends, the time is short, and your march is soon. [*Laughter*] As you give voice to the voiceless I ask you to take comfort from this: The hearts of the American people are good. Their minds are open to persuasion. And our history shows that a cause rooted in human dignity and appealing to the best instincts of the American people cannot fail. So take heart.

Take heart, be strong, and go forth. May God bless you.

NOTE: The President spoke at 9:01 a.m. in the East Room at the White House for later broadcast to march participants on the National Mall in Washington, DC. In his remarks, he referred to Nellie J. Gray, president, March for Life Education and Defense Fund. A tape was not available for verification of the content of these remarks. The related National Sanctity of Human Life Day proclamation is listed in Appendix D at the end of this volume.

Remarks Prior to a Meeting With Congressional Leaders
January 22, 2008

I want to thank the leaders for coming. I initially intended to brief the leaders of the House and the Senate on my trip to the Middle East, and I intend to do so. But we're going to spend some time talking about this economy and the need for us to find common ground for an effective progrowth economic package. We had a good call last Thursday, and I want to thank the Speaker and the leader and other Members. And Secretary Paulson had a good meeting today.

I believe we can find common ground to get something done that's big enough and effective enough so that an economy that is inherently strong gets a boost to make sure that this uncertainty doesn't translate into more economic woes for our workers and small-business people.

And so I really want to thank you all for coming, and I'm looking forward to our discussions. And look, there's a—everybody wants to get something done quickly, but we want to make sure it gets done right and make sure that we're—everybody is realistic about a—the timetable. Legislative bodies don't move as—necessarily in an orderly, quick way. And therefore, these leaders are committed, and they want to get something done. But we want to make sure we're realistic about how fast that can possibly happen. And so when we say, "as soon as possible," that means within the—obviously within the ability of these bodies to effectively do their jobs.

So I have got reasonable expectations about how fast something can happen, but

I also am optimistic that something will happen. And I appreciate very much the leadership being here today. Thank you all.

NOTE: The President spoke at 2:43 p.m. in the Cabinet Room at the White House.

Remarks on the President's Advisory Council on Financial Literacy
January 22, 2008

I appreciate members of my Cabinet joining me today with some of our citizens who care about the future of our country and are willing to do something about it. Earlier today I signed an Executive order establishing the President's Advisory Council on Financial Literacy. I have asked people from the business world, the faith world, the nonprofit world to join this council in order to come up with recommendations as to how to better educate people from all walks of life about matters pertaining to their finances and their future.

Chuck Schwab is the Chairman of this group, and John Hope Bryant is the Vice Chair. These two men have agreed to take time to take the lead, and I appreciate it.

You know, it's interesting that if we want America to be as hopeful a place as it can be, we want people owning assets; we want people investing; we want people owning homes. But oftentimes, to be able to do so requires literacy when it comes to financial matters. And sometimes people just simply don't know what they're looking at and reading. And it can lead to personal financial crises, and that personal financial crises, if accumulated to too many folks, hurts our country.

One of the issues that many of our folks are facing now are these subprime mortgages. I just wonder how many people, when they bought a subprime mortgage, knew what they were getting into. The low

interest rates sounded very attractive, and all of a sudden, that contract kicks in, and people are paying high interest rates. One of the missions is to make sure that when somebody gets a financial instrument, they know what they're getting into; they know what they're buying; they understand.

We want people to own assets. We want people to be able to manage their assets. We want people to understand basic financial concepts and how credit cards work and how credit scores affect you, how you can benefit from a savings account or a bank account. That's what we want. And this group of citizens has taken the lead, and I really thank them—thank you a lot.

There's a—I understand that there are immediate concerns and that one of them has to do with our economy. This administration is monitoring our economy very carefully. Secretary Paulson is frequently giving me updates about conversations he's had with people around the world and obviously with people inside America about our economy.

We have confidence in the long-term strength of America, and so should the American people. This is a flexible, this is a resilient, this is a dynamic economy, and the entrepreneurial spirit is high. But there is some uncertainty that we're going to have to deal with. And one good way to deal with that uncertainty is to work with Congress to pass an economic growth package, a package that is big enough to affect a large economy, a package that will stimulate consumer spending, and a package that will stimulate business, including small business, investment.

Hank had good meetings today with the leadership up there on Capitol Hill, very constructive meetings that lead me to say that I'm confident that we can get an agreement passed, and we can get an agreement passed in relatively short order. All of us want to get something done. All of us want to get something done that will be temporary and effective, and all of us want to get something done as fast as possible.

Earlier today I commented that the legislative process takes time, and I just want to make sure that people's expectations are set right. But I left the meeting that I just had in the Cabinet Room with the leadership in the House and the Senate with a very positive feeling. All of us understand that we need to work together, all of us understand that we need to do some-

thing that will be effective, and all of us understand that now is the time to work together to get a package done.

And that's why Secretary Paulson has taken the lead for our administration. He will be the negotiator for the administration. He too is upbeat that we can get something done.

I appreciate very much you all coming. I appreciate what you're doing. When we look back at this council, and people will say, "Well, we're glad that the administration took the action it took because somebody's life is going to be better as a result of it."

Thanks for serving. God bless. Appreciate you.

NOTE: The President spoke at 4:05 p.m. in the Roosevelt Room at the White House. Executive Order 13455, establishing the President's Advisory Council on Financial Literacy, is listed in Appendix D at the end of this volume.

Message to the Congress Transmitting the Turkey-United States Agreement Concerning Peaceful Uses of Nuclear Energy
January 22, 2008

To the Congress of the United States:

I transmit to the Congress, pursuant to sections 123 b. and 123 d. of the Atomic Energy Act of 1954, as amended (42 U.S.C. 2153(b),(d))(the "Act"), the text of the proposed Agreement for Cooperation between the United States of America and the Republic of Turkey Concerning Peaceful Uses of Nuclear Energy (the "Agreement") together with a copy of the unclassified Nuclear Proliferation Assessment Statement (NPAS) and of my approval of the proposed Agreement and determination that the proposed Agreement will promote, and will not constitute an unreasonable risk to, the common defense and security. The Secretary of State will submit the classified

NPAS and accompanying annexes separately in appropriate secure channels.

The Agreement was signed on July 26, 2000, and President Clinton approved and authorized execution and made the determinations required by section 123 b. of the Act (Presidential Determination 2000–26, 65 *FR* 44403 (July 18, 2000)). However, immediately after signature, U.S. agencies received information that called into question the conclusions that had been drawn in the required NPAS and the original classified annex, specifically, information implicating Turkish private entities in certain activities directly relating to nuclear proliferation. Consequently, the Agreement was not submitted to the Congress and the executive branch undertook a review of the NPAS evaluation.

My Administration has completed the NPAS review as well as an evaluation of actions taken by the Turkish government to address the proliferation activities of certain Turkish entities (once officials of the U.S. Government brought them to the Turkish government's attention). The Secretary of State, the Secretary of Energy, and the members of the Nuclear Regulatory Commission are confident that the pertinent issues have been sufficiently resolved and that there is a sufficient basis (as set forth in the classified annexes, which will be transmitted separately by the Secretary of State) to proceed with congressional review of the Agreement and, if legislation is not enacted to disapprove it, to bring the Agreement into force.

In my judgment, entry into force of the Agreement will serve as a strong incentive for Turkey to continue its support for nonproliferation objectives and enact future sound nonproliferation policies and practices. It will also promote closer political and economic ties with a NATO ally, and provide the necessary legal framework for U.S. industry to make nuclear exports to Turkey's planned civil nuclear sector.

This transmittal shall constitute a submittal for purposes of both section 123 b. and 123 d. of the Act. My Administration is prepared to begin immediate consultations with the Senate Foreign Relations Committee and the House Foreign Affairs Committee as provided in section 123 b. Upon completion of the period of 30 days of continuous session provided for in section 123 b., the period of 60 days of continuous session provided for in section 123 d. shall commence.

GEORGE W. BUSH

The White House,
January 22, 2008.

NOTE: This message was released by the Office of the Press Secretary on January 23. The related Presidential determination of January 22 is listed in Appendix D at the end of this volume.

Message to the Senate Transmitting the Romania-United States Extradition Treaty and Protocols on Mutual Legal Assistance in Criminal Matters
January 22, 2008

To the Senate of the United States:

With a view to receiving the advice and consent of the Senate to ratification, I transmit herewith the Extradition Treaty between the United States of America and Romania (the "Extradition Treaty" or the "Treaty") and the Protocol to the Treaty between the United States of America and Romania on Mutual Legal Assistance in Criminal Matters (the "Protocol"), both signed at Bucharest on September 10, 2007. I also transmit, for the information of the Senate, the reports of the Department of State with respect to the Extradition Treaty and Protocol.

The Extradition Treaty would replace the outdated Extradition Treaty between the United States and Romania, signed in Bucharest on July 23, 1924, and the Supplementary Extradition Treaty, signed in Bucharest on November 10, 1936. The Protocol amends the Treaty Between the United States of America and Romania on Mutual Legal Assistance in Criminal Matters, signed in Washington on May 26, 1999 (the "1999 Mutual Legal Assistance Treaty"). Both the Extradition Treaty and the

Protocol also fulfill the requirements for bilateral instruments (between the United States and each European Union (EU) Member State) that are contained in the Extradition and Mutual Legal Assistance Agreements between the United States and the EU currently before the Senate.

The Extradition Treaty follows generally the form and content of other extradition treaties recently concluded by the United States. It would replace an outmoded list of extraditable offenses with a modern "dual criminality" approach, which would enable extradition for such offenses as money laundering and other newer offenses not appearing on the list. The Treaty also contains a modernized "political offense" clause, and it provides that neither Party shall refuse extradition based on the citizenship of the person sought. Finally, the new Treaty incorporates a series of procedural improvements to streamline and speed the extradition process. The Protocol primarily serves to amend the 1999 Mutual

Legal Assistance Treaty in areas required pursuant to the U.S.-EU Mutual Legal Assistance Agreement, specifically: mutual legal assistance to administrative authorities; expedited transmission of requests; use limitations; identification of bank information; joint investigative teams; and video conferencing.

I recommend that the Senate give early and favorable consideration to the Extradition Treaty and the Protocol, along with the U.S.-EU Extradition and Mutual Legal Assistance Agreements and the other related bilateral instruments between the United States and European Union Member States.

GEORGE W. BUSH

The White House,
January 22, 2008.

NOTE: This message was released by the Office of the Press Secretary on January 23.

Message to the Senate Transmitting the International Convention on the Control of Harmful Anti-Fouling Systems on Ships
January 22, 2008

To the Senate of the United States:

I transmit herewith, for the advice and consent of the Senate to its ratification, the International Convention on the Control of Harmful Anti-Fouling Systems on Ships, 2001 (the "Convention").

The Convention aims to control the harmful effects of anti-fouling systems, which are used on the hulls of ships to prevent the growth of marine organisms. These systems are necessary to increase fuel efficiency and minimize the transport of hull-borne species; however, anti-fouling systems can also have negative effects on the marine environment, including when a vessel remains in place for a period of time (such as in port).

To mitigate these effects, the Convention prohibits Parties from using organotin-based anti-fouling systems on their ships, and it prohibits ships that use such systems from entering Parties' ports, shipyards, or offshore terminals. The Convention authorizes controls on use of other anti-fouling systems that could be added in the future, after a comprehensive review process.

The Convention was adopted at a Diplomatic Conference of the International Maritime Organization in October 2001 and signed by the United States on December 12, 2002. The United States played a leadership role in the negotiation and development of the Convention. With Panama's ratification of the Convention on September 17, 2007, 25 States representing over 25 percent of the world's merchant shipping tonnage have now ratified the Convention. Therefore, the Convention will enter into force on September 17, 2008.

Organotin-based anti-fouling systems are specifically regulated through the Organotin Anti-Fouling Paint Control Act of 1988 (OAPCA), 33 U.S.C. 2401–2410. New legislation is required to fully implement the Convention and will take the form of a complete revision and replacement of OAPCA. All interested executive branch agencies support ratification. I recommend that the Senate give early and favorable consideration to the Convention and give its advice and consent to its ratification, with the declaration set out in the analysis of Article 16 in the attached article-by-article analysis.

GEORGE W. BUSH

The White House,
January 22, 2008.

NOTE: This message was released by the Office of the Press Secretary on January 23.

Message to the Senate Transmitting the Republic of Bulgaria-United States Extradition Treaty and Agreement on Mutual Legal Assistance in Criminal Matters
January 22, 2008

To the Senate of the United States:

With a view to receiving the advice and consent of the Senate to ratification, I transmit herewith the Extradition Treaty between the Government of the United States of America and the Government of the Republic of Bulgaria (the "Extradition Treaty" or the "Treaty") and the Agreement on Certain Aspects of Mutual Legal Assistance in Criminal Matters between the Government of the United States of America and the Government of the Republic of Bulgaria (the "MLA Agreement"), both signed at Sofia on September 19, 2007. I also transmit, for the information of the Senate, the report of the Department of State with respect to the Extradition Treaty and the MLA Agreement.

The new Extradition Treaty would replace the outdated Extradition Treaty between the United States and Bulgaria, signed in Sofia on March 19, 1924, and the Supplementary Extradition Treaty, signed in Washington on June 8, 1934. The MLA Agreement is the first agreement between the two countries on mutual legal assistance in criminal matters. Both the Extradition Treaty and the MLA Agreement fulfill the requirements for bilateral instruments (between the United States and each European Union (EU) Member State) that are contained in the Extradition and Mutual Legal Assistance Agreements between the United States and the EU currently before the Senate.

The Extradition Treaty follows generally the form and content of other extradition treaties recently concluded by the United States. It would replace an outmoded list of extraditable offenses with a modern "dual criminality" approach, which would enable extradition for such offenses as money laundering, and other newer offenses not appearing on the list. The Treaty also contains a modernized "political offense" clause, and it provides that extradition shall not be refused based on the nationality of a person sought for any of a comprehensive list of serious offenses. Finally, the new Treaty incorporates a series of procedural improvements to streamline and speed the extradition process.

Because the United States and Bulgaria do not have a bilateral mutual legal assistance treaty in force between them, the MLA Agreement is a partial treaty governing only those issues regulated by the U.S.-EU Mutual Legal Assistance Agreement, specifically: identification of bank information, joint investigative teams, videoconferencing, expedited transmission of requests, assistance to administrative authorities, use limitations, confidentiality, and grounds for refusal. This approach is consistent with that taken with the other EU Member States (Denmark, Finland, Malta, Portugal, Slovak Republic, and Slovenia) with which the United States did not have an existing mutual legal assistance treaty.

I recommend that the Senate give early and favorable consideration to the Extradition Treaty and MLA Agreement, along with the U.S.-EU Extradition and Mutual Legal Assistance Agreements and the other related bilateral instruments between the United States and European Union Member States.

GEORGE W. BUSH

The White House,

January 22, 2008.

NOTE: This message was released by the Office of the Press Secretary on January 23.

Remarks During a Briefing With Mayors on Free Trade Agreements
January 23, 2008

I'm so honored that mayors from around our country have come. First of all, I want to thank you all very much for serving. I've often said being mayor is a lot tougher than being President—I don't have to fill the potholes and empty the garbage. [*Laughter*] But I thank you for serving our country.

We've got mayors from both political parties here. We didn't have a political discussion; we had a discussion on what's best for America, particularly given the economic uncertainty we face. I talked to them about my desire to work with the Congress to get a stimulus package passed, one that's going to be robust enough to affect the economy, simple enough for people to understand it, and efficient enough to have an impact. And I'm confident that we can get something done. There's a spirit of— that is—that says, we need to take a fundamentally strong economy and help it with a—deal with the uncertainties with a progrowth package.

One way we can also send a message that we can—want to continue to grow is to open up markets for U.S. products and services. We were talking about these trade votes that are coming up in front of the Congress and the importance of getting markets opened up for our workers and entrepreneurs. These trade agreements that we're about to vote on—there are goods coming from their countries coming to our country relatively tariff free; our goods and services going to their country with a tariff on it. In other words, they're not treating us the way we're treating them.

The American people expect us to be— expect America to be treated fairly, and that's what these free trade agreements do. It certainly doesn't make any sense to say in a country like Colombia, your goods can come in our way, but our goods can't come your way—being treated the same way. And by opening up markets, by having us treated fairly, we'll have 100 million new customers. And I like that opportunity for American workers and farmers and businesspeople. See, I believe we can compete with anybody, anywhere, so long as the rules are fair.

And so these mayors who are living close to the people understand that by opening up markets, businesses in their communities and workers in their communities will benefit. And I want to thank you all for coming. We have a good opportunity to get the deal done, and I'm looking forward to working with Congress to get these packages passed. These are progrowth, and they're good for America. And thanks for giving Secretary Gutierrez and I a chance to visit with you.

Thank you.

NOTE: The President spoke at 1:45 p.m. in the Roosevelt Room at the White House.

Statement on Signing an Executive Order To Reform How the United States Reviews National Security Concerns That May Arise From Foreign Investments
January 23, 2008

Today I issued an Executive order reforming how the United States reviews national security concerns that may arise from foreign investments, in light of the Foreign Investment and National Security Act of 2007. The Executive order furthers the goals of the new law by ensuring that the Committee on Foreign Investment in the United States will review carefully the national security concerns, if any, raised by certain foreign investments into the United States. The Executive order reaffirms our commitment to open economies and our policy of welcoming foreign investment and the important economic benefits that such investment brings. At the same time, the Executive order sets forth procedures for protecting our national security, recognizing that our openness is vital to our prosperity and security.

NOTE: The statement referred to Executive Order 13456, which is listed in Appendix D at the end of this volume.

Remarks on a Bipartisan Economic Growth Agreement
January 24, 2008

This morning my administration reached an agreement with Speaker Pelosi and Minority Leader Boehner on an economic growth package. And, Mr. Secretary, thank you for handling negotiations, and appreciate your hard work.

This agreement was the result of intensive discussions and many phone calls, late-night meetings, and the kind of cooperation that some predicted was not possible here in Washington. It also required patience, determination, and good will. I thank the Speaker and I thank Leader Boehner for their hard work and for their leadership and for showing the American people that we can come together to help our Nation deal with difficult economic challenges.

I am pleased that this agreement meets the criterion that I set forth last week to provide an effective, robust, and temporary set of incentives that will boost our economy and encourage job creation. This package has the right set of policies and is the right size. The incentives in this package will lead to higher consumer spending and increased business investment this year. Importantly, this package recognizes that lowering taxes is a powerful and efficient way to help consumers and businesses. I have always believed that allowing people to keep more of their own money and to use it as they see fit is the best way to help our economy grow.

I'm also pleased that this agreement does not include any tax increases as well as unnecessary spending projects that would have little immediate impact on our economy.

I know Americans are concerned about our economic future. Our economy is structurally sound, but it is dealing with short-term disruptions in the housing market and the impact of higher energy prices. These challenges are slowing growth. Yet Americans can also be confident about our long-term outlook. Our economy is strong, it is dynamic, and it is resilient. It has led the world for many decades, and with the right policies in place, including the extension of the tax cuts passed in 2001 and 2003 that have helped our economy, I firmly believe we're going to continue to lead the world.

Because the country needs this boost to the economy now, I urge the House and the Senate to enact this economic growth agreement into law as soon as possible. We have an opportunity to come together and take the swift, decisive action our economy urgently needs.

Secretary Paulson is here to answer any of your questions. At my request, he has taken the lead in negotiations, like I mentioned, and I—you did a superb job, Mr. Secretary. Thank you very much.

NOTE: The President spoke at 2:31 p.m. in the James S. Brady Press Briefing Room at the White House.

Remarks Following a Meeting With Elsa Morejon
January 24, 2008

The President. A while ago I had the honor of presenting the National Medal of Freedom to a patriot of Cuba and a lover of liberty, Oscar Biscet. He was not able to receive the award because he's in a Cuban prison for speaking out on behalf of human rights and human dignity. Today his wife Elsa Morejon is here. She has taken some time from Cuba to come to the United States to visit her son. She came up to the Oval Office to see me, and I'm most honored and most grateful.

We have a comfortable life here in America by and large, and it's hard for us to imagine what it would be like for— to live in a society as repressive as the society of Fidel and Raul Castro. This good woman has had to suffer through days and weeks of deprivation and worry because the love of her life is in a Cuban prison simply because of his beliefs. It's my honor to welcome you here.

My call is for the world to help women such as Elsa. My call is for those who believe that the Cuba of today is a hopeful place to recognize the realities. This is a country that has got political prisoners who are languishing in the jails, who are mistreated in the jails. Our message is, is that political prisoners ought to be free and so should the Cuban people, free to express themselves and free to realize their God-given talents. So I want to welcome you. *Que Dios le bendiga.*

Ms. Morejon. My name is Elsa Morejon. I'm a Cuban woman. I've come here to the United States to visit my son. My husband has spent most of his youth and is now sentenced to 25 more years in jail for defending human rights and for defending civil liberties. He has devoted his life to the cause of defending human rights in Cuba and throughout the world. We do not live in a free country, and I must now return to Cuba.

I want to thank President Bush for inviting me to this meeting today. And I would like to speak to the international community and exhort them to work for the release of all political prisoners, along with my husband, to obtain their immediate and unconditional release from Cuban prisons.

The President. Thank you.

Ms. Morejon. Thank you.

NOTE: The President spoke at 3 p.m. in the Oval Office at the White House. In his remarks, he referred to Yan Valdes Morejon, son of Elsa Morejon; and President Fidel Castro Ruz and Vice President Raul Castro Ruz of Cuba. Ms. Morejon spoke in Spanish, and her remarks were translated by an interpreter.

Statement on Congressional Action on Intelligence Reform Legislation
January 24, 2008

Last August, Congress passed the Protect America Act, which updated our foreign intelligence surveillance law to adapt to today's technology and to meet today's threats. This bipartisan legislation has aided our efforts to monitor the communications of terrorists and other foreign intelligence targets.

Unfortunately, Congress set this legislation to expire on February 1st. That is just 8 days from today, yet the threat from Al Qaida will not expire in 8 days.

If Congress does not act quickly, our national security professionals will not be able to count on critical tools they need to protect our Nation, and our ability to respond quickly to new threats and circumstances will be weakened. That means it will become harder to figure out what our enemies are doing to recruit terrorists and infiltrate them into our country.

Last fall, the Senate Intelligence Committee completed its work on a bipartisan bill to modernize our foreign intelligence surveillance law. I commend Senators Rockefeller and Bond, the committee's chairman and vice chairman, for leading the effort to complete work on this bill.

The Senate Intelligence Committee's bill contains many provisions that our intelligence officials say they need to protect our country. The bill would maintain the vital flow of intelligence on terrorist threats. It would protect the freedoms of Americans while making sure we do not extend those same protections to terrorists overseas. And it would provide liability protection to companies now facing billion-dollar lawsuits only because they are believed to have assisted in efforts to defend our Nation following the 9/11 attacks.

This bill still needs some changes, but I am optimistic that with good will on both sides, we can make those changes quickly. So I ask congressional leaders to follow the course set by their colleagues on the Senate Intelligence Committee, bring this legislation to a prompt vote in both houses, and send me a bill that I can sign before the Protect America Act expires on February 1st.

Congress's action—or lack of action—on this important issue will directly affect our ability to keep Americans safe.

Remarks to the "Congress of Tomorrow" Luncheon in White Sulphur Springs, West Virginia
January 25, 2008

Thank you. I want to thank Tom; he read it just like I wrote it. [*Laughter*] Thanks for your warm welcome. I'm glad to be with you. I'm looking forward to spending some of the afternoon with you, and then I've got to get back to write the State of the Union he was talking about.

Two issues I'm going to talk about in the State of the Union require our immediate attention, and that's an economic growth package that will keep this economy of ours healthy and legislation making sure our professionals—our intelligence professionals have the tools they need to protect the United States of America.

I am confident in the long-term strength of our Nation's economy. I believe that the fundamentals are sound. I know the entrepreneurial spirit is high. We have a flexible, we have a resilient, and we have a dynamic economy. But there are some uncertainties. And after a lot of thought, I called on the Congress, and your leaders responded to enact a growth package so we can reduce the risk of an economic downturn this year.

Speaker Pelosi and Leader Boehner have demonstrated strong leadership. They reached an agreement on a proposal that will have a positive impact on our economy. Congress should move it quickly. And I understand the desire to add provisions from both the right and the left. I strongly believe it would be a mistake to delay or derail this bill.

This package is big enough to affect the economy in positive ways, it will provide immediate help, and it's temporary. The entire package is tax relief. There are no tax increases, no unnecessary spending or regulatory projects; income tax cuts for a lot of people, as well as bonus depreciation for small—for our businesses and small business expensing. It's a sound package. It makes a lot of sense. It's needed, and you need to pass it as quickly as possible to get money in the hands of the people who are going to help this economy stay strong.

Now I want you—I'll make sure you understand in the State of the Union that this package certainly doesn't mean we ought to do something else on taxes. And the best thing we can do to deal with uncertainty in the economy is make the tax cuts we passed permanent. [*Applause*] Thank you. Thank you all.

Our most solemn duty is to protect the American people, and I appreciate the fact that we've worked closely together over the last 7 years to do just that. That is our most solemn duty. Fortunately, we've got a lot of good people working hard to help us protect America, and these professionals need the tools they need to do their jobs.

You know, one of the most important tools is to be able to figure out the intentions of an enemy that still wants to do us harm. If they're making calls into America, we need to know why they're calling, what they're thinking, and what they're planning. We passed the Protect America Act that has aided our efforts to monitor the communications of terrorists and foreign intelligence targets. And I want to thank the—the good work of the people here to get that bill passed last year.

Unfortunately, the bill is set to expire in 7 days. The threat to America does not expire in 7 days. The Senate Intelligence Committee completed work last fall on a bipartisan bill that we can support. It may need some tweaks, but we—it's a good bill in this sense: It will maintain the vital flow of intelligence on terrorist threats to protect the privacy of Americans while making sure we do not extend those same protections to terrorists overseas. It will provide liability protection to companies now facing billion dollars in lawsuits only because they are believed to have assisted the efforts to defend our Nation following the 9/11 attacks.

I'm looking forward to coming before you in Congress and to say as plainly as I can: This bill is important to the security of the United States of America, and the Congress needs to get a good bill to my desk as soon as possible.

Anyway, I'm looking forward to working with you. I thank you. I appreciate the leadership. I appreciate the chance to come and visit with you. Thank you for being friends. Thank you for serving our country.

I also want to thank your families. I understand—I think I've told you this before: I understand what it does to a family to be in public service. You just can't thank our spouses and kids enough for joining in a noble cause of serving the greatest country on the face of the Earth.

I'm proud to be able to thank you and call you friends. I'm proud to be able to thank your families for serving our country as well. God bless.

NOTE: The President spoke at 12:47 p.m. at The Greenbrier. In his remarks, he referred to Rep. Tom Price.

The President's Radio Address
January 26, 2008

Good morning. On Monday night, I will address the American people about the state of our Union. I will report that over the last 7 years, we've made great progress on important issues at home and abroad. I will also report that we have unfinished business before us and we must work together to get it done.

In my speech, I will lay out a full plate of issues for Congress to address in the year ahead. Two of these issues require immediate attention.

First is the economy. I know many of you are worried about the risk of an economic downturn because of the instability in the housing and financial markets. You should know that while economic growth has slowed in recent months, the foundation for long-term growth remains solid. And I believe that with swift action, we can give our economy the boost it needs

to continue expanding and creating new jobs for our citizens.

On Thursday, my administration reached a bipartisan agreement with House Speaker Nancy Pelosi and Minority Leader John Boehner on an economic growth package. This package will deliver direct tax relief to hard-working Americans. It will also include incentives for businesses—including small businesses—to make new investments this year. I ask the House and Senate to enact this package into law as soon as possible. And while I understand the desire to add provisions from both the left and the right, it would be a mistake to undermine this important bipartisan agreement. By working together, we can provide our economy with a shot in the arm when we need it most.

The other urgent issue before Congress is a matter of national security. Congress needs to provide our intelligence professionals with the tools and flexibility they need to protect America from attack. In August, Congress passed a bill that strengthened our ability to monitor terrorist communications. The problem is that Congress set this law to expire on February 1st. That is next Friday. If this law expires, it will become harder to figure out what our enemies are doing to infiltrate our country, harder for us to uncover terrorist plots, and harder to prevent attacks on the American people.

Congress is now considering a bipartisan bill that will allow our professionals to maintain the vital flow of intelligence on terrorist threats. It would protect the freedoms of Americans while making sure we do not extend those same protections to terrorists overseas. It would provide liability protection to companies now facing billion-dollar lawsuits because they are believed to have assisted in efforts to defend our Nation following the 9/11 attacks. I call on Congress to pass this legislation quickly. We need to know who our enemies are and what they are plotting. And we cannot afford to wait until after an attack to put the pieces together.

When I go before Congress on Monday, I will speak more about how we can keep our economy strong and our people safe. I am confident that we can work together to meet our responsibilities in these areas and leave our children a stronger and more prosperous America.

Thank you for listening.

NOTE: The address was recorded at 7:50 a.m. on January 25 in the Cabinet Room at the White House for broadcast at 10:06 a.m. on January 26. The transcript was made available by the Office of the Press Secretary on January 25, but was embargoed for release until the broadcast. The Office of the Press Secretary also released a Spanish language transcript of this address.

Statement on the Situation in Lebanon
January 26, 2008

I strongly condemn the terrorist bombing in Beirut that killed Lebanese Internal Security Forces Captain Wissam Eid and many other Lebanese. I extend condolences to the families of the innocent Lebanese killed in this brutal attack and hope for a rapid recovery for all those wounded.

This bombing, the latest in a series of terrorist attacks targeting those who are working to secure Lebanon's independence and sovereignty, is a part of the continuing assault on Lebanon's institutions. We will not falter in our support for the democratically elected Lebanese Government. We renew our call for the immediate selection of a new President in accordance with Lebanon's Constitution. We demand that Syria, Iran, and their allies end their interference in and obstruction of Lebanon's political process.

The Lebanese people should be able to enjoy security and liberty without the threat of terrorism, violence, and foreign intimidation. I appreciate the U.N.'s efforts to rapidly stand up the Special Tribunal for Lebanon, which will hold accountable those who are responsible for this systematic campaign of murder and intimidation. I urge Lebanon's friends and allies to commit immediately the remaining funds required for the tribunal to commence its work.

Statement on the International Day of Commemoration in Memory of the Victims of the Holocaust
January 27, 2008

On the third International Day of Commemoration, we remember and mourn the victims of the Holocaust.

I was deeply moved by my recent visit to Yad Vashem, Israel's Holocaust museum. Sixty-three years after the liberation of Auschwitz, we must continue to educate ourselves about the lessons of the Holocaust and honor those whose lives were taken as a result of a totalitarian ideology that embraced a national policy of violent hatred, bigotry, and extermination. It is also our responsibility to honor the survivors and those courageous souls who refused to be bystanders and instead risked their own lives to try to save the Nazis' intended victims.

Remembering the victims, heroes, and lessons of the Holocaust remains important today. We must continue to condemn the resurgence of anti-Semitism, that same virulent intolerance that led to the Holocaust, and we must combat bigotry and hatred in all forms in America and abroad. Today provides a sobering reminder that evil exists and a call that when we find evil, we must resist it.

May God bless the memory of the victims of the Holocaust, and may we never forget.

Statement on the Death of Gordon B. Hinckley
January 28, 2008

Laura and I are deeply saddened by the death of our friend Gordon B. Hinckley. While serving for over seven decades in the Church of Jesus Christ of Latter-day Saints, Gordon demonstrated the heart of a servant and the wisdom of a leader. He was a tireless worker and a talented communicator who was respected in his community and beloved by his congregation. As president of his church, he traveled to more than 60 countries to spread a message of love and optimism to the millions of people around the world who shared his faith.

A Mayflower descendent and the grandson of Mormon pioneers, Gordon was a deeply patriotic man. His leadership and service strengthened the board of trustees of Brigham Young University, the Boy Scouts of America, and the 2002 Winter Olympic games in Salt Lake City. In 2004, I was honored to present him with the Medal of Freedom, our Nation's highest civil award, in recognition of his lifelong public service.

Laura and I will miss Gordon's friendship and wisdom. Our thoughts and prayers are with his five children and the rest of the Hinckley family.

NOTE: The statement referred to Kathleen Barnes Walker, Virginia Pearce, Jane Dudley, Richard Hinckley, and Clark Hinckley, children of Mr. Hinckley.

Statement on the Death of Archbishop of Athens and All Greece Christodoulos
January 28, 2008

Laura and I offer our condolences to the people of Greece at this time of mourning for the death of the Archbishop of Athens and All Greece Christodoulos. The late Archbishop was well known as an articulate voice of the Orthodox faith, for his engage-ment in interreligious dialogue, and for his promotion of social programs to help the vulnerable. Our prayers are with the people of Greece and all those who followed his spiritual guidance.

Statement on Senate Confirmation of Edward T. Schafer as Secretary of Agriculture
January 28, 2008

I appreciate that the Senate today unanimously confirmed Ed Schafer to be our next Secretary of Agriculture. As a two-term Governor and business leader, Ed has distinguished himself as an executive with a proven record of results.

Ed will lead a department that oversees our food, agriculture, natural resources, food safety, and health and nutrition programs. He will be an advocate for farmers, ranchers, and consumers as he works to open new markets for their products. And he will work with the Congress to pass a responsible farm bill that will provide a safety net for farmers and protect our lands and the environment while at the same time ensuring Federal tax dollars are spent wisely.

I look forward to seeing Ed take his seat along with the rest of my Cabinet at this evening's State of the Union.

Statement on Signing the National Defense Authorization Act for Fiscal Year 2008
January 28, 2008

Today, I have signed into law H.R. 4986, the National Defense Authorization Act for Fiscal Year 2008. The Act authorizes funding for the defense of the United States and its interests abroad, for military construction, and for national security-related energy programs.

Provisions of the Act, including sections 841, 846, 1079, and 1222, purport to impose requirements that could inhibit the President's ability to carry out his constitutional obligations to take care that the laws be faithfully executed, to protect national security, to supervise the executive branch, and to execute his authority as Commander in Chief. The executive branch shall construe such provisions in a manner consistent with the constitutional authority of the President.

GEORGE W. BUSH

The White House,

January 28, 2008.

NOTE: H.R. 4986, approved January 28, was assigned Public Law No. 110–181.

Address Before a Joint Session of the Congress on the State of the Union
January 28, 2008

Thank you all. Madam Speaker, Vice President Cheney, Members of Congress, distinguished guests, and fellow citizens: Seven years have passed since I first stood before you at this rostrum. In that time, our country has been tested in ways none of us could have imagined. We faced hard decisions about peace and war, rising competition in the world economy, and the health and welfare of our citizens. These issues call for vigorous debate, and I think it's fair to say, we've answered the call. [*Laughter*] Yet history will record that amid our differences, we acted with purpose, and together we showed the world the power and resilience of American self-government.

All of us were sent to Washington to carry out the people's business. That is the purpose of this body. It is the meaning of our oath. It remains our charge to keep.

The actions of the 110th Congress will affect the security and prosperity of our Nation long after this session has ended. In this election year, let us show our fellow Americans that we recognize our responsibilities and are determined to meet them. Let us show them that Republicans and Democrats can compete for votes and cooperate for results at the same time.

From expanding opportunity to protecting our country, we've made good progress. Yet we have unfinished business before us, and the American people expect us to get it done.

In the work ahead, we must be guided by the philosophy that made our Nation great. As Americans, we believe in the power of individuals to determine their destiny and shape the course of history. We believe that the most reliable guide for our country is the collective wisdom of ordinary citizens. And so in all we do, we must trust in the ability of free peoples to make wise decisions and empower them to improve their lives for their futures.

To build a prosperous future, we must trust people with their own money and empower them to grow our economy. As we meet tonight, our economy is undergoing a period of uncertainty. America has added jobs for a record 52 straight months, but jobs are now growing at a slower pace. Wages are up, but so are prices for food and gas. Exports are rising, but the housing market has declined. At kitchen tables across our country, there is a concern about our economic future.

In the long run, Americans can be confident about our economic growth. But in the short run, we can all see that that growth is slowing. So last week, my administration reached agreement with Speaker Pelosi and Republican Leader Boehner on a robust growth package that includes tax relief for individuals and families and incentives for business investment. The temptation will be to load up the bill. That would delay it or derail it, and neither option is acceptable. This is a good agreement that will keep our economy growing and our people working, and this Congress must pass it as soon as possible.

We have other work to do on taxes. Unless Congress acts, most of the tax relief we've delivered over the past 7 years will be taken away. Some in Washington argue that letting tax relief expire is not a tax increase. Try explaining that to 116 million American taxpayers who would see their taxes rise by an average of $1,800. Others have said they would personally be happy to pay higher taxes. I welcome their enthusiasm. I'm pleased to report that the IRS accepts both checks and money orders. [*Laughter*]

Most Americans think their taxes are high enough. With all the other pressures on their finances, American families should not have to worry about their Federal Government taking a bigger bite out of their paychecks. There's only one way to eliminate this uncertainty: Make the tax relief permanent. And Members of Congress should know, if any bill raises taxes reaches my desk, I will veto it.

Just as we trust Americans with their own money, we need to earn their trust by spending their tax dollars wisely. Next week, I'll send you a budget that terminates or substantially reduces 151 wasteful or bloated programs, totaling more than $18 billion. The budget that I will submit will keep America on track for a surplus in 2012. American families have to balance their budgets; so should their Government.

The people's trust in their Government is undermined by congressional earmarks, special interest projects that are often snuck in at the last minute, without discussion or debate. Last year, I asked you to voluntarily cut the number and cost of earmarks in half. I also asked you to stop slipping earmarks into committee reports that never even come to a vote. Unfortunately, neither goal was met. So this time, if you send me an appropriations bill that does not cut the number and cost of earmarks in half, I'll send it back to you with my veto.

And tomorrow I will issue an Executive order that directs Federal agencies to ignore any future earmark that is not voted on by Congress. If these items are truly worth funding, Congress should debate them in the open and hold a public vote.

Our shared responsibilities extend beyond matters of taxes and spending. On housing, we must trust Americans with the responsibility of homeownership and empower them to weather turbulent times in the housing market. My administration brought together the HOPE NOW Alliance, which is helping many struggling homeowners avoid foreclosure. And Congress can help even more. Tonight I ask you to pass legislation to reform Fannie Mae and Freddie Mac, modernize the Federal Housing Administration, and allow State housing agencies to issue tax-free bonds to help homeowners refinance their mortgages. These are difficult times for many American families, and by taking these steps, we can help more of them keep their homes.

To build a future of quality health care, we must trust patients and doctors to make medical decisions and empower them with better information and better options. We share a common goal: making health care more affordable and accessible for all Americans. The best way to achieve that goal is by expanding consumer choice, not Government control. So I have proposed ending the bias in the Tax Code against those who do not get their health insurance through their employer. This one reform would put private coverage within reach for millions, and I call on the Congress to pass it this year.

Congress must also expand health savings accounts, create association health plans for small businesses, promote health information technology, and confront the epidemic of junk medical lawsuits. With all these steps, we will ensure that decisions about your medical care are made in the privacy of your doctor's office, not in the Halls of Congress.

On education, we must trust students to learn, if given the chance, and empower parents to demand results from our schools. In neighborhoods across our country, there are boys and girls with dreams, and a decent education is their only hope of achieving them.

Six years ago, we came together to pass the No Child Left Behind Act, and today, no one can deny its results. Last year, fourth and eighth graders achieved the highest math scores on record. Reading scores are on the rise. African American and Hispanic students posted alltime highs. Now we must work together to increase accountability, add flexibilities for States and districts, reduce the number of high school dropouts, provide extra help for struggling schools.

Members of Congress, the No Child Left Behind Act is a bipartisan achievement. It is succeeding, and we owe it to America's children, their parents, and their teachers to strengthen this good law.

We must also do more to help children when their schools do not measure up. Thanks to the DC Opportunity Scholarships you approved, more than 2,600 of the poorest children in our Nation's Capital have found new hope at a faith-based or other nonpublic school. Sadly, these schools are disappearing at an alarming rate in many of America's inner cities. So I will convene a White House summit aimed at strengthening these lifelines of learning. And to open the doors of these schools to more children, I ask you to support a new $300 million program called Pell Grants for Kids. We have seen how Pell grants help low-income college students realize their full potential. Together, we've expanded the size and reach of these grants. Now let us apply the same spirit to help liberate poor children trapped in failing public schools.

On trade, we must trust American workers to compete with anyone in the world and empower them by opening up new markets overseas. Today, our economic growth increasingly depends on our ability to sell American goods and crops and services all over the world. So we're working to break down barriers to trade and investment wherever we can. We're working for a successful Doha round of trade talks, and we must complete a good agreement this year. At the same time, we're pursuing opportunities to open up new markets by passing free trade agreements.

I thank the Congress for approving a good agreement with Peru. And now I ask you to approve agreements with Colombia and Panama and South Korea. Many products from these nations now enter America duty free, yet many of our products face steep tariffs in their markets. These agreements will level the playing field. They will give us better access to nearly 100 million customers. They will support good jobs for the finest workers in the world, those whose products say "Made in the U.S.A."

These agreements also promote America's strategic interests. The first agreement that will come before you is with Colombia, a friend of America that is confronting violence and terror and fighting drug traffickers. If we fail to pass this agreement, we will embolden the purveyors of false populism in our hemisphere. So we must come together, pass this agreement, and show our neighbors in the region that democracy leads to a better life.

Trade brings better jobs and better choices and better prices. Yet for some Americans, trade can mean losing a job, and the Federal Government has a responsibility to help. I ask Congress to reauthorize and reform trade adjustment assistance so we can help these displaced workers learn new skills and find new jobs.

To build a future of energy security, we must trust in the creative genius of American researchers and entrepreneurs and empower them to pioneer a new generation of clean energy technology. Our security, our prosperity, and our environment all require reducing our dependence on oil.

Last year, I asked you to pass legislation to reduce oil consumption over the next decade, and you responded. Together, we should take the next steps. Let us fund new technologies that can generate coal power while capturing carbon emissions. Let us increase the use of renewable power and emissions-free nuclear power. Let us continue investing in advanced battery technology and renewable fuels to power the cars and trucks of the future. Let us create a new international clean technology fund, which will help developing nations like India and China make a greater use of clean energy sources. And let us complete an international agreement that has the potential to slow, stop, and eventually reverse the growth of greenhouse gases.

This agreement will be effective only if it includes commitments by every major economy and gives none a free ride. The United States is committed to strengthening our energy security and confronting global climate change. And the best way to meet these goals is for America to continue leading the way toward the development of cleaner and more energy efficient technology.

To keep America competitive into the future, we must trust in the skill of our scientists and engineers and empower them to pursue the breakthroughs of tomorrow. Last year, Congress passed legislation supporting the American Competitiveness Initiative, but never followed through with the funding. This funding is essential to keeping our scientific edge. So I ask Congress to double Federal support for critical basic research in the physical sciences and ensure America remains the most dynamic nation on Earth.

On matters of life and science, we must trust in the innovative spirit of medical researchers and empower them to discover new treatments while respecting moral boundaries. In November, we witnessed a landmark achievement when scientists discovered a way to reprogram adult skin cells to act like embryonic stem cells. This breakthrough has the potential to move us beyond the divisive debates of the past by extending the frontiers of medicine without the destruction of human life.

So we're expanding funding for this type of ethical medical research. And as we explore promising avenues of research, we must also ensure that all life is treated with the dignity it deserves. And so I call on Congress to pass legislation that bans unethical practices, such as the buying, selling, patenting, or cloning of human life.

On matters of justice, we must trust in the wisdom of our Founders and empower judges who understand that the Constitution means what it says. I've submitted judicial nominees who will rule by the letter of the law, not the whim of the gavel. Many of these nominees are being unfairly delayed. They are worthy of confirmation, and the Senate should give each of them a prompt up-or-down vote.

In communities across our land, we must trust in the good heart of the American people and empower them to serve their neighbors in need. Over the past 7 years, more of our fellow citizens have discovered that the pursuit of happiness leads to the path of service. Americans have volunteered in record numbers. Charitable donations are higher than ever. Faith-based groups are bringing hope to pockets of despair, with newfound support from the Federal Government. And to help guarantee equal treatment of faith-based organizations when they compete for Federal funds, I ask you to permanently extend charitable choice.

Tonight the armies of compassion continue the march to a new day in the Gulf Coast. America honors the strength and resilience of the people of this region. We reaffirm our pledge to help them build stronger and better than before. And tonight I'm pleased to announce that in April, we will host this year's North American Summit of Canada, Mexico, and the United States in the great city of New Orleans.

There are two other pressing challenges that I've raised repeatedly before this body and that this body has failed to address: entitlement spending and immigration. Every Member in this Chamber knows that spending on entitlement programs like Social Security, Medicare, and Medicaid is growing faster than we can afford. We all know the painful choices ahead if America stays on this path: massive tax increases,

119

sudden and drastic cuts in benefits, or crippling deficits. I've laid out proposals to reform these programs. Now I ask Members of Congress to offer your proposals and come up with a bipartisan solution to save these vital programs for our children and our grandchildren.

The other pressing challenge is immigration. America needs to secure our borders, and with your help, my administration is taking steps to do so. We're increasing worksite enforcement, deploying fences and advanced technologies to stop illegal crossings. We've effectively ended the policy of catch-and-release at the border, and by the end of this year, we will have doubled the number of Border Patrol agents. Yet we also need to acknowledge that we will never fully secure our border until we create a lawful way for foreign workers to come here and support our economy. This will take pressure off the border and allow law enforcement to concentrate on those who mean us harm.

We must also find a sensible and humane way to deal with people here illegally. Illegal immigration is complicated, but it can be resolved. And it must be resolved in a way that upholds both our laws and our highest ideals.

This is the business of our Nation here at home. Yet building a prosperous future for our citizens also depends on confronting enemies abroad and advancing liberty in troubled regions of the world.

Our foreign policy is based on a clear premise: We trust that people, when given the chance, will choose a future of freedom and peace. In the last 7 years, we have witnessed stirring moments in the history of liberty. We've seen citizens in Georgia and Ukraine stand up for their right to free and fair elections. We've seen people in Lebanon take to the streets to demand their independence. We've seen Afghans emerge from the tyranny of the Taliban and choose a new President and a new parliament. We've seen jubilant Iraqis holding up ink-stained fingers and celebrating their freedom. These images of liberty have inspired us.

In the past 7 years, we've also seen the images that have sobered us. We've watched throngs of mourners in Lebanon and Pakistan carrying the caskets of beloved leaders taken by the assassin's hand. We've seen wedding guests in blood-soaked finery staggering from a hotel in Jordan, Afghans and Iraqis blown up in mosques and markets, and trains in London and Madrid ripped apart by bombs. On a clear September day, we saw thousands of our fellow citizens taken from us in an instant. These horrific images serve as a grim reminder: The advance of liberty is opposed by terrorists and extremists, evil men who despise freedom, despise America, and aim to subject millions to their violent rule.

Since 9/11, we have taken the fight to these terrorists and extremists. We will stay on the offense, we will keep up the pressure, and we will deliver justice to our enemies.

We are engaged in the defining ideological struggle of the 21st century. The terrorists oppose every principle of humanity and decency that we hold dear. Yet in this war on terror, there is one thing we and our enemies agree on: In the long run, men and women who are free to determine their own destinies will reject terror and refuse to live in tyranny. And that is why the terrorists are fighting to deny this choice to the people in Lebanon, Iraq, Afghanistan, Pakistan, and the Palestinian Territories. And that is why, for the security of America and the peace of the world, we are spreading the hope of freedom.

In Afghanistan, America, our 25 NATO allies, and 15 partner nations are helping the Afghan people defend their freedom and rebuild their country. Thanks to the courage of these military and civilian personnel, a nation that was once a safe haven for Al Qaida is now a young democracy where boys and girls are going to school, new roads and hospitals are being built, and people are looking to the future with new hope. These successes must continue, so we're adding 3,200 marines to our forces in Afghanistan, where they will fight the terrorists and train the Afghan Army and police. Defeating the Taliban and Al Qaida is critical to our security, and I thank the Congress for supporting America's vital mission in Afghanistan.

In Iraq, the terrorists and extremists are fighting to deny a proud people their liberty and fighting to establish safe havens for attacks across the world. One year ago, our enemies were succeeding in their efforts to plunge Iraq into chaos. So we reviewed our strategy and changed course. We launched a surge of American forces into Iraq. We gave our troops a new mission: work with the Iraqi forces to protect the Iraqi people, pursue the enemy in its strongholds, and deny the terrorists sanctuary anywhere in the country.

The Iraqi people quickly realized that something dramatic had happened. Those who had worried that America was preparing to abandon them instead saw tens of thousands of American forces flowing into their country. They saw our forces moving into neighborhoods, clearing out the terrorists, and staying behind to ensure the enemy did not return. And they saw our troops, along with Provincial Reconstruction Teams that include Foreign Service officers and other skilled public servants, coming in to ensure that improved security was followed by improvements in daily life. Our military and civilians in Iraq are performing with courage and distinction, and they have the gratitude of our whole Nation.

The Iraqis launched a surge of their own. In the fall of 2006, Sunni tribal leaders grew tired of Al Qaida's brutality, started a popular uprising called the Anbar Awakening. Over the past year, similar movements have spread across the country. And today, the grassroots surge includes more than 80,000 Iraqi citizens who are fighting the terrorists. The Government in Baghdad has stepped forward as well, adding more than 100,000 new Iraqi soldiers and police during the past year.

While the enemy is still dangerous and more work remains, the American and Iraqi surges have achieved results few of us could have imagined just 1 year ago. When we met last year, many said that containing the violence was impossible. A year later, high-profile terrorist attacks are down, civilian deaths are down, sectarian killings are down.

When we met last year, militia extremists—some armed and trained by Iran—were wreaking havoc in large areas of Iraq. A year later, coalition and Iraqi forces have killed or captured hundreds of militia fighters. And Iraqis of all backgrounds increasingly realize that defeating these militia fighters is critical to the future of their country.

When we met last year, Al Qaida had sanctuaries in many areas of Iraq, and their leaders had just offered American forces safe passage out of the country. Today, it is Al Qaida that is searching for safe passage. They have been driven from many of the strongholds they once held. And over the past year, we've captured or killed thousands of extremists in Iraq, including hundreds of key Al Qaida leaders and operatives.

Last month, Usama bin Laden released a tape in which he railed against Iraqi tribal leaders who have turned on Al Qaida and admitted that coalition forces are growing stronger in Iraq. Ladies and gentlemen, some may deny the surge is working, but among the terrorists there is no doubt. Al Qaida is on the run in Iraq, and this enemy will be defeated.

When we met last year, our troop levels in Iraq were on the rise. Today, because of the progress just described, we are implementing a policy of return on success, and the surge forces we sent to Iraq are beginning to come home.

This progress is a credit to the valor of our troops and the brilliance of their commanders. This evening I want to speak directly to our men and women on the frontlines. Soldiers and sailors, airmen, marines, and coastguardsmen: In the past year, you have done everything we've asked of you and more. Our Nation is grateful for your courage. We are proud of your accomplishments. And tonight in this hallowed Chamber, with the American people as our witness, we make you a solemn pledge: In the fight ahead, you will have all you need to protect our Nation. And I ask Congress to meet its responsibilities to these brave men and women by fully funding our troops.

Our enemies in Iraq have been hit hard. They are not yet defeated, and we can still expect tough fighting ahead. Our objective in the coming year is to sustain and build on the gains we made in 2007 while transitioning to the next phase of our strategy. American troops are shifting from leading operations to partnering with Iraqi forces and, eventually, to a protective overwatch mission. As part of this transition, one Army brigade combat team and one Marine expeditionary unit have already come home and will not be replaced. In the coming months, four additional brigades and two Marine battalions will follow suit. Taken together, this means more than 20,000 of our troops are coming home.

Any further drawdown of U.S. troops will be based on conditions in Iraq and the recommendations of our commanders. General Petraeus has warned that too fast a drawdown could result in, quote, "the disintegration of the Iraqi security forces, Al Qaida-Iraq regaining lost ground, and a marked increase in violence." Members of Congress, having come so far and achieved so much, we must not allow this to happen.

In the coming year, we will work with Iraqi leaders as they build on the progress they're making toward political reconciliation. At the local level, Sunnis, Shi'a, and Kurds are beginning to come together to reclaim their communities and rebuild their lives. Progress in the Provinces must be matched by progress in Baghdad. We're seeing some encouraging signs. The national Government is sharing oil revenues with the Provinces. The parliament recently passed both a pension law and de-Ba'athification reform. They're now debating a Provincial powers law. The Iraqis still have a distance to travel, but after decades of dictatorship and the pain of sectarian violence, reconciliation is taking place, and the Iraqi people are taking control of their future.

The mission in Iraq has been difficult and trying for our Nation, but it is in the vital interest of the United States that we succeed. A free Iraq will deny Al Qaida a safe haven. A free Iraq will show millions across the Middle East that a future of liberty is possible. A free Iraq will be a friend of America, a partner in fighting terror, and a source of stability in a dangerous part of the world.

By contrast, a failed Iraq would embolden the extremists, strengthen Iran, and give terrorists a base from which to launch new attacks on our friends, our allies, and our homeland. The enemy has made its intentions clear. At a time when the momentum seemed to favor them, Al Qaida's top commander in Iraq declared that they will not rest until they have attacked us here in Washington. My fellow Americans, we will not rest either. We will not rest until this enemy has been defeated. We must do the difficult work today so that years from now, people will look back and say that this generation rose to the moment, prevailed in a tough fight, and left behind a more hopeful region and a safer America.

We're also standing against the forces of extremism in the Holy Land, where we have new cause for hope. Palestinians have elected a President who recognizes that confronting terror is essential to achieving a state where his people can live in dignity and at peace with Israel. Israelis have leaders who recognize that a peaceful, democratic Palestinian state will be a source of lasting security. This month in Ramallah and Jerusalem, I assured leaders from both sides that America will do, and I will do, everything we can to help them achieve a peace agreement that defines a Palestinian state by the end of this year. The time has come for a Holy Land where a democratic Israel and a democratic Palestine live side by side in peace.

We're also standing against the forces of extremism embodied by the regime in Tehran. Iran's rulers oppress a good and talented people. And wherever freedom advances in the Middle East, it seems the Iranian regime is there to oppose it. Iran is funding and training militia groups in Iraq, supporting Hizballah terrorists in Lebanon, and backing Hamas efforts to undermine peace in the Holy Land. Tehran is also developing ballistic missiles of increasing range and continues to develop its capability to enrich uranium, which could be used to create a nuclear weapon.

Our message to the people of Iran is clear: We have no quarrel with you. We respect your traditions and your history. We look forward to the day when you have your freedom. Our message to the leaders of Iran is also clear: Verifiably suspend your nuclear enrichment so negotiations can begin. And to rejoin the community of nations, come clean about your nuclear intentions and past actions, stop your oppression at home, cease your support for terror abroad. But above all, know this: America will confront those who threaten our troops, we will stand by our allies, and we will defend our vital interests in the Persian Gulf.

On the homefront, we will continue to take every lawful and effective measure to protect our country. This is our most solemn duty. We are grateful that there has not been another attack on our soil since 9/11. This is not for the lack of desire or effort on the part of the enemy. In the past 6 years, we've stopped numerous attacks, including a plot to fly a plane into the tallest building in Los Angeles and another to blow up passenger jets bound for America over the Atlantic. Dedicated men and women in our Government toil day and night to stop the terrorists from carrying out their plans. These good citizens are saving American lives, and everyone in this Chamber owes them our thanks.

And we owe them something more; we owe them the tools they need to keep our people safe. And one of the most important tools we can give them is the ability to monitor terrorist communications. To protect America, we need to know who the terrorists are talking to, what they are saying, and what they're planning. Last year, Congress passed legislation to help us do that. Unfortunately, Congress set the legislations to expire on February the 1st. That means if you don't act by Friday, our ability to track terrorist threats would be weakened and our citizens will be in greater danger. Congress must ensure the flow of vital intelligence is not disrupted. Congress must pass liability protection for companies believed to have assisted in the efforts to defend America. We've had ample time for debate. The time to act is now.

Protecting our Nation from the dangers of a new century requires more than good intelligence and a strong military. It also requires changing the conditions that breed resentment and allow extremists to prey on despair. So America is using its influence to build a freer, more hopeful, and more compassionate world. This is a reflection of our national interests; it is the calling of our conscience.

America opposes genocide in Sudan. We support freedom in countries from Cuba and Zimbabwe to Belarus and Burma.

America is leading the fight against global poverty with strong education initiatives and humanitarian assistance. We've also changed the way we deliver aid by launching the Millennium Challenge Account.

This program strengthens democracy, transparency, and the rule of law in developing nations, and I ask you to fully fund this important initiative.

America is leading the fight against global hunger. Today, more than half the world's food aid comes from the United States. And tonight I ask Congress to support an innovative proposal to provide food assistance by purchasing crops directly from farmers in the developing world, so we can build up local agriculture and help break the cycle of famine.

America is leading the fight against disease. With your help, we're working to cut by half the number of malaria-related deaths in 15 African nations. And our Emergency Plan for AIDS Relief is treating 1.4 million people. We can bring healing and hope to many more. So I ask you to maintain the principles that have changed behavior and made this program a success. And I call on you to double our initial commitment to fighting HIV/AIDS by approving an additional $30 billion over the next 5 years.

America is a force for hope in the world because we are a compassionate people, and some of the most compassionate Americans are those who have stepped forward to protect us. We must keep faith with all who have risked life and limb so that we might live in freedom and peace. Over the past 7 years, we've increased funding for veterans by more than 95 percent. And as we increase funding, we must also reform our veterans system to meet the needs of a new war and a new generation. I call on Congress to enact the reforms recommended by Senator Bob Dole and Secretary Donna Shalala so we can improve the system of care for our wounded warriors and help them build lives of hope and promise and dignity.

Our military families also sacrifice for America. They endure sleepless nights and the daily struggle of providing for children while a loved one is serving far from home. We have a responsibility to provide for them. So I ask you to join me in expanding their access to child care, creating new hiring preferences for military spouses across the Federal Government, and allowing our troops to transfer their unused education benefits to their spouses or children. Our military families serve our Nation, they inspire our Nation, and tonight our Nation honors them.

The strength—the secret of our strength, the miracle of America, is that our greatness lies not in our Government, but in the spirit and determination of our people. When the Federal Convention met in Philadelphia in 1787, our Nation was bound by the Articles of Confederation, which began with the words, "We the undersigned delegates." When Gouverneur Morris was asked to draft the preamble to our new Constitution, he offered an important revision and opened with words that changed the course of our Nation and the history of the world: "We the people."

By trusting the people, our Founders wagered that a great and noble nation could be built on the liberty that resides in the hearts of all men and women. By trusting the people, succeeding generations transformed our fragile, young democracy into the most powerful nation on Earth and a beacon of hope for millions. And so long as we continue to trust the people, our Nation will prosper, our liberty will be secure, and the state of our Union will remain strong.

So tonight, with confidence in freedom's power and trust in the people, let us set forth to do their business. God bless America.

NOTE: The President spoke at 9:09 p.m. in the House Chamber of the U.S. Capitol. In his remarks, he referred to President Hamid Karzai of Afghanistan; Usama bin Laden, leader of the Al Qaida terrorist organization; Gen. David H. Petraeus, USA, commanding general, Multi-National Force—Iraq; President Mahmoud Abbas of the Palestinian Authority; and former Sen. Robert J. Dole and former Secretary of Health and Human Services Donna E. Shalala, Cochairs, President's Commission on Care for America's Returning Wounded Warriors. The Office of the Press Secretary also released a Spanish language transcript of this address.

Remarks During a Visit to the Jericho Program in Baltimore, Maryland
January 29, 2008

Thank you all for coming. I'm proud to be standing with you men. Thank you very much. Thank you very much for your hospitality.

Last night in my State of the Union, I highlighted the important work being done by faith-based organizations. This morning I was pleased to visit one of these inspiring groups, the Episcopal Community Services of Maryland, right here in Baltimore. I cannot thank you enough for the chance to take a tour. And, Bonnie, you and your staff have been most hospitable.

I've come to look firsthand at the Jericho Program, which is helping former prisoners make a successful transition back to society. There's no more important goal than to help good souls become—come back to our society as productive citizens. I'm honored to have been with those who have worked hard to deal with their circumstances in such a way that they become productive citizens. I'm standing next to two such men, and I met probably seven others downstairs.

I do want to thank Bonnie Ariano for joining me and the Secretary. I'm going to talk about the Secretary's role here in a minute, in this important program. I thank very much Greg Carpenter, a former prisoner who is now a mentor, a leader in this program. And he's a—I appreciate his heart.

I welcome Jay Hein, Director of the Office of Faith-Based and Community Initiatives at the White House. I do want to thank State Senator David Brinkley for joining us; Senator, proud you're here. I appreciate the Jericho staff. I want to thank

the Episcopal Community Services of Maryland board of directors. I appreciate you all coming. I thank you very much for supporting this program.

When I came into office, the Nation's traditions of religious freedom and equal opportunity were facing unnecessary obstacles. Throughout America, religious and community groups were providing effective assistance to people in need, but there was a great reluctance on the part of the Federal Government to help them. There was the notion that somehow that there needed to be a clear separation of church and state, and therefore, we shouldn't be using taxpayers' money to help programs that were helping to meet important national goals.

Unfortunately, in some instances where there was an interface with Government, people were told that in order to interface, you have to take the cross off the wall or take down the Star of David. In other words, you had to abandon the very principle by which you existed in the first place. And it made no sense. If a program was effective because they were willing to recognize a higher power, if a program was effective because people responded because they felt a call from a higher power, then to deny the higher power really reduced the effectiveness of the program.

And so 7 years ago, my administration created the White House Office of Faith-Based and Community Initiatives to deal with this problem. We wanted to focus our Government and taxpayers' money on solutions, on effective programs, and we recognized that many of the effective programs existed in the faith community. Washington,

DC, oftentimes is a process-oriented town. We need to work hard to make it a results-oriented town. And if one of the compelling national interests is to help good people who have been in prison come back and readjust and learn skills and the attitudes necessary to be a productive citizen, if that's an important national concern, then we ought to turn to programs that are meeting those results. That's what we ought to do.

And that's what's happening right here. That's why I'm here. This is a program that is working, and it is supported by the Federal Government, and it should be.

Since 2001, the Government has leveled the playing field. That's one of our objectives early on in my administration, was to level the playing field, to make it easier for faith-based and community groups to compete for billions of dollars in Federal grants, grants that would help them accomplish their objectives.

With this newfound support, America's faith-based groups are getting results. If you ask people here, is a program working, the answer is, absolutely. It's one thing to ask the director; more importantly, it's another thing to ask those who have benefited. These are men who were, in some ways, lost and lonely and found love and redemption at Jericho. I'm going to talk about them in just a second.

But there are all kinds of programs that are helping meet our national needs and goals. There are programs to help provide mentors for 70,000 children whose parents are incarcerated. There are programs to help deal with drug addiction and alcohol addiction, programs to help young people in our inner cities escape gangs. These are all programs where a faith-based or community group has dedicated their lives to solve a problem. And it makes sense for the Federal Government to give these programs a chance to access taxpayers' money.

When we begin the work, we didn't settle for just opening an office in the White House; we opened 11 offices for faith-based and community initiatives throughout the Federal Government. It's one thing for the White House to have an office, but most of the money—or all the money, for that matter—is appropriated to different Cabinet officers and their secretariats, and then those distribute the money. And so we wanted to make sure that this faith-based initiative was rooted throughout the Government.

And one of the offices is at the Department of Labor, ably headed by Secretary Elaine Chao. She's a member of my Cabinet. Every year, nearly 650,000 men and women are released from prison, and one of her top priorities, along with the Department of Justice, is to help those readjust to our society. And there's a compelling reason to: Half the people getting released from prison go back. And the idea is to help deal with that issue. We don't want people going back to prison; we want to help them readjust in society. And it turns out that faith-based programs are very effective. And this is such a program.

The whole purpose of Jericho is a prisoner reentry initiative. That's why you exist. It's interesting how a program like this works. This is a small program, really, to some of the really large faith-based programs. And by the way, part of our initiative was to encourage what I call "social entrepreneurship." It's to stand side by side with smaller programs, because smaller programs, when they're proved to be successful, turn out to be larger programs. And larger programs obviously help more people, but they also serve as an example.

I like the fact that you call yourselves "the Jericho." After all, the walls came tumbling down. That's what's happening here; old walls are tumbling down, and new lives are being built.

One of the great things about a faith-based program—one of the great aspects of a faith-based program is there's a lot of people in our society who hear the call to love a neighbor. That's, after all, one of the key tenets of faith: Love a neighbor like you'd be—like to love—be loved yourself. And so what you find here is programs supported by people who want to make a difference in our society, and it doesn't require a government law to cause them to do so. You need to pass a law and sign a law that says, you will love your neighbor; there's a higher law that does that. And these programs just gather that love and work to save societies one soul at a time.

And we've got two such souls here. Adolphus Mosely, he came here last summer after having been released from prison, and he graduated from one of Jericho's work training programs. And he started— got him a new job. And he's proud of that.

By the way, first, there's a—people have got to come here and realize that there are people who love them and want to help them. And second, there is the practical application of helping somebody find work. Addiction is hard to overcome. As you might remember, I drank too much at one time in my life. I understand faith-based programs. I understand that sometimes you can find the inspiration from a higher power to solve an addiction problem. This program helps along these folks who have—had been dealing with addictions.

I also appreciate Thomas Boyd. He spent nearly 4 years in prison. He came here September. And thanks to the program, he's got a new dilemma: He had to choose between several job offers. [*Laughter*] That's a good dilemma to have. He's supporting himself. He's—both these men are reunited with their daughters. They find great pride in the fact that they have chosen a path with the help of the folks at Jericho. They shared with me their love for their little girls, and I know the feeling.

And I appreciate the fact that, you know, that you're on your feet and you're feeling good and strong and you're assuming the responsibility of fatherhood.

And so I've come to herald programs such as the Jericho Program. Our Government should not fear the influence of faith in our society. We ought to welcome faith-based programs. Last night I called on the Government to make the charitable choice provisions of our law permanent. We shouldn't say to programs such as this, we'll help you through a Department of Labor and Justice grant, and then turn our back on the program when it's successful. There ought to be consistency of policy. Our Government ought to welcome results. We ought to say, thank God there are people such as this in our neighborhoods and societies helping these good men.

So it's an honor to be here. I'm proud to be in the presence of Americans who care deeply about our country and are willing to do something about the future of the country by helping lost souls find love and hope in their lives. And I want to thank the—I want to thank very much the Episcopal Community Services for sponsoring this program.

Again, I want to thank you all for leading with your hearts. Thank these two good men for joining me today. God bless you. Proud to be with you. Thank you.

All right. Thank you all.

NOTE: The President spoke at 11:45 a.m. at the Robert M. Davis House. In his remarks, he referred to Bonnie Ariano, director, and Greg Carpenter, coordinator for mentoring and training, Jericho Program.

Remarks on Signing the Executive Order on Protecting American Taxpayers From Government Spending on Wasteful Earmarks
January 29, 2008

Director Nussle, thank you. Before I sign the Executive order on earmarks, I do want to congratulate the House of Representatives for overwhelmingly passing a economic growth package that will help our economy. The temptation is going to be for the Senate to load it up. My concerns is that we need to get this bill out of the Senate and on my desk so the checks can get in the hands of our consumers and our businesses can be assured of the incentives necessary to make investments.

Anyway, I do want to thank the Speaker and Leader Boehner for working quickly and working in a bipartisan fashion. This is a very good start.

And now I'm going to sign this Executive order. Last night I said that it's very important for Congress to earn the trust of the American taxpayer, and one way they should do so is to end the practice of earmarks. Now, I said last year that they should voluntarily cut the number in half—not only the number but the amount of earmarks in half. They chose not to do so. So last night I told the Congress that I would veto any bill, appropriations bill, that does not cut the number and the amount of earmarks in half.

Secondly, there's a practice here in Washington—and I'm not sure many of our citizens understand it takes place—where Members just put in special spending projects into what's called report language. That means that these projects never were voted on, never really saw the light of day. And this Executive order says that any such earmarks this year and into the future will be ignored by this administration and, hopefully, future administrations, unless those spending projects were voted on by the Congress.

The American people expect there to be transparency in the process. They expect the people to be—here in Washington to be wise about how they spend their money. And this Executive order will go a long way toward sending that signal to the Congress and, at the same time, earning the trust of the American people.

So, Mr. Director, thank you for your leadership on the issue. It was the right course of action to take, and I am proud to have signed the Executive order. Thank you.

NOTE: The President spoke at 3:38 p.m. in the Oval Office at the White House. In his remarks, he referred to Office of Management and Budget Director James A. Nussle. He also referred to Executive Order 13457, which is listed in Appendix D at the end of this volume.

Remarks Prior to a Meeting With the Joint Chiefs of Staff and Combatant Commanders
January 29, 2008

Mr. Secretary, thank you very much. Mr. Chairman, we're glad you're here. The Vice President and I welcome you all. One of the highlights of my year is to meet with combatant commanders and the Joint Chiefs. We'll have a visit here in the Cabinet Room, talking about the war on terror and the ideological struggle that we're engaged in. We'll talk about our common desire to protect America and how best to do so. And then we're going to have dinner with your spouses, and Laura and I are really looking forward to having you upstairs.

I love our military, and the reason I do is because the character of those who wear our uniform, whether they be the general or the private, is remarkable. We're a nation that has produced people who are willing to volunteer in the face of danger, thank goodness. And as a result, we are a nation in the lead in helping defend this world against extremists who murder the innocent to achieve an ideological objective.

And our military is compassionate as well. I'm looking forward to the stories from our commanders who will share with us the great compassion of our soldiers, whether it's to provide relief from a disaster or to help some child recognize the beauty of going to school.

And so I want to thank you for coming and thank you for serving, and I'm looking forward to hearing from you. Thank you.

NOTE: The President spoke at 5:11 p.m. in the Cabinet Room at the White House.

Statement on the Death of Margaret Truman Daniel
January 29, 2008

Laura and I are saddened by the death of Margaret Truman Daniel. The only child of our 33d President, she supported her father as he confronted the difficult challenges of his Presidency, witnessing firsthand the leadership of Harry Truman in both war and peace. An accomplished author and singer, her life was one of tremendous personal achievement. Our thoughts and prayers are with Margaret Truman Daniel's sons and the rest of the Truman family.

NOTE: The statement referred to Clifton T. Daniel, Harrison G. Daniel, and Thomas W. Daniel, sons of Mrs. Daniel.

Memorandum on Review of Recommendations From the Public Interest Declassification Board
January 29, 2008

Memorandum for the Secretary of State, the Secretary of the Treasury, the Secretary of Defense, the Secretary of Energy, the Secretary of Homeland Security, the Assistant to the President and Chief of Staff, the Director of the Office of Management and Budget, the Director of National Intelligence, the Assistant to the President for National Security Affairs, the Counsel to the President, and the Assistant to the President for Homeland Security and Counterterrorism

Subject: Review of Recommendations From the Public Interest Declassification Board

The Public Interest Declassification Board, an advisory group established by the Public Interest Declassification Act of 2000, as amended (50 U.S.C. 435 note), has submitted a report entitled "Improving Declassification." The report addresses 15 issues and makes 49 recommendations relating to declassification of classified national security information.

Please submit in writing no later than April 15, 2008, through the Assistants to the President for National Security Affairs and for Homeland Security and Counterterrorism, your views on each of the recommendations, including with respect to each recommendation your view of whether and to what extent it should be implemented. Your views with respect to the recommendations should take into account the public interest in declassification of national security information, effective records management, and the effective conduct of United States diplomatic, economic, military, energy, homeland security, and intelligence activities, as well as such other matters as you deem appropriate for consideration.

GEORGE W. BUSH

NOTE: This memorandum was released by the Office of the Press Secretary on January 30.

Remarks at Robinson Helicopter Company in Torrance, California
January 30, 2008

Thank you all. So my daughters are going to be envious I was introduced by Arnold. [*Laughter*] I appreciate you, Governor. Thanks for your strong leadership, thanks for your friendship. You know, California is a really important State for our country, and I think a lot of Californians appreciate the fact that you're steady at the helm. And thank you for having us.

Frank, thank you very much for your hospitality. Some say, "Why do you want to come to Robinson Helicopter Company?" Well, first, I love entrepreneurs and

dreamers. And your boy told me that you dreamt about a company, and you started it in your kitchen. Isn't it interesting? The company was started in the kitchen, and now he's got the Terminator coming by to herald the success. [*Laughter*] I mean, this is—I love America, because we stand for dreams that can be accomplished.

And so the first reason I'm here is I want to congratulate the Robinsons for living a dream and for giving people good work. Arnold and I had the pleasure of working the floor and shaking hands with people who are making a living for their families. And so you're building good helicopters, but more importantly, you're providing people a chance to work, and I appreciate that a lot.

The other reason I'm here is I want to spend a little time talking about the economy and about what we can do to help in the short term and in the long term.

Before I do, I do want to also welcome Congresswoman Jane Harman. This is her district, and I'm proud to have traveled from Washington to California with her. Jane, thank you for coming; appreciate your time being here.

And Dreier and Royce are with us too, as well, and that would be Congressman Dreier and Congressman Royce. I appreciate you all joining us; thank you for your time. Mayor, thanks for coming.

I hope you're confident about our economy; I am. We've got some short-term issues to deal with. Fourth quarter growth slowed to .6 percent. In other words, there are signs that our economy are slowing. There's some uncertainty in the economy, but in the long run, you've got to be confident about your economy. Inflation is down; interest rates are low; productivity is high. Our economy is flexible; it is resilient. We've been through problems before. As a matter of fact, we've been through problems before since I was your President. We've had a recession, corporate scandals, an attack on the United States of America; we've had major national disasters. And every time, we've come through strong, and that what's going to happen this time too.

But the Federal Government can help. We can have some smart policy out of Washington. And the smartest thing we can do is to help deal with the uncertainty by putting about $145 billion into your pockets so you can spend it, which will help this economy stay strong, and at the same time, part of that $145 billion is to provide incentives for businesses, large and small, to invest. See, when you provide an incentive for a company to invest, they go out and

buy a machine. And when they buy that machine, somebody has to put labor into the machine; somebody is working.

So the whole purpose of a stimulus package is to have something robust enough to make a difference, temporary enough that—so that we can balance our budget over time, and simple enough to be effective. And as the Governor mentioned, we reached an agreement with both Democrats and Republicans in the House of Representatives on a package that's simple, robust, and effective. And now the Senate is debating the issue. And I understand people having their points of view, and of course, we welcome points of view in Washington. There appears to be a lot of them up there. [*Laughter*]

But whatever the Senate does, they should not delay this package. They should not keep money out of your pocket. The sooner you get a check, the more likely it is that the stimulus package will kick in and make a difference. So my attitude is, if you're truly interested in dealing with the slowdown of the economy, the Senate ought to accept the House package, pass it, and get it to my desk as soon as possible. That's what I want to talk about.

I also want to talk about trade. Now, people in our country—let's be perfectly frank about it—you hear them say, trade isn't any good; it doesn't help. If I were a worker at Robinson, I'd be arguing against that. You've got good jobs here. People are working, and 70 percent of what you make gets sold overseas. So you can't tell the people at Robinson Helicopter that trade isn't good. When 70 percent of that which you manufacture gets sold somewhere else other than the United States, they ought to have a sign walking in here and say, trade is not only good, it is great, and we want the Federal Government to make it easier for us to sell products.

That's what trade is really about, isn't it? If you're good at something—and you're good at making helicopters—then you ought to have your Government making it easier to sell your product, not harder. Mr. Robinson said 70 percent of the revenues from this company are a result of products being sold overseas. And that happens in a lot of companies in America, by the way. As a matter of fact, it is estimated that our growth last year, a third of that growth was caused by exports. When people are selling something overseas, it means somebody is working. And there's a lot of customers overseas.

And so one of the goals of this administration is to reduce trade barriers. The interesting thing about what I'm about to tell you on three free trade agreements that we're hoping Congress votes on here pretty soon is that we're not treated the same way. In other words, they got their goods and services coming to our country without a lot of tariffs. And when we're trying to sell into their countries, they're taxing it, which makes it much harder to sell.

Reasonable policy says to nations, you treat us the way we treat you. That's all we're asking for. We're saying to countries, if your goods and services are coming here—which, by the way, are good for our consumers; like if you're a consumer, you want a lot of choices, you want a lot of different options. But we want to be treated equally too. Good trade policy is fair trade policy.

And so these trade agreements I'm about to describe to you level the playing field. When I say level the playing field, it means we'll be treated equally. And that's important, because we can compete with anybody, anytime, anywhere, just as long as the rules are fair. That's what I think. I think our workers are the best in the world. I said in the State of the Union the other night, let's open the—level the playing field, open up markets, so the best workers in the world can have the fruits of their labor sold overseas. And that's what trade is all about. You got people in this country saying, "Oh, trade doesn't matter." I'm telling you it matters. It matters to our economy, and it matters to the jobs right here

at Robinson Manufacturer—Robinson Helicopter.

The other interesting thing about trade is if you're working for a company that's selling goods overseas, you're likely to be paid higher wages. Trade yields better pay.

So what are you going to do about it, Mr. President? It's one thing to talk about the benefits of trade. Well, we've negotiated free trade agreements. In other words, we sat down with countries and said, let's get a free trade agreement in place. And we reduced barriers and tariffs through the negotiations, and there are three such agreements before the Congress. There was four; Congress recently passed a deal with Peru. And we want to do the same thing with Colombia and Panama and South Korea.

Now, for the person working here at Robinson, I don't know if you know this, but when you try to sell into Colombia, part of your—part of the helicopter parts face a 5-percent surcharge. That makes it harder to sell something in—when something is taxed, it's harder to sell into a market.

The free trade agreement we've negotiated will eliminate that surcharge. It makes it more likely that these products will be sold to Colombia and Panama. There's a 15-percent tax on the helicopter you manufacture. I've been told there's a 15-percent tax. I believe there's a 15-percent tax, and I know that a free trade agreement will reduce that tax, which means it's more likely you're going to sell a helicopter into Panama. And when you're more likely to sell a helicopter to Panama, it means you're more likely to keep work; that's what that means.

Free trade means jobs for Americans. Free trade means good-paying jobs for Americans. And so Congress needs to pass these agreements for the sake of economic vitality. Now, Arnold talked about the effect for the State of California, you're selling hundreds of billions of dollars' worth of goods out of California to other parts of the world. And we need to keep that trend going. I mean, if we don't want to worry about our economy long term, you need your Government knocking down barriers to our products and on goods and services.

Congress is going to have a vote coming up pretty soon on Colombia. And if it were an easy vote, I wouldn't be talking about it, but it's going to be a tough vote. Some say trade hurts our economy. These are good, decent people. I just beg to disagree; I respectfully disagree and would ask them to think about the example of this company right here. Some say it really doesn't matter. I think it matters a lot to our standing in the world as to whether or not we support a friend.

Colombia is an important country for our interests. They've got a good President, named President Uribe. And he inherited a tough deal, a tough situation, where he's fighting off drug lords and drug traffickers, people who are manufacturing drugs that come and pollute our kids. And he's taking the fight to this enemy. And he's an ally. And he wants this free trade agreement passed. It's in his country's interests.

And if we reject this opportunity to support a friend with good economic policy, if we turn down this free trade agreement, it will hurt our relations in South America. It will give the voices of false populism something to say. It is in our strategic interests that we support democracies in our neighborhood. And it's in our strategic interest and our economic interest that the United States Congress passes this free trade agreement with Colombia.

I'm looking forward to making the case for Panama and South Korea as well. The first vote coming up is Colombia. And I'm looking forward to traveling this country, talking to people about the benefits of free trade and the importance of this free trade agreement. We're also going to try to get a Doha round of trade, in other words, opening up—around the world, opening up trade.

I hope you share the same concern I have about people living in terrible poverty. You know, we're in this ideological struggle against, I called them last night evil men and I meant what I said. There are people that murder the innocent to achieve political objectives. And the only way they can sell their ideology is when they find hopeless people. And you can find hopeless people in places where there's no hope because the economies are sick. The best way to help people is not to give people your taxpayers' money, but to encourage enterprise through commerce and trade. So the Doha round is a great opportunity to advance prosperity around the world and deal a serious blow to those who exploit the hopeless.

The other thing about trade that I want you to know is that sometimes when trade takes place, somebody loses work, and I understand that, and that's not a happy circumstance. And the Government has a— ought to help people. One response is, okay, let's just don't trade at all, which is— would be bad, in my judgment. The other response is, let's have job training to help somebody get the skills necessary to fill the jobs of the 21st century. It's called trade adjustment assistance, and it's a vital program.

And when you combine trade adjustment assistance with our community colleges, what you've got is a great opportunity to help people who've lost a job because of trade find the skills necessary to get a better paying job. And so for the critics who say, "Well, people lose work," my answer is, the benefits for the country as a whole are important, but we will help you, the individual, get your life back together with good education.

And finally, I want to say something about investment. It's very important for our country to be open for investment without sacrificing our national security. There's some countries around the world that have accumulated large amounts of money. Sometimes it's our money. And it

133

makes sense to say to somebody, sure, you can invest in America. I noticed the other day one of these Wall Street firms had a big chunk of foreign money invest on their—in their balance sheet. We ought to say, you bet, absolutely, you're welcome to invest in the United States of America. Investment means jobs and productivity increases.

Now, we're going to do it in a way that doesn't sacrifice national security. We'll analyze investments. But this Nation ought to not close our doors and be fearful. We ought to be confident, because we're a great people. We've overcome problems throughout our history. There will be other problems in the future, and every time, we can overcome them.

And so I appreciate you giving me a chance, Mr. Robinson, to come and visit with you. I especially was pleased to meet your employees. It's a good group of folks, highly motivated and hard-working, and they were very hospitable, and for that, the Governor and I are very grateful.

Governor, I've got my own helicopter driver, thank you. [*Laughter*] But I'm proud to be with you, and more importantly, I'm proud to be with you all. God bless America. Thank you.

NOTE: The President spoke at 11:51 a.m. In his remarks, he referred to Gov. Arnold A. Schwarzenegger of California; Frank Robinson, president and chief executive officer, and his son Kurt Robinson, vice president for product support, Robinson Helicopter Co.; and Mayor Frank Scotto of Torrance, CA.

Remarks on the War on Terror in Las Vegas, Nevada
January 31, 2008

Thanks for the warm welcome. Thank you. So what Ranson didn't tell you is he believes in free speech, and that's what I'm here to give. [*Laughter*] I appreciate the invitation. [*Laughter*] Sharon, thank you very much as well.

I'm honored to be here with the Governor. Governor—the Governor has been a friend of mine for a long time. We served together in Washington. He came back to Nevada—[*laughter*]—to serve the great State. As my wife said, when you get over there, don't mispronounce it again. [*Laughter*] I learned my lesson. But, Governor, thank you for being here. I appreciate all the State and local officials who are here, and I want to thank you for giving me a chance to come by and share some thoughts about the world in which we live.

I do appreciate very much your advocacy of open markets, ownership. I believe the ownership society is necessary for a hopeful America. We want people owning their homes. We want people owning and managing their own health care accounts. We want people managing their pension plans. We ought to trust people. And at my State of the Union—one of the themes at the State of the Union was that government ought to trust people and empower them to make their own decisions about their future. And this institute does that, and I appreciate it very much. I thank you for being on the forefront of good, optimistic thought.

The world in which we live is a dangerous world, but a world full of great opportunity. We're involved in an ideological struggle, the likes of which we have seen before in our history. It's an ideological struggle between those of us who love freedom and human rights and human dignity and those who want to impose their dark vision on how people should live their lives.

This is a—not a political conflict—I mean, a religious conflict. And I'll tell you why: Because the—one of the tactics—and the main tactic of those enemies of freedom—is to murder the innocent to achieve their objectives. Religious people do not murder the innocent.

And so we're facing this ideological struggle of people who use asymmetrical warfare. What distinguishes this ideological struggle from previous ideological struggles, those with—against fascism or communism, is that in this war, individuals use weapons to kill innocent people—car bombs and suicide vests. And they do so to frighten the West. They do so to create chaos and confusion. They do so with the aim of creating vacuums into which their hateful ideology can flow. And that's why you see the September 11th attacks, in London, in Madrid, in Jordan, attacks around the world. Some will say these are just isolated moments of—where all we need is a good, strong law enforcement response. I think they're all part of an ideological struggle.

And the interesting development that is taking place in the beginnings here of the 21st century is the freedom movement is on the march. I'm not surprised, and you shouldn't be either. I believe there is an Almighty. I believe the gift of that Almighty to every man, woman, and child is freedom. I believe that people, if given a chance, will always go to freedom, and that's what you're beginning to see.

And yet every time freedom tries to advance, these ideologues murder innocent people—in Afghanistan, in Iraq, in Lebanon, in Israel, in Palestine. People who can't stand the thought of free societies unleash their hatred by killing innocent people. And the great challenge facing America and the world is, one, will we recognize the challenge? Do we understand the consequences of success and failure? And will the United States be bold and stay in the lead? And my answer is, we have been, we will continue to be, and we must be engaged in making sure we lay the foundation of peace for the sake of our children and grandchildren.

We will prevail. We will prevail in this ideological struggle because liberty is powerful, liberty is hopeful. The enemy we face can only convince people to join their cause is when they find hopelessness. And so our strategy is threefold: one, protect the homeland; two, stay on the offense against these folks; and three, provide an alternative, a hopeful alternative to despair and doubt and hopelessness.

So today I want to spend some time on the strategy. The first—our most important job in government, whether it be the Federal Government, State government, or local government, is to protect you. And remember the lessons of September the 11th, that oceans cannot protect us, that we face coldblooded killers who, in our case, resorted to mass murder to send a message. We've got—you know, thankfully there hasn't been an attack on our homeland since then. That's not for the lack of effort by these evil people.

I hope you take heart in knowing there are a lot of really fine people working long, long hours to get the best information possible to protect the homeland. There's a—unbelievably dedicated folks. And as I said in the State of the Union the other night, we owe these folks a debt of gratitude. And we owe them more; we owe them the tools necessary to protect the American people.

And one such tool in this different kind of war is to fully understand the intentions, the motives, the plans of people who use suicide and bombs to kill the innocent. If these terrorists and extremists are making phone calls into our country, we need to know why they're calling, what they're thinking, and what they're planning. In order to protect the American people, our professionals need to have the tools necessary to do their job you expect them to do. And one such tool is a surveillance program that guarantees the rights of our citizens, but doesn't extend those same guarantees to those who would do us harm.

Congress passed such a bill last year. They recognized that this tool was important to protect America. And yet, unfortunately, the bill they passed is set to expire tomorrow—or was set to expire tomorrow. Now, it's an interesting train of logic, isn't it? The tool was necessary 6 months ago, and yet it was set to expire as if the threat to our country was set to expire. But it's not. There's still ongoing threats.

I will sign today, here in Las Vegas, an extension, 15-day extension to the Protect America Act. This will give people in Congress time to pass a good piece of legislation that makes sure that our professionals have the tools necessary to do their job and provides liability protection to carriers who it is assumed helped us in protecting the American people. This Protect America Act and its strengthening is essential to the security of the United States of America. I will sign the extension, but I expect members from both political parties to get this work done so our professionals can protect the American people.

The second part of our strategy is to stay on the offense against these folks— I mean, every day, stay on the offense, an unrelenting effort to find them and bring them to justice. It's hard to plot, plan, and attack America if you're running and hiding. It's hard to recruit if you're cutting off money. It is hard to spread your poison if other reasonable people join the cause. And so we spend a lot of time doing everything we can to keep the pressure on these folks. And we got some good people working it.

I repeat to you: I know there's some good folks who think this is just simply a law enforcement matter; it is not. This is an effort that requires all assets of the United States and requires coalitions working together. I mean, we need to be sharing intelligence. We need our military on the hunt. We need to be working with allies to keep the pressure on them. And that's exactly what we're doing. America must not relent. If our most important job is to protect the American people, we have got to stay on the offense and defeat the enemy overseas so we do not have to face them here at home.

The third part of our strategy is to spread liberty. I love to tell folks that one of the most unique relationships I had as your President was with the Prime Minister of Japan, Prime Minister Koizumi. He's no longer the Prime Minister, but for a good period of time during my Presidency, he was. You might remember, he's the fellow that Laura and I took to Elvis's place in Memphis. [*Laughter*] He loved Elvis, and he wanted to go to Elvis's place. [*Laughter*] And it was a—we had a—it was a remarkable experience. [*Laughter*]

Even more remarkable was the fact that the United States had no stronger ally in defeating terror, no stronger ally than understanding the power of freedom to be transformative. I say "no stronger ally." Tony Blair was strong; there was a lot, but so was Prime Minister Koizumi. What's ironic about that is that my dad fought the Japanese, and many of your relatives fought the Japanese. They were the sworn enemy of the United States of America. I mean, there was unbelievable hatred in our culture toward the Japanese. After all, they attacked us—the second largest attack on American soil—the first being that on September the 11th, 2001.

And yet 60 years later, the son of a Navy fighter pilot was sitting at the table with the Prime Minister of the former enemy strategizing on how to win this ideological war. I find it ironic. The summary I've come away with is that liberty is transformative. People want to be free, and if given the chance, will be free, do the hard work necessary to be free. And liberty has got the capacity to transform an enemy to an ally.

And therefore, we ought to have confidence in liberty's power to bring the peace we want, and not shy away from helping people realize the great blessings of freedom. We've got to be confident in the transformative powers of liberty, recognizing that deep in everybody's soul is the desire to be free. I recognize that is a—there are some in the world who dismiss the capacity of liberty to take hold in parts of the world. There used to be a foreign policy that advocated stability as the cornerstone of our policy. But stability just masked the hopelessness that seethed beneath the surface. If you believe this is an ideological struggle, like I do, then it's paramount to help people realize a different ideology than that of the enemy. And that's what you're seeing unfold.

And the two most evident places that that's happening right now is in Afghanistan and Iraq. Both those countries are part of the war on terror. These aren't separate, you know, wars; they're part of the same war—different theaters, certainly different circumstances, but the outcome is essential for our security. And so I want to spend a little time on Afghanistan and a little time on Iraq.

In Afghanistan—the interesting lesson on Afghanistan for the world to see is that how the vision of the enemy would be implemented; in other words, these poor folks had the Taliban as their oppressors. The Taliban also, as you might remember, provided safe haven to those who came and attacked us. But if you lived in Afghanistan in those days and were a mom of a child, particularly a female child, you had no hope. These thugs didn't believe in freedoms; they didn't believe in women having equal status; they didn't believe young girls should be educated. And if you dared express your opinion that didn't mesh with theirs, you'd be whipped in the public square or killed. These are brutal people. That's the vision that these folks have for the world. That's what they want. Some Americans probably just missed that and

say, "Oh, that's just a pipedream, pie-in-the-sky on their part."

I think the United States needs to take that vision seriously. I think it's in our interest to liberate people. I think it's in our interest that when we find human suffering, we help deal with it.

In Afghanistan, I am proud to report that the United States of America, thanks to a brave military, liberated 25 million people and gave them a chance to realize the blessings of liberty. Since liberation from the Taliban and since Al Qaida was routed out of that country, where they no longer had safe havens to plot and plan an attack, the people of Afghanistan voted for a President; they voted for a parliament; girls now go to school; highways are being built; health clinics are being constructed around the country.

Is it perfect Government? No, but neither were we. I would remind our fellow citizens that we believed all men were created equal and for a 100 years had slaves. Afghanistan is working on their—on democracy. And it's hard work. It's not easy. It's like, it doesn't happen overnight. But it's in our interest to help them. It's in our interest to help them because we believe that liberty is transformative. And a part of the world that was once a safe haven for an enemy that attacked us will be a more hopeful place when freedom takes hold.

The other night to the Nation I said, we're sending 3,200 marines in to supplement our troops there. And the reason why is because this enemy is relentless in trying to overthrow this democracy, and it's in our interest to stop them. You see, we've got to do the hard work now to make sure that a future generation of Americans can grow up in peace.

In Iraq, the decision to remove Saddam Hussein was the right decision. The world is better off without Saddam Hussein in power, and so are the Iraqi people. There has been some interesting progress in Iraq. They wrote a Constitution. They voted.

Imagine a society going from a brutal tyrant to being able to vote in a short period of time.

And yet the enemy—in this case, Al Qaida as well as militia, militia fighters, some sponsored by Iran, some of them just pure criminals—resented the fact that freedom was moving and in early 2006 began a campaign, and they were looking like they were successful. There was unspeakable violence, and I was concerned about it. I was concerned about it because I understand the consequences of failure for our peace, for the future peace for our children.

I had to make a tough decision. And the decision I made was based on the considered judgment of military people, considered judgment of a lot of folks who were following Iraq. It was not based upon any Gallup poll or focus group. It was based upon what was right for the future of the United States, and that is, as opposed to pulling troops out, send more in. And we went in to—with a counterinsurgency strategy, all aimed at, of course, helping the Iraqis stand up and do the hard work necessary, but in the meantime, making sure that when the enemy was cleaned out of neighborhoods, there was somebody there to provide security for the folks.

Our surge, by the way, was more than just military. We surged diplomats and public service officials, Provincial Reconstruction Teams to make sure that in neighborhoods where an enemy had been routed—and we had folks there, along with the Iraqis, to provide security—that there was also a opportunity to improve life for the average citizen. The Iraqis surged. They created 100,000 new soldiers and police. But curiously enough—and I don't know whether a lot of our citizens understand this—80,000 local citizens stepped up and said: "We want to help patrol our own neighborhoods. We're sick and tired of violence and extremists."

I'm not surprised that that happens. I believe Iraqi moms want the same thing that American moms want, and that is for their children to grow up in peace. That's what I believe. I don't believe that people welcome violence. They got sick of it. People want to be free. People want to live in peace, whether you're Methodist or a Muslim, whether you're American or Iraqi. And what you're watching play out now is that folks are becoming more confident in their capacity to self-govern. They're becoming confident that if they step up and expose these extremists or push these extremists out of their neighborhood, there will be enough muscle to help them.

The surge is working. I know some don't want to admit that, and I understand. But the terrorists understand the surge is working. Al Qaida knows the surge is working. They thought they could live safely in Anbar Province. This was the place from which they were going to launch attacks throughout Iraq and throughout the Middle East. This is a place where they proudly proclaimed, "This is our safe haven." They no longer have a safe haven in Anbar Province; they're on the run. We're going to keep them on the run, and it's in our interests for our own security to keep them on the run.

As a result of our successes, some of our troops are coming home. A Marine expeditionary unit and one Army brigade came home in December. It's not going back. I don't know whether my fellow citizens understand that or not. We surged; we accomplished missions; the Iraqis are more capable. The commanders on the ground say that now we can do the same job with less troops. So folks came home for Christmas. It is anticipated that five [four] ° more Army brigades and two Marine battalions will be coming home by July. That's over 20,000 troops will be coming home because we've been successful, that's why.

° White House correction.

You know, a lot of folks say, "Well, what's next, Mr. President?" And my answer is, we have come too far in this important theater in this war on terror not to make sure that we succeed. And therefore, any further troop reductions will be based upon commanders and conditions. Iraq is important for our security. I will be making decisions based upon success in Iraq. The temptation, of course, is for people to say, "Well, make sure you do the politically right thing." That's not my nature. That's not exactly what we're going to do.

The fundamental question is whether or not democracy can take hold. In other words, the security situation is improving, and therefore, will there be efforts by the Iraqi people to seize the moment? Reconciliation is taking place at the local level. People—as I told you, the basic instinct of people is to want to live in peace, and one way you do that is you put this horrible past as best you can behind you and look forward.

So the two things I look for are, one, economic development—you know, a good economy will lead to a more hopeful future, therefore, causing people to be more likely to reconcile—and politics. On the economic front, the interesting thing about Iraq, as opposed to Afghanistan, is that they've got assets and a lot of money. And we, of course, want to help them build the ministries and the bureaucracies necessary to make sure that money gets spent on people. I know that may sound counterintuitive to you, but governments do need the capacity to take a budget and distribute monies throughout the country in an equitable basis in order for people to say, "Well, this experience in democracy is worthwhile." I just want to make sure the bureaucracy doesn't get too big when you do it.

And so we—you know, we chart business startups and markets. And all I can tell you is, I talk to our Ambassador and General Petraeus on a weekly basis, and they report that markets that were once shut down in dismal places as a result of attacks are beginning to come back and flourish, and life is improving dramatically. Baghdad—the capital of Baghdad is—which was once subject to unbelievable sectarian violence—is improving, and life is returning, and that's positive.

And so we watched a lot about the inflation rates and unemployment rates. And they're doing pretty well—they really are—given the fact that they've come from a tyrannical regime that let the infrastructure of the country fall apart.

The other question is politics. One of the lessons of democracy is a lot of times what happens at the local level informs people who are at the central Government level. And competition is pretty healthy in the democracy. As I told you, the local folks are reconciling; they're getting along better; they understand they have a common future. And the people in Baghdad are beginning to respond. They pass budgets. They're now arguing about their 2008 budget. I'm not sure which Government does their budget work better, ours or theirs. [*Laughter*] I can tell you this: We definitely have an issue with earmarks. [*Laughter*] I don't know if they do yet or not. [*Laughter*]

And by the way, I'm going to do something about earmarks. I signed an Executive order the other day, basically saying if you slip these—slip this spending into bills that don't get debated or voted on, we're not going to spend your money. And this Executive order will—[*applause*]. Let me rephrase that: The money will be spent, but just not on those projects necessarily—[*laughter*]—not on those projects necessarily. And this Executive order goes beyond my Presidency.

But they passed budgets. They're sharing oil revenues. They need to pass a law codifying the oil issue there, but they are sharing oil revenues. And they've got revenues, mainly from oil, and they're distributing those revenues to the Provinces. They passed a pension law and a de-

Ba'athification law, which basically is a part of reconciling with the past. They're now in the process of debating a Provincial powers law.

And what's important about that is the—there's a constant debate in free societies—at least in our free society—about the relationship between the Federal Government and State governments. The Governor is most interested in that debate. [*Laughter*] We believe to the best extent possible that we ought to devolve power. Of course, we even take it—this group here, including me—takes it a step further. We devolve power not only in local government but more importantly to individuals, which help define the political landscape of both State and locals.

But this debate is now ongoing in Iraq. Isn't it interesting? I know 4 years seems like an eternity, particularly in this world of instant news and 24-hour whatever on TV. But it's—but Saddam is removed and now a Government elected by the people debating the proper role between central Government and Provincial government. And that's an important debate. And it's ongoing in the Council of Representatives now, and we anticipate them passing that bill.

What I'm telling you is you're watching a democracy evolve. You're watching people become more confident in their ability to self-govern. And it's important that we help them. It's important we help them for our own security, and it's important that we help them as a part of this freedom movement. People have said, "Freedom can't take hold in the Middle East." I strongly disagree. I believe freedom will take hold in the Middle East, and Iraq is an essential part of this strategy.

We will succeed in Iraq. We will succeed because the Iraqi people want to succeed. And it's in our interest to help them. Success in Iraq will show the world that freedom can take root in the Middle East and inspire others. Success in Iraq will mean that we'll have a ally in this struggle against extremists in the heart of the Middle East. Success in Iraq will send an interesting message to its neighbor, Iran.

Failure in Iraq would cause people to doubt the sincerity of the United States when it comes to keeping commitments. Failure in Iraq would embolden the extremists. Failure in Iraq would say to thugs and killers, the United States is a paper tiger. Failure in Iraq would embolden other extremists in the Middle East. Failure in Iraq would embolden Iran. It's in our strategic interests that we succeed, and we will succeed. We have done this kind of work together.

I said in my speech the other day that it is vital for this generation to do the hard work. It is vital for this generation to assume the responsibilities of peace and take the lead so that when we look back 30 to 40 years from now, people will say, "Thank goodness America didn't lose faith with liberty. Thank goodness they didn't abandon a value system that they believe is universal." And I believe an American President will be sitting down with elected leaders from the Middle East saying the same thing to audiences in Nevada that I said about Prime Minister Koizumi.

I hope that you are inspired by the fact that people are willing to take risks for freedom. I hope these examples of Iraqi citizens who step forward to protect their neighborhoods and their families and children inspire you. They certainly inspire me. I hope you're inspired by political figures who defy killers. They inspire me. And I hope you're inspired by our military.

I want to tell you an interesting story. When I was in Reno, I met a guy—a family named the Krissoff family. They had lost a son in Iraq. He was a marine. And one of my duties is to meet with the families of the fallen. I did so last night in northern California. It's an inspiring experience, by the way. It is a—you know, in many ways, the comforter becomes comforted by the spirit and—of these—and pride of these families.

And so I met the Krissoffs. Mr. Krissoff is a 60-year-old guy—I shouldn't be calling him "mister" because I'm a little older than he is—[*laughter*]—but he's a baby boomer just like me and a successful doctor. He said something very interesting to me. He said that he wanted to honor his country and honor his son by joining the military. I looked at the guy and said, yes, okay. [*Laughter*] I said, "Why don't you?" He said, "Well, some of the folks think I'm a little old." [*Laughter*] I said, "I don't," with him being a younger fella. [*Laughter*] So I helped him. And in the—Laura's box at the State of the Union sat Lieutenant Commander Bill Krissoff, serving the United States of America.

Ours is a fabulous country. We are a dedicated, compassionate people, aiming to lay the foundation of peace for generations to come. I told you early, some see the world and tremble; I see the world and see opportunities. And the great opportunity before us is to lay the foundation of peace, and that is exactly what we're doing. God bless.

Thank you all. Okay, I got a little bit of business to do. If you don't mind sitting down for just a second, I am now going to sign this 15-day extension to give Members of the House and the Senate time to get this bill to my desk for the sake of our security. And thank you for witnessing this.

[*At this point, the President signed the bill.*]

Thank you all very much. God bless.

NOTE: The President spoke at 9:30 a.m. at the Emerald at Queensridge. In his remarks, he referred to Ranson W. Webster, chairman of the board of directors, and Sharon J. Rossie, president, Nevada Policy Research Institute; Gov. James A. Gibbons of Nevada; former Prime Minister Tony Blair of the United Kingdom; and Gen. David H. Petraeus, USA, commanding general, Multi-National Force—Iraq. He also referred to Executive Order 13457, which is listed in Appendix D at the end of this volume; and H.R. 5104, approved January 31, which was assigned Public Law No. 110–182.

Remarks on Signing the American Heart Month Proclamation in Kansas City, Missouri
February 1, 2008

The President. Joyce, thank you for joining me.

Joyce Cullen. Thank you.

The President. Joyce is here to join me as I sign a proclamation declaring February American Heart Month.

Part of the reason she is here is because she understands what Laura understands and what a lot of Americans are coming to understand, is that heart disease is the number-one killer of both women and men——

Ms. Cullen. Yes.

The President. ——and that through awareness of this disease, people are more likely to be able to recognize symptoms and deal with it.

And so there's what we call the Heart Truth Campaign, the Red Dress Campaign. And Laura is very much involved with that. She's in New York today at a fashion show heralding the Heart Truth Campaign. Joyce is with me because when Laura was here last in Kansas City, she went to St. Luke's Hospital and talked about the importance for people to recognize the symptoms of heart disease. Joyce had such symptoms, went to the hospital, and prevented a serious heart disease and heart attack and sits here with the President.

Ms. Cullen. How about that.

The President. But more importantly, she's very much a part of the Heart Truth Campaign here in Kansas City.

Ms. Cullen. Yes.

The President. And she's helping people understand two things: one, to be able to recognize the symptoms, and secondly, be able to prevent the symptoms from happening in the first place.

Now, people need to have screenings and checkups; people need to live healthy lives, through exercise and no tobacco. In other words, the decisions we make will affect whether or not our hearts remain strong.

And so I want to thank you for being a strong leader——

Ms. Cullen. Thank you.

The President.——in the campaign for awareness. And so it's my honor, Joyce, to join you in—as you watch me sign this proclamation declaring February American Heart Month.

[At this point, the President signed the proclamation.]

Thank you. You bet. Thank you for being here. Thank you all.

NOTE: The President spoke at 8:28 a.m. at the InterContinental Kansas City Hotel. The American Heart Month proclamation is listed in Appendix D at the end of this volume.

Remarks at Hallmark Cards, Inc., in Kansas City
February 1, 2008

Thank you all. Thank you for letting me come by to say hello. A couple of observations: One, you work for a fabulous company of caring people. I appreciate, Don, your hospitality. I am still trying to recover from the kindergarten experience. [Laughter] I mean, you talk about sapping a person's energy. [Laughter] But it was a fabulous experience.

I got to see Hallmark cards being made, and the fella kindly made me one that said, "For your daughters." It was sweet; it just didn't have any warning in there about how to conduct myself for the upcoming wedding. [Laughter]

I'm here in Kansas City for a couple of reasons. One, I do want to spend a little time on the economy. I had breakfast this morning with entrepreneurs, small-business owners. I want to find out what's on their mind. I will tell you that there's a sense of optimism, I was pleased to hear. People are confident about the future—at least, these businessowners were—and they should be. Interest rates are low; inflation is low; productivity is high. But there are certainly some troubling signs. There's serious signs that the economy is weakening and that we got to do something about it.

Today we got such a sign when after 52 consecutive months of job creation, we lost 17,000 jobs. The unemployment rate went down, but nevertheless, a serious matter is, is that for the first time in 52 months that we didn't create jobs.

And so the question is, what do we do about it? Does Government have a responsibility, and if so, what is it? I do think Government has a responsibility. I think Government can take decisive action to help us deal with this period of uncertainty.

One such action is to help people stay in their homes. We got—some of our citizens purchased mortgages that they can't afford now. Hopefully, the reason—hopefully, they didn't get deceived, and if they did, the Government has a responsibility to take care of that. In other words, we don't want people buying a mortgage and the person who sold them the mortgage didn't fully disclose the reset inherent in a subprime note.

But we can help people stay in their homes by connecting the borrower with the mortgage industry. Now, what makes it difficult in this day and age is that when I bought a home, I sat down with the savings and loan officer. And had I gotten in a financial bind, I would have gone back to that same officer and said, you own my note; help me refinance so I can stay in my home. Today, that financial institution probably doesn't own the note anymore; somebody else owns the note. And therefore, we're trying to make sure we connect the borrower with somebody in the mortgage industry that will help them refinance.

And that's why we started what's called the HOPE NOW Alliance. Secretary Paulson and Secretary Jackson are bringing people together from the private sector, and they couple that with an information campaign, so that people who have a subprime loan know how to refinance and can find somebody to help them refinance. And it's been a complicated matter, but nevertheless, we're very much engaged in helping people sort through what is definitely a difficult period in their life.

The Government can help. The Federal Housing Administration has got the capacity to help refinance homes, and they need to expand the authority of the FHA to do it. And Congress needs to get that bill passed. I mean, this will be a positive step toward helping people stay in homes. And that's what we want to do. See, you notice I'm not saying, we're going to bail out the lenders. We're going to help the individual person be able to keep their home. It's in the interest of the country we do that.

Secondly, there's bonding authorities, tax-exempt bonding authorities, that are now used to help people buy new homes. States and local governments ought to be able to use that money to help people stay in the home they have. And that will be helpful as well. And so here are some con-structive measures that we can take. There's a cyclicality when it comes to the housing interests—housing industry. But in the meantime, or during this down cycle, we want to help individual Americans.

Secondly, a concern is whether or not our consumers will lose confidence in our economy. You don't want that to happen at Hallmark. You want the consumers to still buy your product on a regular basis. And one way to address that issue is to have a temporary, robust tax rebate. And that's what we're working on in Congress. You hear this discussion of a stimulus package. Well, a key component of that package is to get—give you some of your money back so you can spend it.

And the House of Representatives passed a good package. The administration worked with the House—it may surprise you that Republicans and Democrats can actually get something done in a constructive fashion, but it happened in this case, for the good of the country. And now the Senate is debating the bill, and it's very important for the Senate to finish their work quickly cause the sooner we can get money into our consumers' hands, the more likely it is, is that this economy will get back—recover from this period of uncertainty.

The fundamentals are strong. We're just in a rough patch, as witnessed by the employment figures today. And I'm confident we can get through this rough patch. And one way to do it is to—for Congress and the administration to work collaboratively and get this deal done.

Now, a key component, as well, of a growth package is to encourage businesses to invest. And why would you do that? Well, if Hallmark buys a new piece of equipment, somebody has to make that equipment. In other words, job creation happens when people make investments. And if you, therefore, stimulate businesses, both large and small, to make investments this year, as quickly as possible, it means somebody is more likely to keep work and the economy will continue to be strong.

So the two key components of this package are, one, enhance consumerism by giving consumers money—it's not like a great gift; after all, it's your own money; we're just giving it back to you—and encouraging businesses to invest. I believe we can get this package done. I know it has to be done quickly. I appreciate the fact that the Senate is trying to work through this as quickly as possible. I'm just urging them to get it done, because the sooner this package makes it to my desk, that actually focuses on ways to stimulate growth, the better off our economy is going to be.

Finally, we need to be thinking about how to effect economic growth in the long term. In other words, we'll deal with the short-term issue, but as we do so, we also need to be wise about the policy so that we can continue this period of growth that we've had.

A couple points I want to make to you on that. One is it's important for Hallmark to be able to sell your cards overseas. I mean, the more people that are exposed to the Hallmark product, the more likely it is that they'll buy. You just want a chance to compete. And so trade is an important aspect of—to making sure our economy remains strong. There are some folks who worry about trade. They want to protect America from products from overseas. I am concerned about protectionism, and so should you, because if we end up having trade wars, it's going to be less likely Hallmark products will be sold overseas.

My attitude is, just give us a chance; let's level the playing field. We can compete with anybody, anytime. We've got to have confidence in our capacity to compete in the world. And trade is an important aspect for keeping economic vitality alive.

Education is important. You've got some awfully smart people working here, but they need to be—the future of Hallmark depends upon having an educated workforce. And that's the way it is in most U.S. companies.

And so I'm very much focused on making sure our education system gets it right in the beginning—"right in the beginning" means teaching kids to read and write and add and subtract. I cannot stand a system that refuses to measure. I think it's an appropriate question to ask, can a child read, and if not, what do you intend to do about it?

Accountability is an integral part of making sure this system doesn't leave people behind. I am passionate on the subject of measuring because I used to be a Governor of a State, and I knew who got shuffled through the schools: inner-city kids. I mean, "These are people too hard to educate; let's just move them through"—or parents who—kids whose parents don't speak English as a first language. It's unacceptable to America not to insist that every child gets a good education. And so I'm going to work with Congress on this No Child Left Behind law, which is a very important part of making sure the workforce of the future is educated and ready to compete in a global economy.

Finally, taxes—there is a—you know, I'm sure you've heard that, well, we need more money in Washington; therefore, we're going to raise your taxes. Of course, it's disguised by saying, we're only going to tax rich people, but that's not the way it works. Rich people tend to hire lawyers and accountants, and you get stuck with the bill. We don't need more money. We need to prioritize your money. We need to be wise about how we spend your money.

Raising taxes in a time of economic uncertainty would be bad for the economy, and it would be bad for our people. I believe we ought to trust Americans to spend their money. I mean, the truth of the matter is, you can spend it more wisely than the Government can. And so in my State of the Union the other day, I called upon Congress to make the tax cuts permanent. I want to deal with this aspect of uncertainty. See, if you think your tax bill is fixing to go up—which it is, unless Congress acts; it will be going up in a couple of years—it could change your behavior. It could cause people to pull back and not be confident about the future.

And I also called on them to stop this business about putting special projects in legislation without being voted on. That doesn't make any sense. I mean, our process is one where there should be transparency and—like, if a project is important enough for a Member of Congress to slip into what's called a conference report, that project ought to be important enough for there to be a full vote—Members of Congress get to look at it and see if it makes any sense.

So I've got an agenda for Congress. I'm looking forward to working with them on how to stimulate the economy in the short term, but make sure we remain a strong economy in the long term. And I'm looking forward to working with them. I like the spirit I found up in the Halls of Congress. There's still a little politics in Washington, DC, but that's not to say we can't work for the common good.

And I appreciate you all giving me a chance to come by and visit with you. I hope you can tell I'm optimistic about the future of the country, realistic about the issues we face, and have—got a plan to deal with them. God bless you. Thank you.

NOTE: The President spoke at 10:47 a.m. In his remarks, he referred to Donald J. Hall, Jr., president and chief executive officer, Hallmark Cards, Inc.

Letter to Congressional Leaders Transmitting a Report Relating to the Interdiction of Aircraft Engaged in Illicit Drug Trafficking
January 31, 2008

Dear Madam Speaker: (Dear Mr. President:)

Consistent with the authorities relating to official immunity in the interdiction of aircraft engaged in illicit drug trafficking (Public Law 107–108, as amended, 22 U.S.C. 2291–4), and in order to keep the Congress fully informed, I am providing a report prepared by my Administration. This report includes matters relating to the interdiction of aircraft engaged in illicit drug trafficking.

Sincerely,

GEORGE W. BUSH

NOTE: Identical letters were sent to Nancy Pelosi, Speaker of the House of Representatives, and Richard B. Cheney, President of the Senate. This letter was released by the Office of the Press Secretary on February 4.

Remarks Following a Cabinet Meeting
February 4, 2008

Thank you all for coming. I just met with my Cabinet, where we discussed a lot of issues. And one issue we discussed was the budget. I submitted the budget today to Congress. It's on a laptop notebook, an e-budget. It saves paper, saves trees, saves money. I think it's the first budget submitted electronically.

And it's a good budget. It's a budget that achieves some important objectives. One, it understands our top priority is to defend our country, so we fund our military, as well as fund the homeland security.

Secondly, the budget keeps our economy growing. It's central that we make sure that we deal with the uncertainties—the economic uncertainties we face. And that's why we're working hard with the House and the Senate to get a growth package out quickly that will put money in the hands of consumers and provide incentives to small businesses and large businesses to invest.

Thirdly, we recognize that in order for this economy to grow, it's important to make the tax relief permanent. And that's what this budget reflects. It's a budget that boosts money for education and health and housing. It helps deal with the issue of making the Tax Code more fair for individuals who want to buy health insurance in the individual market.

This budget is one that keeps spending under control; discretionary spending is held to less than 1 percent. It eliminates 151 wasteful or bloated programs, saving the taxpayers $18 billion. It also takes a hard look at entitlement growth over the next 5 years and provides specific recommendations to save $208 billion over those 5 years. At the same time, the budget achieves balance by 2012.

This is a good, solid budget. It's not only an innovative budget, in that it's coming to Congress over the Internet, it's a budget that's balanced—it gets to balance in 2012 and saves taxpayers money.

You know, in my State of the Union, I said to the Congress that there's a lot of talk about entitlement spending. Once again, we've proposed specific reforms and specific measures. And Congress needs to come up with its own ideas. And Congress needs to respond to these looming deficits as a result of unfunded liabilities inherent in Social Security and Medicare. Our budget does that. Our budget protects America and encourages economic growth. Congress needs to pass it.

Thank you very much.

NOTE: The President spoke at 10:57 a.m. in the Cabinet Room at the White House.

Remarks Honoring the 2007 NASCAR Nextel Cup Champion
February 5, 2008

The President. You know, one of the things I love about NASCAR is not only are these great athletes, but they're socially minded folks. And Chandra and Jimmie and I met several times—one time at a place where the folks of NASCAR are putting something back into the community to help the less fortunate. In this case, it happened to be in a place called Victory Junction in North Carolina, and it was a fabulous experience. And I want to thank you all very much for taking your fame and lending it to help somebody in need. It's really what makes America a great place. And you're leaders on the track and leaders off the track.

Jimmie Johnson. Thank you very much.

NOTE: The President spoke at 1:09 p.m. in the Oval Office at the White House. In his remarks, he referred to NASCAR driver Jimmie Johnson and his wife Chandra.

Statement on the Appointment of President Jakaya Mrisho Kikwete of Tanzania as President of the African Union and Foreign Minister Jean Ping of Gabon as Chair of the Commission of the African Union
February 5, 2008

I congratulate President Jakaya Kikwete of Tanzania on his appointment as the new President of the African Union, as well as Foreign Minister Jean Ping of Gabon on his appointment as the new Chair of the Commission of the African Union. I am confident that the African Union and the people of Africa will be well served by the leadership and vision President Kikwete and Minister Ping will bring to these important posts.

The African Continent has experienced important progress in recent years. Economic growth is at historic highs; democracy is taking root in many countries; and efforts to combat HIV/AIDS, malaria, and other infectious diseases are showing results. Difficult challenges remain, including ending genocide in Darfur, restoring peace and stability to Kenya, and bringing freedom to the Zimbabwean people. The United States looks forward to working closely with President Kikwete, Minister Ping, and the African Union to address these challenges and to build on recent achievements to secure a better future for all Africans.

Laura and I look forward to beginning our visit to Africa next week.

Message on the Observance of the Lunar New Year, 2008
February 5, 2008

I send greetings to those celebrating the Lunar New Year, the Year of the Rat.

Throughout our country and around the world, men and women of Asian descent welcome the Lunar New Year with a spirit of giving and renewed hope. This holiday, filled with vibrant traditions, celebrates new beginnings and recognizes the enduring wisdom of ancestors. During this special time of year, millions of people reunite with family and friends, reflect on the past, and look forward to a future of prosperity and opportunity.

The Lunar New Year also reminds us of the richness of Asian culture and the significance of its history. By preserving and sharing their heritage, Asian Americans enhance the American experience and contribute to our country's legacy of diversity.

Laura and I send our best wishes for peace, health, and happiness in the New Year.

GEORGE W. BUSH

NOTE: An original was not available for verification of the content of this message.

Memorandum on Security Clearances
February 5, 2008

Memorandum for the Heads of Executive Departments and Agencies and the Assistant to the President for National Security Affairs

Subject: Security Clearances

The Federal Government needs a qualified, trusted workforce available to successfully execute its missions. However, long-standing practices used in the security processing of individuals and contractors to work for the Government pose challenges to the speed with which these individuals can begin their work or move from one role to another. Specifically, the processes for determining eligibility for access to classified information, determining suitability for Federal employment, determining eligibility to work on a Federal contract, and for granting access to federally controlled facilities and information systems, created for separate purposes, rely on similar background data. Yet the processes for collecting and analyzing this data are not sufficiently standardized or coordinated to allow for individuals to efficiently move between agencies and positions of Government covered by one or more of these processes.

I have determined that the significant opportunities to improve these processes, and the expected benefits of doing so, argue for aggressive efforts to achieve meaningful and lasting reform. Without altering the distinct lines of authority for establishing policies and procedures relating to security clearance, Federal employment suitability, and related determinations, such reform should ensure that the executive branch executes these authorities within a framework that maximizes efficiency and effectiveness while protecting the information collected from unauthorized use or disclosure. Embedding that framework in policies, practices, and infrastructure will ensure that the reform effort and its benefits will continue into the future.

Efforts toward achieving this integration are already underway, sponsored by the Director of National Intelligence, Secretary of Defense, Director of the Office of Personnel Management, and the Assistant to the President for National Security Affairs, and coordinated by the Director of the Office of Management and Budget. These efforts span near-term improvement opportunities up to a blueprint for a transformed clearance process. I direct that their continued close coordination and integration produce a comprehensive reform proposal that:

- Establishes modernized and comprehensive credentialing, security clearance, and suitability processes that employ updated and consistent standards and methods;
- To the extent consistent with applicable law, ensures that investigative standards for security clearance and suitability investigations support and build on each other without requiring duplicative steps;
- Enables these innovations with enterprise information technology capabilities that ensure the most effective and efficient performance across the Federal Government;
- Updates Government information record systems and, as necessary, applicable laws and regulations, to ensure that information maintained by executive departments and agencies and required for investigation and adjudication is available and can be shared rapidly across Government, while still protecting privacy-related information;

- Ensures that a reformed and aligned investigative system maximizes the potential for common ground in the adjudication of those programs whose security and suitability determinations are simultaneous; and,
- Ensures that all resulting decisions are in the national interest, protect national security, and provide the Federal Government with an effective workforce.

Under Executive Order 13381, I assigned to the Director of the Office of Management and Budget responsibility for improving the process for determining eligibility for access to classified national security information. Under Executive Orders 10450 and 10577, as amended, and related statutory authorities, the Office of Personnel Management is assigned various responsibilities related to personnel security investigations and suitability. These and all other current executive orders remain in force. However, recommendations may be made to align or otherwise alter policies and procedures to ensure the effective, efficient, and timely investigation and adjudication of security clearances and suitability for employment for all personnel performing work for or on behalf of the Federal Government.

I hereby direct the Director of the Office of Management and Budget, the Director of the Office of Personnel Management, the Assistant to the President for National Security Affairs, the Director of National Intelligence, and the Secretary of Defense, to submit to the President an initial reform proposal not later than April 30, 2008, that includes, as necessary, proposed executive and legislative actions to achieve the goals of reform described above. This proposal should be followed promptly by any additional proposals this group believes necessary to fulfill its mission.

Nothing in this memorandum alters or impedes the ability to carry out the authorities of the executive departments and agencies to perform their responsibilities under existing law, including, but not limited to, the authority of the Director of the Office of Personnel Management under 5 U.S.C. 1103(a)(7) to recommend executive orders amending the civil service rules governing suitability for employment in the competitive service and the excepted service of the United States, and the authority of the Assistant Attorney General, Office of Legal Counsel, Department of Justice, under 28 C.F.R. 0.25(b) to draft, revise, and advise as to the form and legality all executive orders prior to submission to the President.

The heads of executive departments and agencies are directed to provide all information and assistance requested by the Director of the Office of Management and Budget in this important endeavor.

GEORGE W. BUSH

Letter to Congressional Leaders on Continuation of the National Emergency Blocking Property of Certain Persons Contributing to the Conflict in Cote d'Ivoire
February 5, 2008

Dear Madam Speaker: (Dear Mr. President:)

Section 202(d) of the National Emergencies Act (50 U.S.C. 1622(d)) provides for the automatic termination of a national emergency unless, prior to the anniversary date of its declaration, the President publishes in the *Federal Register* and transmits to the Congress a notice stating that the emergency is to continue in effect beyond the anniversary date. In accordance with this provision, I have sent the enclosed notice to the *Federal Register* for publication, stating that the national emergency and related measures blocking the property of certain persons contributing to the conflict in Cote d'Ivoire are to continue in effect beyond February 7, 2008.

In March 2007, the Ougadougou Political Agreement was signed by the two primary protagonists in Cote d'Ivoire's conflict. Although considerable progress has been made in implementing this agreement, the situation in or in relation to Cote d'Ivoire poses a continuing unusual and extraor-

dinary threat to the national security and foreign policy of the United States.

For these reasons, I have determined that it is necessary to continue the national emergency and related measures blocking the property of certain persons contributing to the conflict in Cote d'Ivoire.

Sincerely,

GEORGE W. BUSH

NOTE: Identical letters were sent to Nancy Pelosi, Speaker of the House of Representatives, and Richard B. Cheney, President of the Senate. The notice is listed in Appendix D at the end of this volume.

Remarks at a Swearing-In Ceremony for Edward T. Schafer as Secretary of Agriculture
February 6, 2008

Thanks for the warm welcome. Before we begin the ceremony today, we turn our thoughts to those suffering from yesterday's tornadoes.

This was a bad storm that affected a lot of people in a variety of States. Our administration is reaching out to State officials. I just called the Governors of the affected States. I wanted them to know that this Government will help them. But more importantly, I wanted them to be able to tell the people in their States that the American people hold them up and—hold those who suffer up in prayer. Loss of life, a lot of loss of property—prayers can help, and so can the Government. And so today, before we begin this important ceremony, I do want the people in those States to know the American people are standing with them.

It's good to be back here at the Department of Agriculture. I am—I first want to say how much I appreciate the hard and good work the people in this Department do on behalf of the American people.

I'm also pleased to witness the swearing-in of an outstanding public servant, the new leader for this Department, Secretary Ed Schafer. I welcome Ed's wife Nancy and all their family members. [*Laughter*] They got four children and eight grandchildren, which means he's got valuable experience when it comes to the food supply. [*Laughter*] I know Ed's family is proud of him, as am I, and I congratulate him on taking his place as America's 29th Secretary of Agriculture.

I appreciate the members of my Cabinet who have joined us. Thanks for coming. I very much appreciate the Members of the Senate and the House who are here, and I know the Secretary does as well: Senator Harkin, Senator Chambliss. These men happen to be the ranking member of the—chairman and ranking member of the agricultural committee in the Senate. I appreciate Collin Peterson, chairman of the House Agriculture Committee, and I want to thank the other Members here as well. I appreciate very much the fact that John

Block, former Secretary of Agriculture, has taken time to join us. Secretary, thanks for coming.

The roots of this Department stretch back to the Presidency of Abraham Lincoln. In 1862, President Lincoln established the first Federal agency devoted to agriculture, and he called it "the people's department." Nearly a century-and-a-half later, the USDA can still be called "the people's department." With your nutrition programs and your support for farmers and ranchers, you help ensure that our people are healthy and well fed. With your food safety measures, you give peace of mind to families across America. With your conservation efforts, you help preserve our natural resources.

Secretary Schafer is going to be a strong and effective leader in all these areas. I know him well; we're members of the ex-Governors club. [*Laughter*] He's a fellow you can trust. He's a skilled manager who knows how to focus and get results. Among his many other distinctions, he is the first North Dakotan to run this Department.

He had an interesting first night on the job; he spent it in the House Chamber listening to me give the State of the Union Address. [*Laughter*] I can report that he didn't go to sleep—[*laughter*]—and applauded just at the right times. [*Laughter*]

Our priorities for this Department are clear. We will work to make our strong agricultural sector even stronger. Ed understands what I know: It makes a lot of sense to make sure that we can grow our own food. It's in our national security interest that we're self-sufficient in food. Farm income, farm equity, and farm exports have reached alltime records. The best way to keep the ag economy growing is to open up new markets for America's crops and farm products around the world.

So Ed is going to join with other members of my administration to work to pass free trade agreements with Colombia and Panama and South Korea. We will support a successful collusion—conclusion of the

Doha round of trade talks. Ed and I are going to work tirelessly to open up foreign markets for U.S. beef.

We recognize that farmers also have the potential to help our Nation solve one of the greatest challenges, and that is our dependence on foreign oil. I'd much rather our farmers be growing energy than trying to buy it from other parts of the world. So we will continue to work on—for renewable fuels and—including a new generation of ethanol and biodiesel.

Finally, Ed understands the importance of a good farm bill. More than a year ago, we proposed a fiscally responsible farm bill that provides a strong safety net and makes important reforms to farm programs. Farm payments would be targeted to farmers who truly need them, especially those involved in production agriculture.

Congress is considering legislation now. It seems like to us it lacks reform. It spends too much money and raises taxes. It's critical for farmers and consumers to have a good farm bill in place. So Ed is going to work with members of both parties on a bill that spends people's money wisely, doesn't raise taxes, reforms and tightens subsidy payments—a farm bill that will benefit the entire economy. I'm confident we can come together to good—get a good farm bill. But if Congress sends me legislation that raises taxes or [does]* not make needed reforms, I'm going to veto it.

In all the work ahead, Ed can count on a strong partner in his Deputy, Chuck Conner. He's a talented public servant. He's devoted his life to agriculture issues, and he did a superb job of running this Department while Ed was being confirmed. And, Chuck, I want to thank you.

We also owe a debt of gratitude to Secretary Mike Johanns. In his 3 years here at this Department, Mike delivered impressive results for farmers and ranchers, from helping to expand trade to promoting biofuels to providing assistance after natural

------

* White House correction.

disasters. I know he's enjoying his time in Nebraska; I hope he'll be back soon. [*Laughter*]

There's no doubt in my mind that Ed Schafer and the good men and women in this Department can build on these achievements. I thank him and his family for answering the call to public service once again. I know he's going to do a fine job here in "the people's department." Congratulations, my friend.

And now I ask Deputy Secretary Conner to administer the oath.

NOTE: The President spoke at 11:07 a.m. at the Department of Agriculture. The transcript released by the Office of the Press Secretary also included the remarks of Secretary Schafer.

Remarks Honoring the 2007 Stanley Cup Champion Anaheim Ducks
February 6, 2008

Thank you all. Thanks for coming. Please be seated. Welcome to the White House. We're glad you're here. Like, have you noticed a lot of security around here? It's because the Vice President heard there were some Ducks around. [*Laughter*]

These Ducks are awfully mighty. It's such an honor to welcome you. I love welcoming champs to the White House, and these are clearly great champs. You know, the playoffs have got to be tough at that time of year, after you've played so long and your legs are a little tired—except you romped through the playoffs. I don't know if many Americans understand that, but this team went 16–5 through the first four rounds, became the first west coast team in the NHL to win the Stanley Cup. And that's a big deal.

And so it's my honor to welcome you to the White House. Glad you're here. I do want to welcome the owner, Henry Samueli; appreciate you coming. Thanks for bringing the girls. I had the privilege of being in pro sports as a baseball owner. I never had the chance to come to the White House as a baseball owner. [*Laughter*] I had a little trouble on the division crowns as a baseball owner. [*Laughter*] But I understand how—what a joy it must be to represent an ownership group, to watch a team you care about win the Stanley Cup,

and win any championship. So we're glad you came. Thanks for coming, Henry.

Michael Schulman, who is the CEO, I'm glad you're here, Mike; Brian Burke, the general manager. I really want to say something about Randy Carlyle, the head coach. It's got to be hard to be a head coach of such great athletes. I don't know if you're ever in the newspaper. [*Laughter*] Yes, I know how you feel. But I'm proud to have you here.

Scott Niedermayer is the MVP. I tend not to try to single out a player, but nevertheless, when you have an MVP in your midst, I'm proud to recognize you; glad you're here.

I do want to welcome the commissioner. Mr. Commissioner, thanks for coming. This isn't the first time we've been together like this; it will probably be the last like this. [*Laughter*] But I know you'll keep coming back to the White House to promote the champs in a sport you love.

I want to thank the mayor of Anaheim, my friend Curt Pringle. Thanks for coming, Mr. Mayor. It must be a big deal when the Ducks win the Stanley Cup for the people of Anaheim, and I'm honored that you're here. I also want to welcome Congressman Eddy Royce. Ed, thanks for coming; appreciate you being here. Of course, we welcome all the players, all the personnel, all the fans.

And how about the Northern Virginia Ice Dog Mites hockey team? Yes. The Ice Dogs—[*laughter*]—are here to see the Ducks. [*Laughter*] I bet you guys want to be Stanley Cup champs some day too, don't you? Well, here they are; you got a chance to see what they look like. I bet you they would tell you that in order to be a Stanley Cup champ, you have to work hard and skate hard and make right choices in life, just like these folks did that are standing up here with me.

The Stanley Cup was awarded 115 years ago, which makes it the oldest trophy in professional sports. The Cup bears the names of not only the teams that won it but more than 2,000 names of the individuals who have raised the Cup in victory. And these men behind me now have their name on the Cup.

The interesting thing about the Stanley Cup, it's the only professional sports trophy that every player on the championship team gets to take home for a day. This Cup has been to some odd places. [*Laughter*] For example, it went to Elvis's place in Memphis, Graceland. [*Laughter*] It has taken a turn on the Indianapolis Motor Speedway. It has seen the inside of an igloo and a New York City jail. [*Laughter*] It stood next to a giant statue of Lenin and a 55-foot Jolly Green Giant in Blue Earth, Minnesota. The Cup has been to countless bars and nightclubs across the world, and I'm sure some of the players are pleased the Cup can't talk. [*Laughter*]

Last year, the Cup made its first visit to a combat zone. Nineteen players— former NHL players—took this cup to Kandahar Air Base in Afghanistan for a ball-hockey game with Canadian and American troops. I promise you, our troops were thrilled to see the Cup. And whoever thought of it, I thank you from the bottom of my heart for supporting those kids.

The Anaheim Ducks also took the Cup on many adventures, traveling with it to Canada, Sweden, Finland, and England. Chris Pronger and Todd Marchant each took it home to use it as a cereal bowl for the kids—[*laughter*]—pretty hungry kids. Sean O'Donnell filled it with dog food so that his Lab, Buddy, could eat from it. You know, I was wondering why Barney and my dogs took such a liking to the Stanley Cup. [*Laughter*]

Ducks players have used their time to help lift the lives of others. This is what I'm particularly grateful for. The Ducks took the Cup to the Mattel Children's Hospital at UCLA and the Children's Hospital in Orange County, where it brought joy to somebody who is suffering. That must have been a fantastic experience, to see somebody's face light up who was having a pretty tough go in life, and I want to thank you for that. I appreciate the fact that you took the Cup to the Orangewood Children's Foundation, where it helped raise the spirits of those who have been— who are victims of abuse and neglect.

Several Ducks took the Cup for a visit to our wounded warriors at Camp Pendleton. The general manager, Brian Burke, said this: "This is the most special moment I've had with the Cup—not being with my family, not being with my friends, but being at Camp Pendleton." He knows what I know: The United States of America is incredibly lucky to have brave men and women volunteer in the face of danger to serve our country. And I cannot thank you enough for honoring those wounded warriors, those marines, and for lifting their spirits and for thanking them for their sacrifice and their service.

I appreciate your talent. These are great athletes, but they've also got big hearts. I congratulate the coaches. I congratulate the family members, the wives, girlfriends who put up with the long, long time away from home. It's got to be tough to be a spouse supporting somebody you love in professional sports, and I want to thank your families for supporting you in this.

I do want to thank all those who make the training room go. You know, a lot of times championships are focused on the players, but these players will be the first to tell you there's the locker room attendants, there's the laundry people, there's the equipment people who deserve just as much of this championship as they do. And I want to congratulate you and those of you who happened to handle this aspect of—for the Anaheim Ducks. Welcome to the White House.

I will remind you that you've achieved something millions of kids dream about—and a couple of oldtimers dream about too.

You set a great example for them, and I congratulate you for your championship. And you'll for always be remembered for the rest of your lives as Stanley Cup champs.

Welcome to the White House, and God bless you.

NOTE: The President spoke at 3:02 p.m. in the East Room at the White House. In his remarks, he referred to Gary B. Bettman, commissioner, National Hockey League; and Chris Pronger and Sean O'Donnell, defensemen, and Todd Marchant, forward, Anaheim Ducks.

Message to the Congress on Continuation of the National Emergency Relating to Cuba and of the Emergency Authority Relating to the Regulation of the Anchorage and Movement of Vessels
February 6, 2008

To the Congress of the United States:

Section 202(d) of the National Emergencies Act (50 U.S.C. 1622(d)) provides for the automatic termination of a national emergency unless, prior to the anniversary date of its declaration, the President publishes in the *Federal Register* and transmits to the Congress a notice stating that the emergency is to continue in effect beyond the anniversary date. In accordance with this provision, I have sent the enclosed notice to the *Federal Register* for publication, which states that the national emergency declared with respect to the Government of Cuba's destruction of two unarmed U.S.-registered civilian aircraft in international airspace north of Cuba on February 24, 1996, as amended and expanded on February 26, 2004, is to continue in effect beyond March 1, 2008.

GEORGE W. BUSH

The White House,
February 6, 2008.

NOTE: This message was released by the Office of the Press Secretary on February 7. The notice is listed in Appendix D at the end of this volume.

Message to the Senate Transmitting the International Convention Against Doping in Sport
February 6, 2008

To the Senate of the United States:

With a view to receiving the advice and consent of the Senate to ratification, I transmit herewith the International Convention Against Doping in Sport, adopted by the United Nations Educational, Scientific, and Cultural Organization on October 19, 2005.

The United States supported the development of the Convention as a means to ensure equitable and effective application and promotion of anti-doping controls in international competition. The Convention will help to advance international cooperation on and promotion of international doping control efforts, and will help to protect the integrity and spirit of sport by supporting efforts to ensure a fair and doping-free environment for athletes.

The International Olympic Movement has been supportive of the promotion and adoption of this Convention by the international community. Ratification by the United States will demonstrate the United States' longstanding commitment to the development of international anti-doping controls and its commitment to apply and facilitate the application of appropriate anti-doping controls during international competitions held in the United States. Ratification will also ensure that the United States will continue to remain eligible to host international competitions. The Convention does not cover U.S. sports leagues.

I recommend that the Senate give prompt and favorable consideration to the Convention and give its advice and consent to ratification.

GEORGE W. BUSH

The White House,
February 6, 2008.

NOTE: This message was released by the Office of the Press Secretary on February 7.

Remarks at the National Prayer Breakfast
February 7, 2008

The President. Gracias, mi amigo.

Senator Kenneth L. Salazar. De nada.

The President. Thank you, friend. Laura and I are honored to join you all here for the 56th National Prayer Breakfast. A lot of reasons to pray, and one, of course, is to strengthen us against temptation, particularly this morning—from temptation to stay in bed. [*Laughter*] Obviously, there's a lot of prayerful people here. [*Laughter*] And I appreciate your warm welcome.

We have a lot of distinguished guests here today: Members of Congress, military leaders, captains of industry. Yet at this annual gathering, we are reminded of an eternal truth: When we lift our hearts to God, we're all equal in His sight. We're all equally precious; we're all equally dependent on His grace. It's fitting that we gather each year to approach our Creator in fellowship and to thank Him for the many blessings He's bestowed upon our families and our Nation. It is fitting that we gather in prayer, because we recognize a prayerful nation is a stronger nation.

I want to appreciate Senators—[*applause*]—I appreciate Senators Salazar and Enzi. Thank you for putting this deal on.

Madam Speaker, Leader Hoyer, Leader Blunt: Thank you all for being here. Welcome the Members of Congress. I appreciate the heads of state who are here. Welcome to America, again. I thank the members of the diplomatic corps who have joined us. Appreciate the distinguished dignitaries, all the members of my Cabinet—don't linger, get back to work. [*Laughter*]

Admiral, thank you for your leadership. Always proud to be with the members of the United States military. I thank the State and local officials. Ward, thanks for your remarks. Those were awesome. I guess that's a Presidential word. [*Laughter*] Proud to be here with Michael W. and Debbie. They're longtime friends of our family. Thank you for lending your beautiful voice. Judge, I'm not going to hold the Texas thing against you. [*Laughter*]

Every President since Dwight Eisenhower has attended the National Prayer Breakfast, and I am really proud to carry on this tradition. It's an important tradition, and I'm confident Presidents who follow me will do the same. The people in this room come from many different walks of faith, yet we share one clear conviction: We believe that the Almighty hears our prayers and answers those who seek Him. That's what we believe; otherwise, why come? Through the miracle of prayer, we believe He listens—if we listen to His voice and seek our presence—His presence in our lives, our hearts will change. And in so doing, in seeking God, we grow in ways that we could never imagine.

In prayer, we grow in gratitude and thanksgiving. When we spend time with the Almighty, we realize how much He has bestowed upon us, and our hearts are filled with joy. We give thanks for our families. We give thanks for the parents who raised us. We give thanks for the patient souls who married us and the children who make us proud each day. We give thanks for our liberty and the universal desire for freedom that He has written in every human heart. We give thanks for the God who made us in His image and redeemed us in His love.

In prayer, we grow in meekness and humility. By approaching our Maker on bended knee, we acknowledge our complete dependence on Him. We recognize that we have nothing to offer God that He does not already have, except our love. So we offer Him that love and ask for the grace to discern His will. We ask Him to remain near to us at all times. We ask Him to help us lead lives that are pleasing to Him. We discover that by surrendering our lives to the Almighty, we are strengthened, refreshed, and ready for all that may come.

In prayer, we also grow in boldness and courage. The more time we spend with God, the more we see that He is not a distant king, but a loving Father. Inspired by this confidence, we approach Him with bold requests. We ask Him to heal the sick and comfort the dying and sustain those who care for them. We ask Him to bring solace to the victims of tragedy and help to those suffering from addiction and adversity. We ask him to strengthen our families and to protect the innocent and vulnerable in our country. We ask Him to protect our Nation from those who wish us harm and watch over all who've stepped forward to defend us. We ask Him to bring about the day when His peace shall reign across the world and every tear shall be wiped away.

In prayer, we grow in mercy and compassion. We are reminded in prayer that we are all fallen creatures in need of mercy. And in seeking God's mercy, we grow in mercy ourselves. Experiencing the presence of God transforms our hearts. And the more we seek His presence, the more we feel the tug at our souls to reach out to the poor and the hungry, the elderly and the infirm. When we answer God's call to love a neighbor as ourselves, we enter into a deeper friendship with our fellow man and a deeper relationship with our eternal Father.

I believe in the power of prayer because I have felt it in my own life. Prayer has strengthened me in times of personal challenge. It has helped me meet the challenges of the Presidency. I understand now clearly the story of the calm in the rough seas. And so at this final prayer breakfast as your President, I thank you for your prayers, and I thank our people all across America for their prayers. And I ask you not to stop in the year ahead. We have so much work to do for our country, and with the help of the Almighty, we will build a freer world and a safer, more hopeful, more noble America.

God bless.

NOTE: The President spoke at 9:16 a.m. at the Hilton Washington Hotel. In his remarks, he referred to Adm. Michael G. Mullen, USN, Chairman, Joint Chiefs of Staff; Edward W. "Ward" Brehm III, Chairman of the Board of Directors, U.S. African Development Foundation; entertainer Michael W. Smith and his wife Debbie; and Carlos F. Lucero, U.S. Circuit Judge for the Tenth Circuit Court of Appeals.

Remarks on Nominations Awaiting Senate Confirmation
February 7, 2008

Thank you all. Please be seated; sit down. Yes, thanks for coming. I appreciate you being here in a timely fashion. After all, Washington traffic is famous for making people late. These days, it seems the worst delays, however, are in the committee rooms of the United States Senate.

Many of the nominees for important Government posts have been waiting for Senate confirmation for way too long. Some of these men and women here—are with us today, and I want to thank you all for joining me. More importantly, I thank you for your willingness to step forward to serve our great country. These folks are qualified, and the Senate needs to give them a prompt vote.

I appreciate very much Members of the Senate who have joined us. These are good, strong leaders, people who share the same spirit about the need to get confirmation done quickly, starting with the Senate minority leader, Mitch McConnell. I appreciate Arlen Specter joining us. You might remember Arlen that when—Arlen was the man, when I named two nominees for the Supreme Court, did a fantastic job of getting those nominees out of the Judiciary Committee and onto the floor of the Senate. And he had good help from Orrin Hatch, his friend and member of the Judiciary Committee.

I'm also here with some of the younger stars—not to call you guys old—but some of the younger stars—[*laughter*]—of the Senate: Richard Burr from North Carolina, Lindsey Graham from South Carolina, and Jim DeMint from South Carolina. Thank you all for coming. Appreciate you guys being here.

I thank members of my administration joining us. Steve, thanks for being here. Chief of Staff Bolten, I appreciate you being here. And thank you all for coming.

As President, I have a constitutional responsibility to nominate qualified men and women for public office. That's my responsibility. I take it very seriously. I have nominated skilled and faithful public servants to lead Federal agencies and sit on the Federal bench. The Constitution also gives Senators an important responsibility. They must provide advice and consent by voting up or down on these nominees. Unfortunately, the Senate is not fulfilling its duty.

The confirmation process has turned into a never-ending political game where everyone loses. With more than 180 of my nominees waiting for the confirmation process in the Senate, it is clear that the process is not working. About half these nominees have been waiting for more than 100 days, more than 30 have been waiting a year or more, and 9 have been waiting for more than 2 years.

That's no way to treat men and women who have stepped forward to serve our country, and it's got to stop. It's in our Nation's interest that this process change. It's not right to treat these good folks this way. These nominees deserve an up-or-down vote. Many of them have had their careers on hold. They've got spouses whose lives are stuck in limbo. They have children waiting to find out where they're going to go to school.

These are real folks making real sacrifices, and they should not be treated like political pawns. Senators should examine every nomination closely, but they should not drag them out indefinitely. If the Senators holding up this process believe my nominees are unworthy for confirmation, the course of action is clear: Hold a vote and see if the majority agree. If these nominees are not approved, they can move on with their lives. If they are approved, they can take office.

The confirmation backlog also places this strain on our Government. Every day nominees are delayed, represents another day without them in office, and that makes it harder for the Government to meet its responsibilities. The nomination before the Senate—these nominations before the Senate are vital positions—or for vital positions affecting issues from the economy to public safety to national security.

The Senate must confirm nominees who help guide our economy during a time of uncertainty. The Senate has stalled nominations for critical economic positions. I mean, we've got—we're dealing with uncer-

tainty, and there are key positions that are not being filled.

The three-member Council of Economic Advisers is down to one person, which makes for lonely Council meetings. [*Laughter*] One of my nominees for the Council withdrew his name after 6 months of waiting without receiving so much as a hearing. My other nominee continues to wait after 7 months of delay. At a time of important decisions for our economy, it is irresponsible for the United States Senate to leave these positions unfulfilled.

One of the most important institutions for the American economy is the Federal Reserve. The Fed decides monetary policy, and it sets key interest rates that have an impact on homeowners and businesses across our country. Yet the Senate is delaying confirmation of three highly qualified nominees for the Fed's Board of Governors. I nominated these individuals nearly 9 months ago. They have valuable experience and skills, and the Senate needs to confirm them as soon as possible.

The Senate also must confirm nominees who will help address issues of public safety. The Federal Aviation Administration plays a vital role in keeping air travelers safe. Yet the Senate has failed to act on my nominee to head this agency. In October, I nominated Bobby Sturgell to lead the FAA. Bobby has nearly 20 years of cockpit experience from his time as a Navy fighter pilot, Top Gun instructor, and commercial airline pilot. He is committed to addressing problems that have caused airline delays, and he has good experience and the skills necessary to get the job done.

I appreciate the Senate commerce committee giving Bobby a hearing today. I urge the Senators to put aside politics and confirm this good man to office. It's important for the country that he be confirmed. If they don't like him, vote him down, but at least give him a vote as soon as possible.

The Senate has also failed to act on my nominations for the Federal Mine Safety and Health Review Commission. As a result of the Senate's ongoing delays, this body can no longer decide cases because it has more vacancies than members. Two of my nominees for the Commission have gone more than a year without even receiving a confirmation hearing. The American people have not forgotten the recent mining tragedies in Kentucky and West Virginia and Utah, and they expect this Commission to have enough members to issue decisions on mine safety.

The Senate must also confirm nominees who will help protect America's national security. In this time of war, we need a strong Department of Justice. Yet the Senate has not voted on seven nominations for senior leadership positions at the Department. I remember being criticized for having too many vacancies at the Justice Department. We stepped up. We sent good names up, and now it's time for those critics to act.

One of the vacancies is for Deputy Attorney General. The Deputy Attorney General helps lead efforts to detect and prevent terrorist attacks here at home. I've selected an outstanding nominee for this position, Judge Mark Filip. I'm sorry that he's not here. He's dealing with a serious family matter. This former prosecutor has earned a reputation for being fairminded and dedicated.

Several years ago, the Senate confirmed him unanimously for a lifetime position on the Federal bench. In other words, this isn't the first time he's gone through a confirmation process. If the Senate can confirm this good man for a lifetime post, there's no reason the Senate cannot confirm him to spend the next year protecting the American people. Yet one Senator has placed a hold on this nomination because of an issue that has nothing to do with the judge. This is unacceptable. Senators need to base their decisions on the judge's qualifications for the job, they need to bring this nomination to the floor for a vote, and they need to confirm this good man.

As Senators confirm these nominees, they also must confirm judges to the Federal bench. I've nominated good men and women who will rule by the letter of the law, not the whim of the gavel. I thank the Senators on both sides of the aisle, like Mitch McConnell, Jon Kyl, and Arlen and Dianne Feinstein and Thad Cochran, for helping confirm fine judges like Leslie Southwick.

Unfortunately, some of their colleagues continue to delay votes for 28 of my other nominees. The Senate has sat on these nominations to the court of appeals for nearly 600 days. And in some cases, the Senate has imposed a new and extra constitutional standard where nominees who have the support of the majority of the Senate can be blocked by a minority of obstructionists. As a result, some judgeships can go unfulfilled for years and justice can be delayed for the American people.

Our courts should render swift decisions. That's what we expect, and so should the United States Senate. Many of my nominees would fill urgent vacancies on courts that are understaffed and overworked. I've sent the Senate three nominees to relieve such a situation on the Fourth Circuit Court of Appeals. Bob Conrad and Steve Matthews and Rod Rosenstein are with us today. These are my nominees. They are accomplished members of the legal community. They will be outstanding members of this court. Yet the Senate has not acted on their nominations. This delay is irresponsible. It undermines the cause of justice. And the United States Senate needs to bring every one of my judicial nominations to the floor for an up-or-down vote.

When men and women agree to serve in public office, we should treat them with respect and dignity. When the Senate fails to do this, it leaves important positions in our Government vacant for months at a time, and it makes it harder for future Presidents to be able to attract good people to serve the United States of America.

We've got to—I'm really grateful for the many talented and dedicated and patriotic men and women who have answered the call to service. And now my call to the United States Senate is this: Rise to your responsibilities, give these nominees the vote they deserve, and confirm them as soon as possible.

Thank you for coming.

NOTE: The President spoke at 10:50 a.m. in the East Room at the White House.

Remarks on Signing the Executive Order To Improve the Coordination and Effectiveness of Youth Programs
February 7, 2008

Thank you all. Thanks. Please be seated. I thank you for joining Laura and me. I've got two jobs. One is I'm going to sign an Executive order here in a minute. I'm making sure that all agencies involved with Helping America's Youth coordinate their activities. And then I've got to introduce Laura. [*Laughter*]

I appreciate very much those of you who are committed to helping our country by saving souls and by giving people hope. I think it's—I can't think of a more noble cause than to serve America. And there's all kinds of ways to serve America. One way is to wear the uniform. Another way is to find—somebody wonders whether or not there's a positive future in their lives, and put your arm around them and say, "I love you; what can I do to help you?"

That happens, by the way, all across America. And it doesn't take one single law to cause somebody to love a neighbor. It does take a law; it's just—it's a higher law. It's a law from a higher inspiration than government. And so today Laura and I welcome those who are neighborhood healers and helpers. We really appreciate your focus on helping our Nation's youth, particularly boys.

In my State of the Union a couple of years ago, I talked about the initiative that we're honoring today, and it's an initiative that says, there is a better future for America's young folks. And we've set some important goals. And one of the goals inside this administration is to make sure that those people who are responsible for spending taxpayers' money on these programs actually coordinate their efforts and set high standards. A lot of times in government we don't do a very good job of measuring, and so the idea is to set standards and to coordinate, but the idea is also to empower those who are on the frontlines of saving lives.

I like to say, government is not really about love. There may be loving people in government, but government itself is laws and justice. Love is found in the hearts of our citizens who are in the neighborhoods.

And so the Executive order I'm going to sign is to—all aimed at kind of leaving behind a structure so that whoever is lucky enough to follow me—[*laughter*]—will see a blueprint on how to help, really, people realize the great promise of the country.

I believe we solve—save souls one person at a time. And I like to remind our fellow citizens, while one person can't save every soul, one person can save a soul. And it's that cumulative effort of love and compassion and work that will define a hopeful future. And somebody who shares that same passion about recognizing the true strength of America lies in the hearts and souls of our citizens, and someone who cares deeply about making sure the young in America have a bright future is our speaker, my wife, the First Lady, Laura Bush.

[*At this point, the First Lady spoke, a video was shown, and the President signed the Executive order.*]

NOTE: The President spoke at 2:54 p.m. in the East Room at the White House. In his remarks, he referred to Executive Order 13459, which is listed in Appendix D at the end of this volume. The transcript released by the Office of the Press Secretary also included the remarks of the First Lady.

Statement on Senate Action on Economic Growth Legislation
February 7, 2008

Two weeks ago, my administration reached an agreement with Speaker Pelosi and Leader Boehner on a short-term economic growth package that would quickly put money into the hands of the American people and provide our economy the boost it needs. Today the Senate amended that bill in ways I can support.

This plan is robust, broad-based, timely, and it will be effective. This bill will help to stimulate consumer spending and accelerate needed business investment.

This economic growth package is an example of bipartisan cooperation at a time when the American people most expect it. I thank members of both parties and both Houses for their efforts to advance this important legislation.

Remarks to the Conservative Political Action Conference
February 8, 2008

The President. Thank you all. Good morning, and thank you all very much. I thank you for coming. I apologize to my friend; he likes to sleep in. [*Laughter*]

I really do want to thank you all for adjusting the schedule. Right after the speech, I'm going to get on an airplane and fly to Tennessee. I'll be taking the prayers of the American people to those who suffered from the devastating tornadoes.

Mr. Leader, thank you for that introduction, and I appreciate your outstanding leadership in the United States Senate. You know, Mr. Leader, I used to think that leading a group of strong-willed Senators was one of the toughest jobs in the country. I may have found one even tougher one: father of the bride. You know, I told Laura I was going to say that, and she said, well, you might add another one: son-in-law to the President. [*Laughter*]

I thank you for the invitation. I appreciate the fact that you've invited our candidates to your forum, and thank you for the hearing you gave them. These are good, honorable people. And I appreciate the fact that you invited Vice President Cheney here. He is the best Vice President in history. Mother may have a different opinion. [*Laughter*] But don't tell her I said this, but my opinion is the one that counts.

Since I spoke with you last, some things have changed. It seems like my hair is little grayer. [*Laughter*] And my jokes are a little older. And some say my speeches are a little windier. Some things haven't changed:

the principles I believe in and my deep, abiding faith in the American people.

It just doesn't seem all that long ago that David invited me here, but it's been about 7 years. And during that time, we have stood together, and we have advanced a philosophy of freedom and responsibility that's made our Nation a better place and a stronger place. And today I want to talk to you about what you and I have achieved together, what it tells us about the stakes in the year ahead, and why it is so important that we keep the White House in 2008.

I thank the leader, David Keene. He's a good guy. You know, this is the 35th—yes—anniversary, which means he started the deal when he was 15. [*Laughter*] At least that's what he claims. [*Laughter*] But thank you for your leadership. I thank you for your board. I've got a lot of friends up here at the head table and a lot of friends in the audience, and I really do appreciate what you've done.

Audience member. We love you, George.

The President. Well, thank you.

A lot has happened over 8 years—that was the last time I spoke to you, was 8 years ago. And we've seen vigorous debates, a lot of debates on nearly every conceivable issue, matters that affected the prosperity and peace.

Our views are grounded in timeless truths. During these debates, we stuck to timeless truths. We believe that the most reliable guide for our country is the collective wisdom of ordinary citizens. We believe our culture benefits from a diversity of faith, a respect for values, and the guidance of a higher power. We believe in personal responsibility. We believe in the universality of freedom. We believe our Nation has the right to defend itself, even if sometimes others disagree. And we believe America remains a force of good in our world.

There's another philosophy, and it's advanced by decent people who see the world differently. They tend to think Washington has the answers to our problems. They tend to believe our country only succeeds under the expansive Federal Government. They tend to be suspicious of America's exercise of global leadership, unless, of course, we get a permission slip from international organizations. [*Laughter*]

Over the past 7 years, we have engaged this opposition with a clear and consistent philosophy. We didn't take polls to decide what to say. We didn't seek the advice of editorial pages to decide what to think. And we darn sure didn't seek the approval of groups like CODEPINK and MoveOn.org before deciding what to do.

We applied our philosophy on issues relating to economic prosperity. When I took office, we inherited a recession, and then we acted. We were guided by this principle: The best way to help our economy grow is to leave money in the hands of those responsible for our prosperity. That, of course, would be the American people. And so with your support, we passed one of the largest tax cuts in American history, and then we cut taxes again. In all, we delivered nearly $2 trillion in tax relief over the past 7 years.

Our critics wanted a different approach. They believed that the best way to keep the economy—to help the economy was to keep taxes in Washington and expand the size and scope of the Federal Government.

Audience members. Boo!

The President. One columnist wrote this—one columnist said this: "Tax cuts—any tax cuts—are the wrong way to go." A prominent newspaper said my administration was on a tax cut rampage and called our tax relief unfair and unaffordable. A think tank expert called our tax relief a reckless gamble.

Despite these dire predictions, the tax cuts we passed contributed to a record 52 months of job creation. They helped produce strong economic growth, and the increased revenues from that growth have put us on track to balance our budget by

2012. Here is the bottom line: Tax relief works.

We're in a period of economic uncertainty, and we've acted again. I want to thank the Members for passing a good piece of legislation, which I will sign into law next week. I want you all to understand that this bill reflects our principles. It is robust. It is progrowth. It stimulates business investment. And it puts money into the hands of American consumers.

In the longer run, the best way to make sure that our economy continues to grow is to make the tax relief we passed permanent. Unfortunately, the other side still hasn't learned the lessons. They want to let the tax cuts expire, and some are claiming, of course, this isn't a tax increase. Yet if they have their way, 116 million American taxpayers would see their taxes rise by an average of $1,800. Listen, I'm not known for my English—[*laughter*]—but in my way of speaking, it sure sounds like a tax increase to me.

You and I know the American people are not undertaxed. The problem is, Washington spends too much of your money. One of the things I have done is, I have set priorities. And you must understand my passion about protecting America. My number-one priority is to protect you. And after 9/11, we have substantially increased spending on defense, intelligence, and homeland security. And we will continue to provide for our troops. We will make sure the men and women who wear the uniform have the best and strongest support they need to do their job.

And so we've worked hard to make sure we hold the line on spending in other areas. For 5 years in a row, my budget requests have kept the growth of nonsecurity discretionary spending below the rate of inflation. I set clear spending limits, told the Congress I was going to veto them if they—veto bills if they exceeded those spending limits. The Democratically controlled Congress, at the end of last year, cut spending plans by billions of dollars.

Last week, I proposed a budget that terminates or substantially reduces 151 wasteful or bloated programs. Those programs total more than $18 billion. And if Congress sends me appropriations bills that exceed the reasonable limits I have set, I will veto the bills.

Last month, I issued an Executive order that directs Federal agencies to ignore any future earmark that is not actually voted on by the United States Congress. This Executive order will extend beyond my Presidency; it will stay in effect unless revoked by a future President. What that means is, any President who wants to return to the old ways of unaccountable and wasteful spending will get to do so publicly. And if that happens, that President will have some explaining to do.

In the long run, you and I know the greatest threat to our fiscal health is the unsustainable growth of entitlement spending. We all know the painful choices ahead if America stays on this path: massive tax increases, sudden and drastic cuts in benefits, or crippling deficits. I have laid out specific proposals to reform and strengthen these programs.

On Social Security, I took the issue head on. That's what you expect a President to do. I proposed a way to make this program solvent without raising taxes and with personal saving accounts that will give individuals more control over their retirement savings.

On Medicare and Medicaid, I sent Congress a budget this week that saves nearly $200 billion over the next 5 years. I hear all the talk from the other side on Capitol Hill about fiscal responsibility, but they haven't put any of their ideas on the table for programs. It is time to stop talking; it is time for them to stop acting and not pass these problems on to future Congresses and future generations.

On matters relating to our economy, our record is clear. You and I succeeded in cutting taxes. We're reducing wasteful spending. On these issues, both sides have made their case. The results are in, and they are proving us right.

We applied our philosophy to questions affecting the moral fabric of our Nation. We believe that all human life is precious and deserves to be protected. In 2001, I had a grave decision to make on the question of embryonic stem cell research. I believed we could empower scientists and researchers to discover cures for terrible diseases without crossing a moral line. So I authorized research on existing stem cell lines and stood against any effort to use Federal tax dollars to support the destruction of human life.

Our critics had a different view. They thought my defense of life was shortsighted and harmful. When I vetoed two bills that sought to use tax dollars to destroy human embryos, some academics described my position as ridiculous and scientifically naive. One publication predicted our plan would not hold up over the long haul.

Then last November, scientists announced a landmark achievement. They found a way to reprogram adult skin cells to act like embryonic stem cells. This discovery has the potential to end the divisive debate over stem cell research. It will allow us to expand the frontiers of medicine while maintaining a culture of life. In the coming year, we will increase funds for this type of ethical research. And I will continue to push for a ban on the buying, selling, patenting, or cloning of human life.

When I took office, our society was grappling with a troubling rate of drug use among our children. A new generation of young people was in danger of being swept up in a cycle of addiction and crime and hopelessness. We believe people should be held responsible for their actions, and we know that people can change their behavior. Sometimes all it takes is the help of a loving soul, somebody who puts their arm around a troubled person and says: "I love you. Can I help you?" We also know that drug——

Audience member. [*Inaudible*]

The President. My soul is not that troubled, but thank you.

We also know that the drug crisis requires us to reduce both supply and demand. And so in 2002, I set our country on an ambitious goal to cut drug use among young people by 25 percent over 5 years. Critics didn't think that was possible. Some thought the drug war had already failed. Some said we focused too much on interdiction and not enough on treatment. An influential magazine and assorted commentators wanted to declare defeat and legalize the drug trade. A left-leaning drug prevention group said that our aggressive strategy was "very unlikely . . . to produce any different result than we have seen so far."

We stood our ground. We worked with international partners to interdict drugs into our country. We increased funds for drug treatment programs. We helped move drug addicts from a culture of victimization to a culture of responsibility. And we have gotten results. Since I took office, the overall use of illicit drugs by young people has dropped 24 percent. Marijuana use fell by 25 percent, steroid by a third, the use of ecstasy by 54 percent. Methamphetamine abuse has plummeted by 64 percent since 2001.

On matters relating to America's moral compass, we have defended human life. We promoted strong families. We confronted the crippling cycle of drug dependency. We challenged the critics, the self-proclaimed experts, and the status quo. Both sides made their case. The results are in, and they're proving us right.

We've also applied our philosophy to issues of national security. Six-and-a-half years ago, our country faced the worst attack in our history. I understood immediately that we would have to act boldly to protect the American people. So we've gone on the offense against these extremists. We're staying on the offense, and we will not relent until we bring them to justice. We recognized that this is a war, not just a matter of law enforcement. We recognize that we're engaged in the decisive ideological struggle of our time.

The first battle in this war against the extremists centered on Afghanistan; the 9/11 attackers had trained and planned in Afghanistan. We believed our military could remove the Taliban from power and that we could help aid the rise of a stable and democratic government.

Critics had a different view. One commentator said most Afghans would oppose an American invasion and fight the foreign occupiers. Another declared, "We're not headed toward a quagmire; we are already in one." Another commentator scoffed, "Afghanistan as a democracy? Forget it."

Well, we stood our ground, and we have seen the results. Al Qaida lost its terrorist camps in Afghanistan and the Taliban was driven from power. The Afghan people braved threats of violence to elect a new President and a new Parliament. Roads and hospitals are being built. Girls who were once forbidden from going to school are now going to school. America, 25 NATO allies, and 15 partner nations are helping the Afghan people secure their country. The Taliban, Al Qaida, and their allies are on the run. Afghanistan has a long road ahead, and they have a future that offers promise and hope. We're going to stand with the Afghan people; we're going to help millions claim their liberty. And we will always work to make sure Afghanistan will never be—again be a safe haven for terrorists and extremists who want to do us harm.

The war against our enemies also brought us to Iraq. Our coalition confronted a regime that defied United Nations Security Council resolutions, violated a cease-fire agreement, attacked its neighbors, sponsored terrorism, and had a history of using and pursuing weapons of mass destruction. Saddam Hussein was a threat to the United States and a threat to the world. My decision to remove Saddam was the

right decision at the time, and it is the right decision today.

Because we acted, 25 million Iraqis are free. We've seen them go to the polls. We've seen them elect a representative government. We've also seen an enemy determined to roll back this progress through horrific acts of violence designed to pit Iraqis one against another.

One year ago, things were not going well in that country. Terrorists and extremists were succeeding in their efforts to plunge Iraq into chaos. You see, they wanted to deny Iraqis their liberty. They can't stand freedom. They wanted to establish safe havens in Iraq from which to launch attacks against America and its allies. I strongly believe that America's security and peace in the world depend upon defeating this enemy. So we reviewed our strategy. Things weren't working; I needed to know why and what it would take to make things better. And that's why you review a strategy.

I made up my mind. I listened carefully to a lot of folks, and I decided to send more troops into Iraq, in a dramatic policy shift. And the policy shift has come—become known as the surge.

Our critics had a different view. They looked at rising violence in Iraq and declared the war was lost.

Audience members. Boo!

The President. Some concluded the surge had failed even before it had fully begun. Two foreign affairs experts proposed, quote, "a well-managed defeat . . . to boost U.S. credibility."

We stood our ground, and we're seeing results. A year after I ordered the surge of forces, high-profile terrorist attacks in Iraq are down, civilian deaths are down, sectarian killings are down. U.S. and Iraqi forces have captured or killed thousands of extremists in Iraq, including hundreds of key Al Qaida leaders and operatives. There is more work to be done. It takes awhile for young democracies to take root, but reconciliation is taking place. I recognize the progress in Iraq is fragile, and there's going to be tough days ahead. Yet even the enemy recognizes the progress we're being making. They recognize they're on the wrong side of events. They are disheartened, they are demoralized, and they will be defeated.

We can have confidence in Iraq's ultimate success because we believe in the transformative power of freedom. We believe there is an Almighty God. And a gift of that Almighty to every man, woman, and child on the face of this Earth is freedom. We have seen that free societies become peaceful societies. We know that a free Iraq will be a friend of America, an ally in this war against the extremists, and a source of hope and stability in a dangerous part of the world.

We'll fight the enemy overseas so we do not have to face them here at home. And as we do so, we must take measures to protect America, the homeland. We must give our intelligence officials the tools they need to uncover terrorist plots and prevent new attacks. And one of the most important tools is the ability to monitor terrorist communications. My most important job is to protect the American people. In order to do that job, we need to know who the terrorists are talking to; we need to know what they're saying; we need to know what they're planning. And so Congress passed the Protect America Act. This law modernized an outdated surveillance law and closed dangerous gaps in our intelligence.

Now, critics had a different view. One liberal interest group called the law an end run around the Constitution. Others falsely claimed law enforcement officials wanted to spy on Americans. Still another summed up the initiative as "a groupthink travesty."

We countered these critics, and we stood our ground. Our ability to monitor the communications of terrorists overseas has helped us gain crucial elements on terrorist cells and helped keep our country safe. The

Protect America Act is working. The problem is that Congress set the law to expire 1 week from tomorrow. I don't think the Al Qaida threat is going to expire 1 week from tomorrow. [*Laughter*] Congress must ensure the flow of vital intelligence is not disrupted. Congress must pass liability protection for companies believed to have assisted in the efforts to defend America. The time for temporary fixes has ended. Congress must pass this law, and they must pass it now.

On matters of war and peace, we have taken the fight to our enemies abroad, and we are defending our people here at home. We're standing with new partners in Afghanistan and Iraq to help them build free nations. We refused to yield when the going got tough. And when the history of our actions is written, it will show that we were right.

We will face other challenges ahead that will require new energy and, before long, new leadership. I'm absolutely confident, with your help, we will elect a President who shares our principles. As we take on the challenges, we must be guided by the philosophy that has brought us success. Our policies are working. The American people support our points of view. They share our philosophy.

And consider our advantage on other great questions before us. On health care, one side says we should expand the Federal Government's control over your private medicine. You and I say we should expand access to health care, empower consumers to make choices, and ensure that medical decisions are left in the hands of patients and their doctors.

On education, one side said—one side says we should spend your tax dollars without measuring whether or not our children are actually learning to read and write and add and subtract. You and I believe in accountability. We believe parents should have more options, and we believe in liberating children from failing public schools.

On the rights of the unborn, the most vulnerable among us, one side supports abortion on demand. You and I believe in the worth of every human being, the matchless joy of adoption, and the right to life.

On the Federal judiciary, one side says we should confirm judges who believe in the "living Constitution," which basically means they can make up laws as they go along. You and I say we need judges who respect our values, do not follow the political winds, and revere the plain meaning of our Constitution. We need more judges like John Roberts and Sam Alito.

On America's role in the world, some believe that our Nation is often the cause of global turmoil, a mentality once called "blame America first." You and I believe that America is a leading light, a guiding star, and the greatest nation on the face of the Earth.

You see, I know of America's greatness because I get to see it up close, and it is a privilege to see it up close. I see it in the foot-soldiers in the armies of compassion, who perform acts of kindness and hope every single day. I see it in the courage of ordinary citizens like those who rushed toward danger when the Twin Towers fell and our Pentagon burned. I see it with military families who've lost loved ones, and every time, I come away moved and inspired by their valor, their grit, their pride, and their love of country. I see it when I exchange salutes with the finest young men and women our country has ever known. These Americans give me endless optimism about our future, and they have made my Presidency a joyous experience.

You know, since I've come to Washington, I've been reading a lot of history. Laura notes it's probably because I'm making up for lost time. [*Laughter*] Over the past few years, I've read three books on George Washington, or as I call him, the original George W.

It is interesting to me that they are still analyzing the record of our first President. My attitude is, if they're still analyzing number 1, 43 doesn't need to worry about it. I'm not going to be around to see the final history written on my administration. The truth is that history's verdict takes time to reveal itself.

But we don't have to wait on history for one thing: In the year ahead, the pundits, the so-called experts, commentator, analysts will offer more gloomy predictions and more big government solutions. And when they do, let us remember their record. This is a group that is seldom correct—[*laughter*]—but never in doubt.

You and I have seen that in our own time. Ronald Reagan was called a "warmonger," an "amiable dunce," a "movie actor detached from reality." Yet within a few years after President Reagan left office, the Berlin Wall came down, the evil empire collapsed, the cold war was won. And over the years, a strange thing has happened. A lot of people who spent the 1980s criticizing President Reagan now tell us they were with him all along. [*Laughter*]

You were with him all along. And over the past 7 years, you've been with me. I appreciate your support.

Audience members. Four more years! Four more years!

The President. Thank you all. I appreciate the chance that you've given me— help me get this opportunity to serve our country. It's been a fantastic experience. I appreciate the countless phone calls you've made. I appreciate the volunteer work you did in two tough campaigns. I'll always—always—be grateful [to each of you]° for supporting our cause, for giving me a chance, and for loving our country. And I thank you for that.

I look forward to working with you this year. My energy is up, my spirit is high, and I will finish strong. And in the meantime, we will elect a new President. We've

---

° White House correction.

had good debates, and soon we'll have a nominee who will carry a conservative banner into this election and beyond. Listen, the stakes in November are high. This is an important election. Prosperity and peace are in the balance. So with confidence in our vision and faith in our values, let us go forward, fight for victory, and keep the White House in 2008.

God bless you, and God bless America.

NOTE: The President spoke at 7:21 a.m. at the Omni Shoreham Hotel. In his remarks, he referred to David A. Keene, chairman, American Conservative Union Foundation and Conservative Political Action Conference; and President Hamid Karzai of Afghanistan. He also referred to H.R. 5140; and Executive Order 13457, which is listed in Appendix D at the end of this volume.

Remarks Following a Briefing on Regional Tornado Damage in Lafayette, Tennessee
February 8, 2008

Listen, I want to thank you for the briefing. People have got to understand here in the region that a lot of folks around America care for them now. And I'm here to listen, to determine, to make sure that the Federal response is compassionate and effective. I don't want people to think something is going to happen that's not going to happen. And therefore, when we say something is going to happen to help them get their feet back on the ground, it will happen.

Secondly, I am here to thank the people that will provide the compassion for people who hurt. I notice we've got the Red Cross sitting over there. They're good responders. They respond to help people in need.

Thirdly, I will make it clear to people here that I have no doubt in my mind this community will come back better than before. Macon County people are down-to-earth, hard-working, God-fearing people, who, if just given a little help, will come back stronger.

And that's what—and so I want to thank you all for the briefing. Governor, again, thank you for being here. Appreciate the Senators and Congressmen joining us too.

NOTE: The President spoke at 10:12 a.m. at the Lafayette Fire Department's Atwell & Scruggs Fire Station. In his remarks, he referred to Gov. Philip N. Bredesen, Jr., of Tennessee.

Remarks Following a Tour of Tornado Damage in Lafayette
February 8, 2008

The President. Phil and June Spears have just—I looked in their eyes and saw incredible sadness and worry.

Phil Spears. It's true.

The President. And I know the Governor joins me in sharing our concerns with you. But I hope a couple of things become evi-

dent to you. One, there's a lot of people who care about you, total strangers showing up here in this community to help you get back on your feet.

And the Government has got a role to play. And I want to thank the Senators and Congressmen for being here, because they know that there is programs available for you. And one of the things the people have got to do is call a phone number. If your life has been turned upside down here, if you've been affected, you ought to call 1–800–621–3362, 1–800–621–3362. And that's where you can find out the help that is available.

What happened is, is that the Governor and his team quickly moved as this storm moved through this—moved through the State of Tennessee, and he made an assessment, and he sent the paperwork up to me. And because he moved quickly, I was able to sign a disaster declaration that then frees help. And so we want the folks to know that there is help from the Federal Government, and he can get the number I just outlined. But there's also going to be a lot of help from loving neighbors.

And we're sorry you're going through what you're going through. You know, life sometimes is unfair, and you don't get to play the hand that you wanted to play.

Mr. Spears. That's true.

The President. But the question is, when you get dealt the hand, how do you play it? And I've come away with this impression of the folks in Macon County: One, they're down-to-earth, good, hard-working people. They have a respect for the Al-

mighty. And this community is going to be as strong as ever. That's what I think.

Mr. Spears. Yes, sir.

The President. I bet you feel the same way.

Mr. Spears. Yes, sir. If it wasn't for my friends, I don't know what I'd do.

The President. And you're going to find you got some new friends showing up too——

Mr. Spears. Appreciate it.

The President. ——people you've never heard of, they don't know who you are, total strangers. But when they know there's a neighbor in need, they'll come and help you.

And I appreciate you giving me a chance to come by, and I know the folks traveling with me appreciate. We're so sorry you're going through what you're going through, but there's help, and that's what you've got to know.

Anyway, God bless. Thank you.

June Spears. Thank you.

Mr. Spears. Appreciate it.

The President. Yes. Hang in there, brother.

NOTE: The President spoke at 12:43 p.m. In his remarks, he referred to Gov. Philip N. Bredesen, Jr., of Tennessee.

The President's Radio Address
February 9, 2008

Good morning. One of the most important jobs of any President is to find good men and women to lead Government agencies, preside over our courts, and provide vital services to the American people. So I have nominated talented individuals for these positions. Unfortunately, the Senate is not meeting its responsibility to consider these nominees in a timely manner. More than 180 of my nominees are waiting for confirmation. Some have been waiting for

more than a year. As a result, careers have been put on hold, families have been placed in limbo, and our Government has been deprived of the service of these fine nominees.

On Thursday, I stood with many of these nominees at the White House. They are decent and talented people. The Senate needs to confirm them to address important issues, from the economy to public safety to national security.

One of the most important institutions for America's economy is the Federal Reserve. The Fed decides monetary policy, and it sets key interest rates that have an impact on homeowners and businesses across our country. Yet the Senate has been delaying three of my nominations to the Fed for nearly 9 months. My nominees have valuable experience and skills, and I urge the Senate to confirm them as soon as possible.

Another important institution is the Federal Aviation Administration. The FAA plays a vital role in keeping you safe when you fly. In October, I nominated Bobby Sturgell to lead the FAA. Bobby has nearly 20 years of cockpit experience from his time as a Navy fighter pilot, Top Gun instructor, and commercial airline pilot. He's committed to addressing problems that have caused airline delays, and I urge Senators to put politics aside and confirm him to office.

In this time of war, we need a strong Department of Justice. Yet the Senate has not voted on nominations for seven senior leadership positions at the Department. One of those vacancies is for Deputy Attorney General. The Deputy Attorney General helps lead efforts to detect and prevent terrorist attacks at home.

I have selected an outstanding nominee for this position, Judge Mark Filip. This former prosecutor has earned a reputation for being fairminded and dedicated. Several years ago, the Senate confirmed him unanimously for a lifetime position on the Federal bench. Now I ask Senators to confirm him once again so he can help keep our Nation safe.

As Senators confirm these nominees, they must also confirm judges to the Federal bench. I have nominated highly qualified individuals who will rule by the letter of the law, not the whim of the gavel. Unfortunately, the Senate continues to delay votes for 28 of my judicial nominees. Three of my nominees for the court of appeals have waited nearly 600 days. These delays are irresponsible, they undermine the cause of justice, and I call on the United States Senate to give these nominees the up-or-down vote they deserve.

When men and women agree to serve in public office, we should treat them with respect and dignity, and that means giving them a prompt confirmation vote. When the Senate fails to give nominees a timely vote, it leaves important positions in our Government vacant, and it makes it harder for Presidents of both parties to attract good men and women to serve in these vital posts.

By working together, Republicans and Democrats can chart a better course. We can bring every nomination to the floor for a vote and give the American people the kind of public servants they deserve.

Thank you for listening.

NOTE: The address was recorded at 2:25 p.m. on February 7 in the Cabinet Room at the White House for broadcast at 10:06 a.m. on February 9. The transcript was made available by the Office of the Press Secretary on February 8, but was embargoed for release until the broadcast. The Office of the Press Secretary also released a Spanish language transcript of this address.

Remarks Honoring President Abraham Lincoln's 199th Birthday
February 10, 2008

Welcome. Laura and I are glad you're here. Rex, thank you for taking the lead for Ford's Theatre. If our—any citizen wants to know how to make a solid contribution to Washington, DC, support Ford's Theatre; it's worth it. Members of my Cabinet, thanks for coming. Members of Congress, we're glad you're here. I've got two tasks. One is to present the Lincoln Medal and invite you to a buffet. [*Laughter*]

I really want to thank Richard for coming. I appreciate your words, Allen; thank you very much—and Craig Wallace. Avery, I've been subject to a few Presidential impersonations myself. [*Laughter*] I'm confident Abe would have liked it. [*Laughter*] I really appreciate you all coming. It's made this a very special evening. I do want to welcome all the Lincoln scholars here and all the Lincoln enthusiasts. We're really glad you're here.

I also am amazed that 200 years have gone by. It just doesn't seem all that long ago, does it? But it's fitting that we honor Abe Lincoln. He—of all the successors to George Washington, he—none had greater impact on the Presidency and on the country. And he remains a presence here in the House. I'm often asked, "Do you ever see Lincoln's ghost?" And I'll tell people, "I quit drinking 22 years ago." [*Laughter*]

But his office is directly above us. At the Center Hall, there's a likeness in marble. His portrait hangs in the Oval Office, and there's a fabulous portrait of Abe Lincoln in the State Dining Room. And that's the way it should be. He was a fabulous man and a great President. His life was one of humble beginnings and steadfast convictions. And so we celebrate his deeds, we lift up his ideals, and we honor this good man.

And it's my pleasure tonight to honor two really fine Americans. Each year, Ford's Theatre presents the Lincoln Medal to recognize high achievement and personal attributes that embody the character of the 16th President.

Dr. Ben Carson is the director of pediatric neurosurgery at Johns Hopkins Hospital. He is one of the most respected surgeons in the world. Twenty years ago, when a 70-member surgical team made history and separated a pair of Siamese twins, the gifted hands leading the team belonged to this good man. Raised with his brother and a single mother—who's here—Ben Carson didn't get much handed to him as he grew up. But his mother pushed him to learn and taught him to trust in the ways of heaven. From his days at Yale and the University of Michigan Medical School, colleagues have known Dr. Carson as both a skilled professional and a deeply reflective man.

His many current duties include service on the President's Council on Bioethics and a tireless commitment to helping young people find direction and motivation in life. He reminds them that all of us have gifts by the grace of the Almighty God. He tells them to think big, to study hard, and to put character first. He tells them to be nice because in his words, "If you're nice to people, then once they get over the suspicion of why you're being nice,"—[*laughter*]—"they will be nice to you." [*Laughter*] His example gives eloquent testimony to the value of perseverance and to the endless promise of America. So tonight we proudly honor Dr. Ben Carson.

President Ronald Reagan called Sandra Day O'Connor a person for all seasons, and few Americans have shown a broader range of talent. She is, after all, the only Supreme Court Justice ever inducted into the Cowgirl Hall of Fame. [*Laughter*] Born in El Paso, Texas, she spent much of her childhood on a ranch in Arizona, where from a young age, she learned to ride horses, mend fences, and shoot a rifle.

She was an academic star, attending Stanford Law School. It was a different era when she got out of law school. After all, not many law firms wanted to hire a woman. But with her intellect, independent spirit, and sense of adventure, Sandra Day O'Connor continued a steady rise in the world. She became a State senator, a State court judge, and the first woman on the highest court in the land.

For 24 years, Justice O'Connor stood out as a careful, fairminded jurist. Sandra Day O'Connor is a great mom to her three sons, and she has been a blessing to her husband John. This lovely lady remains one of the most admired women of our time. She's lived a great American life, and our Nation is proud to honor you once again, Justice. Welcome.

NOTE: The President spoke at 5:54 p.m. in the East Room at the White House. In his remarks, he referred to Rex W. Tillerson, vice-chairman, Ford's Theatre Society; historian Richard Norton Smith; Allen C. Guelzo, professor of history, Gettysburg College; and actors Craig Wallace and Avery Brooks. The transcript released by the Office of the Press Secretary also included the remarks of the First Lady.

Remarks on the 2008 Economic Report of the President
February 11, 2008

The President. I want to thank members of my economic team for submitting this Economic Report of the President. I'm about to sign it. And so I want to—Eddie, thank you for your good work, you and your team.

Council of Economic Advisers Chairman Edward P. Lazear. My pleasure.

The President. This report indicates that our economy is structurally sound for the long term and that we're dealing with uncertainties in the short term. And therefore, what should we do about it? Well, I am so pleased that the Congress and the administration worked closely together to pass a robust progrowth package to deal with the uncertainty. That package is about 160 billion-plus dollars. What that means is, it means that money will be going directly to America: workers and families and indi-

viduals. It also means that there is incentives for American businesses.

I'll be signing this bill soon. But if you're a taxpayer or if you're a—got income up to—earned income—I mean, credited income up to $3,000, you can expect money back. And if you're a businessowner, you're going to get some incentives to invest. And so you ought to be planning upon it—on investing now.

And so I really want to thank the Congress for getting this bill done, and I'm looking forward to signing it. It's going to help deal with the uncertainties in this economy.

Thank you all very much.

NOTE: The President spoke at 1:07 p.m. in the Oval Office at the White House. In his remarks, he referred to H.R. 5140.

Remarks at the Heart Truth Reception
February 11, 2008

Thank you all. Welcome to the White House. Laura and I are glad you're here, and thanks for coming. I welcome members of my Cabinet. I particularly want to thank

all the healers and compassionate folks who help with heart disease. The Vice President sends his best. [*Laughter*]

All of us here are committed to America's heart health. I don't know if our fellow citizens know this, but this is American Heart Month. And it's a good time to remember that an estimated 80 million people across the United States suffer from heart disease. The disease is the number-one killer of American men and women. Many women, however, do not even know they're at risk, and so they don't take simple steps that can protect their health.

And that's where the Heart Truth Campaign comes in. Over the last 5 years, I appreciate the fact that you all have spread the word, and you represent thousands across our country who are doing so as well. You've helped women reduce the factors for heart disease, and that's a noble calling, an important contribution to our country. Every February, you encourage women to wear the red dress, which I appreciate. And I do want to thank the fashion industry for stepping up and—[*applause*].

And the results are measurable. Women's awareness has been raised; women's lives have been saved. Earlier this month, I was in Kansas City, and I met a woman named Joyce Cullen. In 2003, Joyce saw coverage of Laura's visit to a Kansas City hospital. She just talked about the symptoms that— of heart disease in women. It was just a simple explanation of what people should be aware of. She woke up with those symptoms shortly after Laura's visit. She went to the hospital. Her life was saved, and she's now a part of Heart Truth. And that's the effort in which you're involved, simple acts that are spreading across the country and saving lives.

My job today is not only to welcome you and to thank you but to introduce the Heart Truth's national ambassador. Laura is committed to the Heart Truth Campaign. She's a great First Lady, and she's always dear to my heart—the First Lady.

NOTE: The President spoke at 4:40 p.m. in the East Room at the White House. The transcript released by the Office of the Press Secretary also included the remarks of the First Lady. The related American Heart Month proclamation of February 1 is listed in Appendix D at the end of this volume.

Statement on the Death of Representative Thomas P. Lantos
February 11, 2008

Laura and I are saddened by the death of our friend, Congressman Tom Lantos.

Tom was a man of character and a champion of human rights. After immigrating to America more than six decades ago, he worked to help oppressed people around the world have the opportunity to live in freedom. As the only Holocaust survivor to serve in Congress, Tom was a living reminder that we must never turn a blind eye to the suffering of the innocent at the hands of evil men. I appreciate his vision in cofounding the Human Rights Caucus.

I also appreciate his efforts to protect our environment, alleviate the sufferings caused by HIV/AIDS, and strengthen our friendships and alliances around the globe.

We will miss Tom's leadership in the Halls of Congress. Our thoughts and prayers are with his wife Annette, their daughters, and the rest of the Lantos family.

NOTE: The statement referred to Annette Lantos Tillemann-Dick and Katrina Lantos Swett, daughters of Rep. Lantos.

Statement on the Situation in Timor-Leste
February 11, 2008

I strongly condemn the violent attacks against Jose Ramos-Horta, President of Timor-Leste, and Kay Rala Xanana Gusmao, Prime Minister of Timor-Leste. Laura and I offer our condolences to the families of those killed in the attacks, and we send our prayers for a rapid recovery to President Ramos-Horta and the others injured.

Those who are responsible must know that they cannot derail democracy in Timor-Leste, and they will be held accountable for their actions. The United States remains committed to working with the people of Timor-Leste to strengthen democracy there. I also offer my full support to the Government of Timor-Leste, the United Nations Integrated Mission in Timor-Leste, and the International Stabilization Force as they work to maintain calm and security.

Memorandum on Federal Support for the AbilityOne Program
February 11, 2008

Memorandum for the Heads of Executive Departments and Agencies

Subject: Federal Support for the AbilityOne Program

Americans with disabilities make valuable contributions to our country's workforce that help keep our Nation the world's economic leader. Expanding employment opportunities for these individuals will help ensure that our economy is drawing on the talents and creativity of all its citizens and that America remains a place of opportunity for all. Supporting the AbilityOne Program is one good way to achieve this goal.

The AbilityOne Program (formerly the Javits-Wagner-O'Day Program) is a Federal initiative that works with public and private organizations to generate employment opportunities for Americans who are blind or have other disabilities. Nearly 43,000 individuals work in more than 600 community-based nonprofit agencies that serve people with a wide range of disabilities and sell products and services to the Federal Government through the AbilityOne Program.

The AbilityOne Program has taken steps to embrace successful business practices, including e-commerce and performance-based contracting. Strong support from Federal customers is critical to fulfilling this important program's employment mission. Therefore, I encourage you to ensure that your agency's procurement officials acquire products and services provided by the AbilityOne Program, consistent with existing law.

Additional information about the AbilityOne Program may be obtained by contacting the Committee for Purchase From People Who Are Blind or Severely Disabled or by visiting www.AbilityOne.gov.

GEORGE W. BUSH

Remarks Following a Discussion With President Amadou Toumani Toure of Mali
February 12, 2008

President Bush. It's been a honor and a pleasure to welcome the President of Mali here to the Oval Office.

We discussed a variety of issues. I was touched by the President's concern about the life of the average citizen in Mali. We are partners with the President and the people of Mali through the Millennium Challenge Account. And one reason we worked with the Government is because they've agreed to fight corruption and support the education and health of its citizens. This is a country that's committed to the rights of its people, and we're proud to be standing side by side with you.

Two issues that are very important to this administration, Mr. President, were the issues that my wife Laura discussed when she came to your country: One is literacy, and two is the eradication of malaria. And I assured the President that our commitment remains strong to both important issues. And I thank him very much for his hard work in helping his citizens deal with HIV/AIDS.

And finally, the President and I spent a fair amount of time talking about the dangers of radicals and extremists associated with groups like Al Qaida. And we talked about the need for close cooperation to protect the innocent people from those who murder the innocent in order to achieve their dark political vision.

So it's been my honor to welcome a good man here to the Oval Office.

President Toure. Yes. First of all, I would like to convey to the President of the United States the sympathies and solidarity of the people of Mali because of the destruction——

President Bush. Thank you.

President Toure. ——brought by the tornadoes in some of the Southern States of the United States.

And then I told Mr. President that we were sensitive and impressed by the impression that we had from the visit of Mrs. Laura Bush to Mali some time ago. Also, thank the President for the friendship between the people of the United States and the people of Mali and the cooperation between Mali and the United States that we do entertain on both sides since the independence of Mali in 1960.

But I could also come to the United States just to tell Mr. President——

President Bush. Thank you, sir.

President Toure. ——thank you, because the President had some initiatives not only for Mali but also for Africa, which we believe are historical initiatives, and which we do have the Millennium Challenge Corporation, the greater participation against the fight against AIDS through the Global Fund, the initiative of the eradication of malaria, and not to forget the Presidential initiative on literacy in Africa, which is very important in our view, because when you want to develop, you——

President Bush. That's right.

President Toure. ——need to also improve basic education.

President Bush. That's right.

President Toure. So I emphasized to the President that—and I reaffirm—that Mali signed and Mali averred to all different initiatives on the fight against terrorism. So it is humanly inadmissable, unacceptable to see or to assist or to be indifferent to the suggestion that we are seeing to some practices which really do not deserve to exist.

So we had a fruitful exchange of views on our cooperation. So I said to Mr. President that I would like to thank him and also to convey all the gratitude of the people of Mali, but I emphasized also the fact that may God save Mali and the United States. President, thank you very much.

President Bush. Thank you, sir.

NOTE: The President spoke at 10:33 a.m. in the Oval Office at the White House. Presi-

dent Toure spoke in French, and his remarks were translated by an interpreter.

Remarks at a Celebration of African American History Month
February 12, 2008

The President. Thank you all for coming. Good afternoon, and welcome to the White House. Laura and I are honored that you all came as we celebrate African American History Month. This is a month in which we recognize the many African Americans who've made great contributions to our country. We honor the talent and their courage. We renew our commitment to securing liberty and justice for every American. That's why we're here.

I appreciate many of the notables who have joined us. Madam Secretary, appreciate you coming—Mr. Secretary, Alphonso Jackson, and Marcia. Thanks for coming, Mr. Secretary. Proud you're here.

If I skip some of the notables, it's because I'm going to say something about them a little later on. [*Laughter*] So, Congressman, I'll be with you in a minute. [*Laughter*]

I appreciate Dr. Leonard Haynes, who's the Executive Director of the White House Initiative on Historically Black Colleges and Universities. I am proud—Doc, thanks for coming. I'm proud to welcome all the presidents from the Historically Black Colleges and Universities here today; really appreciate your service to the country.

I want to thank Ron Langston, National Director of the Minority Business Development Agency; Roslyn Brock, vice chairman of the NAACP. Roslyn, thank you for coming. Somewhere you are—there you are. I thank John Fleming, president, Association of the Study of African American Life and History. Yes, sir, Reverend Al Sharpton

and his wife Dominique; Reverend, it's good to see you.

Audience member. Daughter.

The President. Daughter. [*Laughter*] Daughter. [*Laughter*] I don't get them right all the time. [*Laughter*] But thank you for coming. And, Dominique, you're sure a lot prettier than your father. [*Laughter*]

Thurgood Marshall, Jr., we're proud you're here. Yes, thanks for coming. Good to see you, sir. State Representative Calvin Smyre of the State of Georgia, who is the president of the National Black Caucus of State Legislators. Sure proud you're here.

Thank you all for coming. There's a lot of other notables here. Just consider yourself welcomed. [*Laughter*]

The theme of this year's African American History Month is a celebration of America's cultural diversity. It is a tribute to a scholar who deepened our appreciation for diversity, Carter G. Woodson. When Dr. Woodson began his career in the early 20th century, most Americans knew little about African American heritage. Dr. Woodson set out to correct that. His scholarship helped pioneer the field of African American studies. And by the time he passed away in 1950, the son of freed slaves had become known as the Father of Black History.

It is important for all our citizens to know the history of the African American struggle for equality. We must remember that the slave trade brought many Africans to America in chains, not by choice. We must remember how slaves claimed their God-given right to freedom. And we must remember how freed slaves and their descendants helped rededicate America to the ideals of its founding.

Our Nation has come a long way toward building a more perfect Union. Yet as past injustices have become distant memories, there is a risk that our society may lose sight of the real suffering that took place. One symbol of that suffering is the noose. Recently, there have been a number of media reports about nooses being displayed. These disturbing reports have resulted in heightened racial tensions in many communities. They have revealed that some Americans do not understand why the sight of a noose causes such a visceral reaction among so many people.

For decades, the noose played a central part in a campaign of violence and fear against African Americans. Fathers were dragged from their homes in the dark of the night before the eyes of their terrified children. Summary executions were held by torchlight in front of hateful crowds. In many cases, law enforcement officers responsible for protecting the victims were complicit in their deeds, and their deaths. For generations of African Americans, the noose was more than a tool of murder; it was a tool of intimidation that conveyed a sense of powerlessness to millions.

The era of rampant lynching is a shameful chapter in American history. The noose is not a symbol of prairie justice but of gross injustice. Displaying one is not a harmless prank. Lynching is not a word to be mentioned in jest. As a civil society, we must understand that noose displays and lynching jokes are deeply offensive. They are wrong, and they have no place in America today.

This afternoon we honor four Americans who understand what this symbol represents and who are leading the way toward ending racial injustice across our land.

Congressman John Lewis earned his place in history long before winning a seat in the United States Capitol. As a young man, he became one of the leaders of the civil rights movement. He organized freedom rides and sit-ins and voter registration drives. One Sunday in 1965, he set out to lead a march from Selma to Montgomery. The marchers never made it past the rows of State troopers outside Selma, but their message made it all the way to Washington, DC. Five months later, Congress passed the Voting Rights Act. And more than 40 years later, John Lewis continues to inspire us, and we're blessed to have him here today.

William Coleman has lived a life of many firsts. After graduating first in his class from Harvard Law School, he went on to become both the first black American to clerk on the Supreme Court and the first to hold a Cabinet post in a Republican administration, as Secretary of Transportation under President Gerald Ford. William Coleman has also helped open doors of opportunities for others. He worked alongside Thurgood Marshall, father of this good man, on the legal team that triumphed in *Brown* versus *Board of Education*. This ruling exposed the fallacy of separate but equal, and it helped return America to the great truth that all men are created equal. For this, we owe William Coleman our lasting thanks. We're honored to have you today, sir.

Three years after *Brown* versus *Board of Education*, nine students in Little Rock stepped forward to test the Supreme Court's ruling. On September 25th, 1957, Federal troops escorted them into the city's all-white Central High School. Once inside, the Little Rock Nine were spit on, harassed, and called names. One of the students was a senior named Ernest Green. As graduation day approached, some suggested it might be safer for Ernest to receive his diploma in the mail. Many people would have taken his—this advice. Not Ernest Green. In May of 1958, Martin Luther King, Jr., was on hand to watch Ernest become the first African American to graduate from Little Rock's Central High School. We're honored to welcome Ernest

Green to the White House during the 50th anniversary—[*applause*].

And finally, as a young boy, Otis Williams remembers his mother packing food for their move from Texas—oh, what a tragic mistake—[*laughter*]—to Detroit. She did so because restaurants along the route refused to serve African Americans. In Detroit, Otis Williams grew up to become the leader of one of the most successful vocal groups in the history of our country, the Temptations. This group has recorded 37 top 40 singles, including 4 number-one hits on the pop charts. Their success paved the way for other African American artists. Their melodies continue bringing Americans of all races together to this day.

Otis can remember performing in a venue in South Carolina where blacks and whites in the crowd were separated by a barrier. The next year when the Temptations returned, the racial divide was gone. As Otis once put it, quote, "The highest achievement for me has been to have our music penetrate all kinds of barriers, for it to be colorless." The music of the Temp-

tations has given countless Americans sunshine on a cloudy day—[*laughter*]—and we cannot help ourselves from loving them. [*Laughter*]

Throughout American—African American History Month, we remember how individuals, African American leaders of all kinds, helped bring our Nation together. We recognize our Nation still has a long way to go. But in the example of the leaders like those we honor today, we see strength greater than any division, and we see hope for a day when freedom rings from every mountainside and every corner of the country.

And now it is my great pleasure to introduce the Temptations.

NOTE: The President spoke at 3 p.m. in the East Room at the White House. In his remarks, he referred to Secretary of State Condoleezza Rice. The related National African American History Month proclamation of January 28 is listed in Appendix D at the end of this volume.

Statement on Senate Passage of the Intelligence Reform Legislation
February 12, 2008

After a full debate, the Senate today cast a strong, bipartisan vote in support of legislation that will ensure that our intelligence professionals continue to have the critical tools they need to protect the Nation.

This good bill passed by the Senate provides a long-term foundation for our intelligence community to monitor the communications of foreign terrorists in ways that are timely and effective and that also protect the liberties of Americans. It will keep closed dangerous intelligence gaps that threatened our security. And this bill improves on the Protect America Act passed last summer by providing fair and just liability protection to those private compa-

nies who have been sued for billions of dollars only because they are believed to have done the right thing and assisted the Nation after the September 11th terrorist attacks.

I commend Senators from both sides of the aisle who came together to pass this important bill. I thank Leaders Reid and McConnell and the leaders of the Senate Intelligence Committee, Senators Rockefeller and Bond, for finishing work on this bill. Today the Senate demonstrated that protecting our Nation is not a partisan issue.

The House of Representatives now has an opportunity to put aside narrow partisan concerns and come together to pass this bipartisan bill and send it to my desk without delay. Our intelligence professionals and private sector partners need the certainty of long-term legislation that will allow us to keep programs in place to protect the Nation, so that the flow of critical intelligence information is not interrupted.

NOTE: The statement referred to H.R. 3773.

Remarks on Intelligence Reform Legislation
February 13, 2008

Director, thank you for joining me. Good morning. At this moment, somewhere in the world, terrorists are planning new attacks on our country. Their goal is to bring destruction to our shores that will make September the 11th pale by comparison. To carry out their plans, they must communicate with each other, they must recruit operatives, and they must share information.

The lives of countless Americans depend on our ability to monitor these communications. Our intelligence professionals must be able to find out who the terrorists are talking to, what they are saying, and what they're planning.

To help our intelligence agencies do this, Congress passed the Protect America Act last year. Unfortunately, Congress set the law to expire on February the 1st and then failed to pass new legislation that would keep these tools in effect over the long run. And so at the 11th hour, Congress passed a temporary 15-day extension of the current law, which will expire at midnight this Saturday. I signed that extension. I did so to give Members of the House and the Senate more time to work out their differences.

Well, the Senate has used this time wisely. I am pleased that last night, Senators approved new legislation that will ensure our intelligence professionals have the tools they need to make us safer, and they did so by a wide, bipartisan majority. The Senate bill also provides fair and just liability protections for companies that did the right thing and assisted in defending America after the attacks of September the 11th.

In order to be able to discover enemy—the enemy's plans, we need the cooperation of telecommunication companies. If these companies are subjected to lawsuits that could cost them billions of dollars, they won't participate, they won't help us, they won't help protect America. Liability protection is critical to securing the private sector's cooperation with our intelligence efforts. The Senate has passed a good bill and has shown that protecting our Nation is not a partisan issue. And I congratulate the Senators.

Unfortunately, the House has failed to pass a good bill. And now House leaders say they want still more time to reach an agreement with the Senate on a final bill. They make this claim even though it is clear that the Senate bill, the bill passed last night, has significant bipartisan support in the House.

Congress has had over 6 months to discuss and deliberate. The time for debate is over. I will not accept any temporary extension. House Members have had plenty of time to pass a good bill. They have already been given a 2-week extension beyond the deadline they set for themselves. If Republicans and Democrats in the Senate can come together on a good piece of legislation, there is no reason why Republicans and Democrats in the House cannot pass the Senate bill immediately.

The House's failure to pass the bipartisan Senate bill would jeopardize the security of our citizens. As Director McConnell has told me, without this law, our ability to prevent new attacks will be weakened, and it will become harder for us to uncover terrorist plots. We must not allow this to happen. It is time for Congress to ensure the flow of vital intelligence is not disrupted. It is time for Congress to pass a law that provides a long-term foundation to protect our country. And they must do so immediately.

Thank you very much.

NOTE: The President spoke at 9:01 a.m. in the Oval Office at the White House. In his remarks, he referred to H.R. 3773.

Remarks on Signing the Economic Stimulus Act of 2008
February 13, 2008

Thank you all. Sit down. Thank you all very much. Thanks for coming. Thanks for the warm welcome. I'm pleased to be joined by leaders of both parties to enact an economic growth package on behalf of the American people.

You know, a lot of folks in America probably were saying that it's impossible for those of us in Washington to find common ground, to reach compromise on important issues. I didn't feel that way; I know the leaders didn't feel that way. And as a result, we have come together on a single mission, and that is to put the people's interests first. And I really do welcome the Members of Congress, and I thank you for your hard work.

Madame Speaker, I thank you for your leadership. Senator Reid, I thank you for your leadership as well. I appreciate very much the fact that the Vice President has joined us, along with Congressman Boehner, Congressman Hoyer, Senator Mitch McConnell, Congressman Roy Blunt, Congressman Jim Clyburn, and other Members of the House and the Senate. You're welcome here in the people's house any time.

I'm very grateful that members of my Cabinet have joined us. Secretary Paulson was the leader in the negotiations on this, and I thank you very much for your hard work, Mr. Secretary. You're earning your pay. [*Laughter*] Appreciate other members of my Cabinet who have joined us as well.

You know, I know a lot of Americans are concerned about our economic future. Our overall economy has grown for 6 straight years, but that growth has clearly slowed. And so in January, I—we had an important phone call with the leaders of the Congress to talk about whether or not we could come together to provide a booster shot for our economy: a package that is robust, temporary, and puts money back into the hands of American workers and businesses.

Congress passed a really good piece of legislation, and they did so in a very expeditious manner. The bill I'm signing today is large enough to have an impact, amounting to more than $152 billion this year, or about 1 percent of GDP. The bill provides temporary tax incentives for businesses to make investments in their companies so that we create new jobs this year. The bill provides individual tax relief in the form of tax rebates. These rebates will amount to as much as $600 for individuals and $1,200 for married couples, with additional rebates for families with children.

The Members resisted the temptation to load up this bill with unrelated programs or unnecessary spending, and I appreciate that. I thank the Members for acting quickly. I thank them for acting to provide immediate tax relief to the American people.

There are other ways we can work together to help our economy through this rough patch. I know many Americans are worried about meeting their mortgages. My administration is working to address this problem. Last fall, for example, we brought together the HOPE NOW Alliance to help struggling homeowners avoid foreclosure. Yesterday Secretaries Paulson and Jackson joined HOPE NOW in announcing what is called Project Lifeline. It's a targeted outreach effort to help more at-risk homeowners.

Congress can also help by passing legislation to reform the regulation of Fannie Mae and Freddie Mac, to modernize the Federal Housing Administration, and to allow State housing agencies to issue tax-free bonds to help homeowners refinance their mortgages. I hope that Congress can act on these matters quickly.

Helping our economy requires us to take action. It is equally important that we not overreact. Our economic success is not the result of the wisdom of politicians in Washington, DC, but of the collective wisdom of the American people. Shopkeepers, farmers, laborers, entrepreneurs in the private sector have given us the most—the strongest and most resilient economic system in the world.

Over the past 7 years, this system has absorbed shocks: recession, corporate scandals, terrorist attacks, global war. Yet the genius of our system is that it can absorb such shocks and emerge even stronger. In a dynamic market economy, there will always be times when we experience uncertainties and fluctuations. But so long as we pursue progrowth policies that put faith in the American people, our economy will prosper, and it will continue to be the marvel of the world.

Now I'm honored to sign the Economic Stimulus Act of 2008.

NOTE: The President spoke at 1:59 p.m. in the East Room at the White House. H.R. 5140, approved February 13, was assigned Public Law No. 110–185.

Message to the Congress Transmitting an Executive Order Blocking Property of Additional Persons in Connection With the National Emergency With Respect to Syria
February 13, 2008

To the Congress of the United States:

Pursuant to the International Emergency Economic Powers Act, as amended (50 U.S.C. 1701 *et seq.*)(IEEPA), I hereby report that I have issued an Executive Order taking additional steps with respect to the Government of Syria's continued engagement in certain conduct that formed the basis for the national emergency declared in Executive Order 13338 of May 11, 2004, including but not limited to its efforts to undermine the stabilization and reconstruction of Iraq.

This order will block the property and interests in property of persons determined by the Secretary of the Treasury, after consultation with the Secretary of State, to be responsible for, to have engaged in, to have facilitated, or to have secured improper advantage as a result of, public corruption by senior officials within the Government of Syria. The order also revises a provision in Executive Order 13338 to block the property and interests in property of persons determined by the Secretary of the Treasury, after consultation with the Secretary of State, to be responsible for or otherwise significantly contributing to actions or decisions of the Government of Syria that have the purpose or effect of undermining efforts to stabilize Iraq or of allowing the use of Syrian territory or facilities to undermine efforts to stabilize Iraq.

I delegated to the Secretary of the Treasury the authority to take such actions, after consultation with the Secretary of State, including the promulgation of rules and regulations, and to employ all powers granted to the President by IEEPA as may be necessary to carry out the purposes of my order.

I wish to emphasize, as well, my ongoing concern over the destabilizing role Syria continues to play in Lebanon, including its efforts to obstruct, through intimidation and violence, Lebanon's democratic processes.

I am enclosing a copy of the Executive Order I have issued.

GEORGE W. BUSH

The White House,
February 13, 2008.

NOTE: The Executive order is listed in Appendix D at the end of this volume.

Remarks on African Development and Upcoming Visit to Africa
February 14, 2008

I've been looking forward to coming to the museum, and there's an added benefit, and that is, I get to be introduced by my wife on Valentine's Day. [*Laughter*] Happy Valentine's.

This morning Laura and I join all Americans in honoring the life of Congressman Tom Lantos. In his remarkable 80 years, Tom Lantos survived the Nazi camps of Hungary to reach the Halls of Congress. As a Representative from California, he was a fearless defender of democracy, a powerful advocate of human rights, and a strong supporter of the fight against HIV/AIDS. Our prayers are with Annette and the Lantos family. We thank God for his service.

Five years ago, Laura and I made our first visit to Africa. Since then, as she mentioned, she's taken three more trips. And every time, she came back with fascinating stories, some of which she just shared with you. And tomorrow, as she mentioned, we're going back, and I'm really looking forward to it.

We're going to Benin, Tanzania, Rwanda, Ghana, and Liberia. Each of these countries is blessed with natural beauty, vibrant culture, and an unmistakable spirit of energy and optimism. Africa in the 21st century is a continent of potential. That's how

we view it. I hope that's how our fellow citizens view Africa. It's a place where democracy is advancing, where economies are growing, and leaders are meeting challenges with purpose and determination.

Our visit will give me a chance to meet with people who are making the transformation on the continent possible. I'm going to witness the generosity of the American people firsthand. It will give me a chance to remind our fellow citizens about what a compassionate people we are. And I will assure our partners in Africa that the United States is committed to them today, tomorrow, and long into their continent's bright future.

And so I thank you for giving us a chance to come and visit with you. You could call this the sendoff speech.

I really want to thank Mark Dybul. I love to support people who are making history. I can't think of any more noble history than to be leading the compassionate effort of the American people to help save lives. And, Ambassador, you're doing a fabulous job.

I also want to welcome Admiral Tim Ziemer. Admiral, good to see you. He's in charge of making sure that we meet our goals in reducing the scourge of malaria.

Thanks for coming. You and Dybul are results-oriented people. Let me say, I'm a results-oriented President, and so when I meet with you, I ask you, what are the results? [*Laughter*] And you'll hear in a minute, they're very positive.

I appreciate very much Dr. Samper and his wife Adriana for welcoming us. Thank you for leading this important institute.

I also want to thank Sharon Patton, the Director of the Smithsonian National Museum of African Art. Thanks for welcoming us. It's not so easy, like, to welcome the President. [*Laughter*] It turns out, the entourages are probably bigger than the visitors to your museum—[*laughter*]—but thank you for coming. This is an important part of the Washington scene. I'd urge our fellow citizens to come to this important museum. I want to thank the board members of the Smithsonian National Museum of Africa Art who have joined us today.

I welcome Jendayi Frazer, Assistant Secretary of State for African Affairs. Are you going on the trip? Yes. Better get home and pack. [*Laughter*] Thanks for coming. I'm proud to work with you.

Henrietta Fore, Administrator of USAID, is with us. Henrietta, thanks for coming.

I better be careful about how I say this for fear of having a huge burst of applause, but I'd like to introduce the Director of the Peace Corps—[*applause*]—Ron Tschetter. Ron, thanks for coming. It's good to see you, sir. And I appreciate you bringing the five-person cheering section with you. [*Laughter*] There seems to be a groundswell here. [*Laughter*]

I welcome the members of the diplomatic corps. Thanks for coming.

And finally, I do also want to do what Mark did, and thank Chuck Dages of Warner Brothers for this trailer. It's good. I appreciate your support.

The museum is a testament to America's long connection to Africa. At least that's how I view it. Africa is the birthplace of humanity, the home of great civilizations, and the source of enduring achievements in culture and art. Africa has also witnessed some of mankind's most shameful chapters, from the evils of the slave trade to the condescension of colonialism. Even the joy of independence, which arrived with such promise, was undermined by corruption, conflict, and disease. Just a decade ago, much of Africa seemed to be on the brink of collapse, and much of the world seemed content to let it collapse.

Today, that's changing. A new generation of African leaders is stepping forward and turning their continent around. International organizations and faith-based groups and the private sector are more engaged than ever. And in one of the major priorities of my Presidency, the United States has fundamentally altered our policy toward Africa.

America's approach to Africa stems from both our ideals and our interests. We believe that every human life is precious. We believe that our brothers and sisters in Africa have dignity and value because they bear the mark of our Creator. We believe our spirit is renewed when we help African children and families live and thrive.

Africa is also increasingly vital to our strategic interests. We have seen that conditions on the other side of the world can have a direct impact on our own security. We know that if Africa were to continue on the old path of decline, it would be more likely to produce failed states, foster ideologies of radicalism, and spread violence across borders.

We also know that if Africa grows in freedom and prosperity and justice, its people will choose a better course. People who live in societies based on freedom and justice are more likely to reject the false promise of the extremist ideology. Citizens who see a future of opportunity are more likely to build hopeful economies that benefit all the people. Nations that replace disease and despair with healing and hope will help Africa do more than just survive, it will help Africa succeed.

For all these reasons, America has dramatically increased our commitment to development in Africa. We have also revolutionized the way we approach development. Too many nations continue to follow either the paternalistic notion that treats African countries as charity cases or a model of exploitation that seeks only to buy up their resources. America rejects both approaches. Instead, we are treating African leaders as equal partners, asking them to set clear goals and expecting them to produce measurable results. For their part, more African leaders are willing to be held to high standards. And together we're pioneering a new era in development.

The new era is rooted in a powerful truth: Africa's most valuable resource is not its oil; it's not its diamonds; it is the talent and creativity of its people. So we're partnering with African leaders to empower their people to lift up their nations and write a new chapter in their history.

First, we are working to empower Africans to overcome poverty by helping them grow their economies. After a long period of stagnation, many of Africa's economies are springing to life. As a whole, sub-Sahara Africa is projected to grow nearly 7 percent this year. The economies of Ethiopia, Mozambique, and Tanzania are among the fastest growing in the world. And across Africa, poverty is beginning to decline. Don't get me wrong, it's still a poor place, but poverty is beginning to decline.

This resurgence shows the strength of the entrepreneurial spirit in Africa. America is working to help unleash that spirit across the continent. Along with our fellow G–8 nations, we have relieved some of—some $34 billion in debt from African nations in the past 18 months. That is roughly the same level of debt that was canceled in the previous 11 years combined. We have also made historic increases in foreign aid. In my first term, we more than doubled development assistance to Africa, part of the largest expansion of American development assistance since the Marshall plan. At

the beginning of my second term, I promised to double our assistance again by 2010. And the budget I sent Congress last week will ensure that we meet this commitment.

And just as important, we're changing the way we deliver assistance. We created what's called the Millennium Challenge Account, which offers financial support to the world's most promising developing nations, nations that fight corruption, nations that govern justly, nations that open up their economies, and nations that invest in the health and education of their people.

America is serving as an investor, not a donor. We believe that countries can adopt the habits necessary to provide help for their people. That's what we believe. And we're willing to invest in leaders that are doing just that. So far, more than two-thirds of the MCA's $5.5 billion is being invested in Africa. And on my trip next week, I will sign the largest project in the program's history, nearly $700 million compact with Tanzania.

Other nations are seeing the benefits of these agreements. They are moving ahead with the tough economic, political, and social reforms necessary to compete for a compact of their own. In fact, there is now more competition for funds than there are funds available, which ought to say two things: One, that this is evidence that the American taxpayers are getting good value for their dollars. In other words, if nations are willing to fight corruption, work on rule of law, support their people and not theirselves, then it makes sense to invest with them. And secondly, it is evidence that Congress needs to fully fund this important initiative.

The best way to generate economic growth in Africa is to expand trade and investment. When businesses in Africa can sell their products and services around the globe, they create a culture of self-reliance and opportunity. One of the most powerful incentives for trade is the African Growth and Opportunity Act. And I appreciate the fact that Congress has extended this good law. Since 2001, exports from sub-Sahara Africa to the United States have tripled. It's also important for our citizens to know that U.S. exports to sub-Sahara Africa have more than doubled.

On my visit to Ghana, I will meet entrepreneurs who are benefiting from new access to U.S. markets. My message to them will be clear, just like it is to the Congress: For the benefit of Africans and for the benefit of Americans alike, we must maintain our commitment to free and fair trade.

Attracting foreign capital is another key to growth. Recent years, African nations have taken impressive steps to improve their investment climates. According to a World Bank report, 16 countries in sub-Sahara Africa recently adopted reforms to make it easier to start a business and to register property. That may sound simple to Americans, but these are important steps to be able to attract capital for investment purposes. When investors look for a promising market, they are increasingly turning to Africa. And in a hopeful sign, private capital flows to sub-Sahara Africa now exceed development assistance.

We've taken several steps to build on this progress. Last year, we launched the Africa Financial Sector Initiative. As part of this effort, our Overseas Private Investment Corporation mobilized $750 million in investment capital for African businesses. Today I'm announcing that OPIC will support five new investment funds that will mobilize an additional $875 million, for a total of more than $1.6 billion in new capital.

And next week, I'm going to sign a bilateral investment treaty with Rwanda. This will be America's first such treaty in sub-Sahara Africa in nearly a decade. It reflects our shared commitment to systems of fair and open investment. It will bring more capital to Rwanda's dynamic and growing economy.

Look, the idea of somehow being able to help people through just giving them money isn't working. That's why I appreciate the efforts of Rob Mosbacher and OPIC, recognizing that when you invest in capital—invest capital, you create jobs. Paternalism has got to be a thing of the past. Joint venturing with good, capable people is what the future is all about.

But in the long run, the best way to lift lives in Africa is to tear down barriers to investment and trade around the world. And we have an opportunity to do that through the Doha round of trade talks. Look, Doha is important to enhance trade, but if you're truly interested in eliminating poverty, we ought to be reducing tariffs and barriers all across the globe. Now, the United States stands ready to cut farm subsidies and agricultural tariffs and other trade barriers that disadvantage developing countries. On the other hand, we expect the rest of the world, especially the most advanced developing countries, to do the same. And if we both make good-faith efforts, we can reach a successful Doha agreement this year.

Secondly, we're working to empower Africans to alleviate hunger, expand education, and fight disease. America is proud to be the world's largest provider of food assistance, including emergency food stocks that have saved lives in places like Ethiopia or Sudan and other African nations. It's a noble effort on our people's part. I don't know if—most Americans don't understand that we're the world's largest provider of food to feed the hungry, but we are.

Yet our ultimate objective is to do more than respond to the hungry, it is to help African countries feed their own people. So I proposed that America purchase crops directly from farmers in Africa, instead of just shipping food assistance from the developed world. This initiative would build up local agriculture markets. It would help break the cycle of famine. And it deserves the full support of the United States Congress.

We're also focusing on education. I'm looking forward to seeing the President of Tanzania. He's a good guy. Here's what he said, he said, "It's an indisputable fact that education is key to development." Across Africa, students are eager to learn, and often they lack quality teachers and just basic supplies. Things we take for granted in America are just lacking in parts of Africa. So in 2002, I launched the Africa Education Initiative, the goal of which is to distribute more than 15 million textbooks, train nearly a million teachers, and provide scholarships for 550,000 girls by 2010. And we're headed to achieving that goal. In other words, this—these just weren't empty words, these were concrete, solid goals being funded as a result of the generosity of the Congress and the American people.

Last year, I also announced a new International Education Initiative, which will help make basic education available to 4 million people in Ghana, Liberia, and other nations. And Laura and I are looking forward to talking to the leaders of Ghana and Liberia about this important, transformative initiative.

With both these steps, we're matching the enthusiasm of African educators with the generosity of our taxpayers, and we believe strongly that this will open up the door of—the door to opportunity for millions. The good news is, so do the leaders of the countries we're going to visit.

The greatest threat to Africa is disease. The greatest threat for a successful Africa is the scourge of HIV/AIDS and malaria. Two out of every three people afflicted with HIV/AIDS live in sub-Sahara Africa. The disease is the leading cause of death in the region. Just a few years ago, there were fears that HIV/AIDS could wipe out much of the continent's population, with death rates that would rival the Black Plague of the Middle Ages.

We responded. We responded with the Emergency Plan for AIDS Relief. It's the largest international health initiative in history to fight a single disease. In 2002, we pledged $15 billion over 5 years to support HIV/AIDS prevention, treatment, and care.

We set some clear principles on how that money would be spent. We put local partners in the lead because they know their people and their needs. We opened the funding to faith-based groups, healers willing to deliver medicine to remote villages by bicycle or on foot. We stressed the importance of changing behavior so that fewer people are infected in the first place.

And the results are striking. When I visited sub-Sahara Africa 5 years ago—or when we visited 5 years ago, 50,000 people were receiving medicine to treat HIV/AIDS. And when we return this week, there will be more than 1.3 million.

One person who knows the benefits of the emergency plan is Tatu Msangi. She's a single mother from Tanzania. She became pregnant. Tatu went to a clinic run by a Christian group, souls showing up to love a neighbor just like they'd like to be loved themselves. You know, it didn't take a Federal law to say, go to Africa to provide love for Tatu; it took a higher calling. These goals responded.

And she learned she was HIV-positive and enrolled in a program designed to prevent mother-to-child transmission. She went on to deliver a healthy, HIV-free girl named Faith. I will see Tatu next week in Tanzania, but it's not going to be the first time I met her. See, a few weeks ago, she and Faith endured a rather windy State of the Union Address. She sat with Laura in the box, here in the Capital of the Nation that helped save their lives.

In all, the Emergency Plan for AIDS Relief has benefited tens of millions in Africa. Some call this a remarkable success; I call it a good start. Last May, I proposed to double our Nation's initial pledge to $30 billion over the next 5 years. The people on the continent of Africa have to know they're not alone. The G–8 has shown leadership by agreeing to match our $30 billion pledge. The private sector has made generous contributions as well. Think of what Warner Brothers has done, for example. And now the time has come for Congress to act. Members of both parties should re-authorize the emergency plan, maintain the principles that have made it a success, and double our commitment to this noble cause.

Malaria is another devastating killer. In some African countries, malaria takes as many lives as HIV/AIDS. And the vast majority of those taken by malaria are children under the age of 5. Every one of these deaths is unnecessary because the disease is entirely preventable and treatable. So in 2005, America launched a 5-year, $1.2 billion initiative to provide the insecticide-treated beds, indoor spraying, cutting-edge drugs that are necessary to defeat this disease. It's not a complicated strategy. It doesn't take a lot of medical research. We know how to solve the problem. That's why I put the Admiral there. He knows how to solve problems. He can get us from point A to point B in a straight line—well, nearly straight line. [*Laughter*] And so we set a historic goal—if you have a treatable problem on hand, then you're able to set measurable goals—and the goal is to cut the number of malaria-related deaths in 15 African nations by half. That's the goal.

Like the Emergency Plan for AIDS Relief, the malaria initiative empowers leaders on the ground to design strategies that work best for their nations. For example, President Yayi of Benin has called the fight against malaria "a fight against misery." With the help of the malaria initiative, he's leading a campaign to deliver insecticide-treated bed nets to children under 5 in Benin. I'm looking forward to hearing how that's going when we meet him on Benin on our first stop. I can't wait to find out how well this initiative is doing.

Like the emergency plan, the malaria initiative has been matched by G–8 nations, which have pledged to cut malaria deaths by half in an additional 15 countries. This initiative has also been greeted with generous support from the private sector, faith-based groups, and Americans who want to do something to save somebody's life. You can buy a $10 bed net and ship it to Africa to save a life. It doesn't take much money, but it takes a big heart. One of the interesting gifts Laura and I got a couple of years ago for Christmas was bed nets in our name. It made us feel great.

Like the emergency plan, the malaria initiative is producing undeniable results. In just over 2 years, the initiative has reached more than 25 million people. According to new data, malaria rates are dropping dramatically in many parts of Africa. If we stay on this path, an extraordinary achievement is within reach: Africa can turn a disease that has taken its children for centuries into a thing of the past. And wouldn't that be fantastic? And so Laura and I are going to spend time with these leaders, saying, what a noble opportunity, what a great goal, what a great way to serve humankind.

Finally, we're working to empower Africans to end conflicts, strengthen democracy, and promote peace. When I took office, Africa was home to six major conflicts: in Angola, Burundi, Congo, Liberia, Sierra Leone, and southern Sudan. We concluded that the best way to broker peace was to support the efforts of African leaders on the ground, instead of dictating solutions from Washington, DC. And today, every one of them has made progress toward peace and stability.

For example, the United States worked closely with Nigeria to help end the Liberian civil war. When the international community called for Charles Taylor to step down in 2003, the President of Nigeria provided a plane to take him in exile. When U.S. marines deployed to Liberia, Nigerian peacekeepers deployed at the same time. And today, Liberia's long war is over. And next week in Monrovia, Laura and I will meet with Africa's first democratically elected woman President, Ellen Johnson Sirleaf.

Even without major conflict or civil war, security challenges remain in Africa, and we're working closely with local partners to address them. The Department of Defense has established a new African Command, which will work closely with African governments to crack down on human trafficking, piracy, and terrorism across the continent. We are employing diplomatic tools as well.

In eastern Congo, we worked with leaders on the ground to broker the recent agreements to demobilize all remaining armed groups. And we stand ready to help all sides to implement them.

In Kenya, we are backing the efforts of former U.N. Secretary-General Kofi Annan to end the crisis. And when we're on the continent, I've asked Condi Rice—that would be Secretary Rice—to travel to Kenya to support the work of the former Secretary-General and to deliver a message directly to Kenya's leaders and people: There must be an immediate halt to violence, there must be justice for the victims of abuse, and there must be a full return to democracy.

In Darfur, the United States will continue to call the killing what it is: genocide. We will continue to deliver humanitarian aid. We will continue to enforce sanctions, tough sanctions, against the Sudanese Government officials, rebel leaders, and others responsible for violence. We expect other nations to join us in this effort to save lives from the genocide that is taking place. We will use all our diplomatic resources to urge full deployment of an effective United Nations force. The decision was made to count on the United Nations to provide the force necessary to protect people, and so we're going to support their efforts. I must confess, I'm a little frustrated by how slow things are moving. And yet we will support their efforts to find forces necessary to make a robust contribution to save lives.

On this trip, I'm going to visit with brave peacekeepers from Rwanda, a nation that knows the pain of genocide and was the first country to send troops into Darfur. Other nations need to follow Rwanda's ex-

ample. Other nations need to take this issue seriously, just like the United States does, and provide more manpower for this urgent mission. And when they do, I pledge America will provide the training and equipment necessary to deploy the peacekeepers to Darfur.

America also stands with all in Africa who live in the quiet pain of tyranny. We will confront tyranny. In Zimbabwe, a discredited dictator presides over food shortages, staggering inflation, and harsh repression. The decent and talented people of that country deserve much better. America will continue to support freedom in Zimbabwe. And I urge neighbors in the region, including South Africa, to do the same. We look forward to the hour when this nightmare is over and the people of Zimbabwe regain their freedom.

These are great challenges, but there is even greater cause for hope. In the past 4 years alone, there have been more than 50 democratic elections in Africa. Thriving free societies have emerged in nations with Islamic majorities, Christian majorities, majorities of other beliefs, which is a powerful rebuke to the ideology of the extremists. In many nations, women have exercised the right to vote and run for office. Rwanda now has the highest percentage of female legislators in the world. Overall, more than two-thirds of the nations of sub-Saharan Africa are free. And for the rest, the direction of history is clear, so long as the United States does not lose its nerve and retreat into isolationism and protectionism. The day will come when a region once dismissed as the "Dark Continent" enjoys the light of liberty.

The United States must remain fully committed to the new era of development that we have begun with our partners in Africa. It's in our national interest we do so. I'm going to work closely with the G–8 nations to ensure that they keep their promises as well. Congress must continue to show its commitment by fully funding the development programs I described today. You see, saving lives is a calling that crosses partisan lines. It remains equally worthy in both good economic times and times of economic uncertainty.

Across Africa, people have begun to speak of the Lazarus effect, where communities once given up for dead are coming back to life. The work of healing and redemption is both a matter of conscience and a wise exercise of American influence. The work is not done. In the face of the needs that remain, it's important for the African people to believe the American people are not going to turn away. That's part of the purpose of our trip. The changes taking place in Africa don't always make the headlines. So don't be frustrated, Mark. That means the work is quiet, but it is not thankless.

Last November, I met a woman from Zambia named Bridget Chisenga. Bridget's husband died of AIDS, and she expected to meet the same fate. Then she went to a clinic operated by Catholic Relief Services, funded by the American people. Today, Bridget is healthy. She has a job at the clinic, where she helps provide AIDS medicine to others. I want our fellow citizens to hear what she said: "This face is alive and vibrant because of your initiative. I would like to thank you."

Americans have heard similar words of gratitude and hope in the past. They were said about the people who liberated the concentration camps and saved the blockaded city of Berlin and stood firm until the prisoners in the gulags were set free. This spirit of purpose and compassion has always defined America. And that is why the people of Africa can be certain they will always have a friend and partner in the United States of America.

God bless.

NOTE: The President spoke at 10:13 a.m. at the National Museum of African Art. In his remarks, he referred to Rear Adm. R. Timothy Ziemer, USN (Ret.), U.S. Malaria Coordinator; Cristian Samper, Acting Secretary, Smithsonian Institution; Chuck Dages, executive vice president of emerging technology, Warner Bros. Home Entertainment Group; President Jakaya Mrisho Kikwete of Tanzania; former President Charles Taylor and President Ellen Johnson Sirleaf of Liberia; former President Olusegun Obasanjo of Nigeria; and President Robert Mugabe of Zimbabwe. The transcript released by the Office of the Press Secretary also included the remarks of the First Lady.

Remarks on Intelligence Reform Legislation and an Exchange With Reporters
February 14, 2008

The President. Good afternoon. This Saturday at midnight, legislation authorizing intelligence professionals to quickly and effectively monitor terrorist communications will expire. If Congress does not act by that time, our ability to find out who the terrorists are talking to, what they are saying, and what they are planning will be compromised. It would be a mistake if the Congress were to allow this to happen.

Members of Congress knew all along that this deadline was approaching. They said it themselves. They've had more than 6 months to discuss and deliberate, and now they must act and pass legislation that will ensure our intelligence professionals have the tools they need to keep us safe.

Earlier this week, the Senate did act and passed a strong bill and did so with a bipartisan majority. The Senate bill will ensure that we can effectively monitor those seeking to harm our people. The Senate bill will provide fair and just liability protection for companies that assisted in the efforts to protect America after the attacks of September the 11th. Without this protection, without this liability shield, we may not be able to secure the private sector's cooperation with our intelligence efforts. And that, of course, would put the American people at risk.

Now it's the House's turn to act. It is clear that the Senate bill would pass the House with bipartisan support. Republicans and Democrats in the Senate can put partisanship aside and pass a good bill. There's no reason why the House cannot do the same and pass the Senate bill immediately.

Our Government has no greater responsibility than getting this work done, and there really is no excuse for letting this critical legislation expire. I urge congressional leaders to let the will of the House and the American people prevail and vote on the Senate bill before adjourning for their recess. Failure to act would harm our ability to monitor new terrorist activities and could reopen dangerous gaps in our intelligence. Failure to act would also make the private sector less willing to help us protect the country, and this is unacceptable. The House should not leave Washington without passing the Senate bill.

Now, I am scheduled to leave tomorrow for a long-planned trip to five African nations. Moments ago, my staff informed the House leadership that I'm prepared to delay my departure and stay in Washington with them if it will help them complete their work on this critical bill.

The lives of countless Americans depend on our ability to monitor terrorist communications. Our intelligence professionals are working day and night to keep us safe, and they're waiting to see whether Congress will give them the tools they need to succeed or tie their hands by failing to act. The American people are watching this debate as well. They expect Congress to meet its responsibilities before they leave town on a recess.

I'll answer a few questions. Ben [Ben Feller, Associated Press], if you've got a question, I'll be prepared to answer.

President's Upcoming Visit to Africa/ Intelligence Reform Legislation

Q. Thank you, Mr. President. It appears with that deadline approaching that the House and the White House might be seen as being engaged in a game of chicken here, playing politics with an important intelligence law.

The President Yes.

Q. If the law expires and something happens, wouldn't you be at least partly to blame? And on your Africa trip, if you have to delay, do you think that you would be shortening your trip at all?

The President. As to the latter, the delay depends on whether the House acts, of course, and they got plenty of time to get this done. But if we have to delay, we'll delay. But I'm going to go to the countries that I said I'd go to.

And to the first case, whether or not this is politics, I certainly hope not. I can assure you, Al Qaida in their planning isn't thinking about politics. They're thinking about hurting the American people again.

Who's to blame? Look, these folks in Congress passed a good bill last—late last summer. In other words, they analyzed the situation, they said there's a threat, and they agreed to give our professionals the tools they needed to do the job. The problem is, they let the bill expire.

My attitude is, if the bill was good enough then, why not pass the bill again? I mean, the threat hasn't gone away. Secondly, they've had plenty of time to think about how to address the issue. Thirdly, the Senate led the way; the Senate showed how to pass a good bill with a bipartisan majority. And the truth of the matter is, if there was a willingness to get this problem solved, all the leadership would have to do is submit the Senate bill for a vote.

So we'll see what happens. My attitude is, now is the time to get the job done. There's been plenty of time to think about it, plenty of time to debate it, and there's a good way forward. And hopefully, the House leadership will put this bill for a vote and let the Members vote as they so desire.

Mike [Mike Emanuel, FOX News].

Terrorist Surveillance Program/War on Terror

Q. Mr. President, I realize this is a sensitive matter, but I'm wondering if there's a way you can spell out for the American public what the practical impact may be, if this law expires, on our intelligence professionals, say, next week.

The President. Well, I hope it doesn't. But clearly, there will be a gap. And of course, we won't be able to assess that gap until the time. Step one is, I guess you got to come to the conclusion that there's a threat to America or not a threat. I mean, evidently, some people just don't feel that sense of urgency. I do. And the reason I do, is I firmly believe that there's still people out there who would do us harm.

Secondly, I know that the tools that I've just described are necessary to protect us. Why? Because we need to know what people are saying, what they're planning, and what they're thinking. And the tool that I have just described has been very effective.

Thirdly, people are wondering why companies need liability protection. Well, if you cooperate with the Government and then get sued for billions of dollars because of the cooperation, you're less likely to cooperate. And obviously, we're going to need people working with us to find out what

the enemy is saying and thinking and plotting and planning.

And so it's a—to me, it's a—I guess one way to look at it is, some may not feel that same sense of urgency I do. I heard somebody say, "Well, this is just pure politics." No, this is what is necessary to protect the American people from harm. And I recognize there hasn't been an attack on our country, but that does not mean that there's not still an enemy that lurks, plans, and plots.

And one of the reasons we've been effective is because we put new tools in place that give our professionals that which is necessary to protect us. This is a different kind of threat than we've ever faced before. It's a different kind of war that we're fighting, and it requires a different approach.

Again, I'll repeat to you that the Congress took a look at this issue and decided that the tools were necessary to give to our professionals last—late last summer. And if it was necessary late last summer, why is it not necessary today? What has changed? Well, the threat hasn't gone away. It's still there, it's still real, and we better be worried about it as a nation. And the House has now got time to go out and get the deal done.

Yesterday, a couple of days—votes ago in the Senate made it abundantly clear that Republicans and Democrats can come together and get a—put a good piece of legislation together and get it passed. And the House leadership has an opportunity to do that now.

Listen, thank you all very much.

NOTE: The President spoke at 1 p.m. on the South Lawn at the White House. In his remarks, he referred to H.R. 3773.

Statement on the Third Anniversary of the Death of Former Prime Minister Rafiq Hariri of Lebanon
February 14, 2008

Today marks the third anniversary of the assassination of former Lebanese Prime Minister Rafiq Hariri. The terrorist attack that killed Prime Minister Hariri, Minister Basil Fuleihan, and many other innocent victims was the spark that launched a transformation in Lebanon, as the Lebanese people demanded an end to the Syrian occupation and the restoration of their sovereignty.

Since the assassination of Prime Minister Hariri, many other Lebanese patriots have been murdered by those who seek to use violence and intimidation to derail progress toward a free, independent, and prosperous Lebanon. It is vital that the perpetrators of these attacks be brought to justice, and I, therefore, call upon the international community to redouble its support for the Special Tribunal for Lebanon. The United States support for the Government and people of Lebanon remains firm and unwavering.

Syria, Iran, and their allies must end their efforts to undermine Lebanon's legitimate Government and to interfere in its political process. The Lebanese deserve a President elected in accordance with their Constitution, without preconditions and in an environment free from fear and intimidation.

The foundation of freedom in Lebanon, which Mr. Hariri helped lay, remains strong. We will continue to support the people of Lebanon as they work to rid the country of terrorism and violence and exercise their democratic freedoms in peace.

Interview With Matt Frei of BBC World News America
February 14, 2008

President's Upcoming Visit to Africa

Mr. Frei. Mr. President, thanks for joining us. You're famous for saying that you don't believe in opinion polls.

The President. Yes.

Mr. Frei. Do you have any idea how you rate in the countries that you're going to be visiting in Africa?

The President. No, sir, I don't.

Mr. Frei. Well, I've got news for you, and it's good news. You rate pretty well, sort of in the average eighties. Is that one of the reasons why you're going there? This is one part of the world where you're still very popular.

The President. I go where needed. And no, I'm going there because I've got a firm, heartfelt commitment to the continent of Africa and had ever since I became President. It's in our interests, national interests, that we help people who are suffering from disease and hunger and hopelessness. The only way a radical can recruit is to find somebody that's hopeless. I mean, their vision is, like, really dark and dim.

Plus, I believe to whom much is given, much is required. And America has been given a lot, and it's required of us to help those who suffer. So mine is a mercy—a mission of mercy and a mission of the cold realism of the world in which we live—based upon the realism in the world in which we live.

President's Emergency Plan for AIDS Relief

Mr. Frei. Your administration has given $15 billion to treat AIDS in Africa, which is an unprecedented amount of money, and you want to double that amount yet again. This is a huge commitment, and yet the administration and you, personally, don't seem to be getting a lot of credit for it.

The President. Yes. You know, this is kind of tied to your first question about polls. Polls are nothing more than just, like, a poof of air. What matters is results. And ultimately, people will be able to make an objective judgment of a President and his administration and, in this case, a country's commitment. And so all I care, really, about is the results of the programs.

I hope by now people have learned that I'm not one of these guys that really gives a darn about elite opinion. What I really care about is, are we saving lives? And in this case, we are. As I mentioned in my speech that you kindly listened to, when I first went to sub-Sahara Africa, 50,000 people were receiving antiretrovirals; today, 1.3 million. And that's a lot in a very quick period of time. But there's still so much more suffering, and that's why I've called for a doubling of aid.

The good news is, it's not just America. As I mentioned in my speech, the G–8 nations also are supporting this very important initiative. And, you know, it's a—it's just—in other words, this isn't a paternalistic effort, this is an effort of mercy.

Mr. Frei. But it has made a huge difference, hasn't it? So why not take some credit for it?

The President. Because it's just not my nature. I really—you just got to understand about me: I'm more interested in seeing results and sharing the credit with the American people. I mean, this is not a George Bush effort. I just happen to be the leader of a nation that's willing to fund this kind of money. And so I praised Congress in my speech; I praised the American

people in my speech. After all, they're the ones who are funding the effort.

Darfur

Mr. Frei. You were very tough in your speech about Darfur, and yet again, you called what's happening there genocide.

The President. Yes.

Mr. Frei. Is enough being done by your administration to stop that?

The President. I think we are, yes. You know, I had to make a seminal decision, and that is whether or not I would commit troops into—U.S. troops into Darfur. And I was pretty well backed off of it by a lot of folks here in America that care deeply about the issue. And so once you make that decision, then you have to rely upon an international organization like the United Nations to provide the oomph, the necessary manpower.

And in my speech today, I did call it genocide again. I think we're the only nation that has done so. Secondly, I did remind people that we're sanctioning leaders, that we have targeted Sudanese companies and individuals, including a rebel leader who have yet to be constructive in the peace process. We're beginning to get a sense that these sanctions are affecting behavior. We're trying to ask others, by the way, to do the same thing, some of whom are reluctant, some who aren't. And then, finally, I pledged that we'll help move troops in. And as I also said—you might remind your listeners—that I'm frustrated by the pace.

U.S. Role in Darfur

Mr. Frei. I'll get onto that in a minute, but, I mean, "genocide" is such a loaded— it's such an important word. And you have committed troops, American troops, around the world in other cases, Iraq, most famously, Afghanistan. Why not in this case?

The President. Well, that's a good question. I mean, we're committing equipment, training, help, movement. I think a lot of the folks were concerned about America into another Muslim country. Some of the relief groups here just didn't think the strategy would be as effective as it was. I mean, I actually, believe it or not, listen to people's opinions and chose to make this decision. It's a decision that I'm now living with, and it's a decision that requires us to continue to rally the conscience of the world and get people to focus on the issue.

You know, you're right. I mean, we sent marines into Liberia, for example, to help stabilize the country there. And Liberia's on my itinerary, where I'll meet with the first woman elected President in Africa's history. But I just made the decision I made.

Steven Spielberg/2008 Beijing Olympics/ China's Role in Darfur

Mr. Frei. Yesterday Steven Spielberg, the Hollywood director, pulled out of the Beijing Olympics over Darfur. He said the Chinese aren't doing enough to stop the killing in Darfur.

The President. Yes.

Mr. Frei. Do you applaud his move?

The President. That's up to him. I'm going to the Olympics. I view the Olympics as a sporting event. On the other hand, I have a little different platform than Steven Spielberg, so I get to talk to President Hu Jintao. And I do remind him that he can do more to relieve the suffering in Darfur.

There's a lot of issues that I suspect people are going to opine about during the Olympics. I mean, you got the Dalai Lama crowd; you've got global warming folks; you've got Darfur. And I just—I am not going to go and use the Olympics as an opportunity to express my opinions to the Chinese people in a public way because I do it all the time with the President. I mean, so people are going to be able to choose—pick and choose how they view the Olympics.

U.S. Foreign Policy/War on Terror

Mr. Frei. The Chinese Government has been saying, in part in response to this, that America is trapped in cold war thinking.

The President. Well, I think that's just a brush-back pitch, as we say in baseball. It's a—America is trapped in this notion that we care about human life; we respect human dignity—and that's not a trap; that's a belief—and that many of us in this country recognize that the human condition matters to our own national security.

See, I happen to believe we're in an ideological struggle. And those who murder the innocent to achieve political objectives are evil people, but they have an ideology. And the only way you can recruit for that ideology is to find hopeless folks.

I mean, who wants to join an ideology that say: women don't have rights; you can't express yourself freely; religious beliefs are—the only religious belief you can hold is the one we tell you. And, oh, by the way, it's great; you can be a suicider. Hopeless people are the ones who get attracted by that point of view. And therefore, it's in the world's interest, from a national security perspective, to deal with hopelessness.

And it happens to be in our moral interest. I repeat to you: I believe to whom much is given, much is required. It happens to be a religious notion, but it should be a universal notion as well. And I believe America's soul is enriched, our spirit is enhanced when we help people who suffer.

Rwanda/Darfur

Mr. Frei. I mentioned the genocide thing also because your predecessor, President Clinton, said that the one thing—one of the key things that keeps him up at night is that he didn't do enough over Rwanda to stop the killing there. Is it possible that Darfur might become your Rwanda?

The President. I don't think so. I hope—I certainly hope not. I mean, Rwanda was, I think, 900,000 people in a very quick period of time of just wholesale slaughter. And I appreciate President Clinton's compassion and concern. And I'm comfortable with making a decision that I think is the best decision and comfortable with the notion that once that decision is made, we're keeping the world's focus as best as we can on that, amongst other issues.

Zimbabwe/South Africa

Mr. Frei. You also had some very strong language today about Zimbabwe——

The President. Yes, I did.

Mr. Frei. ——which is an issue that certain—Britain and the United States care deeply about. Again, this has been going on for years. What can be done to stop the crisis in Zimbabwe?

The President. Yes, I—first is call the— is to speak to the conscience of the world and remind people the facts. I mean, Zimbabwe was the breadbasket of southern Africa, and today, it's in line for food aid. Zimbabwe was a—is now a place where people are repressed because of their beliefs. And you're right; there is not a lot of outcry. And it's a frustrating—look, not everything is perfect in this world, and it just requires constant focus.

And one way to do it is for the American President to speak out or the British Prime Minister to speak out. And, as you know, I mentioned South Africa. I have great respect for the people of South Africa. I just happen to believe their Government can do more to enhance a free society in their region. Yes, it's just—there's a lot of frustrations in this world, and there's a lot of hope in this world as well.

President's Legacy

Mr. Frei. You're nearing the end of your second term and, I guess, one can call is legacy time. Whatever you do and say about Africa, there's only one country, really, that the wider world will associate with you, and that equation is, Bush equals Iraq.

The President. Yes.

Mr. Frei. Are you happy about that?

The President. Well, I mean, that's what the current elite would like everybody to think about, and that's fine. I think history will have a—when history marches on, there will be a little more objective look about the totality of this administration.

Of course, our change in the way we did aid in Africa is substantial and different, and lives will have been saved. Dealing with liberating 25 million in Afghanistan is part of what I hope people think of when they look at my Presidency. Being the first President to propose a two-state solution on Israel and Palestine—I mean, there's a lot of other issues. And I'm happy with Iraq. The right—the decision to move Saddam Hussein was right, and this democracy is now taking root. And I'm confident that if America does not become isolationist and allow the terrorists to take back over, Iraq will succeed.

U.S. Troop Levels in Iraq

Mr. Frei. Are you—do you regret, rather, I should say, that you didn't listen to your—some of your commanders earlier to send more troops to Iraq to achieve the kind of results that we're seeing now to some extent?

The President. You know, my commanders didn't tell me that early. My commanders said, we got the right level of troops. You know, wars—it's easy to second—the tactical decisions of war, and I fully understand and expect that to happen. All I can do is base decisions on the considered judgment of the experts. And I did. And I take full responsibility for every military decision that's been made in Iraq.

But I'm pleased with what's happening now. And the world is beginning to recognize that the decision to send more troops—was a pretty tough decision at the time—is providing enough security for the politics to take place. And this morning—you're the first reporter I've been able to describe these conversations to, but I did speak to the Prime Minister, the Speaker, and two Deputy Speakers to congratulate them on a series of substantial legislative achievements that are beginning to say to the world and, more importantly, the Iraqi people, reconciliation is happening, and the legislative body is beginning to function, which is good news.

U.S. Intelligence Reform Legislation and Interrogation Techniques

Mr. Frei. The Senate yesterday passed a bill outlawing waterboarding. You, I believe, have said that you will veto that bill. Does that not send the wrong signal to the rest of the world?

The President. No, look, that's not the reason I'm vetoing the bill. The reason I'm vetoing the bill—first of all, we have said that whatever we do is for legal—will be legal. Secondly, they are imposing a set of standards on our intelligence communities, in terms of interrogating prisoners, that our people will think will be ineffective.

And to the critics, I ask them this: When we, within the law, interrogate and get information that protects ourselves and possibly others and other nations—to prevent attacks—which attack would they had hoped that we wouldn't have prevented? And so the United States will act within the law, and we'll make sure our professionals have the tools necessary to do their job within the law.

Now, I recognize some say that these terrorists really aren't that big a threat to the United States anymore. I fully disagree. And I think the President must give these professionals, within the law, the necessary tools to protect us. So we're having a debate not only on how you interrogate people; we're having a debate in America on whether or not we ought to be listening to terrorists making phone calls in the United States. And the answer is, darn right we ought to be.

War on Terror/Guantanamo Bay Detainees

Mr. Frei. But given Guantanamo Bay, given also Abu Ghraib, given renditions, does this not send the wrong signal to the world?

The President. It should send the signal that America is going to respect law but is going to take actions necessary to protect ourselves and find information that may protect others. Unless, of course, people say: "Well, there's no threat. They're just making up the threat. These people aren't problematic." But I don't see how you can say that in Great Britain, after people came and blew up bombs in subways. I suspect the families of those victims understand the nature of killers.

And so what people got to understand is, we'll make decisions based upon law. We're a nation of law. Take Guantanamo, look, I'd like it to be empty. On the other hand, there's some people there that need to be tried. And there will be a trial, and they'll have their day in court, unlike what they did to other people.

No, there's great concern about—and I can understand this—that these people be given rights, but they're not willing to grant the same rights to others. They'll murder, but you got to understand, they're getting rights. And I'm comfortable with the decisions we've made, and I'm comfortable with recognizing this is still a dangerous world.

U.S. Foreign Policy

Mr. Frei. Can you honestly say, Mr. President, that today, America still occupies the moral high ground?

The President. Absolutely. Absolutely. We believe in human rights and human dignity. We believe in the human condition. We believe in freedom. And we're willing to take the lead; we're willing to ask nations to do hard things; we're willing to accept responsibilities. And yes, no question in my mind, this is a nation that's a force for good. And history will judge the decisions made during this period of time as necessary decisions. And I firmly believe that we are laying the foundation for peace.

People have written off the Middle East—it's impossible to have—change the conditions there; let's just ignore it, or let's promote stability, which was part of the foreign policy of the past. I chose a different course. Stability didn't work. Stability created the conditions that were ripe for these terrorists to emerge and recruit. I happen to believe free societies provide hope. And I would hope that people in Europe, for example, understand that freedom has led to peace and ought to be supporting the freedom movements and not shy away from the responsibility of the comfortable to help those who long for freedom.

And it's hard work. It's really hard work, and it doesn't happen instantly. You know, we live in a world—like, in all due respect to 24-hour news, we live in a world where everything is, like, instant. But the work we're doing is—it takes patience, but most importantly, it takes faith in the universality of freedom that exists in every heart.

And so yes, I'm not only happy to defend decisions, I'm confident that they will lead to a better tomorrow.

Mr. Frei. Mr. President, I gather we've run out of time. Thanks for doing this.

The President. Thank you, sir. You bet.

Mr. Frei. Thank you.

NOTE: The interview was taped at 11:12 a.m. in the Library at the White House for later broadcast. In his remarks, the President referred to President Ellen Johnson Sirleaf of Liberia; Prime Minister Gordon Brown of the United Kingdom; Prime Minister Nuri al-Maliki of Iraq; and Speaker Mahmud al-Mashhadani, First Deputy Speaker Khalid al-Attiya, and Second Deputy Speaker Arif Tayfur of the Iraqi House of Representatives. He also referred to H.R. 2082. The transcript was released by the Office of the Press Secretary on February 15.

Interview With Foreign Radio Journalists
February 14, 2008

The President. Thank you all. Just a couple of comments. I'm very much looking forward to the trip. This will be my second trip to the continent of Africa, my wife's fifth trip. The reason why I'm looking forward to it is I want the people on the continent of Africa to know that the American people care deeply about the human condition; that when we see suffering, it troubles our conscience, and we want to help. I believe to whom much is given, much is required. A lot has been given to America, and therefore, a lot is required of us to deal with human misery in the form of hunger and disease and hopelessness.

And so this is going to be a trip that I bring the good will of American people, with a strategy to help nations deal with the problems they have. I appreciate the

leadership on the continent of Africa, and I'm looking forward to working with the leaders there as partners in solving some of the problems that I believe can be solved.

And so thank you for coming. I'd be glad to answer questions.

Democracy in Benin/U.S. Foreign Policy in Benin

Q. I'm Jean Jonas from Benin.

The President. Yes, sir. First up.

Q. Well, people from my country are very delighted to welcome you on Saturday. And I wish to say what they are expecting from you and from America. You, President Bush, have said that the best way we can build a peaceful world for the future is to share the principle of freedom with other nations. I took this from the U.S.

Government site—this is a word I appreciate. But we highly appreciate how your Government fight poverty and encourage growth building. But we would like all this take place in a perfectly democratic context. What will be the implication of your trip to Benin, in terms of guaranteeing a perfect democracy for building hope and prosperity?

The President. Democracy is a commitment by government and by people. The people of Benin have committed to democracy. However, to achieve a perfect democracy is very difficult. In my country, we're a great democracy. We were imperfect. After all, we enslaved people. And democracy is work and requires a lot of work. And it requires support from—to help leaders deal with everyday problems.

One such problem in Benin is malaria. Your President has made a strong commitment to help eradicate malaria. Today, in a speech that inaugurated my trip—or kicked off my trip, I talked about your President's commitment to provide nets to every child 5 and under. That's a strong commitment. We have got what's called Millennium Challenge Account programs. These are significant aid programs, but they're given to countries that adhere to rule of law and fight corruption and invest in the health and education of their people.

This is a different type of foreign policy. It's a different type of foreign aid. Foreign aid in the past was just, here, take and spend. This is foreign policy that reinforces the conditions necessary for just and peaceful societies to develop. And Benin is such a country. And so I'm looking forward to confirming our desire to help and reinforcing the President's desire to achieve a democracy in which people have got confidence.

Yes, ma'am, Yvonne.

U.S. Foreign Policy in Africa

Q. I'm Yvonne from Tanzania. I was happy to hear about you congratulating President Kikwete, calling him a good guy, because I agree he's a good guy as well. [*Laughter*]

The President. Well, actually, that's just Texas vernacular, you know, it's not a very—[*laughter*]—it's not diplomatic talk, but, you know—[*laughter*]—he is a good guy.

Q. He's a good guy, yes, and we're happy to receive the MCC money, which we're about to receive when you come down to Tanzania. Now my question is that Tanzania is among 15 countries that have benefited from the U.S. initiative on HIV/AIDS, PEPFAR program, as well as the malaria initiative. But being an undeveloped country, while—would expect that to see more assistance in terms of helping poor countries such as Tanzania develop economically.

So I'd like to know, as you're winding your term in office, what commitment has America made to ensure that developing countries such as Tanzania is assisted in terms of trade and development issues and private sector development as well?

The President. That's good. First of all, just in general, our commitment to the continent of Africa was doubled when I first came into office, and then when I got—started my second term, doubled again.

Secondly, I do agree that the most substantive way to help any developing nation is through the development of commerce and wealth as a result of growing industry and businesses, both small and large. And the best way to foster that is through trade. And that's why AGOA, passed by my predecessor, reauthorized during my Presidency, is a great source of hope for people on the continent of Africa because they now have a market in which to sell.

Today in my speech, I talked about this statistic: Exports to the United States from the continent of Africa, sub-Saharan Africa, have tripled. Exports from the United States to sub-Saharan Africa have doubled. In other words, this trade has been good. One way to firm up the commitment to make sure that our Nation remains non-protectionist—in other words, a free-trading nation—is to complete the Doha round. That's a difficult set of negotiations. The United States has made it clear that we will reduce our agricultural subsidies, but in return, we expect other developed nations—and developing—large developing nations—to also reduce their tariffs and subsidies so that I can come to the Congress and say, here's an agreement that is fair for everybody.

And so the other thing we can do is—so, our assistance aid, by the way, is helping—in some cases helps business. One way to do that is through OPIC. And I announced today a new multimillion dollar—hundreds of millions of dollars of OPIC-type investment funds that will be available for African businesses.

What's interesting is, capital inflows into Africa now exceed grants, development aid. And that's important because capital inflows means jobs and commerce and hope and small businesses. So our plan is a plan that, hopefully, will sustain the gains that have been made. It's not like a one-time shot. It's got structural implications.

The other thing is, is that you can't have a hopeful economy if your people can't read. And so education is a vital link to providing hope. And we've got a strong education initiative on the continent—and started early in my administration; we're following through on it. We're trying to get, I think, like, 12 million textbooks and train 900,000 teachers and provide scholarships to 550,000 girls, all aiming to provide a basis by which these investments and these capital flows will actually be able to take hold—and that is an educated workforce, an educated population.

Albert.

Millennium Challenge Grants/Democracy in Africa

Q. Mr. President——

The President. You're living in Rwanda now?

Q. Yes, I do.

The President. Good.

Q. And I hope I'll be there before you reach, so I can welcome you.

The President. Thank you, sir.

Q. You somehow already replied to the question I wanted to ask you, but I can maybe define it a bit more. It is clear that the increase of support of your administration—your two mandates—increased a lot. And don't you think the U.S. should maybe also develop a higher level political strategy on Africa, that would benefit the U.S. and Africa?

The President. That's a very interesting question. A couple of approaches to aid in the past: One was, "We're feeling terrible for you, here's money," and not much asked in return. The other approach oftentimes has been: "You've got resources; we want them. We'll exploit them and leave behind something that really doesn't benefit the people." I know those are extreme cases, but nevertheless, if you really think about the history of supporting Africa, it's one way to characterize how things were approached. Some of it had to do with the guilt of colonialism; some of it had to do with just the gluttony of need for raw materials. In either case, it didn't work.

So we've taken this approach that said we will invest in countries where leadership has made a firm commitment to some basic principles: rule of law, fighting corruption, investment in people through health and education programs, and adherence to the marketplace. Nations that have received Millennium Challenge grants have met a test. In other words, there is a criterion to qualify for the money.

What's happening, Albert, is that other nations desirous of a Millennium Challenge grant ask, "What did you do to get your grant," to other leaders. And so the habits of a just society become an integral part of the receiving of help. We're more than willing to help, but in this case, we're saying the help has got to be to reinforce those decisions by leaders that'll have a long-lasting impact toward a free society. There's nothing more debilitating to a society than corruption. If the people think that the leadership is there to enrich themselves, they'll have no trust in government. There will be no trust in form of—any form of government.

And so one of the criterion for Millennium Challenge is honesty. We want the leadership and government to be honest with the people. And when we first put out—when I first put out this initiative, I was criticized by some. That's just part of the job, evidently. And it was, "How dare you insist upon conditions for your aid." And my answer is, how can we not? Shouldn't we expect good leadership? Shouldn't we have faith in people from a different part of the world demanding the same things that we expect of our Government?

The answer is, absolutely we should hold people up to a high standard. Absolutely we should expect leaders to adhere to some basic principle. And absolutely we should trust people to want to live in a free society.

And so we changed the policy. Not only did we have a more robust approach to the issues facing Africans than ever before in our Nation's history, by a significant amount, but we have a strategy to do just what you asked. How do we make sure that a free society is lasting, that it's not just a moment—you know, let's just do what old George wants us to do, and then he'll go away and then societies can revert back its norm. And so we have—there's a constant evaluation of results based upon high standards.

Edwin. How are you?

U.S. Role in Africa

Q. Thank you very much. I'm fine.

The President. Yes, good, me too.

Q. Mr. President, I'm impressed by your policy statement on Africa today.

The President. Were you listening?

Q. Yes, for the—yes.

The President. You were the only people in this room; the rest of them fell asleep back there. [*Laughter*]

Q. But just what I've from the—what I've listened to here now, I'm mostly impressed; it's quite encouraging. But I just want to know, what is the motivating factor for the increasing interest in Africa?

The President. Why?

Q. The motivating factor of the interest in Africa. Well, somebody may say it's the new oil finds or the fight against terrorism or we want to promote democracy.

The President. Yes. A couple of things, Edwin. First of all, my passion toward Africa has been sustained throughout 7 years. In other words, my speech today, if you listened carefully to it, indicated a strategy that was first adopted early in my administration.

Secondly, there are two reasons why. Now, one, conditions of life overseas matters to the security of the United States. In other words, if there's hopelessness, then it's liable that extremists who are recruiting people to create havoc not only in their respective countries or neighborhoods but also in our country—if there's hopelessness, they have a better chance to recruit. So it's in our national security interest, Edwin, that we deal with the conditions that enable ideologues—the ideologues of hate to recruit.

Remember that the ideology that is prevalent, that uses murder as a weapon, cannot recruit in hopeful places. I mean, who would want to follow somebody that says: "Follow me; my vision is—if you're a female, follow me; my vision is, you have no rights"? Or, "If you disagree with my religious interpretations, you'll be whipped in the public square." So it's in our national interests.

Equally, if not more important, it is in our moral interests that we help people. I firmly believe—as I said earlier, I firmly believe in the admonition that to whom much is given, much is required. I believe that is a principle by which people should make decisions in their individual lives and for the collective conscience of the United States. It is in our moral interest that we help a brother and sister who's dying of AIDS. And by helping that soul, it really helps ourselves.

America's generosity has been prevalent throughout the decades. And every time America reaches out to help a struggling soul, we find that we're a better nation for it. And so my interest and my focus and my insistence upon results on the continent of Africa are based on those two premises.

The other thing, Edwin, I will tell you is that I've got a lot of resources—or we have a lot of resources at our disposal. And the idea of an entire generation of people dying because of HIV/AIDS troubled my heart. And I felt like America could do something about it. Fifty thousand people were receiving antiretroviral drugs when we first started PEPFAR. Today, 1,300,000 people are receiving antiretrovirals in a very short period of time.

And it's not enough. It's just a beginning. And so you say, "Why, Mr. President, do you feel that way?" It's because I couldn't live with myself if I didn't develop an effective strategy and call upon the American people to help. And the good news is, the American people have responded—$15 billion over 5. We're now going to double our commitment.

Equally important, other nations have stepped up. The G–8 has committed to match the U.S. So all of a sudden, the strategy—and most of these strategies, Edwin, are really based upon—oftentimes when you see human suffering, it's based upon something that affects your heart. And so that's why I've made the decisions I made.

Patience. You've been very patient so far.

Liberian Refugees in the United States

Q. Well, Mr. President, I would like to thank you for considering Liberia as one of the countries you are going to be visiting this time.

The President. Yes, ma'am.

Q. And the Government and the people of Liberia do appreciate all that you've done for us. Now, Mr. President, last year, your administration extended by 1 year the temporary protective status of hundreds of Liberians. Now what happens when you leave office?

The President. Yes.

Q. Is your Government considering anything permanent for them, like what most host countries did for Liberian refugees, integrating them locally, those who wanted to stay? And those who wanted to go back home, taking them back home? Because this might—it will definitely allow these Liberians to continue to contribute to the growth of the economy of the country and also support their families back home.

The President. Interesting; yes, thank you for that. I did extend TPS to Liberians here in America for, I think, 18 months. And there are no plans to make it permanent. I would hope that many of the Liberians who have come and been fine contributors here in America think about going home to help this young country get on its feet after unspeakable violence and terrible times.

You've got a great President, in my judgment. I gave her the National Medal of Freedom. After all, she's the first woman President on the continent of Africa. And she—you know, in my speech today, I said, Africa's greatest resource is not oils or diamonds or rubber, it's really people.

And so, my hope, of course, is that people that have been here trying to save themselves from the violence go help this young—not young, but this country get back on its feet.

Donaig.

Darfur and Chad

Q. Mr. President——

The President. What kind of name is that, Donaig?

Q. Actually, I'm French, but it's a Celtic name.

The President. Really?

Q. Yes.

The President. That's a pretty name.

Q. The situation in Darfur has always been a matter of great concern for you. U.N. officials say that the situation on the ground has been worsening over the last few days. There's also been very heavy fighting in Chad. Do you think there's a link between the two, between Darfur and Chad?

The President. I do, yes.

Q. And where do we go from there?

The President. I appreciate that. I do think there's a link, first of all, and I think that—let me just step back and say that the United States has called the situation in Darfur a genocide. And I made a decision early on that we would work through the United Nations to help expedite troops that would help alleve the suffering and provide some breathing space, hopefully, for the negotiations between rebel groups and the Government.

Unfortunately, the rebel groups that were one time three are now a multiple of three. And unfortunately, a government that could have made a difference early on in Khartoum chose not to do so.

So the United States continues to work with the international community to put pressure on the Sudanese Government. I have issued very harsh sanctions against individuals and Sudanese companies. I also did so against at least one rebel leader I'm aware of, because I wanted to send a signal that your behavior is causing there to be some consequences. We're continually working with other nations to get them to take the same tough approach—nations throughout the world. Some are reluctant to move; some are anxious to help.

In terms of the conditions on the ground, one thing the United States has done is, we're providing enormous amounts of aid and obviously are concerned as to whether or not that aid makes it into the camps.

Secondly is, I have told the folks at the United Nations that we would provide training and equipment to expedite the movement of troops. The question is, will the troops show up? One way I can help call the world to action is when I'm in Rwanda to thank the troops of Rwanda, the Kagame Government, for being so proactive.

I'm frustrated by the pace of development on the ground. I am not pleased that other nations—some other nations don't take necessary steps to pressure the Government. I am—I've named another Envoy to the Sudan, whose job it is to really help bring a negotiating framework that will work.

And again, I'll repeat to you, one of the unfortunate issues has been that the rebel groups have gone from 3 to more than 10—12, I think it is, or 18, if I'm not mistaken. And there needs to be the U.S. and others to pull the groups together so that there is somebody to negotiate with—that can speak with—more likely with a unified voice.

And I do believe that the instability in Darfur affects Chad and French interests. And I do thank the Sarkozy Government for being a responsible nation, rallying EU forces to come and provide some help.

And it's a very unfortunate, sad situation that is frustrating. And on the other hand, there are some hopeful moments, such as the fact that many in the world are providing help for the people in the camps. The problem is the people who are in the camps. And obviously, we'd like them to get back to their villages.

Scott.

Zimbabwe

Q. In your first trip to Africa, you embraced President Mbeki as the honest broker in Zimbabwe. It looks like President Mugabe is a month away from being reelected. So what now?

The President. Well, obviously, we're disappointed that the situation in Zimbabwe since my first trip has gotten worse. And it's very important for people to recognize types of government can affect the well-being and welfare of a country. Zimbabwe used to be a net exporter of food. Today, it is a net importer of food. Mr. Mugabe has ruined a country, and we have—we and frankly Great Britain have been the most vociferous advocates for change, and we still are advocates for change.

I was hoping that the South African Government would have been more proactive in its intercession to help the people of Zimbabwe. It's not anti anybody; it's pro people, and that has yet to happen, admittedly.

One more round here real quick. Yes, Jean.

U.S. Trade With Africa

Q. Thank you, Mr. President.

The President. Is that "Jean"?

Q. Jean Jonas. I will——

The President. Like they say "Juan"— [*laughter*]—where I'm from?

Q. Mr. President, I will recommend you, during your short visit to my country, to have a taste in our juicy, tasty, and nicely perfumed pineapples.

The President. Pineapples.

Q. Yes. And then you will figure out that it will be an opportunity for all the American people to have a taste—[*inaudible*].

The President. Yes, that's a smart move. That's good marketing. [*Laughter*] It's called a taste test. [*Laughter*]

Q. But yet, my country does not benefit much from——

The President. From AGOA?

Q. Yes.

The President. Why? Because fruits are not a part of the AGOA——

Administration official. Pineapples can be imported under AGOA.

The President. So then what we're going to have to do is, I'm going to have to talk to your President and point out the opportunities that pineapples are a part of

the AGOA trade list that can enter into the United States relatively duty free.

Q. Yes, but apart from the pineapple, we have so many things and so many products that can profit from the AGOA but do not——

The President. You need some export credit—I mean, not export credit, you need some help in developing industries that know how to export. Yes, I'll be glad to talk to the President about that. There are several ways the U.S. can help. Some grant money that encourages people to learn how to be an exporting company, microloans can also help. And so can OPIC, which is a way for people to get the capital necessary to be able to develop an infrastructure so that they can take the pineapple from the field, do whatever you're supposed to do, put it in a crate and ship it to the United States for sale—if you know how to market.

In other words, this is a—and so yes, we'd like to help enterprise. The whole purpose of our strategy, which is commerce, is much more effective than aid to governments. It's got a more lasting impact. And one of the things I'm going to do in Ghana is visit entrepreneurs that are taking advantage of marketplace access. And I'm confident I'm going to hear from leaders in the region saying: "That's fine; you're talking about nice things. And we like AGOA, but you've got to do something about your agriculture, because it provides a distinct disadvantage for our farmers."

And my answer is going to be, we're more than willing to do so, but we expect other partners in the world to do the same thing. We expect there to be fairness. And this is a tough issue to get all countries to agree to have equity when it comes to reducing our respective subsidies and tariffs, including African nations.

One of the things I point up to African leaders—point out to African leaders is that oftentimes it is virtually impossible to ship goods from one African country to the next because there are high intra-Africa tariffs and barriers to trade. And so it's a—trade is complicated, and we just want to be treated fairly in America. In order to get something passed, it has to be viewed as a fair and equitable transaction, and I believe we can achieve such a thing. I'm looking forward to that pineapple. [*Laughter*]

Yvonne.

Government Corruption/Millennium Challenge Corporation

Q. Mr. President, your Government has been supporting Tanzania address the issue of corruption as well as good governance through the MCC initiative and through the Threshold Program. And it is now been eligible to receive the funds, but what's going to happen once you step down to make sure what is being done—to make sure that it's going to be sustainable——

The President. That's a good question.

Q. ——it won't end with you.

The President. You're right; my Presidency does end. And that's one of the great things about American democracy: There will be a peaceful transfer of power. And yet I'm hopeful that we leave behind an institution such as the Millennium Challenge Corporation, which has a monitoring device that will more likely assure the people of Tanzania that today's anticorruption measures are for real and lasting.

It's a very interesting question. I mean, you know, today's concern about corruption may not be tomorrow's. I suspect any American President is going to be worried about corruption, particularly since we've changed how aid is granted in the first place. And so the fact that the Millennium Challenge exists will make it more likely future administrations will ask the very same questions we've asked.

Albert.

Democratic Republic of the Congo/Rwanda

Q. Mr. President——

The President. Your thing turned off there, by the way, Yvonne. It clicked off. I think yours did. Anyway, far be it for me to interfere with your——

Q. Mr. President, you will see when you visit Rwanda that 14 years later, after the genocide, Rwanda has incredibly developed. But for development in Rwanda, one of the things that are key—that is key is security. And when you started your first mandate, there was already a threat, and 8 years later, the threat is still there, Mr. President. What do you forecast for the future?

The President. I presume you're referring to those groups that exist——

Q. FDLR.

The President. ——in your neighbor.

Q. Yes. And which are even listed as terrorist organizations, even by the U.S.

The President. Right, right, right. We're working with President Kabila on a disarmament program. We've been very engaged diplomatically in the eastern part of the Congo. I've talked to him about this personally. Our diplomats out of the State Department and on the ground are very actively engaged in getting people to honor the agreement. And I fully understand the issue and the concerns.

Q. Because we don't want to be dragged again——

The President. Back into the—no, no question. First of all, the amazing thing is, is that the recovery of your country. And I'm really looking forward to going. President Kagame has been a very strong leader in the right sense of the word. To be able to come from where you were to where you are today is pretty remarkable. I think I said Rwanda is one of the fastest growing economies in the world, if I'm not mistaken. Now, obviously, that's really good news, and, of course, one of the things that's going to matter is that the people benefit from that economic vitality and growth.

But you're right, it's one of the ongoing issues that I talked about in my speech today, and the reason I did so, is I wanted the President and the people of Rwanda to know that we understand the seriousness of this issue; that nobody wants a replay of a very difficult—very terrible period in your history.

Edwin.

Africa-U.S. Relations/Trade

Q. Yes, Mr. President, your planned visit to Africa shows that the continent has become important to you and your country. Well, that's why the administration has set up AFRICOM for development but not for war——

The President. Africa for development but not for war.

Q. War, war fighting, and then the AGOA, Millennium Challenge Account, all for development—but to the ordinary African, he or she can see these things clearly or feel the impact well, maybe because of the gravity of the situation or poverty. And one way you made mention of it is to trade, not just aid. But we have problem with the African culture produced cotton and all that, because of the subsidies here, the effects are depressed prices back in Africa. What's official—what are you doing to solve this problem of subsidies? Is delicate issue.

The President. Well, thank you. First of all, if you're a mother who's worried about a child dying of malaria, and you see a net provided by an American child, then all of a sudden, the—you get a direct connection between the hearts of Americans and your life. So, in other words, you asked me whether—how does the average person sometimes feel the effects of American commitment to the continent?

And my answer to you—and I'll answer the subsidy thing—but my answer to you is, first of all, it's a very important question, because oftentimes, years ago, aid would never make it beyond the palaces. They would kind of end up in a handful of people's pockets. And our program, Edwin, is really aimed at focusing on individuals. If you believe every human life has dignity, therefore, your programs ought to reflect that concept. And the way you do that is you make sure that the aid gets to the people. In this case, we're focusing on

problems that affect the people most directly.

And so, at Christmas, I got a—a couple years ago, I got nets given in my name or in Laura's name to families on the continent of Africa. I'll never know who they were, and they probably don't know who I am, but the idea that an American family decided to spend money on a Christmas gift aimed at helping a stranger is really an important part of an effective foreign aid policy.

Secondly, our AIDS initiative works very closely with the leaders to design programs that meet the needs of the country—not meet our needs but meet your needs. But the other thing that comes with the AIDS program is a great outpouring of faith-based groups from America. There are thousands of my citizens, Edwin, that would—that long to spend time in parts of Africa delivering help to a total stranger. Other countries—I'm sure that happens, but I happen to say that this is the greatest strength of America.

And so there will be, hopefully, somebody in a village in Ghana that runs into one of these missionaries on a mission of love, that will see the direct help of an AIDS program or a malaria program and education benefits. It may not be that somebody recognizes that a teacher has been trained by U.S. dollars, but our policy is to—we're more focused on the person learning. Maybe there will be a benefit to the United States, a direct benefit, where somebody says, wow, this is great; America did this. On the other hand, our focus is more on making sure that the child learns to read in the first place, because our overall objective is a hopeful society and a peaceful society.

To subsidies, I fully understand the angst about the leadership—by the leadership on U.S. subsidies. And I've said I'm more than willing to—on the Doha round—by the most effective place—first of all, AGOA has helped address that to a certain extent. One way it has—because it's opened up markets. On the other hand, it has not made your farmers feel more comfortable because of the—in their view, that the United States farming is not only efficient, but there's a subsidy to make it even more competitive. I understand that.

In order to deal with this issue, however, there has to be full reciprocity by developing—large developing and developed nations. In other words, the United States farmer is willing to take less of a subsidy if his—can be assured that his product will get a fair hearing in somebody else's market—particularly those that can afford to buy crops on a large scale—and that's not the case. Same thing if we reduce our subsidies on agriculture; we expect other nations to be more opening to manufactured goods and services.

And it's a very complex issue, but it's one that we're trying to work through. And hopefully, if we can get a successful Doha round, your very question will be answered in a way that is hopeful to the farmers there in Ghana.

Patience. Patience, where were you educated? I know I'm not supposed to be asking questions, but—[*laughter*].

Growth of Liberia

Q. Some part of my education was in Nigeria.

The President. Oh, really? Interesting.

Q. Yes. Well, sir——

The President. Are you living——

Q. I'm living in Liberia right now.

The President. Are you? Good. How's it going?

Q. Good.

The President. Is the capital, like, improving——

Q. Well, we're sort of, like, accelerating——

The President. This is off the record, right? [*Laughter*]

Q. ——road construction work, so you can have a safe——

The President. Well, you don't need to worry about me. [*Laughter*]

Q. We're rushing up everything so you can——

The President. You're building things because of my arrival? Maybe I ought to come every other month. [*Laughter*]

Q. Okay. [*Laughter*]

The President. Is there noticeable construction now——

Q. Yes.

The President. ——besides my trip?

Q. Yes. Yes. From 2003 to date, there has been an increase in road construction. We've got infrastructure——

The President. Can you see it, a big difference?

Q. Yes, you can. Yes, you can.

The President. Are people feeling safer?

Q. Yes. People are feeling safer. Those on the ground are feeling safer.

The President. Particularly in the city?

Q. But, like, for Liberians here in America—I have been talking to most of them—for them to go back home and join in this young democracy.

The President. Thank you.

Security Situation in Africa

Q. And some of the things they've been saying is the security. And some of them went back, after the first bout of war and were forced to come back. Now they keep saying security, and each time, I say, we have the U.N. mission down there. But right now the U.N. mission is gradually drawing down faces.

Now, will your Government consider establishing AFRICOM in Liberia, which would consolidate security there? You know, like a couple of the subregions bring in investment into Liberia, which is what mostly Liberia needs right now.

The President. First of all, AFRICOM is a brand new concept aimed at strengthening nations' capacities to deal with trafficking or terror, but also to help nations develop forces capable of doing the peace-keeping that unfortunately too often is needed on the continent.

Secondly, we are in the process of evaluating exactly how AFRICOM will work. Now, because it's a new concept, it was a brand new military-type command—and, by the way, it's going to be more than just military; there will be a State Department component with it, which makes it a very interesting issue. And so we're in the process of determining where and how AFRICOM should be situated on the continent. I'm not avoiding—I guess I'm avoiding your answer, but I don't mean to be avoiding it. I'm just telling you exactly where we are in the process.

And obviously, if there is going to be a physical presence on the continent of Africa in the forms of a headquarters that you just described, obviously, we would seriously consider Liberia. Liberia is a friend. The President has made it abundantly clear to me that she would like us to seriously consider Liberia, and I have told her I would.

I just want to make sure people understand that the makeup and the construct of AFRICOM is still really being thought through, because, as I mentioned to you, this is not—I mean, when you think of, you know, U.S. command structures, you think military, which is fine. But this is a different military mission than Central Command, for example. And as I told you, there's going to be a strong State Department component with it, and we're in the process of making sure we understand what that integration means and then evaluating if and where the facilities will be built. It's on my radar screen.

Donaig.

Kenya's Presidential Election

Q. About Kenya, Mr. President, there's been a month-and-a-half now of continuous ethnic violence. Who won this election? And what should be done to stop this violence?

The President. Yes. I don't think we can say we're certain to who won the election. That's part of the problem. Secondly, there is a way forward, which is for the parties to come together in good faith and work out a way forward until there are new elections, the date of which would be determined by the parties.

I don't think the United States ought to go in, or anybody else, to say, "You must have an election now." But I do think we can go in and help Kofi Annan convince the parties to work together in a cooperative way so that the people can see there's a way forward. And to this end, when I'm in Rwanda, I'm going to ask Condi to go over to Kenya and sit down with the leaders in Kenya to see if we can't help Kofi advance the—Kofi Annan advance the way forward.

Situation in the Horn of Africa

Q. One of the U.S. counterterrorism efforts in Africa has centered on the Horn. Any concern about the continuing instability in Somalia and, again, worsening relations between Ethiopia and Eritrea, the impact that that has not only on stability on the Horn but counterterrorism efforts?

The President. Yes, we're concerned about instability anywhere, really, but instability is what—and confusion and chaos and fear is the conditions under which a group like Al Qaida can thrive. That's why they like to kill people, innocent people, to create doubt about existing security, to create fear among the population. So any time you see that kind of instability, we're deeply concerned about it.

Secondly, there have been Al Qaida—some Al Qaida operating out of Somalia, and therefore, when you know some Al Qaida have been in and out of Somalia and there is some chaos and confusion, the conclusion is, we better be worried about it and do something about it. And we are. We've got cooperative arrangements in the region that will make it more likely for us to be able to provide protections for the people in the region and ourself.

In terms of—yes, and we're also conscious of Ethiopia and Eritrea's border dispute. And I'm constantly talking to Condi about making sure that we're on top of the situation as the best we can make a positive contribution. I feel pretty comfortable that the State Department and our Embassies are fully aware of the issues on the border and are making sure that the respective leaders understand the position of the U.S., which is to solve this thing through mediation and not stack up the troops to the point where they get—where some spark ignites some kind of border dispute.

But the Horn is an area of deep concern for the U.S. We actually happen to have a base there as well, in Djibouti. And we take the issues there seriously and are very engaged with it on a regular basis.

Okay, here's what we're going to do: We'll get a picture, unless you don't want one. [*Laughter*]

NOTE: The interview began at 1:18 p.m. in the Roosevelt Room at the White House. In his remarks, the President referred to President Thomas Yayi Boni of Benin; President Jakaya Mrisho Kikwete of Tanzania; President Ellen Johnson Sirleaf of Liberia; President Paul Kagame of Rwanda; Special Envoy to Sudan Richard S. Williamson; President Nicolas Sarkozy of France; President Robert Mugabe of Zimbabwe; President John Agyekum Kufuor of Ghana; President Joseph Kabila of the Democratic Republic of the Congo; and former Secretary-General Kofi Annan of the United Nations. A reporter referred to President Thabo Mvuyelwa Mbeki of South Africa. The transcript was released by the Office of the Press Secretary on February 15. A tape was not available for verification of the content of this interview.

Remarks Following a Meeting With Congressional Leaders
February 15, 2008

This morning I spoke to the president of Northern Illinois University. I told the president that a lot of folks today will be praying for the families of the victims and for the Northern Illinois University community. Obviously a tragic situation on that campus, and I ask our fellow citizens to offer their blessings, blessings of comfort and blessings of strength.

We also just discussed a serious problem facing our country, and that is the fact that House leaders blocked a good piece of legislation that would give our intelligence community the tools they need to protect America from a terrorist attack.

The American citizens must understand—clearly understand that there is still a threat on the homeland, there's still an enemy which would like to do us harm,

and that we've got to give our professionals the tools they need to be able to figure out what the enemy is up to so that we can stop it.

The Senate passed a good bipartisan bill that makes sure our intelligence community has the tools necessary to protect America from this real threat. And I want to thank you all and thank the Democrats in the United States Senate who worked closely with Mitch and John to get a strong piece of legislation, with a 68-vote majority, out of the Senate.

This bill comes to the House of Representatives, and it was blocked. And by blocking this piece of legislation, our country is more in danger of an attack. By not giving the professionals the tools they need, it's going to be a lot harder to do the job we need to be able to defend America.

People say, "Oh, it doesn't matter if this law hasn't been renewed." It does matter; it matters for a variety of reasons. It matters because the intelligence officials won't have tools necessary to get as much information as we possibly can to protect you. And it matters because these telephone companies that work collaboratively with us to protect the American people are afraid they're going to get sued. And the American people have got to understand, these lawsuits make it harder for us to convince people to help protect you. And so by blocking this good piece of legislation, our professionals tell me that they don't have all the tools they need to do their job.

And so now the House and Senate are off on a 12-day recess without getting the people's business done. And when they come back from that 12-day recess, the House leaders must understand that the decision they made to block good legislation has made it harder for us to protect you, the American people, and we expect them to get a good bill to my desk—which is the Senate bill—as soon as possible.

Thank you.

NOTE: The President spoke at 8:55 a.m. in the Oval Office at the White House. In his remarks, he referred to John G. Peters, president, Northern Illinois University. He also referred to H.R. 3773.

Remarks Following a Meeting With Secretary-General Ban Ki-moon of the United Nations
February 15, 2008

President Bush. Mr. Secretary-General, welcome back to the White House. Thank you for your efforts to make the United Nations a constructive force for good.

I appreciate your tireless work to help solve some of the real humanitarian crises that we face, such as the crises in Sudan, the issues in Burma. I appreciate very much your leadership when it came to Kenya, and thank you for going to support former Secretary-General Annan.

I thank you very much for the leadership that you've shown in Iraq. This young democracy is beginning to gain confidence and make progress, and the U.N. mission there has been very constructive.

I appreciate very much your desire to help the poor and feed the hungry. And on my trip to Africa this week, that's exactly the same message I'll be taking, that the American people are a compassionate people and decent people who want to help moms with—deal with malaria or families

deal with HIV/AIDS, the need to feed the hungry.

So I'm honored you're here. I appreciate your vision. And thank you for your leadership and your friendship.

Secretary-General Ban. Thank you very much. Thank you very much, Mr. President and ladies and gentlemen. Thank you very much for your warm welcome and strong support you have shown me during last 1 year while I was carrying out my duty as Secretary-General. It has been instrumental and very much appreciated.

I've been trying my best to make United Nations more trust-proof, transparent, and accountable and more effective organization. This effort will continue. At the same time, with your strong support and international community, I've been doing my best to address all these regional country issues, starting from the situation in Darfur, Lebanon, Myanmar, and also Kenya. There are so many problems that challenge at this time. I'm committed to address these issues.

At the same time, I've been able to again raise awareness and the political will in addressing global challenges such as climate change. And I need your strong support as we are going through this year, a midpoint year, to realize Millennium Development Goals by 2015. We are going to focus on food situation and agriculture, education, health, and all this, statistical systems, infrastructure of Africa.

In that regard, your visit to African states at this time will be very important and historic. I hope you will be able to discuss with African leaders on how to realize this Millennium Development Goals, how to help people overcome abject poverty and sanitation, access to educational opportunities.

In that regard, I wish you all the best, that this is a very great opportunities. And it would be also very much important for international community to sustain the momentum established in Bali, December last year, in climate change. I'm going to build up on this Bali roadmap so that we will be able to achieve this globally accepted framework, replacing this Kyoto Protocol.

The United States is the country with the most innovative for technology and financing capacities. I count on your leadership and active participation. I do appreciate your constructive engagement in this, starting from high-level meeting September last year and the major economies meeting in September in Washington and in Honolulu this year. I count on your leadership.

All in all, I need your strong support, because I believe a stronger partnership between the United Nations and United States is the crucial, the important element in carrying out this—my duty as Secretary-General and also making United Nations organization more strengthened in carrying out common challenges we share together.

Thank you very much, Mr. President.

President Bush. Thank you, sir. Yes, thank you.

NOTE: The President spoke at 10:09 a.m. in the Oval Office at the White House.

Remarks on Accepting the Grand Cross of the National Order of Benin in Cotonou, Benin
February 16, 2008

Mr. President, thank you. Laura and I are honored to be with you and the First Lady. I gratefully accept this on behalf of the American people. I stand here by your side as a friend, a believer in your vision, and a partner in your willingness to confront the disease and poverty and—that affect mankind.

We would not be standing here if you and your Government was not committed to your people. You mentioned some of the dollar—money we're spending with you, but those dollars come with great compassion from the American people. We care when we see suffering. We believe we're all children of God. And so it's a great honor to accept this award, and the American people send their blessings.

NOTE: The President spoke at 8:28 a.m. at Cadjehoun International Airport. In his remarks, he referred to President Thomas Yayi Boni of Benin and his wife Chantal de Souza Yayi.

The President's News Conference With President Thomas Yayi Boni of Benin in Cotonou
February 16, 2008

President Yayi. Ladies and gentlemen, journalists, on this day, Saturday, February 16, 2008, His Excellency Mr. George W. Bush, President of the United States of America, and his wife Laura Bush have honored my Government and the Beninese people as a whole by deciding to conduct a working visit as part of his second trip to Africa. This visit is a follow-up to the meetings that I had at the White House on December 14, 2006, as part of my working trip to the United States.

Today President Bush and myself have had very fruitful exchanges during our bilateral meeting, as well as during an expanded working meeting with our staffs, in order to review the excellent relations of cooperation which unite the United States and my country, Benin. As you know, during his two terms in office, President Bush showed great concern for Africa, its well-being, and of the development of its people.

I should only mention as evidence the various initiatives on behalf of children, youth, and women, such as the initiative against malaria, the emergency plan against AIDS, the initiative for justice and empowerment of women. For all of these initiatives, Benin was selected by the Government of the United States. Likewise, my country is also benefiting from the President's Millennium Challenge Account initiative, as well as the AGOA, whose ultimate goal is to create the conditions favorable to economic growth on a sustainable manner in order to reduce poverty and build an emerging nation.

During our discussions, we talked about all of the issues of cooperation as well as other international topics, such as settlement of conflicts in Africa, Benin's participation in peacekeeping operations, as well as the reform of the United Nations system.

On behalf of the people of Benin, of my wife, and myself, I'd like to express most sincerely my friendship and all my gratitude to President Bush and to Mrs. Laura Bush for this stay filled with cordiality and conviviality. On behalf of the Beninese people, I would like to thank—wish you a good stay in Africa, Mr. President. Thank you very much.

President Bush. Thank you, sir. Thank you for your friendship; thank you for your vision. Madam, thank you for your warm hospitality. Laura and I are honored to be here.

You know, we've come to talk about our mutual interests, but we would not be talking about this mutual interest if, Mr. President, you didn't believe in certain truths and certain values: that all human beings have dignity; that people need a government that responds to their desires and wishes.

And so I come bringing the warm friendship of the people of the United States and reaffirm our desire to help strengthen your democracy by helping the people here realize their God-given talents.

We spent a little time talking about the malaria initiative and your deep desire to make sure every child has got a mosquito net to protect them. I mean, we can save lives with an aggressive, comprehensive strategy. And that's exactly what you're putting in place here in Benin. And I want to thank you for your leadership on that very important issue. We will continue to help you.

I thank very much your focus on education. You know what I know, that a nation can't be a hopeful place unless its youth are educated. So I'm very pleased to be working with you to expand educational opportunities for the people of your country. Through the African Education Initiative, we've helped train about 30,000 teachers and administrators here. We've provided about 1 million textbooks and teaching guides and workbooks. We've helped young girls get a good education. And we're going to spend another $6 million on these efforts, only because you are focused and your Government is dedicated to making sure the money is spent well and wisely. And so I want to thank you for that, sir.

I appreciate very much your mentioning of the Millennium Challenge Account. That account—those monies are given to countries which fight corruption, which invest in the health and education of their children, which believe in marketplace economies. And that's what you do. And that's why we were more than pleased to provide $307 million over a 5-year period; it's because of your leadership, the commitment of your Government to be a trustworthy partner for the people of Benin. This compact is—should touch the lives of about 5 million people here in Benin and help thousands grow out of poverty.

We also really appreciate the fact that your fight against corruption is visible and easy for the people to see. I mean, after all, you've put auditors in place to make sure the people's money is spent well; that, you know, in so doing—and this is such a good lesson.

And one of the reasons I've come here, sir, is because leaders around the world have got to understand that the United States wants to partner with leaders and the people, but we're not going to do so with people that steal money, pure and simple. And the transparency that you put in place and the strong audits that you've got in your country should give the people of your nation great confidence in your Government, because it gives me confidence to stand side by side with you here.

And so I appreciate your conversation we had. You're right, we spent a lot of time talking about a variety of issues. And

I'm so honored that you would receive us in such a graceful way. Thank you very— *merci.* [*Laughter*]

A couple of questions? Yes, you think? Maybe? Okay.

President's Visit to Benin

Q. Hi, I'm from Beninese television. Mr. President, during this first visit to Benin—this is a first for you, but cooperation between our two countries is been going on for 47 years, but yet it's the first time that we host a President of your great country in our country. So in history, this has been written, but given what has just occurred, is this a diplomatic coup or is it truly a change in the relationships between the—Benin and the United States? Is this a stunt?

President Bush. Well, I can give you my perspective, and of course, the President will give you his. First of all, I am the first President to have come to Benin. I am here to really confirm to the people of Benin and the people on the continent of Africa that the United States is committed to helping improve people's lives.

And I also have come to a country like Benin to remind our fellow citizens that it's in our national interest to support the people of nations, even though we may not have had relations with them in the past, particularly those nations in which the leadership and the government makes a firm commitment to the investment in its people as well as fighting corruption and marketplace economies. And I'm—my trip here is a way to remind future Presidents and future Congresses that it is in the national interest and in the moral interest of the United States of America to help people.

I reject some of the old-style type of grants, which basically said, let's feel better; we'll just give some money out. We believe that rather than making ourselves feel better, that our money ought to make the people of a particular country feel better about their government. And that's why the Millennium Challenge Account, for example, has got certain criterion. And your Government has met those criterion.

And I would say that it's been a change of relationship. But it's been a change of relationship because the leader have changed attitude toward how government ought to relate to its people. And so, Mr. President, I'm proud to be the first President to be in Benin, and I want to thank you for extending me that invitation.

President Yayi. I believe that perhaps for the journalists who are coming from abroad or my compatriots who are also journalists, I think that you know well my position on this issue. And I must tell you that the visit of the President is a symbol. Perhaps it's a signal to us, because as he just said, he conveys who at least—he is attached to virtue. Virtue means a lot to him. He is here to support the countries which strive to be virtuous, the governments which accept to be working on behalf of their people, to serve their people, especially as part of a clear vision where we say, where are we going? Where are we leading our people?

And we were clear about that today. We want to move towards prosperity and sharing—prosperity, sharing, that means using the resources, the work, economic activity, and so on. Of course, this vision cannot be achieved unless you have the behaviors that—which you have defined, namely to ensure that everything that which stains our democracy, which is the—[*inaudible*]—of the people. Everything that would stains democracy will be suppressed—I should say, eliminated—which is why we want to ensure that our democracy will honor us, ensure education, access to water, to roads, to electricity, telephone, to infrastructure—all of these things without which you cannot create jobs and distribute income.

And we identified these ailments that harm democracy, first and foremost, corruption, Mr. President. And behalf of the Beninese people, I would like to reassure you once again—I've did it already last month when I was visiting the United States at the White House—I told you that the people have already defined a mission. The mission that we have defined for ourselves is to guarantee that we can ensure good governance, have the best management of the affairs of a state. And it's at this price that we'll be able to accelerate this march towards prosperity.

So, quite naturally for us, the visit of President Bush is a strong signal, which comforts us in our beliefs. It's an extra support, an extra encouragement in this direction to ensure that this vision will realize itself as quickly as possible for the well-being of our people. And in this regard, during the talks that we have just had, the President himself encouraged us by saying, go ahead, move forward. Do not hesitate. Don't distance yourself from the people. We Americans have to support you, but the issue, the initiatives that we've started in this—in the United States, namely the support against malaria, of course, the fight against HIV/AIDS, the emergency plan against HIV/AIDS, the MCA—because all of these initiatives today which reinforce U.S.—the United States position to help the poor and to fight against poverty.

So I do believe this is a good starting point which takes into account the needs of the 21st century.

President Bush. Oh, I'm sorry. Excuse me.

Situations in Darfur and Kenya/U.S. Foreign Aid

Q. [*Inaudible*]—while it's obvious that Benin is a hopeful example of progress on the African Continent, there are a number of other examples, unfortunately, of violence and strife in other places, most notably Kenya. And I'm wondering, Mr. President, how you go about deciding how best to spend your time here on the continent? It seems a bit of a contrast when there are some hopeful signs, but there obviously are a number of other examples where things are frankly in a very tough position right now.

President Bush. Yes. I've always found, Kevin [Kevin Corke, NBC News], that when you herald success, it's—it helps others realize what is possible. And you're right, there's no question, Sudan is a very difficult situation, which we have labeled a genocide and which we're sanctioning some, rallying others to provide aid in the hopes that there will be a robust U.N. force in Darfur that will help relieve the suffering.

As I said in my speech the other day, that the United States will help facilitate the movement of the force. As I told Ban Ki-moon yesterday in the White House, we want to help you, but you must make sure we have a robust force ready to go.

Secondly, Kenya is an issue, and—we're going to be in the neighborhood in Kenya—in Kenya's neighborhood. And that's why I'm sending Secretary Rice there to help the Kofi Annan initiative, all aimed at having a clear message that there be no violence and that there ought to be a power-sharing agreement. You know, this is—but this is a large place with a lot of nations, and no question, not everything is perfect.

On the other hand, there's a lot of great success stories, and the United States is pleased to be involved with those success stories. I want to remind you, Kevin, that when I first became President, there was about 50,000 people receiving antiretroviral drugs to deal with HIV/AIDS on the continent of Africa. Today, there's about a million three just from the PEPFAR initiative. In other words, there's great progress being made. And there's a lot more work to be done. One of the reasons I've come on this trip is to say, look at the successes we've had—"we," by the way, is not American successes, these are joint successes—and look at the work that needs to be done.

You know, the malaria initiative is an initiative that is very dear to my heart and Laura's heart, because we weep when we think about little babies needlessly dying. And yet now we've got a President who

is committed to distributing a net to every child under 5 years old. But there are still a lot of places that need work on malaria. And so the reason I go to countries in which we've got good relations, where the leaders are making good choices, is to send a clear signal to others that we want to help you, but you've got to have good leadership, you've got to make right choices, and you've got to set a strategy in place in order to benefit your people.

I'm excited to be here, I really am. You know, it's my second trip as President; Laura's fifth trip as First Lady. I hope that sends a clear commitment that the United States—a clear signal that the United States is committed. We're committed for national security reasons, and that being that these ideologues that murder the innocent people can only attract people when there's hopelessness. They have no clear vision that's positive. But we're also committed for moral reasons. As I told you and told people all the time, to whom much is given, much is required. Well, we've been given a lot in the United States, and I believe we're required to help brothers and sisters in need.

And so thank you for your question, and thanks for traveling with us. This is a great trip.

U.S. Trade Policy

Q. Hi, I'm from the Beninese national radio. Mr. President, since you have been in power, you have done trips to the United States and Benin. Last time, you discussed with President Bush of the issue of cotton, American subsidies to their farmers in that country. And we saw with which enthusiasm you tackled this issue because, indeed, cotton is one of the pillars of the Beninese economy. So based on this visit, and up until today, have these things evolved? But is the issue of cotton still a sensitive issue?

President Yayi. I must confess that when we started these discussions, we on purpose did not talk about this, because the President asked us, "What is your country ailing of?" And I didn't bring up cotton. It's he himself who asked: "What about this cotton business? What's going on with cotton?" And I thanked him profusely for that.

So, of course, he shared his vision with us, and he is encouraging us to diversify the sources of solutions to the problem that we have today, namely the cotton industry. He is aware that in our subregion—when we, for example, look at West Africa, and you add Central Africa to that, and a— one citizen out of two lives out of that industry. So I do believe of the workers in Burkina Faso and Mali, Niger and Togo, elsewhere, Senegal—and quite naturally, I think of my compatriots who commit themselves everyday that gives them into this line of business.

So, Mr. President, I was expecting that the press would indeed bring up this issue because anybody who decides to fight on behalf of Africa against poverty cannot be— allow the cotton industry to deteriorate or to disappear. I do believe that there's a strong correlation between the health of the cotton industry and the prosperity of our countries.

So you indeed gave us some advice. I could repeat some of this advice. He said, "Do everything you can to bring added value." That's his first piece of advice. And he asked us to translate this into a vision, and this vision must also be part of a political vision and of a strategy. And I answered him, "You are perfectly right." We ourselves—this was the direction that we have chosen for ourselves. But we are limited by various constraints, such as the shortcomings of some of our infrastructure, which are indispensable.

For example, electricity: I even told him that electricity for the textile industry is basically what blood is for the human body. That we do have basic issues, basic shortcomings, in terms of energy, electricity, water, and so on, truly, and if you could help us in that regard. And he told me

to—recommend to talk to OPIC, in terms of the United States, and to create a partnership between the private and public sectors to allow us to move ahead.

And I reassured him, and I told him that this issue is being discussed within the communities that we have—ECOWAS—so that we can indeed come up with a subregional strategy, because our countries, taken alone, cannot do anything by themself, especially when you look at the difference in the Asian countries, in terms of their textile agencies. And practically no country in the world can compete against them.

So of course, the President did not fail to follow up this question that I asked him when I was at the White House, namely the issue of subsidies. I think you are, indeed, right. Of course, he believed that this was an American issue, and that it's not even at his level that the core issue is being discussed—it's at the Senate; it's in Congress—and that in reality, his concern is to ensure that these efforts towards other countries—in order to resume the Doha cycle. It's through that Doha cycle that we'll come up with a solution. And he said, "If Europe moves, if China moves, and if everyone else moves this, America moves." And I said, "You're absolutely right." But there's one other issue, because when we talked about—with European leaders, they told me, "Well, if America moves, we Europeans, we will move ourselves." So—and he says, "Now, if Europe moves, well, we will move."

So since the America is the great America, I do hope that great America will move, because I wrote to him when this issue was being debated in Congress. And I told him, truly, please intervene personally to ensure that the United States will indeed be the first to make the move.

So today I applaud the fact that he did remember my request, but he did say you can count on him personally, on great America, to ensure that the Doha round will resume. And of course, we will come up with a solution to this—of world governance—to ensure that international trade can truly help the development of the poorest countries, of which we are.

So that's where we are. That's in the update. I would like to thank him very much, because he was the first one, personally, to ask this question.

President Bush. Yes, I brought it up because it was on his mind. And look, the way to solve this issue is for the Doha round to succeed. And the United States has made moves on agricultural subsidies at the—during the negotiations. As a matter of fact, the talks were stalled earlier in my Presidency, and I gave a speech that said, we're going to move on subsidies, and we expect others to, but we'll take the first step—and have.

And so we'll see what happens. These are serious negotiations, but our attitude is, is that we're willing to reduce agricultural subsidies. We just want to have access to people's markets, just like they've got to our markets. And I told the President I was fairly optimistic that we can succeed with the Doha round, and we'll keep working it.

I also said that commodities—whether the United States has subsidies or not, commodities—cotton can be overproduced. There's a lot of cotton producers. And so the best way to deal with commodity swings is to be a value-added processor; take the cotton and convert it into a product people want. And that's why we got into the discussion about electricity needs and, you know, is there investment capital available. And now it's in Washington, DC, that OPIC has got some expanded programs that he ought to look into. So it was a good discussion.

Ann [Ann Compton, ABC News].

U.S. Role in Africa/Situation in Darfur

Q. What specifically do you expect to see coming out of Secretary Rice's visit in Kenya for a few hours on Monday? How much can get done on Monday?

And for both of you, at what point does it take more active intervention by an American President in some of the trouble spots here in Africa?

President Bush. Well, first, you know, I've been very active, in this sense: Every time I meet with a world leader that could affect the outcome of a particular issue, I bring it up and expect there to be, you know, focus and concrete action. For example, I've spent a fair amount of time with Hu Jintao on Darfur, talking about the need for us to work collaboratively on Darfur, same in Burma. In other words, what—these meetings give me an opportunity to talk about ways forward in trouble spots.

In terms of Condi's visit, I will—the key is, is that the leaders hear from her firsthand U.S. desires to see that there be no violence and that there be a power-sharing agreement that will help this nation resolve its difficulties. That's what diplomacy is, and we've been very active on all fronts. Ours—after all, back to Darfur, ours is the first and probably only nation that's declared it a genocide.

And you know, I had a tough decision to make early on, and that is whether to send troops into Darfur. And I think I've discussed this with you all before, that I made the decision not to, upon the recommendation of a lot of the groups involved in Darfur as well as other folks. I've listened very carefully to their—whether we should or shouldn't, but once you make that decision, then there's not many other avenues except for the United Nations and the peacekeeping forces. And that's where we spend a lot of time and energy trying to get there to be an effective response.

The African Union stepped forward initially. And one of the reasons I'm going to Rwanda is to thank President Kagame for his strong efforts in Darfur as a—as one of the real leaders in providing peacekeepers.

But we've been plenty active on these issues. And we'll continue to be active on these issues because they're important issues for the U.S. security and for our interests.

Well, Mr. President, thank you. Like, press conference over. [*Laughter*]

NOTE: The President's news conference began at 9:59 a.m. at Cadjehoun Inter-national Airport. In his remarks, he referred to Chantal de Souza Yayi, wife of President Yayi; Secretary-General Ban Ki-moon and former Secretary-General Kofi Annan of the United Nations; President Hu Jintao of China; and President Paul Kagame of Rwanda. President Yayi and some reporters spoke in French, and their remarks were translated by an interpreter.

The President's Radio Address
February 16, 2008

Good morning. At the stroke of midnight tonight, a vital intelligence law that is helping protect our Nation will expire. Congress had the power to prevent this from happening, but chose not to.

The Senate passed a good bill that would have given our intelligence professionals the tools they need to keep us safe. But leaders in the House of Representatives blocked a House vote on the Senate bill and then left on a 10-day recess.

Some congressional leaders claim that this will not affect our security. They are wrong. Because Congress failed to act, it will be harder for our Government to keep you safe from terrorist attack. At midnight, the Attorney General and the Director of National Intelligence will be stripped of their power to authorize new surveillance against terrorist threats abroad. This means that as terrorists change their tactics to avoid our surveillance, we may not have the tools we need to continue tracking them, and we may lose a vital lead that could prevent an attack on America.

In addition, Congress has put intelligence activities at risk even when the terrorists don't change tactics. By failing to act, Congress has created a question about whether private sector companies who assist in our efforts to defend you from the terrorists could be sued for doing the right thing.

Now, these companies will be increasingly reluctant to provide this vital cooperation because of their uncertainty about the law and fear of being sued by class-action trial lawyers.

For 6 months, I urged Congress to take action to ensure this dangerous situation did not come to pass. I even signed a 2-week extension of the existing law because Members of Congress said they would use that time to work out their differences. The Senate used this time productively and passed a good bill with a strong, bipartisan supermajority of 68 votes. Republicans and Democrats came together on legislation to ensure that we could effectively monitor those seeking to harm our people. And they voted to provide fair and just liability protection for companies that assisted in efforts to protect America after the attacks of 9/11.

The Senate sent this bill to the House for its approval. It was clear that if given a vote, the bill would have passed the House with a bipartisan majority. I made every effort to work with the House to secure passage of this law. I even offered to delay my trip to Africa if we could come together and enact a good bill. But House leaders refused to let the bill come to a vote. Instead, the House held partisan votes that do nothing to keep our country safer.

217

House leaders chose politics over protecting the country, and our country is at greater risk as a result.

House leaders have no excuse for this failure. They knew all along that this deadline was approaching because they set it themselves. My administration will take every step within our power to minimize the damage caused by the House's irresponsible behavior. Yet it is still urgent that Congress act. The Senate has shown the way by approving a good, bipartisan bill. The House must pass that bill as soon as they return to Washington from their latest recess.

At this moment, somewhere in the world, terrorists are planning a new attack on America, and Congress has no higher responsibility than ensuring we have the tools to stop them.

Thank you for listening.

NOTE: The address was recorded at 11:45 a.m. on February 15 in the Cabinet Room at the White House for broadcast at 10:06 a.m., e.d.t., on February 16. The transcript was made available by the Office of the Press Secretary on February 15, but was embargoed for release until the broadcast. Due to the 6-hour time difference, the address was broadcast after the President's remarks in Benin. The Office of the Press Secretary also released a Spanish language transcript of this address.

The President's News Conference With President Jakaya Mrisho Kikwete of Tanzania in Dar es Salaam, Tanzania
February 17, 2008

President Kikwete. Mr. President, welcome. I stand before you with a deep sense of gratitude and satisfaction to once again welcome you, Mr. President, and your entire delegation to our dear country, Tanzania. The outpouring of warmth and affection from the people of Tanzania that you have witnessed since your arrival is a genuine reflection of what we feel towards you and towards the American people.

Welcome, Your Excellency, and your great wife Madam Laura Bush, as enduring partners for our empowerment as we struggle to pull ourselves to prosperity and back from backwardness and undevelopment, infested by poverty, disease, and deprivation of basic social and economic services. We welcome you, Mr. President, as a supportive and understanding partner as we take the necessary measures to promote democracy, human rights, and good governance. You are a dependable partner, indeed, in the pursuit of ensuring national, as well as regional, peace and stability in the African Continent.

Mr. President, you have shown great compassion for Africa and its people. You have personally reached out using different initiatives, instruments, and moral leadership to support Africa's efforts to improve governance, to fight poverty, to seek shared prosperity, to resolve conflict, to improve security, and jointly to fight the scourge of terrorism. Tanzania has been and is committed and poised to continue being an important partner and beneficiary of your empathy and support towards the African peoples.

Mr. President, we thank you for your deep understanding and empathy for the challenges we face on the African Continent. And we truly appreciate what you have done to support us where we needed support for the sake of welfare and dignity of our people.

Ten days ago in Washington, DC, at the 56th National Prayer Breakfast, the keynote speaker and a close friend of Africa, Ward Brehm, Chairman of African Development Foundation, spoke eloquently of the four-fold increase in various forms of support to Africa under your administration. There was immediately an extended applause and standing ovation from the 4,000 people in the audience from the 155 countries. Today I want you to know that we in Tanzania, who have benefited and are continuing to benefit from your commitment to Africa, join in that thunderous applause and standing ovation.

President Bush. Thank you, sir.

President Kikwete. Mr. President, today, there are thousands of women and children who have—would have died from malaria that are alive in Tanzania and all over the country thanks to your malaria support program. I can give the example of Zanzibar. In 2004 in the outpatient clinic, 500,000 malaria patients were treated; in 2007, only 10,000. In 2004 in Zanzibar, 40 percent of the patients tested positive for malaria; in 2007, only 5 percent. When the blood slide is taken, 35 percent tested positive for malaria in 2004; in 2007, only 1 percent.

I can go on and on and say and mention examples, but this is only a very brief press briefing. Today, there are thousands of children who have managed to avoid joining the already long list of orphans and who continue to enjoy the love, guidance, and support of their parents who are alive because of the AIDS care and treatment they get with the support of PEPFAR initiative. Mr. President, thank you. Today, as a result of PEPFAR, parents with AIDS are able to take care of their children.

And here today we have signed the Millennium Challenge compact, the largest ever. This funding will go a long way towards addressing some of our critical infrastructure challenges, which have for a long time been an obstacle to our growth and development. We very much thank you, Mr. President. We thank your esteemed Government for agreeing with us to give the infrastructure sector the priority it deserves.

Your decision that this compact should be signed here in Dar es Salaam today speaks volumes about how deep you have Tanzania in your heart. We are also grateful to the United States Congress for accepting your administration's request to fund the Tanzanian compact package. We also thank the MCC Board and the very able leadership of Secretary Rice. We appreciate the tremendous efforts of Ambassador Danilovich and his staff in making this day possible.

Let me end by saying that different people may have different views about you and your administration and your legacy, but we in Tanzania, if we are to speak for ourselves and for Africa, we know for sure that you, Mr. President, and your administration have been good friends of our country and have been good friends of Africa.

I know you leave office in about 12 months' time. Rest assured that you will be remembered for many generations to come for the good things you have done for Tanzania and the good things you have done for Africa. Your legacy will be that of saving hundreds of thousands of mothers' and children's lives from malaria, preventing new HIV infections and giving hope to those infected through care and treatment, and helping millions of young men and women get education. Last but not least, the legacy of assisting African nations and peoples build capacity for their own growth and development.

And today with the signing of the MCA compact, you are making it possible for the people of Tanzania to chart a brighter future underpinned by growth, opportunity, and democracy. We owe it to you and, indeed, to the American people that this compact meet its objectives and becomes a source of pride and satisfaction for our two governments and peoples.

We owe it to you, Mr. President, and indeed, to our people, that in governing this dear country of ours, we act in a manner that will justify this tremendous trust and confidence you have shown in us. This is my promise. I thank you, and welcome.

President Bush. Thank you, sir. Thanks for your very generous comments. *Vipi mambo?*

President Kikwete. Poa! [*Laughter*]

President Bush. For the uneducated, that's Swahili for, "Howdy, you all." [*Laughter*]

Mr. President, I thank you for your invitation. It's a real pleasure to set foot in your beautiful country. Laura and I are honored that you invited us, and we're so grateful for the warm welcome we received last night. It was very moving, for those of us racing through the streets of Dar es Salaam, to see thousands of people there greeting us. And I really do want to extend my thanks.

Mr. President, I stand next to you advocating to our people strong initiatives on behalf of the people of Tanzania, because you're a strong leader. I'll just put it bluntly: America doesn't want to spend money on people who steal the money from the people. [*Laughter*] We like dealing with honest people and compassionate people. We want our money to go to help the human condition and to lift human lives. We act not out of guilt, but out of compassion, Mr. President. And that's why we're in your beautiful country. I also appreciate the fact that you're—have been elected the Chairman of the African Union; it speaks to your leadership.

We are partners in democracy. We believe that governments ought to respond to the people. We're also partners in fighting disease, extending opportunity, and working for peace. Mr. President, I mentioned I was proud to sign, along with the President, the largest Millennium Challenge Account in the history of the United States here in Tanzania. It will provide nearly $700 million over 5 years to improve Tanzania's transportation network, secure,

reliable supplies of energy, and expand access to clean and safe water.

My hope is that such an initiative will be part of a effort to transform parts of this country to become more hopeful places, Mr. President. We join you in this because of your Government and your personal commitment to fight corruption, to invest in the education and health of your people, and to accept and expand marketplace economics. Those are the conditions of the Millennium Challenge Account. Oh, in the past, countries would give aid and hope for the best. America believes that people can achieve high standards, and therefore, our support to you is based upon our belief and your performance when it comes to achieving high standards.

The United States and Tanzania are working together to fight disease. As the President mentioned—that our efforts are really focused on HIV/AIDS and malaria. Since I've been the President, the number of antiretrovirals extended to people on the continent of Africa have grown from 50,000 to over 1.2 million people. And I tell people in America, that's great, that's good. We've measured it, and it's successful. But it's only a start, Mr. President.

And therefore, I've gone to our Congress to get them to double the amount of HIV/AIDS money for the continent of Africa. The plan we put in place, the strategy we put in place is working. And Congress needs to make sure that this HIV/AIDS plan, PEPFAR, gets reauthorized for a 5-year period of time. We don't want people guessing on the continent of Africa whether or not the generosity of the American people will continue.

I appreciate very much your focus on malaria as well. It breaks my heart to know that little children are dying needlessly because of a mosquito bite. I also fully understand, like you do, Mr. President, that this is a soluble problem. It takes some money, but it also takes organization. It takes the willingness to distribute nets and insecticides and education to the people, and that's what you're doing.

I appreciate the fact that you brought up the example of Zanzibar. It is an example for all on the continent of Africa of what can happen. I mean, this is a place that had been sorely affected by malaria. Today, as Mr. President pointed out, the number of infections have declined dramatically, and that ought to make the people of Tanzania feel good. It also ought to make the American people feel good, to know that their taxpayers' dollars are going to save human lives. And it's in our interests, it's in our moral interest that we continue to do so.

And so, Mr. President, we're so proud of the efforts that you and your Government and the people at the grassroots level have made to distribute nets and insecticides, all in the aim of answering a universal call to protect the most vulnerable amongst us. And we're proud to be your partner.

We also talked about international affairs. I appreciate the President's strong advice. One reason he was elected to be the head of the AU is, he knows what he's talking about. Therefore, it's important for me to listen to him, which I have done. [Laughter]

We talked about Zimbabwe. There's no doubt the people of Zimbabwe deserve a Government that serves their interests and recognizes their basic human rights and holds free and fair elections. That's in the interest of the people of Zimbabwe. It happens to be in the interest of the world as well.

We discussed the genocide in Darfur, and America provides a lot of food aid to the people in Darfur. We're trying to help them. But the truth of the matter is, there are obstacles to peace in Darfur. And that is one of the reasons we've imposed tough sanctions, real, meaningful sanctions against those who are stopping progress toward alleviating the human suffering in Darfur.

I do want to appreciate the fact—to express my appreciation, Mr. President, that you've committed a battalion of Tanzanian troops to go to Darfur. And we're proud to have worked with you to help them train up for the mission.

So we've had a great visit so far, but, like, this is just the beginning of the visit. And I'm looking forward to having dinner with you tonight, looking forward to traveling to parts of your country to see firsthand the great compassionate works that are taking place. And again, I want to thank you for your hospitality. You're a good man, Mr. President, and I'm proud to call you friend. [Laughter]

Moderator. I thank His Excellencies. Thank you. Thank you very much for those excellent statements. And now with your permission, we will invite questions from the media. As we said, it will be two questions from both sides, and I will start with the Tanzanian side. And I will call on—[inaudible]—to ask the first question. Mr.—[inaudible]—please.

President Bush. You better use the mike—[inaudible]. I'm a little old these days. [Laughter] I'm not hearing very well.

U.S. Role in Africa/President's Visit to Africa

Q. My question goes to you, Mr. President. Your visit has come rather late, during the end of your Presidency. And I would like to know, why is it Tanzania and Africa in general so important now?

President Bush. Yes. Thanks, yes. Africa has actually been important from the start of my administration. I'll never forget having a conversation with then my—my then-National Security Adviser Condoleezza Rice. It was early on in the administration, and we were talking about priorities and matters of emphasis.

And she asked me whether or not I really cared about Africa, and my answer to her then is the same answer I will give to you now: Absolutely. It's in our national interests that America help deal with hopelessness, and it's our moral interests that we help brothers and sisters who hurt. It's been the policy of the Bush administration since day one. That's why, in the first 4 years of my administration, I went to Congress, and I asked them to double foreign aid to Africa. And then, as I began the second half of my administration, I asked them to double it again. Why? Because it's in our interests to work on issues such as malaria and AIDS.

It also appalled me very on, sir, in my administration to realize that an entire generation of people could be lost to HIV/AIDS and that those of us who were comfortable weren't doing much about it. I'm a man who believes in certain principles, and I refuse to yield from those principles. And one such principle is that to whom much is given, much is required. And a lot has been given to the United States of America. We're a blessed nation. And therefore, I felt all along it was incumbent upon us to help deal with this pandemic that was—could have literally wiped out an entire generation of Africans and left thousands and thousands of boys and girls orphaned.

And so this has been a priority of mine. Why finally getting to Tanzania? I don't have many excuses, except I've been a pretty busy guy. [*Laughter*] And secondly, it seems like a fortuitous time to come. After all, the results of our efforts are becoming more and more tangible, and there's no better place to come than a place where people achieve results.

Now, there's still a lot of conflict here on this continent; I understand that. I was asked yesterday, "Well, how come you're not going to the places of conflict?" Well, one reason you go to places of success is to show people what's possible. I am going tomorrow [Tuesday]° to a place that had been in serious conflict, however, and that's Rwanda. And one of the reasons I'm going

---

° White House correction.

there is to show that after this horrible situation that occurred, there's life and there's hope and there's progress. And one way to make sure that situations like that don't occur, however, is to deal with the human condition. And that's what this trip is all about. It's heralding good leadership, it's heralding honest government, and it's focusing our help on local folks' efforts to deal with malaria and AIDS. And so thanks for the question.

Q. Jennifer Loven of Associated Press.

President Bush. Yes, Jennifer.

Q. [*Inaudible*]

President Bush. Oops, that's not going to work. Okay, well, you block everybody's view then. [*Laughter*]

Q. Sorry. It's kind of awkward. Thank you.

President Bush. You're handling it well, though.

President's Emergency Plan for AIDS Relief/Senator Barack Obama

Q. I'm trying. On PEPFAR——

President Bush. Yes.

Q. ——there are many Democrats, as well as some medical experts, who say that the abstinence provision—spending such a chunk of the money on abstinence programs is too inflexible and should be dropped. Would you consider doing that?

And then to President Kikwete, I'd like to ask you about American politics. There seems to be a lot of excitement here in Africa and in your country about Barack Obama. And I wonder what you think it says about America, that we might elect a black President with roots in Africa?

President Bush. It seemed like there was a lot of excitement for me—wait a minute. [*Laughter*] Maybe I—maybe you missed it.

Anyway, look, my attitude toward Congress is, look, see what works. PEPFAR is working. It is a balanced program. It is an ABC program: abstinence, be faithful, and condoms. It's a program that's been proven effective. And I understand there's voices on both ends of the political spectrum trying to alter the program. I would ask Congress to listen to leaders on the continent of Africa, find—analyze what works, stop the squabbling, and get the program reauthorized. One of the worst things that can happen is, there's uncertainty. You got a lot of faith-based providers and community organizers here wondering whether or not America will keep its commitment.

And so I—you know, I can understand debates, and those are fine. But they need to end the debates, adopt a reasonable policy—I happen to think the current policy is reasonable; after all, it's working—and get it done.

You want to answer the American political—[*laughter*]. See, she didn't ask me it because she knew I wouldn't answer the question. [*Laughter*]

President Kikwete. Well, I don't think I can venture into that territory either. Of course, people talk with excitement of Obama. Well, our excitement is that President Bush is at the end of his term and the U.S. is going to get a new President. Whoever that one is, for us, the most important thing is, let him be as good friend of Africa as President Bush has been.

President Bush. Thank you. Yes.

Moderator. We will now take the second and final question from the Tanzanian press.

President Kikwete. Of course, if I can—maybe let me just say about PEPFAR, let me just make an appeal: Let PEPFAR continue. This is a passionate appeal from us. It has been quite useful, as I was saying in my speech. There would have been so many orphans to date had it not been for PEPFAR, the care and treatment—so many parents now who have been infected can live. And some of them can live as many years as possible, as long as they adhere to the ABCs of the person infected with HIV living on ARVs.

So can you imagine if this program is discontinued or disrupted? There would be so many people who will lose hope, and certainly, there will be death. You create more orphans. My passionate appeal is for PEPFAR to continue. Through PEPFAR, you know, we did nationwide testing. In 6 months, we have been able to have 3.4 million people tested, and through PEPFAR, we got 2 million test kits. Had it not been for PEPFAR, we would have done less than that. So it's for us—really, for PEPFAR not to continue, well, it's a recipe for disaster for us. That's what I can say.

President Bush. Yes. Thank you.

Q. Thank you, Mr. President.

Moderator. A final question from the Tanzanian side, and I would want to recognize Richard from the Citizen.

U.S. Foreign Policy in Africa

Q. Thank you. President George Bush, you are here with President Kikwete, who was recently elected as the head of African Union. Can you promise the people of Africa—how will you support President Kikwete next 12 months to make sure that the long-end crisis in Darfur, Somalia, and the recent tribal clashes in Kenya are solved effectively?

President Bush. Well, thank you. We have been actively engaged in diplomatic efforts on the continent of Africa for a long period of time and very engaged since I've been the President. You might remember, Liberia was an issue early on in my Presidency. We engaged both diplomatically and, to a certain extent, militarily, in that I sent U.S. marines off the USS *Iwo Jima* onto—into Liberia to help stabilize the situation. As a matter of fact, I'm going to Liberia as my last stop on this very important trip to support the President, the first elected woman President on the continent of Africa, and to remind her that the U.S.'s help will be constant and enduring.

And so step one, you can be assured that we're interested in the affairs of Africa. All you have to do is look at the—at what we've done in this administration.

Secondly, I've always believed that we ought to support African leaders and not impose our views on African leaders. I mean, there's a certain amount of trust that goes with good foreign policy, and we trust your President to make the right decisions to help resolve some of these conflicts, and we'll be active in the process.

So you mentioned Kenya. As a matter of fact, we spent a fair amount of time dealing with Kenya. The President informed me about his discussions with Kofi Annan, and we support the Annan missions very strongly. And to that end, our Secretary of State, Condoleezza Rice, will be going to Kenya tomorrow. And it's just—I find it interesting—I think you ought to find it illustrative—that prior to her trip, she and I spent time discussing a mutual strategy with the President: How best can we help the process? Not what we should do to dictate to the process, but what can America do to help the process move along?

And so our position—and by the way, when it comes to AU efforts in areas where it requires—which requires peacekeepers, we've been very strong about helping to train and transport or arrange transportation for peacekeepers into troubled areas. And so our record speaks for itself, and it—the way we've conducted our foreign policy with Africa is, one, it's been a priority, and two, as I say, we come to the continent not out of guilt but out of compassion. And we come to the continent with confidence that there are leaders here who are very capable of charting the way forward to peaceful resolution of conflicts.

Q. Toby Zakaria [Tabassum Zakaria] of Reuters, please.

President Bush. It's the old reporter shuffle here.

Kosovo/Darfur

Q. Mr. President, do you support Kosovo declaring independence from Serbia? And would the United States recognize it as an independent state?

And, Mr. President, as head of the African Union, how do you get more peacekeepers into Darfur?

President Bush. Well, first, on Kosovo, our position is that its status must be resolved in order for the Balkans to be stable. Secondly, we have strongly supported the Ahtisaari plan. Thirdly, we are heartened by the fact that the Kosovo Government has clearly proclaimed its willingness and its desire to support Serbian rights in Kosovo. We also believe it's in Serbia's interests to be aligned with Europe, and the Serbian people can know that they have a friend in America. Finally, the United States will continue to work with our allies to do the very best we can to make sure there's no violence. And so those are the principles going into the Kosovo issue.

Q. But will the United States recognize it?

President Bush. I suggest you study the Ahtisaari plan. Not to be, like, the, you know, grumpy guy.

President Kikwete. Well, how to get—how do we get more peacekeepers into Darfur? Of course, what has been delaying getting more peacekeepers has been the lack of understanding between the U.N. and the Government of Sudan on the status of forces agreement. Now that one has been signed, I think it has cleared the way. There are many volunteers, and as Chair of the African Union, we certainly seek out more and more volunteers as they are needed. We use our good offices to see more and more African countries contribute. We have volunteered to contribute one battalion. If there is need for another one, we will certainly do that.

NOTE: The President's news conference began at 10:29 a.m. at the State House. In his remarks, he referred to President Ellen Johnson Sirleaf of Liberia; former Secretary-General Kofi Annan of the United Nations; and former President Martti Ahtisaari of Finland, United Nations Special Envoy of the Secretary-General for the Future Status

Process for Kosovo. President Kikwete referred to John J. Danilovich, Chief Executive Officer, Millennium Challenge Corporation.

Remarks During a Visit to Amana District Hospital in Dar es Salaam
February 17, 2008

President Jakaya Mrisho Kikwete of Tanzania. Mr. President, First Lady, my dear wife—Mr. President, welcome again to Amana Hospital. Well, let me use this opportunity to thank you so much, again, for PEPFAR, the President's Emergency Plan for AIDS Relief.

Through PEPFAR, we got these two buildings, a facility we just visited and, again, this clinic. In Dar es Salaam, there are three of these buildings, one in each of the districts, and then we have five smaller ones. About 40 patients have been registered, and 24 are already on ARVs, because they are eligible. I'm not a doctor, but they say the levels of CD4 count, then they reach a certain level above 300, where they say, now they have got to go to start treatment.

Well, the significance of this is the people we have around here. There is Tatu. She has her own story to tell, I'm sure. There is a couple—Steven, where is the wife? Where is your wife? Bring the wife here. Janet? This is Janet; this is Steven. They are a couple. And when she was pregnant, she was diagnosed as being HIV-positive. So then she was—she came under care and treatment. The baby there is healthy.

So we can see, these are some of the typical examples of the success of this kind—this program. Had they not—had there not been a program to test them, well, they might not be there. So one of the advantages is that their son is healthy; they are under treatment; they are healthy; they are doing their own work. So that

son is lucky. He is not orphaned, thanks to the PEPFAR program.

And then we have—Honorati Shirima— yes, and ex-military, I'm told—yes, retired. But I'm told when he came here, he was in very bad shape. He was in bad, bad shape. He was almost dying. So he started the program of ARVs, and you can see how he looks now. He looks healthy; he looks much better than what he was.

So all that I can say, President, is words of appreciation and thanksgiving. It has done a tremendous job. You know Tatu; you know her story. She was in Congress recently. So I can tell you—this is what I can say to welcome you, is to thank you.

President Bush. Thank you, sir.

President Kikwete. Thank you so much for the initiative. It has done so much for our people. It has given a future—as I was saying this morning, many children now have been saved from being orphans, and the example is that man and this girl here. So thank you so much, Mr. President.

President Bush. Well, Mr. President, thanks for having us. I really appreciate you suggesting a stop here at the Amana Hospital District. The American people have built two of the wings of this hospital, and I wanted to come here precisely to let the American people know how important their generosity is to the—to helping save lives.

And, doc, I thank you for setting up this meeting. We're so honored to be with the doctors and the healers as well as those who have been helped by the program. One of the main reasons that I want to make sure the American people know that this program is successful is because I want this program to continue to be funded. It's in our national interests that the American generosity continue beyond my Presidency.

And so, Mr. President, one way to send a clear message to the good people of our country is that their generosity is saving lives. And we really appreciate those whose lives have been saved, to come and share their stories. And, Tatu, it's good to see you again. She was at the State of the Union Address, she and Faith, sitting with Laura and our two daughters. And your smile is bright today as it was then. [*Laughter*] So it's good to see you. And, Doctor, thank you.

President Kikwete. She has hope. Now she has hope for the future.

President Bush. She has hope and Faith. [*Laughter*]

NOTE: The President spoke at 1:35 p.m. In his remarks, he referred to Chalamilla E. Guerino, field director of HIV and AIDS care and treatment, Amana District Hospital; and HIV patients Tatu Msangi and her daughter Faith Mang'ehe, Janet and Steven Rogers and their son Steven, Jr., and Honorati V. Shirima. President Kikwete referred to his wife Mama Salma Kikwete of Tanzania.

Remarks at a State Dinner Hosted by President Jakaya Mrisho Kikwete of Tanzania in Dar es Salaam
February 17, 2008

President Bush. Mr. President, thank you very much, sir, for your gracious and warm hospitality. Madam, thank you very much. Mr. President, thank you for coming back from Germany today. Laura and I are touched. This has been a spectacular trip. It's not over, because tomorrow we're going to tour more of your country.

President Kikwete. You'll be——

President Bush. I'll be—[*laughter*]. But I must say that our trip here has exceeded my expectations. I knew you were an accomplished Government. After all, you've dramatically reduced malaria; you're in the process of dramatically reducing HIV/ AIDS. My country has awarded you the largest Millennium Challenge grant ever in the history of our Nation, all because your

Government is committed to honest, decent government for the people.

I have been extremely touched, as has Laura, by the outpouring of support by the great people of Tanzania. And so, Mr. President, I too would like to propose a toast: To you and your family, to the people of Tanzania, and to our friendship, may it be long lasting.

NOTE: The President spoke at 6:58 p.m. at the State House. In his remarks, he referred to Mama Salma Kikwete, wife of President Kikwete. The transcript released by the Office of the Press Secretary also included the remarks of President Kikwete. A tape was not available for the verification of the content of these remarks.

Remarks Following a Tour of Meru District Hospital in Arusha, Tanzania
February 18, 2008

Habari zenu. We have just toured the hospital here, which is on the forefront of Tanzania's fight against malaria. I want to thank you, doc, for leading the tour, and thank you for your compassion. I appreciate the commissioner welcoming us to the district. I also want to thank Minister Mwakyusa for joining us here in Arusha. I'm grateful for the members of the diplomatic corps who've joined us.

During the visit at this hospital, we met pregnant women who will receive insecticide-treated bed nets. We witnessed a pediatric ward and observed children being diagnosed and treated. We saw how an historic partnership is saving lives across the continent of Africa.

For years, malaria has been a health crisis in sub-Saharan Africa. The disease keeps sick workers home, schoolyards quiet, and communities in mourning. The suffering caused by malaria is needless, and every death caused by malaria is unacceptable. It is unacceptable to people here in Africa, who see their families devastated and their economies crippled. It is unacceptable to people in the United States, who believe every human life has value and that the power to save lives comes with the moral obligation to use it.

In 2005, I announced that the United States would work to save lives through our malaria initiative. Under this 5-year, $1.2 billion program, we're working with 15 African countries to cut malaria-related deaths by half.

Our strategy to achieve this goal is straightforward. First, the initiative supports indoor residual spraying to keep deadly mosquitoes at bay. Here in Tanzania, spraying campaigns have reached hundreds of thousands of homes and have protected more than a million people.

Second, the initiative supports treatment for those who are most vulnerable to ma-laria, especially pregnant women. Here in Tanzania, more than 2,400 health workers have been trained to provide specialized treatment that prevents malaria in expectant mothers.

Third, the initiative provides lifesaving drugs. Here in Tanzania, the program has supported more than 1 million courses of treatment and has trained more than 5,000 health workers in how to use them.

Fourth, the initiative supports the distribution of insecticide-treated bed nets, and Laura and I are about to distribute some of those bed nets. This is one of the simplest technologies imaginable, but it's also one of the most effective. Here in Tanzania, we're working with the Government and partners such as the Global Fund to provide bed net vouchers for infants and pregnant mothers. Women can use these vouchers to buy bed nets at local shops at a huge discount. So far, an estimated 5 million vouchers have been distributed through these programs.

Today I'm pleased to announce new steps in the bed net campaign. Within the next 6 months, the United States and Tanzania, in partnership with the World Bank and the Global Fund, will begin distributing 5.2 million free bed nets. This ambitious nationwide program will provide enough nets to protect every child between the ages of 1 and 5 in Tanzania.

The bed net campaign is supported by Tanzanian manufacturers, including A to Z Textiles, which we will visit later today. So as this campaign protects women and children from malaria, it also boasts—boosts local economies. It helps develop a culture of bed net use that will be sustained long after relief programs have ended.

For the past 2 years, we've applied our strategy here in Tanzania, and we're seeing results. In June 2006, at the district hospital in Muleba, more than 50 people died because of malaria. In June 2007, after a spraying campaign supported by our malaria initiative, the number of deaths had dropped to five. In Zanzibar, the percentage of infants infected with malaria has dropped from about 20 percent to less than 1 percent.

The campaign to fight malaria has the support of government and private citizens alike. In the United States, schoolchildren have raised money to send bed nets to Africa. Houses of worship have sent their prayers and their faithful, compassionate men and women who travel here to confront the suffering and heal the sick.

Tanzanian citizens are stepping forward. In one area, residents launched a campaign called *Kataa Malaria;* for those who don't speak Swahili, it means "Reject Malaria." [*Laughter*] As part of the campaign, workers went door to door to teach people how to use bed nets. They launched TV and radio ads. They spoke in mosques about malaria prevention and treatment. And their efforts are working.

This is a campaign of compassion. This is a practical way to help save lives. It's in the interests of the United States to save lives, and it's in the interests of the Tanzanian Government to put forth an effective strategy. Our interests are combined, and our interests are now making a significant effort.

And so on behalf of the United States of America, we say, God bless you. And to the Tanzanian Government, we say, thank you for your efficient and hard work. And so it's been an honor to be with you. *Asante.*

NOTE: The President spoke at 10:52 a.m. In his remarks, he referred to Aziz Msuya, district medical officer, Meru District Hospital; and Minister of Health and Social Welfare David Homeli Mwakyusa of Tanzania.

Letter to President Fatmir Sejdiu of Kosovo Recognizing Kosovo as an Independent and Sovereign State
February 18, 2008

His Excellency
Fatmir Sejdiu
President of Kosovo
Pristina
Dear Mr. President:

On behalf of the American people, I hereby recognize Kosovo as an independent and sovereign state. I congratulate you and Kosovo's citizens for having taken this important step in your democratic and national development.

On this historic occasion, I note the deep and sincere bonds of friendship that unite our people. This friendship, cemented during Kosovo's darkest hours of tragedy, has grown stronger in the 9 years since war in Kosovo ended. Kosovo has since worked to rebuild its war-shattered society, establish democratic institutions, hold successful elections for a new government, and foster prosperity. As an independent state, Kosovo now assumes responsibility for its destiny. As in the past, the United States will be your partner and your friend.

In your request to establish diplomatic relations with the United States, you expressed Kosovo's desire to attain the highest standards of democracy and freedom. I fully welcome this sentiment. In particular, I support your embrace of multiethnicity as a principle of good governance and your commitment to developing accountable institutions in which all citizens are equal under the law.

I also note that, in its declaration of independence, Kosovo has willingly assumed the responsibilities assigned to it under the Ahtisaari Plan. The United States welcomes this unconditional commitment to carry out these responsibilities and Kosovo's willingness to cooperate fully with the international community during the period of international supervision to which you have agreed. The United States relies upon Kosovo's assurances that it considers itself legally bound to comply with the provisions in Kosovo's Declaration of Independence. I am convinced that full and prompt adoption of the measures proposed by U.N. Special Envoy Ahtisaari will bring Kosovo closer to fulfilling its Euro-Atlantic aspirations.

On the basis of these assurances from the Government of Kosovo, I am pleased to accept your request that our two countries establish diplomatic relations. The United States would welcome the establishment by Kosovo of diplomatic representation in the United States and plans to do likewise in Kosovo.

As Kosovo opens a new chapter in its history as an independent state, I look forward to the deepening and strengthening of our special friendship.

Sincerely,

GEORGE W. BUSH

NOTE: An original was not available for verification of the content of this letter.

Remarks on Kosovo and an Exchange With Reporters in Dar es Salaam, Tanzania
February 19, 2008

The President. Good morning. Sunday, the people of Kosovo declared their independence. They have asked the United States for diplomatic recognition, and yesterday the United States formally recognized Kosovo as a sovereign and independent nation.

In its Declaration of Independence, Kosovo committed itself to the highest standards of democracy, including freedom and tolerance and justice for citizens of all ethnic backgrounds. These are principles that honor human dignity; they are values America looks for in a friend. And soon we will establish full diplomatic relations with the new nation of Kosovo.

We will work with the leaders of Kosovo to carry out a smooth and peaceful transition to independence. America welcomes Kosovo's pledges to fully implement the plan of United Nations Special Envoy Ahtisaari and to accept a period of international supervision. We encourage

Kosovo's leaders to quickly adopt the provisions of the Ahtisaari plan, especially those designed to safeguard the rights of Kosovo's non-Albanian communities.

The independence of Kosovo is an historic step for the Balkans region. It presents an opportunity to move beyond the conflicts of the past and toward a future of freedom and stability and peace. The United States and the European Union must seize this opportunity to offer all the nations of this region the prospect of integration into the political, economic, and security structure of the Euro-Atlantic community. In this way, all the people of the Balkans will be able to see the promise of a better life for themselves and for their children.

Thank you. I'll answer a couple of questions. Mark [Mark Knoller, CBS Radio].

Kosovan Independence

Q. Mr. President, isn't this a poke in the eye to Vladimir Putin and the others who say you're approving of secession movements everywhere implicitly?

The President. Actually, we have been working very closely with the Russians, as we have with the Europeans and other nations on the—on Kosovo's independence, because we believe it's the right thing to do. You know, there's a disagreement, but we believe, as do many other nations, that this is—history will prove this to be a correct move to bring peace to the Balkans.

This strategy has been a long time coming. Yesterday, for example, we had a—worked out with our European allies the sequencing of it to make sure that there was a concerted and constant voice supporting this move. The United States supports this move because we believe it will bring peace. And now it's up to all of us to work together to help the Kosovars realize that peace. And it's important for us to remind Kosovo, which I have just done, that they must honor their commitments to support the rights of non-Albanians, non-Kosovars' rights inside the country.

Q. Mr. President——

The President. Excuse me. Hans [Hans Nichols, Bloomberg News].

Kosovan Independence/Russia

Q. Yes, Mr. President, thank you very much. When you talk about the sequencing of events, did you withhold the endorsement, the recognition, and wait until this morning for any particular reasons or as a favor to the Russians?

The President. No. Hans, as I told you, we worked with the European nations. We had—this strategy was well planned. And the endorsement, by the way, wasn't held until this morning; it was issued last night by the State Department, as I mentioned in my remarks.

But it was a way for us to create an effect that showed that the world was meant—many in the world were very supportive of the independence of Kosovo. Our position has been very clear all along. At the G–8, for example, I expressed—or in Albania, I expressed my position very clearly, so it shouldn't come as a surprise to anybody.

What you may be interested in knowing is that we have been in close consultation with the Russians all along. This wasn't a surprise to Russia. And, you know, today's announcement is simply putting an exclamation point onto a series of announcements that have been made over the last 24 hours.

Thank you all very much. See you in Rwanda.

NOTE: The President spoke at 7:24 a.m. at Kilimanjaro Hotel Kempinski Dar es Salaam. In his remarks, he referred to former President Martti Ahtisaari of Finland, United Nations Special Envoy of the Secretary-General for the Future Status Process of Kosovo. A reporter referred to President Vladimir V. Putin of Russia.

Remarks Following a Visit to Kigali Memorial Centre in Kigali, Rwanda
February 19, 2008

Laura and I have just finished going to a memorial for the—that recognizes the horrors of the genocide that took place here. This is a moving place that can't help but shake your emotions to your very foundation. It reminds me that we must not let these kind of actions take place; that—and that the people of Rwanda need help to reconcile, to move forward, after a brutal period.

It's a—I guess the only thing I can finish saying is that, you know, we ask for God's blessings on those who still hurt and on those who long for help and on the kids whose lives had to have been deeply affected by the trauma of the moment. And we thank the museum officials for their generosity and hospitality and for putting on such an exhibit to remind people that there is evil in the world, and evil must be confronted.

Thank you very much.

NOTE: The President spoke at 10:31 a.m.

The President's News Conference With President Paul Kagame of Rwanda in Kigali
February 19, 2008

President Kagame. President, it's my great pleasure, it's the pleasure of the whole country to welcome you, Mr. President, and Mrs. Laura Bush and your distinguished delegation. We thank you very much for your visit, your friendship, and your support. These have made a substantive difference to many lives in our country.

President Bush. Thank you.

President Kagame. The bilateral investment treaty that we have just signed is further testimony to your commitment and the good will of the American people. Mr. President, your visit is a reflection that the United States and Rwanda have shared values. We believe in investing in our people. We share a commitment to expanding our people's economic and the democratic aspirations. We believe in strong and effective institutions accountable to our respective citizens. But as it is well appreciated, different countries begin their democratic and development agenda from different circumstances.

You saw for yourself there is also decades of bad politics and bad leadership when you visited the genocide memorial that you just saw this morning. The country you are visiting today was vastly different 14 years ago, when the very survival of Rwanda as a nation was in question. But the Rwandan people refused to give up hope, and we have instead embarked on the task of healing, reconstruction, and development.

The results of these efforts may be illustrated by our modest achievements in such areas as education, health, and a general improvement towards sustainable economic growth. Rwandans and the more—especially our youth—have hope in a better future. Primary school enrollment has risen to about 96 percent, spurred by tuition-free education. In our concerted effort to invest in our people, we have extended universal education to the very first 3 years of secondary education. And we intend to do more through the entire value chain of trade.

In the field of health, immunization coverage has risen to 95 percent. Thanks to American support and partnership, thousands of Rwandan children and mothers are alive and have hope because of the President's Emergency Plan for AIDS Relief program. Malaria has almost been eliminated in our country due in large part to the President's Malaria Initiative.

On the economic front, today's agreement will certainly deepen our economic collaboration, Mr. President. Mr. President, we share a deep commitment to democracy and good governance. In this respect, we in Rwanda believe strongly in power sharing and consensus-building as a cornerstone of our political dispensation. This perspective has been made the centerpiece of our Constitution, informed by our particular history and the circumstances that disenfranchised communities and political expressions, often leading to calamities. We know that governance has both universal and homegrown features to allow for greater relevance. We believe we are making progress towards a balance between these imperatives.

Mr. President, the significance of your administration's record is illustrated by your strong leadership in many fields, including health, conflict resolution, promotion of investment and trade, and your insistence that we Africans take ownership of our own development challenges and processes. Permit me to thank you once again for the attention you've paid our continent and our country. It may be stated that you have raised the bar of American-African relations, a level which the next President of the United States will not lower.

We are very happy and honored to have you here, Mr. President and Mrs. Laura Bush. This is the second time Rwanda for the First Lady, and we appreciate that. I thank you for the trust and the confidence you have placed in our country. Mr. President, I thank you very much.

President Bush. Mr. President, thanks. We're proud—[*applause*]—we're honored to be here. Thanks very much for inviting Laura and me to join you and Mrs. Kagame for lunch today in a—what has been, so far, a very important stop. We had good discussions on a variety of subjects. It is really inspiring for us to see people who have endured such suffering respond with such hope.

I really do want to congratulate you and the people in Rwanda for the remarkable recovery you have made. And I assure you, you have a steady friend in the United States. I appreciate the opportunity to visit with your cabinet as well. It's important for my fellow citizens to know that I'm dealing with a respected leader not only here at home but in the region.

And so our discussions not only centered on the issues facing Rwanda but also how we can work together to bring peace to different parts of the continent of Africa.

We're cooperating to address violence and genocide in Darfur. The Rwandan people know the horrors of genocide. I find it— it's not surprising at all that the first nation to step up and say that we want to deploy peacekeepers was Rwanda. And I thank you for your leadership, Mr. President. That's a—it's a strong statement on your part, and you remain one of the largest contributors to stability and peace in Darfur.

And the United States is happy to help. We've trained—or helped train more than 7,000 Rwanda peacekeepers. We've provided more than $17 million to equip and transport these forces into Darfur. The President mentioned something that I agree with, and that is, the role of the United States and others is to help African nations deal with African problems.

And here's an example of a collaborative effort to help solve what our Nation has labeled genocide. The United States is making $100 million available to assist African nations willing to step forward for the cause of peace in Darfur. And up to 12 million of those will help you, Mr. President, do the job that you want to do in Darfur. The United States appreciates the commitments to help bring peace to Darfur made by other African nations as well, such as Ghana, Senegal, Ethiopia, Tanzania, Burkina Faso, and Malawi.

And my message to other nations is, join with the President and help us get this problem solved once and for all. And we will help. We will help through sanctions. We will help through pressure. And we'll help provide money to get these forces in, in an effective manner.

The United States and Rwanda are cooperating to assure long-term stability in eastern Congo. We spent a lot of time talking about that today. I appreciate your guidance and your advice, Mr. President. I hope you could tell from our discussions that Secretary Rice and Jendayi Frazer— Ambassador Frazer—and other people in my administrations takes this issue as seriously as you do. Last month, we helped broker a peace agreement between the Congolese Government and several armed groups. We also helped broker an agreement between the Congolese Government and the Rwanda Government.

And now we've got to make the agreement stick. It's one thing to agree on something; the most important thing is to get results for the agreement. And that's what we discussed today on how to help bring peace to this part of the world.

We also talked about economies. Look, this bilateral investment treaty is important because it sends a signal to U.S. companies that they ought to consider investing in Rwanda. The President has—wisely understands that capital investment is much more effective in the long term than just grant money. And he understands the creation of jobs happens when people are able to attract capital.

And so I was pleased to sign this investment treaty with you, Mr. President. It's a sign of your leadership, and it's a sign that you and I both understand that an agreement such as this will provide legal protections for investors in both our countries, including nondiscriminatory treatment, respect for private property, transparency and governance, and the international arbitration of disputes. In other words, this treaty is a way of saying not only is this a good place to look, but when you invest, there will be certain guarantees: not a guarantee of profit, not a guarantee of return on investment, but a guarantee you'll be treated fairly.

And finally, Mr. President, thank you for mentioning our efforts to help you fight disease. You know, people say, why would you want to come to Africa at this point in your Presidency? Because I'm on a mission of mercy is why.

I want the American people to understand that when it comes to saving lives, it's in our national interest. I firmly believe that, Mr. President. It's in our security interest to help alleve areas of the world from hopelessness. It's in our moral interests to

help save lives. And it's precisely what we're doing, thanks to your leadership and help. This program wouldn't be effective if your Government wasn't committed.

And secondly, I'm frankly not interested in, you know, spending taxpayers' money on governments that end up pocketing the money and not helping citizens live. It's one of the reasons I've come to Rwanda, is the record here is quite extraordinary when it comes to saving lives.

It is irresponsible for nations, to whom much has been given, to sit on the sidelines when young babies are dying because of mosquito bites. And so the United States isn't on the sideline, Mr. President; we're right in the middle of the action with you and proudly so.

The malaria initiative has helped distribute 450,000 bed nets in Rwanda. It's not a very sophisticated strategy, as a matter of fact, just a simple strategy, but when implemented, saves lives. And it starts with having bed nets for citizens throughout your country. And we're just getting started. And I want to thank you for your leadership on this issue.

We've set a goal to help provide indoor spraying in more than 350,000 homes and helped provide more than 900,000 treatments of lifesaving medicines. In my State of Texas, we say, here's a problem, and we're getting after it. That's exactly what's happening here and all across this continent, Mr. President. And we're proud to be your partner in a mission of—that is a mission of the deepest sense of humanity.

Same with HIV/AIDS: our Emergency Plan for AIDS Relief, PEPFAR, has helped deliver 40—antiretrovirals to 44,000 Rwandans. We've helped deliver services to nearly 650,000 pregnant women to help prevent mother-to-child HIV transmission. This is a good beginning, like, a good record, but it should only be viewed as a beginning. And therefore, our United States Congress must double our PEPFAR initiative from 15 billion over 5 years to

30 billion over 5 years, quit the squabbling, and get the bill passed.

And finally, we'll be sending the Peace Corps back into Rwanda, Mr. President; first time it's been here since 1993. These are good, decent folks coming to your country simply to help people realize their God-given talents and realize the blessings of a peaceful, hopeful life.

So I'm proud to be with you. I want to thank you for your record; thank you for being a personal friend.

Moderator. Thank you, Your Excellencies. We are now ready to take questions from the press—four questions, two each from the local press and American press. We'll start with Rwandan press. Yes, Ignatius.

2008 U.S. Presidential Election/Rwandan Elections

Q. Thank you. My name is Ignatius Kabagambe. I work for the New Times newspaper here in Rwanda. My question goes to both of you, Presidents—2008 is a critical year, especially politically, because here in Rwanda, we are going to be having parliamental elections in September, and in the U.S., it's going to be Presidential elections. Presidents, what do you see—how good are your chances to your respective parties? [*Laughter*] And if you wish, you can even—your answers can include what you think are going to be the challenges.

President Bush. Yes, thanks. Yes, this American press has been trying to get me to comment on this for, like, a couple of months. Want me to start? Republicans will win. [*Laughter*] Whoever is the President must understand that this mission on the continent of Africa is in our Nation's interests. But I think my party's nominee will win. Don't be listening to all these pundits here, you know, half of them sitting right here. [*Laughter*]

You know, they—the issues in America are: Who is going to fight terror and protect the homeland, and who is going to keep people's taxes low to make sure that the economy is—grows—really, the issues. And so there's a lot of noise, a lot of movement, but things change rapidly in American politics. It will eventually get down to two people, and then the choice will become very clear. And we'll win.

I don't know about your politics, Mr. President. [*Laughter*] It's probably best not to comment too specifically about it. [*Laughter*]

President Kagame. President, we have something in common, and that is, succeed in what we are doing. So my party will, I think, win these elections on the basis of how this Government, and the party central to it, has performed well, has uplifted the living standards of our people. They have protected—given protection and security and brought in stability to the—this country and restored the rights of every individual citizen of this country. And economic progress is being registered. I think the people of this country will be wanting more of what we are doing.

My prediction is that it will be fine for my party, and we'll do our best to continue the agenda of development of this country. And I think that citizens of this country are willing to give us the chance to continue solving them the way they have been solved. And the challenges are normally just in terms of organization, and it takes time, takes money, takes—but those are easy to overcome. So I think, Mr. President, we are on the same path of succeeding.

President Bush. That's good.

Moderator. From our side, Debbie Charles of Reuters, please.

Cuba/Former President Fidel Castro Ruz of Cuba

Q. Mr. President, can you tell us what it means for the United States that—for the U.S. policy—that Castro has said he's going to step down? And how is that going to change things for the U.S.?

President Bush. Yes, thanks. I heard the reports, several ways: one, reporters yelling it at me, and then, of course, I was briefed.

Not saying you were yelling it at me; I'm saying——

Q. I wouldn't——

President Bush. ——no, no, of course not; you were very polite. More important—you know, the question really should be, what does this mean for the people in Cuba? They're the ones who suffered under Fidel Castro. They're the ones who were put in prison because of their beliefs. They're the ones who have been denied their right to live in a free society. So I view this as a period of transition that—and it should be the beginning of the democratic transition for the people in Cuba.

There will be an interesting debate that will arise eventually. There will be some who say, let's promote stability. Of course, in the meantime, political prisoners will rot in prison, and the human condition will remain pathetic in many cases.

I believe that the change from Fidel Castro ought to begin a period of democratic transition. First step, of course, will be for people put in these prisons to be let out. I've met with many of the—or some of the families of prisoners. It just breaks your heart to realize that people have been thrown in prison because they dared speak out.

The international community should work with the Cuban people to begin to build institutions that are necessary for democracy. And eventually, this transition ought to lead to free and fair elections. And I mean free, and I mean fair, not these kind of staged elections that the Castro brothers try to foist off as being true democracy.

And we're going to help. The United States will help the people of Cuba realize the blessings of liberty. And so those are my initial thoughts.

Moderator. [Inaudible]

U.N. Security Council Sanctions/President's Visit to Kigali Memorial Centre/Rwanda-U.S. Relations

Q. Thank you so much. My name is—[*inaudible*]—from the Reuters news wire.

President Bush. Yes. Wait a minute, back to back—wait a minute. This is a little—[*laughter*]—there seems to be a monopoly here. [*Laughter*]

Q. [Inaudible]

President Bush. That's right, yes. [*Laughter*]

Q. Mr. President, you made what I would describe as an emotional talk or speech on the genocides of Rwanda, especially when you were visiting the memorial. But unfortunately, the perpetrators of the killings are still holed up in several parts of the country—also several parts of the world, especially the Congo. And you just mentioned that we need to see results being done—results being seen, and the civil arguments have been made. So I'm wondering, Mr. President, what is the U.S. going to do about these perpetrators that remain at large and are walking freely?

President Bush. Yes.

Q. And then my other brief question for President Kagame is, what are the details of—can you give us some details about the investment treaty you've just signed with President Bush? What's contained in this treaty, and what's so special about it? Thank you.

President Bush. Yes, just a couple of reactions—thank you very much for that. To specifically answer your question, we support U.N. security sanctions—U.N. Security Council resolutions targeting those who perpetuated the violence and have made our position publicly known. And we'll continue to support.

Secondly, the museum was a profound—it had a profound effect on me. You can't help but walk in there and recognize the—you know, that evil does exist and, in this case, in such brutal form that babies had their skulls smashed. And so the question is, what does the world do to prevent these kinds of incidences? And I came away with two lessons. I'm sure there's many more. One was, we've got to work to prevent it from happening in the first place; when we see issues, that people need not—need to pay attention to the warning signs and prevent crises like this from happening.

We're obviously trying to prevent such a crises from happening in Kenya. Condi Rice briefed the President and me on her meetings yesterday, and we strongly support Kofi Annan's efforts there. Now I'm not suggesting that anything close to—in Kenya has happened—is going to happen— anything close to what happened here is going to happen in Kenya. But I am suggesting there's some warning signs that the international community needs to pay attention to. And we're paying attention to it, as is Kofi Annan, and I know the AU will as well.

And secondly, that when you want— when the people decide to respond, that you go in with enough force that has the proper mandate. In a situation such as that, you don't want to send people in who are observers, you need to send people in who will help deal with the situation. That's why the mandate in Darfur is very important, and we're pleased with the mandate in Darfur. Now we just got to get people in place to be able to save lives.

But those are the lessons I left with. The other thing I came away from, just so you know, is, is how amazing your country has performed given the horror of the genocide. I mean, it is—I just can't imagine what it would have been like to be a citizen who witnessed such horrors and then had to try to gather themselves up and live a hopeful life. And so thanks for your question.

President Kagame. For your question, you asked about the treaty we've just signed. I think central to that treaty, and very importantly, is the fact that it's an invitation to the investors, and information that when they come here, their invest-

ments will be protected, will be in good hands. And when they are in Rwanda, they should be able to reap their returns. Of course, what that means—it means that Rwandans benefit from the capital flows that will be there. They will benefit from technologies that come with such investments. It benefits our laws of employment of a citizen of this country and the skills that will be applied also along with that.

And it's also a commitment by the President and his administration to seeing investors from United States come to Rwanda. And it's also an assurance to them that they will be standing with them, as they come to make investments here, invest adequately. The most important thing to talk about will be this bilateral treaty.

Moderator. All right, last one for us. Sheryl Stolberg with the New York Times, please.

U.S. Role in Africa/Darfur

Q. Thank you. Mr. President, Bill Clinton came here and said he regretted that he wasn't able to do more to stop the genocide here. You have seen the memorial here today, and I'm wondering, what would you tell your successor about America's obligations and also its ability to stop genocide?

And to you, Mr. President, did you raise the issue of Darfur with President Bush? Did you ask him for any further commitment by the United States? And if so, what was it? Thank you.

President Bush. I would say, it's like— as I explained to this fellow here—that one of the lessons of the genocide in Rwanda was to take some of the early warning signs seriously.

Secondly, a clear lesson I learned in the museum was that outside forces that tend to divide people up inside their country are unbelievably counterproductive. In other words, people came from other countries—I guess you'd call them colonialists— and they pitted one group of people against another. And an early warning sign was—

and it's hard to have seen it, I readily admit, but I'm talking earlier than 1994 and earlier than the nineties—was the fact that it became a habit to divide people based upon, you know, in this case, whether they were Tutsi or Hutu, which eventually led to exploitation.

Secondly, I would tell my successor that the United States can play a very constructive role. I would urge the President not to feel like U.S. solutions should be imposed upon African leaders. I would urge the President to treat our—the leaders in Africa as partners. In other words, don't come to the continent feeling guilty about anything, come to the continent feeling confident that with some help, people can solve their problems.

You know, as I told you, I made—yesterday—I made a decision not to unilaterally send troops into the Sudan. And I still believe it was the right decision. But having done that, if you're a problemsolver, you put yourself at the mercy of the decisions of others; in this case, the United Nations. And I'm well known to have spoken out by the slowness of the United Nations. It is—like, seems very bureaucratic to me, particularly with people suffering. And one reason I'm so proud to be standing here with this President is that he didn't wait. He said, "We want to help." And so we're trying to get forces in, and we'll help.

And the third thing is, is that the U.S. will provide—you know, can provide money and help and training. And we have. We've trained their forces—helped train their forces. They're good forces to begin with, and they just need a little added value, and we helped.

So I guess to answer to your questions— it's kind of a long-winded approach—to take problems seriously before they become acute and then recognize that there's going to be a slowness in the response if you rely upon international organizations.

Q. Are you worried that you might have regrets?

President Bush. No, I made a decision. I stand by it. I'm now worried that the rest of the world needs to move as expeditiously, quickly. Therefore, we're—as I've told you in this little address here, we've got $100 million to help move people into Darfur. And nor am I regretful of the fact that we put serious sanctions on leaders in Sudan and companies owned by certain actors in Sudan. It was the right thing to do.

I am trying to get other people to join. As you know, getting a universal sanction regime can be difficult. People sometimes have got different interests, different commercial interests. Our position is, is that human suffering ought to be—preempt commercial interests. And so I'm comfortable with the decision I made. I'm not comfortable with to how quickly the response has been.

And nevertheless, there is a—we'll continue dealing with the issue. Every stop I made, I've talked about Darfur. And the President talked about it too. I've talked so long you probably forgot her question to you. [*Laughter*]

President Kagame. I still remember, President. Certainly, we discussed Darfur, as we discussed other problem areas, especially on our continent. And I do want to agree with the President; problems are there. But I think the best approach is, indeed, to help Africans develop their capacity to deal with these problems. And more importantly, as the President said, we probably also have to invest our time and even resources in the monitoring and also preventing problems coming up, as they keep coming up in different places.

But it is important to understand that, indeed, today we'll have Darfur; maybe tomorrow there will be another problem area, God forbid. But it's important that these problems are not to be seen as if they have to be resolved, attended to, by the United States. They must be attended to by the international community. They must also be attended to by people, if it is in

Africa, by Africans. Primarily, they must develop this capacity. And they should be supported to develop this capacity so that we can prevent and we are prepared to prevent. Then you should be able to cope with these challenges, resolving the problems.

So I think the approach taken by President Bush were realistic, in the sense that you also do not want to see every problem, United States being called upon to be the answer of that problem. And of course, we—the backlash, also, in the sense that, at the same time, they also start blaming the United States, that they are rushing everywhere solving problems and, of course, reading through that to mean they have other interests and so on and so forth.

So I think that will lead the way of helping the people to solve their own problems, but of course, with the support of the United States with its huge capabilities in different areas. And walking together with the rest of the international community is

perhaps more important than just blaming the United States, saying, "Why didn't you go in and solve the problem?" The problems and the solutions to those problems should not be taken away from the responsibilities of their action, should not be taken away from places where they're taking place and the people in those places.

I think that is the best way I could—but we did talk about that. And we did talk about our own contribution and to how that can be enhanced. And the President is willing to support us—support has always been coming—so that we continue to move forward.

NOTE: The President's news conference began at 12:20 p.m. at the Presidency—VIP Building. In his remarks, he referred to Jeannette Nyiramongi, wife of President Kagame; President Raul Castro Ruz of Cuba; and former Secretary-General Kofi Annan of the United Nations.

Remarks During a United States Embassy Dedication Ceremony in Kigali
February 19, 2008

Well, thank you very much. Thank you. Please be seated—unless, of course, you don't have a chair. [*Laughter*] Mr. President, thank you for joining us. Madam Kagame, we're so thrilled you're here. Laura and I are honored to be with you. I appreciate the members of the diplomatic corps joining us as well.

I had a speech; I'm not going to give it. [*Laughter*] Guys like me always like to cut ribbons. There's nothing more special than cutting the ribbon on a new Embassy, particularly in a country like Rwanda.

Rwanda has come—[*applause*]—it's amazing. You know, Laura and I just came from the—well, we came from a beautiful lunch with the President and the First Lady. But we went to the holocaust mu-

seum. It's hard to believe that a country could recover so quickly from such a horrible moment. It's hard to believe that there can be hope after a devastating period of time like that, and yet there is. And so cutting the ribbon here really is a chance for America to say, we stand with you as you hope for a better future.

Plus, I like dealing with strong leaders who care about the people. I like courage and compassion. And that's what I believe your President has, courage and compassion. He cares deeply about the plight of the citizens of—[*applause*].

And I think when people get to know Americans, thanks to people who work here at this Embassy, they will find that we're a nation of courageous and compassionate people too.

So my first call is to thank our fellow citizens for working in Rwanda. And thanks for serving the United States of America. I hope you have as much pride as I do in saying, I represent America. And the reason I do so is because we are a compassionate people. And when we see suffering, we just don't sit around and talk about it; we act upon it. And when we see the hungry, we feed the hungry, not because of its—you know, it's like we want to establish undue influence; it's because we all believe we're children of God.

And so for those of you on the frontlines of saving lives with the malaria initiative, I say, thanks, good job, keep doing it. It's not that hard to spread out nets. It requires a government willing to cooperate with you. It's just not that difficult to figure out how to deal with the disease in which thousands of babies die. It's insecticides and nets and good strategies. And so thanks for working on that.

For those of you who are dealing with HIV/AIDS, you know, people often ask why did I decide to get involved? I couldn't stand by and watch a generation of people eradicated with something that we could help, you see. And so I want to thank my fellow citizens for saving lives. And gosh, I hope it makes you feel good; it certainly makes me feel good to know you're out there working hard. And so thanks for being a part of what I call a mission of mercy. And thanks for showing the good heart of America.

For the Rwandan citizens here, thanks for helping our Embassy go. We can't run our Embassies without the people from the host nations. And the Ambassador tells me that you're really fine people, and I know my fellow citizens thank you for working side by side with the people of the United States of America.

For those of you wearing the uniform, God bless you. There's nothing better than being the Commander in Chief of such an outstanding group of men and women who selflessly serve a cause greater than themselves.

I do want to thank Michael and Lesley for their service. I do want to recognize our great Secretary of State. I thought for a minute you were going to name that road after Secretary Condoleezza Rice. [*Laughter*] When they're talking about great Americans, and they're going on and on and on, I was certain it was going to say "Rice Boulevard." [*Laughter*]

I do want to thank Cheryl Sim and her husband Richard. He's from Texas. Any other Texans that are here? Yes, there you go. You know what it's like. [*Laughter*] Pretty lucky deal to be called Texan, isn't it?

Finally, I do want to end by saying this: To whom much is given, much is required. That's a—Presidents must make decisions based upon certain principles that are timeless and universal. And that's one of the principles that stands in—it stands our Nation in good stead. We're a blessed nation, and I believe it is in our interests, our national interests and our moral interests, to help people like we're helping them here in Rwanda.

And so it's an honor to be here to cut the ribbon for this new Embassy. It's an honor to be in front of people who've got compassion in their hearts and efficiency on their minds and willing to do the right thing to get—to save lives. And it's an honor to be in, a great friend and ally, Rwanda. God bless you.

And now it's my honor to bring to the podium our President—your President and our ally, President Kagame.

NOTE: The President spoke at 2:25 p.m. at the U.S. Embassy Kigali. In his remarks, he referred to Jeannette Nyiramongi, wife of President Paul Kagame of Rwanda; U.S. Ambassador to Rwanda Michael R. Arietti and his wife Lesley; and Deputy Chief of Mission

Cheryl Sim, U.S. Embassy Kigali. The transcript released by the Office of the Press Secretary also included the remarks of President Kagame.

Remarks During a Meeting With President John Agyekum Kufuor of Ghana in Accra, Ghana
February 20, 2008

President Bush. Thank you very much for your hospitality. Mr. President, thanks. First of all, it's an honor to be in your country, and it's an honor to be with you—[*inaudible*]. I don't know if the people of your country truly understand your standing in the international community, but you are one of the most respected international leaders. You have represented your country well; you have represented the continent of Africa well; and you represent certain basic values extremely well. So it's an honor to be with you today.

You're right; you and I are both finishing our term. But you forgot to say that we're both going to finish strong. [*Laughter*]

President Kufuor. That is a politician I talk about. [*Laughter*]

President Bush. You mentioned the Millennium Challenge Account. And I believe you're the first country on the continent of Africa to receive a grant. And we did so because we believe in supporting governments that fight corruption, invest in their children, invest in the health of their citizens, believe in marketplace economies, and that's exactly the way you've led your country.

And so ours is a—it's certainly not a gift. It is given in a cooperative spirit that—[*inaudible*]—people. And we believe that

it is in our national interest to promote freedom and democracy as well as help the citizenry make the—[*inaudible*]. And you've led the way, Mr. President. It's been very easy to support your Government.

And I appreciate you bringing up disease. There's no doubt in my mind that given some help, the Government of Ghana—led by you, sir—will eradicate malaria. It's going to take a lot of work and a lot of organizational skills and support from the international community, which you will have. And I predict to the people of Ghana that when you look back at President Kufuor's leadership, you'll say, this was the beginning of the end of the disease that affected so many lives of young children.

And I appreciate your leadership, my friend, and I want to thank you very much for this warm hospitality. I do want to thank the people of Ghana—at least those we've seen so far—for getting up early, lining the streets, and waving with such enthusiasm. It made us all feel great, and it's a part of the trip I've really been looking forward to. And so grateful for your hospitality. Thank you, sir.

NOTE: The President spoke at approximately 10 a.m. at Osu Castle.

The President's News Conference With President John Agyekum Kufuor of Ghana in Accra
February 20, 2008

President Kufuor. Welcome, Mr. President. I believe we agreed to expose ourselves to the ladies and gentlemen of the media. [*Laughter*] So we are ready for your questions.

President Bush. Let me have a—you want me to say something initially, Mr. President?

President Kufuor. Well, you may, Mr. President.

President Bush. See, he doesn't want to hear what I said upstairs again. But I do want to say a couple of comments. First of all, thank you very much for your warm hospitality. I am really happy to be in Ghana, as is my wife. This is her second time here, Mr. President. And I want to thank you for this grand welcome. And I appreciate your leadership.

Upstairs we talked about the Millennium Challenge Account. And it is a sizeable sum of taxpayers' money, aimed at helping you achieve your objectives, because your Government, led by you, is one that fights corruption and invests in its children, invests in the health of its citizens.

I'm oftentimes asked, "What difference does it make to America if people are dying of malaria in a place like Ghana or anywhere else?" It means a lot. It means a lot morally; it means a lot from a—it's in our national interests. After all, if you believe we're in an ideological struggle against extremism, which I do, the only way these people can recruit is when they find hopeless people. And there's nothing more hopeless than a mother losing a child needlessly to a mosquito bite.

We're going to—we spent time talking about trade, and I'm looking forward to meeting some of your businesses today, Mr. President. I believe firmly in fair trade, and I'm a strong supporter of AGOA. My predecessor put it in office; I've worked to get it reauthorized. And it's an important part of your development. Your businesspeople are making decisions. Your businesspeople are employing people in your country. And your businesspeople should have access to markets.

I do want to announce today that—I am announcing a new initiative dealing with disease, and that is—our plan is to make it available—a total of $350 million over 5 years—to target what they call neglected tropical diseases, such as hookworm or river blindness. This is all part of our initiative—whether it be on HIV/AIDS or malaria—to help save lives. And so, Mr. President, we're looking forward to working with you to help save lives and to bring hope to families.

I want to also announce today that we're going to devote nearly 17 dollars this—million dollars this year to help you on fighting malaria. I firmly believe your Government will do a fine job in getting mosquito nets and—to your people and medicines to your people. And so we're looking forward to helping you.

I also want to thank you for your leadership, Mr. President. As I said upstairs, I don't think a lot of people in Ghana—I hope a lot of people in Ghana understand this—what I'm about to say, but you're really one of the respected leaders around the world because of your firm commitment to peace. I thank you for your leadership here on the continent of Africa. My administration's strategy is to support African leaders to deal with Africa's problems.

I know there's a controversial subject brewing around that's not very well understood, and that's, why would America step—stand up what's called AFRICOM? Let me talk about a couple of points there,

241

Mr. President. First, this is a unique command structure for America. It is a command structure that is aiming to help provide military assistance to African nations, so African nations are more capable of dealing with Africa's conflicts, like peacekeeping training. Obviously, we've got an issue in Darfur that we've got to all work together to solve. And I'm very pleased that the AU and the U.N. hybrid force should be moving in there. I'd like to see it moving quicker, but the whole purpose of AFRICOM is to help leaders deal with African problems.

Secondly, we do not contemplate adding new bases. In other words, the purpose of this is not to add military bases. I know there's rumors in Ghana: "All Bush is coming to do is try to convince you to put a big military base here." That's baloney. [*Laughter*] Or as we say in Texas, "That's bull." [*Laughter*] Mr. President made it clear to me. He said, "Look, we—you're not going to build in any bases in Ghana." I said, "I understand; nor do we want to." Now, that doesn't mean we won't develop some kind of office somewhere in Africa. We haven't made our minds up. This is a new concept.

Now, Mr. President, I appreciate you giving me time to address this issue. I want to dispel the notion that all of a sudden, America is bringing all kinds of military to Africa. It's just simply not true. This is a way of making our command relevant to the strategy that we have put in place. And I feel no more confident than describing—I feel very confident in describing that strategy next to you because I am confident, Mr. President, in your capacity to be a strong leader. You've proved that to be the case.

And finally, he said we're both leaving office together. That's true. But we're going to leave strong with our heads held high, and we're going to sprint to the finish, aren't we, Mr. President?

President Kufuor. Indeed. Thank you.

President Bush. Good, thank you. Questions?

President Kufuor. Thank you, Mr. President. Well, may I just compliment what the President has just said. I am happy, one, for the President dispelling any notion that the United States of America is intending to build military bases on the continent of Africa. I believe the explanation the President has given should put fade to the speculation, so that the relationship between us and the United States will grow stronger and with mutual respect; that's for one.

Two, I should thank the President for the initiative he's just announced of creating a fund to fight the neglected diseases on the continent. My Government, for example, and I would say that for perhaps all African governments, is committed to fighting these diseases, but on a very shoestring budget, so that if our friends internationally would come out and launch initiatives like this to support us fight these diseases, then I will say, "Welcome, and thank you for that initiative."

Then the $17 million you are extending to my Government to help in the fight against malaria. Just this morning I saw in one of our papers that malaria, which perhaps kills more of us than even HIV/AIDS in Ghana, has increased by about 13 percent in our community. So any help that we can get in our fight to contain and eradicate this disease should be most welcome to the people of Ghana. And I thank you for what you've done.

President Bush. Yes, sir. Thank you.

President Kufuor. Thank you. I believe we'll——

President Bush. Want to answer a few questions?

President Kufuor. Yes, we can take questions.

President Bush. All right, good. Why don't you call on somebody in your press, sir.

President Kufuor. Please. Now, you identify yourself. Whoever is going to speak should identify themselves and the papers or radio stations, television stations they are working for.

President's Emergency Plan for AIDS Relief/President's Visit to Ghana

Q. Good morning, Your Excellencies, President Kufuor and President Bush. Thank you for taking my questions. First, a little bias, first to President Kufuor: I would like to know, fighting HIV/AIDS and malaria is the focus of this visit, but can you tell us in what other concrete terms this visit will benefit the economy of Ghana and Ghanaians in particular, since both of you leave office at the end of this year?

And then to President Bush: We know that your support for the fight against HIV/AIDS has been driven by promoting sexual abstinence and fidelity to each other's partner. In African societies, we know that this doesn't really strike a chord because multiple sexual relationships or partner relationships is the reality, though it's not spoken of in public. So how realistic an approach would you want be adopted in fighting HIV/AIDS within this particular context? Thank you.

President Bush. Yes, thanks.

President Kufuor. I answer first. The fight against HIV and malaria is not time bound; I'm sure you'd agree with me. The malaria, for instance, was with us from perhaps time immemorial, and it's still with us. Fortunately, we happen to be living in science and technology times, and solutions are being found quickly to pandemics. So within my time, I am happy the President of the United States of America has come out with large resources, talking of something like $45 billion; it's not something you hear of every day.

So I welcome that. And this money, I hope, will be put to the best uses, in terms of engaging the best scientific and technological means to tackle this disease. The research is still ongoing. Nobody is announcing a find yet, but we shouldn't give up. And within my time, I'm happy this help is coming to infuse the efforts we are already making, so that the researchers will continue. And long after me, perhaps some clever person, scientist, may come out with a solution. This is how I want to look at this. I do not give a time bound to the solution that we seek. Thank you.

President Bush. First of all, obviously, the status quo is not acceptable. One of the reasons that I was motivated to put forth a significant request to our Congress for a comprehensive program to deal with HIV/AIDS is, I felt it was unacceptable to stand by and watch a generation of people, a generation of folks be eradicated.

And so I understand customs and norms, but it seems like to me that if you really want to solve the problem, step one is to have a comprehensive prevention program. And you mentioned abstinence. No question, that's a part of the program—or be faithful. But also, I just want to remind you, there's a third part called condoms. So we have an ABC program that is a comprehensive part of the strategy.

And it's working. Uganda, for example, was the first country to really put the ABC strategy in place, and the results are measurable. All I'm interested in is results. I'm wise enough to set the strategy and change the tactics if they're not working.

Secondly, part of our strategy is to dispense antiretroviral drugs. When I first became President, 50,000 people were receiving ARVs; today, over 1.2 million are. As I said to our country, this is good. These are measurable results, and it's a good start, but it's only a start. And that's why, as the President mentioned, I've asked for Congress to double our budget on HIV/AIDS to 30 billion over 5.

And finally, part of the strategy is to take care of the orphans who have been left behind. Now I don't believe that sometimes bureaucracies are all that effective. And so part of our strategies is to trust the local leadership to devise strategies that best suits their country. And the other part of the strategy is to empower these compassionate folks who want to help, whether they be faith based or otherwise.

And so to answer your question, ma'am, I monitor the results. And if it looks like it's not working, then we'll change. But thus far, I can report, at least to our citizens, that the program has been unbelievably effective. And we're going to stay at it. And the purpose of this trip is to remind the American taxpayers that it's in their interest to help save lives on the continent of Africa. So this program will extend beyond my time in office as well as John Kufuor's time in office.

Ben Feller, Associated——

President Kufuor. May I just add, Mr. President——

President Bush. Yes, sure.

President Kufuor. ——to what you said. Unless we are challenging the statistic given by the AIDS Commission of Ghana, the very reputable establishment, the prevalence rate dropped from 2006, when it was 2.6 percent, to 2.2 percent in 2007. I believe that's considerable. And perhaps some of the credit should be given to the extension of help in terms of resources, including the antiretroviral drugs that we got from development partners like the United States of America.

So even as we agree to perhaps a bit of looseness in our ways, we must also admit that whatever input we are making, are contributing towards enabling us contain the menace; I believe I should add that. From 2.6 percent prevalence rate of HIV in 2007, we got 2.2 percent, a reduction of prevalence in 2006. I believe we should acknowledge that.

President Bush. All right. Ben Feller, Associated Press. I will identify him for you, Mr. President.

President Kufuor. Thank you.

President Bush. Ben Feller. [*Laughter*]

Pakistan/U.S. Aid to Africa

Q. Thank you for covering that, Mr. President.

President Bush. Yes. I was afraid you couldn't handle it.

Q. Thank you. President Bush, I would like to ask you about Pakistan. President Musharraf's party has been routed in parliamentary elections there, and it appears that he's lost the support of his people. Do you see this as the beginning of the end for him? Do you still view him as a credible leader in the fight against terrorism?

President Kufuor, I would like to ask you, President Bush has made a point on this trip of saying that helping Africa is in America's interest, but in the United States, a lot of people are focused on their own families and their own finances. Do you believe Americans see it in their interest to help Africa?

President Bush. Yes. I might try to help you out on the last question. America is wealthy enough to do both.

There was a victory for the people of Pakistan, and that is, there were elections held that have been judged as being fair. And the people have spoken. I view that as a significant victory. I view it as a part of the victory in the war on terror. After all, ideologues can't stand—like these guys we're dealing with—can't stand free societies. That's why they try to kill innocent people. That's why they tried to intimidate people during the election process.

And so I'm—I appreciate the fact that President Musharraf has done exactly that which he said he was going to do. He said he'd hold elections; he said he would get rid of his emergency law. And so it's now time for the newly elected folks to show up and form their Government. And the question then is, will they be friends of the United States? And I certainly hope so.

We view Pakistan as an important ally. We've got common interests. We've got interests in dealing with radicals who killed Benazir Bhutto. We've got interests in helping make sure there's no safe haven from which people can plot and plan attacks against the United States of America and Pakistan. And so that's my take on the elections.

President Kufuor. Thank you, and whether American interests coincides with African interests, I would say, yes. Yes. One should ask what the whole idea of the United States is about. The U.S. is a melting pot of all the races and nationalities of the world. Your country has a large content of African Americans, so that I would expect that constituency of Africa—and incidentally, the African Union has itemized the people of African descent as the sixth region of Africa. And so we look on the African Americans as our kith and kin, and they constitute a sizeable constituency in the United States. It should be in their interest to support any help the United States can extend to Africa. That's one.

Two, we are all moving into a global village, and problems overspill easily, especially with the free movements of people and trade, so that if the United States should lock itself into isolationism and think they are safer there, then I would say, perhaps they don't know what is coming, because global village is a reality. Migration cannot be stopped, and if you do not help, then the vibrant youth of Africa, driven by the technological age forces—they watch television, the Internet, and so forth—they want to move and see what's happening around the world. They will come to you, and if you do not help us to prepare this youth, then whatever youth would land on your shores would come with all the roughness, the hurry, and that would be your headache.

So I believe it's enlightenment for the United States Government to want to support them here. And then we talk terrorism, which has no bounds. As evidence, when the 9/11 happened in your country, it wasn't only Americans who became victims; some Ghanaians died in that event, and shows we have common interests somewhere. So these and other factors should account for why the United States,

perhaps industrially and otherwise the most advanced country in the world, should be concerned about the plight of other peoples. Thank you.

President's Visit to Africa/U.S. Role in Africa

Q. Good morning, Your Excellencies. My question is to President Bush. Looking at Africa from afar, things might look bleak, but all may not be lost yet. A new Africa is emerging. But in your candid view, what do you think Africa must do, and what kind of leadership do you expect to see in Africa? And how will the U.S. help in this regard, to push forward the agenda to transform the continent into a better place for its people?

And secondly, what do you hope to achieve from your five-nation tour, and why have you decided to visit Africa on the last lap of your term? And how do you want to ensure continuity in whatever you hope to achieve?

President Bush. Thanks. I actually went to Africa on the first lap of my Presidency too. This is my second trip to the continent of Africa, and I've come to remind our fellow citizens that it is in our interest to help countries deal with curable diseases like malaria and difficult diseases like HIV/AIDS; that it's in our interest to promote trade between the continent of Africa and the United States of America; that it's in our interest to provide education money so governments will educate children.

And there's no better way of making that point than to be in Ghana, where people will get to see firsthand what I'm talking about. It's one thing to be giving speeches in America, it's another thing to actually come to Ghana and meet different folks that are involved with making the—Ghana a better place.

Secondly, first of all, Africa has changed since I've been the President, in a very positive way. It's not because of me; it's because of African leaders—I want you to know. But there was six regional conflicts when I became the President. Take Liberia, for example. It was a real issue and a real problem, and along with Nigeria and with John's advice, for example, we—I made some decisions, along with other leaders, that helped put in place the first democratically elected woman on the continent's history. And I'm going there tomorrow to herald the successes she's done and to reaffirm our commitment that we'll help.

In other words, conflict resolution has been taking place. And the United States hasn't tried to impose a will. We've just tried to be a useful partner, like in eastern Congo, for example, working with the Presidents of Rwanda and Congo and Burundi.

Secondly, democracy is making progress across the continent of Africa. One reason why is because there are examples like John Kufuor for people to look at. I'm telling you, the guy is a respected person. People look at him, and they say, this is the kind of leader that we respect.

And thirdly, our aid program has changed from one that basically said, here's your money, good luck, to one that said, in return for generosity, we expect there to be certain habits in place, like fighting corruption or investing in the education of children. I don't think that's too much to ask in return for U.S. taxpayers' money. It hasn't been asked in the past. This is a novel approach, interestingly enough. But I feel confident in asking nations to adhere to good principles because I believe in setting high standards for African leaders.

I'm confident in the capacity of the leaders I have met—not every single leader—but on this trip, the leaders I'm with are leaders who have committed themselves to the good of their people, have committed themselves to honest government, have committed themselves to investing in people. They're more interested in leaving behind a legacy of education than leaving behind fancy—a self-serving government. And there's no better way of making that point than coming to the continent. And that's

why I'm here, and I'm glad I am here. It's been a great trip, and it's—and I appreciate the hospitality of my friend, and so does Laura.

Let's see here, John McKinnon. He would be from your Wall Street Journal. Yes, that's a pretty sophisticated paper, no question about that.

Q. Thanks for that plug.

President Bush. Yes. I didn't say, sophisticated reporter, I said, sophisticated paper. But—and a sophisticated reporter as well—yes, Johnny.

China

Q. Thank you, Mr. President. I would like to ask both you leaders about the increasing role of China in Africa's development. What do you think is positive about its role in aid and commerce, and what do you think it could be doing a better job with? In particular, do you think it's ignoring human rights issues and corruption?

President Bush. Well, I might let John start. He's, after all, been engaged with leaders. I have an opinion, but we'll let him start.

President Kufuor. I believe we should all agree, for starters, that the world is opening up and opening up fast. Values are becoming uniform, and the—our multinational efforts agenda, openness and competitiveness and all-inclusiveness. Now China is spreading out, and it's here in Africa and in Ghana too. It's coming not as a colonial power, as far as we can see; it's coming, if I may put it, as a guest and, I believe, on our terms, on the terms of the African nations.

And I can assure you, our nations are not succumbing to dictates and impositions, not from China nor elsewhere. If it's something that Africa wants to buy and it can find it economical, then whatever it is, that's where Africa will buy it from. And China is proving quite competitive. So how do we stop China? We can't stop China. We are relating, and we want to relate on common values. We believe that's what, again, globalization should be all about. We are in the United Nations with China. We talk World Trade Organization, and I believe China is finding its way into that.

President Bush. Yes.

President Kufuor. We want peace around the world. How do we have peace if we do not engage each other peacefully in trade, in common dialogue, and in other respects? So this is China. As to it being useful, and I would say, so far, so good. And I believe Africa is showing awareness because Africa came out of colonialism not too long ago. Ghana, for instance—the first country south of the Sahara to have gained independence—gained independence only 50 years ago. And I don't think the memory is lost to Africa.

So whatever friendships we are engaging in now, we try as hard as possible to turn our new partners around. We try to see if we are engaging on our best terms so we maximize returns for us. Of course, we also care about our partners feeling that they haven't come in here to be short-changed. There should be mutual advantage to all of us, and this is how we are engaging with China. So as far as we are concerned, so far, it's all right with China.

Human rights, well, this would call for knowledge of what obtains in China. I don't pretend that we are too informed of what happens inside China, but we believe that in due course, whatever the situation is, there will be a tendency towards liberalization. Before, the relationship with China was government to government; now it's getting to be people to people. It seems all of us are coming under the influences of the information and communications technology.

So our views are becoming the same. People are beginning to speak for themselves everywhere and standing for their rights. I believe even in China this will come to prevail in due course. And on this basis, I don't think it would be right for people to ostracize. Rather, we should find

ways and means to engage with each other so it becomes a more understanding world for all of us. Thank you.

President Bush. I don't view Africa as zero sum for China and the United States. I mean, I think their—we can pursue agendas that—without creating a great sense of competition. Inherent in your question is that I view China as a fierce competitor on the continent of Africa—no, I don't.

I view—first of all, I just will tell you that our policy is aimed at helping people. Trade helps people. I mean, one reason I'm committed to trying to get the Doha round complete is because the benefits of trade will far exceed monies given. I believe that it's in our Nation's interests— like, I noticed on the seal of the country it says, freedom and justice. There's nothing that promotes justice more than good education.

Now, I do think that it's in the leaders' interests to have some high standards; like, for example, I presume that countries are saying that if you bring your capital, make sure that you employ African workers. I know some of the leaders I've talked to have said that one of the things we're going to do is make sure that our environment is protected, our trees are protected; that we're not going to allow ourselves to become exploited; that we, in fact, want to have relations with different countries, including China, but there is—there will be some high standards. And that's the way it should be, high standards for every country. And the United States, of course, is willing to live with those standards. We believe in those standards.

And so one thing that I hope that we're getting, that we all can do better, is to encourage value-added processing. And one of the things that has been lacking in Africa's past is for the people to really, truly realize the benefits of the resources at home, because those resources are just dug out of the ground or grown and just shipped overseas, when, in fact, if there could be facilities that take advantage of those resources, it will create more employment for people. And I know that John is concerned about that.

And my only point is, there ought to be—you know, these countries ought to set standards and expect countries to live by them. And there's plenty of leaders who are willing to do that.

Anyway, thank you very much, Mr. President. It's been a joyful experience here in the press conference.

President Kufuor. Thank you, Mr. President, for coming.

President Bush. Yes, sir.

President Kufuor. Thank you, ladies and gentlemen.

NOTE: The President's news conference began at 10:38 a.m. at Osu Castle. In his remarks, he referred to President Pervez Musharraf of Pakistan; former Prime Minister and Opposition Leader Benazir Bhutto of Pakistan, who was killed in a suicide attack in Rawalpindi, Pakistan, on December 27, 2007; President Ellen Johnson Sirleaf of Liberia; President Paul Kagame of Rwanda; President Joseph Kabila of the Democratic Republic of the Congo; and President Pierre Nkurunziza of Burundi.

Remarks at the United States Embassy in Accra
February 20, 2008

Thank you all. First, I want to thank Jordin Sparks for taking time out of her busy schedule to join us here in Ghana and for performing such a beautiful version of our national anthem. By prevailing on last season's "American Idol," Jordin showed the world she has a great voice. Raising awareness about malaria means that she has got great compassion and a big heart.

In addition to some great singing, last year's "American Idol" featured a fundraising campaign called Idol Gives Back. The campaign brought in more than $75 million for charities working in the United States and Africa. Seventeen million dollars went to organizations that protect American families—African families from malaria. And one of these charities, Malaria No More, has used the donations to provide bed nets for more than 2 million mothers

and children in Uganda and Angola and Madagascar and Mali and Zambia.

Last spring, Laura and I made an appearance on "American Idol"—not because of our voices. [*Laughter*] We went on the show to thank viewers for participating in the Idol Gives Back campaign. This spring, FOX and "American Idol" will once again appeal to viewers to help defeat malaria. On April 9th, the show will raise money to fight malaria in Africa and support other worthy causes to the second round of Idol Gives Back.

Laura and I hope, and Jordin hopes, that America's generosity will still pour forth. And we ask our fellow citizens to contribute to this worthy cause.

NOTE: The President spoke at 11:36 a.m. in the Ambassador's residence. In his remarks, he referred to entertainer Jordin Sparks.

Remarks During a Lunch With Peace Corps Volunteers in Accra
February 20, 2008

Ambassador, thank you very much for setting up this lunch. Laura and I and Condi are thrilled to be with some of our most notable citizens. These are folks who have left the comfort of America to join the Peace Corps to serve humanity, and we're really looking forward to hearing your stories and hearing what life is like.

And one of the things I tell our country all the time is, our great strength lies in the hearts and souls of our citizens. And I don't think there's any more giving people than the Peace Corps volunteers. And so, Robert, thank you very much for joining us and bringing along some of the—our fellow citizens who are making a huge difference in people's lives.

I'm sure you would like to share a few remarks.

[*At this point, the discussion continued, and no transcript was provided.*]

NOTE: The President spoke at 12:02 p.m. in the Ambassador's residence at the U.S. Embassy. In his remarks, he referred to U.S. Ambassador to Ghana Pamela E. Bridgewater; and Robert W. Golledge, Jr., Country Director, Peace Corps—Ghana.

Remarks Prior to a Tee-Ball Game in Accra
February 20, 2008

Welcome to tee-ball in Ghana. Yes, we're glad you're here. Thanks for coming. I am so honored to be here for—to witness the game between—I want to make sure I get this right—the Little Dragons and the Little Saints.

Yes, I appreciate the Secretary of State coming, Condoleezza Rice. Madam Secretary, thank you. I appreciate very much the Ambassador joining us. Madam Ambassador, thank you. And we got a Major League scout here—yes, Jimmie Lee Solomon from Major League Baseball. He's looking for some talent. Good to see you, Jimmie Lee.

Listen, thank you all for letting us come by. I'm very excited about watching this game. I do want to thank your coaches. Thanks for coaching. Thanks for teaching people the importance of teamwork. I like baseball a lot, so thanks for teaching them how to play baseball too.

And are you ready to start? Are you going to give me that ball? All right, come on over. This is the first ball. Ready? You want to put it on the tee? Play ball.

NOTE: The President spoke at 2:55 p.m. at the Ghana International School. In his remarks, he referred to U.S. Ambassador to Ghana Pamela E. Bridgewater; and Jimmie Lee Solomon, executive vice president, baseball operations, Major League Baseball.

Remarks at a State Dinner Hosted by President John Agyekum Kufuor of Ghana in Accra
February 20, 2008

Mr. President, Mrs. Kufuor, and all the distinguished guests here: Thank you for your warm welcome. And I would like to take this opportunity to thank the good people of Ghana for the wonderful welcome Laura and I received. I don't think I have been to a country where the people have been more friendly, more open. We appreciate so very much your hospitality, and I really appreciate the George Bush Motorway. [*Laughter*] The next time I come and ride on the George Bush Motorway, I promise that we will not shut the highway down. [*Laughter*]

President Kufuor is a close friend. He has earned my respect, and he's earned the respect of leaders all across the world. He is an accomplished man with a good mind and a good heart.

We first met in 2001; we were new Presidents. And here we are, nearly 7 years later, and we're fixing to leave office. [*Laughter*] But we both vow: We will finish strong with our heads held high.

In the remaining months, we will work to strengthen the partnership between our two nations. The ties that bind the United States and Ghana are as long as they are deep. Last year, Ghana commemorated the 50th anniversary of its independence. And when you claimed your liberty in 1957, the United States of America was by your side. Richard Nixon and Martin Luther King, Jr., were among the notable Americans who were here when the Union Jack was replaced by the red, yellow, and green of the Republic of Ghana. Four years later, 51 idealistic young Americans arrived in your beautiful country as Ghana became the first nation to host volunteers from the Peace Corps.

This long tradition of friendship and cooperation continues today. Today, Ghana and the United States are working to strengthen democracy and good government. Together, we're harnessing the power of global trade to alleviate poverty. And, Mr. President, rest assured, I will work to complete the Doha round. Together, we're working to preserve peace, combat disease, and help ensure that all of Ghana's citizens can give their children what we all want for our children, a more hopeful future.

And so, Mr. President, I want to thank you for your friendship. I thank you for your leadership. I thank you for your kindness. And I offer a toast to you, your gracious wife, and to the noble people of Ghana. God bless.

NOTE: The President spoke at 7:58 p.m. in the State Banquet Hall. In his remarks, he referred to Theresa Kufuor, wife of President Kufuor. The transcript released by the Office of the Press Secretary also included the remarks of President Kufuor.

Remarks on Arrival in Monrovia, Liberia
February 21, 2008

President Ellen Johnson Sirleaf of Liberia. Let me say how pleased we are to welcome President Bush, Mrs. Bush, Secretary Rice, and all the members of this delegation. It is a great honor for Liberia to receive them. And they've received a very warm welcome from the Liberian people, from our young people, from our students, who lined the route and waved and showed flags. We're just so pleased and honored. Thank you, President Bush, for making this trip.

President Bush. Madam President, thanks. I've been looking forward to coming here ever since you extended the kind invitation to me. I do want to thank the people of Liberia for the warm welcome that we have received. I loved all the smiles and the enthusiasm along the route.

Most importantly, I want the people of Liberia to know, Madam President, the United States stands with you. We want to help you recover from a terrible period. We want you to build lives of hope and peace. And under your leadership, that's exactly what's happening. It is my honor to have presented you with the National Medal of Freedom. It's the highest civilian award a President can give, and I did so because of your courage and your leadership. And we are so excited to be with you.

Thank you.

President Johnson Sirleaf. Thank you.

NOTE: The President spoke at 10:23 a.m. at the Ministry of Foreign Affairs.

Remarks at a Lunch Hosted by President Ellen Johnson Sirleaf of Liberia in Monrovia
February 21, 2008

Madam President, I want to make sure I've got the following correctly: Here they call you the "Iron Lady," and here they call you "Ma." And I call you friend.

We are honored to be here. Laura and I are thrilled to be here with our delegation to end what has been a very productive trip to the continent of Africa. I can't think of a better place to finish than in—with our dear friend, Liberia.

It is easy to destroy a country; it is hard to rebuild a country. And I—Madam President, I want you to know that the United States of America supports you as you rebuild your country. We share a special history with Liberia. It's a history that is deep, and I want the people of your beautiful country to know that our help is just beginning.

And so, Madam President, I propose a toast to you and the strength of your leadership and the quality of your character. And to the good people of Liberia, may God bless.

NOTE: The President spoke at 12:54 p.m. in the Executive Mansion. The transcript released by the Office of the Press Secretary also included the remarks of President Johnson Sirleaf.

Remarks During a Visit to the Barclay Training Center in Monrovia
February 21, 2008

Madam President, you're right: We have met four times, and every time, I'm the better for it. [*Laughter*] I appreciate the warm welcome we've received from the people of your beautiful country.

We bring with us the greetings and best wishes of the American people. I'm proud to be traveling today not only with a strong delegation, headed by my wife, but also the Secretary of State, Condoleezza Rice.

I'm so honored to be with your troops. I'm looking forward to the display of talent and professionalism we're about to see. I thank those who've worked hard to help them become professional soldiers, all in the cause of bringing peace and security to the people of Liberia.

Though we're over 4,500 miles from the United States, I feel pretty much at home here. In Liberia, you fly the "lone star" flag. [*Laughter*] Of course, I was the former Governor of Texas. [*Laughter*] We call ourselves the Lone Star State. [*Laughter*] Your capital is named for an American President, and, of course, I am an American President. [*Laughter*] The name of your country, Liberia, means "land of the free," and there is no place I feel more welcome than a land where liberty is love and the hope of freedom reigns.

This country was founded by former American slaves who came here seeking the freedom they had been denied in my country. Through hard work and determination, they established the first independent republic on the continent of Africa. The free country they built became a source of pride for her people and a strong ally in the cause of freedom. As the President said, Franklin Roosevelt came here in 1943 to confer with your great President, Edwin Barclay. Together, our two nations helped defeat the forces of fascism. Together, our two nations helped saved millions from lives of tyranny and despair.

In the intervening years, Liberia saw days of challenge and sorrow. You suffered the descent into dictatorship and chaos. Civil wars took the lives of hundreds of thousands of your citizens. Yet even in their darkest moments, the Liberian people never gave up on the hope that this great nation would once again be the land of the free that its founders intended.

In 2005, you reclaimed your liberty. You went to the polls and chose the first woman ever elected to lead an African nation. President Ellen Johnson Sirleaf has been a strong leader for the Liberian people. She has been a strong partner of the United States of America. I'm proud to call her friend, and I'm proud of the work we are doing together to help the people of this nation build a better life.

Together, we're fighting the scourge of disease. It is irresponsible for comfortable nations to stand by knowing that young babies are dying from mosquito bites. It is unnecessary, and the United States will continue to lead the cause to eradicate malaria from the continent of Africa.

We're working to lift the burden of debt so that Liberia can achieve her potential and unleash the entrepreneurial spirit of her citizens. We're working to help the children of Liberia get a good education so they'll have the skills they need to turn their freedom into a future of prosperity and peace. And today, Madam President, I'm proud to announce that the United States will provide 1 million textbooks over the next year, as well as desks and seating for at least 10,000 Liberian schoolchildren by the start of the new school year.

Together, with the help of the United Nations Mission in Liberia, we're working to heal the wounds of war and strengthen democracy and build a new armed forces that will be a source of security for the Liberian people, instead of a source of terror.

In all these areas, we're making good progress. You know, one of the things I've learned and I suspect the people of Liberia have learned, it's easier to tear a country down than it is to rebuild a country. And the people of this good country must understand, the United States will stand with you as you rebuild your country.

And you are making progress, and it's possible because of the iron will of the lady you lovingly refer to as "Ma." That would be you, Madam President. [*Laughter*] I appreciate the fact that you've ushered in an age of reform, and you've opened up a new chapter in the relationship between our country. And as you mentioned, it was my high honor to welcome you to the White House last year and present you with America's highest civil honor, the Presidential Medal of Freedom.

I'm pleased to visit your land. I thank you for the invitation. I thank the Liberian people for courage and steadfastness and enduring faith in the power of freedom. With your continued determination, there is no doubt in my mind that Liberia will become a beacon of liberty for Africa and the world, and you will forever uphold the "lone star."

May God bless you, and may God bless the people of Liberia.

NOTE: The President spoke at 2:34 p.m.

Remarks Prior to a Discussion on Education in Monrovia
February 21, 2008

President Ellen Johnson Sirleaf of Liberia. Mr. President, Mrs. Bush, fellow Liberians: We have been pleased that with the support of the United States Government to our education rebuilding process, we can now say that we're beginning to see the signs of progress.

Mr. President, today you will be listening to some of the beneficiaries who will be sharing their experience with you. They've been supported through the United States Agency for International Development, the President's Africa Education Initiative. Liberia currently receives assistance for adult learners, primary school students, school infrastructure, teacher training, the accelerated learning program, and improvement of higher education.

Thank you for being here with us. And thank you for all that you do, for helping us to rebuild our educational system.

President Bush. Thank you, Madam President. [*Applause*] Does that mean you want me to speak? [*Laughter*]

President Johnson Sirleaf. You speak a little bit, and I'll introduce the——

President Bush. Okay, good, yes. The President said, we have met four times since she's been President. I said out there at the parade grounds that every time, I'm a better person for it, since she's a—[*applause*]. This is the last event on the last stop of what has been a comprehensive trip around the continent of Africa. And it's a fitting—fitting that we talk about education as the last subject to discuss.

First of all, I just want you to know that, Madam President, we admire you, and we appreciate your leadership. I particularly appreciate your commitment to liberty and freedom. Now, the problem is, of course, it's one thing to be for freedom, but it's really important to have a healthy, educated group of folks to be able to realize the blessings of freedom.

And so our desire in the United States is to answer the universal call to love a neighbor and to help those—I believe to whom much is given, much is required. A lot has been given the United States of America, and I firmly believe it's in our national interest to help others not only realize the blessings of liberty but to fight disease when we find it and to deal with illiteracy where we encounter it.

And so our initiative on malaria or the AIDS initiative is all aimed at saving lives, which in essence helps save societies. And same thing with our education initiative. And so we really appreciate you all coming to share your message with us. I hope you're not nervous. [*Laughter*] I bet you're not, because all you got to do is tell us what's on your mind. Just share your stories, and I think people will find that they're most interested.

But what you must know here in Liberia is that the United States of America is with you, and we'll stay with you because we want you to succeed. It's in the interest of the United States of America that Liberia do well. And so, Madam President, we are—[*applause*]—we're proud to stand with you. We're not going to tell you what to do because you're plenty competent. I believe African leaders can run African countries. But I do believe the United States of America can help. And that's exactly what we're going to discuss today, Madam President.

So thank you very much for that introduction. And Laura is thrilled to be here as well. She is the librarian in the family. [*Laughter*]

President Johnson Sirleaf. That's right.

[*At this point, the discussion continued, and no transcript was provided.*]

NOTE: The President spoke at 3:04 p.m. at the University of Liberia.

Interview With Reporters Aboard Air Force One
February 21, 2008

White House Press Secretary Dana Perino. So I thought the President and Mrs. Bush would spend a little bit of time with you, with their reflections, on the record. We don't have a lot of time, especially because Ben Feller [Associated Press] is not feeling well.

The President. I would say this is one of the most exciting trips of my Presidency. Exciting because when we first got to Washington, Africa was—parts of Africa were in turmoil; not much had been to arrest disease; there wasn't intense world focus on the continent. The second trip to Africa for me—the fifth for Laura—was a chance to herald courageous people in their efforts to deal with hopelessness. And what really made me happy was that the people of Africa have come to appreciate the generosity of the American people.

I had a couple of goals. One was to encourage people to continue to make difficult choices—democracy is hard work—but also assure them that we'd stay with them if they made the right choices.

Secondly, I wanted to highlight for the American people what the—that great compassionate work is being done. And I'll give you some—Laura can share some anecdotes too. You know, in the hospital in Tanzania, to see a 3-year-old baby survive a mosquito bite when years earlier probably wouldn't have was a very compelling moment for me.

To have the little orphans in Rwanda put on such a cheerless—a cheery face because somebody is trying to provide them love was inspiring to me. To watch their little guys play tee-ball—all of whom were orphans—against the little school and see how inspired they were. But also see the concern and care of their mentors and coaches was very inspiring to me.

All of these programs are supported by the American taxpayer, and all of them matter. To hear the testimony of these kids and teachers in Liberia about how our aid has helped them regain confidence—I don't know if you all were in there when the mother of three talked about—her husband left her, she said, because she was illiterate, so he just left her with the three kids. And she's a part of this adult literacy program that USAID is helping with. She talked about being able to read, fill out bank checks, her deposit slips, then announced she wanted to go to college, and then announced she wanted to take Ellen Johnson Sirleaf's job. [*Laughter*]

Anyway, it's the human condition that matters. You heard me say a lot on the trip that we're on a mission of mercy, and that's what I think we are. And I think it's in our national interest to do it. I know this: I know that when you volunteer as an individual to help somebody who hurts, it helps you. Well, I believe the same when it comes to collective hearts of America. So it's been a—it's an exciting trip. I mean, you saw the crowds, you saw the enthusiasm.

But that's not what's important. You know, people say—Bob Geldof asked me, he said: "Why don't you take credit for it? Why don't you show what you have done for Africa?" Well, it's not me, for starters. And you don't act out of the desire to enhance your own standing; that's not exactly why one is called into service. It doesn't matter about me. What matters is, are we saving people's lives? That's what matters. And we are.

And so I'm really pleased with it and had great meetings with the leaders. It seems like a couple of months ago that we went to Benin. [*Laughter*] But he's a good guy. He's enthusiastic. And of course, Kikwete in Tanzania and Kagame in—look, the other thing about the Rwanda stop and the Liberia stop is, these are societies that only recently have been ravished by unbelievable and unspeakable violence. And yet they're getting back on their feet. And it's hard work, and we'll help them. That was what I told them. And these were five very strong leaders that we visited with.

Which leads me to conclude this—and Laura can share some thoughts—America should not be dictating to these countries, America ought to be helping leaders make decisions. And that's what we're doing. And we go to Africa with a belief in the capacity of human beings to meet high standards. That's what I kept trying to say to you

out there in code. We didn't go guilt ridden. We go with a positive sense about the capacity of leaders to rise to the challenge and meet certain basic criteria, such as honest government, investing in children, investing in health, and understanding that marketplace economics and trade is more powerful than accepting relief from countries.

Anyway—and how about the Liberian troops? You talk about proud people. Wasn't it unbelievable? "Yeah, Mr. President, it was." [*Laughter*]

Yes, Laura.

[*At this point, the First Lady made brief remarks.*]

The President. Okay, we'll do a round-robin here. Yes, Ann [Ann Compton, ABC News], you're the senior person.

African View of the 2008 U.S. Presidential Election/Texas Presidential Primary

Q. One of the things that we heard from people—I guess they do consider the United States a democracy, a role model. What if an American—African American were elected President? Did they talk to you——

The President. That never came up.

Q. It never came up?

The First Lady. It never came up to us at all. They said they were very fascinated with the election, one group that I talked to.

The President. I'd just like to remind you what Kikwete said. He said, "I hope the next President is as good as this one." Now, I'm not blowing my own horn—[*laughter*]—and I'm sure it was a screaming headline. [*Laughter*]

Q. Are you going to vote in the Texas primary?

The President. Yes, I am.

Q. As a Democrat or a Republican?

The President. I think I'll be in the Republican primary this year.

No, but it never came up. It seemed like a good storyline at the time. Somebody must be putting something out there in the pool, and everybody starts chatting about it.

Q. People would mention it to us.

The President. If you asked them, yes, "What do you think about Obama?" Yes, they mentioned it to you all right. Yes. [*Laughter*]

Q. I asked them—I went out on the street, and two of the four people I asked about—you know, I'd say, Obama——

The President. What?

Q. McCain—they like—they volunteered, two of them——

The President. Really?

The First Lady. What country?

Q. Dar es Salaam.

The President. Look, my mind was not on U.S. politics on this trip; it's just not. It is on yours, not mine. I'm focused on conducting foreign policy. Look, I understand this is the way it's going to be. We'll be having roundtables, and you're going to be fascinated on the latest thing on politics, and I'm going to be fascinated on trying to lay the foundation for lasting foreign policy that will make a significant difference to the United States. I'm not going to be frustrated about it—except every time. No. [*Laughter*]

President's Legacy/U.S. Foreign Policy

Q. A question on that—is this how, in the end, you would like this effort—or this kind of effort, if this not specific one—this is what your Presidency is ultimately about?

The President. We just have to let history be the judge. But we've been a very active—we've had a very active foreign policy, whether it be liberating people from tyranny in order to protect ourselves or liberating people from disease, we've been active and strong and bold. And we'll let history judge the results.

I would just tell you this, and you've heard me say it, and it's true: There's no such thing as short-term political history. I mean, short-term history of an administration—forget "political"—there is such thing as short-term political history because there's an end result, win or lose. There's no such thing as an accurate history of an administration until time has lapsed, unless you're doing little-bitty things.

[*The First Lady made further remarks.*]

The President. The other thing about—one of the things I hope people, when they are able to take an objective look at an administration—which I'm not sure is possible, if you happen to have been living at the time of the administration; maybe you can, I don't think so—is whether or not an administration makes decisions based upon certain fundamental principles from which it will not vary. And you've heard me say over and over again, freedom is universal, or to whom much is given, much is required. Those are fundamental principles on which one can have a foreign policy.

And one of the great dangers for America is to become isolationist or protectionist. And the purpose of—on trips like this is to remind people of the need not to become isolationist. And so it's—I view this as—this was a trip that heralded results. But it was also a trip that gives us an opportunity to explain over and over again the foundations of the foreign policy of the Bush administration.

Yes, Feller. How you feeling, man? I've asked you twice. You look like you're a little pale.

Intelligence Reform Legislation

Q. I'm hanging in there.

The President. Have you vomited yet today? [*Laughter*]

Q. That's off the record. [*Laughter*]

Q. No, that's on the record. [*Laughter*]

Q. I see a big microphone. [*Laughter*]

I'd like to ask you about an issue they're raising back home, and it's not the '08 campaign.

The President. Okay.

Q. On FISA, I understand your position, but what I'm unclear about is whether you're doing something to break the deadlock. Do you see yourself engaging with the other side, compromising? Or where do we go from here?

The President. How do you compromise on something like granting liability for a telecommunications company? You can't. If we do not give liability protection to those who are helping us, they won't help us. And if they don't help us, there will be no program. And if there's no program, America is more vulnerable.

What I'm going to do is continue to remind people that unless they get this program done, we're going to be vulnerable to attack.

Q. Do you see an opportunity to work with the Democrats and——

The President. I mean, there may be one, I don't know. But I will just tell you, there's no compromise on whether or not these phone companies get liability protection. See, what the American people must understand is that without help from the phone companies, there is no program. And these companies are going to be subject to multibillion dollar lawsuits by trial lawyers, plaintiffs' attorneys. And it's going to drive them away from helping us, unless they get liability protection, prospective and retroactive.

It's just so important for people to understand the dangers. If we don't have the capacity to listen to these terrorists, we're not going to be able to protect ourselves.

White House Press Secretary Perino. Just a reminder that they have the votes to pass it in the House.

The President. They've got enough votes to pass the bill in the House. So yes, I'm going to talk about it a lot and keep reminding the American—I'm glad you asked the question, because this will give everybody a chance to know the dangers of the course that some in the House have put us on. And I'll keep talking about it.

You know what? The American people understand that we need to be listening to the enemy.

Situation in Kenya

Q. Back to Africa, on Kenya—on Kenya, I'm trying to understand——

The President. Kenya?

Q. Kenya, yes.

The President. That's why you've got the Secretary sitting here.

Q. Exactly. I mean, are you going to send her back? Where are we? What's next? And how realistic is it—I still don't understand how anyone is really thinking that the Government, which has been so stubborn, is actually going to——

The President. ——the opposition.

Q. Yes.

The President. That's the dilemma; how you get two people to sit down at a table and work on what's best for Africa—I mean, for Kenya.

Q. But realistically, how do you? I mean, are you going to——

The President. She was in the room with them.

Q. Are you going to go back?

The President. We got Frazer, who's plenty competent.

[*Secretary of State Condoleezza Rice made brief remarks.*]

The President. I was going to say that, you know, the most effective way to get these issues resolved is for these leaders to feel pressure from their own people. And it's one thing for Kofi and Condi and people making phone calls, but Kenya is a society; it's got a—for example, Kenya is the economic engine for East Africa. I don't know if you saw all those ships in Dar es Salaam. Those were originally—many of them were originally headed for Nairobi, interestingly enough. And I suspect these leaders are beginning to feel a lot of pressure internal.

Secondly, they're actually hearing from African leaders about the dangers of allowing these kind of conflicts to not be nipped in the bud early, to be prevented from happening. And we will help. We sent people over, and we'll stay engaged. It's really up to the Kenyan society itself and the leaders there to get their leaders with them.

Q. Doesn't it seem to be that they're pressuring with violence?

The President. With what?

Q. The way that they're pressuring, it seems to be with violence.

The President. No, no, no, you're missing it. There is a civil society in Nairobi. You're talking about some of the splinter groups on some of the parties. There is a civil society, and it's a relatively sophisticated civil society that is exerting pressure, that is not resorting to violence.

Secretary Rice. The Kenyan press is very tough on these leaders to resolve this— [*inaudible*]—civil society—[*inaudible*]— people who are pressing for peaceful change and saying, you cannot let our society collapse into anarchy.

Return Trip From Africa

The President. I get to ask a question. Will you be taking a nap on the way back?

Q. I didn't sleep one wink last night, but if I sleep on the flight home, I won't sleep when I get home, and I have to be at the office at 6:15 a.m.

The President. You're going to go around the clock?

Q. Well, I might try.

The President. I'm actually promoting— I've obviously got a nap on my mind. [*Laughter*] I was just trying to, like, plant the seed.

Yes, Rog [Roger Runningen, Bloomberg News].

U.S. View of the President's Visit to Africa

Q. I want to go back to Africa. You talked about Americans and their generosity——

The President. What's that?

Q. Americans and their generosity—what do you think that Americans think of your trip?

The President. I don't have any idea. What are you writing about it? I don't know what they think of it. Ask another question. I really don't know. I'm focused on the trip.

When I get home, I pick up a book and start reading it, and I'm sound asleep shortly thereafter. So I'm not—I don't know. I really don't know.

The First Lady. Depends on what you all are showing.

The President. I don't know. I hope they think—here's what I hope they think: It's worthwhile to be supportive of a robust policy on the continent of Africa. It's worth our national security interest, and it's worth our interest to help people learn to read and write and save babies' lives from mosquito bites. That's what I hope they realize, and that's one of the main—that's a critical reason to go on the trip. I would hope that the country never says, well, it's not worth it over there, what happens over there—or it says, well, we've got to take care of our own first, exclusively.

And my answer is, we can do both. We're a generous country. And we do, do both.

U.S. Aid for Africa

Q. Do you have everything in place so that the next President, who might not look at Africa in the first 6 months—everything is in place to continue?

The President. ——you know, getting this funding from PEPFAR. And I think we will. The PEPFAR program has been great. It's a bipartisan success. Congress funded the thing—not the "thing," Congress funded the program, and they ought to take great pride in the success of PEPFAR. There's a process that goes on to get it reauthorized, and we'll try to get it funded, and will get it funded. I feel pretty good about getting it funded.

Same with the malaria initiative: It's making a huge difference, and the success is unbelievable. In Zanzibar, 20 percent of the kids were infected, had gotten malaria. Now it's one [percent],* in a pretty quick period of time.

Okay, guys.

NOTE: The interview began at 4:42 p.m. en route from Monrovia, Liberia, to Andrews Air Force Base, MD. In his remarks, the President referred to President Ellen John-son Sirleaf of Liberia; musician and activist Robert Geldof; President Thomas Yayi Boni of Benin; President Jakaya Mrisho Kikwete of Tanzania; President Paul Kagame of Rwanda; Sen. Barack Obama; Assistant Secretary of State for African Affairs Jendayi E. Frazer; and former Secretary-General Kofi Annan of the United Nations. A reporter referred to Sen. John McCain. A tape was not available for verification of the content of this interview.

The President's Radio Address
February 23, 2008

Good morning. This Thursday, Laura and I returned from an inspiring visit to Africa. In Benin and Tanzania, we met leaders who are fighting HIV/AIDS and malaria and people whose lives have been saved by the generosity of the American people. In Rwanda, we saw a nation overcoming the pain of genocide with courage and grace and hope. In Ghana, we met entrepreneurs who are exporting their products and building a more prosperous future. And in Liberia, we saw a nation that is recovering from civil war, led by the first democratically elected woman President on the continent. Laura and I returned to Washington impressed by the energy, optimism, and potential of the African people.

Members of Congress will soon be returning to Washington as well, and they have urgent business to attend to. They left town on a 10-day recess without passing vital legislation giving our intelligence professionals the tools they need to quickly and effectively monitor foreign terrorist communications. Congress's failure to pass this legislation was irresponsible. It will leave our Nation increasingly vulnerable to attack, and Congress must fix this damage to our national security immediately.

The way ahead is clear. The Senate has already passed a good bill by an overwhelming bipartisan majority. This bill has strong bipartisan support in the House of Representatives and would pass if given an up-or-down vote. But House leaders are blocking this legislation, and the reason can be summed up in three words: class-action lawsuits.

The Senate bill would prevent plaintiffs' attorneys from suing companies believed to have helped defend America after the 9/11 attacks. More than 40 of these lawsuits have been filed, seeking hundreds of billions of dollars in damages from these companies. It is unfair and unjust to threaten these companies with financial ruin only because they are believed to have done the right thing and helped their country.

But the highest cost of all is to our national security. Without protection from lawsuits, private companies will be increasingly unwilling to take the risk of helping us with vital intelligence activities. After the Congress failed to act last week, one telecommunications company executive was

---

* White House correction.

asked by the Wall Street Journal how his company would respond to a request for help. He answered that because of the threat of lawsuits, quote: "I'm not doing it. I'm not going to do something voluntarily." In other words, the House's refusal to act is undermining our ability to get cooperation from private companies, and that undermines our efforts to protect us from terrorist attack.

Director of National Intelligence Mike McConnell recently explained that the vast majority of the communications infrastructure we rely on in the United States is owned and operated by the private sector. Because of the failure to provide liability protection, he says, private companies who have "willingly helped us in the past are now saying, 'You can't protect me. Why should I help you?'" Senator Jay Rockefeller, the Democratic chairman of the Senate Intelligence Committee, puts it this way: "The fact is, if we lose cooperation from these or other private companies, our national security will suffer."

When Congress reconvenes on Monday, Members of the House have a choice to make: They can empower the trial bar, or they can empower the intelligence commu-

nity. They can help class-action trial lawyers sue for billions of dollars, or they can help our intelligence officials protect millions of lives. They can put our national security in the hands of plaintiffs' lawyers, or they can entrust it to the men and women of our Government who work day and night to keep us safe.

As they make their choice, Members of Congress must never forget: Somewhere in the world, at this very moment, terrorists are planning the next attack on America. And to protect America from such attacks, we must protect our telecommunications companies from abusive lawsuits.

Thank you for listening.

NOTE: The address was recorded at 10 a.m. on February 22 in the Cabinet Room at the White House for broadcast at 10:06 a.m. on February 23. The transcript was made available by the Office of the Press Secretary on February 22, but was embargoed for release until the broadcast. In his address, the President referred to President Ellen Johnson Sirleaf of Liberia. The Office of the Press Secretary also released a Spanish language transcript of this address.

Remarks at a Dinner for the National Governors Association Conference
February 24, 2008

Good evening. Laura and I are honored to have you here, and it's a pleasure to be here with a lot of friends. You know, I've developed a unique perspective on this event. For 6 years, I sat and watched the President speak; for 8 years, I was the President and spoke. [*Laughter*] And next year, I'll be watching on C–SPAN. [*Laughter*]

I appreciate Tim Pawlenty and Ed Rendell, for—serve as the chair and vice chair of the National Governors Association. I congratulate our two newest Gov-

ernors, Kentucky's Steve Beshear and Louisiana's Bobby Jindal. I might add, Jindal is not here, but he's ably represented by the first lady of Louisiana, Supriya. And I congratulate Governor Haley Barbour of Mississippi for his reelection. I want to thank the Vice President and Lynne Cheney for joining us. I also tell you how thankful I am and honored we are that Vince Gill and Amy Grant have come tonight to entertain us.

I value our Governors because our Governors are some of the Nation's foremost policy entrepreneurs. I appreciate what you do. I appreciate the sacrifice your families have made to serve America.

It was in that spirit that Teddy Roosevelt hosted the first Governors meeting here at the White House 100 years ago. I can't imagine what they were thinking about what America would look like 100 years ago, and I'm not sure what people will think 100 years from now. But I do know it makes sense to put wise policy in place

in the meantime so America can remain prosperous and strong and free.

And so tonight it's my honor to welcome you all and to offer a toast to the Nation's Governors.

NOTE: The President spoke at 7:30 p.m. in the State Dining Room at the White House. In his remarks, he referred to Gov. Timothy J. Pawlenty of Minnesota; Gov. Edward G. Rendell of Pennsylvania; and entertainers Vince Gill and Amy Grant.

Remarks During a Meeting With the National Governors Association Conference
February 25, 2008

The President. Thank you very much. I'm supposed to stall to wait for the press corps. [*Laughter*] Chairman, thanks. Let me see your book there, will you? That thing right there, yes. Mr. Vice Chairman, thank you, sir. Hope you enjoyed last night.

Governor Edward G. Rendell of Pennsylvania. Yes, it was great.

The President. It was great, yes. It was fun. I am proud to announce to you that Janet Creighton is running the Intergovernmental Affairs Office for us. She looks forward to working with you. I look forward to hearing from you. There's a lot we can do to—for the next 10 months to work together. I like to tell people, you know, I'm going to finish strong, and I want to work with you as I do so.

A couple of areas I want to talk about, then I'll answer a couple of questions. And then evidently, we're going to have a 100th anniversary picture.

We share a responsibility to protect our country. I get briefed every morning about threats we face, and they're real. Now— and therefore, the question is, what do you do about them? In my judgment, we have got to give the professionals who work hard to protect us all the tools they need. To

put it bluntly: If the enemy is calling to America, we really need to know what they're saying, and we need to know what they're thinking, and we need to know what—who they're talking to.

It's—this is a different kind of struggle than we've ever faced before. It's essential that we understand the mentality of these killers. And so therefore, we worked with Congress to protect—pass the Protect America Act, which everybody knows has expired. And I want to share with you the core of the problem. And the problem is, should companies who are believed to have helped us, after 9/11 till today, get information necessary to protect the country be sued? And my answer is, absolutely not. They shouldn't be sued for a couple of reasons.

One, it's not fair. Our Government told them that their participation was necessary—and it was and still is—and that what we had asked them to do was legal. And now they're getting sued for billions of dollars, and it's not fair. And it will create doubt amongst private sector folks who we need to help protect us.

Secondly, such lawsuits would require disclosure of information, which will make it harder to protect the country. You can imagine, when people start defending themselves, they're going to be asked all kinds of questions about tactics used. It makes absolutely no sense to give the enemy more knowledge about what the United States is doing to protect the American people.

Finally, it'll make it harder to convince companies to participate in the future. I mean, if you've done something that you think is perfectly legal and all of a sudden you're facing billions of dollars of lawsuits, it's going to be hard to provide—with credibility—assurances that we can go forward.

The Senate passed a good bill. You know, there's all kinds of talk about how this is a partisan issue. This is not a partisan issue. There is a very strong bipartisan bill that passed the Senate, and it's a bill that we can live with. And it's a bill that should be put on the House floor for a vote, up or down.

What I do want to share with you is that there's a lot of good folks, and you know it too. And I want to thank you all very much for these counterterrorism cells. I look at the Governor of New York; they got an unbelievably good cell—fusion center in New York City. And around our country, particularly in key areas, the cooperation between the Federal Government and the State government and the local government is superb. And I appreciate you all for providing really good leadership on this issue. It's an important, vital issue for the country.

Secondly, today—and I see that you've been given this book. This is a book which describes the faith-based and community organization initiative. And it breaks out by State the unbelievably good work that's taking place in your States.

Now, as you know, I'm a big believer that government ought to empower people who have got a great capacity to help change people's lives. Sometimes I like to say, government is not a very loving organi-

zation; it's an organization of law and justice. But there are thousands of loving people who are willing, if given help, to interface with brothers and sisters across the country that need help. And so this report is one that describes the Federal-State collaborative that's taken place.

There's 35 faith-based offices set up around—in different States. And for those of you who've got them, I thank you. We want to help you—want to coordinate. If you don't have one, I strongly urge you to take a look at what other Governors have done.

Billions of dollars have now gone into help these different community or faith-based groups meet specific needs. One such need is to help children whose parents may be in prison realize there is hope and love. Seventy thousand kids have been affected by this program. Another one is to help prisoners reenter society. It's a relatively new program and—but so far, we've helped—you've helped 10,000 people readjust.

Another is to provide scrip for somebody who needs help on drugs and alcohol and can redeem this at a regular counseling center or a faith-based center. But the whole purpose is to focus on results. You know, we ought to be asking what works, not the process. And so I appreciate you taking a look at this. Again, I want to thank you for your cooperation, to the extent that you feel comfortable doing so. It's making a huge difference in people's lives, and I congratulate you all.

And finally, I want to spend a little time on health care. This obviously is a—you know, it's a tough issue here in Washington. And I do want to spend just a moment to explain to you the philosophy by which we'll be trying to get legislation passed out of the Congress.

One, we share the same goal: accessible and affordable health care. Secondly, whatever we do must not undermine a health care system that is the best in the world. Our doctors are great; our technology is unbelievable; our hospitals are wonderful. And is it perfect? No, but it is the best in the world. Private medicine has worked in America, and the question is, can we strengthen it, rather than weaken it?

And finally, I believe firmly that any good health care system is one that empowers individuals to be a better consumer, have more choices. And that was the whole spirit of the Medicare reforms. It's quite a controversial act up here in Washington. But time has passed, and there's some interesting news.

First of all, the—inherent in the Medicare reform was, one, it made no sense not to provide prescription drugs for seniors. I mean, you know, people would go get an operation for a heart ailment that would cost the taxpayers thousands and thousands of dollars, but we wouldn't pay for the pills that could prevent the heart operation from being needed in the first place. It just made no sense. Medicare was an old system, and it was antiquated. And I firmly believed it needed reform.

Secondly, inherent in this reform was the idea of giving seniors a variety of choices. For example, now seniors have got choices for a different drug plan. Drug plans are now competing for the seniors' business. Seniors have got different options for other coverage in Medicare. And as a result of the competition, fostered by the fact that folks have got different decision points to make, they say, if you want my business, you're going to have to do better; in other words, a market-oriented approach—the estimated cost of Medicare is down by $240 billion over 10 years. You might remember, there was—when the Medicare debate was started, they were firing out all kinds of numbers. Well, it's 240 billion less than initially anticipated. I believe competition works; markets make sense.

And also in that bill was the health savings account reform, which gives individuals more decisionmaking over their own health care. It allows for a catastrophic policy and health—tax-free savings for monies not

spent on ordinary expenses. It's a way, really, to enhance portability. Somebody told me the other day that if you're under 30 years old, you're likely to have had seven jobs when you reach your 30th birthday. It's a different era. People are moving around. There's a—you know, it's an exciting time, but it's also a time that creates uncertainty, particularly when it comes to somebody being able to carry a good health care policy with them.

So the notion is to empower consumers to be more in charge of their decisionmaking. There's now 4½ million people on HSAs. In other words, when given an opportunity, people are now taking a look at it. It's a difficult thing for people to understand. It's pretty complex. But nevertheless, when the consumers are being given more choices, more opportunities, and they—with more knowledge—just like we're providing for our seniors—people make rational choices.

There is more we can do here in Washington, DC. I don't know if you've studied our Tax Code, but it is biased against people who want to buy an individual policy. If you're working for a company, you get a benefit when it comes to health care. If you're in the individual marketplace, you pay with after-tax dollars. And it's unfair, and it creates discrepancies. And it makes it harder to make sure private insurance is available at reasonable prices—more reasonable prices to the individual, which affects small businesses, sole proprietorships, the people that are really the lifeblood of our economy.

So I think Congress needs to make the Tax Code fair. Everybody ought to be treated the same in the Tax Code in order to encourage the development of a market for private individuals, which will help your small-business owners and obviously help families.

Now, one of the interesting things that has taken place in the States, and one of—I think our jobs is—I said last night, you know, that the Governors are policy entrepreneurs. And I meant what I said. And I find it interesting that in certain States, like in Florida, private companies compete for Medicaid business. Like in Indiana, you know, Mitch has helped uninsured be able to participate in an HSA. Like in Oklahoma, you've helped the uninsured or low-income workers purchase health care through competition from—with Medicaid dollars.

In other words, there's some wonderful things going on, all market driven. And we just want to facilitate those decisions because, in my judgment, the opposite of having the Government here in Washington be the decisionmaker will undermine private medicine, will make quality care more difficult.

And so those are some of the thoughts I wanted to share with you. I appreciate you giving me time. I'll answer a couple of your questions. I thank the national press corps for joining us. See you later. [*Laughter*]

NOTE: The President spoke at 11:10 a.m. in the State Dining Room at the White House. In his remarks, he referred to Gov. Timothy J. Pawlenty of Minnesota, chairman, and Gov. Edward G. Rendell of Pennsylvania, vice chairman, National Governors Association; Janet Creighton, Deputy Assistant to the President and Director of Intergovernmental Affairs; Gov. Eliot Spitzer of New York; and Gov. Mitchell E. Daniels, Jr., of Indiana.

Statement on the Situation in Burma
February 25, 2008

The situation in Burma remains deplorable. The regime has rejected calls from its own people and the international community to begin a genuine dialogue with the opposition and ethnic minority groups. Arrests and secret trials of peaceful political activists continue, such as the recent arrest of journalists Thet Zin and Sein Win Maung. Severe human rights abuses by the Burmese Army, including burning down homes and killing civilians, continue in ethnic minority areas in eastern Burma.

The United States continues to seek a peaceful transition to a democratic government that will promote stability and prosperity in Burma and in the region. We support continued engagement by the U.N. Security Council and United Nations Secretary-General Ban's good offices mission, as well as sustained regional engagement.

As one element of our policy to promote a genuine democratic transition, the U.S. maintains targeted sanctions that focus on the assets of regime members and their cronies who grow rich while Burma's people suffer under their misrule. Therefore, today the Department of the Treasury has applied financial sanctions against Steven Law, a regime crony also suspected of drug trafficking activities, and his financial network, including his wife, father, and 14 companies, pursuant to Executive Order 13448.

Additionally, the Department of the Treasury has applied sanctions to two resorts owned and operated by known regime crony and arms merchant Tay Za, himself designated for sanctions in October 2007. Today's actions add to the 33 individuals and 11 entities previously designated. Furthermore, as a result of the enhanced visa restrictions that I announced in September 2007, 898 Burmese officials and their family members are now subject to visa restrictions.

Concerted international pressure is needed to achieve a genuine transition to democracy in Burma. We encourage Burma's neighbors and other stakeholders in Southeast Asia to impress upon the regime the need to release all political prisoners, including Aung San Suu Kyi, to end military offensives and human rights abuses against ethnic minorities, and to begin a genuine transition to democracy in response to the demonstrated aspirations of all the peoples of Burma.

NOTE: The statement referred to Secretary-General Ban Ki-moon of the United Nations; Cecilia Ng, wife, and Lo Hsing Han, father, of Steven Law; and Aung San Suu Kyi, leader of the National League for Democracy in Burma.

Remarks at the Republican Governors Association Gala
February 25, 2008

Thank you all. Please be seated—unless, of course, you don't have a seat.

Governor, thank you very much for your kind introduction. Thank you all for coming, and thanks for supporting our Republican Governors. If you want to raise money, if you want to get a job done, call on the Texas Governor—and this Governor has delivered.

I appreciate all the other Governors who are here. I particularly want to thank Matt Blunt and Mark Sanford, who are leading the RGA, and all the other Governors that have—on the stage today. I have—I can't thank you enough for your service to the country.

I also want to recognize Laura. She's starring in a new movie: "Mother of the Bride." [*Laughter*] I'm not very objective when I say this, but Laura is a fabulous First Lady. I appreciate the members of the Cabinet who are here.

Republican Governors are smart, capable people. I'd like to read the roster of former Governors who worked in the Bush administration: Thompson, Ashcroft, Ridge, Whitman, Cellucci, Johanns, Leavitt, Kempthorne, and Schafer. Three people that worked in the Bush administration went on to be Governors: Daniels, Huntsman, and Jindal. I'm smart enough to hire Republican Governors, and so are the people in the States that these men are from.

I don't know about you, but I'm confident we'll hold the White House in 2008. And I don't want the next Republican President to be lonely. [*Laughter*] And that is why we got to take the House, retake the Senate, and make sure our States are governed by Republican Governors.

Our ideas are those embraced by the American people. American people want strong national defense, and they want the Government to protect the people from further attack, and that's precisely what Republicans will give them. Americans want lower taxes and less government, and it's precisely what Republicans will give them. Americans want strong, principled leadership, and that is precisely what Republicans will give them.

And so when I say I'm confident, I am so because I understand the mentality of the American people, and I understand the mentality of our candidates. And there's no question in my mind, with your help, 2008 is going to be a great year.

I want to talk about two issues that will affect the upcoming elections. The first is, is that we must elect candidates who understand that this Nation is involved with an ideological struggle against coldblooded killers who would like to do us harm again, and that we better be strong and resolute in the face of this enemy.

Our philosophy is that the best way to defend America is to defeat the enemy overseas so we do not have to face them here at home. And that's precisely what the United States of America is doing.

There are two major fronts in this war: One is in Afghanistan, and one is in Iraq. And I want to spend a little time on Iraq. First of all, the decision to remove Saddam Hussein was the right decision for world peace and for the security of the American people.

One year ago, extremists, coldblooded killers, people who kill innocent men, women, and children to achieve their ideological objectives were succeeding in their efforts to plunge Iraq into chaos. So I had a choice to make. Do I suffer the consequences of defeat by withdrawing our troops, or do I listen to my commanders, the considered judgment of military experts, and do what it takes to secure victory in Iraq? I chose the latter. Rather than retreating, we sent 30,000 new troops into Iraq, and the surge is succeeding.

High-profile attacks are down. Civilian deaths are down. Sectarian killings are down. U.S. and Iraqi forces, who are becoming more capable by the day, have captured or killed thousands of extremists in Iraq, including hundreds of key Al Qaida leaders, the very same people that would like to hurt America once again.

The progress in Iraq is tough, the progress in Iraq is tangible, and the progress in Iraq is enabling this young democracy to begin to make progress under the most modern Constitution written in the Middle East.

I can promise you this: For the next 10 months, I will make the necessary decisions to make sure that we succeed in Iraq. And I believe the American people understand that a success in Iraq is necessary for the long-term security of the American people. And we will elect someone in the White House who will keep up the fight to make sure Iraq is secure and free.

One of the principles by which I have been operating is this: I believe in an Almighty, and I believe a gift of that Almighty to every man, woman, and child is freedom. And I believe it is in the interests of the United States of America to free people from disease and hunger and want and tyranny. It is in our interests to make sure that we defeat the ideologues of hate with an ideology that has worked throughout the centuries. I believe 50 years from now, people will look back at this period of time and say, thank God the United States of America did not lose its faith in the transformative power of liberty to bring the peace we want for our children and our grandchildren.

And we've got to do everything we can to stop attacks on the homeland. There are thousands of people who are working day and night to do the job that the American people expect them to do, and that's to protect you from further attack. Make no mistake about it: There is an enemy that lurks and plots and plans, an enemy that would like to do us harm again.

And therefore, it is incumbent, it is essential that the professionals who are working hard to protect you have the tools they need to be able to do the job we expect them. And one such tool is the ability to listen to the phone conversations or the trafficking of the enemy. We need to know what they're thinking, who they're talking to, and what they're planning in order to do the job the American people expect us to do.

And that is why we worked with the United States Congress last summer to pass the Protect America Act. And the Congress passed the act, giving our professionals the tools they need. The problem is, the act expired recently, and yet to—the threat to America has not expired. And so now we're in a debate about whether or not we ought to pass a good piece of legislation necessary to protect the American people.

And here's the crux of the problem: Companies that were believed to have helped us protect America from attack are now being sued for billions of dollars. That's wrong, it's a mistake, and the United States Congress needs to give those companies liability protection. And let me tell you why.

First, it is not fair to treat these companies this way. Our Government told them that their participation was necessary in order to protect us from further attack. And we asked them—and when we asked them to make those protections, we told them it was legal to do so. And I firmly believe it is legal for them to help us protect the American people. And now they're getting sued. What's more important? Lawyers or protecting the United States of America from further attack?

Secondly, these lawsuits would require disclosure of information which would make it harder to protect the country. If these trials—if these cases go to trial, these companies will have to defend themselves. And they'll be asked all kinds of questions about the tactics they have used to help protect our country. It makes no sense to reveal our secrets to the enemy.

Thirdly, and finally, these—without law, without liability protection for a job that we asked them to do in service to the United States of America, it will make it harder to convince companies to participate in the future. If you've done something that you think is perfectly legal and all of a sudden you're facing billions of dollars of lawsuits, it is going to be hard to provide— with credibility—assurances that you can go forward.

And that's the crux of the problem. People say, "Well, you know, it's a—there's a bunch of folks that just don't see it that way." Well, I want to remind you that a good, bipartisan bill came out of the United States Senate. And there's enough votes in the House of Representatives to pass this piece of legislation. It is time the leadership in the House stops worrying about lawyers and starts worrying more about protecting the United States of America from further attack.

And one thing the American people can be assured of: Our Republican candidates understand the threats facing us, and our Republican candidates will make sure that our professionals have the tools necessary to protect the American people.

Our domestic agenda is based upon this simple principle: We trust the American people, and we will empower them to make the right decisions for their families. We trust in the collective wisdom of the American citizenry.

On health, we trust patients to make their own decisions. And we empower them with HSAs and AHPs, all aimed at making sure health care decisions are made between patients and doctors, not by bureaucrats here in Washington, DC.

We trust parents when it comes to education and empower them with strong accountability. We believe in an ownership society for Americans from all walks of life. When it comes to the economy, this is the basis for our views. We trust America's consumers and farmers and ranchers and producers and small-business people, and we empower them by allowing them to keep more of their own money.

Now, I want you to understand and remind you of the history of our economy, recent history. We've been through a lot. In 7 years, we've been through a recession and attacks on the United States of America and corporate scandals and war and natural disasters and high oil prices. But instead of increasing the size of government, we cut taxes on everybody who pays taxes in the United States of America and had 52 months of uninterrupted job growth, the longest in the history of the American economy.

And at the same time, we were fiscally responsible with your money. Now, I admit, we increased spending in certain areas, and I'm going to continue to increase spending in this important area. We will make sure that our troops have all that is necessary to do the job the United States of America has asked them to do. And you can bet our Republican candidates will do the exact same thing.

On nonsecurity discretionary spending, we reduced it lower than the rate of inflation and have submitted to the United States Congress a budget which will be in balance by 2012.

Now our economy is facing uncertainty again, and the fundamental question is, what do we do? Some in Washington want to increase spending. Fortunately, enough realize that the best way to deal with this economic uncertainty is to empower our consumers and our businesses, both large and small, to make investments that will affect job growth this year.

And so I was pleased to sign a $157 billion progrowth economic package, which should help us deal with these economic uncertainties. People say, "What else should we do?" Well, unless Congress acts, most of the tax reliefs we delivered over the past 7 years will be taken away. We cut taxes on families with children. We cut taxes on small businesses. We cut taxes on capital gains. We cut taxes on dividends. We've put the death tax on the road to extinction. We cut taxes on everybody who paid taxes, and unless the Congress acts, those tax cuts will end.

Some Democrats argue that letting tax relief expire is not a tax increase. Well, they're going to have to explain that to 116 million American taxpayers who would see their taxes rise by an average of $1,800. That may not seem like a lot of people, in Washington, DC, but it's sure a lot of people who are trying to make their mortgages and send their kids to college.

In times of uncertainty, we don't need uncertainty in our Tax Code. And the United States Congress must make the tax relief we passed permanent. And the American people can be assured that our candidates will not be running up taxes.

Those are the two big issues facing us: who best to protect America and who best to keep taxes low. I'm looking forward to this campaign. I'm excited about taking our message to the American people. With your help and hard work, there's no doubt in my mind—no doubt—that we'll win.

And I'm looking forward to finishing my term in office. I want to tell you this: I'm going to finish strong. My vision is clear. My energy is high. My enthusiasm for the United States of America has never waned since I've had the high honor of serving you as President.

I thank you for your prayers. I thank you for your support. God bless America.

NOTE: The President spoke at 6:56 p.m. at the National Building Museum. In his remarks, he referred to Gov. J. Richard Perry of Texas, chairman, Republican Governors Association, who introduced the President; Gov. Matthew R. Blunt of Missouri, vice chairman, and Gov. Mark C. Sanford, Jr., of South Carolina, dinner chairman, Republican Governors Association; former Secretary of Health and Human Services Tommy G. Thompson; former Attorney General John Ashcroft; former Secretary of Homeland Security Thomas J. Ridge; former Administrator of the Environmental Protection Agency Christine Todd Whitman; former U.S. Ambassador to Canada Argeo Paul Cellucci; former Secretary of Agriculture Michael O. Johanns; Secretary of Health and Human Services Michael O. Leavitt; Secretary of the Interior Dirk Kempthorne; Secretary of Agriculture Edward T. Schafer; Gov. Mitchell E. Daniels, Jr., of Indiana; Gov. Jon M. Huntsman, Jr., of Utah; and Gov. Piyush "Bobby" Jindal of Louisiana.

Remarks to the Leon H. Sullivan Foundation
February 26, 2008

Thanks for coming. I appreciate the warm welcome. Last Thursday, Laura and I returned from a 6-day visit to Africa. It happened to be her fifth visit and my second. Without a doubt, this was the most exciting, exhilarating, uplifting trips I've taken since I've been the President. It was an unbelievable experience.

And I want to thank the Sullivan Foundation for letting me come by to visit with you about the trip. And I appreciate the good work they're doing on behalf of the people on the continent of Africa. Hope, thank you very much for introducing me and inviting me back. It's always an honor to be with Andrew Young, chairman of the board of directors of Leon Sullivan.

By the way, I should have recognized Carl Masters, your husband—[*laughter*]. That was a major faux pas, just like I should have recognized that my wife, unfortunately, is not here, but she sends her very best regards.

I do appreciate very much Ambassador Howard Jeter for his service to the United States. I thank the members of the Leon H. Sullivan Foundation who are with us. Pleased to see members of the diplomatic corps who have joined us.

I'm honored that Congressman Donald Payne, who is the chairman of the Africa and Global Health Subcommittee, has joined us today. Thank you for coming, Mr. Chairman. He's knowledgeable about the issues on the continent of Africa, and that's good. And I want to thank you for your interest and your diligence. Sheila Jackson Lee, she's supposed to be here. If she's not here, I'll give her an excused absence; after all, she is from Texas.

I appreciate so very much Jendayi Frazer. She is a—[*applause*]. I probably won't have to say anything else. [*Laughter*] She's been awesome to work with, in putting this strategy in place.

I appreciate very much Rear Admiral Tim Ziemer. He's in charge of the malaria initiative. Admiral Ziemer, he's a no-nonsense guy. I hope people have come to realize I am too. I'm not interested in promises; I'm interested in results. That's why I went to Africa, to see results first-hand. Admiral Ziemer, we're getting great results on the malaria initiative, thanks to your leadership.

Lloyd Pierson, President and CEO of the African Development Foundation—appreciate your leadership, Lloyd. Jody Olsen, Deputy Director of the Peace Corps—[*applause*]—contain yourselves. [*Laughter*] Although, I'll tell you—it's not a part of this speech, but I had a wonderful lunch with Peace Corps volunteers in Ghana. Our Peace Corps is full of compassionate, hardworking, decent people who are serving America on the frontlines of compassion. And I really can't thank the Peace Corps enough.

Last time we met was at your summit in Nigeria, and that was during my first trip to Africa. You know, things have changed in Africa since then, I mean, striking changes. These changes are the result of a new generation of African leaders. They're reformers who are determined to steer their nations toward freedom and justice, prosperity and peace. They're also the result of new American policy and new American commitments.

In my first term, we more than doubled development assistance to Africa. And at the beginning of my second term, I asked the United States Congress to double our assistance again. It is an important commitment that Congress can make. I'm looking forward to working to get these budgets out, Mr. Chairman.

America is on a mission of mercy. We're treating African leaders as equal partners.

We expect them to produce measurable results. We expect them to fight corruption and invest in the health and education of their people and pursue market-based economic policies. This mission serves our security interests. People who live in chaos and despair are more likely to fall under the sway of violent ideologies. This mission serves our moral interests. We're all children of God, and having the power to save lives comes with the obligation to use it.

This mission rarely makes headlines in the United States. But when you go to Africa, it is a visible part of daily life, and there's no doubt that our mission is succeeding. You see it when you hold a baby that would have died of malaria without America's support. You see it when you look into the eyes of an AIDS patient who has been brought back to life. You see it in the quiet pride of a child going to school for the first time. And you see that turning away from this life-changing work would be a cause for shame.

The best argument for our development programs is found in the people they benefit. So with the help of our fabulous White House photographers, I have assembled a slideshow—[*laughter*]—of images from our visit. And this morning it is my pleasure to share it with you.

[*At this point, a slideshow was shown.*]

Our first stop was to the western African nation of Benin, where we touched down on a Saturday morning. Benin is a vibrant democracy with a rich history. It has a wise and determined leader in President Yayi. I was proud to be the first sitting American President to visit the country.

At the airport, we were greeted by women and children wearing traditional dress, and they were dancing and playing drums. And they brought several hand-painted signs that the American people need to look at: "Benin people and his President thank the whole U.S. people." "Beninese people will remember forever."

President Yayi and I had a productive meeting. He told me that the malaria initiative and our $307 million Millennium Challenge compact are helping alleviate poverty and save lives in his country. And I told him that America's support is a reflection of his commitment to govern justly and to tackle problems head on. I congratulated him on his effort to fight malaria, which apparently includes a national awareness day called George W. Bush Day. [*Laughter*] I pointed out to him that hasn't even happened in Texas. [*Laughter*]

While President Yayi and I had our discussion, Laura and Mrs. Yayi met with girls who have received scholarships through our Africa Education Initiative. In Benin, these scholarships cover the cost of school supplies, such as uniforms and books and oil lanterns that allow students to read at night. Many of these girls are the first in their family to complete primary school. And their plans didn't stop there. Three girls told Laura that their goal is to become the first woman President of Benin.

Laura and I left Benin impressed by the energy and determination of its people. Benin is an optimistic, it is a confident, and it is a capable nation. And it was a great place to begin our visit to Africa.

Our next stop was Tanzania. We were met by President Kikwete and Mrs. Kikwete as well as Tanzanians. They were dancing, and they were playing great music. And there was also some unexpected fashion. [*Laughter*] I thought the dresses were pretty stylish. [*Laughter*] But my good wife reminded me that I shouldn't see—expect to see them flying off the shelves in American stores anytime soon. [*Laughter*]

As we drove from the airport to our hotel, there were tens of thousands of people who lined the motorcade route to show their gratitude to the American people. And many of them were smiling, and they were waving, and they were holding flags. It was an unbelievable, unbelievable sight.

Sunday morning began with a meeting with President Kikwete at the State House.

The President told me that relations between our nations are the best they have ever been. He said that America's support is helping Tanzania improve education and fight HIV/AIDS and dramatically reduce malaria. He gave me a memorable gift. Laura said we probably need another pet. [*Laughter*] I'm worried that Barney might be slightly intimidated.

Following our meeting, we signed the largest Millennium Challenge compact in the history of the program. The $698 million agreement will support Tanzania's efforts to improve transportation and energy and its water supply. At a news conference, I again called for Congress to reauthorize the Emergency Plan for AIDS Relief, to maintain the principles that have made it a success and to double our initial commitment to $30 billion over the next 5 years. Then President Kikwete jumped in to say, and I want to quote him on this: "If this program is discontinued or disrupted, there would be so many people who lose hope; certainly, there will be death. My passionate appeal is for PEPFAR to continue." I couldn't agree more with the President. And I hope every Member of the United States Congress hears that appeal.

They should also hear about the HIV/AIDS clinic at the Amana District Hospital, where Laura and I visited with the President and Mrs. Kikwete on Sunday afternoon. The clinic opened in 2004 with the support from PEPFAR. And two thoughts struck me on the visit. First, this program is saving lives; there are tangible results. When I visited sub-Sahara Africa in 2003, 50,000 people were receiving medicine to treat HIV/AIDS. When I visited again last week, the number had grown to more than 1.3 million.

At the clinic, we visited with a man and woman who learned they had HIV while they were dating but went on to get treatment, get married, and have a little baby boy who is HIV-free. We saw many others who have new hope because of PEPFAR, including a 9-year-old girl who is HIV-posi-

tive. She was smiling at the clinic with her grandmother because—or sitting at the clinic with her grandmother because her mom and dad had died of AIDS. For the past year, Catholic Relief Services has been paying for the girl to receive treatment at the clinic. And I want to tell you what her grandmother said: "As a Muslim, I never imagined that a Catholic group would help me like that. I am so grateful to the American people."

The second important point is that PEPFAR is allowing African nations to lay the foundation for a health system that does more than treat HIV/AIDS. When patients report to the clinic, they are given a series of tests, they get results quickly from a laboratory on site, and they can receive treatment in the same place. I was struck by the devotion and the professionalism of the clinic's staff. They spoke proudly about the rigorous training they received and the meticulous way they instruct patients on how to take their medicine. One nurse said PEPFAR funds are helping them to treat more patients while producing—providing more privacy. This is helping extend lives, reduce the stigma of HIV/AIDS, and build the health infrastructure that will save many more lives in the future.

On Monday, we traveled to the northern part of Tanzania. We passed Mount Kilimanjaro and drove past a lot of people who were lining the street on the way to the city of Arusha. Of course, that's where the Sullivan Foundation is going to have its next meeting. You'll like it up there. [*Laughter*] And the people will like seeing you.

It's also on the frontlines of Tanzania's fight against malaria. Laura and I visited the Meru District Hospital, and we saw moms and babies that were overcoming this disease. When new mothers bring their babies, the hospital immediately tests them for malaria and HIV. Nurses distribute bed net vouchers, which mothers can use to buy insecticide-treated bed nets from local retailers at a 75-percent discount. I was concerned about the 75-percent discount, and so I announced a new effort, and that is to distribute an additional 5.2 million bed nets free of charge. And that would be enough for every child in Tanzania between the ages of 1 and 5. It is irresponsible to sit on the sidelines knowing that young babies are needlessly dying across the continent of Africa and elsewhere. And I was really pleased to be able to kick off this new initiative by handing out bed nets to this young mother. After the—[*applause*].

So it made sense to go to the local factory where the bed nets are produced, called A to Z Textiles. On the floor of the newly opened facility, we saw the nets produced in a clean, safe working environment. The owner explained that the factory employs 1,200 local workers. If we're helping projects in Africa, we want those projects to employ people from the country in which we're helping. And the vast majority of those workers are women.

He takes great pride in supplying bed nets to Zanzibar, where the percentage of infants—I want you to hear this—where the percentage of infants infected with malaria has dropped from about 20 percent to less than 1 percent in 2 years. He called America—the American people's efforts to fight malaria "a godsend." And I agree. I thanked him for his good work and was honored to see stacks of these lifesaving nets bearing the name of the United States of America.

In the afternoon, we visited a Maasai girls' school, where we received an unbelievably stirring welcome from the students. This school is led by a Catholic nun—who was on my left—empowers girls who have long lacked education. The girls receive scholarships from our Africa Education Initiative. The girls sang these lyrics: "Look at us. Listen to our voices. Today, we can study because of the American people." It was a stirring anthem. We also met a group of Maasai men. These guys can flag jump. [*Laughter*] Unbelievably powerful experi-

ence for Laura and me, and it was a great way to close our visit to Tanzania.

Early Tuesday morning, we headed to Rwanda. After flying over Lake Victoria, we touched down in the beautiful city of Kigali. We were greeted by Rwanda's thoughtful and effective leader, President Paul Kagame, along with Mrs. Kagame.

Our first stop in Rwanda was to the Kigali Memorial Centre. Laura and I laid a wreath to honor the victims of the 1994 genocide. I don't know if our citizens understand this, but between 800,000 and a million people were murdered in a very short period of time. More than 250,000 are buried at this memorial, and many of them were children, who are depicted in photographs that were donated by their families. This is a moving, moving memorial. One inscription read: "Age 4. Enjoyed singing and dancing." And then it listed the brutal way in which this young girl was murdered. The memorial is a moving reminder that evil is real, and we must confront it wherever it happens.

The memorial centre is also a reminder of how far Rwanda has come in the past 14 years. During our meeting, President Kagame updated me on his country's dramatic and hopeful turnaround. Rwanda has taken bold steps to foster reconciliation, rebuild its devastated infrastructure, and to grow its economy. It is a hopeful country. And to build on this progress, the President and I signed a bilateral investment treaty, which will help attract more capital to Rwanda's dynamic economy.

We're also cooperating on matters beyond Rwanda's borders. I thanked Rwanda for being the first nation to contribute peacekeepers to Darfur. And I announced that the United States has committed $100 million to assist African nations willing to step forward and serve the cause of peace in Darfur. I also had the honor of dedicating a new U.S. Embassy in Kigali, which is a sign of our lasting commitment and our deep friendship.

Our final stop in Rwanda was a hillside school that is supported by PEPFAR, the emergency plan. It was a really interesting experience. We met with a lot of students and their parents. And you know, this is a scene at the most popular club at the school, which is the Anti-AIDS Club. The students told me about their ambitious projects, which include teaching abstinence and providing HIV/AIDS testing and counseling. Abstinence may be controversial in the Halls of Congress; it is not controversial on this campus. As a matter of fact, they put a skit on for us. In it, a girl is approached by a rich man who offers her gifts in exchange for sex. She calls it a "ridiculous" proposition and says, "I'm not that kind of girl."

Laura and I departed Kigali inspired by the courage of the Rwanda people, grateful for their hospitality, and confident in their extraordinary potential for the future.

Our fourth stop was Ghana. We received another warm welcome, with tens of thousands lining the street, including thousands of schoolchildren in their uniforms. I suspect they're really happy I came; they didn't have to go to school—[*laughter*]—at least until the motorcade passed.

President Kufuor and I met at Osu Castle. It's a striking white building on the shore of the Atlantic. For generations, the castle was a post in the slave trade. And today, it is a seat of a proud and democratic Government. During our meeting, President Kufuor and I discussed the wide-ranging cooperation between the United States and Ghana.

After the meeting, I added a new element to our partnership, a $350 million initiative to target neglected tropical diseases like river blindness and hookworm across the globe. Needless to say, the President really welcomed this announcement.

He spoke powerfully about the ideological struggle unfolding around the world, and he stressed the importance of America's continued engagement in Africa. Lis-

ten to his words: "If the United States should lock itself into isolationism and think it is safer, then I would say, perhaps they don't know what is coming." Wise words from a wise man.

Our next stop was a visit to the Embassy staff at the U.S. Ambassador's Residence in Accra. I think the audience was happy to see Laura and me—it seemed that way—but I know they were even more excited to see our surprise guest, reigning "American Idol" Jordin Sparks. This young child can sing. [*Laughter*] And she sang the national anthem that inspired all that were there. And I reminded people there that this spring, "American Idol" will again use its prominence across our TV screens to raise funds for malaria relief in Africa.

After lunch, we went to a trade fair and met local merchants who export their products to the United States through AGOA. And my predecessor gets a lot of credit for getting AGOA out of the United States Congress, and I appreciate the Congress working to extend it again. This is a good program, and it's working.

At the trade fair, we saw how the USAID helps these budding entrepreneurs secure financing and increase their access to the U.S. market. Sometimes we take entrepreneurship for granted. The spirit exists, but sometimes people just need a little help. And that's what we're doing.

One group was called Global Mamas, specializes in helping women entrepreneurs find new places to sell their goods. With USAID help, the company has gone from 7 employees to about 300 employees in 5 years. Those are before Global Mamas.

One woman named Esther runs a dressmaking company called My Redeemer Liveth. Since the trade hub opened, she's increased her exports and more than tripled her number of employees. She told me, "I'm helping other women, and I'm helping my family too."

One of the keys to helping Africa succeed is to empower entrepreneurs. It is in our interest, as well, to open up trade and deal with the subsidies and trade-distorting tariffs. And on the continent, I assured the leaders that I am firmly dedicated to coming up with a successful Doha round to make trade freer and fairer.

After the trade fair, we drove to a local school for one of the best ways you can spend a sunny afternoon, and that's watching a ball game. In this case, it was a tee-ball game. One team featured players from a local orphanage. Americans have got to know, there's a lot of orphans on the continent of Africa as a result of disease and civil strife. It's in our interests to help the orphans, and we are. They were called the Little Dragons, and we played a team from a local school that happened to be called the Little Saints. [*Laughter*] And we saw some very talented players.

We also met great coaches and mentors, many of them from our Embassy, who give their time to help the children improve themselves on the diamond and off. But this is more than a baseball program. This is a hopeful program. This is a program where people realize love. And this is a program where kids are able to develop aspirations and dreams. Some of them, of course, want to be big league players, but a lot of them—and they'll find out, if they can't hit the curve ball, they won't be—but a lot of them want to be doctors and pilots and engineers. One child told me, "I want to be a fashion designer." [*Laughter*] It's in our interests that we help people realize their dreams.

Laura spent time with Ghana's schoolchildren. Here she is with Mrs. Kufuor. They were treated to a kindergarten performance of a song about math, and they listened to a fifth grade debate. And she opened a library. Laura is a librarian. She loves the library; she loves books. And she opened up a reading hut built with support of USAID. And beneath the shade of the hut, she enjoyed some story time with eager young readers and a reading mascot. He's the guy on the left. [*Laughter*]

That evening, the President hosted a spectacular state dinner. The night ended with an impromptu dance to a traditional beat called high life. Some of us put on a better performance than others. [*Laughter*] That is our Ambassador. [*Laughter*] She was somewhat taken aback—[*laughter*]—as was Laura and most everybody else in the audience. [*Laughter*]

I'm impressed by the President of Ghana. He is an example of a leader who has made right choices for his people. And it is in our interests to support such leaders.

Early Thursday morning, we left Ghana for our final stop, which was Liberia. We were met by Africa's first democratically elected woman President, Ellen Johnson Sirleaf. In her office in Monrovia, the President told me about the challenges her country faces and her detailed plan to meet them. She has assembled a wise group of advisers and ministers, many of whom were educated in the United States. And I took a little time there at the meeting to thank them for leaving our wonderful country to go back home and help this young democracy not only survive but to thrive. I told the President that I admire Liberia's recovery from war and that she could count on America to continue to stand by her side. And that's a commitment we must keep.

The spirit of the Liberian people was unmistakable. We drove through the city. Again, there was some—a lot of folks lining the road, and they were cheering, and they were enthusiastic, and they were waving flags. I went to thank those who work at our Embassy. I told them that the desire for freedom is universal. And it was interesting, the response from the Liberians in the audience, and they started shouting back, "Yes!" at the top of their lungs. They wanted America to hear their voices.

When the Liberian troops trained—Liberian troops who were trained with U.S. funds marched past us—the President and me reviewing the troops—it was a proud moment. All of a sudden, you're beginning to see a force take force—place that will be disciplined and serve the people as opposed to intimidating the people. It's worth our interests and efforts to help train people—these governments train force to bring stability to their countries.

But nothing sums up the new Liberia better than its approach to education. We had a roundtable at the University of Liberia. By the way, I'm pretty certain the President was educated at the University of Pennsylvania. The more people who come to be educated in the United States from abroad, the better off our country will be.

This man here is getting U.S. help to train teachers and principals to help rebuild the country's school system. I met a 15-year-old boy who was once reading well below grade level, and he didn't like going to school; that's what he said to the crowd. Both Presidents sitting there, he said, "I just didn't like going to school." And he was falling behind. And yet there's a USAID program to help students like him catch up, and now he wants to go to college. This woman I met told us that her husband left her and three children because she was illiterate. Pitiful excuse for not being—you know, standing up and being a good father. But nevertheless, it's what she said. And now she has learned to read, and she plans to go to college. And like a lot of other people we met, she wants to be the President of Liberia. [*Laughter*]

The progress in Liberia is real, and it is inspiring. As a Liberian official put it during a prayer at one of our ceremonies— and these are prayerful people, and they're not afraid to pray in public—the nation has passed from "the valley of despair to the buoyancy of new hope." The Liberian people have a distance to travel, but they do have an unshakable faith in liberty. And they got a faithful friend in the United States of America.

And so throughout our trip, Laura and I were overwhelmed by the outpouring of warmth and affection for the American people. Again and again, we heard the same words: "Thank you." Thank you for sparing lives from malaria and HIV/AIDS. Thank you for training teachers and bringing books to schools. Thank you for investing in infrastructure and helping our economies grow. Thank you for supporting freedom. And thank you for caring about the people in Africa.

Americans should feel proud, mighty proud, of the work we're doing in Africa. At every stop, I told people that the source of all these efforts is the generosity of the American people. We are a nation of compassionate and good-hearted folks. We recognize the extraordinary potential of Africa. In schoolchildren waving flags on dusty roadsides to nurses caring for their patients at busy clinics to artisans selling their products in scorching heat, we saw people who have been given great challenges and respond to them with clear eyes and big hearts.

In Rwanda, a schoolteacher was discussing the fight to eradicate malaria and AIDS with her class. And she explained her attitude this way: "It can happen here." With those words, she summed up the new spirit of Africa: confident and determined and strong.

This is a spirit worthy of America's support. It is more powerful than any partisan quarrels here in our Nation's Capital. And having given our word, we must not turn back now. Congress needs to make America's commitment clear by fully and promptly funding our development programs. And Presidential candidates of both parties should make clear that engagement with Africa will be an enduring priority of the United States.

Laura and I are going to carry many fond memories from our trips to Africa. We will carry this clear conviction: With the continued support of America, the people of Africa can do more than survive; the people of Africa can succeed. God bless.

NOTE: The President spoke at 9:48 a.m. at the Marriott Wardman Park Hotel. In his remarks, he referred to Hope Masters, special adviser, Leon H. Sullivan Foundation, and her husband Carlton A. Masters; Howard F. Jeter, president and chief executive officer, Leon H. Sullivan Foundation; Assistant Secretary of State for African Affairs Jendayi E. Frazer; President Thomas Yayi Boni of Benin and his wife Chantal de Souza Yayi; President Jakaya Mrisho Kikwete of Tanzania and his wife Mama Salma Kikwete; Anug Shah, owner, A to Z Textiles; President Paul Kagame of Rwanda and his wife Jeannette Nyiramongi; President John Agyekum Kufuor of Ghana and his wife Theresa Kufuor; entertainer Jordin Sparks; and U.S. Ambassador to Ghana Pamela E. Bridgewater.

Remarks Following a Meeting With Former Cabinet Secretaries and Senior Government Officials
February 26, 2008

I've just had a fascinating meeting with folks who have served our country nobly in the past. I thank them for coming. We got Democrats here; Republicans are here; concerned citizens. And our discussion was the trade bill with Colombia.

The trade bill is—with Colombia is a really important piece of legislation for America's national security. A stable neighborhood is in our interests. We want people to be prosperous; we want people to be free; we want people to feel comfortable about making, you know, the tough decisions that democracy requires. And the trade vote with Colombia would say a clear message to a strong democratic ally: We support you; we support you in your efforts.

A defeat of the trade bill with Colombia would send a contradictory message. It would embolden the false populism that exists on the continent. It would send a chilling signal to our allies, and it would harm national security of the United States.

We also talked about the economic benefits. Many of the Colombian goods come into our country duty free. It seems like we ought to be treated the same way by sending our products into their countries. And this will particularly benefit small businesses and farmers and ranchers.

And I want to thank you for your suggestions on how to advance this trade bill, how we can work with both Republicans and Democrats to get this trade bill out soon. It's in the Nation's interests. And a lot of times people think about trade, it's just an economic issue. In this case, it is a national security issue and one that the members of both parties must take seriously. And I repeat: If the trade bill with Colombia is defeated, it will harm the national security interests of the country.

And I thank you all for coming. I appreciate your time. Thank you for your advice.

NOTE: The President spoke at 2:11 p.m. in Room 350 of the Dwight D. Eisenhower Executive Office Building. The Office of the Press Secretary also released a Spanish language transcript of these remarks.

Remarks on the Picturing America Initiative
February 26, 2008

Thank you all for coming. Please be seated. Thank you. Welcome to the White House. Looks like we have a distinguished crowd here today. Most of you are renowned scholars, intellectuals, and writers. You've earned reputations for expressing man's noblest deeds and thoughts in pristine, eloquent English, just like me. [*Laughter*]

Justice, thanks for coming. Appreciate you being here. I thank members of the Cabinet who have joined us. Ambassador, glad you're here.

I want to say a word about Bruce Cole. Bruce is an accomplished art historian, a good man, and he's been a great Chairman of the National Endowment of the Humanities.

Bruce understands what all of you understand: At their best, the arts and humanities express the ideals that define our Nation. The United States is a country defined not by bloodline, race, or creed, but by our character and convictions. We are united by an unyielding principle, and that is, all men are created equal. We firmly believe that each man and woman has the right to make the most of their God-given talents. And we believe that all are endowed with the divine gift of freedom.

These ideals have sustained us throughout the centuries, and as a new generation is called to defend the principles of our democracy, they must understand why these principles are worthy of effort and sacrifice.

The National Endowment for the Humanities is at the forefront of this vital educational mission. One way the endowment fulfills this mission is through the "We the People" program, which we established in 2002 to address gaps in our children's knowledge of history and civics.

In just 5 years, the program has awarded nearly 1,400 grants to projects that preserve historical sites, documents, and artifacts and train future historians. In partnership with the American Library Association, "We the People" has produced an annual bookshelf on enduring American themes such as courage and freedom. More than 6,000 sets of these books have been provided to schools and public libraries across the country.

"We the People" teacher workshops have allowed thousands of educators to discover American history in places where history was made: Ellis Island or the waters of Pearl Harbor. The initiative's National Digital Newspaper Program is making millions of pages of historic American newspapers accessible online. Countless students and teachers and historians will benefit from these important first drafts of history.

In all these ways, "We the People" does an outstanding job of passing America's rich heritage on to future generations. Today I'm pleased to unveil a new project under this program, the Picturing America Initiative. This initiative will educate children about the great people and places and moments in our history using American art and masterpieces that depict them.

It's much better for us to hear about educational programs from someone who's probably more qualified than me—[*laughter*]—like a former teacher or a librarian. [*Laughter*] And so it's my honor to welcome Laura, the First Lady.

NOTE: The President spoke at 2:47 p.m. in the East Room at the White House. In his remarks, he referred to Supreme Court Associate Justice Antonin Scalia; and Italy's Ambassador to the U.S. Giovanni Castellaneta. The transcript released by the Office of the Press Secretary also included the remarks of the First Lady.

Remarks Following a Meeting With Prime Minister Mirek Topolanek of the Czech Republic and an Exchange With Reporters
February 27, 2008

President Bush. We'll have opening statements, and then we'll accept two questions a side. Mr. Prime Minister, welcome. We value our friendship and our partnership with the people of the Czech Republic. I remember well my visit to your beautiful country.

We've had a significant discussion today. It turns out, the year 8 is an important number in Czech history. And we're determined to make the year 2008 a strong chapter in our relationship. We view the Czech Republic as a strategic partner. We've discussed a variety of issues. I want to talk about two issues.

First, visa waiver, I've always felt our visa laws needed to change. I didn't like the idea that we treated our friends in the Czech Republic differently than other friends in Europe. There's new law in place, which requires leadership from the countries, such as the Czech Republic. And, Mr. Prime Minister, you and your Government are providing that leadership.

We signed an important memorandum of understanding. We were able to do so because your negotiators were very smart. They represented your people very well. We still have more work to do, but I'm confident we can get it done. And I hope the people of the Czech Republic understand that your Government and your country is ahead of the line of anybody else when it comes to a visa waiver program. And I congratulate you on your leadership.

Missile defense, it's in our interest to put defenses in place to deal with the true threats of the 21st century. Russia is not a threat to peace. Regimes that adhere to extremist ideologies who—which may have the capability of launching weapons to those of us who love freedom, they're the threats to peace. And a missile defense system is aimed to deal with those threats.

And of course, we want it in the context not only of a bilateral relationship but in the context of NATO. We're both strong partners of NATO. NATO has got to be in a position to deal with the true threats of the 21st century. And so we had a good discussion on this important issue.

In our discussions, I strongly respect the sovereignty of the Government of the Czech Republic. Where they have concerns, of course, we'll listen. And so I want to thank you for that. And at the same time, of course, we discussed very important research and development opportunities, defense cooperation activities.

And finally, I thank the Prime Minister for the courage and sacrifice of the troops that are in Iraq and Afghanistan. The Prime Minister said that there will be a reduction in troops in Iraq, and I fully understand that. After all, we're reducing our troops based upon success. And I thank your willingness to send troops into Afghanistan. It makes sense to help young democracies thrive. They will look back at these decisions, Mr. Prime Minister, and say, thank goodness for the peace that prevailed as a result of the hard decisions we made today.

And I welcome you. You're welcome. Thank you for coming.

Prime Minister Topolanek. Okay. Well, I think that President Bush already mentioned everything that I wanted to mention originally. However, let me revisit or come back to the issue of number 8 and its importance in our history. Number 8 played a very important, nay, a key role in the history of the Czech nation.

In 1918, when the first Czechoslovak republic was founded, it was founded with help and assistance from the American President, Woodrow Wilson. Unfortunately, 1938, which was the time of the Munich agreements, the Americans were not with us, and therefore, it was an unfortunate year. Similarly, as 1948, we commemorated 60 years since the coup d'etat of the Communists in 1948 just on the 25th of February. In 1968, the Prague Spring has occurred, and unfortunately, after a few months of relative liberty and freedom, we were occupied by the Soviet armies.

So what I want to say is, in terms of these number 8 years, it was always very important for the Czech Republic, nay, even decisive, whether we were with the Americans or whether we were on our own. And I really wish that the year 2008 will become a similarly important year both for the Czech Republic and also for the United States of America and our mutual relationship.

And I believe that stationing the missile defense system in our country is, in terms of its importance, similarly important to those events I've been just mentioning in relation to the number eight in our history.

And everybody is, of course, interested to find out whether an agreement has been already done. There are only three words remaining to be resolved and discussed. [*Laughter*] But sometimes one word matters a lot, and sometimes an agreement might fail just because of one word. But this is not the case. These are just minor details, and I'm sure that we're going to finalize it very soon.

And in terms of the Visa Waiver Program, I would like to use this opportunity and thank President Bush for his efforts. And I very much appreciate when a politician or a person says something or promises something and he also delivers on this promise. And this is the case.

So I would like to thank President Bush for his leadership, but I also would like this leadership to become his ownership. [*Laughter*] And of course, there are many politicians in the world, but there are very few politicians who are real statesmen. To have one's principles, to stick to those principles irrespective of—to go against all odds

and adhere to those principles, this is what only very few people can do. We've not spoken about this extensively, but this is what I appreciate the most.

What I believe is of—also of equally significant importance is the starting of the strategic dialogue between the two countries, between the U.S. and the Czech Republic. And I think the outcome of these negotiations is also very good. Both countries, we agreed on research and development in the area of missile defense and, generally, in the defense systems.

Just one marginal note on the Visa Waiver Program and process, I think that the negotiations have been really tough, and the result achieved is a true breakthrough, a breakthrough moment. I think that this is a great achievement, because, first, we joined the Schengen zone, which enabled the Czech citizens to travel from Lisbon as far as Vilnius without the use of any passport or ID. And we did the same for our citizens, in terms of traveling to Canada and the United States of America. So we guaranteed one of the basic human rights, which is freedom of movement.

We, at the same time, are fully aware of the risks and dangers of security nature, which exist all over the world. And therefore, we want to guarantee higher security to our nation. And also, the agreement takes into consideration the reciprocal principle: the principle of reciprocity.

I also would like to mention that a great deal of our discussion revolved around issues of human rights——

President Bush. Yes.

Prime Minister Topolanek. ——in the world. We spoke about Cuba. We spoke about the recent events and our hope for the future. And we also talked about other countries, which so far have not been so fortunate to live in freedom like the Czech Republic.

I'm personally very happy from this meeting. I would like to thank President Bush for his openness and for this wonderful meeting. Thank you very much.

President Bush. Thank you. Good job. A couple of questions. Jennifer [Jennifer Loven, Associated Press]. One second, please.

Q. Thank you, sir.

President Bush. Jennifer.

Missile Defense System

Q. Can you elaborate a little on what's holding up an agreement on the missile defense? And how close are you to getting an agreement with the Polish Government as well?

President Bush. Well, I appreciate that. Obviously, this is a complicated issue that requires the United States, one, to make the case of why a missile defense is needed in the first place; that it is aimed to bring stability to Europe; that it's important for mutual security; that it fits into the concept of NATO and will honor the sovereignty of the Czech Republic or Poland.

And so the discussions revolve around a status-of-forces-type agreement, which requires understanding by the Czech Government of exactly what is meant when it talks about stationing a radar site. We will be coming to their country—under what conditions? How will people conduct themselves? And these are all very legitimate questions that the Prime Minister is asking. The same questions are being asked in Poland.

And I explained to the Prime Minister the following thing: People are wondering, well, is this aimed at Russia? Is this an anti-Russian system? And the answer is, of course not. The system we're developing will be able to deal with one, two, or three types of incoming missiles. Russia could overwhelm a system like this. This is a system to deal with threats that will be evolving in the 21st century.

And so the Prime Minister made it very clear, when it comes to the Russian issue, that his Government will be making the decisions about any so-called presence. Do we want the Russians to be able to, you know, allay their fears by understanding

what's going on? And of course, we do. But he made it clear to me that the Czech Republic will be making decisions about who will be—who gets to come into their country. And I fully understand that.

And so, you know, there's a lot of discussions going on. These aren't easy agreements to put in place, but we feel optimistic that we will get this done. As the Prime Minister said, we're down to a couple of words. What you probably want to know is the three words. I'm not going to tell you. [*Laughter*] I am not going to tell you; that's five words. I tell you, I'm not going to do the three. [*Laughter*]

Q. How close are you, sir? How close are you to——

President Bush. Close. Three words is close. We started off with a blank page, and now we're down to three words. But anyway, look, there is a will to get this done for the sake of mutual security and for the sake of peace.

Prime Minister Topolanek. Just to be more specific regarding these three words or outstanding issue——

President Bush. Wait a minute; you're making me look bad here. [*Laughter*]

Prime Minister Topolanek. It actually relates to environmental protection and the standards that should be adopted. So we're actually looking for the standards, which would be the strictest possible standards, to be applied in terms of ensuring and guaranteeing environmental protection. But that's just a technical matter, which is going to be resolved very soon. It's not any problem.

President Bush. Yes. Why don't you call on somebody from the—from your press corps, if you care to. You call on someone.

Missile Defense System/Russia

Q. Mr. President, would it be acceptable for the United States to have the radar in the Czech Republic without interceptors in Poland, should that——

President Bush. I don't see how. You've got to have interceptors in order to make this system work. The idea is to use a radar system to detect a launch headed toward NATO countries, and then shoot the thing down. And in order to make this system work, there has to be an integrated system.

And of course, what we will work to do is, one, make this system effective, integrated, comprehensive. And the interesting opportunity is for Russia to realize the benefits of such a system by extending the radar coverage into their country, because they will be under the same threat of radicalism that we will be, we collectively.

If some of these countries develop a weapon that's capable of developing a nuclear warhead, free nations, nations such as Russia, do not want to be in a position of political blackmail. And our job as leaders is to deal with the issues of the day, but also deal with the issues of tomorrow in a way that yields a peaceful world. And that's what we're doing.

Stretch [Richard Keil, Bloomberg News].

Kosovan Independence/Intelligence Reform Legislation

Q. Mr. President, thank you. You—I have a national security question in two parts. You just talked about the importance of stability in Europe. How does it serve our national security to support the redrawing of borders in Europe vis-a-vis Kosovo?

And secondly, can you say how has our national security actually been degraded by the lapse of FISA?

President Bush. First, let me talk about Kosovo. We discussed Kosovo. As a consequence of the war that took place during the leaders—during the tenure of Mr. Milosevic, one of the effects has been the desire for the—those of us in the United Nations to promote what's called the Ahtisaari plan, which is a supervised, independent Kosovo.

This is a difficult issue, and I understand it's a difficult issue. But the U.S. Government supports this supervised independence. We believe in free societies, and we believe it will eventually lead to peace. But

there's no—no border has been withdrawn in that sense, Stretch. It's a—Kosovo is a—Kosovo itself's borders have been clearly defined. The type of government has changed. Now, as part of the Ahtisaari plan, we fully expect this independent Kosovo to honor minority rights within their borders. And so my—our position has been clear.

Secondly, you asked about whether or not the United States of America should be able to listen to terrorists' phone calls coming into the United States. And the answer is, absolutely, we should be doing this. There is still an extremist threat. People still want to attack our country, and we better understand what they're thinking and what they're planning and who they're talking to.

And yet unfortunately, a law passed to give our professionals the tools has expired. And it's expired because people want to take class-action lawsuits against private phone carriers and other companies that have—were believed to have helped us protect America. It's not fair to say to a company that was believed to have helped us, it's important for you to help us, and then you get sued for billions of dollars. And such a policy would make it very difficult to get companies to fully cooperate with us in the future.

The law is expired, but my fellow citizens must understand, the threat to America has not expired. And our citizens who are paying attention to this debate must understand, without law, America will be more vulnerable to attack. Democrats and Republicans supported this law, and the House leaders must bring it to the floor, where it will pass with both Republican and Democrat vote. And if this law is allowed to expire, America will be more vulnerable. And that is inexcusable, and it's indefensible.

Czech Opposition Leaders' Visit to Syria

[*At this point, a reporter asked a question in Czech, and no translation was provided.*]

Prime Minister Topolanek. Well, actually, I think the same as you think. Well, if he traveled with Mr. Zaoralek—together with Mr. Zaoralek, then I think it is unforgivable.

Well, first of all, I would like to say that these activities of the opposition leaders and their foreign policy does not really serve the interests of our country. And I would like to remind you that when I was in the opposition—and we were in the opposition—we never created any kind of foreign policy on our own. And therefore, I understand the reasons for this study-visit to Syria. I would be much happier if they traveled as tourists and nothing else.

I would like to actually mention that I got this present from the state Secretary of Commerce, Mr. Gutierrez. It is a bracelet, and there is a simple word on it, which is *cambio*, meaning "change." And in Cuba, you can actually get arrested for wearing this bracelet. But when I come back home, I will wear this just for the sake of Mr. Paroubek and Mr. Zaoralek. [*Laughter*]

President Bush. Thank you. Thank you all.

Prime Minister Topolanek. Thank you very much.

NOTE: The President spoke at 10:54 a.m. in the Oval Office at the White House. In his remarks, he referred to former President Martti Ahtisaari of Finland, United Nations Special Envoy of the Secretary-General for the Future Status Process for Kosovo. Prime Minister Topolanek referred to Parliament Member Lubomir Zaoralek and Leader of the Opposition Jiri Paroubek of the Czech Republic. Prime Minister Topolanek spoke in Czech, and his remarks were translated by an interpreter.

Remarks Following a Meeting With United States Special Envoy to the Organization of the Islamic Conference Sada Cumber and an Exchange With Reporters
February 27, 2008

The President. A while ago, I announced that I would be naming a Presidential Envoy to the Organization of Islamic Conference, and I am pleased to announce it's Sada Cumber. He's a very successful businessman, a person who knows the Islamic world. He's agreed to serve in that capacity, and, Sada, I want to thank you very much.

We just had a discussion about his mission. And the core of his mission is to explain to the Islamic world that America is a friend—is a friend of freedom—is a friend of peace; that we value religion; that, matter of fact, we value it to the point where we believe that anybody should be able to worship the way they see fit, and we respect that.

And his is an important job. There's a lot of misperceptions about America, and Sada is going to be a part of our effort to explain the truth. And when people hear the truth about America, when they know that we're a land full of compassionate people and that we value other people's opinions, that I—they'll slowly but surely begin to better appreciate.

Now, a lot of people love America; don't get me wrong. After all, a lot—there's a lot of people trying to come here because of what we stand for. But we've got work to do in certain areas. And I can't thank you enough for going and really will strongly support you in your work.

Special Envoy Cumber. Thank you.

The President. Thank you very much, sir.

Death of William F. Buckley, Jr.

Q. Any thoughts on Buckley?

The President. I just had the—I just hung up with Christopher Buckley, the son of William F. Buckley. I expressed Laura and my sadness over the passage of this very important figure in American political thought. He was a great author, a great wit, and a leader. And Chris said that his dad died at his desk. And I asked whether it had been a—I know it's a painful experience for Chris's heart, but he said that his dad died a peaceful death. And we got to thank God for that and thank God for his life.

Q. Did you talk to him much during this—[*inaudible*]—sir?

Q. You once said Buckley moved conservatism into the Oval Office, that he moved conservatism from the margins of American society into the Oval Office.

The President. No question, he was a—one of the great political thinkers. He influenced a lot of people, including me. And he was—I can remember those debates they had on TV. And he was so articulate, and he captured the imagination of a lot of folks because he was—he had a great way of defining the issues. It was erudite, and yet a lot of folks from different walks of life could understand it. And he's made—he's a big figure in our history, and he'll be missed. And we ask for God's blessings on his soul. Thank you.

NOTE: The President spoke at 2:01 p.m. in the Oval Office at the White House.

Remarks Honoring the 2007 World Series Champion Boston Red Sox
February 27, 2008

The President. Welcome. Thanks for coming. Please be seated. So Tim Wakefield's batterymate is Doug Mirabelli; mine is the Vice President. [*Laughter*] We're glad you all are here. The mighty Red Sox Nation has stormed the South Lawn.

It's my honor to welcome the owners of the Red Sox. The principal owner is John Henry. Tom Werner is the chairman—and my longtime buddy Larry Lucchino. Thank you all for coming, and congratulations. We appreciate the other owners who are here as well. I'm proud to be here with Terry Francona; the captain of the mighty Red Sox, Jason Varitek; the MVP of the World Series, Mike Lowell. They're mentioned because I'm trying to entice a gift out of them. [*Laughter*]

We appreciate very much members of the administration who are here. Don't linger. [*Laughter*] Welcome to the Members of the United States Congress—Massachu-setts and Connecticut and probably Rhode Island and—[*applause*]—yes. [*Laughter*] Thanks for coming.

I'm real proud for the Red Sox baseball club, its players, the players' families, all those associated with this unbelievably successful franchise. You know, you've—Red Sox Nation extends beyond the South Lawn, extends beyond New England. It obviously goes to the Caribbean and even the Far East. And so we welcome Japan's Daisuke here to the South Lawn. His press corps is bigger than mine. [*Laughter*] And we both have trouble answering questions in English. [*Laughter*]

Two thousand seven was an unforgettable season: fast start; hung on in the end; swept the Angels; had a little trouble with the Indians, but battled back from what a lot of folks were saying sure defeat; and you took on Colorado and swept them. Like, you're 8–0 in the World Series. And I appreciate the fact that, as I mentioned,

Mike Lowell put on an outstanding performance. But it was a team effort that brought the Red Sox here.

I love the fact that you've got some of the game's biggest stars. I mean, Big Papi, the guy lights up the screen. He brings a great personality to it. I'm sorry his running mate, Manny Ramirez, isn't here. I guess his grandmother died again. [*Laughter*] Just kidding. [*Laughter*] Tell Manny I didn't mean it. But I do want to quote him. He said, "When you don't feel good and you still get hits, that's when you know you're a bad man." [*Laughter*] I don't know what that means. [*Laughter*] But if bad man means good hitter, he's a really bad man, because he was clutch in the World Series and clutch in the playoffs, as was my fellow Texan, Josh Beckett. Where's Beckett? There you go. Man, you're looking sharp.

Josh Beckett. A lot better than last time?

The President. Spring, Texas?

Mr. Beckett. Yes.

The President. Spring, Texas. He's a big-game pitcher. He struck out—nine strikeouts a game in the playoffs. I appreciate the—very much that he works hard and throws hard and is a proven winner. And I guess he took some lessons from Curt Schilling, one of the great big-time pitchers.

You can't win the World Series without a good bullpen. I've got to make mention of a guy who is from the—my hometown of Midland, Texas—that would be Mike Timlin. Mike, good to see you again. You did not buy those glasses in Midland, Texas. [*Laughter*]

Mike Timlin. No. [*Laughter*]

The President. Yes. And how about Jonathan Papelbon? The guy pitches almost as well as he dances. [*Laughter*] And I appreciate the dress code. Thanks for wearing pants. [*Laughter*] Good job and congratulations.

I do want to congratulate the ownership and the front office. This is a club that was wise enough to maintain a core of players that knew how to win. Varitek,

Mirabelli, Ortiz, Ramirez, Schilling, Youkilis, Timlin, and Wakefield were all members of the 2004 championship team, and they provided the nucleus to bring some new players and some young players along. I bet you Dustin Pedroia, the American League Rookie of the Year, would tell you it makes a big difference. It makes a big difference to be hanging out with people who know how to win.

And so the ownership gets a lot of credit, the front office gets credit, and so does a really fine manager in Terry Francona. Laura and I had the honor of having Mike Lowell and Mrs. Francona and Terry for dinner earlier this month—earlier this year. And what I was impressed about was the values of this guy and the fact that he honors his family as the first and foremost thing in his life. And I think the ownership made a good deal in signing him to a new contract.

I appreciate the fact the team has overcome adversity. All of America, whether you're a Red Sox fan or not, was moved by the Jon Lester story. Jon had a decisive victory over cancer and in the World Series. And it was an inspiration to a lot of folks who were looking at this good man to determine whether they themselves could overcome adversity. And so, Jon, we want to thank you and congratulate you.

I don't know if you know this or not, but these good folks are headed to Walter Reed after this celebration, and I—[*applause*]. These champs have got a chance to bring some joy in somebody's heart, and I want to thank you for really honoring the true heroes of the United States of America, and those are those who wear the uniform of our country. And I'm really thankful you're going.

I appreciate the work of the Red Sox Foundation and the Jimmy Fund. These are long-lasting charities that this club is committed to, to help improve people's lives. You can be a champion on the field, and you can be a champion off the field.

And a lot of these players are champions off the field.

And I thank you for your commitment. I thank you for your dedication to a great sport. I congratulate and thank your families for hanging in with you in this long, 162-game season. I wish you all the best in the upcoming year, and it's my great honor to welcome you back to the White House as the World Series champs.

NOTE: The President spoke at 3:08 p.m. on the South Lawn at the White House. In his remarks, he referred to Tim Wakefield, Daisuke Matsuzaka, Josh Beckett, Curt Schilling, Mike Timlin, Jonathan Papelbon, and Jon Lester, pitchers, Doug Mirabelli and Jason Varitek, catchers, Larry Lucchino, president and chief executive officer, Terry Francona, manager, Mike Lowell, Kevin Youkilis, and Dustin Pedroia, infielders, David A. "Big Papi" Ortiz, designated hitter, and Manny Ramirez, outfielder, Boston Red Sox; and Jacque Francona, wife of Terry Francona.

Statement on the Death of William F. Buckley, Jr.
February 27, 2008

America has lost one of its finest writers and thinkers. Bill Buckley was one of the great founders of the modern conservative movement. He brought conservative thought into the political mainstream and helped lay the intellectual foundation for America's victory in the cold war and for the conservative movement that continues to this day. He will be remembered for his principled thought and beautiful writing, as well as his personal warmth, wit, and generous spirit. His legacy lives on in the ideas he championed and in the magazine he founded, National Review.

Laura and I send our prayers to Chris Buckley, the Buckley family, and all who loved this good man.

The President's News Conference
February 28, 2008

The President. Good morning. Laura and I, as you know, recently came back from Africa, where we saw firsthand how the Emergency Plan for AIDS Relief is saving lives. I had a chance to go to the—speak to the Sullivan Foundation the other day about our trip, and the reason I did so was to remind the American people about how important it is for our Nation to remain generous and compassionate when it comes to helping people overseas.

I also during my trip urged Congress to reauthorize the emergency plan and increase our commitment, and they did. They approved a good, bipartisan bill that maintains the principles that have made this program effective. And so I want to thank Acting Chairman Howard Berman and Ranking Member Ileana Ros-Lehtinen and all the members of the committee for the action they took. This afternoon they're going to come down, and I'll be able to thank them in person. And I'm going to brief them on the trip. The—obviously, our hope is now that the House will act quickly and send the bill reauthorizing PEPFAR to the Senate. And I'd like to sign it into law as quickly as possible.

Members should also act on a very urgent priority, and that is to pass legislation our intelligence officials need to quickly and effectively monitor terrorist communications. At issue is a dispute over whether telecommunications companies should be subjected to class-action lawsuits because they are believed to have helped defend America after the attacks of 9/11. Allowing these lawsuits to proceed would be unfair. If any of these companies helped us, they did so after being told by our Government that their assistance was legal and vital to our national security.

Allowing the lawsuits to proceed could aid our enemies because the litigation process could lead to the disclosure of information about how we conduct surveillance, and it would give Al Qaida and others a roadmap as to how to avoid the surveillance. Allowing these lawsuits to proceed could make it harder to track the terrorists because private companies besieged by and fearful of lawsuits would be less willing to help us quickly get the information we need. Without the cooperation of the private sector, we cannot protect our country from terrorist attack.

Protecting these companies from lawsuits is not a partisan issue. Republicans and Democrats in the United States Senate came together and passed a good bill protecting private companies from these abusive lawsuits. And Republicans and Democrats in the House stand ready to pass the Senate bill if House leaders would only stop blocking an up-or-down vote and let the majority in the House prevail.

Some in Congress have said we have nothing to worry about because if we lose the cooperation of the private sector, we can use the old FISA law. Well, they're wrong. FISA was out of date. It did not allow us to track foreign terrorists on foreign soil quickly and effectively. And that is why a dangerous intelligence gap opened up last year, and that is why Congress passed legislation that reformed FISA. But they did so only temporarily. The law expired; the threat to America has not expired.

Congress understood last year that FISA did not give our intelligence professionals the tools they needed to keep us safe. The Senate understands that the FISA—old FISA didn't give us the tools needed to protect America. The bipartisan bill it passes provides those tools our intelligence professionals need. Yet the House's failure to pass this law raises the risk of reopening a gap in our intelligence gathering, and that is dangerous.

Another vital priority for protecting the nation is prevailing in Iraq. Unfortunately, this week, the Senate debated yet another bill that threatens to cut off funding and tie the hands of our commanders in Iraq. It seems that no matter what happens in Iraq, opponents to the war have one answer: retreat.

When things were going badly in Iraq a year ago, they called for withdrawal. Then we changed our strategy, launched the surge, and turned the situation around. Since the surge began, high-profile terrorist attacks are down, civilian deaths are down, sectarian killings are down, and our own casualties are down. U.S. and Iraqi forces have captured or killed thousands of extremists, including hundreds of key Al Qaida operatives and leaders. Reconciliation is taking place in local communities across the country. That reconciliation is beginning to translate into political progress in the capital city.

In the face of these changes on the ground, congressional leaders are still sounding the same old call for withdrawal. I guess you could say that when it comes to pushing for withdrawal, their strategy is to stay the course. It's interesting that many of the same people who once accused me of refusing to acknowledge setbacks in Iraq now are the ones who are refusing to acknowledge progress in Iraq.

If we followed their advice a year ago, Iraq would be far different and more dangerous place than it is today, and the American people would be at greater risk. If we follow their advice now, we would put at risk the gains our troops have made over the past year. Congress does need to act when it comes to Iraq. What they need to do is stand by our brave men and women in uniform and fully fund the troops.

Finally, Congress needs to act to help homeowners avoid foreclosure. Unfortunately, the Senate is considering legislation that would do more to bail out lenders and speculators than to help American families keep their homes. The Senate bill would actually prolong the time it takes for the housing market to adjust and recover, and it would lead to higher interest rates. This would be unfair to the millions of homeowners who make the hard choices every month to pay their mortgage on time, and it would be unfair to future homebuyers. Instead, Congress should move ahead with responsible legislation to modernize the Federal Housing Administration and Fannie Mae and Freddie Mac. By taking these steps, we can help struggling homeowners and help our economy weather the difficult time in the housing market.

I'd be glad to take some questions. Terry [Terence Hunt, Associated Press].

National Economy

Q. Mr. President, bad economic news continues to pile up, the latest today, with the GDP barely growing. Are you concerned that a sagging economy and hard times will help defeat John McCain like it did your father in 1992? And how far are you willing to go to prevent that?

The President. I'm concerned about the economy because I'm concerned about working Americans, concerned about people who want to put money on the table and save for their kids' education. That's why I'm concerned about the economy. I want Americans working.

And there's no question, the economy has slowed down. You just cited another example of slowdown. I don't think we're headed to a recession, but no question, we're in a slowdown. And that's why we acted, and acted strongly, with over $150 billion worth of progrowth economic incentives, mainly money going into the hands of our consumers and some money going to incent businesses to invest, which will create jobs.

And so we've acted robustly. And now it's time to determine whether or not this progrowth package will actually work. Now the checks will start going out in the second week of May. There are going to be letters out soon explaining who is eligible for the refunds. Credit will happen in the first week of May. In other words, some people will choose to have their bank accounts credited. And in the second week of May, we anticipate the checks start moving out of Washington.

And the purpose is to encourage our consumers. The purpose is to give them money—their own to begin with, by the way—but give them money to help deal with the adverse effects of the decline in housing value. Consumerism is a significant part of our GDP growth. And we want to sustain the American consumer, encourage the American consumer, and at the same time, we want to encourage investment. So we'll see how the plan works.

Q. But the political context——

The President. Oh, you're trying to get me to be the pundit again. Look, you all figure that out. I mean, we—what I'm dealing with is the situation at hand, and I appreciate that—both Democrats and Republicans in the United States Congress and Senate for getting this bill done very quickly. And it's a substantial piece of legislation, and it's a good sign that we can figure out how to cooperate with each other at times.

And so we'll see the effects of this progrowth package. It's—I know there's a lot of—here in Washington, people are trying to—stimulus package two and all that stuff. Why don't we let stimulus package one, which seemed like a good idea at the time, have a chance to kick in?

Yes.

Turkey and Iraq

Q. Mr. President, Turkey's ground offensive in northern Iraq is now a week old with no end in sight. How quickly would you like to see Turkey end its offensive, its incursion? And do you have any concerns about the possibility of protracted presence in northern Iraq causing further destabilization in the region?

The President. A couple of points on that—one, the Turks, the Americans, and the Iraqis, including the Iraqi Kurds, share a common enemy in the PKK. And secondly, it's in nobody's interests that there be safe haven for people who are—have the willingness to kill innocent people.

A second point I want to make to you, Matt [Matt Spetalnick, Reuters], is that there is a Special Forces presence in northern Iraq, in Kurdistan, now, apart from what you're referring to. In other words—so there is a presence, and there has been a presence for a while.

Thirdly, I strongly agree with the sentiments of Secretary Gates, who said that the incursion must be limited and must be temporary in nature. In other words, it shouldn't be long lasting. But the Turks need to move, move quickly, achieve their objective, and get out.

Q. But how quickly, sir, do they need to move out?

The President. You know, as quickly as possible.

Q. Days or weeks?

The President. Well, as possible.

Russia-U.S. Relations

Q. Mr. President, I'd like to ask you about Russia. The Democratic candidates, when asked about the new Russian leader, Dmitry Medvedev, didn't appear to know

a great deal about him. I wonder what you can say about him; how much power you think he's really got with Putin still in the picture?

And critics would say you badly misjudged Vladimir Putin. So what would be your cautionary tale to your successor about the threat Russia poses and how to deal with this new leader?

The President. I don't know much about Medvedev either. And what will be interesting to see is who comes to the—who represents Russia at the G–8, for example. It will be interesting to see—it will help, I think, give some insight as to how Russia intends to conduct foreign policy over—after Vladimir Putin's Presidency. And I can't answer the question yet.

I can say that it's in our interests to continue to have relations with Russia. For example, on proliferation matters, it's in our interest to be able to make sure that materials that could cause great harm aren't proliferated. It's in our interest to work together on Iran. As I said, I think, in this room the last time I was here, I appreciated the fact that Vladimir Putin told the Iranians that they will provide—they, Russia—will provide enriched uranium to run the Bushehr power plant, thereby negating the need for the Iranians to enrich in the first place. I thought that was a constructive suggestion. And we need to be in a position to be able to work with Russia on Iran.

There's a lot of areas where—yesterday, for example, with the Prime Minister of the Czech Republic, I talked about a missile defense system in Europe. But I believe it's in our interests to try to figure out a way for the Russians to understand the system is not aimed at them but aimed at the real threats of the 21st century, which could be a launch from a violent regime—a launch of a weapon of mass destruction.

So there's areas, David [David Gregory, NBC News], where we need to cooperate and—let me finish—and so it's a—I'm going to try to leave it so whoever my successor is will be able to have a relationship with whoever is running foreign policy in Russia. It's just—it's in the country's interest. That doesn't mean we have to agree all the time. I mean, obviously, we didn't agree on Kosovo. There will be other areas where we don't agree. And yet it is in the interest of the country to have a relationship, leader to leader and, hopefully, beyond that.

Q. But I mean, first of all, are you suggesting or are you worried that, in fact, Medvedev is a puppet for Vladimir Putin? And——

The President. No, I wouldn't say that. I wouldn't—that's your conclusion, not mine.

Q. Well, no, I'm asking the question about whether you're concerned. But isn't there something you took away and that you can offer to your successor about how it's risky in the process of sizing up your Russian counterpart? Don't you think that you learned something from your time with Putin?

The President. Here's what I learned, here's what I learned. I learned that it's important to establish a personal relations with leaders even though you may not agree with them—certain leaders. I'm not going to have a personal relationship with Kim Jong Il, and our relationships are such that that's impossible.

But U.S.-Russian relations are important. It's important for stability. It's important for our relations in Europe. And therefore, my advice is to establish a personal relationship with whoever is in charge of foreign policy in Russia. It's in our country's interest to do so.

Now, it makes it easier, by the way, when there's a trustworthy relationship to be able to disagree and yet maintain common interests in other areas. And so we've had our disagreements. As you know, Putin is a straightforward, pretty tough character when it comes to his interests. Well, so am I. And we've had some headbutts, diplomatic headbutts. You might remember the trip to Slovakia. I think you were there at the famous press conference. But—and yet, in spite of that, our differences of opinion, we still have got a cordial enough relationship to be able to deal with common threats and opportunities. And that's going to be important for the next President to maintain.

Yes, Jonathan [Jonathan Karl, ABC News].

Military Operations in Iraq

Q. Mr. President——

The President. Yes, Jon.

Q. ——do you believe if we had the kind of rapid pullout from Iraq that the Democrats are talking about, that we'd be at greater risk of a terrorist attack here at home? And when Senator Obama was asked a similar question, he said, quote, "If Al Qaida is forming a base in Iraq, then we will have to act in a way that secures the American homeland and our interests abroad."

So I'm wondering if you——

The President. That's an interesting comment. If Al Qaida is securing a Al Qaida base—yes, well, that's exactly what they've been trying to do for the past 4 years. That's their stated intention, was to create enough chaos and disorder to establish a base from which to either launch attacks or spread a caliphate. And the intent of the surge was to send more marines into the area that—where they had proclaimed their desire to set up a base. That was Anbar Province. And so yes, I mean, that's one of the challenges we face, is denying Al Qaida a safe haven anywhere. And their intentions—that's what they said, that they would like to have a base or safe haven in Anbar Province.

Yes, Bill [Bill Plante, CBS News].

Q. But to the second part——

The President. No, next turn.

Q. But the part of the question about——

The President. Nice try. [*Laughter*]

Q. Mr. President——

The President. You obviously haven't been here long, Jon. Where have you been, Jonathan? [*Laughter*]

Q. Across the river.

The President. Yes, okay, yes.

Q. All right.

The President. Welcome to the other side. [*Laughter*]

Terrorist Surveillance Program/Intelligence Reform Legislation

Q. If you can get the Congress to protect telecom companies from lawsuits, then there's no recourse for Americans who feel that they've been caught up in this. I know it's not intended to spy on Americans, but in the collection process, information about everybody gets swept up, and then it gets sorted. So if Americans don't have any recourse, are you just telling them when it comes to their privacy to suck it up?

The President. The—I wouldn't put it that way, if I were you, in public, Bill. I mean, you've been around long enough to—anyway, yes, I—look, there's—people who analyze the program fully understand that America's civil liberties are well protected. There is a constant check to make sure that our civil liberties of our citizens aren't—you know, are treated with respect. And that's what I want, and that's what most—all Americans want.

Now, let me talk about the phone companies. You cannot expect phone companies to participate if they feel like they're going to be sued. I mean, it is—these people are responsible for shareholders; they're private companies. The Government said to those who have alleged to have helped us that it is in our national interests, and it's legal. It's in our national interests because we want to know who's calling who from overseas into America. We need to know in order to protect the people.

It was legal. And now, all of a sudden, plaintiffs' attorneys, class-action plaintiffs' attorneys, you know—I don't want to try to get inside their head; I suspect they see, you know, a financial gravy train—are trying to sue these companies. And first, it's unfair. It is patently unfair. And secondly, these lawsuits create doubts amongst those who will—whose help we need.

I guess you could be relaxed about all this if you didn't think there was a true threat to the country. I know there's a threat to the country. And the American people expect our Congress to give the professionals the tools they need to listen to foreigners who may be calling into the United States with information that could cause us great harm. So, on the one hand, the civil liberties of our citizens are guaranteed by a lot of checks in the system and scrutinized by the United States Congress.

And secondly, I cannot emphasize to you how important it is that the Congress solve this problem. The Senate has solved the problem. And people say, would you ever compromise on the issue? The Senate bill is a compromise. And there's enough votes in the House of Representatives to pass the Senate bill. It's a bipartisan bill. And the House leaders need to put it on the floor. Let the will of the House work. In my judgment, it happens to be the will of the people to give the professionals the tools they need to protect the country.

Elaine [Elaine Quijano, Cable News Network].

Homeland Security and Counterterrorism Adviser Joel Bagnal

Q. Mr. President, you've stressed over and over in recent days particularly the importance of FISA reform to help keep America safe, and yet you have not yet filled a key national security post. Fran Townsend announced her resignation months ago, in November. What is the delay there, and what are Americans to make of that delay? Is America less safe because of it?

The President. We got a fine man named Joel Bagnal working that office right now. He's a professional. I trust his judgment. He's a real good guy. And no, they shouldn't worry about Joel. He knows what he's doing.

John [John McKinnon, Wall Street Journal].

Q. But, sir, the American——

The President. John.

Q. The Homeland Security Adviser is a key post.

Q. Thank you, Mr. President.

Q. What's taking so long?

The President. Joel Bagnal has occupied the position, Elaine. He's doing the job, and I've got confidence in him. And so should the American people have confidence in him. He's a fine professional. He knows what he's doing. And I'm very comfortable in saying, on your cameras, that our staff in the White House, led by Joel Bagnal, knows what they're doing when it comes to advising the President on matters of homeland security.

John.

Trade

Q. Thanks, Mr. President. There's been a lot of criticism on the campaign trail of free-trade policies and even talk about the U.S. opting out of NAFTA. And it doesn't seem that you want to discuss the prospects of Republican candidates on the campaign trail this year, but——

The President. Not yet.

Q. Not yet. But just given all the concerns about the economy that people have, do you feel like you could win in a State like Ohio if you were running again for Presidency?

The President. Landslide, John. [*Laughter*] Look, I am a big believer in free trade. And the reason why is, I firmly believe that free trade is essential to the formation of high-paying, quality jobs. In other words, people who work for industries that export goods to overseas are likely to be paid more than their—other workers.

Secondly, if you look at the—our economic growth recently, particularly last year, a major portion of that growth came

as a result of exports. It's an essential part of our economic picture.

Yes, I heard the talk about NAFTA. One statistic I think people need to know is, I think there's roughly, like, $380 billion worth of goods that we ship to our NAFTA partners on an annual basis. Now, $380 billion worth of goods means there's a lot of farmers and businesses, large and small, who are benefiting from having a market in our neighborhood. And the idea of just unilaterally withdrawing from a trade treaty because of trying to score political points is not good policy. It's not good policy on the merits, and it's not good policy to— as a message to send to our—people who have, in good faith, signed a treaty and worked with us on a treaty.

Thirdly, those of us who grew up in Texas remember what the border looked like when we were kids, and it was really poor. And you go down to that border today, it is prosperous on both sides of the river, to the credit of those who proposed NAFTA and to the credit of those who got NAFTA through the Congress. If you're worried about people coming into our country illegally, it makes sense to help a place like Mexico grow its economy. Most folks would rather be finding a job close to home; most folks would rather not try to get in the bottom of an 18-wheeler to come and put food on the table.

This agreement has meant prosperity on both sides of our borders, north and south. And I believe it's in the interests to continue to seek markets for our farmers, ranchers, and businesspeople. I also know it's in our interest to insist that when people sell products into our countries, that we get treated fairly. In other words, if we treat a country one way—people in a country one way—we expect to be treated the same way, like Colombia.

The Colombia free trade vote's coming up. Many of their products come into our country much easier than our products go into theirs. It makes sense to be treated equally. But on this vote, there's an additional consequence. If the Congress rejects the Colombia free trade agreement, it will sorely affect the national security interests of the United States. It will encourage false populism in our neighborhood. It will undermine the standing of courageous leaders like President Uribe. And I strongly urge the Congress, when they bring this—when the Colombia free trade agreement is brought to a vote, to seriously consider the consequences of rejecting this trade agreement.

Mike [Mike Emanuel, FOX News].

Terrorist Surveillance Program/Intelligence Reform Legislation

Q. Mr. President, on FISA, do you worry that perhaps some House Democratic leaders are playing a high-stakes game of wait and see, in terms of if we get attacked, we all lose; if we don't get attacked, then maybe that makes the case that you don't need all the powers in FISA?

The President. No, I don't think so. I mean, I think that's—that would be ascribing motives that are just—I just don't think they're the motives of the House leaders to do that. I think—look, I think they're really wrestling with providing liability protection to phone companies. I don't think there's—that's cynical or devious, Michael. That's just too risky.

A lot of these leaders understand that there is an enemy that wants to attack. The caucus, evidently, in the House, is—the Democratic caucus is, you know, is concerned about exactly Plante's question, you know. And I just can't tell you how important it is to not alienate or not discourage these phone companies.

How can you listen to the enemy if the phone companies aren't going to participate with you? And they're not going to participate if they get sued. Let me rephrase: less likely to participate. And they're facing billions of dollars of lawsuits, and they have a responsibility to their shareholders. And

yet they were told what they were going to do is legal.

And anyway, I'm going to keep talking about the issue, Mike. This is an important issue for the American people to understand. And it's important for them to understand that no renewal of the PATRIOT Act—I mean, the Protect America Act—is dangerous for the security of the country, just dangerous.

I'm sure people, if they really pay attention to the details of this debate, wonder why it was okay to pass the Protect America Act last summer, late last summer, and all of a sudden, it's not okay to pass it now. And so I will keep talking about the issue and talking about the issue.

Michael [Michael Abramowitz, Washington Post].

President's Foreign Policy

Q. Thank you, Mr. President. I'd like to ask you about another issue that's kind of come up on the campaign trail, in terms of discussion, which is—this is a point of view that has been espoused—that we would be better off if we talked to our adversaries, in particular, Iran and Cuba, you know, without preconditions. And as President, you have obviously considered and rejected this approach. And I'm wondering if you can give us a little bit of insight into your thinking about this, and just explain to the American people what is lost by talking with those when we disagree.

The President. What's lost by embracing a tyrant who puts his people in prison because of their political beliefs? What's lost is, it'll send the wrong message. It'll send a discouraging message to those who wonder whether America will continue to work for the freedom of prisoners. It'll give great status to those who have suppressed human rights and human dignity.

I'm not suggesting there's never a time to talk, but I'm suggesting now is not the time—not to talk with Raul Castro. He's nothing more than an extension of what his brother did, which was to ruin an island and imprison people because of their beliefs.

These wives of these dissidents come and see me, and their stories are just unbelievably sad. And it just goes to show how repressive the Castro brothers have been, when you listen to the truth about what they say. And the idea of embracing a leader who's done this without any attempt on his part to release prisoners and free their society would be counterproductive and send the wrong signal.

Q. But no one is saying embrace him; they're just saying talk——

The President. Well, talking to him is embracing. Excuse me. Let me use another word. You're right, embrace is like big hug, right? That's—you're looking——

Q. Right.

The President. I do embrace people. Mike, one of these days, I'm just thinking about—[*laughter*]. Right, okay, good. Thank you for reminding me to use a different word. Sitting down at the table, having your picture taken with a tyrant such as Raul Castro, for example, lends the status of the office and the status of our country to him. He gains a lot from it by saying, "Look at me, I'm now recognized by the President of the United States."

Now, somebody will say, well, I'm going to tell him to release the prisoners. Well, it's a theory that all you got to do is embrace, and these tyrants act. That's not how they act. That's not what causes them to respond. And so I made a decision quite the opposite, and that is to keep saying to the Cuban people, we stand with you. We will not sit down with your leaders that imprison your people because of what they believe. We will keep an embargo on you. We do want you to have money from people here in the homeland, but we will stay insistent upon this policy until you begin to get free.

And so that's the way I've conducted foreign policy and will continue to conduct foreign policy. I just remind people that the decisions of the U.S. President to have discussions with certain international figures can be extremely counterproductive. It can send chilling signals and messages to our allies; it can send confusion about our foreign policy; it discourages reformers inside their own country. And in my judgment, it would be a mistake, on the two countries you talked about.

Sheryl [Sheryl Gay Stolberg, New York Times].

2008 Presidential Election

Q. Mr. President, thank you. I want to bring you back to Senator Obama's comment on Iraq. Do you believe that his comment was naive?

The President. I believe Senator Obama better stay focused on his campaign with Senator Clinton, neither of whom has secured their party's nominee yet—nomination yet. And my party's nomination hasn't been decided yet either. And so there will be ample time to discuss whoever their candidate for—the positions of whoever their candidate is.

Nice try, Sheryl. Would you like to try another tack, another question?

Q. Well, earlier you said it was an interesting comment. Okay, I'll follow on it. About Iraq, you have said in the past that you want to——

Q. Come on. [*Laughter*]

Q. ——leave a sustainable policy.

The President. Yes.

Q. You said I could have another question.

The President. That's good. Yes, okay.

Q. If you want to leave your——

The President. Well, it was just a little, like—give her—should we vote on whether she gets another question? [*Laughter*]

Military Operations in Iraq

Q. They're for me. [*Laughter*] You've said, Mr. President, that you want to leave Iraq in a sustainable situation——

The President. Yes, I do.

Q. ——at the end of your administration. Can you describe for us specifically, what do you mean by sustainable? Do you have specific goals and objectives that, in your mind, would meet the criteria of sustainability?

The President. Yes, which is to keep enough troops there so we can succeed. And David Petraeus will come as—for example, David Petraeus will come back, along with Ryan Crocker, here later on this spring and will make a recommendation as to what that—what those troop levels ought to be.

The idea of having a request by the Iraqi Government for a long-term security agreement is part of sustainability. And obviously, we're going to be pushing hard at the same time to get the political process moving forward.

I don't know if you noticed yesterday, but it was a very interesting moment in Iraqi constitutional history, when part of the—a member of the Presidency Council utilized his constitutional right to veto one of the three pieces of legislation recently passed. I understand the use of the veto, intend to continue to use it, and I—but I thought it was a healthy sign that the people are thinking through the legislation that's passed, and they're worrying about making sure that laws are constitutional. And I feel pretty good about the fact that they're, of course, going to continue to work to make sure that their stated objective of getting Provincial elections done by October of 2008 will happen.

So there's going to be a lot of work. My only point is, sustainability is political, economic, and security.

Yes, Ed [Edwin Chen, Bloomberg News].

Monetary Policy

Q. Good morning, sir.

The President. Yes, thank you.

Q. If I could get back to the economy—the GDP numbers today show that the—our economy is increasingly relying on U.S. exports to keep growing. How important is a competitive dollar in keeping U.S. exports strong and growing?

The President. We believe in a strong dollar policy, and we believe that—and I believe that our economy has got the fundamentals in place for us to be a—is to grow and continue growing more robustly, hopefully, than we're growing now. And the dollar—the value of the dollar will be reflected in the ability for our economy to be—to grow economically. And so we're still for a strong dollar.

Q. Can I follow up on that, sir?

Price of Gasoline/Taxes/Energy

The President. Maybe.

Q. Thanks.

The President. I guess you are. Yes, I haven't said yes, but please. [*Laughter*]

Q. What's your advice to the average American who is hurting now, facing the prospect of four-dollar-a-gallon gasoline, a lot of people facing——

The President. Wait a minute. What did you just say? You're predicting four-dollar-a-gallon gasoline?

Q. A number of analysts are predicting——

The President. Oh, yeah?

Q. ——four-dollar-a-gallon gasoline this spring when they reformulate.

The President. That's interesting. I hadn't heard that.

Q. Yes, sir.

The President. Yes. I know it's high now.

Q. And the other economic problems facing people—beyond your concern that you stated here and your expectations for these stimulus checks, what kind of hope can you offer to people who are in dire straits?

The President. Permanent tax—keep the tax cuts permanent, for starters. There's a lot of economic uncertainty. You just said that. You just said the price of gasoline may be up to $4 a gallon—or some expert told you that—and that creates a lot of uncertainty. If you're out there wondering whether or not—you know, what your life is going to be like and you're looking at $4 a gallon, that's uncertain. And when you couple that with the idea that your taxes may be going up in a couple of years, that's double uncertainty. And therefore, one way to deal with uncertainty is for Congress to make the tax cuts permanent.

Secondly, it's—people got to understand that our energy policies needs to be focused on a lot of things: one, renewables, which is fine, which I strongly support, as you know; two, conservation. But we need to be finding more oil and gas at home if we're worried about becoming independent—dependent on oil overseas. And this—I view it as a transitory period to new technologies that'll change the way we live. But we haven't built a refinery in a long time. We're expanding refineries, but we haven't built a refinery in a long time. I strongly suggested to the Congress that we build refineries on old military bases, but no, it didn't pass. But if you've got less supply of something as demand continues to stay steady or grow, your price is going to go up.

Secondly, on oil, we—the more oil we find at home, the better off we're going to be in terms of the short run. And yet our policy is, you know, let us not explore robustly in places like ANWR. And there are environmental concerns, and I understand that. I also know there's technologies that should mitigate these environmental concerns.

They got a bill up there in Congress now. Their attitude is, let's tax oil companies. Well, all that's going to do is make the price even higher. We ought to be encouraging investment in oil and gas close to home if we're trying to mitigate the problems we face right now.

And so yes, there's a lot of uncertainty, and I'm concerned about the uncertainty. Hopefully, this progrowth package will help—this 100—I think it's $147 billion that will be going out the door, starting electronically in the first week of May and

through check in the second week of May. And the idea is to help our consumers deal with the uncertainty you're talking about. But yes, no question about it, it's a difficult period.

Yes, Ken [Ken Herman, Cox News].

Presidential Library

Q. Thank you, sir. Now that you've found a location for your Presidential library, you've got to find the money to build it. Reports indicate that you may be trying to collect as much as $200 million. Is that figure accurate? Do you believe it's important for the American people to know who is giving that kind of money to their President? Will you disclose the contributions as they come in? And will you place any restriction on who gives money and how much they can give?

The President. No, yes, no, yes. [*Laughter*] Next question. [*Laughter*] I haven't— phew, man. You obviously haven't asked a question in a long time. It was like, you know, one, I haven't seen the final budget. Two, as Donnie Evans said, who is the chairman of the foundation, we'll look at the disclosure requirements and make a decision. Here's the—well, I—there's a lot of people—or some people; I shouldn't say a lot—some people who like to give and don't particularly want their names disclosed, whether it be for this foundation or any other foundation. And so we'll take that into consideration.

Thirdly—and what was the other?

Q. Any restrictions on who can give? Will you take foreign money for this?

The President. Yes, I'll probably take some foreign money, but don't know yet, Ken. We just haven't—we just announced the deal, and I frankly have been focused elsewhere, like on gasoline prices and, you know, my trip to Africa, and haven't seen the fundraising strategy yet. And so the answer to your question—really, I can't answer your question well.

Q. Where does the people's right to know this fit into all of that?

The President. You know, I don't—we're weighing, taking a look, taking consideration, giving it serious consideration. Nice try, though.

2008 Beijing Olympics/China/Human Rights

Olivier [Olivier Knox, Agence France-Presse].

Q. Thank you, sir. In China, a former factory worker who says that human rights are more important than the Olympics is being tried for subversion. What message does it send that you're going to the Olympics? And do you think athletes there should be allowed to publicly express their dissent?

The President. Olivier, I have made it very clear, I'm going to the Olympics because it's a sporting event, and I'm looking forward to seeing the athletic competition. But that will not preclude me from meeting with the Chinese President, expressing my deep concerns about a variety of issues, just like I do every time I meet with the President.

And maybe I'm in a little different position. Others don't have a chance to visit with Hu Jintao, but I do. And every time I meet with him, I talk about religious freedom and the importance of China's society recognizing that if you're allowed to worship freely, it will benefit the society as a whole; that the Chinese Government should not fear the idea of people praying to a god as they see fit. A whole society, a healthy society, a confident society is one that recognizes the value of religious freedom.

I talk about Darfur and Iran and Burma. And so I am not the least bit shy of bringing up the concerns expressed by this factory worker. And I believe that I'll have an opportunity to do so with the President and, at the same time, enjoy a great sporting event. I'm a sports fan. I'm looking forward to the competition. And each Olympic society will make its own decision as to how to deal with the athletes.

Yes, Mark [Mark Smith, Associated Press Radio].

Price of Oil/Tax Breaks for Oil Companies/Energy

Q. Mr. President, back to the oil price—tax breaks that you were talking about a minute ago. Back when oil was $55 a barrel, you said those tax breaks were not needed; people had plenty of incentive to drill for oil. Now the price of oil is $100 a barrel, and you're planning to threaten a plan that would shift those tax breaks to renewables. Why, sir?

The President. I talked, Mark—I talked about some of the breaks. And this is a—this generally is a tax increase, and it doesn't make any sense to do it right now. We need to be exploring for more oil and gas. And taking money out of the coffers of the oil companies will make it harder for them to reinvest. I know they say, well, look at all of the profits. Well, we're raising the price of gasoline in a time when the price of gasoline is high.

Secondly, we've invested a lot of money in renewables. This administration has done more for renewables than any President. Now, we got a problem with renewables, and that is, the price of corn is beginning to affect food—cost of food, and it's hurting hog farmers and a lot of folks. And the best way to deal with renewables is to focus on research and development that will enable us to use other raw material to produce ethanol. I'm a strong believe in ethanol, Mark. This administration has got a great record on it. But it is a—I believe research and development is what's going to make renewable fuels more effective.

Again, I repeat: If you look at what's happened in corn out there, you're beginning to see the food issue and the energy issue collide. And so, to me, the best dollar spent is to continue to deal with cellulosic ethanol in order to deal with this bottleneck right now. And secondly, the tax—yes, I said that a while ago, on certain aspects. But the way I analyze this bill is, it's going to cost the consumers more money. And we need more oil and gas being explored for; we need more drilling; we need less dependence on foreign oil.

And as I say, we're in a period of transition here in America, from a time where we were—where we are oil and gas dependent to, hopefully, a time where we got electric automobiles, and we're spending money to do that; a time when we're using more biofuels, and we've taken huge investments in that; a time when we've got nuclear power plants and we're able to deal with the disposal in a way that brings confidence to the American people—so we're not dependent on natural gas to fire up our—a lot of our utilities and a time when we can sequester coal.

That's where we're headed for, but we've got to do something in the interim. Otherwise, we're going to be dealing, as the man said, with four-dollar gasoline. And so that's why I'm against that bill.

I thank you. It's been a pleasure. Enjoyed being with you.

Q. Sir, do you think Hillary Clinton is the nominee?

The President. Pardon me?

Q. Do you still think Hillary Clinton will be the nominee?

The President. I'm not talking about politics.

Q. You've said that before, though.

The President. You're trying to get me to be pundit in chief.

Q. Are they qualified to be Commander in Chief?

The President. I appreciate you very—Jackson [David Jackson, USA Today]—Jackson. Nice to see you. [*Laughter*] Thank you.

Q. Thank you.

The President. Glad to see you back. [*Laughter*]

NOTE: The President's news conference began at 10:05 a.m. in the James S. Brady Press Briefing Room at the White House. In his remarks, he referred to Secretary of Defense Robert M. Gates; Russian Presidential candidate Dmitry A. Medvedev; Prime Minister Mirek Topolanek of the Czech Republic; Chairman Kim Jong Il of North Korea; President Alvaro Uribe Velez of Colombia; President Raul Castro Ruz and former President Fidel Castro Ruz of Cuba; Democratic Presidential candidates Barack Obama and Hillary Rodham Clinton; Gen. David H. Petraeus, USA, commanding general, Multi-National Force—Iraq; Donald L. Evans, chairman, George W. Bush Presidential Library Foundation; and former factory worker and human rights activist Yang Chunlin, who was arrested on July 6, 2007, in China. Reporters referred to Republican Presidential candidate John McCain; and former Homeland Security and Counterterrorism Adviser Frances Fragos Townsend. The Office of the Press Secretary also released a Spanish language transcript of this news conference.

Remarks Following a Briefing on the National Economy
February 28, 2008

I want to thank Madam Secretary for hosting this meeting with my economic team. We just had a briefing on what has become very obvious to the American people: that we're in a period of slowness. And it's also a period of uncertainty.

We're optimistic about the long-term economic future of the country, but right now a lot of Americans are facing uncertain times. And we're acting on it.

I want to thank the Members of Congress for quickly passing a economic growth package. And that means that there will be $150 billion or more sent out to American consumers and incentives inherent in that to—for American businesses to invest.

Now, the Secretary briefed us—Secretary Paulson—that we anticipate that the checks will start being sent in the second week of May. And that's going to be very positive news for our consumers. And it's a part of our active plan to help deal with these uncertain times.

One way Congress, if they really want to make a substantial difference in creating certainty during uncertain times, is to make the tax cuts we passed permanent. You see, if you're somebody worried about three-dollar gasoline and you think your taxes may be going up in 2 years, then it—the uncertain price of gasoline creates more uncertainty for you as you plan your future. And Congress needs to make these tax cuts permanent, and they need to think about the American consumer and the American family and the American small-business owner during these times of difficulty and make the tax cuts permanent, send a clear signal to the American people.

Secondly, obviously, the housing issue is one that we're deeply concerned about. We want people being able to stay in their homes. We don't support legislation that will reward lenders—you know, that will bail out lenders—and we don't support legislation that will cause interest rates to go up, like the legislation in the Senate. What we do support is an aggressive plan, led by Secretary Paulson and Secretary Jackson, to help people stay in their homes, to help them refinance their mortgages, to help them make the financial adjustments necessary to help us through this difficult period of time.

And so I want to thank you all for your briefing. I appreciate your concern about our fellow citizens. We share concerns about it. We want them doing well. And we believe that in the long term, we're going to do just fine. This is a resilient economy. We've got good, hard-working people in America. The entrepreneurial spirit is strong. And we'll make it through this period, just like we've made it through other periods of uncertainty during my Presidency. And each time, we came out stronger and better, and that's what's going to happen this time too.

Thank you.

NOTE: The President spoke at 11:41 a.m. at the Department of Labor.

Message to the Congress Transmitting the Denmark-United States Social Security Agreement
February 28, 2008

To the Congress of the United States:

Pursuant to section 233(e)(1) of the Social Security Act, as amended by the Social Security Amendments of 1977 (Public Law 95–216, 42 U.S.C. 433(e)(1)), I transmit herewith the Agreement Between the United States of America and the Kingdom of Denmark on Social Security, which consists of two separate instruments: a principal agreement and an administrative arrangement. The agreement was signed at Copenhagen on June 13, 2007.

The United States-Denmark Agreement is similar in objective to the social security agreements already in force with Australia, Austria, Belgium, Canada, Chile, Finland, France, Germany, Greece, Ireland, Italy, Japan, Korea, Luxembourg, the Netherlands, Norway, Portugal, Spain, Sweden, Switzerland, and the United Kingdom.

Such bilateral agreements provide for limited coordination between the United States and foreign social security systems to eliminate dual social security coverage and taxation, and to help prevent the loss of benefit protection that can occur when workers divide their careers between two countries. The United States-Denmark Agreement contains all provisions mandated by section 233 and other provisions that I deem appropriate to carry out the purposes of section 233, pursuant to section 233(c)(4).

I also transmit for the information of the Congress a report prepared by the Social Security Administration explaining the key points of the Agreement, along with a paragraph-by-paragraph explanation of the provisions of the principal agreement and the related administrative arrangement. Attached to this report is the report required by section 233(e)(1) of the Social Security Act, which describes the effect of the Agreement on income and expenditures of the U.S. Social Security program and the number of individuals affected by the Agreement.

I commend to the Congress the United States-Denmark Social Security Agreement and related documents.

GEORGE W. BUSH

The White House,
February 28, 2008.

Remarks Following a Meeting With Secretary General Jakob Gijsbert "Jaap" de Hoop Scheffer of the North Atlantic Treaty Organization *February 29, 2008*

President Bush. It's my honor to welcome the Secretary General of NATO back to the Oval Office. Last time I was with the Secretary General, I was trying to keep up with him on my mountain bike. He is a dear friend and a strong leader.

I appreciate, Jaap, your helping to transform NATO so it deals with the threats of the 21st century. You've done your job with great dignity and clarity of thought. And I'm looking forward to coming to Bucharest to support your efforts to make sure NATO is a relevant organization aimed at bringing security and peace to the world.

We've had a lot of things to discuss. A couple of key points: one, Afghanistan, the United States is committed to the NATO mission in Afghanistan. We're committed to a comprehensive strategy that helps folks in Afghanistan realize security, at the same time, economic prosperity and political progress.

Secondly, our hope is that nations that have applied to join NATO continue to meet their MAP obligations. And I'm looking forward to getting an assessment of the progress that these three nations have made, from you, before we take the vote on enlargement.

I appreciate very much NATO's role in helping to provide some sense of stability in the Balkans. Thank you for doing a training mission in Iraq. Overall, thanks for being a force for good. And I'm proud to welcome you back here.

Secretary General de Hoop Scheffer. Thank you, Mr. President. Thank you. Thank you, George.

Four working weeks until the Bucharest summit of NATO, I can echo the President's words. First of all, NATO's operations and missions, we have a long-term commitment vis-a-vis Afghanistan. I thank the President for the United States contribution in the NATO framework, which is an essential one. All 26 NATO allies are there, and we are there for the long haul. We are there to support President Karzai and the Afghan people. But we're also there because we're fighting terrorism, and we cannot afford to lose. We will not lose. We are not losing; we are prevailing.

May I mention Kosovo, which will be discussed. The secondary important NATO presence, 60,000 strong, to protect all Kosovars—majority, minority, Albanian, or Serb—so that also Kosovo will have a future.

NATO enlargement, the President mentioned. The nations concerned should go on with their reforms. No tickets are punched yet, but NATO enlargement will be on the agenda of the Bucharest summit, and certainly also what I call NATO finding the answers to modern threats and challenges, be it energy security and NATO's role as a bringer of added value. Cyber

defense: We saw a huge cyber attack on Estonia not that long ago. Missile defense is certainly an issue.

So we have a real full calendar in Bucharest, and that is basically the calendar the President and I discussed. And I'm always very much enjoying the hospitality not only in the Oval but at the Crawford ranch as well.

Thank you very much.

President Bush. Thank you.

Secretary General de Hoop Scheffer. Thanks.

President Bush. Thank you all.

NOTE: The President spoke at 11:48 a.m. in the Oval Office at the White House. Secretary General de Hoop Scheffer referred to President Hamid Karzai of Afghanistan.

Statement on the Resignation of Donald E. Powell as Coordinator of Gulf Coast Region Recovery and Rebuilding
February 29, 2008

Don Powell is an exceptional leader who has worked tirelessly and effectively to help the people of New Orleans and the Gulf Coast region recover and rebuild from one of our Nation's most destructive natural disasters.

Don brought to the job of coordinating our Federal rebuilding efforts the perfect combination of talent, temperament, experience, and compassion. Today, due in part to his leadership and outstanding work with State and local leaders, the Gulf Coast is on the road to recovery. While challenges

remain, the region is open for business, critical infrastructure is being rebuilt, and schools are up and running. People are reclaiming their lives, and our Nation owes Don a debt of gratitude. I appreciate his service to the country and thank him for his dedication.

I am also grateful to Paul Conway, Don's chief of staff, who will assume the duties of the Federal Coordinator for the Office of Gulf Coast Rebuilding in the interim.

Laura and I wish Don well as he returns to Texas.

The President's Radio Address
March 1, 2008

Good morning. Today my administration is releasing our 2008 National Drug Con-

trol Strategy. This report lays out the methods we are using to combat drug abuse in America, and it highlights the hopeful progress we're making in the fight against addiction.

When I took office in 2001, our country was facing a troubling rate of drug abuse, particularly among young people. Throughout America, young men and women saw their dreams disrupted by the destructive cycle of addiction. So I committed our Nation to an ambitious goal. In 2002, we began efforts to cut drug use among young people by 25 percent over 5 years.

Our strategy has three key elements. First, we are working to disrupt the supply of drugs by strengthening law enforcement and partnering with other countries to keep drugs out of the United States. Second, we're working to reduce the demand for drugs through prevention and education programs. And third, we're providing treatment options for those who've fallen prey to addiction.

These efforts have produced measurable results. Since 2001, the rate of youth drug abuse has dropped by 24 percent. Young people's use of marijuana is down by 25 percent. Their use of ecstasy has dropped by more than 50 percent. And their use of methamphetamine has declined by 64 percent. Overall, an estimated 860,000 fewer young people in America are using drugs today than when we began these efforts.

Our drug control strategy will continue all three elements of this successful approach. It will also target a growing problem, the abuse of prescription drugs by youth. Unfortunately, many young Americans do not understand how dangerous abusing medication can be. And in recent years, the number of Americans who have died from prescription drug overdoses has increased.

One of the factors behind this trend is the growing availability of highly addictive prescription drugs online. The Internet has brought about tremendous benefits for those who cannot easily get to a pharmacy in person. However, it has also created an opportunity for unscrupulous doctors and pharmacists to profit from addiction.

One victim of such a doctor was Ryan Haight. The young man from California was only 18 when he overdosed on painkillers that were illegally prescribed over the Internet. With only a few clicks of the mouse, Ryan was able to get a prescription from a doctor he had never met and have the pills sent to his front door. The doctor who wrote Ryan's prescription had previously served time in prison for illegally dispensing controlled substances.

We need to prevent tragedies like this from happening in the future. So I'm asking Congress to work with my administration to put an end to the illegal sale of highly addictive prescription drugs on the Internet. By working together to meet this goal, we can ensure a safer future for our children.

Government action is only one part of the solution to the problem of drug abuse. Others in our society have an important role to play as well. People in the entertainment and sports industries serve as role models to millions of young Americans, and that comes with the responsibility to dispel the notion that drug abuse is glamorous and free of consequences. Teachers, pastors, and parents also have an obligation to help young people develop the character and self-respect to resist drugs. The Federal Government will continue to do its part to keep our young people safe, and I urge all Americans to do the same. Our children deserve nothing less.

Thank you for listening.

NOTE: The address was recorded at 7:50 a.m. on February 29 in the Cabinet Room at the White House for broadcast at 10:06 a.m. on March 1. The transcript was made available by the Office of the Press Secretary on February 29, but was embargoed for release until the broadcast. The Office of the Press Secretary also released a Spanish language transcript of this address.

The President's News Conference With Prime Minister Anders Fogh Rasmussen of Denmark in Crawford, Texas
March 1, 2008

President Bush. Welcome. Thanks for coming. A couple opening statements, and we'll answer two questions apiece.

Mr. Prime Minister, we're really thrilled you're here. Laura and I love having you and Anne-Mette with us. Pretty good guests when you can have a meaningful mountain bike ride at sunset and then at sunrise, and the man not even break into a sweat. You're in incredible condition, and I really have enjoyed my time with you—my time when we talked and my time when we rode. I also appreciate the fact that you're a good personal friend and a strong leader.

I want to share with you some of the things we talked about. First of all, we talked about the war on terror and the ideological struggle of the 21st century. I appreciate your clear vision of the threats we all face and the opportunities that, by working together, we can help young democracies survive and help people realize the blessings of free societies.

I do want to thank you very much for the strong support of the NATO mission in Afghanistan. I know brave Danish soldiers have lost their lives. Our deepest sympathies go for their—to their loved ones. It is painful when anybody loses a life in any time, but—much less in combat. But it's very important for the people of Denmark, like it is for the people of the United States, to understand that, one, we're denying extremist groups safe haven, the very same groups that attacked and killed thousands of innocent people. We're helping young girls go to school. We're helping infrastructure develop. We're helping people find health care. We're helping a hopeful society begin to emerge. And we spent a lot of time talking about that.

I also appreciate very much the Danish contributions to help the people of Iraq. I strongly believe on the policy of return on success. We're returning some of our troops based upon success. That's precisely what the Danish Government did, because they were successful in their mission. And I congratulate you, Mr. Prime Minister, for having a vision.

I also was able to share with you my sense of what's happening in Iraq. We're watching a young democracy grow, much to the amazement of a lot of critics, a lot of people who said, "Well, it's impossible for this to happen in the rocky soils of Iraq." And it's happening today, and there's still more work to be done.

We're looking forward to our summit in Bucharest. We talked about what we intend to do and how to work to have a comprehensive, strategic plan available for Iraq—I mean, for Afghanistan, so our allies can take this plan home, can explain to the people why it's important. We also talked about the need to make sure that there's more civilian-military cooperation, that tangible evidence of a free society begins to become more evident to people and to grassroots in Afghanistan.

We talked about the spirit of NATO's open door policy. And we jointly welcome new nations in the alliance, so long as they meet the standards for membership.

We also talked about other global challenges. We talked about Iran, about how Iran must verifiably suspend its uranium enrichment program and come clean about its nuclear intentions and past actions. I also want Iran to stop supporting terror.

We also talked about Africa. I briefed the Prime Minister on our trip to Africa, talked about our mutual desire to help the folks suffering in Darfur. We talked about what happened in Kenya, and we're most grateful to the leaders there to help reconcile what could have been a very difficult situation.

Finally, we talked about climate change, more than once. We talked about climate change as I showed him my ranch and about how we're conservationists here in Crawford. And then we talked about the need for us to develop alternative technologies. And I really do welcome Denmark's leadership for the 2009 U.N. climate change meeting. And I appreciate very much you taking the lead in this issue.

And look, it was a great visit. And I'm now looking forward to giving the man a hamburger—[*laughter*]—after answering a couple of questions. But welcome, sir.

Prime Minister Rasmussen. Thank you very much, Mr. President. Let me first of all express my gratitude for your invitation to visit your ranch in Crawford. My wife and I are very pleased to be here. We have had a rewarding stay and a challenging stay, I must say. [*Laughter*] You made me work very hard out there on the terrific mountain bike trails on your wonderful ranch. And I can't imagine a better place to spend time talking and enjoying time with good friends. And I can't imagine a better symbol of the close and strong ties between the United States and Denmark.

President Bush. Thank you, sir.

Prime Minister Rasmussen. Mr. President, freedom, democracy, and human rights are the core values that unite us. Freedom and dignity of the individual are universal values. It is values that people living under oppression and brutal regimes strive for. We have an obligation to stand by these people in their struggle for liberty and democracy. This is our common challenge. And you, Mr. President, and the United States have, above anyone else, advanced this vision of liberty and democracy around the world. Allow me to pay tribute to you for this.

President Bush. Thank you, sir.

Prime Minister Rasmussen. And it is no easy task; there are obstacles and opponents. But I do share your vision. Freedom is universal. And in the struggle between democracy and dictatorship, no one can be neutral. It is as simple as that.

That is why we are in Afghanistan to fight the Taliban. That is why we removed the brutal dictator in Iraq. That is why your leadership in the Middle East is crucial. That is why we work for development and against extremism in Africa. That is why we have joined forces in the Balkans, stabilized and recognized Kosovo, and work for Balkan countries to be fully integrated in Europe.

The United States and Europe are key partners in this endeavor. Through NATO and the European Union, we reach out to aspiring countries like Ukraine and Georgia. We support their efforts to reform and develop links with Europe and across the Atlantic. And we will send a strong signal of support from our upcoming NATO summit in Bucharest.

Mr. President, as you mentioned, in 2009 Denmark will host the Global Climate Change Conference in Copenhagen. And it will take place in the land of windmills. We need a comprehensive global agreement, and American leadership is needed to reach that goal. And American leadership is crucial in order to motivate major economies like India and China to contribute.

Climate is a huge international challenge. Many countries are suffering from adverse weather conditions. We need to protect our globe. We need to reduce CO_2 emissions through green technology. We need to reduce our dependency on fossil fuels. And we need to break our addiction to oil, not only to counter climate change, but also to reduce our dependency on unstable and sometimes even undemocratic regimes. And I see the United States and Europe as key partners in the struggle to fight climate change and ensure energy security.

Mr. President, together we have handled the challenges of the past. Now let us together meet the challenges and threats of the future. We owe that to future generations.

Thank you.

President Bush. Thank you, sir.

Deb [Deb Riechmann, Associated Press].

Iraq/Iran

Q. Mr. President——

President Bush. Yes, Deb.

Q. I'd like to ask you about Iraq. General Petraeus and Gates are talking about a pause in troop reductions once we get to the pre-surge levels in July. Will that be it, or is it possible that there will be additional drawdowns before you leave office? And also, does the Iraqi Government's decision to host Ahmadi-nejad in Baghdad undermine your efforts to isolate Tehran?

President Bush. To the latter, I—look, I mean, he's a neighbor. And the message needs to be, quit sending in sophisticated equipment that's killing our citizens, and that the message will be that we're negotiating a long-term security agreement with the United States precisely because we want enough breathing space for our democracy to develop.

My message is for him, stop exporting terror, and that the international community is serious about continuing to isolate Iran until they come clean about their nuclear weapons ambitions. And that's why there will be action in the United Nations here early next week as we work collaboratively to continue to send a clear message.

In terms of troop levels, there is going to be enormous speculation, again, about what decision I will make. I can only tell you, Deb, that it's going to be based upon the recommendations of Secretary Gates, General Petraeus, the Joint Chiefs. My sole criterion is, whatever we do, it ought to be in the context of success.

If we fail in Iraq, the consequences for world peace will be enormous; the consequences for the security of the United States will be enormous. And therefore, my question is, what does it take to succeed? And we're not going to let politics drive my decision—again. If I worried about polls and focus groups, I wouldn't have sent more troops in. I sent more troops in because the situation was unacceptable. And now we're succeeding. And so therefore, Ryan Crocker—the Ambassador—and General Petraeus will be coming back, and they'll report to the country, and they'll report to me. And the decisions—you'll see them evolve.

Q. Can I ask just one follow-up?

President Bush. Maybe. [*Laughter*]

U.S. Troop Levels in Iraq/Iraqi Provincial Elections

Q. Are you worried about reducing U.S. troop presence before the elections in October?

President Bush. Deb, see, that's what I said. I just—politics isn't going to play into it.

Q. You mean the Iraqi politics?

President Bush. Oh, you mean the Iraqi—I thought you meant our——

Q. No, no.

President Bush. I didn't listen.

Q. I'm sorry. [*Laughter*]

President Bush. I apologize.

Q. I believe there's Provincial elections coming up in——

President Bush. There are.

Q. Okay. Which——

President Bush. The 1st of October 2008, that's very observant.

Q. Would you be worried about——

President Bush. And I was not being observant. And it must be because I'm just so relaxed on the ranch, I didn't even bother to listen to your question. [*Laughter*]

Q. Would you be concerned about doing it before then?

President Bush. I think our generals ought to be concerned about making sure there's enough of a presence so that the Provincial elections can be carried off in such a way that democracy advances. But that—I'll wait and hear what they have to say. But yes, I mean, that ought to be a factor in their recommendation to me. I apologize.

Do you want to call on somebody?

Prime Minister Rasmussen. Yup.

Progress in Iraq

Q. Thank you. Mr. President, Mr. Prime Minister, the war in Iraq—if we could stay on that subject for just a minute—I mean, it's been going on for almost 5 years. Is there anything you would have done differently, Mr. President, if you had known back then in 2003 what you know today?

President Bush. That's an interesting question. One thing I wouldn't do differently is leave Saddam Hussein in power. It was the right decision then; it's the right decision today; and it will be viewed as the right decision when history is finally written.

You know, I—look, I mean, there's going to be ample time to second-guess decisions, and I'll let the historians do that. A war is constantly changing, and what appears to have been an easy decision today might have been a lot difficult when you take it—put it in historical context. And so my focus, sir, is moving forward and making sure this progress that we're watching continues.

And there's been some ups and downs, obviously. I mean, the great moments were, of course, the writing of a modern Constitution for the Middle East and votes for a President and a Parliament. And then 2006 came along, and an enemy was able to stir up unbelievable sectarian hatred and violence. And so I had a choice to make, you know, accept it and allow for failure, or do something about it. And obviously, I chose the latter, which was—I wouldn't call that exactly a popular decision. But if you follow popularity as your guide, then you sacrifice principle and vision.

And so, look, this is a—this will be an important chapter of my Presidency, and they'll be analyzing these decisions for a long time. And I just got to tell you, I've got great faith in the capacity of democracy to be transformative, not only for the people of Iraq but for the region. And that's

why we're discussing with the Iraqis a long-term security agreement, to have a—have the kind of effect that will enable people to be confident to make hard decisions when it comes to reconciliation and political progress.

But the historians, I'm sure, will find ample—well, there's some short-term historians already trying to find some ample opportunity to figure out what went right or what went wrong, what we could have done differently. But there's no such thing as accurate short-term history, as far as I'm concerned. There needs to be time for people to be able to see and put things in proper perspective.

Michael [Mike Emanuel, FOX News].

Afghanistan

Q. Thank you, Mr. President. And thank you for bringing us to the great weather.

The President. Yes, back to Texas, man. The guy cut his teeth in Texas. [*Laughter*]

Q. Mr. President, you've had an opportunity to meet with multiple leaders this week to talk about the war in Afghanistan. As you head into the NATO summit next month, what do you anticipate, in terms of, do you think some of the allies may be able to contribute more in terms of trainers and Provincial Reconstruction Teams?

And, Mr. Prime Minister, we've heard the President and other U.S. officials praise Denmark's contribution to Afghanistan. I'm wondering what you think can be done to encourage some other NATO allies to perhaps step up and contribute more.

President Bush. As you know, my administration has made it abundantly clear, we expect people to carry their—to carry a heavy burden if they're going to be in Iraq—Afghanistan. In other words, Secretary Gates made—said, look, if we're going to fight as an alliance, let's fight as an alliance.

Having said that, I understand there's certain political constraints on certain countries. And so we ought to be—I am going to go to Bucharest with the notion that we're thankful for the contributions being made and encourage people to contribute more. The United States is putting in 3,200 additional marines. We are trying to help Canada realize her goal of 1,000 additional fighters in the southern part of the country, as is Anders working toward that.

You know, the key in Bucharest is for people to—from around the world to understand, one, how important the mission is to the successes that are being achieved. Remember last year about this time—it was: The Taliban was going on the offensive; the Taliban was going to be doing this; the Taliban was going to be doing that. Well, the Taliban had a bad year when it came to military operations. And are they still dangerous? Yes, they're dangerous. They're still capable of convincing young kids to go in and blow people up with suicide vests. That's dangerous. Are they overwhelming the Government? No. Do they have a presence in the country? Yes. Do we have the capacity to go after them? Absolutely. Do we need more capacity? Yes, we do, and that's the mission, and that's what we'll work on.

The other thing, as Anders mentioned and I mentioned, was that this is an opportunity to keep an open door policy for NATO, presuming that countries meet certain criterion and meet the obligations to which they signed up.

Prime Minister Rasmussen. Thank you very much. We have to make sure that our mission in Afghanistan will be a success. A lot is at stake for the Afghan people, for international security, and for NATO. Therefore, we need more troops in Afghanistan. This is the reason why Denmark decided to increase our number of troops, equivalent to 50 percent, last autumn.

I feel confident that we can convince partners to contribute with more troops than today. And I think the best way to encourage partners to contribute to a higher degree is to show the good example.

Denmark is a small country, but per capita, Denmark is among the biggest contributors in Afghanistan. And we work together with the British in the southern Helmand Province, really a hot spot. And so I think the good example is a very important thing.

And finally, I think we should be better to tell the positive stories about Afghanistan because, actually, there is a lot of progress: democracy, construction of infrastructure, roads, the health system is in a better condition, not least education. Girls and women have now access to the educational system. We should be better to tell this positive story and, thereby, encourage the international community to step up its efforts.

President Bush. Final question, Anders, I'm getting hungry. [*Laughter*]

Prime Minister Rasmussen. Yes. We have a Danish gentleman over here.

President Bush. Yes.

2008 Presidential Election/Environment

Q. Mr. Prime Minister, you talked about climate. Did these talks make you believe that a bridge can be made so that there will be an agreement at the U.N. climate summit in Copenhagen in 2009?

And, Mr. President, based on what we have heard the two Democratic leading contenders for your job state about foreign policy, what parts of your foreign policy do you see threatened by——

President Bush. Yes. You know, that's a very clever attempt—I'm going to let him answer the climate change thing—but it's a very clever attempt by you to drag me into the middle of the 2008 campaign, similar to what these two fine folks—three fine folks have been doing. So therefore, we'll let it sort out. But I will tell you this: The issue in America is going to be, who will keep taxes low and who will be tough in protecting America. And our candidate for President is going to win because he will have convinced the American people to this truth.

Nice try. [*Laughter*]

Prime Minister Rasmussen. Thank you. Our talks about climate change have really been encouraging. Actually—excuse me, Mr. President—I think the American President is really a convinced environmentalist. And the President has assured me that the United States will take leadership in our endeavors to achieve a comprehensive global deal in Copenhagen in 2009.

And I have commended the President for his initiative to gather the 15 or 17 major economies in the world, because we have to take on board all the major emitters of greenhouse gases. And I consider the American initiative a very valuable input in our preparations for the Global Climate Change Conference in Copenhagen. So based on our talks today, I'm a bit more optimistic than I was before.

President Bush. I know when he says committed environmentalist, it doesn't conform to stereotype. All I ask people is to look at the record.

Thank you all very much for coming. We're thrilled you're here at the ranch. Good to see some of you again. Welcome.

2008 Presidential Election

Q. Did you vote in the Texas primary?

The President. I did, and I'm not telling you who. [*Laughter*] Thank you.

NOTE: The President's news conference began at 12 p.m. at the Bush Ranch. In his remarks, he referred to Anne-Mette Rasmussen, wife of Prime Minister Rasmussen; President Mahmud Ahmadi-nejad of Iran; and Gen. David H. Petraeus, USA, commanding general, Multi-National Force—Iraq.

Remarks to the National Association of Attorneys General
March 3, 2008

General Wasden, thank you, sir. And General Lynch, thank you for having the Attorney General and me here to visit with the Nation's attorney generals. I thank you very much for serving the country. I'm honored that you've stepped forward to say, you know, my family—I'm going to put my family in such a way that we're going to serve together. And I hope you have found the experience to be as enriching as I've found it—my experience in public life to be.

I also know that you're dealing with a wide variety of issues. I was the Governor of Texas. I see my—the attorney general of Texas here. It's been—it was a great joy to work with Greg when I was the Governor. We have a solemn responsibility together, and that's to protect the country. You do it in a variety of ways. And we've got a responsibility here. As a matter of

fact, there's no greater responsibility at the Federal Government than to protect the American people, which means that we must make sure our professionals have the tools they need to do the jobs we've asked them to do.

Now, there's a serious debate here, and some of the attorney generals have written a letter, both Democrats and Republicans, urging that the debate be solved in such a way that the professionals can do the job. And I thank you for wading in. There's a lot of legal complexities on the FISA renewal debate, but the real issue comes down to this: To defend the country, we need to be able to monitor communications of terrorists quickly and be able to do it effectively.

And we can't do it without the cooperation of private companies. Now, unfortunately, some of the private companies have been sued for billions of dollars because they are believed to have helped defend America after the attacks on 9/11. Now the question is, should these lawsuits be allowed to proceed, or should any company that may have helped save American lives be thanked for performing a patriotic service? Should those who stepped forward to say we're going to help defend America have to go to the courthouse to defend themselves, or should the Congress and the President say, "Thank you for doing your patriotic duty"? I believe we ought to say, "Thank you."

I'm really appreciative of the fact that 21 State attorney generals, 7 Democrats and 14 Republicans, wrote a letter stating that assistance from private companies, as they put it, "is utterly essential" and urges the Senate—at the time—to approve FISA reform that protects the companies from lawsuits. I think that represents what most people—how most people think here in the country.

The Senate heard you and heard the voices of other people and passed a really good FISA reform bill by a strong bipartisan majority, 68 to 29. The answer to the question about whether we ought to thank or sue is also clear to the majority in the House of Representatives. If this bill, the Senate bill, were allowed—were given a vote on the floor of the House of Representatives, it would pass. There's enough votes available to pass a good Senate bill that would give our professionals the tools they need to protect the American people from further attack.

Unfortunately, a minority in the House has been holding the bill up. Now, this weekend there was some encouraging news. The chairman of the House Intelligence Committee, Silvestre Reyes, said that he was open to passing a bill with protections for our private sector partners, including those companies who are currently being sued for allegedly helping us after 9/11. I appreciate the chairman's comments, and I urge the full House to pass this legislation as soon as possible.

I feel strongly about this issue, not only because I know we need to have the private carriers available to provide information, but to put it bluntly, if the enemy is calling in to somebody in the United States, we need to know who they're talking to and why they're calling and what they intend to do.

These lawsuits are really unfair if you think about it. If any of the companies believed to have helped us, I'm just going to tell you: They were told it was legal by the Government, and they were told it was necessary by the Government. And here they are getting sued. It would be dangerous—the reason—the danger in all this is that because the private companies are fearful of lawsuits or being besieged by lawsuits, they would be less willing to help in the future.

If your Government has said this is legal and we want your help and then all of a sudden they get sued for billions of dollars, you can imagine how hesitant they'll be with future requests. And yet the threat is ongoing. And that's why we said, failure by the House to act on the Senate bill would create an intelligence gap that is unacceptable.

So I appreciate your interest in the subject. Thank you for giving me and the General a chance to come by, and God bless you. Thank you.

NOTE: The President spoke at 1:22 p.m. in Room 350 of the Dwight D. Eisenhower Executive Office Building. In his remarks, he referred to State Attorneys General Lawrence Wasden of Idaho, Patrick C. Lynch of Rhode Island, and Greg Abbott of Texas.

Remarks Following a Meeting With Lieutenant General Raymond T. Odierno
March 3, 2008

General Ray Odierno served for 30 months in Iraq. He's nominated to Vice Chairman [Vice Chief of Staff]° of the Army. And I asked him to come in for several reasons. One, I wanted to thank him. And in thanking the general, I'm really thanking everybody who has worn the uniform and served in this war against the extremists and terrorists. And in thanking the general, I'm also thanking Mrs. Odierno and every wife or every husband whose spouse has been far away from home and is serving.

And in listening to the general, I was listening carefully to make sure that the decisions that had been made were the right decisions and that the progress that's being made is real. I mean, this is a man who was there when times looked grim and a man who observed firsthand progress that was made as a result of the surge.

He was a straightforward fellow who gave me his candid advice on how best to proceed, not necessarily with troop levels, because that study is going on now, but in making sure that we continue programs such as what's called the CERP money. This is money for our commanders to make—to help these local folks rebuild and reconcile.

And so, general, I want to thank you for your service. And I appreciate the fact that you really snatched defeat out of the jaws of those who are trying to defeat us in Iraq. You were the—you and General Petraeus were a unbelievably strong one-two combination.

And my call and my assurance, sir, is that the gains that you and your teams have made will continue on, because stakes in Iraq are essential for peace, essential for freedom, and essential for the security of this country. I'm honored to be your Commander in Chief.

NOTE: The President spoke at 2:10 p.m. in the Oval Office at the White House. In his remarks, he referred to Linda Odierno, wife of Lt. Gen. Odierno; and Gen. David H. Petraeus, USA, commanding general, Multi-National Force—Iraq.

Remarks on Presenting Posthumously the Congressional Medal of Honor to Woodrow W. Keeble
March 3, 2008

The President. Welcome. Thanks for coming. Mr. Vice President, Mr. Secretary, members of the Dakotan congressional delegations, Senator from Alaska, other Members of Congress, members of my Cabinet, members of the administration, members of the United States Armed Forces, distin-guished guests: Welcome to the White House.

The Medal of Honor is the highest award for valor a President can bestow. And I'm honored recipients of the Medal of Honor have joined us. Thank you for coming.

During my time in office, I've had the privilege of performing this duty on nine

---

° White House correction.

separate occasions. Every ceremony has been inspiring; many have been joyful; some have been poignant. But I'm not sure I can remember many ceremonies quite like this one.

It's taken nearly 60 years for Master Sergeant Woodrow Wilson Keeble to be awarded the medal he earned on the battlefield in Korea. His nominating paperwork was lost, and then it was resubmitted, and then it was lost again. Then the deadline passed, and Woody and his family were told it was too late. Some blamed the bureaucracy for a shameful blunder; others suspected racism. Woody was a full-blooded Sioux Indian. Whatever the reason, the first Sioux to ever receive the Medal of Honor died without knowing it was his. A terrible injustice was done to a good man, to his family, and to history. And today we're going to try to set things right.

Few people worked harder for this day than Woody's family. I thank the members who are with us, including his son Russell, who is accepting this award on their behalf, along with his cousin——

Audience member. Nephew.

The President. ——along with his nephew. I want to welcome you here. Thank you for supporting Woody. Thank you for your understanding, your patience, and, most of all, your persistence.

I also offer special thanks to the determined delegations of North and South Dakota, including the Governor of North Dakota and the former Governor of South Dakota. Woody has ties to both Dakotas. Each State claims him as his own. [*Laughter*] I think I'm going to stay out of the argument. [*Laughter*] I want to thank you for carrying Woody's banner to the Pentagon and to the Halls of Congress. You did the right thing.

It's easy to understand why so many people argued so passionately for the medal once you hear the story of what Woody Keeble did. This story unfolded at an important time in our history. The year was 1951. The world was divided by a cold war.

America was under threat and, some believed, overmatched and out of heart. The great evil of communism was said to be the future of the world. It was on the advance in Europe and in China and on the Asian peninsula of Korea.

On that peninsula, a battle raged between Communist forces in the North and the forces of freedom in the South. And Woody Keeble, a decorated veteran of Guadalcanal, raised his hand to serve his country once again. Woody said he volunteered for Korea because "somebody had to teach those kids how to fight." And that's exactly what he did.

In George Company, he quickly became a mentor, a teacher, and a legend. He was so strong that he could lift the back of a jeep and spin it around. Some people knew he had been scouted by the Chicago White Sox. He had a heck of an arm, and he threw grenades like a baseball. One soldier remembered the time Woody walked through a mine field, leaving tracks for his men to follow. Another recalled the time Woody was shot twice in the arm, and he kept fighting without seeming to notice.

That fall, Woody's courage was on full display during a major offensive called Operation No Man [Nomad].° His company was ordered to take a series of hills protecting a major enemy supply line. High up in those hills and manning machine guns were Chinese Communist forces. After days of fighting, the officers in Woody's company had fallen. Woody assumed command of one platoon, then a second, and then a third, until one of the hills was taken and the enemy fled in wild retreat.

That first advance nearly killed him. By the end of the day, Woody had more than 83 grenade fragments in his body. He had bleeding wounds in his arms, chest, and thighs. And yet he still wanted to fight. So after a day with the medics, he defied

---

° White House correction.

the doctor's orders and returned to the battlefield. And that is where, on October 20th, 1951, Master Sergeant Woodrow Wilson Keeble made history.

Communist forces still held a crucial hill that was the pearl of their defenses. They had pinned down U.S. forces with a furious assault. One soldier said the enemy lobbed so many grenades on American troops that they looked like a flock of blackbirds in the sky. Allied forces had tried heavy artillery to dislodge the enemy, and nothing seemed to be working. The offense was failing, and American boys were dying. But our forces had one advantage; Woody was back, and Woody was some kind of mad.

He grabbed grenades and his weapon and climbed that crucial hill alone. Woody climbed hundreds of yards through dirt and rock, with his wounds aching, bullets flying, and grenades falling all around him. As Woody first started off, someone saw him and remarked, "Either he's the bravest soldier I have ever met, or he's crazy." Soldiers watched in awe as Woody singlehandedly took out one machine gun nest and then another. When Woody was through, all 16 enemy soldiers were dead, the hill was taken, and the Allies had won the day.

Woody Keeble's act of heroism saved many American lives and earned him a permanent place in his fellow soldiers' hearts. Years later, some of those tough soldiers' eyes would fill with tears when they saw Woody again. One said, "He was the most respected person I ever knew in my life." Another said, "I would have followed him anywhere." A third said, "He was awesome." Those brave boys battled tyranny, held the line against a Communist menace, and kept a nation free. And some of them are with us today. We are honored to host you at the White House. We thank you for your courage. We thank you for honoring your comrade in arms. And we thank you for your service to the United States.

As the war ended, Woody went back to North Dakota. In some ways, his return was a sad one. Within a few years, his first wife died. He would suffer from numerous effects of the war. A series of strokes paralyzed his right side and robbed him of his ability to speak. And the wounds he sustained in service to his country would haunt him for the rest of his life.

Yet Woody was not a bitter man. As a member of his family put it, "Woody loved his country, loved his tribe, and loved God." Woody even found love again with a woman named Blossom. Woody may not have been able to speak, but he could still get a message across. He wrote a note asking Blossom to marry him. She told him she needed some time to think about it. So while she was deliberating, Woody put their engagement announcement in the newspaper. [*Laughter*] This is a man who was relentless in love as well as war. [*Laughter*]

In his community, he was an everyday hero. Even in poor health, he would mow lawns for seniors in the summers and help cars out of the snow banks in the winters. He once picked up a hitchhiker who was down on his luck and looking for work. Woody wasn't a rich man, but he gave the man $50. Those who knew Woody can tell countless stories like this, one of a great soldier who became a Good Samaritan.

To his last days, he was a devoted veteran. He proudly wore his uniform at local events and parades. Sometimes folks who loved him would see that uniform and ask him about his missing medal. They felt he was cheated, yet Woody never complained. See, he believed America was the greatest nation on Earth, even when it made mistakes. And there was never a single day he wasn't proud to have served our country.

Woody suffered his eighth and final stroke in 1982. His son, Russell, took him to the hospital and prayed it wasn't the end. But Woody knew, and he wasn't afraid. Woodrow Wilson Keeble died in graceful anonymity, unknown except to the fortunate souls who loved him and those who learned from him. Russell puts it this way: "Woody met death with a smile. He taught me how to live, and he taught me how to die."

I am pleased that this good and honorable man is finally getting the recognition he deserves. But on behalf of our grateful Nation, I deeply regret that this tribute comes decades too late. Woody will never hold this medal in his hands or wear it on his uniform. He will never hear a President thank him for his heroism. He will never stand here to see the pride of his friends and loved ones, as I see in their eyes now.

But there are some things we can still do for him. We can tell his story, and we can honor his memory. And we can follow his lead by showing all those who have followed him on the battlefield the same love and generosity of spirit that Woody showed his country every day.

At the request of the Keeble family and in accordance with the Sioux tradition, two empty chairs have been placed on this stage to represent Woody and Blossom and to acknowledge their passing into the spiritual world. The Sioux have a saying: "The life of a man is a circle." Well, today we complete Woody Keeble's circle, from an example to his men to an example for the ages. And if we honor his life and take lessons from his good and noble service, then Master Sergeant Woody Keeble will serve his country once again.

I want to thank you all for coming. May I ask for God's blessings on you and Woody Keeble and the Keeble family. May God continue to bless our country. And now I ask Mr. Hawkins and Mr. Bluedog to join me. Commander Thompson will read the citation.

NOTE: The President spoke at 2:35 p.m. in the East Room at the White House. In his remarks, he referred to Secretary of Defense Robert M. Gates; Sen. Theodore F. Stevens; former Gov. William J. Janklow of South Dakota; Gov. John Hoeven of North Dakota; and Russell Hawkins, stepson, and Kurt Bluedog, grandnephew, of Mr. Keeble. Following the President's remarks, Maj. Mark Thompson, USMC, Marine Corps Aide to the President, read the citation.

Remarks Following Discussions With King Abdullah II of Jordan and an Exchange With Reporters
March 4, 2008

President Bush. His Majesty and I will take a couple of questions after opening statements.

Your Majesty, I value your friendship, and I value your leadership. And I appreciate you coming back. America has got no stronger friend in the Middle East than Jordan. And we appreciate the—we appreciate your firmness when it comes to dealing with terror and extremism. We appreciate the heart when it comes to people—your heart when it comes to people who suffer.

We spent a lot of time talking about the Middle Eastern peace process. A couple of points I want to reiterate. One is that the United States is engaged and will remain engaged in helping convince the Prime Minister of Israel and President Abbas that now is the time to formulate a vision of what a state will look like.

And secondly, I assured His Majesty this is a major focus of my administration and that I would like to see that vision, the process that we have started in Annapolis, finished prior to my departure from the Presidency. In other words, there is a—people say, "Well, you always set—you're hesitant to set timetables." But there happens to be a timetable, as far as I'm concerned, and that is, I'm leaving office. And Secretary Rice is in the region today, and she is making our views known, that we expect these leaders to step up and make hard decisions. And I told His Majesty I'm optimistic—still as optimistic as I was after Annapolis.

And so we welcome you, sir. And thank you for your passion.

King Abdullah. Thank you very much, Mr. President. It is obviously a great honor to be back here and to be with you. We tremendously appreciate the warm relationship and the great friendship between our two countries.

But as His Excellency, the President, just stated, we are very, very pleased with the continued commitment that the President has to solve the longest, most outstanding issue in the Middle East, the Israeli-Palestinian process. And the words and discussions that we've had this morning will have, I think, a very great response back in our part of the world when I will go back and report to many of my colleagues the President's commitment to bringing a bright future to Israelis and Palestinians and to the whole area.

And we look forward to continuing to work with you, Mr. President, and many of us in the area to finally achieve a peace that will set the Middle East in the right direction.

President Bush. Thank you. A couple of questions apiece.

Ben [Ben Feller, Associated Press].

Middle East Peace Process

Q. Mr. President——

President Bush. Ben.

Q. Mr. President——

President Bush. Hold on a second. Ben.

Q. ——as you have promised—sorry.

Q. Thank you. Thank you, Mr. President. Are you—what are your thoughts about the fact that President Abbas has not resumed peace talks? Are you disappointed? And

very quickly, sir, you said you're still as optimistic as you were after Annapolis.

President Bush. Yes.

Q. What gives you that optimism?

President Bush. I'm optimistic because I am absolutely convinced that Prime Minister Olmert and President Abbas understand that this is now a key moment in achieving peace. Both leaders are committed to a democracy—two democracies living side by side in peace. Both leaders understand that there has to be a vision of what that state will look like. Both leaders fully understand that there has to— you know, have to work out agreements on borders and right of return and other issues. Both leaders understand that a vision that respects people and promotes freedom stands in stark contrast to the extremists who are willing to murder people to stop the advance of democracy and to, you know, dash the ambitions of the Palestinians.

I'm optimistic that they understand that. I understand the difficulties, but I also believe both leaders have—when it—ultimately will have the courage necessary to reach an agreement. And my job as the President and my administration's responsibilities are to help them understand what is possible and to keep them moving on a process. And so I'm optimistic, I am.

Q. Are you disappointed about the lack of resumption in peace talks?

The President. This is a process that, you know, always has two steps forward and one step back. We just got to make sure that it's only one step back. Condi is out there in the region. And sometimes, you know, there's matters going behind the scenes that aren't apparent in the public arena. And so yes, I'm optimistic. And we'll continue to work hard to help achieve the vision.

Step one is to convince the leaders it's necessary and to help them define a vision so that a state can come into being after conditions are met. But a lot of Palestinians are probably—are saying: "We've heard this kind of rhetoric before. Show us what a state looks like." And I said, a state has got to be continuous—a contiguous territory; it can't look like Swiss cheese. You know, the Palestinians have got to understand that this is an option available for them, and it will stand in stark contrast to the vision of Hamas, which has been nothing more than violence and deprivation.

You want to call on somebody?

Q. Mr. President, as you mentioned— you know, as you approach the end of your term in office, you mentioned that you still feel that establishing the Palestinian state is still achievable.

President Bush. Yes.

Q. What is the exact vision that you have, you know, with this short time left?

The President. Sure, I appreciate it. First of all, 10 months is a long time. May seem short to you, but it's—there's plenty of time to get a deal done.

Secondly, I have visited with the leaders, you know, on a one-on-one basis quite frequently, and I understand that it's—this is a difficult subject. But I also feel very comfortable with the commitment they have made to try to work out subjects that have been difficult for other leaders to work out in the past.

The role of the United States—we can't impose peace. We can help leaders come to agreement and come to the table and make hard decisions. We can help facilitate the bridging of gaps, if there are gaps. And that's exactly what our diplomacy is in the process of doing.

And by the way, there is—and one of the reasons why His Majesty is so important in this process, as are other leaders in the Middle East, including my close friend King Abdallah of Saudi Arabia and President Mubarak of Egypt, is that the— both these leaders are going to need the support of the Arab world in order to make tough decisions. But first, it's up to them. And so I'm optimistic that they can con-clude tough negotiations. And we'll try to facilitate that.

Matt [Matt Spetalnick, Reuters].

Organization of the Petroleum Exporting Countries (OPEC)/Oil Prices

Q. Yes, sir. Every indication out of the OPEC meeting of ministers in Vienna is that they will be holding output steady. What is your reaction to that, sir, in light of your recent visit to the Middle East in which you appealed for an increase in output?

The President. Yes. I think it's a mistake to have your biggest customer's economy slow down—or your biggest customers' economies slowing down as a result of high energy prices. It's not the only result—our economy is slowing down. I mean, obviously, we've got a housing issue and some credit issues. But no question, the high price of gasoline has hurt economic growth here in the United States. And if I were a member of OPEC, I'd be concerned about high energy prices causing people to buy less energy over time.

And the other thing high energy prices of course does—which is stimulate alternative fuels, which we're doing a lot here in America. We're spending a lot of money on biofuels and ethanols and new ways to make ethanol. So my advice to OPEC— of course they haven't listened to it—but my advice to OPEC is to understand the consequences of high energy prices and— because I do. And I understand that this is affecting our American citizens. It's making it harder for people to be able to drive, and it's making it tough for families to save.

And so not only is it—high energy prices having an effect on—a macroeffect on our economy; it's affecting a lot of our families, which troubles me as well. And by the way, the higher energy prices stay, the more likely it is countries will quickly diversify. And that's part of our strategy.

You want to call on somebody?

King Abdullah. I think one more.

President Bush. One more?

King Abdullah. Yes—[*inaudible*].

President Bush. Here's a great—ask this lady here; she's good.

Iraqi Refugees/Lebanon/Syria

Q. Thank you, Mr. President. Apart from the Palestinian issue, did you also discuss Lebanon and Iraq and whether there's a common position between you and Jordan regarding the crisis in Lebanon and the situation in Iraq?

President Bush. Yes, thank you. We did. His Majesty—and he, of course, can answer as well—but His Majesty made it very clear to me that stability in Iraq is important for Jordan. He also pointed out something which I knew, but I wasn't exactly sure how it was affecting his country, that there are roughly three-quarters of a million Iraqi citizens who have moved to Jordan. And we talked about a common strategy about how to make sure that those citizens ended up, hopefully, going home to Iraq as the security situation improved, but also, while they're in Jordan, not create terrible issues for the Government.

And of course, we talked about Lebanon. We strongly—I strongly support Prime Minister Siniora and the March 14th coalition. I strongly condemn a Syrian interference in the Lebanese political process.

It is—I am extremely disappointed that the Syrian leader continues to make it hard for the Siniora Government to succeed, and I really don't appreciate the fact that they've made it hard for this Government to elect a President. We had diplomatic success in the past, when the U.N. Security Council passed a resolution seeing to it that Syria left this young democracy to be able to grow on its own. And now here they are once again interfering inside the politics of this country.

And so yes, we discussed the subject.

King Abdullah. And all I can add to that, on the issue of Lebanon, is how we discussed the role of Arab countries and how we can be effective in supporting the process in Lebanon, so that as quickly as possible a government is formed which will be able them—to take them to the future.

President Bush. Thank you all very much. We've got to go have lunch with our wives.

NOTE: The President spoke at 11:47 a.m. in the Oval Office at the White House. In his remarks, he referred to Prime Minister Ehud Olmert of Israel; President Mahmoud Abbas of the Palestinian Authority; Prime Minister Fuad Siniora of Lebanon; and President Bashar al-Asad of Syria.

Remarks on the Situation in Colombia
March 4, 2008

This morning I spoke to President Uribe of Colombia. He updated me on the situation in his country, including the continuing assault by narcoterrorists as well as the provocative maneuvers by the regime in Venezuela.

I told the President that America fully supports Colombia's democracy and that we firmly oppose any acts of aggression that could destabilize the region. I told him that America will continue to stand with Colom-

bia as it confronts violence and terror and fights drug traffickers.

President Uribe told me that one of the most important ways America can demonstrate its support for Colombia is by moving forward with a free trade agreement that we negotiated. The free trade agreement will show the Colombian people that democracy and free enterprise lead to a better life. It will help President Uribe counter the radical vision of those who are seeking to undermine democracy and create divisions within our hemisphere.

Our country's message to President Uribe and the people of Colombia is that we stand with our democratic ally. My message to the United States Congress is that this trade agreement is more than a matter of smart economics; it is a matter of national security. If we fail to approve this agreement, we will let down our close ally, we will damage our credibility in the region, and we will embolden the demagogues in our hemisphere.

The President told me that the people across the region are watching to see what the United States will do. So Republicans and Democrats in Congress need to come together and approve this agreement. By acting at this critical moment, we can show the Colombian people and millions across the region that they can count on America to keep its word and that freedom is the surest path to prosperity and peace.

Thank you very much.

NOTE: The President spoke at 1:05 p.m. on the South Lawn at the White House. The Office of the Press Secretary also released a Spanish language transcript of these remarks.

Message to the Congress on Continuation of the National Emergency With Respect to Zimbabwe
March 4, 2008

To the Congress of the United States:

The crisis constituted by the actions and policies of certain members of the Government of Zimbabwe and other persons to undermine Zimbabwe's democratic processes or institutions has not been resolved. These actions and policies pose a continuing unusual and extraordinary threat to the foreign policy of the United States. For these reasons, I have determined that it is necessary to continue this national emergency and to maintain in force the sanctions to respond to this threat.

Section 202(d) of the National Emergencies Act (50 U.S.C. 1622(d)) provides for the automatic termination of a national emergency unless, prior to the anniversary date of its declaration, the President publishes in the *Federal Register* and transmits to the Congress a notice stating that the emergency is to continue in effect beyond the anniversary date. In accordance with this provision, I have sent the enclosed notice to the *Federal Register* for publication, stating that the national emergency with respect to the actions and policies of certain members of the Government of Zimbabwe and other persons to undermine Zimbabwe's democratic processes or institutions is to continue in effect beyond March 6, 2008.

GEORGE W. BUSH

The White House,
March 4, 2008.

NOTE: The notice is listed in Appendix D at the end of this volume.

Remarks at the Washington International Renewable Energy Conference
March 5, 2008

Thank you all. Thank you for the warm welcome. Thanks for coming. It's my honor to be here. I'm proud to address the Washington International Renewable Energy Conference. Thankfully, you only left it for five words. [*Laughter.*] I appreciate your commitment to renewable energy. I probably didn't help today when I rode over in a 20-car motorcade. [*Laughter.*]

I appreciate the fact that—I hope you understand that you're pioneers on the frontiers of change; that I fully suspect that this conference will seem unbelievably outdated within a decade; that people will marvel about how far technology has helped change our habits and change the world. And I hope you take great pride in being a part of this constructive change. And so thanks for coming to America. We welcome you here.

To my fellow citizens, thanks for being entrepreneurs and forward thinkers. To members of my administration, like Sam Bodman, who just introduced me, or Ed Schafer, the head of the Agriculture Department, or Steve Johnson, EPA, thank you all for serving our country. Thanks for your kind words, Sam. I appreciate all the others who are here from my administration.

Mike Eckhart is the president of the American Council on Renewable Energy. He and I went to Harvard together. I don't know if he is—has had to spend time overcoming that, but I certainly have and— [*laughter*]—particularly in Texas politics. But it's good to be with my friend Mike. I can assure you that when we were at Harvard Business School together, he never envisioned that we would be in our respective positions, like we are today. As a matter of fact, I know in 1975, he never even thought about the word "renewable fuel," much less "President George W. Bush."

I welcome the Ambassadors who are here. I welcome—listen, let me start first by telling you that America has got to change its habits. We've got to get off oil. And the reason why is, first, oil is—dependency on oil presents a real challenge to our economy. As economies grow—and we want all our economies to grow; we want people to be prosperous. We want people who are living in poverty to be able to grow out of poverty. We want there to be general prosperity. But as economies grow, until we change our habits, there is going to be more dependency on oil.

My job, as the President of the country, is to put progrowth policies in place. But we're dependent upon oil, and so as our economy grows, it's going to create more demand for oil—same with China, same with India, same with other growing countries. And it should be obvious to you all that the demand is outstripping supply, which causes prices to go up. And it's making it harder here in America for working families to save and for farmers to be prosperous and for small businesses to grow.

The dependency upon oil also puts us at the mercy of terrorists. If there's tight supply and demand, all it requires is one terrorist disruption of oil and that price goes even higher. It's in our interests to end our dependency on oil because it—that dependency presents a challenge to our national security. In 1985, 20 percent of America's oil came from abroad. Today, that number is nearly 60 percent.

Now, all the countries we import from are friendly, stable countries, but some countries we get oil from don't particularly like us. They don't like the form of government that we embrace. They don't believe in the same freedoms we believe in. And that's a problem from a national security perspective for the United States and any other nation that values its economic sovereignty and national sovereignty.

And finally, our dependence on fossil fuels like oil presents a challenge to our environment. When we burn fossil fuels, we release greenhouse gases. The concentration of greenhouse gases has increased substantially.

We recognize all three of these challenges, and we're doing something about it. I've come today to tell you that America is the kind of country that when they see a problem, we address it head on. I've set a great goal for our country, and that is to reduce our dependence on oil by investing in technologies that will produce abundant supplies of clean and renewable energy and, at the same time, show the world that we're good stewards of the environment.

Now, look, I understand stereotypes are hard to defeat. People get an image planted in their head, and sometimes it causes them not to listen to the facts. But America is in the lead when it comes to energy independence, we're in the lead when it comes to new technologies, we're in the lead when it comes to global climate change, and we'll stay that way.

Overall, over the past 7 years, or since I've been the President, the Federal Government spent more than $12 billion to research, develop, and promote alternative energy sources. Our private sector is investing a lot of money, and I fully understand there needs to be consistent policy out of the U.S. Government that has thus far provided incentives to invest. What the Government doesn't need to do is send mixed signals. I understand private capital, understand how it flows. And so when people look at the United States to determine whether we're committed to new technologies that will change how we live, they not only need to look at the Federal investment, but they've got to understand, there's a lot of smart money heading into the private sector to help develop these new technologies.

Our strategy is twofold: One, we're going to change the way we drive our cars; and two, we'll change the way we power our businesses and homes. In other words, the two most vulnerable areas to economic disruption happens to be automobile use and electric power. The two biggest opportunities to help change the environment is through how we drive our cars and how we power our country. So first, let me talk about automobiles.

I laid out a goal for the United States to reduce gasoline consumption by 20 percent over the next 10 years; that's called 20–10. Now, by the way, that's in the face of a growing economy, to reduce gasoline usage by 20 percent over 10 years.

And we'll work with Congress. For those of you who watch the American legislative process, you think it's probably impossible for the American President to work with Congress these days. Well, it's not true. I was able to sign a good piece of legislation called the Energy Independence and Security Act of 2007. This legislation specifies a national mandatory fuel economy standard of 35 miles per gallon by 2020, which will save billions of gallons of gasoline.

Secondly, the legislation requires fuel producers to supply at least 36 billion gallons of renewable fuel in the year 2022. In other words, these just aren't goals; these are mandatory requirements. I'm confident the United States can meet those goals, and I know we must for the sake of economic security, national security, and for the sake of being good stewards of the environment.

Biodiesel is the most promising of these fuels. Biodiesel refineries can produce fuel from soybeans and vegetable oils and recycled cooking grease, from waste materials. All you out there with waste, you may be in business before you know it as this new technology kicks in. Most Americans—or more Americans are beginning to realize the benefits of biodiesel every year.

Last year, we produced 450 million gallons of biodiesel. That's up 80 percent from 2006. Today, there are more than 650 biodiesel fueling stations in America. There are hundreds of fleet operators that use biodiesel to fuel their trucks, and that's just the beginning of what is going to be a substantial change in our driving habits.

And then there's ethanol. In the 2000 campaign, I strongly supported ethanol. In 2008, it's amazing to think about how far our country has come since the year 2000. Ethanol production has quadrupled from 1.6 billion gallons in 2000 to a little over 6.4 billion gallons in 2007.

And the vast majority of that ethanol is coming from corn, and that's good. That's good if you're a corn grower. And it's good if you're worried about national security. I'd rather have our corn farmers growing energy than relying upon some nation overseas that may not like us. That's how I view it.

In 2005, the United States became the world's leading ethanol producer. Last year, we accounted for nearly half of the worldwide ethanol production. I don't know if our fellow citizens understand that, but there is a substantial change taking place, primarily in the Midwest of our country.

Corn ethanol holds a lot of promise, but there's a lot of challenges. If you're a hog raiser in the United States, you're beginning to worry about the cost of corn to feed your animals. I'm beginning to hear complaints from our cattlemen about the high price of corn. The high price of corn is beginning to affect the price of food.

And so we got to do something about it. And the best thing to do is not to retreat from our commitment to alternative fuels but to spend research and development money on alternatives to ethanol made from other materials. For example, cellulosic ethanol holds a lot of promise. I'm sure there are people in the industry here that will tell you how far the industry has come in a very quick period of time.

I look forward to the day when Texas ranchers can grow switchgrass on their country and then have that switchgrass be converted to fuel. I look forward to the day when people in the parts of our country that have got a lot of forests are able to convert wood chips into fuel. And those days are coming.

The Department of Energy had dedicated nearly $1 billion to develop technologies that can make cellulosic ethanol cost competitive. And the interesting thing that's happened in a relatively quick period of time is that the projected cost of cellulosic ethanol has dropped by more than 60 percent. In other words, new technologies are coming. The job of the Federal Government is to expedite their arrival.

Expanding the use in ethanol and biodiesel requires getting more cars on the road that use these alternative fuels. Now, we expect the private sector to respond. Our consumers are going to demand flex-fuel vehicles when they find out that these new technologies are available. As a matter of fact, there's 5 million flex-fuel vehicles on our roads now. I just saw some new ones here. Amazing joint venture with Mack and Volvo on these giant trucks that are using biodiesel to power them. I said, can you make it more than a couple of miles? The man said, "Not only we can make it more than a couple of miles, we can accelerate out of danger if we need to."

Technology is changing. Five years ago, those trucks would not have been available for people at this exhibit to look at. Today, they're on the road. As a matter of fact, the United States Air Force is using these kinds of trucks. Things are changing.

Another way to reduce our dependence on oil is promote hybrid vehicles. We're providing tax incentives to people to buy these fuel-efficient vehicles. In other words, the Government is saying, if you buy one, we'll give you a little incentive to do so. I've supported those policies. I think it makes sense to create a consumerism for these kinds of vehicles.

When I was first elected, there were virtually no hybrids on the roads. Today, there is nearly a million. We're also investing in plug-in hybrids. We want our city people driving not on gasoline but on electricity. And the goal, the short-term goal is to have vehicles that are capable of driving the first 40 miles on electricity—vehicles that don't look like a golf cart, by the way—vehicles that meet consumer demand. And that day is coming. The battery technologies are amazing, and the United States is investing millions of dollars to hasten the day. The battery technology is more efficient and competitive.

This administration is a strong supporter of hydrogen. We spent about $1.2 billion in research and development to bring vehicles running on hydrogen to the market. A lot of people don't even know what I'm talking about when I'm talking about hydrogen. But the waste product of a hydrogen-powered vehicle is pure and clean water.

This is an amazing opportunity for us. Now, this will be a long-term opportunity compared to ethanol and biodiesel and plug-in hybrids. But it makes sense to invest now and work on the technology so that when it comes—becomes cost competitive, it's available. We're also working for the day when, you know, these new fuels power not only automobiles and trucks but airplanes.

In December, the United States Air Force flew a C–17—that's a huge airplane—from Washington State to New Jersey. For those of you who don't live in America, that is a long way. And they did so on a blend of regular and synthetic fuels. I was interested to see that Virgin Atlantic flew a 747 from London's Heathrow Airport to Amsterdam fueled partly by coconuts and Brazilian babassu nuts. I've never seen a babassu nut, but it's amazing that it helped power an airplane the size of a 747. [*Laughter*]

What I've just described to you is the beginning of a new era. And oh, it's probably hard to equate it to the Model T, but maybe we're not that far off. And the United States believes it's in our interests to promote this new era.

Secondly, we've got to reduce our dependence on oil and fossil fuels and replace them with alternative energy sources to power our homes and our workplaces. Look, you can't have a vibrant economy unless you've got reliable electricity. For those of you in the developing world, you know what I'm talking about. As a matter of fact, the issue is not reliable electricity; the issue is getting electricity to people in the first place. Well, here in the United States, we've overcome those issues. And now we've got to make sure that we have enough of it that enables us to continue to grow. And the truth of the matter is, you've got to be—have a growing economy to be able to afford these technologies in the first place. So here are some ways that we're dealing with the issue of electricity.

One, I strongly believe the United States must promote nuclear power here in the United States. Nuclear power—[*applause*]—if you're interested in economic growth and environmental stewardship, there's no better way to achieve both of them than through the promotion of nuclear power. Nuclear power is limitless. It's one existing source that generates a massive amount of electricity without causing any air pollution or any greenhouse gases.

And yet the United States, we haven't built any nuclear power plants in a long time. What a promising technology available, and yet we're stuck, until recently. All of our citizens probably don't understand, but France, our ally and friend, gets nearly 80 percent of its power from nuclear power. Isn't that an amazing statistic? It's time for America to change.

My administration is working to eliminate the barriers to development of nuclear power plants. Last year, we invested more than $300 million in nuclear energy technologies. We want our people to understand that this generation of nuclear power plants is safe. We want people to feel comfortable about the expansion of nuclear power.

There's regulatory uncertainty when it comes to permitting plants in the United States. You can't expect somebody to invest a lot of money and have the regulatory process at the very end stop that capital from being deployed. It makes no sense. Just like tax policy has to be certain, so does regulatory policy have to create a sense of certainty in order to get people to invest.

So in the energy bill I signed in 2005, we began to address that uncertainty with Federal risk insurance for those who build nuclear power plants. This insurance protects the builders of the first six new plants against lawsuits—we got a lot of them in America, by the way, too many lawsuits, in my judgment—against bureaucratic obstacles and against delays beyond the—that would cause people to hesitate to participate in this program.

We've also launched a program called Nuclear Power 2010. Sam Bodman is in charge of all these. It's a partnership between our industry and the U.S. Government. Since we've started these programs, we've received six applications to build and operate new nuclear power plants in the United States. The paradigm is beginning to shift. And we anticipate that another 13 applications will be submitted this year.

Many of the construction projects will be supported by $18.5 billion in loan guarantees provided by the Government. By the way, that's part of a loan guarantee product—projects that we got out of Congress—18 billion for the nukes, 10 billion for renewable energy expansions in the United States. This will enable our plant owners, guys that are applying for loans— [*laughter*]—the whole purpose is, is we want to expand our nuclear power industry. And we're taking specific actions to do it.

You know, there's a lot of politicians who just talk. I hope when history is written of this administration, we not only talked; we actually did positive things and constructive things.

We're also working with our friends overseas for the Global Nuclear Energy Partnership. I believe developing nations ought to be encouraged to use nuclear power. I believe it's in our interests. I believe it will help take pressure off the price of oil. And I know it's going to help protect the environment. And so we're working with other nations, like Japan and France and Great Britain and Russia and China, to form this energy partnership, the purpose of which is to help developing nations secure cost-effective and proliferation-resistant nuclear power and, at the same time, to conduct joint research on how to deal with the nuclear waste issue through positive, productive reprocessing.

And so the United States of America has got a strategy to help change our electricity mix here at home. And part of that strategy is on nuclear power. Another part of that strategy is based upon wind power. Now, since 2001, America has increased wind energy production by more than 300 percent. This is a new industry for us, and it's beginning to grow. More than 20 percent of new electrical generating capacity added in America came from wind last year. I met some of the wind boys. They're excited about the opportunities in the U.S. market, and they should be because this new technology is taking hold. Last year, America installed more wind power capacity than any other country in the world.

I don't know if you know this or not: When I was the Governor of Texas, I signed a electric deregulation bill that encouraged and mandated the use of renewable energy. Today, Texas is—produces more wind energy than any other State in the Union. If an oil State can produce wind energy, other States in America can produce wind energy. I remember when I signed the bill, I said, "There's a new day coming for wind." And they said, "Well, you're leaving the State, and a lot of hot air is going with it." [*Laughter*]

In addition to wind power, we have spent, since I've been the President, $1 billion on harnessing the power of the Sun. The solar technology folks who are here will tell you there's some amazing changes have taken place in a quick period of time. I mean, I really see a day in which each house can be a little electric generator of their own and feeding back excess power into the grid through the use of solar power.

I told you that we're—and by the way, last year, U.S. solar installations grew by more than 32 percent in the U.S. In other words, I hope you're excited by these statistics. I certainly am. But these are just the beginning. Before I came over here, I really did sit around the Oval Office trying to figure out what a President will be saying 10 years from now. If you really think about what would have been said in 2000 compared to today, imagine what's going to be said 10 years from now compared to today.

I will repeat something I've been saying a lot here in America: The United States is serious about confronting climate change. And the strategies I just laid out for you are an integral part of dealing with climate change. Should there be an international agreement? Yes, there should be, and we support it. But I would remind you, an agreement will be effective, and that's what we want; we want an effective agreement. I think we ought to be results-oriented people, not process people. It's one thing to have a nice conference, but out of those conferences, we should expect results. We want a strategy that works, not sounds good.

And so in order for there to be effective international agreements, it must include— these agreements must include commitments—solid commitments—by every major economy, and no country should get a free ride.

And meeting this goal is going to take some tough choices. I've got a good man named Dan Price on my staff who is leading the U.S. efforts on the major economies conferences that we're hosting. That's, by the way, running parallel to the U.N. process. This is not in lieu of the U.N. process; it is to enable the U.N. process to become effective.

The first step is to get the major economies to agree to a goal. If you want commitment, if you want all folks at the table, the first step has got to be to say, we've got a problem, and here's a goal. I believe in setting clear goals, goals that are easy to understand.

And then it's up to us, each nation, to develop a strategy to help meet those goals. We've got different economies. We've got different electricity mixes. What I've just described to you is a strategy to deal with energy in—dependence as well as climate change. It'll be different from country to country. We've got a different energy mix than a lot of nations do.

And we expect countries that sign up to that goal to develop a strategy to meet that goal. And the United States will do the same thing, see. We're not going to say, okay, you set the goal, and you meet it, but we're not going to join. Once we join, we join. And so you're watching a process unfold to make sure that we have an effective international agreement.

And I fully understand—and by the way, I want to repeat what I said before: An effective agreement is one that recognizes that economies got to grow in order to be able to afford investment in the first place, that you must have economic wealth in order to be able to afford the research and development.

This is an issue that requires substantial commitments of money. And it's hard to commit money if you don't have any, and it's hard to commit money if your economies are hurting. So we ought to make sure we grow our economies and, at the same time, have the money necessary to invest. And I fully understand some nations are incapable of affording these new technologies.

And here's what we intend to do about it. There ought to be an international fund, a clean technology fund from the wealthy nations to help poorer nations clean up their environments. I call on our Congress to commit $2 billion to the fund. And in my travels here in my last year of the Presidency, I'm going to call on other wealthy nations to contribute to this fund.

I want any agreement to be effective. I don't want us just to feel good. I want to be able to say, when it's all said and done, we've done something that's actually going to solve the problem. And if people are truly interested in solving the problem, if you're interested in expanding alternative energy, then we need to come together to eliminate tariffs and other trade barriers to enable clean technologies to move duty free around the world.

There's too many impediments. There's too much protectionism. I mean, if you're truly interested in solving global climate change, then you should insist to your leaders to join the United States and other countries to make it easier to move these products, to eliminate all barriers to trade and technologies that will enable us to be better stewards of the environment.

So here's the strategy to deal with climate change and energy dependence. The United States not only is pursuing this strategy on an international basis, we're also have got bilateral partnerships. With Brazil, for example, we signed a biofuels compact. We signed agreements with China to expand cooperation on biomass and to improve energy efficiencies for vehicles and industrial production. We're working with Sweden—the Deputy Prime Minister is here, and I'm honored you are here—on a very constructive relationship. There's a U.S. company working with United Kingdom's Wave Hub to harness the power of the seas.

This is an ambitious vision I've just described to you. And obviously, you support something ambitious being done; otherwise, you wouldn't be here at this conference. I hope you're excited when you see the exhibits. Just keep in mind how far we have come in a short period of time, and be hopeful about how far we will go in a short period of time.

There was an article in the New York Sun not long after Alexander Bell's famous phone call, his first phone call to a fellow named Thomas Watson. I would like to read to you from that article: "It is to be doubted if the telephone will be used otherwise than locally. It's too sensitive for circuits exceeding a few miles in length." Imagine if that author of that article were alive today. I suspect he would have been sorry he used the words "it should be doubted." After all, he'd see a world where crystal-clear telephone calls are placed over circuits that stretch not miles, but across the globe. He would see a wireless infrastructure developing around the world.

Same thing is going to happen when it comes to energy. Oh, I know there's doubters, but I'm confident that when we look back at this period of time, they will say, how could you have doubted the capacity of mankind to develop the technologies necessary to deal with the real problems of the 21st century?

Leave with one thing in mind: The United States is committed, and we're firm in our commitments to deal with energy problems and to deal with global climate change. And it's been my honor to be with you today.

May God bless you.

NOTE: The President spoke at 10:13 a.m. at the Washington Convention Center. In his remarks, he referred to Deputy Prime Minister Maud Olofsson of Sweden. The Office of the Press Secretary also released a Spanish language transcript of these remarks.

Remarks Following a Lunch With Senator John McCain and an Exchange With Reporters
March 5, 2008

The President. It's been my honor to welcome my friend John McCain as the nominee of the Republican Party. A while back, I don't think many people would have thought that John McCain would be here as the nominee of the Republican Party, except he knew he would be here, and so did his wife Cindy.

John showed incredible courage and strength of character and perseverance in order to get to this moment. And that's exactly what we need in a President, somebody that can handle the tough decisions, somebody who won't flinch in the face of danger.

We also need somebody with a big heart. I have got to know John well in the last 8 years. I've campaigned against him, and I've campaigned with him. Laura and I have spent time in their house. This is a man who deeply loves his family. It's a man who cares a lot about the less fortunate among us. He's a president, and he's going to be the President who will bring determination to defeat an enemy and a heart big enough to love those who hurt.

And so I welcome you here. I wish you all the best, and I'm proud to be your friend.

Sen. McCain. Thank you, sir. Well, I'm very honored and humbled to have the opportunity to receive the endorsement of the President of the United States, a man who I have great admiration, respect, and affection. We—he and I, as is well known, had a very good competition in the year 2000, and I was privileged and proud to have the opportunity to campaign for his election and reelection to the Presidency of the United States.

I appreciate his endorsement. I appreciate his service to our country. I intend to have as much possible campaigning events together, as it is in keeping with the President's heavy schedule. And I look forward to that opportunity. I look forward to the chance to bring our message to America.

Last night, as you know, both Senator Obama and Senator Clinton called to congratulate me. I pledged at that time, and I pledge again, a respectful campaign, a respectful campaign based on the issues and based on the stark differences in vision that we have for the future of America.

I hope that the President will find time from his busy schedule to be out on the campaign trail with me. And I will be very privileged to have the opportunity of being again on the campaign trail with him—only slightly different roles this time. [*Laughter*]

I thank you, Mr. President, and it's a pleasure to be here.

The President. Yes, we'll answer a couple of questions.

Abramowitz [Michael Abramowitz, Washington Post]. Sorry you got such a lousy seat back there. [*Laughter*]

2008 Presidential Election

Q. I wanted to ask about—[*inaudible*]. The voters, according to a lot of the exit polls, seem to be searching for change this year. And I'd like to ask both of you—excuse me—I'd like to ask both of you how the Republican Party, which has been here for 8 years, is going to make the case that you're going to provide the change that the voters seem to want, both on Iraq and on the economy?

The President. Yes. Let me start off by saying that in 2000, I said, vote for me; I'm an agent of change. In 2004, I said, I'm not interested in change; I want to continue as President. Every candidate has got to say "change." That's what the American people expect.

And the good news about our candidate is, there will be a new President, a man of character and courage, but he's not going to change when it comes to taking on the enemy. He understands this is a dangerous world, and I understand we better have steadfast leadership who has got the courage and determination to pursue this enemy so as to protect America.

John McCain will find out, when he takes the oath of office, his most important responsibility is to protect the American people from harm. And there's still an enemy that lurks, an enemy that wants to strike us. And this country better have somebody in that Oval Office who understands the stakes, and John McCain understands those stakes.

Sen. McCain. Thank you, sir. I don't have anything to add. [*Laughter*]

Q. Can I follow up, sir? How would you——

The President. No, you can't follow up. Thank you. [*Laughter*]

Q. Yes, on——

The President. No, no, not you. Going to call Kelly [Kelly O'Donnell, NBC News]. Kelly.

President's Endorsement/2008 Presidential Election

Q. Senator McCain, given President Bush's low approval ratings, will this be a negative or a positive for you? And how much do you hope he'll campaign for you on the trail?

Sen. McCain. I hope that he will campaign for me as much as is keeping with his busy schedule. I'll be pleased to have him with me, both from raising money and the much-needed finances for the campaign and addressing the challenging issues that face this country. I'm pleased to have him as is—as it fits into his busy schedule.

Kelly.

Vice Presidential Candidates/2008 Presidential Election

Q. Mr. President, Senator McCain—sir, how would you counsel Senator McCain to choose a runningmate? How quickly? And given the fact that Democrats will field a nominee who will make some kind of history—a woman, an African American—should Republicans consider that in selecting a Vice Presidential nominee?

The President. I'd tell him to be careful about who he names to be the head of the selection committee. [*Laughter*] Look, now, he's got plenty of experience. He knows what he needs to do, which is to have a process that vets candidates, and the person—it's got to be somebody he's going to be comfortable with and somebody whose advice he relies upon. And he can answer his own question on that, but——

Sen. McCain. Could I just say, Kelly, I didn't think it was appropriate to contemplate this process, as I've discussed before, until after we had secured the nomination of the party. Now we'll begin that process.

Q. Should history make a difference with a woman or an African American on the Democratic side?

The President. People don't vote for Vice Presidents, as much as I hate to say that for those who have been candidates for Vice President. They're going to vote for who gets to sit inside that Oval Office and make decisions on how to protect the country and keep taxes low and how to have a culture that respects the dignity of every human being. And that's what the race is all about. I know there's going to be a lot of speculation on who the Vice President, this and that, but the speculation is over about who our party is going to nominate.

Sen. McCain. Liz [Liz Sidoti, Associated Press].

President's Endorsement/Presidential Campaign

Q. Mr. President, do you—how much do you intend to do for Senator McCain? And do you think, in some cases, that your help could actually hurt him more than help him?

The President. Look, if it—if my showing up and endorsing him helps him, or if I'm against him and it helps him, either way, I want him to win. [*Laughter*] You know, look, this is an age-old question that you— every President has had to answer, and there's an appropriate amount of campaigning for me to do.

But they're not going to be voting for me. I've had my time in the Oval Office. It's been a fabulous experience, by the way. And they're going to be voting for the next person to come in here and make the tough decisions about America: America's security, America's prosperity, and you know, America's hopefulness. That's what this race is about, and it's not about me. You know, I've done my bit.

And by the way, I'm not through, and I'm going to do a lot. And John is right; I do have a day job to keep, and I plan on keeping it. I've told the people that follow me in this press corps that I'm going to sprint to the finish, and I mean what I say. I've got a lot to do. But I'm going to find ample time to help, and I can help in raising money, and if he wants my pretty face standing by his side at one of these rallies, I'll be glad to show up.

But they're going to be looking at him, you know. I'm going to be in Crawford— [*laughter*]—with my feet up. He's going to be sitting in there behind that desk making the decisions on war and peace, and I'm thankful our party has nominated somebody plenty capable of making those decisions. And when the American people take a hard look, they're going to feel comfortable, like I feel comfortable, in recommending him to take my place.

Listen, we thank you.

Wolf [Richard Wolf, USA Today], where's Wolf? No, I'm not calling you. Wolf. No, not you either. Where's Wolf?

Q. Right here.

The President. Well, go ask something, will you? [*Laughter*]

Q. Where do you think you can be most helpful campaigning for him around the country?

The President. You know, look—I mean, if——

Q. And, Senator McCain, where would you like the President to campaign with you?

The President. As I told you, you know, if he wants me to show up, I will. If he wants me to say, "You know, I'm not for him," I will. Whatever he wants me to do, I want him to win. And, you know, Wolf, I don't know where. I mean, look——

Sen. McCain. Could I start out with——

The President. I'm focusing on, you know, protecting America and succeeding in Iraq and dealing with the North Korean and dealing with the Iranian and dealing with the issues around the world where we're making a difference in terms of keeping peace. I want to get this in as good as a position as possible so that when John McCain is the President—and he will be— he can deal with these issues in a way that yields peace.

Sen. McCain. Wolf, could I say, I—one State springs to mind: Texas. [*Laughter*]

The President. He's not going to need me in Texas. He's going to be a landslide in Texas.

Sen. McCain. Could I just say that I do intend to campaign all across this country. I think that literally every section in this country is at play—in play. And I will be glad to have the President with me, in keeping with his schedule, in any part of America. And we're going to go everywhere in America with this campaign.

The President. Listen, thank you all very much for coming.

Q. Did you talk names for Vice President? [*Laughter*]

Q. One press conference every week if you're elected, Senator?

The President. Thank you all very much. It's been a pleasure to see you. Obviously, we've invited some unruly members of the fourth estate here. I'm disappointed in the conduct of some of the people that have come. I told John it would be a nice and polite crowd. Thank you all very much.

Sen. McCain. Thank you.

NOTE: The President spoke at 1:10 p.m. in the Rose Garden at the White House. In his remarks, he referred to Chairman Kim Jong Il of North Korea; and President Mahmud Ahmadi-nejad of Iran.

Remarks Following a Meeting With Frank W. Buckles
March 6, 2008

Sitting next to me is Mr. Frank Buckles, 107 years young, and he is the last living doughboy from World War I. And it has been my high honor to welcome Mr. Buckles and his daughter, Susannah, here to the Oval Office.

Mr. Buckles's mind is sharp, his memory is crisp, and he's been sharing with me some interesting anecdotes. I asked him where he lived, and he said, "That reminds me of what General Pershing asked me." And he told the general that he was raised on a farm in Missouri. And the general said, "Well, you know, as the crow flies, it's 40 miles from where I was raised." So Mr. Buckles has a vivid recollection of historic times.

And one way for me to honor the service of those who wear the uniform in the past and those who wear it today is to herald you, sir, and to thank you very much for your patriotism and your love for America.

So we're glad you're here. Thanks for coming.

NOTE: The President spoke at 11:49 a.m. in the Oval Office at the White House.

Remarks on the Fifth Anniversary of the Department of Homeland Security
March 6, 2008

Thank you very much. Thanks for the warm welcome. Mr. Secretary, thank you for your kind introduction, and I appreciate your outstanding leadership for this Department. I'm really pleased to join you on the fifth anniversary of the creation of the Department of Homeland Security. Man, does time fly. [*Laughter*]

When this Department was established following the September the 11th terrorist attacks, it was hard to imagine that we would reach this milestone without another attack on our homeland. For those of you who were here 5 years ago, if you think back to that time, I don't think we would have predicted that 5 years later there had not been another attack on us. Yet we've been—[*applause*]—and it's your vigilance and your hard work that have helped keep this country safe. And so I want to thank you. I hope you take enormous pride in the accomplishments of this Department, and I hope you know the American people are grateful for your service, and so am I.

On this anniversary, we must also remember that the danger to our country has not passed. Since the attacks of 9/11, the terrorists have tried to strike our homeland again and again. We've disrupted numerous planned attacks, including a plot to fly an airplane into the tallest building on the west coast and another to blow up passenger jets headed for America across the Atlantic Ocean. The lesson of this experience is clear. It's clear to me, and I know it is clear to you. The enemy remains active, deadly in its intent, and in the face of this danger, the United States must never let down its guard.

I thank Tom Ridge for being the first Secretary of the Department of Homeland Security, and it's good to see him again. I appreciate—[*applause*]—I want to welcome the members of my Cabinet who've joined us, the leadership team at the Department. I appreciate the fact that a fine United States Senator and a great patriot has joined us today, Senator Joe Lieberman.

I appreciate the members of the diplomatic corps who've joined us. I appreciate the former DHS employees who are here; I appreciate all the current DHS employees for serving our country. And I want you to thank your families for the sacrifices you're making. I want to thank—[*applause*]—and I appreciate the Homeland Security partners from across the country who've joined us for this fifth anniversary.

The events of September the 11th, 2001, demonstrated the threats of a new era. I say new because we found that oceans which separate us from separate—different continents no longer separate us from danger. We saw the cruelty of the terrorists and extremists, and we glimpsed the future they intend for us. In other words, there's some serious lessons on September the 11th that it's important for all Americans to remember. Two years ago, Usama bin Laden warned the American people, quote, "Operations are under preparation, and you will see them on your own ground once they are finished." All of us, particularly those charged with protecting the American people, need to take the words of this enemy very seriously. And I know you do.

At this moment, somewhere in the world, a terrorist is planning an attack on us. I know that's inconvenient thought for some, but it is the truth. And the people in this hall understand that truth. We have no greater responsibility, no greater charge than to stop our enemies and to protect our fellow citizens.

To protect the American people, we are on the offense against the terrorists around the world. It is better to defeat them over there than to face them here in the United States. Since the enemy attacked us, since they declared war, since we've responded, we've captured or killed hundreds of Al Qaida leaders and operatives in more than two dozen countries. With our allies, we removed dangerous regimes in Iraq and Afghanistan that had harbored terrorists and had threatened our people.

Our men and women in uniform, those in the United States military are helping people of those countries fight the terrorists and build free societies and secure the peace for their children and ours. We owe our military a debt of gratitude, and we owe them something more. We owe them all the tools necessary to do the jobs we expect of them.

This war against these extremists and radicals who would do us harm is the great ideological struggle of our time. We're in a battle with evil men. I call them evil because if you murder the innocent to achieve a political objective, you're evil. These folks have beliefs. They despise freedom. They despise the right for people to worship an Almighty the way he or she sees fit. They desire to subject millions to their brutal rule. Our enemies oppose every principle of humanity and decency that we hold dear. They kill innocent men and women all the time. The only way these terrorists can recruit operatives, the only way they can convince somebody that their dim vision of the world is worth following is to feed on hopelessness and despair.

And so our policy is to oppose this hateful ideology by offering an alternative vision, one based upon freedom and liberty. Across the world, America feeds the hungry; we fight disease; we fight tyranny. We promote the blessings of a free society, not only because it's in our national interest— national security interests, but because it's in our moral interests. You see, by bringing the hope of freedom to these societies, we'll help peaceful people marginalize the extremists and eliminate the conditions that feed radicalism. And so for the sake of our security, for the sake of the peace of our children, the United States of America will stay on the forefront of spreading freedom and liberty around the world.

As we wage this struggle abroad, we're also building the institutions we need here at home to keep our country safe. The second part of the strategy is to protect the homeland. The first part is to stay on the offense, bring people to justice where we find them, and spread liberty as the great alternative to their hateful ideology. The second part of the strategy, of which you're intricately involved, is to protect America. And that's why I'm here to celebrate the fifth anniversary of the Department of Homeland Security, because you're on the frontlines of doing what the American people expect us to do, and that's to protect them.

Before 9/11, there was no single department of Government charged with protecting the homeland. So we undertook the most sweeping reorganization of the Federal Government since the start of the cold war. We merged 22 different Government organizations into a single department with a clear mission: Secure America, and protect the American people from future attacks.

The past 5 years, the men and women of this Department have carried out that mission with skill and determination. In ways seen and unseen, you work each day to protect our people from dangerous and determined enemies. I know how hard you work; a lot of Americans don't. And perhaps on this fifth anniversary, the message will get through that there's a lot of dedicated, decent, honorable folks working their hearts out to protect the country.

The Department of Homeland Security is working to stop terrorists from infiltrating our country. On 9/11, America was attacked from within by 19 men who entered our country, hid among us, and then killed thousands. To stop this from happening again, we've taken important steps to prevent dangerous people from entering America. We made our borders more secure. We've deployed new technologies for screening people entering America.

We're on track to double the number of Border Patrol agents who serve our country. For those of you who—that wear the uniform of the Border Patrol, thanks for what you're doing. We've unified our terrorism databases into one central database. We are enhancing it with biometric capabilities. We've improved the way we evaluate visa applicants. We made it harder to counterfeit travel documents. We want to know who's coming to our country and who's leaving our country, and we take significant steps to be able to tell the American people the answer to those questions.

Secondly, the Department of Homeland Security is working to stop terrorists from smuggling biological and chemical and nuclear weapons into our cities. The Department has deployed a layered system of protections against these dangerous materials that starts overseas, continues along our borders, and extends throughout our country. We've launched innovative programs to protect major metropolitan areas by providing early detection of biological or nuclear or radiological attacks. We are determined to stop the world's most dangerous men from striking America with the world's most dangerous weapons.

The Department of Homeland Security is working to protect our transportation systems and other critical infrastructure from terrorist attacks. Our enemies have declared—they have made it abundantly clear that if they can strike economic targets here in America, they can terrorize our people and do great harm to our economy. So in the face of this threat, the Department of Homeland Security has taken decisive action. Since 9/11, we've worked with the private sector to develop comprehensive security plans for 17 of the Nation's critical sectors, including our food and water supplies, chemical and nuclear facilities, power grids and telecommunications networks.

Under Operation Neptune Shield, the men and women of the Coast Guard are protecting more than 360 ports and more than 95,000 miles of coast guard [coastline].° We've taken action to protect our transportation systems, including a massive overhaul of security at our airports and new steps to protect our railways and mass transit systems.

The message should be clear to the American people: We will protect our country; we will protect our economy from those who seek to do us harm.

The Department of Homeland Security is working to strengthen our defenses against cyber attacks. Our enemies understand that America's economy relies on uninterrupted use of the Internet and that a devastating attack in cyberspace would be a massive blow to our economy and way of life. And so we've taken steps to enhance our cyber security, created a new National Cyber Security Division in this Department charged with protecting against virtual terrorism. We've established a Computer Emergency Readiness Team to provide 24-hour watch, so we can stop cyber attacks before they spread and cripple our economy. The United States Secret Service has established 24 Electronic Crimes Task Forces with a mission to prevent, detect, and investigate cyber attacks on our country.

As we protect our cyber networks, we're also working to deny our enemies the use of the Internet to recruit and train operatives and plan attacks on America. Our strategy is to deny the terrorists safe haven anywhere in the world, and that includes a virtual safe haven on the Internet.

The Department of Homeland Security is working to strengthen cooperation with State and local governments, so we can prevent terrorist attacks and respond effectively if we have to. Before 9/11, the Federal Government sent threat information to authorities—local authorities by fax machine. Today, we've established 21st-century lines of communication that allow us to share classified threat information rapidly and securely. We've helped State and local officials establish intelligence fusion centers in 46 States. These centers allow Federal officials to provide intelligence to our State and local partners and allow locally generated information to get to officials here in Washington who need it.

Even all these steps—with even all these steps, we know that a free society—there's no such thing as perfect security. That's the challenge. To attack us, the terrorists only have to be right once; to stop them, we need to be right 100 percent of the time. And so we're working to ensure that if attack does occur, this country is ready. We'll do everything we can to stop attacks, and we are. I can confidently tell the American people, a lot of folks are working hard to protect them with a good, comprehensive strategy.

But if the enemy is able to make it here and attack us, we want to be able to respond. And so since September of 2001, we've provided more than $23 billion of equipment and training and other critical needs for America's State and local first-responders. We want people at the local level prepared.

° White House correction.

We've worked with officials in 75 major metropolitan areas to improve the ability of first-responders to communicate clearly in an emergency. We've helped establish mutual aid agreements with States and strengthened the Emergency Management Assistant Compact among States, so that when communities need help from their neighbors, the right assistance will get to the right people at the right time.

We've greatly expanded the Nation's stockpile of drugs and vaccines that would be needed in the event of a bioterrorist attack or a mass casualty incident. We now have enough smallpox vaccine for every American in case of an emergency. We've increased our investments in biodefense medical research and development at the National Institutes of Health by more than 3,000 percent since 2001. We launched Project BioShield, an effort to speed the development of new vaccines and treatments against biological agents that could be used in a terrorist attack.

We've learned from our mistakes to improve our response when disaster strikes. When Hurricane Katrina hit our Nation's Gulf Coast, it exposed weaknesses in America's emergency response capabilities, so we retooled and restructured FEMA. Since Hurricane Katrina, we've improved FEMA's logistics management, strengthened its operations planning, augmented disaster assistance programs, and provided the Agency with additional personnel and resources.

And we have seen outstanding results as a result of these efforts. FEMA's response to the California wildfires, to the Minneapolis bridge collapse, and the tornadoes that struck the Mississippi Valley last month were exemplary. Despite these efforts, today, FEMA and the Department of Homeland Security—because of these efforts, FEMA and the Homeland Security are better prepared. There's still work to do, but we're doing it. We're never satisfied here in the Department of Homeland Security. We're constantly assessing weaknesses and needs and constantly adjusting, because there's no greater calling than to protect our country.

The Department of Homeland Security is vital to our safety, and it's just one of the institutions that have been built or transformed to keep our Nation safe. We created the new Office of Director of National Intelligence, which led a broad restructuring of our Nation's intelligence agencies for the threats of the 21st century. We transformed the FBI into an agency whose primary focus is stopping terrorism and reorganized the Department of Justice to help combat the threat.

We created the National Counterterrorism Center, where members of this Department, as well as the FBI and the CIA and other departments and agencies, work side by side to track terrorist threats and prevent new attacks.

At the Department of Defense, we created a new Northern Command responsible for homeland defense and enhanced Strategic Command that is responsible for defending America against long-range attacks.

We created the Proliferation Security Initiative, a coalition of more than 85 nations that are working together to stop shipments of weapons of mass destruction, their delivery systems, and related materials.

And to find out what the terrorists know about planned attacks, we established a program run by the CIA to detain and question key terrorists and operatives.

My administration is determined to ensure those in our Government charged with defending America have the tools they need to fight the terrorists. One of the most important tools is the ability to monitor terrorist communications. To stop new attacks on America, we need to know who the terrorists are talking to, what they're saying, and what they're planning.

We cannot get this vital information without the cooperation of private companies. Unfortunately, some private companies have been sued for billions of dollars because they are believed to have helped defend America after the attacks of September the 11th. Allowing these lawsuits to proceed is—would be unfair because if any of these companies helped us, they did so after being told by the Government that their assistance was legal and their assistance was necessary to defend the homeland.

Allowing these lawsuits to proceed would be unwise because litigation could lead to the disclosure of information about how we conduct surveillance and give Al Qaida and others a roadmap as to how to avoid the surveillance. Allowing these lawsuits to proceed would be dangerous because private companies besieged and fearful of lawsuits would be less willing to help us quickly get the information we need.

The United States Senate passed a good bill that will protect companies from these lawsuits and ensure our intelligence professionals have the tools they need to keep us safe. This bill passed by a strong bipartisan majority of 68 to 29, and a bipartisan majority of the House stands ready to pass the Senate bill if a vote were held. Unfortunately, House leaders blocked a vote on the Senate bill about 3 weeks ago. At the time, House leaders declared they needed 21 more days to work out their differences and get a bill to my desk. The deadline arrives on Saturday. If House leaders are serious about security, they will need to meet the deadline they set for themselves, and pass the bipartisan Senate bill, and get it to my desk this Saturday.

The men and women of the Department of Homeland Security can be proud of all that you have accomplished in 5 years. I've just laid out some of that which you've accomplished, and it took me about 30 minutes. You have built a vital and effective Department that is helping to prevent dangerous enemies from striking our people.

Your efforts and all the institutions we have built since 9/11 are a lasting legacy that will give future generations and future Presidents the instruments they need to keep our country safe.

The most important legacy we can leave behind is a commitment to remain vigilant. With the passage of time, the memories of September the 11th have grown more distant. For some, there is temptation to think that the threats to our country have grown distant as well. They haven't. And our job is to never forget the threat and to implement strategies that will protect the homeland from those who seek us harm.

Under the superb leadership of Secretary Chertoff, that is what the men and women of this Department do each day. And so on behalf of the people, thanks for stepping forward; thanks for shouldering this awesome responsibility. You're working with vital partners in State and local and tribal governments, in the private and nonprofit sectors, and the international community to meet the threats of our time. Many of you serve in dangerous circumstances, and on this anniversary, we remember all those who have given their lives to keep our people safe.

I appreciate every member of the Department of Homeland Security for your dedication and your courage and your resolve. You're helping to ensure that as we wage the war on terror across the world, we never forget where it began: in our homeland.

May God bless you and your families, and may God continue to bless our country.

NOTE: The President spoke at 1:10 p.m. at DAR Constitution Hall. In his remarks, he referred to Usama bin Laden, leader of the Al Qaida terrorist organization.

Statement on the Terrorist Attack in Jerusalem
March 6, 2008

I condemn in the strongest possible terms the terrorist attack in Jerusalem that targeted innocent students at the Mercaz Harav Yeshiva. This barbaric and vicious attack on innocent civilians deserves the condemnation of every nation.

I have just spoken with Prime Minister Olmert to extend my deepest condolences to the victims, their families, and to the people of Israel. I told him the United States stands firmly with Israel in the face of this terrible attack.

Remarks on the Situation in Cuba
March 7, 2008

Sientese. Gracias. Bienvenidos a la Casa Blanca. Mr. Secretary, thank you for being here; Congressman Lincoln Diaz-Balart, members of the diplomatic corps, distinguished officials, honored guests.

We gather today to remember a tragic moment in the history of Cuba. Five years ago this month, Cuban authorities rounded up scores of citizens and charged them with offenses against the regime. Those arrested included teachers and librarians and journalists. They committed no crimes. They simply held views their Government did not like, and they refused to be silent. In all, 75 people were given long prison terms. In the world of Cuban dissidents, that crackdown 5 years ago is remembered as the Black Spring.

A few moments ago, I met with one of the men arrested in that crackdown, Miguel Sigler Amaya, *y su esposa,* Josefa. Miguel was arrested in this crackdown because he and his brothers had long opposed the Castro regime. Over many years, they had been harassed and they had been beaten by Cuban authorities. Miguel once had his ribs cracked by one of the regime's mobs. One of the brothers survived an assassination attempt, and the entire family had received death threats. Now during the Black Spring, Miguel was charged with disobedience. He was sentenced to 26 months

in prison. His brothers, Ariel *y* Guido, each received sentences of 20 years.

When Miguel went to prison, his wife Josefa found common cause with the wives of other political prisoners. They formed a group and chose as their symbol the color white, the color of peace. Every Sunday, these Ladies in White—*las Damas de Blanco*—attend Catholic mass, and then together they walk in silence through the streets. In Cuba, even that simple act is considered dangerous defiance. The women have been subjected to harassment and beatings. Josefa herself was stopped by an assailant who told her that he was sending her a message, and then he clubbed her with a blunt object on the back of her head.

Josefa was ordered to leave Cuba with Miguel once he was released from prison in 2006. In Cuba, they are considered outlaws. In America, they are heralds of freedom, and I'm proud to stand with them in the White House.

Miguel and Josefa tell a compelling story about brutal repression right off the shores of the United States. And I want to thank you for letting us share your stories, and I thank you for your courage.

I've asked Josefa to please tell the Ladies in White—*las Damas de Blanco*—that as they pray for a free Cuba, the American people—many American people will pray for them. And we can be confident that a loving God will listen.

For Miguel and Josefa, the horrors of life in Cuba are behind them, but millions of others are still trapped in the tropical gulag. Miguel's brothers still suffer under inhumane conditions in Cuban jails. The Ladies in White still bravely march for freedom. And most of the Cubans imprisoned during the Black Spring are still in jail, subjected to beatings, inadequate medical care, and long separations from their family.

These prisoners of conscience live in daily torment, and so do hundreds of others. Yet most of the world says nothing. This is a sad and curious pattern.

Last fall, dozens of young Cubans who wore bracelets imprinted with one word, *cambio*, or change, were arrested by Cuban police because of their political beliefs. Yet in the face of this assault on the freedom of expression, much of the world was silent.

Last December, Cuban authorities stormed into a Catholic church, teargassed parishioners, and dragged 18 worshipers out. A Catholic official called the episode, quote, "the worst attack against a church in 45 years." And yet in the face of this assault on religious freedom, much of the world was silent.

And last weekend, Cubans were pushed and shoved and beaten as they distributed copies of the U.N. Declaration on Human Rights. That same week, Cuba signed the International Covenant on Civil and Political Rights. The international community applauded Cuba for signing a piece of paper, but on the abuses that same week, much of the world was silent.

In the face of these abuses, the United States has not been silent, nor will we be silent. We have been consistently joined in condemning the Cuban regime's brutal outrages by a small band of brave nations. Countries such as the Czech Republic, Estonia, Hungary, Latvia, Lithuania, Poland, Slovakia, and Slovenia have placed themselves at the forefront for the fight for human freedom in Cuba. They recently lived through Communist tyranny. They remember what life is like under the boot of the oppressor. They know the daily hardships that ordinary citizens have to endure just to survive. And they refuse to look away.

Unfortunately, the list of countries supporting the Cuban people is far too short, and the democracies absent from that list are far too notable. When a new day finally dawns for Cubans, they will remember the few brave nations that stood with them and the many that did not.

A few weeks ago, reports of the supposed retirement of Cuba's dictator initially led many to believe that the time had finally come for the United States to change our policy on Cuba and improve our relations with the regime. That sentiment is exactly backward. To improve relations, what needs to change is not the United States; what needs to change is Cuba. Cuba's Government must begin a process as peaceful democratic change. They must release all political prisoners. They must have respect for human rights in word and deed and pave the way for free and fair elections.

So far, all Cuba has done is replace one dictator with another. And its former ruler is still influencing events from behind the scenes. This is the same system, the same faces, and the same policies that led Cuba to its miseries in the first place. The United States is isolating the Cuban regime, and we're reaching out to the Cuban people. We've granted asylum to hundreds of thousands who have fled the regime. We've encouraged private citizens and charities to deliver food and medicine and other assistance directly to the people of Cuba. As a result, the American people are the largest providers of humanitarian aid to the Cuban people in the entire world.

This assistance is easing burdens for many Cuban families. But the sad fact is that life will not improve for the Cuban people until their system of government changes. It will not improve by exchanging one dictator for another. It will not improve if we prop up the same tyranny for the false promise of so-called stability.

As I told the Cuban people last October, a new day for Cuba will come. And we will know when it's here. We will know it's here when jailers go to the cells where Cuban prisoners of conscience are held and set them free. We will know it is here when Miguel Sigler Amaya is reunited with his brothers, and they can say what they think and can come and go as they please. And we will know it is here when the Ladies in White no longer make their silent vigils or live in constant fear of assault or arrest.

Until that day comes, the United States will continue to shine a bright and revealing light on Cuba's abuses. We will continue to tell the stories of Cuba's people, even when a lot of the world doesn't want to hear them. And we will carry this refrain in our hearts: *Viva Cuba Libre.*

NOTE: The President spoke at 1:35 p.m. in the Roosevelt Room at the White House. In his remarks, he referred to President Raul Castro Ruz and former President Fidel Castro Ruz of Cuba. The Office of the Press Secretary also released a Spanish language transcript of these remarks.

Remarks on the National Economy
March 7, 2008

Earlier today I spoke with members of my economic team. They updated me on the state of our economy. This morning we learned that our economy lost 63,000 payroll jobs in February, although the unemployment rate improved to 4.8 percent.

Losing a job is painful, and I know Americans are concerned about our economy. So am I. It's clear our economy has slowed. But the good news is, we anticipated this and took decisive action to bolster the economy by passing a growth package that will put money into the hands of American workers and businesses.

I signed this growth package into law just 3 weeks ago, and its provisions are just starting to kick in. First, a growth package includes incentives for businesses to make investments in new equipment this year. These incentives are now in place, and they are starting to have an impact. My advisers tell me that investment in new equipment remains solid thus far in the first quarter.

And as more businesses take advantage of these new incentives as well as lower interest rates, we expect investment will continue to grow and that businesses will begin creating new jobs in the months ahead.

Secondly, the growth package will provide tax rebates to more than 130 million American households. These rebates will begin reaching American families in May. And when the money reaches the American people, we expect they will use it to boost consumer spending, and that will spur job creation as well.

We believe that the steps we've taken, together with the actions taken by the Federal Reserve, will have a positive effect on our economy. So my message to the American people is this: I know this is a difficult time for our economy, but we recognized the problem early and provided the economy with a booster shot. We will begin to see the impact over the coming months. And in the long run, we can have confidence that so long as we pursue progrowth, low-tax policies that put faith in the American people, our economy will prosper.

Thank you.

NOTE: The President spoke at 1:55 p.m. on the Colonnade at the White House. A portion of these remarks could not be verified because the tape was incomplete.

The President's Radio Address
March 8, 2008

Good morning. This week, I addressed the Department of Homeland Security on its fifth anniversary and thanked the men and women who work tirelessly to keep us safe. Because of their hard work and the efforts of many across all levels of government, we have not suffered another attack on our soil since September the 11th, 2001.

This is not for a lack of effort on the part of the enemy. Al Qaida remains determined to attack America again. Two years ago, Usama bin Laden warned the American people, quote, "Operations are under preparation, and you will see them on your own ground once they are finished," end quote. Because the danger remains, we need to ensure our intelligence officials have all the tools they need to stop the terrorists.

Unfortunately, Congress recently sent me an intelligence authorization bill that would diminish these vital tools. So today I vetoed it, and here is why.

The bill Congress sent me would take away one of the most valuable tools in the war on terror: the CIA program to detain and question key terrorist leaders and operatives. This program has produced critical intelligence that has helped us prevent a number of attacks. The program helped us stop a plot to strike a U.S. Marine camp in Djibouti, a planned attack on the U.S. consulate in Karachi, a plot to hijack a passenger plane and fly it into Library Tower in Los Angeles, and a plot to crash passenger planes into Heathrow Airport or buildings in downtown London. And it has helped us understand Al Qaida's structure and financing and communications and logistics. Were it not for this program, our intelligence community believes that Al Qaida and its allies would have succeeded in launching another attack against the American homeland.

The main reason this program has been effective is that it allows the CIA to use specialized interrogation procedures to question a small number of the most dangerous terrorists under careful supervision. The bill Congress sent me would deprive the CIA of the authority to use these safe and lawful techniques. Instead, it would restrict the CIA's range of acceptable interrogation methods to those provided in the Army Field Manual. The procedures in this manual were designed for use by soldiers questioning lawful combatants captured on the battlefield. They were not intended for intelligence professionals trained to question hardened terrorists.

Limiting the CIA's interrogation methods to those in the Army Field Manual would be dangerous because the manual is publicly available and easily accessible on the Internet. Shortly after 9/11, we learned that key Al Qaida operatives had been trained to resist the methods outlined in the manual. And this is why we created alternative procedures to question the most dangerous Al Qaida operatives, particularly those who might have knowledge of attacks planned on our homeland. The best source of information about terrorist attacks is the terrorists themselves. If we were to shut down this program and restrict the CIA to methods in the field manual, we could lose vital information from senior Al Qaida terrorists, and that could cost American lives.

The bill Congress sent me would not simply ban one particular interrogation method, as some have implied. Instead, it would eliminate all the alternative procedures we've developed to question the world's most dangerous and violent terrorists. This would end an effective program that Congress authorized just over a year ago.

The fact that we have not been attacked over the past 6½ years is not a matter of chance. It is the result of good policies and the determined efforts of individuals carrying them out. We owe these individuals our thanks, and we owe them the au-thorities they need to do their jobs effectively.

We have no higher responsibility than stopping terrorist attacks. And this is no time for Congress to abandon practices that have a proven track record of keeping America safe.

Thank you for listening.

NOTE: The address was recorded at 7:50 a.m. on March 7 in the Cabinet Room at the White House for broadcast at 10:06 a.m. on March 8. The transcript was made available by the Office of the Press Secretary on March 7, but was embargoed for release until the broadcast. In his address, the President referred to Usama bin Laden, leader of the Al Qaida terrorist organization. The Office of the Press Secretary also released a Spanish language transcript of this address.

Message to the House of Representatives Returning Without Approval the "Intelligence Authorization Act for Fiscal Year 2008"
March 8, 2008

To the House of Representatives:

I am returning herewith without my approval H.R. 2082, the "Intelligence Authorization Act for Fiscal Year 2008." The bill would impede the United States Government's efforts to protect the American people effectively from terrorist attacks and other threats because it imposes several unnecessary and unacceptable burdens on our Intelligence Community.

Section 444 of the bill would impose additional Senate confirmation requirements on two national security positions—the Director of the National Security Agency and the Director of the National Reconnaissance Office. The National Commission on Terrorist Attacks Upon the United States (9/11 Commission) observed that the effectiveness of the Intelligence Community suffers due to delays in the confirmation process; section 444 would only aggravate those serious problems. Senior intelligence officials need to assume their duties and responsibilities as quickly as possible to address the pressing requirements of national security. Instead of addressing the 9/11 Commission's concern, the bill would subject two additional vital positions to a more protracted process of Senate confirmation. Apart from causing such potentially harmful delays, this unwarranted requirement for Senate confirmation would also risk injecting political pressure into these positions of technical expertise and public trust.

Section 413 would create a new Inspector General for the Intelligence Community. This new office is duplicative and unnecessary. Each intelligence community component already has an Inspector General, and the Inspector General of the Office of the Director of National Intelligence has been vested with all the legal powers of any inspector general to carry out investigations on matters under the jurisdiction of the Director of National Intelligence. There is no reason to commit taxpayer resources to an additional inspector general with competing jurisdiction over the same intelligence elements. Creating duplicative inspectors general, who may have inconsistent views on the handling of particular matters, has the potential to create conflicts and impede the Intelligence Community from efficiently resolving issues and carrying out its core mission. In addition, the creation of a new inspector general would add yet another position in the Intelligence Community subject to Senate confirmation, contrary to the 9/11 Commission's recommendations.

Section 327 of the bill would harm our national security by requiring any element of the Intelligence Community to use only the interrogation methods authorized in the Army Field Manual on Interrogations. It is vitally important that the Central Intelligence Agency (CIA) be allowed to maintain a separate and classified interrogation program. The Army Field Manual is directed at guiding the actions of nearly three million active duty and reserve military personnel in connection with the detention of lawful combatants during the course of traditional armed conflicts, but terrorists often are trained specifically to resist techniques prescribed in publicly available military regulations such as the Manual. The CIA's ability to conduct a separate and specialized interrogation program for terrorists who possess the most critical information in the War on Terror has helped the United States prevent a number of attacks, including plots to fly passenger airplanes into the Library Tower in Los Angeles and into Heathrow Airport or buildings in downtown London. While details of the current CIA program are classified, the Attorney General has reviewed it and determined that it is lawful under existing domestic and international law, including Common Article 3 of the Geneva Conventions. I remain committed to an intelligence-gathering program that complies with our legal obligations and our basic values as a people. The United States opposes torture, and I remain committed to following international and domestic law regarding the humane treatment of people in its custody, including the "Detainee Treatment Act of 2005."

My disagreement over section 327 is not over any particular interrogation technique; for instance, it is not over waterboarding, which is not part of the current CIA program. Rather, my concern is the need to maintain a separate CIA program that will shield from disclosure to al Qaeda and other terrorists the interrogation techniques they may face upon capture. In accordance with a clear purpose of the "Military Commissions Act of 2006," my veto is intended to allow the continuation of a separate and classified CIA interrogation program that the Department of Justice has determined is lawful and that operates according to rules distinct from the more general rules applicable to the Department of Defense. While I will continue to work with the Congress on the implementation of laws passed in this area in recent years, I cannot sign into law a bill that would prevent me, and future Presidents, from authorizing the CIA to conduct a separate, lawful intelligence program, and from taking all lawful actions necessary to protect Americans from attack.

Other provisions of the bill purport to require the executive branch to submit information to the Congress that may be constitutionally protected from disclosure, including information the disclosure of which could impair foreign relations, the national security, the deliberative processes of the Executive, or the performance of the Executive's constitutional duties. Section 326, for example, would require that the executive branch report, on a very short deadline and in accordance with a rigid set of specific statutory requirements, the details of highly classified interrogation techniques and the confidential legal advice concerning them. The executive branch voluntarily has provided much of this information to appropriate members of Congress, demonstrating that questions concerning access to such information are best addressed through the customary practices and arrangements between the executive and legislative branches on such matters, rather than through the enactment of legislation.

In addition, section 406 would require a consolidated inventory of Special Access Programs (SAPs) to be submitted to the Congress. Special Access Programs concern the most sensitive information maintained by the Government, and SAP materials are maintained separately precisely to avoid the existence of one document that can serve

as a roadmap to our Nation's most vital information. The executive branch must be permitted to present this information in a manner that does not jeopardize national security. The executive branch will continue to keep the Congress appropriately informed of the matters to which the provisions relate in accordance with the accommodation principles the Constitution contemplates and the executive and legislative branches have long and successfully used to address information sharing on matters of national security.

GEORGE W. BUSH

The White House,
March 8, 2008.

Remarks Following Discussions With Prime Minister Donald Tusk of Poland and an Exchange With Reporters
March 10, 2008

President Bush. It's been my honor to welcome the Prime Minister of our very close ally and strategic partner, Poland. We'll both have opening statements, and then we'll take two questions a side.

I want to thank you for your candor, thank you for your friendship. The people of Poland stand as a great example of freedom and liberty. This is a nation with a proud history, a nation that has resisted tyranny and now lives as an example of a free society. And there are millions of Americans who are proud of their heritage, Mr. Prime Minister. They're proud to be called Polish Americans. And we welcome you.

I want to thank you for your nation's contributions to the liberation of people in Iraq and Afghanistan. Your troops have performed brilliantly, and they'll be coming home based upon success. And I thank your Government, and I thank the people of Poland for the sacrifices. I also thank you to help the young democracy in Af-

ghanistan survive and thrive and flourish. And someday, Mr. Prime Minister, people are going to say, Afghanistan did exactly the same thing that happened in Poland: The people realized the blessings of liberty, and out of those blessings flowed peace.

The Prime Minister and I had a long discussion about a lot of subjects. One in particular I want to talk about, and that is our mutual security. The United States recognizes the need for Polish—the forces to be modernized. It's important for our allies to—when they are worried about the modernization of their forces, that friends respond, and we're responding. The first part of a response, of course, is to take inventory of needs. And, Mr. Prime Minister, before my watch is over, we will have assessed those needs and come up with a modernization plan that's concrete and tangible.

And along those lines, we talked about the need for mutual security and that the significant threats of the 21st century—or perhaps the most significant is a launch of a missile with dangerous materials in its warhead. Technologies are developing that will enable the free world to be able to defend itself from blackmail and/or strike from these such types of launches.

And we're in discussions with Poland about how we can help the mutual security of the region. I've assured the Prime Minister that any decisions made will reflect the sovereignty of Poland. I've assured the Prime Minister that this system is not aimed at Russia. And I will continue to work with President Putin to give him those assurances as well. This system is designed for the threats of the 21st century.

And so I want to thank you very much for your candor and your friendship. And we're glad you're here. Thank you, sir.

Prime Minister Tusk. I want to thank very much you, Mr. President, for your hospitality and genuine warmth. It doesn't really happen often that people of such a high position are so open and so friendly as you.

President Bush. Thank you.

Prime Minister Tusk. From the very beginning, I was absolutely convinced that this meeting can bring us definitely closer to the work for good solutions.

I am also very glad, Mr. President, that both during our meeting and also here, you appreciate very much the contribution we are making with our troops in Iraq and in Afghanistan. For us Poles, it is really a very big effort, and we really are happy that such an important ally appreciates it.

What really is most important from this meeting, Mr. President, that in the spirit of those talks and also in the agreement, which we have made during this conversation, we can draw the conclusion from that that the United States can count on Poland whenever it needs, and Poland can count on the United States whenever Poland is in need. And this is our belief, the embodiment of the idea of solidarity in the international dimension. And I want to thank you very much for this.

President Bush. Thank you, sir. Thank you.

Prime Minister Tusk. And what is really important for both parties—we came to a conclusion, both during the talks and also the cooperation which we would like to develop together—is that both the missile defense system and the modernization of the Polish forces, as well as the reinforcement of the global security system, which also influences the Polish security system, that all these issues come in one package, and that this is really something which gives us very much good hope for the future. This is a very important declaration for us, and once again, I want to thank you for that.

President Bush. Thank you, sir. Feller [Ben Feller, Associated Press].

Q. Mr. President——

President Bush. Hold on for a second, please.

Q. When——

President Bush. Ben. Excuse me, please. Ben.

Vice President's Visit to the Middle East

Q. Thank you, Mr. President. Secretary Rice was able to help get peace talks restarted in the Mideast during her trip. So what is it now that you want Vice President Cheney to get? What is your specific goal for him?

President Bush. The Vice President will be on an extensive itinerary, as you know. His goal is to reassure people that the United States is committed to a vision of peace in the Middle East; that we expect relevant parties to obligate themselves—uphold their obligations on the roadmap; that we fully see the threats facing the Middle East—one such threat is Iran; and that we will continue to bolster our security agreements and relationships with our friends and allies.

The Vice President will be taking a very hopeful message to the Middle East, that progress in Iraq is necessary for peace in the Middle East. And so it's—I'm looking forward to his trip, and I'm really appreciative of the fact that he's going.

Do you want to call on somebody from the Polish media?

Missile Defense System

Q. Mr. President, is there any breakthrough as far as the missile defense system is concerned?

President Bush. Well, I think there's a commitment to a system that respects Polish sovereignty, will—that will ensure that the people of Poland will not be subjected to any undue security risks, that the system is necessary to deal with the realities of the threats. Obviously, there's a lot of work to do because many times a strategy on paper is a little different from the details. And so our experts are working through the system to make sure that the people of Poland are comfortable with the idea. It's a—look, I mean—you know, I—this is the kind of issue that all kinds of rumors and worries can grow out of. And we just want to assure people that it's necessary, and at the same time, there will be this modernization effort that takes place.

Prime Minister Tusk. What is really very important is what we stressed in the conclusions of this meeting today, that we really want to stop the speculations on intentions expressed by the United States and expressed by Poland. Our joint intention is to cooperate in all aspects of global security, American security, and Polish security. And an element of this security is the missile defense system.

What I would call a breakthrough is my conviction that both the President of the United States and the American party understand quite clearly our expectations. And if I may use this expression, I think that you have set the perspective of Poland on the principle of the cooperation here. And as you said, Mr. President, all the technicalities pertaining to the face of the negotiations and all those technical issues, they will be solved by experts.

President Bush. Thank you, sir. Matt [Matt Spetalnick, Reuters].

Middle East Peace Process

Q. Yes, sir. Back on the Middle East, what do you think of Israel's plan to build 750 new homes in a settlement near Jerusalem? And what, if any, threat or complication do you see to your administration's peace efforts?

President Bush. We expect both parties to—involved in the Middle Eastern peace process to adhere to their obligations in the roadmap. And those obligations are clear. And to this end, the Secretary of State is dispatching the general that we named to be the coordinator of roadmap activities to the Middle East—for him to conduct meetings with the relevant parties.

The key question is whether or not a vision can prevail that will enable people who reject violence and extremists—enable them to see a better tomorrow. That's what we're working toward. And you know, this is a part of the world where people have heard promises before, and they've been vague promises. Now they've got a President and an administration willing to work for two states, two democracies, side by side in peace.

There are three major forces that are— we're now witnessing in the Middle East. Two of those forces adhere to peace: Israel and the forces of President Abbas. And then there's one force in the Middle East, and some suspect that they're funded from outside governments and outside movements, all aiming to destabilize democracy, all aiming to prevent the vision of—where people can live side by side in peace, all wanting to destroy Israel.

And the fundamental question is, will there be enough will and determination to reject those forces of extremism and to stand up and support those who long for peace? And our mission is exactly along those lines. And I'm optimistic that we'll be able to achieve a vision that shows a way forward, and I'm optimistic leaders will step forward and do the hard things necessary so people don't have to live in deprivation and fear. And so that's our focus, and that's our mission.

You want to——

[*At this point, Prime Minister Tusk spoke in Polish, and no translation was provided.*]

U.S. Visa Policy

Q. Mr. President, it's getting to be embarrassing for Polish politicians to talk about visas in the Oval Office, but it's even more embarrassing for my countrymen to apply for visas.

President Bush. Yes.

Q. And it would be really ironic if Poland would become a third missile defense site, and Polish citizens would still have to apply for visas. So can we expect that before your watch is over something will change, and maybe we'll convince the lawmakers on Capitol Hill to do something about this?

President Bush. Well, thank you very much. First of all, the Prime Minister, of course, brought up the issue. And he was very firm about the need for a friend to treat a friend as a friend when it comes to visas.

Look, this is a tough issue. And we changed law. And now there are ways forward for the people applying for visas. A lot of it has to do with rejection rates. And as the Prime Minister noted, the rejec-

tion rates are changing quite dramatically. And so of course, this will be taken into account.

I fully understand the frustrations. And if I were living in Poland, I'd be—and wanted to come to America, I'd be frustrated too. And the truth of the matter is, we're going from one era to the next. We're going from a time when the—during the Soviet era, when there was a different motivation by the people. And we're adjusting. And I fully understand the pace of adjustment doesn't meet expectations inside Poland.

And so I'm very sympathetic. But the law is changing. The paradigm is shifting. And I hope at some point in time, obviously, that the frustrations of our friends and allies are able to be eased with more moderate visa policy.

Thank you, sir. Thank you all.

NOTE: The President spoke at 11:13 a.m. in the Oval Office at the White House. In his remarks, he referred to President Vladimir V. Putin of Russia; Lt. Gen. William M. Fraser III, USAF, U.S. monitor of the Israeli-Palestinian roadmap peace plan; and President Mahmoud Abbas of the Palestinian Authority. Prime Minister Tusk spoke in Polish, and his remarks were translated by an interpreter.

Remarks at a Celebration of Women's History Month and International Women's Day
March 10, 2008

Thank you all. Thank you all. Please be seated. Welcome to the White House for this celebration of Women's History Month and International Women's Day. And we're glad you're here.

Every March, people around the world recognize accomplishments of strong, fearless women. I see a lot of many strong,

fearless women in this room. [*Laughter*] And I feel right at home. After all, I was raised by one, and I married one. [*Laughter*]

My advice to the next President is to surround him or her—[*laughter*]—with strong, fearless women. That's what I've done. People have served—as Laura mentioned, people serving in senior positions in my administration have made great contributions to our country, people like Secretary Rice, Secretary Chao, Secretary Peters, Secretary Spellings, Trade Representative Schwab, White House spokesman Dana Perino.

We've got a lot of strong women throughout our Government, and that's the way it should be. And it's made my job a lot easier, and I appreciate them serving our country with such class and dignity.

I too welcome the Members of the United States Congress. Thank you all for coming. We're honored you're here. Thanks for serving.

Members of the diplomatic corps—Laura and I had a opportunity to meet representatives from our U.S. Armed Services who are here, and we've got representatives of the Army, Marine Corps, Navy, Air Force, and Coast Guard. Thank you all for coming. Thanks for wearing the uniform. Appreciate it.

Appreciate the members of the diplomatic corps joining us. And I too want to congratulate the recipients of the International Women of Courage Award. Thank you all for coming. Why don't we have our award winners stand up. [*Applause*] Yes, thank you all. Thank you all.

During Women's History Month, we honor the courage, foresight, and resolve of women who have strengthened our democracy: pioneers like Amelia Earhart, suffragists like Sojourner Truth, healers like Clara Barton, writers like Harriet Beecher Stowe. These women have helped our Nation live up to its ideals of liberty and justice for all. At the same time, they have changed the way America views its women, the way both men and women view America.

We take pride in the progress women have made here at home, and we know that millions of women abroad are still working to secure their basic rights. And as they do, the United States of America

proudly stands with them. We do so because we know that liberty is the birthright of every person. And we do so because it's in our national interest. Societies where half the population is marginalized, or worse, are less likely to be prosperous and hopeful and more likely to become incubators for hateful ideologies.

So the United States is working to help build more hopeful and just societies for women. In Africa, our Emergency Plan for AIDS Relief, called PEPFAR, and our malaria initiative are saving millions from the disease that devastate women. Our Millennium Challenge Corporation provides microloans that help women start their own businesses. Our international education initiatives have trained thousands of teachers and have provided hundreds of thousands of scholarships to help girls go to school.

The United States works to help build more hopeful and just societies throughout the world and, in particular, the Middle East. In Afghanistan, the Taliban once beat women without reason and executed them without remorse. Today, because we acted, Afghanistan's women serve as teachers and doctors and journalists and judges. More than 80 members of Afghanistan's parliament are women. In Iraq, Saddam Hussein once used rape rooms to brutalize women and dishonor their families. Today, because we acted, Iraq's women voted in a free and democratic elections. They live under a Constitution that protects women's rights. Freedom is powerful, and freedom is precious, and freedom belongs to all, and freedom will yield the peace we long for.

The United States is proud to be a part of the global advance of women's rights. Yet one thing history shows us is that the cause of women's rights is inseparable from the cause of human rights. So on this International Women's Day, we honor the women who work to secure both their liberty and the liberty for others.

America honors women like Madawi Al Hassoun of Saudi Arabia. An educator turned entrepreneur, she was one of the first Saudi women to work alongside men in mixed businesses—in a mixed business environment. Ms. Hassoun was the first female director of the women's branch of one of Saudi's largest banks. She manages her own successful business now. Ms. Hassoun was also one of the first female candidates in Saudi Arabia to run for office. And today, she serves as an appointed member of the Jeddah Chamber of Commerce. As she has broadened the possibilities of Saudi women, Ms. Al Hassoun has also worked to bring greater economic freedom and prosperity to her own nation. She's on the forefront of change, and the United States strongly supports her.

America honors Ellen Johnson Sirleaf of Liberia. Early in her life, this woman waited tables to put herself through school at Harvard. She became an economist who returned to Liberia to serve her country, only to see it destroyed by brutal warlords and dictators. In 2005, Liberians reclaimed their freedom and chose Ellen Johnson Sirleaf to become the first woman ever elected President on the continent of Africa. Laura and I just recently visited the President.

I was impressed by how strong she is as a leader, and she's committed to fighting disease and working to make Liberia's Government more transparent and honest. You know, the Liberians call President Johnson the "Iron Lady" and "Ma." [*Laughter*] I'm proud to call her friend. She's a great lover of liberty, and we will support her.

America honors women like Irina Kozulina. Irina's husband Aleksandr Kozulin is serving a 5-year prison sentence for protesting Belarus's fraudulent 2006 elections. Irina worked relentlessly for her husband's freedom. In doing so, she became a leading voice for all political prisoners held captive by the Lukashenko regime.

Irina was also very prominent in the breast cancer awareness campaign in Belarus. A few weeks ago, the disease claimed her life. The Lukashenko regime refused to release her husband to be with his wife in his final days. That's the definition of brutality. And the United States calls upon that Government to release Aleksandr Kozulin immediately, just like they ought to release every other political prisoner in Belarus. It's important for people to understand that this good woman, Irina, set the stage for what we hope Belarus to become, a free and just and open society.

America honors women like Marta Beatriz Roque Cabello of Cuba. An economist and former math professor, Marta Beatriz is now a leader of a movement for a free Cuba. She spent years in Castro's dungeons for her activism. Because she spoke out about the universality of freedom, she has spent time in jail. She was recently released from her prison term because of her poor health. Yet neither her health nor the threat of danger has deterred this good woman, this pioneer for liberty.

Just last week, Marta was one of the 10 opposition leaders beaten by Cuban police and security forces for distributing copies of the universal declaration for human rights. This courageous woman knows that freedom is not going to come to Cuba by trading one oppressive Castro regime for another. Today I have a message for the people of Cuba: *Viene el dia de su libertad.* Your day of freedom is coming. And until that day, the United States will stand with all the dissidents working together to bring freedom to Cuba, including a brave woman named Marta Beatriz Roque Cabello.

America honors women like Aung San Suu Kyi of Burma. For 12 of the last 18 years, this extraordinary woman has been kept under house arrest by Burma's brutal military regime. Her only crime was to lead a political party that enjoys the overwhelming support of the Burmese people. During the long and lonely years of Daw Suu Kyi's imprisonment, the people of Burma have suffered with her. Aung San Suu Kyi has never wavered. Her courage and her writings have inspired millions, and in so doing, have put fear into the hearts of the leaders of the Burmese junta.

And that's why the regime has called a vote in May to ratify a dangerously flawed constitution, one that bars Suu from ever leading—leaving her country. Aung San Suu Kyi has said to the American people, "Please use your liberty to promote ours." We're doing all we can, and we will continue to do so until the tide of freedom reaches the Burmese shores and frees this good, strong woman.

Americans are inspired by the examples of these women and the women we honor here today. We will continue to support their work and the work of women across the world who stand up for the freedom of their people.

One of America's finest poets was a woman named Emma Lazarus, who is most famous for writing the verses carved into the base of the Statue of Liberty. Those verses describe the copper icon as "a mighty woman with a torch" to light the way for all "yearning to breathe free." During Women's History Month and at this celebration of International Women's Day, we are proud that the most recognizable symbol of America's love for freedom is "a mighty woman." And we reaffirm our commitment to light the way for all—both women and men—"yearning to be free."

And now, I'd like to ask Laura and Secretary Chao and Secretary Peters and the Members of Congress who are here to join me on stage as I proudly sign Women's History Month proclamation.

NOTE: The President spoke at 3:17 p.m. in the East Room at the White House. In his remarks, he referred to White House Press Secretary Dana Perino; President Aleksandr Lukashenko of Belarus; and former President Fidel Castro Ruz and President Raul Castro Ruz of Cuba. The transcript released by the Office of the Press Secretary also included the remarks of the First Lady. The Women's History Month proclamation is listed in Appendix D at the end of this volume.

Remarks on Arrival in Nashville, Tennessee
March 11, 2008

The President. This is Dr. Christian, Dr. Karla Christian, who really symbolizes the best of America. She and a team of hers have performed a surgery on a little Iraqi girl who was discovered by United States marines. People in Nashville raised the money for the family; they were supported by the marines there in Iraq. Some of the marines raised money, and they sent this little girl, whose heart was ailing, to America, right here to Nashville. And Karla and her team healed the little girl, and she's back in Iraq.

And the contrast couldn't be more vivid. We got people in Iraq who murder the innocent to achieve their political objectives, and we've got Americans who heal the broken hearts of little Iraqi girls. Ours is a compassionate nation that believes in the universality of freedom. And ours is a nation full of loving souls that when they find a stranger in need will lend their God-given talents to help that stranger. And that's precisely what happened.

Karla G. Christian. Thank you.

The President. I want you to thank your team there for all the good work you've done.

Dr. Christian. Thank you for all you've done.

The President. God bless.

NOTE: The President spoke at 10:29 a.m. at Nashville International Airport. In his remarks, he referred to Karla G. Christian, associate chief of pediatric cardiac surgery and director of pediatric cardiac surgical education, Monroe Carell Jr. Children's Hospital at Vanderbilt, and her patient Amina Al'a Thabit.

Remarks to the National Religious Broadcasters Convention in Nashville
March 11, 2008

Thank you all. Please be seated. Thank you for the warm welcome. Nothing better than being introduced by a fellow Texan. [*Applause*] And it's good to see some of my Texas buddies here—[*applause*]—like my friend Evans from Dallas. Good to see you, Tony. Thanks for letting me come by.

This is kind of a rambunctious crowd. [*Laughter*] I really am pleased to be with you. For 64 years, this association has brought together some of the most memorable voices of the—our Christian community here in America. You've preached the blessings of grace and understanding and patience. I've needed all three during my time as President. [*Laughter*]

I was very young when I first learned about obedience to a higher power, and my mother sends her best to you. [*Laughter*] I am surrounded by strong women and have been all my wife. [*Laughter*] And speaking about a strong and gracious woman, Laura sends her love and best.

We have something else in common: Each of us has had doors opened to us by the same man. He led the way for America's religious broadcasters. He brought the Gospel to millions, and many years ago, he helped me change my life. And today, this good man is recovering from surgery in North Carolina, and please join me in sending our love and prayers to Billy Graham. A lot of Americans love Billy Graham, and I'm one. So, Billy, we're thinking about you.

He has led countless Americans to the grace and goodness of the Almighty, and each of you performs the same mission every day. You renew the poor in spirit, you bring comfort to those in anguish, and you show millions the path to salvation and the peace of God.

I thank you for guiding the faithful. I thank you for strengthening America's families. I thank you for standing up for our values, including the right to life. And I appreciate your firm belief in the universality of freedom. I believe and I know most of you, if not all of you, believe that every man, woman, and child on the face of the Earth has been given the great gift of liberty by an Almighty God. And today I want to speak about this precious gift, the importance of protecting freedom here at home, and the call to offer freedom to others who have never known it.

But before I do, I do want to thank Dr. Ron Harris and his wife Judy, straight out of Arlington, Texas. Appreciate other members of the National Religious Broadcasters Executive Committee. I thank Dr. Frank Wright and his wife Ruth.

I appreciate Members of Congress who have come today: Congressman Mike Pence of Indiana, Congressman Lincoln Davis of Tennessee, and Congresswoman Marsha Blackburn of Tennessee. Thank you all for coming. Proud to be with you.

This organization has had many important missions, but none more important than ensuring our airways—America's airways—stay open to those who preach the good news. The very first amendment to our Constitution includes the freedom of speech and the freedom of religion. Founders believed these unalienable rights were endowed to us by our Creator. They are vital to a healthy democracy, and we must never let anyone take those freedoms away.

I mention this because there's an effort afoot that would jeopardize your right to express your views on public airways. Some Members of Congress want to reinstate a regulation that was repealed 20 years ago. It has the Orwellian name called the fairness doctrine. Supporters of this regulation say we need to mandate that any discussion of so-called controversial issues on the public airwaves includes equal time for all sides. This means that many programs wanting to stay on the air would have to meet Washington's definition of balance. Of course, for some in Washington, the only options—opinions that require balancing are the ones they don't like. [*Laughter*]

We know who these advocates of so-called balance really have in their sights: shows hosted by people like Rush Limbaugh or James Dobson or many of you in here today. By insisting on so-called balance, they want to silence those they don't agree with. The truth of the matter is, they know they cannot prevail in the public debate of ideas. They don't acknowledge that you are the balance, that you give voice—[*applause*]. The country should not be afraid of the diversity of opinions. After all, we're strengthened by diversity of opinions.

If Congress truly supports the free and open exchange of ideas, then there is a way they can demonstrate that right now. Republicans have drafted legislation that would ban reinstatement of the so-called fairness doctrine. Unfortunately, Democratic leaders in the House of Representatives have blocked action on this bill. So in response, nearly every Republican in the House has signed onto what's called a discharge petition that would require Congress to hold an up-or-down vote on the ban. Supporters of this petition are only 24 signatures away.

I do want to thank Mike Pence, who is with us today, and Congressman Greg Walden for pressing this effort and defending the right for people to express themselves freely. And I urge other Members to join in this discharge petition. But I'll tell you this: If Congress should ever pass any legislation that stifles your right to express your views, I'm going to veto it.

We love freedom in America, and we're the leader of the world not because we try to limit freedom, but because we've helped to spread it. You and I know that freedom has the power to transform lives. You and I know that free societies are more peaceful and more prosperous. You and I know that if given the chance, men and women and children in every society on Earth will choose a life of freedom, if just given a chance. Unless, of course, you don't believe freedom is a gift from the Almighty. The liberty we value is not ours alone. Freedom is not America's gift to the world; it is God's gift to all humanity.

It is no coincidence that the region of the world that is the least free is also the most violent and dangerous. For too long, the world was content to ignore oppression—oppressive forms of government in the Middle East in the name of stability.

The result was that a generation of young people grew up with little hope of improving their lives, and many fell under the sway of violent extremism. The birthplace of three of the world's great religions became the home of suicide bombers. And resentments that began on the streets in the Middle East killed innocent people in trains and airplanes and office buildings around the world.

September the 11th, 2001, was such a day. We saw firsthand how the lack of freedom and opportunity in the Middle East directly affects our safety here at home. Nineteen men killed nearly 3,000 people because someone convinced them that they were acting in the name of God. Murder of the innocent to achieve political objectives is wrong and must be condemned.

These murderers were not instruments of a heavenly power; they were instruments of evil. And we have seen their kind before. It's important not to forget the lessons of history. We must remember the extermination of Jews in Nazi death camps were—was evil. The crimes of Pol Pot were evil. And the genocide in Rwanda was conducted because people's hearts were hardened. This kind of enemy must be confronted, and this kind of enemy must be defeated.

This is the calling of our time. Generations are often called into action for the defense of liberty, and this is such a time. Since 9/11, we're on the offense. My most important duty and the most important duty of those of us who serve you in Government is to protect the innocent from attack. And so we're on the offense. My view is, is that if we press the enemy, if we bring them to justice, if we defeat them overseas, we won't have to face them here—is the best strategy to protect America in the short term.

But that only works in the short term. The best way to defeat the enemy in the long term is to defeat their hateful ideology with a vision based upon hope, and that is, a society is based upon liberty. If you believe in the universality of freedom, then you'll recognize that people, if given a chance—just given a chance—will seize the moment and marginalize the extremists and isolate the radicals.

Hopeful societies are those which will eventually provide the protection we want here in America. And it'll happen, unless America loses its vision and its nerve. It's going to happen, unless we forget the lessons of history.

I want to share one story with you. Some of you may have heard me tell you this before. But one of my best friends in the international community, someone with whom I spent a lot of time talking about how to defeat extremism and defend the peace, was the Prime Minister of Japan. And what I found most interesting was the history of my family. My father, like many of your relatives, signed up to fight the sworn enemy, the Japanese. And 60 years later, his son is at the peace table planning and thinking about how we can confront this form of extremism in the short term and the long term. Something happened between Ensign Bush and Bush President 43. And what happened was, Japan adopted liberty as the core of its political system.

Freedom can transform societies. Freedom can—transforms enemies into allies. And someday, if the United States is steadfast and optimistic, people will—a President will be able to say, amazing thing happened; I sat down at the table with a leader of Muslims' nations, all aiming to keep the peace, to spread freedom, and keep America secure.

We're engaged in this struggle all across the world. And of course, the two most notable theaters in this ideological struggle are Afghanistan and Iraq. Some seem to believe that one of these battles is worth fighting and the other isn't. In other words, there is a good war and a bad war. You know, these—the enemy are fighting hard in both countries to seize power and impose their brutal vision. The theaters are part of the same war, the same calling, the same struggle. And that's why it is essential we succeed.

Seven years ago, Afghanistan was a haven for America's enemies. Under the protection of the Taliban, the September 11th—9/11 hijackers trained and plotted. We worked with—because we worked with brave Afghans, because we upheld doctrine that said, if you harbor a terrorist, you're just as guilty as the terrorist, we removed the Taliban from power, thereby freeing 25 million people from the clutches of a brutal, barbaric regime.

The camps used by the terrorists have been dismantled. The Taliban was removed from power. And then we took on a task that we knew would be as difficult but as essential for keeping our enemies from regaining power, and that is, we offered to help the Afghan people replace tyranny with freedom. We did the short-term job of denying safe haven, but we did something else. We said, we want to help you live lives based upon liberty. And it was a daunting task, when you really put it in perspective. The Afghan people had little experience with democracy. It's a foreign concept. We've grown up in it here. In Afghanistan, you say democracy, they're not exactly sure what you're talking about.

Afghan people under the Taliban didn't have any constitution or any of the normal institutions of a free and stable government. Afghanistan was one of the poorest countries in the world, with few natural resources and a population that thought it was condemned to unspeakable suffering.

In the entire nation, there were only 30 miles of paved road. Only 9 percent of the population had access to health care. Under the strict control of the Taliban, women were treated like chattel, and girls could not attend school. Children lived in hatred and misery, and they were not even permitted an act as simple as flying a kite. It was a backward, brutal society.

But we had better aspirations for the people of Afghanistan. We set our sights high because we believe in the universality of freedom. We trusted in the power of freedom to transform the country, a certain trust that has to go with basic principles in life. And we're seeing the results. Eight million Afghans went to the polls to elect a President for the first time in their history. Afghans drafted a new Constitution and elected a National Assembly. With the support of international partners, the Afghan economy has doubled in size. There are now more than 1,500 miles of paved roads. A majority of the population has access to health care. Women have seats in the parliament. Girls attend school again. And one small but telling sign is this: Afghan children are flying kites again.

A free society is emerging, and the fundamental question facing the United States of America and our friends and allies is, is it worth it and necessary? I believe it is necessary, and I strongly believe it's worth it. Afghanistan has got a lot of challenges. They got to overcome corruption; they got to fight narcotics trafficking; and they got to strengthen the Government at all levels. They face a vicious and brutal enemy that is determined to regain power and deny the people of Afghanistan their freedom.

We saw the nature of this enemy when Taliban extremists invaded an Afghan school. They kidnaped six teachers. They beat the schoolchildren with sticks to scare them away from attending classes. We saw the nature of this enemy when extremists beheaded the principal of an Afghan high school and forced his wife and children to watch. We saw the nature of this enemy last summer when Taliban extremists paid an Afghan boy to push a cart carrying explosives into a crowded marketplace, and the terrorists detonated the cart, killing the boy and Afghan security officials.

This enemy sees no value in human life. And they continue their campaign of bloody and horrific attacks, all attempting to demoralize the people of Afghanistan and all attempting to wait the coalition out. For the sake of humanity and for the sake of the safety of our people, for the sake of human life and human dignity, and for the sake of the security of the United States of America, we will stop this murderous movement now, before it finds a new path to power. The temptation is to say—[*applause*]. I believe it is important for administrations to confront problems now and not pass them on to other people. And that's the choice I have made for the sake of peace and freedom.

Our forces made progress last year in partnering with local Afghans against the enemy in eastern Afghanistan, which was an insurgent stronghold. Now the Taliban and its allies are seeking to launch new attacks against the people. In other words, these are relentless killers. Their methods and their immorality have alienated many of the people who once supported them.

It's amazing what happens when there's a contrast—ideological contrast presented to people with clarity. Do you want to live in freedom, or do you want your little girl denied the opportunity to go to school? Afghans across the country are fighting back. More than 50,000 Afghans have stepped forward to serve the Afghan Army; 76,000 have joined the police force. They've invested in this fight, and they need our help. That's what they're saying: They want help. And we're going to give it to them. It's in our interests that we support these people.

In the year ahead, the United States will work with our allies and the Afghan people in an aggressive effort to counter the enemy. This spring, the United States is increasing our military commitment to the country. We're sending a Marine expeditionary unit and an infantry battalion, totaling more than 3,200 additional marines, to train Afghan forces and to support the offense against the Taliban in southern Afghanistan.

NATO allies and other partners are also in the fight. Many of these allies, particularly the Canadians and the Australians, the Dutch, the Danes, and the British, are taking on some of the most difficult missions in dangerous areas. You may have recently heard about one young Brit who fought against the Taliban. It was Prince Harry of Wales. When he returned to England, he said this: "If you spoke to a lot of the other guys who came off the plane with me, there are plenty of people willing to go back and serve their country." And we admire that spirit, and so do the people of Afghanistan.

In a few weeks, I'm going to attend the NATO summit in Bucharest. I'm going to thank our allies for standing with the people, the brave people of this young democracy. I will remind them that we're not only in a mission to protect our own security, we're on a humanitarian mission that will free young girls to be able to realize their dreams.

I will also ask NATO to join the United States in doing even more. Now is the time for nations to make the hard decisions necessary so our children can grow up in a more peaceful world. I will call upon more international assistance to help Afghanistan on the road to freedom. We know what's at stake, and we know what we have to do. And so we're going to help the people of Afghanistan realize the blessings of liberty.

The other front in this ideological struggle is Iraq. And just as we did in Afghanistan, we removed a lethal threat to our national security. The decision to remove Saddam Hussein was the right decision early in my Presidency, it is the right decision at this point in my Presidency, and it will forever be the right decision.

And again we took on a difficult task that we knew was essential to keeping America's enemies from gaining power. We did not take the easy path of replacing one dictator with another. Instead, we offered Iraqis a chance to build a future of freedom. In that effort, our coalition faced—also faced daunting challenges. Like Afghanistan, Iraq had little experience with true democracy. Iraqis held nationwide votes for President, but it turns out, only one candidate was on the ballot. In 1995, Saddam Hussein received 99 percent of the vote. And 7 years later, he did a little better—[*laughter*]—he got 100 percent of the vote. [*Laughter*]

As Iraqis lived through these grotesque charades, they were rounded up at random by secret police. Women were raped by Iraqi authorities. Citizens were mutilated and dumped into mass graves. And Shi'a and Sunni and Kurds were oppressed and pitted against one another.

Despite the divisions and challenges, I believed, as did many in my administration, that freedom has the power to transform this country, that freedom has the power to provide hope after despair. And so we reached out to the population, and the Iraqi people responded. Together, Shi'a,

Kurds, and an increasing number of Sunnis joined America to advance a bold vision, and that is to build a lasting democracy in the heart of the Middle East.

Twelve million Iraqis braved threats of violence and went to the polls to elect a representative Government. You might remember those days of people waving purple-ink-stained fingers. Iraqis drafted one of the most democratic Constitutions in the Arab world. And hundreds of thousands of Iraqis have raised their hands and risked their lives to defend their nation.

The enemy saw these advances and were determined to stop them. They mounted horrific acts of violence designed to exploit sectarian divisions and incite further killing. And in these acts, we again saw the nature of the enemy. We saw the nature of this enemy when they killed a young boy and then boobytrapped his body so it would explode when his family came to retrieve him. We saw the nature of this enemy when terrorists put children in the backseat of a car so they could pass a security checkpoint and then blew up the car with the children still inside. We saw the nature of the enemy just over a month ago when they sent two mentally retarded, troubled Iraqi women wearing suicide vests into crowded marketplaces. The vests exploded, killing the women and dozens of innocent people.

Anyone who doubts the importance of defeating this vicious enemy need only imagine what would happen if we were driven out of Iraq before the job was finished. What would happen if they seized territory from—to be able to have safe haven? And what would happen if they seized oil fields and used their wealth to attack America and our allies?

These are vicious people who know no bounds of humanity. They would not hesitate to murder. It's essential for our citizens to understand this. And that is why this war must be fought, and that is why this war—this enemy must be defeated.

I wish I didn't have to talk about war. No President wants to be a war President. But when confronted with the realities of the world, I have made the decision that now is the time to confront, now is the time to deal with this enemy, and now is the time to spread freedom as the great alternative to the ideology they adhere to. [*Applause*] Thank you all.

Just over a year ago, things were not going well in Iraq. Terrorists and extremists were succeeding in their efforts to plunge Iraq into chaos. American peace and security required us to defeat this enemy, just as I said. So my administration reviewed our strategy and changed course, with victory in mind. I sent reinforcements into Iraq in a dramatic policy that's now being called the surge.

We also changed the way our troops were used. U.S. and Iraqi forces began living together among the Iraqi people to help drive the terrorists out. Our forces stayed around to ensure the terrorists did not return. We launched a civilian surge to help local governments deliver economic resources in the wake of the security gains. We launched a diplomatic surge, with an expanded and active role for international organizations like the United Nations and the G–8. We've encouraged its neighbors to help this young society flourish and recover from the brutality of a dictator.

The Iraqi people saw these efforts. They had renewed faith in America's commitment to the fight. As you can imagine, during that period of time, a lot of folks were wondering: "Is America going to stay with us? Do they understand our deep desire to live in freedom? Can we count on them?" And when they found out they could, they launched a surge of their own. Increasing numbers of Sunni leaders have turned against the terrorists and begun to reclaim their communities. The Government in Baghdad has stepped forward as well. They've added more than 100,000 new Iraqi soldiers and police during last year. They're beginning to pass laws in

Baghdad. They passed a budget on time. [*Laughter*]

Folks who were involved in the insurgency have now decided they want to be a part of their Government. The Iraqi people have begun to see what freedom offers. They've seen what the enemy plans, and they have chosen to stand on the side of freedom. And America stands with them.

Next month, General Petraeus and Ambassador Ryan Crocker will return to Washington to report on the progress in Iraq and offer their recommendations. And I will carefully consider their recommendations. I can report this to you, though, that since the surge began, sectarian killings are down; Al Qaida has been driven from many strongholds it once held. I strongly believe the surge is working, and so do the Iraqis.

And as a return on our success—in other words, as we get more successful—troops are able to come home. They're not coming home based upon defeat or based upon opinion polls or based upon focus groups or based upon politics, they're coming home because we're successful. And the pace of that withdrawal has been determined, and then the commanders will take a further assessment. But I want to assure you, just like I assure military families and the troops, the politics of 2008 is not going to enter into my calculation; it is the peace of the years to come that will enter into my calculation.

The gains in Iraq are tenuous, they're reversible, and they're fragile. And there is much more work to be done. This enemy is resilient, and they attack. They use asymmetrical warfare; they use suicide vests. Just yesterday the enemy killed eight of our soldiers in two separate attacks. And I know you join me in offering our prayers to their loved ones, that the good Lord will provide them strength and comfort during the ultimate test.

We mourn every loss of life. We also know that the reason why the enemy uses such brutal tactics is they're trying to shake our nerve. And frankly, that's not hard to do in America because we're a compassionate people. We value life, and we care. We really do want to reach out to others, and when we see this kind of horrific killing, it affects us, all of us.

It also must send a message to us that we must be determined and steadfast. We're determined to defeat this enemy, and you just got to know, so are the people of Iraq. Millions who have suffered decades of tyranny and torment now are beginning to see hope. And for the sake of the security and for the sake of peace and for the sake of generation of kids coming up, the United States will help the Iraqis succeed.

And the effects of a free Iraq and a free Afghanistan will reach beyond the borders of those two countries. I believe that success of these two countries will show others the way. It will show others what's possible. And we undertake this work because we believe that every human being bears the image of our Maker. That's why we're doing this. No one is fit to be a master, and no one deserves to be a slave.

People of all faiths and all backgrounds deserve the chance at a future of their own choosing. That's what America believes. After all, those were the ideals that helped create our Nation. Those ideals were an honorable achievement of our forefathers, and now it's the urgent requirement of this generation.

The work before our country is hard, and it has risks. It's just hard work. And yet I don't see that as a reason to avoid it. Our enemies are ruthless, but they're going to be defeated. They've got the capacity to blow people up through these suicides, but you notice none of the leaders ever are the suicide bombers, however. [*Laughter*] But we got something more powerful. We got determination, we got will, and we got freedom at our disposal.

Evil in some form will always be with us, and we must never be afraid to face it. I know you understand that. I also know that you understand that for those who are on the frontlines and for those who struggle against evil, they can be helped through prayer. And I appreciate your prayers. I appreciate your prayers to help comfort millions of people. I appreciate the fact that you pray for our troops and their families. And I appreciate the prayers that you have directed my way. I feel your prayer. I am—I can't tell you how meaningful they have been, to help Laura and me deal with—do our job. And I can report to you this: that the prayers of the people have affected us, and that being the President has been a joyous experience.

And so I thank you for what you do. I thank you for giving me a chance to come and share some of my thoughts with you. God bless you, and God bless America.

NOTE: The President spoke at 11 a.m. at the Gaylord Opryland Resort and Convention Center. In his remarks, he referred to Ronald L. Harris, chairman, National Religious Broadcasters Executive Committee, who introduced the President; Anthony T. Evans, founder and president, The Urban Alternative; evangelist Rev. William F. Graham, Jr.; Frank Wright, president, National Religious Broadcasters; radio show host Rush Limbaugh; James Dobson, radio show host and founder of Focus on the Family; former Prime Minister Junichiro Koizumi of Japan; President Hamid Karzai of Afghanistan; and Gen. David H. Petraeus, USA, commanding general, Multi-National Force—Iraq. The Office of the Press Secretary also released a Spanish language transcript of these remarks.

Statement on the Resignation of Admiral William J. "Fox" Fallon as Commander of United States Central Command
March 11, 2008

Admiral William Fallon has served our Nation with great distinction for 40 years. He is an outstanding sailor, and he made history as the first naval officer to serve as commander of Central Command.

From the Horn of Africa to the streets of Baghdad to the mountains of Afghanistan, the soldiers, sailors, airmen, marines, and coastguardsmen of Central Command are vital to the global war on terror. During his tenure at CENTCOM, Admiral Fallon's job has been to help ensure that America's military forces are ready to meet the threats of an often troubled region of the world, and he deserves considerable credit for progress that has been made there, especially in Iraq and Afghanistan.

With service in Vietnam and as Vice Chief of Naval Operations, commander of Pacific Command, and many other positions, Admiral Fallon has served this country with honor, determination, and commitment. I thank his wife Mary, who knows that military service involves the whole family, and I wish them all the best as they begin the next chapter in their lives.

Message to the Congress on Continuation of the National Emergency With Respect to Iran
March 11, 2008

To the Congress of the United States:

The crisis between the United States and Iran constituted by the actions and policies of the Government of Iran that led to the declaration of a national emergency on March 15, 1995, has not been resolved. The actions and policies of the Government of Iran are contrary to the interests of the United States in the region and pose a continuing unusual and extraordinary threat to the national security, foreign policy, and economy of the United States. Iran remains the world's most active state sponsor of terrorism, and continues to provide lethal support to Lebanese Hizballah, HAMAS, Palestinian Islamic Jihad and numerous other terrorist organizations in the region, as well as to the Taliban in Afghanistan and various Iraqi militant groups. For these reasons, I have determined that it is necessary to continue the national emergency declared with respect to Iran and maintain in force comprehensive sanctions against Iran to respond to this threat.

Section 202(d) of the National Emergencies Act (50 U.S.C. 1622(d)) provides for the automatic termination of a national emergency unless, prior to the anniversary date of its declaration, the President publishes in the *Federal Register* and transmits to the Congress a notice stating that the emergency is to continue in effect beyond the anniversary date. In accordance with this provision, I have sent the enclosed notice to the *Federal Register* for publication, stating that the Iran emergency declared on March 15, 1995, is to continue in effect beyond March 15, 2008.

GEORGE W. BUSH

The White House,
March 11, 2008.

NOTE: This message was released by the Office of the Press Secretary on March 12. The notice is listed in Appendix D at the end of this volume.

Remarks to the United States Hispanic Chamber of Commerce
March 12, 2008

Gracias. Thank you. *Sientese. Gracias mi amigo,* David. Thank you for having me back yet again to speak. This is an opportunity *de practicar mi Espanol.* [*Laughter*] Of course, a lot of people say I ought to be spending more time practicing my English. [*Laughter*] But I'm thrilled to be with you.

I really love the entrepreneurial spirit in all communities. And it's evident in the Latino community. As you know, I'm blessed to be a Texan, and I got to see firsthand, as Governor, the unbelievable initiative and drive of Hispanics who lived in my State. And it's the same thing all across the country. And so part of the purpose for me to come is to thank you for your helping others realize the blessings of owning a small business; thanks for creating jobs, thanks for setting good examples, and thanks for being my friend.

David, as you know, I've been to the Hispanic Chamber, I think this is my third time, but I know a lot of you personally. And this may be my farewell address to the Hispanic Chamber as President, but it's certainly not going to be my farewell to you as a friend.

I thank not only David but Augie Martinez. I thank the directors of the Hispanic Chamber. I thank my old buddy, Hector Barreto, who is here with us, who—[applause]—Michael Barrera, thank you both. Appreciate you, Miguel.

And then there are members of my Cabinet who have come because today I'm going to discuss with you a very serious issue, an issue that matters a lot to your future and the future of this country. And so I welcome Secretary of Defense Bob Gates, Secretary of the Treasury Hank Paulson, Secretary of Agriculture Ed Schafer, Secretary of Commerce Carlos Gutierrez. Elaine Chao, Secretary of Labor, is with us. Susan Schwab of the USTR—Trade Representative is with us. This is not a Cabinet meeting. [*Laughter*]

These are people who are here to put an exclamation point on the subject I'm going to discuss with you today. And so I thank you all for coming. I appreciate your time.

I also want to welcome Carolina Barco, who is the Ambassador from Colombia, and other members of the diplomatic corps that have joined us.

A lot has changed since I first spoke to this group. I had to face some very difficult spending decisions, and I've had to conduct sensitive diplomacy. That's called planning for a wedding. [*Laughter*] *La boda*—[laughter]—*de mi ninita*. [*Laughter*]

I really appreciate the fact that we work together. I just want to review a couple of issues that have made a difference. First of all, we worked together to launch a period of sustained economic growth. I remember meeting with some right after the attacks, and we were wondering whether or not our economy could withstand a terrorist attack. After all, a recession was in place just as I came into office; then the terrorists attacked; then we had corporate scandals.

And a lot of folks were wondering whether or not this economy would be resilient enough to withstand those pressures. And it turns out, it was. And I want to thank you very much for supporting the tax cuts plans that had good effect on small businesses all across the United States during that period of time. I think when people take a look back at this moment in our economic history, they'll recognize tax cuts work. They have made a difference.

And this is what we're doing again. We've entered another period of difficult times. I am confident in the long term for the United States economy. I know we're resilient. I know we're entrepreneurial. I know we'll withstand these times. I want to thank you for supporting the economic stimulus package that we passed, which provides strong incentives for small businesses to expand and will put money into the pockets of the people who earned it.

Secretary Paulson has assured me—and I—he's a can-do guy—that the checks will be coming into the mail in the second week of May. The other thing I do want to assure you of is that if Congress tries to raise taxes, I'm going to veto it. We don't need tax increases.

I appreciate your strong support on No Child Left Behind. We agreed that a system that just simply moves children through without measuring is inexcusable. You recognized early that many Latino kids were denied, you know, the great promise of America because they didn't get the good education that we expect. And so we confronted this business about giving up on kids early. We demand accountability. We spent more money. But in return for the increased money, we expect schools to measure, and we expect schools to correct problems early, before it's too late.

No Child Left Behind is working. We've measured. Fourth grade—Hispanic fourth graders have set new records when it comes to reading and math. So rather than weakening No Child Left Behind, the United States Congress needs to strengthen

No Child Left Behind for the sake of all our children. And I want to thank you for your support.

A Federal contracting process is open to more small and minority-owned businesses, thanks to our SBA guys who have been running the show, Steve and Hector. And we'll continue that practice of making sure that there's fairness when it comes to Federal contracting.

I appreciate your support on immigration law. I'm sorry that—[*applause*]—you know, I'm disappointed that Congress missed a good opportunity to uphold our values and uphold our laws at the same time. And I'm confident that the day will come when a President signs an immigration bill that secures our borders, respect our laws, and treats people with dignity.

And now I want to discuss trade with you. It's a sensitive subject in America, and it's an important subject. As business leaders, you understand that breaking down barriers to trade and investment creates opportunities for our workers, for American workers and employees and employers and consumers. We—trade adds to our prosperity, but as importantly, it adds to the prosperity of our trading partners. We want people who are interested in our goods and services to do well economically. We believe that the world benefits when prosperity is abundant throughout the world.

Trade also serves a broader strategic purpose. When we enter into free trade agreements, we reinforce commitments to democracy and transparency and rule of law. By promoting a future of freedom and progress and hope, we create an alternative vision to those of the terrorists and extremists who prey on societies trapped in poverty and despair. In other words, trade helps democracies flourish; it helps enhance prosperity. And that helps us in our national security concerns.

My administration has made expanding trade a high priority. When I took office, America had free trade agreements in force with just three nations. Isn't that interesting? Just three countries. Today, we have agreements in force with 14, and Congress recently approved another one with Peru. Three more agreements are on Congress's agenda this year: Colombia, Panama, and South Korea. All three are important, and the agreement with Colombia is especially urgent.

For more than a year, my administration has worked with both parties in Congress to seek a path to bring this agreement up for approval. We continue to stand ready to negotiate a bipartisan way forward. But time is running out, and we must not allow delay to turn into inaction. The Colombia agreement is pivotal to America's national security and economic interests right now, and it is too important to be held up by politics. There needs to be a vote on Colombia this year.

And that means that Members of the Congress must be ready to move forward with the agreement when they return from the Easter recess. Members of both parties should work with this administration to bring legislation to implement the Colombia agreement to the floor for approval. And they need to get the job done and get a bill to my desk.

And I'll tell you why: Because this agreement with Colombia will advance our national security and economic interests in these ways. Colombia is one of our closest allies in the Western Hemisphere. Under the leadership of President Uribe, Colombia has been a strong and capable partner, a strong and effective partner in fighting drugs and crime and terror. Colombia has also strengthened its democracy, reformed its economy. It has spoken out against anti-Americanism. This Government has made hard choices that deserves the admiration and the gratitude of the United States.

These actions have required courage, and they've come with costs. As we speak, Colombia is under assault from a terrorist network known as the FARC, which aims to overthrow Colombia's democracy and aims to impose a Marxist vision on the country.

The FARC pursues this objective through bombing, hostage-taking, and assassination, much of it funded by drug trafficking. Since 2003, attacks by the FARC have killed or injured more than 1,500 civilians. Last summer, the FARC executed 11 Colombian lawmakers after holding them captive for 5 years. And the FARC continues to use jungle camps to hold hundreds of kidnaped victims, including three U.S. citizens.

President Uribe has waged an aggressive campaign against FARC terrorists, who do not respect national sovereignty or borders. Earlier this month, Colombian forces killed one of FARC's most senior leaders, a man believed to be responsible for trafficking cocaine and murdering hundreds of people.

And the response to all this action reveals the challenges that Colombia faces. The President of Venezuela praised the terrorist leader as a good revolutionary and ordered his troops to the Colombian border. This is the latest step in a disturbing pattern of provocative behavior by the regime in Caracas. It has also called for FARC terrorists to be recognized as a legitimate army, and senior regime officials have met with FARC leaders in Venezuela.

As it tries to expand its influence in Latin America, the regime claims to promote social justice. In truth, its agenda amounts to little more than empty promises and a thirst for power. It has squandered its oil wealth in an effort to promote its hostile, anti-American vision. And it has left its own citizens to face food shortages, while it threatens its neighbors.

The stakes are high in South America. As the recent standoff in the Andes shows, the region is facing an increasingly stark choice: to quietly accept the vision of the terrorists and the demagogues or to actively support democratic leaders like President Uribe. I've made my choice. I'm standing with courageous leadership that believes in freedom and peace. And I believe when the American people hear the facts, they will make their choice and stand with a person who loves liberty and freedom.

And there is no clearer sign of our support than a free trade agreement. This agreement would help President Uribe show his people that democracy leads to tangible benefits. This agreement would help create new jobs in Colombia, which would make it harder to recruit people to violence and terrorism and drug trafficking. The agreement would signal to the region that America's commitment to free markets and free people is unshakable.

And now it calls on Congress to decide whether this agreement will take effect. People across the hemisphere are watching. They are waiting to see what Congress will do.

Some Members of Congress have raised concerns over the situation in Colombia. Again and again, President Uribe has responded decisively. He's responded to concerns about violence by demobilizing tens of thousands of paramilitary fighters. He's responded to concerns about attacks on trade unionists by stepping up funding for prosecutions, establishing an independent prosecutors unit, and creating a special program to protect labor activists. He's responded to concerns over labor and environmental standards by revising the free trade agreement to include some of the most rigorous protections of any agreement in history. As one Democratic House Member put it, "It's impossible for someone to go to Colombia and not be impressed with the strides they have made." Ladies and gentlemen, if this isn't enough to earn America's support, then what is?

If Congress were to reject the agreement with Colombia, we would validate antagonists in Latin America who would say that the America cannot be trusted to stand by its friends. We would cripple our influence in the region and make other nations less likely to cooperate with us in the future. We would betray one of our closest friends in our own backyard.

In the words of Prime Minister Stephen Harper of Canada, "If the U.S. turns its back on its friends in Colombia, this will set back our cause far more than any Latin American dictator could hope to achieve." Congress needs to listen to those wise words as they consider this important bill. Members of both parties should come together. Members of both parties should demonstrate their support for freedom in our hemisphere. And members of both parties should prove the—approve the Colombian free trade agreement.

These strategic benefits are not the only reason for Congress to approve our trade agreement with Colombia. The agreement will also bring economic gains for both countries. Today, virtually all exports from Colombia enter into the United States duty free, but U.S. exports to Colombia face tariffs up to 35 percent. Now think about that. Goods coming from Colombia to us enter our country virtually duty free, and yet goods going from the United States to Colombia are taxed.

Now, doesn't it make sense to pass an agreement that says, the Colombians will treat us the way we treat them? If you're a farmer or interested in exporting construction equipment or aircraft and auto parts or medical and scientific equipment, your goods will now go into Colombia duty free, which means you're more likely to be able to sell your goods into Colombia. And if you're working for one of those companies, it means you're more likely to be able to keep your job.

I can't understand a mentality that doesn't recognize that causing America to be treated equally is not in our interests. It is in our interests. Every day that Congress goes without approving this agreement is a day that our businesses, large and small, become less competitive. It's missed opportunity.

This agreement is especially important during a difficult period for our economy. Listen, last year, exports accounted for more than 40 percent of growth. Doesn't it make sense to open up markets, to continue to grow our economy with good exports? I think it does. And this is an opportunity for the United States Congress to send a clear message that they are concerned, like I'm concerned, about the state of our economy. They, like me, want to provide opportunities for our producers and our workers to be able to find new markets and expanded markets for U.S. goods and services.

This agreement will also benefit Colombia. It will give Colombian exporters the certainty that comes with permanent access. This will help stimulate investment and economic growth and higher standards of living for families in Colombia. And it will make it clear to the Colombian people, we're partners in prosperity, and we're partners in peace.

The time is coming when Members will get to vote yes or no. My administration is committed to working this agreement hard on the floor of the Congress. I firmly believe it is in our interests that this be passed. It's not in our political interests. We ought to just put politics aside and focus on what's best for the United States of America. And what is best for our country is to get this agreement approved soon.

Congress also ought to approve the other two trade agreements on their agenda after they approve this one. Congress needs to approve the trade agreement with Panama, which will open up U.S. access to one of the fastest growing economies in Central America and support a key democratic partner. Congress also needs to approve the free trade agreement with South Korea, which has the potential to boost U.S. exports by more than $10 billion while strengthening a key ally.

As Congress moves forward with these agreements, we will continue to press for an ambitious, successful Doha round at the WTO. We're prepared to lead to ensure Doha reaches a successful conclusion. We understand the role of the United States. We're not going to shirk our duty to lead.

But we're not going to make unilateral concessions either. We want negotiations to come from—as a result of meaningful contributions by all folks. That's how you reach a successful round.

And so we challenged our trading partners to help forge a deal that opens up global trade flows and creates new opportunities for developed and developing nations alike. Our view is, the time for debating Doha is over. Now is the time for leaders to make tough choices that will allow these negotiations to advance.

Look, I know a lot of folks are worried about trade. There's neighbors worrying about neighbors losing jobs. People say, "Well, trade causes us to lose jobs." And I fully understand that. Sometimes trade causes people to lose jobs. Sometimes the fact that technology hasn't advanced as rapidly or the productivity of workers isn't as good as it should be has caused people to lose jobs.

But nevertheless, there is that concern. And so my question to the American people is, what's the best way to respond? One option is to stop trade, erect barriers, try to wall ourselves off from the world. Those costs of isolationist policies and protectionist policies would far exceed any possible benefit. Closing off our markets would drive up prices for American families. Making it harder for people to sell goods in our country would deny families choices that they've been used to. We want our consumers to have choices when they walk into markets. The more choices available, the better it is for a consumer. The more competition it is for a product, the less likely it is price will rise.

The other nations would retaliate, by the way, if they saw the United States throwing up barriers, and that would push jobs overseas faster. It could hurt millions of Americans who go to work each morning, who work for companies that rely upon exports or companies that rely upon foreign capital as their base of operations.

You know, some have called for a timeout from trade. I guess that's probably popular with the focus group. You know, they toss out the word "timeout" from trade. It's got this kind of catchy little title to it. In the 21st century, a timeout from trade would be a timeout from growth, a timeout from jobs, and a timeout from good results. And retreating from the opportunities of the global economy would be a reckless mistake that our country cannot afford.

And there's a better answer. And one of them shows faith in the American workers instead of trying to stand against the growth of global trade, instead of granting other people access to markets that we ourselves could have. Instead of squandering an opportunity, why don't we help educate people? Why don't we provide educational opportunities so workers will have the skills necessary to fill the high-paying jobs of the 21st century?

One reason I mentioned No Child Left Behind is, it's got to—this program has got to start early, and it is. We're setting high standards and measuring and correcting problems early, before it's too late. But there's more we can do. We provided more than a billion dollars for new initiatives to educate and prepare workers for the jobs of the 21st century. Yesterday Secretary Chao announced more than $100 million in new community-based job training grants. In other words, we're focusing money to help people get the skills necessary to fill the jobs that are available in America. And when you get education, you're a more productive worker, which means you're going to get paid more money. That's what that means.

These grants support community college programs—I'm a big supporter of community colleges—that provide training for jobs in high-growth fields. And that's our strategy. Now, the word you'll hear attached to that is trade adjustment assistance. That's another program aimed at helping people get the skills necessary to find work. We support it. We support reforming and reauthorizing the vital program as a key component of trade policy. And I look forward to working with Congress to sign a good bill that I can sign into law.

These agreements that I've talked about deserve support from both sides of the aisle. And today I want to make a direct appeal to the members of the Democratic Party. From Franklin Roosevelt to John F. Kennedy to Bill Clinton, Democrats have a long history of supporting trade. Opening markets has been a history and a cornerstone of Democratic policy. As President Clinton said when he signed legislation to implement NAFTA 14 years ago, "We're on the verge of a global economic expansion that is sparked by the fact that the United States, at this critical moment, decided we would compete and not retreat." I fully support those strong words, those confident words, those optimistic words about America's ability to compete in the world. Thanks in part to the market-opening set in motion by the President, trade between the United States, Mexico, and Canada has more than tripled since 1993.

I mean, I know there's a lot of criticism of NAFTA, but I will tell you this: I grew up in Texas; I remember what the border was like. And I would ask people to go down to that border today and see the benefits, the mutual benefits of what trade has meant for people who, on both sides of the border, for years grew up in abject poverty. We may have some south Texans here today, and if you're old enough, you know exactly what I'm talking about.

The transformation has been remarkable because both sides have benefited. Both sides have realized the blessings of trade, as has Canada. All three of our economies, by the way, since that agreement was signed, have grown by more than 50 percent. More than 25 million new jobs have been created in the United States. The unemployment rate is lower than in previous decades. Workers, farmers, entrepreneurs have seen real improvements in their daily lives, including many Hispanic-owned businesses on both sides of the border.

Listen, NAFTA has worked. People shouldn't back away from NAFTA. It's been a positive development for a lot of people. And if you're worried about people coming to our country to find jobs, there's no better way to help somebody stay home than for there to be prosperity in their neighborhood. I'm convinced most people don't want to try to sneak into America to work. I'm convinced most people would rather have a job close to their—close to where they live. And trade helps increase prosperity. It's mutually beneficial for Canada, the United States, and America—I mean, and Mexico.

Now, look, I understand supporting free trade agreements is not politically easy. There are a lot of special interest groups that are willing to spend a lot of money to make somebody's life miserable when it comes to supporting free trade agreements. But I believe leadership requires people rising above this empty, hollow political rhetoric. If you're committed to multilateral diplomacy, you cannot support unilateral withdrawal from trade agreements. If you're worried—[applause]—if you are worried about America's image in the world, it makes no sense to disappoint the nations that are counting on us most. If you care about lifting developing nations out of poverty, you cannot deny them access to the world's greatest engine of economic growth. If you're truly optimistic about our country's future, there's no reason to wall our Nation off from the opportunities of the world.

I appreciate your efforts in these matters. I feel strongly that trade is in our national interests. I know it's in your personal interests if you're businesspeople. Of course, as you prosper, people are more likely to find work. After all, 70 percent of the new jobs in America are created by small-business owners just like those present here.

I believe Congress will do the right thing. When it's all said and done, they'll take a hard look at the facts. They will take a look at the consequences of rejecting a trade agreement with our close ally. They'll take a good look at the consequences of sending the wrong message to the false populists of the region. They'll take a simple, logical look at how this can benefit our farmers and small-business owners and employers.

Thanks for helping us work the issue. Thanks for giving me a chance to come and speak to you. May God bless you, and may God bless our country.

NOTE: The President spoke at 10:41 a.m. at the Ronald Reagan Building and International Trade Center. In his remarks, he referred to David C. Lizarraga, chair, Augustine Martinez, interim president and chief executive officer, and Michael L. Barrera, former president and chief executive officer, U.S. Hispanic Chamber of Commerce; Hector V. Barreto, former Administrator, Small Business Administration; Marc Gonsalves, Thomas Howes, and Keith Stansell, hostages held by the Revolutionary Armed Forces of Colombia (FARC); and President Hugo Chavez Frias of Venezuela.

Remarks at the National Republican Congressional Committee Dinner
March 12, 2008

Thanks for the warm welcome. I don't know about you, but I'm excited about the year 2008. I intend to finish strong with my head held high. And I intend to work to see to it that we keep the White House and elect John Boehner Speaker of the House of Representatives. [*Applause*] And evidently, you feel the same way.

Now, I thank you all for coming tonight. I am really pleased that this event has turned out to be as successful as it has been. I send—I bring greetings from First Lady Laura Bush. She's—[*applause*]—yes, thank you. She's doing great. She's wedding planning right now, so I appreciate the invitation to be here. [*Laughter*]

You know, I was just thinking about how next year's dinner is going to be a little different from this one. First, you're going to be welcoming a new keynote speaker, President John McCain. And President McCain will start this dinner by saying, "Thanks for the introduction, Mr. Speaker." And I'll be watching it all on TV in Crawford. [*Laughter*]

I do want to thank my friend John Boehner. He has been a great leader for the Republicans in the House of Representa-

tives. He's a good, solid, strategic thinker. I'm proud to call him friend, and I thank you for your service.

I want to thank the House leaders who are here: Roy Blunt, Adam Putnam, Darrell Issa. Issa, you did a heck of a job tonight. Thank you for doing this. I want to recognize my friend Tom Cole. Tom Cole has the vision and determination to effect change, and that is, elect Republicans to be the Speaker and leaders of the House of Representatives. I appreciate you coming, Tommy.

I want to thank Eric Cantor, David Dreier, Kay Granger, John Carter. I appreciate Sam [Ralph]° Hall, my fellow Texan, and Sam Johnson, my fellow Texan, and Ralph Regula for presenting the awards on all the veterans who are serving in Congress tonight. That'll happen after I leave, but nevertheless, I do want to extend my congratulations.

I thank Trace Adkins for singing here tonight. Trace wondered whether I was going to sing. I told him, no, I didn't think

———
° White House correction.

I'd sing; I thought I'd just do a little tap-dance. [*Laughter*] And I also appreciate my friend, one of the great voices of all time, Sam Moore. Thank you, Sam, for being here.

I also want to welcome all the candidates who are running for office. You know, it's not an easy decision to make to run for the United States Congress, but it's a noble decision. And it's a tough decision for your families. And so I want to thank you for agreeing to run; I want to thank your families for agreeing to support you. My advice is, work hard, talk about what's in your heart, let the people know your values, and win. And I think you will. I think 2008 is going to be a fabulous year for the Republican Party.

And the reason why I believe that is because when the American people look at our ideals versus the ideals of the Democrats, when they look at what we believe versus what they believe, they're with us. We represent the values of the American people. Our ideas are the ones embraced by the folks. They may not be the ones that the pundits listen to, but they're the ones who are out working every single day to make America a great and hopeful place.

We believe in strong national defense, and we will do what it takes to keep our Nation safe from a terrorist attack. We believe in limited government. We believe in the collective wisdom of the American people to make the decisions on behalf of the American Government. We would rather trust you than the people in government to make the decisions for what's best for you.

I'm optimistic about this year because I know John McCain. I've known him for many years. I've seen his character and his leadership up close. I've campaigned with him, and I've campaigned against him. [*Laughter*] And I can tell you this: He's a tough competitor. I've seen in every decision he makes that he is guided by the national interests of the United States, not by self-interest. I know John McCain to

be a man who will make decisions based upon sound principles, not based upon the latest focus group or political poll.

John McCain is running on a clear, consistent, and conservative agenda. He's a man of honor. He's a genuine hero. He has the wisdom and the experience necessary to be the Commander in Chief of our United States military forces. He loves this country. He's ready to lead this country. I'm proud to be his friend. I'm proud to be his supporter. And on Inauguration Day, I'll proud to be—say to John McCain, "Congratulations, Mr. President."

And I can assure you he doesn't want a lonely victory. He needs allies in the Congress to help enact his agenda. And he's going to work hard alongside these candidates and the incumbents to make sure we win. He'll be a great standard bearer. And I'm confident—I hope you go forth from this meeting with confidence because I am confident. I firmly believe that we can retake the House. I know we'll hold the White House. And I know it's necessary for the United States of America that we do both.

Let me talk about some of the issues and why I think we'll win. We trust people. We Republicans believe you can make the best decisions for your life. On health care, we trust patients to make decisions, not bureaucrats in Washington, DC. When it comes to education, we trust parents to make the right decisions for their children, and we believe in strong accountability in our public schools. We refuse to accept mediocrity. We refuse to accept the status quo when not every single child in America is learning to read and write and add and subtract.

The American people need us because we'll appoint judges who will strictly interpret the Constitution and not use the bench from which to write law, judges like John Roberts and Sam Alito.

But I think the biggest issue in this campaign is going to be your taxes. I think the biggest issue in this campaign is which side of the political divide is going to let you keep your money and which side is going to raise your taxes. Now, we've got a record on which side will not raise your taxes. We've been through some tough economic times together. We've been through a recession and a terrorist attack and war and corporate scandal and natural disasters. And up until recently, this economy has been strong. We added jobs for 52 consecutive months. It's the longest uninterrupted job growth in the Nation's history. And the reason we did so in the face of these daunting challenges: We trusted the American people, and we cut taxes on every American who pays taxes.

And we're fixing to do so again. We've hit a rough patch, but we took the lead. We anticipated the problems. And thanks to the leadership of John Boehner and Roy Blunt, they helped shepherd through over $160 billion of tax relief that will be reaching the mailboxes of the American people in the second week of May. Tax relief has worked in the past, and tax relief will work this time, when we get through this rough patch.

Now, apparently, the other side thinks this is a bad thing, because they want to let the tax cuts expire. Let me be clear about this: Milk expires, taxes increase. [*Laughter*] And we know the difference. And so will the American people when they realize that 116 million households will see their taxes rise by an average of $1,800 if the Democrats get their way in the House of Representatives.

Our message is this: We need a Republican President and a Republican Congress to prevent the Democrats from raising your taxes. We need to make the tax cuts permanent.

There's no bigger issue than protecting our country from harm. It is the most solemn responsibility that those of us who have been honored to serve you have. We must do everything in our power to make sure the enemy doesn't strike us again. And I fully understood that after September the

11th, that the temptation would be to dismiss any threat; the temptation would be that, "Oh, perhaps since we haven't been attacked, the threat doesn't exist."

Well, the threat does exist, and it requires steadfast, strong, clear-eyed leadership here in Washington, DC. One of the things that we must do is to make sure that the hundreds of people that are out working for you every night to protect you have the tools they need. If the enemy, if the extremists who want to do America harm, if the radicals who want to kill again, like they did before on our homeland, are making phone calls into the United States of America, we need to know who they're calling, what they're saying, and what they're planning.

The Congress came together last year and passed the Protect America Act to give our professionals the tools they need. Unfortunately, that act expired. But the threat to the United States of America has not expired. Unfortunately, Democratic leaders in the House are continuing to block bipartisan legislation that would give our intelligence officials the tools they need to quickly and effectively monitor terrorist communications.

And they are doing so despite the fact that legislation, good legislation, to give our professionals the tools passed the United States Senate by an overwhelming majority of 68 to 29. Instead of holding a vote on this bill that would pass the House of Representatives, House leaders have introduced a highly partisan and deeply flawed bill of their own. Their bill would put in place a cumbersome court approval process that would make it harder to collect intelligence on foreign terrorists and could reopen dangerous intelligence gaps that we experienced last year.

Their bill fails to provide liability protection to companies believed to have assisted in protecting our Nation after the 9/11 attacks. Instead, the House bill would make matters worse by extending litigation for years to come. In fact, House leaders simply adopted the position that class-action trial lawyers are taking in billions of dollars of lawsuits they have filed.

We're under threat, ladies and gentlemen, and yet the House leaders blocked meaningful, substantial legislation that will help protect America for the sake of class-action trial lawyers. Companies that may have helped us save lives should be thanked for their patriotic service and should not be subjected to billion-dollar lawsuits.

This bill would require the disclosure of state secrets during the litigation process. This could lead to the public release of highly classified information that our enemies could use against us. The Democrat version of protecting America is a bad bill; it is irresponsible. It casts aside the bipartisan consensus that was reached in the United States Senate in favor of a partisan approach that has no chance of becoming law. House leaders know this, yet they're pursuing this anyway. This is bad public policy and another reason to elect Republicans to the House of Representatives.

There's a lot of folks working to protect you at home. But the enemy only has to be right one time, and therefore, the best way to protect the American people from further harm is to defeat the enemy overseas so we do not have to face them here at home. And that's precisely the strategy that we're following.

We're on the offense. Wherever we can find a terrorist who would harm the American people, we'll bring him to justice. We're constantly pressing. And this war against the extremists is now being played out on two major theaters.

First is Afghanistan. I laid out a doctrine that said, if you harbor a terrorist, you're equally as guilty as the terrorists. The Taliban and—didn't believe us, and so the United States of America, after giving the enemy due warning, unleashed the fury of a great military. And in so doing, we cleaned out the terrorist training camps from which they launched attacks on the United States and freed 25 million people from the clutches of a barbaric regime.

This young democracy is struggling for its very existence against coldblooded killers, and it's in the interests of the United States that we stand strongly with these proud Afghan citizens, that we back them in their efforts, and that we make sure Al Qaida or any other extremist can no longer find a safe haven in the country of Afghanistan.

And then, of course, the other theater is Iraq. Removing Saddam Hussein was the right decision early in my Presidency; it is the right decision now; and it will be the right decision ever. And the fight's been tough in Iraq. And for those of you here—who are here who have served in that theater, I can't thank you enough for your sacrifices and your service to the United States of America.

There have been amazing gains made in that country. After all, they wrote one of the most modern constitutions in the history of the Middle East. Iraqis braved the violence to vote. And yet nearly a year ago, the terrorists and extremists were succeeding in their efforts to plunge the country into chaos.

So I had a tough decision to make. I reviewed our strategy. I fully understood that failure in Iraq would make America more vulnerable to attack, that failure in Iraq would create unbelievable chaos in a part of the world that has—that produced suicide bombers in the first place.

And so rather than retreating, I made the considered judgment to send reinforcements into the country, in a dramatic move that's now called the surge. Fourteen months after I ordered the surge of forces, sectarian killings are down, and Al Qaida is on the defense. U.S. and Iraqi forces have captured or killed thousands of extremists in Iraq, including hundreds of key Al Qaida operatives.

Progress in Iraq is fragile, and there's no question, it's going to take strong determination to prevail. Yet even the enemy recognizes they're on the wrong side of events. They're disheartened, they're demoralized, and they will be defeated.

When things were going poorly in Iraq early last year, Democrats called for withdrawal. Today, the situation has turned around, and Democrats are calling for withdrawal. It seems that no matter what happens on the ground, the opponents of the war have only one answer: retreat. You might even say that when it comes to withdrawing from Iraq, the Democrats' policy is, stay the course.

If we followed their advice a year ago, Iraq would be far different and a much more dangerous place than it is today, and the American people would be at greater risk. And if we followed their advice now, we would put at risk all the gains our troops have made over the past year. The United States Congress does need to act when it comes to Iraq, and they need to stand with our brave men and women in uniform and give them all the resources they need to do their job. And it—when it comes to standing with the United States military, there's no greater supporters than the Republicans in the House of Representatives.

The struggle we're engaged in is difficult for the American—some Americans to really understand the scope and the nature of the battle. We're involved in an ideological struggle between folks who murder the innocent to achieve political objectives, folks who have got a vision about what they would like to impose on the rest of the world, and particularly in the Middle East, and those of us who believe strongly in the power of liberty. I believe in the transformative power of liberty. I believe that if the United States of America does not lose its faith in the power of freedom to transform hopeless societies, that we will see the peace that we all want. I believe in the universality of freedom. I believe there's an Almighty, and I believe a gift of that Almighty to every man, woman, and child is freedom.

I love to share the story, and I'm sure some of you have heard this before—but the story about my friendship with Prime Minister Koizumi of Japan. He's the guy that we went down to Elvis's place in Memphis with. He is a good pal. He's no longer in power, but when he was in office, right after the attacks of September the 11th, he clearly saw the dangers and the opportunities. He saw the dangers that hopelessness was the only way that these ideologues could recruit suicide bombers. And he knew that the United States of America and our allies must be firm in our resolve to bring the terrorists to justice and, at the same time, spread the blessings of liberty.

And what's interesting about this story is that he was the leader of a country that my father fought against some 60 years prior. Think about that. Eighteen-year-old Navy Ensign George H.W. Bush, like many of your relatives, signed up to fight the Japanese. As a matter of fact, the war was so bitter that our vocabulary had slur words in it about the Japanese for years after the war ended. They were the hated enemy.

And yet 60 years later, his son, the son of a Navy fighter pilot, was at the table talking with the Prime Minister of the former enemy about the peace. Something amazing took place. And what happened was, Japan adopted democracy, a system of government with liberty at its core.

My friends, freedom is transformative. Freedom can transform an enemy into an ally. And someday, an American President will be thanking this Congress for its steadfast support of liberty, because he'll be sitting down at the table talking about keeping the peace for generations to come, and our children and our grandchildren will be better off for it.

I thank you for coming. I thank you for your prayers. May God bless America.

NOTE: The President spoke at 6:38 p.m. at the Hilton Washington Hotel. In his remarks,

he referred to entertainers Trace Adkins and
Sam Moore.

Remarks at the Kuwait-America Foundation's Stand for Africa Gala Dinner
March 12, 2008

Thank you all. Mr. Ambassador, thank you for the invitation. You've got a beautiful place here. [*Laughter*] Rima, thanks very much. I'm honored to be with you. I'm a little late because Laura had me watching "Father of the Bride." [*Laughter*] And in that I didn't finish it, I'm going to make my remarks short and go home and watch it. It's going to be a big year for us. So the guy comes to see me, and he says, "I want to marry your daughter." I said, "Done deal." [*Laughter*]

It's also a big year for us because I'm absolutely convinced the momentum that we have started on the continent of Africa in dealing with HIV/AIDS or malaria is going to continue on for a long period of time. And I want to thank you all very much for supporting the initiative.

I do want to say something about our Secretary of State. I can remember early on in my administration—she was the National Security Adviser then—and she said, "I presume you're going to pay attention to Africa." And I said, "That's a good presumption because I believe to whom much is given, much is required." And the United States of America has been given a lot. And I firmly believe we're required to respond to human tragedy when we see it.

And there's nothing more tragic than a young baby dying because of a mosquito bite. And so I come to you optimistic about this initiative and thankful for the folks who are supporting Malaria No More. I too want to thank Ray Chambers for his leadership. I like it when people do well in the business world and then, rather than retire, decide to put something back into society.

That's exactly what you've done, and we're very grateful for doing what you're doing.

I see Justice Alito is here. That's good. Hey, Sam, good to see you.

Youssou N'Dour—so, Youssou, I've been practicing my dancing recently—[*laughter*]—and singing. [*Laughter*] And I'm available for a few tips. [*Laughter*]

I appreciate the members of my Cabinet who are here and Members of Congress. I too want to thank Admiral Mike Mullen for serving as the Chairman of the Joint Chiefs, and his wife Deborah. It's amazing to be the Commander in Chief of a group of people that are dedicated, selfless, and courageous like our military. And Admiral Mullen represents the very best of the U.S. military. I thank the diplomatic corps who is here as well.

So my friends in Texas say, "You know, don't we have enough problems here at home?" And my answer is, "We're wealthy enough and we're strong enough and we're good enough to take problems—take on problems here at home as well as in other parts of the world." And then I remind them that we're living in a very difficult period in the history of the world. After all, we're witnessing an ideological struggle between those who kill the innocent to achieve political objectives and those who believe in human dignity and human rights and human freedom.

And it's a tough time, and it's going to take awhile to prevail. But one thing is for certain, that this enemy we face cannot possibly find recruits based upon their vision. Their vision for life is so dark and so dim and so degrading that it's impossible for them to recruit unless they find hopeless situations. And there's nothing more hopeless for a mother to see a baby die needlessly. And there's nothing more hopeless than a pandemic that sweeps through a continent.

And so the initiative, the Malaria No More initiative, first and foremost, is a part of our efforts to make sure that peace prevails in the long term. And it's working; it's amazing. Admiral Ziemer is here. This guy can get the job done. See, I—one of the things that we pride ourselves on in this administration is, we like to not only be talkers; we like to be doers. We like to set out an agenda and then see to it that the agenda is accomplished.

And working on this malaria initiative, we can measure. You can measure how many nets have been purchased and distributed, how many pills have been distributed, how many countries have been affected. When we were in Tanzania, we were told that Zanzibar, which is a part of Tanzania, went from having their babies infected by malaria at the tune of 20 percent to 1 percent in 18 months. And so I am the kind of fellow that says, this is in our interests, and I expect the monies that we're spending to be spent well and to be spent wisely. And they are.

It's also in our moral interest. Our Nation is a better nation when we help people save lives. The collective will of the American people to help somebody who suffers, who they might not ever know, lifts our national spirit. And so on our trip to Africa, I tried to make sure that the people of Africa understood this wasn't a George Bush initiative or a Laura Bush initiative or a Condi Rice initiative; this was an initiative of the most compassionate people on the face of the Earth, the American people.

And you're helping this initiative go forward. And so I've taken a breather from the movie to come by—[*laughter*]—to thank you very much for standing strong with the forces of goodness and light and compassion. And the work you're doing is necessary, and it's important, and it's succeeding. And I hope you take great heart in that.

Thanks for letting me come by to say hi, and God bless you all.

NOTE: The President spoke at 7:22 p.m. at the residence of the Ambassador of Kuwait to the U.S. In his remarks, he referred to Kuwait's Ambassador to the U.S. Salim al-Abdallah al-Jabir al-Sabah and his wife Rima al-Sabah; Raymond G. Chambers, founder, Malaria No More; musician and activist Youssou N'Dour; and Rear Adm. R. Timothy Ziemer, USN (Ret.), U.S. Malaria Coordinator.

Remarks on Intelligence Reform Legislation
March 13, 2008

Last month, House leaders declared that they needed 21 additional days to pass legislation giving our intelligence professionals the tools they need to protect America. That deadline passed last Saturday without any action from the House.

This week, House leaders are finally bringing legislation to the floor. Unfortunately, instead of holding a vote on the good bipartisan bill that passed the United States Senate, they introduced a partisan bill that would undermine America's security. This bill is unwise. The House leaders know that the Senate will not pass it. And even if the Senate did pass it, they know I will veto it.

Yesterday the Attorney General and the Director of National Intelligence sent a leader to the Speaker explaining why the bill is dangerous to our national security. They cited a number of serious flaws in the bill, including the following.

First, the House bill could reopen dangerous intelligence gaps by putting in place a cumbersome court approval process that would make it harder to collect intelligence on foreign terrorists. This is an approach that Congress explicitly rejected last August when bipartisan majorities in both Houses passed the Protect America Act. And it is an approach the Senate rejected last month when it passed a new—new legislation to extend and strengthen the Protect America Act by an overwhelming vote of 68 to 29.

Now House leaders are proposing to undermine this consensus. Their partisan legislation would extend protections we enjoy as Americans to foreign terrorists overseas. It would cause us to lose vital intelligence on terrorist threats, and this is a risk that our country cannot afford to take.

Second, the House bill fails to provide liability protection to companies believed to have assisted in protecting our Nation after the 9/11 attacks. Instead, the House bill would make matters even worse by allowing litigation to continue for years. In fact, House leaders simply adopted the position that class-action trial lawyers are taking in the multibillion-dollar lawsuits they have filed. This litigation would undermine the private sector's willingness to cooperate with the intelligence community, cooperation that is absolutely essential to protecting our country from harm. This litigation would require the disclosure of state secrets that could lead to the public release of highly classified information that our enemies could use against us. And this litigation would be unfair because any companies that assisted us after 9/11 were assured by our Government that their cooperation was legal and necessary.

Companies that may have helped us save lives should be thanked for their patriotic service, not subjected to billion-dollar lawsuits that will make them less willing to help in the future. The House bill may be good for class-action trial lawyers, but it would be terrible for the United States.

Third, the House bill would establish yet another commission to examine past intelligence activities. This would be a redundant and partisan exercise that would waste our intelligence officials' time and taxpayers' money.

The bipartisan House and Senate intelligence and judiciary committees have already held numerous oversight hearings on the Government's intelligence activities. It seems that House leaders are more interested in investigating our intelligence professionals than in giving them the tools they need to protect us. Congress should stop playing politics with the past and focus on helping us prevent terrorist attacks in the future.

Members of the House should not be deceived into thinking that voting for this unacceptable legislation would somehow move the process along. Voting for this bill does not move the process along. Instead, voting for this bill would make our country less safe because it would move us further away from passing the good bipartisan Senate bill that is needed to protect America.

The American people understand the stakes in this struggle. They want their children to be safe from terror. Congress has done little in the 3 weeks since the last recess, and they should not leave for their Easter recess without getting the Senate bill to my desk.

Thank you.

NOTE: The President spoke at 9:20 a.m. on the South Lawn at the White House. In his remarks, he referred to Attorney General Michael B. Mukasey. He also referred to H.R. 3773.

Remarks Following a Briefing By Provincial Reconstruction Team Leaders and Brigade Combat Commanders
March 13, 2008

As you can see here on the screen in front of me, we've got assembled in Afghanistan—thanks to Ambassador Wood—PRTs, which is Provincial Reconstruction Teams, made up of military and civilian personnel, all aiming to help the Afghans recover from unbelievable brutality of the Taliban and have a society that's capable of meeting the needs of its people. We've also got two members of the PRT here present with us.

Our strategy in Afghanistan is, one, to provide enough security so civil society can move forward. Any counter—effective counterinsurgency strategy will require more than just military action; it requires a military-civilian interface. And so if you look on the screen, you see brave and courageous Americans in uniform and not in uniform, because they're a part of this strategy to help Afghans, one, understand the blessings of good governance. In other words, the folks are attempting to fight corruption at the local level so that the local citizens are able to have a positive outlook about their government. We're also working to educate people, build roads, provide good health care. And our fellow citizens are there on the ground, in some difficult circumstances, all aiming to help this young democracy survive and thrive. And there are difficulties, but we're also making progress.

And the best thing we got going for us—not only do we have brave and compassionate citizens willing to serve, but we've also got an ideology based upon liberty, which stands in stark contrast to the ideology of the thugs and murderers called the Taliban. And the job of hand is to help these folks recover, help the Afghans realize there's a better future for them. And it's hard work, but it's necessary work for the security of our country.

And so it's been a great pleasure for senior members of my administration to hear the stories and to hear the issues that they face. I'm enriched by the experience, and I do want to thank you very much for serving our country. And as I mentioned to you earlier, please thank your families for them standing by you during these—during your time of service.

God bless you all, and thank you for your time.

NOTE: The President spoke at 11:27 a.m. in the Roosevelt Room at the White House.

Statement on Farm Legislation
March 13, 2008

The Congress has agreed on legislation to extend current farm programs to April 18, 2008. I will sign this legislation to avoid serious disruptions that might result if the current law is allowed to expire without a responsible farm bill enacted in its place. Farmers and ranchers deserve to know the structure of policies that affect their day-to-day business activities, and right now they face uncertainty.

Throughout this process, my goal has been and remains to sign a good farm bill. Over 1 year ago, following listening sessions across the Nation, the Department of Agriculture unveiled a reform-minded and fiscally responsible approach to supporting

America's farmers and ranchers. My proposal would provide agriculture producers with a safety net that better targets benefits and provides funding for emerging priorities. Today's farm economy is very strong, and Congress should not miss this opportunity to reform current farm programs.

My administration has been eager to work with Congress. We have offered legislative language and a list of potential spending offsets to ensure Congress does not increase taxes. And while insisting on significant program reforms, we have demonstrated flexibility on how to achieve real reform. I have also made it clear that any final farm bill that includes a tax increase or does not include reform will be met with a veto. These negotiations have taken place in good faith with the goal of reaching a final agreement that meets the needs of farmers and enjoys the support of America's taxpayers.

This legislation to extend current farm programs will provide more time for Congress to reach an agreement. If a final agreement is not reached by April 18, I call on Congress to extend current law for at least 1 year. While long-term extension of current law is not the desired outcome, I believe the Government has a responsibility to provide America's farmers and ranchers with a timely and predictable farm program, not multiple short-term extensions of current law. Without a predictable policy, agriculture producers will be unable to make sound business decisions with respect to this year's crop.

I am eager to sign a farm bill that provides a safety net for farmers, includes significant farm program reform similar to the administration's farm bill proposal, and does not include tax increases. I have made clear the framework of an agreement that will garner my signature and urge Congress to pass a bill that meets these criteria.

NOTE: The statement referred to S. 2745.

Statement on the Death of Archbishop Paulos Faraj Rahho of Mosul in Iraq
March 13, 2008

I send my condolences to the Chaldean community and the people of Iraq on the death of Archbishop Rahho. I deplore the despicable act of violence committed against the Archbishop of Mosul. The terrorists will continue to lose in Iraq because they are savage and cruel. Their utter disregard for human life, demonstrated by this murder and by recent suicide attacks against innocent Iraqis in Baghdad and innocent pilgrims celebrating a religious holiday, is turning the Iraqi people against them. We will continue to work with the Iraqi Government to protect and support civilians, irrespective of religious affiliation.

Message to the Senate Transmitting the Protocol Amending the Canada-United States Taxation Convention
March 13, 2008

To the Senate of the United States:

I transmit herewith, for Senate advice and consent to ratification, the Protocol Amending the Convention Between the United States of America and Canada with Respect to Taxes on Income and on Capital done at Washington on September 26, 1980, as Amended by the Protocols done on June 14, 1983, March 28, 1984, March 17, 1995, and July 29, 1997, signed on September 21, 2007, at Chelsea (the "proposed Protocol"). The proposed Protocol would amend the existing income tax Convention between the United States and Canada that was concluded in 1980, as amended by prior protocols (the "existing Treaty"). Also transmitted for the information of the Senate is the report of the Department of State with respect to the proposed Protocol.

The proposed Protocol would eliminate withholding taxes on cross-border interest payments. In addition, the proposed Protocol would coordinate the tax treatment of contributions to, and other benefits of, pension funds for cross-border workers.

The proposed Protocol also includes provisions related to the taxation of permanent establishments, so-called dual-resident corporations, income derived through certain entities that are considered fiscally transparent, and former U.S. citizens and long-term residents. The proposed Protocol further strengthens the existing Treaty's provisions that prevent the Treaty's inappropriate use by third-country residents. The proposed Protocol also provides for mandatory resolution of certain cases before the competent authorities.

I recommend that the Senate give early and favorable consideration to the proposed Protocol and give its advice and consent to ratification.

GEORGE W. BUSH

The White House,
March 13, 2008.

NOTE: This message was released by the Office of the Press Secretary on March 14.

Remarks to the Economic Club of New York and a Question-and-Answer Session in New York City
March 14, 2008

The President. Glenn, thanks for the kind introduction. Thanks for giving me a chance to speak to the Economic Club of New York. It seems like I showed up in a interesting moment—[*laughter*]—during an interesting time. I appreciate the fact that you've assembled to give me a chance to just share some ideas with you. I also appreciate the fact that as leaders of the business and financial community, you've helped make this city a great place, and helped make our country really, in many ways, the economic envy of the world.

First of all, in a free market, there's going to be good times and bad times. That's how markets work. There will be ups and downs. And after 52 consecutive months of job growth, which is a record, our economy obviously is going through a tough time. It's going through a tough time in the housing market, and it's going through a tough time in the financial markets.

And I want to spend a little time talking about that. But I want to remind you, this is not the first time since I've been the President that we have faced economic challenges. We inherited a recession. And then there was the attacks of September the 11th, 2001, which many of you saw firsthand, and you know full well how that affected our economy. And then we had corporate scandals. And I made the difficult decisions to confront the terrorists and extremists in two major fronts, Afghanistan and Iraq. And then we had devastating natural disasters. And the interesting thing: Every time, this economy has bounced back better and stronger than before.

So I'm coming to you as an optimistic fellow. I've seen what happens when America deals with difficulty. I believe that we're a resilient economy, and I believe that the ingenuity and resolve of the American people is what helps us deal with these issues. And it's going to happen again.

Our job in Washington is to foster enterprise and ingenuity, so we can ensure our economy is flexible enough to adjust to adversity and strong enough to attract capital. And the challenge is not to do anything foolish in the meantime. In the long run, I'm confident that our economy will continue to grow because the foundation is solid.

Unemployment is low at 4.8 percent. Wages have risen; productivity has been strong. Exports are at an alltime high, and the Federal deficit as a percentage of our total economy is well below the historic average. But as Glenn mentioned, these are tough times. Growth fell to 0.6 percent in the fourth quarter of last year; it's clearly slow. The economy shed more than 80,000 jobs in 2 months. Prices are up at the gas pump and in the supermarket. Housing values are down. Hard-working Americans are concerned. They're concerned about their families, and they're concerned about making their bills.

Fortunately, we recognized the slowdown early and took action. And it was decisive action in the form of policies that will spur growth. We worked with the Congress. I know that may sound incongruous to you, but I do congratulate the Speaker and Leader Reid, as well as Boehner and Mitch McConnell and Secretary Paulson, for anticipating a problem and passing a robust package quickly.

This package is temporary, and it has two key elements. First, the growth package provides incentives for businesses to make investments in new equipment this year. As more businesses take advantage, investment will pick up, and then job creation will follow. The purpose was to stimulate investment. And the signal is clear: Once I signed the bill, the signal to—folks in businesses large and small know that there's some certainty in the Tax Code for the remainder of this year.

Secondly, the package will provide tax rebates to more than 130 million households. And the purpose is to boost consumer spending. The purpose is to try to offset the loss of wealth if the value of your home has gone down. The purpose is to buoy the consumer.

The rebates haven't been put in the mail yet. In other words, this aspect of the plan hasn't taken to effect. There's a lot of Americans who've heard about the plan; a lot of them are a little skeptical about this "check's in the mail" stuff that the Federal Government talks about. [*Laughter*] But it's coming, and those checks, the Secretary assures me, will be mailed by the second week of May.

And so what are the folks, the experts—guys like Hubbard—anticipate to happen? I'm not so sure he is one now, but the people that have told me that they expect this consumer spending to have an effect in the second quarter and a greater effect in the third quarter. That's what the experts say.

The Federal Reserve has taken action to bolster the economy. I respect Ben

Bernanke. I think he's doing a good job under tough circumstances. The Fed has cut interest rates several times. And this week the Fed—and by the way, we also hold dear this notion of the Fed being independent from White House policy. They act independently from the politicians, and they should. It's good for our country to have that kind of independence.

This week, the Fed also announced a major move to ease stress in the credit markets by adding liquidity. It was strong action by the Fed, and they did so because some financial institutions that borrowed money to buy securities in the housing industry must now repair their balance sheets before they can make further loans. The housing issue has dried up some of the sources of credit that businesses need in our economy to help it grow. That's why the Fed is reacting the way they are. We believe the actions by the Fed will help financial institutions continue to make more credit available.

This morning the Federal Reserve, with support of the Treasury Department, took additional actions to mitigate disruptions to our financial markets. Today's events are fast moving, but the Chairman of the Federal Reserve and the Secretary of the Treasury are on top of them and will take the appropriate steps to promote stability in our markets.

Now, a root cause of the economic slowdown has been the downturn in the housing market, and I want to talk a little bit about that today. After years of steady increases, home values in some parts of the country have declined. At the same time, many homeowners with adjustable rate mortgages have seen their monthly payments increase faster than their ability to pay. As a result, a growing number of people are facing the prospect of foreclosure.

Foreclosure places a terrible burden on our families. Foreclosure disrupts communities. And so the question is, what do you do about it in a way that allows the market to work and, at the same times, helps peo-ple? Before I get to that, though, I do want to tell you that we fully understand that the mounting concern over housing has shaken the broader market; that it's spread uncertainty to global financial markets; and that it has tightened the credit, which makes it harder for people to get mortgages in the first place.

The temptation is for people, in their attempt to limit the number of foreclosures, is to put bad law in place. And so I want to talk about some of that. First of all, the temptation of Washington is to say that anything short of a massive Government intervention in the housing market amounts to inaction. I strongly disagree with that sentiment. I believe there ought to be action, but I'm deeply concerned about law and regulation that will make it harder for the markets to recover, and when they recover, make it harder for this economy to be robust. And so we got to be careful and mindful that any time the Government intervenes in the market, it must do so with clear purpose and great care. Government actions are—have far-reaching and unintended consequences.

I want to talk to you about a couple of ideas that I strongly reject. First, one bill in Congress would provide $4 billion for State and local governments to buy up abandoned and foreclosed homes. You know, I guess this sounds like a good idea to some, but if your goal is to help Americans keep their homes, it doesn't make any sense to spend billions of dollars buying up homes that are already empty. As a matter of fact, when you buy up empty homes, you're only helping the lenders or the speculators. The purpose of government ought to be to help the individuals, not those who, like—who speculated in homes. This bill sends the wrong signal to the market.

Secondly, some have suggested we change the bankruptcy courts, the bankruptcy code, to give bankruptcy judges the authority to reduce mortgage debts by judicial decree. I think that sends the wrong message. It would be unfair to millions of homeowners who have made the hard spending choices necessary to pay their mortgages on time. It would further rattle credit markets. It would actually cause interest rates to go up. If banks think that judges might step in and write down the value of home loans, they're going to charge higher interest rates to cover that risk. This idea would make it harder for responsible first-time homebuyers to be able to afford a home.

There are some in Washington who say we ought to artificially prop up home prices. You know, it sounds reasonable in a speech, I guess, but it's not going to help first-time homebuyers, for example. A lot of people have been priced out of the market right now because of decisions made by others. The market is in the process of correcting itself; markets must have time to correct. Delaying that correction would only prolong the problem.

And so that's why we oppose those proposals, and I want to talk about what we're for. We're obviously for sending out over $150 billion into the marketplace in the form of checks that will be reaching the mailboxes by the second week of May. We're for that. We're also for helping a targeted group of homeowners, namely those who have made responsible buying decisions, avoid foreclosure with some help.

We've taken three key steps. First, we launched a new program at the Federal Housing Administration called FHASecure. It's a program that's given FHA greater flexibility to offer refinancing for struggling homeowners with otherwise good credit. In other words, we're saying to people: We want to help you refinance your notes. Over the past 6 months, this program has helped about 120,000 families stay in their homes by refinancing about $17 billion worth of mortgages. And by the end of the year, we expect this program to have reached 300,000 families.

You know the issue like I do, though. I'm old enough to remember savings and loans, and remember who my savings and

loan officer was who loaned me my first money to buy a house. And had I got in a bind, I could have walked across the street in Midland, Texas, and say: I need a little help. Can you help me readjust my note so I can stay in my house? There are no such things as that type of deal anymore. As a matter of fact, the paper— you know, had this been a modern era, the paper that had—you know, my paper, my mortgage, could be owned by somebody in a foreign country, which makes it hard to renegotiate the note.

So we're dealing in a difficult environment—to get the word to people, there's help for you to refinance your homes. And so Hank Paulson put together what's called the HOPE NOW Alliance to try to bring some reality to the situation, to focus our help on helping creditworthy people refinance, rather than pass law that will make it harder for the market to adjust. This HOPE NOW Alliance is made up of industry—is made up of investors and service managers and mortgage counselors and lenders. And they set industry-wide standards to streamline the process for refinancing and modifying certain mortgages.

Last month, HOPE NOW created a new program. They take a look—they took a look at the risks, and they created a program called Project Lifeline, which offers some homeowners facing imminent foreclosure a 30-day extension. The whole purpose is to help people stay in their houses. During this time they can work with their lender. And this grace period has made a difference to a lot of folks.

An interesting statistic that has just been released: Members of the Alliance report that the number of homeowners working out their mortgages is now rising faster than the number entering foreclosure. The program is beginning to work; it's beginning to help. The problem we have is a lot of folks aren't responding to over a million letters sent out to offer them assistance and mortgage counseling. And so one of the tasks we have is to continue to urge our citizens to respond to the help, to pay attention to the notices they get describing how they can find help in refinancing their homes. We got toll-free numbers and web sites and mailings, and it's just really important for our citizens to understand that this help is available for them.

We've also taken some other steps that will bring some credibility and confidence to the market. Alphonso Jackson, Secretary of HUD, is proposing a rule that require lenders to provide a standard, easy-to-read summary statements explaining the key elements of mortgage agreements. These mortgage agreements can be pretty frightening to people; I mean, there's a lot of tiny print. And I don't know how many people understood they were buying resets or not. But one thing is for certain: There needs to be complete transparency. And to the extent that these contracts are too complex and people made decisions that they just weren't sure they were making, we need to do something about it. We need better confidence amongst those who are purchasing loans.

And secondly, yesterday Hank Paulson announced new recommendations to strengthen oversight of the mortgage industry and improve the way the credit ratings are determined for securities and ensure proper risk management at financial institutions. In other words, we've got an active plan to help us get through this rough period. We're always open for new ideas, but there are certain principles that we won't violate. And one of the principles is overreacting by Federal law and Federal regulation that will have long-term negative effects on our economy.

There are some further things we can do, by the way, on the housing market, that I call upon Congress to do. By the way, Congress did pass a good bill that creates a 3-year window for American families to refinance their homes without paying taxes on any debt forgiveness they receive. The Tax Code created disincentives for people to refinance their homes, and we

took care of that for a 3-year period. And they need to move forward with reforms on Fannie Mae and Freddie Mac. They need to continue to modernize the FHA, as well as allow State housing agencies to issue tax-free bonds to homeowners to refinance their mortgages.

Congress can also take other steps to help us during a period of uncertainty, and these are uncertain times. A major source of uncertainty is that the tax relief we passed in 2001 and 2003 is set to expire. If Congress doesn't act, 116 million American households will see their taxes rise by an average of $1,800. If Congress doesn't act, capital gains and dividends are going to be taxed at a higher rate. If Congress doesn't make the tax relief permanent, they will create additional uncertainty during uncertain times.

A lot of folks are waiting to see what Congress intends to do. One thing it's certain that Congress will do is waste some of your money. So I've challenged Members of Congress to cut the number of— cost of earmarks in half. I issued an Executive order that directs Federal agencies to ignore any future earmark that is not voted on by the Congress. In other words, Congress has got this habit of just sticking these deals into bills without a vote; no transparency, no light of day, they just put them in. And by the way, this Executive order extends beyond my Presidency, so the next President gets to make a decision as to whether or not that Executive order stays in effect.

I sent Congress a budget that meets our priorities. There is no greater priority than to make sure our troops in harm way have all they need to do their job. That has been a priority ever since I made the difficult commitment to put those troops in harm's way, and it should be a priority of any President and any Congress. And beyond that, we've held spending at below rates of inflation; on nonsecurity spending, discretionary spending, we've held the line. And that's why I can tell you that we've submitted a budget that's in balance by 2012, without raising your taxes.

If the Congress truly wants to send a message that will calm people's nerves, they'll adopt the budget I submitted to them and make it clear they're not going to run up the taxes on the working people, and on small businesses, and on capital gains, and on dividends, and on the estate tax.

Now, one powerful force for economic growth that is under—is being questioned right now in Washington is whether or not this country is confident enough to open up markets overseas, whether or not we believe in trade. I believe strongly it's in our Nation's interest to open up markets for U.S. goods and services. I believe strongly that NAFTA has been positive for the United States of America, like it's been positive for our trading partners in Mexico and Canada. I believe it is dangerous for this country to become isolationist and protectionist. I believe it shows a lack of confidence in our capacity to compete. And I know it would harm our economic future if we allow the—those who believe that walling off America from trade to have their way in Congress.

And so I made it clear that we expect for Congress to move forward on the Colombia free trade agreement. And this is an important agreement. It's important for our national security interests, and it's important for our economic interests. Most Americans don't understand that most goods and services from Colombia come into the United States duty free; most of our goods and services are taxed at about a 35-percent rate heading into Colombia. Doesn't it make sense to have our goods and services treated like those from Colombia? I think it does. I think our farmers and ranchers and small-business owners must understand that with the Government finding new markets for them, it'll help them prosper.

But if Congress were to reject the Colombia free trade agreement, it would also send a terrible signal in our own neighborhood. It would bolster the voices of false populism. It would say to young democracies: America's word can't be trusted. It would be devastating for our national security interests if this United States Congress turns its back on Colombia and a free trade agreement with Colombia.

I intend to work the issue hard. I'm going to speak my mind on the issue because I feel strongly about it. And then once they pass the Colombia, they can pass Panama and South Korea as well.

Let me talk about another aspect of keeping markets open. A confident nation accepts capital from overseas. We can protect our people against investments that jeopardize our national security, but it makes no sense to deny capital, including sovereign wealth funds, from access to the U.S. markets. It's our money to begin with. [*Laughter*] It seems like we ought to let it back.

So there's some of the things that are on my mind, and I appreciate you letting me get a chance to come by to speak to you. I'm—you know, I guess the best to describe Government policy is like a person trying to drive a car on a rough patch. If you ever get stuck in a situation like that, you know full well it's important not to overcorrect, because when you overcorrect, you end up in the ditch. And so it's important to be steady and to keep your eyes on the horizon.

We're going to deal with the issues as we see them. We're not afraid to make decisions. This administration is not afraid to act. We saw a problem coming, and we acted quickly with the help of Democrats and Republicans in the Congress. We're not afraid to take on issues. But we will do so in a way that respects the ingenuity of the American people, that bolsters the entrepreneurial spirit, and that ensures when we make it through this rough patch, our driving is going to be more smooth.

Thank you, Glenn, for giving me a chance to come. And I'll answer some questions.

Chairman of the Economic Club of New York R. Glenn Hubbard. Thank you very much, Mr. President.

As is the Club's tradition, we do have two questioners: On my left, Gail Fosler, the president and chief economist of the Conference Board; on my right, literally and metaphorically, Paul Gigot—[*laughter*]—the editorial page editor of the Wall Street Journal.

Gail, the first question for the President is yours.

Gail Fosler. Thank you, very much.

The President. Who picked Gigot? I mean, why does he—[*laughter*]. All right. Excuse me. [*Laughter*]

Ms. Fosler. I'm glad you don't know me, Mr. President.

The President. Yeah, well—[*laughter*]. I'd be more polite, trust me. [*Laughter*] My mother might be watching. [*Laughter*]

Education/Trade/U.S. Foreign Policy

Ms. Fosler. I would like to probe your thoughts on trade. You raised trade in your speech very passionately. And the Conference Board is made up of 2,000 businesses around the world; about a third of them are outside of the United States. And they look at the move toward protectionism in the United States with great alarm, even the shift in the Republican Party toward protectionism. And you mention that a confident nation opens its borders, and there does seem to be a lack of confidence in this country. And I wonder if you would give us a diagnosis of why we find ourselves in the situation we do today?

The President. First of all, a lot of folks are worried about their neighbors losing work. In other words, they fear jobs moving overseas. And the best way to address that is to recognize that sometimes people lose work because of trade. And when that happens, the best way to deal with it is to provide educational opportunities so some-body can get the skills necessary to fill the higher paying jobs here in the United States.

And I think, for example, of what happened to the textile industry in North Carolina. And stories like these really do affect how people think about trade. You know, some companies because of mismanagement, some companies because of trade couldn't survive. And it created a wholesale displacement of workers throughout North Carolina. And what the State of North Carolina did was, they wisely used their community college system to be able to fit needs and skills.

In other words, a community college system—the interesting thing about it, it's probably the most market-driven education system in the United States. Unlike some higher education institutions that are either unwilling or sometimes incapable of adjusting curriculum, the community college system is capable of doing that.

And North Carolina recognized they had a great opportunity to become a magnet for the health care industry. And a lot of their textile workers—with Government help, called trade adjustment assistance—went to community colleges to gain new skills. And it turns out that when you analyze what happened, just the added value, just kind of the increase in productivity and the relevancy of the job training, made the wages higher for those than they were in the textile industry. There's a classic example of how to respond, rather than throwing up trade barriers.

Secondly, a lot of people don't understand this fact: that by having our markets open, it's good for consumers. The more consumers get to choose, the more choice there is on the shelves, the less likely it is there will be inflation. And one of the great things about open markets is that markets respond to the collective wisdom of consumers. And so therefore, it makes sense to have more choice, more opportunities. And yet when you read "made from another country" on the shelves of our stores, people automatically assume that jobs are fragile. And so we've got to do a better job of educating people about the benefits of trade.

Third, it's—sometimes, when times are tough, it's easy to—it's much easier to find a—somebody else to blame. And sometimes that somebody else that's easier to blame is somebody in a distant land.

And so those are some of the fact—and plus it's easy politics. It's easy to go around and hammer away on trade. It's—and I guess if you're the kind of person that followed polls and focus groups, that's what your tendency to be. I'm the kind of person who doesn't give a darn about polls and focus groups, and I do what I think is right. And what is right is making sure that— [*applause*]. And sometimes if you're going to lead this country, you have to stand in the face of what appears to be a political headwind.

So those are some of the dynamics that makes it hard. And I'm troubled by isolationism and protectionism. As a matter of fact, I dedicated part of my State of the Union Address a couple of years ago to this very theme. And what concerns me is, is that the United States of America will become fatigued when it comes to fighting off tyrants, or say it's too hard to spread liberty, or use the excuse that just because freedom hadn't flourished in parts of the world, therefore it's not worth trying. And that, as a result, we kind of retrench and lose confidence in our—the values that have made us a great nation in the first place.

But these aren't American values; they're universal values. And the danger of getting tired during this world is any retreat by the America—by America was going to be to the benefit of those who want to do us harm. Now, I understand that since September the 11th, the great tendency is to say we're no longer in danger. Well, that's false; that's false hope. It's either disingenuous or naive, and either one of those attitudes is unrealistic.

And the biggest job we've got is to protect the American people from harm. I don't want to get in another issue, but that's why we better figure out what the enemy is saying on their telephones, if we want to protect you. Notice how I've deftly taken a trade issue and working in all my other issues. [*Laughter*]

But I'm serious about this business about America retreating. And I've got great faith in the transformative power of liberty, and that's what I believe is going to happen in the Middle East. And I understand it undermines the argument of the stability-ites, people who say, you just got to worry about stability. And I'm saying, we better worry about the conditions that caused 19 kids to kill us in the first place.

And the best way to deal with hopelessness is to fight disease, like we're doing in Africa, and fight forms of government that suppress people's rights, like we're doing around the world. And a retreat from that attitude is going to make America less secure and the world more dangerous, just like a loss of confidence in trade.

And yet the two run side by side, isolationism and protectionism. I might throw another "ism," and that's nativism. And that's what happened throughout our history. And probably the most grim reminder of what can happen to America during periods of isolationism and protectionism is what happened in the late—in the thirties, when we had this America first policy and Smoot-Hawley. And look where it got us.

And so I guess to answer your question: There needs to be political courage, in the face of what may appear to be a difficult headwind, in order to speak clearly about the effects of retreat and the benefits of trade. And so I appreciate you giving me a chance to opine. [*Laughter*]

Mr. Hubbard. Thank you, Mr. President. The second and final——

The President. Never bashful, never short of opinions. Okay, go ahead. [*Laughter*] Just like my mother. [*Laughter*]

Mr. Hubbard. The second and final question for the President is from Paul Gigot.

Monetary Policy/Energy

Paul Gigot. Welcome to New York, Mr. President. And I want to ask you about something you didn't—an issue you didn't address, which is prices.

The President. Which is what?

Mr. Gigot. Prices. Gasoline is selling for $4 a gallon in some parts of the country, but food prices are also rising very fast: grain prices, meat prices, health care prices. And the dollar is weak around the world, hitting a record low this week against the Euro. The price of gold is now about $1,000 an ounce. Many observers say all of this means that we have an inflation problem. Do you agree with them, and what can be done about it?

The President. I agree that the Fed needs to be independent and make considered judgments and balance growth versus inflation. And let me address some of those issues one by one.

We believe in a strong dollar. I recognize economies go up and down, but it's important for us to put policy in place that sends a signal that our economy is going to be strong and open for business, which will—you know, which supports the strong dollar policy, such as not doing something foolish during this economic period that will cause—make it harder to grow; such as rejecting—shutting down capital from coming into this country; such as announcing that—or articulating the belief that making the tax cuts permanent takes uncertainty out of the system.

Energy, our energy policy has not been very wise. You can't build a refinery in the United States; you can't expand a refinery in the United States. The Congress believes we shouldn't be drilling for oil and gas in a productive part of our country like ANWR because it will destroy the environment, which, in fact, it won't. Technology is such that will enable us to find more oil and gas. And so as a result of us not having, you know, been robust in exploring for oil and gas at home, we're dependent on other countries. That creates an economics issue, obviously, and it creates a national security issue.

And, look, I'm very—I'm an alternatives fuel guy; I believe that's important. As a matter of fact, we've expanded—mightily expanded the use of ethanol—a slight consequence if you rely upon corn to grow your hogs. But nevertheless, it's a—it is a policy that basically says that we got to diversify. But diversification does not happen overnight. You know, I firmly believe people in New York City are going to be driving automobiles on battery relatively quickly. And it's not going to be like a golf cart, it'll be a regular-sized vehicle that you'll be driving in. [*Laughter*] And I think it's coming. I think this technology is on its way.

But there's a transition period, and we, frankly, have got policies that make it harder for us to become less dependent on oil. You talk about the price of oil—yeah, it's high. It's high because demand is greater than supply, is why it's high. It's high because there's new factors in demand on the international market, namely China and India. It's also high because some nations have not done a very good job of maintaining their oil reserves, some of it because of bureaucracy, some of it because of state-owned enterprise. And it's a difficult period for our folks at the pump, and there's no quick fix.

You know, when I was overseas in the Middle East, people said, "Did you talk to the King of Saudi about oil prices?" Of course I did. I reminded him two things: One, you better be careful about affecting markets—reminding him that oil is fungible; even though we get most of our oil, by the way, from Canada and Mexico, oil is fungible. And secondly, the higher the price of oil, the more capital is going to come into alternative sources of energy.

And so we've got a plan that calls for diversification, but it's—our energy policy hasn't been very wise up to now.

Anyway, I'm going to dodge the rest of your question. [*Laughter*] Thank you for your time.

NOTE: The President spoke at 11:20 a.m. at the Hilton New York. In his remarks, he referred to King Abdallah bin Abd al-Aziz Al Saud of Saudi Arabia. The Office of the Press Secretary also released a Spanish language transcript of these remarks.

Message on the Observance of Saint Patrick's Day, 2008
March 14, 2008

I send greetings to those celebrating St. Patrick's Day.

On this day, we commemorate the great faith of St. Patrick and celebrate the rich heritage of the Irish people. The Apostle of Ireland was committed to preaching a gospel of peace even in the face of great hardship, and people of all faiths can be inspired by his remarkable example. During St. Patrick's Day, we join together with the many children of Erin who have come to our shores full of hope and purpose, and found success.

Americans are grateful for our country's Irish traditions and the deep friendship that exists between Ireland and the United States. Irish Americans have valiantly defended our Nation, enriched our culture, and contributed to our prosperity. We are reminded, in celebrating, of our history as a Nation of immigrants and of our responsibility to remain a welcoming society.

Laura and I send our best wishes for a blessed and joyous St. Patrick's Day.

GEORGE W. BUSH

NOTE: An original was not available for verification of the content of this message.

The President's Radio Address
March 15, 2008

Good morning. On Friday, I traveled to New York City to talk about the state of our economy. This is a topic that has been a source of concern for families across America. In the long run, we can be confident that our economy will continue to grow. But in the short run, it is clear that growth has slowed.

Fortunately, we recognized this slowdown early and took action to give our economy a shot in the arm. My administration worked with Congress to pass a bipartisan economic growth package that includes tax relief for families and incentives for business investment. I signed this package into law last month, and its provisions are just starting to kick in. My economic team, along with many outside experts, expects this stimulus package to have a positive effect on our economy in the second quarter. And they expect it to have even a stronger effect in the third quarter, when the full effects of the $152 billion in tax cuts are felt.

A root cause of the economic slowdown has been the downturn in the housing market. I believe the Government can take sensible, focused action to help responsible homeowners weather this rough patch. But we must do so with clear purpose and great care, because Government actions often have far-reaching and unintended consequences. If we were to pursue some of the sweeping Government solutions that we hear about in Washington, we would make a complicated problem even worse and end up hurting far more homeowners than we help.

For example, one proposal would give bankruptcy courts the authority to reduce mortgage debts by judicial decree. This would make it harder to afford a home in the future because banks would charge higher interest rates to cover this risk.

Some in Washington say the Government should take action to artificially prop up home prices. It's important to understand that this would hurt millions of Americans. For example, many young couples trying to buy their first home have been priced out of the market because of inflated prices. The market now is in the process of correcting itself, and delaying that correction would only prolong the problem.

My administration opposes these proposals. Instead, we are focused on helping a targeted group of homeowners, those who have made responsible buying decisions and could avoid foreclosure with a little help. We've taken three key steps to help these homeowners.

First, we launched a new program that gives the Federal Housing Administration greater flexibility to offer refinancing for struggling homeowners with otherwise good credit histories. Second, we helped bring together the HOPE NOW Alliance, which is streamlining the process for refinancing and modifying many mortgages. Third, the Federal Government is taking regulatory steps to make the housing market more transparent and fair in the long run.

And now Congress must build on these efforts. Members need to pass legislation to reform Fannie Mae and Freddie Mac, modernize the Federal Housing Administration, and allow State housing agencies to issue tax-free bonds to help homeowners refinance their mortgages.

Congress also needs to take other steps to help our economy through this period of uncertainty. Members need to make the tax relief we passed permanent, reduce wasteful spending, and open new markets for American goods, services, and investment.

By taking these steps and avoiding bad policy decisions, we will see our economy strengthen as the year progresses. As we take decisive action, we will keep this in mind: When you are steering a car in a rough patch, one of the worst things you can do is overcorrect. That often results in losing control and can end up with the car in a ditch. Steering through a rough patch requires a steady hand on the wheel and your eyes up on the horizon. And that's exactly what we're going to do.

Thank you for listening.

NOTE: The address was recorded at 7:20 a.m. on March 14 in the Cabinet Room at the White House for broadcast at 10:06 a.m. on March 15. The transcript was made available by the Office of the Press Secretary on March 14, but was embargoed for release until the broadcast. The Office of the Press Secretary also released a Spanish language transcript of this address.

Remarks Following a Meeting With Economic Advisers on the National Economy
March 17, 2008

Mr. Secretary, thank you very much for coming by today to talk about the economic situation. We'll be meeting later on this afternoon with the President's task force on financial markets.

First of all, you know, the Secretary has given me an update. One thing is for certain: We're under—we're in challenging times. But another thing is for certain, that we've taken strong and decisive action. The Federal Reserve has moved quickly to bring order to the financial markets. Secretary Paulson has been—is supportive of that action, as am I. And I want to thank you, Mr. Secretary, for working over the weekend. You've shown the country and the world that the United States is on top of the situation.

Secondly, you've reaffirmed the fact that our financial institutions are strong and that our capital markets are functioning efficiently and effectively. We obviously will continue to monitor the situation and, when need be, will act decisively, in a way that continues to bring order to the financial markets.

In the long run, our economy is going to be fine. Right now we're dealing with a difficult situation. And, Mr. Secretary, I want to thank you very much for your steady and strong and consistent leadership.

Thank you very much.

NOTE: The President spoke at 9:40 a.m. in the Roosevelt Room at the White House.

Remarks Following Discussions With Prime Minister Bertie Ahern of Ireland
March 17, 2008

President Bush. Taoiseach, welcome, and happy Saint Patrick's Day. It's always a joy to welcome the *Taoiseach* here to the Oval Office. And it's a reminder of the unbelievably powerful influence the Irish have had on the development and prosperity of the United States of America. We're a richer country because of Irish Americans. And, Mr. Prime Minister, Ireland is a great friend and ally, and I want to thank you for your friendship over these years.

We discussed a variety of issues. In particular, we talked about Northern Ireland. And the *Taoiseach* gets a lot of credit for showing a steady hand during a difficult period. And yet as a result of perseverance and hard work, Northern Ireland is a different place than it was last year. And we congratulate the leaders there. And I just want the folks to know, what I told the *Taoiseach* is true, that the United States will continue to stay engaged and will be very supportive of helping the process move forward.

And there's more work to be done, we fully understand, in Northern Ireland. But also, there's a really interesting chance for people from our country to see the investment opportunities available in Northern Ireland. And this May, there's a Northern Ireland investment conference, which the United States will strongly support. And, *Taoiseach*, like I told you, we'll send a strong delegation to look at the opportunities available there.

So thanks for coming. Thanks for your friendship. And once again, happy Saint Patrick's Day.

Prime Minister Ahern. Thank you very much, President. And I want to thank the President. It's the eighth year that he's afforded us an opportunity of representing the Irish people here. And as always, we've had a very fruitful discussion on a range of issues, and obviously important to me is the ongoing process in Northern Ireland. And the President and his people have been really helpful and—as we move now to the remaining issue, the evolution of policing, which we've discussed.

And the investment conference, which is just around the corner—it's a—I've said it several times before: The investment conference is a—really a one-off chance, an opportunity for Northern Ireland to bring some of the big investors of the world to see the opportunities that are there, the opportunities that they had not had a chance of being able to get any benefit from for the last 30 or 40 years. And now they have that. And I think the—it will show Northern Ireland is a place with well-educated people, hard-working people, people who are good at business if given a half a chance.

And it is hugely important to us that in the organization of this, that the President has helped both the British Government and the Irish Government to get this together. We've gone through that today, and I think the—[*inaudible*]—of the President to make sure that there's a high-powered delegation to United States is hugely helpful. I want to thank the President for that.

And I also want to thank him for the assistance that he's given to us on a range of issues that we've had an opportunity of talking about.

President Bush. Thank you, Bertie. Thanks for coming. Thank you all very much.

NOTE: The President spoke at 11:10 a.m. in the Oval Office at the White House.

Remarks at a Saint Patrick's Day Shamrock Presentation Ceremony With Prime Minister Bertie Ahern of Ireland
March 17, 2008

Taoiseach, thanks. Small island, huge impact on the United States of America. [*Laughter*] Laura and I are glad you're here. We welcome you back to the White House on this Saint Patrick's Day. I can't think of a better way to celebrate it than with the *Taoiseach*. Thanks for the bowl of shamrocks. As you said, this is the eighth time I had the honor of receiving this from you. And I want to thank you for your friendship—your personal friendship—and all you've done to strengthen the deep and lasting bond between our two nations.

Also proud to be here with John O'Donoghue, the Speaker of the Dail. Welcome. Members of my Cabinet who are here, thank you for coming. Members of the United States Senate and the United States Congress who've joined us, we're glad you're here. And I know the *Taoiseach* is glad you're here too. [*Laughter*] He was asking me, "Are you in session?" I said, "No, they're out of town." He said, "Well, you must be feeling better about that." [*Laughter*] We'll be having lunch with you soon.

How about members of the fire department of New York's Emerald Society? I thank you for coming. They proudly carry the title "New York's bravest" and rightly so.

And finally, I will be introducing soon Ronan Tynan to entertain us a little bit. He is a wonderful representative of your country. He's a dear friend of the Bush family, and we're so thankful he is here with us today.

You know, *Taoiseach*, you were awfully diplomatic to talk about the fact that the architect came back to rebuild the White House after 1814. What, of course, you didn't say was why the White House needed to be rebuilt in the first place. [*Laughter*] And so I'm proud to welcome the Ambassador from Great Britain, our dear friend. [*Laughter*] Thanks for coming.

I don't know if you know this, but America held its first Saint Patrick's Day celebration in Boston in the year 1737. I don't think you were there, Congressman, but—[*laughter*]—shortly thereafter. [*Laughter*] Nearly 40 years later, in the midst of the Revolution, at least 9 of the 56 signatures on the Declaration of Independence were inked by Irish hands.

We've had a long relationship, *Taoiseach*. Our history has been one where the United States and Ireland have made liberty our common cause, and both of our nations are richer for it. Our partnership is based upon principles, and it's also based upon people. Ireland founded itself—found itself in the grip of poverty and famine in the 19th century, and millions of Irish came here to our soil. They were drawn here by a promise that success would be attainable to all those who were willing to work hard. And that's certainly what happened.

It's an interesting poster that somebody brought to my attention that said this: "In the United States, an industrious youth may follow any occupation without being looked down upon, and he may rationally expect to raise himself in the world by his labor." You know, occasionally, people did look down, but not anymore, because Irish have been unbelievably productive people for the United States of America. They've made a huge contribution. They've become an essential thread in the American fabric.

And that's what we celebrate on Saint Patrick's Day. Our countries are more than just partners; we are family, *Taoiseach*. And today, more than 35 million Americans claim Irish ancestry. America is richer for every Murphy, Kelly, and O'Sullivan. I should have said McCain, but—[*laughter*]. Well, I just did. [*Laughter*] After all this history together, the United States and the Republic of Ireland continue to stand side by side in firm friendship. We were friends in the past, we're friends today, and, *Taoiseach*, I am confident, after my time in office, the next President will be friends with Ireland. We are cooperating to build prosperous economies and—with vibrant trade and sound investment between our countries.

I want to congratulate the *Taoiseach*. He was very generous in his praise about America's role, previous administration's role—hopefully, our role—in helping Northern Ireland have a peaceful future. But, *Taoiseach*, the truth of the matter is, I said on TV in there that you've had a steady hand, and you've been supportive. And I do want to applaud those who are here who've shown great courage, who've been able to put together—put beside—behind them a terrible past and focused on a hopeful future. And it was my huge honor, Martin, to welcome you and Dr. Paisley to the Oval Office. It was an historic moment for me, personally. And it was really, really positive.

But I came away with the impression that obviously the United States needs to help, and we will. But nothing will happen without clear conviction and determination by the folks who live in Northern Ireland. And there's more work to be done, *Taoiseach*. As you said, the devolution of policing is important, and we support that. But we can also help by sending a clear signal that we're interested in investment opportunities. And so the Northern Ireland investment conference in May will be held. And I want to repeat what I told the *Taoiseach*, is that we will send a high-level delegation to not only send a signal that we support the efforts of the folks in Northern Ireland, but we expect our folks to be able to find good investment opportunities—for the good of both.

And so, *Taoiseach*, I, like you, marvel at the success that's taken place since my short time as President and know full well that more progress can and will be made.

You know, there's an old Irish proverb that says, "There is no strength without unity." And so on this Saint Patrick's Day, we can all take pride in the way that the United States and Ireland have come together to enrich each other in the world.

My last time as President to have a Saint Patrick's Day with you, *Taoiseach*. Perhaps when we join the ex-leaders club, we'll sit back and put our feet up—[*laughter*]—and talk about the good old times. In the mean-

time, I know you're going to sprint to the finish, as am I, for the good of our countries.

Thank you for coming. God bless the people of Ireland and the United States. And now I welcome Ronan Tynan.

NOTE: The President spoke at 11:30 a.m. in the East Room at the White House. In his remarks, he referred to Chairman of the Dail Eireann John O'Donoghue of Ireland; FDNY Emerald Society Pipes and Drums, which performed prior to the remarks; the United Kingdom's Ambassador to the U.S. Sir Nigel E. Sheinwald; and First Minister Ian R.K. Paisley and Deputy First Minister Martin McGuinness of Northern Ireland. The transcript released by the Office of the Press Secretary also included the remarks of Prime Minister Ahern.

Remarks at the Jacksonville Port Authority in Jacksonville, Florida
March 18, 2008

Thank you all. Please be seated. Thank you for the warm welcome. It's nice to be back in J-ville. It's an interesting place to come, isn't it? I've been in your stadium. I've been in your church. I've never been on the docks. But if you're interested in trying to figure out one of the reasons why this is one of America's most vibrant cities, you got to come to the docks.

And I want to explain why these docks are important to not only the citizens of Jacksonville, but also why what happens here is important to the overall economy in the United States.

Before I do, I do want to thank *Senor* Morales. Thank you for your leading here as the chairman of the Jacksonville Port Authority. Thanks for being the kind of American we love, somebody who comes from abroad, recognizes the great blessings of the United States of America, and contributes mightily to our success.

I appreciate the executive director, Rick Ferrin. I've just had an interesting tour of this facility by Magnus Lindeback, Captain Magnus Lindeback. [*Applause*] Magnus, it sounds like some of them have heard of you around here. [*Laughter*] I'm going to talk about Magnus a little later on. He's a fellow who came to America with a dream and now employs a lot of good, hard-working folks because of goods that are shipped from here to other parts of the world and for goods that are shipped from other parts of the world to here. See, everybody here is working as a result of trade—trade that happens and occurs right here on these docks.

The Governor of the great State of Florida, Charlie Crist, has joined us. Mr. Governor, proud you're here, thanks for taking time. Two Members from the United States Congress have come—this must be a special occasion—[*laughter*]—Ander Crenshaw, Congressman from this district, doing a find job, and Congresswoman Corrine Brown. Madam Congresswoman, we're proud you're here.

Daniel Davis, president of the Jacksonville City Council, appreciate you coming. A lot of other State and local officials, port authority employees, Coastal Maritime employees, thanks for greeting me here, appreciate you coming.

One thing is for certain: This is a challenging time for our economy. You know that, I know that, a lot of Americans understand that. In the short run, the strains on the economy have been caused by the turmoil in the housing market, which has required focused and decisive action. And that's exactly what the Federal Government's doing.

There are problems, but the key is to recognize problems and to act early, which we have done. For example, we brought together what's called the HOPE NOW Alliance. It's a private sector group that is helping large numbers of homeowners refinance their mortgages. We want to help people stay in their homes. And millions of people are going to be affected by this program. And it makes sense to help some person who is creditworthy find the capacity and understand where to refinance. The more people live in their homes, the better off America is. But no question, there's been a oversupply of housing, and it's going to take time to work through this oversupply.

We also worked with Congress—and I want to thank the Members of Congress—to pass a bipartisan economic growth package. That's Washington-speak for, you're fixing to receive some money. By the way, it's your money to begin with. [*Laughter*] But in the second week of May, there is a substantial amount of money being returned to people in the hopes of encouraging increased consumption. There's also incentives in this piece of legislation passed by both Republicans and Democrats that

will encourage small and large businesses to invest. And when businesses invest, as Magnus will tell you, it makes it easier to give people work. Investment equals jobs.

And so in the second week of May, checks will be coming. And the experts tell me this is going to help with the economic vitality of the country. After all, it's a—over $150 billion that is going to be distributed. The plan was voted on; I signed it into law, but it hadn't been put completely into effect yet.

Our financial markets have also been subjected to stress. And the Federal Reserve and the Treasury acted swiftly to promote stability in our financial markets at a crucial time. It was action that was necessary, and I appreciate the leadership of Chairman Bernanke and Secretary Paulson. And they'll continue to closely monitor the markets in the financial sector. And the point I want to make to you is, if there needs to be further action, we'll take it, in a way that does not damage the long-term health of our economy.

In the long run, Americans ought to have confidence in our economy. I mean, there are some anchors that promote long-term—that should promote long-term confidence. Let me give you a few. First of all, the unemployment rate is relatively low. We've got a low unemployment rate here in Florida, low in most parts of the country. We're an innovative society with a flexible economy. But there's a lot of research and development being spent here in America. There are new technologies being developed. Productivity is on the rise. We have a strong agricultural sector. The small-business sector is vibrant. And people are investing in the United States. And so I understand there's short-term difficulty, but I want people to understand that in the long term, we're going to be just fine. People will still be able to work.

You know, one of the interesting signs of strength is that we're the world's leading exporter of goods and services. I'm not saying we're second place or third place; we're the world's leading exporter. And that's positive, particularly if you're somebody whose job depends upon trade.

Now, we're in the middle of a debate here about trade, whether it's good or not. Well, anybody wondering about the stakes in the trade debate ought to come right here to Jacksonville, Florida, to the docks to see whether or not trade makes sense. According to the most recent data, you move more than 8 million tons of cargo each year. This cargo doesn't move itself. Somebody has to move it from port to port.

I'm sitting in—standing in front of people that are all part of the process, good, hard-working Americans that are putting food on the table for their families because of trade. You handle most—more than— more automobiles than any American port. I don't know if the people of Jacksonville understand that, but think about that. More automobiles are handled at this port than anywhere in the United States of America. You help support more than 45,000 jobs. This port serves as a vital commercial and strategic link to our neighborhood, to our neighbors in Latin America and the Caribbean.

Opening trade has been one of the high priorities of my Presidency. See, I believe trade leads to good jobs. I believe trade is in our interests. When I took office, America had free trade agreements in force with three countries. Today, we have agreements in force with 14 countries. And there are three more agreements pending this year: Colombia, Panama, and South Korea. All three of these agreements are important, and the one with Colombia is especially urgent. And I want to spend a little time talking about the free trade agreement with Colombia and what it means for our national security and what it means for your job security.

We have worked closely with leaders in Congress to seek a path to bring the Colombia agreement up for approval. And we've got a good model to go on. Last year, we worked out a bipartisan approach

on a bill implementing a good free trade agreement with Peru, and it was a good bill. And it was one of those bills where people, when they stepped back from politics, realized it made good sense and overwhelmingly approved it. Both Republicans and Democrats voted for that, two of whom happen to be sitting right here.

The Colombia agreement is almost identical to the agreement with Peru, except that the Colombia agreement has even greater economic potential because Colombia has a larger GDP and even greater national security importance because of Colombia's strategic location. The lesson is clear: If Congress can find a way to vote on and improve the Peru agreement, there's no reason it can't do the same for Colombia.

Now, why is it important? Before I get to the importance, I do want to tell you the time is urgent. There must be a vote on Colombia this year. And this agreement is too important to be delayed any longer. So I am reiterating my call on leaders in Congress to act with urgency. I ask members of both parties to ensure that politics do not get in the way of a vital priority for our Nation and, frankly, a vote that will help people who are working here on the docks. You can think in terms of national security interests, but if that doesn't interest you, think about terms of helping folks just like this make a living.

Let me talk a little bit about the national security implications from this vote. In Colombia, President Uribe is waging an active battle against terrorists who are seeking to overthrow his nation's democracy. This terrorist network is known as FARC. It pursues Marxist objectives through bombing, hostage-taking, and assassination. Much of its funding is derived from drug trafficking. Attacks by the FARC have killed or injured more than 1,000 civilians since 2003. These are brutal people, and they're ruthless people. And they'll use all kinds of means to achieve their objectives. FARC terrorists have held three American citizens hostage in jungle camps for more than 5 years, making them the longest held American hostages anywhere in the world.

The challenge posed by these terrorists is compounded by the hostility and aggression of some of Colombia's neighbors. The regime in Caracas has railed against America, has forged an alliance with Communist Cuba, has met with FARC leaders in Venezuela, has deployed troops to the Colombian border. In the process, regime leaders have squandered their oil wealth and left their people to face food shortages.

Recently, when Colombian forces killed one of the FARC's most senior leaders, they discovered computer files that suggest even closer ties between Venezuela's regime and FARC terrorists than we previously knew. Colombia officials are investigating the ties, but this much should be clear: The United States strongly supports, strongly stands with Colombia in its fight against the terrorists and drug lords.

President Uribe has remained focused on strengthening Colombia's democracy. Over the past 6 years, kidnapings, terrorist attacks, and murders of labor activists have all dropped by more than 75 percent. Police are on the streets. Tens of thousands of paramilitary fighters have been demobilized. And Colombia's murder rate has fallen substantially.

At the same time, Colombia's economy has shown strong growth. Poverty and unemployment have declined. Trade and investment have increased substantially. That's what we want. We want less violence in our neighborhood and more prosperity in our neighborhood. We want our neighbors to be prosperous.

President Uribe has been an unshakeable partner for the United States. He's answered to hundreds of requests to extradite criminals to our country. And with the assistance from Plan Colombia, a program first supported by President Bill Clinton and continued under my administration, he's cracked down on drug trafficking. He constantly speaks out against anti-Ameri-

canism. By any measure, he has been one of the most—our most reliable and effective allies. And this trade agreement is the way to signal our strong support for President Uribe. It's the way to help this country develop more momentum toward peace.

Despite the record of success, some in Congress came—claim Colombia needs to do more before a treat agreement—the trade agreement can be approved. But this is unrealistic, and it is unfair. If Members of Congress truly want Colombia to make further progress, then it makes no sense to block the very measure that would make progress more likely.

Our fellow citizens have got to know that across the hemisphere and across the globe, people are waiting to see what the Members of Congress will do. In other words, this isn't just one of these isolated votes that gets no attention outside of Washington, this is a vote that is being observed very carefully by people across the world. Voices from near and far are urging Congress to make the right decision. Members of Congress from both parties travel to Colombia. They have seen firsthand the progress that President Uribe is making. Business leaders from many backgrounds, along with current and former Senators, Congressmens, mayors, diplomats, National Security Council people, Cabinet members from both parties—I emphasize, from both parties—support this agreement.

In other words, it's just not me talking. There's a lot of people who understand the importance of this agreement. Our allies have made their position clear. I want the Members of Congress to hear what the Prime Minister of Canada, Stephen Harper, said. He said, "If the U.S. turns its back on its friends in Colombia, this will set back our cause far more than any Latin American dictator can hope to achieve." Those are wise words and words worth listening to. Congress needs to listen to the voices, and they need to pass this important piece of legislation.

The national security benefits are only part of the cause for this agreement. Both our economies stand to gain as well. Today, virtually all exports from Colombia enter our country duty free. And yet many U.S. exports going to Colombia face heavy tariffs. Goods coming from Colombia, duty free; our goods going to Colombia get taxed. That doesn't seem fair to me. I know the folks here understand that if you reduce tariffs, it's more likely we'll send more goods. Doesn't it make sense for Congress to say to Colombia, treat America the way we treat you, which is precisely what this trade deal does?

A banana grown in Colombia enters the United States duty free. An apple grown in Pennsylvania or an orange grown in Florida is subject to a 15-percent tariff when it's exported to Colombia. Doesn't it make sense for the Federal Government to try to eliminate that tariff? I think it does. If you're growing oranges, it does. If you're growing apples, it does. And if you're shipping goods and services—or goods from this port to Colombia, it makes sense to make it easier to ship more goods.

That's why I talk about level the playing field. They estimate this will help 9,000 U.S. companies export to Colombia, most of which are small and midsized companies. Level the playing field is going to help hundreds of thousands of employees who work at these companies. And level the playing field will create new opportunities for exporters and dock workers who ship heavy machinery and glass and chemicals and electronics and paper and other products to Colombia from this port, people just like the folks seated right here.

Earlier today I had a chance to tour this company with Magnus Lindeback, Captain Magnus Lindeback. The man is living the American Dream. You talk to Magnus, he's about as proud of American as you can find. He might not have been born here, but he loves it here. And he loves the people that work with him, and he's very proud of the fact that this company has grown from 2 employees to over 250. And he cares about each and every employee.

And here's why the Colombia free trade agreement matters to a—are you small or midsize? I'd call you—oh, midsize. You say small; I say midsize. Okay, small. [*Laughter*] Here's why it matters to a small-sized, midsized company like Coastal Maritime. [*Laughter*] Coastal Maritime—about a quarter of its cargo goes to Colombia. So in other words, if you're somebody wondering whether you're going to have a job and a fellow comes along and says, "Would you like to be able to sell more goods to Colombia? After all, a quarter of your revenues go to Colombia," I think the answer ought to be, yes, we want to be able to access more of Colombia. We're good at what we're doing now.

They send, by the way, mining equipment, bulldozers, and cranes. Magnus doesn't make the cranes and bulldozers and mining equipment. He just ships it. But somebody in America is making the cranes, and somebody in America is making the bulldozers. And so when you think about trade, you're not only thinking about dock workers who are working good jobs because of trade, but somebody has got to make the products that the people in Colombia are buying as well.

If Colombia approves the free trade agreement, Coastal Maritime estimates that the volume of products they ship to Colombia would increase by 20 to 50 percent in a short period of time. Magnus says he's going to use the extra revenues for two purposes: to reinvest in technology and equipment—like that crane we—a guy tried to get me to drive over there—[*laughter*]—I told him I was a history major—[*laughter*]—and he wants to raise wages for his workers.

I want to quote Magnus: "Trade is our entire business. All our workers depend on it. An increased volume of cargo to Colombia would be tremendous from us because the more cargo we have to handle, the more revenue is generated."

American exporters aren't the only ones who will benefit. The free trade agreement will guarantee permanent duty-free access to the U.S. market for businesses in Colombia. And why is that important? Because it will help them attract investment and stimulate growth. It will lead to additional opportunities at a port such as this. The more prosperous our neighborhood, the more commerce there will be. And the more commerce there is, it's more likely to pass through a port just like this. We want people doing well. We want programs that are good for small businesses and farmers. And that's exactly what this vote will be. And it's important. And it's an important vote for the United States Congress to understand. It's in our national security interests and economic security interests.

And during this time of economic uncertainty, when consumer spending and investment is slowing down, it's important to understand the role trade has made for our economy. Last year, exports accounted for more than 40 percent of our total growth. That's good news. Export is continuing. This January, exports were up more than 16 percent over last January. If you're worried about the economy, it seems like you ought to be sending a clear signal that the United States of America will continue to trade, not shut down trade. And that's what this Colombia vote says.

And once Congress approves the free trade agreement with Colombia, they can—then they can approve one with Panama. And once they finish one with Panama, then they can do one with South Korea. All these agreements are important. These agreements to important to enhance our friendship, but these are good for our economy.

Now, I fully understand that trade makes people nervous. It doesn't make these folks nervous because they understand the benefits firsthand. And in a political year, you hear all kinds of things about trade. One of the things people say is that people lose their jobs because of trade. Well, in the manufacturing sector, sometimes that's right, but a lot of times it's a result of productivity increases. In other words, technology changes, and one worker can produce three times as much as he or she used to be able to, and therefore, same output with fewer workers.

But whatever the case is, the question is, what should we do about people who aren't working? One alternative is to say, it's all because of trade, let's quit trading. Then people here lose work. The other opportunity is to focus on good educational programs. You know, we could cut ourselves off, or we could have faith in our capacity to compete and focus on helping individuals. I choose the latter.

I believe strongly that we can help people gain extra skills with smart programs. That's why my budget requests $3 billion to educate and prepare workers for the 21st century. I'm a big believer, Governor, in community colleges. I think our community colleges are great places for people to gain the skills necessary to fill the jobs of the 21st century. So rather than resort to protectionism and say, let's shut down our trading opportunities, why don't we resort to education to give people the skills necessary to fill the jobs for the 21st century here in the United States of America?

Now, you're going to hear the word trade adjustment assistance talked about in Congress. And these two Congress folks understand what I'm talking about. That basically says that we're going to have education programs aimed at helping people find skills. And I'm a supporter. And I believe it's important that trade adjustment be a component of our trade policy. I look forward to working with Congress to reform it and to reauthorize it, to make sure it does the job that it could do—is supposed to do—just like I'm looking forward to signing those trade bills, particularly starting with the one from Colombia.

I—so I've come here as a vivid reminder to people in Congress who wonder whether or not trade is positive for America. It is.

It's economically a good deal for our country. And I do have confidence that Congress will get it right. It may take a little persuading. It's going to take a lot of hard work. Oh, it may take some of you having to write letters to your Senators and Congressmen to remind them that trade is good. Confident nations are free traders.

But trade also means making sure we get treated right, that they treat us the way we treat them. That's all we're asking. That's what this agreement says: Just treat us fairly. Because America can compete with anybody, anytime, anywhere, as long as the playing field is level.

And so I've come to talk about our economy and a key issue facing you. I thank you for giving me the opportunity to be in your midst. I'm proud of the work you do here. And may God bless you and God continue to bless the United States of America.

NOTE: The President spoke at 2:13 p.m. at the Blount Island Marine Terminal. In his remarks, he referred to Ricardo Morales, Jr., chairman of the board of directors, Jacksonville Port Authority; Magnus Lindeback, chief executive officer, Coastal Maritime Stevedoring, LLC; and Marc Gonsalves, Thomas Howes, and Keith Stansell, hostages held by the Revolutionary Armed Forces of Colombia (FARC). The Office of the Press Secretary also released a Spanish language transcript of these remarks.

Remarks on the War on Terror in Arlington, Virginia
March 19, 2008

Thank you all. Deputy Secretary England, thanks for the introduction. One boss may not be here, but the other one is. [*Laughter*] I appreciate your kind words. I'm pleased to be back here with the men and women of the Defense Department.

On this day in 2003, the United States began Operation Iraqi Freedom. As the campaign unfolded, tens and thousands of our troops poured across the Iraqi border to liberate the Iraqi people and remove a regime that threatened free nations.

Five years into this battle, there is an understandable debate over whether the war was worth fighting, whether the fight is worth winning, and whether we can win it. The answers are clear to me: Removing Saddam Hussein from power was the right decision, and this is a fight America can and must win.

The men and women who crossed into Iraq 5 years ago removed a tyrant, liberated a country, and rescued millions from unspeakable horrors. Some of those troops are with us today, and you need to know that the American people are proud of your accomplishment, and so is the Commander in Chief.

I appreciate Admiral Mullen, the Joint Chiefs who are here. Thanks for coming. Secretary Donald Winter of the Navy; Deputy Secretary of State John Negroponte is with us. Admiral Thad Allen of the Coast Guard is with us. Ambassador from Iraq is with us; Mr. Ambassador, we're proud to have you here. Soldiers, sailors, marines, airmen, and coast men—coastguardsmen, thanks for coming; thanks for wearing the uniform. Men and women of the Department of State are here as well.

Operation Iraqi Freedom was a remarkable display of military effectiveness. Forces from the UK, Australia, Poland, and other allies joined our troops in the initial operations. As they advanced, our troops fought their way through sandstorms so intense that they blackened the daytime sky. Our troops engaged in pitched battles with

391

Fedayeen Saddam, death squads acting on the orders of Saddam Hussein, that obeyed neither the conventions of war nor the dictates of conscience. These death squads hid in schools, and they hid in hospitals, hoping to draw fire against Iraqi civilians. They used women and children as human shields. They stopped at nothing in their efforts to prevent us from prevailing, but they couldn't stop the coalition advance.

Aided by the most effective and precise air campaign in history, coalition forces raced across 350 miles of enemy territory, destroying Republican Guard divisions, pushing through the Karbala Gap, capturing Saddam International Airport, and liberating Baghdad in less than 1 month.

Along the way, our troops added new chapters to the story of American military heroism. During these first weeks of battle, Army Sergeant First Class Paul Ray Smith and his troops came under a surprise attack by about a hundred Republican Guard forces. Sergeant Smith rallied his men. He led a counterattack, killing as many as 50 enemy soldiers before being fatally wounded. His actions saved the lives of more than a hundred American troops and earned him the Medal of Honor.

Today, in light of the challenges we have faced in Iraq, some look back at this period as the easy part of the war. Yet there was nothing easy about it. The liberation of Iraq took incredible skill and amazing courage. And the speed, precision, and brilliant execution of the campaign will be studied by military historians for years to come.

What our troops found in Iraq following Saddam's removal was horrifying. They uncovered children's prisons and torture chambers and rape rooms where Iraqi women were violated in front of their families. They found videos showing regime thugs mutilating Iraqis deemed disloyal to Saddam. And across the Iraqi countryside, they uncovered mass graves of thousands executed by the regime.

Because we acted, Saddam Hussein no longer fills fields with the remains of innocent men, women, and children. Because we acted, Saddam's torture chambers and rape rooms and children's prisons have been closed for good. Because we acted, Saddam's regime is no longer invading its neighbors or attacking them with chemical weapons and ballistic missiles. Because we acted, Saddam's regime is no longer paying the families of suicide bombers in the Holy Land. Because we acted, Saddam's regime is no longer shooting at American and British aircraft patrolling the no-fly zones and defying the will of the United Nations. Because we acted, the world is better and United States of America is safer.

When the Iraqi regime was removed, it did not lay down its arms and surrender. Instead, former regime elements took off their uniforms and faded into the countryside to fight the emergence of a free Iraq. And then they were joined by foreign terrorists who were seeking to stop the advance of liberty in the Middle East and seeking to establish safe havens from which to plot new attacks across the world.

The battle in Iraq has been longer and harder and more costly than we anticipated, but it is a fight we must win. So our troops have engaged these enemies with courage and determination. And as they've battled the terrorists and extremists in Iraq, they have helped the Iraqi people reclaim their nation and helped a young democracy rise from the rubble of Saddam Hussein's tyranny.

Over the past 5 years, we have seen moments of triumph and moments of tragedy. We have watched in admiration as 12 million Iraqis defied the terrorists and went to the polls and chose their leaders in free elections. We watched in horror as Al Qaida beheaded innocent captives and sent suicide bombers to blow up mosques and markets. These actions show the brutal nature of the enemy in Iraq, and they serve as a grim reminder. The terrorists who murder the innocent in the streets of Baghdad want to murder the innocent in the streets of America. Defeating this enemy in Iraq will make it less likely that we will face the enemy here at home.

A little over a year ago, the fight in Iraq was faltering. Extremist elements were succeeding in their efforts to plunge Iraq into chaos. They had established safe havens in many parts of the country. They were creating divisions among the Iraqis along sectarian lines. And their strategy of using violence in Iraq to cause divisions in America was working as pressures built here in Washington for withdrawal before the job was done.

My administration understood that America could not retreat in the face of terror. And we knew that if we did not act, the violence that had been consuming Iraq would worsen and spread and could eventually reach genocidal levels. Baghdad could have disintegrated into a contagion of killing, and Iraq could have descended into full-blown sectarian warfare.

So we reviewed the strategy and changed course in Iraq. We sent reinforcements into the country in a dramatic policy shift that is now known as the surge. General David Petraeus took command with a new mission: work with Iraqi forces to protect the Iraqi people, pressure the enemy into strongholds, and deny the terrorists sanctuary anywhere in the country. And that is precisely what we have done.

In Anbar, Sunni tribal leaders had grown tired of Al Qaida's brutality and started a popular uprising called the Anbar Awakening. To take advantage of this opportunity, we sent 4,000 additional marines to help these brave Iraqis drive Al Qaida from the Province. As this effort succeeded, it inspired other Iraqis to take up the fight. Soon similar uprisings began to spread across the country. Today, there are more than 90,000 concerned local citizens who are protecting their communities from the terrorists and insurgents and the extremists. The Government in Baghdad has stepped forward with a surge of its own; they've added more than 100,000 new Iraqi soldiers and police during the past year. These

Iraqi troops have fought bravely, and thousands have given their lives in this struggle.

Together, these Americans and Iraqi forces have driven the terrorists from many of the sanctuaries they once held. Now the terrorists have gathered in and around the northern Iraqi city of Mosul, and Iraqi and American forces are relentlessly pursuing them. There will be tough fighting in Mosul and areas of northern Iraq in the weeks ahead. But there's no doubt in my mind, because of the courage of our troops and the bravery of the Iraqis, the Al Qaida terrorists in this region will suffer the same fate as Al Qaida suffered elsewhere in Iraq.

As we have fought Al Qaida, coalition and Iraqi forces have also taken the fight to Shi'a extremist groups, many of them backed and financed and armed by Iran. A year ago, these groups were on the rise. Today, they are increasingly isolated, and Iraqis of all faiths are putting their lives on the line to stop these extremists from hijacking their young democracy.

To ensure that military progress in Iraq is quickly followed up with real improvements in daily life, we have doubled the number of Provincial Reconstruction Teams in Iraq. These teams of civilian experts are serving all Iraqi—18 Iraqi Provinces, and they're helping to strengthen responsible leaders and build up local economies and bring Iraqis together, so that reconciliation can happen from the ground up. They're very effective. They're helping give ordinary Iraqis confidence that by rejecting the extremists and reconciling with one another, they can claim their place in a free Iraq and build better lives for their families.

There's still hard work to be done in Iraq. The gains we have made are fragile and reversible. But on this anniversary, the American people should know that since the surge began, the level of violence is significantly down, civilian deaths are down, sectarian killings are down, attacks on American forces are down. We have captured or killed thousands of extremists in Iraq, including hundreds of key Al Qaida leaders and operatives. Our men and women in uniform are performing with characteristic honor and valor. The surge is working. And as a return on our success in Iraq, we've begun bringing some of our troops home.

The surge has done more than turn the situation in Iraq around, it has opened the door to a major strategic victory in the broader war on terror. For the terrorists, Iraq was supposed to be the place where Al Qaida rallied Arab masses to drive America out. Instead, Iraq has become the place where Arabs joined with Americans to drive Al Qaida out. In Iraq, we are witnessing the first large-scale Arab uprising against Usama bin Laden, his grim ideology, and his murderous network. And the significance of this development cannot be overstated.

The terrorist movement feeds on a sense of inevitability and claims to rise on the tide of history. The accomplishments of the surge in Iraq are exposing this myth and discrediting the extremists. When Iraqi and American forces finish the job, the effects will reverberate far beyond Iraq's borders. Usama bin Laden once said, "When people see a strong horse and a weak horse, by nature they will like the strong horse." By defeating Al Qaida in Iraq, we will show the world that Al Qaida is the weak horse. We will show that men and women who love liberty can defeat the terrorists. And we will show that the future of the Middle East does not belong to terror. The future of the Middle East belongs to freedom.

The challenge in this period ahead is to consolidate the gains we have made and seal the extremists' defeat. We have learned through hard experience what happens when we pull our forces back too fast: The terrorists and extremists step in; they fill vacuums, establish safe havens, and use them to spread chaos and carnage. General Petraeus has warned that too fast a drawdown could result in such an unraveling with Al Qaida and insurgents and militia

extremists regaining lost ground and increasing violence.

Men and women of the Armed Forces: Having come so far and achieved so much, we're not going to let this to happen.

Next month, General Petraeus and Ambassador Crocker will come to Washington to testify before Congress. I will await their recommendations before making decisions on our troop levels in Iraq. Any further drawdown will be based on conditions on the ground and the recommendations of our commanders. And they must not jeopardize the hard-fought gains our troops and civilians have made over the past year.

Successes we are seeing in Iraq are undeniable, yet some in Washington still call for retreat. War critics can no longer credibly argue that we're losing in Iraq, so they now argue the war costs too much. In recent months, we've heard exaggerated amounts of the costs of this war. No one are—would argue that this war has not come at a high cost in lives and treasure; but those costs are necessary when we consider the cost of a strategic victory for our enemies in Iraq.

If we were to allow our enemies to prevail in Iraq, the violence that is now declining would accelerate, and Iraq would descend into chaos. Al Qaida would regain its lost sanctuaries and establish new ones, fomenting violence and terror that could spread beyond Iraq's borders, with serious consequences for the world's economy.

Out of such chaos in Iraq, the terrorist movement could emerge emboldened, with new recruits, new resources, and an even greater determination to dominate the region and harm America. An emboldened Al Qaida with access to Iraq's oil resources could pursue its ambitions to acquire weapons of mass destruction to attack America and other free nations. Iran would be emboldened as well, with a renewed determination to develop nuclear weapons and impose its brand of hegemony across the Middle East. Our enemies would see an

America—an American failure in Iraq as evidence of weakness and a lack of resolve.

To allow this to happen would be to ignore the lessons of September the 11th and make it more likely that America would suffer another attack like the one we experienced that day, a day in which 19 armed men with box cutters killed nearly 3,000 people in our—on our soil, a day after which, in the following of that attack, more than a million Americans lost work, lost their jobs. The terrorists intend even greater harm to our country. And we have no greater responsibility than to defeat our enemies across the world so that they cannot carry out such an attack.

As our coalition fights the enemy in Iraq, we've stayed on the offensive on other fronts in the war on terror. You know, just a few weeks after commencing Operation Iraqi Freedom, U.S. forces captured Khalid Sheikh Mohammed, the mastermind behind the September the 11th terrorist attacks; we got him in Pakistan. About the same time as we launched Operation Iraqi Freedom, coalition forces thousands of—hundreds of miles away launched an assault on the terrorists in the mountains of southern Afghanistan in an operation called Operation Valiant Strike.

Throughout the war on terror, we have brought the enemy—we have fought the enemy on every single battlefront. And so long as terrorist danger remains, the United States of America will continue to fight the enemy wherever it makes its stand.

We will stay on the offense. But in the long run, defeating the terrorists requires an alternative to their murderous ideology. And there we have another advantage. We've got a singular advantage with our military when it comes to finding the terrorists and bringing them to justice. And we have another advantage in our strong belief in the transformative power of liberty.

So we're helping the people of Iraq establish a democracy in the heart of the Middle East. A free Iraq will fight terrorists instead of harboring them. A free Iraq will be an example for others of the power of liberty to change the societies and to displace despair with hope. By spreading the hope of liberty in the Middle East, we will help free societies take root. And when they do, freedom will yield the peace that we all desire.

Our troops on the frontlines understand what is at stake. They know that the mission in Iraq has been difficult and has been trying for our Nation, because they're the ones who've carried most of the burdens. They're all volunteers who have stepped forward to defend America in a time of danger. Some of them have gone out of their way to return to the fight.

One of these brave Americans is a Marine Gunnery Sergeant named William "Spanky" Gibson. In May of 2006 in Ramadi, a terrorist sniper's bullet ripped through his left knee; doctors then amputated his leg. After months of difficult rehabilitation, Spanky was not only walking, he was training for triathlons.

Last year, at the Escape from Alcatraz swim near San Francisco, he met Marine General James Mattis, who asked if there's anything he could do for him. Spanky had just one request: He asked to redeploy to Iraq. Today, he's serving in Fallujah, the first full-leg amputee to return to the frontlines. Here's what he says about his decision to return: "The Iraqis where—are where we were 232 years ago as a nation. Now they're starting a new nation, and that's one of my big reasons for coming back here. I wanted to tell the people of this country that I'm back to help wherever I can."

When Americans like Spanky Gibson serve on our side, the enemy in Iraq doesn't got a chance. We're grateful to all the brave men and women of our military who have served the cause of freedom. You've done the hard work, far from home and far from your loved ones. We give thanks for all our military families who love you and have supported you in this mission.

We appreciate the fine civilians from many departments who serve alongside you. Many of you served in Iraq and Afghanistan, and some have been on these fronts several times. You will never forget the people who fought at your side. You will always remember the comrades who served with you in combat, [but] ° did not make the journey home. America remembers them as well. More than 4,400 men and women have given their lives in the war on terror. We'll pray for their families. We'll always honor their memory.

The best way we can honor them is by making sure that their sacrifice was not in vain. Five years ago tonight, I promised the American people that in the struggle ahead, "we will accept no outcome but victory." Today, standing before men and women who helped liberate a nation, I reaffirm the commitment. The battle in Iraq is noble, it is necessary, and it is just. And with your courage, the battle in Iraq will end in victory. God bless.

NOTE: The President spoke at 10:04 a.m. at the Pentagon. In his remarks, he referred to Iraq's Ambassador to the U.S. Samir Shakir al-Sumaydi; Gen. David H. Petraeus, USA, commanding general, Multi-National Force—Iraq; Usama bin Laden, leader of the Al Qaida terrorist organization; and Gen. James N. Mattis, USMC, commander, U.S. Marine Corps Forces Central Command, and commanding general, I Marine Expeditionary Force. The Office of the Press Secretary also released a Spanish language transcript of these remarks.

Remarks Following Discussions With President Mikheil Saakashvili of Georgia
March 19, 2008

President Bush. Mr. President, welcome back to Washington. I was just reminiscing with the President about my trip to Georgia, about the unbelievably good food, and about the dancing. He was wondering whether I'd come back and start my dancing career there, and I told him I'd probably better quit while I'm ahead.

We had a good discussion. I admire the President. I admire what Georgia has gone through and what Georgia is doing. We had an interesting talk about a couple of subjects, one of which is the economic opportunities in Georgia. This is a country which has adopted a very simplified tax code. It's easy for people to understand. I told the American people I tried to simplify our Tax Code. It's difficult to do. I congratulate you on simplifying yours, and

I congratulate you about your rates of growth.

We talked about Georgia's contribution to democracy movements, not only her own but to democracy and freedom movements in places like Iraq. The citizens of Georgia must know that the troops that have been provided there are brave, courageous professionals and have made a significant difference. And we want to thank you for that, Mr. President.

We talked about the need for there to be peaceful resolutions of conflicts while recognizing the territorial integrity and sovereign borders of Georgia.

And finally, we, of course, talked about NATO. The Bucharest summit is coming up. Georgia's aspirations will be decided at the Bucharest summit. MAP application, of course, as the President full well knows,

---

° White House correction.

is not membership. MAP is a process that will enable NATO members to be comfortable with a country eventually joining. I believe that NATO benefits with a Georgia membership. I believe Georgia benefits from being a part of NATO. And I told the President the message I'll be taking to Bucharest soon.

And so, Mr. President, thanks for coming. I'm pleased you're here. I'm glad you brought your wife. Turns out, our wives are out having lunch together on the town here in DC. And I just told Laura to keep the tab down. [*Laughter*] I'm working on Government pay these days. But thank you for coming.

President Saakashvili. Thank you. Thank you, Mr. President. I mean, I'm incredibly thrilled to be back in the Oval Office. And you know, we've been essential part of your freedom agenda. I was not President when I heard your speech in Warsaw, when you spoke about freedom between Baltics and Black Sea. And that was extremely visionary speech because you spoke about the Black Sea at the moment when nobody wanted to look in our direction. And I think we are—what we are up to now is to implement this freedom agenda to the end, for the sake of our people, for the sake of our values, for the sake of what United States means for all of us, because the U.S. is exporting idealism to the rest of the world.

And we believe that, you know, we have very, very strong partnerships. We have a very, very strong partnership in democracy building. We have a very strong partnership in our military cooperation, because I'm very proud that Georgian troops in Iraq are not just controlling and are present there protecting people, but are having success in doing so. And certainly this is something that we will state over generations.

I have to thank you, Mr. President, for your unwavering support for our freedom, for our democracy, for our territorial sovereignty, and for protecting Georgia's borders for—and for Georgia's NATO aspira-tions. I think this is a very unequivocal support we are getting from you.

And you know, this is the last year of your administration, but I can tell you, what you've done for—not only for my country but what you've done for all over the region will be remembered greatly and will be remembered as absolutely revolutionary change of way of thinking, of environment, of giving chances to the people who never thought about having those opportunities and chances before. That's what America is all about. That's what Bush freedom agenda is all about. And we are very proud to be part of that agenda, Mr. President.

You should know that this will stay as a photographic memory in our people's mind, and we will always remember it. We'll never—and we are very grateful, of course. You will dance Georgian dance much better than I do. [*Laughter*] You are invited back to come. You've shown considerable talent. [*Laughter*] I know you're not Georgian, you're a Texan. But we are pretty close. [*Laughter*] But deep in your mind, you should have something Georgian. [*Laughter*]

President Bush. That's right. [*Laughter*]

President Saakashvili. That's for sure. And, I mean, we certainly—and if you don't want to dance with us, then you can come and bike with us or do anything. But you're always welcome——

President Bush. Thank you, sir.

President Saakashvili. ——back as somebody who really put Georgia firmly on the world's freedom map—and not only Georgia but many of the countries in the region—and gave us a chance. I think we will continue this cooperation.

I thank you for your support today. We've heard today everything we wanted to hear from the leader of the free world, and I think that's going to give a new opportunities opening to my people. I'm bringing back hope and inspiration.

President Bush. Thank you, buddy.

President Saakashvili. Thanks.

President Bush. Thank you all.

NOTE: The President spoke at 11:58 a.m. in the Oval Office at the White House. In his remarks, he referred to Sandra E. Roelofs, wife of President Saakashvili.

Statement on the 175th Anniversary of Thailand–United States Relations
March 19, 2008

Laura and I join in celebrating the 175th anniversary of relations between the United States of America and the Kingdom of Thailand. The United States and Thailand have long been linked by bonds of trust, appreciation, and friendship. The Treaty of Amity and Commerce, signed on March 20, 1833, solidified our commitment to working together for mutual benefit and marked the first agreement of its kind between the United States and an Asian nation. Over the past 175 years, our two governments have worked together on issues such as economic development, health care, and security. Today, we share a commitment to democracy and to free and fair trade, as well as a respect for human rights. Our tradition of cooperation and support remains strong.

I thank His Majesty the King and the citizens of Thailand for our enduring partnership. This anniversary is an opportunity to underscore our shared ideal of liberty and reinforce our bonds of friendship and understanding. We are proud to celebrate this historic day.

NOTE: The statement referred to King Phumiphon Adunyadet of Thailand.

Statement on the Appointment of Kenneth L. Wainstein as Assistant to the President for Homeland Security and Counterterrorism
March 19, 2008

I am pleased to announce that I have selected Kenneth L. Wainstein to serve as Assistant to the President for Homeland Security and Counterterrorism. Ken is a proven leader and a dedicated public servant with nearly two decades of law enforcement experience, including as United States Attorney for the District of Columbia. As Assistant Attorney General for National Security, he helped improve our ability to confront the threats of a new era. His experience at the Federal Bureau of Investigation as general counsel and Chief of Staff has provided him with a clear understanding of the dangers we face and the importance of ensuring that we have the necessary tools to protect America.

In his new role, Ken will coordinate our Nation's homeland security efforts to ensure that we continue to make progress on combating terrorism, securing our borders, and strengthening our emergency preparedness. I look forward to working with Ken to make America safer.

Message on the Observance of Nowruz
March 19, 2008

I send greetings to those celebrating Nowruz.

For the millions of people who trace their heritage to Iran, Iraq, Afghanistan, Turkey, Pakistan, India, and Central Asia, Nowruz is a time to celebrate the New Year with the arrival of spring. This cherished and ancient festival brings together family and friends to reflect on what has come before and celebrate a season of new beginnings.

Our country is proud to be a land where individuals from many different cultures can pass their traditions on to future generations. The diversity of America brings joy to our citizens and strengthens our Nation during Nowruz and throughout the year.

Laura and I send our best wishes to all those celebrating Nowruz, both here in the United States and abroad. May the year ahead be filled with peace and many blessings.

GEORGE W. BUSH

NOTE: An original was not available for verification of the content of this message.

Interview With Setareh Derakhshesh of VOA Persian News Network
March 19, 2008

Ms. Derakhshesh. Mr. President, let me thank you first on behalf of the Voice of America, on behalf of the Persian News Network for giving us your time. We really appreciate that, sir.

The President. Thank you.

Iran

Ms. Derakhshesh. As you know, Mr. President, this is the eve of Nowruz, the Iranian New Year. What is your message to the Iranian people as they face tough economic circumstances and infringement on their freedoms?

The President. Well, first, *Nowruz a tan Mubarak.* Secondly, that the people of the United States respects the people of Iran, that we respect the traditions of Iran, the great history of Iran. We have differences with the Government, but we honor the people. And we want the people to live in a free society. We believe freedom is a right for all people and that the freer the world is, the more peaceful the world is. And so my message is: Please don't be discouraged by, you know, the slogans that say America doesn't like you, because we do, and we respect you.

Ms. Derakhshesh. What do you say to the regime, sir? What would you say to the regime?

The President. I'd say to the regime that they've made decisions that have made it very difficult for the people of Iran. In other words, the Iranian leaders, in their desire to, you know, enrich uranium, in spite of the fact that the international community has asked them not to, has isolated a great country. And that if—there's a way forward. I mean, the Iranian leaders know there's a way forward. And that is, verifiably suspend your enrichment, and you can have new relationships with people in the U.N. Security Council, for example.

And it's just sad that the leadership is in many ways very stubborn because the Iraqi—the Iranian people are not realizing their true rights. And they're confusing people in Iraq, as well, about their desires.

And you know, it's a tough period if—in history for the Iranian people, but it doesn't have to be that way.

Iran/Uranium Enrichment/Russia

Ms. Derakhshesh. On the nuclear issue, sir, is there a solution to the problem that would both satisfy the United States concern and, at the same time, allow Iran to proceed with nonmilitary nuclear energy research?

The President. Well, part of the problem is that it's very hard for people to trust the Iranian Government because they haven't told the full truth, and that's why the people of Iran have got to understand there's great suspicions right now, not only in the United States but around the world. But there is a better way forward. And I thought, for example, the Russians proposed an interesting way, that says—and I have said publicly, and the Iranian people need to know that I believe Iran has the right to have civilian nuclear power. I believe in civilian nuclear power. Iran is a sovereign country, and they should have it.

The problem is, we just don't trust the Government because they haven't been forthcoming about their enrichment of fuels to go into the reactor. And therefore, Russia's offer to provide fuel on a contractual basis and provide fuel on a consistent basis would help solve the problem. And that is, the Iranians wouldn't need to enrich; they would have fuel for their reactor; and the people would have cheaper electricity. And I support that idea.

Ms. Derakhshesh. Sir, would you allow enrichment inside Iran if there are guarantees and international supervision?

The President. I would have to be convinced that any secret programs, you know, would be disclosed. In other words, I— you know, once you—once a nation hasn't told the truth, it requires a lot of work to convince people that they'll be telling the truth in the future. And my problem is, is that the Iranian Government has not been forthcoming, has not fully disclosed

their programs like the IAEA asked them to. So there's a lot of distrust right now.

And the better way forward is for there to be a contractual, solid obligation to provide fuel for a nuclear reactor, and then the Iranians can have their civilian nuclear power.

Iran/U.S. Foreign Policy

Ms. Derakhshesh. At a time when Iranians are going through very difficult economic circumstances—there's high employment, high unemployment; there are high prices; there are unfilled promises—the United Nations Security Council just passed a new set of sanctions against the regime. Is the United States concerned, sir, that the regime might exploit these circumstances to whip up anti-American sentiments, and also to use those and misuse them?

The President. Sure. No, I appreciate that. Of course we are. We're always concerned about the individual. You know, I'm concerned about the mom trying to raise her child in a hopeful environment. And I'm concerned about a child wanting to gain the knowledge so that he or she can realize her God-given talents. And of course, we're worried about the human condition.

And any time a government is failing to meet the needs of the people—or a lot of times, not any time—but a lot of times governments have failed to meet the needs of their people, particularly in relatively nontransparent, nonfree societies, they always look for somebody to blame. And I'm not surprised that, you know, the leaders would blame the United States for the problems they, themselves, have created.

And so yes, I mean, it enters my mind. On the other hand, the people of Iran must understand that the conditions exist in large part because of either mismanagement by the Government or isolation because of the Government's decisions on foreign policy matters, such as announcing they want to destroy countries with a nuclear weapon.

I mean, it is irresponsible remarks like that which cause great credibility loss with the Iranian Government and the actions of which will—are affecting the country.

Progress in Iraq/Iran

Ms. Derakhshesh. Mr. President, if I may, I want to ask you about Iraq also. Today is the fifth anniversary of the start of the Iraq war, and you had a speech on the war on terror. Are you satisfied with the political situation in Iraq in view of the improving security situation? And also, has Iran played a role in this?

The President. I am pleased, but not satisfied. I am pleased because there's a modern Constitution in Iraq. I am pleased because people have voted in Iraq. I am pleased because there's, you know—they're heading toward Provincial elections in Iraq. I'm pleased to see democracy moving. I'm not satisfied because there's more work to be done.

One of the problems we do have in Iraq is the—there's been some negative Iranian influence, such as the exportation from Iran of certain weapons that have been used by extremists to murder and to kill people. And it's been particularly unhelpful.

Now, look, I understand Iraq and Iran are going to have relations. After all, they've got a long border. But from my perspective, Iran has not been helpful in terms of helping this young democracy survive. I would think it would be in Iran's interests to have a peaceful neighbor. They had been at war at one time with Iraq. I would believe that a peaceful Iraq would be in the long-term interests of the Iranian people. And yet it's hard to have a peaceful Iraq if there are elements inside the country that are trying to use violence and murder to continue to stir up sectarian doubts and raise concerns which will cause more violence.

Iran-U.S. Relations/Iraq

Ms. Derakhshesh. There have been recent contacts between the United States and Iran over Iraq. Some dissidents inside Iran think that these might expand to other areas——

The President. Yes.

Ms. Derakhshesh. ——and they feel that this will undercut their position and that would strengthen the regime's hand. What are your thoughts on that, sir?

The President. My thought is, is that the reformers inside Iran are brave people. They've got no better friend than George W. Bush, and I ask for God's blessings on them, on their very important work. And secondly, that I would do nothing to undermine their efforts. And thirdly, that the talks between Iran—between the U.S. and Iran about Iraq are solely about Iraq, and that the message to the Iranians is: Stop importing your weapons, your sophisticated IEDs, and—or there will be consequences inside of Iraq. And when we find people transporting weapons that are aimed to harm innocent people or to arm militias that are aiming to harm innocent people, then they will be brought to justice—that there's a better way to deal inside of Iraq than the Iranians are now dealing. And so this message is nothing more than limited to Iraq.

Ms. Derakhshesh. Mr. President, thank you very much. And thanks for allowing me to do the interview, sir.

The President. Thank you; yes, ma'am.

NOTE: The interview was taped at 1:11 p.m. in the Map Room at the White House and was released by the Office of the Press Secretary on March 20.

Interview With Parichehr Farzam of Radio Farda
March 19, 2008

Nowruz/Iran

Ms. Farzam. Mr. President, thank you so much for your time in this interview with Radio Farda. On the beginning of Nowruz, the Persian New Year, what message do you wish to share with the people of Iran, especially with the Iranian women, as well as the young generation?

The President. First, that the United States of America wishes everybody a happy New Year. Secondly, that the United States—people of the United States respects the great Iranian history and culture. We have great respect for the people. And we've got problems with the Government. We have problems with the Government because the Government has been threatening, has made decisions that—and statements that really have isolated the people of Iran.

My message to the young in Iran is that someday your society will be free, and it will be a blessed time for you. My message to the women of Iran is that the women of America share your deep desire for children to be—to grow up in a hopeful society and to live in peace.

Iran/Freedom Agenda

Ms. Farzam. Speaking of women of Iran, Mr. President, the majority of population in Iran are women. And even in the Iranian culture they are considered the foundation on which men deeply rely. Is there any plan or could there be one to promote and engage the Iranian women in the U.S. to a unified and centralized movement for a free and democratic Iran?

The President. Well, I think the people of Iran are going to have to come to the conclusion that a free country is in their interest. We, of course, support freedom movements all around the world. We're supporting a freedom movement on the Iranian border in Iraq. We are promoting and helping the Iraqis develop a free society. By the way, a free Iraq will help the Iranians see the blessings of a free society.

There's no doubt in my mind that the women will be leading freedom movements in Iran and elsewhere. And the role of the United States is to provide, you know, moral support without—and other support without undermining their cause.

Iraq/Iran

Ms. Farzam. Mr. President, in this fifth anniversary of the Iraq war, what impact do you think a peaceful solution on the Iranian nuclear crisis and a normalization of our relations with Iran would have on the security and political situation in Iraq and more generally in the whole Middle East?

The President. I think that success in Iraq will first of all depend upon the Iraqis' desire to reconcile their differences and to live in peace, and that's happening. It's hard work to overcome the—a dictatorship like Saddam Hussein's, but nevertheless, most Iraqis want to live in peace with their neighbor.

Secondly, a peaceful Iraq will depend upon making it clear to the Iranians to stop exporting weapons from Iran into Iraq—that arm militias and arm criminal gangs—that cause there to be harm for the innocent people.

Thirdly, it's very important for the neighborhood to understand that the United States is committed to peace and that we're not—that we won't be run out because of violence; that we believe that we're there for the right reason, which is to promote freedom and peace.

The free—you know, there's a chance that the U.S. and Iran can reconcile their differences, but the Government is going to have to make some—make different choices. And one is to verifiably suspend the enrichment of uranium, at which time there is a way forward. And the Iranian people have got to understand that the United States is going to be firm in our desire to prevent the nation from developing a nuclear weapon, but reasonable in our desire to see to it that you have civilian nuclear power without—you know, without enabling the Government to enrich.

And the problem is, is that they have not told the truth in the past. And therefore, it's very difficult for the United States and the rest of the world—or much of the rest of the world—to trust the Iranian Government when it comes to telling the truth. And so I support the Russian proposal to provide Iran with enriched uranium to go into a civilian nuclear power plant.

There's a way forward. In other words, I don't know what the Iranian people believe about the United States, but they must believe that we have proposed a way forward that will yield to peace. And it's their Government that is resisting these changes.

Iran/Uranium Enrichment

Ms. Farzam. Mr. President, as you and your allies launched a global initiative to combat nuclear terrorism, what do you think is your most important challenge to expose and stop the secretive ambition of Iran's Government to enrich uranium, while assuring its citizens that their happiness and prosperity and peace is a benefit within their reach?

The President. Sure, absolutely. Well, one thing is, is to reiterate my belief that the Iranians should have a civilian nuclear power program. It's in their right to have it. The problem is the Government cannot be trusted to enrich uranium because, one, they've hidden programs in the past, and they may be hiding one now, who knows; and secondly, they've declared they want to have a nuclear weapon to destroy people—some in the Middle East. And that's unacceptable to the United States, and it's unacceptable to the world.

But what is acceptable to me is to work with a nation like Russia to provide the fuel so that the plan can go forward, and which therefore makes it—you know, it shows that the Iranian Government doesn't need to learn to enrich.

My only point to the Iranian people is we want you to be able to realize your sovereign rights. The Government has been duplicitous to the world. Very few people trust your Government. And if the Government changes its behavior, there's a better way forward for the Iranian people.

Freedom in Iran

Ms. Farzam. Thank you. Mr. President, world democracy is everyone's rightful way of life. In Iran, on the other hand, there is no respect for the basic rights of Iranian citizen; there is no rule of law; and there is no, certainly, the freedom of speech. Do you believe that the people of Iran stand a chance against this regime, to bring about the positive change in anytime soon with your support?

The President. Well, I would like very much for the Iranian people to realize a society based upon rule of law and free speech and free worship of religion. There's nothing I'd like to see more than a society in which young girls can grow up to realize their dreams with a good education system.

You know, this is a—this regime, however, is one that sometimes when people express themselves in an open way, there can be serious punishment. This is a regime that says they have elections, but they get to decide who's on the ballot, which is not a free and fair election. So this is a regime and a society that's got a long way to go. But the people of Iran can be rest assured the United States, whether I'm President or the next President, will strongly support their desires to live in a free society.

Ms. Farzam. May I have, Mr. President, my last question?

The President. Yes.

Missile Defense System/Russia

Ms. Farzam. Thank you. You said many times that the U.S. missile defense system in Czech and Poland is to defend America and its European allies from attack by rogue states such as Iran. But some—this argument is still between U.S. and Russia. Are you optimistic to solve the problem?

The President. Well, it's interesting you ask that question. We intend to move forward with the—and the Czech Republic and Poland, for the good of NATO. Obviously, it'd be—make life easier if the Russians and the United States cooperated in such a missile defense. Condi Rice and Bob Gates—Secretary Gates, Secretary Rice were in Russia this past couple of days talking about the very subject, as to whether or not we can find grounds to cooperate.

The missile systems, defense systems, would not be aimed at Russia; they'd be aimed at nations that would, you know, try to hold the free world hostage with a nuclear weapon.

And so it's—I'm optimistic. I'm cautiously optimistic. I don't know whether we can find common ground. But we are trying to find common ground, and that's what's—that's the first step, is to make the attempt.

Ms. Farzam. Thank you so much, Mr. President, for your time.

The President. Yes, ma'am, thank you.

NOTE: The interview was taped at 1:24 p.m. in the Map Room at the White House and was released by the Office of the Press Secretary on March 20. A tape was not available for verification of the content of this interview.

Interview With Master Sergeant Erin Roberts of the Pentagon Channel
March 19, 2008

M. Sgt. Roberts. Sir, I want to thank you for this opportunity that you've given us to talk to you.

The President. My honor.

Progress in Iraq

M. Sgt. Roberts. Today is the fifth-year anniversary of U.S. military presence in Iraq. And my first question for you would be, as Commander in Chief, what are the areas you are most focused on and most proud of as U.S. forces and the Iraqi forces continue to work towards stability and security in Iraq?

The President. I'm most proud of the performance of our troops. We have asked a lot of our military and the military families. We've got men and women who have been to both theaters in the war on terror, multiple times. And that's a strain, and it's hard. And I understand it is. On the other hand, our troops know it's necessary.

I am focused on making sure that we do not allow the sacrifice that has gone over the last 5 years to go in vain; that we end up making the hard decisions now, and helping the Iraqis now to develop a peaceful and free society in the heart of the Middle East, which will enable the next generation's children to grow up in a peaceful world—or the next generation to grow up in a peaceful world.

And so I'm pleased with the progress. It's been hard; it's been really hard. It's been hard on our country. It's been hard on the military, but I'm proud of the fact that the military has been so steadfast and courageous.

Wounded Military Personnel/Military Families

M. Sgt. Roberts. Speaking of the military and their families, you meet with many family members, many spouses, on a regular basis——

The President. Yes.

M. Sgt. Roberts. ——of those that are lost and wounded in the conflicts—difficult situation, I'm sure. Could you take a moment and just tell us what it's like meeting with them and what you say to them and what they say to you?

The President. Sure. First of all, obviously, each circumstance is a little different. And you're right, I've met with a lot. Let me first start with the wounded. Generally what happens is, is that, in a place like Walter Reed or Bethesda, you know, a soldier will look at their Commander in Chief and say, "I can't wait to get back in the battle," which obviously—you know, first of all, it's just so inspiring to me, but it also—it's got to change the perspective of their family a little bit.

Secondly, with the wounded, I am obviously always conscious to make sure that these kids, these soldiers—people in uniform—get the best care. And I truly believe they are. And I love our doctors and nurses. It's unbelievable the care they get.

In terms of meeting with the families of the deceased—as you can imagine, it's very emotional. First of all, meeting the President alone can be an emotional experience, and when you put on top of that the Commander in Chief who made the decision of—that got their child in a position where he or she got killed, so, you know, the meetings can be very tearful. I'm a crier, at times. I'm not afraid to hug a mom or hug a wife or hug a husband and cry.

I try to get them to talk about their loved one. I want to learn about each individual person who sacrificed—what they were like, what their interests were—and a lot of times the families love sharing their stories with the Commander in Chief. And to a person, nearly, I have been told that, "Whatever you do, Mr. President, complete this job." Don't—and basically what they're saying is, "Don't let politics, don't let the

Gallup poll, don't let a focus group cause you to make a decision that is not in the best interests of our country and our military." And I assure them that they don't have to worry about that about George W. Bush.

I tell my friends who ask me this question a lot, what—they say: "What's it like? You're the guy who made the decision to put their loved one in harm's way. They didn't come home. What's it like to meet with them?" And I say that oftentimes the comforter in chief is the person who gets comforted, because of the strength and courage and great love of country of these folks.

Progress in Afghanistan

M. Sgt. Roberts. Let's move to Afghanistan. It's been 6½ years——

The President. Right.

M. Sgt. Roberts. ——since we forced the Taliban out of power over there. What do you see the current situation for our troops right now, and how much work do you think needs to be done to sustain the progress that we've made?

The President. Afghanistan obviously is different from Iraq. Afghanistan—I mean, Iraq is a wealthier nation. Afghanistan is broke, and they had a long way to go and—from the days of the Taliban, and, you know, they have made interesting progress. I'm going to get some of these statistics a little wrong, but the point I want to make is that infrastructures change. I mean, it's—I think there was like less than 100 miles of roads, and today, there's over 1,000 miles of road. Young girls weren't going to school, basically, and now there's a lot of young girls going to school. Health care was very rudimentary, and today, a lot of people have got basic health care. In other words, the condition—human condition is changing, which is important.

The Taliban has not been defeated. In other words, they keep coming back. And an enemy such as this gets defeated when two things happen: One, you know, we bring their people to justice, as well as a society develops which marginalizes them—in other words, something that competes with their ideology. Everybody in Afghanistan knows what the Taliban's ideology is like. They had to live under them. And now that—we're trying to help them realize there's another way and a more hopeful life. And until a—you know, a civil society develops that provides hope for the Afghan people, it's going to be—the Taliban will be a factor.

And so they're a factor now. Are they winning? No, they're not winning. Can they beat us militarily? Absolutely not. And so a lot of what—and we're bolstering our troops there, by the way, just to make sure that they're not able to intimidate the people to the point where a civil society and a free society can't develop.

So we've got work to do there. The good news is we're not in there alone. There's a lot of NATO troops—some of whom fight, some of whom don't fight, but all of whom make a contribution. And I'm going to NATO next week and—the NATO meeting in Romania. And I'll, of course, be urging our allies to bolster their presence in Afghanistan because—and I'll remind them that this was the country that had failed so miserably, that not only were people brutalized, but an enemy that hates America and hates free societies developed safe havens from which they launch brutal attack.

And now is the time to deal with them and not hope they change their mind or hope they become better citizens of the world, because they're not.

U.S. Africa Command

M. Sgt. Roberts. Africa——

The President. Yes.

M. Sgt. Roberts. ——the new Africa Command; you just were on a trip to five countries in Africa. Tell me, if you can, briefly, the significance of Africa Command, and—strategically and how it will play in the global war on terror.

The President. Well, first of all, there's some nervousness about the African command in Africa because nations don't want U.S. troops stationed on their border. And so I had to spend time saying, wait a minute, this isn't a typical command. What this is, is a command that will help Africans deal with African problems, such as Sudan. We want well-trained African troops going into places like Sudan, helping the poor folks there who are being brutalized by, you know, thugs, to be able to survive and thrive.

And—first of all, this administration recognizes that Africa is important. That's why we name an African command. Secondly, that hopelessness is the only way radicals can recruit, and therefore, we have programs to, you know, deal with malaria and HIV/AIDS and hunger. But the other source of instability on the continent of Africa is civil unrest, is civil war, is, you know, inflamed passions that break out into violence. And it's in our interests that we help Africans deal with those problems. That's what Africa Command is meant to do.

And so it fits into the broader scope of things, the broader war on terror, and also is a—it's a commitment that we care about the people on the continent of Africa.

NOTE: The interview was taped at 1:37 p.m. in the Map Room at the White House and was released by the Office of the Press Secretary on March 20.

Remarks on the National President's Challenge
March 20, 2008

Thank you all. Please be seated. I'm honored to be joined by members of the President's Council on Physical Fitness and Sports. And today I've got an announcement to make as to how to encourage our fellow citizens to exercise more.

First, I do want to thank the Chairman of this Council, John Burke. His business is to make mountain bikes, Trek mountain bikes. [*Laughter*] I use Trek mountain bikes. [*Laughter*] That's not why he's the Chairman. [*Laughter*] But I like to exercise a lot. And I hope my fellow citizens learn to love exercise as well. It's good for your mind, exercise is good for your body, and it's good for your soul. If you ride mountain bikes, make sure you keep your eyes on the road—[*laughter*]—because sometimes you can go over the handlebars—[*laughter*]—which I have done.

I want to thank the members of the Council for their good work to promote physical fitness. I believe physical fitness is a vital issue for our country. Nearly two-thirds of American adults are overweight or obese. That's too many. More than half of American adults do not get enough physical activity to realize the health benefits. Not enough people are exercising. The benefits include lower risk for many serious conditions, ranging from heart disease to diabetes to depression.

America's young people are three times more likely to be overweight than they were three decades ago. Lack of physical fitness places a huge financial burden on our Nation. Diseases linked to unhealthy habits drive up the price of health care for all Americans.

So we're encouraging Americans to take personal responsibility for their own health. And one way we're doing so is through the HealthierUS Initiative. Now this is an initiative I announced in 2002. And the key—program had four key components.

First, be physically active every day. People say, "I don't have time to be physically active every day." Well, my suggestion is, make time. Secondly, eat well. Thirdly, get preventive screenings. And fourthly, you know, don't do stupid things to your body—like drugs and tobacco and excessive alcohol.

Today we're unveiling a new way to encourage people across the United States to boost their physical activity, and to have some fun doing it. It's called the National President's Challenge. I appreciate very much the Acting Surgeon General Steve Galson is with us, and the person who went to the Press Club and kind of lent a little extra stuff to the announcement, and that would be Eli Manning. You know, he helped kick off this initiative, and he probably thought he'd be—not having to deal with kickoffs anytime after the Super Bowl. [*Laughter*] But I want to thank you all very much for helping to highlight an interesting and exciting and a fun way for people to realize the benefits of physical activity.

So here's how it works. First, you can go online at www.presidentschallenge.org—www.presidentschallenge.org—and you can sign up to participate. You can sign up as an individual, or you can sign up as a group, which would be kind of a fun way to work out together. The deadline, by the way, for signing up is April the third. So get on your web page there and sign up.

Secondly, you get to decide how you're going to meet your physical fitness goal. In other words, you set a goal, and then you pick the exercise or activity. And there's about 100 different activities to choose from, ranging from gardening or skydiving. [*Laughter*] So I suspect my father will be signing up for skydiving. [*Laughter*] Mother wants him to sign up for gardening. [*Laughter*]

Thirdly, start exercising. If you're an adult—and that means 30 minutes of activity a day, 5 days a week; or if you're a kid, 60 minutes. That's—it's not that hard to do if you prioritize and discipline yourself. You've got 6 weeks of activity to meet the challenge; in other words, this ends on May the 15th.

Fourth, you keep track of your activities. In other words, there's the—on the web site there's an activity log that will help make it easier to track whether or not you're accumulating enough points to get an award.

And that's the fifth step. Individuals who meet their fitness goals can receive certificates and medals. Schools that meet their goals will be honored. And when you register, be sure to include the State you're from, because all of us here—up here on the stage will be watching to see which State has the highest percentage of partici-

pants. And of course, there will be proper recognition for the State that does the best. I suspect Texas will do very well. [*Laughter*] I certainly hope so.

I want to thank the members of the President's Physical—Council on Physical Fitness and Sports for leading the effort. I really appreciate your care about the country. I want to thank you for thinking innovatively about how to, you know, encourage our fellow citizens to become active. I wish my citizens the fellow best as they sign up for this exciting new challenge. Have good exercise, have fun, and remember, you'll have a healthy tomorrow when you do so. God bless.

NOTE: The President spoke at 1:09 p.m. in the East Garden at the White House. In his remarks, he referred to Eli Manning, quarterback, National Football League's New York Giants.

Remarks Following Discussions With Prime Minister Hubert Ingraham of the Bahamas, Prime Minister David Thompson of Barbados, and Prime Minister Dean Barrow of Belize
March 20, 2008

President Bush. Secretary Rice and I have had the pleasure of welcoming three of our neighbors—neighborhood's strong leaders: Prime Ministers of the Bahamas, Barbados, and Belize.

And we had a discussion like you would expect neighbors to have: How do we work together for our mutual benefit? We talked about trade and tourism. We talked about how to make sure that our security needs are met without interrupting the ability for our people to travel as freely as possible, and for the ability of people to be able to make a good living as a result of tourism.

We talked about the region. I assured the leaders that the neighborhood is important to the United States of America. We oftentimes are talked about in dealing with

the Middle East or dealing on the continent of Africa. But it was important for these leaders to know that we believe that a good, strong, healthy, vibrant neighborhood is in the interests of the United States. And so we had a good, friendly, important discussion, and I can't thank the leaders enough for coming. I appreciate very much for you being here—two of whom have just recently won elections—good, fair, clean elections.

And I reminded them that there's no stronger advocate for democracy than my administration. And I admire the fact that you agreed to run, had the courage of your convictions, and took your message to the people. And then, of course, there's the old senior man here who's been around quite a while. [*Laughter*] You've seen a lot come and go. And so, Mr. Prime Minister, why don't you say a few remarks, if you don't mind.

Prime Minister Ingraham. Thank you, Mr. President. We've had a wonderful discussion this morning. We're very pleased and grateful that the U.S. President invited us to come. We have discussed with him a number of issues of relevance and concern to ourselves, including the desire on our part to have the Caribbean Basin Initiative act extended. We learned it expires in September of this year. We talked about tourism, the impact that the current in-

crease in the price of oil is having on travel. We talked about security and democracy.

And my two colleagues, who are recent Prime Ministers, David Thompson of Barbados and Dean Barrow of Belize, were able to engage in a full, frank discussion. As for myself, this is my fourth time to have been so fortunate to have come to this place. Thank you, Mr. President.

President Bush. Yes, sir. Thank you all very much.

NOTE: The President spoke at 2:29 p.m. in the Cabinet Room at the White House.

Message on the Observance of Easter 2008
March 21, 2008

"I am the resurrection and the life. He who believes in me will live, even though he dies."

JOHN 11:25

Laura and I send greetings to all those celebrating the joyful holiday of Easter.

The Resurrection of Jesus Christ reminds people around the world of the presence of a faithful God who offers a love more powerful than death. Easter commemorates our Savior's triumph over sin, and we take joy in spending this special time with family and friends and reflecting on the many blessings that fill our lives. During this season of renewal, let us come together and

give thanks to the Almighty who made us in His image and redeemed us in His love.

On this glorious day, we remember our brave men and women in uniform who are separated from their families by great distances. We pray for their safety and strength, and we honor those who gave their lives to advance peace and secure liberty across the globe.

Happy Easter. May God bless you, and may God bless our great Nation.

GEORGE W. BUSH

NOTE: The Office of the Press Secretary also released a Spanish language version of this message. An original was not available for verification of the content of this message.

The President's Radio Address
March 22, 2008

Good morning. This weekend families across America are coming together to celebrate Easter. This is the most important

holiday in the Christian faith. And during this special and holy time each year, millions of Americans pause to remember a sacrifice that transcended the grave and redeemed the world.

Easter is a holiday that beckons us homeward. This weekend is an occasion to reflect on the things that matter most in life: the love of family, the laughter of friends, and the peace that comes from being in the place you call home. Through good times and bad, these quiet mercies are sources of hope.

On Easter, we hold in our hearts those who will be spending this holiday far from home: our troops on the frontlines. I deeply appreciate the sacrifices that they and their families are making. America is blessed with the world's greatest military, made up of men and women who fulfill their responsibilities with dignity, humility, and honor. Their dedication is an inspiration to our country and a cause for gratitude this Easter season.

On Easter, we remember especially those who have given their lives for the cause of freedom. These brave individuals have lived out the words of the Gospel: "Greater love has no man than this, that a man lay down his life for his friends." And our Nation's fallen heroes live on in the memory of the Nation they helped defend.

On Easter, we also honor Americans who give of themselves here at home. Each year, millions of Americans take time to feed the hungry and clothe the needy and care for the widow and the orphan. Many of them are moved to action by their faith in a loving God who gave His son so that sin would be forgiven. And in this season of renewal, millions across the world remember the gift that took away death's sting and opened the door to eternal life.

Laura and I wish you all a happy Easter. Thank you for listening.

NOTE: The address was recorded at 7:10 a.m. on March 20 in the Cabinet Room at the White House for broadcast at 10:06 a.m. on March 22. The transcript was made available by the Office of the Press Secretary on March 21, but was embargoed for release until the broadcast. The Office of the Press Secretary also released a Spanish language transcript of this address.

Statement on the Presidential Election in Taiwan
March 22, 2008

I congratulate the people of Taiwan on the successful conclusion of their March 22 Presidential election. Once again, Taiwan has demonstrated the strength and vitality of its democracy. I also congratulate Mr. Ma Ying-jeou on his victory.

Taiwan is a beacon of democracy to Asia and the world. I am confident that the election and the democratic process it represents will advance Taiwan as a prosperous, secure, and well-governed society.

It falls to Taiwan and Beijing to build the essential foundations for peace and stability by pursuing dialogue through all available means and refraining from unilateral steps that would alter the cross-strait situa-tion. I believe the election provides a fresh opportunity for both sides to reach out and engage one another in peacefully resolving their differences.

The maintenance of peace and stability in the Taiwan Strait and the welfare of the people on Taiwan remain of profound importance to the United States. We will continue to maintain close unofficial ties with the people on Taiwan through the American Institute in Taiwan, in accordance with our longstanding "one China" policy, our three joint communiques with the People's Republic of China, and the Taiwan Relations Act.

NOTE: The statement referred to President-elect Ma Ying-jeou of Taiwan.

Remarks at the White House Easter Egg Roll
March 24, 2008

Laura and I welcome you to the White House for the Easter egg roll. How about the Jonas Brothers? Thanks for coming. We are sure glad you're here. We welcome you to the Easter egg roll.

Pretty soon, after a few remarks, I have the honor of blowing the whistle to start the Easter egg roll. But we've got a lot of other people who are going to make sure today is a special day. We want to thank all our volunteers who have made this event possible. We thank our—[*applause*]—yes, there you are. [*Laughter*] We thank our readers. For you Dallas Cowboy fans, it is a great honor to welcome Troy Aikman here to be one of the readers.

We want to remind you that we're dedicating today's Easter egg roll to our clean oceans. And there's a booth here where you can find out how you can contribute to make sure that we're environmentally sound stewards of our oceans. Ocean conservation is a important aspect of good public service, and it's certainly something that Laura has on her mind, as she comes up to address you. And so now it's my honor to welcome the First Lady of the United States, my dear wife, Laura Bush.

NOTE: The President spoke at 9:23 a.m. from the Blue Room balcony at the White House. In his remarks, he referred to entertainers the Jonas Brothers; and Troy Aikman, former quarterback, National Football League's Dallas Cowboys. The transcript released by the Office of the Press Secretary also included the remarks of the First Lady.

Remarks Following a Briefing at the Department of State
March 24, 2008

Madam Secretary, thank you very much for your hospitality. I just had a very interesting dialogue on how to strengthen the State Department's capacity to bring freedom and peace around the world, how to make sure the State Department works collaboratively with the Defense Department as we deal with some of the more difficult areas and really take advantage of some of the great opportunities that we're faced with.

And so I really want to thank you, Madam Secretary, and I thank the folks who work in this building. Our citizens have really no idea of how competent, cou-rageous, and successful the people here who work at the State Department are. I do. After my—now my eighth year as President, I've gotten to know the people in the State Department well. And I'm impressed, and so should our citizens.

Obviously, we want to expand the reach of the State Department by increasing the size and its efficiencies and to make sure that there's interoperability. And along these lines, of course, I'm fully aware that folks who have worked in the State Department lost their lives and—in Iraq, along with our military folks. And on this day of reflection, I offer our deepest sympathies to their families. I hope their families know that citizens pray for their comfort and their strength. Whether they were the first one who lost their life in Iraq or recently lost their lives in Iraq, that every life is precious in our sight.

And I guess my one thought I wanted to leave with those who still hurt is that one day people will look back at this moment in history and say, "Thank God there were courageous people willing to serve, because they laid the foundations for peace for generations to come." That I have vowed in the past, and I will vow so long as I'm President, to make sure that those lives were not lost in vain; that, in fact, there is a outcome that will merit the sacrifice that civilian and military alike have made; that our strategies going forward will be aimed at making sure that we achieve victory, and therefore, America becomes more secure, these young democracies survive, and peace more likely as we head into the 21st century.

So, Madam Secretary, I'm honored to be here. And I thank you very much for your hard work and your dedication.

Thank you all.

NOTE: The President spoke at 3:03 p.m.

Remarks Following a Meeting With the 2008 Bassmaster Classic Champion and 2007 Women's Bassmaster Tour Champion
March 25, 2008

The President. I've got the fishing champs from this year. And, Judy, thanks for coming.

Judy Wong. Oh, thank you.

The President. She is from Many, Louisiana. She won the Women's Bassmaster. And Alton Jones from Waco, Texas, won the Bassmaster Classic.

And I thought it was important to welcome these champs here to the White House so that—you know, to encourage people to fish. There's nothing better than fishing. I had a fantastic experience with Alton and our friend Charlie Pack. He was a famous local fisherman, and he said, "Do you want to go fishing with a fellow named Jones?" I said: "I've never heard of him. There's a lot people named Jones." [*Laughter*] It turns out, the man I was fishing with is the—wins the Bassmaster Classic.

This is a good, clean sport. It's a sport that requires good conservation in order to make sure our fisheries are good. And I love welcoming the champs here. And so we're glad you're here.

Ms. Wong. Thank you.

The President. The people in Louisiana and Texas are proud of you.

Alton Jones. Well, it's an honor to be here. You know, fishing with you, I've got to say that President Bush is actually a very good fisherman and a great conservationist. And I'm really not sure who's working who here. I'm hoping to get an invite to fish on his lake in Crawford.

The President. That's right.

Mr. Jones. And he's looking for a free fishing guide. [*Laughter*]

Ms. Wong. I would be glad to take you any day on Toledo Bend.

The President. That's good.

Ms. Wong. Okay.

The President. Well, thank you, Judy.

Ms. Wong. And bring Laura as well.

The President. Well, yes, she's—I'm a good fisherman; sometimes I'm a good catcher-man. [*Laughter*]

Mr. Jones. There's a big difference.

The President. Yes, there is. Anyway, thank you all for coming.

NOTE: The President spoke at 10:11 a.m. in the Oval Office at the White House. In his remarks, he referred to TV host and fisherman Charlie Pack.

Remarks Following Discussions With King Hamad bin Isa al-Khalifa of Bahrain
March 25, 2008

President Bush. Your Majesty, welcome back to Washington. It is such a pleasure to see you. I still have such fond memories of our trip to the Kingdom of Bahrain. His Majesty and I were reminiscing about the sword dance that you put on. It was spectacular. And you've got a—not only do you have a beautiful country, but you've got a prosperous country and a country that is a great friend of the United States. It's just such a honor to welcome you back here.

We had a good discussion—and we'll continue our discussion over lunch—on a variety of subjects. First, I do want to thank the Kingdom for sending an ambassador to Iraq. That's a very strong move that indicates a willingness to lead, as well as a willingness to send a signal that when a young democracy like Iraq is beginning to make progress, that it is important for the neighborhood to recognize that progress. And I really do want to thank Your Majesty for that.

We talked about security measures, the need to work together on joint security operations. I congratulated His Majesty on Bahrain's leadership of a joint task force that's—that is enabling nations to learn how to work together in order to keep the peace.

All in all, it's been what you would expect: a visit that's cordial and comfortable and amongst friends. And so, Your Majesty, welcome back, and thank you for coming.

King Hamad. Thank you. Thank you. I would like to thank the President for his kind invitation and his great support to Bahrain and to the stability and prosperity of our region.

And concerning sending back ambassador—an ambassador to Iraq, Iraq is an Arab state. Iraq is a founder of the Arab League, so it deserves all the support that it can get from other brother Arabs.

And the discussion today focused on bilateral relations concerning the free trade agreement, which we have signed, and concerning the energy as well, which yesterday was signed by the Secretary of State and our Foreign Minister. And we talked about security matters, which really are the most important issue for maintaining the development and the prosperity in our region.

And I came all the way to thank the President for what he has done for Bahrain and for our region and for the whole world—stability and security in fighting terrorism and extremism. And we hope we achieve our common goals by having a stable world.

So thank you, Mr. President. Thank you.

President Bush. Thank you, Majesty. Thank you very much.

NOTE: The President spoke at 11:32 a.m. in the Oval Office at the White House. King Hamad referred to Minister of Foreign Affairs Khalid bin Ahmad al-Khalifa of Bahrain.

Remarks at a Celebration of Greek Independence Day
March 25, 2008

Thank you. Your Eminence, thank you very much. Welcome to the White House. I'm always open for a few suggestions. [*Laughter*] You're an easy man to listen to.

And I want to thank you all for coming. Here we are to celebrate the 187th anniversary of Greek independence. And it's an interesting place to celebrate it, isn't it? You know, the White House is a great symbol for independence and freedom and liberty. And it's a fitting place to celebrate the independence of Greece.

Mr. Minister, thank you for coming. We appreciate you coming all the way over for this event, and we're proud you're here. And thanks for bringing your son.

Mr. Ambassador, thanks for coming. Ambassador Mallias is with us today. Mr. Ambassador, there you are, right there, Ambassador. Thank you. It's good to see your wife. Appreciate you all being here. Ambassador Kakouris of—to Cyprus is with us— from Cyprus to U.S. is with us.

Senator, thank you for coming. It's good to see you again. We miss you around these parts. [*Laughter*] I don't know if you've missed these parts, but we miss you around these parts. [*Laughter*]

Father Alex, good to see you again, sir. Thanks. I appreciate very much my Greek American—fellow Greek American citizens coming, as well as those who wear the uniform. We're proud to be in your presence.

Your Eminence, all free people stand on the shoulders of Greece. In the ancient world where political power usually came from the sword, the people of Athens came together around a radical and untried idea: that men were fit to govern themselves. It was this freedom that allowed them to create one of the most vibrant societies in history. And that society deeply influenced America's Founding Fathers when they sought to establish a free state centuries later.

Throughout their history, the people of Greece have been committed to liberty. They've also been committed to the important principle that liberty only survives when brave men and women are ready to come to its defense.

In the years leading up to Greece's war for independence, one of the rallying cries of the Greek people was that it was better to be free for an hour than to be a slave for 40 years. Those are the kind of folks who had their priorities straight.

The United States was by Greece's side from the very beginning of the struggle for independence. In those early days, some Americans volunteered to serve in the Greek army, and many more contributed the funds that were necessary to keep the fight alive. Former Presidents John Adams and Thomas Jefferson and James Madison all spoke in favor of the Greek people's right to self-determination. And after many long years, Greece emerged victorious and free. And that's what we're celebrating today.

And from that time forward, the United States and Greece have been strong allies in the cause of freedom. Today, we continue to work to spread the hope of liberty. Our countries are working together in Afghanistan, where Greek troops are an important part of the NATO forces that are restoring hope to that country. We're also partners in promoting stability in the Balkans and in the Middle East, where Greece provides peacekeepers in Bosnia and Kosovo and Lebanon. Please thank your Governments for this—strong signals that liberty is universal and that liberty will bring the peace we all hope.

Our Nation has been inspired by Greek ideals, and we have been enriched by Greek immigrants. Today, more than 1.3

million Americans trace their ancestry back to Greece, and we're better for having them here. America is a richer place, a better place.

Our two countries also share ties of faith. The Greek Orthodox Church has well over 1 million members in the United States. Under the leadership of this fine man, the Church is a source of strength and inspiration for a lot of our citizens. It's a proud part of our country's tradition of religious diversity and religious tolerance.

For nearly two centuries, the bonds between the United States and Greece have continued to strengthen. And during the earliest days of our friendship, one Greek leader told the American people, quote: "It is in your land that liberty has fixed her abode. In imitating you, we shall imitate our ancestors."

Today, I know that both our countries are making these ancestors proud through our commitment to freedom. And I'm confident that this tradition of friendship between the United States and Greece will continue for many years to come.

And so I ask God's blessings on the people of Greece and the people of America. And now welcome the Metropolitan Youth Choir of the Archdiocese.

NOTE: The President spoke at 3:41 p.m. in the East Room at the White House. In his remarks, he referred to Archbishop Demetrios, Primate of the Greek Orthodox Church in America and his assistant for public affairs Reverend Father Alex Karloutsos; Minister of Development Christos Folias of Greece and his son Sotiris; Greece's Ambassador to the U.S. Alexandros P. Mallias and his wife Francoise-Anne; and Cyprus's Ambassador to the U.S. Andreas S. Kakouris. The related Greek Independence Day proclamation of March 20 is listed in Appendix D at the end of this volume.

Remarks Following a Tour of ColorCraft of Virginia in Sterling, Virginia
March 26, 2008

The President. Jim, thank you very much for your hospitality.

James H. Mayes. Thank you, sir.

The President. Thank you all very much for greeting me here.

ColorCraft is a small, thriving business that will benefit from the stimulus package that the Congress passed earlier this year. And it will benefit from it because if they make—if Jim decides to purchase software or machinery, there is a tax incentive to encourage him to do so. He's made the decision to do so, and his company will be encouraged to do so through the Tax Code.

And that's important because when he buys a machine or when he buys software, somebody has to manufacture that. And therefore, there is a direct link between the stimulus package and jobs. As well—and we talked about this earlier—a lot of the folks who work here at ColorCraft are going to get a check in the second week of May as part of the economic, progrowth stimulus package. And recently, there's been a mailer out to our citizens from the IRS. And this mailer basically describes the benefits from the stimulus package that people will receive.

One of the things that's very important for our citizenry to understand, that is, if you do not file an income tax return, you need to go to your local IRS office and get a form that will show the Government where you live and who you are, so you can get your check. If you file an income tax form, all you got to do is in your '07 income tax, you know, mail it in.

But there's a lot of people eligible for this stimulus package—for the money coming out of the Government to our individual citizens—who don't file income tax forms, and yet they're eligible. And so recently, the IRS has been indicating that this weekend, this Saturday, there's going to be a—there's an opportunity for citizens to go and make it clear who you are, where you live, so you can get your check as well.

The purpose of this is to respond decisively to the economic downturn that we're going through. The Congress, along with the White House, worked very closely to pass a very substantial progrowth package. And I fully recognize that people are concerned about our economy, but they must understand that this package has yet to fully kick in yet. We've taken action, but it's going to take a while for the economy to feel the effects of this good law that I signed. It's going to take a while for these folks standing behind me to get their money.

Now, Jim has already made a decision because the aspects of the stimulus package for small businesses are clear. It is the law. And therefore, when he buys the equipment and software that he's planning on buying, he can rest assured that their tax incentive will be available for him in this year.

Now, small businesses are the backbone of the U.S. economy. Small-business owners and—are dreamers and doers. We want to watch them and help them expand because if they expand, more and more people find work. [*Inaudible*]—a rough patch right now in our economy, but I'm confident in the long term we'll come out stronger than ever before. One of the most decisive actions a government can take is to give people their money back so they can spend it, and that's exactly what we've done. In the second week of May, a lot of folks are going to be getting a sizable check. And I'm looking forward to that day, and I know they are as well.

Mr. Mayes. Yes, sir.

The President. Thank you for coming.

Mr. Mayes. Thank you.

The President. Yes.

Mr. Mayes. Thank you.

The President. Appreciate you having me. Thank you all.

NOTE: The President spoke at 12:25 p.m. In his remarks, he referred to James H. Mayes, president, ColorCraft of Virginia.

Interview With Foreign Print Journalists
March 26, 2008

The President. All right, sit down. How is everybody doing back there? That's what we call the peanut gallery.

I'm looking forward to going to Ukraine and Romania again, Croatia. This will be a—it's a very important trip; important trip to discuss our bilateral relations, and it's an important trip because of NATO. I believe we'll have a successful summit. The definition of success is to make sure NATO stays relevant, and that we work in a collaborative fashion to deal with the threats of the 21st century and the opportunities of the 21st century.

And there's no better opportunity to deal with the threats of terror than in Afghanistan. So part of the mission—part of our collective mission in Romania for the NATO meeting is to encourage people to take our obligations seriously. And the United States, to that end, will make it clear that we do take our obligations seriously. We've committed 3,500 marines—3,200 marines—3,700 marines?

White House National Security Adviser Stephen J. Hadley. Three thousand two hundred.

The President. ——3,200 marines, plus their enablers—[*laughter*]—inside joke— anyway, to—as a part of a stronger commitment, to set an example and encourage others to participate.

Secondly, enlargement of NATO will be on the agenda. And I'm a strong supporter of encouraging the right decision to be made at Bucharest on Croatia and Albania and Macedonia.

Thirdly, we'll be discussing the aspirations of Ukraine and Georgia. I have been public in my statements that I believe that NATO benefits and Ukraine and Georgia benefit, if and when there is membership. I do know that one of the signals we're going to have to send, and must send, is there is a clear path forward for Ukraine and Georgia. The decision will be made, of course, at Bucharest. But I've analyzed the situation, and I believe it's in the interests that there is that clear path forward. It's in the interest of NATO, collectively, and it's in the interest of each individual country.

And finally, we'll be talking about missile defense and cyberterrorism and counterterrorism activities, how we can work together to stay effective in this world in which we live.

And so anyway, I'm looking forward to the trip. And so we'll do a couple rounds of questions.

Alona. Is that an accurate way of saying your name?

Ukraine/North Atlantic Treaty Organization

Q. Yes, Alona.

The President. Alona.

Q. Mr. President, will Ukraine be invited to participate in the Membership Action Plan at NATO summit? And how much, if it gets it, this invitation, how much time will be needed for Ukraine to enter NATO?

The President. Yes——

Q. Nine years as it is for Macedonia, or 5 years as it was for the Baltic States?

The President. Iona, first of all, it's—the decision will be made by NATO members at Bucharest. So when I come to your country, I'll be saying that I believe that Ukraine benefits from not only the process to join NATO but eventually, hopefully, joining NATO. But that decision won't be made until we're all there in Romania.

Secondly, it just depends on the country as to how long events will—the reforms take in order to get offered membership into NATO. So the first step, however, is for there to be a clear path forward, so that people understand. And I believe it's in our collective interest that we offer a clear path forward. But it's very important for the people in your country to understand that the decision won't be made until after I leave Ukraine and make it to Romania.

Are they still talking about the "rainbow speech"? Were you there for that?

Q. Yes.

The President. It was an amazing moment, wasn't it?

Q. Yes. It was amazing moment, yes.

The President. I was giving a speech in the town square where Ceausescu had given his final speech. And it was raining, and just as I got up to speak, a full rainbow appeared.

Q. Yes, and about bridge to a new Russia.

The President. Yes.

Q. You remember that?

The President. I remember the rainbow most of all. It was a startling moment.

Anyway, fire away, Ioana.

Moldova

Q. Johanna.

The President. Johanna.

Q. Mr. President, Moldova is a country between NATO member Romania and possible future NATO member Ukraine. But Moldova still has a lot of problems: poverty, corruption, and Russian troops on its territory without its consent. Washington is currently involved in resolving a breakaway region, Transnistria. But my question is, what do you think the United States can do to help Moldova to become a democratic, independent state and not a failed state under Russian influence, a point of instability at the NATO border?

The President. Right. First is to continue to make our intentions clear, and that is that we want to work to make sure Moldova, which is now an independent nation, has got sovereign borders and is treated like an independent nation. Secondly, we constantly advocate for good, clean, open government. Thirdly, we're a member of a 5-plus-2, which is the process by which, hopefully, the Transnistria issue would be solved.

So our strategy is to work with the relevant parties and to promote, as you said, a independent, open, transparent, good-government Moldova.

Yes, sir.

Croatia

Q. Mr. President——

The President. Yes.

Q. ——how do you see Croatia future in the NATO architecture in southeastern Europe, regarding its capability to host joint military bases, and primarily NATO forces, and the further development of its armed forces and its readiness to take part in NATO missions and contribute to the common security of the alliance?

The President. Yes, thank you.

Q. And how do you see the role of Croatia in promoting peace and stability in southeastern Europe, especially regarding the present situation relating to the establishment of independent Kosovo?

The President. Kosovo, sure. Whew, it's a long question. First of all, just get this off the table: There's no intention to have NATO bases, permanent bases. Secondly, Croatia has served as a very good example, following a very dramatic moment, and that is the breakup of Yugoslavia. And your

Government has made difficult decisions and made those decisions, first and foremost, on behalf of the people. But it turns out, many of the reform decisions, therefore, make it likely that Croatia will be invited into NATO.

Examples are very important. The question is, would people have predicted 15 years ago that we'd be having this kind of discussion about Croatia? And who knows; I don't think many people would have, certainly, 25 years ago. And yet Croatia is a independent, sovereign nation, hopefully, soon to be invited to join NATO, which is a clear example of what is possible if people make the right decisions on behalf of their people.

Part of being a part of NATO means commitment to a modern military. And Croatian troops, which have performed bravely in recent active theaters during this war against extremism, will benefit from being in NATO and benefit from serving side by side with other members of NATO. NATO membership would be a very positive thing for the people of Croatia.

And I'm really looking forward to going to your country. I hope I'm coming with good news, but the decision will be made in this case before I go to Croatia. And they say it's one of the most beautiful coastlines in the entire world.

Q. Yes. Hope you're going to see that.

The President. Am I going to get to see the coastline? I hope I do.

Q. I hope, I hope.

The President. You're not my scheduler, okay.

Thomas.

Progress in Iraq

Q. Thank you, Mr. President.

The President. I do think Great Britain ought to be in NATO, yes. [*Laughter*]

Q. I think we were last time I checked. [*Laughter*]

The President. Yes, you are, and a very good member.

Q. Thank you very much. In a different field of operations, in Iraq, there's been a recent upsurge again in violence, which appears to have emanated in the area of Basra, which Britain used to control. Do you believe recent events there serve as a warning to those in your country and beyond who have counseled you to withdraw rapidly?

The President. My first reaction to watching the Iraqi Government respond forcefully—and to make it abundantly clear that—I think the exact—I can't remember the exact words of the Prime Minister, but "criminal elements," I know, were a part of his declaration—would be dealt with. I thought that was a very positive moment in the development of a sovereign nation that is willing to take on elements that are—you know, that believe they're beyond the law.

And secondly, we are helping, but it's important to know that the Iraqis are in the lead. This is a positive moment in the development of a nation that can govern itself and defend itself and sustain itself. We will provide oversight and, on occasion, support when asked. This is an Iraqi operation.

And one of the things I'll be saying in the runup to the Petraeus-Crocker testimony is that we have made substantial gains, but it's still a fragile situation. Therefore, the decision about our troop levels will be based upon not politics or not who can scream the loudest, but based upon whether or not we can maintain the successes we've had. And I understand there's people here who want us to leave regardless of the situation, but that's not going to happen so long as I'm the Commander in Chief.

British Troop Withdrawal From Iraq

Q. Did we get out too early?

The President. No, you didn't. The British commitment was—first of all, you were there from day one, and you were there during the very heavy fighting. And the

British commitment was to move to the airbase based upon success. And I'm very grateful for the British friendship and alliance and the contributions.

Alona. What do you think, Alona? So where do you live? Kiev?

Ukraine/Kosovan Independence

Q. Kiev, yes.

The President. Yes? So you flew all the way over here just for this interview?

Q. Yes.

The President. I'm very grateful. Oh, so guess what happened to me. I went down to Crawford—that's in Texas—and I went to an event for—to honor some of our soldiers' families. And a local doctor—I think it was a doctor—came and said, "Would you mind meeting a group of people from Ukraine?" I said, "Sure." And there we were in Waco, Texas, with, I think, maybe 20 or 30 health care specialists from Ukraine that were in my home State. And it was sure good to meet them.

Q. And how important is Ukraine's recognition of Kosovo in the U.S. point of view? Do you expect this step from the Ukrainian authorities in the nearest future?

The President. That's going to be up to the Ukranian authorities to make the decisions that they deem are necessary. We hope they will recognize Kosovo's independence, just like we have. It's supervised independence, of course, but we strongly supported that idea from the beginning and supported the U.N. plan that would help lead to a supervised independence and, at the same time, guarantee the minority rights within Kosovo. And we would hope Ukraine would do the same thing.

Ioana.

U.S. Visa Policy

Q. Romania is a U.S. ally in Iraq and Afghanistan, but the Romanians are not met as allies on the United States territory.

The President. Aha. [*Laughter*] You're heading towards the visa issue, aren't you?

Q. Yes. What Romania should do to enter in waiver visa program? And what do you recommend us, bilateral negotiations with the United States or negotiations through European Union?

The President. Yes, thank you. [*Laughter*] Very tricky question. [*Laughter*] You ready? You better turn that thing up, because I'm going to give you a whopper of an answer. [*Laughter*]

Q. Give me the news, I hope. [*Laughter*]

The President. Yes. Now, first of all, it is hard for me to justify to the citizens of Romania that they can serve alongside our troops in major theaters in the war against extremists and not be able to have—be treated like other members of the EU, as far as visa waiver, and I know that. And it's difficult for citizens to understand that.

But we're still dealing with a—you know, it is—we're adjusting law based upon previous practice. And the law needed to change, reflecting the modern era, and it did change. Congress did change the capacity for—to have a new look at visa waiver. But there are some requirements. And my advice is for the Romanian Government to negotiate bilaterally with the United States in order to solve this problem.

There are other countries in your neighborhood that are making good progress toward being granted visa waiver. And I would strongly urge your leaders to take a look at what they have done and then interface with our officials. And I'll, of course, be talking of this with the President and the Prime Minister when I'm there.

Q. Thank you very much.

The President. Yes.

Yes, sir.

Croatia-U.S. Relations

Q. Mr. President, Croatian NATO membership bid and steadfast support of your administration for that ambition was a centerpiece of the bilateral relations between Croatia and U.S.A. last 7 or 8 years. And will it now, if Croatia became a NATO member—and relations will be elevated to the higher level of allies—can we expect to see more importance will be attached to the economic cooperation, U.S. investment in Croatia in the future?

The President. Yes, our relationships tend not to be—they tend to be multidimensional and not just based upon one aspect or another. And I believe strongly in free trade and the movement of investment. And Croatia occupies a crucial part—a crucial space in an important part of the world. And of course, we want to enhance trade.

A lot of Americans need to learn more about Croatia, although there are about a million Croatian Americans here. And there's going to be all kinds of opportunities. Of course, those opportunities will be advantaged if the Government makes rational decisions on, for example, good investment laws. In other words, there's competition for investment dollars, in this case, or investment euros, or investment whatevers. And therefore, the laws need to be transparent, the rule of law consistent, the Government obviously clean, so that the main risk for an invested currency is not government risk, it is the risk of the enterprise itself.

And therefore, to answer your question, yes, of course, we want to have all kinds of different aspects of our relationship flourish with Croatia. But in terms of investing, it's going to be up to the Government to make decisions to make sure the investment climate is good.

Q. Thank you.

The President. Yes.

United Kingdom-U.S. Relations/France-U.S. Relations

Q. Mr. President?

The President. Yes, Thomas.

Q. ——very formal. [*Laughter*]

The President. Okay, Tom.

Q. You mentioned in your preamble that it is important for NATO to honor its obligations to Afghanistan. There has been some criticism of NATO's performance in Afghanistan from Washington. In recent days, Nicolas Sarkozy, your new friend— [*laughter*]—has promised another 1,000 troops for Afghanistan.

The President. Today.

Q. Yes. Is there any sense that on that battlefield and indeed, beyond, France is now emerging as your greatest ally?

The President. I have always said that the relationship with the United Kingdom is a special relationship. And that relationship was never as special as it was during times of conflict, whether it be the relationship in the past between, like, Roosevelt and Churchill, or whether it be the current relationship, more modern relationship between Tony Blair and myself. And so your question, "our greatest ally," it's going to be hard for any nation to trump Great Britain as our—United Kingdom as our greatest ally.

Having said that, no question, the relationship is changing for the better, and President Sarkozy gets a lot of credit for that. I like him personally. He's an interesting man. He is a highly energetic, decisive person, who is not interested in creating divisions between—in the transatlantic alliance, but is interested in making sure that not only are bilateral relations are good, but the transatlantic alliance meets the threats.

And his statement about commitment to—French troops to Afghanistan is a very important preamble to the NATO conference. It will pretty much ensure that this conference is a successful conference, because nations will watch very carefully. When you combine our commitment, the Canadian commitment, the British commitment, and the French commitment of troops that will be in harm's way, it is a strong statement that NATO understands the threats, understands the challenges, and is willing to rise to them.

Okay, everybody, it's been a joyous experience. And for you? It's a beauty. [*Laughter*] Okay.

Russia-U.S. Relations

Q. And about Russia?

The President. I thought we said two questions apiece.

Q. In your opinion, what are the prospects for democracy in Russia, in Medvedev——

The President. I haven't met President Medvedev yet. I may have met him once, but I haven't had a talk to him, President to President, obviously. He's not even the President yet. I'm looking forward to meeting him. I am—have you put out the word yet?

Mr. Hadley. No.

The President. Are you going to today?

Mr. Hadley. I am.

The President. Yes, okay. So I'm going to go to Russia. I've been invited to Russia. President Putin has invited me to Russia. You're the first to hear it, so you can hustle out of here and put it on the wires. This is no longer off the record. Steve is going to come and brief it at 3:30 p.m.—3:15 p.m., President Putin has invited me to go to Sochi. And it's to discuss the strategic agreement, the crucial part of which is missile defense.

Condi Rice and Bob Gates had a good visit with the President and counterparts on this very issue—and hopefully, that we can advance our dialogue, so at some point in time, we can reach an agreement on these important matters, proliferation matters. I know we've got agreement on Iran, and that is that Iran should not have the capacity to enrich, and that I supported the Russian efforts to convince the Iranians that they didn't need to learn how to enrich, because he—Putin—was willing to provide enriched uranium for a civilian nuclear power plant. Therefore, no need to enrich, which I thought was a smart move and supported.

So there's an area where we'll continue to have discussions. And I called President-elect Medvedev and reminded him—and congratulated him for getting elected and reminded him that—of some of the comments he made about rule law and transparency—and can't remember exactly everything he said, but it sounded very progressive. And I said, we're listening very carefully to your words, and I appreciated your speech and looking forward to working with you to help accomplish those objectives.

But I have yet to work with him, obviously, President to President. He hasn't been sworn in. So check back in with me after I've had a couple of meetings with him.

President's Visit to Russia/Missile Defense System

Q. When are you going to Russia?

The President. Day after Croatia. We haven't worked the details yet.

Mr. Hadley. We have not worked the details yet.

The President. My crack adviser here is giving me—[*laughter*].

Mr. Hadley. Clearly, we intend to accept. We're going to have to work the details out.

The President. Yes, we intend to accept. In other words, there's an invitation out there, and this is really—the way to look at this is a follow-up to Condi and Bob Gates's meeting, which is good. Romania and other nations would hope that the United States would have good relations with Russia. And it's important that we have good relations with Russia; we can find common interests.

On the other hand, there are areas where we have been able to be in a position where I've expressed my disagreements with President Putin on different matters related to their democracy. And my strategy all along is to keep relations such that he will actually listen to what I have to say. So when you hear people say, "George Bush has got good relations with Vladimir Putin," there's a reason why. Because if you're—in order to have somebody listen to you, they got to at least have an open

mind. And it's hard to have an open mind if the only thing you're doing is try to blast away on a regular basis about your disagreements publicly. I've chosen not to do that.

Therefore, I'm optimistic we can reach accord on very important matters. I think a lot of people in Europe would have a deep sigh of relief if we're able to reach an accord on missile defense. And hopefully, we can. One of the things that, hopefully, is clear to the Russian side is that this system is not aimed at Russia. After all, it doesn't take many missiles to overwhelm the kind of system we're talking about. And Russia has got plenty of missiles if they want to overwhelm. This is really aimed at a potential missile launch, for example, out of the Middle East. And therefore, I think it makes sense for us to be able to be in a position, if people so choose to share information and fully understand the operational activities of a system, so as to build confidence.

So we'll see how it goes. I'm looking forward to it.

Russia's Leadership

Q. Do you think President Putin continues to pull the strings?

The President. You know, I just don't know. It's an interesting question. That's speculative.

Q. It's what we do for a living. [*Laughter*]

The President. Not me. [*Laughter*]

Thank you all. Enjoyed it.

NOTE: The interview was taped at 1:53 p.m. in the Roosevelt Room at the White House and was released by the Office of the Press Secretary on March 27. In his remarks, the President referred to Prime Minister Nuri al-Maliki of Iraq; Gen. David H. Petraeus, USA, commanding general, Multi-National Force—Iraq; President Traian Basescu and Prime Minister Calin Popescu-Tariceanu of Romania; former Prime Minister Tony Blair of the United Kingdom; and President Nicolas Sarkozy of France. A tape was not available for verification of the content of this interview.

Memorandum on Certification Concerning U.S. Participation in the United Nations-African Union Mission in Darfur Under Section 2005 of the American Servicemembers' Protection Act
March 26, 2008

Memorandum for the Secretary of State

Subject: Certification Concerning U.S. Participation in the United Nations-African Union Mission in Darfur Under Section 2005 of the American Servicemembers' Protection Act

Consistent with section 2005 of the American Servicemembers' Protection Act (Public Law 107–206; 22 U.S.C. 7421 *et seq.*), concerning the participation of members of the Armed Forces of the United States in certain United Nations peacekeeping and peace enforcement operations, I hereby certify that members of the U.S. Armed Forces participating in the United Nations-African Union Mission in Darfur (UNAMID) are without risk of criminal prosecution or other assertion of jurisdiction by the International Criminal Court (ICC) because the United Nations Security Council has permanently exempted members of the U.S. Armed Forces participating in UNAMID from criminal prosecution or other assertion of jurisdiction by the ICC for actions undertaken by them in connection with UNAMID by deciding, in Resolution 1593 (2005), that "personnel from a contributing state outside Sudan which is not a party to the Rome Statute of the International Criminal Court shall be subject to the exclusive jurisdiction of that contributing State for all alleged acts or omissions arising out of or related to operations in Sudan established or authorized by the Council or the African Union, unless such exclusive jurisdiction has been expressly waived by that contributing State."

You are authorized and directed to submit this certification to the Congress and arrange for its publication in the *Federal Register*.

GEORGE W. BUSH

NOTE: This memorandum was released by the Office of the Press Secretary on March 27, and it was not received for publication in the *Federal Register*.

Remarks at the National Museum of the United States Air Force in Dayton, Ohio
March 27, 2008

Thank you all very much. Thank you all. General Metcalf, thanks. Thanks for welcoming me back here. I am really pleased to be back to Wright-Patt, and it's great to be on the inside of the National Museum of the United States Air Force, which is a fabulous place. I hope our fellow citizens come and see it. It is a great tribute to the airmen who've flown the missions and secured the skies and defended America's freedom.

I want to thank the folks who maintain this shrine. I thank you for giving me a place to park Air Force One. [*Laughter*] And I appreciate the hospitality of the people who serve our country here at Wright-Patt. And I want to thank you for coming to give me a chance to share with you an update on the historic work our Nation is undertaking in Iraq.

Over the past year, we have seen significant security gains result from the surge. Less visible are the political and economic changes taking place, from major pieces of legislation being passed to simple signs of normalcy. This progress isn't glamorous, but it is important. And that's what I'm here to talk about today.

But before I do so, I want to thank not only General Metcalf, but I want to thank Congressman Jim Jordan for serving our country. I appreciate the State auditor, Mary Taylor, for joining us today. Thank you for coming. I am grateful that the mayor, Mayor McLin, took time to come by and say hello. Madam Mayor, thank you very much for your—[*applause*]. Appreciate the other State and local officials.

I do want to thank General Bruce Carlson, commander of the Air Force Materiel Command, Colonel Colleen Ryan, and all those who wear the uniform. I'm proud to be with you, and I'm proud to be your Commander in Chief.

I thank very much the fact that Susan Kettering came, vice president of the Kettering Family Foundation. And the reason why she's important and the foundation is important is, they've been strong supporters of this museum.

And finally, I want to recognize Amanda Wright Lane, great grandniece of Orville and Wilbur Wright. Thanks for coming. Nothing wrong with having famous relatives. [*Laughter*]

This museum pays tribute to a—to great aircraft and great airmen and women, from the first fliers of the Great War to the aces of World War II to the daring pilots of Korea and Vietnam. And over the past 6 years, a new generation of American airmen and women have joined that storied history. After all, the Air Force was critical in liberating the people of Afghanistan and the people of Iraq and taking the fight to the enemy overseas so we do not have to face them here at home. On a fateful day in this war, airmen delivered justice to the Al Qaida terrorist Zarqawi in the form of two precision-guided, 500-pound bombs.

The military achievements in Iraq have been accompanied by a political transformation. It can feel like distant history, but it was only 5 years ago that Iraq was one of the most brutal dictatorships on Earth, a totalitarian nightmare where any election was a sham and dissenters often found themselves buried in mass graves. In a matter of 15 months, the Iraqi people reclaimed their sovereignty. They went on to choose an interim Government and to ratify the most democratic Constitution in the Arab world. And in December 2005, 12 million Iraqis elected a Government under that Constitution, a display of courage that defied the terrorists, disproved the critics, and should always inspire the world.

Tragically, the progress threatened to unravel in 2006. The new Government Iraqis elected took months to form. In the meantime, a terrorist attack on a Shi'a shrine in Samarra drove sectarian tensions past the breaking point. Sunni extremists, including Al Qaida terrorists, and Shi'a extremists, some backed by Iran, slaughtered innocent Iraqis in brutal attacks and reprisal killings. And across the country, political and economic activity was set back.

We took a hard look at the situation and responded with the surge. This dramatic shift in policy had two primary goals. The first was to improve security conditions. So I ordered 30,000 additional soldiers and marines into Iraq and gave them a new mission: to focus on protecting the Iraqi people and to hold the gains that had been made.

The other goal of the surge was to open up space for political and economic progress after security returned. So we deployed additional civilian experts and more than doubled the number of Provincial Reconstruction Teams, with a mission to ensure that security gains were followed up by improvements in daily life.

General Petraeus and Ambassador Crocker will provide more details about the progress of the surge when they testify before Congress early next month. But this much is clear: The surge is doing what it was designed to do. It's helping Iraqis reclaim security and restart political and economic life. It is bringing America closer to a key strategic victory in the war against these extremists and radicals.

On the security side, the surge has brought important gains, which I discussed in detail last week in a speech at the Pentagon. In Baghdad, we've worked with Iraqi security forces to greatly diminish the sectarian violence and civilian deaths. We've broken the grip of Al Qaida on the capital. We've weakened the influence of Iranian-backed militias. We've dramatically improved security conditions in many devastated neighborhoods in what some have deemed a reliberation.

In Anbar Province, which 18 months ago was declared lost to Al Qaida, we joined with the brave local sheiks who launched the first large-scale Arab uprising against Al Qaida. Together, we've systematically dismantled Al Qaida in that Province. In just over a year, Ramadi, the capital of Anbar, has seen its average number of attacks plummet from more than 18 per day to less than 1 per week. It's becoming clear that Anbar has not been lost to Al Qaida—that Al Qaida has been—has lost Anbar. And that's important because this is the place where Al Qaida leadership has said they will find safe haven from which to launch further attacks against the United States of America.

In other parts of Iraq, from Baghdad belts to Diyala Province to parts of the south, we've worked with coalition and Iraqi forces to drive the terrorists out of

strongholds and put them on the run. Now Al Qaida's concentrated its efforts in the area of Mosul, which is in northern Iraq. And there's going to be tough fighting in Mosul and in areas around Mosul in the weeks and months. But we are determined, along with the Iraqis, to make sure Al Qaida meets the same fate there that it has met elsewhere in Iraq.

A key factor in these security gains has been new cooperation from the Iraqi people. Ordinary Iraqis have come forward with intelligence tips. Citizens who were once hostile to the coalition have switched sides and are now joining with us. Over the past year, more than 100,000 Iraqis have joined their nation's security forces. In other words, there was an Iraqi surge to match our own. These Iraqis are fighting and sacrificing for their country. They want to live in a free society. Iraqi mothers want their children to grow up in peace, just like American mothers do.

The Iraqi forces are growing in capability. Recently, they planned and executed a highly effective operation to secure nearly 9 million pilgrims celebrating the religious holiday of Arbaeen. And as we speak, Iraqi security forces are waging a tough battle against militia fighters and criminals in Basra, many of whom have received arms and training and funding from Iran.

Prime Minister Maliki's bold decision—and it was a bold decision—to go after the illegal groups in Basra shows his leadership and his commitment to enforce the law in an evenhanded manner. It also shows the progress the Iraqi security forces have made during the surge. Iraqi forces planned this operation, and they deployed substantial extra forces for it. They're leading the operation. Prime Minister Maliki has traveled to Basra to oversee it firsthand.

This offensive builds on the security gains of the surge and demonstrates to the Iraqi people that their Government is committed to protecting them. There's a strong commitment by the central Government of Iraq to say that no one is above the law.

This operation is going to take some time to complete, and the enemy will try to fill the TV screens with violence. But the ultimate result will be this: Terrorists and extremists in Iraq will know they have no place in a free and democratic society.

The surge is yielding major changes in Iraqi political life, and that is important. Before the surge, politics at every level was shutting down. I mean, for leaders, security crisis prevented the routine conduct of government. You know, for ordinary citizens, politics were a distant concern. I mean, after all, they were simply trying to keep their families alive. And for all Iraqis, the violence hardened sectarian attitudes and made tough political compromises impossible.

A year later—1 year later—after we sent additional troops into Iraq, the situation has changed markedly. With security improving, local citizens have restarted the political process in their neighborhoods and cities and Provinces. Let me give you an example. In Ramadi, tribal sheiks who led the uprising against Al Qaida are now leading a revival of politics. With the support of our PRTs, Ramadi now has a fully staffed mayor's office, and neighborhood councils have formed. Judges are presiding over courts and restoring the rule of law.

As the news of the success in Anbar has spread, similar grassroots movements have sprung up all around the country. Today, some 90,000 Iraqis belong to local citizens groups bearing the proud name Sons of Iraq. Many of these groups are Sunnis; some are Shi'a; some are mixed. But whatever their makeup, these groups of citizens are determined to protect their communities; they are determined to fight extremism; and they increasingly participate in civic life. In other words, people have stepped up and said: "We're sick and tired of our families having to live in violence. We can't stand the thought of people who murder the innocent to achieve political objectives, and we intend to do something about it." And they have.

And the central Government is beginning to respond to these Sons of Iraq. And it's not easy. I mean, after all, some of them were former regime members or former insurgents. Yet the Iraqi Government has pledged to incorporate about 20 to 30 percent of the Sons of Iraq into the Iraqi Army and police forces. For the rest, the national Government has now committed $196 million to fund jobs programs so that brave Iraqis who stand up to the extremists and the murders and the criminals can learn the skills they need to help build a free and prosperous nation.

The Sons of Iraq movement is only one element of the bottom-up political process. You know, sometimes it requires grassroots politics to get the folks in central Government to respond. Sometimes that happens in our own country. [*Laughter*] Well, it's happening in Iraq.

You know, another sign of bottom-up political progress is the rebirth of Iraqi civil society. We take civil society for granted in America. But civil society was destroyed during the time of the brutal dictator, Saddam Hussein. And yet it's now coming back to life. Civic organizations are springing up. Institutions that sustain a free nation are strengthening. Our PRT in Karbala, for example, helped local residents establish a women's center that will provide education and promote equality. In Anbar, they just had a 5k race on what used to be the most dangerous streets in Iraq.

I talked to General Odierno; he's the number-two man in Iraq. He just came back after courageously serving our country, and he came to the Oval Office. And here's what he told me. He said he flew over Baghdad 15 months ago, and he couldn't see a single soccer game. On his final flight last month, he counted more than 180. Now, that may sound normal to us, and we take it for granted, but it is a sign that the surge is working and civil society is beginning to grow. It is a sign normalcy is returning back to Iraq.

And over time, these developments at the local level have increased pressure for action at the national level. Leaders in Baghdad are responding. By any reasonable measure, the legislative achievements in Baghdad over the past 4 months have been remarkable.

In December, the Government enacted a pension law that will allow tens of thousands of Sunnis to collect the retirement benefits they were promised. Part of reconciliation is to reach out to groups who may not have trust in central Government, and you build trust by honoring commitments.

In January, leaders enacted a de-Ba'athification law that allows mid-level Ba'ath Party members to reenter political and civic life. There was a period of time that if you were associated with the Ba'ath Party, you couldn't teach in a school, and yet there was a need for teachers. And this law will make it easier for civil society to grow and helps reconcile the past.

In February, leaders enacted a budget that increases spending on security and capital reconstruction projects and Provincial governments. And on the same day, leaders enacted an amnesty law to resolve the status of many Iraqis held in Iraqi custody. Last week, leaders reached agreement on a Provincial powers law that helps define Iraqi federalism and sets the stage for Provincial elections later this year. And that's an important piece of legislation because it will give Iraqis who boycotted the last Provincial election, such as Sunnis in Anbar or Ninawa Provinces, a chance to go to the polls and have a voice in their future.

These pieces of legislation deal with complex issues that are vital for the reconciliation of the country and fundamental for a democratic society. I mean, we've been arguing about the role of the Federal Government relative to the States for a long time here in America. We've been trying to get the balance right. There's a constant struggle between the proper role of State and local government versus the role of the Federal Government. Well, that's what the Iraqis are now struggling through.

You know, they got their budget passed, and sometimes it takes our Congress awhile to get its budget passed. [*Laughter*] Nevertheless, some Members of Congress decided the best way to encourage progress in Baghdad was to criticize and threaten Iraq's leaders while they're trying to work out their differences. But hectoring was not what the Iraqi leaders needed. What they needed was security, and that is what the surge has provided. When the security situation improved and the Iraqi leaders were reassured that America wouldn't leave them, that America would support them, they then made tough compromises necessary to get key pieces of legislation passed.

And it is a lesson worth remembering as Iraq's national Government goes about the substantial work that remains, including implementing the laws it's passed, reviewing its Constitution, drafting a electoral law, and passing laws to reform its oil sector and codify revenue sharing. It's also worth remembering the enormity of what the Iraqis are trying to do. They're striving to build a modern democracy on the rubble of three decades of tyranny in a region of the world that has been hostile to freedom. And they're doing it while under assault from one of history's most brutal terrorist networks.

When it takes time for Iraqis to reach agreement, it is not foot dragging, as one Senator described it during Congress's 2-week Easter recess. It is a revolutionary undertaking that requires great courage. You know, one Iraqi leader recently acknowledged that he's faced four assassination attempts a year since liberation. Yet he proudly serves his nation with strong determination because he wants to live in a free society. And he understands what I understand: Free societies yield the peace we want. And it's in our interests to stand strongly with the leaders like that in Iraq and give them all the support necessary to succeed.

The improvements in security resulting from the surge are also enabling Iraqis to make progress on their economy. Iraq has great economic potential. They've got a young, energetic population; it's got a lot of natural resources. Yet in many ways, the legacy of the tyrant continues to haunt the Iraqi economy. The Government is forced to rely on the centralized food and fuel rationing system that Saddam used to control his population and to punish his enemies. The infrastructure for Iraq's oil sector is still owned and managed by the central Government and suffers from decades of underinvestment. Iraq's economic problems grew worse during the sectarian violence that preceded the surge. Oil revenues declined, businesses closed their doors, and infrastructure was destroyed.

A year later, almost every key economic indicator has turned around. Since the surge began, business registrations have increased by more than 9 percent. Total inflation has fallen by more than 60 percentage points. Investment in the energy and telecom industries has increased. The agricultural sector is improving. Oil production is up, particularly north of Baghdad. The oil fields there have more than doubled production, and exports through Turkey have expanded significantly.

The national Government has announced a plan to reform the food rationing system. Economic growth is projected to be a robust 7 percent this year. And the confidence of Iraqis is rising. They're beginning to see a more hopeful future. More than 75 percent of Iraqi businesses, according to a recent survey, expect the economy continue to growing over the next 2 years.

As the economic situation stabilizes, Iraq's Government has stepped forward to meet more of its own expenses. This is a mark of pride for Iraqis, and it is a point of insistence for us. Early in the war, America funded most of the large-scale reconstruction projects in Iraq, and we've changed our focus. Now we're focused on encouraging entrepreneurship. The Iraqi Government is stepping up on reconstruction projects. They have outspent us in the recent budget 11 to 1, and soon we expect the Iraqis will cover 100 percent of those expenses.

The same is true when it comes to security spending. Initially, the United States paid for most of the costs of training and equipping the Iraqi security forces. Now Iraq's budget covers three-quarters of the cost of its security forces, which is a total of more than $9 billion in 2008. And soon Iraq should, and we expect them to, shoulder the full burden of their security forces.

They have other work to do in their economy. The reforms needed to transition from a command-and-control economy to a modern market-based system are complex, and it's going to take some time. Centralized electricity generation is now above prewar levels, but it is not sufficient to meet the needs of Iraq because demand is growing. Other key infrastructure needs to be upgraded, especially energy pipelines and storage facilities. Unemployment is still too high. Corruption remains a challenge. But the good news is, the Iraqis recognize these shortcomings. They understand what they have to do. And we're going to help them succeed. We're sending experts to help them succeed in their goals.

Listen to the words of Iraq's Deputy Prime Minister: "Last year was the year of security," he said. "This year is the year of reconstruction, it is the year of services, and it's the year of combating corruption." And we're going to help them meet those goals.

The surge is also helping give Iraq's leaders the confidence to expand their international engagement. Iraqi leaders are working hard to meet the criterion required to join the WTO, which would help its entrepreneurs benefit from the opportunities of a global economy. Iraq has taken steps to attract foreign investment, including holding its first Business to Business

Expo since the Gulf war. The Government is meeting its pledge to reform its economy in exchange for development assistance and debt relief through the International Compact for Iraq.

Much of the world is increasing its commitment to Iraq. The United Kingdom, Italy, and South Korea are leading PRTs. The United Nations is playing an expanded role in Iraq and will help prepare for this year's Provincial elections. And next month, the third Expanded Neighbors Conference will meet in Kuwait City to discuss ways the region and the world can further support Iraq's political, economic, and security progress. This is a key diplomatic initiative. It will include all of Iraq's neighbors as well as the permanent members of the U.N. Security Council, the G–8, the Arab League, and the Organization of Islamic Conference.

Iraq's neighbors can do more, and we're constantly sending out diplomatic missions to encourage them to do more. Earlier this week, the King of Bahrain came to visit me in the Oval Office, and his Government announced that he will send an ambassador to Iraq. And I appreciate that and urge other nations in the region to follow his lead. It's in their interest that a peaceful Iraq evolve. At the same time, the regimes in Iran and Syria must stop supporting violence and terror in Iraq.

Iraq also wants to solidify its relationship with the United States. Last year, Iraqi leaders came to us with a request to form a long-term strategic partnership. This partnership would help assure Iraqis that political and economic and security cooperation between our nations will endure. This partnership would also ensure protections for American troops when the U.N. mandate for multinational forces in Iraq expires this December. Now, this partnership would not bind future Presidents to specific troop levels. This partnership would not establish permanent bases in Iraq. It would be similar to partnerships that we have with Afghanistan and other free nations around the world. My administration will work to complete this strategic partnership in the coming months. The Iraqi people have chosen to stand with America against our common enemies, and it's in our interest that we stand with them.

Having witnessed all this progress from the surge, the natural question is, what are the next steps? Well, this week, I've been discussing that question with my national security team in Washington as well as with General Petraeus and Ambassador Crocker in Baghdad. They will discuss that question with Members of Congress when they come and testify in April. They'll outline the achievements of the surge as well as the challenges that remain, including the continued presence of Al Qaida, the violence caused by Shi'a extremists, the destructive influence of Iran, the flow of suicide bombers through Syria, the activities of PKK terrorists.

I'm going to carefully consider the recommendations of Secretary Gates and the Joint Chiefs of Staff and those on the ground, General Petraeus and Ambassador Crocker. And I'll announce my decisions soon after I have fully met with them and heard their recommendations. And as I consider the way forward, I will always remember that the progress in Iraq is real, it's substantive, but it is reversible. And so the principle behind my decision on our troop levels will be ensuring that we succeed in Iraq.

As this debate unfolds, I ask people on both sides to keep an open mind and to take a close look at the situation on the ground. Here is what one scholar and critic of the war recently said: "No one can spend some 10 days visiting the battlefields in Iraq without seeing major progress in every area. If the United States provides sustained support to the Iraqi Government— in security, governance, and development— there is now a very real chance that Iraq will emerge as a secure and stable state."

Some, however, seem unwilling to acknowledge that progress is taking place.

Earlier in the war, they said the political situation wasn't good enough. Then after Iraq held three historic elections, they said the security situation wasn't good enough. Then after the security situation began to improve, they said politics, again, wasn't good enough. And now that political progress is picking up, they're looking for a new reason.

But there's one thing that is consistent. No matter what shortcomings these critics diagnose, their prescription is always the same: retreat. They claim that our strategic interest is elsewhere, and that if we would just get out of Iraq, we could focus on the battles that really matter. This argument makes no sense. If America's strategic interests are not in Iraq—the convergence point for the twin threats of Al Qaida and Iran, the nation Usama bin Laden's deputy has called "the place for the greatest battle," the country at the heart of the most volatile region on Earth—then where are they?

The reality is that retreating from Iraq would carry enormous strategic costs for the United States. It would incite chaos and killing, destroy the political gains the Iraqis have made, and abandon our friends to terrorists and death squads. It would endanger Iraq's oil resources and could serve as a severe disruption to the world's economy. It would increase the likelihood that Al Qaida would gain safe havens that they could use to attack us here at home. It would be a propaganda victory of colossal proportions for the global terrorist movement, which would gain new funds and find new recruits and conclude that the way to defeat America is to bleed us into submission. It would signal to Iran that we were not serious about confronting its efforts to impose its will on the region. It would signal to people across the Middle East that the United States cannot be trusted to keep its word. A defeat in Iraq would have consequences far beyond that country, and they would be felt by Americans here at home.

For the same reason, helping the Iraqis defeat their enemies and build a free society would be a strategic victory that would resound far beyond Iraq's borders. If Al Qaida is defeated in Iraq after all the resources it has poured into the battle there, it will be a powerful blow against the global terrorist movement. If Iran is turned back in its attempt to gain undue influence over Iraq, it will be a setback to the—its ambitions to dominate the region. If people across the Middle East see freedom prevail in multiethnic, multisectarian Iraq, it will mark a decisive break from the long reign of tyranny in that region. And if the Middle East grows in freedom and prosperity, the appeal of extremism will decline, the prospects of peace will advance, and the American people will be safer here at home. The surge has opened the door to this strategic victory. Now we must seize the opportunity and sustain the initiative and do what it takes to prevail.

Realizing this vision is not going to be easy. Yet we should never let the difficulty of the fight obscure the justice of the cause. We should never let the difficulty of the moment cause us to shirk our duty to lay the foundation of peace for generations of Americans to come.

You know, when I mentioned justice of the cause, you see that when Americans in full battle gear hand out books to children, hand out books to total strangers. You see it when they defuse bombs to protect the innocent or help organize a town council meeting. And when you see that, there could be no doubt that America is a force for good and decency.

Four thousand of our finest citizens have sacrificed their lives in this mission. Every one of them was loved; every one is missed. And we thank God for the gifts of these brave Americans, and we ask Him to comfort their families. Every one of them will be honored throughout our history. But the best way to honor the fallen is to complete the mission and lay the foundation of peace.

All those who serve on the frontlines of this struggle, this ideological struggle, this confrontation against those who murder innocent men, women, and children to achieve their political objectives, are patriots who are upholding the highest ideals of our country. Many of them are air men and women. They're adding to the tradition of the great aviators honored by this museum and of others known to us as family, friends, neighbors, or, in my case, dad. The work that today's generation is doing is every bit as challenging, every bit as noble, and every bit as vital to our security as any that came before. When the history of this era is written, it will show that the Air Force and all of Americans' Armed Forces performed with unfailing skill and courage. It will show that the United States of America prevailed, and freedom advanced, and so did peace.

May God bless you, and may God bless our country.

NOTE: The President spoke at 10:21 a.m. at Wright-Patterson Air Force Base. In his remarks, he referred to Maj. Gen. Charles D. Metcalf, USAF (Ret.), director, National Museum of the United States Air Force; Mayor Rhine McLin of Dayton, OH; Col. Colleen M. Ryan, USAF, commander, 88th Air Base Wing, and installation commander, Wright-Patterson Air Force Base; Gen. David H. Petraeus, USA, commanding general, Multi-National Force—Iraq; Prime Minister Nuri al-Maliki and Deputy Prime Minister Barham Salih of Iraq; Lt. Gen. Raymond T. Odierno, USA, commanding general, Multi-National Corps—Iraq; King Hamad bin Isa al-Khalifa of Bahrain; Usama bin Laden, leader of the Al Qaida terrorist organization; and Ayman Al-Zawahiri, founder of the Egyptian Islamic Jihad and senior Al Qaida associate. The Office of the Press Secretary also released a Spanish language transcript of these remarks.

The President's News Conference With Prime Minister Kevin M. Rudd of Australia
March 28, 2008

President Bush. Thank you all. Please be seated. [*Applause*] Thanks for that rousing ovation. [*Laughter*]

Mr. Prime Minister, welcome. We're sure glad you're here. And, Therese, thank you for joining us as well. Laura and I are thrilled to welcome you here to the White House. And I appreciate the opportunity to visit with a leader of one of America's closest allies and friends. And one thing is for sure: That friendship will strengthen and endure under the leadership of Kevin Rudd.

I have found him to be a straightforward fellow. And being from Texas, that's the way I like it. He is thoughtful. He is strategic in thought. And he is committed to the same values that I'm committed to: rule of law, human rights, human decency. And we're sure proud you're here.

We spent a great deal of time talking about the economies. One thing we spent time on is talking about the benefits of trade between our two nations and the benefits of a world that trades freely and fairly. And the Prime Minister was asking me about my views on Doha. I said it's possible to achieve a Doha round. He too believes we should work to achieve a Doha round. However, I informed him that it's—we're willing to make serious concessions on the agricultural front, but we expect other nations to open up their markets on manufacturing as well as services. And to this end,

Prime Minister Rudd—Kevin Rudd decide—said that he would be more than willing to help, and that's—very grateful.

On a bilateral front, not only is the free trade agreement working, but next Monday, we'll be signing an open skies agreement that will further our friendship and further our commercial ties. And I think it's a great success of your administration and ours as well.

We talked about the environment and energy. Here's an interesting moment for all of us to recognize that we can become less dependent, in our case, on foreign oil and, at the same time, be good stewards of the environment. We talked about the need to work collaboratively to achieve an international agreement in which the United States is at the table along with developing nations like China and India. In order for there to be an effective international agreement, China and India must be participants.

Now, we talked about the need to help developing nations improve their environment. And one way that we can do so is to commit ourselves to tariff-free trade and technologies that promote low-carbon energy. And this is something we're spending a lot of money on in the United States. And we'll continue to do so because I happen to believe technologies will enable us to be good stewards of the environment and change our energy habits, which we need to do here in the United States.

So I want to thank you very much for our discussions thus far on our economic interests and our responsibilities. But we also talked about freedom and the need to promote an ideology based on hope and decency, and that's an ideology of liberty. And I want to thank very much the Australian Government and the Australian people for their willingness to help a young democracy such as Afghanistan. The Prime Minister and I discussed how Bucharest can become a success. And I can't thank you enough for going, and I appreciate very much your strong commitment to helping the Karzai Government succeed and thrive. It's in our national interests that we do so.

I also want to thank you very much for being a good, loyal ally on Iraq. Obviously, the Prime Minister kept a campaign commitment, which I appreciate. I always like to be in the presence of somebody who does what he says he's going to do. You know, oftentimes, politicians go out there, and they say one thing on the campaign trail, and they don't mean it. Well, this is a guy who meant it. But he also acted like you'd expect an ally to act, and that is, he consulted closely with his friends. His military commanders consulted closely with our military commanders. But the commitment of Afghanistan is not to leave Iraq alone, it's to change mission.

And so he told me about an interesting story. He met with the Prime Minister, Maliki. Prime Minister Maliki says to Kevin Rudd—or Kevin Rudd says to Prime Minister Maliki, "What can we do to help you?" It wasn't, "What can we do to abandon you?" He said, "How can we help you?" And he said, "How about training some farmers in dry-land farming," something we know something about in west Texas, by the way, Mr. Prime Minister.

And I want to thank you for that. I want to thank you for stepping forward to help Iraq develop a civil society and a strong economy that will enable this young democracy to thrive and help yield peace. People—I'm sure the press corps is going to say, well, aren't you mad at the Prime Minister for fulfilling his campaign pledge? And the answer is, no—just so you don't even need to ask the question now. [*Laughter*]

We talked about Iran and our joint commitment to continue to work together to see to it that the Iranians do not develop the capacity to develop a nuclear weapon. We talked about Burma, and I want to thank you for your commitment to a free Burma. And finally, we talked about North Korea and the six-party talks and Australia's support for those six-party talks.

We're going to have a good lunch too, and we'll continue our discussions on a variety of subjects. He's a easy man to talk to. I appreciate his visions. I particularly appreciate his consultations on China. He's an expert on China. It's clear when you talk to him, he is an expert on China. And all in all, we've had a good start to this important trip.

And we want to welcome you again, Kevin, to the White House. And the podium's yours.

Prime Minister Rudd. Thank you. Thanks very much, George. And it's a pleasure to be here in Washington and—with my wife Therese. And it's great to be here at the White House. And thanks for your hospitality in having us at Blair House. We really appreciate that.

Our alliance doesn't simply reflect our shared past. Our alliance defines our common future as two of the world's great democracies. I was thinking about this, this morning, about the number of Presidents and Prime Ministers who have been party to this alliance, both Republican and Democrat, and both in our country, Labor and Liberal. This alliance has been supported by 12 American Presidents, Republican and Democrat. It's been supported by 13 Australian Prime Ministers, Labor and Liberal. And I'm the 14th.

And I'm confident that this alliance has a strong, robust future. And the reason I'm confident of that is because it's rooted in shared values. We actually take the ideal of democracy seriously. It's not a casual thought; it's not a—it's just not a passing observation; it's something which is part and parcel of who we are as peoples. So when you have an alliance which is rooted in a common set of values, it tends to mean that alliance is going to last for a bit.

And there's the things we've done together right from the Second World War to the present, and there's been many of them. And we've been in the field together, and there are many other areas in wider foreign policy where we cooperate as well.

Turning to the future, the President indicated we discussed the current challenges facing the global economy. And this is, for us in Australia, a global challenge. Obviously, the United States, as the world's largest economy, is fundamentally significant in the way in which this thing plays out. But our response—and we discussed this at some length—is looking at how we can get some better transparency out there in financial markets on some of these particular products, which are causing problems around the world. There's an upcoming meeting of the International Monetary Fund, and we'll be working on our common positions towards that end.

As the President has just indicated, we also spoke about the Doha round. My own view is that if ever the global economy needs a psychological injection of some confidence in the arm, it's now, and that can be delivered by a positive outcome on Doha. Takes more than two to tango. Takes a lot of people to tango when it comes to the Doha round, combination of ourselves and the Cannes Group, the United States, the Europeans, Brazil, India, others. But what we have agreed, again, as strong, long-term supporters of free trade around the world, as one of the best drivers of global economic growth, is to work very closely together in the months ahead to try and get a good, positive outcome for Doha, good for our economy, good for the American economy, good for the global economy.

On foreign policy, the President and I also discussed, of course, Iraq and Afghanistan. I thank him for his remarks in relation to Iraq. And what he said is absolutely right in terms of my discussions with Prime Minister Maliki in Baghdad only in December. We—I've confirmed today to the President, as we'll be confirming to the Government of Iraq in Baghdad, an assistance package of some $165 million, a large slice of which will go to how we assist Iraqis train their people better in agriculture and in the wider economy.

Prime Minister Maliki said: "This is a big need for us. We are a dry continent." We know a fair bit about dry-land farming, so we'll be spending a lot of money training a lot of Iraqi farmers and agricultural scientists in the year ahead.

On Afghanistan, I confirmed to the President that we're in Afghanistan for the long haul. It's a tough fight, but we intend to be there with our friends and partners and allies for the long haul. And I look forward to being with the President in Bucharest soon, so we arrive at a common civil and military strategy with our friends and partners in Europe and elsewhere.

On the other matters which were raised in our discussions, the President has run through them neatly. I won't elaborate on them. But I'll just conclude with this: It was reminding of me—for me when I saw the guest book this morning at Blair House. And one of the first entries, back in 1944, was a page dedicated to the visit by Labor Prime Minister John Curtin to Blair House. FDR was President of the United States at the time. It goes back to remind me how much this alliance has been the product of common nurturing by Presidents and Prime Ministers for a long time.

Mr. President, you said that you had a warm regard for me because, from a Texan point of view, you found me to be a reasonably straight shooter. I therefore designate you as an honorary Queenslander. [*Laughter*] In the great State of Australia, I come from the great State of Queensland. It may surprise you that it's bigger than Texas. [*Laughter*] But can I say quickly—[*laughter*].

President Bush. Can you recover nicely? Yes. [*Laughter*]

Prime Minister Rudd. Yes. The recovery point is this: Queenslanders and Texans have a lot in common——

President Bush. Thank you, sir.

Prime Minister Rudd. ——and they get on well. And so from one Queenslander, one Texan—one Australian to one American, I appreciate the relationship that

we're forming, part and parcel of the relationship between two great democracies.

President Bush. Thank you.

Yes, a couple questions a side. John Yang [NBC News].

Situation in Iraq/Afghanistan/Upcoming NATO Summit

Q. Mr. President, thank you very much. I'd like to ask you about Iraq. Thank you. Yesterday in Dayton, in your remarks, you said that the Iraqi offensive against criminals and militants in Basra was a sign of progress. But it's also triggered clashes with supporters of Muqtada Al Sadr. And this morning, U.S. forces were again fighting the Mahdi army in Sadr City. What does this say about progress in terms of reconciliation in Iraq among the various factions? And what can the United States do, what can you do, what can your administration do to help Prime Minister Maliki make progress in that area?

And, Mr. Prime Minister, if I could ask you, when you're in Bucharest next week at the NATO summit, what's going to be your message to the European allies to try to bring them along, to have the same sort of commitment you just stated here and a commitment to have military operations with their forces in Afghanistan?

President Bush. Yes, John, any government that presumes to represent the majority of people must confront criminal elements or people who think they can live outside the law. And that's what's taking place in Basra and in other parts of Iraq. I would say this is a defining moment in the history of a free Iraq. There have been other defining moments up to now, but this is a defining moment as well. The decision to move troops—Iraqi troops into Basra talks about Prime Minister Maliki's leadership.

You know, one of the early questions I had to the Prime Minister was, would he be willing to confront criminal elements, whether they be Shi'a or Sunni? Would he, in representing people who want to live in peace, be willing to use force necessary to bring to justice those who take advantage of a vacuum or those who murder the innocent? And his answer was, "Yes, sir, I will." And I said, "Well, you'll have our support if that's the case, if you believe in evenhanded justice." And his decision to move into Basra shows evenhanded justice, shows he's willing to go after those who believe they're outside the law.

This is a test and a moment for the Iraqi Government, which strongly has supported Prime Minister Maliki's actions. And it is an interesting moment for the people of Iraq, because in order for this democracy to survive, they must have confidence in their Government's ability to protect them and to be evenhanded.

And so the other thing that's interesting about this, by the way, this happens to be one of the Provinces where the Iraq's are in the lead—Iraqis are in the lead. And that's what they are in this instance. And the United States, of course, will provide them help if they ask for it and if they need it. But they are in the lead. And this is a good test for them. And, of course, routing out these folks who've burrowed in society, who take advantage of the ability to be criminals or the ability to intimidate citizens, is going to take a while. But it is a necessary part of the development of a free society.

Prime Minister Rudd. In answer to your question on Afghanistan, the message I would take to our friends and partners in Europe when we get to Bucharest is, all of us have got to share the burden. And it's built on an assumption that all of us share a common strategy. So the first message, I think, for all of our friends and partners there in Bucharest is, we need to sign up to a common script, both military and civil, in terms of how we actually prosecute and succeed in this conflict. And I believe we can. No point in being there unless you believe you can.

And then the second thing is, once you've signed up to a common script, a common strategy, which has both civilian and military dimensions to it in an integrated fashion, to then say to all of our friends and partners, let's all step up to the plate to make this work—and across the country of Afghanistan, not just in parts of it.

I'm optimistic that we're going to make some progress in Bucharest. I know the President has put in a lot of effort with a lot of European leaders up until now. We've been talking to some ourselves. And I think we should look forward to a good outcome because the people of Afghanistan deserve a good outcome.

If I could ask Mark Kenny for his question.

Australia-U.S. Relations

Q. Mark Kenny from the Advertiser— Mr. President, both sides have stressed that the alliance is in perfect working order and good nick. But how can that be the case? How can the alliance remain unchanged given that Australia has signaled new foreign policy with quite different positions from yours on things like Iraq, climate change, and potentially over China?

President Bush. I guess it depends if you're a half-glass-empty guy or a half-glass-full guy. It sounds like to me our foreign policy interests are aligned. You know, after all, we've committed to an international agreement that will be effective when it comes to greenhouse gases. The Prime Minister just defined his desire to help this young democracy in Iraq succeed. That's what we're for.

So I don't see differences when it comes to foreign policy. As a matter of fact, I see common agreement. And one reason why is, is because we share the same values. And those values are more important than the people who actually occupy the office, by the way. Those are the values that allow 12 U.S. Presidents and 14 Australian Prime Ministers to be united in common goals. And so I disagree with the assessment of whatever expert laid that out.

Steven Lee [Steven Lee Myers, New York Times].

Situation in Iraq/Tibet/China

Q. Thank you, Mr. President. I wonder if you could talk a little bit more about Iraq and how it's—you mentioned criminal elements that are being fought against now. How concerned are you that the violence now reflects, in fact, a deepening political and civil, even ethnic conflict inside of Iraq? How much now are American forces being drawn into the fighting in the last— just few hours even? And how is it going to affect your decision looming on the way ahead?

And if I could ask you both, please, to talk a little bit about the crackdown in Tibet and how you see that affecting relations with China. Thank you.

President Bush. Any other subjects you want to wedge in there? [*Laughter*] Okay. Repeat some of those things. You had about five different things. I'm getting old, Steven. Look, wait a minute. Look, yes, I talked about criminal elements. And one of those things that's been well known is that Basra has been a place where criminality has thrived. It's a port; a lot of goods and services go through there. And there was—from the beginning of liberation, there have been criminal elements that have had a pretty free hand in Basra. And it was just a matter of time before the Government was going to have to deal with it.

And I haven't spoke to the Prime Minister since he's made his decision, but I suspect that he would say, look, the citizens down there just got sick and tired of this kind of behavior. Most people want to have normal lives. Most people don't like to be shaken down. Most mothers want their children to go to school peacefully. And yet that wasn't the case in Basra. And so I'm not exactly sure what triggered the Prime Minister's response. I don't know if it was one phone call. I don't know what— whether or not the local mayor called up

and said: "Help. We're sick and tired of dealing with these folks." But nevertheless, he made the decision to move. And we'll help him.

But this was his decision. It was his military planning. It was his causing the troops to go from point A to point B. And it's exactly what a lot of folks here in America were wondering whether or not Iraq would even be able to do in the first place. And it's happening. Now, they're fighting some pretty tough characters, people who kill innocent people to achieve objectives. And, yes, there's going to be violence, and that's sad. But this situation needed to be dealt with, and it's now being dealt with—just like we're dealing with the situation up in Mosul.

I have said in my remarks, there's been substantial progress, and there has been. But it's still a dangerous, fragile situation in Iraq. And therefore, my decision will be based upon the recommendations of Secretary Gates, the Joint Chiefs, as well as General Petraeus and Ambassador Crocker, all aiming to make sure that we have enough of a presence to make sure that we're successful in Iraq.

And the reason why it's successful—important to be successful in Iraq, because, one, we want to help establish a democracy in the heart of the Middle East, the most volatile region in the world. Two, we want to send a clear message to Iran that they're not going to be able to have their way with nations in the Middle East. Three, that we want to make it clear that we can defeat Al Qaida. Al Qaida made a stand in Iraq. They're the ones who said this is the place where the war will take place. And a defeat of Al Qaida will be a major victory in this war against extremists and radicals. Four, we want to show what's possible to people. There are reformers all over the Middle East who want to know whether or not the United States and friends will stand with these young democracies.

And so this is vital for our national interests. And I'm confident we can succeed, unless we lose our nerve, unless we allow politics to get in the way of making the necessary decisions, which I have vowed to our military and our civilians in Iraq that that's not going to be the case so long as I'm the President. And I'm—as I told you, this is a defining moment, and it's a moment of—where the Government is acting. And it's going to take a while for them to deal with these elements, but they're after it. And that's what's positive.

Tibet, he wants to talk to you about Tibet. [*Laughter*]

Prime Minister Rudd. I'll say one or two things about Tibet, and then we'll flick to an Australian. It's absolutely clear that there are human rights abuses in Tibet. That's clear-cut. We need to be upfront and absolutely straight about what's going on. We shouldn't shilly-shally about it. We've made our positions clear on the public record, the Australian Government has, about the need for restraint in the handling of this. I think it would be appropriate for the Chinese Government to engage the Dalai Lama or his representatives in a informal set of discussions about future possibilities when it comes to internal arrangements within Tibet.

We recognize China's sovereignty over Tibet. But it is difficult, and it's complex. And it certainly will be matters which I'll be raising when I visit China myself at the end of this visit abroad.

President Bush. Mr. Prime Minister, excuse me. Steven Lee is anxious on my view on Tibet. He couldn't have said it better. And that's exactly what I told Hu Jintao a couple of days ago, that it's in his country's interest that he sit down again with representatives of the Dalai Lama—he, not personally, but to have his representatives do so—and that we urged restraint. And I appreciate the Prime Minister's view and advice on dealing with this issue.

Prime Minister Rudd. Paul Bongiorno.

Australian Role in Iraq/War on Terror Strategy

Q. Paul Bongiorno with Ten News—Mr. President, as you noted, Australia will begin withdrawing 500 combat troops from southern Iraq. And I heard that you accept this decision, which did, as you say, play out in our election. But how does it fit with your view, expressed quite strongly again yesterday, that to withdraw troops at this time would be to retreat?

And you've described our former Prime Minister as a man of steel. I'm wondering how you'd describe Mr. Rudd.

President Bush. Fine lad, fine lad.

First of all, I didn't exactly say that. And by the way, we are withdrawing troops. It's called return on success. And our intention is to have pulled down five battalions by July. Troops are coming out—five brigades, excuse me—troops are coming out because we're successful. And so I would view the Australian decision as return on success—returning home on success.

That's fundamentally different from saying, well, it's just too hard, pull them all out. That sends a different signal. This is a signal in which we're working collaboratively with the Iraqi Government. They know our intentions, and they know we're not going to leave them.

In the very same speech, I talked about developing a long-term strategic relationship with Iraq as well. And for those who didn't listen to the full speech, I will remind you that it's in our interests that we enter into such an arrangement. But a long-term strategic arrangement does not commit any future President to any troop level, nor does it talk about permanent bases. But it does talk about a joint strategic relationship to make sure that the Iraqi people know and the Iraqi Government knows that we're not going to leave them in the lurch.

And so we are taking troops out, just like the Australians are, because we're being successful. And his question—Steven Lee's question was, well, are you going to bring any further out? Not, are you going to bring any out, are you going to bring any further troops out from that which we committed to do earlier? And the answer is, it depends on what our commanders say and the folks in Washington say, and it depends upon conditions on the ground. His real question was, have the conditions changed such that you believe your commander is going to make a different recommendation than he might have 2 days ago? And I can't answer that question. I can only tell you what I'm going to do after we get back from NATO.

Thank you for coming. I've enjoyed it.

Q. [*Inaudible*]

President Bush. Yes. Heck, yes. [*Laughter*] Thanks for coming.

Prime Minister Rudd. Good. [*Inaudible*]

President Bush. Appreciate you coming.

NOTE: The President's news conference began at 11:37 a.m. in the East Room at the White House. In his remarks, he referred to Therese Rein, wife of Prime Minister Rudd; President Hamid Karzai of Afghanistan; Prime Minister Nuri al-Maliki of Iraq; Iraqi Shiite cleric Muqtada Al Sadr; Gen. David H. Petraeus, USA, commanding general, Multi-National Force—Iraq; Tenzin Gyatso, the 14th Dalai Lama; and President Hu Jintao of China. A reporter referred to former Prime Minister John W. Howard of Australia.

Remarks Following a Tour of Novadebt in Freehold, New Jersey
March 28, 2008

The President. Thank you very much. I really want to thank Congressman Chris Smith and Vito Fossella for joining me here in Freehold, New Jersey. I'm here at a company called Novadebt. And I really appreciate Joel Greenberg and Jill Feldman for giving me an opportunity to come to this center, this company, and talk with people whose lives are being positively affected as a result of a significant counseling effort to help people stay in their homes. And I really do want to thank you all for your hospitality.

During my tour, I have met with skilled professionals who provide free mortgage counseling for struggling homeowners. And the reason why I'm here is because we have got a issue in housing in America. The value of the houses have gone down in some areas, and people's mortgages are resetting; in other words, the interest rates are going up. And that has caused a consternation and concern and care. A lot of families are facing the frightening prospect of foreclosures. Foreclosures obviously place a terrible burden on a family, as well as they lead to losses for lenders and investors. And this affects our entire economy.

We have a role to play at the Government level, and that is to help lenders and borrowers work together to avoid foreclosure. There's some homeowners who have made responsible buying decisions and who could keep their homes with just a little help—some information and some help. And so to help them, in October, my administration helped bring together a private sector group of lenders, loan servicers, investors, mortgage counselors, which is called the HOPE NOW Alliance. And the members of this group have made some progress. First of all, they agreed to industry-wide standards to streamline the process for refinancing and modifying certain mortgages. HOPE NOW also runs a national hotline to connect struggling homeowners with mortgage counselors just like the folks here at Novadebt.

I also have been—met with some homeowners who've got help. Danny Cerchiaro is with us from Iselin, New Jersey. Thank you for being here, Danny. He owns a home that also serves as a studio for his movie production business. Danny and his wife learned their adjustable-rate mortgage was resetting to a higher rate this past summer, and he became concerned about financial stability. He was worried about staying in his home. He needed a place for his business, and he needed a place to sleep. And he became concerned about whether or not he could afford it.

He got—he called HOPE NOW, and he became working with a mortgage counselor named Penny Meredith. Penny is here. Appreciate you coming, Penny. And in less than 2 months later, Penny helped Danny get a more affordable fixed-rate mortgage. Danny calls Penny, and I quote, the "magic lady." She helped him a lot.

And there's a lot of other Americans who can get the same kind of help. One of the reasons I've come today is to say to people who are worried about staying in their home: There is help available.

I also want to thank Theresa Torres from Kansas City who is with us. She got really worried. She's a mom of three, her husband is a subcontractor, and she was very worried about staying in her home. And the family fell behind on their mortgage payments in December. But fortunately, she knew to call and to get help, and in this case, from Novadebt. They helped her modify her mortgage. And today, as a result of the help she received, she no longer worries about losing her home. And I thought her statement was pretty interesting. She said, "I see my role today to serve as an example for people in a similar situation." So, Theresa, we're glad you're here.

There are hundreds of thousands of homeowners like Theresa and Danny who can benefit from calling HOPE NOW. And so one of my purposes is to make it clear there is a place where you can get counseling. And I want my fellow citizens, if you're worried about your home, to call this number: 1–88–995–HOPE. Let me repeat that again: 1–88–995–HOPE.

HOPE NOW can help homeowners find the right solution. By the way, we've got more work to do in Washington, and one of the things we can do is make sure the Federal Housing Administration gets the reforms it needs. And there's a program called FHASecure, which has given FHA greater flexibility to offer struggling homeowners with otherwise good credit histories a chance to refinance. This program is very helpful. It's, so far, helped 130,000 families refinance their mortgages. And by the end of the year, we expect the program to have reached 300,000 families.

And this is a good start. We want to help people. We're committed to helping our fellow citizens. And I fully understand, as do most Americans, that the housing market problems are complicated, and there's no easy solutions. But in the stories I've heard today, I've seen how Americans are responding with compassion and determination. We will support them with good policies. We will help responsible homeowners weather a difficult period. And in so doing, we will strengthen the dream of homeownership.

Thank you all very much.

Danny Cerchiaro. [Inaudible]

The President. One–eight–eight–eight. Good. Is it two eights or three eights? Okay.

Danny just told me I got to get the number right: 1–888–995–HOPE.

NOTE: The President spoke at 3:30 p.m. In his remarks, he referred to Joel Greenberg, president and chief executive officer, and Jill Feldman, vice president, Novadebt. The Office of the Press Secretary also released a Spanish language transcript of these remarks.

The President's Radio Address
March 29, 2008

Good morning. It's not every day that Americans look forward to hearing from the Internal Revenue Service, but over the past few weeks, many Americans have received a letter from the IRS with some good news. The letters explain that millions of individuals and families will soon be receiving tax rebates, thanks to the economic growth package that Congress passed and I signed into law last month.

Americans who are eligible for a rebate will get it automatically by simply filing their taxes. If you are not a tax filer, you should visit your local IRS office to fill out the necessary paperwork, so you can get your rebate on time.

The growth package also contains incentives for businesses to invest in new equipment this year. On Wednesday, I visited a printing company in Virginia that has decided to use these incentives to purchase new software. As more businesses begin taking advantage of these incentives, investment will pick up and so will job creation. And together with the individual tax rebates, these incentives will help give our economy a shot in the arm.

For many families, the greatest concern with the economy is the downturn in the housing market. My administration has taken action to help responsible homeowners keep their homes. In October, we helped bring together a private sector group called the HOPE NOW Alliance. HOPE NOW has helped streamline the process for refinancing and modifying mortgages, and it runs a national hotline to connect struggling homeowners with mortgage counselors.

On Friday, I visited an impressive mortgage counseling center in New Jersey. At the center, I met with homeowners who have been able to get help, thanks to HOPE NOW. One of them is Danny Cerchiaro. Danny owns a home in New Jersey that also serves as a studio for his movie production company. When Danny and his wife learned that their adjustable-rate mortgage was resetting to a higher rate this past summer, they became concerned about their financial security. So Danny called HOPE NOW for help. Less than 2 months later, he was able to get a more affordable fixed-rate mortgage. And today, Danny calls the mortgage counselor who helped him, quote, "the magic lady."

Theresa Torres from Kansas City is another homeowner who has been helped. Theresa called HOPE NOW after she and her husband fell behind on their mortgage payments in December. A mortgage counselor helped Theresa modify her mortgage. Today, she no longer worries about losing her home.

There are hundreds of thousands of homeowners like Theresa and Danny who could benefit from calling HOPE NOW. If you're a homeowner struggling with your mortgage, please take the first step toward getting help by calling the hotline at 888–995–H–O–P–E. That's 888–995–H–O–P–E.

HOPE NOW can help homeowners find the right solution for them. One solution for some homeowners is a new program we launched at the Federal Housing Administration called FHASecure. This program has given the FHA greater flexibility to offer struggling homeowners with otherwise good credit histories a chance to refinance. So far, this program has helped more than 130,000 families refinance their mortgages, and by the end of the year, we expect this program to have reached nearly 300,000 homeowners in all.

This is a good start, and my administration is committed to building on it. So we're exploring ways this program can help more qualified homebuyers. The problems in the housing market are complicated, and there is no easy solution. But by supporting responsible homeowners with wise policies, we'll help them weather a difficult period, we will help get our economy back on track, and we will ensure America remains the most prosperous nation in the world.

Thank you for listening.

NOTE: The address was recorded at 7:05 a.m. on March 28 in the Cabinet Room at the White House for broadcast at 10:06 a.m. on March 29. In the address, the President referred to Penny Meredith, mortgage counselor, Novadebt. The transcript was made available by the Office of the Press Secretary on March 28, but was embargoed for release until the broadcast. The Office of the Press Secretary also released a Spanish language transcript of this address.

Remarks on Departure for Kiev, Ukraine
March 31, 2008

Good morning. Laura and I are on our way to a very important NATO summit, and Members of the United States Congress are on their way back to Washington. And they have a lot of work to do.

Congress needs to pass FISA reform. Our intelligence professionals are waiting on the Congress to give them the tools they need to monitor terrorist communications. Congress also needs to provide liability protection to companies that may have helped save lives after September the 11th, 2001.

Congress needs to pass legislation to modernize the Federal Housing Administration. Struggling homeowners are waiting on Congress to act, so that the FHA can help more Americans refinance their mortgages and stay in their homes.

Congress needs to act urgently to approve the Colombian free trade agreement. A courageous ally in South America is waiting on Congress to approve an agreement that will strengthen our national security. American businesses, workers, and farmers are waiting on Congress to level the playing field.

These are all vital priorities. And I ask members of both parties to get these important pieces of legislation to my desk as soon as possible.

Thank you very much.

NOTE: The President spoke at 6:56 a.m. on the South Lawn at the White House.

Statement on the Resignation of Alphonso R. Jackson as Secretary of Housing and Urban Development
March 31, 2008

Today Secretary of Housing and Urban Development Alphonso Jackson announced his decision to leave the Department after 7 years of dedicated service. I have known Alphonso Jackson for many years, and I have known him to be a strong leader and a good man. I have accepted his resignation with regret.

Secretary Jackson is a great American success story. The youngest of 12 children—his father was a foundry worker, and his mother was a nurse midwife—Alphonso has always understood the value of hard work and equal opportunity for all Americans.

For more than three decades, he has worked to help more Americans become homeowners and strengthen communities throughout our Nation. While leading the Department of Housing and Urban Development, Alphonso made significant progress in transforming public housing, revitalizing and modernizing the Federal Housing Administration, increasing affordable housing, rebuilding the Gulf Coast, decreasing homelessness, and increasing minority homeownership.

Laura and I treasure our strong friendship with Secretary Jackson, his wife Marcia, their daughters Annette and Lesley, and their granddaughter Lauren. We wish them all the best.

Letter to Congressional Leaders Transmitting a Report on North Atlantic Treaty Organization Enlargement
March 28, 2008

Dear Mr. Chairman:

Pursuant to section 3(2)(E)(i) of the Resolution of Ratification to the Protocols to the North Atlantic Treaty of 1949 on the Accession of Poland, Hungary, and the Czech Republic adopted on April 30, 1998, I am pleased to submit the enclosed report on the Future Enlargement of NATO.

In doing so, I note with appreciation the continued and strong bipartisan support that the Congress has shown on the issue of NATO's next round of enlargement.

The report provides the following information for each of the three current NATO aspirants:

(I)   An evaluation of how each country will further the principles of the North Atlantic Treaty and contribute to the security of the North Atlantic area;

(II) An evaluation of the eligibility of each country for membership based on the principles and criteria identified by NATO and the United States, including the military readiness of each country;

(III) An explanation of how an invitation to each country would affect the national security interests of the United States;

(IV) An up-to-date United States Government analysis of the common-funded military requirements and costs associated with integrating each country into NATO and an analysis of the shares of those costs to be borne by NATO members, including the United States; and

(V)   A preliminary analysis of the implications for the United States defense budget and other United States budgets of integrating each country into NATO.

The report is classified due to the nature of the information it contains assessing aspirants' capabilities and contributions.

Sincerely,

GEORGE W. BUSH

NOTE: Identical letters were sent to Robert C. Byrd, chairman, Senate Committee on Appropriations; Carl Levin, chairman, Senate Committee on Armed Services; Joseph R. Biden, Jr., chairman, Senate Committee on Foreign Relations; David R. Obey, chairman, House Committee on Appropriations; Isaac N. Skelton, IV, chairman, House Committee on Armed Services; and Howard L. Berman, chairman, House Committee on Foreign Affairs. This letter was released by the Office of the Press Secretary on April 1.

The President's News Conference With President Viktor Yushchenko of Ukraine in Kiev, Ukraine
April 1, 2008

President Yushchenko. Dear Mr. President, Excellencies, ladies and gentlemen: This is a great honor for Ukraine and Ukrainian Government to welcome the delegation of—chaired by the U.S. President. We just had one-on-one negotiations and expanded negotiations, and we can make general assessment of our talks. We are very pleased with the frankness and the atmosphere that the talks were carried out in.

And they were about the positions of our bilateral relations, the visit of His Excellency President Bush—is very—[*inaudible*]—documents that were signed. And we also touched upon the issues of the international politics and regional politics. I also want to say that one of the major issues that a lot of attention was paid by us is Ukraine's joining the NATO Membership Action Plan.

And once again, I wanted to prove to Mr. President and the American delegation that when we're speaking about the MAP, we mean political and security essence. The political essence of it is that this country, when we are speaking about the 20th century, has many times announced its independence, but many times this independence failed. For the last 80 years, Ukraine has declared its independence six times, and five times it failed. It failed probably because there were no international signatures—honor our sovereignty. And very often, Ukraine looked like a diversified country, a parted country in an international community. And we are speaking here about the system of political decisions

that fixed it right, and on the other hand, we are speaking about the security context.

In my opinion, there are no alternatives for the—against the idea of collective security. And I believe that collective responsibility for security policy, or defense policy, if you may, is the best response to the challenges that currently exist in this society, that exist in the system of international coordinance.

And we received full-fledged support from the U.S.A. in Ukraine's plan to join the MAP. And in the course of the Bucharest summit, I'm sure that we will receive a positive signal in Bucharest. And that's the spirit that we're going there with. And we're sure that it will be also an advantage for those countries who are only about to determine their way there. And it was very important for us to have the roadmap signed. It will determine, actually, our applicable action plan.

This complex document determines the priorities of our cooperation in many sectors, starting from political dialogue, space exploration, nuclear policy, and ending with ecological and environmental issues.

During Mr. President's visit, we signed a very important agreement, which is a trade and investment framework agreement. It lays the necessary foundation for—to start negotiations on the free trade area between our countries. And in my opinion, it's also—not less important is the framework agreement on research and use of space in peaceful manner. It opens new prospects for our relations. Still, the relations has already had good practices.

And we also touched upon the energy issues and diversification of energy supplies. We paid attention to the energy summit that will take place in Kiev on the 22d, 23d of May, on the issues regarding Odessa-Brody EU pipeline project, in the concept of energy security, and other issues that will be considered in the course of the summit.

We also spoke about the domestic political situation in Ukraine. And I would like to thank very much to Mr. President for this very fruitful and dynamic dialogue and for that open and trustful atmosphere that was during our dialogue. I thank you very much indeed. I really appreciate it.

President Bush. Dobryi den'. Thank you all very much. I am thrilled to be here, as is my wife. And thank you for your gracious hospitality, Mr. President.

I am proud to be sitting next to a leader who has strong convictions and a lot of courage. We come with a message for the people of Ukraine: Your sovereign nation has a friend and a solid partner in the United States.

Our nations have built our friendship on the love of liberty. Our people believe that freedom is the gift of an Almighty to every man, woman, and child. And President Yushchenko and I understand that democracies are the best partners for peace and security in every part of the world. So we spent a lot of time talking about NATO.

First, I do want to remind people that Ukraine and the NATO alliance have built a strong partnership. Ukraine is the only non-NATO nation supporting every NATO mission. In Afghanistan and Iraq, Ukrainian troops are helping to support young democracies. In Kosovo, Ukrainians are—help keep the peace.

Ukraine now seeks to deepen its cooperation with the NATO alliance through a Membership Action Plan. Your nation has made a bold decision, and the United States strongly supports your request. In Bucharest this week, I will continue to make America's position clear: We support MAP for Ukraine and Georgia. Helping Ukraine move toward a NATO membership is in the interest of every member in the alliance and will help advance security and freedom in this region and around the world.

We also share more than security interests; we share democratic values. Ukraine has demonstrated its commitment to democracy and free markets. You've held three elections since the Orange Revolution. Your commitment to open markets has allowed your economy to grow and earned your nation the opportunity to join the World Trade Organization.

I know you're proud of these accomplishments, and you should be, Mr. President, and so should the people of Ukraine.

We're working together to help Ukraine—Ukrainians build a better life. You're on the path to reform, and you can count on our continued support. We work together to fight corruption and support civil society groups and strengthen institutions of a free and prosperous economy. And as you mentioned, Mr. President, we're expanding our economic partnership through a trade and investment cooperation agreement.

And so, Mr. President, we have a deep relationship, an important relationship. And I want to thank you for your friendship. Appreciate what you've done to advance the cause of freedom. And I look forward to continuing to work with you during my time as President to make sure our relationship endures for the years to come.

President Yushchenko. Thank you.

President Bush. Thank you, sir.

North Atlantic Treaty Organization/Missile Defense System

Q. Thank you, Mr. President. Do you think that Russia is applying undue pressure and threats to accomplish its goals at NATO on missile defense and stopping the Membership Action Plans of Ukraine and Georgia?

And, Mr. President Yushchenko, what do you think of Moscow's tactics?

President Bush. Just because there was a bunch of, you know, Soviet-era flags in the street yesterday doesn't—you shouldn't read anything into that. I—look, this is an interesting debate that's taking place. And it's—you know, as every nation has told me, Russia will not have a veto over what happens at Bucharest, and I take their word for it. And that's the right policy to have.

I'm going to work as hard as I can to see to it that Ukraine and Georgia are accepted into MAP. I think it's in our interests as NATO members, and I think it's in Ukrainian and Georgian interests as well.

And on missile defense, we'll see. I've made it abundantly clear to the—President Putin that the missile defense system is not aimed at defending against Russia. After all, Russia could easily overwhelm the missile defense systems that we have in—that we've envisioned. These systems are aimed at a nation out of the Middle East, for example, that could launch an attack against Europe and—just like our systems out in the Far East are aimed at helping protect ourselves from single- or dual-launch regimes.

So obviously, we've got a lot of work to do to allay suspicions and old fears, but I believe we're making pretty good progress along those lines.

President Yushchenko. When we're speaking about Ukrainian politics of joining the MAP and NATO membership, I would like to mention a couple basic things. First, this is not a policy against somebody. We are taking care of our national interest.

Taking a look at our history, it's very rich in many tragedies for Ukrainian state that only the system of collective defense and security—international guarantees of the political sovereignty for Ukraine and territorial integrity will give the full response to the internal question in Ukraine. And I'm sure that for any Ukrainian who takes care of the future for Ukraine, a stable future for Ukraine, the issue of joining MAP is probably the most high-quality response to all the basic and fundamental interests of Ukraine.

Secondly, I would like the debates that are now being carried out in Europe and in the world regarding Ukraine's prospects of joining the MAP and then after, NATO—form any new obstacle. I'm sure that we are going—we're taking the right track, and we are acting within the framework of our national sovereignty. Our nation is determined, and it corresponds to our political reasonability for the security of the state.

I would like the basic and fundamental principle of work of the alliance—I mean, the open door policy would be replaced by the veto right by the country which is not even a member of the alliance. I'm sure that we're witnessing a very hot and overheated emotional discussion where there are few rules or even sometimes very little respect. But at the end of the day, the wisdom should win.

And I want to firmly state that I'm only governed by a single issue. I want to bring calmness, stability, and security stability, in particular we—to this state. We want to be speaking about the Ukrainian presence in the world. We want to speak about the internal country. That's why only through these motives shall we want to have that dialogue, the talks.

And what we have in our society—I mean, the part of the political forces who do not share this opinion—I think that this is all natural, because it's quite natural that today, like, hundreds—some hundreds of people and red flags were in the square. This is a remarkable because the Ukrainian famine was built under the same flags as the Ukrainian oppression. These were the flags that caused totalitarianism and sufferings that caused many deaths of millions of people. And I'm sure that the

Ukrainian Communist Party may also appear one day in Ukraine that will be standing under the flags of the nation. But apparently we still need to have another Moses to bring people over the desert for 40 years, for those who lost national interest and forgot about it and continue living in the past. I don't want this personality, in person, and I just want to show my vision and the ideology.

North Atlantic Treaty Organization/Ukraine

Q. The question to President Bush: Were you able to persuade France and Germany to give positive answer on the Ukrainian issue? And how your visit is remarkable to deciding—to having that decision?

President Bush. Thank you very much. We have been working with all nations in NATO for a positive outcome, because I strongly believe NATO membership is in— for Ukraine and Georgia is in the interest of our organization. And so I have personally talked to quite a few leaders. Secretary Rice has been talking to her counterparts. Mr. Hadley has been talking to his counterparts. And there's a lot of discussions going on. And I wouldn't prejudge the outcome yet. The vote will be taken in Bucharest.

And my stop here is—should be a clear signal to everybody that I mean what I say, and that is, I mean that it's in our interest for Ukraine to join. I mean, that's—and so therefore, one should—but you ought to take more than my stop— more from my stop than just a—trying to send a signal on NATO. I firmly—well, first of all, I was impressed, like most Americans, by the Orange Revolution. You probably don't know this, but a lot of Americans were really, really touched and pleased to see what took place here.

And I told the President that Ukraine is—you know, has caught the imagination of a lot of our fellow citizens over the last decade or so, and that you'll have good friends. The key, of course, is to have government that's open, government that's transparent, government that's noncorrupt,

government that actually listens to the voices of the people as it makes laws, which is what's happening.

But no, this is a good trip, and I'm really thrilled to be here. As the President said, "It took you too long to get here," and I admit it. But nevertheless, better late than never, as they say. And I'm thrilled to be here, and I want to thank you for your hospitality.

North Atlantic Treaty Organization/Missile Defense System

Q. Thank you, Mr. President. How confident are you of resolving your differences over the missile shield with President Putin during your talks in Sochi? And also, sir, there was a growing impression that you are looking, perhaps, at a tradeoff in which the U.S. would soften its push for Membership Action Plans in NATO for Ukraine and Georgia if Russia acquiesces on missile defense. Could you please address that as well?

President Bush. Yes, I'll be glad to address it. That is a misperception. I strongly believe that Ukraine and Georgia should be given MAP, and there's no tradeoffs— period. As a matter of fact, I told that to President Putin on my phone call with him recently. I said: "You just got to know, I'm headed to Bucharest with the idea in mind of getting MAP for Ukraine and Georgia. And you shouldn't fear that, Mr. President. I mean, after all, NATO is a organization that's peaceful, or NATO is an organization that helps democracies flourish. Democracies are good things to have on your border."

And on the second point, on missile defense, it's in his interests that we participate and share information. After all, a missile from the Middle East can fly north just as easily as it could fly west. And the capacity to be able to share information and share technology to be able to deal with these threats is important for a lot of countries, including Russia.

So yes, there's all kinds of rumors about things, but thank you for asking and giving me a chance to clarify. My position is absolutely solid. My position is absolutely solid. Ukraine and Georgia should be given MAP. Thank you.

Missile Defense System/Russia

Q. [*Inaudible*]—what are the chances, in your opinion, of achieving an agreement at Sochi on missile defense?

President Bush. On Sochi, I don't know, but the chances are—advancing my logic is good, since I'll be there talking about it. And we'll see whether or not there's an agreement. But obviously, we've got work to do to convince the President and people around him that the missile defense system is not aimed at Russia. In other words, it's viewed as an anti-Russian device. Well, it's not, and therefore, it requires a lot of time, a lot of discussion. That's what Condi Rice and Bob Gates spent time doing when they were there in Russia, and that is to defuse any notions that this is aiming something at somebody in Europe. This is all aiming to protect people in Europe.

Yes, I mean, the truth of the matter is, the Russian system could overwhelm the missile defense systems we have envisioned. I mean, these systems are designed to deal with, you know, limited launch capabilities. And they've got multiple launch capabilities. And so it's just—it requires a lot of work. We're dealing with a lot of history and a lot of suspicion throughout governments. And so the President and I will try to work through these for our common good. And I'm hopeful we can have some breakthroughs. We'll see.

The other thing is, is that this will be my last chance to visit with him face to face, as you know, and I've worked with him for 8 years. We've had a very interesting relationship. I like him. He's a person that has been a strong leader for Russia. And my view all along has been that it's in our interest—our interests, Ukrainian interests, European interests—to be able to have a working relationship with Russia. And I've had that. And this will be a chance to say, "I appreciate being able to work together," and to be able to try to find some common interests in the waning days of his Presidency.

Ukraine/North Atlantic Treaty Organization

Q. The question to President Yushchenko: Please, Mr. President, say, if the positive decision is not taken in Bucharest on Ukraine, what are the next steps of Ukraine then?

President Yushchenko. If not, the—I'm sure that we will win because the arguments that were just mentioned by Mr. President and the positions that Ukraine is standing with, within the framework of the international debate on this issue—we are every day approaching to the positive final result. This is a colossal international work, and I would like to thank you all—in your presence, I would like to thank President Bush for the work that's been done and that will be done in both public and nonpublic way.

And we fully understand the value of the issue and its importance. Of course, we still have a lot of effort forward to receive a positive answer. I have very good belief that the position of our friends in the EU will play a very important role for tomorrow's decision. And I hope that we will be able to convince those states that still have an opportunity—that will have an opportunity to get more information about it and eliminate all the doubts.

I—frankly speaking, I don't see any other way for Ukraine, no other alternative maybe—emotionally, I would like to say that for the nation, for the political forces, should be more devoted to this way. And the issue of whether Ukraine joins or not—the MAP—is not the complete target, the final target that we have in the Ukrainian society. And I'm sure that in order to avoid speculations on an international level, when somebody refers to the fact that the

Ukrainian nation has not decided yet—I'm sorry, we have decided already. We're not speaking about joining NATO, we are only speaking about MAP.

Why Ukraine should be deprived of that sovereign right is—there is a principle of open doors, which is the basic principle for NATO. Why can't we join MAP, and then let's have a meeting in a year or two, when we explain to the nation that—what the NATO mission is and what the collective security mission is and then how important is—a response for Ukraine it is and why there is no alternative answer for us. If any politician is troubled about this nation and is worried about this future, I am sure that Ukrainian nation is very wise, and it will make positive decision in the course of the referendum that we going to have regarding Ukraine to join NATO.

I recall when, 3 years ago, we started this discussion, I think, from 17 percent of those who are for and who supported the alliance integration—a year ago, we were supported by 33 percent. During the last live debates, we've seen the analytics that raised up to 40 percent. And we haven't started our work yet—I mean, the profound work. So this is the—quite a situation. I mean, the attention to this issue in the parliament for the last 2 months just made that big progress, and the nation started knowing better what NATO is and what its concept is. So I think everything will be fine.

Thank you.

NOTE: The President's news conference began at 11 a.m. in the House with Chimeras at the Presidential Secretariat. In his remarks, he referred to President Vladimir V. Putin of Russia. President Yushchenko and some reporters spoke in Ukrainian, and their remarks were translated by an interpreter.

Remarks at a Luncheon Hosted by President Viktor Yushchenko of Ukraine in Kiev
April 1, 2008

Madam Prime Minister, Mr. Chairman, distinguished guests, thank you for your warm welcome. Laura and I are honored to stand with you on Ukrainian soil, and we bring the greetings of the American people, or as you would say, *Vitayu vas*.

The people of Ukraine have made great contributions to the history of human freedom. During World War II, Ukrainian soldiers helped defeat the armies of fascism and end the deadliest conflict in history. And at the end of the cold war, Ukrainians formed an independent nation and declared your desire to live in freedom and peace.

In 2004, Ukrainians inspired the world with the Orange Revolution, using peaceful demonstrations to protect your right to choose your leaders. Today, Ukrainians are showing courage in helping to advance freedom in many parts of the world. You're helping to train security forces in Iraq, supporting a Provincial Reconstruction Team in Afghanistan. Ukrainians are part of the U.N. mission in Kosovo. Last month in Kosovo, a Ukrainian police officer gave his life and many others were wounded helping to defend the ideals of freedom.

Ukraine is contributing to every mission of the NATO alliance and honoring the ideals that unite the transatlantic community. This week, Ukraine seeks to strengthen its transatlantic ties through a NATO Membership Action Plan. The United States strongly supports your request. We are proud to stand with you in Bucharest and beyond.

Mr. President, our two nations share a common vision for the future. We seek to advance the cause of freedom and help all peoples of Europe live together in security and peace. With great confidence in that future, I offer a toast to you, to your gracious wife, and to a free and sovereign people of Ukraine.

NOTE: The President spoke at 11:57 a.m. at the Presidential Secretariat. In his remarks, he referred to Prime Minister Yuliya Tymoshenko and Verkhovna Chairman Rada Yatseniuk Arseniy Petrovych of Ukraine; and Kateryna Mykhailivna Yushchenko, wife of President Yushchenko. The transcript released by the Office of the Press Secretary also included the remarks of President Yushchenko.

Remarks Following a Tour of School 57 in Kiev
April 1, 2008

Thank you all very much for letting Laura and me come by your school. And thank you all for coming. You did an excellent job. And we love the Peace Corps. They're great, aren't they? Yes.

Listen, Laura and I are very impressed by your country. It's exciting to be in a place that has come through a very difficult period and now heading toward freedom. And the future of your country is going to depend on you. And it's very important for you to be involved with the future of your country.

So how do you do that? Well, one, you demand to make sure that your Government is—doesn't have corruption; that you insist that the Government respond to the will of the people, not to the whims of a few. People will say, oh, your voice doesn't matter. It does matter.

The other thing is, make sure you get— you know, keep your education going and then contribute to your society. And you can do it all kinds of ways. You can be a teacher; you can be a doctor; you can be a small-business owner. You can contribute to the future of your country by just being a good citizen.

So we're very excited for you, and we're excited about your future. And we wish you all the very best. Thank you for your gracious hospitality. Thank you for letting us come by your beautiful school. And may God bless you, and wish you all the very best.

Thank you all.

NOTE: The President spoke at 3:56 p.m.

Remarks in Bucharest, Romania
April 2, 2008

Thank you all. Thank you, and good morning. I appreciate former Presidents Iliescu and Constantinescu for joining us today. I want to thank the President of Latvia and Mrs. Zatlere for joining us. Secretary Rice, ambassadors, Members of the United States Congress, the president of the National Bank of Savings, members of the German Marshall Fund and the Atlantic Council, distinguished guests, ladies and gentlemen: *Buna ziua*.

Laura and I are pleased to be back in Bucharest. The last time we were here, we stood with the people of this city in Revolution Square for a rally celebrating Romania's invitation to join NATO. Tens of thousands came out in the rain to rejoice in this achievement and revel in the promise that, henceforth, no one would ever take Romania's freedom away. It was a moment I will never forget. President Iliescu introduced me in the midst of the drizzling rain. And then the clouds parted, and a rainbow appeared in the sky, heralding a new day for this nation and the Atlantic alliance she was about to join.

Since then, Romania has made strong contributions to the alliance. Romanian soldiers have brought courage to NATO's missions. Romanian leaders have brought moral clarity to NATO's deliberations. And today the Romanian people have brought their famous hospitality to this NATO summit. Laura and I are thrilled to join you for this historic occasion. And the American people are honored to call Romania a friend, an ally, and a partner in the cause of peace.

This is my final NATO summit. The coming days will be a time for hard work, as allies make important decisions regarding the expansion and the missions and the capabilities of NATO. The coming days will also be a time of reflection, a chance to look back on how far we have come in the past 7 years and what this tells us about the challenges ahead.

In June 2001, I came to Europe and spoke to students and faculty at Warsaw University. I reaffirmed America's commitment to a united Europe, bound to the United States by ties of history and trade and friendship. I said that Europe must overturn the bitter legacy of Yalta and remove the false boundaries that had divided the continent for too long. I declared that all of Europe's new democracies, from the Baltic to the Black Sea, should have the same chance for security and freedom and the same chance to join the institutions of Europe.

I spoke those words on the soil of a nation on the Baltic. Today a nation on the Black Sea is where I have come to say, those words have been fulfilled. The NATO alliance that meets here this week now stretches from the shores of Klaipeda to the beaches of Neptun. And here in Bucharest, we will extend the circle of freedom even further by expanding the NATO alliance to include new members from the Balkans.

A decade—the Balkans was a region wracked by war and fanaticism and ethnic cleansing. Today, it is a region growing in liberty and tolerance and peace. These changes are the result of determined actions by NATO and the courageous choices by new Balkan leaders who have worked to overcome the violence and divisions of the past. In recognition of their progress, tomorrow NATO will make an historic decision on the admission of three Balkan nations: Croatia, Albania, and Macedonia. The United States strongly supports inviting these nations to join NATO. These countries have walked the difficult path of reform and built thriving free societies. They are ready to contribute to NATO, and their citizens deserve the security that NATO brings.

As we welcome new NATO allies, we also affirm that the door to NATO membership remains open to other nations that seek it, in the Balkans and beyond. So at this summit, we will also decide whether to accept the requests of two other Balkan nations, Bosnia-Herzegovina and Montenegro, to begin an intensified dialogue with NATO. This is a major step on the road to NATO membership, and it is a step that America fully supports for these two nations. And at our summit tomorrow, we will also make clear that the door to closer cooperation with NATO is open to Serbia as well.

This week, our alliance must also decide how to respond to the requests by Georgia and Ukraine to participate in NATO's

Membership Action Plan. These two nations inspired the world with their Rose and Orange Revolutions, and now they're working to consolidate their democratic gains and cement their independence. Welcoming them into the MATO—into the Membership Action Plan would send a signal to their citizens that if they continue on the path to democracy and reform, they will be welcomed into the institutions of Europe. It would send a signal throughout the region that these two nations are and will remain sovereign and independent states.

Here in Bucharest, we must make clear that NATO welcomes the aspirations of Georgia and Ukraine for their membership in NATO and offers them a clear path forward to meet that goal. So my country's position is clear: NATO should welcome Georgia and Ukraine into the Membership Action Plan. And NATO membership must remain open to all of Europe's democracies that seek it and are ready to share in the responsibilities of NATO membership.

The most important responsibility of NATO is the collective security of our citizens. On my 2001 visit to Warsaw, I said that the United States and Europe share more than an alliance; we share a civilization. Less than 3 months later, that shared civilization came under a monstrous attack. Even now, with the distance of time, it's still difficult to fathom the enormity of what happened on September the 11th, 2001. Thousands of men and women woke up that morning, had breakfast with their families, and left for work, never to return home. Tens of thousands more, including citizens of many NATO nations, still mourn the loss of moms and dads, husbands and wives, brothers and sisters, friends and loved ones who were taken from them in a horrific moment of violence and death.

NATO nations recognize that the attacks were part of a broader ideological struggle. The terrorists who struck America that day murder the innocent in pursuit of a violent political vision. They despise the principles of decency and humanity that are the very foundation of our alliance. They want to impose their brutal rule on millions across the world. They attack our countries and target our people because we stand for freedom and because we hold the power to stop them from achieving their murderous ambitions.

NATO nations recognized that this unprecedented attack required unprecedented action. For the first time in the history of the alliance, Article 5 of the NATO Treaty was invoked. NATO aircraft were soon flying over the United States to provide early warning in case of a follow-on attack. Many NATO nations, including the United Kingdom and France, Canada, Denmark, Germany, Norway, the Netherlands, Italy, and Turkey, deployed forces to fight the terrorists in Afghanistan and to drive the Taliban from power.

Since then, NATO's role in Afghanistan has expanded significantly. In 2003, NATO took over the International Security Assistance Force. And over time, this NATO mission has grown from a small force operating only in Kabul to a force of 47,000 that is now leading operations across all of Afghanistan. Afghanistan is the most daring and ambition mission in the history of NATO. An alliance that never fired a shot in the cold war is now leading the fight on a key battleground of the first war in the 21st century. In Afghanistan, forces from NATO and many partner nations are bringing honor to their uniforms and pride to their countries.

As NATO forces fight the terrorists in Afghanistan, they're helping Afghans take increasing responsibility for their own security. With NATO's help, the ranks of trained Afghan soldiers have grown from 33,000 last year to 55,000 today. And these brave Afghan forces are leading many important combat operations. Thanks to their courage and the skill of NATO personnel, a nation that was once a safe haven for Al Qaida is now a democracy where boys and girls are going to school, new roads and hospitals are being built, and people are looking to the future with new hope.

Afghanistan still faces many challenges. The enemy has been driven from its strongholds and no longer controls a single Afghan city. But as this enemy has been defeated on the battlefield, they have turned increasingly to terrorist tactics such as suicide attacks and roadside bombs. And if we were to let up the pressure, the extremists would reestablish safe havens across the country and use them to terrorize the people of Afghanistan and threaten our own. And that is why we'll stay on the offense, and that is why we'll keep the pressures on these radicals and extremists, and that is why we'll succeed.

Terrorists used safe havens in Afghanistan to launch the 9/11 attacks. Since 9/11, Al Qaida terrorists around the world have succeeded in launching devastating attacks on allied cities such as Madrid and London and Istanbul. They planned more attacks on targets in Europe that never came to pass because of the vigilance of intelligence and law enforcement personnel from many of our nations. For example, in 2006, we stopped an Al Qaida plot to blow up passenger jets departing Europe for the United States. Earlier this year, Turkish authorities broke up an Al Qaida cell that was plotting a series of terrorist attacks on Turkey. This enemy remains dangerous, and that's why our alliance is so important to protecting innocent people.

Two weeks ago, Usama bin Laden issued an audio recording in which he threatened Europe with new attacks. We need to take the words of the enemy seriously. The terrorist threat is real; it is deadly. And defeating this enemy is the top priority of NATO.

Our alliance must maintain its resolve and finish the fight in NATO. As President Sarkozy put it in London last week: "We cannot afford to lose Afghanistan. Whatever the cost, however difficult the victory, we cannot afford it. We must win." I agree completely. To ensure that we do win, France is sending additional forces to Af-

ghanistan. The United States is deploying an additional 3,500 marines. Romania is adding forces, as are several other allies. We ask other NATO nations to step forward with additional forces as well. If we do not defeat the terrorists in Afghanistan, we will face them on our own soil. Innocent civilians in Europe and North America would then pay the price.

The struggle in Afghanistan cannot be won by force of arms alone. We must also help the Afghan Government strengthen democratic institutions, provide essential services, create jobs and opportunity, and show its people that freedom can lead to a better life. But for this to happen, Afghanistan needs security, and that is what NATO is helping to provide.

Many NATO allies are also helping to bring security and stability to the other major front in this war against extremists and radicals: Iraq. At this moment, 10 NATO nations have forces supporting Operation Iraqi Freedom, including the Black Wolves of Romania's 151st Infantry. The battalion has given their base in Iraq a fearsome name: Camp Dracula. Romanian troops are operating unmanned aerial vehicles, protecting critical infrastructure, conducting human intelligence missions, providing medical care, and carrying out combat operations in Iraq.

One Romanian soldier put it this way: "I've been here before and will come back for as many times as needed. I know that what we do is important." Our Romanian allies are serving the cause of freedom in Iraq with skill and honor, and they have earned the respect of my countrymen.

Forces from 14 NATO nations plus Ukraine are also serving in Iraq as part of a NATO training mission. NATO has trained more than 7,000 Iraqi officers so far. The Iraqis have asked us to expand this mission, and we should do so. At our summit this week, we will also expand the NATO-Iraq partnership, so we can allow more Iraqi officers to attend NATO schools and seminars. The purpose is to prepare

Iraqi officers to lead their own troops in battle, so we can help them defend their democracy against the terrorists and extremists who murder their people.

Iraqi forces are fighting bravely in this struggle, and they're risking and giving their lives in the fight against our common enemies. To help them prevail, last year, the United States launched the surge in Iraq. We deployed 30,000 additional soldiers and marines, with a clear mission: help Iraqi forces protect the people; pursue the enemy in its strongholds; and deny the terrorists sanctuary. The Government in Baghdad has stepped forward with a surge of its own, adding more than 100,000 new Iraqi soldiers and police during the past year. And to ensure that military progress in Iraq is quickly followed up with real improvements in daily life, we doubled the number of Provincial Reconstruction Teams in Iraq. These teams are helping to build up local economies, strengthen responsible leaders, and help bring Iraqis together so that reconciliation can happen from the ground up.

The surge has produced results across Iraq. Compared to a year ago, violence is significantly down, civilian deaths are down, sectarian killings are down, and attacks on coalition forces are down. We've captured or killed thousands of extremists in Iraq, including hundreds of key Al Qaida leaders and operatives. With security improving, local citizens have restarted the political process in their neighborhoods and their cities and Provinces. And leaders in Baghdad are beginning to make the tough compromises necessary to get important pieces of legislation passed.

As they do, we will stay on the offense against the enemy. In the north, Iraqi forces backed by American troops are pursuing Al Qaida terrorists who are operating in and around Mosul. In the south, Prime Minister Maliki sent the Iraqi security forces to begin to root out extremists and criminals in Basra, many of whom have received arms and training and funding from

Iran. In retaliation, some of these extremist elements fired rockets into the center of Baghdad hoping to shake Prime Minister Maliki's will. They're not going to succeed. There's tough fighting ahead, but the gains from the surge we have seen are real. And working together with Iraqi forces, our coalition will continue to pursue our enemies and seal their defeat.

The surge has done more than turn the situation around in Iraq, it has opened the door to a major strategic victory in the broader war against extremists. In Iraq, we're witnessing the first large-scale Arab uprising against Usama bin Laden and his grim ideology and his terrorist network. Tens of thousands of ordinary citizens have stepped forward to join the fight against Al Qaida. And when Iraqi and coalition forces defeat this enemy, the effects will reverberate beyond Iraq's borders.

By defeating the enemy in Iraq, we will show people across the Middle East that millions share their revulsion of terrorists' hateful ideology. We will show that free men and women can stand up to the terrorists and prevail against them. We will show that America will not abandon our friends in the fight against terror and extremism. We will show that a hopeful vision of liberty can take root in a troubled region and yield the peace that we all desire. And we will show that the future of the Middle East does not belong to terror, the future of the Middle East belongs to freedom.

As NATO allies fight terror and promote progress in Iraq and Afghanistan, our alliance is taking on other important missions across the world. In the Mediterranean, NATO forces are patrolling the high seas to combat terrorism as part of Operation Active Endeavor. In Kosovo, NATO forces are providing security and helping a new democracy take root in the Balkans. In Darfur, NATO has airlifted African Union peacekeepers and provided them with training to protect the people of that troubled region. The alliance stands ready to provide further assistance to the AU—African Union force.

Each of these missions underscores the changing nature of the NATO alliance. See, NATO is no longer a static alliance focused on defending Europe from a Soviet tank invasion. It is now an expeditionary alliance that is sending its forces across the world to help secure a future of freedom and peace for millions.

To meet the missions of the 21st century, NATO needs 21st-century capabilities. So over the past 7 years, we've taken decisive action to transform the capabilities of this alliance. We created a new NATO transformation command to ensure that NATO is preparing for the threats of the future. We created a new NATO Response Force to ensure that our alliance can deploy rapidly and effectively anywhere in the world. We launched a new Strategic Airlift Initiative to ensure that NATO members have a dedicated fleet of aircraft their forces need to deploy and sustain themselves over great distances. We've created a new NATO special operations coordinator—coordination center in Belgium to increase the interoperability and effectiveness of our special forces.

One of the most important steps we can take is—to protect our citizens is the deployment of new capabilities to defend against a ballistic missile attack. On 9/11, we saw the damage our enemies could do by hijacking planes loaded with jet fuel, turning them into missiles, and using them to strike innocent people. Today, dangerous regimes are pursuing far more powerful capabilities and building ballistic missiles that could allow them to deliver the world's most dangerous weapons to capitals of free nations.

To defend against this emerging threat, the United States has deployed missile defenses in the Pacific that can protect against threats emanating from Northeast Asia. And we're now deploying elements of this system to Europe, so we can defend against

possible attacks emanating from the Middle East.

The need for missile defense in Europe is real, and in my opinion, it is urgent. Iran is pursuing technology that could be used to produce nuclear weapons and ballistic missiles of increasing range that could deliver them. In 2006, Iran conducted military exercises in which it launched ballistic missiles capable of striking Israel and Turkey. Iranian officials have declared that they are developing missiles with a range of 1,200 miles, which would give them the capability to reach us right here in Romania. Our intelligence community assesses that, with continued foreign assistance, Iran could test an intercontinental ballistic missile capable of reaching the United States and all of Europe if it should choose to do so.

Today, we have no way to defend Europe against such an emerging threat, so we must deploy ballistic missile defenses that can help protect. The United States is working with Poland and the Czech Republic to deploy a system that could defend countries in Europe from a limited, long-range attack from the Middle East. We're working with NATO on developing allied capabilities to defend against short- and medium-range attacks from the Middle East. And as we do so, we're inviting Russia to join us in this cooperative effort, so as to be able to defend Russia, Europe, and the United States against an emerging threat that could affect us all.

President Putin has raised the possibility of using radar facilities in Azerbaijan and southern Russia. We believe these sites could be included as part of a wider threat-monitoring system that could lead to an unprecedented level of strategic cooperation between Russia and the NATO alliance. We can only imagine the devastation that would be caused by a ballistic missile attack on one of our cities. So I believe strongly we have a responsibility to work together to ensure that such attack never comes to pass.

This week, President Putin is planning to attend his first NATO summit, and later this week, I plan to travel to Sochi, Russia, for further talks on this and other matters. In our discussions, I will reiterate that the missile defense capabilities we are developing are not designed to defend against Russia, just as the new NATO we are building is not designed to defend against Russia. The cold war is over. Russia is not our enemy. We're working toward a new security relationship with Russia, whose foundation does not rest on the prospect of mutual annihilation.

In Warsaw 7 years ago, I said that the Europe we envision must be open to Russia. During my Presidency, we've acted to make that vision a reality. With our allies, we created the NATO-Russia Council to facilitate greater cooperation between Russia and the Atlantic alliance. The United States and Russia signed the Moscow Treaty, which commits our two nations to historic reductions in our operationally deployed strategic nuclear warheads. And as we look to the future, I believe we can build strong relations with Russia and a strong NATO alliance at the same time.

Building a strong NATO alliance also requires a strong European defense capability. So at this summit, I will encourage our European partners to increase their defense investments to support both NATO and EU operations. America believes if Europeans invest in their own defense, they will also be stronger and more capable when we deploy together.

I have confidence that NATO is ready for the challenges of the 21st century because I have confidence in the courage of allies like Romania. The Romanian people have seen evil in their midst, and they've seen evil defeated. They value freedom because they've lived without it. And this hard experience has inspired them to fight and sacrifice for the liberty of others.

This is precisely what Romanian forces are doing on behalf of this alliance. We see their courage in soldiers like Second Lieutenant Aurel Marcu of Romania's 33d Mountain Battalion. Last fall, Aurel's unit was in Afghanistan when it got word that an American soldiers—American soldiers from the Arizona National Guard had been struck by a roadside bomb. Several were injured, one of them fatally. Aurel and his comrades swung into action and responded to the call for assistance. As his unit sped to the scene of the attack, Aurel's vehicle was struck by a second roadside bomb, killing him instantly. Aurel gave his life rushing to the aid of wounded American soldiers. His example and his valor are an inspiration to all of us. I very much appreciate his wife joining us today, and I want her to know that she and her family have the gratitude and the respect and the prayers of the American people.

Our troops are proud to fight alongside allies like this. We appreciate courage. We appreciate people who love freedom. We appreciate people who understand freedom will yield the peace that we all want. We value our friendship with Romania, and we value the Atlantic alliance that we share. America is united with our European allies by ties of blood that our soldiers have shed together. We're united by ties of conviction, a shared belief that every human life is precious and endowed by our Creator with dignity and worth. We're united by ties of liberty and by an abiding faith in the power of freedom to change the course of history. Strengthened by these convictions, tested in battle, and confident in our future, this great alliance for freedom is ready for all that will come.

Thank you for your time. God bless.

NOTE: The President spoke at 8:45 a.m. at the Casa de Economii si Consemnatiuni. In his remarks, he referred to former Presidents Ion Iliescu and Emil Constantinescu of Romania; President Valdis Zatlers of Latvia and his wife Lilita Zatlere; Radu Gratian Ghetea, president, Casa de Economii si Consemnatiuni; Usama bin Laden, leader of the Al Qaida terrorist organization; President

Nicolas Sarkozy of France; Prime Minister Nuri al-Maliki of Iraq; President Vladimir V. Putin of Russia; and Aurelia Marcu, wife of Romanian Army 2d Lt. Aurel Marcu, who was killed in Afghanistan on September 6, 2007.

The President's News Conference With President Traian Basescu of Romania in Neptun, Romania
April 2, 2008

President Basescu. Well, Mr. President, you will be the first.

President Bush. Well, thank you very much. *Buna ziua.* Mr. President, thank you very much for your warm hospitality. Laura and I are thrilled to be with you and your lovely wife. I can't think of a better place to meet. It's such a beautiful setting, and you're awfully kind to have invited us to be here. After all, that's what friends do, though. And our relationship is very strong, and it's very friendly.

I admire your courage, and I admire your leadership. And I want to thank you for hosting us—hosting NATO in Bucharest. It is—you know, it's a big deal. And what's interesting is, 20 years ago, our nations were separated by a cold war, and Romania was a member of the Warsaw Pact, and the Romanian people suffered under a cruel dictator. Today, think how things have changed. The Romanian people are free; we're strong allies. We appreciate you in NATO, and I want to thank you for your historic contributions to NATO.

I want to thank you and the people of Romania for your contributions to Afghanistan. There are about 600 Romanian troops there. The Afghan people are grateful, as am I. I want to thank you for your contribution to the troops in Iraq. These are tough decisions, but I think they're necessary decisions to keep the peace. You and I have discussed our desire to work closely with those countries to encourage their success, for their sake and for the sake of peace.

I appreciate very much our discussions we had on NATO enlargement. Romania and the United States agree that our alliance must continue to be open to new members that share our values and to make tough choices to reform and—countries that are willing to address our security needs jointly. To this end, I strongly believe that Croatia, Albania, and Macedonia should join NATO as full members, that we ought to extend MAP to Ukraine and Georgia, and that we strongly support the requests of Montenegro and Bosnia-Herzegovina for intensified dialogue with the NATO alliance, and that we ought to open the door to closer cooperation with Serbia. And I thank you for your advice on these issues, and I appreciate your stand.

I also appreciate your leadership in the Black Sea region. Maybe that's why you invited me here, because you're showing such good leadership in the Black Sea region. [*Laughter*] But we share your concerns about enhanced security and making sure this part of the world becomes relevant in a global economy. That's why we've contributed $10 million to the Black Sea Trust, to help fund programs across the region, to strengthen civil society programs, the rule of law, and democratic governance.

I want to thank you very much for your view of the market: that markets flourish and grow when entrepreneurs are encouraged. The Romanian economy is strong. One of the reasons we launched the Romanian-American education foundation and made it go forward is because of the success of your economy and your entrepreneurs. And I want to congratulate you on your rate of growth and on your vision.

And all in all, Mr. President, I am really glad I came. And I thank you and Mrs. for your hospitality. I appreciate the really good lunch. If the American press hasn't eaten Romanian ice cream, I strongly suggest you try it. [*Laughter*]

Thank you very much, sir.

President Basescu. Thank you very much, Mr. President. Firstly, Mr. President, I would like to extend my thanks to you for offering the invitation to reserve a few hours for a visit on the land where I was born, in Dobrogea on the Black Sea shore. Just as we have discussed in Washington 2005, 2006, our partnership has exceeded for long time the stage of a simple partnership, military partnership, a partnership that was envisaged firstly Romanian security.

We're now in the stage of the partnership with a very strong and consistent economic component. Following 2005, Oracle was present in Romania, also Smithfield, with great investment in the food industry, and lastly, also Ford is present here. And this means that the Romanian-American partnership covers practically all the aspects, and we hope to a further development.

I would like to extend my thanks to you for the attention that your administration has been paying to the Black Sea region, for your concern related to the security in the Black Sea region, and for your concern related to the need to guarantee democracy in the Black Sea region.

Moreover, Mr. President, I would like to underline the confidence that United States has had in the Romanian Army by placing under Romanian command important troops in Afghanistan. It was a token of confidence that you have given to us, and we are aware that it is very rare that the United States placed their troops under the command of other countries. Thank you very much.

To conclude, I would like to underline the similarity of approach concerning the region where we find—whether we speak about the Balkans or Ukraine or Georgia. Our approaches envisage mainly Romania's security and the security of the region. And we're glad to see that although the United States are far from this region, they have understood our concerns, the priorities of our country and of our region. Thank you very much, Mr. President, for answering with no hesitation to what we have established.

I would like to assure you at the same time that Romania will respect all its engagements, both the ones related to the relation with NATO and with the European Union, and also the ones related to partnership and our bilateral relation. Thank you.

Questions?

President Bush. Are we starting with the Americans? Who do you think I ought to call on? Okay, I'll call on Roger [Roger Runningen, Bloomberg News].

NATO Troop Levels in Afghanistan

Q. Thank you, Mr. President. On Afghanistan, you're seeking increased commitments from NATO. There are been—have been some new pledges. Are they enough? How many figures—how many troops are needed? Are you satisfied with the pledges, and what are the consequences if those pledges fall short?

President Bush. We expect our NATO allies to shoulder the burden necessary to succeed. And to this end, as you know, I've committed 3,200—3,500 additional marines to send a clear signal that we're willing to do our part.

I was very pleased to listen to the comments of President Sarkozy, where he indicated his willingness to increase troop presence. Other nations have agreed to step up, including Romania. And so we'll see how it goes. That's what summits are for. Summits are for opportunities for people to make clear their intentions about how they intend to support this very important mission.

And obviously, I am grateful for any nation that contributes troops to Afghanistan, as are the Afghan people. And clearly some nations are more capable than others of—in sending troops into combat, into harm's way. We fully understand the politics that prohibit some nations from contributing, but nations need to take this mission seriously because it's in our mutual interests. It's in our interest, of course, to help young democracies survive. But in this case, it's in our interest to help succeed, because we don't want an enemy that has been known to attack people—nations in our alliance—to be able to develop safe haven again, to be able to use a launching pad like Afghanistan to plot, plan, and attack.

So this is a vital mission. And it's hard work. It's a tough mission. And our allies have got to understand it's hard. Taking democracy out of the rubble of this—of the Taliban is hard to do, just like it is in Iraq. So the question nations have to ask: Is it worth it? And my answer is, absolutely, it's worth it—and so is the President—it's worth it for our own security, and it's worth it for the cause of peace.

President Basescu. Thank you. Regarding Afghanistan, we have a main idea that any lack of success of the NATO in Afghanistan will diminish dramatically the credibility of our organization. And for the time being, the civilized world don't have alternatives to the security than NATO. We have to do everything what we can in order to make a success in our action in Afghanistan: granting democratic development of the country, economic development of the country, security of the country, and eliminating the terrorist risks which are generated by this region. Sure, we have a extremely clear idea if we don't keep the terrorists in Afghanistan. If we will let them free, they'll come in Europe, they'll come in United States. For this reason, we have to win; we have to obtain the victory in Afghanistan.

Romania/Black Sea Region

Q. President, getting back to Romania now, behind you there is the Black Sea. Romania has insisted——

President Bush. And a few birds too. [*Laughter*]

Q. ——there is time—has insisted that NATO has to focus its attention upon this region as well. Following the talks today, did you establish a common vision, Romania-United States, as regards the future of this region?

President Basescu. [*Inaudible*]

Q. For both, thank you.

President Bush. Okay, thank you. Your English is better than you let on. [*Laughter*] I take the advice of the President on the Black Sea. He knows it well. After all, he's sailed many a vessel on this—as a matter of fact, I was asking the President about his days as a seafarer, a captain, and he explained to me that recently he got his captain's license renewed. [*Laughter*] So not only does—is he a skillful person, he loves the Black Sea, and he understands the potential of the Black Sea.

And that's why we were happy to contribute to the Black Sea Trust Fund, as a way to help him and other visionary leaders realize the full potential of the Black Sea region. I mean, there's work to be done on regional security matters. Obviously, to the extent that people feel like they can smuggle people or drugs, then there needs to be a strategy to deal with that. The idea of trafficking human beings is abhorrent, and nobody in—any civilized person who accepts that, you know, is just—needs to have their head examined. And yet the President fully understands that cooperation here will help deal with the issue.

We need to promote economic cooperation. There's great potential—economic potential here. We need to promote the scenario where you can promote energy independence. All nations ought to have a variety of sources of energy from which to choose, so it's never become captured by a single supplier.

And so I fully understand the strategic importance of this area, and there's been nobody more clear and articulate on the subject than the President. And I want to thank you for your leadership.

President Basescu. Thank you, Mr. President. As regards the Black Sea, the talks has—have also comprised the idea of supporting the states that have democratic options, of consolidating their institutions. The main idea, this main focus was on combating the asymmetric risks, such as the drug trafficking, persons trafficking, arms trafficking, and not lastly, our objective, the objectives that Romania's allies have endorsed, be it the European Union that has issued the Black Sea Synergy document, be it NATO. Our objective is that this region becomes a secure region, because nobody can be certain about the future if the security is not guaranteed. And this is the major objective that Romania has been promoting, the objective that our allies have endorsed and that we support further on, and that will remain a major foreign policy objective for Romania.

President Bush. Jim [Jim Gerstenzang, Los Angeles Times].

Russia/Missile Defense System/Global Security Cooperation

Q. Mr. President, you pointed out this morning how much the NATO mission has changed. It's changed dramatically over the past decades. Russia still seems to be casting a huge shadow, most recently with missile defense, with NATO expansion. Has some things not changed? Can you avoid a—what would appear to be something of a diplomatic train wreck when you meet with President Putin?

President Bush. I mean, look, I'm going to meet with President Putin to make it clear to him the cold war is over and Russia is not our enemy and that there's common ground. Obviously, I've had my disagreements with the President in the past, and—

but there's also areas where we need to work in common, such as proliferation and dealing with terror. And I've got some convincing to do, but he needs to understand, the missile defense system is aimed at—aimed primarily at rogue regimes coming out of the Middle East that could hold us all hostage. And this is a good—it's a good chance for me to sit down and have yet another heart-to-heart with him. And I'm more than happy to do so.

I made it clear yesterday that NATO needs to look at expansion in our interests, not—and not give any nation a veto power over whether or not NATO ought to extend MAP membership and/or membership. And so it's—you know, I understand Russian concerns about the expanse of NATO. They were concerned when Romania got into NATO, I'm confident. But look what a great partner and a peaceful neighbor Romania is. I mean, Romania has no warlike aspirations. These are people who want to help other democracies thrive and, at the same time, see their economy grow. I've explained to President Putin: Democracies on the border of Russia are in their interest.

And so this is a good opportunity. I don't mind a good, frank discussion with President Putin. He doesn't mind telling me what's on his mind either. We've had 7 years working together, a chance to have some pretty candid exchanges. And secondly—and this is his last—this will be our last face-to-face meeting as his Presidency. And I'll thank him. I'll thank him for being candid with me. I'll thank him for serving his nation. I have no animosity toward President Putin. Just because you don't agree on issues doesn't mean you can't find a cordiality, to be able to discuss things in a frank manner, and that's the way our relationship has been. We—I met with him a lot in the course of my Presidency, and I appreciate the fact that he invited me to Sochi.

And so I have no—I'm not going to set any kind of expectations. I guess you are.

You call it a diplomatic train wreck; I call it an opportunity to sit down and have a good, frank discussion again. And we'll see what happens, what comes out of it. It's a good opportunity for me to say goodbye and to see whether or not we can sign the strategic dialogue that will serve our nations' interest after his Presidency and mine.

President Basescu. From our point of view—and I would like to make a comment here that does not necessarily answer your question—but Romania has a relatively simple approach in relation to its ties with Russia. Firstly, we have to admit that all— we all, and particularly the former Communist states, must equally and perhaps more—to a larger extent, Russia, we all have to overcome the logics of the cold war, because at present, there is nothing to justify this approach, this logic. Each independent state is free to have its options, and nobody can have the right—the veto right upon the options of an independent state.

But apart from this statement that regards more the principles, I would like to point out—to refer to some issues that from our point of view are threats. For example, terrorist is a threat equally for Russia, for America, for Spain, and it can materialize at any time against Ukraine, against Georgia. So I would like to—I could say that in this point, in this respect, we are all at the same level of risk.

The trafficking in arms is an equal threat for the Russian Federation, for the United States, for Romania, for Ukraine, for Georgia, for Albania as well. This is another issue that we have to fight against together. The trafficking in narcotics that transforms into money for arms and into generations of youth that are deeply affected—this threat affects equally the Russian Federation, Romania, America, France, Germany. Trafficking in human beings is another risk that affects equally Russia, America, Ukraine, Romania. And a possible cyber attack can be deployed with an equal risk for Russia, for Romania, for America. Missile attacks that are deployed by countries that do not respect the rules, that are not part of the proliferation treaties—this risk can affect, at any time, the Russian Federation, America, Romania, Ukraine.

Seeing—finding that the risks are the same, are almost similar for everybody, why can't we find a common ground for solidarity between us, among us—NATO member states, Russia Federation, aspiring NATO states—a common ground for generating the same policy? Actually, the only thing that hinders us from acting united against the risks that affect us equally is the fact that some of us are still attached to the logics, to the approach of the cold war, and do not have an equal respect for the democratic rights of the peoples.

U.S. Visa Policy/Romania-U.S. Relations

Q. Mr. President, the Romanian people, the Romanians have a great expectations with regards to the very good ties, political and economic, between the two states. In a very practical manner, they will ask, when will we have the same regime as the other citizens from the European Union with regards to the visas? Could we have a deadline for this when we could travel freely to the United States?

President Bush. First of all, your President was very articulate on the subject of visas. One of the benefits of having a good friendship is that he's not afraid of telling me what's on his mind. [*Laughter*] And he made it abundantly clear that visa policy in America must take into account Romanian past and also Romanian future and present. In other words—and I fully understand the frustrations of the Romanian people. I understand it. I understand that a citizen says: "Wait a minute. We're contributing soldiers in Iraq, and yet we're not necessarily treated like other nations in the European collective or European Union."

And those frustrations are clearly understandable. That's why I went to Congress and tried to get them to modernize the visa law. And all they—although they changed the law, it still creates certain hurdles for nations like Romania. And I assured the President that we will work with him as best as we can to adhere to our law and to, at the same time, understands the contradictions.

It's—hopefully, the new law will—and our cooperation—will make it easier for Romanian citizens to come and visit their relatives. And obviously, to the extent that somebody tries to come and not come back is something we all got to guard about. That's—but the idea of somebody coming to visit a relative or a long-lost cousin to say hello and to see what America is like and then come back to Romania is an issue that we just got to be thoughtful about.

And so yes, I mean, this is—this subject came up. It is clear there's a level of frustration. I explained our new law is in effect, and we'll work closely with the Romanian Government to meet our law and, at the same time, meet the demands of a strong and good ally.

Thank you. Thank you very much.

President Basescu. Thank you very much.

President Bush. Right, you want to go over here?

President Basescu. Just a moment.

President Bush. Oh, you got——

President Basescu. Just a moment.

President Bush. He's not through.

President Basescu. The information I would like to add to refer to two delicate issues, issues that are visible for the Romanian public. We have also approached— we have also addressed the visa issue and also the Teo Peter issue. And we hope to find, in time, the decision taken by President Bush was that, in the near future, we will launch the bilateral mechanism that—apart from the European ones. And referring to the other issue, to find as fast as possible a reasonable solution acceptable for the family of Teo Peter.

Thank you.

President Bush. He's going to show me this wharf out here. [*Laughter*]

NOTE: The President's news conference began at 1:40 p.m. at the Protocol Villas Neptun-Olimp. In his remarks, he referred to Maria Basescu, wife of President Basescu; President Nicolas Sarkozy of France; and President Vladimir V. Putin of Russia. President Basescu and some reporters spoke partly in Romanian, and those portions of their remarks were translated by an interpreter.

Remarks Following a Discussion With Secretary General Jakob Gijsbert "Jaap" de Hoop Scheffer of the North Atlantic Treaty Organization in Bucharest, Romania
April 2, 2008

President Bush. Thank you for your time, and thank you for organizing the Bucharest summit. I appreciate your service very much to the cause of world peace, and I want to thank you for your briefing. I'm, like you, optimistic that this is going to be a very successful summit.

We came in with some objectives in mind. One was to get NATO to continue to support Afghanistan's democracy. And I feel good about what I'm hearing from my fellow leaders about their desire to support Afghanistan. And I think if tomorrow we get clarification on troop support, I think the people of Afghanistan—the way you indicated it may be—the people of Afghanistan are going to be more than grateful. And the people who—whose nations are represented in NATO will be supporting a cause that is worthy, a cause for peace.

Secondly, you and I discussed the need for a comprehensive missile defense regime out of NATO. And it looks like to me that the ingredients are coming together where that could be a distinct possibility. And that would be a very important statement because NATO could assure its members and the people within NATO that there will be defenses available to prevent a Middle Eastern nation, for example, from launching a strike which could harm our security.

We've also talked obviously about enlargement. And we'll see, on enlargement. There's an issue with one country, in particular, but it look—I'm optimistic that this will get solved. And finally, of course, Ukraine and Georgia is a very difficult issue for some nations here; it's not for me. I think that these nations are qualified nations to apply for membership application. And I said so on Ukrainian soil. I also said so in the Oval Office with the President of Georgia. And I haven't changed my mind, because it's—one of the great things about NATO is it encourages the kind of habits that are necessary for peace to exist.

And today in a press conference, I was asked, Mr. Secretary General, about Russia's reactions. I said—I have always told Vladimir Putin, my friend—that it's in his interest that there be democracies on her border, and that he doesn't need to fear NATO; he ought to welcome NATO because NATO is a group of nations dedicated to peace. And so I appreciate your hard work, and I'm excited about tomorrow's—about tonight's meeting and tomorrow's meetings as well.

Secretary General de Hoop Scheffer. Mr. President, thank you for having us and your Afghanistan position. I can share your and echo your optimism, I think, on NATO's key operational priority, which is Afghanistan. We will do well. We will do well in the political sense because we will publish a vision document, as we call it, which is a clear sign of our commitments not only of NATO but of the whole international community; long-term commitment vis-a-vis

Afghanistan, which is important for them, for the Afghan people, but is also important for the reason that said we should not forget that we are on one of the frontlines in a fight against terrorism in Afghanistan. And that is a major argument and a major reason that we cannot afford not to prevail. And we are prevailing in Afghanistan. So I think that's good news. And President Karzai, to whom I spoke this morning, reconfirms that good news.

I'm optimistic about enlargement, Mr. President. I think that enlarging the NATO family of democratic nations, this value-based organization, is a plus. And I hope that tomorrow will see invitations.

I also hope that we'll see a positive and constructive meeting with the—President Putin and the NATO-Russia Council, with the right tone and the right ambition for practical cooperation.

I'm like you, Mr. President, optimism about—optimistic about missile defense. I think the alliance will take a clear position on missile defense, recognizing the threat and working on the answers to that recognized threat.

And last but not least, Mr. President, you mentioned another issue which readily will be discussed: Membership Action Plan for Ukraine and Georgia. I think this can never be a question of "whether." The "whether" is not questionable. If these nations fulfill the criteria and if they would enter—want to enter themselves through NATO's open door, I think that door should be open. So that is a discussion that certainly—we certainly are going to have.

We have a large agenda; we have a full agenda. It will be not only NATO's biggest summit ever, but it will also be a very interesting political summit with, I think, very good results.

Mr. President, once again, thank you for having us.

President Bush. Thank you, sir.

Secretary General de Hoop Scheffer. Thank you.

President Bush. Thank you.

NOTE: The President spoke at 5:15 p.m. at the JW Marriott Bucharest Grand Hotel. In his remarks, he referred to President Mikheil Saakashvili of Georgia; and President Vladi- mir V. Putin of Russia. Secretary General de Hoop Scheffer referred to President Hamid Karzai of Afghanistan.

Remarks at a North Atlantic Council Summit Meeting in Bucharest
April 3, 2008

President Bush. Mr. Secretary General, President Basescu, thank you all very much. For nearly six decades, the NATO alliance has been the hope of a world moving toward freedom and justice and away from patterns of conflict and fear. During times of great challenge, we have advanced our ideals. We've stood form in defending them—firm in defending them, and we have offered NATO's promise to nations willing to undertake the hard work and sacrifices required of its members.

Since the end of the cold war, NATO has welcomed 10 liberated nations to its ranks. These countries have brought new ideas, new enthusiasm, and new vigor. NATO's embrace of these new members has made Europe stronger, safer, and freer. These countries have made our alliance more relevant to the dangers we confront in the new century.

In Bucharest, we're inviting more nations to join us. I'm pleased that the alliance has agreed to invite Albania and Croatia to become members of NATO. Both these nations have demonstrated the ability and the willingness to provide strong and enduring contributions to NATO. Both have undertaken challenging political, economic, and defense reforms. Both have deployed their forces on NATO missions. Albania and Croatia are ready for the responsibility NATO brings, and they will make outstanding members of this alliance.

We regret that we were not able to reach consensus today to invite Macedonia to join the alliance. Macedonia has made difficult reforms at home. It is making major con- tributions to NATO missions all—abroad. The name issue needs to be resolved quickly so that Macedonia can be welcomed into NATO as soon as possible. In the interim, NATO needs to intensify its engagement with Macedonia to make sure that NATO looks forward to the day when Macedonia takes its place among the members of the Atlantic alliance.

Albania, Croatia, and Macedonia all know the difference between good and evil, because they clearly remember evil's face. These nations do not take their freedom for granted, because they still remember life without it. These nations respect the hard work of building democracy, because they brought it to life in their countries.

The United States and all members of the alliance strongly support the aspirations of their people, and we pledge to stand with them as they continue to work on reform. Together, we will continue to help build a Europe that is stable, strong, and free. We'll bring more stability to a once troubled Balkan region. We will be able to demonstrate the benefits that come from siding with the forces of freedom.

NATO's door must remain open to other nations in Europe that share our love for liberty and demonstrate a commitment to reform and seek to strengthen their ties with the transatlantic community. We must give other nations seeking membership a full and fair hearing. As we invite new members today, we're also clear that the progress of enlargement will continue.

The alliance has always welcomed those willing to make the sacrifices necessary to protect our nations and serves as forces for peace. And that is what's made our alliance unbreakable, and that is why NATO remains the most successful alliance in the history on behalf of human freedom.

Congratulations, and thank you.

Secretary General Jakob Gijsbert "Jaap" de Hoop Scheffer of the North Atlantic Treaty Organization. Thank you very much, Mr. President.

NOTE: The President spoke at 2:05 p.m. at the Palace of Parliament. In his remarks, he referred to President Traian Basescu of Romania.

Remarks Following a Discussion With Prime Minister Calin Popescu-Tariceanu of Romania in Bucharest
April 4, 2008

Interpreter. Hello, good day. Of course, our discussion was a very useful and very pleasant one. We discussed both bilateral issues between Romania and the United States. I expressed to the—to President Bush our gratitude for having had the trust to have Romania organize this important NATO summit in Bucharest.

The organization of the NATO summit in Bucharest was very symbolic. It is part of a much larger vision and concept, this vision being that to strengthen and to unify Europe after the fall of the Iron Curtain. And the idea was to foster, to strengthen the alliance in the eastern and southeastern flank, from the Baltic Sea all the way to the Black Sea and the Mediterranean. That is how we have to interpret the membership of Albania and Croatia to NATO, the future membership of Macedonia, and eventual Georgia and Ukraine membership as well.

But our discussion was not limited to that. We also discussed other issues of political and economic relationship between our countries and about the U.S. investments in our country. And I shared with President Bush my ambition, my hope, and actually, my dream that to see a very important industrial investment from the United States in Romania, an investment with which generate common interests and would foster even more our partnership.

And I'm referring to the Ford company, and of course, a common interest like this would make me feel, as a citizen and as a Prime Minister, much more protected by our common interests.

I would like to also mention another initiative which was announced by the President yesterday, which was the creation of an American-Romanian foundation which will set up educational programs and grants for Romanian students. I'm talking about the seed money of $100 million, which could be——

Prime Minister Popescu-Tariceanu. Hundred and fifty.

President Bush. Hundred fifty. Don't shortchange it.

Interpreter. ——$150 million, which in time will arrive at $1 billion investment, which will create—which would be an investment in the future, creating the future—Romanian Ambassadors to United States or the American Ambassadors to Romania—it would be our hope.

Prime Minister Popescu-Tariceanu. Thank you.

President Bush. Yes, thank you, Mr. Prime Minister. We just had a great—we had a good meeting, because we're good friends. All right. Okay, I'll just keep going.

Interpreter. I was actually told that everybody speaks English, so I should not interpret.

President Bush. Okay, fine. I'll speak in Romanian. [*Laughter*] Anyway, we had a very good meeting, Mr. Prime Minister. Thank you for your time. First of all, I want to congratulate the Government, yourself, for hosting a very successful NATO summit. It's not easy to host as many automobiles, bodyguards, world leaders, hanger-on-ers as you did. And yet you did it and you organized well. Everybody who came to the summit was most impressed. I really do want to thank you, and I want to thank the people of Bucharest for their patience. I apologize for the inconvenience, but I do think it was a good sign, and it was important for your country to be the host of this important event. And it was a very successful summit.

We had good discussions about a successful bilateral relationship as well. I told the Prime Minister, one reason why capital comes to a country is because people feel comfortable about taking risk. I also congratulated him on these big investments that are coming; it's a good sign. And the people of Romania ought to be—appreciate the fact that the conditions are such that people are willing to invest. And by the way, investment creates jobs, which is also—will have a direct benefit for the people of Romania.

I also congratulated the Prime Minister on having a 16-percent flat tax. I'm a little envious. I would like to have been able to achieve the same objective for our Tax Code. And it was a smart thing to get done, cause I think those kinds of policies will enable the Romanian folks to have a bright future.

We talked about energy; we also talked about visas. There is a real contradiction here that's hard for the people of Romania to understand in that, on the one hand, how can certain people within the EU be treated one way and Romanians be treated another way, when it comes to visas? And I fully understand that contradiction, Mr. Prime Minister. Our Congress passed new law—it frankly wasn't as good as I thought it should be, but nevertheless, it is the law of the land cause I signed it into law.

And we will work with your Government on a couple of matters: one, to figure out why the rejection rate is so high. There needs to be more transparency, and the Prime Minister made it very clear that we have an obligation to explain why certain folks are not getting visas. And we'll do that. And——

Prime Minister Popescu-Tariceanu. Thank you.

President Bush. ——the other thing is, obviously, we've got law on our books that we need to work with you, to help everybody understand in the process what compliance means.

Overall, the trip here has been great. This is the second time I've come. I didn't have quite the dramatic rainbow scene this time as I did the first time I came, but it's—clearly there's been a lot of progress. The city looks different to me. The spirit is still strong. Freedom has taken hold, and I congratulate you, the Government, and all involved for the progress you've made. Thank you.

Prime Minister Popescu-Tariceanu. Thank you.

NOTE: The President spoke at 2:03 p.m. at the Victoria Palace. Prime Minister Popescu-Tariceanu spoke partly in Romanian, and those portions of his remarks were translated by an interpreter.

Statement on the 40th Anniversary of the Death of Martin Luther King, Jr.
April 4, 2008

Forty years ago today, America was robbed of one of history's most consequential advocates for equality and civil rights. On this day, we mourn the assassination of Dr. Martin Luther King, Jr., and we celebrate his powerful and eloquent message of justice and hope.

Dr. King was a man of courage and vision. He understood that love and compassion will always triumph over bitterness and hatred. His words and deeds inspired Americans of all races to confront prejudice and to work to ensure that our country is a land of opportunity for all its men and women.

We have made progress on Dr. King's dream, yet the struggle is not over. Ensuring freedom and equality for all Americans remains one of our most important responsibilities. As we reflect upon Dr. King's life and legacy, we must recommit ourselves to following his lasting example of service to others.

Remarks at a Dinner Hosted by President Stjepan Mesic of Croatia in Zagreb, Croatia
April 4, 2008

Mr. President and Madam, thank you very much. Mr. Prime Minister, thank you very much. Also good to meet your wife.

Laura and I are thrilled to be in your beautiful country, Mr. President. We appreciate your gracious hospitality, and we celebrate your invitation to become one of America's closest allies. I—you said you're from a small country. I'm impressed by the big hearts and the big basketball team. [*Laughter*]

We are so proud of our relationship, Mr. President. We share common values. We believe in human rights and human dignity. We believe there's a Creator that has given every man, woman, and child on the face of the Earth the great gift of freedom. We believe markets are capable of unleashing the entrepreneurial spirit of our peoples. We understand that freedom requires sacrifice.

I salute the people of your country for your courage and willingness to help a young democracy in Afghanistan not only thrive but succeed. I appreciate the friends who have stared evil in the face and understand there's a better tomorrow.

And so, Mr. President, I bring the greetings of my country to your beautiful land. With the honor due to a trusted ally, I offer a toast to you and to the valiant people of Croatia.

NOTE: The President spoke at 8:04 p.m. at the Pucka Dvorana. In his remarks, he referred to Milka Mesic, wife of President Mesic; and Prime Minister Ivo Sanader of Croatia and his wife Mirjana. The transcript released by the Office of the Press Secretary also included the remarks of President Mesic.

Remarks Following a Meeting With Prime Minister Ivo Sanader of Croatia in Zagreb
April 5, 2008

[Prime Minister Sanader spoke in Croatian, and no translation was provided.]

President Bush. Thank you, Mr. Prime Minister. It's really good to be with you again. I remember very fondly our visit to the Oval Office.

[The interpreter began to translate President Bush's remarks.]

Prime Minister Sanader. No, there is no need.

President Bush. Even though you did a brilliant job. *[Laughter]*

Prime Minister Sanader. They understand; they understand.

President Bush. I understand. But anyway, I—you suggested I come to your country then, and I'm really glad we came. Thanks. It's good news. And the fact that Croatia has been invited to join NATO is a historic moment. And I hope the people of your country are as proud as I am to be here to welcome you into NATO.

The—my only regret is I didn't get to see the coast. But I suspect when more Americans learn of the beauty of your coast, they'll want to come. And that's why the Open Skies agreement that we negotiated is going to be important to open up travel and trade. We will take you up on your request to have a trade mission come. I appreciate the fact that you have an open government, an honest government, a transparent government, which will help attract foreign capital—well-educated, hard-working people that will help attract foreign capital as well.

We talked about the neighborhood, and I appreciate the Prime Minister's advice and counsel on how the United States can help continue to promote stability and freedom. And I want to thank you very much for that.

We talked about an issue that I know is on the minds of the people of Croatia, and that is the visa waiver policy. I fully understand, Mr. Prime Minister, that some in your country wonder why our visa waiver policy is for you—different for you than it is for other people, perhaps, in Europe. After all, you've—you're sacrificing in Afghanistan alongside U.S. troops. And they wonder why they can't go see their relatives in America in an easier way.

I think they should be able to. Congress has passed a law that we now must live with. And we'll work with your Government to facilitate the new law in such a way, hopefully, that people will be able to realize their dreams of going to America to see relatives and loved ones. There's a lot of people in America that have fond memories in—of their homeland, and they want to be able to see their relatives in an easier fashion.

So we'll work government to government to meet our laws and, at the same time, hopefully, facilitate travel. I don't want to create false expectations. On the other hand, people should know that we have committed to working to see to it that the policy is implemented in a way that, hopefully, will ease travel quickly.

All in all, it's been an honor to be with you. I'm so grateful for your Government and for the people of your country for welcoming me and Laura. And I look forward to future visits.

Thank you.

Prime Minister Sanader. Thank you, sir. Thank you.

NOTE: The President spoke at 10:31 a.m. at the Banski Dvori.

Remarks in Zagreb
April 5, 2008

The President. Thank you all. *Dobro jutro.* Mr. Prime Minister, thank you very much. I'm honored to be here with the leaders from Albania, Croatia, and Macedonia. The United States appreciates the leadership you have shown in the cause of freedom. We're pleased Albania and Croatia have been invited to join NATO, and we look forward to Macedonia taking its place very soon in this great alliance for freedom.

Laura, who has joined me today, and I are proud to stand on the soil of an independent Croatia. Our countries are separated by thousands of miles, but we're united by a deep belief in God and the blessings of liberty He gave us. And today, on the edge of a great Adriatic, we stand together as one free people.

Croatia is a very different place than it was just a decade ago. The Croatian people have overcome war and hardship to build peaceful relations with your neighbors and to build a maturing democracy in one of the most beautiful countries on the face of the Earth. Americans admire your courage and admire your persistence. And we look forward to welcoming you as a partner in NATO.

The invitation to join NATO that Croatia and Albania received this week is a vote of confidence that you will continue to make necessary reforms and become strong contributors to our great alliance. Henceforth, should any danger threaten your people, America and the NATO alliance will stand with you, and no one will be able to take your freedom away.

I regret that NATO did not extend an invitation to Macedonia at this week's summit. Macedonia has made difficult reforms at home and is making major contributions to NATO missions abroad. Unfortunately, Macedonia's invitation was delayed because of a dispute over its name. In Bucharest,

NATO allies declared that as soon as this issue is resolved, Macedonia will be extended an invitation to join the alliance. America's position is clear: Macedonia should take its place in NATO as soon as possible.

The NATO alliance is open to all countries in the region. We welcome the decisions of Bosnia-Herzegovina and Montenegro to take the next steps toward membership called intensive dialogue. And we hope that soon a free and prosperous Serbia will find its rightful place in the family of Europe and live at peace with its neighbors.

With the changes underway in this region, Europe stands on the threshold of a new and hopeful history. The ancient and costly rivalries that led to two World Wars have fallen away. We've seen the burning desire for freedom melt even the Iron Curtain. We've witnessed the rise of strong and vibrant democracies and free and open markets. And today, the people of Europe are closer than ever before to a dream shared by millions: a Europe that is whole, a Europe that is at peace, and a Europe that is free.

The people of this region know what the gift of liberty means. You know the death and destruction that can be caused by the followers of radical ideologies. You know that in the long run, the only way to defeat a hateful ideology is to promote the hopeful alternative of human freedom. And that is what our nations are doing today in the Middle East. The lack of freedom and opportunity in that region has given aid and comfort to the lies and ambitions of violent extremists. Resentments that began on the streets of the Middle East have resulted in the killing innocent people across the world. A great danger clouds the future of all free men and women, and this danger sits at the doorstep of Europe.

Together, the people of this region are helping to confront this danger. Today, soldiers from Croatia, Albania, and Macedonia are serving bravely in Afghanistan, helping the Afghan people defeat the terrorists and secure their future of liberty. Forces from Albania and Macedonia are serving in Iraq, where they're helping the Iraqi people build a society that rejects terror and lives in freedom. It's only a matter of time before freedom takes root across that troubled region. And when it does, millions will remember the people of your nation stood with them in their hour of need.

At this great moment in history, you have a vital role. There are many people who don't appear to understand why it takes so long to build a democracy. You can tell them how hard it is to put in place a new and complex system of government for the first time. There are those who actually wonder if people were better off under their old tyranny. You can tell them that freedom is the only real path to prosperity and security and peace. And there are those who ask whether the pain and sacrifices for freedom are worth the costs. And they should come to Croatia, and you can show them that freedom is worth fighting for.

The great church in this square has stood since the Middle Ages. Over the centuries, it has seen long, dark winters of occupation and tyranny and war. But the spring is here at last. This is an era in history that generations of Croatians have prayed for. It is an era that Pope John Paul II envisioned when he came to this land and prayed with the Croatian people and asked for "a culture of peace." Today in this square, before this great church, we can now proudly say those prayers have been answered.

Interpreter. [*Inaudible*]

The President. They can't hear you. Don't worry about it.

May you always remember the joy of this moment in your history. And may the hopeful story of a peaceful Croatia find its way to those in the world who live as slaves and still await a joyful spring.

May God bless Croatia. And thank you for coming.

NOTE: The President spoke at 10:49 a.m. in St. Mark's Square. In his remarks, he referred to Prime Minister Ivo Sanader of Croatia. The transcript released by the Office of the Press Secretary also included the remarks of Prime Minister Sanader.

The President's Radio Address
April 5, 2008

Good morning. I'm speaking to you from Europe, where I attended the NATO summit and witnessed the hopeful progress of the continent's youngest democracies.

The summit was held in Romania, one of the 10 liberated nations that have joined the ranks of NATO since the end of the cold war. After decades of tyranny and oppression, today, Romania is an important member of an international alliance dedicated to liberty, and it is setting a bold example for other former Communist nations that desire to live in peace and freedom.

One of those nations is Croatia, which I'm also visiting on my trip. Croatia is a very different place than it was just a decade ago. Since they attained their independence, the Croatian people have shown the world the potential of human freedom. They've overcome war and hardship to build peaceful relations with their neighbors, and they have built a maturing democracy on the rubble of a dictatorship.

This week, NATO invited Croatia, as well as the nation of Albania, to join the NATO alliance. These countries have made extraordinary progress on the road to freedom, prosperity, and peace. The invitation to join NATO represents the alliance's confidence that they will continue to make necessary reforms and that they will become strong contributors to NATO's mission of collective defense.

I regret that NATO was not able to extend an invitation to a third nation, Macedonia, at this week's summit. Like Croatia and Albania, Macedonia has met all the criteria for NATO membership. Unfortunately, its invitation was delayed because of a dispute over its name. I made clear that the name issue should be resolved quickly, that NATO should intensify its engagement with Macedonia, and that we look forward to the day when this young democracy takes its place among the members of the NATO alliance.

After a century when the great wars of Europe threatened destruction throughout the world, the continent has now entered into a promising new era. Less than two decades ago, Albania, Croatia, and Macedonia suffered under the yoke of Communist oppression. The people in these countries know what the gift of liberty means, because they know what it is like to have their liberty denied. They know the death and destruction that can be caused by the followers of radical ideologies who kill the innocent in pursuit of political power. And these lessons have led them to work alongside America in the war on terror.

Today, soldiers from Croatia, Albania, and Macedonia are serving bravely in Afghanistan, helping the Afghan people defeat terrorists and secure a future of liberty. And forces from Albania and Macedonia are also serving in Iraq, where they're helping the Iraqi people build a society that rejects terror and lives in freedom. These nations have displayed the ultimate devotion to the principle of liberty, sacrificing to provide it for others.

Albania, Croatia, and Macedonia are not alone in discarding the chains to their past and embracing the promise of freedom. Another burgeoning democracy is Ukraine. Earlier this week, I traveled to Kiev to express America's support for beginning the process of bringing both Ukraine and Georgia into NATO. In recent years, both of these nations have seen tens of thousands take to the streets to peacefully demand their God-given liberty. The people of Ukraine and Georgia are an inspiration to the world, and I was pleased that this week NATO declared that Ukraine and Georgia will become members of NATO.

Nearly 7 years ago, I came to Europe and spoke to the students and faculty at Warsaw University in Poland. On that day, I declared that all of Europe's new democracies, from the Baltic to the Black Sea, should have the same chance for security and freedom and the same chance to join the institutions of Europe. Seven years later, we have made good progress toward fulfilling this vision, and more work remains.

In many parts of the world, freedom is still a distant aspiration. But in the ancient cities and villages of Europe, it is at the center of a new era of hope.

Thank you for listening.

NOTE: The address was recorded at 1:30 p.m. on April 3 in Bucharest, Romania, for broadcast at 10:06 a.m., e.d.t., on April 5. The transcript was made available by the Office of the Press Secretary on April 4, but was embargoed for release until the broadcast. Due to the 6-hour time difference, the address was broadcast after the President's remarks in Croatia. The Office of the Press Secretary also released a Spanish language transcript of this address.

Remarks Prior to a Meeting With President Vladimir V. Putin of Russia in Sochi, Russia
April 6, 2008

President Putin. Dear Mr. President, let me once again welcome you here in Sochi. I am very pleased that you've accepted this invitation. And I'm pleased that after the meeting in Bucharest, you now have the opportunity to discuss with me our bilateral relations and security issues.

Yesterday we actually started discussing those issues, and today we'll have to—we have the opportunity to discuss this in a calmer working manner. And on top of all, I am delighted to show you around Sochi, which will be the capital of the Olympic games in 2014.

Welcome, Mr. President.

President Bush. Thank you. I, first of all, was most grateful for the dinner that you gave last night. Secondly, thank you very much for providing fantastic entertainment. I'm only happy that our press corps didn't try—see me trying to dance the dance that I was asked to do. [*Laughter*]

President Putin. We were able to see that you are a brilliant dancer. [*Laughter*]

President Bush. Yes, well, thank you very much. We'll leave it at that, Mr. President. [*Laughter*]

I do want to—you know, it's going to be a very interesting meeting. This is the final meeting that we will have as Presidents of our respective countries. We have met a lot over the past years, and I've come to, you know, respect you. I respect the fact that you love your country. You've been a strong leader. You're not afraid to tell me what's on your mind. And when it's all said and done, we can shake hands.

And so I thank you very much for your wonderful hospitality here. Thank you, sir. Yes.

NOTE: The President spoke at 10:10 a.m. at the Bocharov Ruchei. President Putin spoke in Russian, and his remarks were translated by an interpreter.

Remarks During a Meeting With President-elect Dmitry A. Medvedev of Russia in Sochi
April 6, 2008

President-elect Medvedev. Good afternoon, Mr. President. I'm happy to meet you again. And I would like to once again thank you for warm congratulations on my election——

President Bush. Yes, sir.

President-elect Medvedev. ——as President of the Russian Federation.

President Putin and you, over these last 8 years, did a lot to advance Russian-U.S. relationship. And the relationship between Russia and the United States is a key factor of international security. When I officially assume my duties, I would like to do my best to keep up——

President Bush. And thank you.

President-elect Medvedev. ——that direction that—our relationship, so there will be constructive engagement between us.

President Bush. Yes, sir. Thank you. Look, it seems like there's a lot of interest in you, Mr. President-elect. You've attracted a lot of cameras.

President-elect Medvedev. Surprise, surprise. [*Laughter*]

President Bush. Yes. But I thank you for your kind words. Thank you for meeting with me and my delegation. And I'm looking forward to getting to know you, so we'll be able to work through common problems and find common opportunities.

Thank you, sir.

NOTE: The President spoke at 11:20 a.m. in the President's Office at the Bocharov Ruchei. President-elect Medvedev referred to President Vladimir V. Putin of Russia. President-elect Medvedev spoke in Russian, and his remarks were translated by an interpreter.

The President's News Conference With President Vladimir V. Putin of Russia in Sochi
April 6, 2008

President Putin. Good afternoon, dear ladies and gentlemen. First and foremost, I would like to thank the President of the United States, Mr. Bush, for accepting the invitation to meet here in Sochi in order to, sort of, draw the bottom line of the 8 years of our parallel terms in office. And he will probably agree with me, the result has been positive on the whole.

Since our first meeting in Ljubljana back in 2001, we have had an open and sincere relationship, and this has allowed us, without any circumventions or conventions, to start discussing the most pressing issues on the international and bilateral agenda. This dialogue is not always easy between our two countries. There have been and there remain certain disagreements on a number of issues, but the search of common denominators is going on.

George and I, I have already mentioned, have been able to build our agenda in a way that would prevent our disagreements on one set of issues from negatively influencing the state of play in other areas where we do have progress and where we are converging our positions. This has strengthened the entire architecture of the U.S.-Russian relationship.

In preparing for this meeting and in the course of this meeting, we have taken stock of major issues on the U.S.-Russian agenda, and here in Sochi, we have adopted a declaration on strategic framework. Of course,

it does not provide any breakthrough solutions on a number of issues, but we did not really expect this. It is important that the document sums up the positive achievements of the past few years, these in such areas as security, nonproliferation, including the initiatives that President Bush and I put forward, be it in counterterrorism and building business partnerships.

The declaration also reflects our continuing disagreements, primarily in the political-military field, but we reaffirm our willingness to work towards overcoming those differences. The most important thing is that we are talking about a strategic choice of our nations in favor of developing a constructive relationship that goes beyond the previous model of mutual containment. This declaration is a forward-looking one, and it provides a much more accurate assessment of the level of our partnership than what is normally believed based on stereotypes.

Certainly we have taken advantage of this meeting in order to sincerely, without protocol, discuss the most pressing issues of today, primarily those that influence strategic stability and international security for the long term, which is also very important.

I will not conceal that on a number of the most—one of the most difficult issues was and remains the issue of missile defense in Europe. This is not about language; this is not about diplomatic phrasing or wording; this is about the substance of the issue. I would like to be very clear on this: Our fundamental attitude to the American plans have not changed; however, certain progress is obvious. Our concerns have been heard by the United States. In March at the 2-plus-2 meeting, and earlier today in my conversation with President Bush, we have been offered a set of confidence-building and transparency measures in the field of missile defense, and we can feel that the President of the United States takes a very serious approach here and is sincerely willing to resolve this problem.

We do support this approach, and certainly, in principle, adequate measures of confidence building and transparency can be found. They can be important and useful in addressing this kind of issues. Thus, we now have room for cooperation; we are ready for such interaction. As far as the concrete substance of the U.S. proposals, it is too early to speak about it at this point. It is up to the experts to discuss the technical details of these proposals, and it is up to them to make any final conclusions. And the alternative that we offered last year is still relevant. We hope that it will be an issue for discussion in the future.

As far as strategic offensive weapons are concerned, we do have certain differences, still, in our basic approaches. And of course, both Russia and the United States are in favor of the continuation of a process of nuclear disarmament, and we have found some common ground here.

Last year in Kennebunkport, Mr. Bush and I agreed to start work on a new agreement that would replace the START Treaty, which will expire in 2009. We agreed that it would be necessary to maintain all the useful and necessary parts of the START Treaty. We're going to continue working on this. Our concerns are clear to both sides, in such fields as the development of state-of-the-art technology. And I hope that experts will be able to find some agreement here as well.

We also discussed the CFE Treaty. We discussed the enlargement policy of NATO. We spoke very frankly, in a very substantive fashion. And overall, I am satisfied that our partners are listening to us quite attentively, and I hope that here, as well, we are going to reach some true understanding. Of course, the Sochi declaration had to reflect our cooperation.

In business, we reaffirmed our mutual willingness to ensure Russia's early accession to the WTO on commercially viable terms and commercially justified terms that would not undermine Russia's economic interests. We hope that the United States this year will make Russia exempt from the Jackson-Vanik amendment, and we hope that the United States will establish permanent normal trade relations with Russia. We have also reaffirmed our willingness to continue our business-to-business cooperation. Another relevant issue is the work on a new incremental agreement on the encouragement and mutual protection of investment.

Another important area of our cooperation is energy. Here we do have certain good progress. We hope that our energy dialogue will carry on, and we hope that it will involve major projects that would be in line with the interests of both countries.

This is my last meeting with President Bush in my current capacity, and I would like to mention here that I have always found it rewarding and interesting to deal with the U.S. President. I have always appreciated his honesty and his openness, his willingness to listen to his counterpart. And this is precious. We have been motivated by our sincere willingness to strengthen our partnership and to strengthen mutual understanding between our two nations. We have sought to find new horizons for our cooperation. And I'm grateful to George for the achievement that we can register, and this achievement is very much due to him and his support.

President Bush. [*Inaudible*]—Vladimir, thanks for your gracious invitation. This is the very room where you served an unbelievably good dinner last night, with fabulous entertainments. Thank you for your hospitality. Laura and I are thrilled to be with you. And also, thank you for the briefing on the winter Olympics. I'm sure the people in this area are really excited about the fact that you've been awarded the winter Olympics. I congratulate you and wish you all the very best. And maybe you'll invite me to come as your guest, who knows.

We spent a lot of time in our relationship trying to get rid of the cold war. It's over; it ended. And the fundamental question in this relationship is, could we work together to put the cold war in the past? And I fully recognize there are people in America and Russia that think the cold war still exists. And sometimes that makes relations difficult. But it's very important for leaders to think strategically and not get stuck in the past and be willing to advance agendas.

And so we've worked very hard over the past years to find areas where we can work together and find ways to be agreeable when we disagree. And I think we've done a pretty good job of it. And I want to thank you for your openness as well. It's been a remarkable relationship.

Today the signing of this strategic framework declaration really does show the breadth and the depth of our cooperation. It shows where we differ, as Vladimir mentioned, but it shows that when you work hard, you can find areas where you can figure out how to cooperate. The document speaks of the respect of rule of law, international law, human rights, tolerance of diversity, political freedom, and a free market approach to economic policy and practices.

One of the areas where we've agreed to work together is in missile defense. And obviously, as Vladimir mentioned, this an area where we've got more work to do to convince the Russian side that the system is not aimed at Russia. As the agreement mentioned, we agree today that the United States and Russia want to create a system for responding to potential missile threats, in which Russia and the United States and Europe will participate as equal partners.

This is a powerful and important strategic vision. It's the vision that Vladimir Putin first articulated in Kennebunkport, Maine. For those of you there, you might remember the moment. And this is what we're building on. We're taking the vision that we discussed in Kennebunkport, and now we're putting it in a document form to help not only this administration but future American administrations work with future Russian administrations on this very important issue.

To help counter those threats, the United States is working with the Czech Republic and Poland. And as the President has done consistently, he expressed his concerns about those relationships. There's no doubt where he stands. That's why I like him. You don't have to guess. And he is concerned about it. Yet Russia appreciates the confidence building and transparency measures that we have proposed and declared that if agreed and implemented, such measures will be important and useful in ensuring [assuaging] ° Russia concerns.

He's got doubts about whether or not these systems are aimed at him. My view is, is that the more open we are, the more transparent we are, the more we share technological information, the more likely it will be that people throughout the system understand that this is an opportunity to deal with the threats of the 21st century, such as a launch from the Middle East or elsewhere. And the document shows areas where we agree and where we disagree, but where we can work together in the future. And I appreciate that very much.

We're talk—we're working together to stop the spread of dangerous weapons, and

---

° White House correction.

I appreciate the fact that we're implementing the Bratislava Nuclear Security Initiative, which is an important initiative. We continue to work together to meet the threat of nuclear terrorism, including through the Global Initiative To Combat Nuclear Terrorism. It's an important initiative in which the Russians and the United States have worked cooperatively and have taken the lead.

We talked about Iran. As I told Vladimir, that in the States, when asked about this at the press conferences, I've always told people how much I appreciate his leadership on the Iranian issue. After all, Russia went to the Iranians and said, "You should have civilian nuclear power." I agree. He then went on to say, "And we'll provide the fuel for you; therefore, there's no need for you to enrich." And it's your leadership on this issue, Mr. President, that's very important in making sure that the regime honors the international commitments that we expect it to.

We briefly touched about the six-party talks with North Korea, the need for us to work together to help that nation move forward.

We talked about fighting terror. The United States has suffered terrorist attacks on its soil, as have Russia. And I will tell you, there's been no firmer person in the world who understands the threat of radicalism and the capacity of these radicals and extremists to murder the innocent people. I remember full well when that happened on your soil. I remember our discussions right thereafter.

And I want to thank you for working hard to deal with terrorists and terrorist finance and to share intelligence to protect our people. That's our most important job, and we've improved our relations along these fronts.

We did talk about—Vladimir did talk about economic cooperation. I support Russia's efforts to join the WTO. I support Russia's efforts to join the OECD. I think we ought to get rid of Jackson-Vanik. I

think it's time to move this relationship in a new light. And I look forward to reminding Congress that it's in our interest to do such.

And so we had a—this is a good agreement and a good understanding. And, Mr. President, this is our last meeting as Presidents and—it won't be our last meeting as people, but it will be our last meeting as Presidents of our country. And it's a little bit nostalgic. It's a moment where it just proves life moves on. And I want to thank you for introducing me to the new President. We had a good meeting, and I appreciate you providing the opportunity for us to meet. And I look forward to working with him throughout the rest of my term.

In the meantime, thanks very much for your hospitality and your friendship and for giving me a chance to have yet another press conference with you. [*Laughter*]

Moderator. Dear colleagues, two questions from each side. The first question will be asked by our guests, the United States.

Russian Foreign Policy/President-elect Dmitry A. Medvedev of Russia

Q. President Putin, President Bush has expressed some confusion about who's going to run Russia's foreign policy when you step down and become Prime Minister. And he wondered who was going to represent Russia at the G–8. Who is in charge? And will you represent Russia at the G–8?

And, Mr. President, 7 years ago, you said that you looked into Mr. Putin's soul and that you found him to be trustworthy.

President Bush. Yes.

Q. You met today with his successor. Did you have a similar experience, and what was your take?

President Bush. I did find him to be trustworthy, and he was trustworthy.

Q. No, I mean his successor.

President Bush. No, I know. I'm just setting it up. [*Laughter*] He's going to go first, though.

President Putin. Regarding foreign policy of the Russian Federation, in accordance with the Constitution of the Russian Federation, foreign policy is determined by the President. And the newly elected President of the Russian Federation, Dmitry Anatolyevich Medvedev, will represent Russia at the most important international fora, including the G–8 summit.

Once again, I would like to emphasize that over the past years, as head of the administration, the President of Russian Federation, first Deputy Prime Minister of the Russian Federation, and member of the Security Council of the Russian Federation, Mr. Medvedev has been one of the co-authors of the Russian foreign policy. He is in the course of—he's quite knowledgeable about all the current affairs and our strategic plans. Therefore, this will be a reliable partner, a professional partner, who will be ready for constructive dialogue, with priority given to Russia's national interest, of course.

I don't know if there's anything I can add to what I've just said. Now, as far as your humble servant, myself, if I become Prime Minister, the Prime Minister will have many other issues and problems on his agenda. Those relate mostly to the state of the economy and various social policy issues. And those are issues that the rank and file citizen in any country is concerned with, including in the Russian Federation. And I intend to focus my intention—my attention and my efforts at addressing precisely these tasks.

President Bush. My comments about Vladimir Putin were aimed to say that I found him to be the kind of person—I thought he'd be the kind of person who would tell me what's on his mind. A lot of times in politics you have people look you in the eye and tell you what's not on their mind. He looks you in the eye and tells you what's on his mind. He's been very truthful. And that's—to me, that's the only way you can find common ground and to be able to deal in a way that you don't let your disputes interrupt your relationships.

And you know, I just met the man for about 20 minutes, the President-elect, and it seemed—he seemed like a straightforward fellow, somebody who would tell you what's on his mind. But he is not the President. This man is the President. And so our conversation was—he was very respectful of the fact that he is waiting his time until he gets duly sworn in as President of the Russian Federation, and then he'll act as the President.

And so my first impressions are very positive, a smart fellow. You know, I got to see him at Crawford once before, and then he came to the White House, I think, with Vladimir, and then came on his own one time. But we never really had a full discussion. And I just repeat to you: From my observation, he understands there's a certain protocol, and that he is taking his time; he's studying; he's preparing to assume office. But he is not going to act like a President nor assume Presidential duties until he gets to be the President.

And so you can write down, I was impressed and looking forward to working with him.

Missile Defense System

Q. My first question is to Mr. Putin, Vladimir Vladimirovich. We can see from the declaration what you say about missile defense; the concerns are still there. Issues relating to the third site in Russia are still on the agenda.

And my question to Mr. Bush: You talk about transparency. Will you be able to convince your colleagues in Poland and the Czech Republic to be as transparent as you are going to be in missile defense issues?

President Putin. True, we have not resolved all the problems relating to missile defense and the third site in Europe. However, I have already mentioned, before and today, we have seen once again that our U.S. partners not only understand our concerns but are sincerely trying to overcome our concerns. And another important observation is that I do have certain cautious optimism with regard to mutual agreements. I believe that this is possible. But the devil is in the details, and it is important here that our experts could work at the expert level. It is important for them to agree on the concrete confidence-building measures, and they should see how those measures will be implemented in practical terms.

And the third issue mentioned by President Bush—he said that we should work together on these systems. It would be desirable. I believe that this is the most important thing, if, at the expert level and then at the political level, we are able to start cooperation on a global missile defense system, as we are now talking about—[inaudible]—missile defense in Europe. If we manage to achieve this kind of level of cooperation on a global missile defense system, this will be the best kind of result for all our proceeding efforts.

President Bush. Precisely what he said is true. And that is, is that if we can, first of all, earn enough trust to be able to cooperate regionally and then globally, that's in our interest, because one of the concerns from the Russian side, a clear concern, is that if they believe the system is aimed at them, they're going to obviously do something about it. They'll spend money to avoid the system.

And I view this as defensive, not offense. And obviously, we've got a lot of work to do to convince the experts that the system is not aimed at Russia. It's really to help deal with the threats that we all are going to face. And therefore, the vision about having a global system is something I strongly support, where we're working cooperatively together. Look, there's a lot of—we got a lot of way to go.

And as to your question about the Czech Republic and Poland, it's important for the leaders in those countries—and I've discussed the issue with them—to understand that Russia is not an enemy; Russia is

somebody with whom we need to work. And we'll work through the differences there as well. Transparency is going to require more than just a briefing. Transparency is going to require true openness in a system.

I have no problem with that. I have no problem sharing technologies and information to make sure that all people understand this system is designed to deal with multiple—I mean, single- or dual-launch regimes that could try to hold us hostage. This system is not designed to deal with Russia's capacity to launch multiple rockets.

Now, we got work to do, but we've come a long way since our first discussions. And this document really does express a vision that will make it better for America and Russia when—to work together along these lines. And so yes, I thank you for your question.

Russia-U.S. Relations/Missile Defense System/North Atlantic Treaty Organization

Q. Thank you. Mr. President, your joint statement on missile defense is still far short of a deal for Russian support or even acquiescence on this project. Isn't this just a matter of kicking the can down the road, in the twilight of both of your terms, to a new U.S. administration that may or may not even support it?

And, President Putin, what would it take for you to be convinced that such a system would not be a threat to Russian security? And how would Russia respond if the U.S. went ahead with this anyway, as well as bringing Ukraine and Georgia into NATO?

President Bush. I think I just explained how far we have come on this issue. This is a concept that I talked to Vladimir about a while ago, and we have come a long way. Read the document, and read what it says. It clearly talks about a strategic relationship. It talks about the need for transparency and confidence-building measures. It is a really good opportunity to put a framework in place for our nations to work together.

Now, you can cynically say, it's kicking the can down the road. I don't appreciate that, because this is an important part of my belief that it's necessary to protect ourselves. And I have worked—reached out to Vladimir Putin. I knew this was of concern to him, and I have used my relationship with him to try to get something in place that causes Russia to be comfortable with it.

Is it going to happen immediately? No, it's not going to happen immediately. But is this a good opportunity to work together? You bet it is—for the common good. And so I feel comfortable with it, and I think it is—you know, I happen to believe it is a significant breakthrough, simply because I've been very much involved with this issue and know how far it's come.

President Putin. What could convince Russia that this system is not aimed against our nation? I would like to point out several elements here. First, the first—the best thing to do is to work jointly on a global missile defense, with an equal, democratic-style access to managing such a system. This is what George was just talking about when he said that, at the technological level, certain exchanges made it possible— information exchange may be possible. We can work jointly if we launch such joint work with equal democratic access to managing the system. This will be the best guarantee of the security of all.

If we fail to do it at this point, then we will insist that the system, the transparency that we talk about, verification matters, could be objective and could work on—could function on an ongoing basis, on a permanent basis, with the help of experts that should be present at those sites on a permanent basis. This is the answer to the first part of your question.

As far as NATO enlargement is concerned, we talked about it at length earlier today. I reaffirmed Russia's position on this count. I believe that in order to improve relations with Russia, it is necessary not to pull the former Soviet republics into po-

litical/military blocs, but to develop relations with Russia itself. And then the actions of the bloc, of this or that issue, in a few years will not be perceived so acutely in this country, as is the case today.

As far as enlargement is concerned, technical enlargement of NATO, I believe that this is a policy which is in conformity with a former, old logic, when Russia was perceived as an adversary, which is no longer the case today. As Churchill said, "If you can't change the subject, it is a sign of radicalism."

Global Security/Russia-U.S. Relations/ President-elect Medvedev of Russia

Q. My question is—first to both Presidents—you mentioned that yesterday and today you summed up the 8 years of your cooperation. I would like to ask you, if you assess your work, have there been more pluses or minuses? And please tell me, what have you achieved, and what concrete things will be bequeathed to your successors? Do you think the world has become a safer and more secure place? And how has the U.S.-Russian relationship influenced world politics?

And my question to the United States now—to the President of the United States now—you have met President-elect today— Dmitry Medvedev. You talked about the impression you have of him. I would like to ask you, did you discuss the schedule of your further exchanges with him in the course of this year—for the remaining part of this year?

President Putin. Okay, I will start answering. Has it become better, or has it become worse? We always want to have more of a good thing, and we shouldn't forget that the—as we say, the better is the worst enemy of the good.

Let us remember the world on the brink of a nuclear disaster during the Caribbean crisis, and now let us look at the U.S.-Russia relationship today. A crisis like the Cuban crisis would not be possible now; it would be unthinkable. I agree with

George when he said that Russia and the United States no longer consider each other as enemies. At a minimum, they look at each other as partners, and I believe this is very important.

Of course, a lot of outstanding issues remain. It is true that we do have disagreements on some sensitive areas of our cooperation, but at the same time, we do have enough strength to search for solutions. And as our meeting today has shown, we are capable of achieving positive results—that is, on the whole—in counterterrorism, in fighting proliferation of weapons of mass destruction and missile technology, of fighting the drug threat. All of these create a reliable platform for cooperation, not only between Russia and the United States but a platform that contributes to ensuring international security.

If we mention on top of that our economic cooperation, we can state that in the past 8 years, we have been able to improve the relations between our two countries and in the world as a whole.

President Bush. Yes, I agree with that answer. And secondly, I spent—I told President-elect that I would see him in Japan at the G–8, and that's the only scheduling matters that we discussed. And I'm going to finish out my term—my time with Vladimir, and then I'll turn my attention to the President when he gets to be the President. But the first time I suspect we'll meet will be in the scheduled meeting in Japan.

Thank you.

NOTE: The President's news conference began at 12:07 p.m. in the Press Center at the Bocharov Ruchei. President Putin and some reporters spoke in Russian, and their remarks were translated by an interpreter.

Statement on the Death of Charlton Heston
April 6, 2008

Laura and I are saddened by the death of our friend Charlton Heston. Charlton Heston was one of the most successful actors in movie history and a strong advocate for liberty.

Widely acclaimed for his long, award-winning film career, he also had a profound impact off the screen. He served his country during World War II, marched in the civil rights movement, led a labor union, and vigorously defended Americans' second amendment rights. He was a man of character and integrity, with a big heart. For all these reasons, in 2003, I was proud to award Charlton Heston the Presidential Medal of Freedom, the Nations's highest civil honor.

Our prayers are with his wife Lydia and the entire Heston family during this difficult time.

Remarks on the Colombia Free Trade Agreement
April 7, 2008

Thank you. Please be seated. I want to thank the members of my Cabinet for joining me here today. Madam Ambassador, thank you for coming. I appreciate those who support free trade and fair trade for joining us on this important occasion.

In a few minutes, I will sign a letter to Congress that will transmit legislation implementing the United States free trade agreement with Colombia. This agreement will advance America's national security interests in a critical region. It will strengthen a courageous ally in our hemisphere. It will help America's economy and America's workers at a vital time. It deserves bipartisan support from the United States Congress.

During the 16 months since the Colombia free trade agreement was signed, my administration has worked closely with the Congress to seek a bipartisan path for considering the agreement. We held more than 400 consultations and meetings and calls. We led trips to Colombia for more than 50 Members of the Congress. We've worked closely with congressional leaders from both parties, including the Speaker, Leader Hoyer, and Chairman Rangel, Minority Leader Boehner, Ranking Member McCrery, and Senators Baucus and Grassley.

On May 10th last year, my administration and congressional leaders concluded a bipartisan agreement that provided a clear path for advancing free trade agreements, including the agreement with Colombia. As part of that agreement, we included the strongest labor and environmental provisions of any free trade agreement in history. Those provisions were negotiated with and agreed by, by the leadership of Congress—like the Democratic leadership in Congress.

For the last 16 months, we've worked with congressional leaders to set a schedule for the consideration of the Colombian free trade agreement. While we'll continue to work closely with Congress, the need for this agreement is too urgent, the stakes for our national security are too high, to allow this year to end without a vote. By statute, Congress has 90 legislative days to complete action once I transmit a bill implementing this agreement. Waiting any longer to send up the legislation would run the risk of Congress adjourning without the agreement ever getting voted on.

Transmitting the agreement is neither the beginning nor the end of our cooperative efforts, but instead an important milestone. My administration is eager to work with members from both parties to make sure the vote is a positive one. Congress needs to move forward with the Colombian agreement, and they need to approve it as quickly as possible.

Approving this agreement is urgent for our national security reasons. Colombia is one of our strongest allies in the Western Hemisphere. They are led by a very strong and courageous leader, President Uribe. He's taken courageous stands to defend our shared democratic values. He's been a strong and capable partner in fighting drugs and crime and terror. And he's delivering results. The Colombian Government reports that since 2002, kidnapings, terrorist attacks, and murders are all down substantially, as is violence against union members.

Despite this progress, Colombia remains under intense pressure in the region. It faces a continuing assault from the terrorist network known as FARC, which has seized hostages and murdered innocent folks, including Americans, in an attempt to overthrow Colombia's democracy. Colombia also faces a hostile and anti-American regime in Venezuela, which has met with FARC terrorist leaders and deployed troops to the Colombian border as a means of intimidating the Colombian Government and its people.

President Uribe has stood strong against these threats. And he has done so with the assurance of America's support, because his fight against tyranny and terror is a fight that we share. President Uribe has told Members of Congress, as me—and me as well, that approving the free trade agreement is the best way for America to demonstrate our support for Colombia. People throughout the hemisphere are watching to see what the United States will do. If Congress fails to approve this agreement, it would not only abandon a brave ally, it would send a signal throughout the region that America cannot be counted on to support its friends. As Canadian Prime Minister Stephen Harper has said, "If the U.S. turns its back on its friends in Colombia, this will set back our cause far more than any Latin American dictator could hope to achieve."

Approving the free trade agreement will also strengthen our economy. Today, almost all of Colombia's exports enter the United States duty free, while American products exported to Colombia face tariffs of up to 35 percent for nonagricultural goods and much higher for many agricultural products. In other words, the current situation is one sided. Our markets are open to Colombian products, but barriers exist that make it harder to sell American products in Colombia. I think it makes sense to remedy this situation. I think it makes sense for Americans' goods and services to be treated just like Colombia's goods and services are treated. And so it's time to level the playing field.

As soon as it's implemented, the agreement I'm sending Congress will eliminate tariffs on more than 80 percent of American exports of industrial and consumer goods. Many products in key American sectors, such as agriculture and construction equipment, aircraft and auto parts, medical and scientific equipment, will enter Colombia duty free. If you're an American farmer, it's in your interest that this agreement get passed. After all, farm exports like high-quality beef, cotton, wheat, soybeans, and fruit will enter duty free. And in time, this agreement will eliminate tariffs on all of America's exports to Colombia.

Level the playing field for American exporters is especially important during this time of economic uncertainty. Last year, exports accounted for more than 40 percent of America's total economic growth. With the economy slowing recently, we should be doing everything we can to open up new opportunities for growth. More than 9,000 American companies, most of them small and midsized businesses, export to

Colombia. Approving this agreement will help them increase their sales and grow their businesses and create high-paying jobs.

The economic effects of expanding trade in goods and services are overwhelmingly positive, but trade can also have a negative impact for some of our citizens. In those cases, government has a responsibility to help workers obtain the skills they need to successfully reenter the workforce. My administration is actively engaged in discussions on legislation to improve and reauthorize trade adjustment assistance program. We're committed to advancing the discussions as quickly as possible. I look forward to completing an agreement on trade adjustment that draws on many of the good ideas contained in bills introduced in the House and the Senate. I look forward to signing a good bipartisan piece of legislation.

In discussions about the Colombia free trade agreement, some Members of Congress have raised concerns about the conditions in Colombia. President Uribe has addressed those issues. He's addressed violence by demobilizing tens of thousands of paramilitary figures and fighters. He's addressed attacks on trade unionists by stepping up funding for prosecutions, establishing an independent prosecutors unit, and creating a special program that protects labor activists. He's made clear that the economic benefits the agreement brings to Colombia would strengthen the fight against drugs and terror by creating a more hopeful alternative for the people of Colombia.

If this isn't enough to earn America's support, what is? President Uribe has done everything asked of him. While Colombia still works to improve, the progress is undeniable, and it is worthy of our support.

There's a clear model for Members of Congress to follow as they move forward with this agreement. Just last year, Congress considered a trade agreement with Peru that was almost identical to this one.

The only difference between them is that the Colombian Government has an even greater economic potential because Colombia is a larger market and even greater national security importance because of Colombia's strategic location. Congress passed the Peru agreement with strong bipartisan support and should do the same with this agreement with Colombia.

The stakes are high in South America. By acting at this critical moment, we can show a watching world that America will honor its commitments. We can provide a powerful rebuke to dictators and demagogues in our backyard. We can expand U.S. exports and export-related jobs. We can show millions across the hemisphere that democracy and free enterprise lead to a better life. Congress's path is clear: Members should have a healthy debate, hold a timely vote, and send the bill implementing the Colombia free trade agreement to my desk so I can sign it into law.

And now I would like members of my Cabinet who are here today to join me for the signing of the letter.

[*At this point, the President signed the letter.*]

Thanks for coming.

NOTE: The President spoke at 11:34 a.m. in Room 450 of the Dwight D. Eisenhower Executive Office Building. In his remarks, he referred to Colombia's Ambassador to the U.S. Carolina Barco Isakson. The Office of the Press Secretary also released a Spanish language transcript of these remarks.

Remarks Following a Meeting With Small and Midsize Business Owners
April 7, 2008

I just had a fascinating discussion with fellow citizens who happen to be small-business owners, people who run small businesses. And I'm talking about a variety of small business. We got a meatpacker, an apple processor; we've got a grinder, a large equipment manufacturer, education man. I mean, we got a lot of folks from different backgrounds and different States, all of whom were talking about the effects of the progrowth economic package that was passed by the Congress and how that package is causing them to make capital investments that they might not have made in the year 2008.

And that's important, because in times of economic uncertainty, we want people making investment, so when a person buys an apple press, somebody is going to have to manufacture that press. When somebody manufactures that press, it means there's more likely to be work and income.

And so I'm very pleased to have heard from the small-business owners here that the package is going to cause them to make decisions that will help us recover out of this economic slowdown.

Now, having said that, they did share concerns with me. And I understand those concerns, and I feel the same way. One, there's concern about the high price of fuel. I mean, people have to make a living, and they're driving their cars and their trucks, and it's—fuel is hurting people. And so I fully understand that not only are people worried about their homes, they're worried about the cost of fuel—and one of the reasons why we got to keep taxes low.

As a matter of fact, one of the things that's going to happen with this progrowth package is that not only is it going to affect small businesses like it's affected folks here, but 130 million families are going to get some money, their own money. And of course, the purpose of that is to help boost consumption. We're in a rough time right now. I'm confident we're going to come out of it. And when we do, we're going to be a stronger and better country.

Congress, of course, is contemplating different measures. And my only advice to them is, one, make sure you give the progrowth package that was passed overwhelmingly a chance to work. Let's see what the effects are. Secondly, anything they do should not hurt the economy. And thirdly, I—you know, I think we ought to—in terms of progrowth packages—I think we ought to, again I repeat, give this one a chance to kick in. The experts tell me that this progrowth package is going to add some—you know, a percent, percent-and-

a-half to the economy here in the latter part of this year. If that's the case, it's going to be an important part of recovering.

Anyway, long and short of it is, I thank you all for coming—very useful meeting. I thank you for being entrepreneurs. Thanks for working hard to provide for your families. Thank you for looking after your employees the way you do. Appreciate the fact that you're making investments in the year 2008 which will get this economy going.

Thank you.

NOTE: The President spoke at 1:46 p.m. in the Roosevelt Room at the White House.

Remarks Honoring the 2007 NCAA Football Champion Louisiana State University Tigers
April 7, 2008

Good to see you all. Welcome. Go Tigers! Sit down. Please sit down. Thanks for coming.

So I met some of these men in 2004; they feel pretty comfortable they were going to be back here. Some of them weren't so sure I was going to be back here. [*Laughter*] It's good to welcome you back, proud you're here. Nothing like being called national champs. LSU has the honor of being the first school to win two BCS titles. This year there is no split.

I appreciate Les Miles and Kathy. Thanks for coming. Proud to have met you, coach. It was a great honor for me to have called you after you won that day. And I know you told the team that at least one guy called to congratulate. [*Laughter*] I welcome the LSU administrators, personnel, coaches, trainers, locker room folks, and most of all, the players.

I want to welcome Members of Congress—Jim McCrery. Jim, good to see you, sir. And Scott and Clark, good to see you

boys. Rodney Alexander—Congressman, good to see you. Charles Boustany—I'm glad to see you, Charles. Thanks for coming. I appreciate you taking time to be here.

Out of the State government is State Treasurer John Kennedy. John, thank you for coming. Appreciate you coming up for that. Glad you brought Preston. Is Breaux here? No, he—[*laughter*]—he's working—[*laughter*]—which is a major upset—no. [*Laughter*]

Winning requires very strong leadership; that's what it takes. After 8 years of welcoming national champs, there's always one common denominator, and that is, it requires a strong leader to motivate people toward a common goal. And that's exactly what you have in Coach Les Miles. Coach Miles's 3 years has helped the team compile a 34 and 6 record. And this is a guy who's not afraid to take risks. He tried two fake field goals, fake punt, went for fourth down—went for first down on fourth down

15 times. Made it nearly every time. Of course, he had the players who helped him take that risk.

He also had to deal with some delicate situations away from the field, like inaccurate press stories. [*Laughter*] Coach, let me just say, I know the feeling. [*Laughter*]

This is Coach Miles's first time celebrating here at the White House. And a lot of folks are going to remember it, because it's the first time he's been seen in public without a hat on. [*Laughter*]

LSU fans had an amazing season. They—first of all, in the season, the number one ranking changed hands six times. Of course, LSU was number one on the day it counted; that's why they're here. The—you had to overcome adversity to get here. You played as a team, and you won some dramatic football games. And when you lost, it was pretty dramatic too. You beat Florida in a comeback with the largest crowd ever to watch a game at Tiger Stadium. Two weeks later, you rallied to beat Auburn on a touchdown scored with 1 second left on the clock.

After you lost to Arkansas, a lot of folks counted you out, but you held a team meeting and decided you had something to play for. In other words, you didn't let adversity affect you. You said, "We're going to do something about it." And then you beat Tennessee to win the SEC Championship, and you went from number seven to number two. And you went straight to the national title game, which didn't start off so good. And yet you had 31 unanswered points, like a true champion team, to win 38 to 24. And you're here at the White House representing LSU University as the national champs, and we congratulate you.

Being raised in Texas and growing up in Texas, I've got a lot of friends in Louisiana. And you inspired people across the State. I thought Matt—quarterback Matt Flynn put it best. He said, "You can't dream it any better than that." And that's what a lot of people were saying around your State.

You earned your place in the record books. You scored the most points in school history. And the seniors will go down as LSU's winningest class. No other senior class has had a better record than those who are graduating here. [*Applause*]

I welcome defensive tackle Glenn Dorsey, and so did the team when he turned down—when he decided not to turn pro last year. A lot of fans said, "Thank you, Glenn." [*Laughter*] A lot of opponents said, "No thank you, Glenn." [*Laughter*] After all, he was the defensive player of the year for SEC, Outland Trophy winner, Lombardi Trophy, and Nagurski Award. He'll have his time in the NFL, and a lot of teams are sure anxious to have him play for them. Congratulations, and welcome. Glad you're here.

This is a team of great athletes. Two players were drafted by Major League Baseball. One of the stars, Trindon Holliday, holds the school record in the 100 meters. One of your linemen, Herman Johnson—he holds a different kind of record. [*Laughter*] He was the largest baby ever born in the State of Louisiana, at 15 pounds, 14 ounces. [*Laughter*] That's why he's known as "the House," which puts him in good stead with his fellow teammates known as "Putt" or "Surfer Boy," "L-Crazy," and "Cheese." [*Laughter*] Whatever nickname you prefer to be called, all of us here are calling you champs, and you deserve it. I want to thank you for being champions on the field.

I appreciate you understanding that once you're a champ on the field, means you have a responsibility to be a champ off the field as well. And there's no better inspiration than Les Miles and his wife Kathy. They host events that raise money for the Children's Miracle Network. They're active in cancer fundraising and the Special Olympics, the Baton Rouge Children's Advocacy Center. I told the coach that I was going to mention this, and that is, I'm aware, as the Commander in Chief of the finest military ever assembled on the face of the Earth, that he went to boost our troops in Iraq and Kuwait as part of a USO tour. I want to thank you, coach, for doing your job.

I appreciate the example that Glenn Dorsey has set on the field and off the field to—he works to educate children about the dangers of drugs and encourages them to work hard. His advice is, "Dream big and make things happen." There's nothing better than a champ to help somebody dream big and to encourage them to make something happen.

And so when you leave here, I hope you leave here knowing that you've got a special responsibility, not only to represent your school on the football field but to help make America a better place, just like Ciron Black did when he heard the story of an 8-year-old LSU fan who was suffering from leukemia. And he took time to send an encouraging message. Then he wrote the boy's name, Mikey, on his wristband during the national championship game. Sometimes people say, "I can't help because I can't solve all the problems." But in this case, he showed that you can help one person. And in helping one person,

he helped the Nation as a whole. And I want to thank you, Ciron, for your leadership.

There's a lot of great stories about the character of the people behind me, but it's getting chilly, and I'm looking forward to getting my LSU jersey. [*Laughter*] And so I want to welcome you all to the White House—to the South Lawn of the White House. I'm so honored and proud to welcome the LSU Tigers here as the national champs. God bless you, God bless LSU, and God bless America.

NOTE: The President spoke at 2:08 p.m. on the South Lawn at the White House. In his remarks, he referred to Scott and Clark McCrery, sons of Rep. James O. McCrery III; Preston Kennedy, son of Louisiana State Treasurer John Neely Kennedy; former Sen. John B. Breaux; Jared Mitchell and Trindon Holliday, wide receivers, Chad Jones and Craig Steltz, safeties, Herman Johnson, offensive lineman, Luke Sanders, linebacker, Charles Alexander, defensive tackle, and Ciron Black, offensive tackle, Louisiana State University football team; and LSU football fan Michael Conger.

Message to the Congress Transmitting Proposed Legislation To Implement the United States-Colombia Free Trade Agreement
April 7, 2008

To the Congress of the United States:

I am pleased to transmit legislation and supporting documents to implement the United States-Colombia Trade Promotion Agreement (the "Agreement"). The Agreement represents an historic development in our relations with Colombia, which has shown its commitment to advancing democracy, protecting human rights, and promoting economic opportunity. Colombia's importance as a steadfast strategic partner of the United States was recognized by President Clinton's support for an appro-

priation in 2000 to provide funding for Plan Colombia, and my Administration has continued to stand with Colombia as it confronts violence, terror, and drug traffickers.

This Agreement will increase opportunity for the people of Colombia through sustained economic growth and is therefore vital to ensuring that Colombia continues on its trajectory of positive change. Under the leadership of President Alvaro Uribe, Colombia has made a remarkable turnaround since 1999 when it was on the verge of being a failed state. This progress is in part explained by Colombia's success in demobilizing tens of thousands of paramilitary fighters. The Colombian government reports that since 2002, kidnappings, terrorist attacks, and murders are all down substantially, as is violence against union members.

The Government of Colombia, with the assistance of the United States, is continuing its efforts to further reduce the level of violence in Colombia and to ensure that those responsible for violence are quickly brought to justice. To speed prosecutions of those responsible for violent crimes, the Prosecutor General's Office plans to hire this year 72 new prosecutors and more than 110 investigators into the Human Rights Unit. These additions are part of the increase of more than 2,100 staff that will be added to the Prosecutor General's Office in 2008 and 2009. To support these additional personnel and their activities, Colombia has steadily increased the budget for the Prosecutor General's Office, including by more than $40 million this year, bringing the total outlay for that office to nearly $600 million.

In negotiating this Agreement, my Administration was guided by the objectives set out by the Congress in the Trade Act of 2002. My Administration has complied fully with the letter and spirit of Trade Promotion Authority—from preparation for the negotiations, to consultations with the Congress throughout the talks, to the content of the Agreement itself. In addition, my Administration has conducted several hundred further consultations, led congressional trips to Colombia, and last year renegotiated key labor, environmental, investment, and intellectual property rights provisions in the Agreement at the behest of the Congress. By providing for the effective enforcement of labor and environmental laws, combined with strong remedies for noncompliance, the Agreement will contribute to improved worker rights and higher levels of environmental protection in Colombia. The result is an Agreement that all of us can be proud of and that will create significant new opportunities for American workers, farmers, ranchers, businesses, and consumers by opening the Colombian market and eliminating barriers to U.S. goods, services, and investment.

Under the Agreement, tariffs on over 80 percent of U.S. industrial and consumer goods exported to Colombia will be eliminated immediately, with tariffs on the remaining goods eliminated within 10 years. The Agreement will allow 52 percent of U.S. agricultural exports, by value, to enter Colombia duty-free immediately, with the remaining agricultural tariffs phased out over time. This will help to level the playing field, as 91 percent of U.S. imports from Colombia already enjoy duty-free access to our market under U.S. trade preference programs.

My Administration looks forward to continuing to work with the Congress on a bipartisan path forward to secure approval of this legislation that builds on the positive spirit of the May 10, 2007, agreement on trade between the Administration and the House and Senate leadership, and the strong bipartisan support demonstrated by both Houses of Congress in overwhelmingly approving the United States-Peru Trade Promotion Agreement last year. The United States-Colombia Trade Promotion Agreement represents an historic step forward in U.S. relations with a key friend and ally in Latin America. Congressional approval of legislation to implement the Agreement is in our national interest, and I urge the Congress to act favorably on this legislation as quickly as possible.

GEORGE W. BUSH

The White House,

April 7, 2008.

NOTE: This message was released by the Office of the Press Secretary on April 8.

Remarks on Presenting Posthumously the Congressional Medal of Honor to Petty Officer Michael A. Monsoor
April 8, 2008

Good afternoon, and welcome. Please be seated.

The Medal of Honor is America's highest decoration for military valor. Over the years, many who have received the medal have given their lives in the action that earned it. The name of Petty Officer Michael Anthony Monsoor will now be among them.

September 2006, Michael laid down his life for his brothers in arms. Today we remember the life of this faithful Navy SEAL. And on behalf of a grateful nation, we will present Michael Monsoor's family with the Medal of Honor that he earned.

I welcome the Vice President. Secretary of Defense Gates, thank you for coming; Secretary of Veterans Affairs Peake; Secretary Don Winter of the Navy; Admiral Mike Mullen, Chairman of the Joint Chiefs, and wife Deborah; General James Conway, Commandant of the Marine Corps, and Annette; Admiral Gary Roughead, Chief of Naval Operations, and wife Ellen; Senator John McCain; Congressman Ed Royce; Congresswoman Loretta Sanchez.

Previous Medal of Honor recipients, thank you for joining us.

I appreciate Chaplain Burt, Navy SEALs, the finest warriors on the face of the Earth, the Monsoor family, and everybody else.

The Medal of Honor is awarded for an act of such courage that no one could rightly be expected to undertake it. Yet those who knew Michael Monsoor were not surprised when he did. The son of Orange County, California, grew up in a family where helping others was a way of life. Mike's father was a marine; his mother, a social worker. Together, they raised their four children to understand the meaning of service and sacrifice.

From a very early age, Mike showed the strength of his own convictions. Apparently, going to kindergarten wasn't one of them. Mike had no complaints after the first week of school, until someone broke the news to him that he had to go back the next week. [*Laughter*] Many mornings, Mike refused to put on the nice clothes for school. Instead, he insisted on wearing mismatched outfits. Mike's mother soon discovered there was no stopping the determined young boy from mixing plaids and stripes. And years later, there would be no stopping an even more determined young man from donning a uniform of navy blue.

In some ways, Mike was an unlikely candidate for the Navy. He suffered from terrible asthma as a child. On some nights, his coughing fits would land him in the hospital. But Mike would not lay low for long. He strengthened his lungs by racing his siblings in the swimming pool. He worked to wean himself off his inhaler. He built himself into a superb athlete, excelling from sports like football to snowboarding.

After enlisting in the Navy, he began preparing for the ultimate test of physical endurance: SEAL training. Less than a third of those who begin this training become SEALs. But Mike would not be denied a spot. In September 2004, he earned the right to wear the Navy SEAL trident.

The newly minted frogman became a beloved member of the SEAL team community. His teammates liked to laugh about the way his shiny Corvette would leave everybody in the dust. But deep down, they always knew Mike would never leave anybody behind when it counted. He earned their confidence with his attention to detail and quiet work ethic. One of Mike's officers remembers an instructor once asking after an intense training session, quote: "What's the deal with the Monsoor guy? He just says, 'Roger that,' to everything."

When Mike deployed with his team to Ramadi in the spring of 2006, he brought that attitude with him. Because he served as both a heavy machine gunner and a communications operator, he often had a double load of equipment, sometimes more than 100 pounds worth. But under the glare of the hot desert sun, he never lost his cool.

At the time, Ramadi was in the clutches of Al Qaida terrorists and insurgents. Together, the SEALs and the Army 1st Battalion of the 506 Infantry Regiment took the offense against the enemy. The SEALs carried out a broad range of special operations, including providing sniper cover in tough urban conditions and conducting raids against terrorists and insurgents. Overall, Mike's platoon came under enemy attack during 75 percent of their missions. And in most of these engagements, Mike was out front defending his brothers.

In May 2006, Mike and another SEAL ran into the line of fire to save a wounded teammate. With bullets flying all around them, Mike returned fire with one hand while helping pull the injured man to safety with the other. In a dream about the incident months later, the wounded SEAL envisioned Mike coming to the rescue with wings on his shoulders.

On Saint Michael's Day, September 29, 2006, Michael Monsoor would make the ultimate sacrifice. Mike and two teammates had taken position on the outcropping of a rooftop when an insurgent grenade bounced off Mike's chest and landed on the roof. Mike had a clear chance to escape, but he realized that the other two SEALs did not. In that terrible moment, he had two options: to save himself or to save his friends. For Mike, this was no choice at all. He threw himself onto the grenade, and absorbed the blast with his body. One of the survivors puts it this way: "Mikey looked death in the face that day and said, 'You cannot take my brothers. I will go in their stead.' "

Perhaps the greatest tributes to Mike's life is the way different servicemembers all across the world responded to his death. Army soldiers in Ramadi hosted a memorial service for the valiant man who had fought beside them. Iraqi Army scouts, whom Mike helped train, lowered their flag and sent it to his parents. Nearly every SEAL on the west coast turned out for Mike's funeral in California. As the SEALs filed past the casket, they removed their golden tridents from their uniforms, pressed them onto the walls of the coffin. The procession went on nearly half an hour. And when it was all over, the simple wooden coffin had become a gold-plated memorial to a hero who will never be forgotten.

For his valor, Michael Monsoor becomes the fourth Medal of Honor recipient in the war on terror. Like the three men who came before him, Mike left us far too early. But time will not diminish his legacy. We see his legacy in the SEALs whose lives he saved. We see his legacy in the city of Ramadi, which has gone from one of the most dangerous places in Iraq to one of the most safest. We see his legacy in the family that stands before us filled with grief, but also with everlasting pride.

Mr. and Mrs. Monsoor: America owes you a debt that can never be repaid. This Nation will always cherish the memory of your son. We will not let his life go in vain. And this Nation will always honor the sacrifice he made. May God comfort you. May God bless America.

Come on up. And now George and Sally Monsoor will be here; a Military Aide will read the citation.

NOTE: The President spoke at 3:07 p.m. in the East Room at the White House. In his remarks, he referred to Rear Adm. Robert F. Burt, USN, Chief of Navy Chaplains. Following the President's remarks, Lt. Col. Gina C. Humble, USAF, Air Force Aide to the President, read the citation.

Remarks Following a Meeting With Afghanistan Provincial Governors
April 8, 2008

I've just had a fascinating opportunity to discuss Afghanistan with eight Governors. I started off the meeting by telling them I was a Governor once. And I—and they were then telling me their stories, their concerns. First of all, they universally thanked the American people for standing with them as this new democracy takes hold.

Secondly, there's concerns about unemployment, about economic development. Some Provinces are quiet. And the Governor wondered whether or not, because it's quiet, people remember the people in the Province exist. Other Provinces have got some difficult security problems.

They shared with me very candidly their concerns about different types of operations, their desire to see to it that the police get better training and better equipment.

And I shared with them our desire to help them succeed, because one of the things that really matters in democracy is that local governance is strong and good and honest, that the people are being able to see the benefits of democracy. And it's hard work in Afghanistan, but I told these leaders I think it's necessary work.

And I want to thank them for coming to America. They've got a very busy schedule. They've been to several States. And I think it's going to be very important for our fellow citizens to meet these good men and to understand the problems they face, and their desire to have their families live in peace, and young girls go to school, and be people treated with dignity.

So I want to thank you all for coming. Thank you for the wonderful gift, and I'm proud you're here.

I'm now going to show them the Oval Office, a shrine to democracy. Thank you.

NOTE: The President spoke at 4:18 p.m. in the Roosevelt Room at the White House.

Message to the Senate Transmitting Amendments to the International Telecommunication Union Constitution and Convention
April 8, 2008

To the Senate of the United States:

With a view to receiving the advice and consent of the Senate to ratification, I transmit herewith the amendments to the Constitution and Convention of the International Telecommunication Union (Geneva, 1992), as amended by the Plenipotentiary Conference (Kyoto, 1994) and the Plenipotentiary Conference (Marrakesh, 2002), together with the declarations and reservations by the United States, all as contained in the Final Acts of the Plenipotentiary Conference (Antalya, 2006). I transmit also, for the information of the Senate, the report of the Department of State concerning the amendments.

The Plenipotentiary Conference (Antalya, 2006) adopted amendments that, among other things: clarify the functions of certain International Telecommunication Union (ITU) officials and bodies; reduce the frequency of certain ITU conferences; clarify eligibility for re-election to certain ITU positions; enhance oversight of the ITU budget and provide for results-based (as well as cost-based) budget proposals; expand the scale of available contribution levels for Member States and Sector Members; and, clarify the definition of and role of observers participating in ITU proceedings.

Consistent with longstanding practice in the ITU, the United States, in signing the 2006 amendments, made certain declarations and reservations. Subject to those declarations and reservations, I believe the United States should ratify the 2006 amendments to the International Telecommunication Union Constitution and Convention. These amendments will contribute to the ITU's ability to adapt to changes in the global telecommunications sector and, in so doing, serve the needs of the United States Government and United States industry. It is my hope that the Senate will take early action on this matter and give its advice and consent to ratification.

GEORGE W. BUSH

The White House,
April 8, 2008.

Remarks on Signing the Second Chance Act of 2007
April 9, 2008

The President. Please be seated. Thank you. Please sit down. Thanks for coming. I'm about to sign a piece of legislation that will help give prisoners across America a second chance for a better life. This bill is going to support the caring men and women who help America's prisoners find renewal and hope.

I can't thank the folks who care enough about a fellow citizen to offer their love and compassion. It's through the acts of mercy that compassionate Americans are making the Nation a more hopeful place, and I want to thank you all for joining us today.

And I thank the Members of Congress who have joined us as well: Senator Arlen Specter, ranking member of the Judiciary Committee; Chairman Joe Biden, not of the Judiciary Committee——

Senator Joseph R. Biden, Jr. Thank God. [*Laughter*]

The President. ——but of Foreign Relations; but a key member of the Judiciary Committee, Senator Sam Brownback, as well. So we've got three United States Senators here, and I'm honored they are here. Members of the United States Congress—chairman of the House Judiciary, John Conyers, and Ranking Member Lamar Smith: I want to thank you all for coming.

I appreciate very much Danny Davis joining us as well—bill sponsor. I want to thank Jim Sensenbrenner and Bobby Scott and Howard Coble and Chris Cannon, all good Members and all Members who worked hard to get this piece of legislation here in timely fashion.

I thank the Attorney General, Judge Michael Mukasey, for joining us as well. Elaine Chao—thank you for coming, Madam Secretary; Rob Portman, former Director of the OMB; and all the supporters of the Second Chance legislation. Thanks for caring about your country; thanks for working on this piece of legislation.

The country was built on the belief that each human being has limitless potential and worth. Everybody matters. We believe that even those who have struggled with a dark past can find brighter days ahead. One way we act on that belief is by helping former prisoners who've paid for their crimes. We help them build new lives as productive members of our society.

The work of redemption reflects our values; it also reflects our national interests. Each year, approximately 650,000 prisoners are released from jail. Unfortunately, an estimated two-thirds of them are rearrested within 3 years. The high recidivism rate places a huge financial burden on taxpayers; it deprives our labor force of productive workers; and it deprives families of their daughters and sons and husbands and wives and moms and dads.

Our Government has a responsibility to help prisoners to return as contributing members of their community. But this does not mean that the Government has all the answers. Some of the most important work to help ex-convicts is done outside of Washington, DC, in faith-based communities and community-based groups. It's done on streets and smalltown community centers. It's done in churches and synagogues and temples and mosques.

I like to call the folks who are engaged in this compassionate work members of the armies of compassion. They help addicts and users break the chains of addiction. They help former prisoners find a ride to work and a meal to eat and place to stay. These men and women are answering the call to love their neighbors as they'd like to be loved themselves. And in the process, they're helping prisoners replace anger and suffering and despair with faith and hope and love.

The bill I'm signing today, the Second Chance Act of 2007, will build on work to help prisoners reclaim their lives. In other words, it basically says, we're standing with you, not against you.

First, the act will authorize important parts of the administration's prison reentry initiative. The goal of this initiative is to help America's prisoners by expanding job training and placement services, improving their ability to find transitional housing, and helping newly released prisoners get mentoring, including from faith-based groups.

The past 3 years, congressional appropriations have supported the work in 20 States through a series of pilot programs awarded to community- and faith-based organizations by the U.S. Department of Labor. The early efforts have fielded promising results. In the first 2 years of the program, more than 12,800 offenders have enrolled in the prisoner reentry program. More than 7,900 have been placed in jobs. Only 18 percent of those enrolled in the program have been arrested again within a year; that's less than half the national average. We like to measure results, and the results of these pilot programs are very encouraging.

With the legislation I'll sign today, Congress has recognized the success of this good policy, and I thank them for their good work. Secondly, act will support the Justice Department's ongoing work to help our Nation's prisoners. This bill will help State and local governments and Indian tribes and nonprofit groups implement programs that will improve the prisoner reentry process.

These programs will provide further—former prisoners with essential services, like housing and medical care. It will help develop prisoner drug treatment programs and support prisoner mentoring initiatives. It will support family counseling and other services to help prisoners reestablish their place in the community.

In both these ways, the Second Chance Act will live up to its name. It will help ensure that where the prisoner's spirit is willing, community's resources are available. It will help our armies of compassion use their healing touch so lost souls can rediscover their dignity and sense of purpose.

I recently went to a program in Baltimore, Maryland, called the Jericho. I met a man there, who has kindly joined us today, named Thomas Boyd. He's 53 years old. He spent more than 20 years of his life using drugs and going back and forth to jail. He remembers the day when his daughter sat down, looked him in the eye, and said, "Daddy, I think it's time for you to start doing something with your life."

He took his daughter's advice. He sought out the Jericho reentry program, which is supported by the reentry initiative. When I visited the program, I tried to remind them that the least shall be first. I also reminded him I was a product of a faith-based program. I quit drinking, and it wasn't because of a government program. It required a little more powerful force than a government program in my case.

And he told me that he appreciates the love and compassion he felt—feels on a regular basis. He's working; he's back with his family; he's a good guy. And I want to thank you for coming, Thomas.

I want to thank you for coming, Thomas.

Thomas Boyd. Yes, sir, thank you.

The President. There's a lot of other Thomases out there that we're going to help with this bill. And so I thank the Members of Congress for joining us. Thanks for your hard work. I thank the members of my administration who are going to see to it that the bill is implemented properly.

And now it is my honor to sign this important piece of legislation. May God bless the country, and may God bless those who are trying to help. Thank you very much.

NOTE: The President spoke at 10:31 a.m. in Room 350 of the Dwight D. Eisenhower Executive Office Building. H.R. 1593, approved April 9, was assigned Public Law No. 110–199.

Remarks Following a Meeting With Senior Minister Goh Chok Tong of Singapore
April 9, 2008

President Bush. Welcome the Senior Minister from our very close ally, Singapore, back to the Oval Office. Gosh, I think we must have met, seems like a half a dozen, at least, times since I've been the President.

Senior Minister Goh. Yes.

President Bush. And every time I meet with you, I come away with a better understanding of a lot of issues, particularly in your part of the world. I thank you very much for briefing me and sharing your wisdom.

We spent a lot of time talking about the neighborhood. But before I get to a couple of countries in the neighborhood, I do want to say, one, how much I appreciate your firm stance against extremists and radicals who use the tactics of murder and intimidation to advance their ideologies. Singapore is a very strong ally in the war against the extremists.

And I also am so pleased that the trade agreement that we negotiated during our respective times has kicked in. I'm a believer in free and fair trade, as are you, sir, and our FTA with Singapore was a very positive accomplishment for our two countries.

We did spend time talking about the countries in the neighborhood. We spent time on Burma and the need for the military regime there to understand that they shouldn't fear the voices of people. And yet they do. I'm disappointed with the progress made to date there and would urge the military leadership there to open up and respond to the will of the people.

And the other issue is China and its relations with Tibet. We both agree that it would stand the Chinese Government in good stead if they would begin a dialogue with the representatives of the Dalai Lama. They'll find—if they ever were to reach out to the Dalai Lama, they'd find him to be a really fine man, a peaceful man, a man who is antiviolence, a man who is not for independence but for the cultural identity of the Tibetans being maintained.

And so I want to thank you, sir. You got good knowledge, and you've had a lot of experience, and you're kind to share it with me.

Senior Minister Goh. Well, thank you very much, President, for welcoming me back to Oval Office. It's a joy coming back here and to see you. I was very interested in developments in the Middle East. And the President briefed me on the developments in Iraq, on concerns which he has over Iran, which is still a very big problem, not just for the U.S. but for the region and for the world.

Then President was interested in developments in Asia, so I was able to add some value to his knowledge—[*laughter*]—on Southeast Asia and on Asia.

On Tibet, I agree with the President that the way forward will be for the Chinese leaders to talk to some representatives of the Dalai Lama. And that is to—if they

can—to talk directly to the Dalai Lama. I think that's the only way for them to contain this problem.

On Myanmar, I told the President that while the army is the problem, the army has to be part of the solution. Without the army playing a part in solving problems in Myanmar, there will be no solution. So these are the issues which we discussed.

And of course, I emphasized the importance of keeping the world—having this free trade regime. The Doha round should be encouraged to move forward. It's moving too slowly, but it should move forward.

President Bush. Thank you, sir.

Senior Minister Goh. Thank you.

President Bush. Thanks for coming. Thank you all.

NOTE: The President spoke at 11:36 a.m. in the Oval Office at the White House. In his remarks, he referred to Tenzin Gyatso, the 14th Dalai Lama.

Remarks on the War on Terror
April 10, 2008

Thank you. Please be seated. Good morning. Fifteen months ago, I announced the surge. And this week, General Petraeus and Ambassador Crocker gave Congress a detailed report on the results.

The immediate goal of the surge was to bring down the sectarian violence that threatened to overwhelm the Government in Baghdad, restore basic security to Iraqi communities, and drive the terrorists out of their safe havens. As General Petraeus told Congress, American and Iraqi forces have made significant progress in all these areas. While there is more to be done, sectarian violence is down dramatically. Civilian deaths and military deaths are also down. Many neighborhoods once controlled

by Al Qaida have been liberated. And cooperation from Iraqis is stronger than ever, with more tips from residents, more Iraqis joining their security forces, and a growing movement against Al Qaida called the Sons of Iraq.

Improvements in security have helped clear the way for political and economic developments described by Ambassador Crocker. These gains receive less media coverage, but they are vital to Iraq's future. At the local level, businesses are reopening, and Provincial councils are meeting. At the national level, there's much work ahead, but the Iraqi Government has passed a budget and three major benchmark laws.

The national Government is sharing oil revenues with the Provinces. And many economic indicators in Iraq, from oil production to inflation, are now pointed in the right direction.

Serious and complex challenges remain in Iraq, from the presence of Al Qaida to the destructive influence of Iran to hard compromises needed for further political progress. Yet with the surge, a major strategic shift has occurred. Fifteen months ago, America and the Iraqi Government were on the defensive. Today, we have the initiative. Fifteen months ago, extremists were sowing sectarian violence. Today, many mainstream Sunni and Shi'a are actively confronting the extremists. Fifteen months ago, Al Qaida had bases in Iraq that it was using to kill our troops and terrorize the Iraqi people. Today, we have put Al Qaida on the defensive in Iraq, and we're now working to deliver a crippling blow. Fifteen months ago, Americans were worried about the prospect of failure in Iraq. Today, thanks to the surge, we've renewed and revived the prospect of success.

With this goal in mind, General Petraeus and Ambassador Crocker have submitted recommendations on the way forward. After detailed discussions with my national security team, including the Secretary of Defense, Secretary of State, and the Joint Chiefs of Staff, I've accepted these recommendations.

A recommendation likely to receive the most attention is on troop levels. General Petraeus has reported that security conditions have improved enough to withdraw all five surge brigades by the end of July. That means that by July 31, the number of U.S. combat brigades in Iraq will be down by 25 percent from last year.

Beyond that, General Petraeus says he'll need time to consolidate his forces and assess how this reduced American presence will affect conditions on the ground before making measured recommendations on further reductions. And I've told him he'll have all the time he needs.

Some have suggested that this period of evaluation will be a pause. That's misleading, because none of our operations in Iraq will be on hold. Instead, we will use the months ahead to take advantage of the opportunities created by the surge and continue operations across the board.

All our efforts are aimed at a clear goal: a free Iraq that can protect its people, support itself economically, and take charge of its own political affairs. No one wants to achieve this goal more than the Iraqis themselves. Those who say that the way to encourage further progress is to back off and force the Iraqis to fend for themselves are simply wrong. The Iraqis are a proud people who understand the enormity of the challenges they face and are anxious to meet them. But they know that they still need our help until they can stand by themselves. Our job in the period ahead is to stand with the Iraqi Government as it makes tough choices and makes the transition to responsibility for its own security and its own destiny.

So what will the transition look like? On the security front, thanks to the significant progress General Petraeus reported this week, it is clear that we're on the right track. In the period ahead, we will stay on the offense against the enemy. As we speak, U.S. Special Forces are launching multiple operations every night to capture or kill Al Qaida leaders in Iraq. Coalition and Iraqi forces are also stepping up conventional operations against Al Qaida in northern Iraq, where terrorists have concentrated after being largely pushed from central and western Iraq. And Prime Minister Maliki's Government launched operations in Basra that make clear a free Iraq will no longer tolerate the lawlessness by Iranian-backed militants.

In the period ahead, we'll also continue to train, equip, and support the Iraqi security forces, continue to transfer security responsibilities to them as Provinces become ready and move, over time, into an overwatch role. The Iraqi Army and police are increasingly capable and leading the fight to secure their country. As Iraqis assume the primary role in providing security, American forces will increasingly focus on targeted raids against the terrorists and extremists. They will continue training Iraqi forces, and they will be available to help Iraq's security forces if required.

On the economic front, Iraq is moving forward. With Iraq's economy growing, oil revenues on the rise, and its capital investment expanding, our economic role in the country is changing. Iraqis, in their recent budget, would outspend us on reconstruction by more than 10 to 1. And American funding for large-scale reconstruction projects is approaching zero. Our share of Iraq's security costs will drop as well, as Iraqis pay for the vast majority of their own army and police. And that's the way it should be. Ultimately, we expect Iraq to shoulder the full burden of these costs. In the period ahead, Iraq's economy will increasingly move away from American assistance, rely on private investment, and stand on its own.

On the political front, Iraq has seen bottom-up progress, as tribes and other groups in the Provinces who fought terror are now turning to rebuilding local political structures and taking charge of their own affairs. Progress in the Provinces is leading to progress in Baghdad. As Iraqi leaders increasingly act together, they share power, and they forge compromises on behalf of the nation. Upcoming elections will consolidate this progress. They'll provide a way for Iraqis to settle disputes through the political process instead of through violence. Iraqis plan to hold Provincial elections later this year, and these elections will be followed by national elections in 2009.

On the diplomatic front, Iraq will increase its engagement in the world, and the world must increase its engagement with Iraq. To help in this effort, I'm directing Ambassador Crocker and General Petraeus to visit Saudi Arabia on their trip back to Iraq. I'm directing our Nation's

senior diplomats to meet with the leaders in Jordan, the UAE, and Qatar and Kuwait and Egypt. In each capital, they will brief them on the situation in Iraq and encourage these nations to reopen their Embassies in Baghdad and increase their overall support for Iraq. This will be followed by Secretary Rice's trip to the third Expanded Neighbors Conference in Kuwait City and the second International Compact with Iraq meeting in Stockholm.

A stable, successful, independent Iraq is in the strategic interests of Arab nations. And all who want peace in the Middle East should support a stable, democratic Iraq. And we will urge all nations to increase their support this year.

The regime in Tehran also has a choice to make: It can live in peace with its neighbor, enjoy strong economic and cultural and religious ties, or it can continue to arm and train and fund illegal militant groups which are terrorizing the Iraqi people and turning them against Iran. If Iran makes the right choice, America will encourage a peaceful relationship between Iran and Iraq. If Iran makes the wrong choice, America will act to protect our interests and our troops and our Iraqi partners.

On each of these fronts—security, economic, political, and diplomatic—Iraqis are stepping forward to assume more responsibility for the welfare of their people and the fate of their country. In all these fronts, America will continue to play an increasingly supporting role.

Our work in Iraq will still demand sacrifices from our whole Nation, especially our military, for some time to come. To ease the burden on our troops and their families, I've directed the Secretary of Defense to reduce deployment lengths from 15 months to 12 months for all active Army soldiers deploying to the Central Command area of operations. These changes will be effective for those deploying after August 1st. We'll also ensure that our Army units will have at least a year home for every year in the field. Our Nation owes a special thanks to the soldiers and families who've supported this extended deployment. And we owe a special thanks to all who serve in the cause of freedom in Iraq.

The stress on our force is real, but the Joint Chiefs have assured me that an all-volunteer force—our All-Volunteer Force is strong and resilient enough to fight and win this war on terror. The trends in Iraq are positive. Our troops want to win. Recruiting and retention have remained strong during the surge. And I believe this: I believe the surest way to depress morale and weaken the force would be to lose in Iraq.

One key to ensuring that our military remains ready is to provide the resources they need promptly. Congress will soon consider a vital emergency war funding request. Members of Congress must pass a bill that provides our troops the resources they need and does not tie the hands of our commanders or impose artificial timelines for withdrawal. This bill must also be fiscally responsible. It must not exceed the reasonable $108 billion request I sent to Congress months ago. If the bill meets all these requirements, it will be a strong show of support for our troops; if it doesn't, I'll veto it.

Some in Washington argue that the war costs too much money. There's no doubt that the costs of this war have been high. But during other major conflicts in our history, the relative cost has been even higher. Now, think about the cold war. During the Truman and Eisenhower administrations, our defense budget rose as high as 13 percent of our total economy. Even during the Reagan administration, when our economy expanded significantly, the defense budget still accounted for about 6 percent of GDP. Our citizens recognized that the imperative of stopping Soviet expansion justified this expense.

Today, we face an enemy that is not only expansionist in its aims but has actually attacked our homeland and intends to do so again. Yet our defense budget accounts for just over 4 percent of our economy, less than our commitment at any point during the four decades of the cold war. This is still a large amount of money, but it is modest—a modest fraction of our Nation's wealth, and it pales when compared to the cost of another terrorist attack on our people.

We should be able to agree that this is a burden worth bearing. And we should be able to agree that our national interest require the success of our mission in Iraq.

Iraq is the convergence point for two of the greatest threats to America in this new century: Al Qaida and Iran. If we fail there, Al Qaida would claim a propaganda victory of colossal proportions, and they could gain safe havens in Iraq from which to attack the United States, our friends, and our allies. Iran would work to fill the vacuum in Iraq, and our failure would embolden its radical leaders and fuel their ambitions to dominate the region. The Taliban in Afghanistan and Al Qaida in Pakistan would grow in confidence and boldness. And violent extremists around the world would draw the same dangerous lesson they did from our retreats in Somalia and Vietnam. This would diminish our Nation's standing in the world and lead to massive humanitarian casualties and increase the threat of another terrorist attack on our homeland.

On the other hand, if we succeed in Iraq, after all that Al Qaida and Iran have invested there, it would be an historic blow to the global terrorist movement and a severe setback for Iran. It would demonstrate to a watching world that mainstream Arabs reject the ideology of Al Qaida and mainstream Shi'a reject the ideology of Iran's radical regime. It would give America a new partner with a growing economy and a democratic political system in which Sunnis and Shi'a and Kurds all work together for the good of their country. And in all these ways, it would bring us closer to our most important goal: making the American people safer here at home.

I want to say a word to our troops and civilians in Iraq. You've performed with incredible skill under demanding circumstances. The turnaround you have made possible in Iraq is a brilliant achievement in American history. And while this war is difficult, it is not endless. And we expect that as conditions on the ground continue to improve, they will permit us to continue the policy of return on success. The day will come when Iraq is a capable partner of the United States. The day will come when Iraq is a stable democracy that helps fight our common enemies and promote our common interests in the Middle East. And when that day arrives, you'll come home with pride in your success and the gratitude of your whole Nation. God bless you.

NOTE: The President spoke at 11:24 a.m. in the Cross Hall at the White House. In his remarks, he referred to Gen. David H. Petraeus, USA, commanding general, Multi-National Force—Iraq; and Prime Minister Nuri al-Maliki of Iraq.

Statement on House of Representatives Action on Colombia Free Trade Agreement Legislation
April 10, 2008

Today's unprecedented and unfortunate action by the House of Representatives— led by Speaker Pelosi—to change the rules governing legislation to implement our trade agreement with Colombia is damaging to our economy, our national security, and our relations with an important ally. It also undermines the trust required for any administration to negotiate trade agreements in the future.

By lowering tariffs for products made in America and sold in Colombia, this trade agreement would level the playing field for American workers and provide a boost for our economy at a vital time. Rather than supporting the opening of markets for our farmers and manufacturers, Democratic congressional leaders instead listened to narrow special interests and followed an isolationist path.

Today's action by the House of Representatives also sends a damaging message to the world that Congress cannot be counted on to keep its promises. Colombia is one of our strongest allies in the Western Hemisphere. Colombia's leaders are showing courage in improving the safety of their citizens while battling narcoterrorists that receive support from anti-American forces outside Colombia. The message Democrats sent today is that no matter how steadfastly you stand with us, we will turn our backs on you when it is politically convenient.

In addition, by changing the rules for how it considers legislation to implement trade agreements, the House has severed a bond of trust between the executive branch and the Congress, and with our trading partners, that has served our Nation well for decades. In order to negotiate trade agreements, we empower our trade representatives with the promise that Congress will consider trade agreements with a timely up-or-down vote. By breaking this bond, Democrats have undercut not just this administration, but future administrations as well. This will weaken our Nation's ability to negotiate fair trade agreements for American workers, farmers, ranchers, and service providers.

During the 16 months since the Colombia free trade agreement was signed, my administration has gone above and beyond any reasonable effort to achieve a bipartisan path for considering this agreement. At the expense of our economy and our national security, the House has instead chosen to take a shortsighted and partisan path.

The President's Radio Address
April 12, 2008

Good morning. Fifteen months ago this week, I announced the surge. And this week, General Petraeus and Ambassador Crocker gave Congress a detailed report on the results.

Since the surge began, American and Iraqi forces have made significant progress. While there's more to be done, sectarian violence, civilian deaths, and military deaths are down. Improvements in security have helped clear the way for political and economic progress. The Iraqi Government has passed a budget and three major benchmark laws. And many economic indicators are now pointed in the right direction.

Serious and complex challenges remain in Iraq. Yet with the surge, a major strategic shift has occurred. Fifteen months ago, extremists were sowing sectarian violence. Today, many mainstream Sunni and Shi'a are actively confronting the extremists. Fifteen months ago, Al Qaida was using bases in Iraq to kill our troops and terrorize Iraqis. Today, we have put Al Qaida on the defensive in Iraq, and now we are working to deliver a crippling blow. Fifteen months ago, Americans were worried about the prospect of failure in Iraq. Today, thanks to the surge, we've revived the prospect of success in Iraq.

This week, General Petraeus reported that security conditions have improved enough to withdraw all five surge brigades. By July 31, the number of U.S. combat brigades in Iraq will be down 25 percent from the year before. Beyond that, General Petraeus says he will need time to assess how this reduced American presence will affect conditions on the ground before making recommendations on further reduc-

tions. I've told him he'll have time he needs to make his assessment.

Our job in the period ahead is to stand with the Iraqi Government as it makes the transition to responsibility for its own security and its own destiny. So what would this transition look like? On the security front, we will stay on the offense, continue to support the Iraqi security forces, continue to transfer security responsibilities to them, and move, over time, into an overwatch role.

On the economic front, Iraq's economy is growing. Iraq is assuming responsibility for almost all the funding of large-scale reconstruction projects, and our share of security costs is dropping as well. On the political front, Iraq is planning to hold elections that will provide a way for Iraqis to settle disputes through the political process instead of through violence.

All our efforts are aimed at a clear goal: a free Iraq that can protect its people, support itself economically, and take charge of its own political affairs. And no one wants to achieve that goal more than the Iraqis themselves.

The turnaround that our men and women in uniform have made possible in Iraq is a brilliant achievement. And we expect that as conditions on the ground continue to improve, they will permit us to continue the policy of return on success.

I'm confident in our success because I know the valor of the young Americans who defend us. This week, I commemorated the sacrifice of Michael Monsoor, a Navy SEAL who gave his life in Iraq and became the fourth Medal of Honor recipient in the war on terror. On September 29, 2006, Mike and two teammates had taken a position on a rooftop when an insurgent grenade landed on the roof. Mike threw himself onto the grenade. One of the survivors put it this way: "Mikey looked death in the face that day and said, 'You cannot take my brothers, I will go in their stead.' "

It is heroism like Michael Monsoor's that pays the cost of human freedom. Our prayers remain with Michael's family and with all the men and women who continue this noble fight. We look forward to the day when they return home in victory.

Thank you for listening.

NOTE: The address was recorded at 8 a.m. on April 11 at the Bush Ranch in Crawford, TX, for broadcast at 10:06 a.m. on April 12. The transcript was made available by the Office of the Press Secretary on April 11, but was embargoed for release until the broadcast. In his address, the President referred to Gen. David H. Petraeus, USA, commanding general, Multi-National Force—Iraq. The Office of the Press Secretary also released a Spanish language transcript of this address.

Remarks Following a Cabinet Meeting
April 14, 2008

I want to thank members of my Cabinet for joining me this morning. We discussed a variety of subjects, including the progress being made in the freedom agenda around the world. But we also are reminded that tomorrow is tax day, and our fellow citizens will be paying taxes during a time of economic uncertainty. These are tough economic times.

This administration anticipated these times. We worked with Congress to pass a progrowth package that incensed businesses to invest and a progrowth package that will be sending some of your taxpayers' money back to you. And the Secretary mentioned again that the second week of May, checks and/or credits to your account will start coming to you. And that's going to be an important part of making sure this economy begins to recover in a way that will add confidence and hope.

One way Congress can act is to make the tax cuts permanent. If they really are that concerned about economic uncertainty, they ought to create certainty in the Tax Code.

The other thing we've been very active on is helping people stay in their homes, whether it be the HOPE NOW Alliance or FHASecure. Over a million people have been helped to renegotiate and/or to find ways to stay in a home that they own.

Now Congress can help. Congress needs to modernize FHA; they need to modernize Fannie Mae and Freddie Mac. I mean, there's constructive things Congress can do that will encourage the housing market to correct quickly by encouraging—helping people stay in their homes. I don't think we ought to be bailing out lenders or speculators. I think we need to be helping hardworking Americans who are creditworthy stay in their homes.

And I do want to say something about trade. There's big disappointment around this table about the action that the Speaker took on the Colombia free trade agreement. This free trade agreement is good for American workers, and it's good for American consumers. And this free trade agreement is in our national interests. Yet that bill is dead unless the Speaker schedules a definite vote. This is a unprecedented move, and it's not in our country's interest that we stiff an ally like Colombia and that we don't encourage our goods and services to be sold overseas.

Congress recently has been working on legislation for beach monitoring and landscape conservation. And those are important issues, but not nearly as important as FHA modernization or the Colombia free trade agreement or making the tax cuts permanent.

Thank you very much.

NOTE: The President spoke at 10:14 a.m. in the Cabinet Room at the White House.

Remarks on Presenting the Commander in Chief's Trophy to the United States Naval Academy Midshipmen
April 14, 2008

Sit down, please. Welcome to the Rose Garden. Of course, this is an old habit for a lot of the players standing behind me. After all, this is the fifth year in a row that the mighty Navy football team won the Commander in Chief's Trophy. And we're here to congratulate them on that amazing achievement. As a matter of fact, coming to the Rose Garden is as familiar a place as Bancroft Hall. [*Laughter*]

We welcome you here, and we congratulate you. Coach, thanks for coming, proud you're here. This team has had an historic season. For the third year in a row, had the most rushing yards in the Nation, as well as the Nation's highest graduation rate. You went to your fifth straight bowl game, and of course, you accomplished your most important goal: You beat Army.

I want to thank the House majority leader, Steny Hoyer, strong supporter of the Naval Academy, for joining us. Congressman Hoyer, thanks for being here. Secretary Don Winter, Secretary of the Navy, and Linda; John Dalton, former Secretary of the Navy and a fine Texan, as well as Margaret—thanks for coming. Vice Admiral Jeff Fowler, thanks for being here, sir. Proud you're here. Coach—just Coach—[*laughter*]—like, you call me George; I'll call you Ken. [*Laughter*] Glad you all are here. [*Laughter*]

This team set a school record by scoring 511 points. And with your sixth straight win over Army, you established the longest winning streak against Army in history. You beat Notre Dame for the first time since 1963. I'm probably not going to spend much time talking to the Pope about it. [*Laughter*] You had an interesting game in the great State of Texas against North Texas, when you won 74 to 62—136 combined points were the most scored in a regulation game in the history of NCAA's top division. You earned an invitation to play in the Poinsettia Bowl. Forget the score, but you made an exciting finish. In other words, you brought great credit to a fabulous place of higher institute—of learning.

And I want to thank your head coach and welcome him. He's been a big part of the success over the past 6 years, and no doubt in my mind—more importantly, no doubt in the superintendent's mind—that he's going to be a fabulous head coach for years to come. Congratulations.

I've been reading about some of the standout performers on the team, starting with slot back Reggie Campbell, team captain on offense. He holds—he owns eight school records. He was the MVP of the Army-Navy game. Linebacker Irv Spencer, team captain on defense—he led the team with 95 tackles. Adam Ballard, Texan—[*laughter*]—Lewisville, Texas—he came back from a broken leg in 2006 to score Navy's first touchdown of the season. He's a bruiser. Cornerback Ketric Buffin, Rowlett, Texas—you think I'm only going to talk about Texans, don't you—[*laughter*]—had an interception in each of the first four games. He's the first player in school history to accomplish that feat.

Zerbin Singleton, now there's an inspirational story for all. He faced great challenges growing up. He overcame injuries from a car accident to make it to the Naval Academy. And during the season, he received the Disney Wide World of Sports Spirit Award as college football's most inspirational figure. He's the brigade commander of all 4,200 midshipmen at the Naval Academy. He'll soon begin flight training as a Marine aviator.

Proud to welcome all the individual stars here. But no question, this team played well because you played as a unit. I want to thank every football player for agreeing to put on the uniform of the finest military ever. You've signed up after 9/11. You knew the stakes involved in the war against extremists and radicals. You knew that your country depended on you, and you didn't hesitate to wear the uniform.

I welcome you as stars on the football field, and I welcome you as soon to be sailors and marines who have a major responsibility to protect the United States from harm and spread the great blessings of liberty so we can have peace. I cannot wait to be able to say to you someday, I'm proud to be your Commander in Chief.

And so I welcome you to the Rose Garden. I congratulate you on being fine football players. More importantly, I congratulate you on being patriotic Americans. May God bless you.

NOTE: The President spoke at 1:16 p.m. in the Rose Garden at the White House. In his remarks, he referred to Ken Niumatalolo, head coach, U.S. Naval Academy football team; Vice Adm. Jeffrey L. Fowler, USN, superintendent, U.S. Naval Academy; and Pope Benedict XVI.

Statement on the Death of John A. Wheeler
April 14, 2008

Laura and I are saddened by the death of John Archibald Wheeler, one of America's greatest physicists.

During his distinguished career, Dr. Wheeler collaborated with scientists such as Albert Einstein and Niels Bohr on projects that changed the course of history. His early work with Bohr on how nuclei split apart, his vision of the possibilities of Einstein's curved space, and his work on quantum theory demonstrated his innovation and brilliance. And he will always be remembered for giving the phenomenon of black holes its name.

Dr. Wheeler was also a great teacher who understood that educating young minds would be one of his most significant contributions. As a professor at Princeton University and the University of Texas—Austin, Dr. Wheeler inspired generations of students, such as the late Nobel Prize winning physicist Richard Feynman, to transform their curiosity into scientific discoveries.

Today our thoughts and prayers are with the Wheeler family.

Remarks Honoring President Thomas Jefferson's 265th Birthday
April 14, 2008

Thank you all. Thanks for coming. Please be seated. Welcome to the White House. Laura and I are so honored you are here. I welcome members of my Cabinet, Members of the United States Senate, folks who work in the White House, the Governor of Virginia, and Anne Holton. Thank you all for coming, really happy you're here.

We're here tonight to commemorate the 265th birthday of Thomas Jefferson, here in a room where he once walked and in a home where he once lived. In this house, President Jefferson spread the word that liberty was the right of every individual. In this house, Jefferson sent Lewis and Clark off on the mission that helped make America a continental nation. And in this house, Jefferson was known to receive guests in his bathrobe and slippers. [*Laughter*] Laura said, "No." [*Laughter*] I don't have a bathrobe. [*Laughter*]

With a single sentence, Thomas Jefferson changed the history of the world. After countless centuries, when the powerful and the privileged governed as they pleased, Jefferson proclaimed as a self-evident truth that liberty was a right given to all people by an Almighty.

Here in America, that truth was not fully realized in Jefferson's own lifetime. As he observed the condition of slaves in America, Jefferson said, quote, "I tremble for my country when I reflect that God is just [and] that His justice cannot sleep forever." Less than 40 years after his death, justice was awakened in America, and a new era of freedom dawned.

Today, on the banks of the Tidal Basin, a statue of Thomas Jefferson stands in a rotunda that is a memorial to both the man and the ideas that built this Nation. There, on any day of the week, you will find men and women of all creeds, colors, races, and religions. You will find scholars, schoolchildren, and visitors from every part of our country. And you will find each of them looking upward in quiet reflection on the liturgy of freedom, the words of Thomas Jefferson inscribed on the memorial's walls.

The power of Jefferson's words do not stop at water's edge. They beckon the friends of liberty on even the most distant shores. They're a source of inspiration for people in young democracies like Afghanistan and Lebanon and Iraq. And they are a source of hope for people in nations like Belarus and Burma, Cuba, Venezuela, Iran, Syria, North Korea, and Zimbabwe, where the struggle for freedom continues.

Thomas Jefferson left us on July 4th, 1826, 50 years to the day after our Declaration of Independence was adopted. In one of the great harmonies of history, his friend and rival John Adams died on the very same day. Adams's last words were, "Thomas Jefferson survives." And he still does today, and he will live on forever, because the desire to live in freedom is the eternal hope of mankind.

And now it's my pleasure to welcome Wilfred McClay to the stage.

NOTE: The President spoke at 6:05 p.m. in the East Room at the White House. In his remarks, he referred to Gov. Timothy M. Kaine of Virginia and his wife Anne Holton; and Wilfred M. McClay, SunTrust Bank chair of excellence in humanities and professor of history, University of Tennessee at Chattanooga. The transcript released by the Office of the Press Secretary also included the remarks of the First Lady.

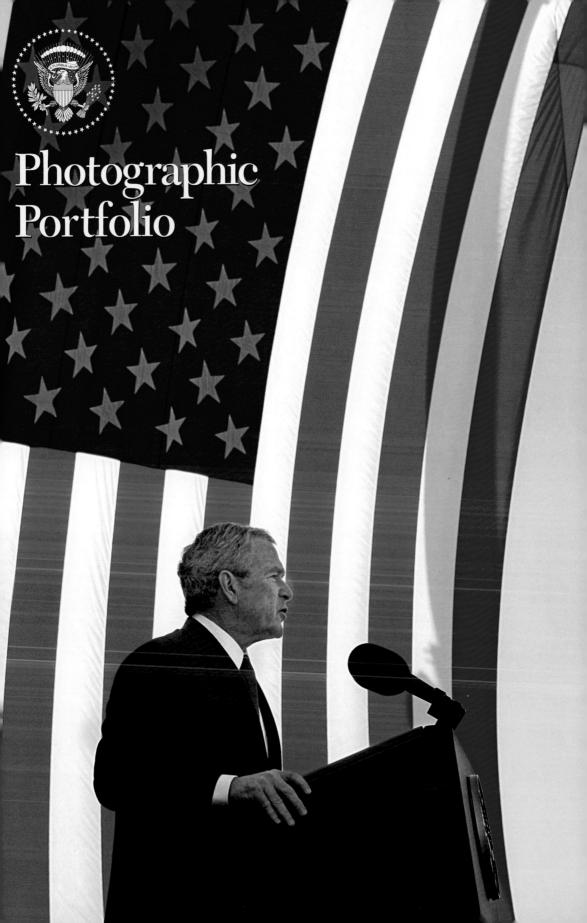

Photographic Portfolio

Overleaf: Addressing military personnel at Camp Arifjan, Kuwait, January 12.

Left: Presenting the Medal of Honor posthumously to M. Sgt. Woodrow Wilson Keeble, USA, in the East Room at the White House, March 3.

Below: Participating in the NATO summit meeting on Afghanistan with President Hamid Karzai of Afghanistan in Bucharest, Romania, April 3.

Right: Touring the Vatican Gardens with Pope Benedict XVI in Vatican City, June 13.

Below right: Arriving at a review ceremony of the 82d Airborne Division with base commander Maj. Gen. David Rodriguez, USA, at Pike Field, Fort Bragg, NC, May 22.

Below far right: Attending a breakfast meeting with business leaders at eggtc. restaurant in Kansas City, MO, February 1.

Above left: Receiving a briefing on Midwest flooding from Dick Hainje, Regional Administrator for the Federal Emergency Management Agency, at Kirkwood Community College in Cedar Rapids, IA, June 19.

Above far left: Attending a tee-ball game between the Little Saints and Little Dragons at Ghana International School in Accra, Ghana, February 20.

Left: Viewing an exhibit with Queen Elizabeth II of the United Kingdom and Prince Philip, Duke of Edinburgh, at Windsor Castle in Windsor, England, June 15.

Above: Accepting a standing ovation during the State of the Union Address at the U.S. Capitol, January 28.

Right: Attending a Memorial Day wreath-laying ceremony at the Tomb of the Unknowns at Arlington National Cemetery with Military District of Washington commander Maj. Gen. Richard J. Rowe, Jr., USA, in Arlington, VA, May 26.

Above: Accepting a team jersey from catcher Jason Varitek of the 2007 World Series champion Boston Red Sox on the South Lawn at the White House, February 27.

Left: Test-driving a lawnmower accompanied by Bill Wright, founder and chief executive officer of Wright Manufacturing, Inc., and Rep. Roscoe G. Bartlett at Wright Manufacturing, Inc., in Frederick, MD, January 18.

Above right: Walking with President Shimon Peres of Israel at the President's Residence in Jerusalem, Israel, May 14.

Above far right: Touring the Saadiyat Island Cultural District Exhibition and Masdar Exhibition with Crown Prince Sheikh Muhammad bin Zayid Al Nuhayyan of Abu Dhabi at the Emirates Palace Hotel in Abu Dhabi, United Arab Emirates, January 14.

Right: Consoling residents affected by tornado damage in Lafayette, TN, February 8.

Overleaf: Posing for a formal portrait with former President George H.W. Bush at Camp David, MD, March 23.

Statement on the Anniversary of the Virginia Tech Shootings in Blacksburg, Virginia
April 15, 2008

April 16, 2007, brought the deadliest day of violence on a college campus in our Nation's history. The horrific crimes committed at Virginia Tech University filled our souls with sadness. One year later, we remember the victims murdered and wounded that day.

We join our fellow Americans in praying for the families and friends whose hearts ache for their lost loved ones. We continue to be amazed by the extraordinary Hokie spirit and inspired by the survivors of this tragedy. Students, teachers, and alumni have overcome evil with good by supporting each other with love and compassion. We are humbled by their resilience and confident in the university's bright future.

We pray that God will continue to comfort and heal the people of the Virginia Tech community.

Remarks at a Welcoming Ceremony for Pope Benedict XVI
April 16, 2008

Holy Father, Laura and I are privileged to have you here at the White House. We welcome you with the ancient words commended by Saint Augustine: *Pax tecum.* Peace be with you.

You've chosen to visit America on your birthday. Well, birthdays are traditionally spent with close friends, so our entire Nation is moved and honored that you've decided to share this special day with us. We wish you much health and happiness today and for many years to come.

This is your first trip to the United States since you ascended to the Chair of Saint Peter. You will visit two of our greatest cities and meet countless Americans, including many who have traveled from across the country to see with you and to share in the joy of this visit. Here in America, you'll find a nation of prayer. Each day, millions of our citizens approach our Maker on bended knee, seeking His grace and giving thanks for the many blessings He bestows upon us. Millions of Americans have been praying for your visit, and millions look forward to praying with you this week.

Here in America, you'll find a nation of compassion. Americans believe that the measure of a free society is how we treat the weakest and most vulnerable among us. So each day, citizens across America answer to the universal call to feed the hungry and comfort the sick and care for the infirm. Each day, across the world, the United States is working to eradicate disease, alleviate poverty, promote peace, and bring the light of hope to places still mired in the darkness of tyranny and despair.

Here in America, you'll find a nation that welcomes the role of faith in the public square. When our Founders declared our Nation's independence, they rested their case on an appeal to the laws of nature and of nature's God. We believe in religious liberty. We also believe that a love for freedom and a common moral law are written into every human heart and that these constitute the firm foundation on which any successful free society must be built.

Here in America, you'll find a nation that is fully modern, yet guided by ancient and eternal truths. The United States is the most innovative, creative, and dynamic country on Earth. It is also among the most religious. In our Nation, faith and reason coexist in harmony. This is one of our country's greatest strengths and one of the reasons that our land remains a beacon of hope and opportunity for millions across the world.

Most of all, Holy Father, you will find in America people whose hearts are open to your message of hope. And America and the world need this message.

In a world where some invoke the name of God to justify acts of terror and murder and hate, we need your message that God is love. And embracing this love is the surest way to save men from falling prey to the teaching of fanaticism and terrorism.

In a world where some treat life as something to be debased and discarded, we need your message that all human life is sacred and that "each of us is willed, each of us is loved"—[*applause*]—and your message that "each of us is willed, each of us is loved, [and] each of us is necessary."

In a world where some no longer believe that we can distinguish between simple right and wrong, we need your message to reject this dictatorship of relativism and embrace a culture of justice and truth.

In a world where some see freedom as simply the right to do as they wish, we need your message that true liberty requires us to live our freedom not just for ourselves but in a spirit of mutual support.

Holy Father, thank you for making this journey to America. Our Nation welcomes you. We appreciate the example you set for the world, and we ask that you always keep us in your prayers.

NOTE: The President spoke at 10:38 a.m. on the South Lawn at the White House. The transcript released by the Office of the Press Secretary also included the remarks of Pope Benedict XVI. The Office of the Press Secretary also released a Spanish language transcript of these remarks.

Joint Statement by the United States of America and the Holy See
April 16, 2008

His Holiness Pope Benedict XVI and President George W. Bush met today in the Oval Office of the White House.

President Bush, on behalf of all Americans, welcomed the Holy Father, wished him a happy birthday, and thanked him for the spiritual and moral guidance, which he offers to the whole human family. The President wished the Pope every success in his Apostolic Journey and in his address at the United Nations, and expressed appreciation for the Pope's upcoming visit to "Ground Zero" in New York.

During their meeting, the Holy Father and the President discussed a number of topics of common interest to the Holy See

and the United States of America, including moral and religious considerations to which both parties are committed: the respect of the dignity of the human person; the defense and promotion of life, matrimony and the family; the education of future generations; human rights and religious freedom; sustainable development and the struggle against poverty and pandemics, especially in Africa. In regard to the latter, the Holy Father welcomed the United States' substantial financial contributions in this area. The two reaffirmed their total rejection of terrorism as well as the manipulation of religion to justify immoral and violent acts against innocents. They further touched on the need to confront terrorism with appropriate means that respect the human person and his or her rights.

The Holy Father and the President devoted considerable time in their discussions to the Middle East, in particular resolving the Israel-Palestinian conflict in line with the vision of two states living side-by-side in peace and security, their mutual support for the sovereignty and independence of Lebanon, and their common concern for the situation in Iraq and particularly the precarious state of Christian communities there and elsewhere in the region. The Holy Father and the President expressed hope for an end to violence and for a prompt and comprehensive solution to the crises which afflict the region.

The Holy Father and the President also considered the situation in Latin America with reference, among other matters, to immigrants, and the need for a coordinated policy regarding immigration, especially their humane treatment and the well being of their families.

NOTE: The Office of the Press Secretary also released a Spanish language version of this joint statement. An original was not available for verification of the content of this joint statement.

Remarks on Energy and Climate Change
April 16, 2008

Thank you. Welcome. I thank you all for coming. I particularly want to thank members of my Cabinet for joining me here today in the Rose Garden.

Tomorrow represents—representatives of the world's major economies will gather in Paris to discuss climate change. Here in Washington, the debate about climate change is intensifying. Today I'll share some views on this important issue to advance discussions both at home and abroad.

Climate change involves complicated science and generates vigorous debate. Many are concerned about the effect of climate change on our environment. Many are concerned about the effect of climate change policies on our economy. I share these concerns, and I believe they can be sensibly reconciled.

Over the past 7 years, my administration has taken a rational, balanced approach to these serious challenges. We believe we need to protect our environment. We believe we need to strengthen our energy security. We believe we need to grow our economy. And we believe the only way to achieve these goals is through continued advances in technology. So we've pursued a series of policies aimed at encouraging the rise of innovation, as well as more cost-effective clean energy technologies that can help America and developing nations reduce greenhouse gases, reduce our dependence on oil, and keep our economies vibrant and strong for the decades to come.

I've put our Nation on a path to slow, stop, and eventually reverse the growth of our greenhouse gas emissions. In 2002, I announced our first step: to reduce America's greenhouse gas intensity by 18 percent through 2012. I'm pleased to say that we remain on track to meet this goal even as our economy has grown 17 percent.

As we take these steps here at home, we're also working internationally on a rational path to addressing global climate change. When I took office 7 years ago, we faced a problem. A number of nations around the world were preparing to implement the flawed approach of Kyoto Protocol. In 1997, the United States Senate took a look at the Kyoto approach and

505

passed a resolution opposing the approach by a 95-to-nothing vote.

The Kyoto Protocol would have required the United States to drastically reduce greenhouse gas emissions. The impact of this agreement, however, would have been to limit our economic growth and to shift American jobs to other countries while allowing major developing nations to increase their emissions. Countries like China and India are experiencing rapid economic growth, and that's good for their people, and it's good for the world. This also means they're emitting increasingly large quantities of greenhouse gases, which has consequences for the entire global climate.

So the United States has launched, and the G–8 has embraced, a new process that brings together the countries responsible for most of the world's emissions. We're working toward a climate agreement that includes the meaningful participation of every major economy and gives none a free ride.

In support of this process, and based on technology advances and strong new policy, it is now time for the United States to look beyond 2012 and to take the next step. We've shown that we can slow emissions growth. But today I'm announcing a new national goal: to stop the growth of U.S. greenhouse gas emissions by 2025.

To reach this goal, we will pursue an economy-wide strategy that builds on the solid foundation that we have in place. As part of this strategy, we worked with Congress to pass energy legislation that specifies a new fuel economy standard of 35 miles per gallon by 2020 and requires fuel producers to supply at least 36 billion gallons of renewable fuel by 2022. This should provide an incentive for shifting to a new generation of fuels, like cellulosic ethanol, that will reduce concerns about food prices and the environment.

We also mandated new objectives for the coming decade to increase the efficiency of lighting and appliances. We're helping States achieve their goals for increasing renewable power and building-code efficiency by sharing new technologies and providing tax incentives. We're working to implement a new international agreement that will accelerate cuts in potent HCFC emissions. Taken together, these landmark actions will prevent billions of metric tons of greenhouse gas emissions from entering the atmosphere.

These objectives are backed by a combination of new market-based regulations, new government incentives, and new funding for technology research. We've provided billions of dollars for next generation nuclear energy technologies. Along with the private sector, we've invested billions more to research, develop, and commercially deploy renewable fuels, hydrogen fuel cells, advanced batteries, and other technologies to enable a new generation of vehicles and more reliable renewable power systems.

In 2009 alone, the Government and the private sector plan to dedicate nearly a billion dollars to clean coal research and development. Our incentives for power production from wind and solar energy have helped to more than quadruple its use. We worked with Congress to make available more than $40 billion in loan guarantees to support investments that will avoid, reduce, or sequester greenhouse gas emissions or air pollutants. And our farmers can now compete for substantial new conservation incentives to restore land and forests in ways that help cut greenhouse gases.

We're doing a lot to protect this environment. We've laid a solid foundation for further progress, but these measures—while these measures will bring us a long way to achieving our new goal, we've got to do more in the power generation sector. To reach our 2025 goal, we'll need to more rapidly slow the growth of power sector greenhouse gas emissions so they peak within 10 to 15 years and decline thereafter. By doing so, we'll reduce emission levels in the power sector well below where they were projected to be when we first announced our climate strategy in 2002.

There are a number of ways to achieve these reductions, but all responsible approaches depend on accelerating the development and deployment of new technologies.

As we approach this challenge, we face a growing problem here at home. Some courts are taking laws written more than 30 years ago to primarily address local and regional environmental effects, and applying them to global climate change. Clean Air Act, the Endangered Species Act, and the National Environmental Policy Act were never meant to regulate global climate. For example, under a Supreme Court decision last year, the Clean Air Act could be applied to regulate greenhouse gas emissions from vehicles. Now, this would automatically trigger regulation under the Clean Air Act of greenhouse gases all across our economy, leading to what Energy and Commerce Committee chairman John Dingell last week called, quote, "a glorious mess."

If these laws are stretched beyond their original intent, they could override the programs Congress just adopted and force the Government to regulate more than just power plant emissions. It could also force the Government to regulate smaller users and producers of energy, from schools and stores to hospitals and apartment buildings. This would make the Federal Government act like a local planning and zoning board. It would have a crippling effect on our entire economy.

Decisions with such far-reaching impact should not be left to unelected regulators and judges. Such decisions should be opened—debated openly. Such decisions should be made by the elected representatives of the people they affect. The American people deserve an honest assessment of the costs, benefits, and feasibility of any proposed solution.

This is the approach that Congress properly took last year on mandatory policies that will reduce emissions from cars and trucks and improve the efficiency of lighting and appliances. This year, Congress will soon be considering additional legislation that will affect global climate change. I believe that congressional debate should be guided by certain core principles and a clear appreciation that there is a wrong way and a right way to approach reducing greenhouse gas emissions. Bad legislation would impose tremendous costs on our economy and on American families without accomplishing the important climate change goals we share.

The wrong way is to raise taxes, duplicate mandates, or demand sudden and drastic emissions cuts that have no chance of being realized and every chance of hurting our economy. The right way is to set realistic goals for reducing emissions, consistent with advances in technology, while increasing our energy security and ensuring our economy can continue to prosper and grow.

The wrong way is to sharply increase gasoline prices, home heating bills for American families, and the cost of energy for American businesses. The right way is to adopt policies that spur investment in the new technologies needed to reduce greenhouse gas emissions more cost effectively in the longer term without placing unreasonable burdens on American consumers and workers in the short term.

The wrong way is to jeopardize our energy and economic security by abandoning nuclear power and our Nation's huge reserves of coal. The right way is to promote more emission-free nuclear power and encourage the investments necessary to produce electricity from coal without releasing carbon into the air.

The wrong way is to unilaterally impose regulatory costs that put American businesses at a disadvantage with their competitors abroad, which would simply drive American jobs overseas and increase emissions there. The right way is to ensure that all major economies are bound to take action and to work cooperatively with our partners for a fair and effective international climate agreement.

507

The wrong way is to threaten punitive tariffs and protective—protectionist barriers, start a carbon-based global trade war, and to stifle the diffusion of new technologies. The right way is to work to make advanced technology affordable and available in the developing world by lowering trade barriers, creating a global free market for clean energy technologies, and enhancing international cooperation and technology investment.

We must all recognize that in the long run, new technologies are the key to addressing climate change. But in the short run, they can be more expensive. And that is why I believe part of any solution means reforming today's complicated mix of incentives to make the commercialization and use of new, lower emission technologies more competitive. Today, we have different incentives for different technologies, from nuclear power to clean coal to wind and solar energy. What we need to do is consolidate them into a single, expanded program with the following features.

First, the incentive should be carbon weighted to make lower emission power sources less expensive relative to higher emissions sources, and it should take into account our Nation's energy security needs.

Second, the incentive should be technology neutral, because the Government should not be picking winners and losers in this emerging market.

Third, the incentive should be long lasting. It should provide a positive and reliable market signal not only for the investment in a technology but also for the investments in domestic manufacturing capacity and infrastructure that will help lower costs and scale up availability.

Even with strong new incentives, many new technologies face regulatory and political barriers. To pave the way for a new generation of nuclear power plants, we must provide greater certainty on issues from licensing to responsible management of spent fuel. The promise of carbon capture and storage depends on new pipelines and liability rules. Large-scale renewable energy installations are most likely to be built in sparsely populated areas, which will require advanced interstate transmission systems to deliver this power to major population centers. If we're serious about confronting climate change, then we have to be serious about addressing these obstacles.

If we fully implement our new strong laws, adhere to the principles I've outlined, and adopt appropriate incentives, we will put America on an ambitious new track for greenhouse gas reductions. The growth in emissions will slow over the next decade, stop by 2025, and begin to reverse thereafter, so long as technology continues to advance.

Our new 2025 goal marks a major step forward in America's efforts to address climate change. Yet even if we reduced our own emissions to zero tomorrow, we would not make a meaningful dent in solving the problem without concerted action by all major economies. So in connection with the major economies process we launched, we're urging each country to develop its own national goals and plans to reduce greenhouse gas emissions.

Like many other countries, America's national plan will be a comprehensive blend of market incentives and regulations to reduce emissions by encouraging clean and efficient energy technologies. We're willing to include this plan in a binding international agreement, so long as our fellow major economies are prepared to include their plans in such an agreement. We recognize that different nations will design different strategies, with goals and policies that reflect their unique energy resources and economic circumstances. But we can only make progress if their plans will make a real difference as well.

The next step in the major economies process is a meeting this week in Paris, and I want to thank my friend President Sarkozy for hosting it. There, representatives of all participating nations will lay the groundwork for a leaders' meeting in conjunction with the G–8 summit in July. Our objective is to come together on a common approach that will contribute to the negotiations under the U.N. framework convention of global climate once the Kyoto Protocol expires in 2012. This approach must be environmentally effective and economically sustainable.

To be effective, this approach will require commitments by all major economies to slow, stop, and eventually reverse the growth of greenhouse gas emissions. To be economically sustainable, this approach must foster the economic growth necessary to pay for investments in new technology and to raise living standards. We must help countries in the developing world gain access to technologies as well as financing that will enable them to take a lower carbon path to economic growth.

And then there will be the major economies leader meeting in July—that's the one I'll be going to—where we will seek agreement on a long-term global goal for emissions reductions, as well as an agreement on how national plans will be a part of the post-2012 approach. We'll also seek to increase international cooperation among private firms and governments in key sectors such as power generation, auto manufacturing, renewable fuels, and aluminum and steel.

We will work toward the creation of an international clean technology fund that will help finance low emissions energy projects in the developing world. We'll call on all nations to help spark a global clean energy revolution by agreeing immediately to eliminate trade barriers on clean energy goods and services.

The strategy I have laid out today shows faith in the ingenuity and enterprise of the American people, and that's a resource that's never going to run out. I'm confident that with sensible and balanced policies from Washington, American innovators and entrepreneurs will pioneer a new generation of technology that improves our environment, strengthens our economy, and continues to amaze the world.

Thanks for coming.

NOTE: The President spoke at 2:45 p.m. in the Rose Garden at the White House. In his remarks, he referred to President Nicolas Sarkozy of France.

Remarks at the President's Environmental Youth Awards Ceremony
April 17, 2008

Thanks for coming. Please be seated, and welcome to the Rose Garden. And thanks for bringing such good weather. [*Laughter*]

Laura and I are thrilled you're here, and we are thrilled to honor young Americans who are helping their communities by safeguarding the environment. I'm really pleased that Steve is with us too. Thanks for coming. Debbie, thanks for being here.

I want to welcome your parents and your sponsors, and I know they're incredibly proud of you. I appreciate the dedication that you've shown to improve neighborhoods. I really thank the fact that you're a person who's willing to be a responsible citizen and take action.

I'm pleased to have all the regional administrators here. It's good to see friends from around the country. Thanks for coming. Thanks for serving the country.

I appreciate the fact that you know that we live in a country of unbelievable splendor and beauty. And no matter which State we call home, we can always find the work of the Almighty in our State. And today we honor 36 young men and women who have devoted their time, energy, and creativity to being good stewards of that creation. And we appreciate the work you're doing to preserve our beauty for generations to come.

Students here today come from all across the country. And your accomplishments are as diverse as your home States. Steve will read out the accomplishments, but I'll just touch on a few.

First, for the people from New York who collected used books that would have ended up in landfills and donated them to schools and nursing homes and homeless shelters.

Got people here from Massachusetts who worked with local fishermen to switch from using lead weights to using substances that didn't have the potential to poison local birds.

Virginia—the good folks from Virginia used—recycled electronic equipment so it wouldn't end up polluting the environment. Makes a lot of sense; it's a rational plan.

Good people from Tennessee who led hundreds of members of the community to switch to more energy-efficient light bulbs, just like Laura insisted we did here at the White House. [*Laughter*]

How about the good folks from Washington State who worked with the school district and helped save more than a half a million dollars by encouraging teachers to reduce their energy use in the classroom.

These are practical ways to help protect our environment. And one way to thank you is to have the Administrator present awards to you. You set a great example for people around the country, and you set a great example for the Government. We're focused on conserving and protecting our environment. I don't know if you know this or not, but in—we created the Northwestern Hawaii Island Marine National Monument, which is the largest single conservation area in our Nation's history and the largest protected marine area in the world. And we did so because there are more than 7,000 species in the monument,

and a quarter of them exist nowhere else on the Earth. And the good news is, Laura went over to dedicate the monument and did a fabulous job.

We're working hard to protect our wildlife. Through the principle of cooperative conservation, which means we bring together different stakeholders—conservationists and sportsmen and local leaders and Federal, State, and tribal authorities—to protect species that are at risk.

We're protecting our—and strengthening our National Park System. One way to dedicate ourselves to conservation is to take that which is already in existence and make it better. And so last year, I announced the National Park Centennial Initiative, which is a great plan to enhance our national parks during the decade leading up to the 100th anniversary in 2016. This is an initiative that's going to allow the Park System to hire more park rangers and to increase the use of technology and upgrade its facilities and its historic buildings. I'm looking forward to working with Congress to make sure this effort's fully funded.

And finally, we're working to ensure that America can develop alternative energy sources and develop new technologies so we can address global climate change without harming the economy. And I believe we can do both. I believe we can be good stewards of the environment, and I believe we can grow our economy, which we're going to have to do to be able to afford the technologies necessary to change.

So yesterday I announced an important national goal, which is stopping the growth in U.S. greenhouse gases emissions by 2025. It's a goal we can achieve. It's important to set realistic goals and then work hard to achieve those goals.

The key to keeping the—making this work is to unleash the entrepreneurial spirit of the country and to develop the new technologies that will allow us to utilize cleaner, more efficient energy sources, which, by the way, will have the beneficial effect of becoming—making us less dependent on oil, particularly oil that comes from parts of the world where the people may not exactly like us. So in other words, we're working on our national security and our economic security and, at the same time, having the beneficial effect of being wise stewards of the environment.

But today you're tired of hearing about an old guy speak. We want to hear the stories of young people, young people who will be the future leaders of the country, young peoples who have laid out a strategy

as to how to protect their local communities and have done so.

And so I welcome you here. I ask Laura and Steve to join me here on the podium to present the awards. Congratulations. Welcome to the Rose Garden, and thanks for coming.

NOTE: The President spoke at 10:03 a.m. in the Rose Garden at the White House. In his remarks, he referred to Stephen L. Johnson, Administrator, Environmental Protection Agency, and his wife Debbie.

The President's News Conference With Prime Minister Gordon Brown of the United Kingdom
April 17, 2008

President Bush. Thank you all. Mr. Prime Minister, welcome to the Rose Garden. Glad you're here. It's a beautiful day. I'm—been a pleasure to welcome a good friend to the Oval Office and had a good discussion.

Appreciate our special relationship with Britain, and I believe that the actions we've taken are making it stronger. We spent time talking about the terrorists and extremists. I would remind my fellow citizens that just days after the Prime Minister took office, his country was attacked by murderers and extremists, and he handled the situation brilliantly. Prime Minister Brown understands our enemies remain determined to strike our countries and to kill our people. He and I share a determination, a fierce determination that these evil men must be stopped and that we can defeat their hateful ideology by the spreading of liberty and freedom.

We're working together in Iraq. I want to—appreciate the sacrifice of the British troops, their families, and the British people. During the recent fighting in the Basra Province, our nations coordinated our support for the Iraqi security forces as they

took on extremists and criminals. I was most thankful for the brilliance of the British helicopter crews that fired under courage and helped evacuate wounded Iraqi soldiers.

I talked to the Prime Minister about my meetings with General Petraeus and Ambassador Crocker and why I made the decision I made about our troop levels in Iraq. I appreciate the fact that the Prime Minister briefed me on what the British commanders are saying about Iraq. The key thing there is that we're working very closely together and that we're making progress.

I also talked about Afghanistan with the Prime Minister. Appreciate the 7,900 British troops that are serving bravely in that country. We talked about the very successful NATO summit that we just concluded in Romania. We talked about our commitment to see to it that we succeed in Afghanistan.

Spent some time on Iran. Our position is clear: that we're going to work together, along with other nations, to make it abundantly clear to the Iranian regime that they must not have the capability of developing a nuclear weapon.

We talked about Zimbabwe, and I appreciate Gordon Brown's strong position on that issue. And I appreciate the fact that he went to the United Nations and made it abundantly clear that—which I feel as well, which is, you can't have elections unless you're willing to put the results out. What kind of election is it if you not let the will of the people be known?

I appreciate those in the region who have spoken out on this issue. Appreciate the fact that some in the region have spoken out against violence. More leaders in the region need to speak out. And the United Nations and the AU must play an active role in resolving the situation in Zimbabwe.

We shared our deep concern about the people in Darfur. And I share frustrations that the United Nations-AU peacekeeping force is slow in arriving. I made the decision not to put our troops in there on the expectation that the United Nations, along with the AU, could be effective. And they haven't been as effective as they should be, and we'll continue to work to help them.

We talked about our joint desire to train health care workers in Ethiopia, Kenya, Mozambique, and Zambia, as well as our continued effort to confront disease, whether it be malaria and HIV/AIDS.

And then, of course, we spent time on our economy—ies. [*Laughter*] That would be two economies. We first spent some time on the global financial markets. And then we spent time talking about what each of us are doing in our respective countries to deal with our financial circumstances.

We spent some time on trade. The worst signal we could send during this global uncertainty is that the world is going to become more protectionist and less willing to open up markets. And I want to thank Gordon Brown for his strong belief that the Doha rounds ought to proceed. I agree with you, sir, and believe we can make good progress toward that end.

We talked about the climate change issue. I gave a speech right here in the

Rose Garden yesterday. I don't know whether any of our press corps read it, but it was a far-reaching speech that talked about our commitment to deal with the issue in such a way that we can develop technologies without wrecking our economy. And it was in clear recognition that unless countries like China and India are at the table, any agreement is not going to work. And I assured the Prime Minister that by the time the G–8 comes, we will work hard to make sure we can reach an international consensus that will be effective.

All in all, we had a fabulous conversation. I'm looking forward to dinner tonight. The Prime Minister is bringing his wife Sarah up here to the White House. And I'm—Laura and I are going to cook you up a meal. [*Laughter*] Well, we'll eat one with you. [*Laughter*] Thanks for coming.

Prime Minister Brown. Thank you very much, sir. Mr. President, let me first of all thank you for your warm welcome, for your hospitality, and for your offer to cook the meal this evening. And let me thank you most of all for your leadership. The world owes President George Bush a huge debt of gratitude for leading the world in our determination to root out terrorism and to ensure that there is no safe haven for terrorism and no hiding place for terrorists.

It's my profound belief that over many decades, no international partnership has served the world better than the special relationship between our two countries, the United States and the United Kingdom. And following our excellent meeting, I'm able to report that the bond between our two countries is stronger than ever.

From the darkest days of the Second World War, when the strongest transatlantic partnership was forged to defend freedom, to the challenges we face together against terrorism in every part of the world, our alliance will remain strong and steadfast in standing for freedom and for justice. And we will continue to work together with the strenuous efforts we are making together in Iraq and Afghanistan.

Today we agreed our determination that in advance of the July G–8 meeting in Japan, where all the major economies will meet together, we will do everything in our power to ensure economic stability and growth. We should be vigilant in maintaining the proactive approach to monetary and fiscal policy to enable our economies to resume their paths of upward growth. We want all our international partners to do the same. To ensure greater confidence in the financial system, all countries should ensure the immediate implementation of the plans for transparency and disclosure and risk management agreed by our finance ministers.

We agreed to work—and President Bush has just referred to this—for an early world trade deal that will give new confidence to the international economy at this time. An enhanced dialogue between oil consumers and oil producers, with rising output from the oil-producing countries, should help stabilize and then cut the price of oil, now at over $110 a barrel.

We want to work with the World Bank and agricultural producers to enhance food supply, tackle food shortages, and increase agricultural production. And both Britain and America are taking action to help the housing market for homeowners and those who want to buy their homes for the first time.

President Bush and I also talked about and agreed new work programs between our two governments on development. And let me acknowledge the pioneering work of President Bush's administration in tackling on the African continent HIV/AIDS and addressing the scandal of avoidable deaths from malaria.

We agreed to work together, as President Bush has just said, to increase the number of doctors, nurses, and midwives in Ethiopia, Kenya, Mozambique, and Zambia, a down payment which, if extended to the whole of Africa, would lead to 1½ million more health service—health care workers.

At the same time, the professionalism and commitment of our brave forces serving alongside America with determination in Iraq and Afghanistan was a subject of much of our discussions. We praise the commitment of the troops of both America and Britain and all who serve in these two countries. And we believe that our program of overwatch in Basra, in the south of Iraq, is making substantial progress. At the same time, we've agreed at the NATO summit in Bucharest measures that we can take so that we match the military effort in Afghanistan with proposals that will enable economic and social development of that country. America and Britain have the first and second largest number of forces in both these countries, and we are determined on the success of our missions.

We reiterated our common stand on Darfur, and we want to see talks from the rebels and the Government working together. We reiterated our common stand also on Burma, where it is important to repeat the call for reconciliation. And on the situation in Zimbabwe, President Bush has made a strong statement that I entirely endorse, calling for full democratic rights of the Zimbabwean people to be respected, and that elections that happen have got to be not only reported but be fair and be seen to be fair in the interest of democracy, not just in Zimbabwe but the reputation of democracy throughout Africa and the world.

We have repeated our common commitments in the fight against terrorism and will continue to work together at every level to defeat terrorism wherever it is. Iran continues to defy the will of the international community. And we are agreed on the need to strengthen the sanctions regime and ensure that these sanctions are effectively implemented. I will be talking to my European colleagues in the next few days about how we can move forward with both these issues throughout Europe. And we want to extend measures to include investment in liquefied national gas.

We also discussed climate change, following President Bush's announcement yesterday. And we agreed we must work internationally to secure progress at the G–8 and towards a post-Kyoto deal on climate change.

President, this is an ambitious agenda that we share together. It can only be achieved by closer cooperation that will happen over these next few months. I look forward to continuing to work with President Bush and his administration in taking it forward. And thank you for your warm welcome and hospitality.

President Bush. Yes, sir. We'll take two questions a side. Hunt. Terry Hunt [Associated Press].

Military Operations in Iraq/2008 Presidential Election

Q. Thank you, Mr. President. You said last week that Iraq was not an endless war, but others have called it an open-ended war and a war with no end in sight. Do you agree with those descriptions?

And, Mr. Prime Minister, you met today with the three candidates who want to succeed President Bush. Did you feel a special kinship with any one of them? And do you think that the transatlantic relationship will improve under the next President? Thank you.

President Bush. One of those three has a good chance of winning. [*Laughter*] Look, I'm interested in succeeding in Iraq. I mean, it's—this is a mission that is succeeding on the security front, it's getting better on the economic front, and it's improving on the political front.

And therefore, my statement has been, we'll have the troops there necessary to succeed. It's—it hasn't been easy; it's been difficult. It's taking longer than I anticipated, but it's worth it. A failure in Iraq would embolden Al Qaida, would give Al Qaida a huge victory, enable them to more likely establish safe haven in a wealthy country from which to launch attacks against us.

And a failure in Iraq would send a message to Iran that the United States and its allies were not intent upon making sure that they stay within the borders of their country and stop promoting terrorism through organizations like Hizballah. And they wouldn't take us seriously when it came to stopping their desires to have a nuclear weapon. Failure in Iraq would send a message to our friends: You can't count on America.

Success in Iraq will be a significant blow to both Al Qaida and Iran's ambitions. And it's worth it, in my judgment, to succeed against Al Qaida, the very country—the very group of people that attacked our country and those who would like to do so again, even on a more massive scale. And it's worth it to say to the theocrats in Iran that you must reform and that we're going to work to prevent you from having a nuclear weapon.

And so when it comes to troop levels and duration, my question is, what does it take to win? And General Petraeus thinks we can win with fewer troops. That's why I accepted the recommendation. General Petraeus and Ryan Crocker know that the troops were necessary to provide stability for the political progress to be made—that's being made and for the economy to improve. And so, so long as I'm the President, my measure of success is victory and success.

Q. [*Inaudible*]

President Bush. I've only got 10 more months left of the Presidency.

Prime Minister Brown. There's no artificial timetable here. Let's not forget that Iraq is now a democracy, that democratic rights have been restored to the Iraqi people, that we're now building schools and hospitals, seeing economic development. And I'm particularly referring to the area where we have responsibility, and that is Basra.

And let us also remember that there is progress in Iraqis now being able to take more control of their own affairs. And we're now in a situation where we've trained up 20,000 Iraqi forces, 22,000 Iraqi police men and women. We've got more to do in that area. And so our role in training the Iraqis, making it possible for them, as they did in the Basra operation, to assume more control of their own affairs is the way that we want to move from combat to overwatch in Iraq. And that's exactly what we're going to do.

And we're going to combine that with building up local government where there will be local government elections that will force militias to make a choice between the democratic process and armed insurrection. And at the same time, economic and social development will be pushed forward. And we are having a conference in London in the next few days where Iraqis and others will look at how we can move forward with the reconstruction and economic development of the area, so that people have a stake in the future, they have jobs, businesses are being created, and Iraq—and Iraqis are now running their own affairs.

It is—if I might ask—answer your second question, it is for Americans to decide who their President is going to be. I was delighted to meet the three Presidential candidates who remain in the field. What I was convinced of after talking to each of them—and talking about the issues that concern them and concern the world—is that the relationship between America and Britain will remain strong, remain steadfast. It will be one that will be able to rise to the challenges of the future. And I look forward to continuing my discussions with all three of them over the next few months.

President Bush. Yes, call on one of these——

Prime Minister Brown. Nick. I thought you usually called Nick. [*Laughter*]

Global Economy/British Government

President Bush. I was afraid Nick might ask me a question this time. [*Laughter*]

Q. The last thing I'd like to do is disappoint you, Mr. President. [*Laughter*]

President Bush. Nick, you need a hat, my boy, you need a hat. [*Laughter*]

Q. I thought of getting one saying "4 more years"——

President Bush. That's right. [*Laughter*]

Q. Mr. President, Prime Minister, Nick Robinson of BBC News. The Prime Minister has repeatedly said that Britain's economic difficulties started here in the United States. Do the solutions to them have to begin here as well?

And, Prime Minister, if I could ask you: You've got a very important agenda here on this trip, and yet at home, increasingly you're being criticized from within your own political party. What is going wrong in your party and Government, and what are you going to do about it?

Prime Minister Brown. I'm sticking to the job, and I'm getting on with the job. And I think people understand that there is a difficult situation around the world. We did have a credit crunch. It did mean that there were problems that started in the financial institutions in America, but these are problems now in Europe. There are problems in Britain. There are problems in every country of the world. And one of the issues that we're dealing with is that the issues that brought about the credit crunch are combined to rising food prices around the world, rising oil prices, and the threat of inflation in certain areas as well.

And I'm satisfied that the discussions we've had today with President Bush, yesterday in Wall Street—I'm meeting Ben Bernanke, the head of the Federal Reserve tomorrow—show the common ground we have in dealing with the issues ahead and in getting the economy to a position where markets are moving again, where growth is restored on an upward path, and where people can feel more safe and more secure about their jobs.

What matters to me is that people feel safe and secure about the future, about their prospects, and about their jobs. And that's why we will not hesitate to take any action that is necessary to keep the economy moving forward.

That's why I've outlined today measures that include what we can do in the housing market, what we can do to tackle food price rises, what we can do to tackle oil price rises. And that's why it's important that there is coordination across the Atlantic—indeed, coordination between all the major industrial powers—so that we can all contribute what each of us can in each continent to the process of restoring both confidence in the world economy and stability and growth. And we will continue to do that.

And as far as the domestic situation back home, is it? I will continue to do the right thing and do what is right for the British economy and the British people.

President Bush. We're in a rough patch right now. We had a pretty good run, as a matter of fact, had the most consecutive months of job growth in the country's history. And our housing market went soft, and it began to affect the financial markets.

So we've done a—taken a variety of steps. First, we're trying to help creditworthy people stay in their homes. I don't know what it's like in Britain, but here, the guy who gave you your mortgage generally doesn't own the paper anymore. They bundled it up and sold it somewhere else, and it's hard to find somebody to renegotiate with. So we put a system in place that helps creditworthy homeowners renegotiate. In other words, we want to help people stay in their homes.

I'm not particularly interested in bailing out lenders or speculators. But I am interested in helping hard-working Americans be able to find a way to stay in their homes. And it's been effective program.

Secondly, we worked with Congress on a progrowth package, over $150 billion of tax cuts, most of which will start hitting people's mailboxes and/or accounts in the second week of May. Some of the incentives in the progrowth package are for small businesses and businesses with accelerated appreciation, incentives to invest. And it's beginning to kick in a little bit, but the program hasn't really taken effect. I mean, the consumers don't have their checks yet. And we feel good that this will help our economy.

And finally, the Fed, which is independent from the White House, I might add, has taken some strong actions to enhance liquidity in the system. And I'm—we'll work with Congress on pieces of legislation that will actually help people, and I'll take a dim view of legislation that will make it harder for the economy to correct.

Yes, Toby [Tabassum Zakaria, Reuters].

Iran/Global Food Prices/Energy

Q. Thank you, Mr. President. Mr. President, Mr. ElBaradei of the IAEA said today that Iran's progress in developing uranium enrichment is slow, and that its centrifuges are older models. So how do you reconcile that with the U.S. view that Iran is a major nuclear threat?

President Bush. Yes.

Q. And, Prime Minister Brown, what concrete measures can Western governments take to address the soaring food prices? And do you think that there should be a rethinking of biofuel policy?

President Bush. Let me start on Iran here. If they learn how to enrich, it is knowledge which can be used to develop a nuclear weapon. They claimed that they've got a civilian program in place, that this is only for civilian purposes. If that's the case, why did they have a secret program? Why have they violated the IAEA? And so our objective is to, on the one hand, recognize they have a sovereign right to have civilian power by joining Russia and providing them with the fuel necessary to run their civilian nuclear facility, and then having them honor the agreements they've signed up to.

They have proven themselves to be untrustworthy. And you know, to say that, well, okay, it's okay to let them learn to enrich, and assume that that program and knowledge couldn't be transferred to a program, a military program, is, in my judgment, naive. And that is why the United States, in working with Britain and France and Germany and the United Nations Security Council, is all aiming to say to the Iranians: Verifiably suspend your program, and there's a better way forward for you.

And so it's—our diplomatic efforts are ongoing, and I appreciate the fact that Great Britain has been a great country to work with on this issue, because Gordon Brown seriously sees the threat, as do I. And now is the time to confront the threat. And I believe we can solve the problem diplomatically, and that is why we're working to verifiably suspend their enrichment.

Prime Minister Brown. Well, I make no apology for saying that we will extend sanctions, where possible, on Iran. Iran is in breach of the nonproliferation treaty. Iran has not told the truth to the international community about what its plans are. And that's why I'm talking to other European leaders about how we can extend European sanctions against Iran over the next period of time and to ensure that what sanctions are taken are effectively implemented and to monitor the effect on the Iranian regime where we see high inflation in Iran that is not properly disclosed by the regime and the effect that sanctions are actually beginning to have on that country.

So in the next few weeks, we want to extend the measures and sanctions to include investment in liquefied natural gas. I believe that sends another signal to the regime that what is happening is unacceptable. I'm pleased Secretary of State Rice is here with us today, because we will support her in the efforts that are being made, working with our other partners, including of course Russia and China, on this to make sure that Iran recognizes that it cannot ignore the international community and its obligations at its—without—with impunity.

You also asked about food prices. I'm calling a meeting in London in the next few days with the head of the World Food Programme to discuss what we can do to deal with the situation that is producing food riots in many countries, the lowest supplies of food for 30 years, shortages of food in many continents and many countries that are making people worried about whether, in some countries, they can actually feed the people.

Now, there are long and detailed causes for why this is happening. In Asia, people's demand for better and higher quality of food means that more agricultural production is needed. Subsidies in some areas have meant that there is less agricultural production in Africa than there should be. The World Food Programme is wanting and has issued an appeal for more support. And we and America have already offered more support to help feed people who are in the greatest of difficulty.

And in the long term, yes, we will look at biofuels, where we've withdrawn some of the subsidies for biofuels. We've got to get it absolutely right, but we're dealing with the environmental issue as well as dealing with the problem of increased production of food. And of course, we've got to increase, generally, our ability to produce more food for more of the world's people over the next few years.

So yes, we must act immediately, and yes, we must have a long-term plan. The world needs to have more supply of food to meet the rising demand of people around the world.

United Kingdom-U.S. Relations/British Economy

Q. Mr. President, I notice your warm words at the start there. Some people would suggest that the special relationship is a little less special than it was under Mr. Brown's predecessor. Is that true or false?

And, Prime Minister, a domestic question: I'm afraid——

President Bush. False. [*Laughter*]

Q. ——a member of your Government appears upset enough tonight about the abolition of the 10p rate to consider resigning. Isn't it time for you to at least consider unraveling that particular change?

President Bush. False, if you didn't hear me. Now, we got a great relationship. And it's—we're working on a variety of issues. Listen, our special relationship has been forged in common values in history, and we're making history together. And we're dealing with a lot of problems. The most severe problem, as far as I'm concerned, is the willingness of people to murder innocent people to achieve their political objectives. I mean, this is the fundamental threat facing civilization in the 21st century.

And Prime Minister Brown sees the threat. I mean, he had to live through the threat. And so it's—our relationship is very special, and it's—I'm confident future Presidents will keep it that way. There's just such a uniqueness in the relationship. That's not to say you can't have other friends, and we do. But this is a unique relationship, truly is. And I value my personal friendship as well as our—the relationship between our countries.

Look, if there wasn't a personal relationship, I wouldn't be inviting the man to a nice hamburger or something—[*laughter*]—well done, I might add.

Prime Minister Brown. I'm very proud to be here today to celebrate a special relationship. In 1941, Winston Churchill met Franklin Roosevelt and inaugurated what is the modern phase of that special relationship. And Churchill said at the time, "Same language, same hymns." He said, "Same ideals, same values, something big is happening." And what was big that happened was that never before has a relationship yielded so much in the 1940s against—in the fight against fascism and the cold war that then followed, where we worked together. In the fight against terrorism, we're—as Tony Blair said, we stand shoulder to shoulder with the American people and with President Bush. And I continue to stand shoulder to shoulder with him in rooting out terrorism wherever we find it, in any part of the world which puts freedom, democracy, and justice at risk.

And what I think is fascinating is that over the next few months, we will be developing that special relationship in new ways, a special relationship of peoples as well as of governments: more cooperation between our universities and more exchanges between young people in Britain and young people in America; more scientific cooperation; more cooperation in the fight against cancer, whether a joint project—the Human Genome Project—where we're working together; environmental action, where the institutes in Britain and America are agreeing this week to have more cooperation; and right across the board, as we take the English language, Britain and America, and make it a gift and then offer it to the rest of the world to make it possible for millions of people in different parts of the world to learn the English language.

So this is a special relationship not just of governments, but of peoples. And I look forward to its enhancement at all levels in the years to come. And I will work as hard as President Bush to make that relationship as strong and as enduring for the future.

You asked also about our economic policies. We have low inflation; therefore, we've brought down interest rates. We have low debt; therefore, we can afford to spend more.

We've made a major tax reform. And you ask about the 10p rate. Let's not forget that this April, the tax rate in Britain, the basic rate of tax is going down from 22 pence to 20 pence. We've virtually doubled child benefit for families over the last 10 years and raised it again this year, and we'll raise it next year. We're raising the child tax credit. We've got a new winter allowance addition for pensioners so that they can meet the fuel bills. And every area where the 10p rate has affected people, whether it be low-paid workers or pensioners or whether it be families with children, we have acted to see that we could do the best by people in our country.

Now, of course, a tax reform is a big thing, but when you're reducing the basic rate from 22 pence to 20 pence—the first time it's been achieved, the lowest tax rate, basic tax rate for 75 years—it is an important thing to do. And I'm satisfied that once people understand the scale of the good things that we have been able to do in reforming the tax system and making it better—and that we're tackling poverty, as they do in America, by introducing and increasing tax credits for the poorest people—then whatever questions people have about these changes can be answered.

Yes, they're important changes. They move the British economy forward. We have just seen this week that despite all the world difficulties, we have the highest employment rates at any time in our history. We have lower unemployment than at any time for 30 years. We have more vacancies in the economy, and that, combined with low inflation, a stable economy, lower interest rates—as we've managed to achieve over the last few weeks—means

that the British economy is well positioned to face the challenges of the future and will continue to be so.

And my answer to people who say what is happening domestically is, we are taking the right long-term decisions for the British economy, whether it's on nuclear power or on housing or on planning or infrastructure. And of course, at some times, people ask questions about whether you're doing the right thing. But we will see these long-term changes through, and these are the right long-term changes for Britain and for the British people.

President Bush. You guys want to sit out here for the afternoon or—[*laughter*]. Thank you, Mr. Prime Minister.

Prime Minister Brown. Thank you very much.

President Bush. Yes. Thank you.

Prime Minister Brown. Thank you.

NOTE: The President's news conference began at 2:43 p.m. in the Rose Garden at the White House. In his remarks, he referred to Gen. David H. Petraeus, USA, commanding general, Multi-National Force—Iraq. Prime Minister Brown referred to Executive Director Josette Sheeran of the World Food Programme; and former Prime Minister Tony Blair of the United Kingdom. A reporter referred to Director General Mohamed ElBaradei of the International Atomic Energy Agency.

Statement on the 25th Anniversary of the Terrorist Attack on the United States Embassy in Beirut, Lebanon
April 17, 2008

On April 18, 1983, the Islamic Jihad organization, known today as the terrorist group Hizballah, detonated a massive car bomb at the American Embassy in Beirut killing 52 people: 17 Americans and 35 Lebanese citizens. The Beirut Embassy bombing was at the time the most deadly

terrorist attack against the United States in our history. On the 25th anniversary of that bombing, we mourn for those who perished, and we honor the sacrifice of their family and friends and of the many who were wounded. This occasion is a timely reminder of the danger our diplomats, military personnel, and locally employed staff bear in their service to the United States.

Since the Beirut attack, we and citizens of many countries have suffered more attacks at the hands of Hizballah and other terrorists backed by the regimes in Tehran and Damascus, which use terror and violence against innocent civilians. All nations should condemn such brutal attacks and recognize that the purposeful targeting of civilians is immoral and unjustifiable.

The people of Lebanon have spent the better part of three decades living under the threat of violence, assassinations, and other forms of intimidation. Despite this, they and their leaders continue to work for a peaceful and democratic future, even as Syria, Iran, and their Lebanese proxies seek to undermine Lebanese democracy and institutions. The United States will continue to stand with the Lebanese Government and the Lebanese people as they struggle to preserve their hard-won sovereignty and independence, endeavor to provide justice for victims of terrorism and political violence, and continue to seek the election of a president committed to these principles.

Message to the Congress on Extending Generalized System of Preferences Benefits to the Solomon Islands
April 17, 2008

To the Congress of the United States:

In accordance with section 502(f)(1)(B) of the Trade Act of 1974, as amended (the "Act"), I am providing notification of my intent to add the Solomon Islands to the list of least-developed beneficiary developing countries under the Generalized System of Preferences (GSP) program. In Executive Order 12302 of April 1, 1981, the Solomon Islands was designated as a beneficiary developing country for purposes of the GSP program. After considering the criteria set forth in sections 501 and 502 of the Act, I have determined that it is appropriate to extend least-developed beneficiary developing country benefits to the Solomon Islands.

GEORGE W. BUSH

The White House,
April 17, 2008.

Remarks at the National Catholic Prayer Breakfast
April 18, 2008

Thank you very much. Good morning. Thank you. Please be seated. Thank you for the gracious welcome. Austin, thanks for your kind introduction. Thanks for giving me this unusual speaking opportunity. I understand that this program builds up to another speech. [*Laughter*] It's not every day you get to be the warmup act to the Holy Father. [*Laughter*] I am honored to be here. I do thank Austin for his leadership for the Catholic Prayer Breakfast. I thank the board of directors for having me. I thank Archbishop Gomez—*Tejano*—for being here. And I want to thank our— Bishop Finn, members of the clergy. Thank you for serving our country. Thank you for being men of faith.

I'm proud to be here with the Chief Justice of the Supreme Court, John Roberts. He's always looking for a free breakfast. [*Laughter*] I'm proud to be here with Members of the United States Senate and Congress. Thank you all for being here. Solicitor General Paul Clement is with us today, members of my administration, members of the diplomatic corps, and distinguished guests.

This has been a joyous week. It's been a joyous time for Catholics, and it wasn't such a bad week for Methodists either. [*Laughter*] You know, the excitement was just palpable. The streets were lined with people that were so thrilled that the Holy Father was here. And it was such a privilege to welcome this good man to the United States.

For those of you on the South Lawn ceremony—who saw the South Lawn ceremony live, it was—what an unbelievable—it was just such a special moment. And it was a special moment to be able to visit with the Holy Father in the Oval Office. He is a humble servant of God. He is a brilliant professor. He is a warm and generous soul.

He is courageous in the defense of fundamental truths. His Holiness believes that freedom is the Almighty's gift to every man, woman, and child on Earth. He understands that every person has value, or to use his words, "Each of us is willed, each of us is loved, [and] each of us is necessary."

The Holy Father strongly believes that to whom much is given, much is required. And he is a messenger of God's call to love our neighbors as we'd like to be loved ourselves.

I've seen how American Catholics are guided by these truths. One of the blessings of being the President is I get to see first-hand how people are motivated by the fundamental truths articulated by the Holy Father. I've watched you live out the Gospel

through countless acts of compassion and courage. I've joined with you in striving to heed the Scriptures' noble calling to see God's image in all mankind and to uphold the dignity of each human being on Earth.

Together, over the nearly 7½ years, we've worked to uphold the dignity of human life. Over the last years, my administration has put a stop to U.S. tax dollars funding foreign groups that perform or promote abortions. We've worked together to protect unborn victims of violence and to end the barbaric practice of partial-birth abortion. We have stood fast in our belief that promising medical advances can coexist with ethical medical practices. Last November, scientists discovered a way to reprogram adult skin cells to act like embryonic stem cells. This is a significant breakthrough, because science—scientists have found a path that can lead beyond the divisive debates of the past and extend the healing potential of medicine without destroying human life.

Together, we've worked to strengthen America's lifelines of learning, including our Nation's Catholic schools. The Catholic Church has a proud educational tradition dating back centuries, and one of the Holy Father's priorities has been maintaining this tradition in the United States. Today, America's Catholic schools serve thousands of students, both Catholic and non-Catholic, in some of our Nation's poorest neighborhoods. They help minority students narrow the achievement gap. They prepare children for lives of character and purpose and success. And yet these schools are closing at an alarming rate. Nearly 1,200 Catholic schools have shut their doors since the year 2000.

In my State of the Union Address, I proposed a new $300 million program called Pell Grants for Kids. And the reason I did so is cause I want to help low-income children in underperforming public schools be able to attend a private or parochial school of their choice. I am concerned about the loss of a major national asset, and that is the decline of Catholic schools, particularly in inner-city America. And to this end, next week we're having a White House Summit on Inner-City Children and Faith-Based Schools. And the purpose of the summit is to highlight the lack of educational options facing low-income urban students. And we're going to bring together educators and clergy and philanthropists and business leaders, all aiming to urge there to be reasonable legislation out of Congress and practical solutions to save these schools and, more importantly, to save the children.

And some of the people trying to save America's Catholic schools are here at this prayer breakfast, and I can't thank you enough for your efforts.

Together, we've worked to foster a culture of tolerance and peace. We believe that religion should be a source of understanding and grace, not a source of extremism and violence. On his visit and throughout his time as the Holy Father, the Pope has worked to foster interreligious dialogue and to heal the wounds of religious conflict. I strongly support the Pope's call for religious freedom around the world. I share his concern for Christians in the Middle East and his desire to see a peaceful and independent Lebanon. I respect his scholarship, which demonstrates that faith and reason can coexist. And I join him in praying for a world at peace, where Christians and Muslims and Jews, believers and nonbelievers, can live side by side. And I thank all of you here who work to make this vision a reality.

Together, we've worked to bring comfort to troubled souls. We believe that where hearts are burdened by destitution and disease and despair, we must answer with hope and love and faith. We know that [no] ° government program can answer the call like our armies of compassion can, but we also know that government programs can support and must support their work. And so I've been a strong believer in the

faith-based and community-based effort to bring healing and hope to people who wonder whether or not there's a bright tomorrow.

I don't know if you really realize this, but in 2006, 3,000 direct Federal grants totaling more than $2 billion were made to faith-based organizations, including many Catholic organizations. And the reason why is because Catholic organizations provide shelter to the homeless in very effective and loving ways. They tutor at-risk youth. They help children of prisoners while, at the same time, they work tirelessly to help prisoners get back on their feet. These groups seek out our society's most vulnerable and fulfill Christ's promise that "the last shall be first."

Abroad, Catholic organizations are a vital part, an integral part of our effort to fight hunger and disease from Latin America to the continent of Africa. In these places, Catholic groups have a hand in what some call the "Lazarus effect," where whole communities that once lay dying are brought back to life.

Oftentimes, people ask me, why is it that you're so focused on helping the hungry and diseased in strange parts of the world? My answer is, we're a wealthy enough nation to take care of people at home and to help those abroad. It is in our moral interests that when we find people suffering, that we do all we can do to help ease the burden. It's in our national interests—[*applause*]—and it's in our national interests that we defeat the ideologues of hate with an ideology of hope.

During these—as President, I've seen some of the great wonders of compassion as a result of our Catholic citizens. I've seen them here in Washington, with the Little Sisters of the Poor. Laura and I had the honor of visiting with the Little Sisters, and, you know, I was struck by how hard they worked to ask [for] ° money to care

---

° White House correction.

for the old and the sick so that the old and the sick don't have to beg for money.

I've seen the wonders of Catholic love on the Gulf Coast. I'm struck by the Catholic educators that, in the face of unprecedented disaster, worked night and day to provide good and stable schools for the children and provide comfort for, you know, people that were just wondering whether or not there was going to be a good tomorrow.

I've seen wonders on the Sea of Galilee during my recent trip to the Middle East. On a recent visit, my guides were joyful Catholic nuns who preserve the holy sites for all mankind, even as they struggle with the dangers to the region's Christian minority.

I've seen the wonders in Africa, in an emergency—in a hospital supported by PEPFAR. In February, I saw a 9-year-old girl who is HIV-positive who had lost both her parents to AIDS. And for the last year, Catholic Relief Services had been playing—had been paying for the girl to receive treatment at the clinic. I want to tell you what her grandmother said: "As a Muslim, I never imagined that a Catholic group would help me like that." She went on to say, "I am so grateful to the American people." And I am grateful for those who provide love and compassion in America and around the world.

This is a prayer breakfast, and this is a perfect place for me to say how much I appreciate the prayers of the people for me and Laura. I can't thank our fellow citizens enough for taking time out of their lives to lift us up for prayer. I have finally begun to understand the story of the calm and the rough seas, and I believe—I believe in my heart of hearts—that it's because of the prayers of my fellow citizens.

And today, with the trust in the Lord's wisdom and goodness, I offer prayers of my own for each gathered in the room, for the safety and success of the Holy Father's visit, and for God's continued blessings on our great land. Thank you.

NOTE: The President spoke at 8:33 a.m. at the Washington Hilton Hotel. In his remarks, he referred to D. Austin Ruse, cofounder and member of the board of directors, National Catholic Prayer Breakfast; Pope Benedict XVI; Most Reverend Jose H. Gomez, Archbishop of San Antonio, TX; and Most Reverend Robert W. Finn, Bishop of Kansas City—St. Joseph, MO. The Office of the Press Secretary also released a Spanish language transcript of these remarks.

Remarks at the America's Small Business Summit
April 18, 2008

Thanks for the warm welcome. I appreciate you being here in the Nation's Capital. I know most of you have come from out of town, which is good. It means you're brave souls to be here on tax week. [*Laughter*] The Holy Father was here as well, which is good, because it will take a miracle to keep the IRS out of your pocket. [*Laughter*]

It's been a fabulous week, and I do welcome you here. And I want to thank you for being dreamers and doers. One of the reasons I spend a lot of time talking about our small-business owners in America is because I truly believe you represent what makes America great, and it's the idea to have your own dreams, form your own businesses, create employment opportunities for citizens in the communities in which you live.

I grew up in Midland, and, gosh, I remember a lot of the—[*applause*]. There you go. I remember—it's not exactly the biggest city in America. On the other hand, it's the kind of place that you know the— you knew the local shop person or the— my friend Jackie Hanks's Uncle Brutus had the local grocery store. And it was just that fabric of the community was the small-business owners.

And so I'm so thrilled you're here. I really appreciate you giving me a chance to come and visit some—talk some policy with you. I appreciate Tom for introducing me—president and CEO of the U.S. Chamber. They do great work in Washington, DC, trying to make sure that there is no harm and that there is good policy in order to encourage people to invest and save.

I want to thank my friend Andy Card who's here. Thanks for being here, Andy— my Chief of Staff in the first 4 years of the Presidency, did a fabulous job. He's a decent, honorable man, a guy I'm proud to call friend.

You know, this summit's occurring at a very trying time for our economy. You know that better than anybody else. We had—we've had a good run. I mean, we had 52 months of uninterrupted job growth, and that's a record. And now our economy has slowed. It's—businesses are being squeezed by high energy prices and high health care prices. Workers and families are anxious on a variety of fronts, including mortgage—making mortgage bills and higher price for food and gasoline. It's a tough time for America.

The—you know, we saw this coming. Last I can remember is talking to our team last year, and they said, there's a slowdown coming. And so we took some action. And I do want to thank Members of the Congress and members of the chamber for working on a—what I believe is going to be a very effective progrowth stimulus package. Now, we actually showed that it's possible for Republicans and Democrats to set aside the political wrangling that takes place here in Washington and focus on what's best for the American people.

And I want to describe this package to you and to remind our fellow citizens that soon, a significant amount of money will be coming in their mailboxes, which is going to help the small-business sector. It's going to help families, and it's going to help the small-business sector, which helps the American economy. After all, you create 70 percent of the new jobs in America. And so the first thing that's going to happen is, is that the consumers will get a boost, in that tax rebates will be sent out to about 130 million American households. Now, these rebates will return up to $600 for individuals, $1,200 for married couples, and $300 per child. When the rebates start to go out in a couple of weeks—which they haven't started to go out yet; Secretary Paulson tells me by the second week of May, the money is going to start moving— a family of four could receive a tax rebate up to $1,800.

Now, here in Washington, that's like— people say, that's not very much money. Well, if you're out there worrying about your—about meeting bills or saving for your kids' education, that's a lot of money. And the purpose is to make a difference to the families and to encourage them and give them confidence so they can go spend, you know, buy products from you.

Secondly, the stimulus package provides incentives for business to invest in new plant and equipment and new technologies. Entrepreneurs like yourself should use this incentive to expand your business; it's the whole purpose of it. And the reason why we're trying to provide incentives for businesses, both large and small, is because when you have the incentive to go purchase a piece of equipment, somebody has got to make the equipment. It has a ripple effect throughout the economy. And this stimulus package has been in place for about 2 months, and small businesses are beginning to use it.

I had the honor of meeting Darlene Miller. You may know Darlene. She's from a—she's got a manufacturing concern in Minnesota called Permac Industries. She is—bought the company 14 years ago, and since then, she's expanded it dramatically. She's nearly doubled her manufacturing space last year, and now she needs some equipment to fill the space. And so thanks to the stimulus package, she told me she's going to purchase much of that equipment this year instead of spacing it out over time. In other words, the incentives have encouraged Darlene to make a purchase this year. She expects these investments to expand manufacturing capacity by 25 percent, and then she plans to hire at least five more workers.

The reason I bring up this example is this how—this is how incentives work. Darlene was incented—received an incentive to purchase machinery, to fill some space, to make sure she becomes more competitive. And in so doing, it not only causes somebody else to have to make the machinery, but she's now going to hire more people. She also had a pretty good achievement at—and she received another good achievement, I understand. After all, she's the Chamber of Commerce's National Small Business Owner of the Year.

And I met a guy named Tom Sawner. Now, he's an old fighter pilot, which means there's no wall he can run through. He's a doer, an achiever, and he's got him a small business called Educational Options. And he provides web-based curricula to schools all across the country. He is purchasing new computers, servers, routers, and cars to expand his business because of the stimulus package, because of the incentives.

He said the stimulus plan has helped give him the confidence to expand his workforce. This year, so far, he has hired four new employees, and he plans to bring on a dozen more. In his words, he said that the stimulus package has made a huge difference. And the stimulus package is making a huge difference because small-business owners, like the two I mentioned, are taking advantage of the stimulus plan to boost investment, which then helps boost jobs.

It's going to take awhile for these changes to be reflected in our economy. The advisers—economic advisers and many outside experts believe that much of the impact of the stimulus will be felt starting in the third quarter, which begins in July. That's what the experts say. There should be no doubt in anybody's mind, though, that we'll recover from this slowdown. And we're going to bounce back strong, and the small businesses of America are going to lead the way.

We designed this package so it would be temporary and robust enough to have an effect. And so we need to be thinking in the longer term as well. And one way that—I mean, one thing Congress has got to understand is that there is—what small-business owners don't need is uncertainty. And one place where there's uncertainty is in the Tax Code, as well as trade. And I want to spend some time on taxes and trade today.

We've—as Tom mentioned, we've cut taxes. And I truly believe in the philosophy that you can spend your own money better than the government can. Obviously, there's a—[*applause*]—we've got needs in Washington, DC. We're fighting a war. We want to make sure our troops are well funded. We want to take care of those who can't help themselves. I mean, there's serious needs. But I also know that the more money that's available in Washington, the more people will figure out how to spend it.

And I truly believe what I mean: I think it's important for government to trust the collective wisdom of the American people. And that's why I was such a strong believer in tax relief. I also knew that we needed to make sure you had more money in your treasuries to help us get out of a recession, to recover from war and corporate scandal and natural disasters.

The—I'm also confident a lot of people in America may have forgotten what it was like before the tax relief. And the problem is, is that we're on schedule for there to be an unpleasant reminder of what it was like before tax relief, because unless Congress acts, almost all the tax relief we delivered will expire in 2010. If Congress were to let this happen, tax rates will rise across the board, the marriage penalty will return in full force, the child tax credit will be cut in half, and every income payer—income tax payer in America will receive a tax hike.

What I don't think a lot of people in Washington fully understand is that small-business owners are going to bear a heavy burden if the tax rates go back up. And the reason why is, is that most small-business owners are subchapter S corporations or partnerships or LLCs that pay their business taxes at individual rates. So if the individual rates go up, it directly affects millions of small businesses in America.

Taxes on capital gains and dividends would go up, which would discourage the investment you need to expand. And the death tax would come back to life. The—overall, it is estimated that small-business owners would face an average tax increase of more than $4,000 per year. That would stifle enterprise; it would hurt workers. The last thing small-business owners need is higher taxes. I believe strongly that to make sure this economy recovers and stays strong, there needs to be certainty in the Tax Code. And the best way for Congress to make sure there's certainty is to make the tax relief we passed permanent.

I want to talk—spend a little time on trade. Last year—and this is important for you to understand—last year, exports accounted for more than 40 percent of our growth. This is a critical contribution to our economy at any time, but especially now. With the economy slowing, exports are providing a valuable contribution to

economic activity. And Congress has an opportunity to expand access to key export markets.

In other words, there's an opportunity for Congress to say that let's continue to have this kind of economic vitality, as a result of exports, permeate throughout our economy. And they've got an opportunity with—to vote on trade agreements with three democratic allies and friends: Colombia, Panama, and South Korea.

I want to spend some time talking about Colombia today because this is the first of these agreements to be considered. Unfortunately, leaders on Capitol Hill seem to have put special interests ahead of the economic and strategic interests of our Nation, because the Speaker of the House recently changed House rules in the middle of the game so she can put off a vote on the Colombia free trade agreement. If this decision stands, it will kill the agreement, and American small-business owners and workers will likely be hurt the most.

And here's why. Almost all of Colombia's exports to the United States enter our country duty free, but the 9,000 American businesses that export to Colombia, including 8,000 small and midsized firms, face substantial tariffs on their products. The Congress has passed laws in the past that enable Colombian goods to come here duty free; the vast majority of our products face taxes to go into their countries. And most of the people facing those taxes are small-business owners.

And this problem is easy to resolve. The free trade agreement would immediately eliminate most tariffs on American exports to Colombia. That's what the free trade agreement does. My attitude is, just treat us the way we treat you. All we want to do is have a level playing field in which to compete. By level the playing field—by leveling the playing field, American products would be more competitive in Colombia, and it would help American businesses.

It turns out that if you're an exporter, your workers are likely to get paid more money. It's good for American workers to be working for companies that export into other markets, and it's good for small businesses. Yet after 500 days that we signed the agreement with Colombia, the one-sided trading relationship remains in place because the Congress has failed to act.

The obstruction has another consequence. Congress is signaling to a watching hemisphere—people in the hemisphere, our own neighborhood, are watching to see how the United States Congress reacts to our friends. They're wondering whether or not America can be trusted to support our friends.

And we've got a friend in President Uribe of Colombia. He's a steadfast ally. He has transformed his country from the brink of a failing state to a stable democracy with a growing economy. He has partnered with the United States of America in the fight against drugs and terror. He has responded to virtually every request of the United States Congress, including revising the free trade agreement to include some of the most rigorous labor and environmental protections in history. He's done all this while under violent assault from a terrorist organization called FARC, and he's done all this facing intimidation from anti-American regimes in the region.

It's hard to imagine any leader in the world who has proven more worthy of our support and friendship. Yet Congress's response is to complain that Colombia still has not done enough. In particular, some Members of Congress have charged that the Colombian Government is not doing enough to prevent violence against unionists. Well, President Uribe has taken historic measures to reduce violence against unionists. As a results, according to the Colombian Government, Colombian unionists are now less likely to be homicide victims than members of the general population. And as President Uribe has made clear, one of the best ways to improve security

even further is to provide more jobs, which is exactly what a free trade agreement will do. By rejecting this agreement after all Colombia has done, leaders in Congress would send a terrible message.

They had an editorial in the Washington Post the other day that summed up Congress's message this way: "Drop Dead, Colombia." Well, the congressional leadership's decision to turn its back on Colombia is especially hypocritical because Democrats are often the loudest voices for more diplomacy and greater sensitivity to our allies. The Colombia agreement is a textbook example of this approach, and yet the Speaker chose to use unprecedented tactics to kill it.

Leaders in Congress have made a serious error. It's a serious error for economic reasons, and it's a serious error for security reasons. They have—it's not too late, however, for them to get it right. This week, a long list of senior officials from Democratic administrations and Democrats from previous Congresses signed a letter urging Congress to approve this agreement this year. And they wrote, "We feel that the treaty should be considered as soon as possible and that any obstacles be quickly and amicably resolved." I couldn't agree more. I urge the leaders in Congress to reconsider their position and recognize the stakes at hand and approve the Colombia agreement as soon as possible.

There are other things we can do to help small businesses weather the difficult time and, equally importantly, remain competitive for a long time to come. One, Congress should work to make health care more affordable and available by expanding health savings accounts, by confronting junk medical lawsuits that are running good doctors out of practice and running up the cost of health care for small businesses, allowing businesses—small businesses to pool together across State lines—it's called association health plans—across State lines to get the same discounts on health insurance that big businesses get.

We're working with Congress, and I've been working with the folks in my administration, to help people who are creditworthy stay in their homes. There's a—I think it's very important that we not help speculators, but there are a lot of people that are wondering how to renegotiate their mortgage. I've explained to people, when I bought my first home in Midland, there was actually things such as savings and loans. And the person that actually lent the money owned the note. Well, these days, the people who are lending the money don't own the notes, and so it's difficult if you want to renegotiate to figure out who to renegotiate with.

And so we've set up a plan called the HOPE NOW Alliance to help creditworthy homeowners renegotiate so they can deal with these reset mortgages and stay in their homes. We want people owning their home. We want people owning a businesses; we want people owning their own homes. We want to help them stay. And Congress can help by passing responsible legislation that modernizes the Federal Housing Administration, reforms Fannie Mae and Freddie Mac, allows State housing agencies to issue tax-free bonds to refinance subprime mortgages. There's a way to help people.

Congress ought to help and, you know, prepare the workforce for the 21st century. One of the concerns of Congress is that trade causes people to lose jobs. I understand that concern. That's why I'm a supporter of trade adjustment assistance. Congress needs to work with leaders of both parties to get a good trade adjustment assistance bill to my desk that I can sign into law.

I also strongly believe that we want to make sure the No Child Left Behind Act continues to work. It's a—you measure every day; that's why you're successful businesspeople. I mean, you know what your business is doing. I believe we ought to extend that same principle to our public schools and ask a simple question: Can a child read at grade level? And in order to determine that, that's why you measure. And if the answer is yes, we all say, great. If the answer is no, the next question ought to be, then what are you going to do about it? And so the principle behind the No Child Left Behind Act is to set high standards, believe every child can learn, and measure to see if we're getting results. And Congress need not weaken such a good piece of legislation.

And finally, one issue that you need to be aware of is that—is the issue on secret ballots when it comes to allowing workers to vote their conscience on whether to form a union or to remain unaffiliated. Congress is now considering—it passed out of the House, and the Senate, I'm told, is going to take this up. And I just want to put this on our collective radar screens, that Congress is considering card check legislation that would strip workers of a fundamental right—that is the right for secret ballot as to—whether to unionize or not. This bill would expose workers to intimidation, it violates the principles of our democracy, and if it were to reach my desk, I will veto it.

The purpose of good policy in Washington should be to unleash the entrepreneurial spirit of the country. You can't make somebody an entrepreneur from government, but you can create an environment which encourages risk-taking and enables people to keep more of what they earn, lets somebody stay more in the shop than in the courthouse, helps people help their workers.

We—and so some of the policies that I've just outlined are all aimed at creating an environment that is conducive to entrepreneurship. I was—I see all kinds of amazing things when I'm President; I read about them, of course. I love meeting with our entrepreneurs, and I love hearing the stories about how businesses get started. And a lot of times, believe it or not, there is—as I'm sure you know, that they all happen, like, at a kitchen table. And sure enough, out of that simple idea and hard work—because I understand as well as anybody how hard it is to build a small business. I mean, it's not—it takes a lot of time and a lot of effort and a lot of focus and patient spouses and sometimes spouses actually watching the money to make sure the other spouse doesn't blow it. [*Laughter*]

So how about this guy. He is a guy who paid his way through college, and he—by diving into water hazards and selling the golf balls that he found. And evidently, he had this dream, and so he graduated and decided to take his idea and make it into an Internet golf shop. And it's a prosperous business, and he's creating jobs.

Now, he didn't need a government program to figure out how to do that, it's his ingenuity. It was his desires to not only pay his own college education but then to convert that into something that would be good for consumers—obviously, if it wasn't good for consumers, he wouldn't have much of a business history—good for the people he's employed. And all he needed

was the ability to dream and willingness to work hard. And this is what defines our country. It's the spirit that makes America so unique and so great. And that spirit is found in the room.

And our—the role of government is to never stifle that spirit, is to encourage the spirit, reward the spirit, and always pay— and always remind our citizens that we are a vibrant and prosperous and hopeful nation, because we are a land blessed with vibrant and hopeful people.

God bless you, and thanks for letting me come by.

NOTE: The President spoke at 11:12 a.m. at the Renaissance Washington, DC Hotel. In his remarks, he referred to Pope Benedict XVI; Thomas J. Donohue, president and chief executive officer, U.S. Chamber of Commerce; Darlene M. Miller, president and chief executive officer, Permac Industries; and Thomas E. Sawner, president and chief executive officer, Educational Options, Inc.

Remarks on the Nomination of Steven C. Preston To Be Secretary of Housing and Urban Development
April 18, 2008

Thank you all. Please be seated. Welcome.

A few weeks ago, my dear friend Alphonso Jackson informed me of his decision to step down as the Secretary of Housing and Urban Development. Secretary Jackson is one of the longest serving members of my administration. I know him well. He's a decent man, he's a dedicated man, and he's a compassionate man. He's worked tirelessly at HUD to help America's homeowners. He has transformed a lot of lives, and America is a better place because of your service. I wish you and Marcia all the very best as you head back to Texas. I'll be right behind you. [*Laughter*]

The Department requires strong leadership at a time when our housing market is experiencing a period of challenge and uncertainty. In seeking to fill this important Cabinet post, I looked for a leader with an impressive background in finance, someone who understands the important role the housing market plays in the broader economy. I sought a reformer who would act aggressively to help Americans obtain affordable mortgages, and I sought a—and be able to keep their homes. I sought a consensus builder who's earned the respect of Republicans and Democrats, who can get things done.

I found these qualities and much more in Steve Preston. Steve is a strong executive with a quarter century of management experience. He's had senior leadership roles at two multibillion-dollar corporations and in the financial services industry. He understands the free enterprise system from every angle.

As the head of the Small Business Administration, Steve has advanced a reform agenda that made the agency more accountable, more effective, and more responsive. Under his leadership, America's entrepreneurs have received improved access to Federal assistance as well as educational resources. Under his leadership, the SBA has increased its focus on supporting business development in areas with high unemployment and poverty rates. And under his leadership, agency efficiency's improved, and America's small-business community has found a trusted friend and partner.

During his tenure at SBA, Steve has managed loan guarantee programs that are similar in structure to those run by the Federal Housing Administration, and he's made these programs run very effectively. When Steve took the reins at the SBA, he streamlined the agency's efforts to disburse loans to small businesses and homeowners devastated by Hurricane Katrina. He matched every loan applicant with a case manager to provide the compassion and expertise that applicants needed to navigate the loan process.

Within months of Steve's reforms, the backlog of loans fell 80 percent and response times improved by 90 percent. Today, more than $6 billion in SBA loans are helping more than 160,000 Gulf Coast families rebuild their homes, their businesses, and their lives.

Steve Preston is an experienced manager who knows what to do. He knows how to tackle a problem, devise a solution, and get results. That's exactly the kind of leadership I was looking for. And that's why I'm going to send his name up to the United States Senate to be the Department's Secretary.

He will play a central role in helping address our Nation's housing challenges. He'll work with Members of Congress to advance responsible legislation that will help millions of American homeowners. He will be entrusted with one of the most rewarding jobs in the Federal Government: helping our fellow Americans have a place to call a home.

These are important responsibilities, and I'm confident I picked the right person for the job. He's a hard-working, dedicated professional. In fact, he was confirmed to his current post by the United States Senate without a single vote in opposition. Let's hope the streak continues. [*Laughter*]

I want to thank Deputy Secretary Roy Bernardi. I appreciate very much your willingness to step forward to serve the country as well as to serve as Acting Secretary of HUD. And I thank you for keeping that position until Steve is confirmed.

I also want to thank Steve's family: Molly, as well as Anna, Madeleine, Gibson, Eleanor, and Steve, Jr. Thank you all for coming to the White House to witness this very important moment.

I ask the Senate to quickly consider Steve Preston and to ratify him on a timely basis. Congratulations.

NOTE: The President spoke at 11:57 a.m. in the Roosevelt Room at the White House. The transcript released by the Office of the Press Secretary also included the remarks of Secretary-designate Preston.

Statement on the Appointment of Douglas V. O'Dell, Jr., as Federal Coordinator of the Office of Gulf Coast Rebuilding
April 18, 2008

Today I am pleased to select Major General Doug O'Dell to serve as Coordinator of Federal support for the recovery and rebuilding of the Gulf Coast.

General O'Dell is an innovative problem-solver with a wealth of experience in helping the people of the Gulf Coast region. As the commanding general of the 4th Marine Division in New Orleans in the aftermath of Hurricane Katrina, he employed over 2,700 marines and sailors to evacuate thousands of civilians, deliver essential cargo, and restore basic functions in more than 30 buildings. His strategic judgment during Hurricane Rita enabled troops to deliver relief almost immediately after the storm. He has earned the trust of many in the region, including State and local officials, and is the right person for this important job.

General O'Dell understands the progress made in the Gulf Coast region, the important work ahead, and the great spirit of the people who call that region home. He will build on the efforts of Don Powell to help the people of the region continue to rebuild their lives and their communities. I also want to thank Paul Conway for doing a fine job as Interim Coordinator.

I am pleased to announce as well that I have signed an Executive order to extend the Federal Coordinator position until February 28, 2009. This extension will ensure a seamless transition into the next administration so that the Federal Government can continue to deliver effective, integrated, and responsible support to the people of the Gulf Coast region.

Message on the Observance of Passover, 5768
April 18, 2008

Then Moses said to the people, "Commemorate this day, the day you came out of Egypt, out of the land of slavery, because the Lord brought you out of it with a mighty hand."

EXODUS 13:3

I send greetings to those observing Passover.

More than 3,000 years ago, God liberated the Children of Israel from the bondage of Egypt and led them on a journey towards the Promised Land. During the holy days of Passover, Jews around the world celebrate this deliverance from oppression and give thanks to a loving God for His many blessings. Passover is an opportunity for Jewish families and friends to gather to read the Haggadah, share the Seder meal, and remember God's mercy through song and prayer. This eight-day observance brings a message of hope and freedom to the Jewish people.

Laura and I send our best wishes for a joyous Passover.

GEORGE W. BUSH

NOTE: An original was not available for verification of the content of this message.

The President's Radio Address
April 19, 2008

Good morning. Next week, I will be hosting the North American Leaders' Summit in New Orleans. This event will give me an opportunity to meet with Canadian Prime Minister Stephen Harper and Mexican President Felipe Calderon to discuss some of the most significant issues facing our hemisphere and the world.

One of the issues I will be discussing with these leaders is the importance of expanding trade in our hemisphere. Recently, I sent Congress an agreement that would expand America's access to markets in Colombia. Unfortunately, the Speaker of the House has chosen to block the Colombia free trade agreement instead of giving it an up-or-down vote that Congress committed to. Her action is unprecedented and extremely unfortunate. I hope that the Speaker will change her mind. If she does not, the agreement will be dead. And this will be bad for American workers and bad for America's national security.

And here is why. Today, almost all of Colombia's exports to the United States enter duty free. But the 9,000 American businesses that export to Colombia, including nearly 8,000 small and midsized firms, face significant tariffs on their products. The situation is completely one sided. Our markets are open to Colombian products, but barriers that make it harder to sell American goods in Colombia remain. If the free trade agreement were implemented, however, most of Colombia's tariffs on American goods would be eliminated immediately.

There's also a strategic imperative to approve the agreement. By obstructing this agreement, Congress is signaling to a watching hemisphere that America cannot be trusted to support its friends. Over the past 6 years, Colombia's President Uribe has been a steadfast ally of the United States. He's transformed his country from a near-failed state to a stable democracy with a growing economy. He has partnered with America in the fight against drugs and terror. And he has addressed virtually every one of Congress's concerns, including revising the free trade agreement to include some of the most rigorous labor and environmental protections in history.

He has done all this while his country is under violent assault from a terrorist organization and facing constant intimidation from anti-American regimes in the region. As Canada's Prime Minister Harper has said, "If the U.S. turns its back on its friends in Colombia, this will set back our cause far more than any Latin American dictator could hope to achieve."

Leaders in Congress have made a serious error, but it is not too late to get it right. This week, a long list of senior officials from Democratic administrations and Democrats from previous Congresses signed a letter urging Congress to approve the agreement this year. They wrote, quote, "We feel that the treaty should be considered as soon as possible and that any obstacles should be quickly and amicably resolved." I strongly agree. I believe that if the Speaker allows a vote on the merits, a majority of the House of Representatives will approve the trade agreement. So I urge leaders in Congress to reconsider their position, recognize the stakes at hand, and approve the Colombia agreement as soon as possible.

Thank you for listening.

NOTE: The address was recorded at 7:35 a.m. on April 18 in the Cabinet Room at the White House for broadcast at 10:06 a.m. on April 19. The transcript was made available by the Office of the Press Secretary on April 18, but was embargoed for release until the broadcast. The Office of the Press Secretary also released a Spanish language transcript of this address.

The President's News Conference With President Lee Myung-bak of South Korea at Camp David, Maryland
April 19, 2008

President Bush. Welcome. We're glad you're here, Mr. President, and we're glad you brought Mrs. Kim. We had a wonderful dinner last night and looking forward to having lunch too today.

We've had great visits. And this is an important visit for me to get to know you. I heard about your background. I admire your strength of character. And this is an important visit to strengthen the relationship between our two countries, and I believe we have done so.

President Lee. Thank you.

President Bush. President Lee is the first Korean President to visit Camp David. And I don't know if the American citizens understand your nickname.

President Lee. Yes.

President Bush. You're known as the Bulldozer. [*Laughter*] He said to make sure that it was a bulldozer with a computer. [*Laughter*] And the reason why is that this is a man who takes on big challenges, and he doesn't let obstacles get in the way. I like his spirit, I like his candor, and I like his optimistic vision. But most of all, I really appreciate his values.

A good relationship is based upon common values, and our countries share common values, values of the rights of each individual to live in a free society. We believe in human dignity and justice.

Now, we discussed a variety of issues. We talked about our defense cooperation. In 2004, our nations began an alliance transformation that has involved realigning U.S. forces in Korea and relocating some of them from the peninsula. We're in constant touch, and we're constantly reas-

sessing our needs. And we have reaffirmed our need to remain in close dialogue. And we reached an agreement to maintain the current U.S. troop level on the peninsula. This is a mutual agreement that benefits both our nations and will strengthen our alliance, and Secretary Gates and Defense Minister Lee will coordinate its implementation.

Korea has asked that—to upgrade its foreign military sales status with the United States and to have the same access to U.S. military technologies as NATO and other key allies. And I strongly support this request and have instructed Secretaries Rice and Gates to work with the Congress to get this done.

Yesterday our nations signed a memorandum of understanding on security improvements necessary for Korea to enter the Visa Waiver Program. This was a very important issue for the President.

President Lee. Yes. Sure.

President Bush. We spent a lot of time talking about this issue. These security enhancements put Korea on the path toward visa-free travel to the United States for its people. We promised that both sides will work hard on this issue so that Koreans will be visiting the United States under the Visa Waiver Program before this year ends.

The United States and Korea are working to improve security and advance freedom in the Asia-Pacific region. Together with China, Russia, and Japan, our nations are pressing North Korea to fulfill its obligations to abandon its nuclear weapons program. Thanks to the six-party framework,

North Korea has begun disabling the plutonium production facilities at Yongbyon. And now North Korea must fulfill its other obligations: provide a full declaration of its nuclear programs and proliferation activities in a verifiable way.

President Lee and I discussed our mutual concern for the human condition in North Korea. I mean, we are—our hearts break when we hear these stories of families that have been torn apart or people being subjected to harsh work camps because of their beliefs. We believe in basic rights, and we believe those rights ought to be extended to the people of North Korea.

We're also thankful for the Koreans' contributions to the young democracies, whether it be Afghanistan or Iraq or Lebanon. And we want to thank you and your people, Mr. President, for those sacrifices.

And then, of course, we talked about our economy. As a former CEO, President Lee understands the importance of trade. First of all, I want to thank you, Mr. President, and I appreciate your decision to reopen the Korean market to American beef, consistent with international standards. This is good news for Korean consumers, and it's good news for American beef producers. As a matter of fact, we had some good American beef last night for dinner. [*Laughter*]

Now, our United States Congress must reject protectionism. It must not turn its back on a friend and ally like Korea and must approve the free trade agreement with Korea this year. So the President was wondering—you see, he's been reading about the decision by our Speaker that effectively killed the Colombia free trade agreement, unless, of course, she gives us a date certain of when there will be a vote. He wonders if this protectionist sentiment is such that it will cause me, for example, not to continue to fight for free and fair trade.

I assured him that the Korea trade agreement is a priority of this administration,

and I assured him that we will press hard with the United States Congress. It's in our country's interests that we approve this agreement, Mr. President. It's in our interests that we stand with our friends and allies. And it's in the interests of the world that we complete the Doha negotiations for the WTO. We spent some time discussing that as well.

And then—and finally, we talked about our mutual desire to have a rational, practical approach to international climate—the international climate issue of global warming. I mean, it's—how can you possibly have an international agreement that's effective unless countries like China and India are not full participants? And that's why I assured him this major economies meeting that's taking place in Paris—I assured him I meant what I said in my speech in the Rose Garden, and that, hopefully, by the time we get to G–8, there's a serious effort by all major economies to become active participants in a effective strategy to deal with this issue.

So we had a great discussion. Really appreciate you coming. And, Mr. President, the podium is yours.

President Lee. Thank you very much, Mr. President. First of all, thank you for inviting me and my wife to this beautiful place called Camp David. I would like to extend my thanks to you, President Bush and Mrs. Laura Bush, for their invitation. And I was warmly welcomed by the American people. If I were to have known I was going to get this warm hospitality, I should have come earlier. [*Laughter*]

Again, I would like to extend my most sincere gratitude to you, Mr. President. And also, we had a very productive discussion. We had a very open and frank discussion. And I believe that today's meeting was very constructive, and I'm very thankful for having this meeting, Mr. President.

The Korea-U.S. alliance was pivotal in ensuring peace and stability of the Korean Peninsula but also that of Northeast Asia. Now, as the international situation as well as the economic and security situation change dramatically, our alliance is also called upon to undergo new changes. And so in order to effectively respond to these need for change, President Bush and I agreed to develop our alliance into an alliance based on freedom and democracy, human rights, and the principle of market economy, otherwise known as the 21st-century strategic alliance, something that will contribute to global peace and security as well.

Furthermore, we both agreed to—based on such mutual understanding and common ideas—to discuss specific ways to realize our vision for this strategic alliance. So we'll discuss this when President Bush visits Korea later on this year.

Just a while ago, President Bush mentioned as for the U.S. forces in Korea, he decided to maintain the current troop levels in Korea. Is that right, Mr. President?

President Bush. Yes, that's an accurate statement.

President Lee. Both of us reaffirmed once again that under no circumstances would we allow North Korea to possess nuclear weapons. Also, we agreed to work together closely within the six-party talks so that North Korea can fully and completely give up all their nuclear weapons program as soon as possible.

Korea and the United States do not harbor any hostile intent towards North Korea. We both agreed to work together to help North Korea escape international isolation and to improve the lives of the North Korean people. President Bush supported our policy towards North Korea, including our denuclearization opening 3000 policy, and also said that the United States will continue to dialogue—seek ways to promote dialogue in exchange with North Korea.

Both President Bush and I agreed that the passage of the KORUS FTA will benefit not only our two economies but also act as a catalyst to substantially improve exchange and cooperation in all areas between our two countries. And so we agreed

to work closely together for the speedy ratification of the KORUS FTA. And, Mr. President, he agreed to work very closely and to convince the United States Congress to pass the KORUS FTA by the end of this year. I would like to thank you for that.

Among the achievements of my visit to the United States—there were a lot of difficulties for Koreans to visit the United States. Most of all, the difficulty they faced was due to the difficulty in getting visas to enter the United States. However, the Republic of Korea has signed a memorandum of understanding for—to take part in the Visa Waiver Program, and we agreed to implement this by the end of this year. Once that happens, our cultural exchange as well as our economic exchange and the exchange in many areas will expand, and I have high hopes for that.

At the same time, President Bush and I agreed to expand exchange programs for our youth and students, which will ensure a brighter future for our bilateral ties.

We reaffirmed that nuclear nonproliferation and the promotion of democracy and human rights are all a vital component in making our world a better, safer place. In this regard, in order to ensure sustainable development, we agreed to work closely on the issues of climate change and energy securities, matters which are very serious and concerns us all.

During the summit meeting today, I was very heartened to hear that the United States and President Bush personally had a very strong interest in fighting global warming and climate change. That's a very important decision, and I hope that the United States—and I have confidence that the United States will take a leading role in this issue, and I have confidence Mr. President Bush will do that as well.

I invited President Bush and Mrs. Laura Bush to visit Korea this summer, and I'm pleased to note that President Bush agreed and readily accepted to come visit Korea with Mrs. Bush.

Once again, today's meeting was an opportunity for us to reaffirm our mutual trust, and that we agreed to work together to solve issues not only of the peninsula but to work closely and cooperate with issues of global concern.

I'm very happy with the results of today's meeting. And we will work very closely together to see the complete dismantlement of the nuclear weapons program of North Korea, and we will work closely within the six-party talks framework. And we must see the satisfactory conclusion, which will lead to helping the North Korean people lead better lives with dignity.

Once again, Mr. President, I'm very happy to have met you, Mr. President, as well as Mrs. Laura Bush. And thank you for the warm hospitality extended to me and my delegation by the people of America. We will work closely together with a future-oriented mind. And I promise you I will do my very best, Mr. President.

President Bush. Thank you. We'll do two questions a side.

North Korea

Q. I have the same question for both of you.

President Bush. I warned him.

Q. [*Inaudible*]—not two questions.

President Bush. Well, no, it's—[*laughter*].

Q. Isn't—first to President Bush—isn't scaling back demands about what the— North Korea has to declare giving in to a country that has repeatedly demonstrated that it can't be trusted? Former U.N. Ambassador Bolton has called it a complete collapse in the deal, and your critics are saying that you're selling out to get an agreement. Why is it not?

President Bush. Look, we're going to make a judgment as to whether North Korea has met its obligations to account for its nuclear program and activities, as well as meet its obligations to disable its reactor. In other words, we'll see. The burden of proof is there. We've laid out— they've made some promises, and we'll

make a judgment as to whether they met those promises. And then we and our partners will take a look at North Korea's full declaration to determine whether or not the activities they promised they could do could be verified. And then we'll make a judgment of our own as to whether or not—you know, we'll—about our own obligations.

Q. So you're not—[*inaudible*]—about what you're asking them?

President Bush. You know, there's all kinds of rumors about what is happening and what's not happening. Obviously, I'm not going to accept a deal that doesn't advance the interests of the region. The whole objective of the six-party talks and framework is to get them to disclose their weapons programs, is to get them to dismantle their plutonium processing, is to get them to talk about activities, nuclear activities. And we'll make a judgment as to whether or not they do that. But somehow, people are precluding—you know, jumping ahead of the game. They have yet to make a full declaration. Why don't we just wait and see what they say before people go out there and start giving their opinions about whether or not this is a good deal or a bad deal.

But one thing is for certain: The most effective way to deal with this issue is to do so with parties like China and Japan and Korea joining the United States and South Korea with a common voice. The whole object of this exercise is to convince the leader of North Korea to give up his nuclear weapons ambitions. That's the whole object.

And so we have yet to come to the stage where he has made a full declaration. And so we'll wait and see what he says, and then we'll make a decision about our obligations, depending upon whether or not we're convinced that there is a solid and full declaration and whether or not there's a way to verify whether or not he's going to do what he says he's going to do.

President Lee. As for the declaration of North Korea, that is in a very important process. I believe if North Korea's declaration is not satisfactory or if the verification is not satisfactory, we could probably have a temporary achievement. But in the long term, that will cause a lot more serious problems. I believe President Bush shares this thought with me.

Mr. President Bush explained just now the declaration, the verification process, has not begun. We are still waiting for North Korea to declare their full program. They should not get away with this temporary measure. The United States is not dealing with the—North Korea alone. There are other parties to the six-party talks, and they must all agree to North Korea's declaration. So in that regard, North Korea's declaration of their nuclear weapons program should be complete and correct, and verification, I'm not sure how long that is going to take, but North Korea must faithfully cooperate with verification process.

All the parties of the six-party talks are with one mind that the verification process must be full and complete and satisfactory. I think it's inappropriate and unconstructive for us to have too many doubts before the process even begins. The process is beginning. We should have trust in the process, and I will watch this process and cooperate fully.

North Korea-South Korea Relations

Q. I have a question for President Lee. Korea and the United States have made many achievements through the summit meeting, especially North Korean nuclear issue and the strengthening of the alliance. As for North Korean nuclear issue, Mr. President Lee suggested setting up a permanent liaison office in both Seoul and Pyongyang. What are some of the follow-up effects, if you do have any follow-up actions? And do you have any thoughts of proposing a meeting with Chairman Kim at an earlier date?

President Lee. The process is not something that we discussed between ourselves during the summit meeting. In fact, when I was staying in Washington, DC, I had an interview with one of the newspapers there, and it came up. Of course, it was not a sudden suggestion. I did have a meeting among my staff and related ministries, and I talked about this in detail before I came to the United States.

We have a new administration in Korea, and we haven't yet to begun dialogue with the North Koreans. Inter-Korean dialogue, there is a need for us to have dialogue all the time. Up until now, we had dialogues whenever the need arose, and then it would stop. However, dialogue should be based on genuine cooperation and sincerity. And so with this in mind, I thought that it would be helpful to set up a permanent liaison office in both Seoul and Pyongyang.

As for the summit meeting between myself and Chairman Kim, I will agree to it when the need is real. And I already said publicly that I am willing to meet with him—not just once, but many times—but if the meeting will yield substantial and real results. I believe only when that is possible, I am ready to meet with him and have sincere dialogue, because that will help to bring about peace and stability of the peninsula.

So basically, I do hold that thought, but I'm not suggesting that—to have a meeting with Chairman Kim anytime soon. If the need arises, again, I'm ready to meet with him.

President Bush. Steven Lee [Steven Lee Myers, New York Times].

North Korea/Six-Party Talks

Q. Thank you very much, Mr. President. If I could follow up a little bit on North Korea, the North Koreans agreed last year to make their disclosure. We're now in April, and we've yet to see this disclosure. There are continued negotiations, a new round next week. Are you concerned that, given this record, they're not prepared to make this full disclosure, that they're stalling the process somehow? And if so, a question for both of you: How do you respond to that?

President Bush. Yes, of course. I mean, they may be trying to stall. One thing about a nontransparent society where there's not a lot of free press, for example, or a lot of opposition voices, it's hard to tell what's going on. Now, he has made declarations, and he's testing the relationship. He's wondering whether or not the five of us will stay unified. And the only thing I know to do is to continue pressing forward within the six-party framework.

The decision—we've made our decision. We, the five of us, have made our decision, and that is, there's a way forward. And obviously, we hope he chooses to honor his commitments in a verifiable way. But it's—when you're dealing with a society in which it's hard to get information out of, you just have to wait and see whether they're sincere or not. Unlike our society, of course, where there's all kinds of people in the administration talking and sharing information with you—some of it authorized, some of it's not—it doesn't happen that way in North Korea. It's a closed society. It's a society in which the will of one person decides the course of the future.

And again, we're very hopeful. We talked about our mutual desire to keep the six-party framework in place to deal with a lot of issues. The first one, of course, is with North Korea. And it's—I can just tell you, Steven Lee, it's much more effective to have more than one voice speaking on this issue than to be the sole voice speaking on the issue. And so if it—if there ever is going to be a breakthrough, it's through the six-party framework.

And look, I'm hopeful. We'll see. This has been a—I've been at this for quite a while. And there's been moments where it looked like the process was going to go very smoothly and everybody's going to honor their commitments, and then for one

reason or another, there's a—there was a setback. But the key thing is, is that we haven't abandoned the efforts to solve this problem peacefully and diplomatically.

President Lee. Thank you. If you correctly understand North Korea and if you do understand North Korean society, you'll probably get a better picture of why we are seeing some delay in the process at the moment. If North Korea wasn't like that, then we would have seen the resolvement of this issue already. We need persistent patience, ladies and gentlemen. And we need time in order to have complete resolution of this issue.

However, it's difficult to convince North Korea to give up their nuclear weapons program, but it's not impossible. It is not impossible. I believe that. So in order to resolve this issue, I believe that the six-party talks is the most effective way and mechanism to resolve this issue, like the President mentioned. And right now we're in the stages of waiting for their declaration, and then we can move on to the verification process.

So I think it's up to you to make the atmosphere so that North Korea can faithfully abide by their promise and make the right declaration, that once North Korea does so, it is also in their interest to make the correct decision to give a full and complete declaration. And it will also help the North Korean people improve the quality of their life, and that is the best strategic choice that they can make.

South Korea-U.S. Relations/China

Q. Chosun Daily News. I have a question for President Bush. The United States has a divergent alliance with countries like the United Kingdom, Japan. In your opinion, President Bush, what kind of alliance do you have with the Republic of Korea? And during your summit meeting today, I believe you agreed to upgrade the Korea-U.S. alliance. In order to upgrade the alliance, what kind of new movement will you take on, for instance, the transfer of wartime operational control? And what will you do, President Bush—do you have any intention to meet with both President Lee and Chairman Kim in order to resolve this issue?

President Bush. No—[*inaudible*]—described the relationship—[*inaudible*]—a 21st-century strategic alliance. That makes sense to me. So what does that mean? Well, it means we work in ways to deal with 21st-century problems, such as proliferation of nuclear materials, such as working to make sure our children are educated with the tools necessary to be productive citizens, such as having a recognition that in the 21st century, a free and fair trading system will be necessary for prosperity. And that's why it's going to be very important for our Congress to ratify the free trade agreement with Korea.

It's going to be very important a 21st-century alliance recognizes that China is a opportunity for both nations to engage in a constructive way. Well, we have our problems with China, of course, whether it be human rights or how the Chinese leadership deals with the Dalai Lama or with Burma, a variety of issues. On the other hand, you can either have a constructive relationship—we can work constructively with China—or we can have a destructive relationship. I've chosen to have a constructive relationship.

And so the step one is to anticipate the issues confronting our peoples in the 21st century, and step two is to develop a practical way to deal with those issues. And that's exactly what our conversation revolved around. And I'm confident that this meeting has strengthened our relationship, and I'm confident that the American people understand how important this relationship is to our own prosperity and our own security.

And so it's been a really good visit, and we're glad you came here too. [*Laughter*] Yes. Thanks for coming. Thank you, sir.

NOTE: The President's news conference began at 11:17 a.m. In his remarks, he referred to Kim Yoon-ok, wife of President Lee; Minister of National Defense Lee Sang-hee of South Korea; Chairman Kim Jong Il of North Korea; and Tenzin Gyatso, the 14th Dalai Lama. A reporter referred to Ambassador John R. Bolton, former U.S. Permanent Representative to the United Nations. President Lee and some reporters spoke in Korean, and their remarks were translated by an interpreter.

Remarks Announcing the Reopening of the Mexican Consulate in New Orleans, Louisiana
April 21, 2008

President Bush. Thank you. *Sientese, por favor.* Mr. President, we are sure glad you're here.

President Felipe de Jesus Calderon Hinojosa of Mexico. Thank you, sir.

President Bush. And thank you for inviting me to be here. Madam Foreign Minister, Consul Garcia Guerra, Ambassador, thanks. Governor, *el alcalde*—Mr. Mayor, Ambassador Garza, I am really glad to be with you on this special occasion. I am

pleased that Mexico has chosen to reopen its consulate in New Orleans, and I'm honored to attend.

New Orleans has had a long tradition of diplomatic ties with Mexico. In 1824, New Orleans, Louisiana, became the first site of the Mexican—where the first Mexican—became the site for the first Mexican consulate in the United States. Isn't that interesting? Unfortunately, the consulate was closed in 2002. And so today we're reopening the consulate. And it's a good sign, because we celebrate the values that cause Mexico and the United States to be friends, values like family and faith and culture.

We celebrate the enduring and close partnership between our countries. Mexico and the United States are working together to build a future of prosperity and opportunity for people on both sides of the border.

And at this ceremony, we also celebrate the comeback of a great American city. You know, I chose New Orleans for our meetings with Mexico and Canada because I wanted to send a clear signal to the people of my country that New Orleans is open for business, and it's a good place to visit, and that after the devastation of Katrina, it's become a hopeful city.

And so on behalf of the people of the United States, Mr. President, *mi amigo*, I thank you for reopening this consulate. I look forward to our meetings. And it's my honor to bring you to the podium.

NOTE: The President spoke at 1 p.m. In his remarks, he referred to Secretary of Foreign Relations Patricia Espinosa Cantellano and Consul Andrea Garcia Guerra of Mexico; Mexico's Ambassador to the U.S. Arturo Sarukhan Casamitjana; Gov. Piyush "Bobby" Jindal of Louisiana; and Mayor C. Ray Nagin of New Orleans, LA. The transcript released by the Office of the Press Secretary also included the remarks of President Calderon Hinojosa. The Office of the Press Secretary also released a Spanish language transcript of these remarks.

Remarks Following a Discussion With President Felipe de Jesus Calderon Hinojosa of Mexico in New Orleans
April 21, 2008

President Bush. Mr. President, thank you very much. We just had a very long and really good discussion on a variety of issues. U.S.-Mexican relations are very important, and sometimes we in America take those relations for granted. But we share a large border; we share the same values. We've got people on both sides of the border who've got friends and family members. And it is fitting that you and I have this kind of conversation.

I want to congratulate you and thank you for your strong leadership. I appreciate the fact that you inherited a very difficult situation. One, you inherited, you know, high demand for drugs in the United States. In other words, people are using drugs, and therefore, people are supplying drugs. And it's caused difficult security problems in your country, and you've responded aggressively. And I think it's in our interests that

we fund the joint initiative. We got to work hard on our side to make sure that we reduce our drug use and, at the same time, work with you in the close coordination to defeat these drug traffickers.

We need to do—continue our initiative that we started with—during your administration, Mr. President, on dealing with arms trafficking—arms coming from the United States into Mexico. We've got a strategy in place, and we're now beginning to implement it. Congress has a chance to send a strong statement that we want to work in a collaborative fashion with the money that's going to be in the supplemental. My hope, of course, is they fully fund the program, and they fund it—a strategy that will be effective.

We talked about trade and how trade has been beneficial to both our countries. When you and I grew up in our respective countries, the border region of Mexico and the United States was very poor. And today, when you go down there, there's prosperity on both sides of the border. A lot of that has to do with trade. Our trade has tripled, and our economies have grown. And this has been a very positive aspect for both our countries. And so we're going to talk about that, of course, with the Canadian Prime Minister in our dinner tonight.

But we also talked about the need to have a successful Doha round. We talked about climate change. We talked about a lot of issues and—but that's what you expect friends to do. So I welcome you.

[*At this point, President Calderon Hinojosa spoke in Spanish, and his remarks were translated as follows.*]

Interpreter. [*Inaudible*]

President Bush. I understood every word. [*Laughter*]

Interpreter. Thank you very much, Mr. President. Thank you so much for your hospitality and for very long and productive discussion we had today. As is fitting for the relationship that Mexico and the United States enjoy, we have been able to discuss a long list of issues today, because we have a very complex and rich relationship.

We talked first of all, as President Bush said, about security. We talked about security along our common border. We talked about the common strategies that we are implementing in order to fight the double scourge of organized crimes and drug trafficking.

President Calderon Hinojosa. The common enemy.

Interpreter. Common enemy. Thank you, Mr. President.

[*The interpreter continued to translate President Calderon Hinojosa's remarks as follows.*]

Interpreter. We discussed the Merida Initiative, a very important initiative that will allow a common strategy that will benefit families on both sides, on the side of Mexico and on the side of the United States.

I also want to express my appreciation for the work the U.S. Government has begun on the problem of arms trafficking. We know that this is a complex issue. We know there is much to be done, but a very important first step has already been made in that direction.

We also discussed the defense of the Mexican administration, of the rights of our Mexican citizens. And we have also discussed the issue of trade and how trade is benefiting both of our peoples. And we have discussed the issue of trade and its benefits. I think that I have made it very clear that as far as I'm concerned, trade is an issue that benefits both sides greatly. It is something that generates jobs both on the U.S. side and on the side of Mexico. We have seen an enormous increase in benefits for consumers as a result of trade as well. We see that the quality of products in general has gone up as a result of increased trade.

And I stress this issue because recently NAFTA has come under criticism, and I do not believe that people are realizing how many benefits NAFTA has brought both to the United States and to Mexico. I can say that hundreds of thousands of jobs have been created on both sides of the border. As far as Mexico is concerned, this increase in jobs has also led to a direct decrease in the amount of immigration from Mexico to the United States. It has generated growth, it has generated jobs, and it is decreasing the flow of immigration.

And we have discussed the defense of the rights of Mexican citizens and the need to increase the way we watch over those rights. This has been—is a very important issue for my administration. We need to continue working on an agenda to find a comprehensive solution for that. I understand that the United States is going through an electoral process, and we respect that process, of course. But I do want to point out that it's very important for my administration, for us to find a solution to this issue, and a solution that will not just find a way to deal with the immigration problem, but one that will do so with respect and responsibility.

We also discussed the concern that we have with regard to the increase of prices of foods around the world and the public policies that are involved in finding alternative fuels and how all of this goes into the mix. We need to face the problem of economies all around the world who have not been able to deal with this problem very well. In Mexico, we have been able to find solutions, but we are concerned about the situation of other countries in Latin America that are not faring quite as well.

And finally, I simply want to say how happy I am to be in the United States. And I don't want to get ahead of myself, but tonight I will be extending an invitation, hopefully, to the next President of the United States to visit us in Mexico next year for this event. And of course, President Bush will always be a welcome visitor in Mexico.

President Calderon Hinojosa. Thank you.
President Bush. Thank you, sir.

NOTE: The President spoke at 2:40 p.m. at the Windsor Court Hotel. In his remarks, he referred to Prime Minister Stephen Harper of Canada. The Office of the Press Secretary also released a Spanish language transcript of these remarks.

Remarks Following a Discussion With Prime Minister Stephen Harper of Canada in New Orleans
April 21, 2008

President Bush. Mr. Prime Minister, thank you, sir, for your personal friendship. Thank you for your leadership. I don't know if the people of Canada understand the leadership role you took in Romania, but it was strong and effective. And I want to congratulate you in front of your media about the job you did. Not only did you represent your country well, you represented universal values, and you spoke clearly about them. And so I thank you for that.

We had a good visit. I'm always interested in making sure that if there's any bilateral tensions or bilateral issues, that I know of them so that we can work collaboratively to deal with them. And in the past, one such issue was whether or not our people could travel back and forth between our respective countries in a way that didn't inconvenience them, or if our borders were—being able to flow smoothly so it

didn't inconvenience trade. And I think we've worked through those issues.

I can remember the last time we visited, there was great concern about whether or not the Western Hemisphere Travel Initiative would be counterproductive to our friendship and relationship. And I thank your government, thank your ministers, and the people in your staff for working hard to find a way that meets our laws and didn't inconvenience the people of Canada or the United States. So I'm pleased with that progress.

We also talked about the importance of trade between Canada and the United States, and Canada and Mexico, and the United States and Mexico. And I assured the Prime Minister that I'm a strong advocate for free trade. I believe it's in our nations' interests that we continue to have a free trade agenda. All of us want to make sure we're treated fairly, and we can do

that. And this summit comes at an oppor-
tune time to reaffirm the benefits of the
trading arrangements between our three
nations.

Canada and the United States have got
a very unique and important relationship,
and I really appreciate the chance to spend
time with you and visit about these—about
the issues of concern.

Finally, the Prime Minister is very articulate on the subject of climate change. And
I assured him that my speech in the Rose
Garden was a sincere speech, a speech that
laid out a strategy that I think will be effective. And I look forward to continuing to
work with you on that issue.

But thanks, good to see you.

Prime Minister Harper. It's nice to see
you again. Thank you for the warm welcome and hospitality.

[*At this point, Prime Minister Harper spoke
in French, and no translation was provided.*]

Prime Minister Harper. I'll just say once
again, delighted to be here in New Orleans,
originally a francophone city, in fact, founded by New France——

President Bush. That's true.

Prime Minister Harper. ——my dad's favorite American city, I was telling him. We
discussed a lot of things to do with the
border, to do with environment, energy,
trade, and commercial relations. And as
you've mentioned, we've made some considerable progress on some of these things.

That said, what I appreciate most, what
I've appreciated in our relationship over the
past couple years, has been the fact that
whether we agree or disagree, we're always
able to talk very frankly, very upfront. The
President has never promised me anything
he couldn't deliver, and that's always appreciative—appreciated.

We have some important joint work
going on, not just in this continent but
around the world, including in Afghanistan.
I appreciate your words about Bucharest,
and I can tell you our armed forces look
very much forward to working in partnership with your people in Kandahar.

So I'm sure we'll have a great summit.
And see you again at the G–8. And I feel
we've got a few more of these to go
through before it's over. [*Laughter*]

President Bush. Thank you, sir.

NOTE: The President spoke at 4:19 p.m. at
the Windsor Court Hotel.

Remarks at a United States Chamber of Commerce Reception in New Orleans
April 21, 2008

I want to thank the band for giving me
a chance to relive my youth. [*Laughter*]
I've had many a fine day here in New
Orleans and a pretty good night too.
[*Laughter*] And it's great to be back. I want
to thank the U.S. Chamber for hosting this
reception in honor of the North American
Leaders' Summit between Canada, the
United States, and Mexico. And for all of
you here from Canada and Mexico, welcome to New Orleans, one of America's
greatest cities.

I chose to host this summit in New Orleans for a variety of reasons, one of which
is, for centuries, this city has been a place
where commerce and culture from across
the globe have come together, one of the
really great international cities in the
United States. And once again, New Orleans now steps on the international scene,
where it should be.

I want to thank Tom for hosting the deal, and I want to thank all the members of the U.S. Chamber for being here tonight. I thank members of the North American Competitiveness Council for being here—looking forward to meeting with you in the morning.

I want to thank the Governor of the great State of Louisiana, Bobby Jindal, and the first lady for being here. My old buddy the mayor—Mayor Nagin is here. Mr. Mayor, it's great to see you. We have spent some quality time together—[*laughter*]—including on the deck of the USS *Iwo Jima*; yes, nonalcohol beer for me. [*Laughter*]

I thank all the State and local officials. I particularly want to say thanks to the Senators from Louisiana for joining us today. Mary Landrieu—thanks for coming, Senator. David Vitter—Senator, it's good to have you here. Thanks for coming. Congressman William Jefferson—thanks for being here, Jeff. Appreciate you being here. I thank the—thanks for coming.

One thing is for certain: New Orleans has come a long way since Hurricane Katrina hit. It—and we've tried to do our part at the Federal level. We spent over $120 billion to help the Gulf Coast recover. The money has helped rebuild a school system, a dilapidated school system, that is now better than before. The money has helped improve the criminal justice system. The money has helped to rebuild highways. The money has helped to strengthen storm surge protection systems so people can feel comfortable living here.

New Orleans faces immense challenges. There's still a lot of work to be done. But there's a lot of hope in this city. I mean, you can see it in the face of the teachers. You can see hope in the jobs that are being created. There's a lot of entrepreneurial spirit in New Orleans. You can see hope in the fact that people are absolutely determined to rebuild this city better than it was before.

And so for all of you who have contributed to New Orleans's resurgence, I want to thank you on behalf of a grateful nation.

This is an important summit. It gives three friends a chance to come together to discuss our commitment to security and prosperity. It's a chance to reconfirm the need for the three of us to work in harmony together for the good of our peoples. It's a chance to talk about how we can best protect our people and extend prosperity. And one of the best ways to do that is through trade.

The people of Louisiana understand the benefits of trade firsthand. While many sectors of the economy were hit hard by Katrina, exports were a source of strength. And they continue to be in the years since. I don't know if a lot of people know this, but exports from Louisiana surpassed $30 billion in the year 2007; that would be $30 billion for the first time ever. And a lot of these exports come through New Orleans, which is a source for jobs and hope.

And the fundamental question is, will we continue to be a nation that believes in free and fair trade? Canada and Mexico are our two most important trading partners. Since the North American Free Trade Agreement took effect, an agreement I strongly support, trade between the United States, Mexico, and Canada has more than tripled, and our economies have grown by more than 50 percent.

One of the challenges for the North American Competitiveness Council is to find unnecessary regulations that prohibit the free flow of trade. And so tomorrow the leaders at the Council will come forth with specific recommendations. And I'm looking forward to hearing them, and I'm looking forward to implementing them.

The United States has an opportunity to continue a trading agenda. As a matter of fact, we have an opportunity with three important countries: Colombia, South Korea, and Panama. Interestingly enough, all 3 of these countries are among Louisiana's top 10 foreign markets for exports.

These agreements will be good for New Orleans's workers and businesses. And the mayor recognized that. He wrote a leader to our Speaker—or wrote a letter to our Speaker, who is the leader in the Congress, and here's what he said: "Each of the future free trade agreements would provide unique opportunities for the city of New Orleans to increase international economic development."

Unfortunately, we had a setback in a very important free trade agreement with Colombia. The Speaker made a decision to block the free trade agreement. It's unfortunate decision, and the deal is dead unless she changes her mind. And that's bad for American workers, and it's bad for our security, and it's bad for the people here in New Orleans, Louisiana.

The economic argument for free trade with Colombia is very clear. Almost all Colombian products now enter America duty free, yet many of our products face steep tariffs in Colombia. Now think about that. All I suggest is that we level the playing field, that we be treated just like we treat others. Our products into Colombia face a tax, a tariff, which makes them more expensive. It makes it harder for our small businesses and farmers to be able to sell into Colombia, yet their products come here virtually duty free. And so by approving this deal, it will level the playing field, but more importantly, it will help our entrepreneurs and help our workers.

There's another cost because of congressional inaction, and that is, Colombia is one of our strongest allies in our neighborhood. And it's important to support our friends. And it's important to send a clear message

that we stand for rule of law and democracy, which is precisely what President Uribe believes in. He's fighting these terrorists and these narcotraffickers. He has strengthened the rule of law. He's protecting his labor leaders. He is a strong, solid leader.

Yet if we turn down this deal or if this deal does not go forward, it would send a variety of messages: One, America can't be counted on to stand next to its friends; two, it will embolden the voices of false populism in our neighborhood; and three, it will make it harder for President Uribe to do what is necessary to make sure Colombia is a safe place for people to live. I fully understand that this is a tough political vote for some, but it's about time America sets aside petty politics and focuses on doing what's right for the United States of America.

So thanks for letting me come by, and thanks for hosting this very important meeting. I am confident the Prime Minister of Canada and the President of Mexico will really enjoy their stays in New Orleans. They will find what I have found, that it's a city not only of good food, good cheer, but it's a city of really fine people. God bless.

NOTE: The President spoke at 6:36 p.m. at Gallier Hall. In his remarks, he referred to Thomas J. Donohue, president and chief executive officer, U.S. Chamber of Commerce; Supriya Jindal, wife of Gov. Piyush "Bobby" Jindal of Louisiana; Mayor C. Ray Nagin of New Orleans, LA; Prime Minister Stephen Harper of Canada; and President Felipe de Jesus Calderon Hinojosa of Mexico.

The President's News Conference With President Felipe de Jesus Calderon Hinojosa of Mexico and Prime Minister Stephen Harper of Canada in New Orleans
April 22, 2008

President Bush. Thank you all. Mr. President, Mr. Prime Minister, welcome to the great city of New Orleans. Thank you all for coming as well. New Orleans is one of America's really top cities. And they, the people of New Orleans, appreciate the help you gave them right after Hurricane Katrina, and so I want to thank you very much for that. New Orleans has always been a crossroads for our continent. And today, there's no better place for our nations to look forward to a bright future, and that's what we're here to do.

I—one of the things our—you know, people ask, well, does it make sense for Mexico, Canada, and the United States to meet? Absolutely, it makes sense. We're neighbors. A prosperous neighborhood is in our interests; a secure neighborhood is in our interests. And we share common values. So I'm not surprised we've had good meetings. Plus, we like each other. It's easy to work with leaders who are straightforward and honest, tell you what's on their mind, and who care deeply about the people of their countries and who are problemsolvers. And that's how I have found this meeting and the previous meetings we've held.

We talked about trade. Mexico, Canada, and the United States made a bold decision in the early 1990s. Our countries decided to reduce our trade barriers through the North American Free Trade Agreement. That was a visionary move by previous leaders, a move that has benefited all three of our countries a lot. Trade has tripled. Our economies have grown by more than 50 percent.

Now is not the time to renegotiate NAFTA or walk away from NAFTA. Now is the time to make it work better for all our people. And now is the time to reduce trade barriers worldwide.

And so we spent time talking about the Colombia free trade agreement. Canada is negotiating a Colombia free trade agreement. Mexico has a free trade agreement with Colombia. And a lot of folks are waiting for the United States Congress to bring this issue up and pass it. It makes no sense to me to say that Colombia goods can come into our country duty free, yet our goods can't go into Colombia duty free. And yet that's the case.

An agreement with Colombia would level the playing field, and a failure to pass an agreement would send a terrible signal to our neighborhood. The Speaker of the United States Congress has killed this bill unless she gives us a date certain for a vote. It is a bad decision on her part, and it's bad for our hemisphere to have the United States of America turn its back on a mutual friend like Colombia.

We're working to make sure we reduce regulations and to add—to make sure that our small businesses and farmers and producers are able to move product in a way without a bunch of government regulations in between. And it's not easy work, because obviously we want to maintain high standards and work for good safety precautions. Yet we're making progress.

And we've charged others to continue to work; like, Carlos Gutierrez and my Cabinet will work on issues with his counterparts for more harmonized standards to reduce the cost of producing cars and trucks throughout our entire market. In other words, you've got different regulations in different countries that make it difficult to compete globally and cause our products to be more expensive than they should be.

We're talking about food and product safety standards to make them compatible in a way that guarantees safety for our consumers. We talked about the need for us to work together to promote clean, efficient, low-carbon energy technologies. Obviously, we talked about global warming and the need to make sure that major economies are all party to an agreement.

People say, well, are you really committed to global—to reducing global warming? Absolutely. As a matter of fact, I gave a speech in the Rose Garden the other day that made it abundantly clear the United States is for an effective climate agreement that includes binding commitments from all major developed and developing economies, and we'll continue to work toward that end.

And then obviously, we're still working to make sure our borders work well. I mean, there's complications on these long borders. I understand that. We're making progress addressing problems and, at the same time, making sure that our people are safe.

For example, we've had an issue with Mexico. The last time—the time before last we met, the President made it abundantly clear that he felt the United States ought to do more to prevent guns from going into the—from the United States into Mexico. I couldn't agree more with him. And we put a process in place that do a variety of things, all aiming to make sure that our neighbors and our neighborhood isn't scourged by these thugs who use guns out of the United States to hold their people hostage, hold the country hostage. And so we've got a lot of tough work to do, but we're doing it.

And finally, in terms of just bilateral relations with Mexico, the Merida project is an important project to help implement a dual strategy to deal with crime and drugs. The President and I have talked about this initiative in a way that benefits the people of Mexico and the United States. The initiative conclude—includes a commitment

this year of $550 million by the United States. And Congress needs to pass the deal—pass the bill. And they need to pass it in such a way that it conforms to the strategy that the President of Mexico thinks will best help deal with this issue.

All in all, it's been a very—it's been a good summit. And I appreciate you all coming. New Orleans is a fun town. I'm looking at the press corps to make sure that they didn't take advantage of it. [*Laughter*] You look well rested.

Anyway, it's a great place. I'm glad you're here. Thanks for coming.

Mr. President.

President Calderon Hinojosa. Thank you, Mr. President. Thank you, President Bush, my friends from the media, from the press, Prime Minister Harper. First of all, I'd like to thank you, Mr. President. I'd like to thank President Bush and the people of the United States for your hospitality. I think that the city of New Orleans has been an ideal venue for this leaders' summit.

And I'd like to say that I congratulate the people of Louisiana for their determination, for their strength. I congratulate the people of the United States, as well, for the recovery they've shown after the effects of Hurricane Katrina. And I repeat that Americans can always count on the solidarity of Mexicans during times of tragedy as a result of, in this case, a natural phenomenon.

I'm pleased because the meeting allowed President Bush, Prime Minister Harper, and myself to work on an agenda that was devoted to improving the welfare of our peoples. President Bush already mentioned some of the issues we talked about. I would simply underscore the following.

First, we reasserted commitments we adopted in Montebello last year, such as that of strengthening the competitiveness of our region, cooperation in the area of imports, products from other areas of North America, food security, and also improving the situation of all the regulation among our three countries. And our Secretary will be spearheading the work on the Mexican side in order to deregulate measures affecting trade.

Second, we talked a lot about the NAFTA, and of course, we agreed that this is not the time to even think about amending it or canceling it. This is the time to strengthen and reinvigorate this free trade agreement among our three countries. Thanks to the free trade agreement, trade exchange went beyond $900 trillion, behind which we have jobs; we have investment; we have goods and services that improve the quality of life of Canadians, Americans, and Mexicans. And we want these benefits to reach more and more of all our citizens.

Third, we agreed on the need to strengthen investments and cooperation among all our nations. And the business leaders of the three countries gave us a very specific agenda that records the progress we've made and also establishes how much more quickly we need to work within the North American Competitiveness Council, where the three leaders agreed we fully need to support the work of this Competitiveness Council.

Fourth, we recognized the progress made within the regulatory framework that's compatible for all three countries.

Fifth, we agreed that the efforts we've made in the area of intellectual property have transferred to major hits against smuggling and the work of pirates. In the case of Mexico, for example, last year, we carried out the biggest seizures in the history of our country. And in fact, last night we had some major efforts carried out against organized crime. And the three countries will continue to work on improving the conditions of law enforcement.

Six, we also talked a lot about border projects. Our three countries want to have safe borders, and we want to have efficient borders, borders that will improve the competitiveness of our various businesses and for the entire region. We talked about how

to make the flow along the borders even better, how to improve trade there.

Of course, there are issues of interest between Canada and the United States. They're working on those issues. In the case of Mexico, we are working very hard on how to expand the border crossings between Mexico and the United States with projects that are already in course: ones in Reynosa, others in Juarez and different points across the border.

We also exchanged viewpoints on the issues that have to do with security in the region. And in this case, we talked to President Bush about the Merida Initiative, an initiative that is focused on facing a joint strategy with regard to a joint—a common enemy, which is organized crime, which operates on both sides of the border and which does not recognize any borders, any limits. And unfortunately, it affects Mexican, Canadian, and U.S. families.

It's very important for our Congresses and Parliaments in our respective countries to strengthen, support the decisive actions that we are carrying out in order to eradicate this scourge that is affecting all of North America.

We also stressed the need to continue to promote growth and development in our entire region. Throughout the continent, and especially in Mexico, we're concerned about Latin America. That's why it's important for this cooperative and collaborative mechanism among the United States, Canada, and Mexico to work. And that's why we also need to redouble the successful cases where trade and cooperation are fruitful and lead to tangible results for our people.

I want to talk about the efforts being made in this country to establish free trade agreements that are much more practical and beneficial for everyone, in particular, the one under discussion now in the U.S. Congress between the United States and Colombia. It's extremely important, I think, to bear in mind that when you provide more opportunities for trade in the Latin

American region, there will be many more opportunities for prosperity. And it needs to be made very clear that the prosperity of Latin America, and particularly that of Mexico, is a crucial factor for the prosperity of the people of North America.

Finally, ladies and gentlemen, I'm convinced, and after this meeting even more so, that after 14 years of a very decisive step, which was the North American Free Trade Agreement, today, the relations between the United States, Canada, and Mexico is more dynamic, more fluid, much more successful than ever before.

In particular, I want to thank President Bush for his leadership in holding not just this meeting here in the United States but the fact that these meetings were established in the year 2005. And President Bush's leadership has been very important for these meetings to be held among the three countries, which don't just affect the leaders attending the meetings themselves but allow all of us to coordinate our policies, our activities, and our objectives in order to ensure greater regional prosperity.

This is the last meeting for President Bush. From now on, the veteran for these meetings is going to be Prime Minister Harper. And I'm sure that whoever the next President of the United States will be, he or she will continue with this regional effort. Independently of the fact that, unfortunately, President Bush will not be with us, we have at least informally invited him to our next meeting personally.

And I'd like to announce formally, on behalf of the Mexican Government, that we have conveyed to the Governments of the United States and Canada a very special invitation to take part at the next leaders' summit of 2009 to be held in Mexico. And of course, from now on, we will be preparing to make sure the summit is memorable and productive, a summit that will offer the taste of the hospitality of the people of Mexico and will also allow us to reach various specific decisions on a number of issues which, as we have shown at

this meeting, have been very carefully analyzed. And the options for the North American Competitiveness Council and the three administrations is very clear.

I hope that we will continue have an even more prosperous North American region, a region where the United States, Canada, and Mexico will gain in competitiveness vis-a-vis other regions of the world which are now leading in terms of growth and productivity. But I'm sure that we can achieve this, especially if we persevere with the good will that has been demonstrated at this New Orleans meeting.

Thank you so much, Mr. President, and thank you to the American people.

Prime Minister Harper. This is the last—we talked about common stakes for our three countries. President Bush, myself, and—we have discussed about commerce and the advantages that NAFTA brings to our three countries and has been doing for 14 years. We talked about the progress that we've made, and we have talked about not only what has been done, but also what needs to be done.

We concluded that it's essential for the prosperity of our countries to continue this effort. And we have emphasized in particular the border crossing, Windsor-Detroit. It is evident that a greater North American cooperation will lead to the creation of jobs and will allow us to compete in a very effective way to other emerging commercial blocs around the world.

I would like—also talked about our concern about the thickening of the border between our countries. The Chambers of Commerce of the United States and Canada are concerned about these border issues for several years. And the council for competitiveness has also talked about their concern about this border issues.

It was a great pleasure to come to New Orleans for this summit. And of course, I want to thank President Bush and the population of New Orleans for their great hospitality. And I'm looking forward to see President Calderon, who will greet us in

Mexico and welcome us to Mexico next year.

[*At this point, Prime Minister Harper continued in English.*]

President Bush, President Calderon, and I have discussed the common issues and challenges facing our three countries. We discussed the importance of cooperation on security and trade and the benefits that NAFTA has produced for each of our three countries over the last 14 years.

We also talked about the progress we've made and are continuing to make to improve North American security. We agreed that continuing to improve and expand trade is the key to greater prosperity for our peoples, and we are putting special emphasis on the Detroit-Windsor crossing.

It's clear that greater North American cooperation is our best option to create jobs and to compete effectively with emerging trading blocs elsewhere in the world. To that end, I specifically raised concerns about the so-called thickening of the Canada-U.S. border. The Canadian and American Chambers of Commerce have been worried about this for several years, and the North American Competitiveness Council raised their concerns at our meeting this morning.

It has been a pleasure to come to New Orleans for this summit. I—my only regret, Mr. President, is that I didn't bring my wife and decide to spend a lot more time here. But it's been wonderful to visit here, to see the rebuilding. I won't say my farewells, because you and I have a few more meetings, including the G–8 this summer, that we're looking forward to.

I also look forward to seeing you, President Calderon, in the future—and for your offer to host us next year. And I can tell you, Canadians are always delighted to visit Mexico in the wintertime, so keep that in mind. [*Laughter*]

President Calderon Hinojosa. Thank you.

President Bush. Okay, a couple of questions.

Trade/2008 Presidential Election/Mexico-Canada-U.S. Relations

Q. Thank you, Mr. President. I want to follow up on your comments about NAFTA. The Democratic Presidential candidates, in fact, are talking about renegotiating that trade agreement if elected. I'm wondering if you're worried that their comments on the campaign trail are perhaps overshadowing your protrade agenda. In essence, do you worry that you're losing the free trade debate in the courts of public opinion?

And to President Calderon and Prime Minister Harper, I'd like to get your thoughts about expanding your trade relationship with the United States. Is there a point at which you shift attention to the people running for the White House and their views and try to reach out to them?

President Bush. Actually, my biggest concern on trade right now is with Colombia. NAFTA exists, and NAFTA—when you analyze it in an objective way, it benefits—beneficial to America. It also happens to be beneficial to Mexico and Canada, which makes it a, you know, a very good, comprehensive agreement.

It's beneficial to us because when you're able to export to your neighborhood, it helps create jobs. Jobs are created when people find outlets for their goods and services. We have found a lot of outlets for our goods and services with our—in our neighborhood. It also helps consumers when you import. In other words, the more choices consumers have, the more options they have, the more—less likely it is there will be price increases, and it's better for your consumers. This agreement's been beneficial in creating wealth in our neighborhood. Our economies have all grown.

I also happen to think it's very important for our citizens. I wish people could remember what the border looked like between Texas and Mexico before NAFTA. I mean, it was poor, really poor, on both sides of the border. If you go down there today, there's prosperity on both sides of the border, and that's in our Nation's interests.

I mean, one way to increase pressure on the border is to—if you do it—away with NAFTA, there's going to be a lot of Mexicans—more Mexicans out of work. It will make it harder on the border. It will make it harder to deal with. So people who say, "Let's get rid of NAFTA," because of a throwaway political line, must understand this has been good for America, and it's also been good for Mexico and Canada, and that's what you want in your neighborhood.

Secondly, my biggest concern is to turn our back on our friends in Colombia. The Speaker of the House made a decision, using an extraordinary procedure, to prevent a vote on a trade bill that had been negotiated in good faith between our respective countries. You heard the—President Calderon say, it's in the region's interest to trade freely and fairly. Well, this agreement we have with Colombia right now is not fair for America, it's not fair for our businesses, it's not fair for our farmers. And all I'm asking the Congress is to make it fair.

And if they—if the Speaker doesn't bring—give us a date certain on the bill, she's effectively killed it. It's her responsibility, and she's going to have to explain why the voices of false populism have been strengthened, why anti-Americanism could flourish, when America turns its back on a strong leader like President Uribe and a friend for democracy like President Uribe.

I'm concerned about protectionism in America. It's not in our interests to become a protectionist nation. And so I'll continue to speak out on it and assure our friends that we will work hard to explain to the people the benefits of why free and fair trade is in our Nation's interest.

President Calderon Hinojosa. First of all, what we have to do—all of us who have responsibilities vis-a-vis our citizens—is to objectively study the facts. What's happened with NAFTA in our three countries? Before NAFTA, there were many businesses, Mexican businesses, that were afraid, and they alleged that it was impossible to compete with the sophisticated and modern U.S. companies. And they weren't going to survive. There were also many U.S. companies who thought it was impossible to compete in more open markets. Now, what was the result? The result has been that trade has grown, and that has led to gains for everyone involved.

Contrary to what they believe—that one was going to win, the other would lose—it was a win-win situation, and NAFTA has benefited the three countries. Trade has grown in all three, jobs have grown in all three, and even wage levels have gone up in all three. Today, the economies of Canada, Mexico, and the United States are bigger and stronger than they were 14 years ago. Income per capita for all three has also grown compared to 14 years ago. The benefits are visible, and all you need to do is to talk based on demonstrated results.

To talk about taking a step backwards, in terms of free trade in the case of Mexico, would effectively provoke considerable damage on the economy. And another factor I was discussing yesterday with President Bush—that he reiterated today, and I will reiterate as well—would be a sudden loss of economic opportunities that would even lead to even greater migratory pressure in the—against—with the United States.

We are doing everything we can in order to create job opportunities in Mexico for people so that Mexicans will not need to seek job opportunities outside their country. And the only way to do it is by creating jobs in Mexico, and the only way is, precisely, multiplying our possibilities of trade.

In the case of the U.S. economy, if you were to take a step backwards with regard to NAFTA or free trade, you would be condemning Americans to have one of the least competitive economies in the developed world. While other parts of the world are accelerating their growth, their integration—China, Japan, India, Asia—in order to have more competitive economies and more complementary situations—and Europe is already becoming a single trade group, and they're adding more and more countries to that bloc every year—here you see protectionist voices arising. And the only thing they would achieve, if they were to prosper, would be to condemn North America as a region to complete backwardness in today's world. And that is the worst possible solution you can provide to your citizens.

It is not my role to talk to the three candidates or precandidates to the Presidency. I'm very respectful of the domestic politics of this country. This is a decision that is solely in the hands of U.S. citizens. And for that reason, I must respect that process completely. It is not my role to talk to any candidates or precandidates. All I would do is speak to the person who will eventually be the President of the United States. And we will speak openly and sincerely about the future of both of our countries or, in this case, our three countries in the trilateral meetings that we hold.

But Mexico will have a respectful relationship with the next President of the United States and will always seek the prosperity of our nations, knowing that through free trade, we have a clear, open, and respectful relationship among all our countries that will achieve prosperity.

If we want to solve common problems, if we want to solve problems like security, problems like immigration, problems like economic growth in the United States and in Mexico, we need to understand that only to the extent that North America is more competitive as a region, only to that extent will we be able to successfully face our problems.

Prime Minister Harper. We have been working with the current U.S. administra-

tion. We've had a very productive relationship with President Bush and his administration. And I trust that this will continue, that it will continue with any of the Presidential candidates here in the United States.

Of course, it's the United States who needs to make a decision about this election. But I think that in the end, Canada really is confident that the next President will also understand the importance of NAFTA and the importance of the commercial relationship between the United States and Canada. And I must emphasize that for energy security, the commercial relationship between our two countries is even more important today than it was 20 years ago. And I think this relationship will be even more important in the future.

[*Prime Minister Harper continued in English.*]

——productive relationship with the current administration, and I anticipate that Canada will have a very productive relationship with the next administration, because I'm confident that when the facts are looked at, any President, just as any Prime Minister of Canada, will quickly conclude how critically important NAFTA and our North American/Canadian-American trade relations are to jobs and prosperity on both sides of our border and, in particular, the importance of energy security that is a particularly critical part of the NAFTA arrangement.

Canada is the biggest and most stable supplier of energy to the United States in the world. That energy security is more important now than it was 20 years ago, when NAFTA was negotiated, and will be even more important in the future.

Mexican Government

Q. Yes, good afternoon. I'd like to ask a domestic question but hear from Mexico. President Calderon, I'd like to ask your ideas about the situation in our Congress and also the spot that was presented lately on the statements made by Mr. Lopez Obrador and comparisons with Hitler and Mussolini. What is your opinion of this? And do you think that this helps the unity you've always called for among Mexicans, with regard to the presentation of the bill on energy in our Mexican Congress?

President Calderon Hinojosa. This kind of attitude can only be compared to the people who are making it. Congress is working normally. There is a responsible attitude on the part of most of the political parties represented therein. People from the PRI, the PAN, the Green Party, the New Alliance, other political parties are working firmly. And I simply deplore this attitude, which only impoverishes the image of those behind it and weakens even more the presence of Mexicans from parties as important as the PRD, which, aside from their own internal crisis, are losing their public image because of the activities of people who simply make them look ridiculous.

I hope that our institutional life will be strengthened and that we strengthen dialogue and the capacity for talking among ourselves.

This issue that you referred to is already in the hands of the authorities. And I'm sure that a new electoral authority, like the IFE, will make a decision according to what it seems—it deems fit based on those TV spots you referred to.

Canadian Campaign Finance Regulations

Q. Prime Minister, if you would respond in both official languages: Canadians have seen the RCMP visit to your party headquarters, they've heard the allegations from Elections Canada, and they're wondering what's going on. Did you know about this scheme, and will you practice it again in the next election?

Prime Minister Harper. Well, this is the same story as before. As you know, Elections Canada view is that some of our local spending should count as national spending. We have a different view. We looked into

this at the time, and that's the view we've taken.

Our position is always that we always follow the law as we understand it, and, more importantly, we always follow the law as it has been interpreted. We were following, in the last election, the interpretations that had been put on that law in the past. If those interpretations change, we'll, of course, conform, but we will expect the same rules for every single party.

[*Prime Minister Harper continued in French, and his remarks were translated as follows.*]

And as I just said, it's always the same thing in this for quite awhile. Elections Canada think that some of our local expenditures should at—should be considered as national expenses. But we do not agree with that, and that's why we went to court with this issue. And in the end, we will respect the law and the interpretations of the law as they are, as we have done in the past.

Price of Gasoline/Energy/U.S. Economy

Q. Thank you, Mr. President. Oil prices today rose above $118 a barrel. It's another record. Are Saudi Arabia and other oil producers, are they our adversaries, or have you had any success with your recent appeals with them? And also, the effect of the gasoline prices, isn't that about to erase or certainly erode the benefit of the economic stimulus package?

President Bush. Yes, no question, rising gasoline prices are like a tax on our working people. And what's happening is, is that we've had an energy policy that neglected hydrocarbons in the United States for a long period of time, and now we're paying the price. We should have been exploring for oil and gas in ANWR, for example. But no, we made the decision: Our Congress kept preventing us from opening up new areas to explore in environmentally friendly ways, and now we're becoming, as a result, more and more dependent on foreign sources of oil. Fortunately, Canada and Mexico are our biggest providers, for which we are grateful. But our energy policy is—wasn't effective over the past decades, and now we're paying the price.

And secondly, there's not a lot of excess capacity in the world. As a matter of fact, unfortunately, a lot of the supplies are coming from parts of the world where there's political instability. Fortunately, again, Canada and Mexico are not included in that group. There are some countries that are not reinvesting in their reserves, which decline without maintenance.

And so I'm obviously concerned for our consumers. All the more reason to have passed a rebate, tax relief, and all the more reason for the United States Congress to keep the tax relief I passed permanent. We got people out there campaigning: "Well, we're just going to tax the rich." You can't raise enough money to meet their spending appetites by taxing the so-called rich. Every one of those so-called tax-the-rich schemes end up taxing the middle class families. And in a time of economic uncertainty, we need tax certainty. In a time of rising gasoline prices, we need to be sending a message to all Americans: We're not going to raise your taxes.

Global Economy/Colombia

Q. Good afternoon, gentlemen. For President Bush, how deep and how long will the economic recession be in the United States, and how will it affect Mexico?

And what is your perspective, Mr. President, of the reform presented by President Calderon in Mexico?

And for all three of you, what's the security context that exists with regard to what's happening to NAFTA and the FTA with Colombia after Colombia carried out a military invasion in Ecuador?

President Bush. First of all, I—we're not in a recession, we're in a slowdown. We grew in the fourth quarter of last year. We haven't had first-quarter growth statistics

yet, but there's no question, we're in a slowdown. And yes, people are concerned about it, obviously. I'm—of all the three of us standing up here, I'm probably the most concerned about the slowdown. After all, it's affecting the people who I have the honor of representing.

That's why we passed, in working with the Congress, a significant progrowth economic package that will pass back rebates to our citizens, starting in the second week of May. Part of that package also included incentives for large and small businesses to invest in the year 2008. I think this is going to have a positive effect on the economy. Experts say it's going to have a positive effect on the economy. And so we'll see what happens there. The key is for Congress not to raise taxes during this period of time and send a signal that they're not going to raise taxes.

You know, the President is plenty capable of handling reform. She's a—he's a good, honest man who cares deeply about the people of Mexico. And he'll do what he thinks is right for the country of Mexico.

And in terms of President Uribe, we got no better friend in South America than President Uribe. He believes strongly in rule of law. He's a reformer, and he's working hard to protect his country from a bunch of narcotraffickers who murder innocent people to achieve their objectives. And he ought to have our support. He has the support of the United States of America in many ways, but if we don't agree to a free trade agreement that we honest—negotiated in good faith with them, it will undermine his efforts, and it will destabilize parts of the world. And it would be a big mistake for the Congress to turn its back on Colombia.

President Calderon Hinojosa. I simply want to stress the measures Mexico is adopting before this situation—this slowdown of economic growth in the United States, which obviously affects us. More than 82 percent of our exports go to the

United States, and we're adopting a number of measures. One of them is a very aggressive program for public expenditure and infrastructure, not just private spending. To give you an idea, Mexico is going from spending 3 percentage points of the GDP per year on infrastructure to over 5½ percent of the GDP on infrastructure.

We're talking about Mexico this year having expenses for infrastructural programs of about $500 billion for private-public programs. That's already showing up in the figures of the first quarter of the year.

We're also working on an anticyclic program with very aggressive tax stimulus package for investment in the poorest regions of Mexico, where whoever invests there will get a 100-percent deduction on all investments, and the Federal Government, for a year and a half, will pay all expenses associated with social security, with labor—all the labor costs associated with social security. And that's a very, very strong stimulus package.

The first data coming in indicates that for Mexico, our economic activity had 4.25-percent growth rate per year. The figures for February and March indicate that industrial activity continues to show about 4 percent growth. So it's a difficult time because of the enormous interconnection among our economies, but we are prepared to face the situation and at a slower place than the one we've had in the past. But we are dealing with the situation. We are moving with everything at the Government's disposal to accelerate the growth of the Mexican economy.

I hope that this situation will not continue for very long and that soon the authorities in the United States will be able to completely overcome the situation. I think that the steps taken so far by the fiscal tax monetary authorities in the United States and the Bush administration—and in general—have been appropriate. They have been the right measures, and we hope that they will very soon demonstrate effects so that we have a quick recovery among all our economies.

Prime Minister Harper. I would just say that in spite of a slowdown of the economy in Canada, the bases of our economy are stable and solid. And we have undertaken measures to ensure the continuous growth in the future.

Now, as far as the Colombia situation is concerned, Canada has negotiated a free trade agreement with Colombia. And it's important also for the United States and for Mexico to benefit from free trade *avec* Colombia.

Last year, in the summit, I said that Colombia can have drug trafficking with our countries without a free trade agreement, but if you want legitimate business for all our economies, we need to pursue free trade agreements with Colombia. And I said in New York a few months ago that I worry if the United States in the end refuses this agreement with Colombia.

We have important alliance in Colombia. Colombia is fighting against political violence, against the FARC. They fight against drug traffickers. And I think that a rejection of or turning our backs to such an ally as Colombia is—could create long-term problems for our countries in South America.

[*Prime Minister Harper continued in English.*]

——free trade agreement to have drug trade with Colombia. You're going to have that anyway. If you want to have legitimate trade and see that country progress economically, we need to have a free trade agreement. We need to have a trade agreement with countries like Colombia.

And I do worry that if the Colombian free trade agreement is rejected, particularly when that country has taken a lot of efforts to fight political violence and corruption and FARC and drug traffickers, if the United States and our allies turn their back on an important ally in this region, that that will have long-term security consequences for all of our countries in North America. So that does worry the Government of Canada.

Trade/Canada-U.S. Relations

Q. If you will allow me, I want to go back to NAFTA. NAFTA is in place for almost 15 years now. Wouldn't it be possible to improve things, perhaps, through renegotiating certain things on NAFTA? Mr. Harper, American President say there's no—we should not renegotiate NAFTA; President Bush says we should not renegotiate. What do you think, Minister?

Prime Minister Harper. We would be ready to do anything that any of our partners wants to do. If one of our partners wants to negotiate NAFTA, we'll do—we'll renegotiate. But this is not the position that we prefer—the Government of Canada. We have an agreement that worked well, that created jobs—lots of jobs in this continent, and I think that the business community is unanimous about the benefits of this agreement.

And I think that the problems that exist really call us to really, perhaps, improve or deepen NAFTA even more. And the problems also justify that we do what we need to do to have trade that works better than it does now. But the right priority is not to renegotiate something that has been decided. This is not the great challenge that we have. When we meet with businessmen and businesswomen, this is not their concern—their main concern. Their concern is in the future, not renegotiating the past. But Canada will always be ready to any possibilities that may happen.

As I said, we have a very dynamic relationship with—relations with the United States. We are the first—or the greatest exporter of energy products towards the United States. And for the United States, we are the main source of energy security for the United States. And we think that now it's even more important—this relation is even more important now than it was

20 years ago, and it will be more important even in the future. So if we have to discuss these possibilities, we'll be in a good position, but we would prefer to talk about the future than the past.

[*Prime Minister Harper continued in English.*]

I just said before, we'll be prepared for any possibility. The American people are going to make a decision. The future American administration may have a different view. I can just tell you, when I meet businesspeople not just from our country but from around the continent, the benefits of our NAFTA relationship are without question. And what all the focus is in our discussions is how to make it work better, how to make the borders thinner, how to make commerce flow more quickly, more freely. That's—how to make our relationship more integrated and deeper—those are the real concerns that I experience in Canada and when I deal with people who are focused on economic development in our trade partners' economies.

But look, as I said, we'll be prepared for any eventuality. Canada is the United States number-one supplier of energy. And we are a secure and stable supplier. That is of critical importance to the future of the United States. And if we had to look at this kind of an option, I think, quite frankly, we would be in even stronger position now than we were 20 years ago, and we'll be in a stronger position in the future. But my preference is not to renegotiate what we discussed in the past; it's to talk about the future. And I think that's what our respective—that's what, at least, the Canadian population wants us to do.

President Bush. Thank you, sir. Good job, Stephen.

NOTE: The President's news conference began at 11:31 a.m. at Gallier Hall. In his remarks, President Bush referred to President Alvaro Uribe Velez of Colombia. President Calderon referred to Secretary of Economy Eduardo Sojo Garza-Aldape of Mexico. Prime Minister Harper referred to his wife Laureen. A reporter referred to former Mexican Presidential candidate Andres Manuel Lopez Obrador. President Calderon spoke in Spanish, and his remarks were translated by an interpreter. Portions of Prime Minister Harper's remarks were in French, and an English translation was provided. Some reporters spoke in Spanish and French, and their remarks were translated by interpreters. The Office of the Press Secretary also released a Spanish language transcript of this news conference.

Joint Statement by President George W. Bush, President Felipe de Jesus Calderon Hinojosa of Mexico, and Prime Minister Stephen Harper of Canada
April 22, 2008

New Orleans

As continental neighbors and partners committed to democratic government, the rule of law and respect for individual rights and freedoms, Canada, Mexico and the United States have shared interests in keeping North America secure, prosperous, and competitive in today's global environment. We met in New Orleans to discuss how we might collaborate further to achieve these goals, as well as to discuss our hemispheric and global interests and concerns.

The Security and Prosperity Partnership (SPP), based on the principle that security and prosperity depend on each other, is a useful mechanism that helps us to identify and pursue practical solutions to shared challenges in North America in a way that respects our individual and sovereign interests. We each remain open and accountable to our own people.

The SPP complements the success of the North American Free Trade Agreement (NAFTA), which has helped to triple trade since 1993 among our three countries to a projected $1 trillion in 2008. NAFTA has offered our consumers a greater variety of better and less expensive goods and services, encouraged our businesses to increase investment throughout North America, and helped to create millions of new jobs in all three countries. NAFTA is key to maintaining North America's competitive edge in an increasingly complex, fast-paced and connected global marketplace.

Our Ministers responsible for security and prosperity met in Los Cabos, Mexico on February 27, 2008 to advance the five priority areas we identified last year in Montebello. In New Orleans, we decided that our Ministers should renew and focus their work in the following areas:

- To increase the competitiveness of our businesses and economies, we are working to make our regulations more compatible, which will support integrated supply chains and reduce the cost of goods traded within North America. In the auto industry, for example, we are seeking to implement compatible fuel efficiency regimes and high safety standards to protect human health and the environment, and to reduce the costs of producing cars and trucks for the North American market. We also are strengthening efforts to protect our inventors, authors, performers and other innovators by advancing our Intellectual Property Action Strategy. We have forged stronger relationships to support more effective law enforcement efforts to combat the trade of counterfeit and pirated goods.

- To make our borders smarter and more secure, we are coordinating our long-term infrastructure plans and are taking steps to enhance services, and reduce bottlenecks and congestion at major border crossings. In this regard, we are working to coordinate the efforts of federal agencies to enhance capacity at major border crossing points, such as Detroit-Windsor and San Diego-Tijuana. We are deepening cooperation on the development and application of technology to make our border both smarter and more secure, as well as strengthen trusted traveler and shipper programs. We will seek to allocate resources efficiently so as to avoid unnecessary inspections. We are exploring new customs procedures, such as a more uniform filing procedure, with the aim of reducing transactional costs while enhancing the security of our borders. We are cooperating to install advanced screening equipment at ports of entry to deter and detect the smuggling of nuclear and radiological materials. The United States and Canada are working to finalize a framework agreement to govern cross-border maritime enforcement operations in shared waterways. All of these efforts will help us more effectively facilitate the legal flow of people and goods across our shared borders while addressing threats to our safety.
- To strengthen energy security and protect the environment, we are seeking to develop a framework for harmonization of energy efficiency standards, and sharing technical information to improve the North American energy market. Together we intend to create an outlook for biofuels for the region, work to enhance our electricity networks, and make more efficient use of our energy through increasing fuel efficiency of our vehicles. Building on the gains in technology over the last 5 years, we are exchanging information and exploring opportunities for joint collaboration to further reduce barriers to expanding clean energy technologies, especially carbon dioxide capture and storage to mitigate greenhouse gas emissions. We are working to better North America's air quality and working together to improve the safety of chemicals in the marketplace.
- To improve our citizens' access to safe food, and health and consumer products in North America, we are increasing cooperation and information sharing on the safety of food and products. We are working to strengthen our respective regulatory and inspection systems to protect consumers, while maintaining the efficient flow of food and products among our three countries. We are working to make our food and product safety standards more compatible. We are also working to improve continental recall capacities and are engaging the private sector to ensure that our efforts are complementary.
- To improve our response to emergencies, we are updating our bilateral agreements to enable our local, State, Provincial, and Federal authorities to help each other quickly and efficiently during times of crisis and great need, including responding to threats posed by cyber or chemical-biological attacks. We have made significant progress in discussions for new bilateral emergency management agreements to help manage the movement of goods and people across the border during and after an emergency. We will explore ways to expand cooperation in North America to the trilateral level.

Our efforts in these areas have been informed by the insights of interested parties, in particular the North American Competitiveness Council (NACC), representatives from the business community who have helped us identify and develop solutions to the most pressing issues affecting North American competitiveness.

Our citizens represent the true promise and potential of North America. Our governments help best when they act to promote the conditions necessary for the liberty, safety and success of our people. We believe that we should continue and strengthen our regular dialogue and ongoing cooperation. The partnership among Canada, Mexico and the United States is broader than the sum of our many bilateral and trilateral activities. We share the goals of strengthening democratic governance and reducing barriers to trade within our region and beyond. We also share a common purpose to strengthen our hemispheric institutions and consultative processes.

We will continue working to fight transnational threats that pose challenges to our countries and to the well being of our people, such as organized crime; trafficking in arms, people, and drugs; smuggling; terrorism; money laundering; counterfeiting; and border violence. The transnational nature of these threats makes it imperative that our domestic efforts be complemented and strengthened by our cooperation together, and in international fora.

We reiterate our support for the Bali Action Plan and stress the urgency of reaching agreement to ensure the full, effective and sustained implementation of the U.N. Framework Convention on Climate Change now, up to and beyond 2012. We believe that the Major Economies Leaders Meeting should make a contribution to that outcome. All should redouble efforts to address climate change and to establish nationally appropriate programs and goals to be reflected in binding international commitments based on the principle of common but differentiated responsibilities and respective capabilities, to contribute to ensuring global greenhouse gas emission reductions, adaptation measures, energy security, and sustainable development. We are determined to work together to further explore regional cooperation in climate change efforts, including, but not limited to, advancing innovative and suitable clean energy technologies, building the capacity to adopt and deploy them and developing appropriate financial and technical instruments. We reaffirm our shared conviction that increased trade in environmental goods, services, and technologies can have a positive impact on global climate change efforts and encourage the removal of barriers to such trade.

We welcome the invitation of President Calderon to host the next meeting of North American leaders in 2009.

NOTE: The Office of the Press Secretary also released a Spanish language version of this joint statement. An original was not available for verification of the content of this joint statement.

Remarks Following a Meeting With Community Leaders in New Orleans
April 22, 2008

I want to thank the Governor, thank the mayor, thank the parish presidents, Congressmen. Thank you all very much—city council leaders, compassionate citizens from New Orleans. Thank you very much for briefing me and my team and the new Coordinator from the White House, Doug O'Dell, for keeping us abreast of progress that has been made down here and challenges that remain.

You know, one of the things—I came to New Orleans and spoke about the Federal commitment, and I said, it's been a devastating period, and the Federal Government is committed and will remain committed to helping. Thus far, the Federal Government's committed $120 billion—little more than that—of taxpayers' money to help all along the coast. I think it's money well spent. I think it's important for our country that the Gulf Coast region and the great city of New Orleans recover as quickly as possible.

My impression is that—you know, that there's a lot more hope now than there was even from a year ago. I mean, there's just—people have a little different bounce in their step. But there are some significant problems. One is we got to make sure these levees meet the obligations and meet the standards.

Secondly, I am concerned about the health care system that was torn up and needs to be rebuilt in a way that encourages there to be good health care and in a way that recognizes the changing population of New Orleans.

Thirdly, I have been concerned about the stories on crime, just like the citizens have been worried about the stories on crime. And I appreciate the Federal attorney giving me an update, and I appreciate the mayor's efforts to work hard to hold people to account for breaking the law. That's what the average citizen expects; that's what the taxpayers who are helping the people down here want to see.

All in all—and then, finally, public housing restoration—it's a big issue in New Orleans. It's—but it's an issue where there is a plan, and we just need to follow through on the plan.

So there are some hurdles, but this city has come a long way and—to the point where I felt very comfortable hosting the international conference with the President of Mexico and the Prime Minister of Canada. And I will tell you that not only did the leaders feel welcomed in New Orleans and feel comfortable in New Orleans and feel relaxed in New Orleans, but so did the delegations they brought with them. New Orleans is a great city to host a meeting or host a convention. They know what they're doing down here. The city is recovered, it's on its feet, and it's bouncing back. And it is an honor to be back here.

And I want to thank you all for sharing your thoughts with me. And thank you for being leaders and helping this part of the—vital part of the country recover.

NOTE: The President spoke at 2:07 p.m. at Galatoire's Restaurant. In his remarks, he referred to Gov. Piyush "Bobby" Jindal of Louisiana; Mayor C. Ray Nagin of New Orleans, LA; Douglas V. O'Dell, Jr., Federal Coordinator, Office of Gulf Coast Rebuilding; Jim Letten, U.S. Attorney for the Eastern District of Louisiana; President Felipe de Jesus Calderon Hinojosa of Mexico; and Prime Minister Stephen Harper of Canada.

Remarks on Arrival in Baton Rouge, Louisiana
April 22, 2008

The President. First of all, it's good to be back in Baton Rouge, home of the LSU Tiger national championship football team. I had the honor of welcoming the team and Coach Les Miles to the White House,

and it was a great honor for me, and I enjoyed it. And I do want to congratulate the good folks of Louisiana for supporting a football team that brought great credit to the game.

I'm here with the Governor—the great Governor of Louisiana to lend my support to John Kennedy for the United States Senate. I thank Becky and Preston for joining us as well. John Kennedy will make a fine Senator for the people of Louisiana. He's a fiscal watchdog. He cares about the tax-payers' money. He's made a career out of making sure that whenever government spends money, it's spent wisely, and that's the kind of Senator Louisiana needs.

He'll support the troops. He'll support those who wear our Nation's uniform. And he'll see our troops are funded without the United States Senate telling our military how to conduct the war. So I appreciate your strong support for our military, John.

You know, one of the issues that the Senate will be faced [with] ° is whether or not to raise people's taxes. John Kennedy has pledged to keep taxes low. We want the people here in Louisiana to have more of their own money to spend. And we can meet our priorities at the Federal Government without getting into the pockets of the people of Louisiana.

And finally, John Kennedy understands that our most important task is to protect the American people from harm. And if Al Qaida is making a phone call into the United States, he understands we need to know who they're talking to and why they're making the call.

So I look forward to having a man in the Senate who understands the priorities have got to be to protect the American people and understands that the same civil liberties given to our people shouldn't be extended to terrorists who want to do us harm.

So I wish you all the best, Senator-to-be. We got a good fundraiser for you. I'm honored that you would invite me here. And I look—ask the people of Louisiana to give this good man a fair hearing—more importantly, give him their vote, because he'll do a fine job as the United States Senator.

Thank you and congratulations.

John N. Kennedy. Thank you, Mr. President. Thank you so much.

The President. Good to see you. Let's load up and get going.

NOTE: The President spoke at 3:19 p.m. at Baton Rouge Metropolitan Airport. In his remarks, he referred to Gov. Piyush "Bobby" Jindal of Louisiana; and Becky, wife, and Preston, son, of senatorial candidate John N. Kennedy.

Statement on Farm Legislation
April 22, 2008

I am disappointed that Congress has failed to put forward a good farm bill, leaving farmers and ranchers in a state of continued uncertainty as to how they will be affected by Federal policies.

The farm bill proposal currently being discussed by conferees would fail several important tests that I have set forth. With record farm income, now is not the time for Congress to ask other sectors of the economy to pay higher taxes in order to increase the size of Government. The proposal would increase spending by at least $16 billion, masked in part by budgetary gimmicks and funded in part by additional tax revenues. These tax revenue provisions are unacceptable, including tax compliance initiatives being considered by the House

----
° White House correction.

and Senate conference committee. As important, the proposal also lacks the important reforms I've repeatedly called for.

After last week's short-term extension of the farm bill, Congress now has only 4 days to provide certainty to America's farmers and ranchers. Despite the passage of more than a year since my administration unveiled a responsible and forward-looking farm bill proposal, there are no signs that the conference committee will reach agreement on an acceptable farm bill by Friday. I therefore call on Congress to provide our agricultural producers with the certainty to make sound business and planting decisions about this year's crop by extending current law for at least 1 year.

Statement on the No Child Left Behind Act
April 22, 2008

Today Education Secretary Margaret Spellings took an important step towards strengthening and improving the No Child Left Behind Act. In the 6 years since its enactment, this law has delivered real results for students across the country. Students are achieving record math and reading scores, and African American and Hispanic students are making significant progress, posting alltime high scores in a number of categories.

No Child Left Behind was a bipartisan achievement. Unfortunately, at this time, Congress hasn't made noteworthy progress toward strengthening the law. In January, I indicated that the Secretary should move forward on reforms she can undertake administratively if Congress fails to act.

Secretary Spellings's announced package of regulations and pilot programs will address the dropout crisis in America, strengthen accountability, improve our lowest performing schools, and ensure that more students get access to high-quality tutoring. Her actions build on a series of administrative steps we've taken to provide additional flexibility to strengthen and improve the law to ensure continued progress toward the goal of every child reading and doing math at grade level by 2014.

Remarks on Presenting the Congressional Gold Medal to Michael E. DeBakey
April 23, 2008

Madam Speaker, Mr. Leader, Members of Congress, fellow Texans, distinguished guests, Dr. and Mrs. DeBakey: I'm honored to join you on this day of celebration. Throughout our Nation's history, the Congressional Gold Medal has been awarded sparingly, in recognition of the tremendous accomplishments that it takes to earn this high honor. The recipients of this medal who have come from the world of science are few, but they are iconic. They include Thomas Edison, Walter Reed, and Jonas Salk. Today we gather to recognize that Michael DeBakey's name belongs among them.

I appreciate the members of the Texas delegation, Senator Hutchison, Representative Green, and others, who sponsored this legislation.

As the chancellor emeritus of the Baylor College of Medicine and the director of the DeBakey Heart Center, Dr. DeBakey has given the citizens of the great State of Texas one more reason to be proud. It's a good thing too, because we're usually such a quiet bunch—[*laughter*]—unassuming people.

In the year that Michael DeBakey was born, Theodore Roosevelt sat in the White House, Henry Ford produced the first Model T automobile, and the average American's life expectancy was a little more than 51 years. That last point is worth noting, because the number today is nearly 78 years. Our lifetimes have been extended by more than 50 percent within the course of a century, and the man we're honoring today is part of the reason why.

It was Hippocrates, the author of the doctor's sacred oath, who said, "Wherever the art of medicine is loved, there also is a love of humanity." Truer words could not be spoken of Michael DeBakey. Growing up in the small town of Lake Charles, Louisiana, he learned the power of compassion at the early age. Every Sunday, as the Speaker noted, Michael's parents and siblings would load the family car with clothes and food for children who lived in an orphanage on the outskirts of town. One weekend, the donations included one of his favorite ball caps. When Michael complained, his mother simply told him, "You have a lot of caps. Those children have none." It was a lesson that he never forgot, and Michael DeBakey has been giving to the world ever since.

The other gift that Dr. DeBakey's parents gave him was a love of learning. In fact, young Michael's mother and father required their children to check a book out of the library every week. One week, Michael returned home frustrated, and he told his father that he had found a fascinating book, but that the librarians refused to lend it to him. The book was actually a part of a series called the Encyclopedia Britannica. [*Laughter*] And when his father

bought the set for him, Michael read every word of every article in every volume.

The charitable spirit and disciplined mind that Michael developed in his youth have lasted throughout his life. It was his selflessness that caused him to volunteer for World War II, even though he was a successful surgeon and professional. It was his intellect that caused him to help develop the idea of the MASH unit during his service. It was his power of his mind that led him to become one of the pioneers of the heart transplant, bypass surgery, and the artificial heart. And it was his sense of compassion that led him to help create a magnet school in Houston for young people pursuing careers in science.

It's been nearly 40 years since President Lyndon B. Johnson awarded Dr. DeBakey the Presidential Medal of Freedom. At that point four decades ago, he'd already proven himself to be one of the great scientific minds of his generation. In the years since, that status is being reaffirmed by many honors he has received, including the National Medal of Science, induction into the Health Care Hall of Fame, a lifetime achievement award from the United Nations, and a Living Legend citation from the Library of Congress.

But I was most interested in another distinction. It is this: that Dr. DeBakey was the first foreign physician made an honorary member of the Russian Academy of Sciences. That took quite an act to get into the Russian Academy of Sciences; all it took was him saving the life of a President. [*Laughter*] In 1996, only 5 years after the cold war ended, Dr. DeBakey traveled to Moscow and arranged Boris Yeltsin's quintuple bypass. President Yeltsin spoke for many of Dr. DeBakey's patients when he called him "a man with a gift of performing miracles."

Dr. DeBakey has an impressive resume, but his truest legacy is not inscribed on a medal or etched into stone, it is written on the human heart. His legacy is the unlost hours with family and friends who are still with us because of his healing touch. His legacy is grandparents who lived to see their grandchildren. His legacy is holding the fragile and sacred gift of human life in his hands and returning it unbroken.

For nearly 100 years, our country has been blessed with the endless talents and dedication of Dr. Michael DeBakey. And he has dedicated his career to a truly noble ambition: bettering the life of his fellow men.

So, Dr. DeBakey, on behalf of all those you've healed and those you've inspired, we thank you. May God bless you.

And now I ask the Speaker and Senator Reid to join me for the gold medal presentation.

NOTE: The President spoke at 11:33 a.m. in the Rotunda at the U.S. Capitol. In his remarks, he referred to Katrin DeBakey, wife of Michael E. DeBakey.

Remarks on Small Business Week
April 23, 2008

Welcome. I'm glad you're here. Thanks for coming. Nothing better, being in the East Room of the White House with successful entrepreneurs, small-business owners, dreamers, and doers who really add such richness to our country. So I welcome you here. I'm glad you're here. It's exciting to be here, isn't it? Yes, after 7½ years, it's still exciting for me too. And I'm really glad you're here.

I want to thank Steve Preston. He's done a fantastic job as the head of the SBA, so good that I named him to be the Secretary of Housing and Urban Development. And I congratulate you, Steve, for taking the job. I'm looking forward to getting the Senate to take up your nomination quickly and get you approved.

So Small Business Week—the truth of the matter is, every day ought to be small business day in America because—[applause]. Of course, people say, why? Well, first of all, small businesses create over two-thirds of all new jobs in America. And if you want your economy to grow, and if you want the country to be hopeful, it seems like you ought to be celebrating the talent and the energy of our small-business owners daily. But we've decided to do it week—yearly—Small Business Week. I pre-

sume that's 1 week out of the year. [*Laughter*]

And so the first thing I've got to do is congratulate all the award winners who are here. Thanks. It's—owning a small business is hard; it's not an easy experience. I've had the pleasure of getting to meet a lot of small-business owners during my time as, first, Governor of Texas and then President of the country. And you'll be amazed at how many times people have said, well, you know, it all started around the kitchen table. You'll also be amazed at how many family members are involved in the creation and the operation of a small business. And our fellow citizens wouldn't be amazed to know that the number of hours required to make sure the business is going is a lot. But the thing that struck me the most, besides the fact that people are willing to dream and work hard, is how proud the small-business owner is of the employees with whom the person works and how caring the owner is to make sure that those who've helped the business succeed are treated well.

I have the pleasure of welcoming and recognizing one Shawn Christopher Boyer, who happens to be the recipient of the Small Business Owner of the Year. Now, Shawn started off by helping a friend search online for an internship, and he got an idea for a business right there. Sometimes that happens. You know, it's just, like, click. And the idea was to create a web site to help unemployed Americans with job opportunities. And actually, I asked him to leave a business card, because it seems like I might be looking here after a while. [*Laughter*]

He started his business with just two employees. I bet you a lot of the winners here can say, "I started my business with one or two employees." He has grown— got 100 employees now. He is—earnings have grown from almost $900,000 in '03 to over $11 million 4 years later. And as I just told you, he was named National Small Business Person of the Year. I met with Shawn, the CFO David Bosher, Tennille, as well as his dad. And I want to congratulate you, Shawn. Welcome to the White House, and I really wish you all the very best.

Angela Timm, where's Angela? Oh, there you are. Thank you, Angela. She started a company in her home that sells music boxes and framed messages that offer words of hope and inspiration. She's gone through what a lot of other small-business owners go through, which is good times and bad times. And the fundamental question is, do you have the perseverance to endure the bad time and the humility to handle the good times?

In 2004, her business hit hard times. She had a good idea, but sometimes everything doesn't go well for you in the business world. The company's line of credit was maxed out. They had to let managers go, and her home was hit by a tornado. Her family and Angela held on through the adversity. They recovered. They hired back employees. In recent years, they have seen sales in the millions, with healthy profits. And that is why she's the runner-up Small Business Owner of the Year.

And the reason I bring up these 2 stories—we could be here for the other 48 stories, which would have a lot of similar-

ities. I appreciate you all coming together to share stories, to reach out to others who wonder what it's like to be an entrepreneur, to help others realize the great wonders of ownership, and to make sure that as you tell the story, that people are realistic about what it takes to succeed.

Government has a role to play as well, and that is to create an environment in which the entrepreneurial spirit flourishes. I mean, as I remind people, that Government doesn't create success in a small business. Matter of fact, Government can pass policies that make it harder to succeed in small business. Government has got to be mindful of the contribution of the entrepreneur and make sure that the environment is such that people feel comfortable dreaming and owning and expanding.

And so I know you're going to be speaking to elected officials, and I've got a few suggestions about what you might offer them in the way of advice. First, you might suggest to Members of Congress that they let you keep your money, in other words, to keep taxes low. This is obviously a difficult time for the economy, and I like to say it's a rough patch. And the reason I call it that is because I'm confident that with good policies and hard work, we'll come out stronger than we were entering. But nevertheless, it's tough. And it's tough on small-business owners.

We did take action in which, rather than just analyzing the situation, we saw this coming and moved swiftly with Members of Congress from both parties, believe it or not—actually got something done in a constructive way without feeling like they had to call each other names. And it's a progrowth package which will provide tax rebates to more than 130 million American households. And that ought to help—that ought to help stimulate consumption. The money hasn't hit yet. It's going to be there—start moving in the second week of May.

The stimulus package also provides incentives for businesses like yours to invest in new equipment and technology this year. In other words, it's a temporary stimulus package aimed at dealing with the rough patch that we've entered into, but it's got to be robust enough to matter. So when you're affecting 130 million households, that's robust. And when you're affecting all the businesses in the United States, that's a robust message.

And the reason why it's important to stimulate investment is because if tax policy can encourage you to buy a piece of equipment, one, it helps your business be more productive, but also somebody has got to make the equipment. And if somebody is making the equipment, then somebody has got to buy the supplies to make the equipment, and it kind of ripples throughout the economy.

So the idea was to provide stimulus to businesses and to provide—give money to the taxpayers so that they can go out and purchase things and remain active consumers. And it's going to take awhile for this to have an effect. The experts tell me that—you got these economists that say, on the one hand, and on the other hand—if they had three hands, it would be three opinions, but nevertheless—all due respect to some of my economist friends here. [*Laughter*] But pretty well consensus that the stimulus package, when it takes full effect, will affect our growth in the third quarter, which begins in July of this year.

There's other work to be done on taxes. One of my concerns about tax policy is that it creates uncertainty. In other words, when you're trying to figure out a 5-year projection about your companies, you've got to be certain that the tax load that you now bear isn't going to increase. It's hard to plan. It's hard to have a successful small business if there's uncertainty in the environment. And one place where there can be a lot of uncertainty is whether or not your taxes are going to remain low. And the reason why that's the case is because the tax relief we passed is going to expire, some of it beginning in 2010.

Now, the tax relief we passed, you might remember, cut taxes on all people who pay taxes. Now, we have—and emphasis on families with children, for example. We tried to get rid of the death tax forever. A small-business owner has got to be saying to Members of Congress, "I don't want to be taxed twice, once when I'm alive, and once after I die"—particularly if you own a small business. It's an unfair tax. Yet that tax, which is on the road to extinction, is going to come back to life.

And equally damaging, as far as I'm concerned, is the fact that people are saying, we're going to let the personal income tax rates go back up. And, of course, the language is, "only on the rich people." Well, the sad fact is, is that many of our small businesses are subchapter S corporations, LLCs, limited partnerships that pay tax at the individual income tax level. And so the tax relief we provided was in many ways—should have been called a small-business tax relief plan. And the idea of saying that we're going to raise individual income tax rates really is counterproductive to making sure that the economy remains strong.

If you're creating over two-thirds of the new jobs, why would we want to be taking money out of the treasuries of those job creators? Less money in your treasury means it's going to be harder for you to create the jobs necessary for this economy to be strong. If Congress truly cares about keeping this economy strong, they ought to have certainty in the Tax Code by making all the tax cuts we passed permanent.

A couple other issues, now that I got you stuck here. [*Laughter*] Health care, I fully understand that you're concerned about affordable health care. You're concerned, obviously, because it affects your bottom line, but you're also more concerned because it affects the people you work with. And I understand that. And there's a choice that we can make in Government. One is, do we have kind of a wholesale plan sponsored by, executed by the Federal Government, or do we put policy in place that encourages the decisionmakers to be directly in touch with the providers? That's what I have tried to propose, and have proposed, such as health savings accounts.

For those of you who have not explored health savings accounts, I strongly urge you to do so. It's a very powerful way for you to better afford health insurance and, at the same time, empower your employees.

I believe Congress should change the Tax Code. If you're working for a big company in America, you get a better tax break than if you're working for—on your own or you're on a contract, employee. And so there ought to be a standard deduction for health insurance so that the bias in the Tax Code is eliminated.

We ought to confront junk lawsuits that drive good docs out of practice and run up the cost of your health care.

And finally, I strongly believe that Congress should allow small businesses to pool risk across jurisdictional boundaries. Those are long words. Like, if you're a restaurant guy in Texas, you ought be able to put your employees in the same risk pool as a restaurant person in Maryland. Those are called association health plans that will enable small businesses to be able to buy insurance at the same discounts that big businesses get. But what we shouldn't do is have a health care system where the decisions are made in Washington, DC, not made in your offices or between patients and doctors.

I want to talk about an interesting issue that is getting a lot of attention these days, and that is the issue of trade and markets. And as you know by now, I hope, that I'm—I believe that it's in our interests to open up markets for U.S. products and goods and services. I also know it's in our interest to say to the world, treat us the way we treat you. In other words, all we want to do is be treated fairly. And one of the interesting votes coming up here soon—hopefully, if the Speaker doesn't

change her—does change her mind—which would be on the Colombia free trade agreement. And let me tell you why I think this is important.

First of all, there are about 9,000 American businesses that export to Colombia. Most of those businesses, by far the vast majority, are midsized and small businesses. The problem is, is that that which they export generally faces significant tariffs. In other words, the product that they're selling is more expensive because of the tariffs. On the other hand, as a result of congressional policy over the years, products coming from Colombia into the United States don't face tariffs. So American goods and services, mainly provided by midsized and small-sized businesses, are taxed going into Colombia, making it harder for those products to gain market access. On the other hand, as a result of years of policy, Colombian goods come here duty free.

Now, doesn't it make sense to say to Colombia, we value our friendship, but we would like to be treated the way we treat you? And that's what the Colombia free trade agreement says. It—this is a bill that is beneficial to our small businesses and midsized businesses. It makes eminent sense to level the playing field. Yet, unfortunately, the leadership in the House of Representatives chose a unusual procedure to block a vote. I believe the bill will pass. I know that when people really analyze whether it's fair or not to be treated one way and yet Colombia be treated beneficially—say, well, why don't we just level the playing field?

The other thing is this vote has got enormous national policy implications. First of all, it's in our interest to have a neighborhood that's free—when people who believe in rule of law and human rights—support leaders in our neighborhood that are tough on dealing with narcotraffickers.

In Colombia, there's a group called FARC, which is funded by, in large part, drugs, that are willing to use violence to advance their agenda. And they're threatening our ally. And President Uribe is taking them on in a way that doesn't violate the human rights of his people. He's a strong, strong leader. And yet if Congress turns down this agreement, it's like turning our back to an ally, which will encourage the voices of false populism in our neighborhood.

And so I—this is an important vote. It's important for small businesses, it's important for our economy, and it's important for our national security interests. And the United States Congress must give it a vote on the floor of the House.

So those are some of the things that are on my mind. [*Laughter*] You know, it's interesting, there's a portrait of a fellow that hangs here in the White House who—he failed at nearly every enterprise he started. He invested in a zinc mine, but lost his money. He invested in an oil company, but the company sold the lease to a—and it turned out to be a gusher, but he didn't own any of it at that point in time. He ran a store with a friend, but it went bankrupt after a few years. And yet he was arguably one of the finest Presidents we had, and that was Harry Truman.

I'm convinced—I've never had a visit with Harry at all, but I'm convinced that he would say, "The lessons I learned in trying to be a small-business owner are lessons that are important for a decisionmaker in the White House." And although it's hard to say he was a successful businessperson, he learned about hard work and determination and resilience and willing to face adversity with good spirit.

And that is why I am honored to be with you today, because I'm confident that's what you've done. What you've chosen to do is not easy, but what you've chosen to do is important for our country. It's the collective decisions by our small-business owners that make America the envy of the world in many ways.

I love it when people can say, "I have a idea, and I am going to apply all my talent and all my effort to see the idea come to fruition." It is what made us great in the past, it's what makes us great today, and what is going to make us great in the future. And I hope you take great pride in the contributions that you're making to your community, your family, and your Nation.

Thanks for coming, and may God bless you.

NOTE: The President spoke at 3:50 p.m. in the East Room at the White House. In his remarks, he referred to Shawn C. Boyer, president and chief executive officer, David Bosher, senior vice president and chief financial officer, and Tennille Boyer, national account executive, SnagAJob.com, Inc.; J. Hardin Boyer, father of Mr. Boyer; and Angela Timm, founder and chief executive officer, Cottage Garden Collections. The Small Business Week proclamation of April 17 is listed in Appendix D at the end of this volume.

Statement on National Donate Life Month
April 23, 2008

During National Donate Life Month, we show our appreciation for our fellow Americans who have saved lives by becoming organ, tissue, marrow, and blood donors, and we honor the health care professionals, researchers, and others involved in this life-saving work. I was pleased today to meet with organ donors, medical professionals, and organ recipients, all of whom participated in a historic six-recipient kidney transplant in which six patients received

new organs from six unrelated living donors. This history-making medical event
took place 3 weeks ago at Johns Hopkins
Comprehensive Transplant Center. These
people are all firsthand witnesses to the
gift of life, or, in this case, lives.

We are blessed to have a health care
system that is the best in the world and
includes skilled medical professionals like
those I met with today. We are also blessed
to be a nation filled with generous and
compassionate people. The selflessness of
those who are donors is an inspiration.

Unfortunately, thousands of Americans
are on waiting lists for an organ or tissue
transplant. I urge all Americans to make
the decision to donate. For information
about becoming an organ and tissue donor,
go to organdonor.gov. Talk to your family,
talk to your friends, and register. You can
give a transforming gift of life.

NOTE: The National Donate Life Month
proclamation of April 1 is listed in Appendix
D at the end of this volume.

Remarks at the White House Summit on Inner-City Children and Faith-Based Schools
April 24, 2008

Thank you all. Aysia, thanks for the introduction. You did a fabulous job. I'm told
that you're a very hard worker who loves
school, and it's clear you always wear a
smile. She's a member of her school's student advisory group, has performed in plays
ranging from Shakespeare to "The Lion
King," writes short stories, and as you just
heard her explain, she loves all language
arts. Well, that's good. Some people say
I'm pretty artful with language as well.
[*Laughter*]

It is clear she has a promising future
because of the education she is receiving
at Saint Ann's. Unfortunately, thousands of
other children like her are missing out on
these opportunities because America's
inner-city faith-based schools are closing at
an alarming rate. And so that's why we've
convened this summit, to discuss how we
can extend lifelines of learning to all America's children. And I want to thank you
for coming.

I take this summit seriously. Obviously,
you do as well. My administration looks
forward to working with you. This is a national objective, to make sure every child

gets a good education. And I really appreciate you coming.

I want to thank my friend and the Secretary of Education, Margaret Spellings, for
joining with us today. I thank the Acting
Secretary of HUD, Roy Bernardi.

Archbishop Wuerl, thank you very much,
sir, for being here. We were just talking
about what a glorious week it was to welcome His Holiness to America. It was an
extraordinary moment for all who were directly involved and, I think, an extraordinary moment for all of America.

I got to know Archbishop Wuerl in Pittsburgh. I hope I conveyed to him my sense
that providing a sound education for every
child is one of the really important challenges for America. I happen to believe
it is one of the greatest civil rights challenges. I am fully aware that in inner-city
America, some children are getting a good
education, but a lot are consigned to inadequate schools.

And I believe helping these children
should be a priority of a nation. It's certainly a priority to me. I married a teacher
who has worked in inner-city schools; I
helped raise one as well. And helping

inner-city children receive the education they deserve is so important as we head into the 21st century, to make sure every child has got the skills necessary to succeed. That's what a hopeful country is all about.

Over the past 7 years, we have worked to strengthen the public school system. In other words, we haven't given up on public schools. Quite the contrary, we've tried to help them succeed by passing the No Child Left Behind Act. In some circles, it's controversial. I don't think it should be controversial, however, to demand high standards for every child. I don't think it should be controversial to insist upon accountability to see if those children are meeting those standards. And I don't think it should be viewed as controversial to say to a public school, if children are falling behind, here's supplemental services to help that individual child catch up.

As a result of accountability measures, I can now say that eighth graders set a record high for math scores. In other words, in order to be able to say that, you have to measure in the first place. When I was Governor of Texas, I didn't like a system where we just simply guessed—you know, "Do you think the child is learning?" "I don't know. Maybe, maybe not." [*Laughter*] That's unacceptable, particularly when a child's life is at stake.

We've learned that scores for minority and poor students are reaching alltime highs in a number of areas, and that's great. As a matter of fact, there's an achievement gap in America that is unacceptable. The good news is, it's beginning to narrow. The problem is, is that while the No Child Left Behind Act is helping to turn around many struggling schools, there are still children trapped in schools that will not teach and will not change.

Today, nearly one-half of children in America's major urban school districts do not graduate on time; one-half of our children in major urban school districts do not get out of school on time. In Detroit, one student in four makes it out of the public school system with a diploma. When schools like these fail our inner-city children, it is unfair, it's unacceptable, and it is unsustainable for our country.

And so there are a variety of solutions. One is to work hard to improve the public school system. But also another solution is to recognize that there is a bright future for a lot of children found in faith-based schools.

The faith-based school tradition is not a 21st-century phenomenon. A Quaker school opened in Philadelphia in 1689. A Jewish day school opened in New York more than 40 years before the American Revolution. And during the 19th century, Catholic schools in our biggest cities welcomed children of poor European immigrants. Can you imagine what it would—what it's like to be an immigrant coming to America, can't hardly speak the language, and find great solace in two institutions: one, church; and two, schools? And generations of Americans have been lifted up. Generations of the newly arrived have been able to have hopeful futures because of our faith-based schools. It's been a—it's a fact. It's a part of our history. Frankly, it's a glorious part of our history.

Today, our Nation's poorest—in our poorest communities, religious schools continue to provide important services. And as they carry out their historic mission of training children in faith, these schools increasingly serve children, you know, that don't share their religious tradition. That's important for people to know, that there's a lot of students who, for example, may not be Catholic who go to the schools and get a great education. That's what we ought to be focused on, how to get people a great education.

In neighborhoods where some people say children simply can't learn, the faith-based schools are proving the naysayers wrong. These schools are—provide a good, solid academic foundation for children. They also help children understand the importance of discipline and character.

Yet for all their successes, America's inner-city faith-based schools are facing a crisis. And I use the word crisis for this reason: Between 2000 and 2006, nearly 1,200 faith-based schools closed in America's inner cities. It's affected nearly 400,000 students. They're places of learning where people are getting a good education, and they're beginning to close, to the extent that 1,200 of them have closed. The impact of school closings extends far beyond the children that are having to leave these classrooms. The closings place an added burden on inner-city public schools that are struggling. And these school closings impoverish our country by really denying a future of children a critical source of learning not only about how to read and write, but about social justice.

We have an interest in the health of these institutions. One of the reasons I've come is to highlight this problem and say to our country, we have an interest in the health of these centers of excellence. It's in the country's interest to get beyond the debate of public/private, to recognize this is a critical national asset that provides a critical part of our Nation's fabric in making sure we're a hopeful place.

And so I want to spend a little time talking about what can be done to help preserve these schools and provide, more importantly, a hopeful future. And that's what you're going to do after I leave as well.

First, ensuring that faith-based schools can continue to serve inner-city children requires a commitment from the Federal Government. Federal funds support faith-based organizations that serve Americans in need. So we got beyond the social service debate by saying, you know, it's okay to use taxpayers' money to provide help for those who hurt. My whole theory of life was, we ought to be asking about results, not necessarily process. When you focus on process, you can find all sorts of reasons

not to move forward. If you, say, focus on results, it then provides an outlet for other options than state-sponsored programs, which is okay.

I mean, what I'm telling you is, is that we're using taxpayers' money to empower faith-based organizations to help meet critical needs throughout the country, critical needs such as helping a child whose parents may be in prison understand there's hope; a critical need is helping a prisoner recently released realize there's a hopeful tomorrow; a critical need is to help somebody whip drugs and alcohol so they can live a hopeful life. And we do that in the social services.

We also provide Federal funds—funding support for institutions of higher learning. We're using taxpayers' money to enable somebody to go to a private university, a religious university. It's a long tradition of the United States of America.

So my attitude is, if we're doing this, if this is a precedent, why don't we use the same philosophy to provide Federal funds to help inner-city families find greater choices in educating their children.

There is a precedent for this called the DC choice initiative act. And we've got some advocates here for the DC Choice Incentive Act—I know; I've worked with them—and I'm surprised they're not yelling again. [*Laughter*] The law created Washington's opportunity scholarship program, which has helped more than 2,600 of the poorest children in our Nation's Capital find new hope at a faith-based or other nonpublic school. In other words, one way to address the closings of schools is to empower parents to be able to send their children to those schools before they close.

And this is a successful program, I think it's safe to say. One way to judge whether it's successful is to look at the demand for the scholarship relative to the supplies of the scholarship. And there's a lot of people who want their children to be able to take advantage of this program. As a matter of fact, demand clearly outstrips supply, which says to me we ought to expand the program and not kill the program. I mean, when you have a—[*applause*].

So we'll continue to work with Congress to not only reauthorize the program as it exists, but hopefully, expand it so that parents will be able to—[*applause*].

I also proposed an idea that I really hope Congress takes seriously, and that is Pell Grants for Kids. We—this would be a $300 million initiative that would help as many as 75,000 low-income children that are now enrolled in troubled public schools to be able to go to a school of the parents' choice. See, one of the—what's very important to make sure that an accountability system works is there's actual consequences and outlets.

And one of the outlets would be, if you're in a public school that won't teach and won't change, and you're—qualify— here's a scholarship for you to be able to have an additional opportunity. And to me, this is a good way to help strengthen the schools that I was talking about that are losing. I mean, one way to make sure you don't lose schools is you have people that are able to afford the education sustain the cashflow of these valuable American assets.

Pell grants—I want to remind our citizens, Pell grants have helped low-income young adults pursue the dream of a college education. And it is time to apply the same spirit to liberate poor children trapped in public schools that aren't meeting expectations.

State and local governments can help. Today, more than 30 State constitutions include so-called Blaine amendments, which prohibit public support of religious schools. These amendments have their roots in 19th-century, anti-Catholic bigotry, and today, the legacy of discrimination continues to harm low-income students of many faiths and many backgrounds. And so State lawmakers, if they're concerned about quality education for children and if they're concerned about these schools closing, they ought to remove the Blaine

amendments; they ought to move this part of history.

There are other things State and local governments can do. I would call people's attention to the Pennsylvania Educational Improvement Tax Credit—P-E-I-T-C— PEITC—[*laughter*]—which allows businesses to meet State tax obligations by supporting pre-K through 12 scholarships for low-income students. It's an innovative way to use the Tax Code to meet a national— in this case, State—objective. The scholarships then allow children to attend the school of their choice, including religious schools. Since 2001, these tax credits have yielded more than $300 million to help Pennsylvania families. It's an innovative use of the Tax Code to meet social objectives. All 12 high schools in the diocese—in Pittsburgh, Bishop—have seen increased enrollment each year the program has been in place. That's positive.

And so I would call upon State leaders to listen to what comes out of this conference and to think of innovative ways to advance education for all children. Faith-based schools can continue to serve inner-city children requires a—to see that that happens requires a commitment from the business community. It's in corporate America's interest that our children get a good education, starting in pre-K through 12th grade.

In Chicago, a group of Jesuit priests found an innovative way to finance children's education called Cristo Rey, and they convinced Chicago's businesses to become involved. It's interesting that the Jesuits took the initiative. I would hope that corporate America would also take initiative. [*Laughter*] But 4 days of the week, the children go to class, and then on the fifth, they report for work at some of Chicago's most prestigious firms.

The businesses get energetic, reliable workers for high-turnover jobs. The students get a top-notch education plus real work experience. They feel a sense of pride when they leave some of the city's most dangerous neighborhoods for the city's tallest skyscrapers. It's a program that is working, and many of the students take that same sense of pride and accomplishment to higher education.

It's interesting to note that Cristo Rey is now involved in 19 cities. In other words, the good ideas can take hold. The job of this conference is to provide a kind of go-by for people who share a sense of concern about our Nation's future. And hopefully, from this summit, good ideas will be spawning other good ideas—at the Federal level, the State and local level, at the corporate level, and then, of course, at the citizen level.

Citizens are—you know, we are a compassionate nation. What I see is America at its very best, which is these millions of acts of kindness and generosity that take place, and it doesn't require a government law. Sometimes it takes a little higher authority than government to inspire people to acts of kindness and mercy. But it happens all the time in America, it truly does. About one-third of Americans who volunteer do so through religious organizations. Many of them happen to be faith-based schools, by the way. When you hear about an America that volunteers, many of the volunteers are at faith-based schools.

I was struck by a interesting story that came out of Memphis, Tennessee. Ten years ago, private donors gave approximately $15 million to the church in Memphis to help revive Catholic schools in the city's poorest neighborhoods. Assets exists; they're worried about them going away. So rather than just watch schools close, somebody—individuals did something about it by putting up $15 million. With the seed money, the diocese launched the Jubilee Schools initiative and reopened Catholic schools that had been shuttered actually, in some cases, for decades. Today, 10 Jubilee schools serve more than 1,400 students. Eighty-one percent of these children are not Catholic; nearly 96 percent live at or below poverty level.

With the help from Jubilee scholarship donors, tuition becomes whatever the family can afford. And the schools happen to be working as well, which is really important. The program—and the reason I can tell you is because test scores are up; like, they're not afraid to measure. You've got to be a little worried in our society when somebody says, "I don't think I want to measure." That's like saying, "I don't want to be held to account." The problem with that line of reasoning when it—is that when you're dealing with our children, it's unacceptable. Of course, you should be held to account. We ought to praise those who achieve excellence and call upon those who don't to change so they can achieve excellence.

And so this school system is willing to measure, and it has been a great joy for the people of Memphis to watch excellence spread. And I want to thank those who have put forth the money and call on all citizens to find ways they can contribute with their hearts to help educational entrepreneurs succeed—is really what we're talking about, isn't it? Kind of innovation—the willing to challenge the status quo if it's not working. I call it educational entrepreneurship, so I'd consider yourself entrepreneurs, social entrepreneurs.

Faith-based schools can continue to serve inner-city children, and sometimes they can get a good boost from higher education. It seems like to me it's—when I was Governor of Texas, I tried to get our higher education institutions to understand that rather than becoming a source of remediation, they ought to be a source of added value. And one way to do so is to help these schools early on to make sure that children don't slip behind in the basics.

I was impressed by Notre Dame's Alliance for Catholic Education, known as ACE, which prepares college graduates to work as teachers in underserved Catholic schools. It's an interesting way to participate in making sure the Catholic schools and the faith-based schools stay strong, and that is to educate teachers, actually go in the classrooms, and make sure that there's adequate instruction available. The people at Notre Dame commit to teach for 2 years as they earn their master's degree in education. And turns out that when you get a taste for being a teacher, that you tend to stay. And so today, there are about 650 ACE teachers and graduates who work at Catholic schools across the country.

And there's a—I like the idea of these higher education institutions saying, okay, here's what I can contribute to making sure that elementary school and junior high school and high school education has high standards and excellence. And one way to do it is to support our faith-based schools all across the country.

And so that's what I've come to talk to you about. Here are some ways—I mean, these are levels of society that ought to all be involved, and hopefully, out of this meeting, that there's concrete action. We didn't ask you to come to Washington just to opine; we came and asked you to Washington to set good ideas out there for others to go by, because there's a lot of people in our country who share the same concern you share. People understand what we're talking about here. This is pretty practical stuff. This isn't—these are just down-to-earth ideas on how to solve some of our Nation's critical problems.

And so I'm—let me end with a story here about Yadira Vieyra. Yadira's here. She goes to Georgetown University, and she said—I heard—I was asking if Yadira was going to be here so I could ask her to stand here in a minute, and a fellow told me she's a little worried about missing class. So whoever Yadira's teacher is, please blame it on me, not her. [*Laughter*]

She is a—she was born in Mexico—*Mexicana*. And they moved to Chicago, probably to try to realize a better life—I'm confident, to try to realize a better life. Mom and dad had a dream to give their family hope. There's no more hopeful place in the world, by the way, than the

United States of America. We shouldn't be surprised when people come to America for a hopeful life. And that's what America has been and should be.

And then we shouldn't be surprised when the parents hope that their children get a great education, because there's nothing more hopeful for a parent than to know their child is receiving a good education. Well, that's what Yadira's folks wanted for her. And so when the time came—time for her to go to high school came—they wanted something better than a low-performing high school. You know, one of the interesting things about the accountability system—a lot of people think that their child goes to the finest school ever, until the results get posted. [*Laughter*]

And it's—the whole purpose, by the way, is not to embarrass anybody; it's not to scold anybody. The whole purpose is to achieve excellence for every person. And so Yadira's parents, I'm sure, took a look at the school system and said, there's a better way. And so guess what? She went to Cristo Rey, the program I just described to you. And she was challenged by the school's rigorous academics.

If you set low standards, guess what you're going to get—low results. If you believe in every child's worth and every child can learn, it's important to set high standards and challenge the children. And that's what happened in the school she went to. She was inspired by great teachers. She said she was motivated by the school's amazing job program. And she is now at Georgetown University, one of the great schools—universities in America. And guess what she wants to do when she leaves Georgetown? She wants to enroll in Notre Dame's ACE program. Yadira, thanks for coming.

You either just got an A—[*laughter*]— or an F. [*Laughter*] Either case, we're glad you're here—[*laughter*]—and I love your example. And the reason why it's important to have examples—so that we get beyond the rhetoric and realize that we're dealing with the human potential. Someday, no telling what Yadira's going to be in life, but one thing is for certain: It's going to be a productive citizen, and America will be better for it. And so we're glad you're here. Thank you for your spirit. Tell your parents thank you.

And so let me close with what happened at Nationals stadium with His Holy Father. He—when he celebrated Mass there, one of the objects he blessed at the end of the Mass was the new cornerstone of the Pope John Paul the Great High School in Arlington, Virginia. Isn't that interesting? I mean, I'm sure there was a lot of demands on His Holy Father, but he took time to bless the cornerstone of a school.

And my hope is, is that we're laying cornerstones for new schools here or revived schools; that we take the spirit of the Holy Father and extend it throughout the country and work for excellence for every child,

to set high standards, and when we find centers of excellence, not let them go away, but to think of policy that will enable them to not only exist, not only survive, but to thrive. It's in our Nation's interests. It's an important summit for America.

I thank you for bringing your talents, your energies, and your efforts. I thank you for caring deeply about our young. And I thank you for being a part of what I believe is a necessary strategy to make sure America continues to be a hopeful place for all.

God bless you. Thank you all.

NOTE: The President spoke at 10:23 a.m. at the Ronald Reagan Building and International Trade Center. In his remarks, he referred to Aysia Mayo-Gray, student, St. Ann's Academy, Washington, DC; Archbishop Donald W. Wuerl of Washington, DC; and Pope Benedict XVI.

Remarks Following a Discussion With President Mahmoud Abbas of the Palestinian Authority
April 24, 2008

President Bush. Thanks for coming, Mr. President. I appreciate your chance to talk about peace. I assured the President that a Palestinian state's a high priority for me and my administration—a viable state, a state that doesn't look like Swiss cheese, a state that provides hope. It's in—I believe it's in Israel's interest and the Palestinian people's interest to have leaders willing to work toward the achievement of that state.

People that can deliver that state, that vision, to the Palestinian people were sitting right here in the Oval Office, led by the President. The President is a man of peace. He's a man of vision. He rejects the idea of using violence to achieve objectives, which distinguishes him from other people in the region. I'm confident we can achieve

the definition of a state. I'm also confident it's going to require hard work.

To that end, I'm going back to the Middle East. I'm looking forward to meeting you, sir. And thank you for making time. I consider you a friend. I also consider you a courageous person. And I'm also will consider—believe strongly that when history looks back at this moment and a state is defined, that the Palestinian people will thank you for your leadership.

There are a lot of issues we discussed, issues of importance: the security of the Palestinian people and the Israeli people, the economic advancement of the Palestinian people. The thing that I'm focused on, and you are: how to define a state that is acceptable to both sides. I'm confident it can get done. I want to thank you for coming. I appreciate your time.

President Abbas. Thank you. Mr. President, thank you very much for receiving us here at the White House these days. And I also would like to thank you very much for the initiative that was launched during the Annapolis conference.

We believe that you actually are truly seeking a true, genuine, and lasting peace in the Middle East. And I am certain that you would like to see an agreement and settlement before the end of your term. And at the same time, we are doing everything we can in order to seriously negotiate and reach a peace that will be satisfactory to both the Palestinian side and the Israeli side, a peace that would be promoted around the world.

There are many parties also that are working very hard to support our efforts and to help us reach that peace. When I talk about your initiative, Mr. President, I also have to praise the Arab peace initiative that simply states that peace will be achieved after the Israeli withdrawal from the occupied Arab and Palestinian Territories. As a result of that, I believe strongly that more than 57 Arab and Islamic countries will normalize their relations with Israel. I believe very strongly that time is of the essence. We are working very hard and hope not to waste any time and continue these efforts to achieve peace.

Mr. President, your efforts, the efforts of your administration, the various visits—your previous one and your upcoming visit to Sharm el-Sheikh and to the region—all of this is a strong indication that you are very keen to continue to work very hard and to achieve your vision.

I cannot say that the road to peace is paved with flowers; it is paved with obstacles. But together we will work very hard in order to eliminate those obstacles and achieve peace.

President Bush. Thank you, sir. Thank you all. *Shukran jazeelan.*

NOTE: The President spoke at 1:51 p.m. in the Oval Office at the White House. President Abbas spoke in Arabic, and his remarks were translated by an interpreter.

Remarks to Participants of the Wounded Warrior Project Soldier Ride
April 24, 2008

Thanks for coming. Doocy, thanks for the introduction. This has got to be one of the most inspiring athletic events in our Nation's history. At least it is for me, and I hope it is for you.

I was going to ride with the guys today, but Laura told me I probably wouldn't be able to keep up. [*Laughter*] I'm—there is no doubt in my mind the people behind me are some of the most bravest people in our country's history. I admire their courage; I admire their determination. We're honored to have you here.

I'm also joined by the Secretary of State, Condoleezza Rice. Thank you for coming, Madam Secretary. Secretary Jim Peake of the Department of Veterans Affairs is with us. Deputy Secretary Gordon England is with us. Admiral Mike Mullen, Chairman of the Joint Chiefs, are here—other members of my administration and Members of Congress. The reason they're there is the same reason I'm here: We love and respect our military. And I thank you for coming.

I want to thank Granger Smith and the band for joining us today. Thanks for being here.

I appreciate those who wear the uniform who have joined us. I'm proud of you. Thanks for serving. I want to thank the wounded warriors. I want to thank their caregivers from Walter Reed and Bethesda. I appreciate the members of the Wounded Warrior Project. And I want to thank the family members and friends who are here today. Welcome to the White House.

Four years ago, Chris Carney decided to ride coast to coast to raise awareness and money for our wounded warriors. In the first year, he biked more than 5,000 miles from Long Island to the Pacific Ocean and raised more than a million dollars for the Wounded Warrior Project. He started what's called the annual Soldier Ride.

Next year, wounded vets started coming along. In 2006, 75 wounded warriors took turns riding portions of the cross-country journey. These service men and women rode to raise money for their fellow soldiers, including those who were hurt too much to ride. And they also rode to show themselves what they could do. And in so doing, they showed the world what they could do.

Americans came out to cheer. More soldiers and supporters came out to ride. More Americans then came out to show their support, so the Soldier Ride started doing different races around the country so even more of our citizens could participate. Today hundreds of people have gathered here on the South Lawn to kick off this ride, and I want to thank you all for being here.

The 3-day bike ride you're starting today at the White House says a lot. It says that you're showing that even when you're wounded, you're not done fighting. One of the riders today is Marine Corporal Chad Watson. I've gotten to know Chad. I met him when I was at Walter Reed 3 weeks after his Humvee was hit with an IED on patrol in Fallujah. He lost his right leg; he shattered his left ankle and foot; he took shrapnel to his face. And when I went into his room, he wanted to stand at attention and shake hands with the Commander in Chief, as well as salute.

He got up to his walker—his daddy helped him and so did his brother—he held himself upright with his arm strength while a fellow marine read his accommodation, and I had the honor of giving him the Purple Heart.

I told him to sit down. He didn't want to; he was a marine. And now he's here. He's got a new leg, and thanks to that leg, Chad will be able to start on even a greater journey than the one he begins today. This summer, he's going to walk down the aisle to get married to his beautiful bride. We're glad you're here.

The technology that you're witnessing today is helping our troops regain their lives. And it's state of the art, and that's the way it should be. We owe those who wear the uniform all the support they can possibly have. We'll give them the best medical care. And for the docs and nurses here, there's no doubt in my mind, our troops get the best medical care possible.

We owe them the best prosthesis. And if there's a new advance, it will be made available for our folks. We owe them a Veterans Health Administration that's seamless and works well. We owe them our thanks.

These servicemembers are focused on what you have to give than what you've lost. I appreciate the spirit of those in the Soldier Ride.

I thank my fellow citizens for supporting our troops. I appreciate the fact that the families have stood by those who wear the uniform. I appreciate your loved ones who are here today to cheer you on. The riders represent the spirit of the strongest military in the world and the greatest country on Earth. I'm thankful that we have brave men and women like you who step forward to protect America. I'm proud to be your Commander in Chief.

And now let us get started. God bless you.

NOTE: The President spoke at 3:26 p.m. on the South Lawn at the White House. In his remarks, he referred to Steve Doocy, anchor, FOX News Channel's "Fox and Friends"; Chris Carney, founder, Wounded Warrior Project Soldier Ride; and Jillian Kinsella, fiancee of Cpl. Chad M. Watson, USMC.

Statement on Armenian Remembrance Day
April 24, 2008

On this day of remembrance, we honor the memory of the victims of one of the greatest tragedies of the 20th century, the mass killings and forced exile of as many as 1.5 million Armenians at the end of the Ottoman Empire. I join the Armenian community in America and around the world in commemorating this tragedy and mourning the loss of so many innocent lives.

As we reflect on this epic human tragedy, we must resolve to redouble our efforts to promote peace, tolerance, and respect for the dignity of human life. The Armenian people's unalterable determination to triumph over tragedy and flourish is a testament to their strength of character and spirit. We are grateful for the many contributions Americans of Armenian heritage have made to our Nation.

We welcome the efforts by individuals in Armenia and Turkey to foster reconciliation and peace and support joint efforts for an open examination of the past in search of a shared understanding of these tragic events. We look forward to the realization of a fully normalized Armenia-Turkey relationship.

The United States is committed to a strong relationship with Armenia based on shared values. We call on the Government of Armenia to take decisive steps to promote democracy and will continue our support for Armenia to this end. We remain committed to serving as an honest broker in pursuit of a lasting and peaceful settlement of the Nagorno-Karabakh conflict.

On this solemn day of remembrance, Laura and I express our deepest condolences to Armenian people around the world.

Remarks on the National Economy
April 25, 2008

Good morning. It's obvious our economy is in a slowdown. But fortunately, we recognized the signs early and took action. I signed an economic growth package that will provide tax rebates to millions of American families and workers to boost consumer spending.

On Monday, the Treasury Department will begin delivering the first of these tax rebates by direct deposit. During the first week alone, nearly 7.7 million Americans will receive their tax rebates electronically.

Then on May 9, the IRS will begin mailing checks to millions more across America.

By this summer, the Treasury Department expects to have sent rebates to about 130 million American households. These rebates will provide eligible Americans with payments of up to $600 a person, $1,200 for couples, and $300 per child.

If you've already filed your income tax return, your rebate is on the way. Even if you don't owe any income taxes, you may still be eligible for a check, but you need to file a form with the IRS. And it's not too late to do so. Now, you can find out information as to how to proceed by calling your local IRS office, or go to the IRS web site.

We want to make sure everyone who's eligible for a check gets one on a timely basis. This money is going to help Americans offset the high prices we're seeing at the gas pump, at the grocery store. And it will also give our economy a boost to help us pull out of this economic slowdown.

I'm pleased that the Treasury Department has worked quickly to get the money into the hands of the American people. Starting Monday, the effects of the stimulus will begin to reach millions of households across our country.

Thank you very much.

NOTE: The President spoke at 9:16 a.m. on the South Grounds at the White House.

Remarks During a Visit to the Northwest Boys & Girls Club in Hartford, Connecticut
April 25, 2008

Entertainer Melinda Doolittle. We need you speaking up here right now. I would love—actually, Mr. President, I know that you went to Africa. I got a great chance to go to Africa with your wife and kind of see firsthand in Zambia what the disease does to people and how much they are appreciative of getting these bed nets. I know you got to travel, so I'd love it if you'd share some things—[*inaudible*]—of that.

The President. Sure. I think the thing that I would start with was how appreciative people in Africa were of the fact that total strangers cared about their lives. You see, if you are a mother who is holding a baby that is sick because of a mosquito bite, it creates a lot of hopelessness, and you really wonder whether anybody cares. And the fact that total strangers would come together—in Boys & Girls Clubs or basketball teams or singers—and care about them really lifts their spirits.

And so it's been a—been really interesting to travel to Africa and see how appreciative the people in Africa are of the United States and the citizens. Isn't it interesting that there's a call to love your neighbor like you'd like to be loved yourself?

And that's what you're doing. And I'm here really to thank all the people, not only here, but across the country, for being so supportive of a humanitarian effort that is worthy of a great nation.

So the trip was great. It was really a lot of fun. You know what it's like there.

Ms. Doolittle. I do, I do.

The President. It's a bit exciting, isn't it?

Ms. Doolittle. Yes, and I think the thing that struck me the most is that in the midst of all of that devastation that you may see in any country, they are the most joyful people you will ever meet in your entire life. And that also is infectious. So that is one thing that I wanted to catch going out of Africa, is that joy that they had in the midst of all that they were going through. So these are people that absolutely love life, they cherish it. And we get to help them cherish that life a little longer. So it's a wonderful, wonderful thing to do.

I would love to have you two come up and look at these bed nets and kind of——

The President. Yes, why don't we get a team picture?

Ms. Doolittle. ——kind of see——

The President. I don't think there's enough cameras here. [*Laughter*]

NOTE: The President spoke at 11:30 a.m.

Remarks on Malaria Awareness Day in Hartford
April 25, 2008

Thank you all. Thank you very much. Thank you for the kind introduction, Roxanne. She wrote it—read it just like I wrote it. [*Laughter*] It's good to be with you. I appreciate the—being here at the Boys & Girls Club here in Hartford. I really enjoyed being with the boys and girls of the Boys & Girls Club. Thank you for greeting us.

I—we do have something in common—at least I do—with the Boys & Girls Club. As Roxanne noted, the Boys & Girls Club were born in Connecticut. Well, so was I, just a little different date, you know. [*Laughter*] The Boys & Girls Clubs are 102. My daughters think I act like I'm 102 at times. [*Laughter*] But I really thank you all for greeting me.

I want to thank the members of this club for your compassionate work in the fight against malaria. And that's what I want to spend some time talking about today. I appreciate being joined by Melinda Doolittle of "American Idol." I've gotten to know Melinda because Melinda is not only a great talent, Melinda has got a huge heart. And it's interesting, isn't it, that she has garnered all this publicity and acclaim, all to channel it into helping other people. And I love your example, and I thank you for your leadership.

And I'm also honored to be up here with Tamika Raymond, as well as Charlie Villanueva. They know something about the State of Connecticut because they were stars on their respective University of Connecticut Husky basketball teams. They are professional athletes, one with the Milwaukee Bucks and the other with the Connecticut Sun. But more importantly, they're using their presence on the court to be able to advance important issues. And in my judgment, a great issue to advance is saving people's lives. And that's what we're here to celebrate today.

Sorry my wife isn't with me. She is a huge supporter of the malaria initiative. She cares a lot, like the people on this stage care a lot, about the human condition here in America and elsewhere. She's getting ready to be the mother of the bride—[*laughter*]—which I guess that means I'm getting ready to be the father of the bride.

I want to thank Admiral Tim Ziemer. He is the Coordinator for the U.S. Malaria Initiative. You notice I said "admiral." He's—when it comes to picking people to get a job done, you want somebody who can go from point A to point Z and plow ahead through the obstacles. You know, I'm really not interested in policies that are long on rhetoric and short on results. I think the taxpayers, as well as the people we're trying to help, need to know our strategy is well defined, with clear goals, and we hold people accountable. And the great thing about Admiral Ziemer is, he's willing to hold people to account and willing to be held to account himself. And you're about to hear some of the progress we've made, and a lot of it has to do with his leadership. And I'm proud you're here. Thanks for coming.

I also thank Sam Gray—[*applause*]—not just your family members who are cheering; that's good. [*Laughter*]

So I've come to herald the Boys & Girls Clubs all across America, and they do fine work. And Roxanne is right: They're saving lives. And I want to thank you for the—

for those of you who support the Boys & Girls Clubs here in Hartford and around the country.

But today also marks the second annual Malaria Awareness Day in the United States. And here to help celebrate that day with us is the Congressman from Connecticut, Christopher Shays. Thank you for coming.

On this day, we remember those who've died from malaria. In other words, an awareness day is one in which you recognize the consequences, in this case, of this disease. And so we mourn the loss of life, especially and including the children who have needlessly died on the continent of Africa and elsewhere. They died because of a mosquito bite. Also, this is a day of hope, however, as well. And the reason it is, because nations once trapped in fear because of malaria are now tackling malaria head on. And they're doing so with our help.

It is a day of hope because more Americans are recognizing the timeless truth: To whom much is given, much is required. It should be the corner—and is—the cornerstone of American foreign policy. Some people say, "Well, what about our own people?" And my answer is, we're plenty rich to help our own and to help others. We've been a blessed nation, and it's in our interest to share our blessings with other. It's a day of hope because compassionate souls are acting on the truth and helping to wipe out malaria in Africa and beyond.

A few moments ago, I presented three Dragonfly Awards. So, like, you say, "Why call some—an award a Dragonfly Award?" Well, the award is named for the natural predator of the mosquito. And each one of this year's winners has shown great determination in working hard and in creative ways to eradicate the disease.

The first Dragonfly Award winner went to Roxanne, who accepted on behalf of the Boys & Girls Club of America. A year and a half ago, Roxanne attended a White House summit on malaria hosted by Laura

and me, and she was touched by the suffering that malaria inflicts on African children. And so she pledged to rally American children to help. And she acted on the pledge. Sometimes in life, you get the pledgers and not doers; in this case, it was the pledger and the doer.

More than 150 Boys & Girls Clubs have joined the campaign to raise funds and spread awareness. Local clubs have held events ranging from car washes to bake sales to walkathons. All together, Boys & Girls Clubs have raised some $25,000, more than enough to buy 2,500 bed nets for families in Africa.

I know the boys and girls will probably never meet any of the lives who are being saved. I had the honor of traveling to Africa, and I can assure all who've been helping, the people of Africa are most grateful to the American citizens for their help.

The second Dragonfly Award winner is Zachary Ellenthal, who happens to be from Connecticut. When Zach celebrated his bar mitzvah last October, he asked family and friends not to give him money. Instead, he wrote a letter with facts about malaria in sub-Sahara Africa and asked his guests to consider donating to Malaria No More. He even set up a web page so they could make donations online. As a result of this man's compassion and decency, he raised more than $11,000 to purchase bed nets. And Zachary—[*applause*].

The final Dragonfly Award winner is Allyson Brown from Florida. Allyson came up with an innovative way to combine two of her passions: one, fighting malaria in Africa, and school dances. She put together a fundraising dance with the theme Stayin' Alive and came away with more than $1,600 in donations. Then she built upon her success by working with Malaria No More to start a nationwide Stayin' Alive campaign. So far, more than 100 schools in 30 States have joined. Together, they've raised more than $30,000 to purchase bed nets. Allyson will be graduating from high school this year, and she's on her way to Florida State University.

The interesting thing is, there are countless stories like this across America. From major corporations, to the NBA and WNBA, to small-town faith-based groups, the American people are rallying to stop a preventable and treatable disease. I try to explain to people that the great compassion of America is defined by the thousands of acts of kindness that take place on a daily basis.

The Federal Government is doing our part; we have a role to play. In 2005, I launched what we've called the President's Malaria Initiative, which is a 5-year, $1.2 billion initiative to cut the number of malaria-related deaths in 15 African nations by half. In other words, we're focusing our attempt with a clear goal. It's an ambitious goal, but the program is off to a very strong start. In just 2 years, the initiative has helped provide bed nets and antimalaria medicine, insecticide sprays, and prenatal drugs to an estimated 25 million people in sub-Sahara Africa.

Behind these numbers are whole communities looking to the future with renewed hope. Laura and I saw this. As I've mentioned, we went to Africa in February. It was such a touching moment to hold babies in our arms who might have died without the support of our fellow citizens. We visited children your age who can go to school because they're free of malaria. And the good news is, we listened to determined African leaders described how life is being transformed for their people and how they want to help, how they thank the American people for their great compassion, but understand it's their responsibility to put strategies in place and to see that they're followed through.

I want to tell you an amazing statistic, and this is what's going to happen all across Africa where we're focusing our efforts. In Tanzania, the percentage of infants in Zanzibar infected with malaria has dropped from about 20 percent to less than 1 per-

cent in 2 years. There are thousands more children who can grow up healthy, who will be able to contribute to their society and reach their potential. Here's—one man said, when he summed up America's efforts to fight malaria, he called it "a godsend."

America is proud to lead the way, and we are urging other nations to join us. Last summer, we had a meeting, what's called the G–8, and I called upon them to join the United States and match our commitment to cut malaria deaths in half in an additional 15 countries. So we're willing to take the lead on 15 countries where we're needed—where help is needed the most, but we expect you as well, as nations to whom much is given, to be joining us. And they made their pledges; they made their promises. And we're going to have a meeting in July, another G–8 meeting in July, and they need to make sure that they meet their pledges. There are babies dying needlessly on the continent of Africa, and if they have made a pledge to support the efforts to fight malaria, they need to write the checks. And I, of course, will be reminding them of that in a very gentle way—[*laughter*]—diplomatic fashion.

Our efforts to fight malaria means that we're answering a moral imperative. It's in our Nation's moral interests to do this. We're a better nation, collectively a better nation, that when we help people, when we save lives—but it's also a strategy that advances our security interests as well. From experience, we understand that the terrorists and extremists can only find fertile recruiting grounds where they find hopelessness. Their ideology is so backwards, so distorted, so hateful, nobody really wants to follow it unless you're so hopeless that it becomes appealing. And so the best way to defeat this ideology of hate is with acts of compassion and love. The best way to defeat an ideology of darkness is to spread the light of hope.

And that's exactly what we're doing. So to my fellow citizens, I not only say it's in our moral interests to help, it's in our strategic interest to help defeat these ideologues who murder the innocent to achieve their political objectives.

America is fully committed to this mission of mercy. The United States of America is doing the right thing, and your Government and the people of this country are showing their kindness and compassion and decency. Any American who wants to become involved in this mission can go to fightingmalaria.gov. It's pretty easy. All you got to do is type in fightingmalaria.gov, and you can find out how you can help a worthy and noble and necessary cause.

I thank you for coming and giving me a chance to explain our initiative. God bless you.

NOTE: The President spoke at 11:44 a.m. at the Northwest Boys & Girls Club. In his remarks, he referred to Roxanne Spillett, president and chief executive officer, Boys & Girls Clubs of America; entertainer Melinda Doolittle; and Samuel S. Gray, Jr., president and chief executive officer, Boys & Girls Clubs of Hartford, Inc. The Malaria Awareness Day proclamation is listed in Appendix D at the end of this volume.

The President's Radio Address
April 26, 2008

Good morning. As we approach graduation season, many American students are looking forward to beginning college in the fall. This new chapter of life is a time of great expectation but can also be a time of anxiety. And that anxiety is being heightened by the recent credit crunch, which has raised concerns about the potential availability of student loans.

Recently, some lenders have dropped out of the Federal program that provides college loans to students who have often little or no credit. Without an adequate response, this means that many students may approach the upcoming school year uncertain of when they will be able to get their loans or where they will come from.

A slowdown in the economy shouldn't mean a downturn in educational opportunities. So we're taking decisive action now to ensure that college is accessible and affordable for students around the country.

One way we're helping is through the Department of Education's lender of last resort program, which works to provide loans for students who are unable to secure one from a lender. The Department is taking steps to ensure that the agencies involved in this program are ready and able to meet their responsibilities. If necessary, the Government will help fund these loans. With these actions, we will help ensure that a college education is not unnecessarily denied to those who have earned it.

These are important first steps, but more needs to be done. Congress needs to pass legislation that would give my administration greater authority to buy Federal student loans. By doing so, we can ensure that lenders will continue to participate in the guaranteed loan program and ensure that students continue to have access to tuition assistance.

A bill that would do this has already passed the House of Representatives. It is called the "Ensuring Continued Access to Student Loans Act." This bill provides the necessary tools for safeguarding student loans without permanently expanding the Government's role in their financing. The authority the bill grants is temporary and would be used only if it became apparent there was a shortage of loans available to students.

Ensuring the stability of student loans is essential to keeping educational opportunities open to all Americans. Last year alone, Federal loans provided more than $60 billion of aid to American students. This money helped pay for tuition, textbooks, and the lifetime of opportunity that comes with holding a college degree. Members of Congress now have a chance to preserve this opportunity, and they should take it.

I urge Congress to get the "Ensuring Continued Access to Student Loans Act" to my desk as soon as possible. A delay of even a week or two may make it impossible for this legislation to help students going to school this fall. By working together to improve and enact this legislation quickly, we can ensure that higher education remains within the reach for all those who've earned it, and we can ensure that America's college students can spend more time next fall thinking about their textbooks than their pocketbooks.

Thank you for listening.

NOTE: The address was recorded at 7:10 a.m. on April 25 in the Cabinet Room at the White House for broadcast at 10:06 a.m. on April 26. In his address, the President referred to H.R. 5715, the "Ensuring Continued Access to Student Loans Act of 2008." The transcript was made available by the Office of the Press Secretary on April 25, but was embargoed for release until the broadcast. The Office of the Press Secretary also released a Spanish language transcript of this address.

Remarks at the White House Correspondents' Association Dinner
April 26, 2008

Thank you, ladies and gentlemen. Please excuse me if I'm a little sleepy—3 a.m. this morning, the red phone rang. [*Laughter*] It was the damn wedding planner. [*Laughter*]

Two weeks from tonight is Jenna's wedding, so I'm a little wistful this evening. Plus, this is my last White House Correspondents' dinner as President. You know, I'm not sure what I'm going to do next. After he left office, Vice President Gore won an Oscar and the Nobel Peace Prize. [*Laughter*] Hey, I don't know, I might win a prize—Publishing Clearinghouse or something. [*Laughter*]

But thanks for inviting me. Our entertainment tonight is Craig Ferguson. You know, this is a small world. Craig was once in a punk band called Bastards from Hell, which is what Dick and I are going to call our band. [*Laughter*] Craig is Scottish by birth; so is Barney. [*Laughter*] Two months ago, Craig became an American citizen. I'm honored to call you fellow American.

Ladies and gentlemen, surprisingly, I've enjoyed these dinners. [*Laughter*] So tonight I thought we'd reminisce a bit. The first couple of years I came to this dinner, I was really into slide shows.

[*At this point, a video was shown.*]

Next year, a new President will be standing up here. I have to say, I'm kind of surprised we don't have more Presidential candidates here tonight, like, any. [*Laughter*] Senator McCain is not here. He probably wanted to distance himself from me a little bit. [*Laughter*] You know, he's not alone; Jenna's moving out too. [*Laughter*]

The two Democratic candidates aren't here either. Senator Clinton couldn't get into the building because of sniper fire, and Senator Obama's at church. [*Laughter*]

But I'm sure whoever the next President is will show up at these dinners, especially like the dinners in 2005 and 2006, when we had a couple of surprises up our sleeves.

[*A video was shown.*]

We've had a lot of fun nights over the years. Do you remember the year I mentioned Ozzy Osbourne, and he stood up on a chair and blew me a kiss? [*Laughter*] So few leaders get that kind of experience. [*Laughter*] You know, I love the mixed crowds here. It's an interesting crowd. You know, just think: Pamela Anderson and Mitt Romney in the same room. [*Laughter*] Isn't that one of the signs of the apocalypse? [*Laughter*]

Which brings me to Dick. [*Laughter*] For 8 years as Vice President, Dick has ridden shotgun. That's probably not the best analogy. [*Laughter*] But he is a dear friend, and he's been the greatest straight man in the history of the world. [*Laughter*] Dick, I don't know what I would have done for material without you. [*Laughter*]

[*A video was shown.*]

What I like best about these evenings is the laughter and the chance to thank you for the work you do for the country. I also view this as a good chance to put aside our differences for a few hours.

And one thing we all share, whether we're native citizens or new citizens like Craig, is a tremendous appreciation for our people in uniform, an appreciation symbolized by the United States Marine Band, which is celebrating its 210th anniversary this year. I love the band, and so I'm going to say my farewell to you by doing something I've always wanted to do. And I do it in the spirit of our shared love for this country.

[*The remarks concluded as President Bush conducted the United States Marine Band.*]

NOTE: The President spoke at approximately 8 p.m. at the Washington Hilton Hotel. In his remarks, he referred to entertainers Craig Ferguson, Ozzy Osbourne, and Pamela Anderson; and former Gov. W. Mitt Romney of Massachusetts. The transcript was released by the Office of the Press Secretary on April 28.

Remarks Following a Discussion With President Alvaro Colom Caballeros of Guatemala
April 28, 2008

President Bush. It's been my honor to welcome to the Oval Office the President and First Lady of a close friend of the United States. Mr. President, thank you for coming.

We've had a good discussion about a variety of issues. We discussed bilateral relations between Guatemala and the United States, which are very strong. We are friends. We treat each other with respect. Our objective is—with U.S. foreign policy—is to have a neighborhood that is peaceful and prosperous, where social justice is important; want to achieve social justice through good health policy, good education policy, and good judicial policy. The United States is pleased to help this Government, as best as we possibly can, help the average citizen get a good education and have good health care.

We talked about how CAFTA is working. Exports to the United States have increased; exports from the United States have increased. And that's good.

We talked about security and the need for the region—Mexico, the United States, and the countries of Central America—to fight drug trafficking. I told the President that we are working hard to reduce demand for drugs here in America. And at the same time, we want to work in conjunction with strong leaders to make sure these drug traffickers don't get a stronghold. And that's why it's very important for Congress to fund the Merida project.

We talked about the reforms that the Government is instituting inside of Guatemala, including tax reform and reform to make sure that people who break the law are held to account.

I was particularly pleased to note that the Guatemalan Government and its leadership is promoting laws to make sure women are treated well and that violence against women is prosecuted.

And so—and we're going to talk a little later on about the Millennium Challenge Account. And by the way, we were talking about blueberries, and—so that blueberries are able to come off-season here to the United States, which is a positive development for Guatemalan farmers.

And finally of course, the President brought up the issue of immigration. And he wanted to urge me to think about TPS—TPS for citizens, as well as comprehensive immigration reform. I assured him that I will consider his request. And I assured him that I believe comprehensive immigration reform is in our Nation's best interests.

And so we've had a good discussion, and right after this press availability, I'll be taking he and the First Lady to lunch. And I'm looking forward to serving them lunch, and I bet you're looking forward to eating lunch. [*Laughter*] Thanks for coming.

President Colom Caballeros. I want to thank President Bush for his hospitality. We've spent a couple of days working here, and we are very happy to hold this meeting in which we have discussed strengthening our relationship with an—already a strong relationship, in fact.

We discussed, as the President mentioned, the fight against drug trafficking. We are doing everything necessary to eliminate drug trafficking and drug traffickers from our territory.

We discussed the issue of social investment. We have received support from USAID. We—our two countries have common aims in this regard.

We also discussed the issue of our migrants. We brought up TPS with the President. We will be awaiting a response on that.

We described our recent tax reform to the President. That is something we're starting in Guatemala because we need to ensure that we have the public funds to be able to carry out the reforms in the areas of social justice and others that we have discussed.

We want to express our appreciation for the support that we have received from the United States to combat drug trafficking. Recently, we received four helicopters. This has been extremely helpful to us. We've also achieved good success on this front with the recent cocaine seizures. In fact, an operation was just carried out last night, a very large one, very successful. And on that, we are working not just with the United States but also with Mexico and the entire neighborhood in Central America, because all of us must be involved, as President Bush said, in order to combat that scourge at all levels.

And so we are very happy to be here and very happy to be moving forward. Thank you.

President Bush. Gracias, senor.

President Colom Caballeros. Si. Gracias.

NOTE: The President spoke at 11:41 a.m. in the Oval Office at the White House. In his remarks, he referred to Sandra Torres de Colom, wife of President Colom Caballeros. President Colom Caballeros spoke in Spanish, and his remarks were translated by an interpreter. The Office of the Press Secretary also released a Spanish language transcript of these remarks.

Remarks Prior to a Meeting With United States-Brazil CEO Forum Officials
April 28, 2008

It is my honor to welcome the U.S.-Brazil CEO Forum here to Washington. First of all, I want to thank my friend President Lula for encouraging this forum to go forward. It's an indication of the importance that we both place on our bilateral relations. Brazil is a very powerful, very important country in our neighborhood. And it's really important for this administration and future administrations to work closely with the Brazilian Government, like it is important for our respective business communities to work closely together.

I do want to thank you all very much for putting forward a list of recommendations. I'm looking forward to our discussion. As I understand, the list of recommendations includes a successful Doha round as well as a bilateral tax treaty and a bilateral investment treaty. One of the things I will share with the Brazilian CEOs is that I strongly support a successful Doha round, and our Government will work closely with Brazil to get that done. And secondly, in terms of our bilateral policy, I also strongly, as does my administration, support a bilateral tax treaty and a bilateral investment treaty.

I'm—relations between our two countries are very positive, and they're very important. And so thank you all for coming. Please give my best regards to President Lula. Thank you for being here.

NOTE: The President spoke at 1:57 p.m. in Room 350 of the Dwight D. Eisenhower Executive Office Building. In his remarks, he referred to President Luiz Inacio Lula da Silva of Brazil.

The President's News Conference
April 29, 2008

The President. Thank you. Good morning. This is a tough time for our economy. Across our country, many Americans are understandably anxious about issues affecting their pocketbook, from gas and food prices to mortgage and tuition bills. They're looking to their elected leaders in Congress for action. Unfortunately, on many of these issues, all they're getting is delay.

Americans are concerned about energy prices, and I can understand why. I think the last time I visited with you it was like—I said it was like a tax increase on the working people. The past 18 months, gas prices have gone up by $1.40 per gallon. Electricity prices for small business and families are rising as well.

I've repeatedly submitted proposals to help address these problems, yet time after time, Congress chose to block them. One of the main reasons for high gas prices is that global oil production is not keeping up with growing demand. Members of Congress have been vocal about foreign governments increasing their oil production, yet Congress has been just as vocal in opposition to efforts to expand our production here at home.

They've repeatedly blocked environmentally safe exploration in ANWR. The Department of Energy estimates that ANWR could allow America to produce about a million additional barrels of oil every day, which translates to about 27 millions of gallons of gasoline and diesel every day. That would be about a 20-percent increase of oil—crude oil production over U.S. levels, and it would likely mean lower gas prices. And yet such efforts to explore in ANWR have been consistently blocked.

Another reason for high gas prices is the lack of refining capacity. It's been more than 30 years since America built its last new refinery, yet in this area too, Congress has repeatedly blocked efforts to expand capacity and build more refineries.

As electricity prices rise, Congress continues to block provisions needed to increase domestic electricity production by expanding the use of clean, safe nuclear power. Instead, many of the same people in Congress who complain about high energy costs support legislation that would make energy even more expensive for our consumers and small businesses.

Congress is considering bills to raise taxes on domestic energy production, impose new and costly mandates on producers, and demand dramatic emissions cuts that would shut down coal plants and increase reliance on expensive natural gas. That would drive up prices even further. The cost of these actions would be passed on to consumers in the form of even higher prices at the pump and even bigger electric bills.

Instead of increasing costs and imposing new roadblocks to domestic energy production, Congress needs to clear away obstacles to more affordable, more reliable energy here at home.

Americans are concerned about rising food prices. Unfortunately, Congress is considering a massive, bloated farm bill that would do little to solve the problem. The bill Congress is now considering would fail to eliminate subsidy payments to multimillionaire farmers. America's farm economy is thriving. The value of farmland is skyrocketing, and this is the right time to reform our Nation's farm policies by reducing unnecessary subsidies. It's not the time to ask American families who are already paying more in the checkout line to pay more in subsidies for wealthy farmers. Congress can reform our farm programs, and should, by passing a fiscally responsible bill that treats our farmers fairly and does not impose new burdens on American taxpayers.

Americans are concerned about making their mortgage payments and keeping their homes, and I don't blame them. Last year, I called on Congress to pass legislation that would help address problems in the housing market. This includes critical legislation that would modernize the Federal Housing Administration, reform Fannie Mae and Freddie Mac, and allow State housing agencies to issue tax-free bonds to refinance subprime loans. Yet they failed to send a single one of these proposals to my desk. Americans should not have to wait any longer for their elected officials to pass legislation to help more families stay in their homes.

Americans are concerned about the availability of student loans. The recent credit crunch makes it uncertain that some students will be able to get the loans they need. My administration is taking action through the Department of Education's lender of last resort program, which works to arrange loans for students who are unable to secure one from a lender on their own. In other words, we're helping. Congress needs to do more by passing a bill that would temporarily give the Federal Government greater authority to buy Federal student loans. This authority would safeguard student loans without permanently expanding the Government's role in their financing.

In all these issues, the American people are looking to their leaders to come together and act responsibly. I don't think this is too much to ask, even in an election year. My administration will reach out to Congress. We will work to find areas of agreement so that we can deal with the economic pressures that our American taxpayers and American families are feeling. I ask Congress to do its part by sending me sensible and effective bills that I can sign, instead of issuing or sending bills that simply look like political statements. We can work together. We can help Americans weather this difficult period. We can keep our country moving forward.

Now I'll be glad to take some of your questions. Jennifer [Jennifer Loven, Associated Press].

National Economy/Energy

Q. Thank you, sir. You have said that we need to wait until the first stimulus has taken effect to act again. But since it was passed, gas prices have gone up, foreclosures have gone up, there have been layoffs, news just this morning that consumer confidence is down yet again.

President Bush. Yes.

Q. Isn't it time to think about doing more?

And on another issue, would you support a summer moratorium on the Federal gas tax?

The President. First of all, the money is just now making it into people's bank accounts. And I applaud the Speaker and the leader of the Senate and minority leaders there to—for working together to get this done. And now, after a period of time, the money is beginning to arrive, and we'll see what the effects are.

And we'll look at any idea in terms of energy, except I will tell you this: that if Congress is truly interested in solving the problem, they can send the right signal by

saying, we're going to explore for oil and gas in the U.S. territories, starting with ANWR. We can do so in an environmentally friendly way. They ought to say, why don't we—I proposed, you might remember, taking some abandoned military bases and providing regulatory relief so we can build new refineries. I mean, if we're generally interested in moving forward with an energy policy that sends a signal to the world that we're not—we're going to try to become less reliant upon foreign oil, we can explore at home as well as continue on with an alternative fuels program.

Yes, sir.

National Economy/Energy/Oil Supply

Q. So was that a yes on the moratorium?

The President. No. I'm going to look at everything they propose. We'll take a look.

Q. Thank you, Mr. President. Were you premature in saying that the U.S. economy is not in a recession when food and energy prices are soaring so high?

And what more can you do to persuade Saudi Arabia during your upcoming visit to reconsider output levels and cut prices?

The President. Yes. Look, I mean, you know, the words on how to define the economy don't reflect the anxiety the American people feel. The average person doesn't really care what we call it. The average person wants to know whether or not we know that they're paying higher gasoline prices and that they're worried about staying in their homes. And I do understand that. That's why we've been aggressively helping people refinance their homes. That's why I continue to call upon Congress to pass legislation that will enable people to stay in their homes.

These are tough times. People—economists can argue over the terminology. But—and these are difficult times, and the American people know it. And they want to know whether or not Congress knows it. I think an important signal to send on energy, just like I said, is to say, okay, we're going to go find oil here at home.

We can—we're transitioning to a new era, by the way, a new era where we're going to have batteries in our cars that will power—enable people to drive 40 miles on electricity. There's going to be more ethanol on the market, more alternative fuels. It would be—our driving habits will change. But in the meantime, we need to be sending a signal to the world markets that we intend to explore here in America. We can also send a clear signal that we understand supply and demand. And then when you don't build a refinery for 30 years, it's going to be a part of restricting supply, and therefore, we ought to expand our refining capacity by permitting new refineries and getting after it quickly.

On the electricity front, as you know, I'm a big believer in nuclear power, except we keep getting mixed signals out of Congress, and the regulatory system sends mixed signals.

And so—and then to your question on the Saudis, look, I have made the case that the high price of oil injures economies. But I think we better understand that there's not a lot of excess capacity in this world right now. Hopefully, high prices will spur more exploration to bring excess capacity on, but demand is rising faster than supply. And that's why you're seeing global energy prices rise. And that's why it's important for us to try to take the pressure off by saying, we're going to start exploring here at home.

John [John Yang, NBC News].

Alternative Fuel Sources/Price of Food

Q. Thank you, Mr. President. I'd like to ask you about an area——

The President. You're welcome.

Q. ——where food prices and energy policy come together; that's biofuels.

The President. Yes.

Q. The World Bank says about 85 percent of the increase in corn price since 2002 is due to biofuel—increased demand for biofuels. And your Secretary of State

said that—indicated yesterday that she thought that might be part of the problem. Do you agree with that? And what can the United States do—what more can the United States do to help make food more affordable around the world?

The President. Yes, actually, I have a little different take. I thought it was 85 percent of the world's food prices are caused by weather, increased demand, and energy prices—just the cost of growing product—and that 15 percent has been caused by ethanol—or the arrival of ethanol.

By the way, the high price of gasoline is going to spur more investment in ethanol as an alternative to gasoline. And the truth of the matter is, it's in our national interests that we—our farmers grow energy as opposed to us purchasing energy from parts of the world that are unstable or may not like us.

In terms of the international situation, we are deeply concerned about food prices here at home, and we're deeply concerned about people who don't have food abroad. In other words, scarcity is of concern to us. Last year, we were very generous in our food donations, and this year, we'll be generous as well. As a matter of fact, we just released about $200 million out of the Emerson Trust as part of a ongoing effort to address scarcity.

One thing I think that would be—I know would be very creative policy is if we would buy food from local farmers as a way to help deal with scarcity, but also as a way to put in place an infrastructure so that nations can be self-sustaining and self-supporting. It's a proposal I put forth that Congress hasn't responded to yet, and I sincerely hope they do.

That would be Jim [Jim Axelrod, CBS News].

Price of Gasoline/National Economy/2008 Presidential Election

Q. Good morning, Mr. President. Thank you. I just want to follow up on the idea of the gas tax moratorium, if I may, because you're indicating that perhaps you'd be open to it. You mentioned in your opening remarks that——

The President. I'm open to any ideas, and we'll analyze everything that comes our way, but go ahead.

Q. Well, we're talking about perhaps the most immediate relief to people who are buying gasoline every day, because it would be an 18.4-cents-a-gallon tax cut. Senator Clinton and Senator McCain are in favor of it; Senator Obama is not.

The President. Yes.

Q. But Americans are hearing about this every day. So could you flesh out, perhaps, some of your thinking about why this would be a good idea or not, why you would agree with Senator McCain or Senator Obama?

The President. No, I appreciate you trying to drag me in the '08 race. And this is the first attempt to do so, and I can understand why you would want to do that.

I will tell you that, first of all, the American people have got to understand that here in the White House, we are concerned about high gasoline prices. We're concerned about high food prices. We're concerned about people staying in their homes. And we're concerned about student loans, just like I described. And Congress can be helpful. Congress, they can show leadership by dealing with these issues.

And we'll consider interesting ideas. But, Jim, what I'm not going to do is jump right in the middle of a Presidential campaign. We'll let the candidates argue out their ideas.

Q. Well, would——

The President. I just told you, I'll consider the ideas. If it's a good idea, we embrace it; if not, we're analyzing the different ideas coming forward.

Wendell [Wendell Goler, FOX News Channel].

Alternative Fuel Sources/Energy

Q. Mr. President, you just said there's not a lot of excess supply out there. Some energy experts think we may have already passed or be within a couple of years of passing the maximum oil pumping capability. In other words, we may be close to tapping all we've got. Do you think that's the case? And if you do, why haven't you put more resources into renewable energy research, sir?

The President. Wendell, we've put a lot into ethanol. And we're—matter of fact, the solution to the issue of corn-fed ethanol is cellulosic ethanol, which is a fancy word for saying we're going to make ethanol out of switchgrasses or wood chips. And we're spending a lot of money along those lines.

But energy policy needs to be comprehensive. And we got to understand, we're in a transition period. The problem is, there's been a lot of focus by the Congress in the intermediate steps and in the long-term steps—the long-term steps being hydrogen; the intermediate steps being biofuels, for example, and researching the biofuels and battery technology—but not enough emphasis on the here and now.

And so you ask—you say that people think we can't—there's not any more reserves to be found. Well, there are reserves to be found in ANWR. That's a given. I just told you that there's about 27 million gallons of diesel and gasoline that could be—from domestically produced crude oil that's not being utilized. And not only that, we can explore in environmentally friendly ways. New technologies enables for—to be able to drill like we've never been able to do so before—slant hole technologies and the capacity to use a drill site, a single drill site, to be able to explore a field in a way that doesn't damage the environment. And yet this is a litmus test issue for many in Congress. Somehow if you mention ANWR, it means you don't care about the environment. Well, I'm hoping now people, when they say ANWR, means you don't care about the gasoline prices that people are paying.

Yes, sir. Rog [Roger Runningen, Bloomberg News].

Strategic Petroleum Reserve

Q. Thank you, Mr. President, and good morning.

The President. Good morning. [*Laughter*] I like a friendly guy here in the Rose Garden.

Q. Sir, 14——

The President. Would that be you, Rog, a friendly guy here in the Rose Garden? [*Laughter*]

Q. Thank you.

The President. Yes. Mr. Sunshine, they call you. [*Laughter*]

Q. Fourteen Senators, including your own Senator, Kay Bailey Hutchison from Texas, calling on you to stop filling the Strategic Petroleum Reserve. You've been asked that several times over the past few years.

The President. Yes.

Q. I know what your answer has been. But do you think now, with the rising prices, the record high oil prices, it's time to change course?

The President. In this case, I have analyzed the issue. And I don't think it would affect price for this reason: We're buying, at the moment, about 67,000 to 68,000 barrels of oil per day, fulfilling statutory obligations to fill up the SPRO. World demand is 85 million barrels a day. So the purchases for SPRO account for one-tenth of one percent of global demand. And I don't think that's going to affect price, when you affect one-tenth of one percent. And I do believe it is in our national interest to get the SPRO filled in case there's a major disruption of crude oil around the world.

I mean, one of the—for example, one of the things the—Al Qaida would like to do is blow up oil facilities. Understanding we're in a global market, a attack on an oil facility in a major oil exporting country would affect the economies of their

enemy—that would be us and other people who can't stand what Al Qaida stands for. And therefore, the SPRO is necessary, if that's the case, to be able to deal with that kind of contingency. And if I thought it would affect the price of oil positively, I'd seriously consider it. But when you're talking about one-tenth of one percent of global demand, I think the—if you—on a cost-benefit analysis, I don't think you get any benefits from making the decision. I do think it costs you oil in the case of a national security risk.

Martha [Martha Raddatz, ABC News].

Afghanistan/War on Terror

Q. Thank you, Mr. President. I'd like to switch to Afghanistan. There was another attempt on President Karzai's life. There are operations going on there right now. Is the strategy succeeding? Are we winning in Afghanistan?

The President. Yes, I think we're making progress in Afghanistan, but there's a very resilient enemy that obviously wants to kill people that stand in the way of their reimposition of a state that is—which vision is incredibly dark. I mean, it's very important for the American people to remember what life was like in Afghanistan prior to the liberation of the country. We had a government in place that abused people's human rights. They didn't believe in women's rights, they didn't let little girls go to school, and they provided safe haven to Al Qaida. In the liberation of this country, we've achieved some very important strategic objectives: denying Al Qaida safe haven from which to plot and plan attacks and replacing this repressive group with a young democracy.

And it's difficult in Afghanistan. I mean, it's—if you know the history of the country, you understand it's hard to go from the kind of society in which they had been living to one in which people are now responsible for their own behavior. But I am pleased with a lot of things. One, I'm pleased with the number of roads that have been built. I'm pleased with the number of schools that have opened up. I'm pleased a lot of girls, young girls, are going to school. I'm pleased health clinics are now being distributed around the country. I'm pleased with the Afghan Army, that when they're in the fight, they're good.

I wish we had completely eliminated the radicals who kill innocent people to achieve objectives, but that hasn't happened yet. And so I think it's very much in our interests to continue helping the young democracy, and we will.

Yes. Obviously, you've got a follow-up.

Q. But do you think we're winning? Do you think we're winning?

The President. I do. I think we're making good progress. I do, yes.

Q. Can I just add to that? A couple of weeks ago——

The President. No, you can't. This is the second follow-up. You usually get one follow-up, and I was nice enough to give you one. I didn't give anybody on this side a follow-up, and now you are trying to take a second follow-up.

Q. They didn't try.

The President. I know you try.

Yes.

Q. Can I just say that——

The President. No, they just cut off your mike. You can't, no.

Q. A couple of weeks ago, you said——

The President. Now she's going to go without the mike. This is awesome. [*Laughter*]

Q. A couple of weeks ago, you said that in Iraq, in 2006, you said we were winning and the strategy was working to keep up troop morale.

The President. Yes.

Q. How can we believe that you're not doing the same thing here?

The President. Oh, you tried to ask me that question before. It's a repeat. Look, I said——

Q. No, I'm talking——

The President. Can I finish, please? The question you asked me before at the exclu-

sive I gave you on the ranch was, "You said that we were winning in the past." I also said that there was tough fighting. Now, make sure you put the comments in place.

So what I'm going to tell you now is, we're making progress in Afghanistan, but there's tough fighting. I'm under no illusions that this isn't tough. I know full well we're dealing with a determined enemy. I believe it's in our interest that we defeat that enemy. And so yes, we're making progress, but it's also a tough battle. We're facing people who are willing to strap bombs on themselves and walk into places where the innocent dwell or the innocent shop and kill them.

Is it in our interest to confront these people now, whether it be in Afghanistan or Iraq or Europe or anywhere else? And the answer is, absolutely, it's in our interest. And the notion that somehow we can let these people just kind of have their way, or, you know, let's don't stir them up, is naive or disingenuous, and it's not in our Nation's interests. We are in a global struggle against thugs and killers, and the United States of America has got to continue to take the lead.

And so in Afghanistan, yes, we're making progress. Does that mean that we're—that it's over? No, it doesn't mean it's over. We're in a long struggle, as I've told you many a time, against these jihadists. You defeat them ultimately by the advance of democracy. See, this is an ideological struggle. These aren't isolated, kind of, law enforcement moments. We're dealing with a group of ideologues who use asymmetrical warfare—that means killing innocent people—to try to achieve their objectives. And one objective is to drive us out of Afghanistan, Iraq, the Middle East, or anywhere else where we try to confront them.

And so yes, I mean, look, is it tough? Yes, it's tough. Is it difficult? Absolutely. Is it worth the fight? In my judgment, yes, it is.

Yes, ma'am.

Syria/North Korea/Iran

Q. Thank you, Mr. President. What is the impact—[*inaudible*]?

The President. I can't hear you too well. Sorry, got a flawed mike. Martha, what did you do to the mike? [*Laughter*]

Q. Thank you, sir.

The President. She wanted an exclusive again. Anyway. [*Laughter*]

Q. Mr. President, thank you, sir. And previously, when asked about Israel's September bombing of the Syrian facility, you refused aggressively to discuss it. Then suddenly last week, your administration released classified photos and details of that bombing, intelligence officials claiming that it showed that this facility was a North Korean-designed nuclear facility being actually built with the help of Pyongyang. Why the turnaround, sir? What did you hope that that would accomplish? And what do you say to lawmakers of both parties on Capitol Hill who are quite concerned that, indeed, if this was what this facility was, that it took some 8 months for you to inform them, sir?

The President. Thank you. Let me correct the record. We briefed 22 Members of Congress on what I'm about to tell you. First, we were concerned that an early disclosure would increase the risk of a confrontation in the Middle East or retaliation in the Middle East. As I mentioned to you early on, we did notify 22 Members of Congress, key committee chairmen. And I was—I'm mindful that there was going to be this kind of reaction. And we—of course, we wanted to include more Members of Congress at a time when we felt the risk of retaliation or confrontation in the Middle East was reduced. And so that moment came upon us and then extended the briefings.

We also wanted to advance certain policy objectives through the disclosures. And one would be to the North Koreans, to make it abundantly clear that we may know more about you than you think, and therefore, it's essential that you have a complete disclosure on not only your plutonium activities but proliferation as well as enrichment activities.

And then we have an interest in sending a message to Iran, and the world for that matter, about just how destabilizing a—nuclear proliferation would be in the Middle East, and that it's essential that we work together to enforce U.N. Security Council resolutions aimed at getting Iran to stop their enrichment programs. In other words, one of the things that this example shows is that these programs can exist and people don't know about them and—because the Syrians simply didn't declare the program. They had a hidden program.

And finally, we wanted to make it clear to Syria and the world that their intransigence in dealing with—helping us in Iraq or destabilizing Lebanon or dealing with Hamas, which is a destabilizing force in our efforts to have a Palestinian state coexist peacefully with Israel, that those efforts are—it gives us a chance to remind the world that we need to work together to deal with those issues. So that's why we made the decision we made.

Yes, sir.

Congress/Legislative Priorities

Q. Mr. President, you've expressed frustration with Congress, obviously, over the economic—wanting them to do more on the economy. They've blocked you on Colombia. They've blocked you on the FISA issue. Are you frustrated? Are you angry? And do you have any real hope of being able to work with this Congress this year?

The President. Yes. I am—I believe that they're letting the American people down, is what I believe. The—on the FISA issue, it is hard to believe that it's okay to pass the Protect America Act in August of 2007, and that act—and that people in Congress can't—don't believe that act is relevant in 2008. I mean, the act was set to expire; it did. And yet this threat hasn't gone away.

And I can only—it's either lack of leadership or a lack of understanding of the issue. And either way, it's not good for the country. We need to make sure our professionals have the tools to protect the American people from attack.

The Colombia free trade agreement—this economy is—as I mentioned to you, it's a sour time. It's tough for the American people. And yet the Colombia free trade agreement would benefit our economy. And the reason why is, is that many goods from Colombia come into our country duty free. And yet our goods going to Colombia are taxed through tariff. And the American people expect the President and the Congress to at least insist that a foreign country treat us the way we treat them. And in this case, the benefits will be more exports, more midsized and small businesses exporting into Colombia. About 9,000 exporters into Colombia today; 8,000 are midsized and small businesses. And when you can export more, it helps the economy. And one of the bright lights of the economy has been the amount of exports going overseas.

So rather than playing politics or whatever rationale that they have made for Colombia, they ought to be saying, this is good for our economy, it's good for workers, it's good for small businesses.

And so I'm perplexed, I guess is the best way to describe it, about why there's no action, inactivity on big issues. And because the two issues you mentioned—FISA, protecting America, and Colombia, protecting America's economy by encouraging growth—are important to people whether they be Republicans, Democrats, or Independents.

Sheryl [Sheryl Gay Stolberg, New York Times].

National Economy/Energy/Taxes

Q. Thank you, Mr. President.
The President. You're welcome.
Q. I'm still waiting for my exclusive at the ranch.

The President. Yes. [Laughter]
Q. Mr. President, today I'm—[laughter].
The President. I'm at a loss for words. If only you'd have been at the White House Correspondents' dinner, I would have invited you. [Laughter] Anyway, please, go ahead.
Q. Well said.
The President. It's an inside joke, for everybody listening. [Laughter]
Q. Mr. President, you have spoken today about opening ANWR for drilling and also refineries. But these are clearly long-term solutions to the problem of rising gas prices. What can you tell Americans about what your administration is doing in the short term?

And secondly, have you been briefed on tomorrow's GDP numbers, and are you concerned——
The President. No, I haven't been.
Q. Okay—and are you concerned that they will show us to officially be in a recession?
The President. I think they'll show that we're—it's a very slow economy. I can't guess what the number will be, and I haven't been shown, truly.

And by the way, opening up ANWR is not long term, it's intermediate term. But it sends a clear signal, is what it does. It sends a clear signal to the markets that the United States is not going to restrict exploration, the United States is going to encourage exploration.

And in the meantime, we have done—increasing CAFTA, for example. But the market's going to do as much for encouraging conservation as anything else is now. And so I firmly believe that—you know, if there was a magic wand to wave, I'd be waving it, of course. It's—I strongly believe it's in our interest that we reduce gas prices—gasoline prices. I mean, it would be like a major tax cut for people. And——
Q. But what——

The President. But let me finish, please, Sheryl. Strike one on the exclusive. [*Laughter*] Excuse me, strike two. [*Laughter*]

That—you made me lose my train of thought, of course. Maybe that's what you were attempting to do. No, I think that if there was a magic wand and say, okay, drop price, I'd do that. And so part of this is to make—set the psychology right that says to the world, we're not going to become more beholden on your oil; we're going to open up and be aggressive and have an aggressive energy policy. Secondly, we're going to be—send the signal we're going to be building new refineries.

But there is no magic wand to wave right now. It took us awhile to get to this fix. That's why I told you that if Congress had responded—as a matter of fact, Congress did pass ANWR in the late 1900s—I mean, 1990s—and the 1900s—1990s, but it didn't go forward. And it's in my considered judgment, given the technological advances, to say, this is—we'll destroy the environment is just—I don't think it's an accurate statement.

And so I think it's very important, Sheryl, for Congress. The other thing Congress can do, if you want to send a good signal during these uncertain times, is make the tax cuts permanent, is to let people—send the signal that people are going to be able to keep their money. And I think that will help the psychology of the country.

Yes, Mark [Mark Knoller, CBS Radio].

Hamas/Situation in the Middle East

Q. Mr. President, do you feel——

The President. Yes, you can use a mike.

Q. Do you feel your foreign policy in the Middle East has been undermined by Jimmy Carter's meeting with Hamas leaders? What harm does it do for him to have met with Hamas leaders?

The President. No. Foreign policy and peace is undermined by Hamas in the Middle East. They're the ones who are undermining peace. They're the ones whose foreign policy objective is the destruction of Israel. They're the ones who are trying to create enough violence to stop the advance of the two-party state solution. They are a significant problem to world peace—or Middle Eastern peace.

And that's the reason I'm not talking to them. And that's the reason why—it's just important for people to understand that this is a—we're in a—we're witnessing a struggle between those who understand liberty and believe in the advance of liberty and those who want to stop the advance of liberty. And Hamas has made their position very clear.

Unfortunately, they're getting help. In Syria, they get help. There's rumors about Iranian help. And these countries that I just named are—take, for example, Lebanon. I talked to Prime Minister Siniora today. Here's a struggling democracy in the heart of the Middle East that is—whose internal politics are being influenced by Syria, Hizballah—as a result of Iranian influence with Hizballah, all aiming to destabilize the country, which should be a clear signal about the intents of—the intentions of groups like Hizballah and Hamas.

And so when you want to talk about peace being difficult in the Middle East, it's going to be difficult. But it's even made more difficult by entities like Hamas, who insist upon lobbing rockets into Israel, trying to provoke response and trying to destabilize—even destabilize the region more.

And anybody can talk to who they want, but I just want the people to understand that the problem is Hamas. And until Hamas changes or until there's a competing vision in the Middle East for President Abbas, Prime Minister Fayyad to offer to the Palestinian people, that's all the more reason to try to define a state. And that's why I'm going to the Middle East, besides going to the 60th anniversary of Israel.

Yes, Ann [Ann Compton, ABC News].

Hamas/Middle East Peace Process

Q. Thank you, sir. Did any good come out of President Carter's talks with Hamas?

And did anyone in your administration ask him not to do it? And will it have any impact on your trip to the Middle East?

The President. I didn't talk to him, and I don't know. I don't know what the conversations were, and I don't see Hamas changing. It's up to Hamas to change. And you get these meetings with these people, and they say one thing and do another. And this is the way it's been now for 7½ years in this administration, watching Hamas be a destabilizing influence.

And I supported the elections, by the way. And curiously enough, they won the elections against Fatah because they ran on a noncorruption campaign. The sad situation is, now they've been given power, they haven't delivered for the people in Gaza.

And my mission is to—when I go to the Middle East—is to continue to work with both Israelis and the—President Abbas and his Government on a variety of fronts: one, coming up with the vision, helping them find the common ground on the vision; but also working with the Israelis to empower the Palestinians in the West Bank to be more in charge of security, to have less obstacles with which to deal with, to help the Palestinians with economic vitality and growth. There's some very interesting initiatives that are being developed there.

I'm still hopeful we'll get an agreement by the end of my Presidency. Condi is heading back out there. I've been in touch with President Abbas here in the Oval Office, and I talk to Prime Minister Olmert, and the attitude is good. People do understand the importance of getting a state defined.

But Hamas is—look, when you're Israel and you've got people lobbing rockets into your country, you're going to take care of business. But you got to ask, why is Hamas lobbing rockets? And one reason why is because they're trying to destabilize and create chaos and confusion. And to answer whether or not the people's conversations with them were more effective: That's all we got to do, is watch and see how Hamas behaves.

Richard [Richard Wolf, *USA Today*].

Congressional Action on Supplemental Appropriations/Veterans' Benefits

Q. Thank you, Mr. President. Congress is preparing to add a couple of things to your supplemental spending request for Iraq. And I'm wondering, some of these seem like things you could support: extending unemployment benefits and, particularly, additional help for Iraq and Afghanistan war veterans in terms of educational benefits. Are these things you might agree to, even though you have set a $108 billion ceiling on the package?

The President. Richard, 108 is 108. And I made my position very clear to Congress, and I will not accept a supplemental over 108 or a supplemental that micromanages the war, ties the hands of our commanders.

We will work with Congress and—on these veterans' benefits. I'm a firm believer that we ought to treat our veterans with respect. In the State of the Union, I talked about the idea of transferring—a soldier being able to transfer educational benefits to spouse or children. We've sent legislation to that effect up to Congress; we would like for them to move on it quickly. But the 108 is 108.

Michael [Michael Allen, *Politico*].

2008 Presidential Election/U.S. Foreign Policy

Q. Thank you, Mr. President. I wonder if there's a big, urgent problem facing the country, coming down the road, that you worry your successor will neglect or postpone. That is, when the politics are done, after the war on terror, what do you think should be at the top of the list of the person who moves into that office?

The President. Yes. I don't think John McCain is going to neglect the war on terror, and I do think he'll be the President. Here I am interjecting myself in the '08 campaign, just like I told you I wouldn't. That's unfair, isn't it?

He—it's very important for the President to understand that America is still in danger of attack and that we're dealing in—with an ideological struggle that can only be solved with the spread of liberty. And a concern of mine, as you've heard me say, is that the Nation has had the tendency in the past to become isolationist and correspondingly protectionist. And I would hope whoever the President is—and I do believe it will be John—will be willing to resist the impulse, the temptation to say, well, it's not worth it anymore to confront an enemy; it's not worth it to try to do the hard work of helping democracies thrive and succeed. Because not only is it worth it; we will succeed in laying the foundation for peace if we have faith in the capacity of liberty to be transformative.

I'm also concerned about protectionism. This lad right here asked me about Congress's intransigence on Colombia. I think it reflects the fact that there is a strong protectionist sentiment in the United States. People—good people—believe it is not in our interest to be opening up markets. You might remember the CAFTA trade vote. We won by one vote, and it was a tough vote to get. And now the Speaker pulled a unique maneuver to stop the Colombia from moving forward. And it's a sign of—that the country is losing its confidence to a certain extent, that protectionist policy is better than confidently trading and treating unfairness in the marketplace.

And so my worry—not worry—my hope is, is that whoever the President is understands that America is a force for good in the world, that we're—that in the spread of liberty, we're adhering to a universal value. It's not an American value, it's a universal value, the notion of liberty. And you've heard me say it a lot. I do believe it's a gift from the Almighty to every man, woman, and child. And if you believe in that and act on that, you're really acting

on a platform of peace, because ultimately, liberty yields the peace you want. It's transformative and powerful. And I believe that people will be making a mistake if they say, we can't compete economically, and therefore, let's throw up walls. And yet the tendencies here in America are pretty strong right now.

There's a lot of concern around the world, by the way, about America's retreat. They're wondering whether or not America is going to remain a leader. They're wondering whether or not, for example, will capital be welcomed back into our country. And so it's the "isms" that bother me—isolationism and protectionism.

April [April Ryan, American Urban Radio Networks].

National Economy/Zimbabwe

Q. Thank you, Mr. President.

The President. Yes. You're looking good in yellow.

Q. Thank you.

The President. How's the baby?

Q. She's good.

The President. Good. Yes.

Q. Thank you. You're trying to get me off.

The President. No.

Q. But it's okay.

The President. Is it true you named her Georgia?

Q. No. Is that okay with you?

The President. It's your baby. [*Laughter*]

Q. Anyway, moving on to the subject of the day, I talked to James Clyburn before this press conference. He said, "As a man thinketh, so are we." And Americans believe we are in a recession. What will it take for you to say those words, that we are in a recession?

And also, on Zimbabwe, what's the next step? And does South Africa play a part in that?

The President. Yes, thank you. I've answered my—the question on the words and terminologies. I will tell you that these are very difficult economic times—very difficult. And we'll let the economists define it for what it is. I would hope that those who worry about recession, slowdown—whatever you want to call it—make the tax cuts permanent as a way of helping to address this issue. Because if you're somebody out there trying to plan your future and you're worried about the future and you think your taxes are going to go up, it's going to cause different behavioral patterns.

Secondly, I do want to thank the Members of Congress. And the man you talked to is a leader and did a very good job of helping shepherd through this billions-of-dollar package that is now beginning to hit America's pocketbooks. And we'll see how that goes. I hope it's as stimulative as we think it will be. But you can tell the good man you talked to, who is a good guy, that I fully understand that people are concerned. And they're concerned about high gasoline prices. They're worried about high food prices, worried about staying in their homes.

The new issue, of course, is student loans. The House of Representatives passed a bill that—sponsored by Mr. Miller, George Miller, that is a—that we think can do the job. I hope the Senate moves a version of it very quickly so that we can help address this issue. I mean, one of the things that Government can do is either create more anxiety or less. And if you think your taxes are going to go up, that's going to make you anxious. If you think the Government is going to step in with a good policy that will help your child get a student loan, that will make you less anxious.

One of the things we've done on home-ownership is the HOPE NOW Alliance, which, hopefully, makes people less anxious. Hopefully, it helps—has kind of brought some sense of not only concern but action into the marketplace. And I was told this morning that HOPE NOW has affected about 1.4 million homeowners and helped a lot of them refinance, get refinancing, or helped a lot of them get different interest payment schedules, all aiming for creditworthy people to be able to stay in their homes during this difficult period.

Zimbabwe—first of all, the will of the people needed to be respected in Zimbabwe. And it is clear that they voted for change, as they should have, because the—Mr. Mugabe has failed the country. It's a country that used to be an exporter of food; it's now got terrible human conditions there.

Secondly, the violence and the intimidation is simply unacceptable. The Government is intent upon—and is—intimidating the people there.

We support the U.N. Security Council discussions that are going on. But the truth of the matter is, April—and you mentioned this—it's really incumbent upon the nations in the neighborhood to step up and lead and recognize that the will of the people must be respected and recognize that that will came about because they're tired of failed leadership.

Thank you all for your interest. Enjoyed it.

NOTE: The President's news conference began at 10:31 a.m. in the Rose Garden at the White House. In his remarks, he referred to Prime Minister Fuad Siniora of Lebanon; President Mahmoud Abbas and Prime Minister Salam Fayyad of the Palestinian Authority; Prime Minister Ehud Olmert of Israel; and President Robert Mugabe of Zimbabwe. Reporters referred to former President Jimmy Carter; and Rep. James E. Clyburn.

Remarks Following a Discussion With Special Representative of the United Nations Secretary-General for Afghanistan Kai Eide
April 29, 2008

President Bush. I have just had a very constructive and important dialogue with the United Nations envoy to Afghanistan. Mr. Ambassador, thank you so very much for coming to the Oval Office, and thank you so much for serving the cause of peace.

Ambassador Eide. Thank you.

President Bush. You've been given a very difficult job, which is to help coordinate world—the world's efforts to help this young democracy succeed. And I want to assure you that the United States Government and I personally support you in everything you're going to do.

We've supported this—the creation of this position. We supported your nomination because you're a man of action, a man of determination, and a man willing to sacrifice to help the Karzai Government, but more importantly, help the people of Afghanistan realize the blessings of liberty.

The Afghan theater in this war against the extremists is a vital part of making sure that peace prevails. And no question, there's challenges. As I told the Ambassador, if this were easy, we wouldn't have selected a man of his caliber to—or the U.N. wouldn't have selected a man of his caliber to take on the task.

And so I appreciate your time. This is our first meeting, and I hope that—I know it won't be the last. He's given me good advice. He's given me a picture of what—on how the United States Government can help him accomplish his missions, and we're more than willing to help.

And so I welcome you to the Oval Office. And thank you for your great service.

Ambassador Eide. Thank you very much, Mr. President. For me, it's been an honor to be here and also to feel the support and confidence that you have shown me as I now take on this very difficult assignment. That support is very important to me; that I know that I have the confidence of the international community and also the confidence of the Afghan Government and the President of Afghanistan, which I feel very strongly——

President Bush. Yes, sir.

Ambassador Eide. ——after my first few weeks. That's—those are important tools for me in order to perform my duties effectively.

We also discussed one important event that lies ahead of us, which is the Paris conference on the 12th of June, and the importance of doing everything we can to mobilize support, mobilize donors, and also see to it that our efforts are as coordinated and as effective as they possibly can.

So thank you very much, Mr. President, for this occasion and for the support you give me.

President Bush. Thank you, sir. Glad you're here.

Ambassador Eide. Thank you.

NOTE: The President spoke at 1:48 p.m. in the Oval Office at the White House. In his remarks, he referred to President Hamid Karzai of Afghanistan.

Remarks on National Volunteer Week
April 29, 2008

Be seated. Welcome. What a great day for the White House. I am pleased to welcome volunteers from the—around the United States who have given of their time to help those who need help. And we're sure glad you're here. Those of you today who perform acts of kindness do so out of love, and you do so out of the desire not to be recognized. But anyway, you're going to be recognized. We have the opportunity today to thank you and the opportunity today to celebrate the difference that volunteers have made all across America.

I want to thank Jean Case, who's the Chairman of the President's Council on Service and Civic Participation. And I want to thank the members of the Council who are here.

And I thank David Eisner, the CEO of the Corporation for National and Community Service; Jack Hawkins, the Director of Volunteers for Prosperity, USAID; Ron Tschetter, Director of the Peace Corps; and other Peace Corps volunteers who are here—about which I'm going to say something a little later. [*Laughter*] This tends to be an enthusiastic bunch, and so I would ask you to—[*laughter*]—keep your enthusiasm in check for just a minute. [*Laughter*]

The spirit of charity that is celebrated here has been a part of our character, our Nation's character, ever since before we were an independent nation. In 1736, for example, Benjamin Franklin organized the citizens of Philadelphia to form a volunteer fire company. Isn't that interesting? A lot of our—a lot has changed since then, but the principle that inspired Benjamin Franklin is still true today all throughout the communities in America.

Those of you who are here today understand the lesson, how you can gain by giving. You can understand how volunteering can transform the souls, both who give and those they help. When you teach a child

to read, for example, you not only improve their chances for success in the world, but you become invested in the progress of a young life. When you visit the elderly, you remind them that they are loved, and you remind yourself of how deeply we all feel the need for compassion. When you help the homeless find shelter, you remove the pain of need and rediscover the resiliency of the human spirit.

While there are many ways that Government can help society's least advantaged—and we try to do our best here in Washington—it can never replicate the private acts of goodness and the ties of affection they create between Americans. And that is why our administration has focused on empowering citizens with open hearts, not just Government programs by opening up checkbooks.

I strongly support the faith-based and community-based initiative. I believe it is in Government's interest to empower those neighborhood healers and helpers, social entrepreneurs to be able to complete their acts of love and compassion. Government is love in—Government is justice and law; it's not love. Love is found in the hearts of our fellow citizens. And the true strength of America truly is found in the hearts and souls of Americans who hear the universal call to love a neighbor.

One of the ways that we have tried to encourage volunteerism is through the creation of the USA Freedom Corps. The Freedom Corps is an attempt—and a successful attempt, I might add—to create a culture of service and citizenship and responsibility. And so one way to be useful in the Government level is to provide a way for citizens to become connected to service opportunities in their communities. And it's working, it really is. Last year alone, more than 60 million—60 million volunteers from all across America provided social services and aid to those in need, both here at home and abroad.

The volunteers oftentimes work for large charitable organizations, or they find individual opportunities in their own community. But it always requires someone willing to say, "I want to help somebody else." And so Americans, if they want to find out how they can help, if you're motivated by Volunteer Week, or if you're motivated by hearing this message—you're motivated by a neighbor saying, "Gosh, it's really made my life better to help somebody in need," why don't you go to the web site of USA Freedom Corps. And you can look it up at volunteer.gov. It's not all that hard. You just get on there and type volunteer.gov. [*Laughter*] And you can find opportunities to be able to serve your country by helping somebody who needs some help.

Another step we've taken is the creation of the Presidential Council on Service and Civic Participation. And one of the Council's initiatives is awarding the President's Volunteer Service Award, which is a distinction that honors hard work and dedication. It's a way to say thanks. We can't give everybody an award; I wish we could. So we try to herald people who can set a good example for others.

And this year, we focused on recognizing volunteer programs that are started in corporate America. I believe corporate America has got an enormous responsibility to give back to their communities—and so too those who are being honored today. Paul Otellini and Barry Salzberg are with us. I'm going to talk about each one of them individually.

First, Barry Salzberg. He's the CEO of Deloitte, and he is—he understands the need to be a good corporate citizen. He understands corporate giving is an essential part of being a good citizen in the United States of America. He himself has been a board member of several charitable organizations, including the College Summit, the YMCA of Greater New York, and the Committee for Encouraging Corporate Philanthropy.

Under his leadership, Deloitte has committed to providing pro bono services worth up to $50 million for the nonprofit sector over the next 3 years. And Barry, thank you very much for being here.

And then there's Paul Otellini. Glad you're here, Paul. He happens to be the CEO of a little mom and pop operation called Intel. [*Laughter*] Intel will be celebrating its 40th anniversary this year. The company could have chosen to mark this occasion by simply looking back on its four decades of impressive accomplishments, but instead, as a result of Paul's leadership, the company has chosen to celebrate with a great act of compassion: Intel has committed to 1 million hours of volunteer service by its employees. This is a huge effort, and I can't tell you how appreciative we are of your generosity, but more importantly, those who you will help are more appreciative of your generosity. Please thank your employees for their—[*applause*].

There is a lot of volunteer work here in America. Every day, there are just countless acts of compassion. And interestingly enough, it doesn't require one Government law. As a matter of fact, oftentimes people are inspired by a higher law.

And there are also countless acts of compassion overseas. One of the great joys for Laura and me is to—as we travel, is to be able to see ordinary citizens from the United States helping save babies' lives as a result of the malaria initiative or working with orphans who have been left alone because of HIV/AIDS. And also, it's a chance for us to really run into one of the great organizations that Government has sponsored. It's called the Peace Corps.

Forty-seven years ago, President John F. Kennedy, in the Rose Garden, sent the first team of Peace Corps volunteers to Africa. And in the intervening years, more than 190,000 Peace Corps volunteers have carried our country's great spirit of generosity and compassion throughout the world.

Laura and I met with Peace Corps volunteers in Ghana recently, and they are some kind of fired up. [*Laughter*] And a matter of fact, it is exciting to be with those good souls who are motivated to put—to go help, and in so doing, it really is the best foreign policy America could possibly have.

And today I just had my picture taken with a group of spirited volunteers—[*laughter*]—who are headed to Guatemala. And I thank you all for your service. And I'm glad you're here, and thanks for coming.

I believe strongly in the admonition to whom much is given, much is required. Those of you here today are living up to that noble calling, and you carry on the best traditions of American citizenship. In my first Inaugural Address, I said, it's im-portant to be a citizen, not a spectator. And there's no better way to be a citizen [than] ° to be a soldier in the armies of compassion, a foot soldier.

And so today we commemorate your work and the work of volunteers all across the country, here at the White House. I appreciate the lasting legacy that you've helped create in the hearts of our fellow citizens. I thank you for what you do. And I ask for God's blessings on your work. Thanks for coming.

NOTE: The President spoke at 2:58 p.m. in the East Room at the White House. The National Volunteer Week proclamation of April 22 is listed in Appendix D at the end of this volume.

Remarks Honoring the 2008 National and State Teachers of the Year
April 30, 2008

The President. Good morning. Good morning. Welcome to the White House. Welcome to the Rose Garden. We're walking out of the Oval Office, Mike turns to me and says, "I like what you've done with the place." [*Laughter*] All I did was mow the lawn. [*Laughter*] Glad you're here.

I'm really glad to be taking a part of an event that honors America's teachers. It's a tradition that started with Harry Truman. It's a tradition that Laura and I have really enjoyed carrying on. She's not here, unfortunately. She sends her best. You know, I like to tell people that, you know, one of the interesting questions you get in my line of work is, "Can you name a teacher who had influenced you?" I said, "Yes, my wife." [*Laughter*]

But she and Jenna are out promoting a new book that they wrote called "Read All About It." I'm not suggesting that people buy it, of course. That would be un-seemly here in the Rose Garden. [*Laughter*] But it is a book they're attempting to promote literacy. She sends her love. She understands what it means to be a teacher. We were so honored that our little girl chose to be a teacher as well. It made her dad feel really well. I'm sure—I just hope you know the influence you have on children. I suspect you do; that's why you're such a good teacher.

Good teachers hear a call. Good teachers are empathetic souls. And really, the best teachers have a special intuition and, I suspect, a little potential, and so the ability to see potential and the ability to have the patience necessary to watch it grow. I want to thank you for nurturing young minds. I thank you for providing such wonderful examples. And I thank you for inspiring the imaginations and unleashing the talents of our Nation's young.

° White House correction.

I'm up here with not only the Teacher of the Year, but with Margaret Spellings, the Secretary of Education. I do want to welcome Senator Gordon Smith and Senator [Congressman]° Greg Walden. Turns out they're both from the State of Oregon. [*Laughter*] I wonder why you're here? But anyway, I'm glad you're here. Thank you for being strong supporters of the teachers in your State.

I welcome the State Teachers of the Year. I really enjoyed seeing you in the Oval Office. It's fun for me to be able to greet you and say thank you. And I can't thank you enough for serving as such great role models for other teachers in your States. And we're sure glad you're here.

I do want to thank the National Teacher of the Year finalist: Lewis Chappelear, who is with us—thank you, Lewis—from California; June Teisan, from Michigan; as well as Tommy Smigiel, from Virginia—that would be Norfolk, Virginia.

I am obviously up here with the Teacher of the Year. I'll spend a little time talking about Michael in a minute, but I am so proud that his mom and dad have joined us, as is he. Thank you for coming. I know it brings you great pride to have raised a son who is dedicated to helping others. His wife is with us, for whom I'll say something else a little later; son and daughter is with us, as well as brother. Thanks for coming.

Finally, we got Ken James, president-elect, Council of the Chief State School Officers, who administers the Teacher of the Year program. Thanks for coming. And the rest of you are welcome here too. [*Laughter*]

One of the things that Margaret and I have tried to do is help teachers be able to set high standards and achieve accountability. And that was the spirit behind passing No Child Left Behind Act. It basically—if you really think about the act, it, one, refuses to, what I used to call—still

———
° White House correction.

call—refuses to accept the soft bigotry of low expectations. I firmly believe that if you have low expectations, you'll achieve them. I believe that when you say to people, we want you to achieve high expectations, you really have got this great faith in the human potential. I also believe that if you're a teacher that you ought to welcome a law that says we trust you in your ability to set high expectations.

And secondly, behind that law is a notion that we'd like at least to know whether or not people can read, write, and add and subtract. Good teachers understand that. As a matter of fact, the Teacher of the Year understands that, and I suspect you all do as well. I'm often told that the accountability system is a—is meant to punish. I don't think so. I think it's meant to diagnose and correct and reward. And you're Teachers of the Year because you've got kids in your classroom who are excelling. And the reason we know is because we measure.

And so I want to thank you for being people willing to set high standards. Curiously enough, because we do measure, we have learned this fall that fourth graders and eighth [graders]° earned the highest math and reading scores in the history of our Nation's Report Card. That's a positive sign. Eighth graders set a record in math scores. In other words, because we are people who believe in accountability, we're beginning to get a sense for whether or not the achievement gap in America is closing. And it must close in order for this country to realize its full potential.

We understand that there's been some tough, tough neighborhoods, but that should not be an excuse for mediocrity. And I know our Teachers of the Year understand that and are willing to challenge the status quo and expect the best. And so we appreciate very much your work. And we hope Congress would reauthorize the No Child Left Behind Act. It's—and we're committed to working with Members of Congress to do it. The good news is the act doesn't go away without reauthorization; it still exists.

And so what—last week, what Secretary Spellings did, because the act hasn't been reauthorized, is that she announced a package of reforms that the Department of Education is now implementing to improve the No Child Left Behind Act, reforms that support our teachers and provide help to struggling students.

One thing about No Child is that when you find somebody struggling, it's important to get extra resources to help that child get up to speed now, before it's too late. The reforms are going to deal with—help schools deal with dropouts, increase accountability, and ensure that more students get the tutoring we want.

And so I want to thank you, Margaret, for being a leader, realizing the situation needs to be constantly improved, and improving it. And I think you'll find these additional tools and these measures will help you, not hurt you, and make it easier to do your job.

And I hope Senators in Congress—we don't give up on reauthorization. I understand it's an election year and sometimes things don't get done, but this is a brilliant, important piece of legislation. And I thank you all for supporting us the first round. And I hope we can work together on this round as well.

One person who believes very strongly in the potential of each child is our Teacher of the Year, Michael Geisen, who happens to be from Prineville, Oregon. Before he entered teaching—interesting enough, if you're from Prineville, one of the options for you is to be a forester. And he loves nature. He's an outdoors guy, and yet he really longed to be with his fellow citizens. There's no better way to do so than teaching. And so 7 years ago, after being a forester, he got in the classroom at Crook County Middle School.

It was not an easy time for that school when he entered. Crook County had gone through five principals in 6 years. Students' test scores had flatlined. In other words, kind of, they were just maintaining, which is unacceptable. It's unacceptable to Michael; it should be unacceptable to everybody if we're just kind of maintaining.

And so Mike saw his challenge, and he rose to it. You raised a good guy. Great teachers like Mike are optimists who believe in setting high standards. He believes that every child can learn if given a chance. And so when he became head of the science department, he created assessments for the students, and he put a system in place to measure results. That's what confident, optimistic people do; they say, "I'm not afraid to measure." And if you believe every child can learn, then you want to assess to make sure they are.

He knew the importance of parental involvement, so he created family-oriented school projects that would enlist moms and dads in their children's work. I suspect a lot of the Teachers of the Year understand how important that is, and that's why you're sitting out there. And he saw results. In his first 2 years as the department chair, the school State achievement scores in science rose from 55 percent to 72 percent, and they're still rising.

Great teachers like Mike instill a love of learning in young people. And so he captivates his students. I told you about his humor, right? [*Laughter*] "Did a fine job out here, President." [*Laughter*] Well, that—he takes that humor into the classroom.

He also loves to use music in his classroom, and he has a hands-on science curriculum. So, like, on the music deal—so he turns to songs to get people to pay attention. One of the greatest hits he's used is about gravity. One I like was a blues song written from the perspective of a lonely bacterium. [*Laughter*] Mike, you can sing it here in the Rose Garden if you want to. [*Laughter*]

Michael Geisen. You got a band? [*Laughter*]

The President. Yes, I probably suggest you don't. But—[*laughter*]—I tried to dance here one time, and it made a—[*laughter*]—it didn't work. [*Laughter*]

But here's what one of his students said, "Mike Geisen is such an awesome teacher"—actually called him Mr. Geisen—"[he's] an awesome teacher. He could make watching grass grow interesting." No wonder you're Teacher of the Year. One of his signature achievements is the annual science fair where the students create everything from electric cars to electric hot-dog cookers. The fair culminates with what Mike calls "a legendary evening of science, creativity, food, and wackiness." It's not what a lot of people think as a science class, to be frank with you, but nevertheless, it's a reason he's the Teacher of the Year.

He's found innovative ways to use his innate humor and creativity to encourage students to take science seriously. And we need a lot of scientists in America.

He also is a role model. You all are all role models. He teaches his students the—about the importance of service by demonstrating it in his own life. One of the things he's done is he's volunteered a lot of time to raise money for rock—for a rock-climbing wall. He's an outdoorsman, as I told you. He strongly has a—respects the environment. And he's a family man. He's a role model because he's a good family man.

Jennifer is here—thank you for coming—as is Aspen and Johanna. And as Mike says, he calls them his favorite teachers. Isn't that an interesting concept? They are—I know they're proud of their dad, as is his family, and so am I. And so we join the Geisen family in congratulating Mike on his well-deserved recognition as the 2008 National Teacher of the Year. [*Applause*] Not yet—[*applause*]—maybe.

I do want to say one final thing, and then we'll get Michael up here and let him give a speech. This is the last Teacher of the Year ceremony I get to do as President. And as I told you, I'm sorry Laura is not here, because she would share in this sentiment. This has really been one of the favorite events of ours during our time in Washington. You're probably just saying, of course, he says that to every event. [*Laughter*] It's always the favorite.

Actually, this is a fabulous opportunity for us to thank our teachers, people who could be doing something else in life and have chosen to go in the classroom to lift somebody's life up, to make a difference in the future of the country.

And so I know you know this: You represent teachers from all over America. So when I thank you, I'm teaching—I'm thanking teachers from all across our country. I appreciate you making our experience here in the White House a joyful experience. I thank you for making America a more hopeful place. And I ask God's blessings on your work and the work of teachers all across America.

And now the Secretary and I will give Michael his award.

NOTE: The President spoke at 11:20 a.m. in the Rose Garden at the White House. In his remarks, he referred to Jennifer, wife, Lisa and Ken, parents, Aspen and Johanna, children, and David, brother, of 2008 National Teacher of the Year Michael Geisen. The transcript released by the Office of the Press Secretary also included the remarks of Mr. Geisen.

Remarks Honoring the 2008 Super Bowl Champion New York Giants
April 30, 2008

The President. Welcome. It's my honor. Thank you for coming. Please be seated. Welcome to the White House. It's an honor to recognize the Super Bowl champs, the New York football Giants.

I appreciate you all coming. Mr. Vice President, thank you for joining me up here as we welcome the Giants to the South Lawn. I want to thank John Mara and his mom Ann, who's joined us; Steve Tisch and his mother Joan; of course, their head football coach, Tom Coughlin, and his wife Judy. He got the extension; that's a good thing. [*Laughter*] Makes it a little easier to be standing up here. [*Laughter*]

I appreciate all the players who have joined us today and the coaches and the personnel that make the club function.

I thank members of my administration who have joined us. I welcome Members of the Congress, Senate, particularly from New Jersey and New York, State elected officials from New Jersey and New York— that's a good thing to be here.

I welcome those from Walter Reed who have joined us today. And of course, welcome to all the Giants fans. [*Applause*] Behave yourselves. [*Laughter*]

First, it's good to be up here with the Super Bowl MVP, Eli Manning. We have a few things in common. [*Applause*] We got some things in common. Eli has a father and a brother in the same business he's in. [*Laughter*] Sometimes the press are skeptical. [*Laughter*] And he just survived a big wedding. So I asked him coming in, "Any advice?" He said, "I wasn't father of the bride." [*Laughter*]

New York Giants have one of the great storied histories of—in pro football. And this club carried on that great tradition. And perhaps—many would say this is probably the most exciting chapter ever written in the New York Giants' football history. After all, you started off the season and

allowed 80 points in the first two games. That would be called a lousy start. [*Laughter*] And then you're playing the Redskins——

Audience members. Boo!

The President. It's okay, you know. [*Laughter*] And the game wasn't going very well, as I recall. And then you rallied, and you won.

And a lot of the people that know something about football said that was the turning point. And the winning streak—what's interesting is—six straight games, as I understand, on two different continents. You also had a great road record. I don't know if the fans understand this, but you piled up more away-game victories than—in NFL history. And the good news is, your fans still loved you at home. [*Laughter*] They really loved you.

You got into the—you secured a wild card. And it was interesting, in the last game of the season, a lot of folks thought the coach would just kind of lay down and let New England cruise to a perfect season—I remember a lot of people speculating about that last game of the season— and yet you didn't, Coach. Your team didn't win on the scoreboard, but you won the hearts of a lot of Americans for contesting the game. And you also—your team—[*applause*]—and it clearly gave your team some self-confidence, because you stormed through Tampa Bay and then went into Dallas——

Audience members. [*Applause*]

The President. Okay, look, I'm a good sport. [*Laughter*] We're going to send Jessica Simpson to the Democrat National Convention. [*Laughter*]

Packers was one of the coldest games in NFL history. You lit up the field like you were on fire. And Lawrence Tynes, who's with us here, came through with a 47-yard fieldgoal in overtime, putting you in Super Bowl XLII. Yes, I knew you were going to make it. [*Laughter*] I don't know if everybody else did, but I knew you were going to make it. And you knew you were going to make it.

Lawrence Tynes. I did.

The President. And all of a sudden, a 0–2 team was about to square off against the 18–0 New England Patriots. Now they've got a lot of experts in our society—Coach, you might know what I'm talking about—and in looking back, it's hard to find many of the experts who predicted a Giants victory. Most people were calling it a cakewalk; you know, be prepared to turn off your television sets early because this isn't much of a game you're about to watch; when, in fact, it turned out to be really one of the great, legendary football games in our country's history.

First of all, your defense was awesome, Coach, and they deserve a lot of credit. And so does your offense. It was the 83-yard comeback drive in the fourth quarter that a lot of folks will remember for a long time coming. Eli Manning started one of the great plays called the Great Escape; it ended on David Tyree's helmet. [*Laughter*] So, like, I'm going to take you in the White House, and you can show me how you did it. [*Laughter*] And then Plaxico Burress, of course, caught the winning touchdown with 35 seconds left.

This is a great team that worked together. You won the Vince Lombardi Trophy, and you won the deep gratitude of the 1972 Miami Dolphins. [*Laughter*]

First of all, you've won the gratitude of your fans. New York Giants fans love these Giants. So we congratulate you all, but we're also congratulating your families, your loved ones, those who make the locker room work, the trainers, the people who clean up after you. We want to—we know you played for some—ones who lost loved ones, like the Tyrees and the Maras and the Tisches. I know you loved going down the Canyon of Heroes for the first ticker-tape parade since before the attacks of Sep-

tember the 11th, 2001. And I guarantee you, there was a lot of New York firefighters and police who were really thrilled to see you.

I like the fact that this team, the coaches and players, offer free camps for kids. Some of them run life-changing ministries. They raise money for children who have cancer. This is a team that supports the Ronald McDonald House and the United Way, promotes family literacy through Read Across America. It's even helped run a charter school program in inner-city Newark.

I appreciate the fact, Coach, that you and your players support our troops, but more importantly, our troops appreciate the fact that you support them. You've come to know the story like I have of Lieutenant Colonel Greg Gadson. He lost both of his legs while in Iraq. He first met up with the Giants in September, when you invited him to address a pregame meeting that helped inspire the comeback over the Redskins.

Then you saw him in Tampa, when he was trying out his legs that he walked on today to be on the stage with you. He was an honorary captain in Green Bay. He never left the sidelines, despite the 23-below windchill. In your last team meeting before the Super Bowl, Lieutenant Colonel Greg Gadson urged you to have pride in your team and believe in yourselves, which is exactly what you did.

I'm proud to be on the stage with this man. To me, it's a symbol of your respect for our country and your patriotism that you would let Greg Gadson be a part of this team. He has got the Purple Heart and three Bronze Stars, and now he's got a Super Bowl ring minted for a true "giant."

So while you're still on your feet: The Super Bowl New York Giants.

NOTE: The President spoke at 3:14 p.m. on the South Lawn at the White House. In his remarks, he referred to John K. Mara, president and chief executive officer, Steven Tisch, co-owner, Lawrence Tynes, kicker, and Plaxico Burress, wide receiver, New York Giants; E. Archibald Manning III, father, and Peyton Manning, brother, of Eli Manning, quarterback, New York Giants; and entertainer Jessica Simpson. The transcript released by the Office of the Press Secretary also included the remarks of New York Giants head coach Tom Coughlin.

Statement on North Korea Freedom Week
April 30, 2008

Laura and I send greetings to all those observing North Korea Freedom Week. I am deeply concerned about the grave human rights conditions in North Korea, especially the denial of universal freedoms of speech, press, religion, assembly, and association and restrictions on freedom of movement and workers' rights. I have met in the Oval Office with some of the brave individuals who have escaped from that country. I am deeply concerned by the stories of divided families, harsh conditions, and suffering. The United States stands with the North Korean people in their call for freedom. We believe it is every person's basic right to live in freedom and dignity. We will continue to support the North Korean people as they strive to achieve the rights and freedoms to which they are entitled as human beings. We look forward to the moment when we can celebrate the blessings of liberty with the North Korean people.

Message to the Congress Reporting on Blocking Property and Prohibiting Certain Transactions Related to Burma
April 30, 2008

To the Congress of the United States:

Pursuant to the International Emergency Economic Powers Act (50 U.S.C. 1701 *et seq.*) (IEEPA), I hereby report that I have issued an Executive Order (the "order") that takes additional steps with respect to the national emergency declared in Executive Order 13047 of May 20, 1997, and expanded in Executive Order 13448 of October 18, 2007.

In 1997, the United States put in place a prohibition on new investment in Burma in response to the Government of Burma's large scale repression of the democratic opposition in that country. On July 28, 2003, those sanctions were expanded by steps taken in Executive Order 13310, which contained prohibitions implementing sections 3 and 4 of the Burmese Freedom and Democracy Act of 2003 (Public Law 108–61) (the "Act") and supplemented that Act with additional restrictions. On October 18, 2007, I determined that the Government of Burma's continued repression of the democratic opposition in Burma, manifested at the time in the violent response to peaceful demonstrations, the commission of human rights abuses related to political repression, and engagement in public corruption, including by diverting or misusing Burmese public assets or by misusing public authority, warranted an expansion of the then-existing sanctions. Executive Order 13448, issued on that date, incorporated existing designation criteria set forth in Executive Order 13310, blocked the property and interests in property of persons listed in the Annex to that Executive Order, and provided additional criteria for designations of certain other persons.

The order supplements the existing designation criteria set forth in Executive Order 13310, as incorporated in and expanded by Executive Order 13448. The order blocks the property and interests in property in the United States of persons listed in the Annex to the order and provides additional criteria for designations of persons determined by the Secretary of the Treasury, after consultation with the Secretary of State, to be owned or controlled by, directly or indirectly, the Government of Burma or an official or officials of the Government of Burma; to have materially assisted, sponsored, or provided financial, material, logistical, or technical support for, or goods or services in support of, the Government of Burma, the State Peace and Development Council of Burma, the Union Solidarity and Development Association of Burma, any successor entity to any of the foregoing, any senior official of any of the foregoing, or any person whose property and interests in property are blocked pursuant to Executive Order 13310, Executive Order 13448, or the order; or to be owned or controlled by, or to have acted or purported to act for or on behalf of, directly or indirectly, any person whose property and interests in property are blocked pursuant to Executive Order 13310, Executive Order 13448, or the order.

The order leaves in place the existing prohibitions on new investment, the exportation or reexportation to Burma of financial services, and the importation of any article that is a product of Burma, which were put into effect in Executive Order 13047 and Executive Order 13310.

The order authorizes the Secretary of the Treasury, after consultation with the Secretary of State, to take such actions, including the promulgation of rules and regulations, and to employ all powers granted to the President by IEEPA and section 4 of the Burmese Freedom and Democracy Act of 2003 as may be necessary to carry out the purposes of the order.

I am enclosing a copy of the Executive Order I have issued.

GEORGE W. BUSH

The White House,
April 30, 2008.

NOTE: This message was released by the Office of the Press Secretary on May 1. The related Executive order is listed in Appendix D at the end of this volume.

Remarks on the National Day of Prayer
May 1, 2008

Good morning. Welcome to the White House. And I am honored to join you for the National Day of Prayer. I'm sorry Laura's not here. She's out selling her book. [*Laughter*]

Shirley, thank you very much for being the chairman of the National Day of Prayer. Glad you brought old Jim with you. [*Laughter*] Dr. Zacharias, thank you for being the honorary chairman. I appreciate the members of my Cabinet who are here today. Thank you all for coming. It's good to see Members of the United States Senate and the House of Representatives. Appreciate you all taking time out of your busy schedule to come by. It's always good to be with you.

I want to thank our military chaplains who are with us. Thank you for doing the Lord's work with our troops. I'm proud to have prayer leaders here. Rabbi Fishman, thank you; it's good to see you again, sir. Father Coughlin, from the United States House of Representatives, it's good to see you, sir. I want to thank Pastor Mays, who will be following me here shortly, for coming. I'm looking forward to hearing the choir of Saint Patrick's Cathedral, New York City, New York. It's going to be a great moment to have this East Room filled with joy of song. And so I welcome them here today.

On this day, Americans come together to thank our Creator for our Nation's many blessings. We are a blessed nation. And on this day, we celebrate our freedoms, particularly the freedom to pray in public and the great diversity of faith found in America. I love being the President of a country where people feel free to worship as they see fit. And I remind our fellow citizens, if you choose to worship or not worship, and no matter how you worship, we're all equally American.

I think one of the interesting things about a National Day of Prayer is it does help describe our Nation's character to others. We are a prayerful nation. A lot of citizens draw comfort from prayer. Prayer is an important part of the lives of millions of Americans. You know, it's interesting, when you think about our faith, you can find it in the Pledge of Allegiance, you can find an expression of American faith in the Declaration of Independence, and you can find it in the coins in our pockets. I used to carry coins—[*laughter*]—about 10 months, I'll be carrying them again. [*Laughter*]

The fidelity to faith has been present in our Nation's leaders from its very start. Upon assuming the Presidency, George Washington took the oath of office and then added the famous plea, "So help me

God." On John Adams's first day in the White House, he wrote a prayer that is now etched in marble on the fireplace in the State Dining Room. And he prayed, "May none but honest and wise men ever rule under this roof." Now, we'll leave it to the historians to judge whether or not that happened throughout our history. [*Laughter*]

During the Civil War, Abraham Lincoln turned to prayer. His second Inaugural Address quoted from Scripture. He stood before the United States people and quoted from Scripture. And he sought to heal a people who "read the same Bible and prayed to the same God," his words.

As William McKinley lay dying from an assassin's bullet, one of his final words on Earth focused on the Almighty. On his deathbed he was heard to say, "Nearer, my God, to thee."

As American forces risked their lives on D-day, Franklin Roosevelt delivered a Presidential prayer over the radio. He asked God to protect our troops as they liberated "a suffering humanity," and he prayed for "a peace that will let all men live in freedom." When Roosevelt died, his successor, Harry Truman, said he "felt like the Moon, the stars, and all the planets" had fallen on him. He told reporters, "Boys, if you ever pray, pray for me now."

John F. Kennedy attended Mass in Florida during the last week of his Presidency—and during the last week of his life. It was at that Mass that he heard the parable where the—our Lord compared the Kingdom of Heaven to a mustard seed that grew into a large tree and offered shelter to God's creatures.

Three days after the worst terrorist attack on American soil, Laura and I joined our fellow citizens in prayer before the Lord. It was in the middle hour of our grief. We prayed for those who were missing. We prayed for the dead. We prayed for those who loved them. I recall the words of a woman from New York, who said, "I prayed to God to give us a sign that He is still here."

Well, sometimes God's signs are not always the ones we look for. And we learn in tragedy that His purposes are not always our own. But we also know that in adversity, we can find comfort through prayer.

Over the last 7 years, our country has faced many trials. And time and time again, we have turned to prayer and found strength and resilience. We prayed with those who've lost everything in natural disasters and helped them heal and recover and build. We prayed for our brave and brilliant troops who died on the field of battle. We lift up their families in prayer. And as we pray for God's continued blessings on our country, I think it makes sense to hope that one day there may be a international day of prayer, that one day the national prayer—[*applause*]. It would be a chance for people of faith around the world to stop at the same time to pause to praise an Almighty. It would be a time when we could pray together for a world that sees the promise of the Psalms made real: "Your love is ever before me, and I walk continually in your truth."

I want to thank you all for coming. I particularly want to thank you for your prayers. You know, somebody asked me one time when I was there—over seeing the Sea of Galilee, they said, "What did you think about when you were there, Mr. President?" I said, "I have finally understood the story of the calm on the rough seas." I may have been a little hardheaded at times, but I'm absolutely convinced it was the prayers of the people who helped me understood: In turbulence, you can find calm and strength. And I thank you for those prayers.

NOTE: The President spoke at 10:12 a.m. in the East Room at the White House. In his remarks, he referred to Shirley Dobson, chairman, National Day of Prayer Task Force, and her husband James; Ravi Zacharias, honorary chairman, National Day of Prayer Task Force; Rabbi Lyle Fishman, Ohr Kodesh Congregation in Chevy Chase, MD; and Pastor Steve Mays, senior pastor, Cavalry Chapel South Bay in Gardena, CA. The Office of the Press Secretary also released a Spanish language transcript of these remarks. The National Day of Prayer proclamation of April 28 is listed in Appendix D at the end of this volume.

Remarks on the Observance of Asian Pacific American Heritage Month
May 1, 2008

Thank you all. Please be seated. Thank you. Good afternoon, and welcome to the White House. The East Room is a fitting place to celebrate Asian Pacific American Heritage Month. I say fitting because in 1860, this was where James Buchanan first—became the first President to receive an official delegation from Japan. It was a great meeting, except for one slight wrinkle. The interpreter the Japanese brought with them couldn't speak English. [*Laughter*] So he translated Japanese into Dutch— [*laughter*]—and then another interpreter translated Dutch into English. [*Laughter*] I thought that was pretty interesting. People say when I speak, it sounds like Japanese translated into Dutch translated into English. [*Laughter*] I'm just upholding a diplomatic tradition. [*Laughter*]

During Asian Pacific American Heritage Month, we honor citizens whose families have come from halfway around the world, but who are now an integral part of America. I want to thank former Secretary and my dear friend Norm Mineta, who, when he was in Congress, introduced legislation that led to this celebration. And I thank each of you for coming to be a part of it.

Madam Secretary, we're proud you're here. Elaine Chao has been a member of my Cabinet since day one, and I think America is better off for it. So thank you for coming, Madam Secretary. Members of Congress—Congressman Wu, thank you for being here, sir. Members of my administration, I'm glad you all are here. Members of the diplomatic corps, it's so kind of you to take time out of your day to come. We got our veterans here and, of course, members of the United States military. Proud to call you Commander in Chief, and thank you for being here today.

More than 15 million Americans claim Asian or Pacific ancestry. They make America's culture more vibrant, and we're a better place—and a more lively place, I might add—from Songkran celebrations in Los Angeles to Chinese New Year parties in Chicago to Diwali festivals right here at the White House.

Asian Pacific Americans make our country more competitive. It turns out there's a great entrepreneurial streak that runs throughout the citizens whom we honor today. Small-business owners all over America are creating new jobs and are living the dream. They enrich America because of their love for America.

And many Asians have settled in this country after fleeing oppressive regimes. They looked at America as a hopeful place. They include the boat people of Vietnam, men and women who escaped the killing fields of Cambodia, those who endured the Cultural Revolution in China, and victims of the regime in North Korea.

America must always remember that we are a place of hope and freedom for people who live in oppressive societies. Throughout the Asian American community, there is a special appreciation of liberty known only to those who've been denied it. If

you've been denied freedom, if freedom is something you long for, you understand how to treasure it. Asian Americans are committed to advancing the cause of freedom—and I can't thank you enough for that—both in their ancestral nations and in our own.

Together, we work to expand economic freedom and prosperity in the Asian-Pacific region. It's in our interest that we enter into trading agreements with nations throughout the world, starting with South Korea. I negotiated a free trade agreement last June with South Korea. This agreement is going to create opportunities for American businesses and workers. It will increase trade between our countries by about $17 billion. It's going to strengthen America's relationship with one of our closest, closest allies. When President Lee visited the United States a few weeks ago, I promised him that I would encourage Congress in as many ways as I could to get this agreement passed, that I'd work hard to remind people that this is a mutually beneficial agreement.

The Asian community efforts have supported free trade agreements throughout the Asian-Pacific area. And I want to thank you for working to educate Members of Congress about why we ought to improve this agreement as soon as possible.

We're working to increase security and reduce the threats to freedom in the Asia-Pacific region. Thank you for coming, Chris Hill. He's very much involved in what we've called the six-party talks, which is where we've joined with Korea, Japan, and Russia and China to convince North Korea to abandon its nuclear weapons program. Nations have come together to send a clear message that it's important to abandon those nuclear weapons ambitions. We want a Korean Peninsula that is nuclear weapons free.

We've put together what's called the Proliferation Security Initiative. It works with more than 85 countries, including many in the Asia-Pacific region, to stop the shipment of the world's most dangerous weapons. In other words, this is just kind of a quest for security and freedom. And we're working with nations all throughout the world, including those in the Asian-Pacific region, to protect our peoples from the true threats of the 21st century. We're working with Pakistan and Indonesia and Malaysia and the Philippines and other partners, and Singapore and other partners, to dismantle terrorist networks and to combat the ideology of the extremists.

You can always defeat an ideology of hate with an ideology of hope. And there's nothing more hopeful than a system based upon human rights and human dignity and a system based upon the freedom for people to worship and speak their minds freely.

We're working with India to promote democracy and the peace it yields throughout the continent. We're working together to extend the hope of liberty throughout Asia.

I know you share my concerns about the situation in Tibet. I welcome the recent statements by the Chinese Government expressing its willingness to meet with representatives of the Dalai Lama. It's precisely what I have suggested President Hu Jintao do. I think it's important that there be a renewed dialogue, and that dialogue must be substantive, so we can address the real way—in a—including—can address in a real way the deep and legitimate concerns of the Tibetan people.

In Burma, the brutal military regime continues to reject the clear will of the Burmese people to live under leaders of their own choosing. So over the past 8 months, my administration has tightened sanctions on the regime. We've imposed visa bans on the junta's generals and their families and their cronies. We're trying to send a clear message, and we hope the rest of the world follows as well.

Today I've issued a new Executive order that instructs the Treasury Department to freeze the assets of Burmese state-owned companies that are major sources of funds that prop up the junta. These companies, in industries such as gems and timber, exploit the labor of the downtrodden Burmese people but enrich only the generals. And today I'm sending yet another clear message that we expect there to be change, and we expect these generals to honor the will of the people.

We're also working to address the humanitarian crisis in Burma. The U.S. has resettled tens of thousands of Burmese refugees in the last few years, and this year, we expect to admit as many as 18,000 more. Last December, I signed legislation to ease restrictions that have prevented ethnic minorities involved in the struggle against the Burmese regime from entering the United States.

And I applaud the Asian Americans who have helped these refugees get settled once they come to the United States of America. It's got to be hard to come here not knowing the language. It's got to be hard to come here as a stranger. And I thank those of you and those around the country who have opened up their arms and said, "Welcome to America. How can we help you settle in?" I urge others, especially those who share the customs of these newest Asian Americans, to help them feel at home here in their adopted country.

We're working together to strengthen our partnership with Japan, which is really one of the great success stories of freedom. Six decades ago, my dad fought the Japanese. They were the sworn enemy of the United States of America. And now his son sits down with Prime Ministers of Japan talking about how to keep the peace. Isn't that interesting? What a great irony it is that the father served to fight and the son serves to work with the Prime Minister of the former enemy to keep the peace. Freedom is transformative. Freedom and democracy are powerful instruments of change.

The lesson learned in this example is one that we can apply elsewhere around the world to yield the peace that we all want.

And this friendship was made possible by Americans who understood the power—the transformative power of freedom years ago. I wasn't the first person to think of that. Fortunately, predecessors of mine understood with great faith that freedom is universal, that freedom is widespread, that people long to be free, and if given the chance to be free, peaceful societies develop.

With us today are veterans from the 442d Regimental Combat Team. This was a segregated Army unit composed mostly of volunteers recruited from internment camps in the United States. Isn't that interesting? People whose love of the country was such that they were over—able to overcome the bitterness of being interned by a country they called home. And they were willing to put on the uniform, and not only put on the uniform, they served America with distinction in eight battle campaigns in Europe. In 1945, members of the 442d helped liberate the concentration camp at Dachau. They went from an intern camp, to wear the uniform of the United States Army, to liberate camps in Europe.

Yet the 442d is best known for their mission to rescue the trapped soldiers of the Texas National Guard's "lost battalion." A lot of Texans thanking you guys for that, by the way. [*Laughter*] In the mountains of eastern France, the 442d went up against the heavily entrenched Germans and suffered devastating casualties. But their courage saved more than 200 of their brothers. Their valor helped earn them several Presidential Unit Citations and helped make their unit one of the most highly decorated in U.S. military history. Their sacrifice earns the gratitude of the Nation they defended, and an attitude we express today to the men of the 442d. Thank you for coming.

I do want to point out one soul who's joined us—and Ben is not going to be happy about it—Ben Kuroki. He probably doesn't want to be called out, but I'm going to do it anyway, Ben. I got the podium, and you don't. [*Laughter*]

Two days after Pearl Harbor, Ben volunteered to join the Army, where there is no doubt he met prejudice at nearly every turn. Still, he became one of the few Nisei admitted to the Army Air Corps. He flew 58 missions over Europe and Japan, and he earned three Distinguished Flying Crosses.

When he came back home, he turned to another mission: working to overcome the intolerance he had experienced during his early days in the Army. Ben edited newspapers. He spoke to audiences around the country. He became a strong advocate of racial equality. He knew something, and he knew the subject well, unfortunately.

Sixty years after the Japanese surrender, Ben received the U.S. Army Distinguished Service Medal. And at the ceremony, here's what he said: "I had to fight like hell to fight for my country, and now I feel completely vindicated."

We are glad you feel vindicated, but I am proud to tell you, America is a better place because of you, Ben. Thank you for coming.

And so during Asia Pacific American Heritage Month, we thank you all for helping make America a better place. We thank you for loving our country the way you do. The way—thank you for being great contributors to the life of our fellow citizens.

We ask for God's continued blessings on you, your family, and all the citizens of our great land. Thanks for coming. God bless.

NOTE: The President spoke at 2:53 p.m. in the East Room at the White House. In his remarks, he referred to former Transportation Secretary Norman Y. Mineta; President Lee Myung-bak of South Korea; Assistant Secretary of State for East Asian and Pacific Affairs Christopher R. Hill; Tenzin Gyatso, the 14th Dalai Lama; President Hu Jintao of China; and Prime Minister Yasuo

Fukuda of Japan. The Asian/Pacific American Heritage Month proclamation of April 29 is listed in Appendix D at the end of this volume.

Remarks on Emergency Food Aid Programs
May 1, 2008

In recent weeks, many have expressed concern about the significant increase in global food prices. And I share that concern. In some of the world's poorest nations, rising prices can mean the difference between getting a daily meal or going without food.

To address this problem, 2 weeks ago, my administration announced that about $200 million in emergency food aid would be available through a program at the Agriculture Department called the Emerson Trust. But that's just the beginning of our efforts. I think more needs to be done, and so today I am asking Congress to provide an additional $770 million to support food aid and development programs. Together, this amounts to nearly $1 billion in new funds to bolster global food security. And with other security assistant programs already in place, we're now projecting to spend nearly—that we will spend nearly $5 billion in 2008 and 2009 to fight global hunger.

This funding will keep our existing emergency food aid programs robust. We have been the leader for providing food to those who are going without in the past, and we will continue to be the leader around the world. It will also allow us to fund agricultural development programs that help farmers in developing countries increase their productivity. And of course, this will help reduce the number of people who need emergency food aid in the first place.

As America increases its food assistance, it's really important that we transform the way that food aid is delivered. In my State of the Union Address this year, I called on Congress to support a proposal to purchase up to nearly 25 percent of food assistance directly from farmers in the developing world. And the reason you do that is, in order to break the cycle of famine that we're having to deal with too often in the modern era, it's important to help build up local agriculture. I ask Congress to approve this measure as soon as possible. It's a commonsense way to help deal with food emergencies around the world.

Now, other countries have a role to play as well. America is in the lead; we'll stay in the lead. And we expect others to participate along with us. We're working with our G–8 partners and other developed nations to secure commitments from their governments for additional food aid.

We're also working toward the conclusion of a successful Doha agreement that will reduce and eliminate tariffs and other barriers as well as market-distorting subsidies for agricultural goods. And the reason why getting a Doha round done is important is it'll end up reducing the cost of food, importing food; it'll make it cheaper for consumers all around the world. In other words, we want to change the system to make it easier for people to get less expensive food.

We're also urging countries that have instituted restrictions on agricultural exports to lift those restrictions. Some countries are preventing needed food from getting to market in the first place, and we call upon them to end those restrictions to help ease suffering for those who aren't getting food.

We're also urging countries to remove barriers to advanced crops developed through biotechnology. These crops are safe, they're resistant to drought and disease, and they hold the promise of producing more food for more people.

Now, here at home, we're working to ensure that our poorest citizens get the food they need. Since 2001, the administration, in working with Congress, has increased funding for nutrition assistance programs by 76 percent. We've adjusted food stamp benefits annually to cover price increases at the checkout counter. And last month, the Agriculture Department made available an additional $150 million to respond to the food needs of those who depend on WIC, the Special Supplemental Nutrition Program for Women, Infants and Children. With this new funding, we will have increased our support for WIC by 18.6 percent this year.

The American people are generous people, and they're compassionate people. We believe in the timeless truth to whom much is given, much is expected. And so therefore, at home we will work to ensure that the neediest among us can cope with the rising food prices. And with the new international funding I'm announcing today, we're sending a clear message to the world that America will lead the fight against hunger for years to come.

Thank you very much for your interest. God bless.

NOTE: The President spoke at 3:13 p.m. in the Diplomatic Reception Room at the White House.

Statement on the Situation in Burma
May 1, 2008

The people of Burma have long awaited the opportunity to live in a true democracy. The referendum vote scheduled for May 10, 2008, could have been that opportunity. However, Than Shwe and his regime are ensuring that the referendum vote will be on a dangerously flawed Constitution and will not be free, fair, or credible. They continue to ignore calls from the Burmese people and the international community for a genuine process that could result in a legitimate Constitution reflecting the will of the people, and they continue to carry out a campaign to intimidate voters and to arrest those who dare speak out against the flaws of the referendum and draft Constitution.

The regime has not acted on any of the measures called for by the United Nations Security Council and does not cooperate with Special Adviser Ibrahim Gambari. We have called for the early release of all political prisoners; implementation of measures to address the political, economic, humani-

tarian, and human rights issues that are of concern; and the creation of necessary conditions for a genuine dialogue with Daw Aung San Suu Kyi and all concerned parties and ethnic groups in order to achieve an inclusive national reconciliation. Furthermore, the regime has refused offers from Mr. Gambari to provide technical assistance or international monitors for the pending referendum.

Laura and I are committed to work for the people of Burma and help in their struggle to free themselves from the regime's tyranny. I have signed a new Executive order that will block all property and interests in property of designated individuals and entities determined to be owned or controlled by, directly or indirectly, the Government of Burma or an official or officials of the Government of Burma. This Executive order expands existing authorities that allow the United States Government to target those who are responsible for supporting, empowering, and enriching the Burmese regime, a regime that exploits and oppresses the people of Burma.

The United States will continue to pressure Burma's rulers until they respond to the legitimate calls of the Burmese people for a genuine dialogue leading to a democratic transition.

NOTE: The statement referred to Senior Gen. Than Shwe, Chairman, State Peace and Development Council of Burma; United Nations Special Envoy to Myanmar Ibrahim Gambari; and Aung San Suu Kyi, leader of the National League for Democracy in Burma.

Statement on World Press Freedom Day
May 1, 2008

May 3 marks World Press Freedom Day. Just and open societies protect and rely on the freedom of the press. That freedom is enshrined in the first amendment to the United States Constitution, because freedom of speech is integral to a free society.

Brutal regimes and others who seek to stifle liberty often do so by closing down private newspapers and radio and television stations. They kidnap, arbitrarily jail, and beat journalists. Some journalists have been taken from their families for years, and others have been killed for speaking out. Many were killed by terrorists, extremists, and insurgents who seek to deny people even basic access to information as well as the right to free speech.

Journalists should be able to report without fear of persecution. In countries such as Belarus, Burma, China, Cuba, Eritrea, Iran, Libya, North Korea, Syria, Venezuela, and Zimbabwe, repressive laws severely restrict freedom of speech, and those who attempt to report are often imprisoned. In 2007, for the ninth consecutive year, China remained the world's top jailer of journalists, followed by Cuba, Eritrea, Iran, and Azerbaijan.

The United States condemns the harassment, physical intimidation, persecution, and other abuse that journalists, including bloggers and Internet reporters, have faced in China, Cuba, Egypt, Tunisia, Venezuela, and Vietnam, as well as the unsolved murders of journalists in Belarus, Lebanon, and Russia. We call on all governments to guarantee the inalienable rights of their people, including, consistent with article 19 of the United Nations Universal Declaration of Human Rights, the right to freedom of speech and the press.

America stands with those who struggle for their liberty, including those in the press who continue their work in spite of risks. During fiscal year 2007, the United States provided $78 million in approximately 40 countries to promote media freedom and freedom of information. As President, I have met with many journalists and editors who are struggling against forces that seek to suppress media freedom. We salute these courageous individuals, and we recognize the importance of the right to a free press in spreading freedom around the world.

Statement on Congressional Passage of Student Loan Access Legislation
May 1, 2008

Earlier today Congress passed the "Ensuring Continued Access to Student Loans Act" with overwhelming bipartisan support. I am pleased by Congress's swift action to address this vital issue. In particular, I want to thank the committee chairs and ranking members for their hard work. Millions of students around the country could potentially benefit from this important piece of legislation.

In order to ensure that Americans can continue to compete in the global marketplace, the Federal Government has an obligation to encourage and support people pursuing higher education. By granting the Department of Education greater authority to purchase Federal student loans, today's action should ease the anxiety many students may feel about their ability to finance their education this fall. Thanks to quick and decisive action by my administration and the Congress, Federal student aid will be available in a more timely fashion.

NOTE: The statement referred to H.R. 5715.

Remarks on the National Economy and a Question-and-Answer Session in Maryland Heights, Missouri
May 2, 2008

The President. Thank you very much. Please be seated. Thank you. What he said was, "It's about time you made it." [*Laughter*] Dave was right: I was scheduled here at World Wide, and then the fires hit in California, and I went out there to help the people try to recover from the natural disaster. And I told him at the Christmas party there at the White House, I said, "I'm coming back." I've always felt like if you're a politician and you make a promise, you better keep it. [*Laughter*] And so I have.

And the reason why I wanted to come then and wanted to come back is, I think it's very important for the President to recognize success and for the President to herald entrepreneurship. And so in meeting with Dave and Jim and the employees of this company, really what I'm saying is that the entrepreneurial spirit is alive and well here at World Wide.

You heard the man say that over the past 7 years, revenues have tripled, and they've expanded the job base by 500 people. And what's relevant for America is that it's the small-business sector—I don't know if you call yourself small anymore; you're probably a medium-sized business sector—[*laughter*]—that creates jobs. Seventy percent of new jobs in America are created by small and medium-sized businesses. And if you're worried about the economy like I'm worried about the economy, then it makes sense to put policy in place that encourages investment and growth with the job creators.

And that's what I want to spend a little time talking to you about. But before I do so, I do want to thank the World Wide Technology employees. The truth of the matter is, this company is doing well cause you've got imaginative leadership, but you've also got great employees who are well motivated, taken care of, inspired. And it's been my honor to meet some of your employees, and I look forward to answering some of your questions here in a minute.

I do want to thank the Governor of the State of Missouri for joining us. Governor Blunt, I'm proud you're here. Thank you for taking time out of your schedule. The Governor and I discussed the recent storms that have hit parts of Missouri. I assured him that we will stay in touch with his office and the emergency teams to make sure that if there needs to be a Federal response, we will be ready to give one. And obviously, for those who've lost their property today, we send our heartfelt condolences, and just want you to know that when natural disaster strikes, if the disaster is—merits it, there will be a ample and robust government response. So thanks for coming, Governor.

I'm also proud to be here with the United States Senator, Kit Bond from Missouri. Needless to say, he used his time on Air Force One to make sure I understood the issues that were facing the State of Missouri. We spent a little time talking about the Missouri River. And Todd Akin is with us too. Congressman, I'm proud you're here. Thanks for coming.

So we're getting economic news. There's a lot of data beginning to move. On Wednesday, the—they talked about the fact that the economy in the first quarter grew at 0.6 percent. That's the same as it grew in the fourth quarter of last year. That's not good enough for America. It's positive growth, but we can do better than that. Today there was another report out that showed that we lost 20,000 jobs last month, even though the unemployment rate dropped to 5 percent. In other words, the unemployment rate went down. And again, that's a sign that this economy is not as robust as any of us would like it.

The good news is, is that we anticipated this. Last fall, we started to get indications that the economy was going to slow down. And so I—believe it or not, you can actually work with Congress sometimes on— with people on both sides of the aisle, which is what we did; these two Members were incredibly constructive—to pass a stimulus package, progrowth package.

There's two aspects to that package I want to spend some time talking about. One of them is, is that you're going to get some money—turns out, it's your own money, but you're going to get it back. [*Laughter*] Six hundred dollars per person, $1,200 per couple, $300 per child; a family of four will be getting a $1,800 check. And the reason why—and by the way, it's going to affect 130 million families. And the reason why that is good policy, first of all, it's a temporary tax relief, recognizing that we're going to recover. And this is to help stimulate that recovery.

Secondly, we wanted to make sure that people were encouraged to be consumers. We wanted there to be consumption in our society, and no better way to stimulate consumption than to let you have some of your own money back.

Thirdly, it turns out that this money is going to be very helpful in helping people deal with high energy prices and food price. I'm going to spend a little time on energy here in a minute.

And fourthly, it's big enough. In other words, we didn't want to make a political statement. We wanted to make a statement that will affect this economy. When you're affecting 130 million households, with over $150 billion of progrowth package, it's going to affect us positively. The experts say that beginning—toward the end of this quarter and the beginning of next quarter, we should see some positive signs as a result of the progrowth economic package.

Now, some of you are saying, "You think I'm ever going to see my money? We've heard 'the check is in the mail' deal before." Well, it's coming. They started hitting last Monday. And Secretary of the Treasury Paulson is on top of this, and so you'll start seeing—if you're not—if you didn't get your money electronically, you're going to start seeing it come in the check form.

And for those people in Missouri and around the Nation that do not file income taxes, you need to contact the local IRS office because you're likely to be eligible. And therefore, you got to make sure you sign up for the program in order to get the money. We want you to get the money. And so if you're involved in a church group that's worried about helping people, then make sure that parishioners, or make sure people in the community centers understand that if you're not a filer, you're still eligible to get a check.

Now, the other aspect of the program was to stimulate investment for companies like World Wide. In other words, there's a—you can affect the Tax Code that provides incentives for the CEOs to say, "I think we need—we ought to buy some equipment." And that's important for a couple of reasons: One, it makes you more productive; it makes you more competitive; it gives the employees a better chance to keep this company on a cutting edge.

Secondly, somebody has to make that which you purchase. So if the Tax Code says it's in your interest to buy a piece of equipment or to buy software or to buy something to make this company a better company, then somewhere in the economy somebody is going to make it for you. And that also creates jobs. There's a ripple effect for using the Tax Code to stimulate investment.

I was talking to Dave and Jim, and they were telling me that the incentives built in the progrowth plan for businesses will—have—are causing them to make new investments for you that they may have put off for later years. And the effects of this aspect of the progrowth plan are beginning to kick in as well; in other words, it's just starting. We passed the deal in February.

The point I'm trying to tell you is, is that we worked well with Congress, and that the effects of a robust attempt to inject life hasn't really kicked in yet. And I'm—if you believe these economists, if they had three hands they'd say, "On the one hand,

on the other hand, and then on the third hand." [*Laughter*] But we've got some smart folks around that are analyzing what this means, and they feel confident about it.

I've been—since I've been your President, I want to remind you, we have been through a recession, we have been through a terrorist attack, we have been at war, we have had corporate scandals, we have had major natural disasters, and yet this economy always recovers. We're a resilient economy because we've got good, capable, smart, hard-working people in America. And I know it's tough times, and I know you're having to pay more at the fuel pump than you want, but this economy is going to come on. I'm confident it will. And I want to thank the folks at World Wide for being a part of the leading edge of optimism here in America and the leading edge in making sure that people can find good, hard—paying jobs.

Let me talk about energy very quickly. I'm fully aware that people are paying dearly at the pump. The other day at a press conference I said it's like a tax; it's a tax on you. The more that gasoline goes up, the more you're paying for the pump, the less money you have in your pocket to spend for your family. I will tell you, it's taken us awhile to get in this fix, and therefore, it's going to take us awhile to get out of the fix. But I want to remind you that an energy policy that basically prohibits America from finding oil in our own land is an energy policy that has led to high gasoline prices.

When I first got to the Congress, I suggested that we have a comprehensive energy policy: one that recognizes the short-term effects of being reliant upon foreign oil; one that says we can use new technologies that will enable us to power our automobiles in different kinds of ways, using ethanol, for example, or battery technology; and one ultimately that will allow hydrogen to power the car.

So we worked well with Congress on the interim step. As you know, ethanol is beginning to take off. And I'm convinced we're going to be able to make ethanol out of something other than corn here relatively quickly, like wood chips or grasses grown in the desert, which will be very exciting for the American people. Hydrogen, we're doing a lot of research on your behalf to have hydrogen-powered automobiles, which means you're running on hydrogen, the waste product of which is water.

But in the meantime, in the short run, we didn't allow exploration for oil and gas in places like Alaska or Outer Continental Shelf. And guess what happened? World demand exceeded supply, and now you're paying for it. If Congress truly is interested in helping relieve the price of gasoline, they would do two things. They would recognize that we can drill for oil and gas in environmentally friendly ways here in the United States, where there is good reserves. And they would build refineries; they would encourage the construction of refineries. Do you know that there hasn't been a new refinery built in America since 1976? No wonder there's constricted supplies. If you want more of something, in this case, you got to build the additional manufacturing capability. And so our gasoline supplies are restricted as well.

My attitude is, I understand the pain, but I also understand if we don't allow us to explore in environmentally friendly ways for oil and gas reserves in the United States of America, we'll remain dependent in the short term on foreign oil. And that's not good for us.

I want to talk about housing very quickly. The key to the housing market is for the market to adjust—you know, built too many houses. We just got to work through the system. But there's things Government should and can do that is responsible—mainly, is to help creditworthy people stay in their home. That's the best thing we can do, is to help somebody who is capable of paying the mortgage, and if they just

need a little help to be able to stay in the home, is to help provide that help.

And here's the dilemma: If you got a—bought yourself a mortgage, in the old days when you—the originator of your mortgage, like a savings and loan, was somebody that you could go and talk in the office, say, "Listen, man, I got a little bit of a problem. I'm in a bind. I need a little help on my interest payment. Or can you extend my note out a little bit?" The originator of the mortgage, the guy who loaned you the money, still owned the paper. In this day and age, the person that loaned you the money for the mortgage may not own the mortgage anymore.

And so we came together—the Treasury Department and groups that help people understand the mortgage market and refinancing experts—and put together what's called the HOPE NOW Alliance, which enables people to go and renegotiate loans. That's what we want to do. We want to help people stay in their homes. The market is going to correct. And what we want to do is to say, here's a way for you to stay in your home. They go to these lenders, big lenders and say, look, just help them out a little bit—delay interest or renegotiate the interest rates or extend the payments. We've helped about 1,400,000 homeowners stay in their homes.

I know there's all kinds of proposals coming out of Congress. I mean, one such proposal was: Why don't you use your money to buy empty houses? Well, that doesn't help the person who's no longer in the house. That may help the lender; that may help the speculator. I'm interested in helping the homeowner. And so I—we'll work with Congress on legislation, but in my judgment, the best kind of legislation focuses on the person that actually owns the home.

Now, look, some people were in there speculating. I don't think Government ought to help speculators. And Government—you know, the truth of the matter is, some folks probably shouldn't have tried to buy a home in the first place. But there's a lot of good, creditworthy people; they just need a little relief to stay in the home.

The other thing I'm worried about is these reset mortgages. What I'm very concerned about is somebody went out and got them a mortgage, and the person that sold them the mortgage said, "Boy, this is a good, low interest rate for you." They forgot to tell them the second half: that in a couple of years, it's going to bump up. These resets, as you know, you buy a low interest rate, and you get on the paper, and then by a couple of years later, all of a sudden, the interest rate booms up.

And I'm—what I'm really concerned about is fraudulent tactics that didn't tell people that didn't really quite understand what was going on, the full story. And it's a Federal responsibility to make sure if that stuff goes on, people are held to account. We don't want people being cheated in America.

The other thing that the Government can do is to reform what's called these GSEs. These are big Government-backed lending institutions. And we can reform them and get them focused on their core mission, which is to help the mortgage industry move forward, help people in homes.

And finally, another interesting idea is to let the States' housing authorities issue tax-free bonds, which will then provide more money for refinancing.

Finally, I do want to talk about trade. It's an interesting subject here in America. There's a lot of people who say trade is bad for our country. We shouldn't be a nation that opens up markets, that's what they're saying. Unless, of course, you're a Missouri farmer who's selling your product into foreign markets. Unless, of course, you're World Wide Technology, which is expanding in a robust way and is looking for new markets. By the way, it's in your interests if you're working for World Wide that markets be open. If you're good at what you're doing—and you are, obviously; otherwise, you wouldn't be successful—then trade policy ought to make it easier for you to enter foreign markets.

All I want is for America to be treated the way we treat other nations. I think that's a reasonable thing to ask. And so let me talk about the Colombia free trade agreement. You might have been reading about that lately. It's one of these issues that has created consternation, at least in Washington. Most goods from Colombia come into the United States duty free. That's a result of longstanding congressional policy. Most of our goods and services are taxed going into Colombia. Most goods coming here come in duty free; most goods produced in the United States, or services like yours, pay a tariff. That means a tax. It's more expensive. It's harder to get into the market because what you charge is upped by tax.

I think it makes sense to have Congress say, "We want Colombia to treat us just the way we treat Colombia." It turns out, 9,000 businesses export into Colombia in the United States, 8,000 of which are small and midsized businesses. Isn't that interesting? Many of the people benefiting, people working for companies that export into Colombia, work for small businesses and medium-sized businesses.

But Congress doesn't see it that way right now. A lot of Members of Congress do, but they have absolutely shut down the vote on the Colombia free trade agreement. And I think it's irresponsible. If you're worried about the state of the economy, we ought to be opening up markets, not shutting down markets. We ought to be insisting we're treated fairly.

And I'll tell you another problem. In not moving the Colombia free trade agreement, we are turning our back on a very strong ally of the United States of America. There's a President of Colombia named Uribe, and he's got a tough situation down there because he's dealing with what's called FARC, which is an extremist group that uses drug dollars to perpetuate violence and to move their products mainly to here. And here's a man who says, "I'm going to deal with them, and I'm going to be tough with them." And then all of a sudden, the United States Congress turns its back on him. What kind of message is that?

And so I'm—I strongly urge the Congress to understand that opening up markets is good for our economy. But I also strongly urge the Congress to understand, whether it would be Colombia or Panama or Korea, that we can't be turning our backs on our allies. This is good economics, and it's good national security.

Those are some of the things on my mind. I've got a lot on my mind, by the way. [*Laughter*] Getting ready to march down the aisle and—[*laughter*].

What I thought I'd do is answer some questions—any question, any topic. I've been around long enough to dodge them if I can't figure out the answer. [*Laughter*] I can ask myself one.

Yes, sir, Mr. Chairman—oh, Mr. President. Fine. [*Laughter*]

Health Care

Q. So as Dave mentioned, we're doing very well as a company. Had a very good first quarter, best first quarter ever. Last year, last 3 years, we've grown about 29 percent. One of the challenges that we have is managing the cost of health care. So with all of our employees here, can you give some of your thoughts in regards to how do we manage the continuing increased cost of health care?

The President. Absolutely. In essence, there's two paths. One is for the Government to basically make most of the decisions. In other words, say, we're going to make sure you have health care, and we'll make sure it's available for you. And the problem with that system is, they basically make decisions for you.

I happen to believe in private medicine. I think it is by far the best route to go

because private medicine has made American health care the best in the world. I don't care what people tell you, America's health care is on the leading edge of change, and our American people get really good health care.

Now the question is, who pays for it? The question is, is it available and is it affordable? And so the approach I've taken is to, one, remember the most important element in any system is the buyer, is the consumer, is the customer. That would be you, if you're a patient. And therefore, the policies that I've articulated have been all aimed at empowering you to have more decisionmaking in the health care system, so as to help deal with costs. If there's no decisionmaking in the system—in other words, there's no shopping, there's no consumerism—price goes up. It's just—it's an economic fact.

And so I'm a strong believer in health savings accounts. I don't know if you have them here, but they are very empowering instruments. They let you make the decisions. They let you save when you don't spend money. They let you roll the money over, tax free. They let you pull it out, tax free, for medical care. It's your money, and it grows.

The other thing is, is that it's portable. When you go from one job to the next, it follows you. So I think it's a very important aspect in a society in which, if you're under 30 years old, you're likely to have worked for seven or eight jobs. In other words, this is a very highly mobile workplace we have now.

Secondly, if you're a small business, you ought to be allowed to pool risk, just like big companies can do. But you ought to be able to do it across jurisdictional boundaries. That's fancy words for, if you're a restaurant in Missouri, you ought to be able to put your employees in a risk pool with a restaurant in Texas. The larger the risk pool—in other words, the more people involved in the insurance—the less price goes up, the easier it is for somebody to find affordable product. But now it's against the law to do that. So small businesses ought to be allowed to pool risk. That's what big companies do. And I believe we ought to treat World Wide just like—give World Wide the same advantages in the marketplace that big companies get to do. Those are called association health plans.

The Tax Code is discriminatory. It says that if you work for a company, you get tax benefits. If you don't, you don't get tax benefits. If you're a very small company trying to provide health care, the Tax Code discriminates against your employees. We ought to change the Tax Code. We ought to treat everybody the same in the Tax Code, all aiming to drive the establishment of an individual market so that people can better afford health care.

Now, look, we spend a lot of money, by the way, on people who need help. My view of America is that we're rich enough to take care of people who can't help themselves, and we do. We got a robust Medicare system, which, by the way, my administration reformed for the first time since Lyndon Johnson—substantially reformed it since Lyndon Johnson was the President. And now you get a prescription drug benefit. So for all you guys my age, get yourself a prescription drug benefit pretty soon. [*Laughter*]

We take care of the—through Medicaid—community health centers all throughout the country, and we're expanding them so that people can get primary care in a place other than an emergency room.

Thirdly, there needs to be transparency in pricing. How many of you ever asked a doctor how much something costs? Have you ever shopped? And the answer is, no, you likely haven't. It's because the system—somebody else pays your bill in a third-party payer system. And so when somebody else pays the bill, there is no incentive to worry about cost. "Hey, what do I care? Somebody else is paying the bill," you think, until your benefit structure starts to change because of inflation in the health care system.

And so the whole purpose is to have transparency in the system. One of the things we're doing—you know, we're a big purchaser of health care, thanks to you—like, veterans, Medicare, Medicaid. And so we're now saying that if you participate with the Government, post price, let people see what the different prices are; post quality ratings. It's nice to know, if you're a consumer, isn't it? Whether or not you got a—whether or not somebody you're thinking about paying has got a good record.

The other thing is, is that one of the real cost drivers—there are other cost drivers I want to discuss—so in other words, consumerism helps deal with cost; transparency helps deal with cost. This is a system in which there's been no cost consciousness whatsoever.

Thirdly, there—information technology—the best way to describe this in health care is that people are still taking handwritten files, putting them under their arms, and delivering it from one office to the next. And that means oftentimes there's medical errors because the files get lost. Doctors can't write very clearly anyway. And so you—something gets illegible.

Most industries—your industry is using high-tech to modernize. There's a lot of cost efficiencies that can be wrung out of the system by the advent of information technology. The dream is that someday you've got a medical record, your own medical record—by the way, tamper proof, in other words, protected—that you can use from one office to the next. It's a sign that efficiencies in the system have taken hold.

I'll tell you an interesting story about that. The Veterans Administration in New Orleans was clobbered during Katrina. And so you had a lot of veterans leaving the New Orleans area—many of them going to Houston, for example—but they had electronic medical records. It turns out, the Veterans Affairs is generally ahead of the rest of the field. And all they did was take their chip and they plugged it into the computers in Houston, and the whole medical records was available. That's—not only it's good for the customer, the patient, but what I'm telling you is, it'll help wring out the inefficiencies in the system. Health care is an inefficient system right now.

And finally—it's a long answer, sorry. [*Laughter*] I've thought a lot about it. [*Laughter*] I've analyzed what's best on how to deal with this. It's a very—it's a tough issue for you, and it's a tough issue for small businesses. It's a tough issue. But one of the cost drivers, just so you know, is lawsuits. And if you're an attorney, I don't mean to be stepping on your toe. Well, everybody needs a good attorney, you know—particularly me, since I'm getting sued all the time. But it's a—[*laughter*]— I think I am.

If you're a doctor and you're afraid you're going to get sued, you practice additional medicine. It's called defensive medicine. You prescribe tests and procedures and perhaps medications that really may not be necessary, but are necessary if you're getting sued, and the suit could drive you out of business. I—and therefore, I'm a big believer in medical liability reform. If you've got an egregious suit, you should be able to take it to the courthouse.

But it's these junk lawsuits that are doing two things around America. They're running good doctors out of practice. I mean, people say, "I can't afford liability insurance," and when they can, they're going to pass it on to you in higher bills. But since you're not paying the bills—somebody else is—it's okay by you. The problem is, it's part of a cost driver. It's making medicine more expensive than it should be.

I really think, at the core of this issue, America has got to be very careful about what kind of health care system to embrace. It's essential that we not undermine private medicine. If you really think about the health care advances in America relative to the rest of the world, they've been

phenomenal. And to me it's that entrepreneurial spirit that's important to maintain on the kind of forefront here in America, and at the same time, make sure we've got a rational approach to health care. There's a long answer to a short question.

Any other questions?

Yes, sir. Everybody gets nervous. I used to hate to ask questions in class. [*Laughter*] "I hope he doesn't call on me." [*Laughter*]

Domestic Agenda/War on Terror

Q. I have a statement and a question.

The President. Okay.

Q. First of all, I want to thank you for encouraging World Wide to sell more CISCO equipment. [*Laughter*] As an employee at CISCO, we greatly appreciate it.

The President. Yes. There's a marketing genius. [*Laughter*] The guy has got the national TV cameras on him, and he's going to leave here on his cell phone and say, "Hey, boss, did you see me on C–SPAN?" [*Laughter*]

Q. And the question is, outside of the economy, what do you see as your single biggest domestic challenge through the end of your term?

The President. The biggest domestic challenge is to protect America from attack. That's the biggest domestic challenge.

I wish I didn't have to say that. You know, it's—but that's reality. The President doesn't have the luxury of dealing with the world the way he wished it was. My job is to do everything I can to rally forces to protect you. And I never thought I would be a war President, never wanted to be a war President, didn't campaign in 2000 saying, I'm going to be a war President. The interesting thing about life is that sometimes you get dealt a hand you didn't expect—oftentimes you do. And the question isn't whether you get dealt the hand. The question is, how do you play it? And here's how I'm playing it.

First, I expect the Congress to give our professionals all the tools they need to protect you again. Let me just start—let me just take a step back. There must be some in the country who don't believe that the enemy is a threat. I just completely disagree with you. And I would remind people, since September the 11th, a day which affected me deeply, there have been a lot of attacks on innocent people by extremists who use murder as a tool to advance their ideology.

The Government—and this is—the reason I say it's the biggest domestic challenge is because it's our most important responsibility. I mean, there's a lot of important issues, but protecting the people is by far the most important thing. It's the thing I think about the most. This is a different kind of war, and it's hard for some Americans to get their hands around it.

This is a war where we're dealing with nonstate actors. World War II, there was Germany and Japan and Italy. Cold war, there's a big standoff between the Soviet and the United States. There is no nation involved in this war. These are people who, however, share an ideology. Just think about what life was like in Afghanistan under the Taliban with Al Qaida driving the agenda. This is where girls have no rights. You can't worship freely. This is a very dark, grim vision that they believe they must spread far and wide. That's what they think.

And they—one way they achieve their objectives, of course, is to intimidate by death. There's no rules with these people. There's just—so America has got to understand that in order to find them, we've got to get in their heads. If you're facing a nation, you can find the nation. If you're facing people that bury in failed states, you've got to understand how to find them.

One of the interesting debates in Washington, DC, is whether or not we ought to be using modern technologies to understand how this enemy thinks and to get in and figure out what they're planning. And a lot of times that comes over communications companies. The way I put it, just so people can understand in plain English:

If Al Qaida is making a phone call into the United States of America, we better know why. If you're interested in protecting an attack and there's a dirty number being called, the Government of the United States better understand the intentions and why that phone call is being made. And so—and we had that bill passed, thanks to Senator Bond, and yet, curiously enough, the Congress decided to allow the bill to expire. It's called the Protect America Act. And now the Protect America Act is expired, as if the enemy has gone away.

And so I—one huge issue for us is to make sure that the American people understand the facts. You see, what's happened is, is that these phone companies which have allegedly helped the United States monitor conversations are now being sued for billions of dollars of lawsuits. Isn't that interesting? All I'm asking for is the Congress to provide liability protection for patriotic companies that are serving to help you. And yet we can't get them to do it. They're not going to let it vote. They passed it out of the Senate—Kit did a really good job of working with his Democrat counterpart—and they buried that bill in the House of Representatives.

And this is bad for America. I'm telling you, if you expect me to do my job, you better make sure Congress gives our professionals the tools. And we can do this, by the way, in a way that, I promise you, guarantees your civil liberties. We just shouldn't be extending the same liberties to you—to a bunch of thugs that want to murder the American people.

This is another long answer. [*Laughter*] But I—it's very important for you to understand my thinking. I spend a lot of time on this issue, as you can imagine. Second aspect—so in other words, we'll give our professionals tools. We got a lot of really good people working. We meet all the time, Government is meeting constantly, ferreting out any information.

And by the way, just so you know, we're picking up people on the battlefield, and the battlefield is varied. I mean, we're finding Al Qaida in Iraq. That's—they're trying to kill people in Iraq to drive us out. We're finding them in remote regions of Afghanistan. And a lot of times, they're carrying computers. And so you say, "Where do you get numbers?" We're getting them off the computers of the people we're capturing or bringing to justice. And if there's a phone number on one of those computers of one of these thugs and it links to a phone number somewhere in America, I really think it's in our interest to find out why.

The other thing is just to keep the pressure on them. It's hard to plot and plan if you're moving, if there's enormous pressure, which really is important that we deny safe haven. You hear a lot of discussion about safe haven. Well, safe haven means that these nonstate actors are able to find breathing space to be able to plot. And they're sophisticated. You know, 19 kids on 3 airplanes, it's a sophisticated operation—4 airplanes, excuse me. This is a sophisticated operation. And they're good communicators. These people are—they're a tough enemy.

And so we're pressuring all the time. You probably read your newspaper today. I can understand if you didn't, but you probably—[*laughter*]—there's—well anyway, there was a strike in Somalia, and the headline says "Al Qaida operative." We're constantly trying to find these people before they hurt you and pressuring all the time.

Finally—and by the way, Afghanistan was denial of a safe haven, and—as well as I saw an existential threat, as did most of Congress, in Saddam Hussein. I understand there's a lot of looking back. But getting rid of Saddam Hussein was the right thing.

And now the question is, will we help the 50 million people in Afghanistan and in Iraq that we liberated realize the blessings of freedom? I'm telling you, it's essential that we do so. This is an ideological war. The people we face have an ideology. Those that came and killed nearly 3,000

citizens on our soil, in the largest attack in American history on U.S. soil, believe something, and so do we.

We believe in human rights and human dignity. We believe in the right to a person to worship or not worship and be equally American. We say loud and clear, "It doesn't matter whether you're Christian, Hindu, Muslim, Jewish, don't believe in anything, you're equally American." They say, "We'll kill you if you don't worship the way we tell you to." And so it's the advance of liberty and freedom which will ultimately achieve the peace we want for our children.

Someday, an American President is going to be saying, this is not that big an issue anymore. But it's going to take an ideology to spread. And so when you see hopelessness as an American President, you got to understand that the only way these thugs can recruit is when they find hopeless people. I mean, who wants to be a suicide bomber except a hopeless person. You notice none of the leaders ever become suicide bombers, by the way. [*Laughter*]

And so it's—so what you're watching is, you're watching democracy unfold. And some say: "It's not worth it. Who cares how they live?" I'm telling you that we better care how people live. That's why, for example, the HIV/AIDS initiative in Africa is a cornerstone of Bush foreign policy; or helping moms whose little babies are needlessly dying because of mosquito bites is a cornerstone of Bush foreign policy; just like helping Afghan citizens and Iraqi citizens realize the blessings of a free society is a cornerstone of my policy—because in all cases, we're helping people deal with hopelessness. And it's worth it, and it's necessary.

And I operate on this principle—it's a cornerstone principle: I believe in an Almighty, and I believe a gift of that Almighty to every man, woman, and child—every man, woman, and child—is freedom. That's what I believe. I believe deep—[*applause*]. And if you believe that and you happen to be the President of the most influential nation, shouldn't you use the influence to help people realize the blessings of freedom? And that's what you're watching happen. And it's going to happen, unless, of course, America grows tired and weary; unless we say it's not worth it and we become isolationist and protectionist.

And so to answer your question, I thank you for giving me a chance to share that with you; it's a big issue for the American people. It's a—what you just asked about is a really important thing for our people to understand. We've been in ideological struggles before.

Let me end—finish this really long answer with—[*laughter*]—I want to tell you something interesting about my Presidency. One of my best buddies in this war against extremists was the Prime Minister of Japan, Prime Minister Koizumi. You might remember, he's the guy that Laura and I took to Elvis's shop—Elvis's place in Memphis. [*Laughter*] People go: "So what? So what's the big deal? Other Presidents have had relations with the Japanese Prime Minister." Yes, but other Presidents haven't necessarily been in this kind of struggle before.

And my dad fought the Japanese—that's what's interesting—just like many of your relatives did. They were the sworn enemy of the United States of America. If you think back to 1940—forties, midforties—if you'd have thought an American President would stand up and say, "My close buddy in dealing with the threats to our countries would be the Prime Minister of Japan," they'd say, "Man, you're nuts, hopelessly idealistic." Except the truth is, 60 years after 19-year-old Navy fighter pilot George H.W. Bush took off on a mission serving his country, his son sits down with Prime Minister Koizumi talking about how we can spread freedom as the great alternative to these jihadists that kill. And I have found that to be one of the really ironic twists of history.

What happened between 41—that's what they call the old man, 41; I'm the 43d President, 43—something happened: Democracy took hold. What I'm telling you is, liberty is transformative, freedom is powerful, and if you believe in the universality of freedom, then it makes sense to encourage others to realize the blessings of freedom for the sake of peace.

Any other questions? Look, as you can tell, I can talk all day long. [*Laughter*]

Yes, sir. Name—[*laughter*]—in case I'm a talk show host afterwards, you know? [*Laughter*]

Price of Food

Q. [*Inaudible*]—I'm Japanese.

The President. And American?

Q. Yes.

The President. Well, then you're American first.

Q. That's right. [*Laughter*] Good point. And I ask this partly because I'm hungry, but your thoughts on rising food prices?

The President. Yes, thank you. [*Laughter*] By the way, that's a polite way of saying, "Hey, man, how about cutting it short." [*Laughter*]

You know, it's a very interesting debate that's taking place. There's two aspects of rising food prices: one, how it affects our own citizens. And again, I'm—we're spending billions of dollars on people who can't afford food, and that's good. We don't have a scarcity issue in America, interestingly enough; we got a price issue. Our shelves aren't going empty, it's just costing more money. And it's why, for example, we've expanded Women and Infants with Children's program to make sure we can help the poor.

Secondly, there is scarcity in the world, and I happen to believe when we find people who can't find food, we ought to help them find it. I just told you why. There's nothing more hopeless than to be a mom wondering whether or not their child is going to get food the next day. And so I announced a major initiative.

By the way, just so you know, America is by far the most generous nation when it comes to helping the hungry, no contest. We're an unbelievably compassionate nation. And so I asked Congress to put some more money out. It will be over—it's about $5 billion, over a 2-year period of time, of food. Now, keep in mind, we're spending about 19 billion here at home.

Secondly, I think we ought to change our food policy in Africa and other third— developing countries. I think we ought to be buying food directly from farmers as opposed to giving people food. I think we ought to be saying, why don't we help you be able to deal with scarcity by encouraging your farmers to grow and be efficient growers. Otherwise, we're going to be in this cycle forever.

Now, let me talk about price. As you know, I'm a ethanol person. I believe, as I told you, the interim step to getting away from oil and gas is to go to ethanol and battery technologies for your automobiles. I think it makes sense for America to be growing energy. I'd much rather be paying our farmers when we go to the gas pump than paying some nation that may not like us.

And so—but most of ethanol now—or nearly all of ethanol now is produced as a result of corn. And the price of corn is real high now. And so people say, "Well, it's your renewable fuels policy that is causing the price of food to go up." I've looked at this issue a lot. Actually, the reason why food prices are high now is because, one, energy costs are high. And if you're a farmer, you're going to pass on your cost of energy in the product you sell; otherwise, you go broke. And when you're paying more for your diesel, paying more for your fertilizer, because it's got a lot of natural gas in it—in other words, when your basic costs are going up, so does the cost of food.

Worldwide, there is increasing demand. There turns out to be prosperity in the developing world, which is good. It's going to be good for you, because you'll be selling products into countries—big countries perhaps—and it's hard to sell products into countries that aren't prosperous. In other words, the more prosperous the world is, the more opportunity there is.

It also, however, increases demand. So, for example, just as an interesting thought for you, there are 350 million people in India who are classified as middle class. That's bigger than America. Their middle class is larger than our entire population. And when you start getting wealth, you start demanding better nutrition and better food. And so demand is high, and that causes the price to go up.

And finally, there's been weather-related problems. Some of the major producers of food have had drought. That's what happens. Weather patterns change. And so there's a lot of reasons why the price of food is high. And no question that ethanol has had a part of it, but I simply do not subscribe to the notion that it is the main cost driver for your food going up.

Anyway, it's a good question. You don't look hungry. [*Laughter*]

Yes.

President's Legacy/Faith-Based and Community Organizations

Q. First off, I would like to thank you for—[*inaudible*].

The President. Thank you.

Q. Secondly, maybe on a more lighter note, what are your plans after you—[*inaudible*]?

The President. Thank you. Yes. I'm heading home. I tell people that, first of all, it's been a huge honor to serve the country, and I'm really glad I did. And I thank the American people for giving me a chance to serve. It's—as you can imagine, it's been a remarkable experience.

A couple of points on that—what's probably counterintuitive to you is that this has been a great experience for our family. I've lived in the White House now for 7½ years, and the furniture is interesting—

[*laughter*]—but it's like a museum. [*Laughter*] And there's love in that White House, thanks to a good wife. She's great. Laura is a—[*applause*]—which is one of the reasons this has been a fabulous experience.

You know, obviously, there's some good days and some bad days. I feel so strongly about my principles and my values, and I'm an optimistic guy, that what may appear to be really difficult to deal with—like my buddies from Midland, Texas—that, for me, it's just part of the job. Interestingly enough, it is a lot harder to have been the son of the President than to be the President.

And so it's been a joyous experience. You know, one of the great, really fun things we do is we welcome our pals from west Texas to the White House, and they come to the Oval Office. And they're walking around, they say, "Man, I can't believe I'm here." And then they take a look at me—[*laughter*].

So the first thing is, I'm heading home. I came from Texas with a set of values, and I'm going to go home with the same set of values. In order to be making consistent decisions in this complex world, you can't be shifting your principles in order to be the popular guy. I guess I'll go home and mow the lawn. I don't—[*laughter*].

I'm interested in promoting the whole—what I talked to you about—the whole philosophy behind the freedom agenda. I think it's going to be very important to be kept in the forefront of American philosophical thought. And I'm going to build a Presidential library at SMU. It's where Laura went to university, there in Dallas. And I'd like to have a think tank. This isn't a political precinct; this will be a place where we get the thinkers from around the world to come and write about and articulate the transformative power of freedom, abroad and at home.

One of the initiatives that I'm very proud of is the interface between government and faith-based and community groups. I believe that government ought to empower people who have been called to serve for reasons other than just government law. And there are thousands, by the way, of social entrepreneurs all throughout the country, little healers and helpers that just can make a difference in somebody's lives. And I think it's in our interests to empower groups through the use of your—taxpayers' money, without using your money to proselytize. And let me give you an example.

If you're a drug addict or a heavy boozer, sometimes it requires more than a psychological counseling session to convince you to quit. As a matter of fact, a lot of people have turned to a higher power, which is not part of a government program. And so I'm—strongly support taxpayers' money going to an individual that seeks help and allowing that person, if he or she so chooses, to seek the redemptive power of a higher being as part of a government program.

And so I'd like to—and that's something else I'd like to foster. But other than that, I mean, that's as far as I've—I got a lot to do. I mean, I really do have a lot to do. It's—which makes the job exciting.

Now that you didn't ask, I'll tell you something interesting about—so if you walk in the Oval Office, I hope you'd be struck by a beautiful rug that's there. And so I was getting ready to be sworn in as President. And we're at the Blair House, which is right across the street from the White House. And as you can imagine, it was a slightly nerve-wracking moment, when I was preparing the Inaugural Address to be sworn in as your President. And the guy calls and says, like, "You're supposed to pick the rug." I said, "Huh?" [*Laughter*] He said, "So you're supposed to pick the color rug you want in the Oval Office." And the first lesson there is, when you're short on a subject—and I'm short on rugs—delegate. [*Laughter*]

And I think it's going to be very important, as you pay attention to the Presidential race, to try to come up with not only who you agree with, obviously, but whether that person knows how to delegate, knows how to set up a structure so that good information can make it into the Oval Office in a way that enables good decisionmaking. The temptation, of course, is to walk in the Oval Office and say, "Oh, man, you're looking beautiful." And the President doesn't need somebody—because generally he's not looking beautiful. The President needs somebody to walk in and say, "Here's what I think."

So when you think about good, solid advisers—at least in my case—think about somebody like Condoleezza Rice or Hank Paulson—used to run Goldman Sachs—or Bob Gates. These are strong, capable people. And my job is to make sure that the environment is such that they can walk in and say, "Mr. President, here's what I'm thinking; here's my advice." And their job, by the way, once the President makes up his mind, is say, "Yes, sir, Mr. President." [*Laughter*] And so in this case, I delegated to Laura. [*Laughter*] And I should—and it's—and by the way, it's not "Yes, sir, Mr. President," it's—[*laughter*]—"Yes, ma'am, First Lady." [*Laughter*]

I said—here's an interesting lesson about the Presidency and life in general if you're delegating. I said to Laura—I said, "I want the rug to say 'optimistic person comes to work.' " I didn't say, "Here are the colors." In other words, I left the tactics to her, and the strategic thought was mine. The strategic thought is—behind that is that you can't possibly lead unless you're optimistic that tomorrow is going to be better. And just so you know, I hope at least one thing you come away from this is, I am absolutely optimistic, in my very soul and very core, that in the defense of America, we're laying the foundation for peace.

And so the rug looks like the sun. And you walk in, man, I'm telling you, it is optimistic. [*Laughter*] It's a fabulous rug. Yes.

Faith-Based and Community Organizations/ Pope Benedict XVI/President's Visit to Romania

Q. I just want to start by saying that my mom prays for you every day.

The President. Yes. Thank you.

Q. All right. I'm Dan Buck. I'm with St. Patrick's Center, and we help end homelessness for thousands of folks in St. Louis.

The President. There you go.

Q. But your Faith-Based and Community Initiative has truly broken down walls between government and faith-based organizations.

The President. Thank you for saying that.

Q. We have grown from 4 million to 12 million. We serve more people more effectively because of that partnership. How do we grow it after your administration? Will this continue, and is there plans in place that the FBCI will continue?

The President. Well, I think—thank you for asking that, and thanks for your kind words. It's just going to be very important for organizations that understand the power and the leverage that can be gained by the use of money that could be going elsewhere to stay in the program. It's going to require Governors to open up faith-based offices, as well, and just get it ingrained in the system. And then your elected officials have to understand how powerful this has been. It's—again it recognize—there's some great Federal programs, some State programs, but there's a lot of programs that are really effective that can be helped by empowering individuals to have a script or money that they can redeem at their services.

And so thanks for saying—are you a Catholic? Yes. So here's one of the great moments of the Presidency: the Holy Father coming to the South Lawn. I'm telling you, it was a magnificent moment. It's the largest crowd we've ever had on the South Lawn. And it was really interesting, from this Methodist's perspective, was to watch the reaction for our fellow citizens to His Holy Father. And it was a magnificent moment. The day—it was a beautiful day, and the Army choir sang "The Battle Hymn of the Republic." That was just great. Anyway, we had a wonderful trip, and it was such an honor.

I mean, you get to do some fabulous things as President. You asked about the— and one of them is welcoming the Holy Father to the south ground of the White House. You know, we—Laura and I went out to Andrews Air Force Base to see him, and then his first public event was there, and then he went on from there for the rest of his trip.

It was—you know, representing our country has been a fabulous experience— I want to conclude by one story, and then I got to—I'm heading out of here. And this guy is hungry. [*Laughter*] So am I. Yes. [*Laughter*]

I'm going to tell you an interesting story about this experience in—so I was going to Bucharest, Romania. Romania had just been admitted into NATO. And the big deal there for the Romanian citizens that had come under the—come out from underneath the clutch of a brutal dictator named Ceausescu was, if you're a member of NATO, there's a clause that says, "An attack on one is an attack on all." In essence, if there's—they get the—they have the United States of America, the great United States of America, as somebody to help them, as an ally. And that's really important for a lot of countries. And they had just been accepted into NATO, and the President asked me and Laura to go. And there was 225,000 people, more or less, in the town square to see the American President, and it was raining.

Now the interesting thing from my perspective was that I was here, and there was a balcony lit in the town square, and I was told this was where the tyrant Ceausescu and his wife had made their last public appearance. And the story has it that he—somebody started chanting, "Liar," and he realized his power was slipping away, and then he tried to get out of there. And anyway, he was done in by the people. They were tired of him. He was a brutal guy.

And so that was my line of sight. And the President introduced me, and just as I got up to speak, a full rainbow appeared. And it was a startling moment. And I turned back—Laura was, like, from me to you back there—I went, "Look, baby, look up there." And so when I pointed up, 225,000 heads whipped around to look at the rainbow. I then ad-libbed, "God is smiling on Bucharest." And the reason I did is because the rainbow ended right behind the balcony where the tyrant had given his last speech. Liberty is transformative, and it will yield the peace we want.

Thanks for coming by. God bless.

NOTE: The President spoke at 11:11 a.m. at World Wide Technology, Inc. In his remarks, he referred to David L. Steward, chairman of the board, James P. Kavanaugh, chief executive officer, and Joseph G. Koenig, president, World Wide Technology, Inc; President Alvaro Uribe Velez of Colombia; Pope Benedict XVI; and former President Ion Iliescu of Romania.

Message on the Observance of Cinco de Mayo, 2008
May 2, 2008

I send greetings to those celebrating Cinco de Mayo.

Cinco de Mayo is a joyful day in Mexican history and an important milestone in the history of freedom. On May 5, 1862, an outnumbered band of Mexican soldiers defeated a large European power against overwhelming odds at the Battle of Puebla. Emboldened by victory and yearning for independence, Mexican patriots ultimately won independence on September 16, 1867. Today, we remember these heroic accomplishments and all those working to advance peace and liberty around the globe.

This holiday is also an opportunity to recognize the strong ties of family, economy, and culture that bind the United States and Mexico. Through a shared commitment to economic liberty and the universal right of freedom, the United States and Mexico continue to build a future of prosperity and opportunity for all people.

Laura and I send our best wishes. *Que Dios los bendiga.*

GEORGE W. BUSH

NOTE: The Office of the Press Secretary also released a Spanish language version of this message. An original was not available for verification of the content of this message.

Letter to the Speaker of the House of Representatives Transmitting a Request for Fiscal Year 2009 Supplemental Appropriations for Ongoing Military and Intelligence Operations and Selected Other International Activities
May 2, 2008

Dear Madam Speaker:

I ask the Congress to consider the enclosed amendments to my FY 2009 Budget that provide the necessary resources for ongoing military and intelligence operations, as well as foreign assistance activities in support of Operation Iraqi Freedom and Operation Enduring Freedom. They also provide the necessary resources for selected other international activities that advance our national security, including food assistance to address the global food crisis.

These amendments distribute by account $70 billion of discretionary budget authority included as an allowance in my FY 2009 Budget for the Global War on Terror. This amount is already factored into the FY 2009 Budget projections and would not increase the deficit.

I hereby designate the specific proposals in the amounts requested herein as emergency requirements. This request represents urgent and essential requirements. The details of the request are set forth in the enclosed letter from the Director of the Office of Management and Budget.

Sincerely,

GEORGE W. BUSH

The President's Radio Address
May 3, 2008

Good morning. This week, the Commerce Department reported that GDP grew at an annual rate of six-tenths of a percent in the first quarter. This rate of growth is not nearly as high as we would like. And after a record 52 months of uninterrupted job growth, April was the fourth month in a row in which our economy lost jobs, although the unemployment rate dropped to 5 percent.

My administration has been clear and candid on the state of the economy. We saw the economic slowdown coming. We were upfront about these concerns with the American people, and we've been taking decisive action.

In February, I signed an economic growth package to put more than $150 billion back into the hands of millions of American families, workers, and businesses. This week, the main piece of that package began being implemented, as nearly 7.7 million Americans received their tax rebates electronically. Next week, the Treasury Department will begin mailing checks to millions more across the country. And by this summer, it expects to have sent rebates to more than 130 million American households. These rebates will deliver up to $600 per person, $1,200 per couple, and $300 per child.

This package will help American families increase their purchasing power and help offset the high prices that we're seeing at the gas pump and the grocery store. It will also provide tax incentives for American businesses to invest in their companies, which will help create jobs. Most economic experts predict that the stimulus will have a positive effect on the economy in this quarter and even a greater impact in the next. And Americans should have confidence in the long-term outlook for our economy.

While getting more money back in the hands of Americans is a good start, there are several additional steps that Congress needs to take to ease the burdens of an uncertain economy. Americans are concerned about energy prices. To increase our domestic energy supply, Congress needs to allow environmentally safe energy exploration in northern Alaska, expand America's refining capacity, and clear away obstacles to the use of clean, safe nuclear power.

Americans are concerned about rising food prices. Yet, despite this growing pressure on Americans' pocketbooks, Congress is considering a massive farm bill. Instead, they should pass a fiscally responsible bill.

Americans are concerned about making their mortgage payments and keeping their homes. Yet Congress has failed to pass legislation I have repeatedly requested to modernize the Federal Housing Administration that will help more families stay in their homes, reform Fannie Mae and Freddie Mac to ensure they focus on their housing mission, and allow State housing agencies to issue tax-free bonds to refinance subprime loans.

Americans are concerned about their tax bills. With all the other pressures on their finances, American families should not have to worry about the Federal Government taking a bigger bite out of their paychecks. So Congress should eliminate this uncertainty and make the tax relief we passed permanent.

America is now facing a tough economic period, but our long-term outlook remains strong. This week, we saw evidence that our economy is continuing to grow in the face of challenges. This should come as no surprise. No temporary setbacks can hold back the most powerful force in our economy: the ingenuity of the American people. Because of your hard work and dedication, I am confident that we will weather this rough period and emerge stronger than ever.

Thank you for listening.

NOTE: The address was recorded at 8:55 a.m. on May 2 in the Cabinet Room at the White House for broadcast at 10:06 a.m. on May 3. The transcript was made available by the Office of the Press Secretary on May 2, but was embargoed for release until the broadcast. The Office of the Press Secretary also released a Spanish language transcript of this address.

Commencement Address at Greensburg High School in Greensburg, Kansas
May 4, 2008

Thank you all. Thank you very much. Superintendent, thank you for that kind introduction. Governor Sebelius, thank you for being here; Senator Brownback; Senator Roberts; Congressman Tiahrt; Mayor Janssen; Mayor-elect Dixson; City Administrator Hewitt; Principal Fulton; members of the administration; faculty and staff; distinguished guests; family, friends, and most importantly, the class of 2008.

I am honored to be at Greensburg High School, home of the Rangers. As some of you may know, I used to be one of the owners of a baseball team with that name. [*Laughter*] So from one Ranger fan to another, I give you this message: Beat 'em up, beat 'em up, GHS.

And I thank you for rescheduling this ceremony so I could make it. [*Laughter*] I know you originally planned to hold the commencement next weekend. It's the same weekend as my daughter's wedding. I could have suggested changing the date of the wedding instead. [*Laughter*] I think we all know how that would have turned out. [*Laughter*] So, thanks so very much.

It is fitting that we hold the commencement on this day, because it marks the 1-year anniversary of the tornado that forever changed your lives. Those of you who lived through the storm remember your ears popping from the change in the air pressure. You remember huddling with your loved ones in basements. And when it was safe to come out, you remember the shock of seeing your entire town in ruins.

At this ceremony, we celebrate your yearlong journey from tragedy to triumph. We celebrate the resurgence of a town that stood tall when its buildings and homes were laid low. We celebrate the power of faith, the love of family, and the bonds of friendship that guided you through the disaster. And finally, we celebrate the resilience of 18 seniors who grow closer together when the world around them blew apart. When the class of 2008 walks across the stage today, you will send a powerful message to our Nation: Greensburg, Kansas, is back, and its best days are ahead.

To reach this day, the class of 2008 has overcome challenges unlike those faced by any other graduating class. You've spent a year in portable classrooms that look very different from the red book—brick school you attended as freshmen. Many of you have gone home to trailers that lack the comforts of the houses you had. All of you have had to juggle a full load of schoolwork and activities while also working to help this community rebuild. Through it all, you've shown determination and perseverance, and today you have earned the right to call yourselves graduates of Greensburg High School. And I congratulate you all on a tremendous achievement.

To reach this day, the class of 2008 depended on the support of loving families. Your families are proud of what you've accomplished, and I know you are grateful for their unconditional love. I ask all the parents to stand and receive the thanks of the class of 2008.

To reach this day, the class of 2008 also relied on the guidance and wisdom of your teachers and administrators. They have known many of you since your first day of kindergarten, and they were determined to help you graduate in the town where your education began. Less than 4 months after the storm, they managed to reopen classes for the start of the new school year. Under the leadership of your superintendent and the principal, the faculty and staff of Greensburg High School have given this community stability and strength in a time of desperate need. And today we give them all our thanks.

Over the past year, your—the members of your class have relied on fundamental values that have given you strength and comfort as you deal with hardship and you heal your community and you rebuild your lives. You've learned some important lessons that will serve you for whatever you do next.

The Greensburg class of 2008 has learned that America's communities are stronger than any storm. The tornado tore apart the beams and boards that held your houses together, but it could not break the bonds of family and faith that hold your town together.

We see the strength of those bonds in the way that you held commencement last year on a golf course just weeks after the storm. We see the strength of those bonds in congregations that have stuck together despite losing their church buildings. We see the strength of those bonds in the caravan of cars that follow your school sports teams wherever they go. Because the storm destroyed your athletic facilities, you had a full schedule of away games. And even though you're always on the road, they tell me you always had a home crowd.

When your boys basketball team made it to the sub-State finals, nearly every person in this town turned out. The team even got a police escort. They say it was bigger than the one I got. [*Laughter*] Your fans rushed to the court after you won on a buzzer beater to advance to the State tournament for the first time in 30 years. And I have been told that the first person to spring out of the stands was Principal Fulton. [*Laughter*] The basketball team finished with a great record, and along with all your other school teams, it has given this good town a lot to cheer about.

As the class of 2008 ventures into the world, your hometown will always be a source of stability and comfort and pride. Greensburg is where many of your parents and grandparents grew up. It's where you went to church with your neighbors on Sundays. It's where you wanted home to be after the storm. So wherever you go, you will be able to rely on the ties of family and your faith and your friends that were forged here, and you'll always carry Greensburg, Kansas, in your heart.

The Greensburg class of 2008 has learned that Americans will always rebuild stronger and better than before. Often in life, you're dealt the hand that you did not expect. The test of a community and the test of an individual is how you play the hand. Over the past 7 years, I've seen Americans in communities across our country overcome some tough hands. I've seen the resolve of American spirit in the wake of the terrorist attacks of 9/11, the flood waters of Hurricane Katrina, eight hurricanes in Florida, tornadoes in States like Missouri, Tennessee, and Alabama, wildfires in southern California and in Oregon. I saw the same resolve and the same determination in the people of Greensburg, Kansas.

When I visited Greensburg last year, I remember walking your streets, and I remember meeting Kaye Hardinger. She was standing outside the wreckage of her home. She took a look at me and said, "I would have invited you in for coffee," but she didn't have time to dust. [*Laughter*] Today, Kaye lives in a trailer with her family in a nearby town, but she continues to plan for the day when she and her family move back to Greensburg and rebuild. And, Kaye, when that day comes, fire up the coffeepot. [*Laughter*]

When I visited Greensburg, I also met a man named Kelly Estes. Kelly is a John Deere dealer. I remember so very well walking with Kelly and his wife and his family through the rubble after that storm hit. He lost more than $18 million worth of equipment, but he was ready to look for the future. After caring for his employees who had lost their homes, he began making plans to bring his business back to Greensburg. Earlier this year, he broke ground on a new dealership that will be a model of energy efficiency, create more than two dozen new jobs, and inject new vitality into Greensburg economy.

People like Kaye and Kelly are part of a more hopeful future for your city. The leaders of your town understand that out of the devastation of the storm comes an opportunity to rebuild with a free hand and a clean slate. They envision a future where new jobs flourish, where every public building meets the highest environmental standards, and where the beauty of rural America meets the great possibilities of new technology. The community is dedicated to putting the "green" in Greensburg. And as you work to achieve this vision, the Federal Government will honor its commitments and continue to stand by you.

Ultimately, the future of Greensburg and the future of our Nation will belong to the young. The education that you've received at this school will prepare you for a lifetime of opportunity and achievement. And the lessons you have learned in this town will give you the strength to rise above any obstacle in your path. You've seen life at its most difficult. You have emerged stronger from it. Now I call on you to take this spirit forward and help our country in a way that makes us more resilient and more courageous as a people.

And finally, the Greensburg class of 2008 also understands what it means to serve a higher cause. The hours—in the hours after the storm, your concern was not for what you'd lost, it was for the safety of the people you loved. As senior class president Jarrett Schaef said, he'd look for his friends in the dark of night. And I appreciate that kind of leadership. When someone suggested that he leave town, he refused. Here is what he said: "I hadn't found nearly enough of my friends, and I wasn't going to leave until I had."

Jarrett wasn't alone that night. As you well know, many of your family members rushed to Greensburg from nearby counties and other States to offer love and support.

Other folks came from towns as well, compassionate citizens who came to do their duty to help a neighbor in need.

And you'll always remember these generous and caring souls. And you will always remember the thousands of other volunteers who descended upon Greensburg in the months that followed. The volunteers came from all across America.

One of them was a student named Christopher Skrzypczak. Last year, Christopher almost lost his life when a tornado tore through his high school in Enterprise, Alabama. So when he saw the news reports about Greensburg, he wanted to help. He raised money to purchase hundreds of new books for your library. He drove with his family all the way from Enterprise to Greensburg to deliver the books in person. Volunteers like Christopher brought hope to this community, and they set an inspiring example for our country.

Over the past year, students in Greensburg have also answered the call to serve others. Despite all that you lost, each of you has discovered that you have far more to give. Over the summer, many of you worked with AmeriCorps to clear debris and help the needy. On Greensburg Make a Difference Day, you helped plant new trees and flowers in the parks. When a tornado hit Jackson, Tennessee, in February, elementary and middle school students worked with their teachers to raise more than $5,000 in aid for the victims. In these acts of service, we are reminded that as much as Greensburg changes, the compassion of its citizens is a constant source of strength.

One member of your class who represents the spirit of service is Aaron Widner. This fall, Aaron decided to enlist in the Marine Corps. Like many other courageous young men and women across America, he has stepped forward to defend our freedom during a time of war, and we honor him today. And, Aaron, I wish you the best of luck at boot camp, and

I look forward to serving as your Commander in Chief.

On this graduation day, I ask every member of your class to devote your lives to a cause larger than yourselves. Over the past year, you've learned that you can never predict what tomorrow will bring. Wherever the winds of life take you, you can be certain that serving others will always make your lives more fulfilling.

As we watch the class of 2008 graduate today, the dark clouds from 1 year ago have parted and have made way for a brighter future. We'll always hold in our hearts those who lost their lives. But with faith in He who rides above the mighty storm, we go forth with confidence that Greensburg will rise again.

I thank you for having me today. God bless you. God bless you, and may God bless the class of 2008. Thank you.

NOTE: The President spoke at 3:28 p.m. In his remarks, he referred to Darin Headrick, superintendent, Greensburg USD 422; Gov. Kathleen Sebelius of Kansas; Mayor John Janssen, Mayor-elect Bob Dixson, and City Administrator Steve Hewitt of Greensburg, KS; and Randy Fulton, principal, Greensburg High School.

Remarks at a Cinco de Mayo Celebration
May 5, 2008

Welcome. *Sientese.* [*Laughter*] Laura and I welcome you to the Rose Garden for what is going to be a spectacular evening. We are so glad you are here. Ambassador Garza, thank you for coming. Ambassador Sarukhan, thank you for being here as well. I appreciate Members of the United States Senate for joining us, Members of the House of Representatives for joining us, members of my Cabinet, members of the Hispanic American community.

I want to thank the Mariachi Campanas de America from San Antonio, Texas, for joining us here today. After dinner, we are so fortunate to have Shaila Durcal, who will be singing for us. Hold your applause for Shaila until after she sings. I will tell you, however, that she has interrupted her honeymoon to come to the Rose Garden tonight, for which we are very grateful.

Cinco de Mayo is a joyous celebration. It commemorates a joyful moment in the history of Mexico. It's when Mexican soldiers defended their independence against what appeared to be an elite and insurmountable army from Europe. Nearly a century and a half later, Cinco de Mayo is celebrated by Americans and Mexicans alike. After all, it is a symbol of determination and great—against great odds, and it is a source of inspiration for all who love freedom.

For me, Cinco de Mayo is a chance to say that Mexico and the United States are connected by more than geography. Sure, we show a—share an important border, but we're also united by values, our love of family and faith and freedom. We share an interest in making sure our people are prosperous and safe.

In America, we deeply value the culture and the contribution of Mexican Americans. The United States is a richer place, a more vibrant place, because people who have—claim Mexican heritage now are called United States citizens. And today we honor those Mexican Americans who live in America, and we consider ourselves fortunate to have Mexico as a friend and a neighbor.

And so my toast is to Mexico and to the United States and the people therein. *Que Dios los bendiga. Feliz Cinco de Mayo.*

NOTE: The President spoke at 7:51 p.m. in the Rose Garden at the White House. In his remarks, he referred to Mexico's Ambassador to the U.S. Arturo Sarukhan Casamitjana.

The Office of the Press Secretary also released a Spanish language transcript of these remarks.

Remarks on Signing a Bill To Award the Congressional Gold Medal to Aung San Suu Kyi
May 6, 2008

I just signed a bill passed by the leaders of the Senate and the House, who have joined me, to honor Daw Aung San Suu Kyi the—with the Congressional Gold Medal.

This is a fitting tribute to a courageous woman who speaks for freedom for all the people of Burma and who speaks in such a way that she's a powerful voice in contrast to the junta that currently rules the country.

Burma's been hit by a terrible natural disaster. Laura and I and Members of the Senate and the House here express our heartfelt sympathy to the people of Burma. The United States has made an initial aid contribution, but we want to do a lot more. We're prepared to move U.S. Navy assets to help find those who've lost their lives, to help find the missing, and to help stabilize the situation. But in order to do so,

the military junta must allow our disaster assessment teams into the country.

So our message is to the military rulers: Let the United States come and help you help the people. Our hearts go out to the people of Burma. We want to help them deal with this terrible disaster. And at the same time, of course, we want them to live in a free society.

I want to thank you for your leadership. Thank you for your determination to send a message that America stands with this courageous woman. Thank you.

NOTE: The President spoke at 8:49 a.m. in the Oval Office at the White House. In his remarks, he referred to Aung San Suu Kyi, leader of the National League for Democracy in Burma. H.R. 4286, approved May 6, was assigned Public Law No. 110–209.

Remarks on Military Spouse Day
May 6, 2008

Thank you very much, Phil. I appreciate you and your band members being here today. Thanks for entertaining us here on the South Lawn of the White House. And we are so glad you have come.

We're honoring six recipients of the President's Volunteer Service Awards. And as we do so, we celebrate the contributions and achievements of our military spouses all across the country.

Laura sends her very best. She's heading down to Texas for—[*applause*]. She left behind a DVD—[*laughter*]—with Steve Martin; said, you might want to watch this before you head down there yourself. [*Laughter*] But she sends her love. And I'm very fortunate to have married such a kind and decent, compassionate woman.

I appreciate the Secretary of Defense. Secretary Bob Gates is with us. I'm proud you're here, Mr. Secretary. Secretary Pete Geren of the United States Army is with us. Secretary Don Winter, U.S. Navy, and his wife Linda have joined us. Vice Chairman of the Joint Chiefs of Staff Hoss Cartwright—General Hoss Cartwright and his wife Sandee have joined us. General Dick Cody, Vice Chairman of the—Vice Chief of Staff of the U.S. Army, and his wife Vicki is with us. Thanks for coming, General Cody; Master Chief Petty Officer of the Coast Guard Skip Bowen.

Members of the United States Congress—John Carter, Susan Davis, Dutch Ruppersberger—we're so honored you all have come to pay tribute to the military spouses. I'm really pleased that Mary Jo Myers, who is a member of the President's Council on Service and Civic Participation, is with us. She's the wife of General Richard Myers, former Chairman of the Joint Chiefs. Appreciate the winners' families joining us here today. But thank—most of all, thank you all for coming.

So here's why this event is happening. Twenty-four years ago, President Ronald Reagan signed a proclamation recognizing Military Spouses Day. And my own judgment is, is that we need to recognize military spouses every day. But this is the time of year that we honor the wives and husbands who support our men and women in uniform. And today it's my honor to welcome you here to the White House. I can't think of a better place in which to say thanks.

Whether you're signed up for military life at the recruiting station or at the altar rail, each person—[*laughter*]—each person is a volunteer. And when you married your soldier, sailor, airman, marine, or coastguardsman, you became more than just part of a family, you became part of our Nation's military family.

It's not an easy life being in the military, particularly when we're at war, and I understand that. For many of you, it means packing up your belongings and moving on short notice. I suspect a lot of you have

been on the move much more than you thought you would be on the move. [*Laughter*] For others, it means living in a foreign land, which can be exciting, but it also means you're far away from your extended family, and that's hard. And for many of you, it means missing a spouse as he or she serves on the frontlines in this battle to secure our country and to spread freedom for the sake of peace.

Being left behind when a loved one goes to war has got to be one of the hardest jobs in the United States military. I've talked to a lot of folks who have been in the theater and—as well as spouses, and it is clear to me the harder job, in many ways, is to be the person at home taking care of the kids and having sleepless nights as you pray for safe return.

You're carrying out the burdens. You're serving our country. And it's noble service, and it's necessary service. And the United States [of] ° America owes you a huge debt of gratitude. And so on behalf of our people, thank you for what you're doing.

One of the things I have learned in 7½ years as the President is, as you've served our country, you also serve each other. I've spent a lot of time visiting our military bases here in America and across the world, and it's been a great experience. What I've found is that there's always a close-knit community, people who are sharing a special bond and people who take time to look out after people. It's a—it's been an amazing experience to see the fabric of our military communities firsthand. And today we're going to honor six military spouses who've done a little extra to serve their communities and serve the Nation.

First, we honor an Army wife named Colleen Saffron. In May 2004, Colleen's husband Terry, who is with us, was severely injured while serving in Iraq. And Colleen learned firsthand the challenges facing the families of wounded warriors. So last year,

---

° White House correction.

she helped found Operation Life Transformed, which is a nonprofit that helps family members and caregivers of our wounded troops get the training they need so they can work from home while caring for their loved ones. To date, Operation Life Transformed has helped more than 30 spouses and caregivers get the funding and support they need for new and flexible careers. And one of those she helps is Maria Baez, and she was the mom whose marine son was paralyzed by a sniper bullet in Fallujah. Here's what Maria said about Operation Life Transformed: "I can't thank you enough for helping me and trusting me and also for not giving up."

And so, Colleen, America can't thank you enough to help our wounded troops and their families. And we're so pleased to have you here at the White House. First, stand up. Thank you. Good job.

Today we honor a Coast Guard wife named Ramona Vazquez. Several years ago, while stationed in Miami, Ramona got to know an enlisted coastguardsman named Nate Bruckenthal. Then in 2004, she learned that Nate had been killed by a suicide bomber in Iraq, the first coastguardsman killed in military action since the Vietnam war. Nate left behind a wife, who was expecting their first child. And when she gave birth to a daughter named Harper, Nate's dad was quoted as saying, "When one door closes, another door opens."

He inspired Ramona to start Nate's Open Door Baby Pantry, a program that provides diapers and formula and clothing and toys and furniture to military members and civilians at no charge. The motto of this organization is, "Unconditional love and support." And so, Ramona, America is proud of you; I'm proud of you. I have a feeling that Nate is looking down on great pride today as well. Thank you for joining us.

Today we honor Air Force husband Bob Davison. Since his wife Lisa joined the Air Force nearly 12 years ago, Bob has lived on bases across the country and across the world. And everywhere Bob goes, he's made a difference.

When Lisa and Bob were stationed at Lackland Air Force Base in Texas, Bob raised $10,000 for the local Fisher House. When they were stationed at Lakenheath, England, Bob established the Airman's Food Pantry, raising nearly $120,000 in donations to provide short-term food aid for our military families facing financial difficulties. When they were stationed at Scott Air Force Base in Illinois, Bob began volunteering with Operation Home Front, which is a national nonprofit that assists our military families in need. He has continued working with Operation Home Front at his wife's current duty station at Columbus Air Force Base in Mississippi.

To date, he's raised donations worth more than $350,000 for the organization, including more than 1 million phone card minutes for distribution to our servicemembers. Lisa Davison is a leader in the United States Air Force. Bob Davison is a leader in America's armies of compassion. And I welcome you today to the White House. Good job. Thanks for serving.

We honor Navy wife Ellen Patton. Ellen's husband Mark is a captain in the Navy, and her son Erik is a cadet at West Point. She loves our military, she loves her boys, and she loves to sew. [*Laughter*] So she put these two loves together—or three loves together—and began to volunteer with Quilts of Valor Foundation. The organization has taken on a mission to provide wartime quilts to every single servicemember wounded in the war against these extremists. So far, she has made and sent more than 80 quilts to veterans and wounded troops. She also tracked down many of the sailors injured during the attack of the USS *Cole* and made quilts for them as well. Ellen says that when she sees troops coming home with terrible wounds, she wants to provide them with some "healing in knowing that they are appreciated." So,

Ellen, we thank you for what you do to wrap our soldiers in quilts made with such loving hands. And welcome to the White House.

We honor Army Reserve wife Dawnle Scheetz. In 2006, Dawnle's husband Major Larry Scheetz deployed to Iraq with the U.S. Army Reserve. When he arrived, Larry saw terrible conditions of young Iraqi children and told Dawnle about it. So Dawnle started Operation School House, a project to collect school supplies and clothing and toys for poor children in Afghanistan and Iraq. During an 8th-month span, she collected 5 tons of supplies, which were packaged and shipped to the frontlines and distributed by our troops. Here's something even more impressive: She's doing it while fighting breast cancer.

And so, Dawnle, your service has changed young lives in Iraq and Afghanistan; your service has inspired the whole Nation. We all pray for a speedy recovery, and we honor you here at the White House.

We honor a Marine wife named Kaprece James. Kaprece has been married for 2 years to Second Lieutenant Rodney James. She's living at her first duty station, the Marine Corps Air Ground Combat Center in Twentynine Palms. She's been a force of nature since she's arrived.

When she moved on the base, Kaprece immediately began volunteering with the American Red Cross. She's assisted with more than 100 Red Cross communications messages that have provided our deployed servicemembers with notification or assistance in emergency situations. Kaprece developed the first year-round youth leadership program on base to help young people learn from professional—learn professional leadership and interviewing skills. She raised funds for a program that will allow young people to assemble 500 disaster kits for enlisted servicemembers and their families. She developed a special newsletter for distribution to 250 families of deployed personnel. And on top of all that, she serves as a cheerleading coach for the children of marines and civilian personnel on base. Whew. [*Laughter*]

So today, Kaprece, we honor you. We honor your enthusiasm. We admire your dedication to the corps. And we thank you for the example you've set.

The six individuals we honor here today have earned the respect of our Nation. They represent thousands of other military spouses who make significant contributions to our country. So we honor six, but we say thanks to millions.

Our country appreciates the service and devotion. Our country owes you something else in return. One way we can repay the service of our spouses is by making the burdens of military life a little easier. So this year, I signed into law a change in the Family and Medical Leave Act, which allows a spouse, parent, child, or next of kin to take up to 26 workweeks of leave to care for a servicemember with a certain—serious injury or illness who is undergoing therapy or treatment. I hope that helps.

When we find substandard housing, we'll take care of it. We want to make sure that the sacrifice you're making is one that at least you understand that the Government appreciates what you're doing.

I sent up some legislation—I certainly hope Congress moves on it quickly—that will make it easier to expand access to child care, create new authorities to appoint qualified spouses into civil service jobs, provide educational opportunities and job training for our military spouses, and finally, allow our troops to transfer their unused education benefits to spouses or children. This legislation's moving. I hope to be able to sign it as quickly as possible. It is the absolute right thing to do. It should send a clear message that we care for you, we respect you, and we love you.

Thanks for coming to the White House. May God bless you, your families, your loved ones, and the United States of America.

NOTE: The President spoke at 9:55 a.m. on the South Lawn at the White House. In his remarks, he referred to entertainer Phil Vassar; Cpl. Visnu Gonzalez, USMC, son of Maria Baez; and Patricia, wife, and Ric, father, of PO 3d Class Nathan B. Bruckenthal, USCG, who was killed in the northern Persian Gulf on April 24, 2004. The Military Spouse Day proclamation of May 5 is listed in Appendix D at the end of this volume.

Remarks in a Discussion With President Martin Torrijos Espino of Panama
May 6, 2008

President Bush. It's been my pleasure to welcome my friend, the President of Panama. Mr. President, welcome back. It's good to see you, sir. I can't thank you enough for your friendship and your leadership. Under your leadership, relations between the United States and Panama are strong and healthy and vibrant.

I'll never forget being your guest in your beautiful country and going to see the Panama Canal. It's a engineering marvel. And then when you shared with me your vision about the expansion of the Canal, I said, now here's a man who thinks big. And, in fact, not only do you think big, but you act. And the President has shared with me the expansion plans, the progress being made, and I congratulate you very much for that progress.

Secondly, we talked about trade. The Panamanian free trade vote is a priority of this Government. It is—it should be a priority of the United States Congress. The President has heard a lot of talk about whether or not trade bills will move or not. And I assured him that we will do everything in our capacity to move the trade bills, not only the Panamanian bill but the Colombian bill and the Korean bill. It's in this country's interest, Mr. President. I want to thank you for going up to the Hill to work the issue.

We talked about food prices. The President is deeply concerned about the cost of food for the citizens of his country. I expressed the same concerns. I told him that if there's any way that we can help with food shortages, we'll try to help. And—but I appreciate your compassion and *corazon grande*.

And finally, we talked about drugs—*drogas*. And I assured him I understood that the drug issue is two way. One, that because too many of our citizens use drugs, it provides an avenue for the movement of drugs. And we've got to do a better job in America of reducing the demand for drugs. And we must also help our friends in the neighborhood deal with the suppliers of drugs. The President is committed to sharing intelligence and working closely—and so are we—working closely together to prevent drugs from being transshipped through Panama, which is bad for his country and bad for ours.

And there's a bill, a funding issue up on Congress called the Merida project, that not only works with Mexico but also works with our Central American friends, including Panama. It's a strategy designed by experts on both sides. It's a strategy that we're convinced will work. And I ask Congress to pass the Merida project in whole, as written.

And, Mr. President, I'm honored you're here, and I thank you again for coming.

President Torrijos. Thank you, Mr. President.

President Bush. Bueno hombre.

President Torrijos. Thank you, Mr. President. I want to thank you for your interest in the region—in Latin America. You have not only studied the problems of Latin

America, but you have visited Latin America. It's been part of your concern. And I want to thank you for your commitment on free trade and on the hopes that we can successfully conclude the—[*inaudible*]—trade that we have together.

I want to thank you for the cooperation that we are experience in this difficult time regarding food prices and exchanging ideas, the projects that we have on the bilateral agenda—projects on education, projects on health—and of course, a mutual commitment of fighting drug trafficking in benefit of both countries and building the capacity of the region to be able to handle the problems related to drugs and crime.

So thank you, President. It's been really a privilege, the friendship that Panama has with the United States. And we hope that this success story of Panama and the United States solving the issue of the Panama Canal, and now looking forward for the future of the canal expansion, it's something that we always keep in mind of how we can build a mutual future.

President Bush. Thank you, sir. *Gracias.*

President Torrijos. Thank you.

President Bush. Yes. Thank you.

NOTE: The President spoke at 3:07 p.m. in the Oval Office at the White House.

Message to the Senate Transmitting the Iceland-United States Taxation Convention
May 6, 2008

To the Senate of the United States:

I transmit herewith, for Senate advice and consent to ratification, the Convention Between the Government of the United States of America and the Government of Iceland for the Avoidance of Double Taxation and the Prevention of Fiscal Evasion with Respect to Taxes on Income, and accompanying Protocol, signed on October 23, 2007, at Washington, D.C. (the "proposed Treaty"). The proposed Treaty would replace the existing income tax Convention with Iceland that was concluded in 1975 (the "existing Treaty"). Also transmitted for the information of the Senate is the report of the Department of State with respect to the proposed Treaty.

The proposed Treaty contains a comprehensive provision designed to prevent so-called treaty shopping. The existing Treaty contains no such protections, resulting in substantial abuse of the existing Treaty's provisions by third-country investors. The proposed Treaty also reflects changes to U.S. and Icelandic law and tax treaty policy since 1975.

I recommend that the Senate give early and favorable consideration to the proposed Treaty and give its advice and consent to ratification.

GEORGE W. BUSH

The White House,
May 6, 2008.

Remarks Following a Meeting With the House Republican Conference
May 7, 2008

I'm pleased to be joined by the Republican House leadership. These are dear friends of mine who are committed to doing what's right for the country.

I just met with the Republican caucus, the House, and I want to share some thoughts with you. First of all, we are committed to a good housing bill that will help folks stay in their house, as opposed to a housing bill that will reward speculators and lenders. There's a House alternative that will do the right thing for the American people when it comes to housing.

I will veto the bill that's moving through the House today if it makes it to my desk. And I urge Members on both sides of the aisle to focus on a good piece of legislation that is being sponsored by Republican Members.

Secondly, we talked about gasoline prices. No doubt about it, we're deeply concerned about the high price of gasoline, which means that the United States Congress should not pass legislation that makes it harder to increase the supply of crude oil as well as increase the supply of gasoline. What they should do is allow for the construction of refinery and for environmentally friendly domestic exploration.

And if—the truth of the matter is—Congress were that concerned about the consumers, they ought to make sure that they make the tax relief we passed a permanent part of the Tax Code.

We talked about the supplemental that's moving. I told the Members I support $108 billion supplemental without any strings and that we're going to work toward that goal.

I talked about the Colombia free trade agreement. The Speaker stopped the bill from moving. All we ask is that it be given an up-or-down vote. The bill is in our economic interests. If you're worried about the economy, then you got to recognize that opening markets for U.S. goods and services will help strengthen the economy. And if you're worried about the security in our neighborhood, turning our back on a strong ally like President Uribe will be—is bad national security policy. And the Speaker has got to let this bill come to the floor for an up-or-down vote.

And finally, we talked about FISA. That's the ability for our intelligence folks and folks on the frontline of protecting America to have the tools necessary to stop Al Qaida from attacking us. And the fact that the Democrat leadership refuses to let this vote come to the floor is bad for our national security. This vote will pass—this bill would pass. It has passed the Senate, will pass the House, thanks to the leadership of the Members up here as well as discerning Democrats. And yet the leadership refuses to let it come up. And the country is at greater risk as a result of not having a modernized FISA bill.

And so those are the issues we discussed. It's a positive agenda. It's an agenda that speaks to the economic interests of the people. It's an agenda that speaks to the national security interests of the people. And it's agenda that recognizes that we can find the wisdom of the American people in their souls, in their hearts. We listen carefully to what they think, and we respond in a way that meets their needs.

And so thank you all for coming. Proud to work with you, and enjoyed visiting today. Thank you.

NOTE: The President spoke at 10:06 a.m. on the North Portico at the White House. In his remarks, he referred to President Alvaro Uribe Velez of Colombia.

Remarks to the Council of the Americas
May 7, 2008

Thank you all. Please be seated. Bill, thank you for the kind introduction. Thanks for giving me a chance to come by and see that the Secretary of State's dining room is a lot better than the President's dining room. [*Laughter*] I'm honored to be here. I'm pleased to be with the Council of Americas again. I appreciate what you do to promote personal and economic freedom throughout the region, throughout the Americas. I appreciate your strong concern about the need for liberty to be spread, liberty in forms of government and liberty in forms of economies.

I am honored to be here with the Secretary of State, Condoleezza Rice, better known in the neighborhood as *Senorita Arroz.* [*Laughter*] I'm pleased to be with Carlos Gutierrez, the Secretary of Commerce, Susan Schwab, the U.S. Trade Representative. I'm thrilled to be here with Susan Segal, the president and CEO of the Council of Americas; a dear family friend, former member of the Cabinet of—in 41, Robert Mosbacher; Mack McLarty as well—people who care a lot about the region. Thank you for joining us here. I'm also pleased to be here with Ministers, representatives, Ambassadors from the Governments of Canada, Colombia, Mexico, and Peru. Honored you all are here.

The foundation of a good foreign policy is good relations with your neighbors. A peaceful and secure neighborhood is in the interest of the United States of America. And so I want to talk to you about the hemisphere we share, the challenges we face, and the aggressive work that the United States is doing to help make the Americas a place of hope and liberty.

In recent decades, there have been positive developments in Latin America. Countries have moved away from an era of dictatorships, era of civil strife. Unfortunately, today, some countries in the region are seeing a resurgence of radicalism and instability. And one nation in the region remains mired in the tyranny of a bygone era, and that is Cuba.

Yesterday I had a fascinating opportunity to speak with a leading Cuban dissident, a former political prisoner, and a wife of a man who is held in a Cuban prison simply because he expressed his belief that all people should live in a free society. Video conferencing is one of the great wonders of the 21st century. And to be able to sit in the White House and talk to these three brave souls in Havana was a inspiring moment for me. It reminded me about how much work the United States has to do to help the people in Cuba realize the blessings of liberty.

It also reminded me of a couple of things: One, that there's an eternal truth when it comes to freedom; that there is an Almighty, and a gift of that Almighty to every man, woman, and child, whether they be American, *Cubano*, or anywhere else, is freedom; and that it's going to take the courage and determination of individuals such as the three I met with to help inspire the island to embrace freedom.

The Cuban Government recently announced a change at the top. Some in the world marveled that perhaps change is on its way. That's not how I view it. Until there's a change of heart and a change of compassion and a change of how the Cuban Government treats its people, there's no change at all. The regime has made empty gestures at reform, but Cuba is still ruled by the same group that has oppressed the Cuban people for almost half a century. Cuba will not be a land of liberty so long as free expression is punished and free speech can take place only in hushed whispers and silent prayers. And Cuba will not become a place of prosperity just by easing restrictions on the sale of products that the average Cuban cannot afford.

If Cuba wants to join the community of civilized nations, then Cuba's rulers must begin a process of peaceful democratic change. And the first step must be to release all political prisoners. They must respect the human rights in word and in deed. And they must allow what the Cuban people have desired for generations: to pick their own leaders in free and fair elections. This is the policy of the United States, and it must not change until the people of Cuba are free.

We will face other challenges in the hemisphere as well. I'm deeply concerned about the challenge of illicit drug trade. First, I fully understand that when there is demand, there will be supply. And the United States of America is implementing a strategy to reduce—a comprehensive strategy to convince our people to stop using illegal drugs. I talk to my counterparts all the time in the region. And I talk about how we can work together—and I'll explain some strategies here in a minute— but I also remind them that so long as the United States uses illegal drugs, you know, drug dealers will find a way to get their products here.

We made some progress on reducing demand. Since 2001, the rate of drug use among the young has dropped by 24 percent. Young people's use of marijuana is down by 25 percent. The use of ecstasy has dropped by more than 50 percent. Methamphetamine use is down by 64 percent. Overall, it's estimated that 860,000 fewer young people in America are using drugs today than when we began. But obviously, we still have a lot of work to do. And so my commitment to our friends in the neighborhood is, the United States will continue to implement its comprehensive strategy to do our part to reduce demand for illegal drugs.

Secondly, we're working to intercept illegal drugs before they reach our citizens. Every day, the men and women of the DEA, the Coast Guard, the Border Patrol, and other law enforcement organizations are working tirelessly to intercept drugs, to stop money laundering, and to bust the gangs that are spreading this poison throughout our society. We've had some success. We've seized record amounts of cocaine coming into the United States. Last year, these efforts resulted in a significant disruption of the availability of cocaine in 38 major cities. We still have more work to do.

And a final leg of our strategy is this: We will work with our partners, Mexico and the countries of Central America, to take on the international drug trade. I am deeply concerned about how lethal and how brutal these drug lords are. I have watched with admiration how President Calderon has taken a firm hand in making sure his society is free of these drug lords. And the tougher Mexico gets, the more likely it is they—these drug families and these kingpins—will try to find safe haven in Central America.

And that is why I committed my administration to the Merida Initiative. It's a partnership, a cooperative partnership with Mexico and Central America that will help them deal with the scourge of these unbelievably wealthy and unbelievably violent drug kingpins. And I want to work with Congress to make sure that, one, they fully pass our requests in the upcoming supplemental debate, and also remind Members of Congress that the strategy that we have put forth is a strategy designed with the leadership of the Central American countries as well as with Mexico. It's a strategy designed to be effective. And so when Congress passes our supplemental request, they also got to make sure that they implement the strategy we proposed in full.

Another challenge is to—promoting social justice in the region. Nearly one out of four people in Latin America lives on $2 a day. Children never finish grade school. Mothers have trouble finding a doctor. In the age of growing prosperity and abundance, this is a problem that the United States must take seriously. As the most prosperous country in the world, the United States is reaching out to help our partners improve the lives of their citizens.

Social justice requires access to decent health care. And so we're helping meet health care needs in some of the most remote parts of Latin America, primarily by using the United States military's medical personnel to treat local citizens.

I'll never forget going to Guatemala and seeing the clinics run by our troops. America is a compassionate country. We're plenty strong when we need to be. But our military has provided unbelievably good care for a lot of people who have never seen health care before. The missions last year provided treatment for 340,000 individuals in 15 countries. And this year, a new series of humanitarian assistant missions will treat an additional 320,000. I mean, it's so important when people think of America and think of the neighborhood that they understand social justice is at the forefront of our agenda.

Social justice requires access to decent education as well. And since 2004, the taxpayers of the United States have provided more than $300 million for education programs throughout the region, with a special emphasis, a special focus, on rural and marginalized populations.

Last year as well, the Secretary and I announced a new partnership for Latin American youth to help train thousands of young people in the Americas with their English and to provide opportunity to study here in the United States. And the reason why is simple: We want people in our neighborhood to have the skills necessary to take advantage of the opportunities of the 21st century. It's in the interest of the United States that we promote good health policies and good education policies.

Social justice also requires institutions that are fair, effective, and free of corruption. It's hard to have a hopeful society when leadership steals the taxpayers'

money. It's hard to have a hopeful place when the people aren't comfortable with the nature of government. And so we'll continue our bilateral aid, and I'm proud of the amounts of money we're spending in the region. But we've also changed the way that we're providing aid by insisting upon rules of governance, rule of law, the education—the investment in education and health of its people, and governments to embrace marketplace economies.

And we do this what's called—through what's called the Millennium Challenge Account. It is a new way to say that, yes, we're going to provide taxpayers' money, but we expect something in return from the governments that we help. I don't think it's too much to ask a government that receives U.S. aid to fight corruption. A matter of fact, I think it's a request that's long overdue. I don't think it's too much to ask a government that we help to invest in the health and education of their children. Nor do I think it's too much to ask for a government to accept marketplace economics.

The Millennium Challenge Account has invested $930 million in the—our region thus far to assist the countries of El Salvador, Guyana, Honduras, Nicaragua, Paraguay, and Peru. And let me talk about just some of the initiatives to give you a sense for the types of programs we're talking about.

In Honduras, the United States is providing assistance to nearly 1,300 farmers so they can develop their farmland and provide for their families. In Nicaragua, we've helped small farmers and entrepreneurs increase their productivity in rural communities. In Paraguay, we're working to—with local leaders to reduce the cost of starting new businesses.

See, the whole purpose is to encourage enterprise, infrastructure that'll help people get goods to markets; to provide the capacity—increase the capacity of these countries to be able to provide hope for their people.

This is a really good program, and the Congress needs to fully fund it as they debate the appropriations bills this year.

The Millennium Challenge Account is one way to promote prosperity, but perhaps the most—not perhaps—the most effective way is through trade. Trade brings increased economic opportunities to both the people of Latin America and the people of the United States.

Congress recognized these opportunities. I mean, Congress took a look at whether or not we ought to have free trade agreements in our neighborhood, and they started doing so with Peru. And the bill, thankfully—the trade bill with Peru passed by a large bipartisan majority. It's a good agreement. It's good for Peru; it also happens to be good for the United States. And now my call on Congress is to take that same spirit by which they passed the Peruvian trade agreement and do the same thing for Colombia and Panama.

About 17 months ago, the United States signed a free trade agreement with Colombia. Ever since, my administration has worked closely with Congress to seek a bipartisan path for considering this agreement. I understand trade votes are hard. And that's why we continually reached out with—to Congress. We've had more than 400 consultations, meetings, and calls. We've led trips to Colombia for more than 50 Members of Congress. We've worked closely with congressional leaders from both parties. We've responded to concerns over labor and environmental standards by including some of the most rigorous protections of any trade agreement in the history of the United States. We have bent over backwards to work with members from both parties on the Hill.

And despite this, Congress has refused to act. One month ago, I sent the bill to implement the agreement to the Congress. Yet the Speaker chose to block it instead of giving it an up-or-down vote that the Congress had committed to. Her action is unprecedented. It is extremely unfortunate.

I hope the Speaker is going to change her mind. I hope you help her to change her mind. If she doesn't, the agreement is dead, and this will be bad for our workers, our businesses, and it'll be bad for America's national security.

Approving the agreement would strengthen our economy. Today, almost all of Colombia's exports enter the United States duty free. Yet American products exported to Colombia face tariffs of up to 35 percent for nonagricultural goods and much higher for many agricultural products. Think about that. They export into the United States duty free, and we don't have the same advantage. I would call that a one-sided economic agreement.

Failure to pass the free trade agreement, therefore, is making it much harder to sell our products into Colombia. To try to put this in perspective for you: This weekend we reached an unfortunate milestone when the tariffs imposed on U.S exports to Colombia reached an estimated $1 billion since the free trade agreement was signed. There's a—that's 1 billion good reasons why the United States Congress ought to pass this bill. Passing the agreement, we could create the—[*applause*].

Members of Congress need to think about this. Once implemented, the Colombia free trade agreement would immediately eliminate tariffs on more than 80 percent of American exports of industrial and consumer goods. Many American exports of agriculture and construction equipment, aircraft and auto parts, and medical and scientific equipment would immediately enter Colombia duty free. So would farm exports like high-quality beef and cotton and wheat and soybeans and fruit. And eventually, the agreement would eliminate all tariffs on U.S. goods and services.

Opening markets is especially important during this time of economic uncertainty. Last year, exports accounted for more than 40 percent of America's total economic growth. Forty percent of the growth was as a result of goods and services being sold from the United States into foreign markets. With our economy slowing, it seems like to me that we should be doing everything possible to open up new markets for U.S. goods and services. More than 9,000 American companies, including 8,000 small and midsized firms, export to Colombia. And approving this agreement, opening up markets for their goods and services, would help them increase sales, would help them grow their businesses, and would help them pay good-paying jobs.

If you're interested in work in America, if you're interested in economic vitality, you ought to be doing everything you can to make it easier for U.S. companies to be selling overseas.

And finally, approving this agreement is a urgent national security priority. Colombia is one of our strongest allies in the Western Hemisphere. I admire President Uribe a lot. He is courageous. He shares our values. He is a strong, capable partner in fighting drugs and crime and terror. The Colombia Government reports, since 2002, kidnapings in Colombia have dropped 83 percent, terrorist attacks are down 76 percent, murders have dropped by 40 percent. He's got a strong record of doing what he said he was going to do.

And despite the progress, Colombia remains under intense pressure in the region. It faces a continuing assault from the terrorist group known as FARC, which seizes hostages and murders innocent civilians. Colombia faces a hostile and anti-American neighbor in Venezuela, where the regime has forged an alliance with Cuba, collaborated with FARC terrorists, and provided sanctuary to FARC units.

President Uribe has stood strong. He has done so with the assurance of American support. Congress's failure to pass the Colombia free trade agreement has called this support into question. President Uribe told Members of Congress that approving this agreement is one of the most important ways that America can show our unwavering commitment to Colombia. Congres-

sional leaders need to send a message that we support this brave and courageous leader and that we will not turn our back on one of our most steadfast allies.

Yesterday I met with the President of Panama. I assured him our efforts to get the Panamanian trade bill passed will be just as vociferous and vigorous as our efforts to get the Colombia trade bill passed. Congress must understand: They have a chance to spread prosperity in our neighborhood; they have a chance to support friends in our neighborhood. And there's no better way to express that friendship than to support the Colombia free trade agreement, the Panamanian free trade agreement, and while they're at it, to send a clear message around the world that the South Korean free trade agreement is good for the U.S. economy as well.

The ties between the people of the United States and the people of Latin America are important to our country. They're important to our prosperity, and they're important to the national security interests of the country. We share a deep bond, a bond between friends and a bond between neighbors. And because of this bond, the United States will, and must, remain committed to making sure that Latin America is a place of opportunity, a place of hope, a place of social justice, a place where basic necessities like health care and education are not too much for any child to dream about, or a place where poverty gives way to prosperity, and a place, above all, where freedom is the birthright of every citizen.

I want to thank you for taking on the cause. I thank you for your vision. I thank you for your steadfast support of doing what's right in our neighborhood. And it's been my honor to come and share some thoughts with you. God bless.

NOTE: The President spoke at 1:14 p.m. at the State Department. In his remarks, he referred to William R. Rhodes, chairman, Council of the Americas; former White

House Chief of Staff Thomas F. "Mack" McLarty; Cuban dissident Martha Beatriz Roque Cabello; former Cuban political prisoner Jorge Luis Garcia Perez; Berta Soler Fernandez, wife of Cuban political prisoner Angel Moya Acosta; President Felipe de Jesus Calderon Hinojosa of Mexico; and President Martin Torrijos Espino of Panama. The Office of the Press Secretary also released a Spanish language transcript of these remarks.

Message to the Congress on Continuation of the National Emergency Blocking Property of Certain Persons and Prohibiting the Export of Certain Goods to Syria
May 7, 2008

To the Congress of the United States:

Section 202(d) of the National Emergencies Act (50 U.S.C. 1622(d)) provides for the automatic termination of a national emergency unless, prior to the anniversary date of its declaration, the President publishes in the *Federal Register* and transmits to the Congress a notice stating that the emergency is to continue in effect beyond the anniversary date. In accordance with this provision, I have sent to the *Federal Register* for publication the enclosed notice, stating that the national emergency declared in Executive Order 13338 of May 11, 2004, and expanded in scope in Executive Order 13399 of April 25, 2006, and Executive Order 13460 of February 13, 2008, authorizing the blocking of property of certain persons and prohibiting the exportation and re-exportation of certain goods to Syria, is to continue in effect beyond May 11, 2008.

The actions of the Government of Syria in supporting terrorism, interfering in Lebanon, pursuing weapons of mass destruction and missile programs including the recent revelation of illicit nuclear cooperation with North Korea, and undermining U.S. and international efforts with respect to the stabilization and reconstruction of Iraq pose a continuing unusual and extraordinary threat to the national security, foreign policy, and economy of the United States. For these reasons, I have determined that it is necessary to continue in effect the national emergency declared with respect to this threat and to maintain in force the sanctions I have ordered to address this national emergency.

GEORGE W. BUSH

The White House,
May 7, 2008.

NOTE: The notice is listed in Appendix D at the end of this volume.

Message to the Congress Transmitting the Czech Republic-United States Social Security Agreement
May 7, 2008

To the Congress of the United States:

Pursuant to section 233(e)(1) of the Social Security Act, as amended by the Social Security Amendments of 1977 (Public Law 95–216, 42 U.S.C. 433(e)(1)), I transmit herewith the Agreement Between the United States of America and the Czech Republic on Social Security, which consists of two separate instruments: a principal agreement and an administrative arrangement. The Agreement was signed in Prague on September 7, 2007.

The United States-Czech Republic Agreement is similar in objective to the social security agreements already in force with Australia, Austria, Belgium, Canada, Chile, Finland, France, Germany, Greece, Ireland, Italy, Japan, Korea, Luxembourg, the Netherlands, Norway, Portugal, Spain, Sweden, Switzerland, and the United Kingdom. Such bilateral agreements provide for limited coordination between the United States and foreign social security systems to eliminate dual social security coverage and taxation, and to help prevent the lost benefit protection that can occur when workers divide their careers between two countries. The United States-Czech Republic Agreement contains all provisions mandated by section 233 and other provisions that I deem appropriate to carry out the purposes of section 233, pursuant to section 233(c)(4).

I also transmit for the information of the Congress a report prepared by the Social Security Administration explaining the key points of the Agreement, along with a paragraph-by-paragraph explanation of the provisions of the principal agreement and the related administrative arrangement. Annexed to this report is the report required by section 233(e)(1) of the Social Security Act, which describes the effect of the Agreement on income and expenditures of the U.S. Social Security program and the number of individuals affected by the Agreement. The Department of State and the Social Security Administration have recommended the Agreement and related documents to me.

I commend to the Congress the United States-Czech Republic Social Security Agreement and related documents.

GEORGE W. BUSH

The White House,
May 7, 2008.

Memorandum on Designation and Sharing of Controlled Unclassified Information (CUI)
May 7, 2008

Memorandum for the Heads of Executive Departments and Agencies

Subject: Designation and Sharing of Controlled Unclassified Information (CUI)

Purpose

(1) This memorandum (a) adopts, defines, and institutes "Controlled Unclassified Information" (CUI) as the single, categorical designation henceforth throughout the executive branch for all information within the scope of that definition, which includes most information heretofore referred to as "Sensitive But Unclassified" (SBU) in the Information Sharing Environment (ISE), and (b) establishes a corresponding new CUI Framework for designating, marking, safeguarding, and disseminating information designated as CUI. The memorandum's purpose is to standardize practices and thereby improve the sharing of information, not to classify or declassify new or additional information.

Background—The Current SBU Environment

(2) The global nature of the threats facing the United States requires that (a) our Nation's entire network of defenders be able to share information more rapidly so those who must act have the information they need, and (b) the United States Government protect sensitive information, information privacy, and other legal rights of Americans. A uniform and more standardized governmentwide framework for what has previously been known as SBU information is essential for the ISE to succeed. Accordingly, this memorandum establishes a standardized framework designed to facilitate and enhance the sharing of Controlled Unclassified Information.

Definitions

(3) In this memorandum, the following terms have the meaning indicated:

a. "Controlled Unclassified Information" is a categorical designation that refers to unclassified information that does not meet the standards for National Security Classification under Executive Order 12958, as amended, but is (i) pertinent to the national interests of the United States or to the important interests of entities outside the Federal Government, and (ii) under law or policy requires protection from unauthorized disclosure, special handling safeguards, or prescribed limits on exchange or dissemination. Henceforth, the designation CUI replaces "Sensitive But Unclassified" (SBU).

b. "CUI Council" is a subcommittee of the Information Sharing Council (ISC), created by the Intelligence Reform and Terrorism Prevention Act of 2004 (Public Law 108–458) (IRTPA).

c. "CUI Framework" refers to the single set of policies and procedures governing the designation, marking, safeguarding, and dissemination of CUI terrorism-related information that originates in departments and agencies, regardless of the medium used for the display, storage, or transmittal of such information.

d. "CUI Framework Standards Registry" (the "CUI Registry") refers to the official list of, and recognized standards for, CUI markings including "safeguarding," and "dissemination" maintained by the Executive Agent.

e. "Departments and Agencies" means executive agencies as defined in section 105 of title 5, United States Code; the United States Postal Service; but not the Government Accountability Office.

f. "Enhanced Safeguarding" is a handling requirement that means the information so designated is subject to measures more stringent than those normally required because inadvertent or unauthorized disclosure would create a risk of substantial harm. This requirement is indicated by the marking "Controlled Enhanced."

g. "Executive Agent" means the National Archives and Records Administration (NARA).

h. "Information" means any communicable knowledge or documentary material, regardless of its physical form or characteristics, that is owned by, is produced by or for, or is under the control of the Federal Government.

i. "Information Sharing Environment" means an approach that facilitates the sharing of "terrorism information," as defined by section 1016 of IRTPA.

j. "Safeguarding" means measures and controls that are prescribed to protect controlled unclassified information.

k. "Sensitive But Unclassified" refers collectively to the various designations used heretofore within the Federal Government for documents and information that are sufficiently sensitive to warrant some level of protection from disclosure but that do not warrant classification.

l. "Specified Dissemination" is a handling instruction that means the information so designated is subject to additional instructions governing the extent to which dissemination is permitted.

m. "Standard Dissemination" is a handling instruction that means dissemination is authorized to the extent it is reasonably believed that dissemination would further the execution of lawful or official mission purpose, provided that individuals disseminating this information do so within the scope of their assigned duties.

n. "Standard Safeguarding" is a handling requirement that means the information so designated is subject to baseline safeguarding measures that reduce the risks of unauthorized or inadvertent disclosure. This requirement shall be indicated through the use of the marking "Controlled."

o. "Terrorism-Related Information" means (i) information, as defined by Implementing Recommendations of the 9/11 Commission Act of 2007, Public Law 110–53, section 504; (ii) homeland security information, as defined by 6 U.S.C. 482(f); and (iii) law enforcement information relating to terrorism.

Policy—The CUI Framework

(4) The uniform use of CUI is essential to fostering an effective ISE. All departments and agencies shall apply the CUI Framework, which consists of the following policies and standards, as outlined in paragraphs 5–19 for the designation, marking, safeguarding, and dissemination of any CUI terrorism-related information within the ISE that originates in departments and agencies, regardless of the medium used for its display, storage, or transmittal.

(5) All CUI shall merit one of two levels of safeguarding procedures: standard (marked "Controlled") or enhanced (marked "Controlled Enhanced").

(6) All CUI shall merit one of two levels of dissemination controls: "Standard Dissemination" or "Specified Dissemination."

(7) All CUI shall be (a) categorized into one of three combinations of safeguarding procedures and dissemination controls, and (b) so indicated through the use of the following corresponding markings:

(i) "*Controlled with Standard Dissemination*" meaning the information requires standard safeguarding measures that reduce the risks of unauthorized or inadvertent disclosure. Dissemination is permitted to the extent that it is reasonably believed that it would further the execution of a lawful or official purpose.

(ii) "*Controlled with Specified Dissemination*" meaning the information requires safeguarding measures that reduce the risks of unauthorized or inadvertent disclosure. Material contains additional instructions on what dissemination is permitted.

(iii) *"Controlled Enhanced with Specified Dissemination"* meaning the information requires safeguarding measures more stringent than those normally required since the inadvertent or unauthorized disclosure would create risk of substantial harm. Material contains additional instructions on what dissemination is permitted.

(8) Any additional CUI markings may be prescribed only by the Executive Agent. Use of additional CUI markings is prohibited unless the Executive Agent determines that extraordinary circumstances warrant the use of additional markings.

(9) Departments and agencies shall apply the CUI Registry's standards. The originator of CUI may not impose any additional safeguarding or dissemination requirements upon the recipient(s). No department or agency shall create CUI categories or rules outside the CUI Framework.

(10) Recipients of CUI shall report any unauthorized or inadvertent disclosures to the designating agency.

(11) All CUI shall be marked in a clear manner and conform to statutory and regulatory requirements, if any, regarding markings. Recipients of CUI that is not marked shall mark the information appropriately and inform the originator that it has been so marked.

(12) Wherever possible, it is expected that departments and agencies will re-mark archived or legacy material when it is incorporated into the ISE.

(13) CUI markings may inform but do not control the decision of whether to disclose or release the information to the public, such as in response to a request made pursuant to the Freedom of Information Act (FOIA).

(14) Originating departments and agencies shall retain control of decisions regarding whether to disseminate CUI materials beyond their Standard or Specified Dissemination instructions, including any dissemination to the media or general public.

(15) Material that contains both CUI and non-CUI information, or that contains multiple categories of CUI, should be marked accordingly by portions such that those categorical distinctions are apparent.

(16) The CUI markings shall be incorporated into ISE-related information technology (IT) projects under development or developed in the future and shall be reflected in plans for new information technologies.

(17) The CUI markings shall be used regardless of the medium through which the information appears or conveys. Oral communications should be prefaced with a statement describing the controls when necessary to ensure that recipients are aware of the information's status.

(18) Departments or agencies shall not impose safeguarding requirements or dissemination controls on information in the ISE that is neither classified nor CUI.

(19) When a department or agency receives CUI originating from a State, local, tribal, private sector, or foreign partner, any nonfederal legacy markings shall be retained, unless the originator authorizes its removal.

(20) Implementation of the CUI Framework shall commence upon the date of this memorandum and shall be completed within 5 years.

CUI Framework Implementation

(21) The Executive Agent shall be responsible for overseeing and managing implementation of this CUI Framework.

(22) The Executive Agent shall have the following authorities and responsibilities:

a. Develop and issue CUI policy standards and implementation guidance consistent with this memorandum, including appropriate recommendations to State, local, tribal, private sector, and foreign partner entities for implementing the CUI Framework. As appropriate, establish new safeguarding and dissemination controls, and, upon a determination that extraordinary circumstances warrant the use of additional CUI markings, authorize the use of such additional markings;

b. Establish and chair the CUI Council;

c. Establish, approve, and maintain safeguarding standards and dissemination instructions, including "Specified Dissemination" requirements proposed by the heads of departments and agencies;

d. Publish the CUI safeguarding and dissemination standards in the CUI Registry;

e. Monitor department and agency compliance with CUI policy, standards, and markings;

f. Establish baseline training requirements and develop an ISE-wide CUI training program to be implemented by departments and agencies;

g. Provide appropriate information regarding the CUI Framework to the Congress, to State, local, tribal, and private sector entities, and to foreign partners;

h. Advise the heads of departments and agencies on the resolution by the CUI Council of complaints and disputes among such departments and agencies concerning the proper designation or marking of CUI; and

i. Establish, in consultation with affected departments and agencies, a process that addresses enforcement mechanisms and penalties for improper handling of CUI.

(23) A CUI Council is hereby established as a subcommittee of the ISC. Its members shall be drawn from the ISC's membership. The CUI Council shall:

a. Serve as the primary advisor to the Executive Agent on issues pertaining to the CUI Framework;

b. Advise the Executive Agent in developing procedures, guidelines, and standards necessary to establish, implement, and maintain the CUI Framework;

c. Ensure coordination among the departments and agencies participating in the CUI Framework;

d. Advise the Executive Agent on the resolution of complaints and disputes among departments and agencies about proper designation or marking of CUI; and

e. As appropriate, consult with the ISC's State, Local, Tribal, and Private Sector Subcommittee.

(24) The head of each department and agency with possession of terrorism-related information shall:

a. Ensure the implementation of the CUI Framework within such department or agency;

b. Promulgate guidance for the implementation of the CUI Framework within such department or agency, consistent with ISE-wide CUI policies issued by the CUI Executive Agent, as established in paragraph 21;

c. Adopt markings listed in the CUI Registry maintained by the Executive Agent as the exclusive CUI markings used by such department or agency, consistent with paragraphs 5–8 of this memorandum;

d. Propose any necessary "Specified Dissemination" instructions to the Executive Agent for approval and listing in the CUI Registry;

e. Designate an appropriately qualified senior official from within the department or agency as its representative on the CUI Council;

f. Implement a CUI training program for their respective department or agency, based on the ISE-wide training program established by the Executive Agent, and ensure all appropriate personnel (i) understand CUI policies and procedures, and (ii) can apply them when creating, disseminating, or safeguarding CUI material;

g. Establish a process that enables their respective department or agency to address noncompliance with the new CUI Framework within the agency, and ensure management and oversight issues or concerns can be elevated to the appropriate department or agency decision-makers;

h. Establish a process within their respective department or agency that, where appropriate, promptly raises to the Executive Agent matters of concern regarding the Framework; and

i. Ensure full implementation of the CUI Framework, consistent with policies, guidance, and standards established by the Executive Agent, within 5 years of the date of this memorandum.

Designating CUI

(25) Information shall be designated as CUI and carry an authorized CUI marking if:

a. a statute requires or authorizes such a designation; or

b. the head of the originating department or agency, through regulations, directives, or other specific guidance to the agency, determines that the information is CUI. Such determination should be based on mission requirements, business prudence, legal privilege, the protection of personal or commercial rights, safety, or security. Such department or agency directives, regulations, or guidance shall be provided to the Executive Agent for review.

(26) Notwithstanding the above, information shall not be designated as CUI:

a. to (i) conceal violations of law, inefficiency, or administrative error; (ii) prevent embarrassment to the Federal Government or any Federal official, any organization, or agency; (iii) improperly or unlawfully interfere with competition in the private sector; or (iv) prevent or delay the release of information that does not require such protection;

b. if it is required to be made available to the public; or

c. if it has already been released to the public under proper authority.

Exceptions to CUI

(27) This memorandum requires that all CUI originated by departments and agencies and shared within the ISE shall conform to the policies and standards for the designating, marking, safeguarding, and disseminating established in accordance with this memorandum. However, infrastructure protection agreements not fully accommodated under the CUI Framework (and its associated markings, safeguarding requirements, and dissemination limitations) shall be considered exceptions to this CUI Framework. Infrastructure protection exceptions include and apply to information governed by or subject to the following regulations:

a. 6 CFR Pt. 29—PCII (Protected Critical Infrastructure Information);

b. 49 CFR Pts. 15 (Department of Transportation) & 1520 (Department of Homeland Security/Transportation Security Administration)—SSI (Sensitive Security Information);

c. 6 CFR Pt. 27—CVI (Chemical Vulnerability Information); and

d. 10 CFR Pt. 73—SGI (Safeguards Information).

(28) The CUI Framework shall be used for such information to the maximum extent possible, but shall not affect or interfere with specific regulatory requirements for marking, safeguarding, and disseminating.

(29) The affected department or agency is authorized to select the most applicable CUI safeguarding marking for the regulation. Any additional requirements for the safeguarding beyond that specified under the CUI Framework shall be appropriately registered in the CUI Registry. Any regulatory marking shall follow the CUI marking, and a specified dissemination instruction shall articulate any additional regulatory requirements.

General Provisions

(30) This memorandum:

a. shall be implemented in a manner consistent with applicable law, including Federal laws protecting the information privacy rights and other legal rights of Americans, and subject to the availability of appropriations;

b. shall be implemented in a manner consistent with the statutory authority of the principal officers of departments and agencies as heads of their respective departments or agencies;

c. shall not be construed to impair or otherwise affect the functions of the Director of the Office of Management and Budget relating to budget, administrative, and legislative proposals; and

d. is intended only to improve the internal management of the Federal Government and is not intended to, and does not, create any rights or benefits, substantive or procedural, enforceable at law or in equity by a party against the United States, its departments, agencies, or entities, its officers, employees, or agents, or any other person.

GEORGE W. BUSH

NOTE: This memorandum was released by the Office of the Press Secretary on May 9.

The President's Radio Address
May 10, 2008

Good morning. Today is my daughter Jenna's wedding day. This is a joyous occasion for our family as we celebrate the happy life ahead of her and her husband Henry. It's also a special time for Laura, who, this Mother's Day weekend, will watch a young woman we raised together walk down the aisle.

Mother's Day is a special time for mothers all across America. On this holiday, we pause to celebrate the love and compassion of the women who have raised us and to thank them for the many years of patience and selflessness. Throughout our lives, mothers are there with an encouraging word, a sympathetic ear, and a tender heart. They set our direction in life, and from time to time, they have been known to correct our course.

Like many of you, my life has been blessed by a mother who is a source of unconditional love. Those of us who have been so fortunate are forever in debt to these caring women. So on this holiday weekend, we celebrate all those mothers who help make our country a better place.

On this Mother's Day weekend, we think of the mothers who are celebrating this holiday for the very first time. Few blessings can compare to starting a new family, and few bonds are stronger than those between a mother and her newborn baby. This is also a special time for new adoptive mothers, who have welcomed their children into their homes with open arms and an open heart. We wish all these new parents many happy Mother's Days to come.

On this Mother's Day weekend, we think of the many mothers who raised the brave men and women serving our country in uniform. And to those mothers, I offer the thanks of a grateful nation. Your sons and daughters are defending our freedom with dignity and honor. And America appreciates the sacrifices that your families make in the name of duty.

On this Mother's Day weekend, we remember the mothers grieving a son or daughter lost in the service to their country as well as the children who have lost a mother in uniform. We share their pride in these wonderful Americans who have given everything to protect our people from harm. Nothing we say can ever make up for their loss. But on this special day, we hold them in our hearts, and we lift them in our prayers.

I wish every mother listening this morning a blessed Mother's Day, including my own. And I have a message for every son and daughter listening this morning: Remember to tell mom, the first thing tomorrow, how much you love her.

Thank you for listening.

NOTE: The address was recorded at 7:20 a.m. on May 8 in the Cabinet Room at the White House for broadcast at 10:06 a.m. on May 10. The transcript was made available by the Office of the Press Secretary on May 9, but was embargoed for release until 6 a.m. on May 10. In the address, the President referred to Henry Hager, fiance of Jenna Bush. The Office of the Press Secretary also released a Spanish language transcript of this address.

Remarks on Departure From Waco, Texas
May 11, 2008

Laura and I want to wish everybody a happy Mother's Day. It's just a special day for—to give thanks to our moms, to appreciate the hard work that moms do. And I understand that for some, however, Mother's Day is a sad day for those who lost their lives in Oklahoma and Missouri and Georgia because of the tornadoes—are wondering whether or not tomorrow will be a bright and hopeful day.

We send our prayers to those who lost their lives, the families of those who lost their lives. And the Federal Government will be moving hard to help. I'll be in touch with the Governors to offer all the Federal assistance we can.

This Mother's Day weekend was awfully special for Laura and me. Our little girl Jenna married a really good guy, Henry Hager. The wedding was spectacular. It's just—it's all we could have hoped for. The weather was—cooperated nicely, and just as the vows were exchanged, the sun set over our lake. And it was just a special day and a wonderful day, and we're mighty blessed.

Anyway, thank you all.

NOTE: The President spoke at 11:52 a.m. at Texas State Technical College. In his remarks, he referred to Gov. C. Bradford Henry of Oklahoma; Gov. Matthew R. Blunt of Missouri; and Gov. George E. "Sonny" Perdue of Georgia.

Interview With Nadia Bilbassy Charters of Al Arabiya Television
May 12, 2008

Ms. Bilbassy Charters. Mr. President, thank you very much for your time, sir.

The President. I am honored to be with you again. Thank you.

Situation in Lebanon

Ms. Bilbassy Charters. Thank you. And of course, we're going to focus on Lebanon. You have been a strong supporter of Prime Minister Siniora. Yet when he came under attack, he seems to be abandoned—not the U.S. and not the U.N., not Arab countries came to his aid. How do you explain that?

The President. Well, I don't think it's an accurate description that the United States hasn't stayed in contact with him, has listened to him, has listened to his requests. I mean, we're in contact with him a lot. And the reason why is because I personally admire Prime Minister Siniora, and the Lebanese democracy is essential to a peaceful Middle East in many ways. And so we're—we will help him. We will help him particularly and primarily through strengthening his armed forces, the Lebanese Armed Forces. It's probably the most practical way that we can get some help to him quickly.

Ms. Bilbassy Charters. Just to follow up on that, during the fight with Fatah al-Islam, you have helped the Lebanese Army, but in this particular case, it doesn't seem to be coming. So what—can you just give us some details——

The President. Yes, we probably got some more work to do, Nadia. I mean, we've got—it's interesting, the situation has evolved from one where Hizballah supposedly was protecting the Lebanese people from Israel; now we're going to need—inherent in your question is a desire for the Lebanese Armed Forces to protect the Lebanese people from Hizballah. And the roles are seemingly reversed. And so Condi, in particular, has been in touch—Condi Rice has been in touch with the Prime Minister a lot to assess needs and to help and see how we can help.

Safety of Lebanese Leaders

Ms. Bilbassy Charters. Three of your closest allies, which is Sa'ad al-Hariri, Walid Jumblatt, and Prime Minister Siniora, are under siege. They're under house arrest. Is this any guarantee that you—their life or—is safe or that they're not going to be attacked? And if they are attacked, what the United States can do?

The President. Well, we're constantly looking at options, of course. And we're monitoring the situation very closely by staying in touch with these leaders, particularly Prime Minister Siniora. And the best solution is for the Lebanese Armed Forces to be—is to be capable of protecting the leaders. And that's what we expect. And our Ambassador evidently was in with the Prime Minister when he gave

instructions to the military to protect the—these leaders.

And the Lebanese Armed Force is pretty good. They're not great yet, but they're pretty good. And we want to make them better so that they can respond.

Ms. Bilbassy Charters. But you're confident that their safety is not going to be touched?

The President. I hope so. I'm not confident the—I was hopeful that Hizballah would become patriotic—patriots to Lebanon and not respond every time to Syrian or Iranian demands. And so we'll see what happens. As you know, there's been a lot of confusing stories coming out. But one thing that we're concerned about is obviously the safety of our friends and leaders.

U.S. Troop Movements/Situation in Lebanon

Ms. Bilbassy Charters. One other thing we have seen was the USS *Cole* has moved from the Suez Canal opposite the Lebanese shores. Is this just a show of force, or are they able to do something?

The President. Well, this is a part of a routine training mission that had been scheduled a long time before. Again, I repeat to you: The best way for us to help stabilize the situation and eventually allow this Lebanese democracy to go forward is, one, keep the pressure on Syria and, two, bolster the capabilities of the Lebanese Armed Forces so that they respond to the Government—and the Government says, okay, you need to go protect these people, or go take care of business here, they'll be able to do so.

Lebanese Armed Forces

Ms. Bilbassy Charters. So you're satisfied with their role so far, the army?

The President. Satisfied with?

Ms. Bilbassy Charters. With the army.

The President. No, I'm not satisfied with the army, but I'm satisfied that, given their equipment, they've done a good job. And the question then is, can we help them get better equipment and better training in the short run? In other words, we want it to be better than today. I was satisfied with the earlier incursion that you talked about. I thought they handled themselves very well.

Meeting With Prime Minister Fuad Siniora of Lebanon/Situation in Lebanon

Ms. Bilbassy Charters. You wanted to meet with Prime Minister Siniora in Sharm el-Sheikh, but he's under siege. How he's going to get out of Lebanon?

The President. Yes. I don't know, we'll see. I'd like to meet him. And we'll just have to deal with that when I get over there.

Ms. Bilbassy Charters. Is there any plans?

The President. No, I haven't—there may be; I just haven't talked to anybody about it today, Nadia. In terms of—you know, I'd love to see him. I think it would be a good message if I could see him and stand with him, side by side, and say my— say the truth, which is, I admire his courage. And I think the Arab world needs to support him stronger, and I think the Arab world needs to make it clear to the Iranians and Syrians that—allow this good man to govern his country without interference.

Situation in the Middle East/Iran

Ms. Bilbassy Charters. Sir, a former Israeli Army—Amnon Shahak—said that it's better if Hizballah is in control of Lebanon. It will make it easier for Israel to attack. Would you agree with this man?

The President. I'm a peace man. I think—I don't know who this guy is, and I haven't read about it, but I will tell you that I would much rather have the Siniora Government succeed and survive and that there be peaceful—a peaceful process. I think we ought to all work to prevent the necessity for armed conflict in order to solve problems. Obviously, look, I believe that using the military as a last option is

important to keep on the table. But I would hope that we—through better policy that we would create the conditions—that we would not create the conditions that would enable another war inside Lebanon. These people have suffered too long.

Ms. Bilbassy Charters. I hope so.

The President. So have the Palestinians, by the way, and that's why I'm for a Palestinian state.

Ms. Bilbassy Charters. Well, we're going to follow up on the Palestinian issue in a minute, but do you see what's happening in Lebanon as a proxy war between Iran and the U.S., fought this time on Lebanese territory?

The President. I think that it's a part of a larger ideological struggle where people are willing to use agents of violence in order to achieve their political objectives. And so whether it be Lebanon, Iraq, or the Palestinian Territories, you're seeing this type of strategy play out, and a lot of it is fueled by Iran.

Syria/Iran

Ms. Bilbassy Charters. What measures would you take to pressurize Syria or Iran regarding the action of Hizballah in Lebanon?

The President. Well, we're taking pressures, as you know, through sanctions, which sometimes are effective, sometimes aren't. And what's very important during this period, Nadia, is to remind people of the truth and the realities on the ground, to encourage them to be more tough on implementing these U.N. Security Council resolutions.

And obviously, we're trying to solve problems diplomatically. I mean, it's important that we work with friends and allies to see if we can't convince the Iranians to stop funneling monies to these violent groups or to stop their enrichment—suspend their enrichment activities; or in Syria's case, to put financial pressure on them to adhere to the U.N. Security Council resolutions regarding Lebanon.

And we've been successful sometimes, as I mentioned, and sometimes we haven't, because sometimes commercial interests don't take the threats nearly as seriously as you do or I do. And so it's just a lot of work to keep the pressure. But to me, that's the best way to try to solve these problems, is through diplomacy.

Ms. Bilbassy Charters. So there is no selective military strike that could be considered?

The President. Well, there's always—as you know, there's always that option. I made it very clear during my Presidency that option is on the table. And of course—and I've also always said diplomacy is our first choice.

Iran/Middle East Peace Process

Ms. Bilbassy Charters. Some will say that Iran is establishing a foothold in the Mediterranean, whether it's happening in Lebanon now, and this issue of Gaza, to a certain extent, by Hamas. How would you, sir, kind of react to Iranian influence in the region?

The President. Well, it's clearly there. And the first thing is to tell the truth. That's why I'm glad you're asking me about this question, because I want people who are listening to understand that it's the Iranian influence that is creating problems for the Palestinians trying to have a state. I mean, isn't it interesting that there's a two-state solution on the table that needs to be negotiated. I readily understand that, that you can negotiate the boundaries, negotiate the refugee issue, negotiate the other issues. But as those negotiations go forward, there are Iranian-backed groups trying to kill people to stop it, trying to create enough violence and confusion so that the peace talks don't go forward.

And it's just a clear example of why the Iranian influence needs to be dealt with. And the United States is very much involved with doing that through, for example, success in Iraq. And we're trying to stand with our friend—not trying—we are standing with our friend Siniora. We're analyzing ways that we can continue to do so. And I'm going to the Middle East to talk very clearly about the Palestinian state and how I'd like to get it defined before I leave office. And I think we can. I think we can.

United States-Israel-Palestinian Authority Meeting

Ms. Bilbassy Charters. But the fact that you don't have a trilateral meeting between yourself, Abbas, and Olmert——

The President. I don't think——

Ms. Bilbassy Charters. ——as some would say, it's like——

The President. Yes, I know, but don't read into that. I mean, it's—look, I think I can be plenty effective meeting with these leaders. And remember, Condi is over there meeting—the main negotiators, by the way, happen to be Tzipi and Abu Ala. And they're talking all the time, and we're trying to get their data, get to where they are, and bring it to the leadership level at times. And the leaders are meeting as well. So it's a very complicated process. And I don't think necessarily not having a trilateral meeting should be read as anything other than that it just didn't work out. It's not a sign that the talks aren't going forward.

Ms. Bilbassy Charters. My time is over. They give me the two x's. But can I—do I—can I——

The President. Yes, fire away. Of course you can.

Middle East Peace Process

Ms. Bilbassy Charters. Okay. Thank you, sir. You know, I mean, some will say that you were the first President to call for a Palestinian state, yet people do not see a tangible results on the ground. You're going now in a very tough time. Prime Minister Olmert is facing corruption charges. You're celebrating 60 years of Israel independence; for the Palestinians, 60 years of misery.

What can we offer tangibly, on the ground, to the Palestinians that will say, George Bush did this for us?

The President. No, I appreciate that very much. One is a security force that can respond to the—Prime Minister Fayyad's work and President Abbas's desires. I mean, it's—in other words, people want to see whether or not the state is capable of protecting them. And therefore, as this Palestinian force gets more capable, we expect the Israelis to move back, and move back to the point where the state can actually begin to function a little bit in the West Bank.

Secondly, economic development—I mean, people are wondering, okay, it's great; Bush shows up; he talks about a Palestinian state, but where are the tangible benefits? And so the idea of working these entrepreneurial programs or some of these programs that my friend Tony Blair is doing—who I will meet with, by the way, just to get a sense for how we can advance them.

But I fully understand your question. And your question is: All we hear is talk; when are we going to see action? Well, part of the plan is for people to see better life. And the other part of the plan is for there to be a clearly defined state, so it's no longer just a two-state solution, it's: "Here's what the borders will look like; here's how we're going to deal with the refugees; here's how we're going to deal with the different, complicated issues"—so people could actually see and analyze, do I want this, or do I want what's happening in Gaza, for example. And given that choice, I'm confident, having met a lot of Palestinians and know the Palestinians fairly well, about how people just want peace. They want their children to grow up in peace, and they want to be able to make a living.

Look, the Palestinians are very entrepreneurial and—people. They know how to make a good living, and that's all they want. And moms want their kids to go to schools—and without fear of violence and fear of poverty and fear of disease. And believe me, I understand that there needs to be a lot of work, but from my perspective, the definition—a clear definition of a state would be a major step forward of providing hope and a different vision, a different way forward.

Ms. Bilbassy Charters. So the agreement still can be reached by the time you leave office?

The President. Yes, I think so. That's what I'm aiming for, absolutely. We're pushing hard.

President's Upcoming Visit to the Middle East/Saudi Arabia

Ms. Bilbassy Charters. Just on the Saudis—also, you're visiting Saudi Arabia to celebrate 75 years of—[*inaudible*]—nations.

The President. I am going to go to Saudi. See, I'm going to go to Israel, but I'm also going to two other important stops, which is Saudi Arabia as well as Egypt.

Ms. Bilbassy Charters. And what do you hope to achieve in your visit with the Saudis?

The President. Well, first of all, His Majesty—it's always a pleasure to be in his company. He's a dear friend of mine, and he's kindly invited me back to his farm, which is a great—it's an honor. And we'll talk about a lot of bilateral relations, visas, and different relations. And of course, he'll be very interested in a lot of other subjects too. He'll be interested in knowing about progress in the Palestinian issue. He'll be——

Ms. Bilbassy Charters. Iraq?

The President. Yes, Iraq. He'll be interested in Iran. He'll be interested in a lot of issues. And I'm looking forward to briefing him in person.

Price and Supply of Oil

Ms. Bilbassy Charters. Right. And the price of oil, would you raise it with him?

The President. Yes. I mean, I raise it with him every time I see him. And it's gotten higher. And, yes, of course, I will. It's—the interesting thing for people to understand, though, is that there's not just—there's not a lot of excess capacity in the world now. Demand has risen so fast relative to supply that it's very tight. And there is no easy solution. It took us a while to get to where we are, and it's going to take us a while to get out of where we are.

The Presidency and the Middle East

Ms. Bilbassy Charters. Finally, what would be your advice to the next President regarding the Middle East? How would you——

The President. Take the Middle East seriously because that's the center of—that's the place where people are—get so despondent and despair that they're willing to come and take lives of U.S. citizens.

On the other hand, be hopeful, because the Middle East is full of really decent, honorable people that want to live in peace. And use our influence to promote peace, whether it would be in Iraq, Lebanon, Palestinian Territories, or elsewhere.

Ms. Bilbassy Charters. Thank you very much.

The President. Yes, ma'am.

Ms. Bilbassy Charters. Thank you for your time. Thank you.

NOTE: The interview was taped at 12:09 p.m. in the Map Room at the White House for later broadcast. In his remarks, the President referred to Deputy Prime Minister and Minister of Foreign Affairs Tzipora "Tzipi" Livni of Israel; former Prime Minister Ahmed Qurei (Abu Ala), Prime Minister Salam Fayyad, and President Mahmoud Abbas of the Palestinian Authority; former Prime Minister Tony Blair of the United Kingdom, Quartet Representative in the Middle East; and King Abdallah bin Abd al-Aziz Al Saud of Saudi Arabia. Ms. Bilbassy Charters referred to Parliament Members Sa'ad al-Din al-Hariri and Walid Jumblatt of Lebanon; former Israeli Defense Force Chief of Staff Amnon Lipkin-Shahak; and Prime Minister Ehud Olmert of Israel.

Statement on the Earthquake in China
May 12, 2008

I extend my condolences to those injured and to the families of the victims of today's earthquake in China's Sichuan Province. I am particularly saddened by the number of students and children affected by this tragedy. The thoughts and prayers of the American people are with the Chinese people, especially those directly affected. The United States stands ready to help in any way possible.

Statement on the Situation in Lebanon
May 12, 2008

I strongly condemn Hizballah's recent efforts, and those of their foreign sponsors in Tehran and Damascus, to use violence and intimidation to bend the Government and people of Lebanon to their will. The United States will continue to firmly support the Government of Lebanon, led by Prime Minister Siniora, against this effort to undermine the hard-fought gains in sovereignty and independence the Lebanese people have made in recent years. The international community will not allow the Iranian and Syrian regimes, via their proxies, to return Lebanon to foreign domination and control. To ensure the safety and security of the people of Lebanon, the United States will continue its assistance to the Lebanese Armed Forces to ensure they are able to defend the Lebanese Government and safeguard its institutions.

It is critical that the international community come together to assist the Lebanese people in their hour of need. I plan to consult with regional leaders on my upcoming trip to the Middle East to coordinate efforts to support the Lebanese Government and implement U.N. Security Council Resolutions 1559 and 1701, among others, which seek to bolster Lebanon's sovereignty against external efforts at destabilization and interference. The Lebanese people have sacrificed much for the sake of their freedom, and the United States will continue to stand with them against this latest assault on their independence and security.

Interview With Jacob Eilon and Gil Tamari of Channel 10 TV of Israel
May 12, 2008

Q. Mr. President, thank you for speaking with Channel 10.

The President. Yes, sir.

Jenna Bush Hager's Wedding

Q. First of all, congratulations on your daughter's wedding this weekend. [*Laughter*]

The President. Thank you. It was—as my Jewish friends tell me, there was *mazel tov.* And it was a beautiful experience. It was very emotional, and it was—to see your little girl marry a good guy. And Laura and I were thrilled.

Q. Made you proud?

The President. Yes, I was very proud of her. It was a wonderful time. And we did it on our ranch, which was—we didn't do it here in the White House because Jenna wanted a more low-key, kind of homey environment. And she loves the ranch, and so do we, so it was perfect. It was wonderful. Thanks for asking.

Q. Great. Now to business.

The President. Yes. [*Laughter*]

Middle East Peace Process

Q. Israeli Prime Minister Ehud Olmert just said a couple days ago that he would resign if he was indicted with some new corruption charges. Does that change in any way your strategy on the peace process in the Middle East?

The President. No. The vision of the peace process still is the same. I have come to the conclusion that it is essential for Israel to have a Palestinian partner that is a democracy committed to peace. I fully understand not all Palestinians agree with that vision. But I also believe, over time, that when confronted with life in Gaza, what that's like, or life in a place where you can raise your child in peace, most of the Palestinians will choose peace, and that the best way to marginalize these radicals who murder the innocent to achieve their political objectives is through Palestinian democracy.

Q. And you can do that with Olmert and Abbas?

The President. Well, the Prime Minister's—as I understand it, the legal issue goes on, and I fully understand that and respect Israeli rule of law. I will just tell you, in my—I have great relations with the Prime Minister. I find him to be a frank man, an honest man, an open man, a guy easy to talk to, and somebody who has—understands the vision necessary for Israeli security.

And so we will continue working hard. And I do believe we can get a state defined by the end of my Presidency. A state won't exist until certain obligations are met by everybody, but to have it defined is very important.

Middle East Peace Process/Hamas

Q. So that's the goal? By the end of the year, a defined—what borders of a Palestinian state?

The President. Well, that and refugee issue as well as the other key security issues that are necessary for a state to come into being. But the roadmap has obligations for all parties. And so my goal is to get the state defined.

Look, I firmly believe that—first of all, I supported the Sharon move on Gaza and still think it was the right move; and that I supported the elections, because there needs to be clarity. Everybody's got to see the truth. And the truth is that Hamas can't deliver promised—promises for the Palestinian people. And the truth is, is that there's an opportunity now to offer a different vision from theirs. Their vision is, destroy Israel. How about a vision that says, we want to coexist with Israel so we can raise our children in peace?

Now, they—I'm sure people say, oh, Bush, man, he sounds hopelessly idealistic. But the truth of the matter is, in order for peace to secure, it's that kind of idealism that has got to prevail.

Iran

Q. Mr. President, you have said that the bombing of the Syrian/North Korean facility by Israel sent a message to Iran. What was the message? You are next?

The President. No, it's just that people are going to take care of their security needs. And the message to Iran is that your desire to have a nuclear weapon, coupled with your statements about the destruction of our close ally, has made it abundantly clear to everybody that we have got to work together to stop you from having a nuclear weapon.

I mean, to me, it's the single biggest threat to peace in the Middle East, is the Iranian regime, not only because of their desire to have the technologies to build a weapon—the technologies necessary to build a weapon, but it's also to—their funding of Hizballah. Look what's happening in Lebanon now, a young democracy trying to survive. By the way, it's in Israel's interests that the Lebanese democracy survive.

Q. So what's going to stop them?

The President. Well, pressure, sanctions, diplomacy, all options on the table. They're trying to destabilize the young Iraqi democracy. And what stops them there is when we catch them moving their weapons in, they're brought to justice. That's what stops them.

Israel/Iran

Q. Many Israelis think that the only thing that would stop them would be a military attack. Have you considered that?

The President. I've always told people that all options are on the table. I've also learned that in my 7½ years as President, it's probably best not to be talking about the specifics of any option.

Q. If Israel does that, would you understand?

The President. You're becoming very hypothetical in your questions. I fully understand Israel's concerns about Iran. That's going to be my message when I come to Israel, and that is that you need to be concerned about Iran, and you are concerned about Iran, and so are we. And part of our job is to—you know, look, we want to solve anything—I mean, stopping them enriching is—the first choice is to do it diplomatically, of course. And that's why we're working on the sanction regime, and that's why we're trying to affect their money flows.

But it's hard because not everybody shares the same anxiety as Israel and the United States does. And—but it's a tough issue, and I fully understand it. And I will continue to pressure as best I can.

Jonathan Pollard Case

Q. Mr. President, did you get any official request to pardon Jonathan Pollard, and if yes, would you consider it? And do you know, many people in Israel think that the arrest of Ben-Ami Kadish in another spy case tended to influence you?

The President. We are constantly analyzing cases. There's been no change in the Government's attitude at this point.

Q. So——

The President. No change.

Q. What is your—did you get such a request from Israel?

The President. Oh, yes, constantly.

Q. Constantly?

The President. Sure.

Q. So for our 60th birthday, any new presents?

The President. We'll analyze every request, but there's been no change of attitude.

Situation in the Middle East/Middle East Peace Process

Q. Mr. President, it took, like, 7 years before you got involved in the Middle East.

The President. No, but that's not an accurate statement, please.

Q. Well, it is in the Israeli-Palestinian peace process, maybe to be more accurate.

The President. No, that is an inaccurate statement too. But, anyway, go ahead. I will let you finish your question.

Q. Would you recommend the next President to start earlier?

The President. Look, I inherited—when I came in office, there was an intifada. It's hard in the middle of the intifada to be talking peace. I mean, you had people scrambling for their security. But I gave a speech in June 2002—remember, I was sworn in in 2001—which really helped define the two-state solution. It talked about who we would or not deal with. I've been—I know, we've been very much engaged in terms of setting the conditions. Remember, the roadmap was done during my time. Anyway, no, we've been very much involved in the Middle East. It's a——

Q. And should the next President start early?

The President. Like me?

Q. You're not the next President.

The President. No, no, you mean, start it early like I did? Sure, yes——

Q. No. Okay——

The President. ——you can't help it. Look, this is the—one of the accomplishments—or one of the interesting things that's happened in this administration is we have placed American foreign policy—a top priority of our foreign policy is squarely in the Middle East. We got Iraq, we got Lebanon, we got Iran, and of course, we got the Middle Eastern—the peace process between the Palestinians and Israelis, which frankly is moving down the road pretty good. And I hope during my time, before it's over, we get the vision defined. But it's—I think any American President is going to be committed to Israel's existence and understand the realities and threats in the Middle East.

President's Upcoming Visit to Israel

Q. Finally, Mr. President, you are coming to Israel for your second visit as President of the United States. What do you expect from this visit?

The President. I expect a chance to speak in the Knesset, which I'm excited about, and I'm thankful. And I'm looking forward to telling people that I fully understand that—the nature of the world, and that there are ideologues who murder innocent people to achieve their political objectives. And we must do—we must stand strong against those ideologues, and we must, on the one hand, be strong in our security measures, and on the other hand, offer a competing vision. And that's what I'm going to talk about.

It's a hopeful speech. It's an optimistic speech. And it's one that I hope assures Israelis that during the Bush administration and the subsequent administrations, they'll have a strong friend and ally in the United States of America.

Q. Mr. President, we wish you a pleasant trip to Israel. Thank you very much.

The President. I'm looking forward to it. Thank you, sir.

Q. Thank you very much for this interview.

The President. Yes, thanks. Good to see you guys.

NOTE: The interview was taped at 11:30 a.m. in the Map Room at the White House for later broadcast. In his remarks, the President referred to Henry Hager, husband of Jenna Bush Hager; and former Prime Minister Ariel Sharon of Israel. The interviewers referred to President Mahmoud Abbas of the Palestinian Authority; former civilian U.S. Navy intelligence analyst Jonathan Pollard, who was convicted of treason and espionage in 1987; and former civilian U.S. Army mechanical engineer Ben-Ami Kadish, who was arrested on April 22. The transcript was released by the Office of the Press Secretary on May 13.

Interview With Mona Shazli of Egypt's Dream TV
May 12, 2008

Ms. Shazli. Mr. President, it's not an easy thing to interview the President of the most powerful state on—in the world. However, what is more difficult is to size down your questions to fit in the minutes.

The President. In the timeframe. [*Laughter*]

Egypt-U.S. Relations

Ms. Shazli. Yes. My first question is, people in Egypt, sometimes they get confused. On one hand, they hear the U.S. statements, speeches that stress on the long-lasting relationships with Egypt, the strategic importance of Egypt to the U.S. and to the Middle East, Egypt as the major player in the peace process. On the other hand, they could see indications that contradicts with this: U.S. depending on other parties in the region, your snatching visit to Sharm el-Sheikh last January, the partial cutting of the U.S. aid. How would you comment on that?

The President. Yes. I would comment this, that from my perspective, the Egyp-

tian-U.S. relationship is a very important part of our Middle Eastern foreign policy, for these reasons: One, Egypt has got a proud history and a great tradition, and a lot of people look to Egypt for help.

Now, the United States can't solve a lot of problems on our own, has to have allies be a part of it. And so on the Palestinian issue, for example, Egypt can be very constructive and has been constructive and helpful. Egypt has got a society that honors diversity and gives people a chance to realize their talents, like you. I mean, you're a very smart, capable professional woman who has showed the rest of the Middle East what's possible in the Middle East. And Egypt has been on the forefront of modernization. Egypt is a—strategically located.

And so our relationship is strong and good. We've had our differences—on elections, for example. But nevertheless, to answer your question, I would say the relationship is very solid and very important.

Democracy Efforts in Egypt

Ms. Shazli. Then how would you perceive the state of democracy in Egypt?

The President. I would say, fits and starts; good news and bad news. In other words, there's been some moments where it looked like Egypt was going to continue to lead the Middle East on the democracy movement, and there's been some setbacks. But I guess that just reflects the nature of the administration and their—on the one hand, their desire for democracy; on the other hand, their concerns about different movements. My view is, is that democracy is a powerful engine for reform and change and leads to peace.

Ms. Shazli. But the public opinion—sometimes they perceive the U.S. criticism to the development of democracy in Egypt as an unacceptable intervention in the internal affairs.

The President. Yes, I can understand that. Look, nobody wants the big, influential guy to come from the outside and tell them what to do. I'm sensitive to that. On the other hand, I do believe it's important for a leader in a country to adhere to certain values, universal values. I think the idea of giving people a chance to vote and a chance to participate freely in society is a universal value. And so it's—I try to balance, on the one hand, my beliefs, and on the other hand, a friendship with the Government and friendship with President Mubarak.

Middle East Peace Process

Ms. Shazli. It's a matter of hours, and you will be in Tel Aviv celebrating the 60th anniversary of the establishment of the State of Israel. This celebration might be perceived by Palestinians and Arabs like—it is criticized, because it's ignoring the flip side, which is the 60 years of agony, pain, and struggle in the area, in the region. What would you tell Palestinians and Arab concerning this?

The President. Well, I am going to talk to the Palestinians face to face when I come to Sharm el-Sheikh. And I will say that there's been 60 years of struggling on both sides, and it's time that the struggle has got to end. And now for—is the time for the development of a Palestinian state that has got defined borders, that doesn't look like Swiss cheese; in other words, it's contiguous territory, where the refugee issue is dealt with. And that's what my message is, is that I'm going to—I fully recognize the agony and pain that have been lived by everybody in the region, and that here's one way forward. And it's a—and we will continue to work, and hopefully, by the end of my Presidency, we'll get the definition of a state. And so I'll talk to President Mubarak about how we can work together.

Palestinian State

Ms. Shazli. Is this—some people would consider this as getting the ceiling lower and lower. Before, you said this—your administration will witness the declaration of the Palestinian state. Now we are talking about only the definition of the state.

The President. No, no, it's always been the definition, cause I always said that the state won't come into being until certain obligations are met through the roadmap. And so the whole purpose was to define—it's a semantical difference, but I really haven't changed my position.

Middle East Peace Process

Ms. Shazli. Former President Jimmy Carter was in Cairo weeks ago, and he was really trying to tell how he was seeing things. He said with a simple comparison between the victims from the Israeli side and the Palestinian side, you can see who is suffering more.

The President. Yes. Well, everybody has got their opinions. I just happen to believe that I'm in a position to help move the definition of a state, which will help solve the problem in the long run. I'm the first President ever to have articulated a two-state solution, two states living side by side in peace. And my only thing I want to tell your listeners is that I'm going to drive hard, along with Secretary Rice and other people in my administration, to see if we can't get the Palestinians and Israelis to agree on what that state will look like.

War on Terror

Ms. Shazli. Mr. President, do you still believe that who's not with us is against us?

The President. Yes. Yes, in the war on terror, I do. Yes. When you kill innocent people to achieve political objectives, I think they're against civilized people. We've witnessed this kind of ideological——

Ms. Shazli. But minutes ago, you said we have differences. We have——

The President. Of course, we have differences.

Ms. Shazli. ——it's normal to have differences.

The President. It is, but killing people to achieve political objectives is—it's one thing to have differences of opinion, it's another thing to have differences of action. And my comments about that—what—the line you just quoted was in the context of dealing with these extremists, like Al Qaida or Hamas, who just murder innocent people. And, yes, I still feel very strongly about that. Most people don't believe in using murder as a political tool. Most people want to live in peace, and so do I.

President's Image Abroad

Ms. Shazli. I have only just a chance for one question.

The President. Sure.

Ms. Shazli. You will be in the region very soon: Israel, Saudi Arabia, and then Egypt. The question is, maybe there are 250 million Arabs who think that President Bush has added to their sufferings and

problems during his administration. How would you adjudicate this?

The President. I would just ask them to wait for history to answer the question. There's an advent of a young democracy in Iraq. Ask those people what it's like to live under a freer society, rather than the thumb of a tyrant or a dictator; or the people that we're trying to help in Lebanon by getting the Syrians out through a U.N. Security Council resolution; or the Palestinians who—for whom I've articulated a state.

In other words, I understand people's opinions. All I ask is that when history is finally recorded, judge whether or not I've been a contributor to peace or not.

President's Legacy

Ms. Shazli. You think history will be in your side?

The President. I think history will say, George Bush clearly saw the threats that keep the Middle East in turmoil and was willing to do something about it, was willing to lead, and had this great faith in the capacity of democracies and the great faith in the capacity of people to decide the fate of their countries; and that the democracy movement gained impetus and gained movement in the Middle East. Yes, I think people will say, "Well, he had a difficult set of circumstances to deal with, and he dealt with them with a sense of idealism."

Ms. Shazli. Mr. President, thank you for this interview.

The President. Yes, thanks for coming.

NOTE: The interview was taped at 11:42 a.m. in the Map Room at the White House for later broadcast. In his remarks, the President referred to President Mohamed Hosni Mubarak of Egypt. The transcript was released by the Office of the Press Secretary on May 13.

Interview With Lukman Ahmed of BBC Arabic
May 12, 2008

Jenna Bush Hager's Wedding

Mr. Ahmed. Thank you so much, Mr. President, for this. And first, I must congratulate you for your daughter's wedding. And how does it feeling, being a father? I know you are listening to your mom; I know you are a father, and you are having a daughter's wedding. How does it feel?

The President. You know something, I was emotional, and—because I was so happy and proud. And she's marrying a good guy, Lukman. And we were out there on our ranch, which is a part of the world Laura and I love, and it was just a special evening, and it was great. I feel great. Thank you.

Lebanon/Iran

Mr. Ahmed. All right. You have given— we are going to Lebanon. You are giving Hizballah the choice of being terrorist organization or a political party. What do you think would prompt Hizballah to abandon its—[*inaudible*]? Why Hizballah claim the existence of legitimate concern for these weapons?

The President. Yes. I don't know. I mean, it's hard for me to get inside Hizballah's head. I do know that they are destabilizing Lebanon. I do know that they were viewed at one time as the protectors against Israel, and now, in fact, they're turning against the Lebanese people themselves.

And I do know that Lebanon's success is very important for peace in the Middle East. And so our position—the—my Government's position is to support the Siniora Government, is to beef up his army so that he can have a chance to respond to people who are acting outside the confines of government.

And you know, Hizballah wouldn't be— would be nothing without Iranian support. And Iranian is the crux of many of the problems in the Middle East, whether it

be funding of Hizballah, funding of Hamas, or obviously, actions within the young democracy of Iraq. And so a lot of my trip is going to be to get people to focus not only on Lebanon and remember Lebanon, but also to remember that Iran causes a lot of the problems around the Middle East.

Lebanese Armed Forces

Mr. Ahmed. We are going to touch that Iranian support and Syrian support to Hizballah. Many supporters of the U.S. policy in Lebanon criticize the lack of practical American support to the Siniora Government. That's what we are seeing right now. The USS *Cole* is now heading to the region, in what you call a—or previously mentioned, the support of an American ally. Does this mean the USS *Cole* is willing to offer this practical assistance?

The President. Well, the most practical assistance, really, is to help the Lebanese Armed Forces become effective. And that's what we're doing. A couple years ago, I sent one of our top admirals to Lebanon to assess the needs of the military. And as well as I've been watching very carefully to assess the courage of the leadership, like Prime Minister Siniora. I'm impressed by the Prime Minister. He's a good guy who cares deeply about the future of his country. And he needs a military that has got the practical equipment necessary to deal with elements in this society that are destabilizing. And that's really where our practical help is going to be.

Situation in Lebanon

Mr. Ahmed. And as supporting the Lebanese military, that means they should go, or do you think would go, to disarm Hizballah?

The President. Well, of course, I don't see how you can have a society with

Hizballah armed up the way they are. I mean, any time they feel like moving, they try to do it. In this case, though, they moved against the Lebanese people. They're not moving against any foreign country; they're moving against the Lebanese people. And it should send a signal to everybody that they're a destabilizing force. And—but the first step, of course, is to make sure that the Siniora Government has got the capacity to respond with a military that's effective, that can move point A to point B in a quick fashion, and that's got the capacity to get the job done.

Syria/Iran

Mr. Ahmed. You are calling both Iran and Syria to halt their support to Hizballah. But in the absence of any direct contact with Iran and Syria, your administration—how do you think both countries should stop doing this? You are not negotiating with them. You are not exploring other means to have them halt their support.

The President. So what's there to negotiate? I mean, they know my position. Early on in my administration, we sent the word to the Syrians, with top administrative officials, that if you want better relations with the United States, stop supporting these extremist groups that are trying to stop the advance of free societies. And every time, their response was nothing. So they know our position, the Syrians and the Iranians.

I have made it abundantly clear there's a better way forward. If the Iranians want to have relations with us, they ought to verifiably suspend their enrichment, and then they will—they can visit with us and other nations involved with the—through the U.N. process.

But they—both sides, both countries have made the decision to not take up offers. And they're very destabilizing influences. And they're—I truly believe that the Middle East is where the world ought to spend a lot of time, attention, and focus to help bring prosperity and peace, and that when people do pay attention closely, they'll recognize the destabilizing influence that the Iranians and the Syrians are having.

U.S. Foreign Policy/Iran

Mr. Ahmed. So what are the other means that you think you could take to have them stop their support?

The President. Well, you know, there are sanctions, of course. There's international—working with the international community to send common messages, working with the financial community. And we're doing that. The problem is, some folks just don't see the same—the threat that Iran poses in the Middle East, for example, as others do. I view them as a serious threat to peace, and therefore, I spend a lot of time trying to convince other nations, other leaders to join in this common concern.

Palestinian State

Mr. Ahmed. We are going to the Palestinian and Israeli issue. And we know that you are going there to commemorate the 60th anniversary of the establishment of Israel, and you are the President who put the idea of the two-state solution. There are the other sayer in the Palestinian side. They call this anniversary as *Nakba*, or disaster. What do you say to them, Mr. President?

The President. I say to them that I care deeply about the Palestinian people and their future. They're going to have a choice to make, hopefully, and that choice is, here's what a state's going to look like, or do you want the kind of state that Hamas has brought you? And there needs to be a vision that people can see, that's clearly spelled out, with defined borders and the refugee issue settled and something on how to move forward on the holy sites, security discussions.

And those discussions are ongoing right now. And our job in the United States, it seems like to me, is to encourage the parties to come and reach a common solution so that they can then say, the world can say, here's what a state will look like, and now you suffering Palestinians have a choice to make: You can accept that, or you can continue to follow or accept in your presence these extremists who murder innocent people.

Isn't it interesting that as the talks begin to emerge, there's more rockets flying into Israeli neighborhoods? Why? Because they want to stop the advance of a Palestinian state. And so no, I got a good message for the people of the Palestinian Territories.

Middle East Peace Process

Mr. Ahmed. In fact, I'm going to carry on that message. I'm given 30 seconds, so I hope if you could allow me to ask this question here. In your last meeting with Abu Mazen here in the White House, you stated, as I quote here, that "I'm confident we can achieve the definition of a state." Actually, Abu Mazen, he expressed some concern after that meeting that he couldn't see anything that would suggest that the possibility of establishing the state before the——

The President. Yes.

Mr. Ahmed. ——end of your term. And he's hoping, and you are hoping, right now you are heading there. Are you willing to tell me that before the end of your administration, there will be an agreement to be concluded, based on the assurance you get from the—both sides?

The President. I think we can; I really do. We're going to work hard for that end. Look, it's hard. I understand that. And Abu Mazen was expressing frustrations with the process, and that's okay. He's sending a message. He wasn't speaking necessarily to the American people. He was sending a message back home that he's frustrated, and he expects there to be more progress made to his liking. I understand that. That's what negotiations are all about.

Abu Mazen and Olmert are, of course, necessary to get a good deal, but there's still—Tzipi Livni and Abu Ala are talking now. There's a lot of discussions going on.

And it's just a process. And the fundamental question is, when it gets down to it, will they be able to agree? They've closed the gap, closed the gap. Will they be able to agree at that last minute? And that's why Condi Rice and Hadley and others are going out there all the time to encourage them to get a deal done. It's in their interests. It's in the Israelis' interests that there be a state living side by side with them in peace, and it's in the Palestinians' interest. The status quo is unacceptable; Gaza's unacceptable. What they need is a state that responds to the will of the people. And the first step is to define what the state looks like. And we'll work hard for the next months to see if we can't get it done.

Palestinian State

Mr. Ahmed. And the agreement that you are trying to get it done, is it going to be a description of the state or the establishment of the state?

The President. No, it will be a description of the state. Remember, I told everybody earlier that there's got to be some roadmap obligations that have to be met. Everybody understands that. Step one is the description. And the state can't look like Swiss cheese. It has to be contiguous territories with defined borders—and the refugee issue concluded as well.

Mr. Ahmed. And that's what we're going to get before the end of your administration——

The President. I think so.

Mr. Ahmed. ——is a description of the state?

The President. I'm working hard to get there.

Iran

Mr. Ahmed. Thank you so much. With regard to Iran, President——

The President. Yes.

Mr. Ahmed. ——Bush, it's very vital, as you say it always, that their cooperation to have stability in Iraq. Do you think that it—you consider one day that—talking direct to them to have them achieve that goal to——

The President. They know—look, if I thought talks would matter, we'd talk. But they know our position. We have had talks between our Embassy and their Embassy. They know, and they know that the Iraqi Government, along with the U.S. Government, wants them to stop sending their weapons from Iran into Iraq, all aiming to kill innocent people. That's what they're doing. They're being very—they're not being constructive at all. But they absolutely know our position. And when we catch them doing it, they'll be brought to justice. And we are catching them doing it right now.

Syria/North Korea

Mr. Ahmed. And the issue of the possible cooperation between Syria and North Korea on the weapon of—nuclear weapons, actually——

The President. Yes. Well, their—yes, that was a troubling development, wasn't it? That all of a sudden, out of the blue, there's—in the middle of a kind of a remote area, a reactor is there, built with the help of Koreans—North Koreans. And it just goes to show, unless there's transparency and openness, unless there's a strong inspection regime, what could happen. And that's why it's very important that the world stay diligent and pay attention to what goes on in the Middle East, and not hope for the best, but remain active.

Mr. Ahmed. But thus, the evidence is seriously being—my last question, last question. This evidence, Mr. President, seriously being questioned. Obviously, the people have in mind that—the presentation at the U.N. with regard to the Iraqi weapon of mass destruction. So how do you see that, how——

The President. Yes, look, I mean, it's—the difference was, in this case, there was concrete examples. I mean, everybody that analyzed the data realized it was true. I mean, are people saying that it didn't exist? Is that what the line of reasoning is? Well, I just—just not the case or the truth. The truth is, is that out of nowhere was discovered this reactor that nobody talked about. The Syrians didn't tell anybody about it. The North Koreans didn't tell anybody about it. And it was discovered, and now it's destroyed.

Mr. Ahmed. Mr. President, thank you so much.

The President. You're a good man.

Mr. Ahmed. Thank you so much for this opportunity.

The President. Yes, sir.

NOTE: The interview was taped at 11:52 a.m. in the Map Room at the White House for later broadcast. In his remarks, the President referred to Henry Hager, husband of Jenna Bush Hager; Prime Minister Fuad Siniora of Lebanon; President Mahmoud Abbas (Abu Mazen) and former Prime Minister Ahmed Qurei (Abu Ala) of the Palestinian Authority; and Prime Minister Ehud Olmert and Deputy Prime Minister and Minister of Foreign Affairs Tzipora "Tzipi" Livni of Israel. The transcript was released by the Office of the Press Secretary on May 13.

Message to the Congress Transmitting the Proposed Russia-United States Agreement on Cooperation in the Field of Peaceful Uses of Nuclear Energy
May 12, 2008

To the Congress of the United States:

I am pleased to transmit to the Congress, pursuant to sections 123 b. and 123 d. of the Atomic Energy Act of 1954, as amended (42 U.S.C. 2153(b), (d)) (the "Act"), the text of a proposed Agreement Between the Government of the United States of America and the Government of the Russian Federation for Cooperation in the Field of Peaceful Uses of Nuclear Energy. I am also pleased to transmit my written approval, authorization, and determination concerning the Agreement, and a Nuclear Proliferation Assessment Statement (NPAS) concerning the Agreement (in accordance with section 123 of the Act, as amended by title XII of the Foreign Affairs Reform and Restructuring Act of 1998 (Public Law 105–277), a classified annex to the NPAS, prepared by the Secretary of State in consultation with the Director of National Intelligence, summarizing relevant classified information, will be submitted to the Congress separately). The joint memorandum submitted to me by the Secretary of State and the Secretary of Energy and a letter from the Chairman of the Nuclear Regulatory Commission stating the views of the Commission are also enclosed.

The proposed Agreement has been negotiated in accordance with the Act and other applicable law. In my judgment, it meets all applicable statutory requirements and will advance the non-proliferation and other foreign policy interests of the United States.

The proposed Agreement provides a comprehensive framework for peaceful nuclear cooperation with Russia based on a mutual commitment to nuclear non-proliferation. It has a term of 30 years, and permits the transfer of technology, material, equipment (including reactors), and components for nuclear research and nuclear power production. It does not permit transfers of Restricted Data, and permits transfers of sensitive nuclear technology, sensitive nuclear facilities, and major critical components of such facilities by amendment to the Agreement. In the event of termination, key non-proliferation conditions and controls continue with respect to material and equipment subject to the Agreement.

The Russian Federation is a nuclear weapon state party to the Treaty on the Non-Proliferation of Nuclear Weapons. Like the United States, it has a "voluntary offer" safeguards agreement with the International Atomic Energy Agency (IAEA). That agreement gives the IAEA the right to apply safeguards on all source or special fissionable material at peaceful nuclear facilities on a Russia-provided list. The Russian Federation is also a party to the Convention on the Physical Protection of Nuclear Material, which establishes international standards of physical protection for the use, storage, and transport of nuclear material. It is also a member of the Nuclear Suppliers Group, whose non-legally binding Guidelines set forth standards for the responsible export of nuclear commodities for peaceful use. A more detailed discussion of Russia's domestic civil nuclear program and its nuclear non-proliferation policies and practices, including its nuclear export policies and practices, is provided in the NPAS and in the classified annex to the NPAS submitted to the Congress separately.

I have considered the views and recommendations of the interested agencies in reviewing the proposed Agreement and have determined that its performance will promote, and will not constitute an unreasonable risk to, the common defense and security. Accordingly, I have approved the Agreement and authorized its execution and urge that the Congress give it favorable consideration.

This transmission shall constitute a submittal for purposes of both sections 123 b. and 123 d. of the Atomic Energy Act. My Administration is prepared to begin immediately the consultations with the Senate Foreign Relations Committee and House Foreign Affairs Committee as provided in section 123 b. Upon completion of the 30-day continuous session period provided for in section 123 b., the 60-day continuous session period provided for in section 123 d. shall commence.

GEORGE W. BUSH

The White House,
May 12, 2008.

NOTE: This message was released by the Office of the Press Secretary on May 13.

Statement on Farm Legislation
May 13, 2008

In January 2007, I was hopeful that leaders in Washington could come together on a good farm bill. At that time, my administration had completed more than 50 listening sessions across the country and developed a reform-minded farm bill based on the thousands of comments received. Our proposal would make wise use of the people's money by reforming farm programs, funding emerging priorities, and providing a safety net that better targets benefits for farmers.

I am deeply disappointed in the conference report filed today, as it falls far short of the proposal my administration put forward. If this bill makes it to my desk, I will veto it.

Today's farm economy is very strong, and that is something to celebrate. It is also an appropriate time to better target subsidies and put forth real reform. Farm income is expected to exceed the 10-year average by 50 percent this year, yet Congress's bill asks American taxpayers to subsidize the incomes of married farmers who earn $1.5 million per year. I believe doing so at a time of record farm income is irresponsible and jeopardizes America's support for necessary farm programs.

Congress claims that this bill increases spending by $10 billion, but the real cost is nearly $20 billion when you include actual Government spending that will occur if this bill becomes law. Instead of fully offsetting the increased spending, the bill resorts to a variety of gimmicks, such as pushing commodity payments outside the budget window. Adding nearly $20 billion in additional costs to the current 10-year spending level of approximately $600 billion is excessive, especially when net farm income is at a record high and food prices are on the rise. My administration clearly identified numerous reforms as essential to justify even a $10 billion increase in spending, yet this bill includes none of those reforms in full.

Crop prices have averaged a 20-percent increase since just last year. Still, Congress wants to raise payment rates for most crops and create new subsidies which can be triggered even at very high prices. The bill fails to stop the practice of collecting subsidies even when crops are sold later at a higher price, it restricts our ability to redirect food aid dollars for emergency use in the midst of a global food crisis, and it falls short of the administration's conservation proposals. By increasing trade-distorting subsidies, the bill undermines our ability to open foreign markets to American agricultural goods. The bill creates an egregious new sugar subsidy program that will keep sugar prices high for domestic consumers, while making taxpayers subsidize a handful of sugar growers. These are just a few of the reasons why I cannot support this bill.

In the absence of a good farm bill, I call on Congress to extend current law for at least 1 year. The administration's reform-minded proposal would be preferable to current law, but in light of the bill produced by conferees, an extension is now the better policy for American agriculture and American taxpayers. It is a far superior option than supporting a bill that increases farm subsidy rates, spends too much, and fails to reform farm programs for the future.

Remarks at a Welcoming Ceremony in Tel Aviv, Israel
May 14, 2008

Mr. President and Mr. Prime Minister, Mrs. Olmert, thank you very much for your warm welcome. It's good to be back again. We're proud to reaffirm the friendship of our peoples, and we're delighted to join you in celebrating the 60th anniversary of the State of Israel.

Our two nations both faced great challenges when they were founded, and our two nations have both relied on the same principles to help us succeed. We've built strong democracies to protect the freedoms given to us by an Almighty God. We've welcomed immigrants who've helped us thrive. We've built prosperous economies by rewarding innovation and risk-taking and trade. And we've built an enduring alliance to confront terrorists and tyrants.

Americans and Israelis can be proud of our past, and the best way to honor our founders is to continue the work they started. Tomorrow I'm going to address the

members of the Knesset and the people of Israel. I look forward to discussing how I believe our two nations can continue to advance our ideals and approach our next 60 years of partnership with confidence and with hope.

Laura and I appreciate your invitation, your kind invitation to share these days of celebration with you. We consider the Holy Land a very special place, and we consider the Israeli people our close friends.

Shalom.

NOTE: The President spoke at 11:32 a.m. at Ben Gurion International Airport. In his remarks, he referred to President Shimon Peres and Prime Minister Ehud Olmert of Israel; and Aliza Olmert, wife of Prime Minister Olmert. The transcript released by the Office of the Press Secretary also included the remarks of President Peres and Prime Minister Olmert.

Remarks During a Meeting With President Shimon Peres of Israel in Jerusalem, Israel
May 14, 2008

President Peres. Mr. President, Secretary of State, distinguished delegation: I got permission from the Americans to be a—and Miss Tzipi Livni, our Foreign Minister—I got permission to be, all my life, an optimist. And you bring with you optimism, so I feel a sort of competition. [*Laughter*] But let me say that I know you have elections sometimes, by the end of this year, and maybe there will be a change of administration, a change of guards. I think before you will leave office, you will see a change of guards here in the Middle East.

President Bush. Yes.

President Peres. What looks today so gloomy may be the last effort by some very extremist group to remain alive. Because it's concentrated, it becomes sharp and clear, particularly in two places. In Lebanon, Hizballah is simply destroying Lebanon. It's a matter that concerns not only the United States or Israel; it concerns the Arab world. For them, the destruction of Lebanon is the destruction of statehood in many other places. And it's a protest without a message. And the second goes to Gaza, where Hamas is responding to the establishment of a Palestinian state. I think you, and may I say the Secretary of State, invested so much effort to enable the Palestinians to correct the historic mistakes in—from 1947, because would they then accept an Arab state, we wouldn't have all these troubles. But never the mind, we cannot change the past.

But today, the real obstacle, when I consider everything else for—before creation of—the—[*inaudible*]—recreation of a Palestinian state, is Hamas. And talking with the Palestinians, I know that's their view. We are not their enemies, as we are not enemies of Lebanon. On the contrary, I think we would like to see a united, integrated Lebanon living in peace, who don't have any ambitions neither to their water, nor to their land, nor to their politics. We would like to see the Palestinians living together. They suffered a great deal of their life. The separation is a tragedy for them and for the rest of us.

Now the Arab world will have to take a stand, not about the conflict between us and them, but about their own destiny, where are they moving. And that will affect us.

Your 8 years were very moving years for all of us.

President Bush. Thank you.

President Peres. [*Inaudible*]—that you can really watch a friendship without any bad mood. And I know that we are not the—[*inaudible*]—half the time. But you never interrupted your understanding, your support——

President Bush. Thank you.

President Peres. ——and really trying to do whatever you, your administration, and the lady who is on the State Department really did then to help us negotiate a difficult time.

So for us, it's a celebration not only because we're a little bit older—60 years, it's not too much—but also because we feel that our efforts are not in vain. And it is in this optimistic view that I welcome you here.

President Bush. Thank you, sir.

President Peres. Thank you.

President Bush. Mr. President, it's great to be with you. You're known as a wise soul, and your comments reflect your wisdom. I am delighted to be here for the 60th birthday party. As a person who is 61 years old, it doesn't seem that old. [*Laughter*]

But I suspect if you looked back 60 years ago and tried to guess where Israel would be at that time, it would be hard to be able to project such a prosperous, hopeful land. No question, people would have said, "Well, we'd be surrounded by hostile forces." But I doubt people would have been able to see the modern Israel, which is one reason I bring so much optimism to the Middle East, because what happened here is possible everywhere.

And the objective of the United States must be to, one, support our strongest ally and friend in the Middle East that won't— only true democracy against the forces of terror that you just described—and at the same time, talk about a hopeful future.

So I'm really looking forward to my time here. I want to thank you for giving me a chance to speak to the Knesset. I hear it's quite an experience. It'll be a huge honor to represent my country for your 60th birthday.

In the meantime, we will continue to work toward a vision of—where the— where people who are just reasonable and want a chance to live at peace with Israel have that opportunity, and at the same time, speak clearly about those forces of terror who murder innocent people to achieve their political objectives and how the world must stand against them.

And so I want to thank you for giving me a chance to come by and see you again. And you're looking good. [*Laughter*] I hope you're feeling well.

Thank you, sir.

President Peres. Thank you very much.

NOTE: The President spoke at 2:29 p.m. at the President's residence.

Remarks Following a Meeting With Prime Minister Ehud Olmert of Israel in Jerusalem
May 14, 2008

Prime Minister Olmert. I am delighted to honor President George W. Bush on his second visit. This time, President came to celebrate with Israel the 60th anniversary of the State of Israel.

We are particularly excited by the fact that the President chose to come this week, which is a very meaningful and very exciting week in his private life. And I congratulate you again, President——

President Bush. Thank you.

Prime Minister Olmert. ——for the marriage of your daughter Jenna this last weekend. We are very happy to host you here.

We had a long discussion about a variety of issues. The first of the issues was the attempts made by Iran to acquire nuclear capabilities. This is a danger of the highest order to the safety of the region—of course, Israel is part of it—and many other countries in the world. And there is an international effort, led by the United States of America, to try and stop Iran from acquiring nuclear power. And the discussions between our two countries will continue on this issue. And of course, Israel will try to join the main forces, led by the United States of America and the President, to try and stop the Iranians from continuing their efforts, which are going on and which are clearly dangerous and threatening for the stability of the world.

We also discussed the situation in Lebanon. We observed the events in Lebanon, and we are very much concerned that there will be an attempt to upset the democratic process, which has to take place properly in Lebanon. And we will continue to observe the situation, and hopefully, the situation will stabilize in Lebanon and the Government of Prime Minister Siniora will prevail against the provocations and the efforts made by Hizballah and the Iranians, which are obviously heavily involved in the attempts to upset the situation over there.

We also discussed the situation in Gaza. A couple of days ago, I had a visit of General Omar Suleiman, the head of the Egyptian military intelligence, and we discussed possible terms for what may emerge as a cease-fire in the Gaza district. The fact is that while General Suleiman was visiting here, Qassam rockets were still shot at innocent people in the south of Israel, and two people were killed. And this is a very threatening signal. An organization which pretends to want to stop terror can't continue to shoot at innocent people. We will make exceptional efforts that we will not explain. But Israel naturally will not be able to tolerate continuous attacks on innocent civilians.

We hope that we will not have to act against Hamas in other ways, with the military power that Israel hasn't yet started to use in a serious manner in order to stop it. But it entirely depends on responding positively to the principles set forth by me and by the Israeli Cabinet in order to stop these operations.

We also briefed the President on the negotiations between us and the Palestinians. We are genuinely interested in meeting the time framework that we talked about in Annapolis. I still remember the very eloquent presentation of President Bush prior to the public meeting in Annapolis, in which he described the difficulties, the sensitivities, the complexities, and also the opportunities that the Annapolis process proposes for both sides. The Israeli side is making an exceptional effort on all fronts. We need to reach an understanding that will define accurately the parameters for the realization of the vision of you, Mr. President, of a two-state solution that will relate to the issue of borders, to the issue of refugees, to the issue of the security arrangements, and will set forth also, at the end of the day, the framework for how to deal later with the issue of Jerusalem.

We will continue this discussion. And I'm sure that America will continue the extraordinary efforts made by Secretary Rice and President Bush to try and influence the process so that it will end up in a positive way.

Again, this is not just a ceremonial visit. I thank you, Mr. President, for your friendship, for your dedication to the basic principles which are shared by our two countries, and for your great friendship. You are a great person, you are a great leader, and you are a great friend. And it's a great honor for me to have the opportunity to host you in the home of the Prime Minister of the State of Israel on the 60th anniversary of the State of Israel. Thank you very much.

President Bush. Mr. Prime Minister, thank you for your friendship, and thank you for your hospitality. Laura and I are looking forward to having dinner with you and Mrs. Olmert tomorrow night, as well as the celebrations tonight and tomorrow.

I'm honored to be representing our country here for the 60th anniversary of the existence of the State of Israel. It's just a great honor, and it's a chance for me to express the enduring friendship of the American people with the Israeli people. It's also an interesting time to come because, you know, here we are in the heart of a thriving democracy, and yet that democracy, as are other democracies, are being challenged by extremists and terrorists, people who use violence to try to advance their dark vision of the world.

I happen to believe it's an important role of the United States to stand with democracies and to stand strong against terrorists, whether it be to stand with Israel against the existential threat of a nuclear weapon with Iran or whether it be to stand with the Siniora Government.

What's interesting—what took place in Lebanon—is that Hizballah, the so-called protector of the Lebanese against Israel, has now turned on its own people. And as you mentioned, Hizballah is supported by Iran. This is an Iranian effort to destabilize that young democracy. And the United States stands strongly with the Siniora Government.

You brought up Hamas. Hamas's objective—stated objective is the destruction of the State of Israel. And therefore, the United States will stand strongly with Israel, as well as stand strongly with the Palestinians who don't share that vision.

And so I thank you very much for your efforts to describe what's possible for the millions of Palestinians who simply want to live side by side with Israel in peace.

We've had an—extensive discussions on a variety of issues, and there's no better person to discuss those issues with than you. You clearly see the threats; you clearly see the opportunities. And I want to thank you for your strong leadership, and thank you for your friendship.

NOTE: The President spoke at 5:35 p.m. at the Prime Minister's Residence. In his remarks, he referred to Aliza Olmert, wife of Prime Minister Olmert; and Prime Minister Fuad Siniora of Lebanon.

Remarks in Jerusalem
May 14, 2008

Thank you all. President Peres, thank you, sir, for your hospitality. Mr. Prime Minister and Mrs. Olmert, it's great to be with you. We consider you friends. Heads of state, thank you all for coming. I think it's a great tribute to this conference, as well as to Israel, that so many heads of state have come. Ex-heads of state and ex-leaders, thanks for being here. Save a seat in the ex-leader's club. [*Laughter*] Citizens of Israel: Laura and I loved coming to your beautiful country, and thank you for your warm hospitality. Citizens of the United States, my fellow Americans: Spend freely and behave yourselves. [*Laughter*]

Distinguished guests, I really appreciate your warm welcome. And we are thrilled to be here with one of America's closest friends. Laura and I are honored to represent the American people on the 60th anniversary of your independence. Happy birthday.

As we celebrate the anniversary, it is useful to look back at the story of your founding. It is the story of how faith guided the Jewish people through centuries of bitter exile. It is a story of how those living behind ghetto walls and barbed wire never

lost sight of Jerusalem. It is a story of how brave pioneers risked everything to redeem the promise of this land. It is a marvelous story.

When Israel's founders gathered in Tel Aviv to sign your Declaration of Independence, the threat of war loomed. But it could not overshadow the joy of people who had lived to see their prayers answered. Celebrations broke out all across this land, and of course, they broke out in America as well. In New York, young men and women danced the *hora* in the streets. In Washington, a crowd gathered to watch a flag-raising ceremony outside the building that would become Israel's first Embassy. After one man saw the flag bearing the Star of David, he said, "I never thought I'd live to see this day."

Looking back 60 years later, it is important to remember what the founders of Israel had to overcome at every stage of the journey. They established one of the world's great democracies in a region where democracy had few roots. They formed a unified army out of immigrants and refugees from many different countries. They planted the seeds of a modern economy in the sands of an ancient desert. In these accomplishments, we see the visionary leadership of men and women like Herzl and Weizmann and Ben-Gurion and Golda Meir and Rabin and Sharon, and we honor each of them this evening.

And looking back 60 years later, we've also got to remember the courage of President Harry S. Truman. As Israel prepared to declare independence, President Truman faced a tough choice over whether to recognize a new state. The future of Israel hung in the balance. As Chaim Weizmann told the President, he said, "History and Providence have placed this issue in your hands." And today, we know that the forces of Providence could not have chosen a better man than America's 33d President.

Eleven minutes after Israel came into existence, the United States became the first nation to recognize its independence. And because Harry Truman did what was right instead of following the conventional wisdom, we can say today that America is Israel's oldest and best friend in the world.

With every passing year, the bonds of friendship between America and Israel have grown stronger. America stands for peace, and so does Israel. And as we stand in peace, we must understand the realities of the world in which we live. We must be steadfast and we must be strong in the face of those who murder the innocent to achieve their objectives. And in the long run, we share a powerful belief in a powerful weapon against the terrorists. We believe that the surest way to defeat the enemies of hatred is to advance the cause of hope through the cause of freedom, liberty as the great alternative to tyranny and terror.

Mr. President, Mr. Prime Minister, thank you for inviting me to speak at the Knesset tomorrow. I hear it's a place of many a sharp elbow. [*Laughter*] I'm looking forward to giving my speech. [*Laughter*] I'm not going to be throwing any elbows. But I will talk about the day when I believe every child in the Middle East can live in peace and live in freedom. With trust in the Rock of Israel, we know that day will come. And when it does, the United States of America will be at your side.

God bless Israel, and God bless America.

NOTE: The President spoke at 9:20 p.m. at the ICC Jerusalem International Convention Center. In his remarks, he referred to President Shimon Peres, Prime Minister Ehud Olmert, and former Prime Minister Ariel Sharon of Israel; and Aliza Olmert, wife of Prime Minister Olmert.

Remarks to Members of the Knesset in Jerusalem
May 15, 2008

Thank you. President Peres and Mr. Prime Minister, Madam Speaker, thank you very much for hosting this special session. President Beinisch, Leader of the Opposition Netanyahu, Ministers, members of the Knesset, distinguished guests: *Shalom.* Laura and I are thrilled to be back in Israel. We have been deeply moved by the celebrations of the past 2 days. And this afternoon, I am honored to stand before one of the world's greatest democratic assemblies and convey the wishes of the American people with these words: *Yom Ha'atzmaut Sameach.*

It is a rare privilege for the American President to speak to the Knesset. [*Laughter*] Although, the Prime Minister told me there is something even rarer: to have just one person in this chamber speaking at a time. [*Laughter*] My only regret is that one of Israel's greatest leaders is not here to share this moment. He is a warrior for the ages, a man of peace, a friend. The prayers of the American people are with Ariel Sharon.

We gather to mark a momentous occasion. Sixty years ago in Tel Aviv, David Ben-Gurion proclaimed Israel's independence, founded on the natural right of the Jewish people to be masters of their own fate. What followed was more than the establishment of a new country. It was the redemption of an ancient promise given to Abraham and Moses and David, a homeland for the chosen people: *Eretz Yisrael*.

Eleven minutes later, on the orders of President Harry Truman, the United States was proud to be the first nation to recognize Israel's independence. And on this landmark anniversary, America is proud to be Israel's closest ally and best friend in the world.

The alliance between our governments is unbreakable, yet the source of our friendship runs deeper than any treaty. It is grounded in the shared spirit of our people, the bonds of the Book, the ties of the soul. When William Bradford stepped off the *Mayflower* in 1620, he quoted the words of Jeremiah: "Come let us declare in Zion the word of God." The Founders of my country saw a new promised land and bestowed upon their towns names like Bethlehem and New Canaan. And in time, many Americans became passionate advocates for a Jewish state.

Centuries of suffering and sacrifice would pass before the dream was fulfilled. The Jewish people endured the agony of the pogroms, the tragedy of the Great War, and the horror of the Holocaust—what Elie Wiesel called "the kingdom of the night." Soulless men took away lives and broke apart families, yet they could not take away the spirit of the Jewish people, and they could not break the promise of God. When news of Israel's freedom finally arrived, Golda Meir, a fearless woman raised in Wisconsin, could summon only tears. She later said: "For 2,000 years, we have waited for our deliverance. Now that it is here,

it is so great and wonderful that it surpasses human words."

The joy of independence was tempered by the outbreak of battle, a struggle that has continued for six decades. Yet in spite of the violence, in defiance of the threats, Israel has built a thriving democracy in the heart of the Holy Land. You have welcomed immigrants from far—from the four corners of the Earth. You have forged a free and modern society based on the love of liberty, a passion for justice, and a respect for human dignity. You have worked tirelessly for peace; you have fought valiantly for freedom.

My country's admiration for Israel does not end there. When Americans look at Israel, we see a pioneer spirit that worked an agricultural miracle and now leads a high-tech revolution. We see world-class universities and a global leader in business and innovation and the arts. We see a resource more valuable than oil or gold: the talent and determination of a free people who refuse to let any obstacle stand in the way of their destiny.

I have been fortunate to see the character of Israel up close. I've touched the Western Wall; I've seen the sun reflected in the Sea of Galilee; I have prayed at Yad Vashem. And earlier today I visited Masada, an inspiring monument to courage and sacrifice. At this historic site, Israeli soldiers swear an oath: "Masada shall never fall again." Citizens of Israel, Masada shall never fall again, and America will be at your side.

This anniversary is a time to reflect on the past. It's also an opportunity to look to the future. As we go forward, our alliance will be guided by clear principles, shared convictions rooted in moral clarity and unswayed by popularity polls or the shifting opinions of international elites.

We believe in the matchless value of every man, woman, and child. So we insist that the people of Israel have the right to a decent, normal, and peaceful life, just like the citizens of every other nation.

We believe that democracy is the only way to ensure human rights. So we consider it a source of shame that the United Nations routinely passes more human rights resolutions against the freest democracy in the Middle East than any other nation in the world.

We believe that religious liberty is fundamental to a civilized society. So we condemn anti-Semitism in all forms, whether by those who openly question Israel's right to exist or by others who quietly excuse them.

We believe that free people should strive and sacrifice for peace. So we applaud the courageous choices Israeli's leaders have made. We also believe that nations have a right to defend themselves and that no nation should ever be forced to negotiate with killers pledged to its destruction.

We believe that targeting innocent lives to achieve political objectives is always and everywhere wrong. So we stand together against terror and extremism, and we will never let down our guard or lose our resolve.

The fight against terror and extremism is the defining challenge of our time. It's more than a clash of arms; it is a clash of visions, a great ideological struggle. On the one side are those who defend the ideals of justice and dignity with the power of reason and truth. On the other side are those who pursue a narrow vision of cruelty and control by committing murder, inciting fear, and spreading lies.

This struggle is waged with the technology of the 21st century, but at its core, it is an ancient battle between good and evil. The killers claim the mantle of Islam, but they are not religious men. No one who prays to the God of Abraham could strap a suicide vest to an innocent child or blow up guiltless guests at a Passover seder or fly planes into office buildings filled with unsuspecting workers. In truth, the men who carry out these savage acts serve no higher goal than their own desire for power. They accept no God before

themselves, and they reserve a special hatred for the most ardent defenders of liberty, including Americans and Israelis.

And that is why the founding charter of Hamas calls for the elimination of Israel. And that is why the followers of Hizballah chant: "Death to Israel! Death to America!" That is why Usama bin Laden teaches that the killing of Jews and Americans is one of the biggest duties. And that is why the President of Iran dreams of returning the Middle East to the Middle Ages and calls for Israel to be wiped off the map.

There are good and decent people who cannot fathom the darkness in these men and try to explain away their words. It's natural, but it is deadly wrong. As witnesses to evil in the past, we carry a solemn responsibility to take these words seriously. Jews and Americans have seen the consequences of disregarding the words of leaders who espouse hatred. And that is a mistake the world must not repeat in the 21st century.

Some seem to believe that we should negotiate with the terrorists and radicals, as if some ingenious argument will persuade them they have been wrong all along. We've heard this foolish delusion before. As Nazi tanks crossed into Poland in 1939, an American Senator declared, "Lord, if I could only have talked to Hitler, all this might have been avoided." We have an obligation to call this what it is: the false comfort of appeasement which has been repeatedly discredited by history.

Some people suggest if the United States would just break ties with Israel, all our problems in the Middle East would go away. This is a tired argument that buys into the propaganda of the enemies of peace, and America utterly rejects it. Israel's population may be just over 7 million, but when you confront terror and evil, you are 307 million strong, because the United States of America stands with you.

America stands with you in breaking up terrorist networks and denying the extremists sanctuary. America stands with you in firmly opposing Iran's nuclear weapons ambitions. Permitting the world's leading sponsor of terror to possess the world's deadliest weapons would be an unforgivable betrayal for future generations. For the sake of peace, the world must not allow Iran to have a nuclear weapon.

Ultimately, to prevail in this struggle, we must offer an alternative to the ideology of the extremists by extending our vision of justice and tolerance and freedom and hope. These values are the self-evident right of all people, of all religions, in all the world because they are a gift from the Almighty God. Securing these rights is also the surest way to secure peace. Leaders who are accountable to their people will not pursue endless confrontation and bloodshed. Young people with a place in their society and a voice in their future are less likely to search for meaning in radicalism. Societies where citizens can express their conscience and worship their God will not export violence; they will be partners in peace.

The fundamental insight that freedom yields peace is the great lesson of the 20th century. Now our task is to apply it to the 21st. Nowhere is this work more urgent than here in the Middle East. We must stand with the reformers working to break the old patterns of tyranny and despair. We must give voice to millions of ordinary people who dream for a better life in a free society. We must confront the moral relativism that views all forms of government as equally acceptable and thereby consigns whole societies to slavery. Above all, we must have faith in our values and ourselves and confidently pursue the expansion of liberty as the path to a peaceful future.

That future will be a dramatic departure from the Middle East of today. So as we mark 60 years from Israel's founding, let us try to envision the region 60 years from now. This vision is not going to arrive easily or overnight. It will encounter violent resistance. But if we and future Presidents and future Knessets maintain our resolve and have faith in our ideals, here is the Middle East that we can see.

Israel will be celebrating the 120th anniversary as one of the world's great democracies, a secure and flourishing homeland for the Jewish people. The Palestinian people will have the homeland they have long dreamed of and deserved, a democratic state that is governed by law and respects human rights and rejects terror. From Cairo to Riyadh to Baghdad and Beirut, people will live in free and independent societies, where a desire for peace is reinforced by ties of diplomacy and tourism and trade. Iran and Syria will be peaceful nations, with today's oppressive—oppression a distant memory and where people are free to speak their minds and develop their God-given talents. Al Qaida and Hizballah and Hamas will be defeated, as Muslims across the region recognize the emptiness of the terrorists' vision and the injustice of their cause.

Overall, the Middle East will be characterized by a new period of tolerance and integration. And this doesn't mean that Israel and its neighbors will be best of friends. But when leaders across the region answer to their people, they will focus their energies on schools and jobs, not on rocket attacks and suicide bombings. With this change, Israel will open a new, hopeful chapter in which its people can live a normal life, and the dream of Herzl and the founders of 1948 can be fully and finally realized.

This is a bold vision, and some will say it can never be achieved. But think about what we have witnessed in our own time. When Europe was destroying itself through total war and genocide, it was difficult to envision a continent that six decades later would be free and at peace. When Japanese pilots were flying suicide missions into American battleships, it seemed impossible that six decades later Japan would be a democracy, a linchpin of security in Asia, and one of America's closest friends. And when waves of refugees arrived here in the desert with nothing, surrounded by hostile armies, it was almost unimaginable that Israel would grow into one of the freest and most successful nations on the Earth.

Yet each one of these transformations took place. And a future of transformation is possible in the Middle East, so long as a new generation of leaders has the courage to defeat the enemies of freedom, to make the hard choices necessary for peace, and stand firm on the solid rock of universal values.

Sixty years ago, on the eve of Israel's independence, the last British soldiers departing Jerusalem stopped at a building in the Jewish quarter of the Old City. An officer knocked on the door and met a senior rabbi. The officer presented him with a short iron bar, the key to the Zion Gate, and said it was the first time in 18 centuries that a key to the gates of Jerusalem had belonged to a Jew. His hands trembling, the rabbi offered a prayer of thanksgiving to God, "who had granted us life and permitted us to reach this day." Then he turned to the officer and uttered the words

Jews had awaited for so long: "I accept this key in the name of my people."

Over the past six decades, the Jewish people have established a state that would make that humble rabbi proud. You've raised a modern society in the promised land, a light unto the nations that preserves the legacy of Abraham and Isaac and Jacob. And you have built a mighty democracy that will endure forever and can always count on the United States of America to be at your side.

God bless.

NOTE: The President spoke at 2:55 p.m. at the Knesset. In his remarks, he referred to Prime Minister Ehud Olmert, Speaker of the Knesset Dalia Itzik, and former Prime Minister Ariel Sharon of Israel; Dorit Beinisch, president, Supreme Court of Israel; Holocaust survivor, Nobel Prize winner, and author Elie Wiesel; Usama bin Laden, leader of the Al Qaida terrorist organization; and President Mahmud Ahmadi-nejad of Iran. The Office of the Press Secretary also released a Spanish language transcript of these remarks.

Remarks at the Israel Museum in Jerusalem
May 15, 2008

Thank you all for coming. Never a man to shy away from a microphone. [*Laughter*] I didn't realize it got so cold here in Jerusalem in May. [*Laughter*] Yes, but thanks for coming.

I first want to thank James Snyder and the museum of—folks for hosting this fantastic reception. Mr. President, thanks for joining us, and Mr. Prime Minister, I'm so honored that you all would take time to be here, as I am—members of your cabinet, members of the Knesset. We've got leaders from around the world who are here to share in this fantastic celebration. Laura and I really wanted to come by and

say thanks to our fellow Americans for coming as well.

So I'm driving in the limousine, waving at friendly faces, half of whom seem to be from California or—[*laughter*]. I hope you're having as much fun as we are. It's been a—it's been such a fantastic couple of days for us, and what a fitting way to end with our buddies from the United States of America. You know, Israel has got no closer ally than America, and one of the reasons why is because of the connections between our—citizens of the U.S. and the citizens of Israel.

And so we're thrilled to be with you. We're also honored to be steps away from some of the oldest Biblical texts. I don't know if you've had a chance to go through the museum. I strongly urge you to do so—if they open it up for you like they did—[*laughter*]. But these documents tell the story of the righteous—of a righteous God and His relationship with an ancient people.

There's no doubt in my mind that the patriarchs of ancient Israel and the pioneers of modern Israel would marvel at the achievements of this nation. I mean, if you really think about it, I doubt few of the prognosticators would have projected Israel to be what it is today: a modern, thriving democracy in the heart of the Middle East. It's been an amazing transformation of dry valleys to fertile lands. And the new technologies being nurtured here are a great testimony to the truest resource of the Israeli people, and that's the brainpower and ingenuity and drive.

I gave a speech today in the Knesset. It was such an honor to stand in that hallowed hall. One of the things I wished I would have projected maybe more clearly was the fact that this is a land of courageous people, people who have had to withstand bombings and suiciders but never lost faith, people who have shown incredible resilience. And it's a nation worthy of our support and a nation worthy of our friendship.

As I said in my speech, I'm—I truly believe that if we stay firm in our resolve, resist the temptation to give in to the terrorists, and believe in the transformative capacity of liberty, someday other nations in the region will share the blessings of democracy and liberty. Someday they'll know that they'll have governments that respond to the people. They'll build schools instead of bombs; that they'll not want a war with their neighbors, but want to live in peace. And that's the dream, and that's the hope. And I firmly believe it can come true.

I do want to pay tribute to one brave soul, and that is Liviu Librescu. I don't know if you remember him, but he was the teacher at Virginia Tech. His folks live in Israel. I bring him up because it was a courageous act of selflessness—he blocked the doorway to his classroom with his body to allow his students to escape. And I think it's a fitting final statement here in Israel for me to make—to say that, isn't it amazing that a survivor of the Holocaust gave his life for others in the Virginia countryside? And I just want his family to know that we appreciate his courage and that his legacy lives on.

And so thanks for coming. Thanks for honoring a great nation and a worthy friendship. I'm proud to be here on Israeli soil as the President of the United States of America. I'm proud to carry our banner of liberty around the world. And I'm proud to proclaim our deep desire for peace.

Thanks for coming. God bless you. God bless Israel. And God bless America.

NOTE: The President spoke at 7:40 p.m. In his remarks, he referred to James S. Snyder, director, the Israel Museum; and President Shimon Peres and Prime Minister Ehud Olmert of Israel.

Remarks in a Discussion With Israeli Youth in Jerusalem
May 16, 2008

The President. Please sit down. First of all, Laura and I are honored that you'd join us. Thanks very much for sharing some thoughts with us. As you know, we're parents of young professional women. We're interested to know what's on your mind. And if you've got any questions of me, I'll be glad to answer them.

What's on my mind is peace. I hope someday that everybody will be able to co-exist and respect each other's religions and work together for harmony. And I believe it's possible. And I know it's going to happen when young people put a—get their minds together and say, "Listen, let's make this work."

So I'm interested in your thoughts, and so is Laura. And we're pleased to be joined by Condoleezza.

And perhaps you'd like to say something to begin with?

Participant. Mr. President, Mrs. Bush, thank you so much for choosing to spend this time with us. This is an amazing opportunity, and I'm very honored and glad to be here. Congratulations, *mazel tov* for your daughter's wedding. [*Laughter*]

I think this museum comes to show how unique this land and this region is. It's so rich with history, the Cradle of Civilization. While on the other hand, we see that Israel is such a new, vibrant country, only 60 years old. And we're still building our country; nothing is for certain here. And we—I, my friends, we want peace; we want to see the world like—live in peace, especially in this region. And I do hope—and I guarantee that myself as, hopefully, a future leader will do the best I can, the best of my abilities in order to make it happen.

I think that it's for now. [*Laughter*]

The President. Thank you. You want to share some thoughts?

[*At this point, another participant made brief remarks.*]

The President. Thanks.

NOTE: The President spoke at 10:30 a.m. at the Bible Lands Museum Jerusalem. In his remarks, he referred to Secretary of State Condoleezza Rice.

Message to the Congress on Continuation of the National Emergency With Respect to Burma
May 16, 2008

To the Congress of the United States:

Section 202(d) of the National Emergencies Act (50 U.S.C. 1622(d)) provides for the automatic termination of a national emergency unless, prior to the anniversary date of its declaration, the President publishes in the *Federal Register* and transmits to the Congress a notice stating that the emergency is to continue in effect beyond the anniversary date. I have sent the enclosed notice to the *Federal Register* for publication, stating that the Burma emergency is to continue beyond May 20, 2008.

The crisis between the United States and Burma arising from the actions and policies of the Government of Burma, including its engaging in large-scale repression of the democratic opposition in Burma, that led to the declaration of a national emergency on May 20, 1997, and its expansion on October 18, 2007, and April 30, 2008, has not been resolved. These actions and policies are hostile to U.S. interests and pose a continuing unusual and extraordinary threat to the national security and foreign policy of the United States. For this reason, I have determined that it is necessary to continue the national emergency with respect to Burma and maintain in force the sanctions against Burma to respond to this threat. This action does not inhibit any efforts on the part of the United States to provide humanitarian assistance to the people of Burma in the aftermath of Cyclone Nargis.

GEORGE W. BUSH

The White House,

May 16, 2008.

NOTE: This message was released by the Office of the Press Secretary on May 17. The notice is listed in Appendix D at the end of this volume.

Remarks Following a Meeting With President Hamid Karzai of Afghanistan and an Exchange With Reporters in Sharm el-Sheikh, Egypt
May 17, 2008

President Bush. Mr. President, good to see you. Thanks. President Karzai and I have had a lot of meetings together, and this was a very upbeat meeting. And I want to thank you for coming. I appreciate your courage. Appreciate you taking on a very tough assignment, which is helping your young democracy survive amidst the threats from the radicals and extremists.

I really appreciate the briefing you gave me on how you're going to approach the Paris donors' meeting. This is a great opportunity for the world to help Afghanistan grow and prosper. His strategy is a smart strategy. And part of his strategy is to—is for the world to help Afghanistan's agricultural community grow and prosper, so that they can not only become self-sufficient in food but become net exporters of crops that people need in order to be able to eat and survive.

And so I thought it was a smart approach. I hope the world rallies to your behalf. We'll certainly help. I appreciate you being here.

President Karzai. Thank you very much.

President Bush. Yes, sir.

President Karzai. Thank you very much. Well, Mr. President, thank you very much for this very good meeting once again. We have always had very good meetings with you in the past. This one was one more of such meetings. And thank you very much once again, Mr. President, for the help that

you have given us in the past 6 years— 6½ years in Afghanistan.

I told you about a story earlier, that we, for the first time after 30 years, were able to give diplomas to the graduates of Afghanistan's universities, the medical colleges, economics, law, and all that. That would have not been possible without your help and the help of the rest of the world.

And thank you very much for the support on Paris. We'll be going to Paris to ask for more help for Afghanistan's agriculture, so that Afghanistan can become self-sufficient in agriculture and also be an exporter to the rest of the world. And we'll be asking for help on energy resources in Afghanistan and the—better irrigation and hydro projects.

Afghanistan once again thanks the people of the United States. Mr. President, thank you very much, and please convey that gratitude to the American people. And please do visit us very, very soon. The Afghan people want to be there to greet you and to express their gratitude for your leadership and help.

President Bush. Thank you, sir. Thank you. I'll take two questions. Terry [Terence Hunt, Associated Press].

Middle East Peace Process

Q. Mr. President, Egypt's state-owned media says that you have tilted too far toward Israel. One of them, the newspaper, says that you aim to do nothing but appeasing Israel. Did you encounter that attitude today, and what do you say to this?

President Bush. Actually, in my meeting with the President of Egypt, he wanted to make sure that my approach toward the Middle Eastern peace is firm, and that we work hard to get the Palestinian state defined. And in my speech tomorrow, I'll make it clear that I believe we can get a state defined by the end of my Presidency, and we'll work hard to achieve that objective. I had conversations with Prime Minister Olmert and others in his Government to that effect. I will have conversations with President Abbas and people in his Government tonight.

Every one of these meetings helps advance the process. Every one of these meetings helps us inch toward the goal of getting a state defined with borders and the refugee issue as well as security concerns defined by the end of my Presidency. And I believe we can do that, and I know it's going to be important for the peace in the Middle East.

John [John McKinnon, Wall Street Journal], yes.

Saudi Arabia/Oil Production

Q. Mr. President, can you talk a little bit more about your meetings with officials in Saudi Arabia? And are you satisfied with the response that they gave you on oil?

President Bush. Look, my—with—His Majesty is—he kindly called in the Energy Minister, who, I think, was in Korea. And the man flew back to talk with us. I said very plainly, I said, you've got to be concerned about the effects of high oil prices on some of the biggest customers in the world. And not only that, of course, high

energy prices is going to cause countries like mine to accelerate our move toward alternative energy.

And as the Minister said yesterday, that Saudi Arabia, this year, has increased the number of barrels of oil per day by 300,000 a day, and they're increasing refining capacity, which is not enough. It's something, but it doesn't solve our problem. Our problem in America gets solved when we aggressively go for domestic exploration. Our problem in America gets solved if we expand our refining capacity, promote nuclear energy, and continue our strategy for the advancement of alternative energies as well as conservation.

And one of the interesting things about American politics these days is, those who are screaming the loudest for increased production from Saudi Arabia are the very same people who are fighting the fiercest against domestic exploration, against the development of nuclear power, and against expanding refining capacity. And so I was pleased that they had increased production by 300,000. But I'm also realistic to say to the American people, we've got to do more at home, and we need a Congress who will be responsive to those requests.

Thank you all very much for your interest.

NOTE: The President spoke at 3:14 p.m. at the Hyatt Regency Sharm El Sheikh. In his remarks, he referred to President Mohamed Hosni Mubarak of Egypt; Prime Minister Ehud Olmert of Israel; President Mahmoud Abbas of the Palestinian Authority; and King Abdallah bin Abd al-Aziz Al Saud and Minister of Petroleum and Mineral Resources Ali Ibrahim al-Naimi of Saudi Arabia.

The President's Radio Address
May 17, 2008

Good morning. I'm speaking to you from the Middle East, where Laura and I are on a trip to Israel, Saudi Arabia, and Egypt.

When Air Force One touched down at Ben Gurion Airport in Tel Aviv, I was greeted by Israel's President and Prime Minister. I joined them in celebrating an historic milestone: Israel's 60th anniversary as an independent nation. And I assured them that Israel could count on America as a strong and steady ally long into the future.

During our visit, I had conversation with Israel's leaders about their efforts to forge peace with the Palestinians and our shared belief that a peace agreement is possible this year. I also had the opportunity to address members of the Knesset, Israel's elected legislature. I reminded these democratic leaders that America was the first nation in the world to recognize Israel's independence. I told them that 60 years later, America is proud to be Israel's best friend in the world. I reaffirmed the principles that make our alliance strong: a love of liberty, a devotion to justice, and a respect for human dignity. And I said that standing firm on these ideals is the surest way to defeat the extremists and build a future of peace for people throughout the Middle East.

For Laura and me, this visit to Israel was an especially moving experience. We toured the Bible Lands Museum, saw the Dead Sea Scrolls, and visited Masada, an inspiring shrine to Jewish courage and sacrifice in the first century. From the window of our hotel room, we had a magnificent view of the Old City of Jerusalem, home to some of the holiest sites in Judaism, Christianity, and Islam. And on our final morning in the city, we met some of Israel's young people, talented and hopeful citizens who gave me confidence in Israel's future.

On Friday, we visited another of America's friends in the Middle East, Saudi Arabia. I had a series of productive meetings with King Abdallah at his farm. We celebrated the 75th anniversary of diplomatic relations between the United States and Saudi Arabia. We reaffirmed our shared objectives of peace in the Holy Land, a secure and united Iraq, and a sovereign, independent Lebanon that is free of outside interference. We talked about oil production and gasoline prices. We discussed the King's efforts to diversify his nation's economy and the importance of political reform. And I thanked him for Saudi Arabia's strong commitment to fighting terror.

Our final stop is Egypt, where we are visiting the beautiful resort city of Sharm el-Sheikh. I am meeting with a number of key leaders from the region, including President Mubarak of Egypt, President Abbas of the Palestinian Authority, King Abdullah of Jordan, President Karzai of Afghanistan, Prime Minister Gilani of Pakistan, and several senior officials from Iraq's democracy.

I will also address the World Economic Forum in the Middle East. I will stress the importance of building dynamic and diverse economies that unleash the creativity and enterprise of citizens throughout the region, especially women and young people. I will make clear that the only way to ensure true prosperity is to expand political and economic freedom. And I will urge leaders across the region to reject spoilers such as the regimes in Iran and Syria, move past old grievances, and embrace the changes necessary for a day when societies across the Middle East are based on justice, tolerance, and freedom.

Reaching that day will not be easy. But with continued leadership from America and our friends in the region, I am confident that it can happen. And when that day arrives, the Middle East will be more hopeful, the world will be more peaceful, and the American people will be more secure.

Thank you for listening.

NOTE: The address was recorded at 7 p.m. on May 15 at the King David Hotel in Jerusalem, Israel, for broadcast at 10:06 a.m. e.d.t., on May 17. The transcript was made available by the Office of the Press Secretary on May 16, but was embargoed for release until the broadcast. Due to the 7-hour time difference, the address was broadcast between the President's meetings with President Hamid Karzai of Afghanistan and President Mahmoud Abbas of the Palestinian Authority in Sharm el-Sheikh, Egypt. In his address, the President referred to President Shimon Peres and Prime Minister Ehud Olmert of Israel; and King Abdallah bin Abd al-Aziz Al Saud of Saudi Arabia. The Office of the Press Secretary also released a Spanish language transcript of this address.

Remarks Following a Meeting With President Mahmoud Abbas of the Palestinian Authority in Sharm el-Sheikh
May 17, 2008

President Bush. Mr. President, thank you for your time, and thank you for your courage.

We talked about two issues primarily. First, I do want to discuss Lebanon. The President is deeply concerned about Lebanon, the fate of the Siniora Government, as am I. We're concerned about radical elements undermining the democracy. It is clear that Hizballah, which has been funded by Iran, can no longer justify its position as a defender against Israel when it turns on its own people. This is a defining moment. It's a moment that requires us to stand strongly with the Siniora Government and to support the Siniora Government. And the President was quite articulate about his concerns. And I appreciate you sharing your strategy with me.

And then we talked, of course, about the Palestinian state. I told the President that I am absolutely committed to working with he and his negotiators, as well as the Israelis, to get a state defined. And I do so for a couple of reasons. One, it breaks my heart to see the vast potential of the Palestinian people really wasted. These are good, smart, capable people that, when given a chance, will build a thriving homeland. It'll be an opportunity to end the suffering that takes place in the Palestinian Territory.

And the second reason I am for it is because it's the only way for lasting peace. The President and his team are committed to peace. They stand squarely against those who use violence to stop the peace process. And for that I admire you and your team, Mr. President. And I commit to you once again that my Government will help achieve a dream, a dream that you have, and the truth of the matter is, a dream that the Israelis have, which is two states living side by side in peace.

So thank you for coming.

President Abbas. Thank you.

President Bush. Appreciate you.

President Abbas. Mr. President, thank you very much for receiving us today. Of course, we have talked about the peace process and the negotiations that are taking place these days between us and the Israeli side. We know very well that you personally, as well as your administration, are committed to reach peace before the end of 2008. Therefore, we are working very seriously and very aggressively with the hope that we will be able to achieve this objective before the end of the year.

We have talked with the President about the details of the negotiations that are taking place between our side and the Israeli side. And of course, we also talked about a wide range of issues that affect the entire region, but also affect the Palestinian people, because it is very important for us that the entire Arab region will be living in stability in order to be able to achieve peace in our Palestinian Territory.

So we are very delighted that the President is following all the details of everything and every discussion that is taking place in the Palestinian negotiations as well as issues in the region.

Therefore, we're delighted to continue our engagement with you, Mr. President, in order to be able to achieve all the objectives which are ours and yours at the same time.

Thank you.

NOTE: The President spoke at 6:39 p.m. at the Hyatt Regency Sharm El Sheikh. In his remarks, he referred to Prime Minister Fuad Siniora of Lebanon. President Abbas spoke in Arabic, and his remarks were translated by an interpreter.

Remarks Following a Meeting With Prime Minister Syed Yousuf Raza Gilani of Pakistan in Sharm el-Sheikh
May 18, 2008

President Bush. Mr. Prime Minister, thank you for coming. It's the first time we've had a chance to visit. I appreciate the very candid discussion we had. I appreciate the fact that you're committed to working to make sure that relations between the United States and Pakistan are strong and vibrant and productive.

And one area where our relations can be productive is to cooperate on economic matters, because the truth of the matter is, in a population that has got hope as a result of being able to find work is a population that is going to make it harder for extremists and terrorists to find safe haven.

And so I appreciate very much our candid discussion about the economy. I fully understand that you're dealing with serious food prices. I appreciate the compassion you showed for the people of Pakistan. I told the President—the Prime Minister that one thing we can do, having talked to the President of Afghanistan, is help Afghanistan grow wheat, help Afghanistan become self-sufficient, which will take the pressure off of the people of Pakistan.

The Prime Minister and I talked, of course, about our common desire to protect ourselves and others from those who would do harm. And I want to thank your steadfast support and your strength of character and your understanding of the problems we face. Relations are good between our two countries, and they will continue to be good. And I want to thank you for coming and to—and advancing those relations.

Prime Minister Gilani. Thank you.

President Bush. Welcome.

Prime Minister Gilani. Thank you. Thank you very much, Mr. President, for this opportunity. I want to take your call to confidence that, with the change of the new Government in Pakistan, with a new democratic Government in this country, there's a change for the system. And I've been unanimously elected as the Prime Minister of Pakistan; that's the first time in the history of Pakistan. And we have discussed in detail on a few issues like economics, like the food problems, like the energy problems.

And the common problem—and that is the biggest threat to the world—is terrorism and extremism. And our Government is committed to fight for terrorism and extremism. It is against the humanity; it's against the world. And I have lost my own great leader, Benazir Bhutto, because of terrorism. Therefore, I pledge and I stand by the world to fight against extremism and terrorism.

I appreciate the support of Mr. President for our concerns on both social sectors: economic sectors, energy sectors. And we want to work together on all these issues. And I once again thank Mr. President for extending this opportunity.

President Bush. Yes, sir, Mr. Prime Minister. Thank you, Mr. Prime Minister.

Prime Minister Gilani. Thank you so much.

President Bush. Thank you very much. I appreciate it.

NOTE: The President spoke at 9 a.m. at the Hyatt Regency Sharm El Sheikh. In his remarks, he referred to President Hamid Karzai of Afghanistan.

Remarks Following a Meeting With Iraqi Leaders in Sharm el-Sheikh
May 18, 2008

President Bush. I just had a discussion with the Vice President, the Deputy Prime Minister, Foreign Minister of the sovereign nation of Iraq. I told them that I'm impressed by the progress that's taking place, the security progress. We talked about Basra and the success of the Iraqi Government in Basra in dealing with Shi'a extremists.

We talked about the economic progress that is being made. We also talked about the fact that there's—more work needs to be done, that this is—you know, there's still problems. But the good news is, is that these three leaders recognize the problems, and they have got solutions to deal with the problems.

And finally, we talked about the need for the people in the Middle East to understand the importance of a successful Iraq. And these three men are courageous men. They're smart, capable people who are—who represent the Iraqi people with a lot of dignity.

And I welcome you here, Mr. Vice President. Thank you for coming.

Vice President Abd Al-Mahdi. Thank you, Mr. President. We had a very good meeting with President Bush, who always supported Iraq. And we assessed the progress that we did on all levels: security, politics, even economical progress. It's a regular relationship, and international community progress has been marked all of the—on those levels.

We also assessed the future, what we should do in the future, the long-term relationship, other issues of economic kind, and also the regional issue.

So we are working together, really, Iraq with the United States. And we were always optimistic, even in the worst days. And we now—today, we realize how—the importance of our work, of the cooperation between the United States and Iraq, and we'll continue that.

President Bush. Thank you all.

Vice President Abd Al-Mahdi. Thank you.

NOTE: The President spoke at 1:43 p.m. at the Hyatt Regency Sharm El Sheikh. Participating in the meeting were Vice President Adil Abd Al-Mahdi, Deputy Prime Minister

Barham Salih, and Minister of Foreign Affairs Hoshyar Mahmud Zebari of Iraq.

Remarks to the World Economic Forum in Sharm el-Sheikh
May 18, 2008

Klaus, thank you very much. Thanks for inviting me. Klaus said, "It's about time you showed up." Proud to be here. Laura and I are so honored that, Klaus, you gave us a chance to come. I do want to thank President Mubarak and Mrs. Mubarak for their wonderful hospitality. I want to thank the Members of Congress who are here. I appreciate the heads of state who've joined us. I thank the foreign ministers who are here, including my own, Secretary of State Condoleezza Rice. And I want to thank the members of the diplomatic corps.

Laura and I are delighted to be in Egypt, and we bring the warm wishes of the American people. We're proud of our long friendship with your citizens. We respect your remarkable history. And we're humbled to walk in the ancient land of pharaohs, where a great civilization took root and wrote some of the first chapters in the epic story of humanity.

America is a much younger nation, but we've made our mark by advancing ideals as old as the pyramids. Those ideals of liberty and justice have sparked a revolution across much of the world. This hopeful movement made its way to places where dictators once reigned and peaceful democracies seemed unimaginable, places like Chile and Indonesia and Poland and the Philippines and South Korea.

These nations have different histories and different traditions, yet each made the same democratic transition, and they did it on their own terms. In these countries, millions every year are rising from poverty. Women are realizing overdue opportunities. And people of faith are finding the blessing of worshiping God in peace.

All these changes took place in the second half of the 20th century. I strongly believe that if leaders, like those of you in this room, act with vision and resolve, the first half of the 21st century can be the time when similar advances reach the Middle East. This region is home to energetic people, a powerful spirit of enterprise, and tremendous resources. It is capable of a very bright future, a future in which the Middle East is a place of innovation and discovery driven by free men and women.

In recent years, we've seen hopeful beginnings toward this vision. Turkey, a nation with a majority Muslim population, is a prosperous, modern democracy. Afghanistan, under the leadership of President Karzai, is overcoming the Taliban and building a free society. Iraq, under the leadership of Prime Minister Maliki, is establishing a multiethnic democracy. We've seen the stirrings of reform from Morocco and Algeria to Jordan and the Gulf States. And isolation from the outside world is being overcome by the most democratic of innovations: the cell phone and the Internet. America appreciates the challenges facing the Middle East, yet the light of liberty is beginning to shine.

There's much to do to build on this momentum. From diversifying your economies to investing in your people to extending the reach of freedom, nations across the region have an opportunity to move forward with bold and confident reforms and to lead the Middle East to its rightful place as a center of progress and achievement.

Taking your place as a center of progress and achievement requires economic reform. This is a time of strength for many of your nations' economies. Since 2004, economic growth in the region has averaged more than 5 percent. Trade has expanded significantly. Technology has advanced rapidly. Foreign investment has increased dramatically. And unemployment rates have decreased in many nations.

Egypt, for example, has posted strong economic growth, developed some of the world's fastest growing telecommunications companies, and made major investments that will boost tourism and trade. In order for this economic progress to result in permanent prosperity and an Egypt that reaches its full potential, however, economic reform must be accompanied by political reform. And I continue to hope that Egypt can lead the region in political reform.

This is also a time to prepare for the economic changes ahead. Rising price of oil has brought great wealth to some in this region, but the supply of oil is limited, and nations like mine are aggressively developing alternatives to oil. Over time, as the world becomes less dependent on oil, nations in the Middle East will have to build more diverse and more dynamic economies.

Your greatest asset in this quest is the entrepreneurial spirit of your people. The best way to take advantage of that spirit is to make reforms that unleash individual creativity and innovation. Your economies will be more vibrant when citizens who dream of starting their own companies can do so quickly, without high regulatory and registration costs. Your economies will be more dynamic when property rights are protected and risk-taking is encouraged, not punished, by law. Your economies will be more resilient when you adopt modern agricultural techniques that make farmers more productive and the food supply more secure. And your economies will have greater long-term prosperity when taxes are low and all your citizens know that their innovation and hard work will be rewarded.

One of the most powerful drivers of economic growth is free trade. So nations in this region would benefit greatly from breaking down barriers to trade with each other. And America will continue working to open up trade at every level.

In recent years, the United States has completed free trade agreements with Jordan, Oman, Morocco, and Bahrain. America will continue to negotiate bilateral free trade agreements in the region. We strongly supported Saudi Arabia's accession to the World Trade Organization, and we will continue to support nations making the reforms necessary to join the institutions of a global economy. And to break down trade barriers and ignite economic growth around the world, we will work tirelessly for a successful outcome to the Doha round this year.

As we seek to open up new markets abroad, America will keep our markets open at home. There are voices in my country that urge America to adopt measures that would isolate us from the global economy. I firmly reject these calls for protectionism. We will continue to welcome foreign investment and trade. And the United States of America will stay open for business.

Taking your place as a center of progress and achievement requires investing in your people. Some analysts believe the Middle East and North Africa will need to create up to 100 million new jobs over the next 10 to 15 years just to keep up with population growth. The key to realizing this goal is an educated workforce.

This starts early on, with primary schools that teach basic skills such as reading and math rather than indoctrinating children with ideologies of hatred. An educated workforce also requires good high schools and universities where students are exposed to a variety of ideas, learn to think for themselves, and develop the capacity to innovate.

Not long ago, the region marked a hopeful milestone in higher education. In our meeting yesterday, President Karzai told me he recently handed out diplomas to university graduates, including 300 degrees in medicine and 100 degrees in engineering and a lot of degrees to lawyers. And many of the recipients were women.

The people of the Middle East can count on the United States to be a strong partner in improving your educational systems. We're sponsoring training programs for teachers and administrators in nations like Jordan and Morocco and Lebanon. We sponsored English language programs where students can go for intensive language instruction. We've translated more than 80 children's books into Arabic. We've developed new online curricula for students from kindergarten through high school.

It is also in America's interest to continue welcoming aspiring young adults from this region for higher education to the United States. There were understandable concerns about student visas after 9/11. My administration has worked hard to improve the visa process. And I'm pleased to report that we are issuing a growing number of student visas to young people from the Middle East. And that's the way it should be. And we'll continue to work to expand educational exchanges, because we benefit from the contribution of foreign students who study in America, because we're proud to train the world's leaders of tomorrow, and because we know there is no better antidote to the propaganda of our enemies than firsthand experience with life in the United States of America.

Building powerful economies also requires expanding the role of women in society. This is a matter of morality and of basic math. No nation that cuts off half its population from opportunities will be as productive or prosperous as it could be. Women are a formidable force, as I have seen in my own family—[*laughter*]—and my own administration. As the nations of the Middle East open up their laws and their societies to women, they are learning the same thing.

I applaud Egypt. Egypt is a model for the development of professional women. In Afghanistan, girls who were once denied even a basic education are now going to school, and a whole generation of Afghans will grow up with the intellectual tools to lead their nation toward prosperity. In Iraq and in Kuwait, women are joining political parties and running campaigns and serving in public office. In some Gulf States, women entrepreneurs are making a living and a name for themselves in the business world.

Recently, I learned of a woman in Bahrain who owns her own shipping company. She started with a small office and two employees. When she first tried to register her business in her own name, she was turned down. She attended a business training class and was the only woman to participate. And when she applied for a customs license, officials expressed surprise because no woman had ever asked for one before.

And yet with hard work and determination, she turned her small company into a $2 million enterprise. And this year, Huda Janahi was named one of the 50 most powerful businesswomen in the Arab world. Huda is an inspiring example for the whole region. And America's message to other women in the Middle East is this: You have a great deal to contribute; you should have a strong voice in leading your countries; and my Nation looks to the day when you have the rights and privileges you deserve.

Taking your place as a center of progress and achievement requires extending the reach of freedom. Expanding freedom is vital to turning temporary wealth into lasting prosperity. Free societies stimulate competition in the marketplace. Free societies give people access to information they need to make informed and responsible decisions. And free societies give citizens the rule of law, which exposes corruption and builds confidence in the future.

Freedom is also the basis for a democratic system of government, which is the only fair and just ordering of society and the only way to guarantee the God-given rights of all people. Democracies do not take the same shape. They develop at different speeds and in different ways, and they reflect the unique cultures and traditions of their people. There are skeptics about democracy in this part of the world. I understand that. But as more people in the Middle East gain firsthand experience from freedom, many of the arguments against democracy are being discredited.

For example, some say that democracy is a Western value that America seeks to impose on unwilling citizens. This is a condescending form of moral relativism. The truth is that freedom is a universal right, the Almighty's gift to every man, woman, and child on the face of the Earth. And as we've seen time and time again, when people are allowed to make a choice between freedom and the alternative, they choose freedom.

In Afghanistan, 8 million people defied the terrorist threats to vote for a democratic President. In Iraq, 12 million people waved ink-stained fingers to celebrate the first democratic election in decades. And in a recent survey of the Muslim world, there was overwhelming support for one of the central tenets of democracy, freedom of speech: 99 percent in Lebanon, 94 percent here in Egypt, and 92 percent in Iran.

There are people who claim that democracy is incompatible with Islam. But the truth is that democracies, by definition, make a place for people of religious belief. America is one of the most—is one of the world's leading democracies, and we're also one of the most religious nations in the world. More than three-quarters of our citizens believe in a higher power. Millions worship every week and pray every day, and they do so without fear of reprisal from the state. In our democracy, we would never punish a person for owning a Koran. We would never issue a death sentence to someone for converting to Islam. Democracy does not threaten Islam or any

religion. Democracy is the only system of government that guarantees their protection.

Some say any state that holds an election is a democracy. But true democracy requires vigorous political parties allowed to engage in free and lively debate. True democracy requires the establishment of civic institutions that ensure an election's legitimacy and hold leaders accountable. And true democracy requires competitive elections in which opposition candidates are allowed to campaign without fear or intimidation.

Too often in the Middle East, politics has consisted of one leader in power and the opposition in jail. America is deeply concerned about the plight of political prisoners in this region as well as democratic activists who are intimidated or repressed, newspapers and civil society organizations that are shut down, and dissidents whose voices are stifled. The time has come for nations across the Middle East to abandon these practices and treat their people with dignity and the respect they deserve. I call on all nations to release their prisoners of conscience, open up their political debate, and trust their people to chart their future.

The vision I have outlined today is shared by many in this region, but unfortunately, there are some spoilers who stand in the way. Terrorist organizations and their state sponsors know they cannot survive in a free society, so they create chaos and take innocent lives in an effort to stop democracy from taking root. They are on the wrong side in a great ideological struggle, and every nation committed to freedom and progress in the Middle East must stand together to defeat them.

We must stand with the Palestinian people, who have suffered for decades and earned the right to be a homeland of their own—to have a homeland of their own. I strongly support a two-state solution, a democratic Palestine based on law and justice that will live with peace and security alongside a democrat Israel. I believe that the Palestinian people will build a thriving democracy in which entrepreneurs pursue their dreams, and families own their homes in lively communities, and young people grow up with hope in the future.

Last year at Annapolis, we made a hopeful beginning toward a peace negotiation that will outline what this nation of Palestine will look like, a contiguous state where Palestinians live in prosperity and dignity. A peace agreement is in the Palestinians' interests, it is in Israel's interests, it is in Arab States' interests, and it is in the world's interests. And I firmly believe that with leadership and courage, we can reach that peace agreement this year.

This is a demanding task. It requires action on all sides. Palestinians must fight terror and continue to build the institutions of a free and peaceful society. Israel must make tough sacrifices for peace and ease the restrictions on the Palestinians. Arab States, especially oil-rich nations, must seize this opportunity to invest aggressively in the Palestinian people and to move past their old resentments against Israel. And all nations in the region must stand together in confronting Hamas, which is attempting to undermine efforts at peace with acts of terror and violence.

We must stand with the people of Lebanon in their struggle to build a sovereign and independent democracy. This means opposing Hizballah terrorists, funded by Iran, who recently revealed their true intentions by taking up arms against the Lebanese people. It is now clearer than ever that Hizballah militias are the enemy of a free Lebanon. And all nations, especially neighbors in the region, have an interest to help the Lebanese people prevail.

We must stand with the people of Iraq and Afghanistan and other nations in the region fighting against Al Qaida and other extremists. Bin Laden and his followers have made clear that anyone who does not share their extremist ideology is fit for murder. That means every government in the Middle East is a target of Al Qaida. And

America is a target too. And together, we will confront and we will defeat this threat to civilization.

We must stand with the good and decent people of Iran and Syria, who deserve so much better than the life they have today. Every peaceful nation in the region has an interest in stopping these nations from supporting terrorism. And every peaceful nation in the region has an interest in opposing Iran's nuclear weapons ambitions. To allow the world's leading sponsor of terror to gain the world's deadliest weapon would be an unforgivable betrayal of future generations. For the sake of peace, the world must not allow Iran to have a nuclear weapon.

Changes I have discussed today will not come easily. Change never does. But the reform movement in the Middle East has a powerful engine: demographics. Sixty percent of the population is under 30 years old. Many of these young people surf the Web, own cell phones, have satellite televisions. They have access to unprecedented amounts of information. They see what freedom has brought to millions of others and contrast that to what they have at home.

Today I have a message for these young people. Some tell you—some will tell you change is impossible, but history has a way of surprising us, and change can happen more quickly than we expect. In the past century, one concept has transcended borders, cultures, and languages: in Arabic, *hurriyya*; in English, freedom. Across the world, the call for freedom lives in our hearts, endures in our prayers, and joins humanity as one.

I know these are trying times, but the future is in your hands, and freedom and peace are within your grasp. Just imagine what this region could look like in 60 years. The Palestinian people will have the homeland they have long dreamed of and deserved: a democratic state that is governed by law, respects human rights, and rejects terror. Israel will be celebrating its 120th anniversary as one of the world's great democracies, a secure and flourishing homeland for the Jewish people.

From Cairo, Riyadh, Baghdad to Beirut, people will live in free and independent societies, where a desire for peace is reinforced by ties of diplomacy and tourism and trade. Iran and Syria will be peaceful nations, where today's oppression is a distant memory and people are free to speak their minds and develop their talents. Al Qaida, Hizballah, and Hamas will be defeated, as Muslims across the region recognize the emptiness of the terrorists' vision and the injustice of their cause.

This vision is the same one I outlined in my address to the Israeli Knesset. Yet it's not a Jewish vision or a Muslim vision, not an American vision or an Arab vision. It is a universal vision based on the timeless principles of dignity and tolerance and justice, and it unites all who yearn for freedom and peace in this ancient land.

Realizing this vision will not be easy. It will take time and sacrifice and resolve. Yet there is no doubt in my mind that you are up to the challenge, and with your ingenuity and your enterprise and your courage, this historic vision for the Middle East will be realized.

May God be with you on this journey, and the United States of America will be at your side.

Thank you for having me.

NOTE: The President spoke at 3 p.m. at the Maritim Sharm El Sheikh International Congress Center. In his remarks, he referred to Klaus Schwab, founder and executive chairman, World Economic Forum; President Mohamed Hosni Mubarak of Egypt and his wife Suzanne Thabet; Huda Janahi, managing director, Global Cargo & Traveller's Services; and Usama bin Laden, leader of the Al Qaida terrorist organization.

Interview With Richard Engel of NBC News in Sharm el-Sheikh
May 18, 2008

Mr. Engel. Mr. President, thank you very much for joining me.

The President. Richard. Thank you, sir.

President's Remarks at the Knesset in Jerusalem, Israel

Mr. Engel. In front of the Israeli parliament, the Knesset, you said that negotiating with Iran is pointless. And then you went further, you saying—you said that it was appeasement. Were you referring to Senator Barack Obama? He certainly thought you were.

The President. You know, my policies haven't changed, but evidently the political calendar has. People need to read the speech. You didn't get it exactly right ei-

ther. What I said was, is that we need to take the words of people seriously. And when, you know, a leader of Iran says that they want to destroy Israel, you got to take those words seriously. And if you don't take them seriously, then it harkens back to a day when we didn't take other words seriously.

It was fitting that I talked about not taking the words of Adolph Hitler seriously on the floor of the Knesset. But I also talked about the need to defend Israel, the need to not negotiate with the likes of Al Qaida and Hizballah and Hamas, and the need to make sure Iran doesn't get a nuclear weapon. It was a—but I also talked about a vision of what's possible in the Middle East.

Iran

Mr. Engel. Repeatedly, you've talked about Iran and that you don't want to see Iran develop a nuclear weapon.

The President. Yes.

Mr. Engel. How far away do you think Iran is from developing a nuclear capability?

The President. You know, Richard, I don't want to speculate, and there's a lot of speculation. But one thing is for certain: We need to prevent them from learning how to enrich uranium. And I have made it clear to the Iranians that there is a seat at the table for them if they would verifiably suspend their enrichment. And if not, we'll continue to rally the world to isolate them.

U.S. Foreign Policy/Iran

Mr. Engel. You've been rallying the world. Have you had some success on this Arab tour to try and—and Israeli tour—to mobilize this community against Iran? Is that part of your mission?

The President. No, it's not so much; actually, the place where I'm spending time, in terms of dealing with serious economic isolation, is with our European friends. They're the ones who have had significant trade with the Iranians. We're dealing with it not only in goods and services, trying to convince them to hold back goods and services until there's a verifiable suspension, but also dealing with the Iranian finances.

I don't have to spend too much time in the world—in this part of the world creating concerns about Iran. There is big concern about Iran, given the fact that Hizballah is destabilizing Lebanon, Hamas is trying to prevent the creation of a Palestinian state, and, of course, Iranian action inside of Iraq.

Iraq/Iran

Mr. Engel. A lot of Iran's empowerment is a result of the war in Iraq. How do you feel——

The President. Yes.

Mr. Engel. ——that Iran is—its position in the world is rising because of your actions in Iraq?

The President. See, I'm not so sure I agree with that. That's a premise I don't necessarily agree with. As a matter of fact, I think Iran is troubled by the fact that a young democracy is growing in Iraq. I—you know, this notion about somehow if Saddam Hussein were in power, everything would be fine in the Middle East is a ludicrous notion. Saddam Hussein was a sponsor of terror. And can you imagine what it'd be like to see an arms race between Saddam Hussein and Ahmadi-nejad, in terms of creating instability in the Middle East? As a matter of fact, the way to ultimately defeat those who use terror to destabilize young democracies is to help the young democracies succeed.

Progress in Iraq

Mr. Engel. I've watched Iran's influence grow in Iraq. It's been very steady over the years. What are you going to do to try and counteract——

The President. Yes.

Mr. Engel. ——Iran's influence?

The President. Well, Basra, for example, is—we stood by the Prime Minister's decision to move into Basra and to—continue to encourage the Prime Minister to go after Shi'a criminals and Shi'a armed militias that are doing harm to the average Iraqi and, at the same time, encourage him to use some of the Iraqi wealth to improve conditions of life. And that's what's happening. Basra is—it's still obviously got work to be done, but it was a successful operation, as you know better than me. He's now heading into Sadr City—he, the Iraqi Government—all aiming to protect innocent people from people who are operating outside the law. And to the extent that those are folks who are supported by Iran, it will serve as a defeat to Iran.

Iraq is changing. You know it better than anybody; you've been spending a lot of time there. And it's in the interest of the

United States that we help it continue to change to the better.

Freedom Agenda/Iran

Mr. Engel. You talked about Iran being a major threat to American policies in the region, with Hamas, Hizballah, militia groups in Iraq. Do you intend to finish your term in office with a military action of some kind against Iran?

The President. Richard, that's highly speculative. I've always made it clear that options are on the table. But, you know, the biggest weapon we have against those who can't stand freedom is the advance of freedom. I'm going to give a speech here in a minute that talks about the need to advance the freedom agenda in the Middle East.

And my—you know, Iran is a threat to people who want to live in peace. That's what they've clearly shown. I mean, the interesting thing in Lebanon is that Hizballah, which had sold itself as a protector against Israel, all of a sudden turned its weapons on the people of Lebanon and all the—the true colors. And sometimes in life there needs to be clarity in order for people to rally to solve a problem.

And so the best way to deal with the Iranians in the Middle East is to help the young democracy of Lebanon survive, is to stand up a Palestinian state—obviously, subject to the roadmap—which we intend to do before my Presidency, and succeed in Iraq.

Lebanon

Mr. Engel. How are you going to prevent Hizballah from taking over in Lebanon? They had a small coup. The army didn't do anything. And they proved that they are clearly in control of the streets when they want to be.

The President. Yes. Well, that's a problem. And obviously, one thing to do is to help strengthen the Lebanese Army, which I sent General Dempsey to Beirut—I don't know if he was there when you were there,

but he was there precisely to help inventory the Lebanese Army—is to make it clear to Prime Minister Siniora, we stand strongly with you. We'll see what happens out of this agreement and how—whether it sticks or not. But we strongly support the March 14th Coalition.

Perhaps one way to help deal with the situation is to get the U.N. tribunal up and running that's investigating the death of Mr. Hariri. But you know, no question, it's a tough situation. It's not as if Lebanon has been a stable situation forever either. I mean, this is—and yet the Lebanese people deserve a peaceful democracy, and our aim is to help them.

President's Remarks at the Knesset in Jerusalem

Mr. Engel. It sounded like, when you were addressing the Israeli Knesset, you gave a green light to Israel to take action against Hizballah and Hamas.

The President. I don't—Richard, you can read into it what you want to read into it. That certainly wasn't my intention. My intention was to say that all of us need to understand that radical groups are the threat to peace, whether it be Al Qaida or Hamas or Hizballah.

Iran

Mr. Engel. Negotiations with Iran—is that appeasement? Is that like——

The President. No.

Mr. Engel. ——appeasing Adolph Hitler?

The President. My position, Richard, all along has been that if the Iranians verifiably suspend their enrichment, which will be a key measure to stop them from gaining the know-how to build a weapon, then we—they can come to the table, and the United States will be at the table. That's been a position of my administration for, gosh, I can't remember how many years, but it's a clear position. We've stated it over and over again.

But I've also said that if they choose not to do that—verifiably suspend—we will continue to rally the world to isolate the Iranians. And it is having an effect inside their country. There's a better way forward for the Iranian people than to be isolated, and their leaders just need to make better choices.

U.S. Troop Levels in Iraq

Mr. Engel. In Iraq, I recently met a soldier. He was medevaced out on his first tour. He's now back on his second tour—was already medevaced to the green zone. How many more tours do these soldiers have to do? Is there an exit strategy for Iraq?

The President. Well, first of all, the fact that this person volunteered again speaks to the great bravery of our troops. And we need to honor them and will honor them. And one way to do so is to have more set tours: in for 12, out for 12.

The other thing is to take care of their families, and when they're veterans, take care of the vets. You know, the fact that you told me about a guy who got medevaced twice only says to me that we've got a courageous military.

In terms of success, we're returning troops on success. You might remember, I had to make a difficult choice to put more troops in. Those troops are coming home by July. And then, of course, General Petraeus and his successor will assess the situation on the ground, and we will end up having the troops necessary to help the Iraqis succeed.

U.S. Troop Levels in Iraq/Progress in Iraq

Mr. Engel. So it doesn't sound like there's an end anytime soon. It just sounds like we need to support them as much as we can and keep them there for as long as we can.

The President. I think the end, Richard, is, I told you, return on success. The more successful Iraq is, the fewer troops we'll need. And there's no question, Iraq is becoming successful. The security situation has changed; the political situation is a lot

better; the economic situation—unlike other parts of this world—are pretty strong. And now the question is, are they going to be able to get the resources in an efficient way to the people, so the people see the benefits of democracy? And they're doing a better job of that.

Progress in Iraq

Mr. Engel. You still view Iraq as a success. Because on the ground, it looks very bleak. People still want to leave the country, and people are——

The President. Well, that's interesting you said that. That's a little different from the surveys I've seen and a little different from the attitude of the actual Iraqis I've talked to, but you're entitled to your opinion.

Mr. Engel. The Iraqi Government, I think, has one position, which is that it's seeing a lot of progress. But Sadr City has been up in revolt. There's major battles in Mosul. I was just in a major firefight in Sadr City, hit by an EFP. It is still very much a war zone.

The President. Richard, no question, it's violent. But there's no question that the Iraqi Government are dealing with the violent people. It's like this attitude about Basra. I can remember, you know, a good reporter saying, "Basra is a disaster." I'm not suggesting you did, but people said, "It's a disaster." And lo and behold, it wasn't; it was successful.

What you're watching is an Iraqi Government take care of extremists in their midst so that a democracy can survive. And it's essential that this democracy survive for our own security as well as the stability of the Middle East.

Middle East Peace Process/Lebanon

Mr. Engel. You've talked about having a Israeli-Palestinian peace agreement by the end of this year.

The President. Right.

Mr. Engel. What gives you hope that that is not overly ambitious? Why do you think that's possible?

The President. Because, first of all, people in Israel understand that in order for them to have long-term security, there has to be a democratic state. People in Palestine want a democratic state. Now, there are people opposing that—Hamas, in particular—trying to create the violence and fear to stop the state from progressing.

Secondly, I know their leaders. I spent a lot of time with Prime Minister Olmert and President Abbas. They are dedicated to doing the hard work.

And thirdly, I've seen the progress being made on issues like——

Mr. Engel. What about Hamas? Hamas was elected——

The President. Excuse me for a minute, please—on issues like the border and refugees and security. And yes, Hamas was elected, and they've done a disaster in— of running Gaza. And there will be an interesting contrast between the vision of Hamas and their record and the vision of President Abbas and Prime Minister Fayyad and the Palestinian state. And it's that vision, the competing visions that will be put forth to the Palestinian people at some time.

And I believe a state will exist, and I know it's necessary for peace in the Middle East. And I think—I feel good that we can get it defined during my Presidency and implemented subject to roadmap.

Freedom Agenda/Al Qaida

Mr. Engel. Going back to your vision and the message you've been pushing about democracy and supporting moderates across the region, if you look back over the last several years, the Middle East that you'll be handing over to the next President has—is deeply problematic. You have Hamas in power, Hizballah empowered, taking to the streets, more—stronger than the Government, Iran empowered, Iraq still at war. What region——

The President. Richard.

Mr. Engel. ——are you handing over?

The President. Richard, those folks were always around; they were here. What we're handing over is a Middle East that, one, recognizes the problems—and the world recognizes them. There's clarity as to what the problems are. To say all of a sudden that Hamas showed up is just not factual. They have been around, and they have been dangerous. Hizballah has been around, and they are dangerous. They have been—that's why we put them on the terrorist list before my Presidency.

And what you're beginning to see is new democracies. You'll see a Palestinian state. You'll see a—Iraq emerging. And it doesn't happen overnight. The freedom movement is not a instant. The freedom movement is a challenge to a system that said, the status quo is acceptable, when underneath was brewing all kinds of resentments.

We've taken on Al Qaida in the Middle East. It was from here that they recruited people to launch attacks. And while they're still existing, they've been hurt. And they're going to be hurt even more as liberty advances and freedom advances.

Al Qaida/Iran

Mr. Engel. Do you believe that Iran is now more of a threat in Iraq than Al Qaida?

The President. You know, that's an interesting question. I believe—yes, I bet—I think they've both been seriously hurt in Iraq. And you know, Al Qaida thought they were going to have a stronghold in Anbar Province. They proudly proclaimed this was going to be their capital from which they were going to launch missions around the world and throughout the region, and they failed.

And in Iran [Iraq],* Shi'a groups funded by Iran have tried to take on the Government. And the Government is succeeding, and it's—but it's going to take a while.

———————
* White House correction.

War on Terror/Freedom Agenda

Mr. Engel. The war on terrorism has been the centerpiece of your Presidency. Many people say that it has not made the world safer, that it has created more radicals, that there are more people in this part of the world who want to attack the United States.

The President. Yes. That theory says, by confronting the people that killed us, therefore, there's going to be more; therefore, we shouldn't confront them.

Mr. Engel. Or creating more people who want to kill us, one could also say.

The President. Well, you can say that, but the truth of the matter is, there's fewer Al Qaida leaders; the people are on the run; they're having more trouble recruiting in the Middle East. Saudi Arabia, our partner, has gone after Al Qaida. People now see Al Qaida for what it is, which is a group of extremists and radicals who preach nothing but hate. And no, I just—it's just the beehive theory. We should have just let the beehive sit there and hope the bees don't come out of the hive.

My attitude is, the United States must stay on the offense against Al Qaida—two ways. One from——

Mr. Engel. But haven't you just smashed the bees——

The President. ——two ways——

Mr. Engel. ——in the hive and let them spread?

The President. Excuse me for a minute, Richard, two ways: One, find them and bring them to justice—what we're doing; and two, offer freedom as an alternative to their vision. And somehow to suggest that bees would stay in the hive is naive. They didn't stay in the hive when they came and killed 3,000 of our citizens.

Mr. Engel. Thank you very much for your time, Mr. President.

The President. Yes, sir. Yes.

Mr. Engel. Thank you.

NOTE: The interview was taped at 2:02 p.m. at the Hyatt Regency Sharm El Sheikh for later broadcast. In his remarks, the President referred to President Mahmud Ahmadinejad of Iran; Prime Minister Nuri al-Maliki of Iraq; Lt. Gen. Martin E. Dempsey, USA, acting commander, U.S. Central Command; Prime Minister Fuad Siniora of Lebanon; Gen. David H. Petraeus, USA, commanding general, Multi-National Force—Iraq; Prime Minister Ehud Olmert of Israel; and President Mahmoud Abbas and Prime Minister Salam Fayyad of the Palestinian Authority. The transcript was released by the Office of the Press Secretary on May 19.

Remarks Following a Meeting With Secretary of the Treasury Henry M. Paulson, Jr.
May 19, 2008

Secretary Paulson, thanks for coming. And I just got back from the Middle East, and the Secretary came over to talk about the economy and how he sees it. And we're working through tough times, and I appreciate the leadership you're providing.

He did assure me that the refund checks are heading out; people are getting that money. And that's good. It should help our economy and, more importantly, help people pay their bills. And we hope people use that money and take care of their families and shop.

I also asked him how he was doing in helping people stay in their homes. We spent time talking about the housing industry. And one of the really impressive programs has been the HOPE NOW program. Secretary Paulson has taken the lead in—to help people refinance and help people get the financial help necessary to stay in homes. And that help comes in all different kinds of ways, but generally, it just means that the lending institutions are—help a creditworthy person stay in their home, and that's what we want to have happen.

Since the program started, 1.4 million people got mortgage relief so they can stay in their homes. And in the first quarter of this year, 500,000 households, 500,000 families were helped.

And I appreciate your leadership on that, Hank. It's been—our policy in this administration is, we—laws shouldn't bail out lenders; laws shouldn't help speculators; the Government ought to be helping creditworthy people stay in their homes. And one way we can do that—and Congress is making progress on this—is the reform of Fannie Mae and Freddie Mac. That re-form will come with a strong, independent regulator.

The Secretary is briefing me on the progress being made on the Hill on this very important subject. Our fellow citizens have got to know that these major players in the mortgage markets, if reformed properly by Congress, will really help stabilize the markets and make it easier for people to stay in their homes.

And we look forward to working with Congress to get a good piece of legislation to my desk that helps our fellow citizens and helps us get through this housing issue.

So, Mr. Secretary, thank you for your briefing. I appreciate very much your leadership on the issue.

NOTE: The President spoke at 11:15 a.m. in the Oval Office at the White House.

Remarks on the Earthquake in China
May 20, 2008

Laura and I have come to the Chinese Embassy. Mr. Ambassador, thank you very much. Madam, thank you very much. We've come to express our country's condolences for those who mourn for the loved ones.

We stand ready to help in any way that the Chinese Government would like. We know there's great courage being displayed, Mr. Ambassador, as rescue workers search for those who may still be living.

This natural disaster is very hard on many of your people, and we understand that. And we extend our deepest sympathies and pray for recovery and pray for the strength of those who are—whose lives have been torn apart during this terrible tragedy.

Thank you.

NOTE: The President spoke at 10:13 a.m. at the Embassy of China. In his remarks, he referred to China's Ambassador to the U.S. Zhou Wenzhong and his wife Xie Shumin.

Statement on Senator Edward M. Kennedy
May 20, 2008

Laura and I are concerned to learn of our friend Senator Kennedy's diagnosis. Ted Kennedy is a man of tremendous courage, remarkable strength, and powerful spirit. Our thoughts are with Senator Kennedy and his family during this difficult period. We join our fellow Americans in praying for his full recovery.

Statement on Senate Confirmation of G. Steven Agee as United States Circuit Judge for the Fourth Circuit
May 20, 2008

Today Members of the Senate voted unanimously to confirm Justice Steven Agee to serve on the United States Court of Appeals for the Fourth Circuit. I appreciate their work on his nomination. Justice Agee is a man of integrity who is respected for his sound legal judgment and commitment to equal justice for all Americans. His work on the Supreme Court of Virginia and the Virginia Court of Appeals demonstrates that his rulings are based on the letter of the law. I am confident that he will serve on the fourth circuit with the same level of dedication and professionalism.

After I nominated Justice Agee on March 13, 2008, he received a hearing and a confirmation vote in less than 3 months. Unfortunately, many of my other judicial nominees have not received a timely confirmation process, and their nominations have been pending before the Senate Judiciary Committee for significantly longer.

Since the beginning of the 110th Congress, the Senate has only confirmed eight circuit court nominees. In the last 2 years of the past 3 administrations, the Senate has confirmed an average of 17 circuit court judges. I encourage the Senate to provide all judicial nominees with a swift and fair confirmation process.

Message to the Congress on Continuation of the National Emergency With Respect to the Stabilization of Iraq
May 20, 2008

To the Congress of the United States:

Section 202(d) of the National Emergencies Act (50 U.S.C. 1622(d)) provides for the automatic termination of a national emergency unless, prior to the anniversary date of its declaration, the President publishes in the *Federal Register* and transmits to the Congress a notice stating that the emergency is to continue in effect beyond the anniversary date. In accordance with this provision, I have sent the enclosed notice to the *Federal Register* for publication. This notice states that the national emergency declared in Executive Order 13303 of May 22, 2003, as modified in scope and

relied upon for additional steps taken in Executive Order 13315 of August 28, 2003, Executive Order 13350 of July 29, 2004, Executive Order 13364 of November 29, 2004, and Executive Order 13438 of July 17, 2007, is to continue in effect beyond May 22, 2008.

Obstacles to the orderly reconstruction of Iraq, the restoration and maintenance of peace and security in the country, and the development of political, administrative, and economic institutions in Iraq continue to pose an unusual and extraordinary threat to the national security and foreign policy of the United States. Accordingly, I have determined that it is necessary to continue the national emergency with respect to this threat and maintain in force the measures taken in response to this threat.

GEORGE W. BUSH

The White House,
May 20, 2008.

NOTE: The notice is listed in Appendix D at the end of this volume.

Remarks on the Situation in Cuba
May 21, 2008

Thank you all. *Bienvenidos*. Thanks for coming to mark this Day of Solidarity with the Cuban People. This is a day of pride, as we honor the culture and history of a noble nation. It's a day of sorrow, as we reflect on the continued oppression of the Cuban people. Most of all, this is a day of hope. We have hope because we see a day coming when Cubans will have the freedom of which they have dreamed for centuries, the freedom that is the eternal birthright of all mankind. And many of you here are working to hasten that day, and I thank you for your efforts.

I particularly thank the members of my Cabinet who've joined us. Madam Secretary, thank you for coming and being a staunch friend of the Cuban people. *Mi amigo* Carlos Gutierrez *y su familia*—for those of you in Cuba who are listening to this broadcast, I think it is important for you to know that Carlos is a Cuban American. He's now in the Cabinet of the President of the United States. All things are possible in a free society. Secretary Kempthorne, Secretary Chao, and Secretary Leavitt: Thank you all for coming as well. I appreciate Acting Secretary Bernardi of the Department of Housing and Urban Development.

I'm particularly thankful for Members of the United States Congress: Mel Martinez—all things are possible in a free society; Ileana Ros-Lehtinen; *los hermanos* Balart, Lincoln Diaz-Balart *y tambien* Mario Diaz-Balart. Thank you for coming. Congressman Chris Smith, Congressman

Darrell Issa, Congressman John Campbell, Congressman Gus Bilirakis: Thank you all for coming. Appreciate you all coming.

I appreciate the members of the diplomatic corps who've joined us. Thank you for being such good friends of the Cuban people. I want to thank the family members of the Cuban dissidents who are here. Welcome to the White House. Thank you for coming. *Y por fin*, Willy Chirino and his wife Lissette Alvarez, thank you all for coming.

This time of year holds great significance for the Cuban people. One hundred and thirteen years ago this week, Cuba lost its great poet and patriot Jose Marti. And 106 years ago this week, Cuba achieved the independence for which Marti gave his life. Jose Marti knew that true liberty would come to Cuba only with a just government of its people's choosing. He warned, "A regime of personal despotism would even be more shameful and more calamitous than the political despotism [Cuba] now endures."

Marti's warning proved truer than anyone could have imagined. Today, after nearly a half-century of repression, Cuba still suffers under the personal despotism of Fidel and Raul Castro. On the dictators' watch, Cuba's political freedoms have been denied. Families have been torn apart. The island's economy has been reduced to shambles. Cuba's culture has been drained of artists and scholars and musicians and athletes. And like the once grand buildings of Havana, Cuba's society is crumbling after decades of neglect under the Castros.

A few months ago, when Fidel handed over many of his titles to his brother Raul, the Cuban regime announced a series of so-called reforms. For example, Cubans are now allowed to purchase mobile phones and DVD players and computers. And they've been told that they will be able to purchase toasters and other basic appliances in 2010.

If the Cuban regime is serious about improving life for the Cuban people, it will take steps necessary to make these changes meaningful. Now that the Cuban people can be trusted with mobile phones, they should be trusted to speak freely in public. Now that the Cuban people are allowed to purchase DVD players, they should also be allowed to watch movies and documentaries produced by Cuban artists who are free to express themselves. Now that the Cuban people have open access to computers, they should also have open access to the Internet. And now that the Cuban people will be allowed to have toasters in 2 years, they should stop needing to worry about whether they will have bread today.

There is another problem with the regime's recent announcements. It is the height of hypocrisy to came—claim credit for permitting Cubans to own products that virtually none of them can afford. For the regime's actions to have any impact, they must be accompanied by major economic reforms that open up Cubans' inefficient state-run markets to give families real choices about what they buy and institute a free enterprise system that allows ordinary people to benefit from their talents and their hard work. Only when Cubans have an economy that makes prosperity possible will these announcements lead to any real improvements in their daily lives.

Real change in Cuba also requires political freedom. In this area too, the regime has made grand commitments. One of Raul's first acts after receiving his new titles was to sign a major United Nations treaty on human rights. Yet when it comes to respecting human rights on the island, the regime has not attempted even cosmetic changes. For example, political dissidents continue to be harassed, detained, and beaten, and more than 200 prisoners of conscience still languish in Castro's tropical gulag.

Recently, I received a letter from a man who spent 17 years in these dungeons. He described them as "dens of torture and pain and death." This is an undeniable violation of the U.N. treaty that Cuba just signed. If the regime views this document as anything more than a worthless piece of paper, it must immediately stop its abuse of political dissidents and release all political prisoners.

The world is watching the Cuban regime. If it follows its recent public gestures by opening up access to information and implementing meaningful economic reforms, respecting political freedom and human rights, then it can credibly say it has delivered the beginnings of change. But experience tells us this regime has no intention of taking these steps. Instead, its recent gestures appear to be nothing more than a cruel joke perpetuated on a long-suffering people.

America refuses to be deceived, and so do the Cuban people. While the regime embarrasses and isolates itself, the Cuban people will continue to act with dignity and honor and courage. In Cuba, advocates of liberty use this week to honor political prisoners who have sacrificed for the cause of freedom, like the brave writer named Pedro Luis Boitel. On May 17th, 1972, while on a hunger strike in prison, Boitel said: "They can kill and destroy my body, but never my spirit. This can never bend." Eight days later, Boitel died. He was 41 years old.

We see the same unbending courage in Cuba's political prisoners today. We see it in a man named Luis Enrique Ferrer Garcia. Luis Enrique is a peaceful prodemocracy advocate who was rounded up during the 2003 Black Spring. Luis Enrique received the longest sentence of all those arrested during the crackdown, condemned to 28 years in Castro's prisons. At times, this brave man has been trapped in a dark cell too small for him to stand. He suffers from high blood pressure and severe gastrointestinal illnesses. As his health obviously deteriorates, he has little access to his family.

We see this courage in a doctor named Oscar Elias Biscet. Dr. Biscet is a healer, a man of peace, and a determined activist for human rights. For all this, Dr. Biscet serves a 25-year sentence under the worst conditions. He was once put into solitary confinement for nearly 8 months, trapped in a small, dark, underground cell. He lost nearly 50 pounds and has lost almost all his teeth. He is in poor health. He is allowed very few visitors.

We see this courage in Cuba's *Damas de Blanco*. Every Sunday, these ladies in white march in silent and peaceful protest demanding the release of their loved ones. A few weeks ago, when about a dozen of these women held a peaceful sit-in at a public park, they were dragged from the area by a large proregime mob. One of the women was Berta Soler, whose husband Juan Angel Moya Acosta, is serving a 20-year sentence. Earlier this month, Berta told me personally: "Despite the torture, Cuba's political prisoners will not give in."

Recently, a former political prisoner asked me to remember his brothers languishing in Castro's jails. Through this Day of Solidarity with the Cuban People, we honor that request by speaking the names of Cuba's prisoners of conscience. They include men I have just mentioned. They include others, such as Ricardo Gonzalez Alfonso, Jose Luis Garcia Paneque, Normando Hernandez, Jorge Luis Gonzalez Tanquero, and Ariel *y* Guido Sigler Amaya. They include other names that many of you keep in your hearts and in your prayers.

These names are being whispered in Cuban cities from Pinar del Rio to Santiago de Cuba. These names are being echoed at Solidarity events across the world, as people from South America to Eastern Europe demand the release of all Cuban prisoners—political prisoners. Today these names are being recognized by the nation that will always be a friend of Cuban freedom, *los Estados Unidos*.

This is the first Day of Solidarity with the Cuban People, and the United States must keep observing such days until Cuba's freedom. We will continue to support the Cubans who work to make their nation democratic and prosperous and just. Since 2001, the United States has dramatically stepped up our efforts to promote freedom and democracy in Cuba. This includes our increased efforts to get uncensored information to the Cuban people, primarily through Radio *y* TV Marti.

Today I also repeat my offer to license U.S. NGOs and faith-based groups to provide computers and Internet to the Cuban people, if Cuban rulers will end their restrictions on Internet access. And since Raul is allowing Cubans to own mobile phones for the first time, we're going to change our regulations to allow Americans to send mobile phones to family members in Cuba. If Raul is serious about his so-called reforms, he will allow these phones to reach the Cuban people.

Through these measures, the United States is reaching out to the Cuban people. Yet we know that life will not fundamentally change for Cubans until their form of government changes. For those who've suffered for decades, such change may seem impossible. But the truth is, it is inevitable.

The day will come when Cubans freely receive information from many sources. The day will come when popular blogs are no longer blocked and broadcasts from the United States are no longer jammed. The day will come when Cuban leaders live up to the international human right documents they have signed, instead of making a mockery of them. The day will come when Cubans can speak their dissent and change their jobs and leave their country and return to it. And the day will come when they can worship the God Almighty without fear. The day will come when all political prisoners are offered unconditional release. And these developments will bring another great day, the day when Cubans choose their own leaders by voting in free and fair elections.

Today, 113 years after Jose Marti left us, a new postpatriot expresses the hopes of the Cuban people. With us this morning is songwriter Willy Chirino. Willy will perform a song that is on the Cuban people's lips and in their hearts. And here are some of the lyrics: *Nuestro dia ya viene llegando*.

As I mentioned, today my words are being broadcast directly to the Cuban people. I say to all those listening on the island today: Your day is coming. As surely as the waves beat against the Malecon, the tide of freedom will reach Cuba's shores. Until it does, know that you are in our prayers. And know that the Author of Liberty hears those prayers, *y que, con su ayuda, veremos a Cuba libre. Gracias, y que Dios los bendiga.*

NOTE: The President spoke at 10:28 a.m. in the East Room at the White House. In his remarks, he referred to former President Fidel Castro Ruz and President Raul Castro Ruz of Cuba; and former Cuban political prisoners Jorge Luis Garcia Perez and Miguel Sigler Amaya. The Office of the Press Secretary also released a Spanish language transcript of these remarks. The related proclamation of May 20, A Day of Solidarity With the Cuban People, is listed in Appendix D at the end of this volume.

Remarks on Signing the Genetic Information Nondiscrimination Act of 2008
May 21, 2008

I want to thank the Members of Congress who've joined us as I sign the Genetic Information Nondiscrimination Act. It's a piece of legislation which prohibits health insurers and employers from discriminating on the basis of genetic information. In other words, it protects our citizens from having genetic information misused. And this bill does so without undermining the basic premise of the insurance industry.

I also want to pay homage today to—and not only to Members of the Congress who are behind me but also to Senator Ted Kennedy, who has worked for over a decade to get this piece of legislation to a President's desk. All of us are so pleased that Senator Kennedy has gone home, and our thoughts and prayers are with him and his family.

Now it's my honor to sign the Genetic Information Nondiscrimination Act.

[*At this point, the President signed the bill.*]

Thank you.

NOTE: The President spoke at 2:05 p.m. in the Oval Office at the White House. H.R. 493, approved May 21, was assigned Public Law No. 110–233.

Statement on the Death of W. Hamilton M. Jordan
May 21, 2008

Laura and I are saddened by the death of Hamilton Jordan. Hamilton Jordan was a man whose love for American politics and his country took him at a young age from the State capitol in Georgia to the White House. As President Carter's close adviser, Hamilton played an important role in shaping our Nation's policies. We value his service to our country.

Hamilton Jordan was also a great community leader, using lessons learned during his personal struggle against cancer to encourage other cancer survivors to remain optimistic and embrace the blessings of each day. Through their work with Camp Sunshine, he and his wife Dorothy have helped thousands of children enjoy life as they cope with the challenges of cancer.

Our thoughts and prayers are with the Jordan family.

Message to the House of Representatives Returning Without Approval the "Food, Conservation, and Energy Act of 2008"
May 21, 2008

To the House of Representatives:

I am returning herewith without my approval H.R. 2419, the "Food, Conservation, and Energy Act of 2008."

For a year and a half, I have consistently asked that the Congress pass a good farm bill that I can sign. Regrettably, the Congress has failed to do so. At a time of high food prices and record farm income, this bill lacks program reform and fiscal discipline. It continues subsidies for the wealthy and increases farm bill spending by more than $20 billion, while using budget gimmicks to hide much of the increase. It is inconsistent with our objectives in international trade negotiations, which include securing greater market access for American farmers and ranchers. It would needlessly expand the size and scope of government. Americans sent us to Washington to achieve results and be good stewards of their hard-earned taxpayer dollars. This bill violates that fundamental commitment.

In January 2007, my Administration put forward a fiscally responsible farm bill proposal that would improve the safety net for farmers and move current programs toward more market-oriented policies. The bill before me today fails to achieve these important goals.

At a time when net farm income is projected to increase by more than $28 billion in 1 year, the American taxpayer should not be forced to subsidize that group of farmers who have adjusted gross incomes of up to $1.5 million. When commodity prices are at record highs, it is irresponsible to increase government subsidy rates for 15 crops, subsidize additional crops, and provide payments that further distort markets. Instead of better targeting farm programs, this bill eliminates the existing payment limit on marketing loan subsidies.

Now is also not the time to create a new uncapped revenue guarantee that could cost billions of dollars more than advertised. This is on top of a farm bill that is anticipated to cost more than $600 billion over 10 years. In addition, this bill would force many businesses to prepay their taxes in order to finance the additional spending.

This legislation is also filled with ear-marks and other ill-considered provisions. Most notably, H.R. 2419 provides: $175 million to address water issues for desert lakes; $250 million for a 400,000-acre land purchase from a private owner; funding and authority for the noncompetitive sale of National Forest land to a ski resort; and $382 million earmarked for a specific watershed. These earmarks, and the expansion of Davis-Bacon Act prevailing wage require-ments, have no place in the farm bill. Rural and urban Americans alike are frustrated with excessive government spending and the funneling of taxpayer funds for pet projects. This bill will only add to that frus-tration.

The bill also contains a wide range of other objectionable provisions, including one that restricts our ability to redirect food aid dollars for emergency use at a time of great need globally. The bill does not include the requested authority to buy food in the developing world to save lives. Addi-tionally, provisions in the bill raise serious constitutional concerns. For all the reasons outlined above, I must veto H.R. 2419, and I urge the Congress to extend current law for a year or more.

I veto this bill fully aware that it is rare for a stand-alone farm bill not to receive the President's signature, but my action today is not without precedent. In 1956, President Eisenhower stood firmly on prin-ciple, citing high crop subsidies and too much government control of farm programs among the reasons for his veto. President Eisenhower wrote in his veto message, "Bad as some provisions of this bill are, I would have signed it if in total it could be interpreted as sound and good for farm-ers and the nation." For similar reasons, I am vetoing the bill before me today.

GEORGE W. BUSH

The White House,
May 21, 2008.

Remarks at a Division Review Ceremony at Fort Bragg, North Carolina
May 22, 2008

The President. I want to thank you for the warm welcome to Fort Bragg. It is good to be at the home of the Airborne and Special Operation Forces. This is my fourth visit to Fort Bragg since I have been honored to be the President. Somehow I always find my way back to the "center of the universe." And every time I come, I look forward to saying, "Hooah!"

Audience members. Hooah!

The President. I'm pleased to be with the paratroopers of the all-American 82d Airborne Division. You know, you and my dad have something in common: You both enjoy jumping out of airplanes. [*Laughter*] He's jumped with the Golden Knights at Fort Bragg six times. Dad is America's only skydiving President, and that's a distinction he's going to keep as far as I'm concerned. [*Laughter*] Speaking of which, he has a message for all of you—of those of you jumping tomorrow: "Airborne, all the way!"

This is the first time since 2006 that five brigades from your division have assembled together. Most of you recently returned from extended 15-month deployments to the frontlines in Afghanistan and Iraq. We've asked a lot of you. You've achieved difficult objectives in a new kind of war. You've performed with skill and valor, and on behalf of a grateful nation: Welcome home.

I thank General Dave Rodriguez for his service to our country. I thank Pete Geren, Secretary of the Army, for joining us today. I appreciate Brigadier General Art Bartell,

Colonel Victor Petrenko. I want to thank Sergeant Major Tom Capel.

I'm honored to be here with the military families. I particularly want to say hello to Maureen McNeill, wife of General Dan McNeill. I know he'll be pleased that I recognized you here at this event when I see him. [*Laughter*]

I want to thank all the families of the paratroopers from the 82d Airborne Division who are here today. I welcome the families of the fallen heroes here today. It's such an honor to see the veterans of the 82d Airborne Division and other veterans who have joined us today.

I want them—to pay a special tribute to the wounded warriors from the 82d Airborne. Thank you for your courage.

I welcome the State and local elected officials and members of the Fort Bragg community. Thank you for supporting these troops.

Looking out on the units this morning, I see why the 82d Airborne is known as America's Guard of Honor. In your ranks, I see the strength of the greatest military the world has ever known. And in the families of Fort Bragg, I see the love and support that makes your service possible. The United States of America owes our troops in uniform a debt of gratitude, and we owe our military families the strong support necessary to make sure that they understand that we appreciate their sacrifices.

Every trooper in the 82d is a triple volunteer. You volunteered to join the Army, you volunteered to attend jump school, and you volunteered to undertake some of our military's most difficult missions by joining this elite division. Each of you is proud to wear the all-American patch of the 82d. And I am incredibly proud to be the Commander in Chief of such noble, courageous men and women.

As members of the 82d Airborne Division, you belong to a storied military tradition. When Allied forces landed in Normandy, their paratroopers of the 82d were among the first boots on the ground. When

Saddam Hussein invaded Kuwait in 1990, this division was among the first units to deploy to Operation Desert Shield. When our Nation announced that the 82d Airborne was flying toward Haiti in 1994, the country's oppressive leader began to make plans to fly out. Across the world, the 82d has come to represent the vanguard of freedom. And we salute all the brave veterans with us today who have ever marched in your ranks.

At the beginning of a new century, the men and women of the 82d Airborne have once again stepped forward to advance the cause of liberty. Since the attacks of 9/11, you have deployed on more missions than any other division in the United States Army. You've taken the battle to the terrorists abroad so we do not have to face them here at home. And you've shown the enemies of freedom that the 82d Airborne will never give any ground and will always fight all the way.

From the frontlines in Afghanistan, we welcome home the 4th Brigade Combat Team, which brought "Fury from the Skies" to America's enemies. We welcome home units of the Combat Aviation Brigade, which flew on "Pegasus Wings." We welcome home your Division Headquarters, your Special Troops Battalion, your commander, Major General Dave Rodriguez— "All-American Six."

During your deployment in Afghanistan, you served under NATO commander and longtime Fort Bragg resident General Dan McNeill. Under his leadership, and because of your courage, you took the fight to the enemy. And thanks to you, the Taliban no longer controls the Sangin Valley. And thanks to you, the Taliban's stronghold in the town of Musa Qala has fallen and a flag of a free Afghanistan has risen. Thanks to you, hundreds of insurgents have been captured in eastern Afghanistan; many others have been killed. And thanks to you, a nation where Al Qaida once plotted the attacks of 9/11 is now a democracy and an ally in the war against these extremists.

From the frontlines in Iraq, we welcome home the "Falcons" of the 2d Brigade, the "Panthers" of the 3d Brigade, the "Providers" of the 82d Sustainment Brigade, and units of the Combat Aviation Brigade.

When Operation Iraqi Freedom began, members of the 82d Airborne helped remove Saddam Hussein from power. The decision to remove Saddam Hussein was the right decision at the time, and it remains the right decision today.

With Saddam gone, our job was to help the Iraqi people defend themselves against the extremists and to build a free society. In 2006, that mission was faltering. I knew a victory was essential to our security, so we implemented a new strategy. Instead of retreating, we sent in more troops. And the first troops in as part of that surge were the troops of the Falcon Brigade of the 82d Airborne. Together with the Panther Brigade and other units of the 82d Airborne, you pursued the enemy in its strongholds; you denied the terrorists sanctuary; you brought security to neighborhoods that had been in the grip of terror. And across Iraq, violence is down, civilian deaths are down, sectarian killings are down, and attacks on American forces are down. You did the job we sent you to do. You have returned home on success. And all of America is proud of the 82d Airborne.

When I was looking for a commander to lead the surge, I turned to a former commander in the 82d Airborne, General David Petraeus. He's done a brilliant job leading our troops in Iraq. And when it came time to name a new leader for Central Command, he was my first and only choice. The United States Senate must give him a fair hearing, and they must confirm him as quickly as possible.

General Petraeus has reported that security conditions have improved enough in Iraq to return by the end of July to the pre-surge level of 15 combat brigade teams. So far, three brigades, including the Falcon Brigade, have redeployed without replacement as part of this drawdown. Two more brigades will follow in the months ahead. When we complete this drawdown, we will have reduced our combat brigades in Iraq by 25 percent from the year before. General Petraeus and our commanders will continue to analyze the situation on the ground and report back to me with their recommendations for future troop levels. But my message to our commanders is this: You will have all the troops, you will have all the resources you need to win in Iraq.

Often I've been asked, "What will success look like in Iraq?" So I want to share some thoughts with you. Success will be when Al Qaida has no safe haven in Iraq, and Iraqis can protect themselves. Success will be when Iraq is a nation that can support itself economically. Success will be when Iraq is a democracy that governs itself effectively and responds to the will of its people. Success will be when Iraq is a strong and capable ally in the war on terror. And when our country succeeds in Iraq, generations of Americans will be more secure.

The first condition for success in Iraq is a country that can protect its own people. Paratroopers gathered here have seen the Iraqis in action. They're brave people. They're courageous people. And with our training, they're becoming better soldiers. They're assuming greater responsibility for fighting the terrorists and policing the streets and defending their territory. And as a sign of their commitment to this mission, the Government in Baghdad launched a surge of 100,000 new troops.

In Mosul and other areas in northern Iraq, Iraqi forces have launched operations to drive Al Qaida from one of its few remaining major strongholds in the country. In Basra and Sadr City, Iraqi forces have led operations to clear out Iranian-backed special groups, illegal militias, and criminal gangs. The capability of the Iraqi security force is improving. They're winning battles.

In this fight, they have been joined by about 100,000 Iraqis who belong to citizens groups bearing the proud name of Sons of Iraq. Many of these groups are Sunni; some are Shi'a; some are mixed. But whatever their makeup, these groups are determined to expel the enemies of freedom and secure their communities and build a more hopeful future.

The enemies of free Iraq are determined to deny that future, and that means we can expect more violence. We can also expect the Iraqi security forces to be better equipped, better trained, and better able to take the fight to the enemy. And as they do, they can count on the United States of America.

The second condition for success in Iraq is a country that can support itself economically. Iraq's economy has made tremendous strides since the beginning of the surge. Inflation is declining. Economic growth is increasing. Investment in the energy and telecom industries is increasing. Energy production is on the rise. Listen, there are many challenges that remain, and there is work to be done to overcome decades of oppression and mismanagement. Yet Iraqis can take pride in the economic progress their country has made.

And they can take pride in the fact that they're paying a greater share of their own expenses. The—we provided critical help to Iraq early on. And now that the economy expands, the Government in Baghdad has a solemn responsibility to invest in its people, pay for its infrastructure, and pay for its own security.

The third condition for success in Iraq is a democracy that governs itself effectively and responds to the will of its people. Security has improved, and Iraqis have realized they don't have to rely on militias or other extremists for protection. And they're taking a growing interest in their country's political future.

In local communities, Iraqis are increasingly demanding reconciliation. They're demanding a better life for their families. In the Provinces, the tribes that rose up to cast off Al Qaida now look forward to casting votes and rebuilding their neighborhoods.

And in Baghdad, the Government is responding to these developments with an impressive string of legislative achievements. They passed a pension law, de-Ba'athification reform, a new budget, an amnesty law, and Provincial powers law. And while there's still a distance to travel, they have come a long way. Their legislative accomplishments would be notable in any country, but they're even more impressive considering the conditions the Iraqis have had to overcome.

As we look ahead, we cannot expect Iraq to suddenly put aside all their political differences. Sometimes we have a few of our own in the United States. We can't expect them to reach agreement on every issue. But we can expect Iraqis of all backgrounds to take an increasingly active role in the democratic process, share power, and settle disputes by debating in the halls of government rather than fighting in the streets.

The fourth condition of success in Iraq is a country that is an ally in the war on terror. The people of Iraq have seen the dark vision the enemy offers; they've rejected it. The Iraqis understand firsthand how the terrorists murder and maim with no respect for innocent life. It is no coincidence that a nation that has suffered mightily at the hands of terror is becoming a strong ally in the war against the terrorists.

And now the leaders of Iraq want to solidify their country's relationship with the United States. Last year, America and Iraq agreed to sign a long-term strategic partnership. This partnership would support future cooperation between our countries, without establishing permanent bases or without binding a future President to specific troop levels. Part of this agreement would provide legal protection for American troops in Iraq similar to those in other countries where our forces are deployed. And it would show our friends across the world that America will stand with them as they stand against terror.

The vision for success in Iraq that I just outlined will not come easily. There will be tough fighting ahead. But the progress is undeniable. Because of your bravery and your courage, the terrorists and extremists are on the run, and we are on our way to victory.

I know there have been some disagreements on the war on terror. But whenever—whatever—wherever Members of Congress stood on the decision of—to remove Saddam Hussein, we should be able to agree that our troops deserve America's full support. And that means the United States Congress needs to pass a responsible war funding bill that does not tie the hands of our commanders and gives our troops everything they need to complete and accomplish the mission.

Some of our fellow citizens wonder whether the mission in Iraq is worth the cost. I strongly believe it is. And here is why: The enemy has made clear that Iraq is the central battleground of the great ideological struggle of our time. This is a struggle between those who murder the innocent to advance their hateful objectives and those of us who love liberty and long for peace. We saw that these enemies—what these enemies intend for our country on September the 11th, 2001, and we must do everything in our power to stop the enemy from attacking us again.

Withdrawal from Iraq before we have achieved success would embolden Al Qaida and give them new safe havens from which to plot attacks on the American homeland. Withdrawal before success would embolden Iran in its nuclear weapons ambitions and its efforts to dominate the region. Withdrawal before success would send a signal to terrorists and extremists across the world that America is weak and does not have the stomach for a long fight. Withdrawal before success would be catastrophic for our country. It would more likely—be more likely that we would suffer another attack like the one we experienced on September the 11th. It would jeopardize the safety of future generations. And we must not, and we will not, allow that to happen.

By contrast, success in Iraq would deny Al Qaida a safe haven and hand Usama bin Laden a strategic defeat in the land where his terrorist movement has chosen to make a stand. Success in Iraq would deal a devastating blow to Iran's ambitions to dominate the region. Success in Iraq would show the people of the Middle East that democracy and freedom can flourish in their midst. And success in Iraq would send a signal to the world that America does not withdraw, does not retreat, does not back down in the face of terror. And that will make us safer here in the United States of America.

America is fortunate to have courageous men and women who volunteer to protect us during these dangerous time. We've seen that courage in the story of Sergeant First Class Benjamin Sebban of the 82d Airborne. As a senior medic in his squadron, Ben made sacrifice a way of life. When younger medics were learning how to insert IVs, he would always offer up his own arm for practice. And when the time came, Ben did not hesitate to offer his fellow soldiers far more.

On March 17, 2007, in Diyala Province, Ben saw a truck filled with explosives racing toward his team of paratroopers. He ran out in the field to warn them, exposing himself to a blast. Ben received severe wounds, but this good medic never bothered to check his own injuries. Instead, he devoted his final moments on Earth to treating others. This morning, it was such a great honor to be able to present Ben's mom the Silver Star.

We pray that a loving God comforts his family. We pray that a loving God comforts the families of all the fallen. We will always honor their memory. And we pledge that their sacrifice shall not be in vain.

Our mission in Iraq has been long and trying. But when the history books are written, they will show that this generation of heroes was as great as any in the history of our Nation. They will show that America refused to shrink in the face of terror. They will show that freedom prevailed.

Thank you for who you are. Thank you for what you do. Yesterday, today, and tomorrow, you are America's Guard of Honor. May God bless you, and may God bless America.

NOTE: The President spoke at 10:54 a.m. In his remarks, he referred to Maj. Gen. David Rodriguez, USA, commander, Col. Victor Petrenko, USA, chief of staff, and CSM Thomas Capel, USA, command sergeant major, 82d Airborne Division; Brig. Gen. Arthur M. Bartell, USA, deputy commanding general, XVIII Airborne Corps and Fort Bragg; Gen. Dan K. McNeill, USA, commander, NATO International Security Assistance Force, Afghanistan; former leader Raoul Cedras of Haiti; Gen. David H. Petraeus, USA, commanding general, Multi-National Force—Iraq; Usama bin Laden, leader of the Al Qaida terrorist organization; and Barbara Filik Walsh, mother of Sfc. Benjamin L. Sebban, USA.

Remarks on World Trade Week
May 23, 2008

Thanks for coming. Please be seated. Welcome to the White House and the South Lawn. It's a joy to welcome entrepreneurs and business leaders and folks who understand the importance of this country being confident enough to work to open up markets for our goods and products and services. I'm—obviously, some of the exporters are pretty good sales men and women. After all, they let you drive a tractor here on the South Lawn. [*Laughter*] Imagine what the Secret Service was saying.

I'm really pleased to welcome Members of the Congress; Congressmen Petri and Herger are here. Thanks for coming. Petri is here because he's a—he believes in— the Harley-Davidson is a product that people around the world ought to be able to drive by making it more affordable—I suspect that's why you're here—as well as some other trucks made in your State.

I want to thank the members of the Cabinet. Thank you all for being such strong advocates of free and fair trade. We've got the Secretary of Agriculture here, Secretary Schafer. His being here sends a message that the American farmer and rancher expects us to work hard to open up markets for the products they grow. So if you're a farmer out there in the heartland, it seems like you'd want somebody working on your behalf here in Washington to be able to make it easier for you to sell your crops. And that's exactly what we're doing in this administration. Mr. Secretary, thanks for coming.

Carlos Gutierrez is the Secretary of Commerce. Trade means commerce. Elaine Chao is here from the Department of Labor. Madam Secretary, thank you. Your presence here is clear recognition that the more products we sell overseas, the more likely it is somebody's going to work.

And today I'm going to spend some time so our fellow citizens understand the importance of trade by connecting trade with products with jobs. Good jobs policy is a good trade policy.

I appreciate very much Sue Schwab here. She's the U.S. Trade Representative. Her job is to open up markets. And I'm going to talk about three trade agreements that she's worked hard to put in place that open up markets for U.S. goods and services. I really appreciate John Veroneau joining us as well. He's the deputy. His job is to also work with the Ambassador to open up markets.

I want to thank Federico Humbert, the Ambassador *de* Panama. I want to thank Lee Tae-sik, Ambassador from South Korea. I want to thank Mariana Pacheco, who is the Deputy Chief of Mission for the Embassy of Colombia. These are three nations I'm going to be talking about. I want to thank you all for coming. It's a— I really appreciate you giving me a chance to talk about your countries in your presence, because I want your leaders to understand the Bush administration and a lot of Members of Congress believe it's in our national interest that we have free and fair trade with your nations.

I thank the representatives of the companies whose products are here. I want to thank the members of the business community. And thanks for your caring about your country.

But first of all, the—you know, it's a rough economic times. Small-business owners know what I'm talking about; large-business owners know what I'm talking about. It's a period of uncertainty. And one way to deal with uncertainty in the economy is to work from your strengths. One strength, of course, is to trust the American people. And the best way to trust them is to keep your taxes low. I mean, we really don't need to be sending—[*applause*]. If there's uncertain times, there's no worse signal to send, that, you know, we may be raising your taxes. That creates even more uncertainty. There's got to be consistency in the Tax Code so people can plan, so individuals can plan and small business can plan and large businesses can plan. Congress needs to make the tax relief we passed permanent in order to deal with the uncertainty in the economy.

Of course, they got a huge appetite for spending your money, so it shouldn't surprise you that some up there really do want to raise your taxes. And we'll do everything we can and—that we're not going to let them raise your taxes. But the best signal that Congress could send, for the sake of economic growth and vitality, is that we're going to keep your taxes low by making the tax cuts permanent.

Another thing Congress can do is pass trade agreements that open up markets. You know, 40 percent of our growth last year—during a time of economic uncertainty, 40 percent of the growth came as a result of exports. So when I say, play to our strength, one of the strengths during this period of time is to continue to export products. If the growth that we had during some quarters, recent quarters was as a result of exports, it seems like we ought to be working to create more exports to be able to sell our goods and services into more markets.

And we have an opportunity to do that by opening up markets with Colombia, Panama, and South Korea. You know, we trust you to create jobs. The Government ought to trust you by opening up more markets, by making sure the playing field is level for our producers. That's all we want. We just want to be treated fairly in the world.

For some in Washington, trade is a good political issue. In other words, people think it makes good politics to say, "We're not going to let you trade." But what they've got to understand—those voices of pessimism and voices of protectionism must understand that oftentimes, opening up markets means the difference between giving employees a pay raise or a pay cut. The politicians in Washington who use trade as an issue to frighten voters must understand that opening up markets can mean the difference between expanding the number of workers, as opposed to shrinking the number of workers.

And our fellow citizens, I understand, you know, have got concerns about trade. And the reason why we've asked you to bring some of your products here is to remind people that that motorcycle is made by American workers, and that if we're able to more likely sell those motorcycles into

Colombia, for example, or Panama or South Korea, that the worker who made that is more likely to get a pay raise or have somebody else join him or her on the floor. That's the practicality of trade.

The interesting thing about trade as an issue, if you really study the issue of free and fair trade, leaders from both parties have been strong advocates for opening up markets. They really have been. I mean, generally this has been a—not nearly as bitter an issue in the past as it is today. You know, I remember reading about John F. Kennedy's stand on trade. He was a strong believer in free and fair trade. My predecessor, President Clinton, worked hard to open up markets. It's interesting that a lot of the people that worked with the President have been here to the White House to, I guess, first, test my temperature to determine whether I really was willing to strongly advocate opening up markets. And then when they realized that they had a steady ally, were willing to go out and declare publicly that they believed that we ought to open up markets.

And yet today, there's just a different attitude, evidently. But I want to thank you for helping to try to change that attitude by bringing a practical—some practical thoughts to this debate, kind of fight through all the rhetoric and remind our fellow citizens that—of some of the facts. One, our economy grows better when we export; two, there are jobs. When we talk about trade, we're talking about helping people keep work. And it turns out, if you're working for a company that exports goods and services, you make better money. Isn't that an interesting fact? If you're working for a company that sells goods and services overseas, you're going to make more money than your neighbor in a comparable industry.

If you're a farmer—we got some products here, grown right here in the United States of America. If you're a farmer, it seems like you want people to work hard to make it easier for you to sell that orange

somewhere else. Increased demand means it's more likely you'll be able to sell your crop.

Trade is in the interests of the working people here in America, pure and simple. Trade is in the interests of small-business owners and farmers and ranchers, pure and simple. And that's why I'm a strong believer that the United States Congress needs to pass trade agreements with Colombia, Panama, and South Korea.

Now, let me give you some of the practical lessons of why. Take dairy products: There's a 20-percent tariff on dairy products from the United States into Colombia; 36 percent into Korea. That means that the cost of that dairy product—chunk of cheese—you know something about cheese, Petri, in Wisconsin—a chunk of cheese is going to be 20 percent more expensive, which makes it harder to sell that product.

When you say, level the playing field, what I'm talking about is reducing tariffs on goods and services, which makes it easier to sell product. In other words, it's less expensive. The quality is the same. We're really good at what we make and what we grow. The quality is the same, but the price is less, which makes it more likely something is going to be purchased.

Fruits, oranges—these oranges right here are taxed at 15 percent going into Colombia—they're 15 percent more expensive, 30 percent more in South Korea, and 15 percent more in Panama. Broccoli, they got a really high tariff on broccoli at my father's house. [*Laughter*] But there also happens to be one: 15 percent in Colombia, 27 percent in South Korea, and 15 percent in Panama.

So those are percentages, but you need to think about the percentage in terms of, it's that much more expensive to buy. And sometimes if you're shopping for an orange, that 15-percent differential means you're not going to buy it. Motorcycle—that motorcycle right there is 20 percent more expensive in Colombia, 8 percent more in Korea, and 15 percent more in Panama.

And so the purpose of a trade agreement is to reduce those tariffs, is to make the products less expensive. So if we get the deal done with Colombia, that motorcycle will be $4,000 less expensive. The great quality of Harley will be the same. There will be no diminution of how cool one is when they drive a Harley. [*Laughter*] But it's going to be easier for somebody to buy it.

This Case tractor—by the way, manufactured in Fargo, North Dakota—called a Case IH, will be $15,500 cheaper in Colombia. That could be a significant difference when it comes to somebody buying that tractor. And I hope the Case workers hear me loud and clear: The cheaper that is for somebody to buy in Colombia, the more work you're going to have.

The reason I brought these products here is, it means somebody is making them today and is going to be able to make them tomorrow if we'd level that playing field. And let me tell you why I talk about leveling the playing field. The first vote coming up is Colombia. I say, the first vote coming up is Colombia—you might remember, the vote has never been allowed to come up. The Speaker of the House pulled a parliamentary maneuver that sent a bad signal, and so it hasn't come up yet.

Our job is to say, let the people vote, let the Members of Congress vote. I like our chances if they let the Members of Congress vote. Congress has a way of sorting through all the noise and all the pessimism and oftentimes reaches the right conclusion.

Most of the goods coming from Colombia enter America duty free—isn't that interesting?—as a result of actions of Congress in the past. Most goods that Colombia makes comes to our country without any tax. And I've just described to you, the goods and services we send to Colombia are taxed. And that frankly doesn't seem very fair to me. It didn't seem fair to the Colombian Government either. They all—

they agree with me: Let's just treat each other fairly.

Their goods are not taxed; our goods are. It seems unfair to me. And people of Congress should understand how unfair it is to the workers in their districts or the farmers in their districts or the people who are working hard for a living in their districts that count upon selling goods overseas.

So the agreement we reached basically says that those oranges will go in duty free. Some of the products will go in duty free immediately; some of them will be phased in over time; but nevertheless, the playing field will be level. So here you hear, free and fair trade; that's the definition of free and fair trade. Colombia treats us just like we treat them. That's fair.

Secondly, the Colombia free trade vote, like these other free trade votes, have got national security implications. Colombia has got a very bold leader named President Uribe, who is a reformist. Panama has got a strong leader, who, by the way, went to Texas A&M University. He's a reformist. I had the honor of meeting the South Korean President at Camp David—first South Korean President to have come to Camp David—and I did so for a reason. Because I wanted to send a strong signal about our friendship with the people of South Korea. He's a strong, strong leader. All these leaders have got a clear vision about enhanced prosperity in their country. They care deeply about their people.

President Uribe has got a unique challenge in Colombia. He's facing a group of narcotraffickers who are violent, who use force to achieve political objectives, who are supported by some of the countries in the neighborhood. They're a threat to peace inside Colombia, and they provide a threat to the United States, in the sense that they—to the extent that they facilitate drug trafficking. It makes it here. And yet the President has stood strong in dealing with these folks. He is a clear example of a leader who has set the—an agenda that is bold, and he's following through with that agenda.

If we were to turn our back on Colombia by rejecting the free trade agreement, it would send a terrible signal to leaders willing to be courageous. It would send a bad signal to our friends. And in the case of Colombia, it would send a bad signal to the voices of false populism in South America. It's in our economic interest that we pass trade agreements. Oh, I know there's great debate about that. But I hope that people listen to the facts and understand the practical consequences of opening up markets for the products made here in the United States. Then they'll understand why all of us are so passionate about making sure we're treated fairly.

There's also a significant national security concern when it comes to America turning its back on friends. The region needs democracy; the region needs rule of law; the region needs stability; and the region needs strong leaders like President Uribe. And a rejection of the free trade agreement with Colombia will undermine that which the leader—the region needs.

It's interesting, I've been—you know, I constantly talk to fellow leaders on the telephone, and as you know, I've been traveling as well. And the—I've been asked quite frequently, "Why is it that your Congress won't pass a free trade agreement with Colombia, for starters?" And they ask that question first with amazement. They can't believe the great United States of America is not confident enough or wise enough to level the playing field when it comes to U.S. goods and services.

And once the tone of amazement passes, then there's this serious tone of concern— concerned about the United States becoming protectionist, concerned about the United States losing its confidence when it comes to the entrepreneurial spirit that

has made us great, concerned that we really don't seem to care about the plight of others. Because trade helps lift people out of poverty, trade is a powerful engine for change.

And all I can tell them is, is that politics is too strong right now. But I also tell them, I haven't given up hope. I haven't given up hope that that Colombia free trade agreement is going to make it to the floor of the Congress, and with your help, I hope you get it there. I haven't given up hope that the people will recognize that obstructionism is not leadership, that obstructing an important piece of legislation, not even allowing it to come to the floor for a vote, is not what the people expect.

And so my call on the leadership in the House is to let this trade agreement get to the floor; let the representatives of the people decide; let there be an open and honest debate about the merits of this piece of legislation, the merits from an economic perspective and the merits from a national security perspective. And then when you pass a Colombia free trade bill, we go to South Korea and Panama and get those bills passed. And then we can go to the people who are making these products here and say, we did the job you expected us to do.

Thank you all for coming. May God bless you.

NOTE: The President spoke at 10:54 a.m. on the South Lawn at the White House. In his remarks, he referred to President Martin Torrijos Espino of Panama; and President Lee Myung-bak of South Korea. The Office of the Press Secretary also released a Spanish language transcript of these remarks. The World Trade Week proclamation of May 15 is listed in Appendix D at the end of this volume.

The President's Radio Address
May 24, 2008

Good morning. This Memorial Day weekend, kids will be out of school, moms and dads will be firing up the grill, and families across our country will mark the unofficial beginning of summer. But as we do, we should all remember the true purpose of this holiday: to honor the sacrifices that make our freedom possible.

On Monday, I will commemorate Memorial Day by visiting Arlington National Cemetery, where I will lay a wreath at the Tomb of the Unknowns. The tomb is the final resting place of three brave American soldiers who lost their lives in combat. The names of these veterans of World War I, World War II, and the Korean war are known only to God, but their valor is known to us all.

Throughout American history, this valor has preserved our way of life and our sacred freedoms. It was this valor that won our independence. It was this valor that removed the stain of slavery from our Nation. And it was this valor that defeated the great totalitarian threats of the last century.

Today, the men and women of our military are facing a new totalitarian threat to our freedom. In Iraq, Afghanistan, and other fronts around the world, they continue the proud legacy of those who came before them. They bear their responsibilities with quiet dignity and honor. And some have made the ultimate sacrifice in defense of their country.

One such hero was Sergeant First Class Benjamin Sebban of the Army's 82d Airborne Division. As the senior medic in his squadron, Ben made sacrifice a way of life. When younger medics were learning how to insert IVs, he would offer his own arm for practice. And when the time came, Ben did not hesitate to offer his fellow soldiers far more.

On March 17, 2007, in Iraq's Diyala Province, Ben saw a truck filled with explosives racing toward his team of paratroopers. He ran into the open to warn them, exposing himself to the blast. Ben received severe wounds, but this good medic never bothered to check his own injuries. Instead, he devoted his final moments on this Earth to treating others. Earlier this week, in a ceremony at Fort Bragg, North Carolina, I had the honor of presenting Sergeant Sebban's mom with the Silver Star that he earned.

No words are adequate to console those who have lost a loved one serving our Nation. We can only offer our prayers and join in their grief. We grieve for the mother who hears the sound of her child's 21-gun salute. We grieve for the husband or wife who receives a folded flag. We grieve for a young son or daughter who only knows dad from a photograph.

One holiday is not enough to commemorate all of the sacrifices that have been made by America's men and women in uniform. No group has ever done more to defend liberty than the men and women of the United States Armed Forces. Their bravery has done more than simply win battles; it has done more than win wars; it has secured a way of life for our entire country. These heroes and their families should be in our thoughts and prayers on a daily basis, and they should receive our loving thanks at every possible opportunity.

This Memorial Day, I ask all Americans to honor the sacrifices of those who have served you and our country. One way to do so is by joining in a moment of remembrance that will be marked across our country at 3 p.m. local time. At that moment, Major League Baseball games will pause, the National Memorial Day Parade will halt, Amtrak trains will blow their whistles, and buglers in military cemeteries will play

"Taps." You can participate by placing a flag at a veteran's grave, taking your family to the battlefields where freedom was defended, or saying a silent prayer for all the Americans who were delivered out of the agony of war to meet their Creator. Their bravery has preserved the country we love so dearly.

Thank you for listening.

NOTE: The address was recorded at 10:06 a.m. on May 23 in the Cabinet Room at the White House for broadcast at 10:06 a.m. on May 24. The transcript was made available by the Office of the Press Secretary on May 23, but was embargoed for release until the broadcast. In his address, the President referred to Barbara Filik Walsh, mother of Sfc. Benjamin L. Sebban, USA. The Office of the Press Secretary also released a Spanish language transcript of this address.

Remarks During a Meeting With Leaders of Rolling Thunder, Inc.
May 25, 2008

The President. [*Inaudible*]—to get to know the leaders of Rolling Thunder. For our fellow citizens who don't know Rolling Thunder, Rolling Thunder is a—the moment in time here in Washington, on Memorial Day weekend, when thousands of motorcyclers come to the Nation's Capital to pay tribute to those who have died in service, those who sacrifice, and those who serve. And it's a magnificent sight.

We just choppered in, Artie, and I saw your brothers and sisters cranking up their machines and driving through the Nation's Capital. Many of them have got the flag on the back. And I am just so honored to welcome you back. I want to thank you and all your comrades for being so patriotic and loving our country as much as you do. And I think this is the—I don't know if this is the eighth time we've been together here, but pretty close.

Artie Muller. Pretty close, sir. Maybe one more.

The President. Yes, one more. [*Laughter*] Anyway, Artie is the main man, and this is his board of directors who have continued to rally people around the country.

I went to Greensburg, Kansas, Artie, and I came into this town that had been destroyed by a tornado. I was going to give the high school graduation speech, and rode in from the airport, and the motorcyclers were all lining the streets with the flags. And it made me feel great.

When people go to protest at the funeral of one of our brave soldiers that died in combat, Artie's folks are there to make sure that those protestors don't denigrate the moment.

And so you're doing a lot for the country.

Mr. Muller. Thank you.

The President. And our troops appreciate you, the veterans appreciate you, and your President appreciates you.

Mr. Muller. Thank you, Mr. President.

The President. Welcome.

NOTE: The President spoke at 12:54 p.m. on the South Lawn at the White House. Participating in the meeting was Artie Muller, national executive director, Rolling Thunder, Inc.

Statement on the Presidential Election in Lebanon
May 25, 2008

I congratulate Michel Sleiman on his election as President of Lebanon. I am confident that Lebanon has chosen a leader committed to protecting its sovereignty, extending the Government's authority over all of Lebanon, and upholding Lebanon's international obligations under U.N. Security Council resolutions, including 1559, 1701, and 1757.

I am hopeful that the Doha agreement, which paved the way for this election, will usher in an era of political reconciliation to the benefit of all Lebanese. We look forward to working with President Sleiman in pursuit of our common values of freedom and independence.

Remarks at a Memorial Day Ceremony in Arlington, Virginia
May 26, 2008

Thank you. Mr. Secretary, thank you for the kind introduction. Members of my Cabinet, members of the administration, Admiral Mullen, Members of the United States Congress—Senator Warner and Congressman Skelton—members of the military, our veterans, honored guests, families of the fallen: Laura and I are honored to be with you on Memorial Day, and thank you for coming.

A few moments ago, I placed a wreath upon the tomb of three brave Americans who gave their lives in service to our Nation. The names of these honored are known only to the Creator, who delivered them home from the anguish of war, but their valor is known to us all. It's the same valor that endured the stinging cold of Valley Forge. It is the same valor that planted the proud colors of a great nation on a mountaintop on Iwo Jima. It is the same valor that charged fearlessly through the assault of enemy fire from the mountains of Afghanistan to the deserts of Iraq. It is the valor that has defined the Armed Forces of the United States of America throughout our history.

Today we gather to honor those who gave everything to preserve our way of life.

The men and women we honor here served for liberty, they sacrificed for liberty, and in countless acts of courage, they died for liberty. From faraway lands, they were returned to cemeteries like this one, where broken hearts received their broken bodies. They found peace beneath the white headstones in the land they fought to defend.

It is a solemn reminder of the cost of freedom that the number of headstones in a place such as this grows with every new Memorial Day. In a world where freedom is constantly under attack and in a world where our security is challenged, the joys of liberty are often purchased by the sacrifices of those who serve a cause greater than themselves. Today we mourn and remember all who have given their lives in the line of duty. Today we lift up our hearts, especially to those who've fallen in the past year.

We remember Army Specialist Ronald Tucker of Fountain, Colorado. As a young man, Ronnie was known for having an infectious smile and a prankster's sense of humor. And then he joined the United States Army, which brought out a more mature side in him. Ronnie transformed from a light-hearted teenager into a devoted soldier and a dutiful son who called his mother every day from his post in Iraq. In his final act of duty, less than a month ago, he worked with other members of his unit to build a soccer field for Iraqi children. As he drove back to his base, an enemy bomb robbed him of his life. And today our Nation grieves for the loss of Ronnie Tucker.

We remember two Navy SEALs: Nathan Hardy of Durham, New Hampshire, and Michael Koch of State College, Pennsylvania. Nate and Mike were partners in the field, and they were close friends in the barracks. Through several missions together, they had developed the unique bond of brotherhood that comes from trusting another with your life. They even shared a battlefield tradition. They would often head into battle with American flags clutched to their chests underneath their uniform. Nate and Mike performed this ritual for the last time on February the 4th. They both laid down their lives in Iraq after being ambushed by terrorists. These two friends spent their last few moments on Earth together doing what they loved most, defending the United States of America. Today Nathan Hardy and Mike Koch lay at rest next to each other right here on the grounds of Arlington.

The men and women of American Armed Forces perform extraordinary acts of heroism every single day. Like the Nation they serve, they do not glory in the devastation of war. They also do not flinch from combat when liberty and justice are embattled. Ronald Tucker, Nathan Hardy, and Mike Koch make clear: They do not waver, even in the face of danger.

And so today, here in Washington and across our country, we pay tribute to all who have fallen, a tribute never equal to the debt they are owed. We will forever honor their memories. We will forever search for their comrades, the POWs and MIAs. And we pledge—we offer a solemn pledge to persevere and to provide the security for our citizens and secure the peace for which they fought.

The soil of Arlington and other sites is filled with liberty's defenders. It is nourished by their heroism. It is watered by the silent tears of the mothers and fathers, and husbands and wives, and sons and daughters they left behind. Today we pray for God's blessings on all who grieve and ask the Almighty to strengthen and comfort them today and every day.

On this Memorial Day, I stand before you as the Commander in Chief and try to tell you how proud I am at the sacrifice and service of the men and women who wear our uniform. They're an awesome bunch of people, and the United States is blessed to have such citizens.

I am humbled by those who've made the ultimate sacrifice that allow a free civilization to endure and flourish. It only remains for us, the heirs of their legacy, to have the courage and the character to follow their lead and to preserve America as the greatest nation on Earth and the last, best hope for mankind.

May God bless you, and may God bless America.

NOTE: The President spoke at 11:15 a.m. in the Amphitheater at Arlington National Cemetery. In his remarks, he referred to Secretary of Defense Robert M. Gates; Adm. Michael G. Mullen, USN, Chairman, Joint Chiefs of Staff; and Susan Arnold, mother of Spc. Ronald J. Tucker, USA. The Office of the Press Secretary also released a Spanish language transcript of these remarks. The Prayer for Peace, Memorial Day proclamation of May 22 is listed in Appendix D at the end of this volume.

Remarks Following a Meeting With NCAA Football Head Coaches
May 26, 2008

The President. I just welcomed five of our Nation's university coaches to the Oval Office to thank them for going overseas to boost the morale of our troops. It was very interesting listening to them. Charlie Weis is going to say a few comments about what they saw and heard. But I wanted them to know how much I appreciate—and the—of going to say to these young men and women, "Thanks for what you're doing."

This is Memorial Day. It's a day to honor not only those who have died in combat, but it's to honor those who continue to serve. And these men make a living motivating young men on the football field, and I am absolutely confident that when our soldiers and sailors and marine and airmen and Coast Guard men and women met them, that they inspired them.

And most importantly, I'm confident what they heard was America appreciates what they do. We can't thank our troops enough for the sacrifices they're making on behalf of the Nation. And so I want to—I'm so grateful for you all for going, and I'm really grateful that you expressed the gratitude of the American people.

Now, Charlie, you may want to say a few things.

Charlie Weis. Thank you, Mr. President.

The President. Notre Dame man.

Mr. Weis. I think that Mr. President definitely had the inspired part right, but that inspire part definitely worked both ways. Now, we went over there to help motivate the morale of the troops, but I think we came home probably more inspired than even they were. I mean, it was just an unbelievable experience to watch the enthusiasm and the pride and the teamwork over there.

And I mean, I can't—we saw thousands and thousands of troops, and when they heard that we were coming to the White House on Monday, to a man and to a woman, almost everyone said, "Could you just pass on one message to the President," and asked us to thank him for them—for him supporting them. I mean, think about it. They're there for 4 months, 6 months, a year—it was just unbelievable—from Germany, you watch—you know, seeing guys and girls that had gotten injured in battle and the—you know, their framework, their psyche—it was just an unbelievable experience.

And I think all five of us said we just wish we could have brought our players over there, you know, the 18-to-23-year-olds that we deal with, so they could see what maturity looks like at a young age and teamwork at its utmost. And I tell you what, on behalf of all five coaches—I can tell—it was just an invigorating experience, one that we'll always treasure the rest of our lives.

And we got something special going on over there, because there wasn't one person, of the thousands and thousands of soldiers we met, that had one negative thing to say. And that's almost overwhelming to think about it—not one. And there were a couple at the end of their year tours that were very much looking forward to getting their call to go home. But I'll tell you what, it was great. And what a perfect way to end up our trip, to end up at the White House on Memorial Day.

Thank you.

The President. Thank you very much. Thank you all.

NOTE: The President spoke at 1:17 p.m. on the South Lawn at the White House. Participating in the meeting were Tommy Tuberville, head coach, Auburn University football team; Mark Richt, head coach, University of Georgia football team; Randy Shannon, head coach, University of Miami football team; Charlie Weis, head coach, University of Notre Dame football team; and Jack Siedlecki, head coach, Yale University football team.

Remarks Following a Tour of Silverado Cable Company in Mesa, Arizona
May 27, 2008

The President. I've come to Silverado for a couple of reasons: one, to remind our fellow citizens how important small businesses are to the backbone of our economy. These two brothers started this company with five employees.

Robert Simpson. Five employees.

The President. How many you got now?

Robert Simpson. We have 70.

The President. Seventy. One of the things that's important in law is to encourage certain behavior, and the stimulus package we passed encouraged investment. And so the—these guys were showing me a new laser machine they purchased this year. And they purchased it this year because the stimulus package provided a tax incentive to do that. And the reason why that's important is when the economy slowed down, we wanted to stimulate activity.

And so the fact that they purchased the machine meant somebody had to make the machine. And when somebody makes a machine, it means there's jobs at the machine-making place. Plus, their employees are more productive; they're more competitive. It makes it more likely they're going to keep their business and expand their business.

And so the first thing I want to do is, one, thank you for being entrepreneurs, and two, remind our citizens that this stimulus package that we passed in Congress is just beginning to kick in. And it's going to make a positive contribution to economic growth.

The other thing that's important to remember is that a company such as these—as this one pays taxes at the individual income tax rate. So when you hear these politicians campaign and say, "We're going to raise taxes, oh, just on the rich people," they're raising taxes on companies like Silverado.

What you don't want to do is take money out of the treasuries of these small businesses across America. If you're interested in economic vitality and growth, you want these—owners of these small businesses to have more money to invest. It's good for their employees, it's good for their growth, and it's good for our Nation.

And so I strongly urge the United States Congress to make the tax relief we passed permanent so that companies such as Silverado don't have to worry about what their tax burden is going to be in 2 years come. See, we're in—we have times of economic uncertainty right now, and what creates more uncertainty for owners of businesses like these is whether or not their taxes are going to go up.

And Congress ought to just declare once and for all: We're going to make the tax cuts we passed permanent. It will be—add peace of mind for these business leaders. It'll make it easier for their employees to keep a job. It'll make it easier for them to do what they want to do and take care of their—people that work here.

And so I'm thrilled to be with you. Congratulations on——

Robert Simpson. It's our pleasure. Thank you so much, Mr. President.

The President. Congratulations on being dreamers and doers.

Mitch Simpson. Thank you, Mr. President. Thank you.

The President. Yes, sir. I loved meeting your employees too.

Robert Simpson. Well, if you have just a minute, I have a few more back there.

The President. All right, good. Thank you.

NOTE: The President spoke at 3:07 p.m. In his remarks, he referred to Robert Simpson, president, and Mitch Simpson, vice president, Silverado Cable Co.

Statement on the Situation in Burma
May 27, 2008

I am deeply troubled by the Burmese regime's extension of National League for Democracy general secretary and Nobel Peace Prize winner Aung San Suu Kyi's house arrest on May 27. Aung San Suu Kyi's current house arrest dates back to May 2003, when she was detained following the murderous assault by regime-sponsored thugs on her motorcade in Depayin. The United States calls upon the regime to release all political prisoners in Burma and begin a genuine dialogue with Aung San Suu Kyi, the National League for Democracy, and other democratic and ethnic minority groups on a transition to democracy.

The United States will continue to help the people of Burma recover from the devastation of Cyclone Nargis and will continue to support the Burmese people's long-term struggle for freedom. Laura and I look forward to the day when the people of Burma know true liberty and democracy.

Commencement Address at the United States Air Force Academy in Colorado Springs, Colorado
May 28, 2008

Thank you. Mr. Secretary, thank you for the kind introduction. General Moseley, General Regni, Mr. Congressman: Thank you. Academy staff and faculty, distinguished guests, and proud family members: I am so pleased to stand before the future leaders of the United States Air Force.

I have something I'd like to say to the Cadet Wing: Class of 2008! [*Applause*] Yes, that's good. I was a little worried you we're going to yell, "Give him the Bird!" [*Laughter*]

You're the 50th graduating class in the history of the Air Force Academy. Each of you has worked hard to reach this mo-
ment. You survived "Beast," "Terrazzo sailing," "fatty bags" at Mitch's. [*Laughter*] You earned your "prop and wings" at Pinnacle. And today you will receive your degree and commission as Air Force officers. Your teachers are proud of you, your parents are proud of you, and so is your Commander in Chief. Job well done.

The superintendent informs me that some of you are still on restriction. [*Laughter*] It might be because you were caught running from the "lightning van." [*Laughter*] Or it might be because of "Jimmy Chad's apple." [*Laughter*] Whatever the reason you got your form 10, help has arrived. [*Laughter*] In keeping with a long-standing tradition, I hereby absolve all cadets who are on restriction for minor conduct offenses. As for your grades, well, some things are even beyond the powers of the President. [*Laughter*]

In becoming officers of the United States Air Force, you have chosen a vocation that is both hazardous and rewarding. As a former F–102 pilot, I know the exhilaration of flight. As the son of an aviator who was shot down in combat, I know its perils. Whether you serve in the skies above or on the ground below, each of you has stepped forward to defend your country. You've chosen to face danger in foreign lands so your fellow citizens do not have to face danger in our own land. And I want to thank you for making this courageous choice. And all of America is grateful to the class of 2008.

When you put on your second lieutenant bars in a few moments, you will become part of a great history, a history that is still only beginning to unfold. By any standard, air power is still a relatively new phenomena. Men have been fighting on land and at sea for thousands of years, yet there are still Americans among us who were born before man ever flew. In the lifetime of one generation, our Nation has seen aviation progress from that first tentative lift-off at Kitty Hawk to an age of supersonic flight and space exploration.

And as flight has progressed, it changed the face of war. In the 20th century, air power helped make possible freedom's victory in great ideological struggles with fascism and communism. In those struggles, our Nation faced evil men with territorial ambitions and totalitarian aims who murdered the innocent to achieve their political objectives. Through a combination of military strength and national resolve and faith in the power of freedom, we defeated these adversaries and secured the peace for millions across the world.

And now in the 21st century, our Nation is once again contending with an ideology that seeks to sow anger and hatred and despair, the ideology of Islamic extremism. In today's struggle, we are once again facing evil men who despise freedom and despise America and aim to subject millions to their violent rule. And once again, our Nation is called to defeat these adversaries and secure the peace for millions across the world. And once again, our enemies will be no match for the men and women of the United States Air Force.

You know, what's remarkable about this class is that each of you knows the stakes in the war on terror. You applied to this Academy after seeing the attacks of September the 11th, 2001. You came to this Academy knowing that the responsibility of our military is to protect the American people. And you now leave this Academy to take your place in this great struggle. Today I've come to talk to you about the battle you're about to join, the lessons we can learn from the conflicts of the past, and what they can teach us about the challenges we face in the war on terror that will dominate your military careers.

First lesson is this: In both the 20th century and today, defeating hateful ideologies requires all elements of national power, including the use of military power. The military power that you will wield in your military careers is much more precise and effective than in past generations.

When the United States entered World War II, the age of long-range bombing was just beginning. There were no computer guidance, no GPS targeting, or laser-guided munitions. The allied bombing raids against Germany and Japan resulted in horrific civilian casualties and widespread destruction. It took nearly 4 years before the regimes in Berlin and Tokyo finally capitulated, with difficult battles from the deserts of North Africa to the forests of France to the islands of the Pacific.

Today, revolutionary advances in technology are transforming warfare. During

Operation Iraqi Freedom, for example, we employed military capabilities so precise that coalition air crews could take out a tank hiding under a bridge without damaging the bridge. With this military technology, we can now target a regime without targeting an entire nation. We've removed two cruel regimes in weeks instead of years. In Afghanistan, coalition forces and their Afghan allies drove the Taliban from power in less than 2 months. In Iraq, with the help of the United States Air Force, our troops raced across 350 miles of enemy territory to liberate Baghdad in less than 1 month, one of the fastest armored advances in military history.

These facts create both opportunities and challenges. One opportunity is that if we have to fight our enemies, we can now do so with greater precision and greater humanity. In the age of advanced weapons, we can better strike—we can better target strikes against regimes and individual terrorists. Sadly, there will be civilian casualties in war. But with these advances, we can work toward this noble goal: defeating the enemies of freedom while sparing the lives of many more innocent people, which creates another opportunity, and that is, by making war more precise, we can make war less likely.

For hostile dictators, it is a powerful deterrent to know that America is willing and able to target their regimes directly. When rulers know we can strike their regimes while sparing their populations, they realize they cannot hide behind the innocent. And that means they are less likely to start conflicts in the first place.

Our unmatched military power also creates challenges. Because no adversary can confront and defeat our military directly, the enemies of the 21st century will increasingly turn to the use of asymmetric warfare. We've seen this in Afghanistan and Iraq. In those countries, our adversaries did not lay down their arms after the regime had been removed. Instead, they blended into the civilian population and with the

help of stateless terrorist networks continued the fight through suicide bombings and attacks on innocent people. In the 21st century, this Nation must be prepared to fight this new kind of warfare.

To meet this new challenge, we need to continue to develop technologies that put unprecedented speed and precision and power in your hands. And that's what we're doing. Since 2002, the number of unmanned aerial vehicles in our arsenal has increased nearly 40-fold to more than 5,000, and we're increasing them even more. We've transformed the Special Operations Command and more than doubled its budget. We're improving our intelligence and surveillance and reconnaissance capabilities. We're transforming our ground forces for the wars of the 21st century, making them faster and more agile and more lethal.

And you'll see the impact of these changes in your own Air Force careers. Instead of serving at 10,000 feet, some of you will serve on the ground as battlefield airmen, deploying behind enemy lines and using laser technology to fix targets on—for aviators circling above. Instead of sitting in jet fighter cockpits, some of you will sit before computer consoles at bases here in the United States, where you'll guide Predator UAVs half a world away and use them to strike terrorist hideouts. These and other changes will increase your ability to prevail in asymmetric warfare. They will make you more effective in the defense of freedom.

Another challenge of asymmetric warfare is that it requires patience. Our new enemies know they can't defeat us militarily. So their strategy is to cause us to lose our nerve and retreat before the job is done. They take advantage of the information age and the 24-hour news cycles, creating images of chaos and suffering for the cameras in the hope that these images will horrify the American people and undermine resolve and morale here at home. This means that to win the first war of the 21st century, we need to prevail not just in the battle of arms but also in the battle of wills. And we need to recognize that the only way America can lose the war on terror is if we defeat ourselves.

The second lesson is this: In both the 20th century and today, defeating hateful ideologies requires using our national resources to strengthen free institutions in countries that are fighting extremists. We must help these nations govern their territorial—territory effectively so they can deny safe haven to our common enemies. And in Afghanistan and Iraq, where we removed regimes that threatened our people, we have a special obligation to help these nations build free and just societies that are strong partners in the fight against these extremists and terrorists.

We've assumed this obligation before. After World War II, we helped Germany and Japan build free societies and strong economies. These efforts took time and patience, and as a result, Germany and Japan grew in freedom and prosperity. Germany and Japan, once mortal enemies, are now allies of the United States. And people across the world have reaped the benefits from that alliance. Today, we must do the same in Afghanistan and Iraq. By helping these young democracies grow in freedom and prosperity, we will lay the foundation of peace for generations to come.

We face a number of challenges in undertaking this vital work. One challenge is that in the past, in Germany and Japan, the work of rebuilding took place in relative quiet. Today, we're helping emerging democracies rebuild under fire from terrorist networks and state sponsors of terror. This is a difficult and unprecedented task, and we're learning as we go.

For example, in Iraq, we learned from hard experience that newly liberated people cannot make political and economic progress unless they first have some measure of security. In 2006, Iraqis did not have this security, and we all watched as their capital descended into sectarian violence.

So this year, we changed our strategy. Instead of retreating, instead of pulling back and hoping for the best, I made the decision to send in 30,000 additional troops with a new mission: Protect the American people—Iraqi people from terrorists and insurgents and illegal militias. Together, U.S. and Iraqi forces launched new offensives across the country to clear the enemy out of its strongholds. And as this military surge brought security to neighborhoods that were once in the grip of terror, it was followed by a civilian surge, with Provincial Reconstruction Teams deploying to work with Iraqis to ensure military progress was quickly followed by real improvements in daily life.

And today, we're seeing the fruits of the new strategy. Violence in Iraq is down to the lowest point since March of 2004. Civilian deaths are down; sectarian killings are down. And as security has improved, the economy has improved as well. Political reconciliation is taking place at the grassroots and national level. The surge is working. Our men and women in Iraq are performing with skill and valor, and they have earned the respect of the people of the United States of America.

This experience will help shape your careers as officers in the United States Air Force. During your time in uniform, some of you will have to help young democracies build free institutions amid chaos and confusion. You'll have to work with civilians on the battlefield in ways generations never imagined. To support your efforts, to help you make young democracies transition from tyranny to freedom, one thing is for certain: The United States Congress better make sure you have all the resources you need to do your job.

Another challenge in this new and unprecedented era is defining success. In the past, that was relatively easy to do. There were public surrenders, a signing ceremony on the deck of a battleship, victory parades in American cities. Today, when the war continues after the regime has fallen, the definition of success is more complicated. So in Iraq and Afghanistan, we set a clear definition of success. Success will come when Al Qaida has no safe haven in those countries and the people can protect themselves from terror. Success will come when Iraq and Afghanistan are economically viable. Success will come when Iraq and Afghanistan are democracies that govern themselves effectively and respond to the will of their people. Success will come when Iraq and Afghanistan are strong and capable allies on the war on terror. Men and women of the Air Force: These successes will come, and when they do, our Nation will have achieved victory, and the American people will be more secure.

The third lesson is this: For all the advanced military capabilities at our disposal, the most powerful weapon in our arsenal is the power of freedom. And we can see this story in the 20th century. In 1941, when Nazi bombers pounded London and Imperial Japan attacked Pearl Harbor, the future of freedom appeared bleak. There were only about a dozen democracies in the world. It seemed that tyranny, not liberty, was on the march. And even after Japan and Germany were defeated in World War II, freedom's victory was far from clear. In Europe, the advance of Nazi tyranny was replaced by the advance of Soviet tyranny. In Asia, the world saw the Japanese Empire recede and communism claim most of its former territory, from China to Korea to Vietnam.

Imagine if a President had stood before the first graduating class of this Academy five decades ago and told the Cadet Wing that by the end of the 20th century, the Soviet Union would be no more, communism would stand discredited, and the vast majority of the world's nations would be democracies. The cadets probably would have said he had done one too many "chariot races." [*Laughter*]

Many throughout history have underestimated the power of freedom to overcome tyranny and transform whole societies. Yet in the end, despite challenges and setbacks, freedom ultimately prevails because the desire for liberty is written by our Creator in every human heart. We see that desire in the citizens of Georgia and Ukraine who stood up for their right to free and fair elections. We see that desire in the people of Lebanon who took to the streets to demand their independence. We see that desire in the Afghans who emerged from the tyranny of the Taliban to choose a new President and a new parliament. We see that desire in the jubilant Iraqis who held up ink-stained fingers and celebrated their freedom. And in these scenes, we see an unmistakable truth: Whenever men and women are given a real choice, they choose to live in freedom.

The enemies of freedom understand this, and that is why they're fighting desperately to deny this choice to men and women across the Middle East. But we understand some things too. We understand that freedom helps replace the conditions of hopelessness that extremists exploit to recruit terrorists and suicide bombers. We understand that free societies are peaceful societies and that people who live in liberty and hope do not turn to ideologies of hatred and fear. And that is why, for the security of America and the peace for the world, the great mission of your generation is to lead the cause of freedom.

This is the last time I'll address a military academy commencement as a President. Over the past 8 years, from Annapolis to West Point to New London to Colorado Springs, I have looked out at the best young men and women our Nation has to offer, and I have stood in awe. And I stand in awe again today. Each of you is a volunteer who stepped forward to accept the burdens of war, knowing all the dangers you would face upon graduation. You willingly risk your lives and futures so that our country can have a future of freedom and peace. Our enemies say that America is weak and decadent and does not have the stomach for the long fight. Our enemies have never set foot on the campus of the United States Air Force Academy.

A nation that produces citizens of virtue and character and courage, like you, can overcome any challenge and defeat any adversary. So I'll leave this campus today filled with the confidence in the course of our struggle and the fate of our country because I've got confidence in each of you.

We see the strength and spirit of this class in a cadet named Erik Mirandette. In 2003, Erik felt a tug at his heart from the Almighty to take time off from the Academy and do humanitarian work in Morocco. After nearly 2 years there, Erik and his brother Alex and two childhood friends decided to ride across the African continent on dirt bikes. The last stop in their journey was Cairo, where a suicide bomber attacked them by exploding a bucket filled with nails. The blast killed Erik's brother, injured his two friends, and left Erik bleeding on the street. Doctors did not think he'd ever walk again. He never gave up his dream of coming back to this Academy. And 14 months ago, after surviving the blast, Erik returned to this campus. Today he begins his career as a proud officer in the greatest Air Force known to man.

He still has got dozens of nails in his body, but he has a fierce determination in his heart to protect his country, defeat the forces of terror. Erik puts it this way: "I'll live the rest of my life scarred inside and outside. But I've got a sense of calling. I want to prevent attacks on other good people."

Each of you gathered here this morning has answered that same call. I want to thank you for stepping forward to serve. The security of our citizens and the peace of the world will soon be in your hands— the best of hands. Be officers of character and integrity. Keep your wings level and true. Never falter, do not fail. And always know that America stands behind you.

Thank you. May God bless. And congratulations to the class of 2008.

NOTE: The President spoke at 10:15 a.m. at Falcon Stadium. In his remarks, he referred to Secretary of the Air Force Michael W. Wynne, who introduced the President; Gen. T. Michael Moseley, USAF, chief of staff, U.S. Air Force; Lt. Gen. John F. Regni, USAF, superintendent, U.S. Air Force Academy; Rep. Doug Lamborn; and President Hamid Karzai of Afghanistan.

Statement on the Fifth Anniversary of the Proliferation Security Initiative
May 28, 2008

Members of the international community are gathered in Washington, DC, today on the fifth anniversary of the Proliferation Security Initiative (PSI). Since former Polish President Kwasniewski and I first announced the initiative on May 31, 2003, in Krakow, Poland, PSI partner nations have been taking cooperative action to stop the proliferation trade and to deny terrorists, rogue states, and their supplier networks access to weapons of mass destruc-

tion (WMD), their delivery systems, and related materials.

Five years ago, the world became aware that an international black market network, headed by A.Q. Khan, had for many years supplied a clandestine nuclear weapons program in Libya. Recently, the discovery of Syria's covert nuclear reactor demonstrated that proliferators are capable of pursuing dangerous objectives even as the world becomes more vigilant. And today, in violation of United Nations Security

Council resolutions, Iran continues to enrich uranium and develop missile systems that could eventually deliver WMD. These proliferation activities undermine peace and security and remind us of the continued need for cooperative action.

The PSI has responded to this challenge and achieved a solid record of success. Beginning in 2003 with only 11 states, the PSI has grown to more than 90 nations from every region of the world committed to conduct interdictions and deter those engaged in this dangerous trade. As a result of the collaborative efforts and training it sponsors, PSI is an increasingly effective tool to carry out real-world WMD-related interdictions, from shutting down front companies to disrupting financial networks, prosecuting proliferators, and stopping shipments of sensitive materials from reaching their intended destination.

I commend all PSI partners for the work they have undertaken and pledge continued U.S. leadership and support for the effort. I urge all responsible nations to join this global initiative to end WMD proliferation.

Memorandum on Potential Pearl Harbor National Monument
May 28, 2008

Memorandum for the Secretary of Defense and the Secretary of the Interior

Subject: Potential Pearl Harbor National Monument

Pearl Harbor is well known as the site of Imperial Japan's attack on December 7, 1941. Its historical significance, however, both preceded the Japanese attack and spanned World War II, during which it served as the central base for our Pacific naval forces. While the USS *Arizona* Memorial serves as the final resting place for many of that battleship's brave crew members who lost their lives on December 7, 1941, other objects of historic and scientific interest in the area of Pearl Harbor and other sites in the Pacific remain outside this Memorial.

I have been advised that there are objects of historic and scientific interest at Pearl Harbor, including on Ford Island, and at other sites across the Pacific that may be appropriate for recognition and possibly protection through the designation of a National Monument under the Antiquities Act of 1906 (16 U.S.C. 431). These objects of historical and scientific interest may tell the broader story of the war, the sacrifices made by America and its allies, and the heroism and determination that laid the groundwork for victory in the Pacific and triumph in World War II.

Accordingly, please provide to me your assessment, with relevant supporting information, of the advisability of providing additional recognition or protection to historic landmarks, historic sites, or other objects of historic or scientific interest at Pearl Harbor and other sites associated with the war in the Pacific and America's ultimate victory in the Pacific theater during World War II, through designation and management as part of a National Monument. Because much of the Pearl Harbor area lies within an active military base, and other World War II historic resources lie within areas of the Pacific that are of strategic importance to the United States, please consider in your assessment that any proposed actions should not limit the Department of Defense from carrying out the mission of the various branches of the military stationed or operating anywhere within the Pacific.

GEORGE W. BUSH

NOTE: This memorandum was released by the Office of the Press Secretary on May 29.

Letter to Congressional Leaders Transmitting Designations Under the Kingpin Act
May 30, 2008

Dear _____ :

This report to the Congress, under section 804(b) of the Foreign Narcotics Kingpin Designation Act, 21 U.S.C. 1901–1908 (the "Kingpin Act"), transmits my designations of the following four foreign persons and three foreign entities as appropriate for sanctions under the Kingpin Act and reports my direction of sanctions against them under that Act:

Haji Asad Khan Zarkari Mohammadhasni
Hermagoras Gonzalez Polanco
Cumhur Yakut
Marcos Arturo Beltran Leyva
Beltran Leyva Organization
PKK (KGK, Kongra-Gel, formerly Kurdistan Workers' Party)
'Ndrangheta Organization

Sincerely,

GEORGE W. BUSH

NOTE: Identical letters were sent to John D. Rockefeller IV, chairman, Senate Select Committee on Intelligence; Patrick J. Leahy, chairman, Senate Committee on the Judiciary; Joseph R. Biden, Jr., chairman, Senate Committee on Foreign Relations; Carl Levin, chairman, Senate Committee on Armed Services; Max S. Baucus, chairman, Senate Committee on Finance; Silvestre Reyes, chairman, House Permanent Select Committee on Intelligence; John Conyers, Jr., chairman, House Committee on the Judiciary; Howard L. Berman, chairman, House Committee on Foreign Affairs; Isaac N. Skelton IV, chairman, House Committee on Armed Services; and Charles B. Rangel, chairman, House Committee on Ways and Means.

The President's Radio Address
May 31, 2008

Good morning. Next week, Congress will return to Washington after its Memorial Day recess. I hope Members of Congress return rested, because they have a lot of work left on important issues and limited time to get it done.

Congress needs to pass a responsible war funding bill that puts the needs of our troops first, without loading it up with unrelated domestic spending. Our troops in Afghanistan are performing with courage and honor, delivering blows to the Taliban and Al Qaida. Our troops in Iraq have driven Al Qaida and other extremists from sanctuaries they once held across the country and are chasing them from their last remaining strongholds. Our men and women in uniform are risking their lives every day, and they deserve the resources and flexibility they need to complete their mission.

Congress needs to support our military families by passing an expansion of the GI bill that makes it easier for our troops to transfer unused education benefits to their spouses and children. It is critical for this legislation to support the All-Volunteer Force and help us recruit and retain the best military in the world.

Congress needs to ensure that our intelligence professionals have the tools to monitor terrorist communications quickly and effectively. Last year, Congress passed temporary legislation that provided these tools. Unfortunately, the law expired more than 3 months ago. Congress needs to pass long-term legislation that will help our intelligence professionals learn our enemies' plans before they can attack and put an end to abusive lawsuits filed against companies believed to have assisted the Government after the attacks of September the 11th. And Congress needs to act soon so we can maintain a vital flow of intelligence.

Congress needs to approve the Colombia free trade agreement so we can open a growing market for American goods, services, and crops. Unfortunately, the House of Representatives is blocking a vote on this vital agreement. Unless this agreement is brought up for a vote, it will die. This will hurt American workers, farmers, and businessowners, and it will hurt our Nation's strategic interests in a vital region of the world.

Congress needs to confirm the good men and women who have been nominated to important Government positions. There are now more than 350 nominations pending before the Senate. These include highly qualified people I have nominated to fill vacancies on the Federal bench. And they include talented nominees who are needed to help guide our economy during a time of uncertainty. For example, three nominees to the Federal Reserve have been waiting for confirmation for more than a year. And because of Senate inaction, the Council of Economic Advisers is now down to a single member. This confirmation backlog makes it harder for Government to meet its responsibilities, and the United

States Senate needs to give every nominee an up-or-down vote as soon as possible.

One nominee who needs to be confirmed right away is Steve Preston. A month has passed since I nominated Steve to be the next Secretary of Housing and Urban Development. Unfortunately, Senators have stalled this nomination over an issue that has nothing to do with Steve or his qualifications for the job. With all the turbulence in the housing market, this is no time to play politics with such a critical appointment. So I call on the Senate to give Steve Preston a prompt vote and confirm this good man without further delay.

At a time when many Americans are concerned about keeping their homes, Congress needs to pass legislation to modernize the Federal Housing Administration, reform Fannie Mae and Freddie Mac to ensure they focus on their housing mission, and allow State housing agencies to issue tax-free bonds to refinance subprime loans.

And at a time when Americans are concerned about rising gas prices, Congress needs to pass legislation to expand domestic energy production.

In all these areas, Congress has failed to act. The American people deserve better from their elected leaders. Congress needs to show the American people that Republicans and Democrats can compete for votes and cooperate for results at the same time. You sent your representatives to Washington to do the people's business. And you have a right to expect them to do it, even in an election year.

Thank you for listening.

NOTE: The address was recorded at 11 a.m. on May 30 in the Cabinet Room at the White House for broadcast at 10:06 a.m. on May 31. The transcript was made available by the Office of the Press Secretary on May 30, but was embargoed for release until the broadcast. The Office of the Press Secretary also released a Spanish language transcript of this address.

Commencement Address at Furman University in Greenville, South Carolina
May 31, 2008

Thank you. Thank you very much. Mr. President—President Shi, thank you for that kind introduction. Governor Sanford, Senator Graham, Congressman Inglis, members of the board of trustees, faculty, staff, members of the Furman community, parents, and most important, the class of 2008: Thank you for this kind invitation to be with you.

I congratulate the parents here who have sacrificed to make this day possible. When your child graduates from college, it is a glorious day for your family and a pretty good day for your bank account. [*Laughter*] I know the graduates will join me in thanking you for your love and support.

And I thank the members of the Furman faculty. I appreciate your devoting your career to improving the lives of young people. I know this is an institution where folks are encouraged to make their voices heard. I too am a strong believer in free speech. And to prove it, I'm about to give you one. [*Laughter*]

For 4 years, this campus has been your life. You've studied hard, and I suspect some of you may have played hard. [*Laughter*] Along the way, some of you may have wondered whether this day would ever come. Well, it's finally here, and Laura and I send our heartfelt congratulations to the class of 2008.

I'm glad to be joined with my friend and outstanding leader of South Carolina, Governor Mark Sanford, class of 1983. Governor, I'm not going to ask if you ever got caught swimming in the fountains. [*Laughter*]

As the president said, 25 years ago, the Governor sat where you now sit, as a member of the graduating class. As it happens, as he mentioned, the commencement speaker that day was my dad. Now, that means some at Furman will have heard graduation speeches from two generations of Bushes. It's a great step forward for the Bush family and a great step backward for your English department. [*Laughter*]

And as the president mentioned, I have other family ties with Furman. In the early 1930s, a student named Willa Martin graduated from the women's college that was soon to become part of Furman. She went on to marry my mother's father. She also spent time as a columnist for the Associated Press, thus beginning the long history of warm relations between the Bush family and the media. [*Laughter*]

My administration also has another Furman connection. One of the first people I see almost every morning is a Furman grad and my Director of National Intelligence, Admiral Mike McConnell, class of 1966. I asked Mike if he ever took part in the "midnight serenade." He said, I'd like to tell you, but the information is classified. [*Laughter*]

It's a special time of your life. It's—you're going to find it's a time when you get a lot of free advice—some of it helpful, some of it not—like that one graduation speaker who urged the students to keep their ears to the ground, their shoulders to the wheel, and their noses to the grindstone. All I could think was, that's a hell of a position to be in. [*Laughter*]

I also remember what it was like to graduate from college and look out at the world before me. At the time, I must confess, the last thing on my mind was how to be a model citizen. Just ask my mother. [*Laughter*] Yet I found, as you will, the world has a way of helping you to grow. Soon many of you will be earning a living and getting married and raising families. As you move ahead in life, you will find temptations and distractions that can take you off course. You might also find that years may pass before you learn some important truths: that who you are is more important than what you have, and that you have responsibilities to your fellow citizens, your country, your family, and yourself.

In my first speech as the Governor of Texas, I talked about the importance of a responsibility society. In my last commencement address as President, it seems a fitting subject to return to.

I'm heartened today to see that our country is seeing a resurgence of personal responsibility. I'm pleased that this resurgence is being led by many young people who are embracing bedrock values of faith and family. These are values on which Furman and many other great universities were founded. And as you leave this campus today, my call to you is this: Strengthen this rising culture of responsibility in America by serving others, contributing to our civic life, and being accountable to yourself and your families.

A culture of responsibility does mean serving others. Through the toil of generations and the grace of an Almighty, our Nation has been given a lot. And more and more Americans are recognizing our obligations to help those who have little.

One of the most uplifting trends in our country is that volunteerism is at near all-time highs. And we see this spirit here at Furman. I was impressed when I heard that nearly two-thirds of you balanced your studies this year with outreach to your community. You helped children with disabilities realize they have a place in our communities and in our hearts. You helped Habitat for Humanity give people a home of their own. Through such works of compassion, you've learned early in life that nothing is more fulfilling than putting the needs of others ahead of your own. And I thank you for what you've done for this community and for our country.

I saw the spirit of service in Greensburg, Kansas, which was destroyed by a tornado last year. In the aftermath, a Greensburg resident simply said, "My town is gone." And it was. But after the storm receded, a wave of compassion arrived. First, family members rushed in with aid. Then folks came from nearby towns doing their duties to help their neighbors in need. And soon citizens across our country rallied to help the people of Greensburg. I recently went to Greensburg High School to deliver their commencement address, and I'm pleased to report to you, the town of Greensburg is recovering, and the spirit of determination and compassion is alive and well in America's heartland.

I've seen the spirit of service in good Americans who work to heal troubled communities across our country. Much of this good work is carried out by community and faith-based groups who lift up struggling souls one at a time. They serve in soup kitchens and help former prisoners rejoin society, inspire young people in inner-city classrooms, ensuring they have the skills they need to live lives of hope and opportunity.

I've seen the spirit of service in Americans who are changing lives on the continent of Africa. Our citizens are teaching children in Ghana, helping villagers fight malaria and HIV/AIDS in Tanzania, and helping war-ravaged people recover and rebuild in Liberia. These citizens are showing the world the true face of our country, a kind and generous nation that is meeting its responsibility to help the poor and the sick and the hungry.

I've seen the spirit of service in those who proudly wear the uniform. America is blessed to have citizens who volunteer in times of danger, and that includes some of you here today. You will leave Furman with more than a degree—[*applause*]—you'll leave this fine university with more than a degree; you will also receive your commission as an officer in the United States military. I thank you for making the noble decision to serve. Your country's proud of you, and so is your Commander in Chief.

To all of you, my call is to make service to others a way of life. Wherever you live, whatever you do, find a way to give back to your communities. And however you choose to serve, you're going to learn a great lesson: that the more you give, the more you'll benefit.

A culture of responsibility means contributing to our civic life. I ask you to be citizens, not spectators, and help to build a nation of virtue and character. You can strengthen our country by participating in the democratic process. In recent years, we've seen millions of people in places like Afghanistan, Iraq, and Georgia and Ukraine risk their lives for the right to cast a ballot. These courageous people should inspire us to take our votes just as seriously. I know the democratic spirit is alive in our country because there was a big vote recently. The new American Idol got about 55 million votes. [*Laughter*] I hope we see even a bigger turnout this November. For some of you, this will be your first Presidential election. I ask you to get involved in the process and do your duty and vote. By the way, if you're wondering who to vote for, the Governor and I would be happy to offer a few suggestions. [*Laughter*]

You can strengthen our country by showing fiscal discipline in your lives. It may sound funny coming from a visitor from Washington, DC, but it's important to your futures and to the future of our country. Many of you have debts from student loans. It's an investment that I expect you will find worthwhile. In the next few years, you may find it tempting to amass more debt, particularly from credit cards, on expenses that bring little long-term benefit. My advice to you is to—not to dig a financial hole that you can't get out of. Live within your means, and bear in mind that there are no shortcuts to the American Dream.

Your Furman degree will open the door to a wide variety of career options. One of the most noble paths you can take is a career in public service. I know you probably look at the debates in Washington and conclude that public service isn't worth it. That's a mistake. I've had my fair share of critics, but no criticism can overcome the satisfaction of serving your fellow citizens and pursuing great goals for our Nation. If you choose a career in public service, maintain the highest ethical standards, bring honor to whatever position you hold, and always put the people you serve ahead of yourself.

But public service is not just politics. It can include social work and teaching and careers in the nonprofit sector. There are countless organizations across our country that devote themselves to improving the lives of others, such as the American Red Cross or Teach for America or the Boys and Girls Clubs. These groups fulfill a noble mission, and they're a vital part of the responsibility society.

Others of you will make your careers in the private sector. If you choose this path, take pride in what you do, work hard, and bring value to the enterprise you work for. And remember this: Our country needs corporate responsibility as well as personal responsibility. So if you enter the business world, be honest with your shareholders, be truthful to your consumers, and give back to the communities in which you live. And all of us have a responsibility to be good stewards of the environment.

Finally, a culture of responsibility means being accountable to your families and to yourself. I found family to be a source of great comfort and strength. When people talk about my family, they often say I inherited my dad's eyes and my mother's mouth. [*Laughter*] But I got far more from them than that. From my dad, I learned that a gentle soul can also be strong. From my mother, I saw the blessings of humor and honesty and unqualified love. And from the two of them, I got an inspiring example of how a strong marriage can carry you through any challenge. And what has carried me through the challenges in my life have been the love and support of a wonderful woman named Laura Bush.

My wish is that you find a partner in life who loves you and challenges you and comforts you and gives your life meaning. And if you have the blessings of becoming a parent, I would like for you to remember that the most important job you will ever have is to love your child with all your heart.

In life, there's going to be many temptations to distract you from your responsibilities. Popular culture can give you the impression that alcohol, drugs, or promiscuity can lead to fulfillment in life. It's an illusion, and I urge you to reject it.

If you do fall short, know that it is never too late to recover and get back on the right track. There was a time in my life when alcohol competed for my affections, but I found salvation in my family and my faith. There's no shame in recognizing your failings or getting help if you need it. Tragedy comes when we fail to take responsibility for our weaknesses and surrender to them.

Finally, you probably don't realize it, but you're role models for others in your life, whether it's a little brother or sister who looks up to you or someone else who admires you. Positive role models are greatly needed in this society. And I urge you to set a hopeful example by leading lives of character and integrity. And if you do, you'll be proud of who you are; you'll teach others around you that a life of responsibility leads to a life of fulfillment.

In all these ways, your generation has an opportunity to show how timeless values can be applied in a modern world. And as you do so, history offers noble examples to follow, including many from right here in South Carolina. From this State came a signer of the Declaration of Independence who lost his fortune fighting for our freedom, but never regretted the fight. From this State came the brave colonel who drew a line in the sand against oppressive rule at the old Spanish mission called the Alamo. And from this State came the child of slaves who was among the first black women to be an adviser to Presidents.

And from this State came a young man who went off to serve his country in World War II. His last name was Smith, and it happens his first name was Furman. Private Furman Smith, he never attended this school, but he grew up right down the road. While on duty in Italy, Private Smith's unit came under heavy fire. He fended off 80 enemy soldiers to defend his wounded buddies. He died at the age of 19, with his rifle still clutched in his hand. For the acts of courage and character that cost him his life, Furman Smith was awarded the Medal of Honor. Sixty-four years ago this very day, that young man carried the Furman name into history. And now, in a very different way, so will each of you.

May the values you learned here always guide your course. May you always make the right choices. And may you always look in the mirror and be proud of what you see.

Congratulations. God bless you.

NOTE: The President spoke at 8:09 p.m. at Paladin Stadium. In his remarks, he referred to David E. Shi, president, Furman University.

Remarks at the Ford's Theatre Gala
June 1, 2008

Thank you all. Hal, thanks for the introduction. And I want to thank you all for supporting Ford's Theatre. Laura and I have been coming here now for 8 years to the Ford's Theatre gala, and this is by far the best.

We want to thank our choir and our orchestra and all the fabulous performers for taking time out of your busy schedules to help—to support this really important part of Washington. And Gatlin is probably saying, of course, I said that for the crowd last year. [*Laughter*] But no, it really was fantastic. And it's such an uplifting performance and a reminder of what a great President Abraham Lincoln was.

I do want to thank Paul Tetreault for being a really fabulous director of the Ford's Theatre. And I want to thank the gala cochairs and all the people who support the Ford's Theatre. I know you're ex-

cited about the opening of the renovated Ford's Theatre in February 2009. Laura and I are excited too. Just send the pictures down to Crawford. [*Laughter*]

Thanks for a fabulous evening, and God bless.

NOTE: The President spoke at 7 p.m at the National Theatre. In his remarks, he referred to actor Hal Holbrook; musician Larry Gatlin; and Paul R. Tetreault, producing director, Ford's Theatre. The transcript released by the Office of the Press Secretary also included the remarks of the First Lady. The transcript was released by the Office of the Press Secretary on June 2.

Remarks on Presenting Posthumously the Congressional Medal of Honor to Private First Class Ross A. McGinnis
June 2, 2008

Good morning. Welcome to the White House. A week ago, on Memorial Day, the flag of the United States flew in halfstaff in tribute to those who fell in service to our country. Today we pay special homage to one of those heroes: Private First Class Ross Andrew McGinnis of the United States Army. Private McGinnis died in a combat zone in Iraq on December the 4th, 2006, and for his heroism that day, he now receives the Medal of Honor.

In a few moments, the Military Aide will read the citation, and the Medal will be accepted by Ross's mom and dad, Romayne and Tom. It's a privilege to have with us as well, Becky and Katie, Ross's sisters.

I also want to thank the other distinguished guests who have joined us: Mr. Vice President; Secretary Jim Peake of Veterans Affairs; Secretary Pete Geren of the Army; Secretary Michael Wynne of the Air Force; General Jim "Hoss" Cartwright, Vice Chairman of the Joint Chiefs. I appre-

ciate other members of the administration for joining us.

I want to thank Members of the United States Congress who have joined us today: Steve Buyer, John Peterson, Louie Gohmert. Thank you all for coming. I appreciate the chaplain for the prayer. We welcome friends and family members of Ross, as well as members of the 1st Battalion, 26th Infantry, including Charlie Company, that's with us today.

We're also joined by Private McGinnis's vehicle crew, the very men who witnessed his incredible bravery. We welcome Sergeant First Class Cedric Thomas, Staff Sergeant Ian Newland, Sergeant Lyle Buehler, and Specialist Sean Lawson.

A special welcome to the prior recipients of the Medal of Honor, whose presence here is—means a lot to the McGinnis family. Thank you for coming.

The Medal of Honor is the Nation's highest military distinction. It's given for valor beyond anything that duty could require or a superior could command. By long tradition, it's presented by the President. For any President, doing so is a high privilege.

Before he entered our country's history, Ross McGinnis came of age in the town of Knox, Pennsylvania. Back home, they remember a slender boy with a big heart and a carefree spirit. He was a regular guy. He loved playing basketball. He loved working on cards—cars. He wasn't too wild about schoolwork. [*Laughter*] He had a lot of friends and a great sense of humor. In high school and in the Army, Ross became known for his ability to do impersonations. A buddy from boot camp said that Ross was the only man there who could make the drill sergeant laugh. [*Laughter*]

Most of all, those who knew Ross McGinnis recall him as a dependable friend and a really good guy. If Ross was your buddy and you needed help to—or you got in trouble, he'd stick with you and be the one you could count on. One of his friends told a reporter that Ross was the type who would do anything for anybody.

That element of his character was to make all the difference when Ross McGinnis became a soldier in the Army. One afternoon 18 months ago, Private McGinnis was part of a Humvee patrol in a neighborhood of Baghdad. From his position in the gun turret, he noticed a grenade thrown directly at his vehicle. In an instant, the grenade dropped through the gunner's hatch. He shouted a warning to the four men inside. Confined in that tiny space, the soldiers had no chance of escaping the explosion. Private McGinnis could have easily jumped from the Humvee and saved himself. Instead, he dropped inside, put himself against the grenade, and absorbed the blast with his own body.

By that split second decision, Private McGinnis lost his own life, and he saved his comrades. One of them was Platoon Sergeant Cedric Thomas, who said this: "He had time to jump out of the truck. He chose not to. He's a hero. He was just an awesome guy." For his actions, Private McGinnis received the Silver Star, a posthumous promotion in rank, and a swift nomination for the Medal of Honor. But it wasn't acclaim or credit that motivated him. Ross's dad has said: "I know medals never crossed his mind. He was always about friendships and relationships. He just took that to the ultimate this time."

When Ross McGinnis was in kindergarten, the teacher asked him to draw a picture of what he wanted to be when he grew up. He drew a soldier. Today our Nation recognizing—recognizes him as a soldier and more than that because he did far more than his duty. In the words of one of our commanding generals, "Four men are alive because this soldier embodied our Army values and gave his life."

The day will come when the mission he served has been completed and the fighting's over and freedom and security have prevailed. America will never forget those who came forward to bear the battle. America will always honor the name of this brave soldier who gave all for his country and was taken to rest at age 19.

No one outside this man's family can know the true weight of their loss. But in words spoken long ago, we are told how to measure the kind of devotion that Ross McGinnis showed on his last day: "Greater love hath no man than this, that a man lay down his life for his friends."

Gospel also gives this assurance: "Blessed are they that mourn, for they shall be comforted." May the deep respect of our whole Nation be a comfort to the family of this fallen soldier. May God always watch over the country he served and keep us ever grateful for the life of Ross Andrew McGinnis.

And now I'd like to invite Mr. and Mrs. McGinnis to please come forward for the presentation, and the Military Aide will read the citation for the Medal of Honor.

NOTE: The President spoke at 9:50 a.m. in the East Room at the White House. In his remarks, he referred to Maj. Gen. Douglas L. Carver, USA, Chief of Army Chaplains.

Following the President's remarks, Lt. Cmdr. Daniel Walsh, USCG, Coast Guard Aide to the President, read the citation.

Remarks During a Meeting on the National Economy
June 2, 2008

The President. Thank you all for coming. I want to thank Dr. Lindsey and Bob Carroll and John and Marty. Thank you all for talking about the benefits and wisdom of keeping taxes low. I do want to remind people what life was like in the years 2001 and 2003. The country was having some pretty tough economic times in 2001. Larry, you might remember that period.

Lawrence B. Lindsey. I do, painfully.

The President. Yes, we had a period of— we had a couple of meetings in Austin, Texas, prior to me getting sworn in as the President, and people from industry were saying, "You're going to inherit a really tough period." I mean, the—clearly the economy was slowing, and so we had to strategize on how to deal with it.

And Larry and others in—agreed that the best way to deal with economic uncertainty is to let people have more of their own money. Because we believe that the economy benefits when there's more money in circulation, in the hands of the people who actually earned it. I know that's probably not as sophisticated a concept as some of you all up here have articulated, but it's a concept that worked.

And then when you couple the economic slowdown with an attack on our Nation and our firm response to that attack, it created more economic uncertainty. And that's why the tax cuts of 2001 and 2003 were necessary. And the facts are that we had 52 months of uninterrupted job growth, the longest in the history of the United States.

And I know you believe, and I firmly believe, that those tax cuts were part of that engine for that economic vitality. And the economy is not doing as well as we'd like to do—like it to do today. But there's no question that the tax cuts provided economic vitality.

And the—and now the question is, what will the Congress do? Given the facts that tax cuts have worked, what will be the congressional response? Our response is, let's make those tax cuts permanent. Let's make sure that there is certainty during uncertain times in our economy. Imagine if you're trying to plan—plan your life, plan the future for your small business—and you don't know whether or not Congress is going to keep your taxes low. It makes your environment more uncertain.

You hear a lot of talk out of Congress about, you know, the economic slowdown. And we understand there's an economic slowdown, and we're concerned about the economic slowdown. And—but one of the things that they can do to help make sure that this economy is a—recovers like we believe it will—is to cut—make the tax cuts permanent.

Now, our fellow citizens have got to understand that those tax cuts aren't permanent. In other words, if Congress allows them to expire, here are the consequences. Now, first of all, taxes go up by an average of $280 billion a year. And I promise you, there's going to be a $280 billion expansion of government to couple that—those tax increases. And the fundamental question is, who would you rather have spending your money, you or the Congress? I would strongly suggest the answer is you. [*Laughter*]

A family of four with $50,000 in income will pay $2,155 more in taxes. That may not sound like a lot to folks who are throwing around a lot of big numbers in Washington. It means a lot if you're trying to save for your family. It means a lot if you're worried about gasoline prices. It means a lot if you're a hard-working American family. That's a lot of money.

If you're a family of four with a $60,000 income, you'll pay $1,900 more in taxes. Overall, 43 million families with children will face a tax increase of $2,323 on average.

Our philosophy is, not only does the economy benefit when taxes are low, we believe American families benefit when they have more money to spend. And it's that collective wisdom of individual Americans that really define the course for our country. And there really is, kind of, talks about the philosophical divide we face. Who is more wise, the Congress or the individual? We trust the individual. We trust that individual to make the proper decisions for their family.

Now, people say, there's got to be basic services out of government. Absolutely. But we got plenty of money in Washington. What we need is more priority. People got to set the priorities. Government can't try to be all things to all people. Government has got to also understand that when someone's working hard, the more money they have in their pocket, the better off the country is.

I want to talk about small businesses. Seventy percent of new jobs are created by small businesses. It's really an important part of the American economic scene. As a matter of fact, it's an important part of a hopeful America. Isn't it wonderful to have a country where people can come and have a dream and work hard and own their own business?

And so that's why throughout this administration we've been promoting the ownership society. I love it when I mean—I meet owners of a business. Many of them happen to be formed around a kitchen table. And you meet these men and women, and they just—with such pride, they tell you about their company, and they tell you about their employees, and they tell you how proud they are of being able to make it.

Well, it just turns out that 75 percent of the taxpayers who benefited from the reduction of the top bracket were small-business owners. So when you hear people say, "We're just going to tax the rich," American citizens have got to understand, because of the way these small businesses are set up, that they pay taxes at the individual income tax rate. And so when you hear "tax the rich," you're really talking about taxing mom-and-pop businesses. If 70 percent of the new jobs in America are created by small businesses, why would you want to take money out of their treasury? Why wouldn't you want to encourage them to thrive by letting them keep more of their hard-earned dollars?

If Congress doesn't act, 27 [sic] small-business owners will face a tax increase of $4,066 on average. In other words, that $4,000, on average, for the small businesses won't be available for investment, won't be available for programs that help their employees, will make it harder for them to compete.

And so I want to thank you all for your steadfast support of the American people and the American small-business owner by working to keep taxes low.

Today the Senate is debating a bill called the Warner-Lieberman bill, which would impose roughly $6 trillion of new costs on the American economy. There is a much better way to address the environment than imposing these costs on the job creators, which will ultimately have to be borne by American consumers. And I urge the Congress to be very careful about running up enormous costs for future generations of Americans.

We'll work with the Congress, but the idea of a huge spending bill fueled by taxes—increases—isn't the right way to proceed. And the right way for Congress to proceed on taxes in general is to send a clear message that these tax relief we passed need to be made permanent.

Thank you for your interest. Thank you for your concern about our fellow citizens. God bless you.

NOTE: The President spoke at 11 a.m. in Room 450 of the Dwight D. Eisenhower Executive Office Building. In his remarks, he referred to Lawrence B. Lindsey, president and chief executive officer, the Lindsey Group; Robert Carroll, vice president for economic policy, the Tax Foundation; John Rutledge, chairman, Rutledge Capital; and Martin A. Regalia, vice president for economic and tax policy and chief economist, U.S. Chamber of Commerce.

Statement on the Situation in Zimbabwe
June 2, 2008

The continued use of Government-sponsored violence in Zimbabwe, including unwarranted arrests and intimidation of opposition figures, to prevent the Movement for Democratic Change from campaigning freely ahead of the June 27 Presidential runoff election is deplorable. We call on the regime to immediately halt all attacks and to permit freedom of assembly, freedom of speech, and access to the media. We urge the Southern African Development Community, the African Union, the United Nations, and other international organizations to blanket the country with election and human rights monitors immediately.

We also are concerned by reports that misguided Government policies are projected to result in one of the worst crop harvests in Zimbabwean history. While Robert Mugabe makes political statements in Rome, his people continue to face empty markets at home. The United States currently feeds more than 1 million Zimbabweans and spent more than $170 million on food assistance in Zimbabwe last year. We will continue these efforts to prevent Government-induced starvation in Zimbabwe.

NOTE: The statement referred to President Robert Mugabe of Zimbabwe.

Remarks Honoring the 2008 NCAA Men's Basketball Champion University of Kansas Jayhawks
June 3, 2008

The President. Please sit down. Welcome. It's an honor to welcome the 2008 NCAA men's basketball champs, the Kansas Jayhawks. So when Kansas fans come to the Rose Garden, they don't come to admire the flowers—[*laughter*]—they come to

"wave the wheat." I just wish Big Jay and Baby Jay could have come with you. Barney was looking forward to meeting them. [*Laughter*]

I want to congratulate this team. You brought new glory to one of our Nation's most storied basketball programs, and you gave your fans all across America one more reason to chant, "Rock Chalk Jayhawk!"

I appreciate Bob Hemenway, the chancellor, and his wife Leah. Thanks for coming. Head coach Bill Self, Cindy; daughter Lauren, and son Tyler: We're sure glad you all are here.

I called Coach after the championship. I think I might have woke you up.

Bill Self. By a hair. [*Laughter*]

The President. Yes. I said, "Would you like to come to the White House?" He said, "When?" [*Laughter*] And I'm glad you're here, Coach, and congratulations.

I want to thank all the folks who represent KU: the personnel, coaches, and players.

Proud to welcome the United States Senators from Kansas—Senator Pat Roberts, honored you're here; KU Law School alum Senator Brownback—Sam Brownback—and Mary, who happened to be a KU undergrad and law school. KU undergrad and law school alum Jerry Moran; KU undergrad alums Dennis Moore and Stephene—thank you all for coming; Doug Lamborn from the great State of Colorado—KU undergrad and law school alum; Senator Bob Dole, one of the great KU citizens.

This team got off to an incredibly fast start. They won their first 20 games. They managed to beat Yale, my alma mater. I don't—[*laughter*]—I'm not sure how you did it, but nevertheless—[*laughter*]—it was a great victory. You won the Big 12 title. You were the number-one seed in the Midwest region. God, blew through the competition early, and then you won a thriller against Davidson, which propelled you to the Final Four in San Antonio, Texas. By the way, to my fellow Texans on the team: Nice to see you. [*Laughter*]

The interesting thing about the tournament in San Antonio was that all number-one seeds made it to the Final Four. That's never happened before. It meant the competition was pretty tough. And this championship team gave America an unforgettable show, it really did.

In the semifinal matchup against North Carolina, you took a big lead, and you held on. It was a team effort, but you got to note that Brandon Rush did score 25 points in the game. [*Laughter*]

In the finals, you made a great comeback against Memphis. You overcame a 9-point deficit. Mario Chalmers, of course, hit the 3-pointer to send you into overtime. The guy is known as Super Mario. [*Laughter*] Then he became known as MVP. [*Laughter*]

I know you got to be excited about winning an incredibly tough tournament. And your fans are excited, and I'm excited to welcome you to the Rose Garden. It's a big deal, as far as I'm concerned, to welcome KU to the Rose Garden.

Most of the players on this team have little or no memory of the last time Kansas won a national title, which would be 1988. As a matter of fact, I'm sure some of the players weren't even born yet. It's really hard to envision when you're an old guy like me and Roberts. [*Laughter*] The 1988 team became known as Danny and the Miracles. And, Danny Manning, welcome back to the White House.

This 2008 team will be remembered a little differently. More than any one player, Americans will remember the way you played as a team. They'll remember stifling defense. They'll remember the way seven different players led your team in scoring during the course of the season. Teamwork is a testament to the leadership of six seniors. It's a testament, as well, to a coach. Bill Self has proven himself to be one of the finest coaches in the land. And I'm sure—[*applause*]—and I am sure KU fans are delighted to know that he's going to keep coming back for a while.

Good move, Chancellor, good move. [*Laughter*]

The greatest testament to this team is also the character it showed not only on the court, but off. It turns out—I often say this when I welcome championship teams here to the White House, but character matters a lot in order to become a champion. This is a team that when teammates lost loved ones, they had players-only meetings to help to rally their friends through a difficult time.

It's a team that reached out to others in need. Coach Self set the example by launching a foundation to help children in Lawrence build healthier and more wholesome lives. During the holiday, players purchased gifts for needy families. You signed hundreds of balls for charity auctions. You ran free basketball clinics for children. And I'm very thankful that you went to Walter Reed to spend time with America's real heroes, our courageous wounded warriors.

I wish those of you going to pro ball all the very best. Some of us are going to be out of work soon. We may be looking for loans. [*Laughter*] I welcome you to the White House. Good luck next season. And may God bless you all.

NOTE: The President spoke at 10:06 a.m. in the Rose Garden at the White House. In his remarks, he referred to Cindy Self, wife of University of Kansas men's basketball head coach Bill Self; Mary Brownback, wife of Sen. Sam D. Brownback; Stephene Moore, wife of Rep. Dennis Moore; former Sen. Robert J. Dole; and Brandon Rush and Mario Chalmers, guards, and Danny Manning, assistant coach, University of Kansas men's basketball team.

Remarks Prior to a Meeting With Prime Minister Ehud Olmert of Israel
June 4, 2008

President Bush. Mr. Prime Minister, welcome back. First of all, I want to thank you and your good bride for being such gracious hosts to Laura and me. I loved my trip to Israel. It was really a meaningful trip, and a lot of it had to do with your gracious hospitality. So I welcome you back here to Washington. You come back as my friend; I'm glad to see my friend.

I'm looking forward to our discussions on the issues that we have spent a lot of time discussing up to now. We'll be, of course, talking about the Palestinian issue, the peace process. Now, we'll be talking about Lebanon. I'm looking forward to your wisdom about how you see the Syrian issue. And finally, we're going to spend a lot of time talking about Iran. Iran is an existential threat to peace, and it's very important for the world to take the Iranian threat seriously, which the United States does, as the Prime Minister will tell you. And we will continue our discussions about that subject as well.

So glad you're here. Good to see you.

Prime Minister Olmert. Thank you very much, President.

President Bush. Yes, sir.

Prime Minister Olmert. Thank you. Well, I am delighted to be again at the Oval Office as a guest of my friend President Bush. We enjoyed tremendously your visit in Israel. From a national point of view, people of Israel were absolutely excited and moved by your spectacular speech in the Knesset, which was the best expression of the United States commitment to the security and the well-being of the State of Israel, which was appreciated by everyone in the State of Israel.

And we had many discussions, that you have mentioned, on the main issues: the peace process with the Palestinians, situation in Lebanon, the contacts that, hopefully, may lead to pull out Syria from the axis of evil, which is very important; and also, naturally, about the main threat to all of us, which is Iran. And as you said, President, indeed we talked all about this.

From a personal point of view, I can only say that I admire your friendship and your commitment and your emotions, as they were expressed in such a powerful manner in your visit to the State of Israel.

President Bush. Thank you.

Prime Minister Olmert. And they loved you and Laura very much. And part of my mission is to make you feel this way. Thank you very much.

President Bush. Thank you very much.

Prime Minister Olmert. Thank you.

President Bush. Thank you all.

NOTE: The President spoke at 1:54 p.m. in the Oval Office at the White House. In his remarks, he referred to Aliza Olmert, wife of Prime Minister Olmert.

Message to the Senate Transmitting the Bulgaria-United States Taxation Convention
June 4, 2008

To the Senate of the United States:

I transmit herewith, for Senate advice and consent to ratification, the Convention Between the Government of the United States of America and the Government of the Republic of Bulgaria for the Avoidance of Double Taxation and the Prevention of Fiscal Evasion With Respect to Taxes on Income, with accompanying Protocol, signed at Washington on February 23, 2007 (the "Proposed Treaty"), as well as the Protocol Amending the Convention Between the Government of the United States of America and the Government of the Republic of Bulgaria for the Avoidance of Double Taxation and the Prevention of Fiscal Evasion With Respect to Taxes on Income, signed at Sofia on February 26, 2008 (the "Proposed Protocol of Amendment"). The Proposed Treaty and Proposed Protocol of Amendment are consistent with U.S. tax treaty policy. Also transmitted for the information of the Senate is the report of the Department of State with respect to the Proposed Treaty and Proposed Protocol of Amendment.

The Proposed Treaty generally reduces the withholding tax on cross-border dividend, interest, and royalty payments. Importantly, the Proposed Treaty generally eliminates withholding tax on cross-border dividend payments to pension funds and cross-border interest payments made to financial institutions. The Proposed Treaty also contains provisions, consistent with current U.S. tax treaty policy, that are designed to prevent so-called treaty shopping. The Proposed Protocol of Amendment further strengthens these treaty shopping provisions.

I recommend that the Senate give early and favorable consideration to the Proposed Treaty and give its advice and consent to ratification to both the Proposed Treaty and the Proposed Protocol of Amendment.

GEORGE W. BUSH

The White House,
June 4, 2008.

Remarks at a Groundbreaking Ceremony for the United States Institute of Peace
June 5, 2008

Thank you all. Please be seated. Mr. Secretary, thank you for your kind introduction. And thank you for inviting me to join you to break ground for the United States Institute of Peace's new home. I'm really pleased to be here. I appreciate what you do to resolve conflict and support new democracies and to build peace by promoting effective diplomacy. And speaking about effective diplomacy, it seems like you used some to get this special piece of land. I congratulate you on picking a wonderful site.

I thank Robin West, the Chairman; Dick Solomon, the President. Members of the Board of Directors, thank you for being here. I'm so pleased to be with the Secretary of State, Condoleezza Rice, and some of her predecessors. Thank you for being here. I appreciate Admiral Mullen joining us. I want to thank members of my administration for coming. Madam Speaker, you grace us with your presence. Thank you for coming. I also want to pay homage to Ted Stevens for helping to secure the funding for this important site, as well as Members of the United States Senate who have joined him here and Members of the House. I appreciate Reverend Lovett, Father Hesburgh, members of the diplomatic corps, ladies and gentlemen.

The Institute of Peace was founded in 1984. It was during the last great ideological struggle of the 20th century. This was the struggle against Soviet communism, a struggle that was eventually won by freedom because of peace through strength and because of the help of the Institute of Peace.

We're in a different struggle today, but we're in an ideological struggle against violent extremism. The U.S. Institute of Peace is playing an important role, and I thank you for that. In Afghanistan, you're helping a young democracy establish the rule of law and strengthen public education and build a civil society. In Iraq, you're helping the nation overcome the legacy of decades of tyranny by strengthening government institutions and promoting peaceful engagement. And although the struggle against violent extremism is in its early years, there's no doubt in my mind, freedom will again prevail, and your help is going to be important.

In this struggle, we're guided by a clear principle: Freedom is universal. We believe that freedom is the birthright of every man, woman, and child. Free societies are peaceful societies. Freedom helps supplant the conditions of hopelessness that extremists exploit to recruit terrorists and suicide bombers. People who live in liberty are less likely to turn to ideologies of hatred and fear. And that is why the United States is leading and must continue to lead the cause of freedom for the sake of peace.

September the 11th, we saw how the lack of freedom in other lands can bring death and destruction to our own land. Our most solemn obligation is to protect the American people. That is why we're pursuing and bringing to justice terrorists. We're fighting them overseas so we don't have to face them here in the United States of America.

But the effort requires more. It requires using the power of liberty to marginalize extremists. And the best way to do so is to use our national resources to strengthen the institutions of freedom. That's what I want to talk to you about today, briefly, you'll be pleased to hear.

Institutions, of course, include a democratic system of government, a vibrant free press, independent judiciary, a free enterprise system, places of worship where people are free to practice their faith. These institutions include an education system that provides citizens a link to the world, health infrastructure that combats plagues like HIV/AIDS and malaria, and women's organizations that help societies take advantage of the skills and talents of half their population.

We're helping nations across the world build these institutions, and we face three challenges as we do so. First of all, there are developing nations, many on the continent of Africa, that are facing extreme poverty and health epidemics and humanitarian catastrophes and are therefore vulnerable to extremists who take advantage of chaos and instability.

Secondly, there are nations like Colombia and Lebanon and Pakistan that are facing transnational threats from drug cartels or terrorist networks that seek safe haven on their territory and threaten to overwhelm their institutions.

And thirdly, there are nations like Afghanistan and Iraq, where we removed dangerous regimes that threatened our people and now have a special obligation to help them build free societies that their— that become allies in the fight against these extremists.

It's in America's vital interest to help all these nations combat ideologies of hate. It's in our security interest to eliminate safe havens for terrorists and extremists. It's in our national interest to develop institutions that allow them to govern their territories effectively and improve their lives.

We've been making transformations over the last 8 years to make these capabilities more real and more effective. We're transforming the United States military so we can deliver justice to the terrorists in a more effective way. We're transforming America's capabilities to help poor and struggling societies become healthy and prosperous.

And we've seen those effective transformations through the Emergency Plan for AIDS or malaria initiative or the Millennium Challenge Account. The Millennium Challenge Account represents a different approach to development. It rewards nations that govern responsibly and fight corruption and invest in the health and education of their people and use the power of free markets and free trade to lift the people out of poverty.

One thing in common for all these programs is, we insist upon results, and we measure. And the results are coming in, and millions of people are benefiting from this foreign policy initiative. And they deserve to be fully supported by the United States Congress.

We're also transforming America's capabilities to helping emergency—emerging democracies build free institutions while under fire from terrorists and under pressure from state sponsors of terror. And this is a new challenge that we face at the start of the 21st century. And as we've adopted to meet these new circumstances, there have been successes and setbacks, and we've learned some lessons.

One lesson is that before nations under fire from terrorists can make political and economic progress, their populations need basic security. Sometimes local security institutions, with training and equipment and support from the outside, can handle the task. Take, for example, Colombia. Colombia and America launched an ambitious program that helped rescue that country from the brink of becoming a failed state. Plan Colombia, which started under my predecessor, made it clear that the United States would help the Colombian Government modernize its military and fight the FARC terrorists, expand education opportunity, provide Colombians with alternatives to a life of terror and narcotrafficking. Congress has an opportunity to strengthen these efforts, and I strongly urge them to send a clear and sound message to the people of Colombia and the region that we stand with them by passing the Colombia free trade agreement.

In other situations, America is training international peacekeepers so they can deploy to provide security in troubled regions. We've started what's called the Global Peace Operations Initiative. The whole idea is to work to train international peacekeeping forces so they can do the work necessary to provide stability and security, so institutions can advance. So far, we've trained more than 40,000 peacekeepers, and the plan is to train 75,000 additional.

These instances where America has removed regimes that threaten us, American troops may need to play a direct role in providing security. In Iraq, 2006, the country was descending into sectarian chaos. So we launched the surge, 30,000 additional troops to work with Iraqi forces to protect the Iraqi people from terrorists, insurgents, and illegal militias. Today, because we acted, violence in Iraq is down to its lowest point since late March of 2004. Civilian deaths are down. Sectarian killings are down. Security has improved, as well as the economy. Political reconciliation is taking place at the grassroots and Federal level. And as the Iraqi security forces are becoming more capable, our troops are beginning to come home under a policy of return on success.

A lesson we've learned is that civilian expertise is vital to strengthening the institutions of freedom. In Iraq and Afghanistan, we've developed an important tool to tap into civilian expertise called Provincial Reconstruction Teams. PRTs bring together civilian, diplomatic, and military personnel. They move into communities that our military has cleared of terrorists. They help ensure that security gains are followed with real improvements in daily life by helping local leaders create jobs and deliver basic services and build up local economies.

PRTs are uniquely suited to situations like Afghanistan and Iraq. In the future, civilian expertise will be needed in other countries where we do not have ongoing military operations. At the moment, we lack the capability to rapidly deploy civilian experts with the right skills to trouble spots around the world. We launched what's called a Civilian Stabilization Initiative, which is being run out of the State Department in the Office of Reconstruction and Stabilization.

One element of the new office is an Active Response Corps, made up of civilian experts from many Government agencies who deploy full time to at-risk countries. This corps will eventually include 250 personnel from the Departments of State and Justice, Agriculture, Commerce, AID, and other civilian agencies with relevant expertise.

Another element is the Standby Reserve [Response] * Corps, which is a reserve force of current and former Government employees who volunteer to be an on-call supplemental force that can deploy for reconstruction and stabilization missions on short notice.

And finally, this initiative will include a new Civilian Reserve Corps that will function much like our military reserve. It will be made up of American citizens with critical skills, such as police officers and judges and prosecutors and engineers and doctors and public administrators. The corps will give people across America who do not wear the uniform a chance to serve in the defining struggle of our time.

Legislation authorizing the Civilian Reserve Corps has passed the House of Representatives. It's awaiting action in the Senate. And I strongly urge Congress to pass this bipartisan legislation as soon as possible.

Another lesson is, is that in aiding the rise of strong and stable democracies requires that—the efforts of much more than Washington, DC. It requires the efforts of other governments and nonorganizational— nongovernmental organizations and people around the world.

---

* White House correction.

The work of democratic development is the work of all free nations. This is precisely the message that Secretary Rice and I have been carrying around the world. We're rallying other nations to train peacekeepers to support Afghanistan and Iraq and to act boldly to alleviate hunger and poverty.

I'm going to the G–8 in Japan in the month of July. The last G–8, our partners stood up and made strong commitments to help Africa deal with malaria and HIV/AIDS. They have yet to make good on their commitments. And I will remind them, it's one thing to make a promise; it's another thing to write the check. And the American Government expects our partners to live up to their obligations.

The work of democratic development sometimes requires young democracies under siege to band together with partnerships to deal with common threats. And this is the approach we're taking in Central America. We've encouraged nations threatened by narcotraffickers to cooperate in protecting their people. The supplemental that's being debated in the Congress will help further this effort by linking Mexico and Central America with U.S. to have a joint strategy: protecting our hemisphere from narcotraffickers and the terrorists that they ultimately yield. I asked Congress to approve the request quickly in the supplemental without putting unreasonable conditions on the vital aid.

One thing is for certain: that if we expect democracies to prevail, to marginalize the extremists, countries—it requires countries to have good, strong democratic leaders. And the best way to encourage that is to have them come to our colleges and universities. We've made good progress about changing the student visa regime after 9/11. We've increased the number of students coming here. And it's in our interest that we continue to increase the number of students coming to study in the United States.

And finally, the work of democratic development is the work of nongovernmental organizations, like the U.S. Institute of Peace. Obviously, these organizations can go into countries where it's harder for governments to operate. So it's very important for this Government and future Governments to always be a strong and steady partner to nongovernmental organizations and groups like the U.S. Institute of Peace.

The work of democratic development is the great cause of our time, and we shouldn't shy away from it. And we must be confident in our ability to help others realize the blessings of freedom. My big concern is that the United States becomes isolationist and nervous; we don't support those values that have stood the test of time. The Institute of Peace, I hope, will make sure that never happens.

Our fellow citizens can help in many ways. They can join an organization like this one. They can join the civilian reserve. They can become—like thousands of other compassionate citizens—become soldiers in the armies of compassion by helping HIV/AIDS victims or help educate people around the world. Or they can make the noble choice that has sustained freedom for generations and join the United States military. However they choose to serve, advancing the cause of liberty is necessary to advance the cause of peace.

I'm honored to be with you today. Looking forward to coming back someday to see this building when it's built. Thanks for your efforts. Thanks for your mission. May God bless you all.

NOTE: The President spoke at 10:49 a.m. at Navy Hill. In his remarks, he referred to former Secretary of State George P. Shultz, who introduced the President, and Rev. Theodore M. Hesburgh, cochairs, Building for Peace Campaign, U.S. Institute of Peace; J. Robinson West, Chairman of the Board of Directors, Richard H. Solomon, President, and Rev. Sidney Lovett (Ret.), former member of the Board of Directors, U.S. Institute of Peace; and Adm. Michael G. Mullen, USN, Chairman, Joint Chiefs of Staff. The Office of the Press Secretary also released a Spanish language transcript of these remarks.

Remarks Following a Meeting With Prime Minister Jan Peter Balkenende of the Netherlands
June 5, 2008

President Bush. Mr. Prime Minister, thanks for coming back. I enjoyed being with you. You represent a great country. You're a good friend of the United States of America, and I appreciate our candid discussion of a variety of issues.

First, I want to thank you and your folks for helping the people of Afghanistan realize the blessings of liberty. There is a— we're engaged in a struggle against ideologues who use murder to achieve their political objectives. One way to help—and defeat those folks and marginalize them is to help others realize the blessings of a free society. And I appreciate your courage, and I appreciate the troops, and—but the people of Afghanistan appreciate them more.

We had a good discussion on a variety of issues. We talked about the need for— to continue our close cooperation on a series of issues. I appreciate very much your concern about the people on the continent of Africa, your concern about people needlessly dying because of HIV/AIDS. I share those same concerns with you.

Talked about completing the WTO round, the Doha round. The Prime Minister and I both agree, a world that trades freely is a world that is a more hopeful world and, certainly, a way to help people grow out of poverty.

And we talked about the climate issue. I assured him that the United States is concerned about the issue. We're concerned about being dependent on oil. And the two happen to go hand in hand. And we've developed a strategy to encourage the advent of new technologies that will change our habits; at the same time, allow us to empower our economy in a way that will help us be good stewards in the environment. I want to thank you for your candid discussion on that.

Relations—bilateral relations with our countries are very strong and very good. And I can't thank you enough for coming. Welcome.

Prime Minister Balkenende. Mr. President, thank you very much for the hospitality and the friendship. It is true what you're saying about the bilateral relations between the United States and the Netherlands; they are very good. And also next year—and we have the 400-year celebration of the fact that Henry Hudson came, on behalf of the Dutch East Indian Company, to Manhattan.

President Bush. That's right.

Prime Minister Balkenende. And they'll be celebrated then. And just an example of the long tradition we have.

At this moment, we're working together. And you referred to that, by example, in Africa. In the struggle against HIV/AIDS, we are working together. We also are working together on the issue of deforestation in Latin America. There will be a meeting in Suriname in September, and we are supporting that event. And thanks for your remarks about our cooperation and the activities of our military people in Afghanistan. It's necessary to work together.

Of course when you are friends, sometimes there are issues you do not agree about, but because you have a friendship, then you can talk about finding solutions and talk about critical aspects. We also talked about the European Union, and I'm convinced that the United States and the European Union share the same values. You talked about it: freedom, human rights and democracy, economic dynamism, sustainable development. And I think we— if we work together, we really can make a difference. And I think it's necessary.

So I'm really looking forward of the new administration also to have a good cooperation between the European Union and the United States.

It was also important what you said about role of multilateral channels, the United Nations; but also, we talked about the NATO. And it is important to make progress on the issues of climate change and energy. We have so many things in common.

So I want to thank you very much for hospitality, the cooperation. You know, there are really close ties between the people of the United States and the Netherlands. And I'm sure that will continue in the—in future. And when we talk about these issue—important issues like human rights, freedom, democracy—they—we have, really, a common responsibility.

I wish you all the best. I presume this will be the last time here in the White House when you're in office. I wish you all the best, and thanks again for the hospitality.

President Bush. Thank you, sir. Thank you.

Prime Minister Balkenende. Thank you.

NOTE: The President spoke at 2:13 p.m. in the Oval Office at the White House.

Statement on Senate Confirmation of Steven C. Preston as Secretary of the Department of Housing and Urban Development
June 5, 2008

I am pleased that the Senate unanimously confirmed Steve Preston to serve as Secretary of the Department of Housing and Urban Development.

Steve is a strong leader whose understanding of our financial markets and strong management skills make him highly qualified to serve in this important position. He will aggressively work to ensure that the Department remains focused on its mission of making housing more affordable and helping Americans keep their homes. Steve is also a consensus builder who will build on our efforts to work with Congress on responsible legislation addressing our Nation's housing policies.

Directive on Biometrics for Identification and Screening To Enhance National Security
June 5, 2008

National Security Presidential Directive/NSPD–59

Homeland Security Presidential Directive/HSPD–24

Subject: Biometrics for Identification and Screening to Enhance National Security

Purpose

This directive establishes a framework to ensure that Federal executive departments and agencies (agencies) use mutually compatible methods and procedures in the collection, storage, use, analysis, and sharing of biometric and associated biographic and contextual information of individuals in a lawful and appropriate manner, while respecting their information privacy and other legal rights under United States law.

Scope

(1) The executive branch has developed an integrated screening capability to protect the Nation against "known and suspected terrorists" (KSTs). The executive branch shall build upon this success, in accordance with this directive, by enhancing its capability to collect, store, use, analyze, and share biometrics to identify and screen KSTs and other persons who may pose a threat to national security.

(2) Existing law determines under what circumstances an individual's biometric and biographic information can be collected. This directive requires agencies to use, in a more coordinated and efficient manner, all biometric information associated with persons who may pose a threat to national security, consistent with applicable law, including those laws relating to privacy and confidentiality of personal data.

(3) This directive provides a Federal framework for applying existing and emerging biometric technologies to the collection, storage, use, analysis, and sharing of data in identification and screening processes employed by agencies to enhance national security, consistent with applicable law, including information privacy and other legal rights under United States law.

(4) The executive branch recognizes the need for a layered approach to identification and screening of individuals, as no single mechanism is sufficient. For example, while existing name-based screening procedures are beneficial, application of biometric technologies, where appropriate, improve the executive branch's ability to identify and screen for persons who may pose a national security threat. To be most effective, national security identification and screening systems will require timely access to the most accurate and most complete biometric, biographic, and related data that are, or can be, made available throughout the executive branch.

(5) This directive does not impose requirements on State, local, or tribal authorities or on the private sector. It does not provide new authority to agencies for collection, retention, or dissemination of information or for identification and screening activities.

Definitions

(6) In this directive:

(a) "Biometrics" refers to the measurable biological (anatomical and physiological) and behavioral characteristics that can be used for automated recognition; examples include fingerprint, face, and iris recognition; and

(b) "Interoperability" refers to the ability of two or more systems or components to exchange information and to use the information that has been exchanged.

Background

(7) The ability to positively identify those individuals who may do harm to Americans and the Nation is crucial to protecting the Nation. Since September 11, 2001, agencies have made considerable progress in securing the Nation through the integration, maintenance, and sharing of information used to identify persons who may pose a threat to national security.

(8) Many agencies already collect biographic and biometric information in their identification and screening processes. With improvements in biometric technologies, and in light of its demonstrated value as a tool to protect national security, it is important to ensure agencies use compatible methods and procedures in the collection, storage, use, analysis, and sharing of biometric information.

(9) Building upon existing investments in fingerprint recognition and other biometric modalities, agencies are currently strengthening their biometric collection, storage, and matching capabilities as technologies advance and offer new opportunities to meet evolving threats to further enhance national security.

(10) This directive is designed to (a) help ensure a common recognition of the value of using biometrics in identification and screening programs and (b) help achieve objectives described in the following: Executive Order 12881 (Establishment of the National Science and Technology Council); Homeland Security Presidential Directive-6 (HSPD–6) (Integration and Use of Screening Information to Protect Against Terrorism); Executive Order 13354 (National Counterterrorism Center); Homeland Security Presidential Directive-11 (HSPD–11) (Comprehensive Terrorist Related Screening Procedures); Executive Order 13388 (Further Strengthening the Sharing of Terrorism Information to Protect Americans); National Security Presidential Directive-46/Homeland Security Presidential Directive-15 (NSPD–46/HSPD–15) (U.S. Policy and Strategy in the War on Terror); 2005 Information Sharing Guidelines; 2006 National Strategy for Combating Terrorism; 2006 National Strategy to Combat Terrorist Travel; 2007 National Strategy for Homeland Security; 2007 National Strategy for Information Sharing; and 2008 United States Intelligence Community Information Sharing Strategy.

Policy

(11) Through integrated processes and interoperable systems, agencies shall, to the fullest extent permitted by law, make available to other agencies all biometric and associated biographic and contextual information associated with persons for whom there is an articulable and reasonable basis for suspicion that they pose a threat to national security.

(12) All agencies shall execute this directive in a lawful and appropriate manner, respecting the information privacy and other legal rights of individuals under United States law, maintaining data integrity and security, and protecting intelligence sources, methods, activities, and sensitive law enforcement information.

Policy Coordination

(13) The Assistant to the President for Homeland Security and Counterterrorism, in coordination with the Assistant to the President for National Security Affairs and the Director of the Office of Science and Technology Policy, shall be responsible for interagency policy coordination on all aspects of this directive.

Roles and Responsibilities

(14) Agencies shall undertake the roles and responsibilities herein to the fullest extent permitted by law, consistent with the policy of this directive, including appropriate safeguards for information privacy and other legal rights, and in consultation with State, local, and tribal authorities, where appropriate.

(15) The Attorney General shall:

(a) Provide legal policy guidance, in co-ordination with the Secretaries of State, Defense, and Homeland Security and the Director of National Intelligence (DNI), regarding the lawful collection, use, and sharing of biometric and associated biographic and contextual information to enhance national security; and

(b) In coordination with the DNI, ensure that policies and procedures for the consolidated terrorist watchlist maximize the use of all biometric identifiers.

(16) Each of the Secretaries of State, Defense, and Homeland Security, the Attorney General, the DNI, and the heads of other appropriate agencies, shall:

(a) Develop and implement mutually compatible guidelines for each respective agency for the collection, storage, use, analysis, and sharing of biometric and associated biographic and contextual information, to the fullest extent practicable, lawful, and necessary to protect national security;

(b) Maintain and enhance interoperability among agency biometric and associated biographic systems, by utilizing common information technology and data standards, protocols, and interfaces;

(c) Ensure compliance with laws, policies, and procedures respecting information privacy, other legal rights, and information security;

(d) Establish objectives, priorities, and guidance to ensure timely and effective tasking, collection, storage, use, analysis, and sharing of biometric and associated biographic and contextual information among authorized agencies;

(e) Program for and budget sufficient resources to support the development, operation, maintenance, and upgrade of biometric capabilities consistent with this directive and with such in-structions as the Director of the Office of Management and Budget may provide; and

(f) Ensure that biometric and associated biographic and contextual information on KSTs is provided to the National Counterterrorism Center and, as appropriate, to the Terrorist Screening Center.

(17) The Secretary of State, in coordination with the Secretaries of Defense and Homeland Security, the Attorney General, and the DNI, shall coordinate the sharing of biometric and associated biographic and contextual information with foreign partners in accordance with applicable law, including international obligations undertaken by the United States.

(18) The Director of the Office of Science and Technology Policy, through the National Science and Technology Council (NSTC), shall coordinate executive branch biometric science and technology policy, including biometric standards and necessary research, development, and conformance testing programs. Recommended executive branch biometric standards are contained in the Registry of United States Government Recommended Biometric Standards and shall be updated via the NSTC Subcommittee on Biometrics and Identity Management.

Implementation

(19) Within 90 days of the date of this directive, the Attorney General, in coordination with the Secretaries of State, Defense, and Homeland Security, the DNI, and the Director of the Office of Science and Technology Policy, shall, through the Assistant to the President for National Security Affairs and the Assistant to the President for Homeland Security and Counterterrorism, submit for the President's approval an action plan to implement this directive. The action plan shall do the following:

(a) Recommend actions and associated timelines for enhancing the existing terrorist-oriented identification and screening processes by expanding the use of biometrics;

(b) Consistent with applicable law, (i) recommend categories of individuals in addition to KSTs who may pose a threat to national security, and (ii) set forth cost-effective actions and associated timelines for expanding the collection and use of biometrics to identify and screen for such individuals; and

(c) Identify business processes, technological capabilities, legal authorities, and research and development efforts needed to implement this directive.

(20) Within 1 year of the date of this directive, the Attorney General, in coordination with the Secretaries of State, Defense, and Homeland Security, the DNI, and the heads of other appropriate agencies, shall submit to the President, through the Assistant to the President for National Security Affairs and the Assistant to the President for Homeland Security and Counterterrorism, a report on the implementation of this directive and the associated action plan, proposing any necessary additional steps for carrying out the policy of this directive. Agencies shall provide support for, and promptly respond to, requests made by the Attorney General in furtherance of this report. The Attorney General will thereafter report to the President on the implementation of this directive as the Attorney General deems necessary or when directed by the President.

General Provisions

(21) This directive:

(a) shall be implemented consistent with applicable law, including international obligations undertaken by the United States, and the authorities of agencies, or heads of such agencies, vested by law;

(b) shall not be construed to alter, amend, or revoke any other NSPD or HSPD in effect on the effective date of this directive;

(c) is not intended to, and does not, create any rights or benefits, substantive or procedural, enforceable by law or in equity by a party against the United States, its departments, agencies, instrumentalities, or entities, its officers, employees, or agents, or any other person.

GEORGE W. BUSH

Remarks at the Congressional Picnic
June 5, 2008

The President. Welcome. Thank you for coming. Laura and I are thrilled you're here. Vice President and Lynne Cheney are happy you're here as well. This is a chance for us to thank the Members of Congress and their families for serving the United States of America. I hope you have found it as great a joy serving our country as we have. The South Lawn is full of anticipation and excitement. There's square dancing and trains and obviously balloon hats. [*Laughter*]

Audience member. It's a cowgirl hat.

The President. Cowgirl hat. Madam Speaker, thank you for coming. I'm—appreciate you bringing your family. Leaders of the House and the Senate, thanks for serving. I'm really thrilled to be able to introduce a friend of my family's—friends of my family for a long period of time. We're really lucky to have with us today the Oak Ridge Boys. I'm honored they are here.

Thank you all for coming. Please enjoy yourselves. May God bless you and your families. And may God continue to bless the United States of America. Thank you for coming.

NOTE: The President spoke at 6:43 p.m. on the South Lawn at the White House.

Remarks Following a Meeting on Earthquake Relief Efforts in China
June 6, 2008

Thank you very much, Bonnie, for inviting me here. I'm proud to be here with Secretary of State Rice, Secretary of Treasury Paulson. Ambassador, thank you for being here.

I've just been briefed about how the United States private sector, faith-based community, NGO community's responding to what is a horrible human disaster in China—estimated 70,000 people have died, 18,000 people missing, 15 million people homeless, and the tally is still being counted. There's no question, this is a major human disaster that requires a strong response from the Chinese Government, which is what they're providing, but it also responds—a compassionate response from nations to whom—for—that have got the blessings—good blessings of life, and that's us.

I told the folks assembled here that I'm not surprised that the American people have responded to this challenge. And the reason I'm not surprised is, we're a compassionate, decent nation that cares deeply about a stranger who hurts. And so the response of the—so far of our American citizens have been impressive—unprecedented and unparalleled in its compassion.

There'll be more work that needs to be done. My message to the Chinese Government is, thank you for welcoming our aid, thank you for taking a firm response to this disaster, and just know the American people care about the people of China. When a brother and sister hurts, we care about it.

And so that's why our response has been so robust and so compassionate to date. I want to thank you all from the bottom of my heart for showing the great compassion of America.

Thank you.

NOTE: The President spoke at 11:43 a.m. at the American Red Cross National Headquarters. In his remarks, he referred to Bonnie McElveen-Hunter, chairman of the board of governors, American Red Cross; and China's Ambassador to the U.S. Zhou Wenzhong.

Remarks at a Swearing-In Ceremony for Steven C. Preston as the Secretary of Housing and Urban Development
June 6, 2008

Thank you all. Please be seated. Thank you. Welcome. Thank you. It's a—so glad to be here at the Department of Housing and Urban Development. And I've come to introduce you to your new boss, Secretary Steve Preston. I want to thank

Steve's wife Molly, five children, and his mom and dad, Lee and Ursula.

Mr. Secretary, thanks for coming—Secretary Kempthorne; and Director John Walters. It's good to see two of your predecessors here, Steve—Alphonso Jackson and Jack Kemp. Thank you all for coming.

This is a time of turbulence in the housing market and slow growth for our overall economy. This morning the Labor Department reported that our economy lost 49,000 jobs in May and the unemployment rate rose to 5.5 percent. This rise was caused, in part, by a surge of new, young entrants into the job market, but it's clearly a sign that is consistent with slow economic growth.

To help keep this economy growing, we did pass an economic stimulus package that provides tax rebates for American families and incentives for businesses to invest in new equipment. We're beginning to see the signs that the stimulus may be working. And now the Congress needs to take the next steps. At a time when Americans are concerned about higher gas prices, Congress needs to pass legislation that expands—it will allow for the expansion of American energy production.

In this period of economic uncertainty, the last thing the Americans need is a massive tax increase. So Congress needs to send a clear message that the tax relief that we passed will be made permanent.

Unfortunately, these policies are being blocked by the Democratic Congress. So I call on congressional leaders to put partisanship aside and work with me to enact these important initiatives for the American people.

This Department is also critical to meeting the challenges we face in our economy. We need strong leadership in the Secretary's office. Steve Preston is the right man for the job. He's a financial expert who understands how the housing market impacts our broader economy. He's a skilled manager. He's a person of character and integrity.

Secretary Preston will work to strengthen homeownership with the same dedication he brought to his previous job of strengthening the American small-business community. As the head of the SBA, Steve presided over loan guarantee programs that are similar in structure to those run by the Federal Housing Administration. And just as entrepreneur across our Nation found a trusted friend in Steve Preston, so will America's homeowners.

Before coming to the SBA, Steve gained valuable financial and leadership experience in the private sector. His impressive career has taken him from investment banking to senior financial posts at major corporations. Wherever he's gone, Steve has earned the admiration of his colleagues. He takes on this new challenge with my full confidence and my trust.

Steve takes over for a good man, my longtime buddy, Secretary Alphonso Jackson. I thank you for your compassion and your hard work. You helped change a lot of lives. And I wish you and Marcia all the very best. See you back in Texas. [*Laughter*]

I also want to thank Deputy Secretary Roy Bernardi for his service. He filled in as the Acting Secretary during this transition. He spent nearly 7 years of his life here at this Department. And I appreciate your hard work on behalf of all Americans.

As Steve takes office, his first priority will [be] ° to help lead my administration's response to the challenges in the housing market. We've taken aggressive action to help responsible homeowners to keep their homes by giving the FHA greater flexibility to offer refinancing options. We're also helping to bring together what's now called the HOPE NOW Alliance. By working together, participants in the mortgage industry have helped more than 1 million—1½ million families stay in their homes. HOPE

° White House correction.

NOW is working, but we've got more to do.

Yesterday we learned that the foreclosure rates continued to rise in the first quarter. So Steve will work with Democrats and Republicans in Congress to address this challenge. We need to pass legislation to reform Fannie Mae and Freddie Mac. We need to pass legislation to modernize the Federal Housing Administration and allow State housing agencies to issue tax-free bonds to help homeowners refinance their mortgages. By taking these steps, we'll help more responsible homeowners weather this rough patch and, at the same time, strengthen the dream of homeownership for generations to come.

I've got confidence that we're going to meet these challenges, and I got confidence in the people who work in this Department. I appreciate what you do every day to expand the dream of homeownership. I thank you for your efforts to provide low-income Americans with access to affordable housing. You work hard to make sure our communities are more vibrant and hopeful. The United States is fortunate to have such devoted public servants in this Department, and I'm grateful for your service.

You're going to have a worthy leader in Steve Preston. I thank the Senate for confirming Steve as your new Secretary. I now ask the Senate to confirm the three remaining HUD nominees to help him lead this Department.

Steve, I appreciate your stepping forward to serve your country once again. I congratulate you. And now I ask my Chief of Staff, Josh Bolten, to administer the oath of office.

NOTE: The President spoke at 1:55 p.m. at the Department of Housing and Urban Development. In his remarks, he referred to Marcia Jackson, wife of former Secretary of Housing and Urban Development Alphonso R. Jackson. The transcript released by the Office of the Press Secretary also included the remarks of Secretary Preston.

Message to the Congress on Continuation of the National Emergency With Respect to the Actions and Policies of Certain Members of the Government of Belarus and Other Persons Undermining Democratic Processes or Institutions in Belarus
June 6, 2008

To the Congress of the United States:

Section 202(d) of the National Emergencies Act (50 U.S.C. 1622(d)) provides for the automatic termination of a national emergency unless, prior to the anniversary date of its declaration, the President publishes in the *Federal Register* and transmits to the Congress a notice stating that the emergency is to continue in effect beyond the anniversary date. In accordance with this provision, I have sent to the *Federal Register* for publication the enclosed notice stating that the national emergency and related measures blocking the property of certain persons undermining democratic processes or institutions in Belarus are to continue in effect beyond June 16, 2008.

The actions and policies of certain members of the Government of Belarus and other persons pose a continuing unusual and extraordinary threat to the national security and foreign policy of the United States. These actions include undermining democratic processes or institutions; committing human rights abuses related to political repression, including detentions and disappearances; and engaging in public corruption, including by diverting or misusing

Belarusian public assets or by misusing public authority. For these reasons, I have determined that it is necessary to continue the national emergency and related measures blocking the property of certain persons undermining democratic processes or institutions in Belarus.

GEORGE W. BUSH

The White House,

June 6, 2008.

NOTE: The notice is listed in Appendix D at the end of this volume.

Interview With Gianni Riotta of Italy's Rai TV
June 6, 2008

Iraq/Afghanistan/Iran

Mr. Riotta. Mr. President, the world has known tremendous change during your tenure, and three areas of concern remain: Iraq, Iran, Afghanistan. What's your assessment of those three theaters? And looking back in perspective, would you do anything different?

The President. Well, that's an interesting question on doing anything different. Of course, history is going to be the judge of that. But the decision, for example, on Iraq, to remove Saddam Hussein, was the right decision then, and it's the right decision now.

The progress in Iraq has been substantial. For a period of time, it—the democracy was in doubt, primarily because sectarian violence was really unacceptable. I decided to put more troops in, rather than pull back, and now the violence is the lowest it's been since March of 2004. And politics is beginning to happen. So I'm encouraged about Iraq.

Afghanistan is also difficult because of new democracy emerging from the shadows of a brutal regime. Last year, of course, the Taliban announced they were going to go on the offense. In fact, our coalition went on the offense and, from a security perspective, made some progress against the Taliban. The best progress, though, is the advance of better trained police

forces—and I thank the Italian Government for helping—as well as a better Afghan Army, which over time needs to provide the security for the country. Iraq will probably—progresses quicker cause it's got wealth. Afghanistan is broke.

Iran—the free world must continue to send a clear message to the Iranians that their ability to enrich, which could be transferred to a program to develop a nuclear weapon, is unacceptable. And so I will continue to work on this trip to talk about the dangers of a nuclear Iran—not civilian nuclear power, but a program that would be aimed at blackmail or destruction—and that we've got to work to stop them from learning how to enrich. And there's other ways to approach it.

Iran

Mr. Riotta. Should Iran resist the international pressure, military option remains open?

The President. Yes, it does.

Iran/Italy

Mr. Riotta. Italy wants to join the 5-plus-1 group of contacts negotiating with Iran. Germany is skeptical; they don't want us. What do you say?

The President. I say that whatever is effective in terms of sending a clear message to Iran. I will be spending time talking to this with the Prime Minister, Silvio

Berlusconi. I've talked to Condi about this issue. I said, look, whatever works. Let's make sure we're effective. Italy can be an effective voice in sending a message to the Iranians. And that you don't have to choose isolation; there's a better way forward. Verifiably suspend your enrichment program, and there's a better way forward for you and your people.

And Italy can be a critical part of that. And so we'll work—I haven't really taken the temperature that much, but my judgment is, Italy can be a very important contributor.

U.S. Foreign Policy/Energy/Food Prices

Mr. Riotta. The relationship between the United States and Europe has been strained sometimes in the recent past. During your trip, what do you suggest we can do together vis-a-vis the oil crisis, food crisis, and the recession coming?

The President. Yes, you know—first of all, let me talk about strained relations. Look, I've had great relations with many of the leaders. America and Italy remain incredibly close. Do we agree on every issue? No. But do we agree on common values? Absolutely. We believe in human rights and human dignity and free press and free religion. And so what unites us is a heck of a lot stronger than those moments where we don't necessarily agree on every single issue. And so I will remind people of that. I'll remind people that we've got a lot of work to do.

In terms of the current energy issue, look, we're too dependent on hydrocarbons. World demand is such, relative to supply, that the price of energy is high. And therefore, we need to be spending monies on new technologies to enable us to become less dependent on oil. And I'm a big nuclear power guy. I believe the United States must be much more aggressive expanding nuclear power for two reasons: one, less dependency on hydrocarbons; and two, it will make us better stewards of the environment. I mean, if you're concerned about global warming, one thing you ought to be concerned about then is making sure that we've got power generated from a clean source of energy, a renewable source of energy, which is nuclear power.

The food prices concern me, obviously. But the truth of the matter is, one reason why food prices are so high is because energy prices are high. I mean, when you think about it, farming is a pretty energy-intensive business: fertilizer is an energy; driving a tractor is an energy; crops to markets require energy. And so the crux of a lot of the problem is the energy prices.

Italy-U.S. Relations

Mr. Riotta. Talking to Prime Minister Berlusconi, what areas do you—will you encourage Italy to work with the United States, especially?

The President. Well, Iran, of course, because I just happen to see it as a major threat. We—look, we got a lot of common areas: Afghanistan—and I will thank the Italian people for their sacrifices to help this young democracy. Silvio Berlusconi and I worked a lot of big issues together in the past. I know him well, I trust him, I like him. I'm—I find him to be one of the really interesting world leaders. And I'm really looking forward to seeing him again in his capacity, once again, as the Prime Minister.

We ought to work on trade matters. We ought to work on diseases like HIV/AIDS and malaria on the continent of Africa, for example. I mean, there's a lot we can do together.

Pope Benedict XVI

Mr. Riotta. You met the Pope while in the United States, and how do you see his role in trying to reopen the dialogue between different civilizations and religions?

The President. Yes, I think it's—look, the Holy Father is a significant world figure. And we had a fabulous visit here, and it was such an honor to welcome him to the

South Lawn of the White House. I wish you could have seen it. But you—maybe you did see it. I wish your viewers could have seen the reception he was given here. I think it was one of the largest crowds ever on the South Lawn, like 13,000 people. And my own personal visit with him was so uplifting.

And we did talk about the interfaith dialogue, that I think is really important for people to find common ground through religion to, like, deal with the violence that is used by some in the name of religion, to perpetuate an ideology, and to remind people that peace—religion is peace. And there's no better person to carry that message than His Holy Father.

I talked to the King of Saudi Arabia about his visit with the Holy Father, and those are two very important figures when it comes to obviously Christianity and Islam. And I think it's just—I think it's great that he's reaching out.

2008 Presidential Election

Mr. Riotta. I know you don't want to comment on the Presidential elections, but the world is watching and is very excited because——

The President. Yes.

Mr. Riotta. ——there is a former war hero, there is an African American candidate, there's been Italian Americans, there's been a lady running for President. How do you see vitality of the American democracy, looking at this?

The President. Well, look, I'm for McCain, and everybody knows that. On the other hand, I thought it was a really good statement, powerful moment when a major political party nominates a African American man to be their standard bearer. And it's good for our democracy that that happened. And we also had a major contender being a woman. Obviously, Hillary Clinton was a major contender. So I think it's a good sign for American democracy.

Now the debate begins as to who could be the best President. And I'm in an inter-

esting position. I ran hard for the Presidency twice; I campaigned hard in the off years, and now I'll be passing the mantle on to Senator McCain, particularly at the convention when he becomes the official nominee of our party. Obviously, he's going to be the nominee, but there's a moment at the convention where it's, "Here he is." And I'll do my part to help him win, and—but it's going to be up to him. That's—he'll be the man sitting in the Oval Office making the tough decisions for peace and security.

Iraq

Mr. Riotta. You mentioned history at the beginning of this interview. And you know—you're aware that history will ask you about Iraq. What do you think now, when you look back to Iraq, especially after the report yesterday? Are you still happy with all these positions?

The President. Look, I want to remind people, the report yesterday was one of many reports that—everybody thought Saddam Hussein had weapons of mass destruction. I will remind people—and one of the things that's important about history is to remember the true history. And so the Security Council resolution was 15 to nothing on Saddam Hussein: disclose, disarm, or face serious consequences. European nations—France, Great Britain—supported that—1441, because everybody thought he had weapons of mass destruction, including many of the people who—of the Democratic Party here in the United States. You should listen to their words and listen to their quotes.

And so, absolutely, getting rid of Saddam Hussein was the right thing. And it was—we're all disappointed the intelligence wasn't what it was. But now the challenge is to help this young democracy survive. And a democracy in the heart of the Middle East is going to be, in my judgment, a powerful part of change. And we've got to work to free people in the Middle East from tyranny, because that is from—the place from which the terrorists have launched their attacks.

President's Future

Mr. Riotta. In the few seconds that are left, what will you do next?

The President. You know, good question. I haven't had much time to think about it, because I've got a lot to do. But I will probably write a book talking about the decisions I had to make, precisely to make sure that history understands the conditions and the environment during which I had to make decisions; start a freedom institute at what's called Southern Methodist University in Dallas to talk about the universal values of freedom abroad and at home. And other than that, I'm open for suggestions.

Mr. Riotta. Thank you, Mr. President.

The President. Yes, sir. Thanks. Looking forward to going back to Rome. It's a fabulous city, one of the great cities of the world.

Mr. Riotta. Especially after you leave the White House, come and I will take you around. [*Laughter*] Without the constraint of official——

The President. I'd love to.

NOTE: The interview was taped at 10:28 a.m. in the Map Room at the White House for later broadcast. In his remarks, the President referred to Prime Minister Silvio Berlusconi of Italy; Pope Benedict XVI; King Abdallah bin Abd al-Aziz Al Saud of Saudi Arabia; Democratic Presidential candidate Barack Obama; former Democratic Presidential candidate Hillary Rodham Clinton; and Republican Presidential candidate John McCain. The interviewer referred to former Republican Presidential candidate Rudolph W. Giuliani. The transcript was released by the Office of the Press Secretary on June 7. A portion of this interview could not be verified because the tape was incomplete.

The President's Radio Address
June 7, 2008

Good morning. Congress will soon vote on legislation to fund our troops serving on the frontlines of the war on terror. This is an opportunity for Congress to give our men and women in uniform the tools they need to protect us, and Congress should approve these vital funds immediately.

Congress has had this funding request for more than a year, and there is no reason for further delay. This money is urgently needed to support military operations in Afghanistan and Iraq. I put forward some reasonable requirements this bill must meet. First, this bill must give our troops the resources they need to defeat the terrorists and extremists. Second, the bill must not tie the hands of our commanders. And third, the bill must not exceed the reasonable and responsible funding levels I have requested.

Congress has had 16 months to decide how they will meet these requirements, and now the time has come for them to support our troops in harm's way. If Congress does not act, critical accounts at the Department of Defense will soon run dry. At the beginning of next month, civilian employees may face temporary layoffs. The Department will have to close down a vital program that is getting potential insurgents off the streets and into jobs. The Pentagon will run out of money it needs to support critical day-to-day operations that help keep our Nation safe. And after July, the Department will no longer be able to pay our troops, including those serving in Afghanistan and Iraq.

Our men and women in uniform and their families deserve better than this. Around the world, our troops are taking on dangerous missions with skill and determination. In Afghanistan, they're delivering blows to the Taliban and Al Qaida. In Iraq, they've helped bring violence down to its lowest point since late March of 2004. Civilian deaths are down; sectarian killings are down. As security has improved, the economy has improved as well, and political reconciliation is taking place at the grassroots and national levels. The Iraqi security forces are becoming more capable, and as they do, our troops are beginning to come home under a policy of return on success.

Each day, the men and women of our Armed Forces risk their lives to make sure their fellow citizens are safer. They serve with courage and honor. They've earned the respect of all Americans, and they deserve the full support of Congress. I often hear Members of Congress say they oppose the war but still support the troops. Now they have a chance to prove it. Congress should pass a responsible funding bill that gives our men and women in uniform the resources they need and the support they have earned.

Thank you for listening.

NOTE: The address was recorded at 10:30 a.m. on June 6 in the Cabinet Room at the White House for broadcast at 10:06 a.m. on June 7. The transcript was made available by the Office of the Press Secretary on June 6, but was embargoed for release until the broadcast. The Office of the Press Secretary also released a Spanish language transcript of this address.

Statement on the Death of Jim McKay
June 7, 2008

Laura and I were saddened to learn of the passing of Jim McKay. For a generation of Americans, Jim was more than the much-honored host of "Wide World of Sports" and ABC's Olympic coverage. He was a talented and eloquent newsman and storyteller whose special gift was his ability to make the viewers at home genuinely care about more than just who won or lost.

Jim was at his best during what had to be his most difficult assignment, hosting with skill and sensitivity ABC's blanket coverage of the 1972 Munich Olympics hostage crisis.

Off camera, he was a compassionate and generous person and devoted family man.

We are also grateful for Jim's service to his country as a naval officer aboard a minesweeper during World War II.

Our thoughts and prayers are with Jim's wife Margaret, his children Sean and Mary, and all of his family and friends.

Interview With Natasa Briski of Slovenia's POP TV
June 6, 2008

Ms. Briski. First of all, I would like to thank you very much for this opportunity and for your time, Mr. President. Thank you very much.

The President. You're welcome.

President's Visit to Slovenia

Ms. Briski. Your first—7 years ago—and what just might be your very last trip to

Europe as President include both—includes both times a stop in Slovenia. Excellent choice, I might add. [*Laughter*]

The President. I don't blame you for saying it. First of all, my first trip was consequential because that's where I first met Vladimir Putin. This trip is consequential because, of course, we're going to have an EU-U.S. summit. And my impressions of Slovenia—I've told this to a lot of people— is first of all, it's a beautiful country.

Ms. Briski. It is.

The President. Probably somewhat undiscovered in America, but my fellow citizens ought to go and explore Slovenia cause it's, I think, not only—it's got—I mean, you can ski, you can play golf.

Ms. Briski. It's a lot of opportunities for mountain biking.

The President. You can fish, mountain biking. So it's beautiful. And plus, the people are incredibly friendly.

EU-U.S. Summit

Ms. Briski. You are coming for the U.S.-EU summit.

The President. Right.

Ms. Briski. To—no dramatic announcements expected. But it will be the last summit for you.

The President. Yes.

Ms. Briski. What outcome would you like to see?

The President. Well, you know, look, the important thing about these summits is that it reaffirms our mutual values of human rights and human liberty, of our desire to work together on some key issues. And the United States and Europe has had its differences on certain issues, and—but we've always had the same common values. And it's important for me to signal to the Europeans, as well as my fellow citizens, that this relationship is an important relationship. And I'm confident the next President will see it as an important relationship as well. But we'll discuss a lot of important issues there too.

North Atlantic Treaty Organization/Europe-U.S. Relations

Ms. Briski. You're also coming to celebrate the 60th anniversary of Marshall plan and Berlin Airlift, the historic role U.S. had after World War II in supporting Europe. And you know, Europe has changed a lot recently: Western Balkans, two new states; Kosovo high on a priority list for Slovenia's Presidency. I would like to hear, what do you think are the most memorable events, Europe-wise, that your administration helped to achieve in the past 7 years?

The President. Well, one, of course, is the expansion of NATO. And it's a—I'll never forget going to Romania right after nations—some nations were admitted into NATO and talking about Article 5—an attack on one is an attack on all. And a lot of countries had come from a different style of government and a different type of security arrangements to one in which free nations were bound together. And so the expansion of NATO and the offering of—sending a positive signal to Georgia and Ukraine recently has been an incredibly positive accomplishment.

I think working together in Afghanistan is a—is going to be an historic achievement; helping a young democracy recover from a society in which women, for example, were treated as unbelievably second-class citizens. I mean, it was just a barbaric regime.

Hopefully, in terms of trade, that we'll fight off protectionism and keep trade open. I know there's some trade disputes going on, but that shouldn't prevent us from being active in terms of perpetuating free and fair trade. And so one of the things, of course, we'll be discussing is the Doha round of the WTO.

Iran/U.S. Foreign Aid

Ms. Briski. That's true. And it probably— Iran might be also high on the agenda at the summit?

The President. Yes, Iran—kind of the common threats will be on the agenda. For me—as you know, I'm a big believer in freedom. Interesting that Europe is now whole, free, and at peace, and there's a reason why. And we got to, in my judgment, extend that same concept to the Middle East, from which a lot of violence comes. And obviously, one of the problems that we face is preventing Iran from developing the know-how as to how to make a nuclear weapon.

And so we'll be discussing that kind of joint efforts, multilateral efforts. But you know, I also want to emphasize that—but the United States—and I personally feel very strongly about helping people realize the blessings of life by freeing them from HIV/AIDS or malaria or hunger. And I'm very proud of our Nation's accomplishments in terms of those agenda items. And I'm looking forward to working with our European colleagues to see if we can't make it even more robust.

Visa Waiver Program

Ms. Briski. Next question would be on visa waiver.

The President. Yes. [*Laughter*]

Ms. Briski. It's an issue, I know. It's an issue in Europe.

The President. It is an issue. It is an issue.

Ms. Briski. And you know that currently, United States enforces two different systems for travelers from——

The President. Yes.

Ms. Briski. ——European countries. Plus, you just announced new, stricter rules for countries that are part of the Visa Waiver Program. I wanted to hear your opinion on that, and maybe your answer to those in Europe who say that America is not as welcoming a place that it used to be.

The President. Yes. No, look, I'm concerned about that impression, because we are a welcoming place. We want our friends to come. We want investment to be open.

You know, first of all, I can understand why many of our friends in Europe who aren't treated like other nations within the EU are treated on visas are concerned. They say: "Wait a minute. We're very supportive of the United States. We like the United States. And yet we're treated differently when it comes to visas." And this is a hangover from the old visa system, which I have been assiduously working to change. And we are making good progress. As a matter of fact, there—I think there's going to be quite a few nations that were—will get visa waiver.

As to whether or not we've made it harder for visa waiver countries to come to the United States, actually not; we've made it easier. In other words, you file your paperwork online before you come to the United States, which should actually facilitate travel, we hope. But look, I am concerned that people say, "Well, America no longer wants us to come," when it's the exact opposite of my personal point of view and the view of my government.

U.S. Image Abroad

Ms. Briski. Sure. And I have to ask you this: Public surveys taken globally indicate kind of anti-Americanism, and——

The President. Yes.

Ms. Briski. ——Europe is no exception in that. Do you believe that the American brand needs a makeover?

The President. No. I mean, we stand for liberty and human rights and freedom. Look, I've had to make some tough decisions that some people didn't like. But the truth of the matter is, when you really look at—like, for example, our relations in the Far East, we got great relations with Japan, China, and Korea—South Korea. Or India, for example—we got new relations with India that no administration has ever pushed—South America, and Central America.

My attitude is this—this is what I tell people: First of all, you can't make decisions based upon opinion polls. Secondly, that a lot of people like America; they may not sometimes necessarily like the President, but they like America. They like what

America stands for. Otherwise, why would so many people wanting to be—come here, for example, which we welcome. And so I don't—I hear just stuff like that, and I just—I dismiss it as kind of like what happens when there's, kind of, gossip and rumors and—because the truth of the matter is, America, just like many nations in Europe, stands for what's right, which is decency and freedom of speech and freedom to worship. And I'm very proud of my country, obviously.

2008 Presidential Election

Ms. Briski. Okay. And on American Presidency, actually on elections, international policies are the aspects where the President's work—that—where the Commander in Chief has an opportunity to change the history's course.

The President. Yes.

Ms. Briski. And that is why people around the world follow the American elections very, very closely. It's been very interesting so far.

The President. Yes, it has.

Ms. Briski. The Democrats—Democratic candidates have not been very easy on you.

The President. Of course not. They got me—look, if you're—that's what happens. I mean, they say, "We want change." Of course—and I tell people, every time I ran for politics I said, "We want change," unless, of course, I was the incumbent, in which case I was not for change; I was for myself. But what you'll see is a lot of rhetoric, and I understand that. It's—and,

you know, I'm in an unusual position because for the past 14 years, I've been an active candidate myself, and now I'm kind of getting to be a senior—kind of senior status. And I'll help my party, and of course, I'm for John McCain. But there will be a lot of debate, and it will be interesting to watch these candidates.

Ms. Briski. Sure. So your message to the 44th President of the United States would be?

The President. Stand on principle, stay strong, promote freedom, defend America, and work with our friends and allies to achieve common objectives.

Ms. Briski. Mr. President, thank you very much for this interview. I hope you will have a safe flight to Europe. And as you referred to Slovenia 2 years ago, on our Prime Minister's visit to the White House, as an "interesting slice of heaven," I hope you will have a heavenly stay.

The President. I'll bet I do.

Ms. Briski. Thank you very much.

The President. Thank you so much. Good to see you.

NOTE: The interview was taped at 10:15 a.m. in the Map Room at the White House for later broadcast. In his remarks, the President referred to Prime Minister Vladimir V. Putin of Russia, in his former capacity as the President of Russia; and Republican Presidential candidate John McCain. Ms. Briski referred to Prime Minister Janez Jansa of Slovenia. The transcript was released by the Office of the Press Secretary on June 8.

Remarks on Departure for Kranj, Slovenia
June 9, 2008

Good morning. I'm just about to leave for Europe. I'm looking forward to my trip. I'm looking forward to meeting with our friends and allies. We've got strong relations in Europe, and this trip will help so-

lidify those relations. And we got a lot to talk about.

First, I'm looking forward to talking about the freedom agenda with the European nations. You know, we've got a lot of work to do in Afghanistan. And the countries I'm going to have committed troops to Afghanistan, and of course, I want to thank them and remind them there's a lot of work to be done.

I talked to Laura yesterday, who, as you now know, took a trip to Afghanistan. I want to thank her for going. She gave me a good assessment about what she saw. She saw progress, but she also saw there needs to be a lot of work to be done—there's a lot of work to be done. And so she's going to go to the Paris conference, along with Secretary Rice, on our behalf to ask nations to contribute to the development of Afghanistan, which will mean they'll be contributing to peace.

And then, of course, we'll be talking about the economy. A lot of Americans are concerned about our economy. I can understand why. Gasoline prices are high; energy prices are high. I do remind them that we have put a stimulus package forward that is expected to help boost the economy. Of course, we'll be monitoring the situation.

We'll remind our friends and allies overseas that we're all too dependent on hydrocarbons and must work to advance technologies to help us become less dependent on hydrocarbons. I'll also remind them, though, that the United States has an opportunity to help increase the supply of oil on the market, therefore, taking pressure off gasoline for hard-working Americans, and that I've proposed to the Congress that they open up ANWR and open up the Continental Shelf, and give this country a chance to help us through this difficult period by finding more supplies of crude oil, which will take the pressure off the price of gasoline.

These are global issues we'll be discussing. Secretary Paulson will be also discussing issues at the G–8 ministers in Japan this week.

As well, I'll talk about our Nation's commitment to a strong dollar. A strong dollar is in our Nation's interests; it is in the interests of the global economy. Our economy is large, and it's open and flexible. Our capital markets are some of the deepest and most liquid. And the long-term health and strong foundation of our economy will shine through and be reflected in currency values.

U.S. economy has continued to grow in the face of unprecedented challenges. We got to keep our economies flexible. Both the U.S. economy and European economies need to be flexible in order to deal with today's challenges.

I'm looking forward to my trip, and I'm looking forward to seeing Laura. Thank you.

NOTE: The President spoke at 6:55 a.m. on the South Lawn at the White House.

Letter to the Speaker of the House of Representatives Transmitting Budget Amendments
June 9, 2008

Dear Madam Speaker:

I ask the Congress to consider the enclosed amendments to my FY 2009 Budget requests for the Departments of Agriculture, Energy, Homeland Security, Housing and Urban Development, the Interior, Labor, Transportation, and the Treasury; as well as the Corps of Engineers, the National Aeronautics and Space Administration, and the Office of Personnel Management. These amendments will decrease by $3 million the overall discretionary budget authority in my FY 2009 Budget.

These amendments are necessary to correctly reflect policies proposed in my FY 2009 Budget. The details of these amendments are set forth in the enclosed letter from the Director of the Office of Management and Budget.

Sincerely,

GEORGE W. BUSH

NOTE: This letter was released by the Office of the Press Secretary on June 10.

Letter to the Speaker of the House of Representatives Transmitting Budget Amendments
June 9, 2008

Dear Madam Speaker:

I ask the Congress to consider the enclosed amendments to my FY 2009 Budget for the Departments of Agriculture, Commerce, Health and Human Services, Homeland Security, the Interior, Labor, and the Treasury. Overall, the discretionary budget authority proposed in my FY 2009 Budget would not be increased by these requests.

I am requesting an additional $546 million for the Department of Commerce to cover increased costs to conduct the 2010 Decennial Census. I am also requesting $275 million for the Department of Health and Human Services to improve food and medical product safety and $1 million for the Department of Homeland Security to continue operations of the Office of the Federal Coordinator for Gulf Coast Rebuilding through February 28, 2009. These amounts are fully offset by reductions to other accounts.

The details of these amendments are set forth in the enclosed letter from the Director of the Office of Management and Budget.

Sincerely,

GEORGE W. BUSH

NOTE: This letter was released by the Office of the Press Secretary on June 10.

Letter to the Speaker of the House of Representatives Transmitting a Supplemental Budget Request for the Legislative Branch for Fiscal Year 2008
June 9, 2008

Dear Madam Speaker:

As a matter of comity, I am transmitting to the Congress, without modification, the enclosed supplemental proposal from the legislative branch for FY 2008.

The details of this request are set forth in the enclosed letter from the Director of the Office of Management and Budget.

Sincerely,

GEORGE W. BUSH

NOTE: This letter was released by the Office of the Press Secretary on June 10.

The President's News Conference With European Union Leaders in Kranj, Slovenia
June 10, 2008

Prime Minister Jansa. Good afternoon, and welcome to Slovenia. Welcome to Brdo, where we have just concluded this year's summit meeting between the EU and the U.S.A. I welcome in our midst the President of the United States of America, Mr. George W. Bush, and the President of the European Commission, Mr. Jose Barroso.

For the U.S. President, this is the eighth summit and his second visit to Slovenia. It happened on the same spot; also, the press conference was held here. This is a historic event. On my visit to Washington 2 years ago, Mr. President, you welcomed us by saying that Slovenia is a piece of heaven on Earth, and we enjoyed your excellent hospitality. I hope we are returning that hospitality to some extent today.

Our discussions at this summit were very good and open. We confirmed that the transatlantic partnership is solid and dynamic. This message carries special weight in the historic context of this summit. Sixty years ago, the U.S. offered the ravaged and divided Europe hope through the Marshall plan and through courage, solidarity, and vision. The first U.S. President, George Washington, once said that there will be a united states of Europe. This has not happened yet, but European Union has been created, an area of freedom and progress uniting 500 million Europeans.

The European Union and the U.S. share the most important fundamental values: democracy, free entrepreneurial initiative, respect for human rights and fundamental freedoms, and the respect for the principles of the rule of law. The EU and the U.S. together represent 10 percent of the world's population. The trade in goods and services amounts to 3 billion euros a day, and they together produce almost 60 percent of the world's GDP. And together they

contribute 75 percent of development aid to poor countries. However, they also emit the majority of greenhouse gases.

Because of all these reasons, they also share a significant joint responsibility impacting the key global challenges. Our views on certain paths differ. Our views are different on, for example, the death penalty or the mandatory restriction on CO_2 emissions, but we are openly discussing these differences and looking for solutions.

We spoke at length about the issues of climate change and energy security. These issues affect all humanity and our well-established habits and our way of life. We confirmed our readiness to face this challenge together. We in the European Union consider it necessary to define the mandatory objectives for reducing CO_2 emissions and to reach a global agreement. We must cooperate in protecting the environment, in searching new sources of energy, and in developing new technologies.

High oil prices have forced us to intensify our search for new energy solutions. We are on the threshold of a new industrial revolution. Low carbon production and transport are becoming an economic necessity in addition to an environmental one. We need the most efficient solutions to the benefit of the present and future generations as soon as possible. The European Union and the U.S. will lead the new industrial revolution.

We must also create broad alliances. Several important meetings are ahead of us this year. We have great expectations concerning the G–8 summit and the U.N. conference on climate change in Poland.

We spoke about the most topical issues of the world economy. Our goals include a secure future, preservation of jobs, and combating protectionism. We are determined to cooperate in eliminating the global imbalances and to attract to the this— to this task the new, fast-growing economies. We are committed to continuing discussions on the Doha development agenda within the framework of the WTO and to the realization of the Millennium Development Goals.

We also discussed a series of regional issues. We focused in particular on the Western Balkans. In the European Union, we value greatly the role the U.S. played in the 1990s in putting an end to the violence in the region. Today we are united and firm in our support of the prospect of these countries joining the Euro-Atlantic structures. This is the path which leads to peace and stability, as well as to the necessary democratic and economic reforms.

We were informed of the work carried out by the Transatlantic Economic Council. We remain committed to the elimination of barriers to mutual trade, a process which will bring economic growth and create new jobs. We are in favor of establishing the Transatlantic Economic Council as a mechanism for bringing tangible results that will benefit both consumers and producers in the EU and the U.S. The European Commission and its President, Barroso, are making every effort to this end.

The concrete results also includes the Air Transport Agreement. The first stage of the agreement has already entered into force. It liberalizes conditions for mutual investment and enables a freer access to air services. And in the middle of the former months, we launched the negotiations on the second stage. The work on the Aviation Safety Agreement has also been completed, and I hope it will be signed by the end of the month.

We also spoke about visa-free travel to the U.S. for all EU citizens. I am pleased that we are close to seeing new countries join the Visa Waiver Program soon. We are aware that certain restrictions are necessary for security reasons. Nevertheless, we remain determined to ensure that the need for enhanced security will not restrict the visa-free travel for our citizens.

[*At this point, Prime Minister Jansa continued in English.*]

Mr. President, European Union and United States are most developed democracies. Last big EU enlargement, which included Slovenia and other center and Eastern European countries, has been one of the great—greatest achievements in terms of promotion of democracy. Today, almost whole Europe is free and united. This is very strong message for 21st century. The world is now complex. Nobody alone can solve all problems. War, peace, security, and promotion of democracy, climate change, and fight against poverty are global challenges today. Even together, we are not able to solve all of them, but if we don't work together and we are not able to form even stronger alliance, then I'm afraid we won't succeed.

I'm glad that we can conclude after last few and also after today's EU-U.S. summit that we indeed work together. Although we might have different approaches in some aspects, it should never overshadow the depth and quality of our cooperation. We covered, as I said, a wide range of issues during our talks, from foreign policy to economic cooperation. Many strategic projects are underway. Maybe we need to develop also a common name for them. Symbols and names are important in the world's politics.

Mr. President, we led strongly to the rich story of your—this time's European tour— 60th anniversary of the Berlin Airlift and the Marshall plan. United States engagement did not only bring rehabilitation to Europe by promoting integration, it set an irreversible process in motion. Today Slovenia is hosting EU-U.S. summit, something that seemed impossible 60 years ago, something that seemed impossible even 20 years ago, during the Slovenian Spring, when our streets were full of people fighting for freedom and democracy.

Our history teach us that we must be ambitious. It's time to be ambitious. We have to create stronger alliance based on our democratic values—ever to protect them, but also to share them with others. Alliance of democracies is strong and credible toward inside and open to outside world. Alliance able to lead, to change, and to help—a new hope for those who suffer. Who else can start the work if the biggest and most developed democracies can't?

Now I invite the President of United States, Mr. George Bush, to take the floor, and then the President of the European Commission.

Thank you.

President Bush. Mr. Prime Minister, thank you. Commission President Barroso, it's good to see you. Thank you for your time and friendship. Let me correct the record, Mr. Prime Minister. I said, "Slovenia was a little slice of heaven." I'd like to, with your indulgence, change my remarks. Slovenia is a big slice of heaven. [*Laughter*] And I'm——

Prime Minister Jansa. Thank you.

President Bush. ——honored to be back in your beautiful country. One of these days, I'm going to come back as a tourist. As you know, I'm close to retirement. [*Laughter*] And I'm looking forward to seeing more of your beautiful country and meeting more of your really gracious and hospitable people. So thank you very much.

This is my eighth EU-U.S. meeting. My message at the end is that it's really important for the United States to stay close with the EU. It's in our interest that the EU be strong, vibrant, and it's in our interests to work hard to have a partnership that solves problems.

And we discussed a lot of problems today. First, we discussed the freedom agenda. I find it ironic—not ironic, just interesting—that 20 years ago, Mr. Prime Minister, you were in jail—[*laughter*]—because of your beliefs, because——

Prime Minister Jansa. Not very happy times. [*Laughter*]

President Bush. You shouldn't have been happy about it. But because you had the courage to stand up and speak out clearly for freedom for all people, you were put in jail. And it seems like that any time we find people who were put in jail because they're willing to speak up for freedom, those of us who live in free lands ought to work to liberate them, Mr. Prime Minister.

And we spent a lot of time talking about how to help others realize the blessings of liberty, whether it be in the Balkans, and whether it be a Palestinian state, whether it be to use the EU as a way to encourage people to develop the habits of reformist societies.

And by the way, one subject we didn't spend a lot of time on that I'd like to clarify the U.S. position on is, we strongly believe Turkey ought to be a member of the EU. And we appreciate Turkey's record of democratic and free market reforms in working to realize its EU aspirations.

We spent a lot of time on the Middle East. Besides the Palestinian state, we talked about Lebanon, Iran, and Syria. One thing is for certain: If more people lived in free societies in the Middle East, the Middle East would be a more hopeful and more peaceful place. And so we strategized as to how to do that, Mr. Prime Minister, and I want to thank you for that.

I thank you for your support in Iraq and Afghanistan. It's amazing how these countries have gone from tyrannical situations to hopeful, young democracies. And I believe it's in our mutual interest to work hard to help these democracies survive for the sake of peace and for the sake of human rights and human dignity.

We talked about Cuba. I want to thank very much your leadership—both of your leadership in having the EU summit in South America. Obviously, it's in the U.S. interest that you do so. We've got a lot of relations with countries in our neighborhood.

I want to thank you very much for your expressions on Cuba. They said, before relations should go forward, all political prisoners ought to be freed. If the Castro administration really is different, the first way to show that difference to the world is to free the political prisoners. That's something, Mr. Prime Minister, that I'm sure you can relate to.

We talked about Zimbabwe, Darfur, and Burma. We talked about how to make sure we have travel in a way that comforts our societies. I understand the visa waiver issue very well. I spend a lot of time talking to people that are worried about not being able to be treated like other members of the EU. I know the problem. We're on our way to solving it in a way that, I think, will satisfy countries as well as the EU itself, Jose.

We spent a lot of time on Iran. And I appreciate the Foreign Minister, Solana, going to Iran to deliver a clear message: There is a better way for you to move forward than a way that, so far, has led to isolation. And a—Iran with a nuclear weapon would be incredibly dangerous for world peace. And so we've got to continue to work together to make it clear, abundantly clear to them, that it's their choice to make. They can either face isolation, or they can have a—better relations with all of us if they verifiably suspend their enrichment program.

We talked about trade and the Doha round. We're committed to a successful Doha round. It's not going to be easy, but it's, in our judgment, necessary that we continue to work together. I appreciate Ambassador Schwab and Commissioner Mandelson's cooperation in trying to get an agreement that we all can live with. It's really important to defeat the voices of protectionism now. And if you're truly worried about global development, if you're worried about poverty, one of the best ways to help poor people is through trade. And so we're committed to the global round.

I thought our discussions today were very good. And we don't—we spent time talking about HIV/AIDS and malaria on the continent of Africa. The United States is—looks forward to working with EU nations to helping alleviate folks from needless death. We've got a strategy in place that's effective, and we look forward to having partners join us.

And then finally, of course, we talked about energy and global climate change. I assured the leaders we have a strategy that we think will be effective at addressing global climate change and, at the same time, dependence on hydrocarbons, and that is through a major economies meeting, a series of meetings, all aimed at getting the major developing—the major economies to agree to a firm goal and to commit to strategies to achieve that goal. The United States is more than willing to engage in those discussions. I will just tell you that unless China and India are at the table, unless they agree to a goal, unless they agree to firm strategies to achieve that goal, then I don't see how any international agreement can be effective.

And so therefore, our strategy is to be realistic and to understand that the process is important but not nearly as important as the results. And so we've had good engagement, Mr. Prime Minister and Commission President Barroso. Thank you for your friendship. I'm—you know, it's interesting, my first visit as U.S. President to Europe included a—my first stop in Slovenia. My last visit as U.S. President to Europe includes first stop in Slovenia. It's a fitting circle. [*Laughter*]

Thank you.

Prime Minister Jansa. Thank you. Please.

President Durao Barroso. Thank you. Thank you, Prime Minister Jansa, President Bush. I'll start by this point. I think it's very symbolic and important that this summit, here with President Bush, the last one you will be present as President of the

United States, with European Union is in Slovenia, a country that, more or less, 25 years ago was not yet free and independent. And today, it's the Presidency of the European Council, is a member of the euro zone, is a member of the Schengen area, and assuming full its responsibilities.

And let me underline this point, because it really deserves to be underlined: That would not have been possible without European Union and without strong transatlantic relationship, because during the cold war, we have always had the support of the United States of America.

And this is very important to understand, for the public in Europe and, I believe, also in United States, that the support of the United States of America to freedom and democracy and, indeed, to the European integration process was very, very important, and that this great project of European integration is well and running. Fifty years ago, we were 6 member states; now we are 27 countries. And this country where we were was not a free country. My own country, 45 years ago, was not a democracy. And now we have from the Atlantic to the Black Sea, from the Mediterranean to the Baltic Sea, democratic countries living together in peace and freedom.

This is indeed a great achievement. And this achievement was possible thanks to the commitment of the founding fathers of the European Union to a united Europe, but also thanks to support of the United States of America. That's why I think it's fair to say to the United States sometimes, "Thank you." Thank you for all the support you have been giving to the integration and progress of democracy also in Europe.

So I believe it's important that we put all our relations in this perspective: a community of values, a community of values not only for our respective nations but beyond, promoting and supporting a world based on human rights and democracy.

President Bush and Prime Minister Jansa already spoke about the main subjects. I will not repeat what—everything they said. Let me just underline one or two points that are more in the competence of the European Commission.

On trade issues, we must work hard to achieve a fair and balanced outcome to the current round of WTO talks. The deal remains there to be done if the political will is there. I believe the deal will be good for developing countries in terms of new opportunities. It will also give a needed boost to the global economy, including the European Union and the U.S. economies. Time to move is now. We have a fair and balanced deal in our grasp that will help us face the challenges of globalization.

So I believe together the United States and European Union can make a difference trying to bring others to a more realistic position so that we can achieve that deal on Doha trade and development talks.

One year ago, we have adopted a framework for advancing transatlantic economic integration, and I was proud, together with President Bush and Chancellor Merkel—then President of the Council—to create a Transatlantic Economic Council. We have put in place a new working method. Today I'm happy to say that in just 1 year of existence, this body has brought more and steadier progress on some issues than in many years before. We have made progress on open investment, on accounting standards, on finding alternative methods to animal testing, on certification of electrical equipment.

This might be seen as rather technical, but all of these developments add up to major cost savings for European Union companies and United States companies as well. This is understood by all parties. There were reports made by the transatlantic business community as estimated economic benefits of the items on our TEC—on our Transatlantic Economic Council agenda—as $10 billion in terms of savings for business on both sides of the Atlantic.

So it is fair to say that Transatlantic Economic Council has given new momentum to the bilateral economic agenda. Indeed, the European Union and the United States of America count for the largest bilateral trade relationship in the world. Transatlantic trade in goods and services totals over 1.9 billion euros a day, and the figures of all bilateral trade and investment show the high degree of interdependence of our economies. The European—the United States remains the largest export destination for the European Union. In a time of important challenges to our economies, we have reaffirmed our commitment to free trade, open economies in the face of protectionist voices on both sides of the Atlantic.

The challenging economic situation makes the partnership ever more important. As we see with rising fuel and food prices, we, now in Europe, are discussing what are the right policy choices to increase energy diversification, energy efficiency, and also to improve food management. And we believe that these developments make it even more urgent to find a global agreement on climate change, and we spent a lot of our time discussing this.

What we have in common? The will to come to that agreement. We need that agreement to be global, so, of course, to add also China, India, and others. And I believe it is important now to move ahead.

We have discussed some of the events that we are preparing, like that major economies meeting and also the G–8 meeting. And we hope that the United States and Europe can work even closer in this matter, because we—European and American leadership—it's quite clear for me that it will be easier to get that global agreement. We are trying to get it by 2009 in Copenhagen, a United Nations agreement that could, of course, create the right response—global response for a global problem in terms of climate change. We need that not only because of a responsibility towards our planet, but we need also be-

cause of energy security concerns and also because of the rising food prices and the pressure that those prices are putting on our economies and the competitiveness of our economies.

So those were two of the subjects that we have discussed—economic—more in detail: the economic and trade and investment relations and also climate change. There were many others that President Bush and Prime Minister Jansa also referred, but let me congratulate you, Prime Minister Jansa, for a very successful meeting and for the high quality of the debate and the open debate that you had today.

Prime Minister Jansa. Thank you. Now we have time for a few questions.

EU-U.S. Relations

Q. Hello, Mr. President, here I am—Slovenian public television. Mr. President, as you mentioned before, this is probably your last visit in Slovenia and Europe.

President Bush. As President. [*Laughter*]

Q. As President, of course. With your past experience of last, let's say, 8 years, how can you see the future of the European Union and its relations with United States? There are certain problems.

President Bush. Yes, there are problems. On the other hand, there is much more that unites us than divides us. Of course, there is going to be problems and differences. That's normal.

First of all, there's going to be differences within the EU. You got—you have 27 nations all trying to come together to forge a common agenda. That's why I'd much rather have my job than Jose's job. [*Laughter*] But there will be differences. But somehow they managed to forge a common position on a lot of key issues, and that's where we discuss these issues.

And—but the thing that unites us—and this is important for all of us to realize—is that we share common values. And people say, oh, that's just corny, that doesn't mean anything. It means a lot if you believe in human rights and human dignity and rule of law and freedom to speak and freedom to worship. That's a lot. That's a foundation for a very firm and lasting relationship.

And so I am confident that whoever succeeds me as President will understand the importance of the EU in regards to United States foreign policy and will work hard to make sure ties, you know, remain strong. But make no mistake about it, there will be differences of—on how to approach certain issues, and that's okay, just so long as we let those—don't let those differences divide us permanently, and I don't believe they possibly can.

Press Secretary Dana Perino. All right, we'll take a question from the American side, Steven Lee Myers of the New York Times, please.

Iran

Q. Thank you, gentlemen. I wonder if I could ask about your statement on Iran and the communique today. And you described a combination of incentives as well as additional measures that you might take. And I wonder if you think that that is enough—the idea of the prospect of future action is enough or sufficient to get the Iranians to change their point of view?

And for you, President Bush, sir, are you frustrated at all by the pace of the diplomatic negotiations underway, particularly in light of the IAEA findings and Iran's insistence that it's going to continue to enrich? Thank you.

President Bush. I'll start. We've always made it clear to the Iranians there's a better way forward, that if they want to have a relationship with the EU–3 and the United States and other countries, they— all they've got to do is verifiably suspend their enrichment program. And the reason why that's important is that they learn to enrich, it means they've learned to—a key part of developing a nuclear weapon. And if they end up with a nuclear weapon, the free world's going to say, why didn't we do something about it at the time, before

they developed it? And so now is the time for there to be strong diplomacy.

You know, the fundamental question is not ours to make; it's theirs to make, and that is, are they going to continue on their path of obstruction? Will they continue to isolate their people? Are they going to continue to deny the people of Iran a bright future by basically saying, we don't care what the world says.

And that's the position they're in. I'll leave behind a multilateral framework to work this issue. I think the Prime Minister said it's—you know, one country can't solve all problems. I fully agree with that. A group of countries can send a clear message to the Iranians, and that is, we're going to continue to isolate you; we'll continue to work on sanctions; we'll find new sanctions if need be if you continue to deny the just demands of a free world, which is to give up your enrichment program.

They've ignored IAEA in the past, and therefore, they can't be trusted with enrichment. And I thought we had a very fruitful discussion. We're on the same page. And I want to thank both leaders up here and Foreign Minister Solana as well.

Iran/Israel/Environment

Q. [*Inaudible*]

President Bush. This is "Ask George" day. [*Laughter*]

Moderator. A question from the European side.

Q. Yes. I would have a question for both of—President and the Prime Minister.

President Bush. Which President? [*Laughter*] Let me guess.

Q. The President of the United States.

President Bush. Yes, all right. [*Laughter*] Sorry, Jose. Just trying to work you in the deal here, you know? [*Laughter*]

Q. As you said, he's the Commission's President.

President Bush. Okay, fine.

Q. On Iran, I would like to ask you, Mr. President, there is—seems to be an emerging debate in Israel about a military option against the nuclear installations in Iran. How do you see that debate?

And, Prime Minister Jansa, I would like to ask you on climate change, how do you rate the chances that in the following years there will be an agreement with the U.S. on this issue?

President Bush. First of all, if you were living in Israel, you'd be a little nervous too if a leader in your neighborhood announced that they—he'd like to destroy you. And one sure way of achieving that means is through the development of a nuclear weapon. Therefore, now is the time for all of us to work together to stop them. There's a lot of urgencies when it comes to dealing with Iran, and the Israeli political folks—and if you go to Israel and listen carefully, you'll hear that urgency in their voice—one of many urgencies. And I'm hopeful we can get it done.

And by the way—I don't want to preclude the Prime Minister's answer—I think we can actually get an agreement on global climate change during my Presidency, just so you know.

Prime Minister Jansa. I believe in a global agreement for a joint fight against climate change. This is, as a matter of fact, the only solution. An agreement or a self-commitment of the most developed or industrial countries to reduce greenhouse gas emissions is not enough, especially because some developing countries are developing really fast. China will, in a few years, become the first in terms of the greenhouse gas emissions. And a global agreement without the developing countries would be a short-term solution.

So, as a matter of fact, we really need that everybody who is a key stakeholder sits at the table. And I have mentioned already in my introduction, those who are most developed should take the leading role. And therefore, this alliance, these agreements, these discussions on bringing closer the standpoints is of such significance.

As President Bush has mentioned, the commitment of the most developed economies—which is mandatory to reduce emissions by a certain deadline—this is a key commitment: how individual economies this reach is less important. However, the goals must be set, and we must have mandatory goals, and this is of key importance. And in this way, we will reduce the threat of climate change.

And of course, we should also attract to this task the other countries. Without the leading role of the European Union and the United States of America and without close cooperation, it is not possible to reach a global agreement in short term. Therefore, this discussion is of extreme importance. And the G-8 summit in Japan in next month should represent an important step forward if we wish, in time, before the U.N. conference in Copenhagen, reach this agreement. There is not much time left. The time is running out.

Press Secretary Perino. All right, we'll take the last one from John McKinnon of the Wall Street Journal.

President Bush. It's called technology. [*Laughter*]

Q. Thanks again.

President Bush. Yes. [*Laughter*] Glad to help out, you know.

U.S. Monetary Policy/European Economy/ EU-U.S. Relations

Q. I'd like to ask each of you leaders about economic issues. For President Bush, will the United States intervene to support the dollar if your current efforts to talk it up don't succeed? And what also is your reaction to the Saudi Arabian proposal for a summit on energy prices?

For Prime Minister Jansa, what effects are you feeling in Eastern and Central Europe from the rising energy prices and the rising value of the euro? Did those factors pose a risk to growth and integration for those countries, for your countries?

And for President Barroso, given the proliferation of disputes between Europe and the United States over food safety issues, is there a concern that the EU is being too restrictive on those issues?

President Bush. Okay, John, interesting idea by the—His Majesty, the King of Saudi Arabia. Secondly, I articulated a policy that I had been articulating ever since I have been the President. It's the same policy, which is, we believe in a strong dollar and that relative value of economies will end up setting the proper valuation of the dollar.

Prime Minister Jansa. Past growth, or growth with little comparison in the history—this is the growth of energy and food prices. And the food prices are going up due to high cost of energy or oil, and this has a significant effect on the economy in Slovenia and throughout Europe. This is one of the key questions being dealt with at the national level and at the level of the European institutions, as has been mentioned by President Barroso. This is a serious problem. It will, on the one hand, make us search long-term solutions. I have mentioned this in part before. And on the other hand, it will make us search short-term solutions, and one of these is energy efficiency.

We have also discussed this at today's summit, and this is a strong message. The investment in research and development, the investment into what the economy can do, an economy that is less dependent on carbon, less dependent on fossil fuels, this will have a long-term strategic effect on the price.

So the key is the technology. I remember the President of the United States saying 2 years ago at the summit meeting in Vienna that the key thing is investment in the development of new technologies. This is the key strategic reply to these challenge. And as far as the euro is concerned, on the one hand, we are satisfied and happy that euro is a strong currency. And since the 1st of January of last year, Slovenia is also part of the euro zone. And I can say that in the majority, the effects are

positive. When calculating the high prices of oil in dollars, this slightly mitigates this jump. And on the other hand, this is also a problem for importers in the European Union. We wouldn't like to see a weak euro and a strong dollar.

Moderator. The press conference is nearly completed.

President Durao Barroso. Honestly, I don't see the proliferation of difficulties with the United States on food. On the contrary, some of the issues that we have been discussing for some time have now known some progress. What I believe is that on food and energy in general, there are issues that we have to address together. And some of those challenges are really global by nature, and we need to have a structured responses to them.

There will not be quick fixes. Some of those developments are long-term structural challenges. What is important, by the way, is that in the short term, we do not take measures against what is the long-term solution for those problems—namely, once again, we need a global agreement on climate change, is best way to fight some of the problems of energy prices and also to address some of problems of food security, namely in some developing countries.

But I don't see a proliferation of specific problems now on United States regarding food. On the contrary, I see a very cooperative position, and negotiations on the specific issues are going on with a very constructive mood.

Moderator. Thank you very much. The press conference has finished. And now I give the concluding words to the Prime Minister, Mr. Janez Jansa, the President of the Council of the European Union.

Prime Minister Jansa. Mr. President, before we conclude this press conference, let me repeat once again how much we appreciate your visit here after 7 years, concluding the circle, as you said. And our bilateral meeting, which we had in this morning, confirmed that Slovenia and the

United States have established sound foundations for building excellent relations. And I want just to repeat the words from the President of the European Commission, that without the vital support of United States for this positive changes in Europe, before the fall of Berlin Wall and after it, maybe we wouldn't be here today at Brdo. And I surely wouldn't be here in this capacity. [*Laughter*]

But I also want to say thank you because of one other thing. Sir, hundreds of thousands of Slovenes driven from homeland by the economic and political hardship of our history have found open hands and hearts in the United States. Some of them are making great contributions their walks of life in the United States. We are proud of them here in Slovenia. We are also pleased that the progress that Slovenia has made since independence gives them pride. And I'm sure that today, as we host this summit, there is a lot of proud Slovenes in the States.

President Bush. Yes, sir.

Prime Minister Jansa. Mr. President, this was your eighth EU-U.S. summit. During this last 8 years, our EU-U.S. strategic partnership has developed significantly. It has faced also some serious challenges, which we have successfully overcome. Today, we are closer to common position to our most important global challenges than ever. It is not too early, but it's not too late either. Thank you, Mr. President, for your leadership.

President Bush. Thank you, sir. Thank you. I appreciate you. Good job.

NOTE: The President's news conference began at 2:35 p.m. at Brdo Castle. Participating in the event were Prime Minister Janez Jansa of Slovenia, in his capacity as President of the European Council; and President Jose Manuel Durao Barroso of the European Commission. President Bush referred to President Raul Castro Ruz of Cuba; Foreign Minister Javier Solana Madariaga and Commissioner for Trade Peter Mandelson of the European Union; and King Abdallah bin Abd al-Aziz Al Saud of Saudi Arabia. President Durao Barroso referred to Chancellor Angela Merkel of Germany. Prime Minister Jansa spoke partly in Slovenian, and those portions of his remarks were translated by an interpreter.

The President's News Conference With Chancellor Angela Merkel of Germany in Meseberg, Germany
June 11, 2008

Chancellor Merkel. Well, good morning, ladies and gentlemen. I see that there are quite a number of you who have made the trouble to come here today. I would like to welcome you very warmly. Let me say that I'm delighted to be able to have this press conference together with the American President after our talks here today. Yesterday we had very intensive talks over dinner. We had intensive talks this morning. We're going to continue them over lunch later on. Let me say that I'm very, very pleased to have the President of the United States here as our honored guest in this guest house of the Government.

We had a very good atmosphere. This atmosphere shows—I think shows very clearly that we have constructive dialogue at virtually all levels on virtually all issues. We've had that for quite some time, and we're going to continue this dialogue in the next few months to come.

We debated on the issues that are of global importance. First, the world trade round—Doha—I'm very glad to note that we have a common interest in seeing this Doha round to come to a successful conclusion. Free trade—particularly looking at the problems that developing countries have, as regards food, for example, food supplies, food prices—I think this trade round is absolutely essential for a balanced situation in the world at large. We have every chance to come to a successful outcome. We will see to it. We will pool all our efforts in order to bring this about, and also in the period leading up to the G–8, we will, hopefully, be able to activate all of our efforts.

This G–8 meeting in Japan will deal with very important issues, for example, with climate change. During the G–8 meeting, there will be also a so-called meeting of the major emitters. And we do hope that all of the issues that we started to talk about in Heiligendamm can be brought forward and—in the sense that it is made clear we need a global agreement under the roof of the United Nations. But each and everyone has to take his or her share of that particular issue, and developing countries obviously will be in on this too.

The Heiligendamm process will also be continued. That is to say, the O–5 will be in on this, and what will be in the foreground here are food prices, energy prices. We also discussed this here in our meeting. There are basically two things that I think we need to do. On the one hand, there are a lot of speculations that are possible because—as regards energy prices—because the consumption and the demand is not yet sort of safely predictable. So we need to tell those countries how they intend to make themselves independent of gas and oil supplies—to these emerging economies. How can we actually further develop technology? What could we as industrialized country provide these emerging economies as regards technology, modern technology?

We in the European Union have initiated a number of activities. Particularly, Germany has held a very intensive discussion also on what renewables and new technology means in this respect.

We talked about the transatlantic dialogue, about projects that are also quite difficult. Yesterday there was the EU-U.S. summit, or rather 2 days ago, and a lot of these issues were also on the agenda there.

As regards transatlantic economic cooperation, I would like to see us work together close also on biofuels. We have taken over very clear commitments here. We also know we need to have certain standards. We must not come into competition with food production, for example, here.

Then on international issues, Afghanistan was discussed, progress in the Middle East, Iran—the offers we put on the table to Iran, but also the fact that if Iran does not meet its commitments, then further sanctions will simply have to follow. We again said we want to give room for diplomatic solutions. We want to give diplomacy a chance, but we also have to stay on that particular issue.

These were constructive, very intensive talks, talks that were characterized by a friendship between us. And I think this can lend a contribution towards solving a number of issues that are outstanding in the world at large, and we show at the same time transatlantic cooperation between Germany and the United States is working very well. Thank you again, Mr. President, for coming, and a very warm welcome.

President Bush. Madam Chancellor, thank you for the invitation to this beautiful place, a modest little cottage by the lake. It is—I'm really glad you thought of this location. Laura and I loved our dinner last night. For those in the German press who thought I didn't like asparagus, you're wrong. [*Laughter*] The German asparagus are fabulous.

But anyways, it's a great place for—to relax and have a good discussion. Our relationship is strong, and our relationship is active. And I assured the Chancellor that when I say I'm going to sprint to the finish, that's what I mean. And that we had a lot of—we've got a lot of issues that we can talk about.

I first want to thank the German people for their contributions to helping the people of Afghanistan realize the blessings of a free society. I know this is a controversial subject here, but I hope when the Afghanistan debates go forward, I hope people here think of young girls who couldn't go to school in the past but now can, or think of mothers who bring their babies to health clinics for the first time; think about farmers who now have got access to markets to help deal with food shortages. This is hard work—I understand that—to help a young democracy grow after years of tyranny, but I believe it's necessary work. And, Madam Chancellor, I appreciate your leadership on this issue.

I also want to thank you for the contributions you're making to the young democracy in Iraq as well. This has obviously been a contentious issue between our countries in the past, but what shouldn't be contentious is the mutual desire to help advance freedom in the Middle East as the great alternative to the ideology of the haters and the murderers, those who espouse violent extremism to advance their agendas.

We talked about, you know, progress in the Holy Land for the establishment of a Palestinian state. I'm still optimistic that we can get a state defined, clearly understood by both parties before the end of my Presidency.

We talked about Iran, of course. I told the Chancellor my first choice, of course, is to solve this diplomatically. All options are on the table, and that—but the first choice is to solve this problem by working closely together, by sending a dual message, which has been the consistent policy of this administration, that if you verifiably suspend your enrichment programs, you'll end your isolation, and there's a way forward for you.

The Iranian regime has made a choice so far, and it's a bad choice for the Iranian people. The Iranian people deserve better than being isolated from the world. They deserve better from having, you know, their Government held up as, you know, unsafe and not trustworthy. And so the message from the EU Foreign Minister, Solana, will be, there's a better choice for you. And we'll see what choice they make.

We talked about Lebanon and the need for that young democracy to survive. We did talk about global climate change, of course. The Chancellor started a very good process here in Germany nearly a year ago. As a result of her leadership, the United States is working very closely with, you know, other major economies to develop a common goal. Step one of solving a problem is for nations who actually emit carbon dioxide to agree to a goal. And that's just not European nations, that's the United States along with China and India. Once that goal is agreed to, then develop long-term and interim strategies that are binding strategies to meet those goals.

And so that's the process we're going forward. It turns out, the major economies meeting is working concurrently with the G–8, meeting at the same time as the G–8. And the objective is to be able to announce a long-term binding goal at the G–8 as well as the major economies meeting, Madam Chancellor, on a process that you started.

We talked about Doha. You know, it's—I'm a free trader; the Chancellor is a free trader. The question is, you know, is there a commitment to free trade in the face of protectionism? A lot of protectionism in the American political scene these days. I'm sure there's some protectionism here in Germany. I happen to think it would be, you know, disastrous for the world economy and disastrous for poor nations if we didn't trade freely and fairly.

And so one way to make that commitment is for the Doha round to succeed.

I assured the Chancellor that we're committed to the Doha round. We will work hard to achieve it. The Transatlantic Economic Council is a very important council that we started together as a way to resolve our differences to make sure that trade is fair and free.

All in all, I—relations with Germany are strong, as I told you. And that's good, and that's important. And, Madam Chancellor, I want to thank you for your friendship as well.

Chancellor Merkel. Well, we now have the possibility to take questions. Maybe we ought to start with a German correspondent.

Q. [*Inaudible*]

Chancellor Merkel. You will get a microphone, don't worry.

Iran/Germany-U.S. Relations

Q. Mr. President, Madam Chancellor, you spoke about Iran at some length. In Israel, the press writes that Israel might well contemplate action against this threat that Iran poses to them. What would be your—what are you saying, Mr. President, to the Israeli Government? And you said, Chancellor, give diplomacy a chance. Madam Chancellor, Mr. President, how long would you say diplomacy has to be given a chance? Can we exclude that during your term in office military action will be taken—will take place against Iran, Mr. President?

And you, Chancellor, how do you assess the era of George Bush? In your party, one of your leading party members said that you will not miss George Bush. Will you miss him?

And a question directed to both of you. Why do you, Mr. President——

Chancellor Merkel. I think—don't ask for too long.

Q. ——but why do you—why are you seen as so unpopular, Mr. President, in Germany?

President Bush. I just told you that all options are on the table, and my first choice is to solve this diplomatically. And the best way to solve it diplomatically is to work with our partners, and that's exactly what we're doing. And the message to the Iranian Government is very clear: that there's a better way forward than isolation, and that is for you to verifiably suspend your enrichment program. And the choice is theirs to make. Obviously, we want to solve this issue peacefully, and so we'll give diplomacy a chance to work. And I want to thank the message that came out of the EU meeting yesterday, which is that if they choose to be—continue to be obstinate, there will be additional sanctions.

Chancellor Merkel. We talked just now at some length about this. I very clearly pin my hopes on diplomatic efforts. And I believe that diplomatic pressure actually already has taken effect. If you look at the situation in Iran on the ground, you see that quite clearly. These efforts can have a success, but this presupposes, obviously, that the global community is sort of unified. Both in the European Union and in the world Security Council, we have to continue this common approach. We cannot exclude either that there may well be a further round of sanctions, and those need to be negotiated in the Security Council of the United Nations.

What's important now is to see to it that this last round of the sanctions is actually implemented and can take effect, because the effectiveness of sanctions is actually then proved only once they are taken seriously. And we are under certain—quite a considerable pressure to act together and in concert. And we in the European Union will do everything to see to it that this actually happens.

As regards our relationship, you know that this is a relationship characterized by friendship. It's a direct and candid relationship. When there are differences of opinion—whenever there were differences of opinions, we actually called a spade a spade. It's actually nice about the President that you can actually call a spade a spade with him. And when, for example, I had—as regards to the climate change discussion last year, this year, when we—ever we had differences of opinion, there was a way forward; there was a constructive way forward.

And I think that this initiative on climate by the European Union is a very important initiative. The President himself took, actually, forward action on this, apart from our military action that we do together, for example, in Afghanistan, in the general international negotiating processes.

We also need on other areas between the European Union and the United States, not only Germany and the United States, a lot of close cooperation in many areas. And there was always greater—great openness here between us. This cooperation is fun, I must say. And as the President said, it is going to be a sprint to the last day of his office. And I trust—often trust that we shall have other similar meetings of this kind, candid and open and constructive.

I'm looking forward to the G–8 summit in Japan. I hope that we can make further progress on climate protection, which—talking about targets now—that is to say, some kind of binding targets—I think is already great success.

Iran

Q. Thank you, sir. Mr. President, back on Iran, can you talk a little bit about—well, Iran has signaled that it seems likely to reject Mr. Solana's offer, presenting on behalf of you and the EU. What have you and your European counterparts agreed upon in terms of new measures against Iran if that is indeed the case?

And to Chancellor Merkel, what is Germany willing to do specifically, whether in implementing the sanctions already in place or taking further measures beyond those?

President Bush. That's exactly what we discussed: How do you implement sanctions that are already in place, and should we levy additional sanctions? Our position is, is that we ought to enforce the sanctions that are in place, and we ought to work with our allies to levy additional sanctions if they choose—if the Iranians choose to continue to ignore the demands of the free world.

Chancellor Merkel. I personally have always come out very strongly in favor of seeing to it that sanctions are decided at the level of the United Nations Security Council too, because including China and Russia obviously makes for much greater effectiveness of such sanctions. But that doesn't exclude that within the European Union too, we may discuss, for example, are further possibilities open, for example, in the banking sectors? But these further possibilities, these further measures, must not lead to a situation where at the greater—the bigger stage, so to speak, we then relent, because the more countries are in on this, the more the effect—the more effective the impact will be on Iran, for example.

We always think that quite often, on the one hand, people like to reject certain measures to be taken, but let us think of the people in Iran. This is what is essential. I think these people deserve a much more—sort of a better outlook also, as regards their economic prospects. And we would hope for the leadership in Iran to finally see reason. I mean, just look at the reports of the IAEA. They—it says clearly—the report states clearly that certain violations of agreements that were entered into have taken place. And we—it means that we need to react to this, even if it—with further sanctions, if that's necessary.

Military Operations in Iraq

Q. Mr. President, on the way to Europe, you gave a very interesting interview for the Times newspaper in which you basically said that you regret your war rhetoric. Now I'm wondering, do you actually just regret your war rhetoric, or do you regret having gone to war with Iraq?

President Bush. I don't regret it at all. Removing Saddam Hussein made the world a safer place. And yes, I told the guy—

the guy said, "Now what could you do over?" First of all, you don't get to do things over in my line of work. But I could have used better rhetoric to indicate that, one, we tried to exhaust the diplomacy in Iraq; two, that I don't like war. But, no, the decision to remove Saddam Hussein was the right decision.

Myers [Steven Lee Myers, New York Times]. I mean—no, no, Eggen [Dan Eggen, Washington Post], Eggen, excuse me. I called you yesterday, Myers. What's the difference? [*Laughter*]

Iraq-U.S. Security Agreement/German Role in Iraq

Q. Thank you, Mr. President. Thank you, sir.

President Bush. Yes, no problem. [*Laughter*]

Q. Speaking of Iraq, there are increasing controversy in Iraq over the security agreement that's being negotiated. Some top Iraqi officials are calling for a dramatic reduction in the U.S. presence. Does this concern you that the direction that those negotiations are going in?

And, Madam Chancellor, does this have any impact on your approach towards Iraq?

President Bush. First of all, I think we'll end up with a strategic agreement with Iraq. You know, it's all kinds of noise in their system and our system. What eventually will win out is the truth. For example, you read stories, perhaps in your newspaper, that the U.S. is planning all kinds of permanent bases in Iraq. That's an erroneous story. The Iraqis know—will learn it's erroneous too. We'll be there at the invitation of the sovereign Government of Iraq.

And I strongly support the agreement because I think it helps send a clear message to the people of Iraq that, you know, that security you're now seeing will continue. And one of the lessons of Iraq is, is that in order for a democracy to develop or in order for an economy to develop, there has to be a measure of security,

which is now happening. And so I think we'll get the agreement done.

And as I said clearly in past speeches, this will not involve permanent bases, nor will it bind any future President to troop levels. You know, as to—look, Eggen, you can find any voice you want in the Iraqi political scene and quote them, which is interesting, isn't it? Because in the past you could only find one voice, and now you can find a myriad of voices. It's a vibrant democracy; people are debating. There's all kinds of press in the Iraqi scene, of course, to the benefit of the Iraqi society.

And I deal with Prime Minister Maliki. He appreciates our presence there, and he understands that we're returning on success. As the situation merits and the situation improves, we're bringing our troops home. And I'm pleased with the progress. I don't know whether or not it's—the progress has made it here to Germany or not yet, but the progress in Iraq is substantial, and it's going to help change the Middle East for the better. And I love the idea of having—giving people a chance to live in a free society. The blessings of freedom are—shouldn't be just in a regional blessing. I believe freedom is universal, and I believe freedom yields peace.

Madam Chancellor.

Chancellor Merkel. Well, obviously, from the German side too, and the European side for that matter, we have every interest, indeed, a vital interest in seeing Iraq taking a turn for sort of a good kind of development. I invited the Iraqi Prime Minister here to Germany, and I think he will pay us the honor of a visit. We have been trying to have economic relations. We've also, outside of Iraq, also trained security personnel, and we're ready to continue that.

So everything we can do beyond a sort of military presence, everything we can do as regards civilian building up of the country, assisting them, is something that we're continuing to doing. And I would like to very much look forward to the visit of the Prime Minister. We're glad to see progress happening there on the ground, because it's in our vital interest to see to it that this region takes a turn for the better, and it's in the interest of the region too.

Thank you very much.

NOTE: The President's news conference began at 11:34 a.m. at Schloss Meseberg. In his remarks, he referred to European Union

Foreign Minister Javier Solana Madariaga; and Prime Minister Nuri al-Maliki of Iraq. Chancellor Merkel referred to Outreach 5 (O–5), a group of five important emerging economies that works with the G–8. Chancellor Merkel and a reporter spoke in German, and their remarks were translated by an interpreter.

Interview With Christian Malard of France 3 TV
June 6, 2008

President's Legacy

Mr. Malard. Mr. President, after 8 years at the White House, how does President George W. Bush judge President George W. Bush? What are your good points, according to you, and your negative points?

The President. Well, you know, I think that people will say he's a decisive person who took action when necessary to protect his country and to address the problems of the world. Bad points are probably sometimes my rhetoric was a little—was misunderstood. I mean, I can remember saying, you know, "dead or alive," which sent—it sent signals that could be easily misinterpreted.

I think people will say that he was tough when he needed to be tough and compassionate when he needed to be compassionate, because our agenda was not only dealing with terror but freeing people is a compassionate act, but freeing people not only from forms of tyranny but from diseases like HIV/AIDS or malaria or hunger. And the United States is proudly in the lead on these issues.

War on Terror/Global Economy

Mr. Malard. Today, the world is struck by economic crisis.

The President. Yes.

Mr. Malard. Instability, terrorism still prevail in Middle East. Don't you feel your

successor might face the risk of a major conflict, another September 11?

The President. You know, it's interesting, I think that's always a threat. No question that there's an enemy out there that would still like to harm America and, I believe, other free nations. But what has changed is, one, we've got the pressure on Al Qaida. The very ones who attacked us are now on the defense. We're dismantling them. We're working hard to find them. Our intelligence is better; our intelligence sharing is better. But no question, it's still a dangerous world when it comes to that, and—but there's tools now in place—that we put in place, that will help the next President deal with the security issue.

And in terms of the economy, yes, look, economies go up and down, and right now it's a difficult period for all of us. Energy prices are high. Food prices are high. In our country, we've got a mortgage issue. But I do believe that we'll come out of this, and we'll come out of it stronger. And it's just that—it's what happens in free markets.

Middle East Peace Process

Mr. Malard. Israel-Palestinian conflict is the cancer of all evils in Middle East. Your predecessors tried to get a solution; you tried to get a solution. But it seems that the two sides don't want to make the necessary concessions and political sacrifices. So does that mean that the tragedy—I don't say "the show"—but the tragedy goes on?

The President. I don't—[*laughter*]—that's a good way of putting it. I don't think so. I think they'll come to—first of all, I'm the first President to have articulated two states, because I believe it's in the interest of the Palestinians to have a state of their own that is whole, that doesn't look like Swiss cheese. And I firmly believe it's in Israel's interest to have a state, a democratic state, as a neighbor.

I know these leaders well, Prime Minister Olmert and President Abbas. I know they're committed to working out the differences on a variety of issues, such as what the borders look like, the refugee issue, security issues. I was confident when I went to the Middle East last time that there's still that desire to get something done. I feel—still feel good about it.

Obviously, the politics in Israel is a little different right now. But nevertheless, in my visit with Prime Minister Olmert at the Oval Office recently, he understands the importance of reaching an agreement with President Abbas on what the state looks like and how to deal with these very difficult issues.

Condi is going to go during the European trip—is going to go back to the Middle East and continue to work on it. And I'm very hopeful that we can get that vision defined.

Iran

Mr. Malard. Iranian President Ahmadinejad is gaining influence in Iraq, in Lebanon with Hizballah, no doubt. He doesn't show any sign of flexibility——

The President. Yes.

Mr. Malard. ——on nuclear—on his nuclear program. Mr. President, is there any space left still for discussion with him?

The President. Well, there will be definitely space for discussion when he verifiably suspends his enrichment program. First of all, I disagree with the premise that he is succeeding in Iraq. Quite the contrary. Iraq is becoming a democracy, a functioning democracy. They understand Iranian influence is destabilizing. Obviously, there is some influence inside of Iraq, but—Iranian influence inside Iraq—but it's less than it has been and will continue to lessen, in my judgment, as its economy and as its political society begins to develop.

The—therefore, in speaking with my friend President Sarkozy or any other European leaders, we've still got to continue to send that message to the Iranian leadership that you're isolated; you'll continue to get pressured unless you verifiably suspend your enrichment program. And the reason why that's important to continue the pressure on is that if they can enrich, they could easily transfer that knowledge to a weapons program, which would destabilize the Middle East.

Mr. Malard. There's no military option in the air?

The President. Yes, it's still there. Absolutely it's got to be on the table. But, of course, I've always said to the American people, we want to solve this problem diplomatically, and we're going to work to solve it diplomatically. But the Iranians have got to understand all options are on the table.

U.S. Foreign Policy

Mr. Malard. When you see the big push of China, India, Russia on the international stage today, do you think that in 10 years from now, America will still be the superpower of the world?

The President. You know, I—that's an interesting question. I think that—I would rather define us as a very influential nation that is willing to work with others to achieve common objectives. You mentioned those three nations, and my approach has been to have strong bilateral relations with all three. We've got strong bilateral relations with China, even though we differ on issues. I've had strong bilateral relations with Russia, a lot of it having to do with my personal relationship with Vladimir Putin. We've had our differences, but nevertheless, we found a lot of common ground to work together on, including Iran. And in India, I've changed the relationship between India and the United States in a way that we're partners as opposed to, you know, being antagonistic.

And therefore, if the United States is active diplomatically in maintaining good bilateral relations with these countries, I think we'll still be in a position to use our influence for the common good. And these relationships don't have to be antagonistic. They can be—I've worked hard to get to know these leaders individually so that we can be able to discuss matters, delicate matters, in open and honest ways without rupturing relations. And I hope it serves as a go-by for future Presidents, that you can have disagreements, but you don't have to have this kind of zero-sum attitude about life.

2008 Presidential Election

Mr. Malard. Last two short questions. I don't want to put you in trouble, interfering in American elections. But today, do you have the feeling that the barriers of— and the game is not over, far from being over, I know—but do you think the barriers have fallen down, to have a potential black citizen to become President of the United States?

The President. You know, look, I—my attitude about that is I think it's a good statement about American democracy that a major political party would nominate Senator Obama. Now that that process has ended, the fundamental question is, who can be the best President? That's the question.

And I'm obviously for John McCain. I think he'll be a really good President. And the American people will make that decision. And it's going to be up to each person to be able to describe how they're going

to handle the pressures of the job, how they'll be making decisions, what principles they'll be standing on, because this is a job—that I'm sure you can imagine—where there's all kinds of pressures. And if you don't believe something in your soul, if you don't stand on principle and you're on shifting ground, you'll be very unpredictable. And the world doesn't need unpredictability, it needs predictability out of the United States.

France-U.S. Relations

Mr. Malard. Last point, Mr. President. You and President Sarkozy put on the right track the Franco-U.S. relationship. We were a bit of trouble between you and President Jacques Chirac. With your next successor, whoever it is, do you think it will go on very well between France and United States?

The President. I do. Look, France and the United States have had a fabulous history together. And I remind my friends that it was the French that stood strong with the American patriots in the Revolutionary War. It was the French that determined the balance of power when it came to whether or not the United States would even be the United States of America, an independent republic.

And we've had a great relationship. And of course, we've had our differences, but that's okay. There have been differences throughout our history. The fundamental question is, do we understand there are— common values unite us? And we do. The French love freedom and human rights and human decency, and so do Americans. And so the relationship—and the—plus, there's a lot of personal relationship, a lot of friendship between individuals here in our country and French citizens that make it— there's no question in my mind, we'll have good relations with the French.

Q. Mr. President, I want to thank you very much, and I wish you the very best.

The President. Well, thank you, sir. I'm looking forward to going to beautiful Paris.

Q. Great to see you again.

The President. Thank you, sir. Good to see you.

NOTE: The interview was taped at 10:39 a.m. in the Map Room at the White House for later broadcast. In his remarks, the President referred to Prime Minister Ehud Olmert of Israel; President Mahmoud Abbas of the Pal-estinian Authority; President Nicolas Sarkozy of France; Prime Minister Vladimir V. Putin of Russia, in his former capacity as the President of Russia; Democratic Presidential candidate Barack Obama; and Republican Presidential candidate John McCain. Mr. Malard referred to former President Jacques Chirac of France. The transcript was released by the Office of the Press Secretary on June 12.

Remarks in a Discussion on Italy-United States Business Exchanges in Rome, Italy
June 12, 2008

Ambassador Ronald P. Spogli. Mr. President, good morning. Good morning to everyone. First of all, I'd like to welcome you to the American Academy, and thank you for having so graciously agreed to be with us here this morning. I'd like to also welcome all of our fellow roundtable participants.

As you know, we have eight students, five of whom have been to the United States on our BEST program, three of whom will shortly depart. And then we do have a couple of gentlemen who are slightly older than our researchers and scientists who are here—not that old, certainly, but a bit older—Michele and Marco, who have been successful entrepreneurs, have overcome the difficulties that we've talked about for some time in the Italian system, and who have graciously created an NGO that works on helping young entrepreneurs overcome difficulties. I'd like to also recognize our sponsors and welcome them this morning, and I'll have occasion to come back to you in a second.

[*At this point, Ambassador Spogli continued his remarks, concluding as follows.*]

Ambassador Spogli. Clearly, economic growth is the key question facing the country today, and so the Partnership for Growth was conceived as a way to make a contribution toward the economic growth of Italy. And we focused on three fundamental areas.

The first was commercializing research. Italy does a tremendous amount of high-quality research in nanotechnology and biotechnology and in other fields, but unfortunately, a relatively small amount of that research ever becomes commercialized. And so we wanted to fundamentally address that question.

Second issue is one of a scarcity of financing for risk-taking capital enterprises. Italy is a country of great savers, has a very high savings rate; yet unfortunately, very little is channeled into venture capital and private equity. We wanted to address this particular question as well. So we've had over 200 events in the course of almost 3 years focusing on ways that we could share information and enhance not only our bilateral economic relationship but, hopefully, address some of these fundamental questions.

Which brings me to the third and most important element of the Partnership for Growth, and that is our BEST student exchange program. Many companies came to us and said: It's great that you're focusing on technology transfer; it's great that you're focusing on venture capital; but there's one very important element that we'd like you to make a contribution to, and that is helping to change and add to the entrepreneurial culture of our country. You need to send high-quality researchers and scientists and engineers to the United States, give them a full immersion opportunity in a place like Silicon Valley, have them come back, take some of those experiences and then begin to create here in Italy a wonderful, unique entrepreneurial ecosystem.

And so we did just that; we created the BEST program: Business Exchange and Student Training. And in that program, we send young, promising scientists and engineers to the United States. They study for 6 months in Silicon Valley, 3 months at the University of Santa Clara in their entrepreneurship center, and then they do a 3-month apprenticeship in a high-tech startup company to see literally how you can go from the creation of an idea to the—to, hopefully, the formation of the next great business here in Italy. The researchers must come back to Italy and share their experiences here and, hopefully, develop their research ideas.

The program started last year with a five-person contingent, all of whom are here today. This year it's 15; it's grown to 15, 3 of whom are here. And next year, we hope to grow the program to 25 and, hopefully, more into the future.

One final comment, sir, before I turn it over to you, and that is, the program would not have been possible without our many sponsors and supporters who are in the audience this morning. One hundred percent of this program was financed here in Italy by the generosity and forward thinking of our sponsors. Who do we have? We had Italian businesses, we had American companies who have subsidiaries in Italy, we had a number of associations that are interested in economic growth and development, we've had cities, and we've had regions participate.

So, for example, the city of Milan was a very early supporter of our program, Mr. President, and we have the mayor of Milan,

Mayor Moratti, who is here this morning representing her fine city. We've had tremendous support from the Italian postal system, and we have the Chief Executive Officer this morning, Massimo Sarmi, who is the head of that organization, certainly. And then we've had wonderful support from a number of American businesses, such as IBM, who is represented by Dr. Martucci this morning, who has been, again, a great supporter of our program. We're delighted they're here. They contribute over a million dollars to this program. We'd like them to contribute a lot more going forward so we can send more high-quality students.

And, sir, I'd like to turn it over to you, and thank you again.

President Bush. Mr. Ambassador, thank you. Now, first of all, I do want to thank the folks here at the American Academy for welcoming me and what generally is a rather large entourage. I'm real proud of the fact that my fellow citizens have contributed to the restorations building— it turns out, someone from the great State of Texas, notably Mercedes Bass. And I want to thank them and thank my citizens for supporting this important institute.

I want to thank you all for giving me a chance to come by and listen to you. I want to hear your impressions of America. I want to hear what you think of the challenges as this really important country moves ahead. And I really want to hear how you intend to contribute to the future of your country.

I want to thank you all for sponsoring these exchanges. Madam Mayor, I'm particularly pleased that you're here. You know, one of the best diplomacy—the best diplomacy for America, particularly among young folks, is to welcome you to our country. You get to see firsthand the truth about America, you know, like a lot of images. There's a lot of, in my view, misinformation and propaganda about our country. We're a compassionate, we're an open country.

We care about people, and we're entrepreneurial. And we love the entrepreneurial spirit. We love it when somebody has a dream and then is—works hard to achieve the dream, thereby contributing to the society and creating jobs for people so they can realize their aspirations as well.

And so I want to thank you, Ambassador, for getting this program going. And thank you all for coming to share your thoughts with me. I really am looking forward to hearing from you.

We'll have—Marco, do you want to say a few words?

Marco Palombi. Well, yes, Mr. President.

President Bush. Marco, what do you do?

Mr. Palombi. I actually sold my company a year-and-a-half ago. I was——

President Bush. Oh, so you retired?

Mr. Palombi. Well, no, no. [*Laughter*] Not yet, no.

President Bush. Okay.

Mr. Palombi. We actually created, with Michele, the NGO the Ambassador was referring us for.

President Bush. Oh, that's good. Thank you.

Mr. Palombi. Yes. So basically, I created the largest blogging platform in Italy.

President Bush. Really?

Mr. Palombi. Yes, yes, yes. And then I sold it to one of the largest media company in Italy.

President Bush. Well, congratulations.

[*Mr. Palombi made brief remarks, concluding as follows.*]

Mr. Palombi. So what we did was basically introduce our friends who have achieved something in Italy too. We call them first generation entrepreneurs, because we think that the best role model will be someone who started from zero, who doesn't have his parents' money behind, and he really started from scratch; he risked. And we chose these guys, and we had these video chats on the Internet, which we—which are now there. And it's one of the best, probably, entrepreneurship

material that you have in Italy right now. It's funny because right now, talking to people who have watched this video chats, they really are motivated by what they see. And this is amazing because you can change things by showing them that someone like them did it.

President Bush. Absolutely. That's good. Thanks, Marco.

Mr. Palombi. Sure.

President Bush. You ready?

Micol Macellari. Yes, I'm ready. [*Laughter*]

President Bush. Micol.

Ms. Macellari. I'm Micol, yes.

President Bush. Yes, thank you.

[*Ms. Macellari made brief remarks, concluding as follows.*]

Ms. Macellari. I really think—I strongly believe that in Italy, we have everything we need to make a success and to turn a good scientific project in business and bring greatest scientific idea to the market. We have a strong example of entrepreneurs that did so. So on our own, we can follow——

President Bush. Absolutely.

Ms. Macellari. ——his example. And we can represent, as the first people who've gone there, a good example for all the other students for the future years.

President Bush. Thank you.

NOTE: The President spoke at 10:55 a.m. in the Villa Aurelia at the American Academy. In his remarks, he referred to philanthropist Mercedes T. Bass; and Mayor Letizia Moratti of Milan. Ambassador Spogli referred to Luciano Martucci, president and chief executive officer, IBM Italy. Participating in the discussion were U.S. Ambassador to Italy Ronald P. Spogli; 2007 BEST program participants Abramo Barbaresi, Elisabetta Capezio, Valentina Coccoli, Micol Macellari, and Emanuele Orgiu; 2008 BEST program participants Francesco Cattaneo, Chiara Giovenzana, and Michela Piacenti; and

BEST program participant mentors Michele Appendino and Marco Palombi.

The President's News Conference With Prime Minister Silvio Berlusconi of Italy in Rome
June 12, 2008

Prime Minister Berlusconi. Good evening to all of you, and welcome to our American guests. And of course, I would like to extend my warmest welcome to President Bush, who is a friend—a personal friend of mine and also a great friend of Italy's. I also wish to thank him because Rome has the very great privilege of being the European capital that President Bush has visited more than any other capital in Europe. If I'm not mistaken, this is the sixth time that he's here in Rome. And we are certainly delighted to have always seen that he is an ally who has always helped our country have strong relations with the United States. And I must say that this has never been the case.

I also wish to thank him for all the efforts which he has undertaken during his administration in order to safeguard democracy and freedom. We have been the first Government to support one of his initiatives within the U.N., i.e., the Community of Democracies, which aims at spreading democracy throughout the world. We are both fully convinced that it is only through a real democracy that we can have true freedom. And it is only through freedom that individuals can tap their potentials fully, and this is how we can all help our families overcome any poverty. And obviously, this is how peoples can overcome poverty and, therefore, become evermore prosperous. And this is what we need to aim for in order to establish long-lasting peace throughout the world. This, in fact, is one of the issues that we have worked on and which we continue to pursue in the future.

We've discussed many issues this afternoon, and we've also had the opportunity to discuss two programs, two initiatives, which I think have commonalities. The university for liberal thinking, we think—or are thinking of establishing one of these universities here in Italy in fact. And I had the opportunity to show President Bush some of these photographs which I already have. And President Bush is thinking of doing something very similar in Texas, and therefore, we've decided that we'll perhaps have a professor exchange program. And obviously, I've also invited President Bush to come to act as visiting professor, and I've already told him that many of our colleagues, Prime Ministers and heads of states, in fact, have okayed that as well.

I know that you'll all have questions. You obviously are curious about what we've discussed, and that's very legitimate. We've gone over the international situation, and we've also reported some of the decisions taken by our Government with regard to our presence in Afghanistan, Kosovo, Lebanon and also our position vis-a-vis in some international developments. And of course, Iran is a very, very sensitive issue and is one of—is among these.

Now, we are certainly in agreement on all these issues, as we always have been. And I wish to wind up by thanking President Bush wholeheartedly. I thank America, and I again was able to address the U.S. Congress a couple of years ago, and this is something that I'll never forget. And the Italians, especially those who are members of my generation, will never forget that this is a country that has sacrificed many lives to save us from totalitarianism, communism, fascism, nazism, and this is a country that has given us back our dignity and has ensured freedom and well-being for all Italians. Now this is something that I shall never, ever forget.

President Bush. [*Inaudible*]—you're right, we're good friends, and I appreciate that very much. I also have enjoyed coming to Rome. I always leave with a little extra culture and a little fatter. Thank you for your hospitality. Before I——

Prime Minister Berlusconi. President Bush doesn't know what's for dinner yet this evening.

President Bush. Turning to the meeting, I want to say something about the severe weather that has affected so many of the citizens back in the United States. There's been some terrible storms and a lot of destruction and some death. Throughout the trip, I've been updated on the devastation.

I've spoken with the Governors of three affected States: Iowa, Wisconsin, and Indiana. Our Government is in touch with the authorities. We will assist these States in any way we can to help people recover from the devastation. My thoughts and prayers are with the victims of the terrible tornadoes and flooding, especially those who lost loved ones. We've been inspired by the stories of heroism, neighbors helping neighbors, and communities coming together. It's a really tough time for the people in the Midwestern part of the United States. And they'll have the prayers of the American people, and we'll help them recover.

We did have a wide-ranging discussion. I appreciate very much the fact that Italy is meeting international obligations. I don't think the citizens at home really understand how many troops Italy has deployed to help troubled spots of the world, and we thank you for that, Mr. Prime Minister. You've got about 8,700 troops in places like Kosovo, Chad.

You've got a very significant presence in Afghanistan. And I appreciate very much

the fact that the Government announced to the Parliament, with your instructions, Mr. Prime Minister, that the caveats that had restricted your forces in Afghanistan are—have been removed, and that you've committed additional Carabinieri to help train the Afghan police. Your Carabinieri are excellent professionals, and they're needed. And I want to thank you for that commitment.

We talked about Iraq and how Iraq is changing for the better, how people are beginning to realize the blessings of a free and peaceful society. And you're—you've been very helpful through the NATO mission there, of training, as well.

And I want to thank you very much for our discussion on Iran. We discussed how we can work effectively together to solve this issue diplomatically. I told the Prime Minister what I said yesterday in Germany, that all options are on the table, but the first choice, of course, is to convince the Iranians that they must give up their ambitions to develop the capacity to make a nuclear weapon, for the safety—for our own safety and for the sake of peace. And I'm confident we can continue to work together in a constructive way.

We did talk about the climate change issue. I talked to him about our strategy for the major economies meeting, which will run concurrently with the G–8. The United States is committed to convincing those of us that have got economic development and produce greenhouse gases to agree to a long-term goal.

Now, I reminded the Prime Minister our objective is to get nations like China and India to sign up to the goal, and that we'll develop our own strategies that will be firm strategies within the U.N. framework.

Over dinner, we'll talk about the Doha round, how the United States is committed to completing a successful round of Doha.

And finally, today I was real proud that Laura represented us at the food agency—the food summit. The United States is committed to helping people who don't have food. Over the next—in '07 and '08, we'll have committed about $5 billion to help. I really think our strategy can be a lot more effective than just giving people food. I think we ought to be buying food from affected nations so they develop their own agriculture. I firmly believe it's in the world's interest that nations that prevent the export of food stop doing so.

And we ought to let sound science make the decision about genetically modified crops, be really interested in helping people in dry areas develop agriculture so they don't have to rely upon the world. And we ought to look at these GMAs with science in mind so that agriculture, sustainable agriculture, can be developed in the places that are—where the people are suffering.

And so we've had a good agenda, Mr. Prime Minister. It's great to be with you again. And looking forward to one of your famous meals, after we answer a few questions. [*Laughter*]

Ready to answer some questions?

Prime Minister Berlusconi. Thank you, yes. We've been told that we'll have two questions from our U.S. guests and two questions from Italian journalists. And I would ask the President to just go ahead and start with the American journalists.

President Bush. [*Inaudible*]—oh, there you are, yes.

U.S. Supreme Court Ruling on Guantanamo Bay Detainee Rights/2008 Presidential Election

Q. Mr. President, also back home, the Supreme Court ruled that Guantanamo detainees have rights under the Constitution to challenge their detention in U.S. civilian courts. Doesn't this rebuke of your policy on detainees validate the criticism that Gitmo has gotten all over the world, especially here in Europe?

President Bush. Yes.

Q. And for the Prime Minister, sir, who do you want to come see you as the next U.S. President?

President Bush. First of all, it's the Supreme Court decision. We'll abide by the Court's decision. That doesn't mean I have to agree with it. It's a deeply divided Court, and I strongly agree with those who dissented that. And their dissent was based upon their serious concerns about U.S. national security.

Congress and the administration worked very carefully on a piece of legislation that set the appropriate procedures in place as to how to deal with the detainees. And we'll study this opinion, and we'll do so with this in mind, to determine whether or not additional legislation might be appropriate so that we can safely say—or truly say to the American people, we're doing everything we can to protect you.

Prime Minister Berlusconi. As far as my question is concerned, well, of course, I cannot express any preference with regard to an electoral campaign going on in another country. However, I suppose I could express my own personal preference for one of the candidates, the Republican candidate. And this is for a very selfish reason, and that is that I would no longer be the oldest person at the upcoming G–8, because McCain is a month older than me, 29th of August, 1936—29th of September, which is when I was born. There you go. [*Laughter*]

The second question now from the American journalist, please.

President Bush. Let's see.

Prime Minister Berlusconi. [*Inaudible*]

President Bush. Yes, Jeff Stinson [USA Today].

Upcoming Middle East Oil Summit/Energy

Q. First of all, for you, Mr. President, the Saudis, in about 10 days, will be hosting a summit on oil prices and supplies. Prime Minister Gordon Brown has said that he will go to this. With four-dollar-a-gallon gasoline back home, would you go?

President Bush. You know, I'm going to go back home and take a look at the intentions and purpose of the meeting. There will be a high-level official, for certain, from my administration. We ought to be at the table as producers. My call on Congress is to recognize the seriousness of the problem and pass law that encourages exploration for oil and gas in the United States so that down the road, an American President will go as a producer, not a consumer.

And our policies frankly have been—are now coming home to roost. For 8 years, I have been saying to the Congress, we ought to be exploring in ANWR; we ought to be drilling on the Outer Continental Shelf. And the Democratically led Congress has prevented that from happening. And now the prices of gasoline are high, and the American people don't like it, and I can understand why they don't like it. In the interim term, we'll—we need to be finding more oil and gas. In the longer term, we ought be diversifying away from our reliance upon oil.

And so yes, I'm interested in the meeting. I said it's an interesting idea. And I'm going to get home and take a look, and we'll send somebody high level there.

Thank you.

Prime Minister Berlusconi. Thank you very much. And now to the Italian journalists. Firstly, we have a journalist from Channel One news, our Susanna Petruni.

Iran/Italian Role in the War on Terror and the Middle East Peace Process

Q. Two very quick questions, one for President Bush and the other for Prime Minister Berlusconi. Now, we know that you are in sound agreement. And, President Bush, I think that you were recently interviewed by my newscast, and you said that you were in favor of Italy being part of the 5-plus-1 group, which is handling the Iranian crisis issue.

Now, Stephen Hadley said today that your position is that of waiting to see what might happen. Now, the White House was backing Italy's participation in the 5-plus-1 group. So an answer on that.

And, Prime Minister Berlusconi, will there be changes in Italy's presence in Afghanistan and other trouble spots after your talks with President Bush this afternoon?

President Bush. [*Inaudible*]—the P–5-plus-1. And I told Silvio I'd seriously consider it. I also made it clear, however, that all of us, P–5-plus-1 or not, need to be sending the same message to the Iranians, which is, verifiably suspend your enrichment program or else you will face further sanctions and further isolation. And the sad thing about this issue is that the Iranian people are suffering. They could be doing a lot better. Their lives could be much more hopeful, except their Government has made the decision to defy the demands of the free world, has made the decision to ignore the IAEA, and has continued to enrich in a way that we think is dangerous.

And so the choice is theirs to make. Foreign Minister Solana is going to see the Iranian here very shortly, and his message is one that—is the one I just delivered. And it's—I hope for the sake of the Iranian people that their Government changes course. There is a better way forward.

I want to remind you something about this Iranian issue. Vladimir Putin, our mutual friend, went to the Iranians and said, you have a right to have civilian nuclear power. I have said the same thing publicly as well. I mean, I'm a big believer in nuclear power. I think the best way to deal with climate change is the spread of nuclear power. The best way to become less dependent on foreign sources of energy is nuclear power. And I believe Iran should have a civilian nuclear power. I don't believe they can be entrusted to enrich.

And therefore, Vladimir Putin went and said—and he believes that—and he said, we'll provide the fuel for you, and we'll not only provide the fuel, we'll gather the spent fuel, so you don't need to enrich. So the argument of the Iranian Government that "we have a right to have civilian nuclear power" has been undermined by the Russian proposal.

And so it will be interesting to see their decision. But what they need to hear is, is that we are firm in our resolve to prevent them from having the capacity to make a nuclear weapon.

Prime Minister Berlusconi. And with regard to the question addressed to me, we've offered to join the other European countries, plus China, plus Russia, in order to make our contribution to the negotiations which are underway with the Iranian Government. Now, our offer is based on the fact that we know Iran very well from the inside. We have some leading companies that are operating in these countries, and therefore, we think that this would be very useful in helping President Bush and Vladimir Putin to pursue the strategy that they've determined for that country.

Now, we obviously need to make sure that nuclear energy is being used for only peaceful reasons. With regard to the sanctions proposed by the United Nations, we have always abided by those. And the presence of our businesses have to do with agreements and contracts which date back several years.

Now, with regard to our willingness to remove or lift any caveats with regard to Afghanistan, we discussed that. And we also said that we are willing to keep our troops in other fronts, as it were, in other areas—in Kosovo and Lebanon and wherever it is that our Italian soldiers are today.

And I thank President Bush for his appreciation and acknowledgment of the Italian commitment in these international fronts. And in fact, there are 40,000 troops that are currently operating in our foreign missions. And we—there—we obviously have a turnover, and we always manage to keep that very large number of troops there. And we will continue, therefore, to pursue this, because we are fully convinced that it is extremely important to be able to establish democracy in Iraq. This is a very important country in that region, and we'll obviously continue to pursue our other efforts. And we obviously back any agree-

ment that will help us to overcome any divisions in Lebanon.

And we're also working on the agreements—on the negotiations for an agreement in Israel and the Middle East. And we are hoping that in all these countries it will be possible to establish peace and that they will certainly be able to become fully established democracies.

The second Italian journalist is from ANSA, the leading news agency.

U.S. Troop Levels in Iraq/Italian Foreign Policy

Q. Good evening to all of you. I also have a couple of questions, one for President Bush—good evening, sir—and it is about Iraq. You've spoken about a change in the country. Do you think it might be at all possible to have a withdrawal, maybe a partial withdrawal, of U.S. troops? And if so, when do you think that might be?

My second question is for you, Prime Minister Berlusconi. Today the President talked about the fact that Italian foreign policy might change pace, as it were, thanks to the dialogue that has been established among the political forces in Italy. Do you think that is so, and if you do, how do you think you can uphold the dialogue with the opposition in Italy?

President Bush. The progress is such on the security front that we're—are bringing troops home. We anticipate having the troops that went in for this—what's called the surge—back home by July. General Petraeus will come back; he'll assess the situation—come back to the United States—and make further recommendations. I don't know what those recommendations will be. I have told the American people, though, that conditions on the ground, the situation in Iraq, should determine our troop levels.

And so we are in the process of what's called return on success. And I had the honor of going to see the 82d Airborne that had been in Iraq, and they came home. And it was—I was—I am constantly amazed at the courage and the commitment of our troops. And I'm also pleased with the courage and commitment of the Iraqi Government and the people of Iraq. The situation is dramatically different than what it was a year ago. And United States and our allies must send a clear message to the Iraqis: We'll stand with them as their democracy continues to evolve and their economy continues to grow.

Prime Minister Berlusconi. And now my question: I'm very happy to acknowledge the forecast made by the President of Italy with regard to the attitude being shown by the opposition. And we are happy to think that the opposition might like to support our foreign policy, and our foreign policy will go along the same lines that we pursued in our previous Government for those 5 years.

And this is a pro-European integration foreign policy. It is a foreign policy which is based on the idea that we don't have two Western worlds, we don't have Europe on one side and the U.S. and Canada on the other. When we talk about the West, we mean only one West. And our foreign policy aims at being based on cordial relations with an important country such as the Russian Federation.

So our policy is going to require our effort to strengthen the ties and the cooperation between the European Union and the Russian Federation. And it is a policy that will consider NATO to be the vehicle which will help to maintain and uphold peace throughout the world, as it has done over the past decades.

Now, what about the wounds in the world, at—where we know that they're going to need our generosity? Democracies are going to have to help those people who cannot establish freedom on their own. And as I said earlier, we think that this is the only way that we can possibly pursue in order to enable and ensure peace throughout the world after having fully eliminated terrorism.

Now let me also acknowledge your vision, Mr. President, your policy, and the courage that you have shown throughout all the years, of hard work on behalf—on the part of your administration. You've always expressed your ideas with great courage, your ideals for the future, your vision for the future. I have gotten to know President Bush very well. I consider him to be a very close friend, a very unique person. And when he says no, he means no; when he says yes, it means yes. And he's always known—he's always shown that he has been able to be very close to those friends of his who have shared his ideals.

I thank you very much, Mr. President, for your friendship between the two of us, on a personal level, your friendship shown to our country. And I thank you for the very courageous role that you have always taken as the leader of the most important country in the world and—which is able to determine peace and freedom throughout the world.

Thank you once again. Thank you for being here this evening. And thank you to all our American friends who are accompanying the President.

NOTE: The President's news conference began at 7:39 p.m. in the Loggia di Raffaello at the Villa Madama. In his remarks, the President referred to Gov. Chester J. Culver of Iowa; Gov. James E. Doyle of Wisconsin; Gov. Mitchell E. Daniels, Jr., of Indiana; European Union Foreign Minister Javier Solana Madariaga; Minister of Foreign Affairs Manuchehr Motaki of Iran; Prime Minister Vladimir V. Putin of Russia; and Gen. David H. Petraeus, USA, commanding general, Multi-National Force—Iraq. Prime Minister Berlusconi referred to U.S. Republican Presidential candidate John McCain; and President Giorgio Napolitano of Italy. A reporter referred to Prime Minister Gordon Brown of the United Kingdom. Prime Minister Berlusconi and some reporters spoke in Italian, and their remarks were translated by an interpreter.

Remarks to the Organisation for Economic Co-operation and Development in Paris, France
June 13, 2008

Thank you. Thank you very much. Mr. Secretary-General, thank you for your hospitality. It's good to see you again. I remember our days together in the *la frontera de Tejas y Mexico*, when I was the Governor of Texas and you were one of the leading officials of Mexico. And it's great to see you here in Paris, *tambien su esposa*. Madam Secretary, thank you; Ambassadors, World War II veterans, and distinguished guests. Laura and I have— are having a wonderful trip through Europe, and we are so pleased to be back in Paris. It's been a little more than 4 years since we were last in Paris together, and a lot has changed. Laura wrote a book. [*Laughter*] Our daughter got married. [*Laughter*] My dad jumped out of an airplane. [*Laughter*] And my hair is a lot grayer. [*Laughter*]

What has not changed is the friendship between America and France. Recent history has made clear that no disagreement can diminish the deep ties between our nations. France was America's first friend. And over the centuries, our nations stood united in moments of testing, from the Marne to Omaha Beach to the long vigil of the Civil War [cold war].° After September the 11th, 2001, a major French newspaper published a headline my Nation will never forget: *Nous sommes tous Americains*. America is grateful to the people of France. We're proud to call you friends, and our alliance will stand the test of time.

We gather to commemorate a landmark in the moment of that alliance, and that's the 60th anniversary of the start of the Marshall plan. In 1948, the United States Congress passed and President Harry Truman signed legislation to fund this unprece-

_____
° White House correction.

dented effort. And just steps from here, at the Chateau de la Muette—the headquarters for the organization that implemented the Marshall plan and worked with our allies to promote open economies and strong free market policies across Europe.

Through this building flowed friendly aid that helped renew the spirit of the continent, what one magazine called "the D-day for peace." From this building came money for fuel and vehicles and machinery that helped bring Europe's economies back to life. And in this building were written the first chapters of European unity, a story of cooperation that eventually resulted in institutions like NATO and the European Union and the organization that carries the spirit of the Marshall plan into a new century, the OECD.

The Marshall plan was the source of aid and assistant, and it wisely gave Europeans a leading role in reconstruction. By doing so, the plan conveyed a message of partnership and respect. And by offering help to nations across Europe, including Communist nations, the plan also had the effect of clarifying the new ideological struggle that was unfolding.

When he announced the plan, Secretary Marshall made it clear it was "directed not against any country or doctrine, but against hunger and poverty and desperation and chaos." With these words, he showed that we stood for a future of unity and prosperity and freedom throughout Europe. Yet the leaders in the Kremlin denied the Marshall plan aid to the suffering people of the Soviet Union and its captive nations. What followed was nearly a half century of repression and fear in the East, until at last freedom arrived. In an ironic final scene, the Soviets did accept some Western assistance after all. As the last Secretary General sat down to sign the papers ending the Soviet Union, he discovered that his pen was out of ink, so he borrowed one from an American news crew. [*Laughter*]

In the years since the cold war ended, Europe has taken inspiring strides toward a continent whole, free, and at peace. Over the past 8 years, we have watched nations from the Baltics to the Balkans complete the transition from the Soviet bloc to the European Union. We've seen former members of the Warsaw Pact proudly sign the treaty to join NATO. We witnessed an Orange Revolution in Ukraine, a Rose Revolution in Georgia, a Declaration of Independence in Kosovo, and the rise of a democratic movement in Belarus. America admires these brave stands for liberty. We look forward to the day when all free people on this continent take their rightful place in the institutions of Europe.

With these changes has come a revitalization between the relationship—of the relationship between Europe and the United States. Instead of focusing on issues within Europe, we're increasingly looking to matters of global reach. Instead of dwelling on our differences, we're increasingly united in our interests and ideals.

On my first trip abroad of my second term as President, I traveled to Brussels and called for "a new era of transatlantic unity." This week, I have seen the outlines of that new era. In leaders like Berlusconi and Brown and Merkel and Sarkozy, I see a commitment to a powerful and purposeful Europe that advances the values of liberty within its borders and beyond. And when the time comes to welcome a new American President next January, I will be pleased to report to him that the relationship between the United States and Europe is the broadest and most vibrant it has ever been. We see this broad and vibrant relationship in the expansive agenda for our meetings this week.

America and Europe are cooperating to open new opportunities for trade and investment. And we're determined to help make this the year the world completes an ambitious Doha round.

America and Europe are cooperating to address the twin challenges of energy security and climate change while keeping our economies strong. We will continue working to diversify our energy supplies by developing and financing new clean energy technologies. We will continue working toward an international agreement that commits every major economy to slow, stop, and eventually reverse the growth of greenhouse gases.

America and Europe are cooperating to widen the circle of development and prosperity. We lead the world in providing food aid, improving education for boys and girls, and fighting disease. Through the historic commitments of the United States and other G–8 countries, we are working to turn the tide against HIV/AIDS and malaria in Africa. And to achieve this noble goal, all nations must keep their promises to deliver this urgent aid.

America and Europe are cooperating on our most solemn duty of all: protecting our citizens. From New York and Washington to London and Madrid to Copenhagen and Amsterdam, we've seen terrorists and extremists rejoice in the murder of the innocent. So America and Europe are applying the tools of intelligence and finance and law enforcement and diplomacy, and, when necessary, military power to break up terror networks and deny them safe havens. And to protect the people of Europe from the prospect of ballistic missile attacks emanating from the Middle East, we're developing a shared system of missile defense.

These measures are critical to the success in the fight against terror. Yet as in the cold war, we must also prevail in a wider struggle, the battle of ideas. On one side are all who embrace the fundamental tenets of civilization: the natural right to liberty, freedom of conscience and dissent, and the obligation of the strong to protect the weak. On the other side are men who place no value on life, allow no room for dissent, and use terror to impose their harsh ideology on as many people as possible.

Ultimately, the only way to defeat the advocates of this ideology is to defeat their ideas. So the central aim of our foreign policy is to advance a more hopeful and compelling vision, especially in the broader Middle East, a vision on the ideals of liberty and justice and tolerance and hope. These ideals are the foundation of France's Declaration of the Rights of Man and America's Declaration of Independence. Yet these ideals do not belong to our nations alone. They are universal ideals. And the lesson of history is that by extending these ideals—it's more than just a moral obligation—that by expending these—extending these ideals is the only practical and realistic way to protect—to provide our security and to spread the peace.

The rise of free and prosperous societies in the broader Middle East is essential to peace in the 21st century, just as the rise of a free and prosperous Europe was essential to peace in the 20th century. So Europe and America must stand with reformers and democratic leaders and millions of ordinary people across the Middle East who seek a future of hope and liberty and peace.

In Afghanistan, we must stand with a brave young democracy determined to defeat Al Qaida and the Taliban. NATO has accepted an historic mission in Afghanistan. And I applaud the leadership of President Sarkozy, who hosted an international support conference yesterday and will soon deploy additional forces to Afghanistan. President Sarkozy has said, "What is at stake in that country is the future of our values and that of the Atlantic alliance." He is right. Our nations must ensure that Afghanistan is never again a safe haven for terror.

In Lebanon, we must stand with those struggling to protect their sovereignty and independence. We must counter the dangers posed by Hizballah terrorists supported by Iran and Syria. And together, we must show the people of Lebanon that they will have the lasting support of the free world.

In the Holy Land, we must stand with Palestinians and Israelis and all others committed to a two-state solution, a permanent peace based on two democratic states, Israel and Palestine, living side by side in security and peace. I firmly believe that with leadership and courage, a peace agreement is possible this year.

In Iran and Syria, we must stand with the decent people of those two nations who deserve much better than the life they have today. We must stand—we must firmly oppose Iran and Syria's support for terror. And for the security of Europe and for the peace of the world, we must not allow Iran to have a nuclear weapon.

In Iraq, we must stand with the courageous people who have turned the momentum against Al Qaida and extremists. From Anbar Province to mixed neighborhoods in Baghdad to the cities of Basra and Mosul, Iraqis of all backgrounds have made it clear they reject extremism and terror. Today, violence in Iraq is down to the lowest point since March of 2004. Civilian deaths are down; sectarian killings are down. And as security has improved, economic life has been revived. Reconciliation is taking place in communities across that country. And the Government in Baghdad is showing strong leadership and progress on the path to a free society. With the terrorists on the run and freedom on the rise, it is in the interests of every nation on this continent to support a stable and democratic Iraq.

Since 2001, the freedom movement has been advancing in the Middle East. Kuwait has had elections in which women were allowed to vote and hold office for the first time. Algeria held its first competitive Presidential elections. Citizens have voted in municipal elections in Saudi Arabia, in competitive parliamentary elections in Jordan and Morocco and Bahrain, and in a multiparty Presidential election in Yemen.

Liberty takes hold in different places in different ways, so we must continue to adapt and find innovative ways to support those movements for freedom. The way to do so is to stand with civil society groups, human rights organizations, dissidents, independents, journalists and bloggers, and others on the leading edge of reform. We have taken important steps in this area, such as the Broader Middle East and North American [North Africa]* Initiative led by the United States, the Forum for Freedom [Forum for the Future]* led by the G–8, and the Partnership for Democratic Governance led by the OECD.

Spreading the hope of freedom is the calling of our time. And as we look ahead to the great task, we can be guided by four key principles: unity, confidence, vision, and resolve.

We must go forward with unity. Over the course of the cold war, the transatlantic alliance faced moments of serious tension, from the Suez crisis in the 1950s to the basing of missiles in Europe in the 1980s. Yet with the distance of time, we can see these differences for what they were, fleeting disagreements between friends. We'll have more disagreements in the decades ahead, but we must never allow those disagreements to undermine our shared purposes. Dividing democracies is one of our enemies' goals, and they must not be allowed to succeed.

We must go forward with confidence. Our vision of freedom and peace in the Middle East and beyond is ambitious, and of course, there will be voices that will say it will never arrive. And that's natural, and it's not new. There were times when it seemed impossible that there could ever be peace between Britain and France, or France and Germany, or between Germany and Poland. Yet today, all those nations are at peace, and war in Europe is virtually unimaginable. Something happened in Europe that defied the skeptics and the pat-

---

* White House correction.

tern of the centuries, and that was the spread of human freedom.

In truth, this is a strange time to doubt the power of liberty. Over the past 30 years, the number of democracies has grown from 45 to more than 120, which is the fastest advance of freedom in history. As some of the world's oldest democracies, we should never be surprised by the appeal of freedom. We should stand against the moral relativism that views all forms of government as equally acceptable. And we should be confident that one day, the same determination and desire that brought freedom to Paris and Berlin and Riga will bring freedom to Gaza, Damascus, and Tehran.

We must go forward with a clear vision. In the cold war, we laid out a vision of liberty and trusted its power to transform societies. And that transformation took place in ways almost no one could foresee. In the late 1970s, for example, many in the West worried we were losing. And then one October afternoon, there came a sign as bright as the white smoke above the Sistine Chapel. Onto the balcony of St. Peter's stepped the first Polish Pope in history, who inspired millions behind the Iron Curtain with his call: "Be not afraid." John Paul's election was followed by the elections of Margaret Thatcher and Ronald Reagan, who helped restore confidence in freedom's power and pursued a policy of peace through strength. And soon other remarkable events began unfolding: Shipyard workers in Gdansk brought down a government, a jailed playwright in Prague touched off a Velvet Revolution, and citizens of Berlin prayed for the end of a wall and then found the strength to tear it down.

In today's struggle, we have again laid out a clear vision of freedom, and it will transform lives in the Middle East and beyond in ways we cannot fully predict. But we can see some of the sources of change. Sixty percent of the Middle East population is under 30 years old, and over time, these young people—surfing the Internet and watching satellite television and studying abroad—will demand that their societies fully join the free world. The women's movement in the region is growing, and over time, this movement will spark reform, as mothers and daughters make clear that it is costly and unwise to keep half the population from fully contributing to the life of a nation. Middle Eastern immigrants here in Europe are seeing the benefits of freedom, and over time, they will insist that the liberty of their adopted homelands also belongs in the lands of their birth. The future of the region is the hands of its people, and those of us who live in free societies must continue to encourage these early stirrings of reform.

And finally, we must go forward with resolve. In the years ahead, there will be periods of difficulty, yet history shows that freedom can endure even the hardest of tests. Picture what the future of Europe must have looked like for leaders meeting here in Paris 60 years ago. Moscow had occupied much of Central and Eastern Europe after World War II. Communist parties had threatened Governments in Italy and here in France. A severe Soviet threat imperiled Greece and Turkey. A Communist coup had toppled the elected Government of Czechoslovakia. Stalin ordered the blockade of Berlin.

Yet in America and in free capitals of Europe, we summoned the resolve to prevail. We launched the Marshall plan and the Berlin Airlift. Then came the signing of the North Atlantic Treaty and the formation of West Germany. Looking back over the decades, we can see that these brave, early measures put us on the path to victory in the cold war.

There are moments today when the situation in places like the Middle East can look as daunting as it did in Europe six decades ago. Yet we can have confidence that liberty once again will prevail. We can have confidence because freedom is the longing of every soul, and it is the direction of history. We can have confidence because men and women in the Middle East and beyond are determined to claim their liberty, just as the people of Europe did in the last century.

Near the end of his life, George Marshall made a final trip to Europe. He came not for a military meeting or a diplomatic summit, but to accept the Nobel Peace Prize. In his address, Marshall offered a bold prediction: "Tyranny inevitably must retire before the tremendous moral strength of the gospel of freedom." Sixty years ago, the faith in liberty helped the gospel of freedom ring out in nations devastated by war. Today, freedom rings out across this continent. And one day, freedom will ring out across the world.

Thank you for having me. God bless.

NOTE: The President spoke at 3:36 p.m. at the Organisation for Economic Co-operation and Development headquarters. In his remarks, he referred to Secretary-General Angel Gurria of the Organisation for Economic Co-operation and Development and his wife Lulu Quintana; Secretary of State Condoleezza Rice; Prime Minister Silvio Berlusconi of Italy; Prime Minister Gordon Brown and former Prime Minister Margaret Thatcher of the United Kingdom; Chancellor Angela Merkel of Germany; President Nicolas Sarkozy of France; and former President Vaclav Havel of the Czech Republic.

Statement on the Death of Timothy J. Russert
June 13, 2008

Laura and I are deeply saddened by the sudden passing of Tim Russert. Those of us who knew and worked with Tim, his many friends, and the millions of Americans who loyally followed his career on the air will all miss him.

As the longest serving host of the longest running program in the history of television, he was an institution in both news and politics for more than two decades.

Tim was a tough and hard-working newsman. He was always well informed and thorough in his interviews, and he was as gregarious off the set as he was prepared on it.

Most important, Tim was a proud son and father, and Laura and I offer our deepest sympathies to his wife Maureen, his son Luke, and the entire Russert family. We will keep them in our prayers.

Letter to Congressional Leaders Reporting on the Deployments of United States Combat-Equipped Armed Forces Around the World
June 13, 2008

Dear Madam Speaker: (Dear Mr. President:)

I am providing this supplemental consolidated report, prepared by my Administration and consistent with the War Powers Resolution (Public Law 93–148), as part of my efforts to keep the Congress informed about deployments of combat-equipped U.S. Armed Forces around the world. This supplemental report covers operations in support of the war on terror and in Kosovo.

THE WAR ON TERROR

Since September 24, 2001, I have reported, consistent with Public Law 107–40 and the War Powers Resolution, on the combat operations in Afghanistan against al-Qaida terrorists and their Taliban supporters, which began on October 7, 2001, and the deployment of various combat-equipped and combat-support forces to a number of locations in the Central, Pacific, European, and Southern Command areas of operation in support of those operations and of other operations in our war on terror.

I will direct additional measures as necessary in the exercise of the right of the United States to self-defense and to protect U.S. citizens and interests. Such measures may include short-notice deployments of special operations and other forces for sensitive operations in various locations throughout the world. It is not possible to know at this time the precise scope or the duration of the deployment of U.S. Armed Forces necessary to counter the terrorist threat to the United States.

United States Armed Forces, with the assistance of numerous coalition partners, continue to conduct the U.S. campaign to pursue al-Qaida terrorists and to eliminate support to al-Qaida. These operations have been successful in seriously degrading al-Qaida's training capabilities. United States Armed Forces, with the assistance of numerous coalition partners, ended the Taliban regime and are actively pursuing and engaging remnant al-Qaida and Taliban fighters in Afghanistan. The total number of U.S. forces in Afghanistan is approximately 31,122, of which approximately

14,276 are assigned to the International Security Assistance Force (ISAF) in Afghanistan. The U.N. Security Council authorized ISAF in U.N. Security Council Resolution 1386 of December 20, 2001, and has reaffirmed its authorization since that time, most recently for a 12-month period from October 13, 2007, in U.N. Security Council Resolution 1776 of September 19, 2007. The mission of ISAF under NATO command is to assist the Government of Afghanistan in creating a safe and secure environment that allows for continued reconstruction and the exercise and extension of Afghan authority. Currently, more than 40 nations contribute to ISAF, including all 26 NATO Allies.

The United States continues to detain several hundred al-Qaida and Taliban fighters who are believed to pose a continuing threat to the United States and its interests. The combat-equipped and combat-support forces deployed to Naval Base, Guantanamo Bay, Cuba, in the U.S. Southern Command area of operations since January 2002 continue to conduct secure detention operations for the enemy combatants at Guantanamo Bay.

The U.N. Security Council authorized a Multinational Force (MNF) in Iraq under unified command in U.N. Security Council Resolution 1511 of October 16, 2003, and reaffirmed its authorization in U.N. Security Council Resolution 1546 of June 8, 2004, U.N. Security Council Resolution 1637 of November 8, 2005, U.N. Security Council Resolution 1723 of November 28, 2006, and U.N. Security Council Resolution 1790 of December 18, 2007, set to expire on December 31, 2008. Under Resolutions 1546, 1637, 1723, and 1790, the mission of the MNF is to contribute to security and stability in Iraq. These contributions have included assisting in building the capability of the Iraqi security forces and institutions as the Iraqi people drafted and approved a constitution and established a constitutionally elected government. The U.S. contribution to the MNF fluctuates over time, depending on the conditions in theater as determined by the commanders on the ground; the current U.S. contribution to the MNF is approximately 155,230 U.S. military personnel.

In furtherance of our efforts against terrorists who pose a continuing and imminent threat to the United States, its friends and allies, and our forces abroad, the United States continues to work with friends and allies in areas around the globe. These efforts include the deployment of U.S. combat-equipped and combat-support forces to assist in enhancing the counterterrorism capabilities of our friends and allies. United States combat-equipped and combat-support forces continue to be located in the Horn of Africa region.

In addition, the United States continues to conduct maritime interception operations on the high seas in the areas of responsibility of all of the geographic combatant commanders. These maritime operations have the responsibility to stop the movement, arming, or financing of international terrorists.

NATO-LED KOSOVO FORCE (KFOR)

As noted in previous reports regarding U.S. contributions in support of peacekeeping efforts in Kosovo, the U.N. Security Council authorized Member States to establish KFOR in U.N. Security Council Resolution 1244 of June 10, 1999.

The original mission of KFOR was to monitor, verify, and when necessary, to enforce compliance with the Military Technical Agreement between NATO and Serbia (formerly the Federal Republic of Yugoslavia), while maintaining a safe and secure environment. Today, KFOR deters renewed hostilities and, with local authorities and international police, contributes to the maintenance of a safe and secure environment that facilitates the work of the United Nations Interim Administrative Mission in Kosovo (UNMIK), the European

Union (EU)-led International Civilian Office, and the evolving EU Rule of Law Mission (EULEX).

Currently, there are 25 NATO nations contributing to KFOR. Eight non-NATO contributing countries also participate by providing military and other support personnel to KFOR. The U.S. contribution to KFOR is about 1,500 U.S. military personnel, or approximately 9 percent of KFOR's total strength of approximately 16,000 personnel.

The U.S. forces participating in KFOR have been assigned to the eastern region of Kosovo, but also have operated in other areas of the country based on mission requirements. For U.S. KFOR forces, as for KFOR generally, helping to maintain a safe and secure environment remains the principal military task. The KFOR operates under NATO command and control and rules of engagement. The KFOR currently coordinates with and supports UNMIK within means and capabilities and, pending decision by the North Atlantic Council, may offer this same cooperation to EULEX. The KFOR provides a security presence in towns, villages, and the country-side and organizes checkpoints and patrols in key areas to provide security, to protect all elements of the population living in Kosovo, and to instill a feeling of confidence in all ethnic communities throughout Kosovo.

NATO continues periodically to conduct a formal review of KFOR's mission. These reviews provide a basis for assessing current force levels, future requirements, force structure, force reductions, and the even-tual withdrawal of KFOR. NATO adopted the Joint Operations Area plan to regionalize and rationalize its force structure in the Balkans.

The UNMIK international police and Kosovo Police Service (KPS) have primary responsibility for public safety and policing throughout Kosovo. The UNMIK international police and KPS also have assumed responsibility for guarding some patrimonial sites and operating border crossings. The KFOR supports these police forces when requested and augments security in particularly sensitive areas or in response to particular threats as events on the ground dictate. The relationship among UNMIK police, EULEX, KPS, and the Government of Kosovo will likely be adjusted after June 15, 2008, when the constitution of the Republic of Kosovo comes into force.

I have directed the participation of U.S. Armed Forces in all of these operations pursuant to my constitutional authority to conduct the foreign relations of the United States and as Commander in Chief and Chief Executive. Officials of my Administration and I communicate regularly with the leadership and other Members of Congress with regard to these deployments, and we will continue to do so.

Sincerely,

GEORGE W. BUSH

NOTE: Identical letters were sent to Nancy Pelosi, Speaker of the House of Representatives, and Richard B. Cheney, President of the Senate. This letter was released by the Office of the Press Secretary on June 14.

The President's News Conference With President Nicolas Sarkozy of France in Paris, France
June 14, 2008

President Sarkozy. Ladies and gentlemen, thank you for coming to work with us on this Saturday morning. I wanted to thank President Bush for his visit to Paris on his European tour. I see there how much importance he attaches to Franco-American relations and the transatlantic relation. And I think everyone should firmly bear in mind the importance of this transatlantic relation between the United States and Europe, especially as we celebrate the 60th anniversary of the Marshall plan. This is an opportunity for me to extend the same sort of hospitality, warm hospitality that was extended to me last November when I went to Washington and to Mount Vernon.

It's also an opportunity to continue to pursue this confident, trusting, regular dialogue between France and the United States on all issues that we have in common—and there are so many of them. We had an extended discussion on the international situation on the Middle East, but also on economic and trade matters. We checked that—once again saw that there were many areas of convergence, although perhaps slight differences, and that's only right and normal. Friendship should not prevent France or the United States from expressing independent views. But if there are differences, we can discuss them calmly in a level-headed manner. And this is once again an opportunity for me to say to the American people the deep gratitude of the French people and our friendship.

President Bush. Yesterday I reminded the world, really, Nicolas, that America's first friend was France. And frankly, we wouldn't be where we are today without French support early in our Revolution. You are not only our first friend, you've been a consistent friend. And the meetings here have reconfirmed and strengthened our friendship between our countries and our personal friendship.

I really enjoy being with President Sarkozy. He's an interesting guy. [*Laughter*] He is full of energy, he's full of wisdom, he tells me what's on his mind, and we've had—every time I've met with him, we've had very meaningful discussions. We discussed Afghanistan. And thank you very much for supporting the Paris support conference. It made a big difference for that young democracy. And I do thank the people of France for supporting the women and children and the young democrats in Afghanistan. And thank you too, Nicolas.

We talked about Lebanon, of course. Talked to him about the Holy Land, about our deep desire for there to be two states living side by side in peace: two democracies, a Palestinian democracy and Israel, having a—resolving this conflict which creates so much difficulty for not only the Palestinians and the Israelis but for much of the Middle East.

And we talked about Darfur. And I want to thank you very much for having your troops there in Chad.

We talked about Iran—spent a lot of time talking about Iran. And I will tell you that we both have a mutual desire to prevent the Iranians from gaining the knowledge so that they could build a weapon. And we do that for the sake of peace and security of the world.

We talked about Doha, the importance of a Doha round. And frankly—and then we spent some time on climate change. We had a meaningful, good discussion. And I thank you very much for the dinner last night. And it's a great pleasure to have been able to meet your wife too. She's a really smart, capable woman, and I can see why you married her. [*Laughter*] And I can see why she married you too. [*Laughter*]

Anyway, thanks. It's been a good visit. We'll be glad to take some questions.

President Sarkozy. Thank you, George. Perhaps a first question from the French press.

Syria/Iran/Lebanon

Q. To both of you, what specific, concrete requests do you wish to make or send to the Syrian President, Bashar al-Asad, so that he normalize his relations with the West, and of course, to achieve stability in Lebanon and in the rest of——

President Bush. Well, my message would be, stop fooling around with the Iranians and stop harboring terrorists. Serve as a constructive force in the Middle East to help the advance of a Palestinian state. Make it clear to Hamas that their terror is a—should stop for the sake of peace; and make it clear to their Iranian allies that the West is serious when we talk about stopping them from learning how to enrich, which would be the first—a major step for developing a bomb; and to make it clear to their Iranian allies that Hizballah is a destabilizing force for not only Lebanon but elsewhere.

That would be my message. I'd make it clear to him that there is a better way forward for Syria. And Nicolas and I talked about this subject today.

President Sarkozy. Well, George and I totally agree on the need to guarantee Lebanon's independence. Lebanon is entitled, like any other country anywhere in the world, to its independence and to remain independent. And this is one of the preconditions that I have laid down: the election of a new President for Lebanon. That is exactly what happened. It was done with the election of General Sleiman.

Second point, we will go through with the process—the procedure of the international tribunal to track down those who assassinated Mr. Rafiq Hariri. But once I have said to Bashar al-Asad to let the Presidential process take—run its course, we would go back—get back into contact with them, and that is exactly what we've done. We have to let Lebanon stand free.

I also share the view of the United States of America on the fact that the Iranian question—and the fact that they might get their hands on a nuclear weapon—is of the essence; it is a major issue. Syria has to peel off, as much as possible, from Iran in its desire to lay its hands on a nuclear weapon. Once that has happened, then the process will continue.

Lastly, I told the President of the United States that we have taken the initiative of convening a summit for the Mediterranean, and to my knowledge, Syria is part of the Mediterranean region—is a Mediterranean country. Now if you go around the Mediterranean region and start picking and choosing and simply inviting those who correspond to exactly our criteria, then we'll probably have a meeting with very few people attending it.

President Bush. I want to call on Bill Plante from CBS, but before I do, I want to say something about one of your colleagues.

America lost a really fine citizen yesterday when Tim Russert passed away. I've had the privilege of being interviewed by Tim Russert. I found him to be a hardworking, thorough, decent man. And Tim Russert loved his country, he loved his family, and he loved his job a lot. And we're going to miss him all, and we send our deepest sympathies to Maureen, his wife, and Luke, his son. I know they're hurting right now, and, hopefully, the prayers of a lot of Tim's friends and a lot of Americans will help them during this time of difficulty.

Plante.

Iran

Q. Mr. President, Iran's Government spokesman, shortly after the package had been presented by the Europeans, dismissed it out of hand, saying that if it does not—if it includes suspension of enrichment, it absolutely will not fly. Can you convince the rest of your allies and partners to enforce the sanctions which are envisioned in that package? It seems that many of them are reluctant.

President Bush. That's probably a question you ought to ask the President of France, but let me just give you my impressions of the situation. We have worked hard—"we" being our allies—have worked hard to say to the Iranian people, there is a better way forward for you. You've got a Government that has isolated you. You've got a Government that is creating the conditions so that you can't live a full and hopeful life. And the reason why that's happening is because your Government has defied the demands—the just demands of the free world. In other words, they refuse to abandon their desires to develop the know-how which could lead to a nuclear weapon.

Now, they say, "Well, we want a civilian nuclear power." And as I explained to Nicolas today, I agree, they should have the right to have civilian nuclear power. As a matter of fact, Vladimir Putin delivered that very message to the Iranian regime. He also delivered this message: That because you have been untrustworthy, because you haven't fully disclosed your programs to the IAEA in the past, that we can't trust you to enrich. And therefore, Russia will provide the fuel necessary for the civilian nuclear reactor. And therefore, you don't need to rich [enrich]. *

And so our demands are just and fair. And, Bill, we have been implementing the sanctions through the United Nations. And we're working with our friends and allies. As a matter of fact, much of my discussions on this trip have been dominated by this subject because our allies understand that a nuclear-armed Iran is incredibly destabilizing, and they understand that it would be a major blow to world peace.

And so I'm disappointed that the leaders rejected this generous offer out of hand. It's an indication to the Iranian people that their leadership is willing to isolate them further. And our view is, we want the Iranian people to flourish and to benefit. We want their economy to be strong so people can grow up in peace and hope. And yet they've got a—this Ahmadi-nejad is obviously—takes a different position from that and—so his policies are what's creating the deprivation inside Iran.

President Sarkozy. Well, I think France's position is well known. If Iran gets a nuclear bomb, that is totally unacceptable. I

———

* White House correction.

mean, that's very clear. It is an unacceptable threat to world stability, especially when you think of the repeated statements made by the President of Iran right now. Anyone is entitled—including Iran—to access to civilian nuclear energy. We will help them to do so if they act in good faith. If the Iranian authorities are in good faith, then they should let inspections run their course. If they have nothing to hide, then they have nothing to hide; let's show it.

And meanwhile, the only solution in order to persuade the Iranians of this is a faultless, seamless sanction system, you see? The door is wide open to access to civilian nuclear technology—straightaway, now. But as far as military nuclear energies—nuclear access is concerned, this is "no" on the part of the international community. And as the President just said, Vladimir Putin has, with us, sung from the same hymn sheet, and our position will not change. The Iranian people—which is a— who are great people and a major civilization—they need economic progress; they need growth; they deserve better than the impasse, the dead-end into which some of their leaders are leading them.

European Union/Lisbon Treaty

Q. President, good morning.

President Sarkozy. Hold it the other way around, madam.

Q. Well, I should actually know what— how to hold a microphone, but thank you. President—to you, Mr. Sarkozy, it would appear that the building and shaping of Europe has been seriously shaken yesterday by the Irish "no." In fact, some have called for the ratification procedure to be suspended. Can this not be the case? And secondly, do you want your Presidency, the French Presidency to be one which, as you called for, continues to push Europe forward? And do you not think that the Irish "no" is going to hinder this?

President Sarkozy. Well, it's going to make things more difficult, but when you're a head of state and when the bubble—

you take over the Presidency of the Union, if you like easy jobs, then you should step down straightaway.

Now, the Irish "no" is a political reality. It's a fact; it's happened. But the issue is not whether we like or not. It's a fact; we have to live with it. The Irish people said what they had to say, and we have to accept that. Now, having said that, we, with Angela Merkel, believe that we have to continue with the ratification process, because at this stage, 18 European states have ratified the treaty. We have to continue doing so, and that is Gordon Brown's intention, as he explained to me yesterday over the telephone, so that this Irish hiccup not become a major crisis.

So, despite that, let's continue to ratify. But at the same time, we have to put our heads together, all of us. It is no coincidence, it is no surprise to a certain extent—in fact, I spoke yesterday with the Irish *Taoiseach*, the Irish Prime Minister. A lot of Europeans do not understand how we are shaping Europe right now and building Europe, and we have to take account of that. And we have to do so very fast. We have to change our way of building Europe.

The idea of a European construct, it was one of the most wonderful ideas that the founding fathers had some half a century ago. We are not allow—we shouldn't sabotage it. But perhaps we should do it differently. Europe was set up to protect, and yet it worries so many Europeans. We can't not take account of this. We have to do so, and we have to do so now. So I have every intention of taking initiatives. I'm thinking, for instance, of a European immigration policy. I'm thinking of a European response to this endless increase in oil prices. It seems to me that we have a duty to be more effective and look at what the daily lives of our citizens—fellow citizens—look like. And I take the Irish "no" as a call for us to do things differently and do things better.

Now, of course, it's not going to simplify the work and the task of the French Presi-dent—Presidency of the European Union, but——

President Bush. Olivier [Olivier Knox, Agence France-Presse]. Tossing a bone to somebody who's got a French name. [*Laughter*] Might want to use the mike, Olivier.

Iraq/France-U.S. Relations

Q. Yes, I will. Thank you, Mr. President. *Merci, Monsieur President.* First——

President Bush. Speaks the language too. [*Laughter*]

Q. Just wait. [*Laughter*] I'd like to ask you each a question.

President Bush. In the great tradition of David Gregory [NBC News].

Q. Who?

President Bush. Yes, just trying to work him in the news here.

Q. I'd like to ask you a question first, Mr. President. *Et ensuite une au President de la Republique.*

Interpreter. I'm going to question the President of the Republic.

Q. President Bush, Iraqi Prime Minister Nuri al-Maliki says that talks on a status of forces agreement are at an impasse, or a dead end—not dead, but in trouble. How do you break this impasse, and are the conditions that the United States have set forward in support so far nonnegotiable?

[*At this point, the reporter asked a question in French, and it was translated as follows.*]

Q. And to you, President, is the Franco-American relationship the privilege, the priority number-one relationship in the trans-atlantic context?

President Bush. Olivier, if I were a betting man, we'll reach an agreement with the Iraqis. And it's—you know, of course we're there at their invitation; this is a sovereign nation. And therefore, we're working hard with the elected Government of Iraq about, you know, U.S. presence and coalition presence in a way that the elected Government is comfortable.

And it's interesting to be in—working with a democracy where, you know, people are trying to prepare the ground to get something passed through Parliament, for example, or the free press is vibrant. But we're going to work hard to accommodate their desires. It's their country.

And at the same time, we believe that a strategic relationship with Iraq is important. It's important for Iraq; it's important for the United States; it's important for the region. And I repeat to you that whatever we agreed to, it will not commit future Presidents to troop levels, nor will it establish permanent bases.

Anyway, we'll see how it goes. And thanks for the question in English. [*Laughter*]

President Sarkozy. Well, the Americans and the French have had a privileged relationship for two centuries now. I mean, when the United States of America was born, France made a choice. It was not a European choice, because we chose to side with the Americans or the United States of America as opposed to Britain at the time. And in two World Wars, we've been together. We share the same values.

So yes, it is a privileged relationship, but it's not privileged since I came to be elected; it's been privileged for two centuries now. You can't neglect that. Now, through this—throughout that, we have had ups and downs—hiccups—because two peoples— I'm talking about the French and the American peoples—that actually resemble one another. We express our feelings. The American people can be heard, and likewise for the French people. We have to be careful about this. We have to be mindful of this when we talk to one another in our relations.

I have always seen American leaders— and thank you to President Bush—for accepting European originality and independence and, of course, French originality and independence. And I've always noted that we can talk very frankly when we had points of disagreement. But we have to do

so in—as allies and as friends, and be mindful of not hurting one another. We can agree on an issue, on the substance of issue, but we don't have to say so in an unpleasant manner. It so happens that today we have a lot of areas of convergence. But yes, maybe on such and such an issue, we don't totally agree, but it doesn't in any way undermine the basis of what I have to say, which is that the Americans are our friends and our allies. They know they can count on us.

Might I add that it seems to me that the more you trust somebody, the more trust there is on both sides of the Atlantic, the more leeway we have. We don't ask the United States to apologize to us because they have their own vision of their strategic interests, and they don't ask us to apologize for the fact that we are defending our own strategic interests, precisely because the relationship is a strong one; it is a calm one. And when a relationship is that strong, you accept one's divergences or differences. And that is my whole point. You've got to understand, if you're in a strong relationship, then you have more room for freedom, more room for maneuver. That's what this is all about.

Perhaps one last question?

President Bush. Oh. [*Laughter*]

President Sarkozy. One more, last.

Middle East Peace Process

Q. You have set the target before leaving the White House that, by the end of this year, you will, hopefully, achieve an historical peace between the Israelis and the Palestinians. However, in light of what's happening to the fragile position of Ehud Olmert—Prime Minister Ehud Olmert and the continuous process of building illegal settlements in the—in eastern Jerusalem and certain parts of the occupied territories, do you think that peace is far away right now in light of those obstacles?

President Bush. Yes. Thank you. First of all, I view the concept of a Palestinian state and the idea of a Palestinian state for

Israeli security, as well as Palestinian security and hope, as bigger than the political process. And I fully recognize there's a lot of uncertainty in the Israeli political scene now.

On the other hand, what is not uncertain is that most people—or many people in Israel understand that for their own security, there has to be a Palestinian state with clearly defined borders, a state that doesn't look like Swiss cheese, a resolution of the refugee issue and the security issue, and of course, issues surrounding Jerusalem.

Most Palestinians want to coexist in peace with Israel. And that peace must be in a state that is clearly visible, well-defined, and in actuality is a state. And so in other words, the concept—and by the way, this is newly arrived. I'm actually the first President ever to have articulated a two-state solution, two democracies living side by side with peace—in peace. And during my time as President, I've seen a notable shift amongst folks in the Middle East that recognize the importance of having that state.

So my point to you is, is that, you know, it's been a—there's always difficulties in democracies, but the notion is a—of getting this work done is important. And therefore, our diplomacy is to remind all the parties involved that they have now an opportunity to get a state negotiated. And I think it can be done by the end of the year. Condi is very much involved with it on a—you know, a nearly weekly, it seems like, basis. And of course, I'm in touch with the leaders. The Palestinians are discouraged by the settlement activity—all the more reason to get the borders clearly defined as quickly as possible.

I want to thank Nicolas and the EU, for example, for helping build civil society in the Palestinian Territory as well as helping Prime Minister Fayyad with security measures.

I'll also remind you that it's essential that we get a state defined as quickly as possible so that leaders such as President Abbas and Prime Minister Fayyad can say to their people, here's an alternative vision to what's taking place in Gaza. You support us, and you're going to get a state. You support Hamas, and you're going to get Gaza. Take your pick.

And therefore, there it's imperative that we, you know, convince the parties to get this done. Now, I know some say, "All America has got to do is say, 'Do it.'" No, the way it works is, is that the parties have got to come to this agreement. Our job, along with the EU through the Quartet, is to keep the process moving.

And so I'm optimistic. I understand how difficult it is, but difficulty should not cause people to do the right thing. If you believe in your soul something is right, then you have an obligation to work. And in this case, I firmly believe that the establishment of the Palestinian state will bring hope and peace to the Israelis and the Palestinians.

Thank you.

NOTE: The President's news conference began at 11:45 a.m. at Elysee Palace. In his remarks, he referred to Carla Bruni-Sarkozy, wife of President Sarkozy; Timothy J. Russert, moderator of NBC's "Meet the Press," who died on June 13; Prime Minister Vladimir V. Putin of Russia, in his former capacity as President of Russia; President Mahmud Ahmadi-nejad of Iran; and Prime Minister Salam Fayyad and President Mahmoud Abbas of the Palestinian Authority. President Sarkozy referred to President Michel Sleiman of Lebanon; Chancellor Angela Merkel of Germany; Prime Minister Gordon Brown of the United Kingdom; and Prime Minister Brian Cowen of Ireland. A reporter referred to Prime Minister Ehud Olmert of Israel. President Sarkozy and some reporters spoke in French, and their remarks were translated by an interpreter.

The President's Radio Address
June 14, 2008

Good morning. This week, I'm traveling in Europe. In the past few days, I have visited Slovenia, Germany, Italy, and the Vatican. I'm spending this Saturday in France, and I will conclude my trip in the United Kingdom.

In my meetings, I've discussed our shared efforts to advance peace and prosperity around the world. America has strong partners in leaders like Italy's Silvio Berlusconi, Germany's Angela Merkel, France's Nicolas Sarkozy, and Britain's Gordon Brown. And together we're pursuing an agenda that is broad and far reaching.

America and Europe are cooperating to open new opportunities for trade and investment. We're working to tear down regulatory barriers that hurt our businesses and consumers. We're striving to make this the year that the world completes an ambitious Doha trade agreement, which will open up new markets for American goods and services and help alleviate poverty around the world.

America and Europe are cooperating to address the twin challenges of energy security and climate change, while keeping our economies strong. We're working to diversify our energy supplies by developing and financing new clean energy technologies. And we're working toward an international agreement that commits every major economy to slow, stop, and eventually reverse the growth of greenhouse gases.

America and Europe are cooperating to widen the circle of development and prosperity. We're leading the world in providing food aid, improving education for boys and girls, and fighting disease. Through the historic commitments of the United States and other G–8 countries, we're working to turn the tide against HIV/AIDS and malaria in Africa. And to achieve this noble goal, all nations must keep their promises to deliver this urgent aid.

America and Europe are cooperating on our most solemn duty: protecting our citizens. Our nations are applying the tools of intelligence, finance, law enforcement, diplomacy, and when necessary, military power to break up terror networks and deny them safe havens. And to protect against the prospect of ballistic missile attacks emanating from the Middle East, we're developing a shared system of missile defense.

We're also working together to ensure that Iran is not allowed to acquire a nuclear weapon. This week, America and our European allies sent a clear and unmistakable message to the regime in Tehran: It must verifiably suspend its enrichment activities or face further isolation and additional sanctions. Together, America and Europe are pursuing strong diplomacy with Iran, so that future generations can look back and say that we came together to stop this threat to our people.

In the long run, the most important way we can protect our people is to defeat the terrorists' hateful ideology by spreading the hope of freedom. So America and Europe are working together to advance the vision of two democratic states, Israel and Palestine, living side by side in security and peace. We're working together to protect the sovereignty of Lebanon's young democracy. And we're working together to strengthen the democratically elected Governments in Iraq and Afghanistan.

In all of these areas, the United States and Europe have agreed that we must take action and that we must go forward together. The level and breadth of the cooperation between America and our European allies today is unprecedented. And together we're making the world a safer and more hopeful place.

Thank you for listening.

NOTE: The address was recorded at 9:15 a.m. on June 13 in Rome, Italy, for broadcast at 10:06 a.m., e.d.t., on June 14. The transcript was made available by the Office of the Press Secretary on June 13, but was embargoed for release until the broadcast. Due to the 6-hour time difference, the address was broadcast after the President's news conference in Paris, France. The Office of the Press Secretary also released a Spanish language transcript of this address.

Interview With Ned Temko of the Observer in Rome, Italy
June 13, 2008

Progress in Iraq/Remarks to the Organisation for Economic Co-operation and Development in Paris, France

Mr. Temko. You're giving a major speech in Paris in a few hours' time on what you describe as a new era of transatlantic union. And obviously, the picture in Europe is much more encouraging, it would seem, than a few years ago. What's changed, in your view, and what needs to be fixed?

The President. This is the—what's changed is the—we've gone beyond the Iraq period for two reasons. One is that Iraq is—democracy is succeeding. People are beginning to see progress. And therefore, people that—at least governments that felt like they didn't want to participate in the liberation of Iraq have now wanted to participate in the reconstruction of Iraq. And their people are beginning to see some success. Maliki has moved things—Stockholm—and comports himself like a leader would, and he speaks hopefully about the future.

Secondly, that there are a lot of issues that we're focused on that kind of send a signal that cooperation is necessary to change the conditions of the world for the better—cooperation on AIDS, cooperation on malaria, cooperation on trade, hopefully, discussion about climate change, cooperation in Afghanistan. In other words, the agenda is varied, and it's profound.

And my speech basically says that by focusing on these issues and by working together in a unified way, we can be trans-formative, just like we were in the past. Europe used to be inward looking right after World War II—necessarily so—to rebuild. America helped. Now we can be outward looking as we help others.

I also have a—I'm a believer that liberty is transformative—the power of liberty is universal, that moral relativism must be rejected, and that we've got to have confidence in liberty to help others so that we're more secure ourselves. And that's what the speech is. It's a hopeful speech.

Russia-U.S. Relations

Mr. Temko. And one of the areas of Europe where liberty has been sort of partly transformative is clearly post-Soviet Russia. And you've had very strong personal relationship with Putin. First of all, is your assessment that Putin is still basically in charge? And how important is your personal relationship?

The President. Let me start with the second. My personal relationship is important because we had differences. And therefore, if you work hard to establish a relationship of trust, that you're then able to air out your differences in a way that's respectful of the other person, and at the same time, find common ground.

One area of common ground that has really not been given much attention is Iran. I agreed that the Iranians should have—they have the sovereign right to have civilian nuclear power. Putin obviously believes they should; witness the cooperation on Bushehr. We both agree, however, that they can't be trusted with the knowledge that comes from enrichment. And therefore, Putin suggested to the Iranians that Russia provide the enriched uranium necessary to run their fuel plant. I agree. And as I said yesterday in the press conference, that this really undermines the argument for the Iranians because if, in fact, their only focus is on civilian nuclear power, they readily accept the plant, the fuel, and the offer of Russia to pick up the spent fuel.

So there are areas where we cooperate, and there are areas where we have disagreements. And yet I believe the best foreign policy for the American President is to be in a position to earn the trust of those where there's not a hundred-percent agreement. And by the way, any American President will find out there's never a hundred-percent agreement, even with your closest friends.

Mr. Temko. I'm sure that's right. [*Laughter*]

The President. And so the first part of the question—yes, look, I think it's—I went to Sochi. Putin introduced me to Medvedev. And he, in not only his body language, but in his words to me—that Medvedev is going to be in charge of foreign policy. And their relationship is being sorted out, and the world is fascinated to watch what's happening. I think it's—I'll take him for his word, and then we'll watch and see what happens.

Religious Freedom

Mr. Temko. How concerned are you about issues like human rights in Russia? And what degree of influence does any outside country—even the United States or——

The President. Oh, I think it matters. I think it matters when people speak up, whether it be in Russia or China or anywhere else. In Russia's case, there was— early on in my Presidency, I remember talking to Vladimir Putin on behalf of the Catholic Church, where there were concerns about the Church being able to have a robust presence.

Vladimir Putin is sensitive to religious issues. He's a religious guy himself. He has a beautiful little Orthodox church on his own property, which he proudly showed me and Laura one time. He made sure I met some of the Jewish community when I was there in Russia. And so he is sensitive to religious liberty, more so than some other countries.

Natural Resources/Multilateral Relations

Mr. Temko. And is Western leverage reduced by the fact that Russia has a good chunk of the world's natural energy resources?

The President. I think it certainly changes the equation on a lot of foreign policy. It's interesting to watch the European Union wrestle with energy independence. Early in my Presidency, nations were saying they were going to get rid of nuclear power. And I questioned them quietly, on an individual basis, about that decision, because if you get rid of one source of power, you have to find another source of power, unless, of course, you don't care whether your economy grows. Most leaders end up caring whether their economy grows.

So I predicted to some of these leaders that there would be an issue in terms of having a sole source supplier, particularly of natural gas from Russia. And now there's great consternation within the EU. And my only point is, is that this energy issue complicates a lot of foreign policy issues, including that between the EU and Russia, as well as that between the United States and Venezuela, or the world and Iran. And the question is, what do you do about it?

Energy Policy

Mr. Temko. Well, that was going to be my next question.

The President. What we need to do about it in the United States is to get this Democratically controlled Congress to allow us to explore for oil and gas. We did an energy study when I first became President that predicted it would be an issue if we did not explore for oil and gas. And what people don't understand is hydrocarbons are necessary as we transition to a new era, based upon new technologies. But new technologies don't arrive overnight. I mean, they just don't suddenly appear. It takes time and money to develop these technologies. The world is in the process of doing that. The United States is spending a lot of money on research, both privately and publicly. Japan is as well.

And yet we forgot the notion of transitioning. And so we don't explore in ANWR, we don't explore for oil shale, we don't explore off the coast of America, and we should be.

Oil Prices/Upcoming Middle East Oil Summit

Mr. Temko. In terms of the oil price, which is obsessing most of the world now, is there anything individual governments can do, in your view?

The President. There's no magic wand. It took us a while to get to where we are; it's going to take us a while to get out of it. And the truth of the matter is that there's either got to be more supply or less demand. And demand doesn't decline overnight, although patterns and habits are beginning to change in the United States. You notice some of these car manufacturers are now announcing they're going to be manufacturing smaller automobiles.

I think that people have got to recognize that, I mean, our policy in America has been robust on the development of new technologies and weak on finding enough hydrocarbons so that we can become less dependent on foreign sources of oil.

Mr. Temko. In terms of the short term, fixing the oil price——

The President. You mean the magic wand?

Mr. Temko. Yes.

The President. No, there's not one.

Mr. Temko. And in terms of these conferences, I notice there's going to be a conference in Jeddah, and your national security staff——

The President. That would be Hadley, the spokesman.

Mr. Temko. Yes, indeed—not unreasonably said that you would want to know what such a conference——

The President. I was asked this at a press conference last night. I said it's an interesting idea. Of course, I'm going to go home and take a look at what it all means, and I'll decide who's going to attend on our behalf. But if I might repeat, the solution to the price of hydrocarbons is either more hydrocarbons or less usage of hydrocarbons.

During my trips to the Middle East—I've got great relations with the leaders there, and I talked to King Abdallah about increasing the supply of oil, on the theory that if you harm your consumers with high price, they will find other ways to power their economies as quickly as possible. And secondly, he should not want to see kind of a worldwide contraction as a result of consumers spending money on energy that ends up overseas, as opposed to spending money on opportunities in their respective economies.

So I think people, if they take a sober look at the world's supply, there's just not a lot relative to demand.

One of the things that could help is that if some countries, big consumers of hydrocarbons stop subsidizing their populations so that there is a response to price on the demand side.

Iran

Mr. Temko. Iran has been very much on the agenda again, all this week——

The President. Yes, it is. It should be.

Mr. Temko. ——and should be. Ahmadinejad has all but said no to the latest incentive package. If that stands, what's the next step in your view?

The President. More sanctions. The next step is for the Europeans and the United States and Russia and China to understand diplomacy only works if there are consequences. And sometimes the world tends to focus on the process as opposed to the results. And I have tried during my Presidency to say, we need to focus on the results. And for diplomacy to be consequential, there has to be a statement that says to the Iranians: Here's your way forward; if you choose not to, there will be a consequence. And the consequence in this case, in the diplomatic channel, is sanctions that are effective. So we will work with our partners on implementation of the sanctions thus far in place through the U.N., and work with them on additional sanctions, including through the U.N. process, as well as through the financial process.

Mr. Temko. What's at stake here? Sorry, go on.

The President. On the theory that there are people inside Iran who, one, are suffering as a result of the decisions their Government made; but secondly, leaders inside of Iran who are sick and tired of the isolation brought about by this regime. In 2003, the Iranians had agreed to verifiably suspend; we had agreed to say, there's a way forward, working with our European partners. In other words, there was a—looked like a successful way forward for both sides of this debate. Then Ahmadi-nejad gets elected, changes the tone and changes the policy.

And so my only point there is that— and this is the point I make to our partners—is that the Iranians had adopted a different attitude during my Presidency— in other words, in the relatively near past— and that's not to say they can't do it again. And now is the time. And the consequences of Iran having a nuclear weapon are substantial. They're substantial in the Middle East. If the people in the Middle East do not think that the United States and Europe, for example, are going to work to provide security, they will find their own

ways to secure themselves. And what the Middle East does not need is a nuclear arms race. It does not need the instability that comes from an innate fear that the West is not strong enough or willing enough to take on the problem.

Situation in the Middle East

Mr. Temko. So there's a lot at stake here, in your view.

The President. In my judgment, it's the international issue that faces all of us. And therefore, success in Iraq is important; it has consequences for the Iranian issue. It is important for us to have security agreements with our friends. We, the United States, has security agreements with UAE, for example. When you go to the Middle East and you sit in my seat and listen, yes, there's concern about the Palestinian state. But the dialogue has shifted dramatically from solve the Palestinian state and you've solved the problems in the Middle East, to now solve the Iranian issue and you solve the problems in the Middle East.

Iran

Mr. Temko. Let's assume that Ahmadi-nejad does not respond to this latest package, that there are additional sanctions. You clearly feel very strongly about this issue.

The President. That's why I put all options on the table.

Mr. Temko. And there are other options, obviously. What happens if at the end of the year, you have tougher sanctions, but you still have no resolution?

The President. I don't want to speculate on that. My hope is, is that let's get the tough sanctions in place. That's the task.

Mr. Temko. But there's always an alternative on the table; there has to be.

The President. Oh, yes, absolutely.

Mr. Temko. And you——

The President. And alternatives not just for the United States, alternatives for a lot of other countries, some of which the world needs to think about as we head into this arena. We don't want a nuclear arms race in the Middle East. That's an alternative.

U.S. Foreign Policy

Mr. Temko. But you would be willing to hand over a status quo which was slightly improved, i.e., tougher sanctions?

The President. Actually, it's not status quo because there's a multilateral forum in place that will enable Presidents to more likely deal with this issue.

I have made it clear that it's difficult for the United States to achieve an issue in a one-on-one situation with people like Ahmadi-nejad or Kim Jong Il. I have changed the foreign policy of the United States to make it more multilateral because I understand that diplomacy without consequences is ineffective. And the only way to achieve consequences through diplomacy is for there to be a universal application, in this case, of sanctions. Unilateral sanctions don't work.

You know, I tell my partners, we're asking you to sanction. I know you're sitting there saying to yourself, "Well, it's easy for him to say because they've already sanctioned." And the question facing countries is, does money trump effective diplomacy for the sake of peace and security?

Progress in Iraq

Mr. Temko. Iraq, you mentioned. Postsurge, are things heading in the right direction, in your view?

The President. Absolutely.

Mr. Temko. And how is——

The President. Violence is down. And as a result of violence being down, the economy is growing and political reconciliation is taking place. And the lesson learned in this postconflict period in both Iraq and Afghanistan is, you got to have security.

I gave a speech at the Air Force Academy that said it's a different set of issues that we face now than we faced 60 years ago in postconflict. First of all, the conflicts took longer to resolve in World War II, and yet the reconstruction was done in rel-ative peace and security. Here it took little time to accomplish the initial military objective, and reconstruction had to be done in the face of a lot of violence.

And in 2006, it became apparent that our strategy of training and encouraging the Iraqis to take the lead was not working; sectarian violence was severe. As you know, I made the decision to send 30,000 more in because we recognized that—and had belief that security would yield this kind of evolution of democracy, and it is. The number of laws they passed, the Iraqi Parliament have passed, have been—I would say it certainly exceeded expectations. And they passed their budgets faster than we have passed our budgets.

British and U.S. Troop Levels in Iraq

Mr. Temko. I'm sure that's true. [*Laughter*]

The British Government, Gordon Brown had said yesterday, I think, that he will announce sometime in the coming weeks future plans for British deployment in Iraq. British officers have acknowledged that in the recent fighting in Basra, the American military role was crucial to making sure that there was a response. Is there not a concern that, whatever the justifications for a British withdrawal, that a British pullout of troops could have an effect either on American deployment or on the situation as a whole? Or are you relaxed about it?

The President. I'm, first of all, appreciative of the fact that Gordon Brown is constantly in dialogue with us about what he and his military are thinking. Secondly, we ourselves are bringing out troops based upon return on success. And thirdly, I am confident that he, like me, will listen to our commanders to make sure that the sacrifices that have gone forward won't be unraveled by drawdowns that may not be warranted at this point in time. I'm looking forward to discussing with him.

We've had some discussions. He was going to be at 3,500, I think, if I'm not mistaken; he's now at 5,000.

National Security Adviser Stephen J. Hadley. I think he's at 4,200.

The President. Forty-two-hundred, I don't know, whatever, but it's——

Mr. Temko. But it did roll back on an——

The President. It's greater than he thought, in other words——

Mr. Temko. Yes, that's right.

The President. In other words, the Government took a look and said, "Well, maybe we ought to leave more troops in." My only point is, is that timetables—you say, timetable for withdrawal, and our answer is, there should be no definitive timetable; there ought to be obviously a desire to reduce our presence, but it's got to be based upon success.

All I can tell you is, from my perspective, the British response has been that way. They've said, we're going to have—we think we'll be at 3,500, but then adjusted their plans based upon the conditions.

Iraq/President's Decisionmaking

Mr. Temko. Weapons of mass destruction in Iraq obviously is——

The President. Still looking for them.

Mr. Temko. Still looking for them, exactly. [*Laughter*]

The President. That was a huge disappointment.

Mr. Temko. And the obvious question your critics ask, particularly in Britain, is if we'd known at the time there weren't any WMD, would there have been this war?

The President. Well, you know, that's one of those great hypotheticals that we didn't know. Now having said that, I still strongly defend the decision. The world is better off without Saddam Hussein in power. But Presidents don't get to do redos; they don't get to do look-backs, ifs. All I can tell you is, is that we thought for certain there was weapons of mass destruction, as did the nations that voted for 1441.

See, the interesting thing about history is that—short-term, kind of momentary his-

tory, is that people forget what life was like at the moment that this decision was made. One, people forget that we tried to solve this problem diplomatically. You might remember, there was a great debate: Will Bush go to the United Nations, or will they move without trying to solve this problem diplomatically? Well, we did go to the United Nations; I insisted we go to the United Nations. And we worked diligently from the summer of 2002 until March of 2003 to see if we couldn't have solved this. We went back to the United Nations for a resolution.

Mr. Temko. For a second resolution, yes.

The President. And in the meantime, we're working with our allies and friends. We didn't realize, nor did anybody else, that Saddam Hussein felt like he needed to play like he had weapons of mass destruction. It may have been, however, that in his mind all this was just a bluff. After all, there had been 17 United Nations Security Council resolutions, the world wasn't serious, which leads me back to the point that when the world says something, it better have—it better mean what it says, otherwise people who are destabilizing just don't take it seriously. "Who cares?" they say.

And so I was asked in Germany—one of the guys said, "You making any mistakes?" "Of course," I said. One of the mistakes was my language made it look like that I was anxious for war; that because of my language, I didn't understand the consequences. Well, of course I understand the consequences. And I understand better than anybody that the Commander in Chief has got an obligation to comfort those who have lost a loved one because of his decision. And then the man went on and said, "Well, was it a mistake to get rid of Saddam Hussein?" The answer is absolutely not.

President's Decisionmaking

Mr. Temko. You very movingly described in one interview this week that—how difficult it is to put young American men and women in harm's way and how much time and energy you've tried to devote to doing what you can, obviously, to comfort the families of someone who has been killed——

The President. And making sure they understand that the sacrifice won't go in vain. Nothing worse than a politician making decisions based upon the last Gallup poll when people's lives are at stake, or where they have made a sacrifice. And I tell these folks—and they want to know—look, there's a lot of them, and I haven't visited with all the families. But I will tell you this: Many, many families look at me trying to determine whether or not, one, I believed that it was necessary; and two, whether or not I'm going to let their son or daughter kind of lie in an empty grave when it comes to the sacrifice they made. They want to know whether or not the President—if he believes it was necessary, whether or not he's going to see this thing through, regardless of what they're screaming on the TV sets.

President's Image Abroad

Mr. Temko. You're flying into Britain where your public awaits you, and you know there's a tough public there sometimes. One of the questions——

The President. Do I care? Only to the extent that it affects people's view of my—the citizens I represent. Do I care about my personal standing? Not really.

Iraqi Civilians/U.S. Military Casualties/Freedom Agenda

Mr. Temko. One of the questions, of course, they ask, is, do you feel a sense of personal pain——

The President. Course I do.

Mr. Temko. ——over the Iraqi civilians who have——

The President. I feel a sense of pain for those who were tortured by Saddam Hussein, by the parents who watched their daughters raped by Saddam Hussein, by those innocent civilians who have been killed by inadvertent allied action, by those who have been bombed by suicide bombers. I feel a sense of pain for death. I feel a sense of pain for the families of our troops. I read about it every night, or I used to read about it every night. The violence has changed.

But I get a report every day about whether or not the U.S. has suffered casualties. And when I get those reports, I think about those mothers and fathers. And I meet with a lot of families—a lot—in order to be able to—it's my duty to try to console and comfort. And many times, the comforter in chief ends up being comforted, by the way, by the families, the strength of the families.

This is a volunteer army, and these kids are in this fight because they want to be in the fight. And they believe in it. And yet these poor parents are looking at—oftentimes looking at negativity, just people quick to report the ugly and the negative. But it's hard to report on the schools that are opening or the clinics that are opening or the playgrounds that are filling up. The society is coming back.

I have great faith in the power of liberty. First of all, I wasn't surprised when people went to vote in defiance of the killers. I was pleased, but not surprised, because I believe in the universality of freedom. I don't believe it is a Western value. And I say to people, I am concerned about the comfortable isolating themselves and saying, who cares whether somebody over there lives in a free society?

And I'll say in my speech, moral relativism must be challenged, this notion that it doesn't matter what forms of government are—I think it does matter. I think it also matters, along these lines, that when I talk about freedom, it's just not freedom from tyranny, it's freedom from HIV/AIDS; it's freedom from malaria; it's freedom from hunger—for two reasons. One, it's in our national interests that we defeat hopelessness. The only way a suicide bomber can recruit is when he finds somebody hopeless. And secondly, it's in our moral interests. A nation is a better nation when it feeds the hungry and takes care of the diseased.

And therefore, when I go to the G–8, my message to the G–8 is, yes, we'll talk about the environment, and that's important. But George W. Bush is going to be talking about those people who are needlessly dying because of mosquito bites. And I expect them to honor their obligations. We came to the G–8 last year, and I said: "Why don't you match what the United States of America does? We're putting up $30 billion for HIV/AIDS, $1.6 billion for malaria. And why don't you match us?" And they said, "Okay."

And so we're going to go to the G–8 and we're going to sit down and say, "Have we matched?" Because there are people needlessly dying today. And we'll come up with a good solution for greenhouse gases by getting China and India at the table. And it's going to take time to evolve, but I'm going to remind people we can act today to save lives for the good of the world.

White House Press Secretary Dana Perino. Okay, we're about 25 minutes.

The President. That means shorten my answers.

Former Prime Minister Tony Blair of the United Kingdom

Mr. Temko. No, no, I'll shorten my questions. [*Laughter*]

Just three very brief questions. First of all, your relationship with Tony Blair—I'm struck, in your last question, that you seem to share with him a genuine passion for ideas and that politics matter. How would you describe your relationship with Blair?

The President. I would say, first of all, it's a relationship forged by fire. We

share—as you can tell, I have this idealistic streak, and so does Blair. But we also understand that this idealism is a practical response to the world. See, this is an— he understands, like I understand, this is an ideological struggle. These acts are not isolated acts of lawlessness. We're in a war.

A lot of people hope this wasn't the war—you know, just kind of dismiss it as, oh, there's some irritated guys, you know, just kind of making some moves. We viewed it as an ideological struggle that requires response through good intelligence, sometimes military, obviously, sometimes law enforcement, all aiming to dismantle and protect our people—dismantle the cells and protect our people, but that ultimately, freedom has to defeat the ideology of hate.

Mr. Temko. Was Tony Blair your poodle, to use the——

The President. You know, look, this is the convenient—one of the great things about Western press is that they oftentimes retreat to the convenient rather than trying to, you know, probe the depths of a relationship or the depths of somebody's feelings or the basis of philosophy. And so it's convenient. It's convenient to say, you know, "warmonger," "religious zealot," "poodle." I mean, these are just words that people love to toss around foolishly.

President's Legacy

Mr. Temko. How do you think and how do you hope that you and Blair—but particularly yourself—how would you hope that the achievement—what's your greatest achievement or your greatest pride as President? And what's your greatest regret?

The President. Well, first of all, just so you know, I'm not going to be around to see it. There's no such thing as objective short-term history. It takes a while for history to have its—you know, to be able to have enough time to look back to see why decisions were made and what their consequences were.

So you know, I'd hope it'd be somebody who would use the influence of the United

States to help transform societies by working on disease and hunger and freedom. And the liberation of 50 million people from the clutches of barbaric regimes is noteworthy, at the minimum.

President's Beliefs

Mr. Temko. Does this job take its toll on you? I mean, can you——

The President. My spirits are pretty high. I mean, I'm—you got to believe, you know? You got to have a set of beliefs that are the foundation for your very being. Otherwise these currents and tides and 24-hour news and politics will kind of leave you adrift. And I tell people that when I get home, I'm going to look in that mirror and say, I didn't sacrifice my core beliefs to satisfy critics or satisfy pundits or, you know——

President's Future

Mr. Temko. And what next—a foundation, a book?

The President. Yes, I'm going to think about that, yes—writing a book. I'm going to build a Presidential library with a freedom institute at SMU—Southern Methodist University—all aimed at promoting the universal values that need to be defended. I'm very worried about isolationism and protectionism. The world has gone through these "isms" before. And you watch and see, the protectionist debate is mounting in the United States; it's mounting in Europe, certainly. It was much easier to kind of blame the economic woes on external forces, and therefore, the response would be, okay, let's quit trade, let's make sure our jobs aren't going elsewhere, and that's—some of those concerns are legitimate.

On the other hand, it is a forerunner of isolationism, and you know, I remind people that we've been through a period of isolationism and protectionism right before World War II. And, by the way, curiously enough, at that period of time, there was nativism as well. And I find it interesting that the immigration debate is now

pretty pronounced around. And so I'm going to set up a—this isn't, like, you know, a headquarters for the Republican Party.

And by the way, just so you know, the foreign policy I've just outlined for you is—you know, it's not a hundred percent received amongst conservative thinkers in the United States either.

NBC's "The West Wing"

Mr. Temko. Yes, I know, yes. Do we have 90 seconds?

Ms. Perino. Yes.

Mr. Temko. Okay, so——

Ms. Perino. I would say 90 seconds.

Mr. Temko. Ninety seconds, okay. Just one very quick—this is going to seem slightly flippant, but you're going to the greatest fan club of "The West Wing" television show in the world on Sunday. Since you're the only person who can review that program from experience——

The President. I've never watched it.

Mr. Temko. You're kidding. Why not?

The President. Because I don't watch network TV. I read.

Mr. Temko. You read. Okay. And then the——

The President. I seriously don't watch TV. You know, I watch sports, but I'd much rather read books. And I do, I read a lot. I may even read yours. [*Laughter*]

Progress in Iraq

Mr. Temko. And then the last question——

The President. But I won't be able to find it because it's written by—so-called written by the other guy. [*Laughter*]

Q. Certainly true. Last question, which comes back to Iraq again. Gordon Brown—and I thought your question on the pain you feel personally was quite clear and absolutely strong. Gordon Brown a couple weeks ago phoned a voter who was upset about Iraq, and apologized on behalf of the Government, not for the war, which he still thinks was the right thing, but for the kind of suffering of the Iraqi people. Do you think that's a wise thing to do?

The President. I think the Iraqi people—yes, some have suffered, no question. But they're living in a free society. Everybody is going to have to handle their own internal business the way they want to. I'm not going to second-guess one way or the other. But my view is, is that when you talk to Iraqis, they're thrilled with the idea of living in a free society. Do they like the fact that violence is still there? No. But every society reaches a level of violence that's tolerable.

And has that reached Iraq? I don't know yet. But I do know life is improving. I do know they live under a Government that they helped elect, or they elected. And there's still a lot of work to be done, don't get me wrong, but—and you know, the thing that people ought to focus on is the courage of the Iraqis. They put up with a lot of violence, Muslims killing Muslims. But first of all, there have been some accidents, but nobody can claim that the United States or Great Britain are intentionally killing innocent people. We're not. As a matter of fact, warfare has changed a lot.

Mr. Temko. But the existence of the war has led to the deaths of innocent people, and the fact is——

The President. It has, but before the war, hundreds of thousands were discovered in mass graves.

Freedom Agenda

Mr. Temko. So on balance, you have——

The President. Freedom trumps tyranny every time. And it's hard for people to see

that. It's hard for people sitting afar to say, "Isn't that beautiful, somebody lives in a free society?" And my point is, is that I think it's important for those of us who do live in free societies to understand that others want to live in free societies. And it takes time and sacrifice and effort to get that done. But one of the lessons of history is, is free societies yield of peace.

I remind people, 60 years ago isn't all that long. And to say that Europe would be whole, free, and at peace prior to the end of World War II would have been, you know, you would have been viewed as a hopeless idealist. Well, I'm making the point that I—when I gave my speech at the Knesset, if you read what I said, here's what 60 years from now the world can look like, and I believe will look like, unless we all retreat. It's not worth it, you know. And my point is, it's working.

Mr. Temko. Good. Thank you very much. And thank you for taking so much time.

NOTE: The interview was taped at 9:45 a.m. at the Villa Taverna. In his remarks, the President referred to Prime Minister Nuri al-Maliki of Iraq; Prime Minister Vladimir V. Putin and President Dmitry A. Medvedev of Russia; King Abdallah bin Abd al-Aziz Al Saud of Saudi Arabia; President Mahmud Ahmadi-nejad of Iran; Chairman Kim Jong Il of North Korea; and Prime Minister Gordon Brown of the United Kingdom. The transcript was released by the Office of the Press Secretary on June 15. A tape was not available for verification of the content of this interview.

Remarks to Reporters in Paris, France
June 15, 2008

Midwest Flooding/Father's Day

Laura and I had the joy of worshiping here in Paris.

My thoughts and prayers go out to those who are suffering from the floods in our country. I know there's a lot of people hurting right now, and I hope they're able to find some strength in knowing that there is love from a higher being.

I also want to wish all the fathers in America happy Father's Day. So, Dad, if you're listening, happy Father's Day.

Thank you all.

NOTE: The President spoke at 12:13 p.m. at the American Cathedral of the Holy Trinity.

The President's News Conference With Prime Minister Gordon Brown of the United Kingdom in London, England
June 16, 2008

Prime Minister Brown. I'm delighted to welcome President Bush and the First Lady back to London. And his visit today is an opportunity to celebrate the historic partnership of shared purpose that unites the United Kingdom and the United States of America. We both share a great love of history and about how we have forged the ideas of democracy and liberty over centuries. And the special partnership that President Bush and I both agree today is a partnership not just of governments but of peoples, is driven forward not simply by mutual interests but by our shared values. Both countries founded upon liberty, our histories forged through democracy. Our shared values expressed by a commitment to opportunity for all, putting into practice what Churchill called the "joint inheritance of the English-speaking world."

So let me thank President Bush for being a true friend of Britain and for the importance he attaches to enhancing our transatlantic partnership, from the work we do in Afghanistan and Iraq to every part of the world. And let me thank him for the steadfastness and the resolution that he has shown in rooting out terrorism in all parts of the world; in working for a Middle East peace settlement; in bringing hope to Africa; in working for a free trade world where, in spite of today's current difficulties with oil and food prices, there is and should be a wider and deeper prosperity in future for all.

Now, in our substantive and wide-ranging talks last night and this morning, the President and I have discussed a number of central issues. We have discussed Iran's nuclear ambitions. We have discussed Iraq and Afghanistan, where our forces are working side by side. We have discussed the criminal cabal that now threatens to make a mockery of free and fair elections in Zimbabwe. We have discussed what we can do about democracy in Burma.

We have resolved, first of all, as we did some years ago, that it is in the British national interest to confront the Taliban in Afghanistan, or Afghanistan would come to us. And so today Britain will announce additional troops for Afghanistan, bringing our numbers in Afghanistan to the highest level. And let me thank our troops and the troops of America and 42 other countries who are in Afghanistan, as I thank our forces in Iraq for their courage and for their professionalism. And let me acknowledge the bravery of the five members of the 2d Paratroop Regiment, British men who have in the last few days sacrificed their lives for freedom.

Eighteen months ago, the Taliban boasted that they and their paid foreign fighters would drive our forces out of southern Helmand. Now most agree that security is on the way to being transformed. Last week in Paris, a total of 80 countries pledged 20 billions, with nearly a billion from the United Kingdom, to support the Afghan National Development Strategy.

Our aim is to generate progress where the fourth poorest country in the world, laid low by decades of conflict, can as a democracy enjoy peaceful social and economic development, with our forces, over time, moving from a direct combat role to train and support Afghanistan's own Army and police.

In Iraq, there is still work to be done, and Britain is playing and will continue to play its part. Where we have over 4,000 troops in Basra, we will continue the shared policy of Iraqis taking more control over their own affairs, moving from combat to overwatch in Basra. Our policy is showing success as we continue the task we have set ourselves: strong and well-trained Iraqi forces capable of securing the peace, firm commitments to new local government elections soon, and speeding up the social and economic development of Iraq so that people have a stake in the future.

Our message today to the Iranian people is that you do not have to choose the path of confrontation. The latest rounds of talks with the Iranians took place over the weekend. Once again, we put our enhanced offer on the table, including political and economic partnership and help with nuclear technology for civilian use. We await the Iranian response, and we'll do everything possible to maintain the dialogue. But we are also clear that if Iran continues to ignore united resolutions, to ignore our offers

of partnership, we have no choice but to intensify sanctions. And so today Britain will urge Europe, and Europe will agree, to take further sanctions against Iran.

First of all, we will take action today that will freeze the overseas assets of the biggest bank in Iran, the Bank Melli.

And second, action will start today for a new phase of sanctions on oil and gas. And I will repeat that we will take any necessary actions so that Iran is aware of the choice it has to make: to start to play its part as a full and respected member of the international community or face further isolation.

We discussed the deteriorating situation in Zimbabwe. In recent weeks, under Robert Mugabe's increasingly desperate and criminal regime, Zimbabwe has seen 53 killings, 2,000 beatings, the displacement of 30,000 people, the arrest and detention of opposition leaders, including Morgan Tsvangirai, and this is wholly unacceptable. Mugabe must not be allowed to steal the election that is now less than 2 weeks away. And that is why we call for Zimbabwe to accept a United Nations human rights envoy to visit Zimbabwe now and to accept the international monitors from all parts of the world who are available to ensure that this is a free and fair election.

We agreed that at the G–8 in Japan, the United Kingdom and the U.S.A. would propose a plan to recruit and train health workers for the poorest countries. To save the lives of mothers who needlessly die in childbirth, we are developing proposals to tackle the diseases that bring needless death and suffering, including malaria, AIDS, and neglected tropical diseases. And we agreed also to work together to ensure G–8 commitment to scale up funding on education and get the remaining 72 million children who do not go to school today into school.

The world oil prices trebled in recent months. In the right of this, I welcome Saudi Arabia's initiative to host a producer-consumer summit in Jeddah on the 22d of June. And we will all work together to ensure an enhanced dialogue between oil producers and consumers.

And the President and I also agreed that over the next few weeks, we need to press hard to achieve a world trade deal. Both of us are ensured that this could unlock new opportunities for the world economy. It would also help reduce high global food prices.

Finally, we go from here to Northern Ireland. The United States has played an essential role in securing peace in Northern Ireland and helping the people of Northern Ireland move away from conflict to, potentially, a new prosperity. And I want to thank President Bush for his personal efforts to speed up the Northern Ireland peace process and to make sure that there is investment in Northern Ireland, not just from the rest of the United Kingdom but from America.

And I thank him for his work to ensure that the recent investment conference in Northern Ireland was a huge success. And there will be further announcements of jobs in Northern Ireland today. America has played a huge role in this peace process, and President Bush is to be thanked by all the people of the United Kingdom for what he has done.

So, Mr. President, I thank you again for your friendship, for your leadership, for your commitment to us continuing to work together to solve the challenges facing the world. I'm pleased you're here. I value the gains we've made together, and I look forward to our continued friendship.

President Bush. Thank you, Mr. Prime Minister. I thank you very much for your friendship. Thank you for your hospitality. This is—this has been a good trip. By the way, some are speculating this is my last trip. Let them speculate. Who knows? [*Laughter*] But it's been a—we had a great dinner last night. I want to thank you and Sarah. And thanks for calling together the historians. It's a—you know, Great Britain has produced great historians. And I am—

I love reading a lot of their works, and it was so kind of you to have them over. And the food was good too. [*Laughter*]

And also, we had a great visit yesterday. Laura and I went to see Her Majesty the Queen. And I thank her for her hospitality. And then yesterday at the Embassy, thanks to our Ambassador, I had the opportunity to speak to some of your soldiers. And I was—listened to their stories of courage and bravery and sacrifice, and it was so—really touching. And I really appreciate the British people supporting the people who wear the uniform. And I am looking forward to going to Northern Ireland this evening. You've taken the lead. We're just pleased to help. And hopefully, this visit will help keep the process moving.

First thing about Gordon Brown, he's tough on terror. And I appreciate it, and so should the people of Great Britain and the world. He fully understands that while some want to say that the terrorist threat is gone or there's nothing to worry about, it is something to worry about. And he was—you were tested early in your Prime Ministership. You dealt with the challenge. And I appreciate your continued focus and your understanding that we've got to work together to protect our people and your understanding that freedom is transformative, and the ultimate way to succeed against these extremists who use murder as a way to achieve their political objectives is to marginalize them through the advance of liberty.

And that's what we're doing in places like Afghanistan and Iraq. And it is tough work. It's hard to take a society that had been ravished by brutality and convince people to take the risk necessary to work for civil society and freedom for women and to educate their children. But I believe it's necessary work for the sake of peace and for our security. And I believe it's in the moral interests of comfortable nations to help others realize the blessings of liberty. Oh, for some that sounds like hopeless idealism. For those of us involved with making public policy necessary to protect our people, it is the only realistic way to guarantee the peace for our people.

And so you've been strong on Afghanistan and Iraq, and I appreciate it. But more importantly, the people of Afghanistan and Iraq appreciate it. The march to democracy is never smooth. We've had our own history. America is viewed as a great democracy. Just remember, many of our citizens were enslaved for a long period of time before we finally got it right.

But it's in our interests to help these folks. It's in our interests little girls go to school in Afghanistan. It's in our interests that there be free elections in Iraq. And it's in our interests that we help these governments survive. And it's taken sacrifice from our people; I understand that. The fundamental question history is going to look back on is, did we understand the duty that we've been called to do to protect ourselves and help others? And this Prime Minister has understood the duty.

No, I know there's a lot of discussion here in the British press about, well, you know, is there going to be enough troops or not enough troops and all that business. Is he trying to distance this, that, and the other? It's just typical. But I just want to remind you that he has left more troops in Iraq than initially anticipated. And like me—we'll be making our decisions based upon the conditions on the ground, the recommendation of our commanders, without an artificial timetable set by politics.

I thank you for your troop announcement today in Afghanistan as well. Then you issued a strong statement on Iran. It was a clear statement, and it was a strong statement, and it was a necessary statement, because the free world has an obligation to work together in concert to prevent the Iranians from having the know-how to develop a nuclear weapon. And now is the time to work together to get it done, and I appreciate your statement.

Hopefully, the Iranian leadership will take a different position than the one they've taken in the past, which is basically, who cares what the free world says; we're going to—we'll go our own way. And now has faced—they face serious isolation, and the people who are suffering are the Iranian people. We have no qualms with the Iranian people. As a matter of fact, we want the Iranian people to thrive. It's in our interests that there be a hopeful society. It's their Government who has denied them their rightful place in the world.

And so I want to thank you very much for working hard to, you know, to help keep this coalition together to provide pressure necessary so we can solve the problem diplomatically. That's my first choice. Iranians must understand all options are on the table, however.

Thank you for your strong words on Zimbabwe. And I—you know, you obviously are emotional on the subject. And I don't blame you, because the people of Zimbabwe have suffered under Mugabe leadership. And we will work with you to ensure these good folks have free and fair elections to the extent—best extent possible, which obviously Mr. Mugabe does not want to have.

We talked about Darfur. We talked about Burma. I strongly support your health care worker initiative. I'm looking forward to going to the G–8 to articulate that. And we expect the people of the G–8—the leaders of the G–8 countries to fulfill their obligations, because last year we met, and we had a—we discussed a lot of issues, including HIV/AIDS and malaria on the continent of Africa. And they all came forth and said, we'll match the United States. Except most nations haven't matched the United States to date except for Great Britain. You know, they haven't done their part in matching the United States.

And so my message at the G–8 is: Looking forward to working with you; thanks for coming to the meeting; just remember, there are people needlessly dying on the continent of Africa today. And we expect you to be more than pledge makers; we expect you to be checkwriters for humanitarian reasons.

Now, we did talk about energy and Doha. I'm concerned about Doha. I'm concerned that while we're making some progress on the agricultural side, that nations such as Brazil and India and China are not making corresponding openings on manufacturing and service—and the service sector on their part. And in order to have a successful round, which I believe is essential, and so does Gordon—to fight off protectionism and to help poor nations develop, that now is the time to get a Doha round completed. And in order to do so, there has to be more movement on the manufacturing and service sector so there can be a fair and equitable deal.

Finally, we talked about global climate change. And I briefed Gordon on our strategy for the major economies meeting to, hopefully, reach an international goal for 2050 that will have intermediate strategies that are binding on each nation within the U.N. framework. And the reason why I believe this is the right approach to take— that unless China and India are a part of a binding international agreement—and the United States—then we will not have effective policy in dealing with climate change. It might make us all feel good, but the results won't be satisfactory. And so hopefully, in Seoul, South Korea, coming up, there will be a major economy meeting agreement on a long-term goal with binding commitments.

Mr. Prime Minister, all in all, it's been a great meeting. Thank you for the conversation, and thank you for your friendship.

Prime Minister Brown. Thank you. Questions.

British and U.S. Troop Levels in Iraq/ Afghanistan

Q. Nick Robinson, BBC News.

President Bush. Who? Can you say his name again, please? [*Laughter*]

Q. Good to have you here.

President Bush. Yes. Missed the hat. [*Laughter*]

Q. Prime Minister, isn't it time to withdraw British troops from Iraq in order to send them where the military really needs them, to Afghanistan, or are you too worried about his reaction if you do?

And, Mr. President, are you prepared——

President Bush. We miss you, Nick. We miss you, buddy.

Q. Are you prepared to see British troops withdrawn from Iraq while you're still in office, or are you concerned about the symbolic significance of that?

Prime Minister Brown. Can I just say that in Iraq, there is a job to be done, and we will continue to do the job. And there's going to be no artificial timetable. And the reason is that we are making progress—making progress in the Iraqis themselves being trained up to run their own armed forces and, of course, to be the police men and women in their areas. And we're making progress also because we hope local government elections will happen later this year. We hope to return the airport that we are responsible for in Basra to civilian use as well. And most of all, in the next stage, we want to see the economic and social development of Basra and the southern part of Iraq proceed so that people have a stake in the future.

So yes, we are moving from what we call combat to overwatch, and that's been announced many months ago. Yes, as a result of what happened in Basra a few months ago, we have kept higher the level of troops that are necessary, but yes, also, we have a job that's still to be done. And that job is to train up the forces; that job is to speed up economic and social development; and that job is to have local government elections so that Iraqis can take control of their own democracy. And I'm determined that we continue to do that job.

And that will happen not at the cost of lesser troops for Afghanistan, but with more troops going to Afghanistan. The Defense Secretary will announce later this afternoon that we will send more troops to Afghanistan. The reason is that we want to help the Afghans train up their own Army and their own police forces. And the reason is, we want to have better equipment in Iraq—in Afghanistan in future. And therefore, there's going to be a reconfiguration of our troops. There will be some coming out and some more going in, and that— an overall increase in the numbers so that we will have the highest level of troops in Afghanistan. You cannot trade numbers between the two countries.

There is a job to do in Iraq, and I've described it. And there is a job to do in Afghanistan, and we will continue to do it. And the fact that 43 countries are helping us in Afghanistan and 80 countries are supporting the economic and social development of Afghanistan shows how in this country, which is one of the poorest in the world, we are trying to make progress more quickly. So the announcement will come later today from the Defense Secretary.

President Bush. We're withdrawing troops. We anticipate the 30,000 surge troops will be coming home by July—more or less 30,000. And so the plan is, bring them home based upon success. That's what we expect the British Prime Minister to do. That's what I'm doing—that as the Iraqis are trained up, as they're taking more responsibility, as the security situations decline, as the economy is improved, as political reconciliation is taking place, we can bring more troops home. That's the whole purpose of the strategy. And so give the Iraqis more responsibility. Let them take more—be in more charge of their own security and their own Government, and that's what's happening.

And so yes, I mean—look, the key thing for me is that I have—you know, is that Gordon shares with me his plans. He listens to—and he talks to his commanders, and he picks up the phone and says,

"Here's what we're thinking." So there's no surprises. And as I said yesterday on TV here, I have no problem with how Gordon Brown is dealing with Iraq. He's been a good partner and—but, as I told you, we're bringing ours home too.

Military Operations in Afghanistan/Oil Supply

Q. Mr. President, I'd like to ask you about recent events along the Pakistan-Afghanistan border. Do you back President Karzai when he says he may send his troops into Pakistan to take care of some of the militants who are launching attacks on his territory? And do you think that the agreements that the new Government of Pakistan is pursuing with some of the militant tribes in that area amount to the sort of appeasement that you talked about in your speech last month?

And, Mr. Prime Minister, I'd like to ask you about the meeting—upcoming meeting in Saudi Arabia. What do you expect to come out of that meeting? And do you think it would be helpful if your friend there, standing there, Mr. Bush, were to see you in Jeddah at that meeting?

President Bush. Our strategy is to deny safe haven to extremists who would do harm to innocent people. And that's the strategy of Afghanistan. It needs to be the strategy of Pakistan. It's in all our interests to prevent those who murder innocent people to achieve political objectives to gain safe haven.

And so we'd look forward to working— I mean, one thing that can happen is, there can be, you know, more dialogue between the Pak Government and the Afghan Government. Now, there was—in the past, they had a jirga amongst tribal leaders in the region on both—from both sides of the border that made a difference. And I think that would be a good idea to restart the jirga process.

I know there needs to be dialogue between the intel services between the respective countries. And I know there needs to be better cooperation, and there needs to be trilateral cooperation on the border—trilateral being Pak, Afghan, and coalition border patrols—to prevent people from coming back and forth across the border.

And there's a lot of common ground. I repeat: It is in no one's interest that extremists have a safe haven from which to operate. And I'm, you know—I mean—and obviously, it's a testy situation there. And if I'm the President of a country and people are coming from one country to another—allegedly coming from one country to another—to kill innocent civilians on my side, I'd be concerned about it. But we can help. We can help calm the situation down and develop a strategy that will prevent these extremists from, you know, from developing safe haven and having freedom of movement.

Prime Minister Brown. Can I say, I'm traveling to Jeddah next Sunday at the invitation of the King of Saudi Arabia. And I want a long-term dialogue, and this is part of a process, not an event, between oil producers and oil consumers. I think there is a view developing that the price of oil is increasingly dependent not just on today's demand and supply factors but on what people perceive as demand outstripping supply next year, in the medium term, and in the long term.

And I want to tell the King of Saudi Arabia and others who are there that the world will build more nuclear power. And I have suggested that on present trends, it would be about 1,000 nuclear power stations over the next 30 years. The world will increase its use of renewables. The world will increase its use of coal. It will lessen its dependence on oil, and that the world is determined to make a more efficient use of oil.

And I think this dialogue between producers and consumers is absolutely essential. President Bush has just been in Saudi Arabia. I have not been there recently. I want to go and talk to the King and talk to others there about what I believe should

be a process whereby we understand what are the pressures on demand in future years, as well as we understand the pressures on supply. And I believe that that long-term debate about the future can have an effect on today's markets.

Now, that's what the debate is about. And that is part of a process that I hope will continue, if necessary, with a meeting in London later and with further meetings, so that there is a genuine dialogue between producers and consumers about what is the most worrying situation in the world at the moment, and that is the trebling of the price of oil.

President's Decisionmaking/Freedom Agenda/Lisbon Treaty

Q. Mr. President, in his last major speech, Tony Blair said on Iraq: "Hand on heart, I did what I thought was right. But if I got it wrong, I'm sorry." Is it possible you got it wrong? Would you share, at this point, those slightly more reflective sentiments? And in particular, should you, in retrospect, perhaps have concentrated a little more on Afghanistan?

And could I ask the Prime Minister, is the Lisbon Treaty dead in the water now? And if so, what happens next for Europe?

President Bush. History will judge the tactics. History will judge whether or not, you know, more troops were needed earlier, troops could have been positioned here better or not. Removing Saddam Hussein was not wrong. It was the right thing to do. It was the right thing to do for our security, right thing to do for peace, and the right thing to do for 25 million Iraqis.

And now the fundamental question is, will we have the willpower and the patience to help the Iraqis develop a democracy in the heart of the Middle East? It's a democracy that's not going to look like America. It's not going to look like Great Britain. But it's a democracy that will have government responsive to the people. People say: "Was that worth it? Is it necessary?" Absolutely, it's necessary, if you believe we're in an ideological war being—the theaters of which right now—the most notable theaters are Afghanistan and Iraq.

The strategic implications of a free Iraq are significant for our future. For example, a free Iraq will make it easier to deal with the Iranian issue. A free Iraq will send a clear signal to reformers and dissidents, would-be journalists throughout the Middle East that a free society is available for you as well. And the question facing the Western World is, will we fall prey to the argument that stability is more important than forms of government, that what appears to be stable and peaceful—is that more important than how people live their lives, what kind of government? You just heard the Prime Minister speak eloquently about Zimbabwe. The lesson there is, forms of government matter.

Freedom has had a transformative effect in Europe, in the Far East. And the fundamental question is, will we work to see it have a transformative effect in the Middle East? Now, there are many doubters. I understand that, because there is some who say that perhaps freedom is not universal. Maybe it's only Western people that can self-govern. Maybe it's only, you know, white-guy Methodists who are capable of self-government. I reject that notion. I think that's the ultimate form of political elitism, and I believe an accurate reading of history says that freedom can bring peace we want. And it'll bring peace to the Middle East, unless of course we become isolationist, unless of course we lose our confidence, unless of course we quit.

And so yes, I'm sure there's—people will say, they could have done things better here and there. But I'm absolutely confident that the decision to remove Saddam Hussein was the right decision.

Prime Minister Brown. And can I just emphasize: The passion for freedom, I think, is a universal value, and I believe that Iraq is a democracy today because of the action that we have taken. And our next task is to make sure that all Iraqis feel that they have an economic stake as well as a democratic stake in the future of the country. And that's why the work continues.

On Europe, I'll meet Brian Cowen, the *Taoiseach* of Ireland, when I'm in Belfast later today. The legal position on the European treaty is very clear, that all 27 members must sign and, therefore, ratify the treaty before it comes into force. It is for each member to decide its own process for doing so. And we will continue our process of debating this in the House of Lords and then royal assent during the course of this week.

I think a short period of reflection is necessary for the Irish to put forward their proposals about how they will deal with this, and we look forward to the Irish coming to the European Council on Thursday with a view of what should be done. I believe that when David Miliband makes a statement to the House this afternoon following a meeting of the European foreign ministers, he will be able to say that all the European Union members believe that Ireland should be given this time to reflect on what they need to do and then make their proposals about how the situation can be resolved.

Iran/North Korea/Six-Party Talks

Q. Good morning, Mr. President, Prime Minister. I'd like to ask you both about Iran. President Bush, you've talked about it at every stop. A similar process, it seems, that is deterring North Korea from its nuclear ambitions has basically allowed North Korea to make progress toward nuclear weapons. At what point are you willing to draw a line here with Iran? And isn't Iran seemingly learning a lesson from the North Korea experience?

President Bush. Ed [Edwin Chen, Bloomberg News], I just strongly disagree with your premise that the six-party talks has encouraged Iran to develop nuclear weapons. I don't know why you have even come to that conclusion because the facts are, the six-party talks is the only way to send a message to the North Koreans that the world isn't going to tolerate them having a weapon.

I mean, in other words, they are—we'll see what they disclose, but we, hopefully, are in the process of disabling and dismantling their plutonium manufacturing. We're, hopefully, in the process of getting them to disclose what they have manufactured and eventually turning it over. We're, hopefully, in the process of disclosing their proliferation activities, and it's a six-party process. I mean, the only way, in my judgment, to diplomatically solve these kinds of problems with nations like Iran and North Korea, nontransparent nations, is through a multilateral process where there's more than one nation sending the same message to the leaders of these respective countries.

And so I disagree with your premise. As a matter of fact, the Iranians must understand that when we come together and speak with one voice, we're serious. That's why the Prime Minister's statement was so powerful, and that's the lesson that the North Koreans are hearing. And so it's— I said the other day that, you know, one of the things that I will leave behind is a multilateralism to deal with tyrants, so problems can be solved diplomatically.

And the difficulty, of course, is that sometimes economics and money trumps national security interests. So you go around asking nations—by the way, it's not a problem for Great Britain—so you say to your partners, don't sell goods; you know, let's send a focused message, all aiming to create the conditions so that somebody rational shows up. In other words, people, hopefully, are sick of isolation in their respective countries, and they show up and say, we're tired of this; there's a better way forward.

And in order for that to be effective, Ed, there has to be more than one voice. So if I were the North Koreans and I were looking at Iran, or the Iranians looking at North Korea, I'd say, uh-oh, there are coalitions coming together that are bound tightly, more tightly than ever, in order to send us a focused message.

And you know, let me just say one thing about the Iranian demand for civilian nuclear power: It's a justifiable demand. You just heard the Prime Minister talk about the spread of civilian nuclear power, which I support—starting in my own country, by the way. We need to be building civilian nuclear power plants.

And so when the Iranians say we have a sovereign right to have one, the answer is, you bet. You have a sovereign right; absolutely. But you don't have the trust of those of us who have watched you carefully when it comes to enriching uranium because you have declared that you want to destroy democracies in the neighborhood, for example. Therefore—and this is the Russian proposal, by the way—therefore, we'll provide fuel for you, and we'll collect the fuel after you've used it so you can have your nuclear—civilian nuclear power, which undermines what the Iranians are saying, and that is, we must enrich in order to have civilian nuclear power. You don't need to enrich to have civilian nuclear power. The Russian proposal is what we support. This proposal wouldn't have happened had there not been a multilateral process.

And so what these nations need to see is, we're serious about solving these problems. And the United States spends a lot of time working with our partners to get them solved.

Thank you very much.

Prime Minister Brown. Thank you all very much.

NOTE: The President's news conference began at 11 a.m. in the Locarno Treaty Room of the Foreign & Commonwealth Office Building. In his remarks, he referred to Sarah Brown, wife of Prime Minister Brown; Queen Elizabeth II of the United Kingdom; U.S. Ambassador to the United Kingdom Robert H. Tuttle; and President Robert

Mugabe of Zimbabwe. Prime Minister Brown referred to Secretary of State for Defense Desmond Browne and Secretary of State for Foreign and Commonwealth Affairs David Miliband of the United Kingdom; King Abdallah bin Abd al-Aziz Al Saud of Saudi Arabia; and Prime Minister Brian Cowen of Ireland. Reporters referred to President Hamid Karzai of Afghanistan; and former Prime Minister Tony Blair of the United Kingdom.

Remarks Following a Meeting With First Minister Peter Robinson and Deputy First Minister Martin McGuinness of Northern Ireland in Belfast, Northern Ireland
June 16, 2008

President Bush. Mr. First Minister, Mr. Deputy Minister, thank you for your hospitality. I'm excited to be here in Northern Ireland. And one of the reasons why is because I'm impressed by the progress that is being made toward peace and reconciliation. As a matter of fact, the world is impressed by the progress being made toward peace and reconciliation. And that obviously takes a commitment by leadership. And I want to thank you all for giving me time to hear your thoughts and to visit with you.

We talked about a lot of issues. We talked about the devolution of police and justice. We talked about the successful investment conference that took place here. And I want to thank my fellow citizens for coming, and I want to thank those from around the world who are paying attention to Northern Ireland. And the truth of the matter is this, is, you know, people who have come here and looked at the Government, looked at the situation and gotten to know the people realize this is a good place to invest. And ultimately, investment is going to help Northern Ireland realize its full potential.

And then finally, I was able to thank the leaders for their work in helping others reconcile their differences. The interesting thing about the progress being made here in Northern Ireland is that it's attracted the attention of societies around the world that wonder whether reconciliation is possible for them. And Martin was telling me about his talks with some of the Iraqi leaders, about his—sharing his stories about how folks can reconcile. Northern Ireland is a success story. Obviously, there's more work to be done, but the progress made to date has been unimaginable 10 years ago.

And I want to congratulate you, thank you for serving your communities. And I wish you all the very best as you continue your journey.

First Minister Robinson. Thank you very much, indeed. Can I say that I'm delighted that President Bush, of his own choice, has recognized that Belfast is one of the major cities of Europe and has included it in this tour. It is a personal commitment that the President has shown towards Northern Ireland. And we are really grateful, not just for him coming today but for the work that has been done by the President and his ambassadors over the previous years, and particularly the work that has been done most recently for the investment conference.

The endorsement of the President for our investment conference goes a long way, and it lets people throughout the world know that Northern Ireland truly is open for business.

Deputy First Minister McGuinness. Can I say, just to echo what Peter has said, that this is an opportunity for us to express our thanks and appreciation for the tremendous work that has been done, in terms of the United States of America, and what is now undoubtedly one of the most successful peace processes in the world today. Beginning with the work of President Clinton, the contribution of Senator George Mitchell, the envoys that were sent by President Bush, such as Richard Haass and Mitchell Reiss and now Paula Dobriansky, all of whom have played a very important role in contributing to our process, which I do believe is, as the President has identified, a role model for how other conflicts can be resolved in other parts of the world.

And really we're having a tremendous amount of interest in our work. We've had two delegations of Iraqi Parliamentarians to Parliament buildings here in Belfast, just a few yards up the road. And there is no doubt whatsoever that other places that have suffered from conflict are anxious to learn from our experiences. We don't believe that we have got all of the answers, but what we can certainly do is outlay our experiences for others to consider.

We also are very appreciative of the width of support that has been put behind the economic investment conference by the President and by Paula Dobriansky as Ambassador. And we're very hopeful in the time ahead. And, in fact, I think we're confident that jobs, much needed jobs, will flow from that. And I think providing good jobs, a decent standard of living, facing up to the economic difficulties that are—people have to endure is a very important part of the workload which Peter and I, as First and Deputy First Minister, need to take forward in the time ahead.

President Bush. Thank you all very much.

NOTE: The President spoke at 4:14 p.m. at Stormont Castle. In his remarks, Deputy First Minister McGuinness referred to former Sen. George J. Mitchell; former U.S. Special Envoys for Northern Ireland Richard N. Haass and Mitchell B. Reiss; and Ambassador Paula J. Dobriansky, U.S. Special Envoy to Northern Ireland.

Remarks Following a Briefing on Flooding in the Midwest
June 17, 2008

I've just assembled my—many people in my domestic policy team to discuss the current flooding in the Midwest. First, our hearts and thoughts go to those who lost life. And of course, we're concerned about those whose—who've lost their homes or lost their businesses.

I've been briefed by Secretary Chertoff and Secretary Schafer and Director Paulison about the response. First task at hand is to deal with the flood waters, to anticipate where the flooding may next occur, and to work with the State and local authorities to deal with the response.

For example, in the case of Iowa, one of the issues was the need for fresh drinking water—or drinking water, and so Director Paulison informed me that we've provided about 2 million liters of drinking water. When I was overseas, I spoke to the Governor, and he said, "Listen, I—the Federal—we need Federal help on drinking water." So I sent the word to David, and he responded well.

My only point to you is, is that we're in constant contact with people on the ground to help make sure that we save lives. Now that the water is beginning to recede, the question is, how do we help with the recovery? And Secretary Chertoff briefed me on plans, particularly when it comes to housing. A lot of people are going to be wondering, is there short-term help for housing? And there is, and we'll provide that help.

And secondly, what's going to happen in the long term to the homes? And so Michael's going to set up a housing task force, similar to the kind we set up in California for the wildfires, to work with State and local authorities to have an orderly strategy to help people get back in their homes.

I fully understand people are upset when they lose their home. A person's home is their most valued possession. And we want to work with State and local folks to have a clear strategy to help people find—get back into a place they—that—where they can live.

Secondly, we're worried about farmers and ranchers. The country that's being affected by these floods has got a lot of farm country, a lot of people raising livestock. And the Secretary of Agriculture has briefed me on the conditions—and we're still assessing how widespread the damage is on the farmlands—and assures me that his team's in place to help farmers and ranchers with the Federal aid available.

And finally, Director Nussle's here from the Budget Office. We've got what we called a Disaster Relief Fund. There's enough money in that fund to take care of this disaster, but what we're concerned about is future disasters this year. And therefore, we're going to work with the Congress—Jim Nussle is going to go up to work with Congress to get enough money in the upcoming supplemental to make sure that fund is—has got enough money to deal with a potential disaster—another disaster this year.

Congress doesn't need to worry about working with the White House on this, because we think the supplemental is the way to go. What they do need to worry about is making sure that there is enough, but not too much, money in the fund, so we can say we have done our job.

I want to thank the members of my administration for working hard on this issue. I want to thank the Governors in the affected States for being so compassionate in caring for their citizens. I want to thank the folks at the local level for loving a neighbor like they'd like to be loved themselves.

This Thursday, I'm going to take our team down there to meet with the folks in Iowa. And I, unfortunately, have been to too many disasters as President. But one thing I've always learned is that the American citizen can overcome these disasters. And life, while it may seem dim at this point in time, can always be better because of the resiliency and care of our citizens.

Thank you.

NOTE: The President spoke at 10:21 a.m. in the Roosevelt Room at the White House. In his remarks, he referred to Secretary of Agriculture Edward T. Schafer; R. David Paulison, Administrator, Federal Emergency Management Agency; Gov. Chester J. Culver of Iowa; and James A. Nussle, Director, Office of Management and Budget.

Remarks Following a Briefing on the Security Situation in Afghanistan
June 17, 2008

The President. It's been my privilege to have served with two really fine Americans, General Dan McNeill and Maureen McNeill. I've gotten to know the General well. He's a tough, no-nonsense patriot who was our commander in Afghanistan. I want to thank you very much for the briefing you just gave me about the issues that we face, your optimism about success.

I was telling the Secretary and the General, I just—about my trip to Europe, where I was pleased with the strong commitments of our allies to helping us succeed in Afghanistan. They know that what happens in Afghanistan matters to their own internal security.

They fully understand as well that helping young girls go to school and helping moms raise their babies in a—you know, in a better environment, helping rebuild this society after years of tyranny is in all our interests. And it's also a moral duty we have.

And so I'm pleased, Mr. Secretary, that your hard work in working with the allies is paying off.

And, General, I know you're moving on, but the country thanks you for what you did. The world is better off because of your service. I'm proud to have you here.

Gen. Dan K. McNeill. Thank you, Mr. President.

The President. Yes, sir. Thank you.

NOTE: The President spoke at 10:44 a.m. in the Oval Office at the White House. In his remarks, he referred to Gen. Dan K. McNeill, USA, former commander, NATO International Security Assistance Force, Afghanistan, and his wife Maureen; and Secretary of Defense Robert M. Gates.

Remarks at a Reception for Black Music Month
June 17, 2008

Thanks for coming. Please be seated. Thank you. Welcome to the White House. I really appreciate you coming to celebrate Black Music Month. Music has been a part of this house since its beginning. Some of our Presidents themselves were skilled musicians; some were not. [*Laughter*] As a matter of fact, after the Temptations came here a couple of months ago, I was so inspired that I thought I would take up singing. [*Laughter*] Laura said, "You might just stick with practicing your speaking." [*Laughter*] So thanks for giving me a chance to do it today. And thanks for coming. We're going to have a pretty special day here at the White House.

I want to thank my friend Alphonso Jackson and Marcia. It's good to see you. Appreciate you being here.

Rod Paige, former Secretary of the Education, celebrating his 75th birthday today. Yes. You're looking good, Rodney.

Dr. Dorothy Height—honored you're here, Dr. Height. Proud to be with you.

Roslyn Brock, vice chairman of the NAACP—Roslyn—yes, good to see you, Roslyn. Thanks for coming. Marc Morial, president and CEO of the National Urban League, proud to have you here, Marc. Thanks for coming.

John Styll, president and CEO of the Gospel Music Association—thanks, John. Dr. Bobby Jones, television host—where are you, Bobby? There you are, Bobby. Dyana Williams, cofounder and president of the International Association of African American Music—Dyana, thank you for coming—and everybody else. [*Laughter*]

As we honor black music in America, our thoughts turn to one of its legends, Bo Diddley. Bo was one of the pioneers of rock and roll. And during his more than five decades as a singer, songwriter, and performer, he changed the face of music; he really did. We mourn his loss, yet we know this: that his memory will live on the songs and the joy he brought to millions, including a little fellow like me. So all of us here today send our thoughts and prayers to Bo Diddley's family.

Over the years, the White House has been home to many memorable events in black music. I suspect that 30 years from now, when a President is speaking, he's going to say, this is going to be one of the memorable events. In 1882, President Chester A. Arthur invited to the White House the first black choir ever to perform here, the Jubilee Singers from Fisk University in Tennessee. Of course, during those days they had trouble finding a place to stay. But they were welcomed warmly here at the White House, just like everybody here is welcomed warmly at the White House. Their music was so powerful that it moved President Arthur to tears.

In the ensuing decades, other Presidents followed this example, recognizing the contributions of black musicians when many other Americans would not. Benjamin Harrison welcomed the daughter of a former slave, an opera singer named Sissieretta Jones. President Franklin Roosevelt called on the talented Maria [Marian]° Anderson to sing "Ave Maria" for the King and Queen of England.

In 1979, President Jimmy Carter welcomed the legendary Chuck Berry in his first official celebration of Black Music Month at the White House. Ever the performer, Chuck Berry changed the lyrics in one of his famous songs from "Oh Carol" to "Oh Amy," in honor of the little girl sitting on the White House lawn. The day's finale came when the entire audience rose to its feet, swaying and clapping to the gospel song "Jesus is the Answer."

° White House correction.

For this year's Black Music Month, we return to the theme of gospel music. The gospel music tradition was born from great pain. Slaves sang spirituals to communicate with one another in the fields, and songs of faith helped black Americans endure the injustice of segregation. Today, gospel is more than an anchor for black culture and history; it's a source of inspiration for the whole Nation.

Gospel has influenced some of the legends of other forms of American music. Louis Armstrong once said that when he sang in church, his heart went into every song. Aretha Franklin wowed crowds in her dad's church in Detroit. Elvis Presley listened to gospel music after rock concerts to calm his mind. And Bob Dylan won a Grammy for his song—for his album of gospel hymns.

Today, gospel music continues to provide strength for our communities, and it is making the "good news" sound sweeter than ever. I know you're looking forward to three great gospel performers we have in store. So I'd like to now turn the podium over to the founder of Gospel Today magazine, our outstanding emcee this evening, Teresa Hairston.

NOTE: The President spoke at 3:01 p.m. in the East Room at the White House. In his remarks, he referred to former Secretary of Housing and Urban Development Alphonso R. Jackson and his wife Marcia; civil rights leader Dorothy I. Height; and Amy Lynn Carter, daughter of former President Jimmy Carter. The Black Music Month proclamation of May 30 is listed in Appendix D at the end of this volume.

Joint Statement by President George W. Bush and President Dmitry A. Medvedev of Russia on the Fourth Meeting of the Global Initiative To Combat Nuclear Terrorism
June 17, 2008

We are pleased to be working closely together with our Global Initiative Partners to combat nuclear terrorism. That so many nations have joined the Global Initiative to Combat Nuclear Terrorism demonstrates a true commitment to defeat this threat to our peace and security.

The Russian Federation and the United States launched the Global Initiative on July 15, 2006 and we can now call more than 70 nations Global Initiative partners. We will continue to stand upon the principles at the heart of this Initiative, attract others to our ranks and realize our goal of making this a truly global effort. Gathering as partners in Madrid is an important reminder to one another of the commitments we have to each of our citizens to see clearly the concrete steps we can take together to prevent nuclear terrorism and ensure our peace and security.

NOTE: An original was not available for verification of the content of this joint statement.

Message to the Congress on the Designation of the Chairman and Vice Chairman of the United States International Trade Commission
June 17, 2008

To the Congress of the United States:

Consistent with the provisions of 19 U.S.C. 1330(c)(1), this is to notify the Congress that I have designated Shara L. Aranoff as Chairman and Daniel Pearson as Vice Chairman of the United States International Trade Commission, effective June 17, 2008.

GEORGE W. BUSH

The White House,
June 17, 2008.

Remarks on Energy
June 18, 2008

Good morning. I want to thank Secretary Kempthorne and Secretary Bodman for joining me here. For many Americans, there is no more pressing concern than the price of gasoline. Truckers and farmers, small-business owners have been hit especially hard. Every American who drives to work, purchases food, or ships a product has felt the effect. And families across our country are looking to Washington for a response.

High oil prices are at the root of high gasoline prices; behind those prices is the basic law of supply and demand. In recent years, the world's demand for oil has grown dramatically. Meanwhile, the supply of oil has grown much more slowly. As a result, oil prices have risen sharply, and that increase has been reflected at American gasoline pumps. Now much of the oil consumed in America comes from abroad—that's what's changed dramatically over the last couple of decades. Some of that energy comes from unstable regions and unfriendly regimes. This makes us more vulnerable to supply shocks and price spikes beyond our control, and that puts both our economy and our security at risk.

In the long run, the solution is to reduce demand for oil by promoting alternative energy technologies. My administration has worked with Congress to invest in gas-saving technologies like advanced batteries and hydrogen fuel cells. We've mandated a large expansion in the use of alternative fuels. We've raised fuel efficiency standards to ambitious new levels. With all these steps, we are bringing America closer to the day when we can end our addiction to oil, which will allow us to become better stewards of the environment.

In the short run, the American economy will continue to rely largely on oil. And that means we need to increase supply, especially here at home. So my administration has repeatedly called on Congress to expand domestic oil production. Unfortunately, Democrats on Capitol Hill have rejected virtually every proposal, and now Americans are paying the price at the pump for this obstruction. Congress must face a hard reality: Unless Members are willing to accept gas prices at today's painful levels—or even higher—our Nation must produce more oil. And we must start now. So this morning I ask Democratic congressional leaders to move forward with four steps to expand American oil and gasoline production.

First, we should expand American oil production by increasing access to the Outer Continental Shelf, or OCS. Experts believe that the OCS could produce about 18 billion barrels of oil. That would be enough to match America's current oil production for almost 10 years. The problem

is that Congress has restricted access to key parts of the OCS since the early 1980s. Since then, advances in technology have made it possible to conduct oil exploration in the OCS that is out of sight, protects coral reefs and habitats, and protects against oil spills. With these advances—and a dramatic increase in oil prices—congressional restrictions on OCS exploration have become outdated and counterproductive.

Republicans in Congress have proposed several promising bills that would lift the legislative ban on oil exploration in the OCS. I call on the House and the Senate to pass good legislation as soon as possible. This legislation give—could get—should give the States the option of opening up OCS resources off their shores, provide a way for the Federal Government and States to share new leasing revenues, and ensure that our environment is protected. There's also an executive prohibition on exploration in the OCS. When Congress lifts the legislative ban, I will lift the executive prohibition.

Second, we should expand oil production by tapping into the extraordinary potential of oil shale. Oil shale is a type of rock that can produce oil when exposed to heat or other process. One major deposit—the Green River Basin of Colorado, Utah, and Wyoming—there lies the equivalent of about 800 billion barrels of recoverable oil. That's more than three times larger than the proven oil reserves of Saudi Arabia. And it can be fully recovered—and if it can be fully recovered, it would be equal to more than a century's worth of currently projected oil imports.

For many years, the high cost of extracting oil from shale exceeded the benefit. But today the calculus is changing. Companies have invested in technology to make oil shale production more affordable and efficient. And while the cost of extracting oil from shale is still more than the cost of traditional production, it is also less than the current market price of oil. This makes oil shale a highly promising resource.

Unfortunately, Democrats in Congress are standing in the way of further development. In last year's omnibus spending bill, Democratic leaders inserted a provision blocking oil shale leasing on Federal lands. That provision can be taken out as easily as it was slipped in, and Congress should do so immediately.

Third, we should expand American oil production by permitting exploration in the Arctic National Wildlife Refuge, or ANWR. When ANWR was created in 1980, Congress specifically reserved a portion for energy development. In 1995, Congress passed legislation allowing oil production in the small fraction of ANWR's 19 million acres. With a drilling footprint of less than 2,000 acres—less than one-tenth of 1 percent of this distant Alaskan terrain—America could produce an estimated 10 billion barrels of oil. That is roughly the equivalent of two decades of imported oil from Saudi Arabia. Yet my predecessor vetoed this bill.

In the years since, the price of oil has increased sevenfold and the price of American gasoline has more than tripled. Meanwhile, scientists have developed innovative techniques to reach ANWR's oil with virtually no impact on the land or local wildlife. I urge Members of Congress to allow this remote region to bring enormous benefits to the American people.

And finally, we need to expand and enhance our refining capacity. Refineries are the critical link between crude oil and the gasoline and diesel fuel that drivers put in their tanks. With recent changes in the makeup of our fuel supply, upgrades in our refining capacity are urgently needed. Yet it has been nearly 30 years since our Nation built a new refinery, and lawsuits and red-tape have made it extremely costly to expand or modify existing refineries. The result is that America now imports millions of barrels of fully refined gasoline from abroad. This imposes needless costs on American consumers. It deprives American workers of good jobs. And it needs to change.

So today I'm proposing measures to expedite the refining—refinery permitting process. Under the reformed process that I propose, challenges to refineries and other energy project permits must be brought before the DC Circuit Court of Appeals within 60 days of the issuance of a permit decision. Congress should also empower the Secretary of Energy to establish binding deadlines for permit decisions, and to ensure that the various levels of approval required in the refining—refinery permitting process are handled in a timely way.

With these four steps, we will take pressure off gas prices over time by expanding the amount of American-made oil and gasoline. We will strengthen our national security by reducing our reliance on foreign oil. We will benefit American workers by keeping our Nation competitive in the global economy, and by creating good jobs in construction and engineering and refine—refining, maintenance, and many other areas.

The proposals I've outlined will take years to have their full impact. There is no excuse for delay—as a matter of fact, it's a reason to move swiftly. I know the Democratic leaders have opposed some of these policies in the past. Now that their opposition has helped drive gas prices to record levels, I ask them to reconsider their positions. If congressional leaders leave for the Fourth of July recess without taking action, they will need to explain why four-dollar-a-gallon gasoline is not enough incentive for them to act. And Americans will rightly ask how high oil—how high gas prices have to rise before the Democratic-controlled Congress will do something about it.

I know this is a trying time for our families, but our country has faced similar strains before, and we've overcome them together. And we can do that again. With faith in the innovative spirit of our people and a commitment to results in Washington, we will meet the energy challenges we face and keep our economy the strongest, most vibrant, and most hopeful in the world.

Thank you for your time.

NOTE: The President spoke at 10:30 a.m. in the Rose Garden at the White House. The Office of the Press Secretary also released a Spanish language transcript of these remarks.

Remarks Following a Meeting With Prime Minister Sergei Stanishev of Bulgaria
June 18, 2008

President Bush. Mr. Prime Minister, welcome to the Oval Office. It was about a year ago that I had the great pleasure of visiting your beautiful country, and I want to thank you for the warm hospitality you showed. And thank you for giving me a chance to welcome you here to the Oval Office. We had a very extensive conversation.

Prime Minister Stanishev. Indeed.

President Bush. And that's what you'd expect among friends.

First, I want to congratulate you and thank you and the Government for the role you have played in the Western Balkans. You've been a constructive force for stability, a constructive force for hope. You've projected a hopeful future and—for the people in Kosovo and Serbia. And I want to thank you for that. It's really important that there be leadership in the neighborhood, and you've provided it.

Secondly, I want to thank you very much for your nation's strong contributions to helping others realize the blessings of liberty, whether it be in Afghanistan or Iraq. I fully understand how difficult these issues can be. On the other hand, you understand how hopeful the world can be when people live in free societies. So I want to thank you and I want to thank the people of your country for the sacrifices that you have made.

Thirdly, we talked about our—a mutual concern, and that's energy. How do we get more energy on the market? How do we help others—our respective countries and others realize the blessings of additional energy supply? I mean, we're in a world that is—where supply has exceeded—where demand has exceeded supply. There's high prices. Both our countries—the people in our countries are wondering, what do we intend to do about it?

And so we had a good discussion about the diversification of energy supply. I really appreciate the Prime Minister's discussion about nuclear power. Prime Minister, we're trying to expand nuclear power here in the United States of America because it's clean, it's renewable, and it'll help us become less dependent on hydrocarbons.

We talked about two other issues that are of importance to the Prime Minister and the people of his country. First, we talked about visas. I fully understand the concerns of your people when it comes to visas. People say, on the one—we're helping, we're part of a very important coalition, we're allies, and yet we don't get treated the same as other people within the EU.

Prime Minister Stanishev. It was a good breakthrough.

President Bush. And today, because of the Prime Minister's hard work, there has been a breakthrough on the visa waiver, as an important step toward achieving the same status as other countries in the EU. And I want to congratulate you on that. Thank you for your hard work, and thank you for your care about the people of your country.

Now, finally, I applauded the Prime Minister for his and his Government's work on dealing with corruption. I reminded the Prime Minister that all of us have got a responsibility to deal with corruption. When we find corrupt officials in the United States, we expect them to be—within the rule of law—be dealt with. And that's what you're doing. And the people who ultimately benefit from that decision are the people of your country. I mean, they—I know they appreciate your tough stand. Nobody wants to have a government where it looks like a few benefit at the cost of many.

And so your tough stance have made a big difference. I'm proud that you're here. I want to thank you for it. You're a good, young, strong leader, and that's said from an old guy.

Prime Minister Stanishev. Thank you, Mr. President.

President Bush. Welcome.

Prime Minister Stanishev. Thank you.

President Bush. Yes.

Prime Minister Stanishev. Well, thank you, Mr. President, for the good words about Bulgaria, indeed. And my assessment is that our relations have reached the level of strategic partnership. And I see no contradiction in this with our good behavior and our contributions to the European Union.

President Bush. That's right.

Prime Minister Stanishev. I think Bulgaria proved in the last several years that we can be good contributors of stability for NATO, we can be active in the European Union, and we can develop our excellent relations with the United States—because it is amazing that in 18 years, our countries have reached this level of trust, confidence. And from this point of view, I appreciate your very strong leadership role in the support of the reform process in Bulgaria.

President Bush. Yes, sir.

Prime Minister Stanishev. It is never easy. It requires a lot of efforts, persistence.

Results do not always come overnight, but they develop. And everyone who comes to Bulgaria after several years of absence is saying the country has made great progress. And the United States have always been very helpful in this process.

I must say that we see our role in the region as a country which is bridging and guaranteeing stability both for the Western Balkans and for the broader Black Sea area, which are very important, because without stability in the Balkans, without European perspective and NATO perspective for these countries, we cannot speak about real prosperity and democracy in the region. The region has many wounds from the war in former Yugoslavia, and they have to be healed. And the international presence is very important and European perspective as well.

And we also see the importance of the Black Sea area, both politically, from the point of view of security issues and from the point of view of energy issues. And I appreciate the dialogue which we had on diversification of energy supply, on nuclear energy. Bulgaria will be developing our nuclear facilities, not only the new ones, but there are many other projects where American companies can participate in nuclear issues, but also in thermal power plants, many other energy projects, because we want to be, indeed, a hub of energy stability in the region. We want to be enough independent. We want to be exporter of energy.

We are good partners in Afghanistan, in Iraq, in Kosovo. And Bulgaria really is not simply a beneficiary of our membership in NATO or the European Union, but we are a contributor because we know our responsibilities. And we shall not give up from these responsibilities because there are many challenges around the world. We have to overcome them together with our friends and partners.

I thank you very much for this support and for the American experts who worked on this declaration on visa waiver. You, Mr.

President, were the first to say that this is not a normal situation, when two nations have such confidence, when we have 200,000 Bulgarians living in the United States, more and more Americans coming to Bulgaria, to have this obstacle for normal human contacts. There is a way to go; there is work to do. But we shall do it together, and I believe that the sooner we achieve— make our business, the better for the citizens of the two countries.

And finally, thank you also for the supporting the reforms in the fight against organized crime and corruption. Bulgaria is a nation which became member of the European Union, which is modernizing. Our economic growth is excellent. Our performances in economy are good. And we see the reforms in fight against organized crime

and corruption, the judiciary reform, as a very important further precondition for our economic growth and for the development of the nation.

And I remember that last year, you supported the establishment of the new State Agency for National Security. I can say with satisfaction that it is already operational. It works excellently with American services, and it has operations which are bringing concrete fruits. But there is work to do.

President Bush. Thank you for coming.

Prime Minister Stanishev. Thank you, Mr. President.

President Bush. Yes. Thank you. Thank you all.

NOTE: The President spoke at 11:48 a.m. in the Oval Office at the White House.

Message to the House of Representatives Returning Without Approval the "Food, Conservation, and Energy Act of 2008"
June 18, 2008

To the House of Representatives:

I am returning herewith without my approval H.R. 6124, the "Food, Conservation, and Energy Act of 2008."

The bill that I vetoed on May 21, 2008, H.R. 2419, which became Public Law 110–234, did not include the title III provisions that are in this bill. In passing H.R. 6124, the Congress had an opportunity to improve on H.R. 2419 by modifying certain objectionable, onerous, and fiscally imprudent provisions. Unfortunately, the Congress chose to send me the same unacceptable farm bill provisions in H.R. 6124, merely adding title III. I am returning this bill for the same reasons as stated in my veto message of May 21, 2008, on H.R. 2419.

For a year and a half, I have consistently asked that the Congress pass a good farm bill that I can sign. Regrettably, the Congress has failed to do so. At a time of

high food prices and record farm income, this bill lacks program reform and fiscal discipline. It continues subsidies for the wealthy and increases farm bill spending by more than $20 billion, while using budget gimmicks to hide much of the increase. It is inconsistent with our objectives in international trade negotiations, which include securing greater market access for American farmers and ranchers. It would needlessly expand the size and scope of government. Americans sent us to Washington to achieve results and be good stewards of their hard-earned taxpayer dollars. This bill violates that fundamental commitment.

In January 2007, my Administration put forward a fiscally responsible farm bill proposal that would improve the safety net for farmers and move current programs toward more market-oriented policies. The bill before me today fails to achieve these important goals.

At a time when net farm income is projected to increase by more than $28 billion in 1 year, the American taxpayer should not be forced to subsidize that group of farmers who have adjusted gross incomes of up to $1.5 million. When commodity prices are at record highs, it is irresponsible to increase government subsidy rates for 15 crops, subsidize additional crops, and provide payments that further distort markets. Instead of better targeting farm programs, this bill eliminates the existing payment limit on marketing loan subsidies.

Now is also not the time to create a new uncapped revenue guarantee that could cost billions of dollars more than advertised. This is on top of a farm bill that is anticipated to cost more than $600 billion over 10 years. In addition, this bill would force many businesses to prepay their taxes in order to finance the additional spending.

This legislation is also filled with earmarks and other ill-considered provisions. Most notably, H.R. 6124 provides: $175 million to address water issues for desert lakes; $250 million for a 400,000-acre land purchase from a private owner; funding and authority for the noncompetitive sale of National Forest land to a ski resort; and $382 million earmarked for a specific watershed. These earmarks, and the expansion of Davis-Bacon Act prevailing wage require-

ments, have no place in the farm bill. Rural and urban Americans alike are frustrated with excessive government spending and the funneling of taxpayer funds for pet projects. This bill will only add to that frustration.

The bill also contains a wide range of other objectionable provisions, including one that restricts our ability to redirect food aid dollars for emergency use at a time of great need globally. The bill does not include the requested authority to buy food in the developing world to save lives. Additionally, provisions in the bill raise serious constitutional concerns. For all the reasons outlined above, I must veto H.R. 6124.

I veto this bill fully aware that it is rare for a stand-alone farm bill not to receive the President's signature, but my action today is not without precedent. In 1956, President Eisenhower stood firmly on principle, citing high crop subsidies and too much government control of farm programs among the reasons for his veto. President Eisenhower wrote in his veto message, "Bad as some provisions of this bill are, I would have signed it if in total it could be interpreted as sound and good for farmers and the nation." For similar reasons, I am vetoing the bill before me today.

GEORGE W. BUSH

The White House,
June 18, 2008.

Remarks at the President's Dinner
June 18, 2008

Thank you very much. Thank you for the warm welcome. Good evening. I appreciate that kind introduction, Jeb, and I thank you for bringing Melissa too.

It's my honor to be with you. I can't thank you enough for coming to support our candidates running for the United

States House, the United States Senate, and for the White House.

I appreciate my friends from the Congress who are here. I especially want to pay tribute to Senator Mitch McConnell, Senate Republican leader; Congressman John Boehner, House Republican leader; Senator John Ensign, the chairman of the

NRSC, who, by the way, brought his son Michael; Congressman Tom Cole, chairman of the NRCC, a man who deserves a lot of credit, along with Jeb, for tonight's success; my friend from the State of Utah, Senator Orrin Hatch. I thank the RNC chairman, Mike Duncan; all those here at the head table for their leadership in making this an incredibly successful event.

Most of all I want to thank you all for coming, for giving of your time and your money to help us achieve a big victory in November of 2008.

This is my eighth President's Dinner, also known as my last dinner before mandatory retirement. [*Laughter*] I can't say for sure what I'm going to be doing next year. I suspect I'll be in Crawford, watching the Rangers on TV. But I know what you'll be doing. You'll be holding this dinner in honor of a new guest: President John McCain.

I know John McCain well. I have worked with him, and I have run against him. Take it from me: It's better to have him on your side. [*Laughter*]

The stakes in this election are high. I know the pressures of the Oval Office: the daily intelligence briefings, the unexpected challenges, and the tough decisions that can only be made at the President's desk. In trying times, America needs a President who has been tested and will not flinch. We need a President who has the experience and judgment to do what is right, even when it is not easy. We need a President who knows what it takes to defeat our enemies. And this year, there is only one man who has shown those qualities of leadership, and that man is John McCain.

Sending John to the White House is a great goal, but it's not our only goal. As President, he's going to need strong conservative allies on Capitol Hill. And that means we need to put the House and the Senate back where they belong, into Republican hands. And I appreciate you coming tonight to see that is exactly what happens.

You know, this election season is just beginning. The real campaign will be in the fall. And the American people will take the measure of the candidates running and their vision for the future. And when they do, they're going to find some big differences between our parties.

On issues that matter the most, from taxes and spending to confirming good judges and building a culture of life to protecting our people and winning the war on terror, the American people will have a clear choice. And after the speeches and the debates and when the American people focus on what matters to their future, they're going to send Republican candidates to the House, Republican candidates to the Senate, and John McCain to the White House.

This November, the American people are going to have a clear choice when it comes to taxes and spending. Republicans believe American families can spend their money far better than the Federal Government can. We've restrained spending in Washington. We delivered the largest tax cuts since Ronald Reagan was the President of the United States. We cut taxes for married couples. We cut taxes for families with children. We cut taxes for small businesses. We cut taxes on dividends and capital gains. We put the death tax on the road to extinction. We eliminated income taxes for nearly 5 million families in the lowest tax bracket. And as a result, the American people have more money in their pocket, and that is the way it should be.

Our opponents take a different view. The Democratically controlled Congress refuses to make the tax relief permanent. And when tax relief expires, every income tax rate in America will go up. The marriage penalty will return in full force. The child tax credit will be cut in half. Taxes on capital gains and dividends will increase significantly. The death tax will return to life. A typical family of four with an income of $40,000 will face a tax increase of more than $2,000.

At a time when the American people are struggling with high food [prices],° high gas prices, and economic uncertainty, the absolute last thing they need is a tax increase. And in order to make sure that doesn't happen, the American people need to elect a Congress and a President that will make the tax relief permanent.

Now, there's a reason why the Democrats want to raise taxes. They need more money to pay for all the new spending they have in mind. When the Democrats campaigned in 2006, they promised fiscal responsibility. But when they took control of the Congress, they tried to go on a spending spree and stick the American people with the tab. Over the past 17 months, Democrats in Congress have routinely filed legislation with excessive spending. But there was an important thing that stood between them and the American people paying more in taxes, and it's called a veto pen.

You know, when it comes to taxes and spending, our opponents offer a lot of soothing words. But keep this in mind: While their talk may be cheap, their agenda isn't. And here's the bottom line: If you want a bigger tax bill and bigger government, put the Democrats in charge of both the White House and Capitol Hill. But if you want to keep your taxes low and stop wasteful spending, elect John McCain and a Republican Congress.

This November, the American people will have a clear choice when it comes to confirming good judges and building a culture of life. Republicans aspire to build a society where every human being is welcomed in life and protected in law. We've funded crisis pregnancy programs and supported parental notification laws. We outlawed the cruel practice of partial birth abortion. We defended this good law all

---

° White House correction.

the way to the Supreme Court, and we won.

This victory shows how important it is to put good judges on the bench. Republicans have a clear view of the role of the courts in our democracy. We believe that unelected judges should strictly interpret the law and not legislate from the bench. I've nominated and Congress has confirmed good judges, including the two newest members of the Supreme Court, Justice Sam Alito and Chief Justice John Roberts.

And our opponents have a different view. There's no clearer illustration of their differences in our judicial philosophies than this: John McCain voted to confirm these eminently qualified Supreme Court Justices; his opponent voted against them.

We received a fresh reminder of the importance of the courts last week. A bare majority of five Supreme Court Justices overturned a bipartisan law that the United States Congress passed, and I signed, to deliver justice to detainees at Guantanamo Bay. With this decision, hardened terrorists—hardened foreign terrorists now enjoy certain legal rights previously reserved for American citizens. This is precisely the kind of judicial activism that frustrates the American people. And the best way to change it is to put Republicans in charge in the Senate and John McCain in the White House.

This November, the American people will have a clear choice when it comes to protecting our country and winning the war on terror. Republicans believe that our most solemn duty is to protect the American people. Since September the 11th, 2001, we have worked day and night to stop another attack on our homeland.

Here at home, we've strengthened our defenses, reformed our intelligence community, and launched a new program to monitor terrorist communications. Around the world, we have gone on the offense against the terrorists. We've advanced freedom as the great alternative to the ideology of hatred and violence. In a time of war, we need a President who understands that we must defeat the enemy overseas so we do not have to face them here at home, and that man is John McCain.

In Afghanistan, we destroyed Al Qaida training camps and removed the Taliban from power. And today, we're helping a democratic society take root, ensuring that Afghanistan will never again be a safe haven for the terrorists planning an attack on America.

And in Iraq, we removed the dangerous regime of Saddam Hussein. Removing Saddam Hussein was the right decision at the time, and it is the right decision today. Early last year, when the situation in Iraq was deteriorating, we launched what's called the surge. And since the surge, violence in Iraq has dropped. Civilian deaths and sectarian killings are down, and political and economic progress is taking place. A democracy is taking root where the tyrant once ruled.

In Iraq and Afghanistan and around the world, our men and women in uniform are performing with skill and honor. And our country needs a Commander in Chief who will respect and fully support the United States military, and that man is John McCain.

The war on terror is the great challenge of our time. And on this vital issue, the Democratic Party has repeatedly shown it would take America down the wrong path. Democratic leaders in Congress have yet to renew a surveillance law that our intelligence professionals say is critical to protecting America. They tried to shut down a CIA program for questioning terrorists, a program that has saved American lives. They've repeatedly delayed funding for our troops in the field.

On Iraq, the Democrats declared the surge a failure before it began. And now that the surge has turned the situation around, they still call for retreat. The other side talks a lot about hope, and that sums up their Iraq policy pretty well. They want to retreat from Iraq, and hope nothing bad

happens. But wishful thinking is no way to fight a war and to protect the American people. Leaving Iraq before the job is done would embolden our enemies and endanger our citizens. The only path to victory is to support the Iraqi people, support our commanders, support our troops, support Republicans for Congress, and elect John McCain as the next Commander in Chief.

Over the next few months of this campaign, you're going to hear a lot of talk about change. Democrats say they're the party of change. There was a time when they believed that low taxes were the path to growth and opportunity, but they've changed. There was a time when they believed in commonsense American values, but they have changed. There was a time when they believed that America should pay any price and bear any burden in the defense of liberty, but they have changed. These days, if you want to know how a Democrat in Congress is going to vote tomorrow, just visit the web site of MoveOn.org today.

This is change all right, but it's not the kind of change the American people want. Americans want change that makes their life better and our country safer, and that requires changing the party in control of the United States Congress. So with your efforts and with your hard work, I am confident that the American people will send Republicans to Congress—and to send our friend John McCain to the White House.

This is the final time I'm going to speak to this event. And when I ran for President 8 years ago, as Jeb mentioned, I promised to uphold the dignity and honor of this office. And to the best of my ability, I have tried to live up to that promise. Next January, I will leave with confidence in our country's course and the proud work we have done together.

We've worked together to make our country safer and to spread prosperity throughout our land. I've been strengthened by your support and lifted up by your prayers. I've also been blessed to share these years with a strong and loving family, including a fabulous woman named Laura Bush. I believe she's the finest First Lady in our Nation's history. Just don't tell mother. [*Laughter*] And in this job, I have had no finer example of character, decency, and integrity than the first man to be called President George Bush.

This isn't a farewell speech, because we've got a lot to do this year. I want you to know my energy is up, my spirits are high, and I am going to finish this job strong. So with confidence in our vision, strong belief in our philosophy, faith in our values, let us go forward, reclaim the Congress, and elect John McCain as President in 2008.

God bless you, and God bless America.

NOTE: The President spoke at 7:29 p.m. at the Walter E. Washington Convention Center. In his remarks, he referred to Rep. Jeb Hensarling, chairman, 2008 President's Dinner, and his wife Melissa.

Message to the Congress on Continuation of the National Emergency With Respect to the Risk of Nuclear Proliferation Created by the Accumulation of Weapons-Usable Fissile Material in the Territory of the Russian Federation
June 18, 2008

To the Congress of the United States:

Section 202(d) of the National Emergencies Act (50 U.S.C. 1622(d)) provides for the automatic termination of a national emergency unless, prior to the anniversary date of its declaration, the President publishes in the *Federal Register* and transmits to the Congress a notice stating that the emergency is to continue in effect beyond the anniversary date. In accordance with this provision, I have sent to the *Federal Register* for publication the enclosed notice stating that the emergency declared in Executive Order 13159 of June 21, 2000, with respect to the risk of nuclear proliferation created by the accumulation of a large volume of weapons-usable fissile material in the territory of the Russian Federation is to continue beyond June 21, 2008.

It remains a major national security goal of the United States to ensure that fissile material removed from Russian nuclear weapons pursuant to various arms control and disarmament agreements is dedicated to peaceful uses, subject to transparency measures, and protected from diversion to activities of proliferation concern. The accumulation of a large volume of weapons-usable fissile material in the territory of the Russian Federation continues to pose an unusual and extraordinary threat to the national security and foreign policy of the United States. For this reason, I have determined that it is necessary to continue the national emergency declared with respect to the risk of nuclear proliferation created by the accumulation of a large volume of weapons-usable fissile material in the territory of the Russian Federation and maintain in force these emergency authorities to respond to this threat.

GEORGE W. BUSH

The White House,

June 18, 2008.

NOTE: This message was released by the Office of the Press Secretary on June 19. The notice is listed in Appendix D at the end of this volume.

Remarks on Presenting the Presidential Medal of Freedom
June 19, 2008

The President. Welcome to the White House for what is going to be a joyous occasion. Mr. Vice President, Justice Scalia, members of my Cabinet and administration, Members of Congress, Medal of Freedom recipients and their families and friends: Thanks for coming. Laura and I are honored to welcome you here.

The Medal of Freedom is the highest civil honor a President can bestow. The award recognizes outstanding individuals who have been leaders in their chosen fields, have led lives of vision and character, and have made especially meritorious contributions to our Nation and the world. Today we add the names of six remarkable Americans to that select list.

The story of our first recipient begins in a poor neighborhood in the heart of Detroit. This was an environment where many young people lost themselves to poverty and crime and violence. For a time, young Ben Carson was headed down that same path. Yet through his reliance on faith and family, he turned his life into a sharply different direction. Today, Dr. Carson is one of the world's leading neurosurgeons. He is renowned for his successful efforts to separate conjoined twins and his expertise in controlling brain seizures. He has worked to be a motivating influence on young people. He and his wife Candy have started an organization that offers college scholarships to students across America. The child of Detroit who once saw a grim future became a scholar, a healer, and a leader.

Ben would be the first to tell you that his remarkable story would not be possible without the support of a woman who raised him and is at his side today. Some moms are simply forces of nature who never take no for an answer. [*Laughter*] I understand. [*Laughter*] Ben Carson's mom had a life filled with challenges. She was married at the age of 13 and ultimately to—was left to raise her two sons alone. She made their education a high priority. Every week, the boys would have to check out library books and write reports on them. She would hand them back with check marks, as though she had reviewed them, never letting on that she couldn't read them. Even in the toughest times, she always encouraged her children's dreams. She never allowed them to see themselves as victims. She never, ever gave up. We're so thrilled you're here. Sonya Carson, welcome to the White House.

Ben has said that one of his role models is Booker T. Washington, who inspired millions and who was one of the first African American leaders ever to visit this house as a guest of a President. He walked on this very floor a little more than a century ago. Today, Ben Carson follows in his footsteps in more ways than one. He's lived true to the words that was once uttered by this great man: "Character, not circumstances, makes the man." Ben, you demonstrate that character every day through the life you lead, the care you provide, and the family that you put at the center of your life. Murray, B.J., and Rhoeyce, I know how proud your dad is of each of you. I'm delighted that you have a chance to see how proud our Nation is of him.

For his skills as a surgeon, high moral standards, and dedication to helping others, I am proud to bestow the Presidential Medal of Freedom on Dr. Benjamin S. Carson, Sr. [*Applause*] The bestowing part will take place a little later, Ben. [*Laughter*]

Three decades ago, a mysterious and terrifying plague began to take the lives of people across the world. Before this malady even had a name, it had a fierce opponent in Dr. Anthony Fauci. As the Director of the National Institute of Allergy and Infectious Diseases for more than 23 years, Tony Fauci has led the fight against HIV and AIDS. He was also a leading architect and champion of the Emergency Plan for AIDS Relief, which over the past 5 years has reached millions of people, preventing HIV infections in infants and easing suffering and bringing dying communities back to life.

The man who would lead the fight against this dreaded disease came from an Italian American family in Brooklyn. Even as a boy, Tony was distinguished by his courage. In a neighborhood full of Brooklyn Dodgers fans, he rooted for the Yankees. [*Laughter*] Tony earned a full scholarship to Regis High School, a Jesuit school in Manhattan. And he still quotes what he learned from Jesuit teaching: "Precision of thought, economy of expression." And now you know why he never ran for public office. [*Laughter*]

Those who know Tony do admit one flaw. Sometimes he forgets to stop working. He regularly puts in 80-hour weeks. And from time to time, he's even found notes on his windshield left by his coworkers that say things like: "Go home. You're making me feel guilty." [*Laughter*] A friend once commented that Tony was so obsessed with work that his wife must be a pretty patient woman. The truth of the matter is, she's very busy herself. Christine Grady is a renowned bioethicist. And together they raised three talented daughters: Jennifer, Megan, and Alison. And I hope each of you know that for all Tony has accomplished, he considers you to be one of his— not one of his—his most important achievement. Your love and support have strengthened him as he works to save lives across the world.

For his determined and aggressive efforts to help others live longer and healthier lives, I'm proud to award the Presidential Medal of Freedom to Dr. Anthony S. Fauci.

When Tom Lantos was 16 years old, Nazi troops occupied his hometown of Budapest. During that bitter occupation, young Tom was active in the resistance. He twice was sent to a Nazi labor camp; both times he escaped. Tom and his wife Annette survived the Holocaust. Others in their family did not.

Their experiences amid Nazi terror shaped the rest of their lives. After they left Hungary and made California their home, Tom put his name on the ballot for a seat in the House of Representatives and became the only survivor of the Holocaust ever elected to Congress. One of his early acts was to establish the Congressional Human Rights Council [Caucus].° Annette served as the Caucus's director. Tom earned the respect from both sides of the aisle, and he rose to become the chairman of the Foreign Affairs Committee. One colleague put it this way: "Tom was at the forefront of virtually every human rights battle over nearly three decades in the Congress."

On Capitol Hill, Tom displayed the energy and enthusiasm of people half his age. When he was in his seventies, he said that he was at the midpoint of his congressional career. [*Laughter*] When he was diagnosed with a fatal form of cancer, he responded with typical grace. As he announced his decision to retire from the job he loved, his words were not of despair but of gratitude for a nation that had given him so much. "Only in America," he said, "could a penniless survivor of the Holocaust receive an education, raise a family, and have the privilege of serving in the Congress." That dying servant of the people then said this: "I will never be able to express fully my profoundly felt gratitude to this great country."

America is equally grateful to Tom Lantos. We miss his powerful voice and his strong Hungarian accent. [*Laughter*] We miss his generosity of spirit. And we miss

---

° White House correction.

his vigorous defense of human rights and his powerful witness for the cause of human freedom.

For a lifetime of leadership, for his commitment to liberty, and for his devoted service to his adopted nation, I am proud to award the Presidential Medal of Freedom, posthumously, to Tom Lantos. And proud that his loving wife Annette will receive the award on behalf of his family.

One of my great privileges as the President has been to meet so many outstanding Americans who volunteer to serve our Nation in uniform. I've been inspired by their valor, selflessness, and complete integrity. I found all those qualities in abundance in General Pete Pace. As Chairman of the Joint Chiefs of Staff, Pete Pace was a skilled and trusted adviser in a time of war. He helped transform our military into a more efficient and effective force in America's defense.

General Pace experienced the blessings America offers at an early age. He was born in Brooklyn to an Italian immigrant father who sometimes worked two or three jobs at a time to make ends meet. He was raised by a mom who instilled in him the sustaining power of faith. Together, his parents raised four children; each went on to great achievements in their chosen fields. That childhood gave young Pete Pace an early glimpse of what he would later call "the incredible benefits that our Nation bestows on those who come to our shores."

Pete Pace attended the Naval Academy and, as a young marine, soon found his way to Vietnam. At the age of 22, he took command of a platoon engaged in heavy fighting against the enemy during the Tet offensive. Pete quickly won the respect and the trust of his unit and formed a bond with all those who served with him. That bond only strengthened throughout his military career.

He was the first marine to serve as Chairman of the Joint Chiefs of Staff. And he performed his duties with a keen intellect, a sharp wit, and a passionate devotion to our country. He won the admiration of all who knew him. And that includes a soldier in Afghanistan who came up to General Pace last year during his farewell visit to that country and said simply: "Sir, thanks for your service. We'll take it from here."

On his final day in uniform, General Pace took a quiet journey to the Vietnam Veterans Memorial. He searched the names engraved in the sleek granite and then found a spot where he placed his four stars that had adorned his uniform. Along with those stars he attached notes addressed to the men who died under his first command some four decades ago. The notes said: "These are yours, not mine. With love and respect, your platoon leader, Pete Pace." General Pace ended his military career the same way that he began it, with love for his country and devotion to his fellow marines.

For his selfless service to his country and for always putting the interests of our men and women in uniform first, I am proud to award the Presidential Medal of Freedom to General Pete Pace.

When Donna Shalala was 10 years old, a tornado struck her house and her neighborhood near Cleveland. Her parents searched throughout the house for young Donna, but couldn't find her anywhere. She was finally spotted down the road, standing in the middle of the road directing traffic. [*Laughter*] Even at a young age, she was ready to take charge. [*Laughter*]

Donna was always an enthusiastic participant in life. She once played on the girls' softball team coached by George Steinbrenner. [*Laughter*] She also joined the Peace Corps and was stationed in the Middle East. I really wonder which one of those two experiences was more challenging. [*Laughter*]

In 1993, President Clinton nominated Donna as the Nation's Secretary of Health and Human Services. She served for a full two terms, longer than any other person who held that position. During her tenure, she developed a reputation for fairness and a willingness to hear both sides of an issue. Former Republican Governor who worked closely with Donna called her cooperative and pragmatic. The late Texas columnist Molly Ivins once called her "almost disgustingly cheerful." [*Laughter*] I knew Molly; that's a high compliment. [*Laughter*]

As a college president, Donna has demonstrated her commitment to education. And as Cochair of the Dole-Shalala Commission on Care for America's Returning Wounded Warriors, she has worked to ensure that we provide the best possible care for America's veterans, especially those who have borne the scars of battle. I came to know Donna in the course of the Commission's work. She believes deeply that our Nation has no more important responsibility than to make sure that we provide our veterans with all the love and care and support they deserve. Donna, you helped America move closer to realizing that noble goal, and your country is deeply grateful.

For her efforts to help more Americans live lives of purpose and dignity, I am proud to award the Presidential Medal of Freedom to Donna Edna Shalala.

Few men have played roles in as many memorable moments in recent American history as Laurence Silberman. He was a senior official in the Justice Department in the aftermath of Watergate and helped to restore America's confidence in the Department. As Ambassador to Yugoslavia, he was a vigorous representative of America's values behind the Iron Curtain. He was a fierce advocate for the "peace through strength" policies that helped win the cold war.

As a Federal judge on the DC circuit—often called the second-highest court in the land—Judge Silberman has been a passionate defender of judicial restraint. He writes opinions that one colleague has described as always cutting to the heart of the matter—sometimes to the jugular. [*Laughter*] His questioning is crisp and incisive, and at least one lawyer who was subjected to his inquiries actually fainted.

[*Laughter*] Judge Silberman was a particularly important influence on two other members of that court: Antonin Scalia and Clarence Thomas. When each was nominated to the Supreme Court, Judge Silberman, in typical fashion, was not sad to see them go. That's because when Scalia left the court, Judge Silberman gained seniority, and when Thomas left the court, Judge Silberman gained his furniture. [*Laughter*]

In a new and dangerous era for our country, Larry Silberman has continued to answer the call to service. He served with distinction on the Foreign Intelligence Surveillance Court of Review. He took a year off from the Federal bench to serve as Cochairman of a bipartisan commission on intelligence reform. And in all his work, he's remained a clear-eyed guardian of the Constitution. He continues to leave his distinctive mark in the opinions he issues and the generations of bright and talented lawyers he has trained.

For his resolute service to the Nation and his stalwart efforts to advance the cause of ordered liberty, I am proud to bestow the Presidential Medal of Freedom on Laurence H. Silberman.

My congratulations to each of the recipients. And now the military aide will read the citations for the Presidential Medals of Freedom.

[*At this point, Lt. Cmdr. Robert A. Roncska, USN, Navy Aide to the President, read the citations, and the President presented the medals.*]

The President. In honor of these distinguished men and women, Laura and I invite you to stay for a reception in the State Dining Room. Please enjoy yourselves. Congratulations. May God bless you all.

NOTE: The President spoke at 9:45 a.m. in the East Room at the White House. In his remarks, he referred to George M. Steinbrenner III, chairman, Major League Baseball's New York Yankees; and former Gov. Tommy G. Thompson of Wisconsin.

Remarks in a Briefing on Flooding in the Midwest in Cedar Rapids, Iowa
June 19, 2008

The President. Our job is to come down here—and I want to thank the Senator and Congressman and members of the Cabinet—just to listen to what you got on your mind. Obviously, to the extent that we can help immediately, we want to help, and then plan for recovery.

I know a lot of farmers and cattlemen are hurting right now, along with the city people. The other thing I think is just very important is that—and the Senator and Governor have made it clear—that as we worry about Cedar Rapids, we also got to worry about the little towns. A lot of folks are wondering whether or not the government hears about them too. And I can assure you that I know the Governor cares deeply about it, and so do we.

Paulison, who is the head of FEMA, tells me that there are 600 FEMA people moving around the State, and that ought to help the people in the smaller communities know that somebody is there to listen to them and care about them.

Our hearts and prayers are—from around the Nation go out to people here. It's a tough time for you.

Mayor Kathleen "Kay" Halloran of Cedar Rapids, IA. It is.

The President. The good news is, the people in Iowa are tough-minded people. I mean, you'll come back better. Sometimes it's hard to see it when you're this close to the deal.

Mayor Halloran. Well—and it's going to take time.

The President. A lot of people aren't getting much sleep these days, but—[*laughter*]. You're exhausted; I understand that.

But we want to—Congress passed a—is about to pass a big chunk of disaster money, which will put—help put people's mind at ease, and that will—we're going to help people—going to help you recover.

Anyway, thanks for letting me come by and see you.

Governor Chester J. Culver of Iowa. Thank you, Mr. President.

The President. Yes.

Gov. Culver. If I could, just very quickly, I want to thank the President on behalf of the people of Iowa——

The President. Get those cameras back in here. [*Laughter*]

Gov. Culver. And I want to make sure they get in trouble. [*Laughter*] But I also want to thank this incredible team, all of these people in this room, just an amazing team. All the people standing up here: Thank you. And we will rebuild this State and this city, and it will be even better and even stronger as a result. Thank you.

NOTE: The President spoke at 12:01 p.m. in the Lynn County Training and Response Center at Kirkwood Community College. In his remarks, he referred to Sen. Thomas R. Harkin; and Rep. David W. Loebsack. A portion of these remarks could not be verified because the tape was incomplete.

Remarks to Reporters in Iowa City, Iowa
June 19, 2008

The President. Let me thank the mayor, thank the Governor. Mr. Congressman, thanks for flying down from Washington with us. And Senator Harkin, thanks for being here.

Senator Thomas R. Harkin. Thank you, Mr. President.

The President. You know, these are tough times for the people of Iowa City and Cedar Rapids and a lot of other communities in Iowa. Some of them are, you know, real tiny communities. And this—obviously, as you can see here, they're still going through a recovery phase. The mayor was telling me that she had the—part of the city evacuated and now some folks are able to come back in.

I brought a lot of Federal officials with me because it's really important that as the rebuilding phase begins, there's a coordinated effort between the Federal Government and the State and the local governments. And Michael Chertoff is going to be handling the coordinating effort with the Governor. And the Governor will make sure that the affected communities are represented as well.

We passed a—or the Congress is contemplating passing a supplemental, and a big chunk of that supplemental will be disaster relief money. And I want to thank the Members of Congress—hope we can get that done quickly.

Representative David W. Loebsack. It will get done.

The President. The—one of the things that happens in a disaster such as this is that citizens from around the country want to know how they can help. They see the picture of this kind of flooding on TV and they know that people are hurting and they want to know how they can participate in helping the rebuilding. Well, one way that the people can do is they can go on their computers and dial up volunteer.org [volunteer.gov]. *

And you know, if you want to try to figure out how to send something, you can—there will be ways to—ways to direct your compassion. If you want to give money, there are organizations that could use your contributions; organizations such as the Red Cross. And I'm—again, I'll repeat to you: volunteer.gov; I think I might have said "org," I meant "gov."

And I really again want to congratulate the local folks here for really showing great compassion and working hard and hugging people and giving people hope. And, Governor, you've been out front. You and your first lady are working hard, and the mayor has been very much engaged in helping people deal with the initial response. And now we all got to come together and help people deal with the rebuilding of Iowa.

Anyway, thank you for your hospitality. I'm sorry we're going through this. I tell people that oftentimes you get dealt a hand you didn't expect to have to play, and the question is not whether you're going to get dealt the hand; the question is, how do you play it? And I'm confident the people of Iowa will play it really well.

Anyway, thank you.

NOTE: The President spoke at 2 p.m. In his remarks, he referred to Mayor Regenia Bailey of Iowa City, IA; and Gov. Chester J. Culver of Iowa and his wife Mari.

Message on the Observance of Juneteenth
June 19, 2008

I send greetings to those celebrating Juneteenth.

On Juneteenth, we commemorate the arrival of Major General Gordon Granger in

---

* White House correction.

Galveston, Texas, and his declaration that slavery had been abolished and the blessings of liberty were finally extended to African Americans.

On this occasion, we recognize the many contributions that African Americans have made to our great Nation and honor the legacy of diversity that America has embraced. Today is an opportunity to recommit ourselves to confronting injustice wherever we find it and upholding the dignity of all people. By doing so, we protect the freedom and democratic ideals that will keep America strong for generations to come.

Laura and I send our best wishes on this memorable occasion.

GEORGE W. BUSH

NOTE: An original was not available for verification of the content of this message.

Remarks at a Celebration of American Jazz
June 19, 2008

Welcome to the East Room of the White House. I welcome members of my Cabinet and my administration; a music lover, Senator Orrin Hatch from the great State of Utah; distinguished guests. We're so pleased you're here to celebrate a great American art form: jazz. And we hope you're jazz lovers, because you're going to hear some good music tonight.

The story of jazz mirrors the story of our Nation. This proud musical tradition was born of the songs brought here by African slaves. Decades later, it absorbed the waltzes that accompanied immigrants from Europe. Over time, jazz helped break down barriers of prejudice between blacks and whites and even defined an age that brought new liberty to America's women.

In a twist of history, the music that came to America in chains ultimately helped America spread freedom abroad. In 1956, the State Department sent American jazz musician Dizzy Gillespie around the world on a mission to trumpet American values. He was in Turkey when word came that a group of Cypriot students stoned the U.S. Embassy in Athens. And so he was sent to the Greek capital to soothe anti-American hostility with a jazz performance. The concert atmosphere was tense. The students stormed the stage. People were nervous, until the students put Dizzy Gillespie on their shoulders and shouted "Dizzy! Dizzy! Dizzy!" [*Laughter*]

With its spontaneity and energy and innovation, jazz expresses the best of America's character. And through a—its role in fostering freedom and equality, jazz reflects the best of America's ideals. Tonight this magnificent art form will be brought to life by some jazz masters. Grammy award winning guitarist Earl Klugh will play for us after dinner. And before dinner, we're honored to hear from saxophonist Davey Yarborough, vocalist Esther Williams from the Washington Jazz Arts Institute.

Before Davey and Esther take the stage, please join me in a toast to American jazz, but more importantly, to the United States of America.

NOTE: The President spoke at 7:36 p.m. in the East Room at the White House. A portion of these remarks could not be verified because the tape was incomplete.

Remarks on Congressional Action on the Legislative Agenda
June 20, 2008

Good morning. This week, Congress moved forward on two important issues affecting the national security of our country.

Yesterday the House passed a responsible war funding bill that will provide vital resources to our men and women on the frontlines in the war on terror. This legislation gives our troops the funds they need to prevail without tying the hands of our commanders in the field or imposing artificial timetables for withdrawal.

The bill also supports our military families by passing an expansion of the GI bill that makes it easier for our troops to transfer unused education benefits to their spouses and their children. I want to thank the Members of Congress for their action on this legislation, and I urge the Senate to pass it as soon as possible.

Members of the House and Senate also reached a bipartisan agreement yesterday on legislation to allow our intelligence professionals to quickly and effectively monitor the plans of terrorists abroad, while protecting the liberties of Americans here at home.

My Director of National Intelligence and the Attorney General tells me that this is a good bill. It will help our intelligence professionals learn our enemies' plans for new attacks. It ensures that those companies whose assistance is necessary to protect the country will themselves be protected from liability for past or future cooperation with the Government.

The enemy who attacked us on September the 11th is determined to strike this country again. It's vital that our intelligence community has the ability to learn who the terrorists are talking to, what they're saying, and what they are planning.

I encourage the House of Representatives to pass this bill today, and I ask the Senate to take it up quickly so our intelligence professionals can better protect Americans from harm.

I'm pleased with the bipartisan cooperation on both these bills, and I thank the Members for their efforts.

Thank you.

NOTE: The President spoke at 9:11 a.m. from the Oval Office Patio at the White House. In his remarks, he referred to Attorney General Michael B. Mukasey.

Letter to Congressional Leaders Transmitting a Report on North Atlantic Treaty Organization Enlargement
June 20, 2008

Dear Mr. Chairman:

Pursuant to section 3(2)(E)(ii) of the Resolution of Ratification to the Protocols to the North Atlantic Treaty of 1949 on the Accession of Poland, Hungary, and the Czech Republic adopted on April 30, 1998, I am pleased to submit the enclosed report.

In doing so, I reiterate with appreciation the bipartisan support that the Congress has shown for NATO's next round of enlargement.

As provided in the Resolution, for each of the two current NATO invitees (Albania and Croatia) as well as for Macedonia (in the event an invitation is issued by the Alliance before the signing of accession protocols), the enclosed report includes:

(I) updated information contained in the report required under clause (i) with respect to that country; and

(II) an analysis of that country's ability to meet the full range of the financial burdens of NATO membership, and the likely impact upon the military effectiveness of NATO of the country invited for accession talks, if the country were to be admitted to NATO.

This report is in both classified and unclassified forms, as provided in the Resolution.

Sincerely,

GEORGE W. BUSH

NOTE: Identical letters were sent to Robert C. Byrd, chairman, Senate Committee on Appropriations; Carl Levin, chairman, Senate Committee on Armed Services; Joseph R. Biden, Jr., chairman, Senate Committee on Foreign Relations; David R. Obey, chairman, House Committee on Appropriations; Isaac N. Skelton IV, chairman, House Committee on Armed Services; and Howard L. Berman, chairman, House Committee on Foreign Affairs.

The President's Radio Address
June 21, 2008

Good morning. Americans are concerned about the high price of gasoline. Everyone who commutes to work, purchases food, ships a product, or takes a family vacation feels the burden of higher prices at the pump. And families across our country are looking to Washington for a response.

The fundamental problem behind high gas prices is that the supply of oil has not kept up with the rising demand across the world. One obvious solution is for America to increase our domestic oil production. So my administration has repeatedly called on Congress to open access to new oil exploration here in the United States. Unfortunately, Democrats on Capitol Hill have rejected virtually every proposal. Now Americans are paying the price at the pump for this obstruction. So this week, I asked Democratic congressional leaders to take the side of working families and small businesses and farmers and ranchers and move forward with four steps to expand American oil and gasoline production.

First, we should expand American oil production by increasing access to the Outer Continental Shelf, or OCS. Experts believe that the OCS could produce enough oil to match America's current production for almost 10 years. The problem is that Congress has restricted access to key parts of the OCS since the early 1980s. So I've called on the House and Senate to lift this legislative ban and give States the option of opening up OCS resources off their shores, while protecting the environment. There's also an executive prohibition on exploration in the OCS, which I will lift when Congress lifts the legislative ban.

Second, we should expand American oil production by tapping into the extraordinary potential of oil shale. Oil shale is a type of rock that can produce oil when exposed to heat and other processes. One major deposit in the Rocky Mountain West alone would equal current annual oil imports for more than 100 years. Unfortunately, Democrats in Congress are standing in the way of further development. In last year's omnibus spending bill, Democratic leaders inserted a provision blocking oil shale leasing on Federal lands. That provision can be taken out as easily as it was slipped in, and Congress should do so immediately.

Third, we should expand American oil production by permitting exploration in northern Alaska. Scientists have developed innovative techniques to reach this oil with virtually no impact on the land or local wildlife. With a drilling footprint that covers just a tiny fraction of this vast terrain, America could produce an estimated 10 billion barrels of oil. That is roughly the equivalent of two decades of imported oil from Saudi Arabia. I urge Members of Congress to allow this remote region to bring enormous benefits to the American people.

Finally, we need to expand and enhance our refining capacity. It has been 30 years since a new refinery was built in our Nation, and lawsuits and redtape have made it extremely costly to expand or modify existing refineries. The result is that America now imports millions of barrels of fully refined gasoline from abroad. This imposes needless costs on American families and drivers. It deprives American workers of good jobs, and it needs to change.

I know Democratic leaders have opposed some of these policies in the past. Now that their opposition has helped drive gas prices to record levels, I ask them to reconsider their positions. If congressional leaders leave for the Fourth of July recess without taking action, they will need to explain why four-dollar-a-gallon gasoline is not enough incentive for them to act.

This is a difficult time for many American families. Rising gasoline prices and economic uncertainty can affect everything from what food parents put on the table to where they can go on vacation. With the four steps I've laid out, Congress now has a clear path to begin easing the strain high gas prices put on your family's pocketbook. These proposals will take years to have their full impact, so I urge Congress to take action as soon as possible. Together, we can meet the energy challenges we face and keep our economy the strongest, most vibrant, and most hopeful in the world.

Thank you for listening.

NOTE: The address was recorded at 7:40 a.m. on June 20 in the Cabinet Room at the White House for broadcast at 10:06 a.m. on June 21. The transcript was made available by the Office of the Press Secretary on June 20, but was embargoed for release until the broadcast. The Office of the Press Secretary also released a Spanish language transcript of this address.

Memorandum on the 2008 Combined Federal Campaign
June 19, 2008

Memorandum for the Heads of Executive Departments and Agencies

Subject: 2008 Combined Federal Campaign

Admiral Thad W. Allen, Commandant of the U.S. Coast Guard, has agreed to serve as the Honorary National Chairman of the 2008 Combined Federal Campaign. I ask you to enthusiastically support the CFC by personally chairing the campaign in your agency and by exhorting top agency officials around the country to do the same.

The Combined Federal Campaign is an important way for Federal employees to support thousands of worthy charities. Public servants not only contribute to the campaign but also assume leadership roles to ensure its success.

Your personal support and enthusiasm will help positively influence thousands of employees and will guarantee another successful campaign.

GEORGE W. BUSH

NOTE: This memorandum was released by the Office of the Press Secretary on June 23.

Remarks Honoring the 2007 Women's National Basketball Association Champion Phoenix Mercury
June 23, 2008

The President. Thanks for coming. Please be seated. Welcome to the White House. And it is fitting that we use the East Garden because, one, this is rarely used; and two, it is an opportunity for me to welcome a lot of people to the—that are here to see the WNBA champs, Phoenix Mercury. And we're glad you came.

People who follow sport in America will know that the Phoenix Mercury played together as a great team, and they brought new glory to women's athletics and the sport of basketball. As they like to say, "Mighty Mercury, we are number one!" [*Laughter*] And these women proved it.

I want to thank Jay Parry, president and COO of the Phoenix Mercury, for joining us. Ann Meyers Drysdale, the general manager of the Phoenix Mercury—where is your son? There he is. Kind of looks like the big right-hander. You're right. [*Laughter*]

Corey Gaines, the head coach—Coach, thanks for coming, proud you're here. I particularly want to pay my respects to the cocaptains of the team, Cappie Pondexter and Diana Taurasi.

Now, this is not the first time that Diana has been here to the White House. She came with the mighty UConn Huskies. And she told me she was going to amount to something in life when I saw her. [*Laughter*] She said, "I will be back," and she is, as the champion. Welcome. Glad you're here.

And I wish these two great athletes all the best at the Olympics in Beijing. They're going to be carrying on the great tradition of women's basketball here in the United States. And even though it's going to be tough—a lot of teams are getting ready for them—they're going to come back with the gold. And America will be proud.

I welcome the other athletes on the stage and the newly—the new athletes who have joined the Phoenix Mercury. Must be pretty cool to be playing with champs. I bet it's wearing off on you, what it means to make the sacrifices necessary to win the title and be invited here in the White House.

I want to welcome Congressman Trent Franks. Congressman, thanks for coming. Thanks for taking an interest in the Phoenix Mercury. I know they're proud to have your support.

I welcome members of the Jr. WNBA that have joined us. Thanks for coming. Thanks for taking an interest in women's basketball. I want to—do thank—do want to thank the WNBA representatives and personnel who've joined us; appreciate you promoting women's athletics. As the father of twin girls, there's nothing better than having good role models for girls to look at. And there are no better role models than women basketball players. They're great athletes; they're well-conditioned people; they're disciplined.

I want to welcome the Phoenix fans here, professionally known as the X-Factor. I know these women really love the fact that they play in a city that supports them. And I hope the fans that, you know, aren't here recognize that even here in Washington, DC, we've heard of the Phoenix Mercury, and proud to have them come.

The team's playoff slogan was, "One team, one city, one goal." And they've fulfilled the goal. You became the first WNBA team in history to win a championship on the road. For the second year in a row, you set the record for the highest scoring average in WNBA history.

You were led ably by Coach Paul Westhead. I know he is proud of the women. And Corey Gaines was the assistant coach, so he had the pleasure of being part of a championship program. And he knows what it takes to get you in a position where you can win this year as well. Of course, I'm not going to be around to welcome you, but play hard anyway. [*Laughter*]

A thing I love about this team—and a lot of champions that I get to recognize here at the White House—is the fact that they understand you're a champ on the courts and you're a champ off the courts. The—this team spent weekends on a Habitat for Humanity program called Women Build. They served meals at homeless shelters. They honored breast cancer survivors. They helped sign up runners for Race for the Cure. They collected water bottles from fans and donated them to the Salvation Army's Extreme Heat Emergency Project. They participated in Read to Achieve. They helped stuff backpacks with supplies for underprivileged children.

They support the Jr. WNBA program, fully understanding that promoting healthy lifestyles is good for America. And there's no better way to have a healthy lifestyle than to participate in athletics. They've done their duty as citizens of the United States. I'm honored to welcome you. I'm proud of your championship trophy. I thank you for what you do for the country. May God bless you all.

Ann Meyers Drysdale. Mr. President, on behalf of the 2007 WNBA champion Phoenix Mercury, we'd like to thank you for your invitation to the White House. The Phoenix Mercury and the WNBA is all about leadership, being a strong role model, teamwork, and making a difference in others' lives.

This team accomplished a lot last year and had a lot of firsts. The coaches, fans, and players never stopped believing in themselves. Mr. President, we know your support for the Phoenix Mercury is genuine because of the influence of the women in your life.

The President. Yes.

Ms. Meyers Drysdale. All First Ladies—your graceful mother, your classy wife——

The President. Thank you.

Ms. Meyers Drysdale. ——your very strong-willed daughters. [*Laughter*] You think?

The President. Yes, that's why my hair is white. [*Laughter*]

Ms. Meyers Drysdale. We are very proud of this team. And on behalf of the Phoenix Mercury, we'd like our two Olympians, Diana Taurasi and Cappie Pondexter, to present you with a Phoenix Mercury jersey and a replica banner of our championship.

NOTE: The President spoke at 11:02 a.m. in the East Garden at the White House.

Remarks Following a Meeting With President Gloria Macapagal-Arroyo of the Philippines
June 24, 2008

President Bush. Madam President, it is a pleasure to welcome you back to the Oval Office. We have just had a very constructive dialogue. First, I want to tell you how proud I am to be the President of a nation that—in which there's a lot of Philippine

Americans. They love America, and they love their heritage. And I reminded the President that I am reminded of the great talent of the—of our Philippine Americans when I eat dinner at the White House. [*Laughter*]

President Macapagal-Arroyo. Yes.

President Bush. And the chef is a great person and a really good cook, by the way, Madam President.

President Macapagal-Arroyo. Thank you.

President Bush. We talked about our friendship, our bilateral relations, and we spent some time on foreign policy.

First, I expressed our deep condolences to those who suffered as a result of the typhoon. And I know there's some families that are hurting. Some are wondering whether or not their loved ones will, you know, reappear. We, the American people, care about the human suffering that's taking place, and we send our prayers.

Secondly, I informed the President—Secretary Gates informed the President, through me, that the United States will move the USS *Ronald Reagan*, a large aircraft carrier, to help with the assistance, along with other U.S. Navy assets. Madam President, we're happy to do it. We want to help our friends in a time of need.

We talked about, you know, food, and I assured the President we'll continue to help. We helped with rice in the past. And, you know, I'm proud of my country. We give a lot of food aid. And this is a time where America needs to step up, and we will, Madam President.

We talked about our mutual desire to advance—how important it is to move forward bilateral and multilateral trade agendas. I'm a—I believe trade is beneficial to both our countries. I'm hopeful we can get a Doha round done; we strategized together about how we can move the process.

I congratulated the President on her strong stand on counterterrorism—more than strong stand—effective stand on counterterrorism as well as laying out a vision for peace. The President's been very

strong in having a carrots-and-sticks approach. "Sticks," of course, say we're not going to allow for people to terrorize our citizens; the "carrot" approach is that there's peace available.

And we talked about Burma—the area, the region. The President's been a very strong leader when it comes to the freedom agenda and human dignity.

And so all in all, we had a very constructive talk. I'm proud you're here.

President Macapagal-Arroyo. Thank you.

President Bush. Thanks for coming.

President Macapagal-Arroyo. Thank you. Thank you. Mr. President, with your permission, I'd like to address our countrymen in our native language.

[*At this point, President Macapagal-Arroyo spoke in Tagalog, and her remarks were translated as follows.*]

Interpreter. Fellow countrymen, America is a strong ally in supporting our efforts to strengthen our economy and reinforce our democracy. The Philippines and the United States have a strong relationship, and we are here today to discuss important bilateral issues with President Bush, members of his administration, and congressional leaders. As President Bush mentioned, we will focus our discussions, now more than ever, on food shortages, defense cooperation, and economic aid. Together with our friends, such as America, let us join forces and move our country forward towards the company of First World, developed nations over the next 20 years.

Long live the Philippines, and long live the friendship between the Philippines and the United States.

President Bush. I couldn't have said it better myself. [*Laughter*] Thank you, Madam President.

President Macapagal-Arroyo. Thank you. Thank you.

President Bush. Thank you all.

NOTE: The President spoke at 10:25 a.m. in the Oval Office at the White House. In his remarks, he referred to White House Executive Chef Cristeta Comerford.

Remarks Following a Meeting With Prime Minister Nguyen Tan Dung of Vietnam
June 24, 2008

President Bush. Mr. Prime Minister, welcome to the Oval Office. I fondly remember my trip to your country. I remember the wonderful hospitality that you and your Government gave to Laura and me. I remember the thousands of people lining the street in Ho Chi Minh City and Hanoi, and it was just a memorable trip. So it's my honor to welcome you back here.

We had a good dialogue. We talked about economic cooperation, and we talked about educational cooperation. We talked about the need to work together on the environment. I thanked the Prime Minister for his work on accounting for the POWs and MIAs. We discussed the neighborhood and the region. We talked about the freedoms—religious and political freedom. And I told the Prime Minister that I thought the strides that the Government is making toward religious freedom is noteworthy, and I appreciated the efforts that he and his Government are making.

All in all, we had a very good discussion. Our relationship with Vietnam is getting closer, in a spirit of respect. And I thank you for coming to help make that relationship even stronger. Welcome.

Prime Minister Dung. Mr. President, ladies and gentlemen, I would like to thank you, Mr. President and American friends, for your warm hospitality.

I would like to tell you that Mr. President and I have just had successful talks in a friendly, constructive, and understanding spirit. And we took note, with great pleasure, of rapid development in the Vietnam-U.S. relationship toward a friendly and constructive partnership, multifaceted

cooperation on the basis of equality, mutual respect, and mutual benefit. We agreed with each other on a wide range of issues, which will be fully reflected in our adjoined statement.

And now I would like to give you some highlights of our conversation. Mr. President and I agreed to establish a new dialogue mechanism at the senior level on the strategic matters of economics, education, environment, science, defense, and security. And President Bush reiterated his support for Vietnam's sovereignty, security, and territorial integrity.

We agreed to establish a high-level education task force to effectively advance the education cooperation between our two countries. The two sides also agreed to set up a new subcommittee to assist Vietnam in conducting researches to respond to the climate change and the rising sea level.

And President Bush reaffirmed that the U.S. is actively reviewing Vietnam's request to join the GSP program and acknowledged Vietnam's request to be accorded the market economy status. The U.S. is also considering the import of fruits from Vietnam. Also, the two sides agreed to commence negotiations on a bilateral investment treaty.

Both sides also agreed to strengthen cooperation to address humanitarian issues left over by the war, such as the American MIA issue, mine clearing, remediation of the Agent Orange consequences, the Vietnamese MIA issue.

Ladies and gentlemen, my visit to the U.S. this time is the follow-up of the foreign policy of independence and sovereignty, diversification and multilateralization of our external relations. Vietnam wants to be friends with all country and trusted partners with all nations and nationalities in the international community. And along that line, with—Vietnam will continue to strengthen the fine relationship between Vietnam and the United States under the framework defined by the two countries' leaders.

I hope that with the fruitful outcome of my visit, the Vietnam-U.S. relationship will be elevated to new heights in the interest of both peoples, of peace, stability, and development cooperation in the region and the world.

Thank you, Mr. President.

President Bush. Thank you. Yes, sir.

NOTE: The President spoke at 1:53 p.m. in the Oval Office at the White House. Prime Minister Dung spoke in Vietnamese, and his remarks were translated by an interpreter.

Remarks Honoring 2007 and 2008 NCAA Championship Teams
June 24, 2008

Thank you all. Please be seated. Welcome to the White House. It is an honor to be here with so many fine student athletes now known as national champs.

It seems like the South Lawn is a fitting place to hold champions day. After all, we have a swimming pool, a tennis court, a running track, a putting green, and a basketball court, just in case any of our athletes here want to squeeze in a little friendly competition. [*Laughter*]

I appreciate the fact that you showed incredible discipline, skill, perseverance. It's hard to become a champ, and that's why we love to honor people here at the White House when you become one. And one of the things I tell people is, is that if you work hard and become a repeat champion, I look forward to welcoming you back to the White House. However, this time around it's not going to work. My eligibility has run out. [*Laughter*] But I do wish you all the very best. So the next President can welcome you to the White House, but in the meantime, we're going to honor the folks here today.

I welcome the members of the Cabinet. Mr. Secretary, thanks for coming. Members of Congress, thank you all for being here;

United States Senators, United States Congressmen, student athletes, coaches, school officials, and fans.

Today we honor 20 teams from 15 campuses in 13 States. These athletes excelled from tee boxes in California to ski slopes in Colorado to parallel bars in Oklahoma to bowling alleys on Maryland's Eastern Shore. You're represented by a wide variety of mascots: the Orange and the Golden Bears; the Hawks, the Eagles, and the Ducks; the Bruins, the Buckeyes, and two different types of Bulldogs. Despite these differences, you all share the right to call— be called champs, a title you'll keep for the rest of your life.

We have two first-time champions here today: UCLA women's tennis and the University of Maryland Eastern Shore women bowling Hawks. We have two teams that have spent a long time waiting to reclaim their national crowns. The University of Oregon men's cross country team brought the national title to Eugene for the first time in 30 years. I know you're proud, Senator. And the UCLA men's golf Bruins earned their first national championship in 20 years.

Even more impressive than winning the national title is becoming a repeat champion. Some of the teams here have accomplished that feat. Cal's men water polo team, University of Tennessee women's basketball, University of Georgia men's tennis—they're all repeat champs. Congratulations to you.

And then we've got two teams that have achieved the rare four-peat, the University of Georgia women's gymnastics, affectionately known as the Gym Dogs. And two Senators are here to honor them. UCLA women's water polo Bruins are here.

On the road to the championship, some teams recorded particularly memorable achievements. The University of North Carolina women's field hockey team compiled a perfect 24–0 record, making them just the fifth team in the sport history to— sport's history to finish undefeated. Penn State men's volleyball and Penn State women's volleyball pulled off a rare double championship, winning both the men's and women's title in the same year. Charlie Dent is here representing the team.

The University of Denver men's and women's ski team competed with one fewer skier than their rivals, making them only the second ski team in NCAA history to win the title shorthanded. And we congratulate you.

The USC women's golf team set a school record with five All-Americans on their championship team. [*Applause*] And all five just yelled. [*Laughter*]

Some of the champs here are building on long legacies of excellence. Ohio State men's and women's fencing finished in the top five for the seventh consecutive year and earned the third fencing championship in school history. And we welcome you here.

Boston College men's ice hockey prevailed in the Frozen Four for the third time in school history and the second time in this decade.

The University of Minnesota Duluth women's ice hockey Bulldogs—the Senator—earned their fourth championship in the past 8 years. It's good to see you again.

The University of Oklahoma men's gymnastics upset the top seed to win their fifth national title in the past 7 years.

And the Syracuse men's lacrosse team claimed their 10th national championship, which sets a new NCAA lacrosse record.

We honor you all, and we welcome you to the White House. And as importantly, we thank you for your contributions to the communities in which you live. These athletes have volunteered at food banks during holidays. They have visited schools to inspire children with disabilities. They've encouraged literacy and good health. They've raised money to fight cancer. What I'm telling you are—is, they're great athletes and good citizens. And for that, our country is grateful.

We're glad that you're here. We congratulate you and your families and your schools for your achievements. We ask for God's blessings on you and on our country. Thank you for coming.

NOTE: The President spoke at 4:08 p.m. on the South Lawn at the White House. In his remarks, he referred to Secretary of Agriculture Edward T. Schafer; Sens. Gordon H. Smith, Saxby Chambliss, Johnny Isakson, and Amy Klobuchar; and Rep. Charles W. Dent.

Message to the Congress on Continuation of the National Emergency With Respect to the Western Balkans
June 24, 2008

To the Congress of the United States:

Section 202(d) of the National Emergencies Act (50 U.S.C. 1622(d)) provides for the automatic termination of a national emergency unless, prior to the anniversary date of its declaration, the President publishes in the *Federal Register* and transmits to the Congress a notice stating that the emergency is to continue in effect beyond the anniversary date. In accordance with this provision, I have sent the enclosed notice to the *Federal Register* for publication stating that the Western Balkans emergency is to continue in effect beyond June 26, 2008.

The crisis constituted by the actions of persons engaged in, or assisting, sponsoring, or supporting (i) extremist violence in the Republic of Macedonia and elsewhere in the Western Balkans region, or (ii) acts obstructing implementation of the Dayton Accords in Bosnia or United Nations Security Council Resolution 1244 of June 10, 1999, in Kosovo, that led to the declaration of a national emergency on June 26, 2001, in Executive Order 13219 and to Executive Order 13304 of May 28, 2003, has not been resolved. The acts of extremist violence and obstructionist activity outlined in Executive Order 13219, as amended, are hostile to U.S. interests and pose a continuing unusual and extraordinary threat to the national security and foreign policy of the United States. For these reasons, I have determined that it is necessary to continue the national emergency declared with respect to the Western Balkans and maintain in force the comprehensive sanctions to respond to this threat.

GEORGE W. BUSH

The White House,
June 24, 2008.

NOTE: The notice is listed in Appendix D at the end of this volume.

Remarks Following a Meeting With President Jalal Talabani of Iraq
June 25, 2008

President Bush. It's been my honor to welcome a friend, President Talabani, back to the Oval Office. He is the President of a free Iraq. He is a man who's been on the frontlines of helping to unify Iraq and to help Iraq recover from a brutal regime, that of Saddam Hussein.

I complimented the President on the progress that the Government has made. I complimented the President on the fact that as security has improved, he and his fellow officials are reaching out to all aspects of society to help people realize the blessings of a free life.

There's still a lot of work to be done; we recognize that. We talked of a variety of subjects. We talked about a strategic framework agreement that suits the Iraqi Government. We talked about elections and different laws that have been passed. I did compliment the President on working hard to see to it that the legislative session this year has been very successful. We talked about the fact that the economy's improving and that the attitude of the people there has improved immeasurably over the years.

And so I welcome you here. I'm proud of what you've done, and I thank you for the tough decisions, so that the people of a free Iraq can realize hopes and dreams. Welcome.

President Talabani. Well, I am proud to have the honor of meeting President George Bush, whom we consider the liberator of Iraq from the worst kind of dictatorship, as a great friend of Iraqi people. I am grateful for what he said about me. But I agree with him that we are going to work together for having this agreement—security agreement between United States and Iraq and also to continue our cooperation in our struggle against terrorism, for promotion of democracy in Iraq and Middle East.

We are proud to have such a good friends here in this great country. And I think we can—I can say that we can pass, this year, two important laws, oil and election. And we are now going to reunite our Government by bringing Tawafuq also to the—I mean, Sunni representatives—to the Iraqi national unity Government headed by our Prime Minister, Nuri Maliki.

I also briefed our good friend about the achievements which Iraq had done in struggle against terrorism and, again, militias, who were making troubles for Iraq and threatening civil war. Now I can say that Iraq—big part of Iraq is stable and is secured and liberated from the danger of terrorism and militia.

Yes, some places still—there are some groups that remain here and there, but I think big achievement we have done this year with the support of the United States Army and Government and with the friendly advices from President Bush. I can say that we are proud to achieved good successes in Iraq. And our economy is growing.

We have also—big steps forward for national reconciliation. We improved our relation with our neighbors, with Turkey, with Egypt, with Jordan, with Kuwait. We normalized our relation with Iran and with Syria also. So Iraqi Government is now going to play its role in the Arab world as one—a founder of the Arab League. And there is no—I think, no more—any kind of isolation of our Government.

We are doing our best for this agreement. That this agreement with the United States of America—I think we have—we had very good, important steps towards reaching to finalize this agreement. And we continue our struggle to—our efforts to reach—*inshallah*—very soon this agreement.

And again to thank—here I am again here to thank here our great friends, President Bush and American great people, for their sacrifice and their support for Iraqi people. Thank you very much.

President Bush. Thank you, Mr. President. Thank you.

NOTE: The President spoke at 10:43 a.m. in the Oval Office at the White House.

Remarks in a Meeting With United Nations Security Council Permanent Representatives
June 25, 2008

The President. Mr. Ambassador——

Ambassador Zalmay Khalilzad. Sir.

The President. ——it's good to see you again.

Ambassador Khalilzad. It's good to see you.

The President. Thank you very much for bringing your colleagues from the United

Nations Security Council. And first, I want to thank you all very much for serving your respective countries. And thank you for being voices for peace and freedom.

We've had a really good discussion. We talked about a U.N. Security Council role for Darfur and Burma. We talked a little bit about Iran and how the United Nations Security Council is sending a focused message that the world really offers Iran a better way forward than isolation if they will verifiably suspend their enrichment programs.

And then we talked about Zimbabwe. Friday's elections, you know, appear to be a sham. You can't have free elections if a candidate is not allowed to campaign freely and his supporters aren't allowed to campaign without fear of intimidation. Yet the Mugabe Government has been intimidating the people on the ground in Zimbabwe, and this is an incredibly sad development.

I hope that the EU—I call—AU will, at their meeting this weekend, continue to highlight the illegitimacy of the elections, continue to remind the world that this election is not free and is not fair.

I want to thank very much the leaders in the region, those who have stepped up and spoke clearly. I appreciate them doing their—taking their responsibility seriously. And I want to thank the members here around the table of the United Nations Security Council for your strong Presidential statement. It was a powerful statement for fairness and decency and human dignity. And I suspect you'll still be dealing with this issue. And as you do, I hope you continue to speak with the same clarity that you spoke with last Monday.

People of Zimbabwe deserve better than what they're receiving now. People there want to express themselves at the ballot box, yet the Mugabe Government has refused to allow them to do so. This is not just, and it is wrong.

Thank you very much.

NOTE: The President spoke at 2:31 p.m. in the Roosevelt Room at the White House. In his remarks, he referred to Ambassador Zalmay Khalilzad, U.S. Permanent Representative to the United Nations; and President Robert Mugabe of Zimbabwe.

Remarks at the Max M. Fisher National Republican Leadership Award Dinner in Livonia, Michigan
June 25, 2008

The President. Thank you. Please be seated. Thanks for the——

Audience member. We love you! [*Laughter*]

The President. Thank you for the warm welcome. I'm fresh in from Washington, bringing greetings from First Lady Laura Bush, who's done a fabulous job. And I'm so pleased to be back in Michigan. I've spent some quality time in your State. I've enjoyed it every time I've come. I remember—you know, we've got a lot of fond memories here, such as the time when the

Republican Party nominated a really good guy to be the Vice Presidential candidate with Ronald Reagan. That would be the first President George Bush.

You might remember, that was in Detroit. And I remember the night—the time that Ronald Reagan reminisced about that evening. As he told the story, a friend of his was watching the convention proceedings in a hotel lounge in California. And he was on the stage and my dad was on the stage and all the supporters were on the stage. And then he heard someone ask this question: "Who are all those people up on the podium with Max Fisher?" [*Laughter*]

Everybody who knew Max Fisher loved Max Fisher. He was a man of uncommon grace. He was a person that could speak to the folks on the assembly line as well as to Presidents. He is a generous soul who gave to his community, his country, and the city of Detroit. He was a man of great courage. After all, he lived some 40 miles from Ann Arbor, but always reminded people he went to Ohio State. [*Laughter*]

I'm proud to join you in honoring Max Fisher's legacy. And if he were with us today, here's what he would say. He'd say, "Stop talking about me and getting to work." And our message is, is that we're going to get to work. We will return the Republican Party to the majority of the Michigan House of Representatives. We will take control of the Senate, and we—House, and we will elect John McCain the next President.

Mr. Chairman, thank you for leading the party. And I believe, with your hard work, John McCain is going to carry Michigan.

Today I had the privilege of flying down on Air Force One with Thaddeus McCotter, United States Congressman. This is the town in which he was raised. This is the district he represents. He is a smart, capable Member of the House of Representatives. And you—those of you who live here are lucky to have him as your Congressman.

I'm proud to be here with Attorney General Michael Cox; Mike Cox, who happened to marry a woman named Laura. [*Laughter*] Thanks for serving, Mike. I appreciate your leadership.

I'm proud to be here with Sheriff Mike Bouchard. Mike's been a friend of mine for a long time. And I know—the folks he represents through law enforcement really appreciate his dedication and hard work.

I appreciate State Representative Jack Hoogendyk and wife Erin. And I wish Jack all the best in his run for the United States Senate. Thanks for running; appreciate—wish you all the very best.

I thank my friend Chuck Yob, who's the Republican national committeeman from Michigan. And thank you all for coming.

The last time I attended this dinner, I was the Governor of Texas, running for President of the United States. Maybe some of you are old enough to remember that. [*Laughter*] Since then, some things have changed: My daughter got married, my hair is grayer, the entourage is bigger, and I haven't seen a traffic jam in 8 years. [*Laughter*] But some things that haven't changed: the principles that are etched in my soul and my faith in the American people.

Over the past 8 years, we've endured a lot together. When you think about what has taken place, it's been a challenging time for the American people. We've had a recession, high energy prices, housing downturn, unprecedented attack on our homeland, wars in Afghanistan and Iraq, and devastating natural disasters. The reason I bring that up is because you can't know what the future will bring, but you can bet there's going to be some unexpected challenges facing our country. And that is why the United States must elect a leader who has the experience and judgment necessary to handle those challenges.

I know a lot about the Oval Office—the daily intelligence briefings, the unexpected challenges, and the tough decisions that can only be made at the President's desk. In trying times, America needs a President who has been tested and will not flinch. We need a President who will do what is right, even when it's not easy. And we need to elect a President who knows what it takes to defeat our enemies. And this year, there is only one man who has shown those kind of leadership qualities, and that man is John McCain.

And a President McCain is going to need allies on Capitol Hill. That means we need to put the House and the Senate back where they belong, in Republican hands. And a President McCain will need people he can work with in this State on behalf of the people of Michigan, and that needs—means we need to put the Michigan House of Representatives where it belongs, back into Republican hands.

And I want to thank you all for helping make that reality come true. Thanks for your hard work that you're going to do, and thanks for your contributions that will help make this party vibrant and competitive coming down the stretch. After all, the campaign season really hasn't begun. It may seem like it's begun to you, but it really hasn't, because the main campaign is going to be in the fall. And that's the time most Americans are going to take measures of the candidates, and they're going to be wondering about what they believe for the future. And when the people start paying attention, and when they start looking at the philosophical differences, they're going to find that there's a wide chasm. There really are fundamental differences between what Republicans believe and what Democrats believe.

On the issues that matter most, from taxes and spending to confirming good judges and building a culture of life to protecting our people and winning the war on terror, the American people are going to have a very clear choice. When they get in that voting booth on election day, when they think about what really matters to them, they're going to vote Republican. They're going to vote Republican for Congress, they're going to vote Republican for the Michigan statehouse, and they're going to vote Republican for President of the United States.

This November, the American people are going to have a clear choice when it comes to taxes and spending. Republicans believe that American families can spend their own money far better than the government can.

We've worked hard to restrain spending in Washington. We delivered the largest tax cuts since Ronald Reagan was the President. We cut taxes for married couples. We don't think you ought to penalize marriage in the Tax Code. We cut taxes for families with children. We cut taxes for small businesses. We cut taxes for capital gains and dividends. We put the death tax on the road to extinction. We eliminated income taxes to nearly 5 million families in the lowest tax bracket, and as a result, the American people have more of their own money in their pocket, and that is the way it should be.

Now, our opponents have a different view on taxes, as you well know here in Michigan. After all, you've seen the Democrats propose and pass millions of dollars in new taxes. And if they increase their numbers in Lansing, we all know that that tax burden is likely to continue to grow.

And in Washington, the Democratically controlled Congress refuses to make the tax relief we passed permanent. When the tax relief expires, every income tax rate in America will grow—go up. The marriage penalty will return in full force. The child tax credit will be cut in half, and taxes on capital gains and dividends will increase significantly. The death tax will return to life. A typical family of four with an income of $40,000 will face a tax crease [increase] ° of more than $2,000. At a time when our citizens are struggling with high food prices and high gas prices and economic uncertainty, the last thing we need is a tax increase. That is why we must elect Republicans to the Congress and John McCain to the Presidency to make the tax relief permanent.

Now, there's a reason why the Democrats want to raise taxes. It's because they need more of your money to increase—to pay for all the new spending they have in mind. This is a well-thought-out plan

---

° White House correction.

on their part. You've seen this on the Federal level. When the Democrats campaigned for Congress in 2006, they promised fiscal responsibility. And since they took office, they've been acting like teenagers with a new credit card. [*Laughter*]

When those bills to increase spending and raise taxes reach my desk, I answer them with my favorite veto pen, and the famous words of Elvis Presley: "Return to Sender." [*Laughter*]

And one area where the Democrats in Congress has failed to lead is on energy policy, and that's becoming more and more apparent to the American people. You know, I know that you're concerned about rising gasoline prices, and so am I. I've repeatedly proposed ways to boost America's domestic oil supply, and the Democrats have rejected virtually all of them.

It puts them in an interesting position. They say they want lower prices at the pump, but they're against measures that would actually do that. You might say, when it comes to energy policy, the Democrats in Congress are running on empty.

This November, the American people have a clear choice when it comes to confirming good judges and building a culture of life. Republicans aspire to build a society where every human being is welcomed in life and protected in law. We funded crisis pregnancy centers and supported parental notification laws. We outlawed the cruel practice of partial-birth abortion, and we defended this good law all the way to the Supreme Court, and we won.

And that victory shows how important it is to put good judges on the bench. Republicans have made it—they made it clear what our view is about the judiciary, the role of our courts in our democracy. We believe that judges should strictly interpret the law and not legislate from the bench. We need more judges like Justice Sam Alito and Chief Justice John Roberts.

Our opponents see things differently. There's no clearer illustration of the differences than this: The Democrats' chosen candidate for President voted against both these good men. And our candidate for President, John McCain, voted for them.

And we recently received a fresh reminder of the importance of the courts. A bare majority of five Supreme Court Justices overturned a bipartisan law that Congress passed and I signed to deliver justice to the detainees at Guantanamo Bay. With this decision, hardened terrorists now enjoy the same legal rights previously reserved for Americans.

This is precisely the kind of judicial activism that frustrates the American people. And the best way to change it is to put Republicans back in charge of the United States Senate and John McCain in the White House.

And the best way to keep judges in Michigan from substituting their own political views for the clear principles of the Constitution is to elect more judges like Cliff Taylor on the Michigan Supreme Court.

This November, the American people are going to have a clear choice when it comes to protecting our country and winning the war on terror. Republicans believe that our most solemn duty is to protect the American people. And since September the 11th, 2001, we have worked day and night to stop another attack on our homeland.

At home, we've strengthened our defenses, we've reformed our intelligence community, and we've launched a new program to monitor terrorist communications. Around the world, we have gone on the offense against the terrorists and advanced freedom as the great alternative to their ideology of hatred and violence. In a time of war, we need a Commander in Chief who understands that we must defeat the enemy overseas so we do not have to face them here at home, and that man is John McCain.

In Afghanistan, we destroyed Al Qaida training camps and removed the Taliban from power. And today, we're helping a democratic society take root and ensuring that Afghanistan will never again be a safe haven for terrorists planning an attack on America.

And in Iraq, we removed a dangerous regime run by Saddam Hussein. The decision to remove Saddam Hussein was the right decision at the time, and it is the right decision today.

Early last year, when the situation in Iraq was deteriorating, we launched what's called the surge. And since the surge, violence in Iraq has dropped, a lot. Civilian deaths and sectarian killings are down, and political and economic progress is taking place. A democracy is taking root where a tyrant once ruled.

In Afghanistan, Iraq, and around the world, our men and women are performing with skill and honor. Some of these brave troops have come from Michigan. We honor their sacrifices. We are grateful to their families. And every single American should be proud of their noble work.

The war on terror is the great challenge of our time. The Democratic Party has repeatedly shown that it would take America in the wrong direction, starting with the fact that many don't consider this to be a war at all. In their view, this is a—primarily a matter of law enforcement. In the war on terror, our focus should not be on prosecuting criminals after they have committed a crime. Our job is to find the terrorists and stop new attacks before they happen.

To stop new attacks, we need to know what the terrorists are planning. And the best source of information about terrorist attacks is the terrorists themselves. After 9/11, we established a program at the CIA to detain and question key terrorist operatives and their leaders. This program has stopped new attacks on our country and has saved American lives. And despite these successes, Democratic leaders in Congress have tried to shut it down.

To stop new attacks, we also need to deny terrorists safe haven, including in Iraq. And that's why we launched the

surge. Yet the Democrats declared the surge a failure before it even began. And now that the surge has turned the situation around, they still call for retreat.

The other side talks a lot about hope, and that sums up their Iraq policy pretty well: They want to retreat from Iraq and hope nothing bad happens. But wistful thinking is no way to fight a war and to protect the American people. Leaving Iraq before the job is done would endanger our citizens and embolden the enemies who have vowed to attack us again. When it comes to the war on terror, our Democratic leaders should pay more attention to the warnings of terrorists like Usama bin Laden and spend less time heeding the demands of MoveOn.org and CODEPINK.

Over the next few months, you're going to hear a lot of talk about change. The Democrats say they're a party of change. Let me review the history of the Democratic Party. There was a time when they believed that low taxes were the path to growth and opportunity, but they've changed. There was a time when they believed in commonsense American values, but they have changed. There was a time when they believed that America should pay any price and bear any burden in the defense of liberty, but they have changed.

This isn't the kind of change the American people want. Americans want change that makes their lives better and their country safer. And that requires changing the party in control of the Congress. And that requires having a Commander in Chief who will support our military and will fight and win the war against those who would do us harm, and that Commander in Chief will be John McCain.

And so I thank you for coming tonight. I just want you to know that we've got a lot of work to do together. I don't know about you, but my energy is up and my spirits are high, and I'm going to finish my job with a sprint to the finish line.

So with confidence in our vision and faith in our values, let's go forward together. Let's put Republicans back in control of the Congress and the Senate. Let's make sure Republicans run the statehouse here in Michigan, and let's do all we can to put John McCain in the Oval Office.

May God bless you, and may God bless our country.

NOTE: The President spoke at 5 p.m. at Laurel Manor. In his remarks, he referred to Saulius Anuzis, chairman, Michigan Republican Party; Michigan State Attorney General Michael Cox; Michael J. Bouchard, sheriff, Oakland County, MI; Democratic Presidential candidate Barack Obama; Chief Justice Clifford W. Taylor, Michigan State Supreme Court; and Usama bin Laden, leader of the Al Qaida terrorist organization.

Statement on Senate Confirmation of Judges for the United States Courts of Appeals and District Courts
June 25, 2008

Yesterday the Senate confirmed Raymond Kethledge and Helene White to the U.S. Court of Appeals for the Sixth Circuit and Stephen Murphy to the U.S. District Court for the Eastern District of Michigan. I appreciate the Senate's work on filling these important seats, which had been declared judicial emergencies.

For the first time in my administration, the Sixth Circuit will now have a full court to address important issues facing the residents of Kentucky, Michigan, Ohio, and Tennessee. Unfortunately, too many other

Federal judgeships across America remain vacant. This is unacceptable and inexcusable. Since the beginning of the 110th Congress, the Senate has confirmed only 10 circuit court nominees. In the last 2 years of the past three administrations, the Senate has confirmed an average of 17 circuit court judges. I strongly urge the Senate to hold hearings and votes on the 28 pending circuit and district court nominations to ensure that our Nation has a fully functioning judicial system.

Joint Statement by the United States of America and the Socialist Republic of Vietnam
June 25, 2008

President George W. Bush welcomed Prime Minister Nguyen Tan Dung to the United States of America and to the White House yesterday for the fourth bilateral meeting between leaders of our two countries in as many years. The President and the Prime Minister discussed the progress made since they last met in Vietnam in 2006 and committed to specific efforts to carry this increasingly robust bilateral rela-

tionship forward. The two leaders agreed the relationship is based on a positive, growing friendship, mutual respect, and a shared commitment to pursuing constructive and multifaceted cooperation on a wide range of issues that will contribute to the development of the depth of the relationship, which is in the long-term interests of both countries. They also shared their vision and goals for a stable, secure, democratic, and peaceful Asia-Pacific region and discussed future U.S.-Vietnam contributions to that end.

The leaders welcomed the deepening economic ties, noting that two-way bilateral trade topped $12 billion in 2007 and that the United States is Vietnam's top export market. Prime Minister Dung affirmed Vietnam's resolve to maintain macroeconomic stability and determination to implement its commitments under the World Trade Organization, the Bilateral Trade Agreement, and the Trade and Investment Framework Agreement; improve its legal system; and create conditions favorable for foreign investors and trade growth.

The two leaders agreed that trade and economic ties are significant to the bilateral relationship. They announced that the United States and Vietnam would initiate negotiations toward a Bilateral Investment Treaty, signaling our commitment to open investment regimes and fair, non-discriminatory, and transparent treatment of foreign investment. President Bush affirmed that the United States is seriously reviewing Vietnam's request to be designated as a beneficiary of the Generalized System of Preferences program, and he acknowledged Vietnam's request to be accorded Market Economy Status. They noted the importance of efforts within the Asia-Pacific Economic Cooperation (APEC) forum to promote free and open trade and investment, including the prospect of a Free Trade Area of the Asia-Pacific. President Bush reiterated the United States' general opposition to restrictions on food exports at a time of rising prices. The two leaders called on all countries to join in the effort to solve the world food problem. President Bush reaffirmed the United States' commitment to pursuing actions to maintain or expand existing assistance levels and to address the underlying conditions contributing to high food prices.

The two leaders discussed expanding and strengthening our senior-level dialogues.

They endorsed the creation of new political-military and policy planning talks, which will allow for more frequent and in-depth discussions on security and strategic issues. The two leaders noted the benefit of an open and candid dialogue on issues relating to human rights and fundamental freedoms. President Bush and Prime Minister Dung agreed on the importance of the rule of law in modern societies, and President Bush underscored the importance of promoting improved human rights practices and conditions for religious believers and ethnic minorities. Prime Minister Dung informed President Bush of the policies and efforts made by Vietnam in this area, and President Bush took note of Vietnam's efforts to date and encouraged further progress. On the occasion of the 60th anniversary of the Universal Declaration on Human Rights, the two leaders reaffirmed their commitment to promoting and securing fundamental human rights and liberties.

The two leaders were pleased with the successes of Vietnamese Americans and noted their contribution to the promotion of the relationship between the two countries. President Bush welcomed these contributions and reiterated the U.S. government's support for Vietnam's national sovereignty, security, and territorial integrity.

President Bush expressed appreciation for Vietnam's cooperation in our joint humanitarian effort to achieve the fullest possible accounting for Americans who remain missing in action and Vietnam's willingness to carry out additional measures, noting that the Joint Field Activities have allowed for the identification and repatriation of the remains of 629 U.S. soldiers and reaffirmed the U.S. government's continued assistance in obtaining information for Vietnam's own accounting efforts. Prime Minister Dung highlighted the United States' assistance in this area as well. Prime Minister Dung applauded bilateral progress in addressing environmental contamination near former dioxin storage sites in Vietnam, particularly the ongoing implementation of $3 million in U.S. funding for environmental remediation and health projects.

President Bush congratulated Prime Minister Dung on his country's two-year membership on the United Nations Security Council. The two leaders reaffirmed that the two countries will continue consultations on the pressing issues that will face the Security Council. The Prime Minister informed the President that Vietnam is completing the preparatory process for its effective participation in UN peacekeeping operations. Prime Minister Dung thanked President Bush for the invitation for Vietnam to participate in the Global Peace Operations Initiative (GPOI), through which Vietnam will participate in training courses and other activities on peacekeeping operations. President Bush noted the ongoing visit of the humanitarian ship the USNS Mercy to Vietnam.

The two leaders expressed their wish to enhancing further U.S. relations with the Association of Southeast Asian Nations (ASEAN), and President Bush expressed his appreciation for Vietnam's active role in ASEAN. The two leaders discussed the areas of cooperation with ASEAN, including humanitarian assistance and Cyclone Nargis. President Bush reiterated that the United States is willing to work with ASEAN, the United Nations, and other non-governmental organizations to bring additional, much-needed humanitarian assistance to those affected by the devastating cyclone, and they discussed the need for entry and prompt access to all international aid workers to the disaster area.

The two leaders underscored the importance of cooperation on education and agreed to launch a high-level bilateral Education Task Force that will chart a roadmap and identify effective modalities for enhanced U.S.-Vietnam education cooperation. The two leaders also welcomed the continued success of the Fulbright Program in Vietnam and the growing number of Vietnamese students who choose to study in the United States. President Bush underscored the importance of a future Peace Corps program in Vietnam. Prime Minister Dung agreed in principle to the President's proposal on such a program and that the two sides will continue discussion to finalize related arrangements.

Prime Minister Dung thanked President Bush for assistance under the President's Emergency Plan for AIDS Relief (PEPFAR), noting that many people in Vietnam, including vulnerable children, are now receiving care, support, antiretroviral treatment.

The President expressed his commitment to continue the development of inter-country adoption cooperation between the United States and Vietnam that ensures the best interests of the child, respects his or her fundamental rights, and prevents the abduction and trafficking of children. The Prime Minister underscored that Vietnam shares these goals and stressed that Vietnam will speed up preparations for an early accession to the Hague Convention on Intercountry Adoptions. The Prime Minister also welcomed U.S. technical assistance in facilitating this step.

Prime Minister Dung thanked President Bush for the United States' assistance on Vietnam's Atomic Energy Law as well as for technical information and training on nuclear safety.

Finally, the two leaders discussed cooperation on climate issues. Prime Minister Dung and President Bush welcomed the commencement of the Delta Research and Global Observation Network (DRAGON) project in Vietnam, which will establish an institute at Can Tho University to cooperate on training and research to produce healthy ecosystems and sustainable deltas. The two leaders also agreed to work together to promote Vietnamese climate change adaptation and mitigation efforts, including the formation of a new subcommittee under the bilateral Science and Technology Agreement to discuss and coordinate joint initiatives.

NOTE: An original was not available for verification of the content of this joint statement.

Remarks on the Situation in North Korea and an Exchange With Reporters
June 26, 2008

The President. Good morning. The policy of the United States is a Korean Peninsula free of all nuclear weapons. This morning we moved a step closer to that goal when North Korean officials submitted a declaration of their nuclear programs to the Chinese Government as part of the six-party talks.

The United States has no illusions about the regime in Pyongyang. We remain deeply concerned about North Korea's human rights abuses, uranium enrichment activities, nuclear testing and proliferation, ballistic missile programs, and the threat it continues to pose to South Korea and its neighbors.

Yet we welcome today's development as one step in the multistep process laid out by the six-party talks between North Korea, China, Japan, Russia, South Korea, and the United States.

Last year, North Korea pledged to disable its nuclear facilities. North Korea has begun disabling its Yongbyon nuclear facility, which was being used to produce plutonium for nuclear weapons. This work is being overseen by officials from the United States and the IAEA. And to demonstrate its commitment, North Korea has said it will destroy the cooling tower of the Yongbyon reactor in front of international television cameras tomorrow.

Last year, North Korea also pledged to declare its nuclear activity. With today's declaration, North Korea has begun describing its plutonium-related activities. It's also provided other documents related to its nuclear programs going back to 1986. It has promised access to the reactor core and waste facilities at Yongbyon, as well as personnel related to its nuclear program. All this information will be essential to verifying that North Korea is ending its nuclear programs and activities.

The six-party talks are based on a principle of action for action. So in keeping with the existing six-party agreements, the United States is responding to North Korea's actions with two actions of our own.

First, I'm issuing a proclamation that lifts the provisions of the Trading With the Enemy Act with respect to North Korea.

And secondly, I am notifying Congress of my intent to rescind North Korea's designation as a state sponsor of terror in 45 days.

The next 45 days will be an important period for North Korea to show its seriousness of its cooperation. We will work through the six-party talks to develop a comprehensive and rigorous verification protocol. And during this period, the United States will carefully observe North Korea's actions and act accordingly.

The two actions America is taking will have little impact on North Korea's financial and diplomatic isolation. North Korea will remain one of the most heavily sanctioned nations in the world. The sanctions that North Korea faces for its human rights violations, its nuclear test in 2006, and its weapons proliferation will all stay in effect. And all United Nations Security Council sanctions will stay in effect as well.

The six-party process has shed light on a number of issues of serious concern to the United States and the international community. To end its isolation, North

Korea must address these concerns. It must dismantle all of its nuclear facilities, give up its separated plutonium, resolve outstanding questions on its highly enriched uranium and proliferation activities, and end these activities in a way that we can fully verify.

North Korea must also meet other obligations it has undertaken in the six-party talks. The United States will never forget the abduction of Japanese citizens by the North Koreans. We will continue to closely cooperate and coordinate with Japan and press North Korea to swiftly resolve the abduction issue.

This can be a moment of opportunity for North Korea. If North Korea continues to make the right choices, it can repair its relationship with the international community, much as Libya has done over the past few years. If North Korea makes the wrong choices, the United States and our partners in the six-party talks will respond accordingly. If they do not fully disclose and end their plutonium, their enrichment, and their proliferation efforts and activities, there will be further consequences.

Multilateral diplomacy is the best way to peacefully solve the nuclear issue with North Korea. Today's developments show that tough multilateral diplomacy can yield promising results. Yet the diplomatic process is not an end in itself. Our ultimate goal remains clear: a stable and peaceful Korean Peninsula, where people are free from oppression, free from hunger and disease, and free from nuclear weapons. The journey toward that goal remains long, but today we have taken an important step in the right direction.

I'll take a couple of questions.

Mike [Mike Emanuel, FOX News].

Six-Party Talks/Message to North Korean People

Q. Mr. President, thank you very much. After declaring them a member of the axis of evil, and then after that underground nuclear tests that North Korea conducted in 2006, I'm wondering if you ever doubted getting to this stage. And also, I'm wondering if you have a message for the North Korean people.

The President. I knew that the United States could not solve or begin to solve this issue without partners at the table. In order for diplomacy to be effective, there has to be leverage. You have to have a— there has to be consequential diplomacy.

And so I worked hard to get the Chinese and the South Koreans and the Japanese and the Russians to join with us in sending a concerted message to the North Koreans, and that is that if you promise and then fulfill your promises to dismantle your nuclear programs, there's a better way forward for you and the people. In other words, as I said in the statement, it's action for action.

It took a while for the North Koreans to take the six-party talks seriously. And it also took there to be concerted messages from people other than the United States saying that if you choose not to respond positively, there will be consequences.

And so I'm—it's been a—multilateral diplomacy is difficult at times. It's hard to get people heading in the same direction. And yet we were able to do so along— our partners helped a lot, don't get me wrong.

The message to the North Korean people is, is that we don't want you to be hungry; we want you to have a better life; that our concerns are for you, not against you; and that we have given your leadership a way forward to have better relations with the international community.

This is a society that is regularly going through famines. When I campaigned for President, I said, we will never use food as a diplomatic weapon. In North Korea, we have been concerned that food shipments sometimes don't make it to the people themselves. In other words, the regime takes the food for their own use.

So my message to the people is, is that we'll continue to care for you and worry about you and, at the same time, pursue a Korean Peninsula that's nuclear weapons-free. And today we have taken a step, and it's a very positive step, but there's more steps to be done.

Deb [Deb Riechmann, Associated Press].

Six-Party Talks/Abduction of Japanese Citizens

Q. Mr. President, what do you say to critics who claim that you've accepted a watered down declaration just to get something done before you leave office? I mean, you've said that it doesn't address the uranium enrichment issue, and of course, it doesn't address what North Korea might have done to help Syria build its reactor.

The President. Yes. Well, first, let me review where we have been. In the past, we would provide benefits to the North Koreans in a hope that they would fulfill a vague promise. In other words, that's the way it was before I came into office.

Everybody was concerned about North Korea possessing a nuclear weapon; everybody was concerned about the proliferation activities. And yet the policy in the past was, here are some benefits for you, and we hope that you respond. And of course, we found they weren't responding. And so our policy has changed—that says, in return for positive action, in return for verifiable steps, we will reduce penalties. And there are plenty of restrictions still on North Korea.

And so my point is this, is that we'll see. They said they're going to destroy parts of their plant in Yongbyon. That's a very positive step. After all, it's the plant that made plutonium. They have said in their declarations—if you read their declarations of September last year, they have said specifically what they will do. And our policy and the statement today makes it clear we will hold them to account for their promises. And when they fulfill their promises, more restrictions will be eased. If they don't fulfill their promises, more restrictions will be placed on them. This is action

for action. This is, we will trust you only to the extent that you fulfill your promises.

And so I'm pleased with the progress. I'm under no illusions that this is the first step. This isn't the end of the process; this is the beginning of the process of action for action. And the point I want to make to our fellow citizens is that we have worked hard to put multilateral diplomacy in place, because the United States sitting down with Kim Jong Il didn't work in the past. Sitting alone at the table just didn't work.

Now, as I mentioned in my statement, there's a lot of more verification that needs to be done. I mentioned our concerns about enrichment. We expect the North Korean regime to be forthcoming about their programs. We talked about proliferation. We expect them to be forthcoming about their proliferation activities and cease such activities. I mentioned the fact that we're taking—beginning to take inventory, because of our access to the Yongbyon plant, about what they have produced. And we expect them to be forthcoming with what they have produced and the material itself.

So today I'm just talking about the first step of a multistep process. And I want to thank our partners at the six-party talks. It's been incredibly helpful to achieve—the beginnings of achieving a vision of a nuclear-free Korean Peninsula, to have the Chinese to be as robustly involved as they are. You notice that the North Koreans passed on their documents to the Chinese. After all, we're all partners in the six-party talks.

The other thing is—I want to assure our friends in Japan—is that this process will not leave behind—leave them behind on the abduction issue. The United States takes the abduction issue very seriously. We expect the North Koreans to solve this issue in a positive way for the Japanese. There's a lot of folks in Japan that are deeply concerned about what took place. I remember meeting a mother of a child who was abducted by the North Koreans, right here in the Oval Office. It was a heart-wrenching moment to listen to the mother talk about what it was like to lose her daughter. And it is important for the Japanese people to know that the United States will not abandon our strong ally and friend when it comes to helping resolve that issue.

Today is a positive day; it's a positive step forward. There's more work to be done, and we've got the process in place to get it done in a verifiable way.

Thank you.

NOTE: The President spoke at 7:40 a.m. in the Rose Garden at the White House. In his remarks, he referred to Chairman Kim Jong Il of North Korea; and Sakie Yokota, mother of Megumi Yokota, who was abducted by North Korean authorities.

Message to the Congress on Continuing Certain Restrictions With Respect to North Korea and North Korean Nationals and the Termination of the Exercise of Authorities Under the Trading With the Enemy Act
June 26, 2008

To the Congress of the United States:

Pursuant to the International Emergency Economic Powers Act, as amended (50 U.S.C. 1701 *et seq.*) (IEEPA), I hereby report that I have issued an Executive Order continuing certain restrictions on North Korea and North Korean nationals imposed pursuant to the exercise of authorities under the Trading With the Enemy Act (50 U.S.C. App. 1 *et seq.*) (TWEA). In the order, I declared a national emergency to deal with the unusual and extraordinary threat to the national security and foreign policy of the United States posed by the current existence and risk of the proliferation of weapons-usable fissile material on the Korean Peninsula. I ordered the continuation of certain restrictions on North Korea and North Korean nationals as we deal with that threat through multilateral diplomacy.

These restrictions were first imposed pursuant to authorities found in section 5(b) of TWEA, following the declaration of a national emergency in 1950 in Proclamation 2914 (15 *FR* 9029), and continued annually, after the enactment of IEEPA in 1977, in accordance with section 101(b) of Public Law 95–223 (91 Stat. 1625; 50

U.S.C. App. 5(b) note). The most recent continuation of such TWEA authorities is found in Presidential Determination 2007–32 of September 13, 2007. In a proclamation, which I signed the same day as the order, I terminated, effective the following day, the exercise of TWEA authorities with respect to North Korea.

The order I have issued continues the blocking of certain property and interests in property of North Korea or a North Korean national that were blocked as of June 16, 2000, and that remained blocked immediately prior to the date of my order. Absent this order, my proclamation terminating the exercise of TWEA authorities with respect to North Korea would have resulted in the unblocking of that property.

The order also continues restrictions relating to North Korea-flagged vessels that would otherwise have been terminated by my proclamation. These restrictions prohibit United States persons from owning, leasing, operating, or insuring any vessel flagged by North Korea and from registering vessels in North Korea or otherwise obtaining authorization for a vessel to fly the North Korean flag. For the reasons set forth above, I found that it was necessary to continue these restrictions.

I delegated to the Secretary of the Treasury, after consultation with the Secretary of State, the authority to take such actions, including the promulgation of rules and regulations, and to employ all powers granted to the President by IEEPA as may be necessary to carry out the purposes of my order.

I am enclosing a copy of the Executive Order and proclamation I have issued.

GEORGE W. BUSH

The White House,
June 26, 2008.

NOTE:The Executive order and proclamation are listed in Appendix D at the end of this volume.

Remarks at the National Hispanic Prayer Breakfast
June 26, 2008

The President. Gracias. Sientese. [*Laughter*] Luis, thank you, sir. So he asked, would I come to the prayer breakfast. My answer was, *por supuesto.* [*Laughter*] I am honored to join you. I was proud to stand with you in 2002 at the first National Hispanic Prayer Breakfast, and today I am proud to stand with you at the—for the final time as your sitting President.

This happens to be an important event, in my view. It's an important event because it reminds us that no matter what our status in life might be, that we have a duty to respond to a higher power.

Audience member. Amen!

The President. You know, next year in Crawford, Laura and I are going to have a different kind of prayer breakfast. I'll be cooking the eggs, and she'll be praying I don't burn them. [*Laughter*]

I do want to welcome the First Lady of Panama, Vivian Fernandez de Torrijos. Thank you for coming. As some of you may or may not know, the—*mi ninita* lived in Panama for a while, and the government and the people there were so kind and hospitable, and I can't—and I'll never be able to repay you for that. So thank you very much. Please give your *esposo* my best regards, *el Presidente de Panama. Si*, thank you.

Proud to be here with pastors and community leaders. Thank you for doing what you're doing.

Each of you here this morning is here to celebrate a simple and powerful act, prayer to an Almighty God. You know the comfort that comes from placing our worries in the hands of a higher power. You know the humility that comes from approaching our Maker on bended knee. And you know the strength that comes from lifting our thoughts from worldly cares and focusing on the eternal.

Today I ask all to join together to pray that God continues to bestow His blessings on our wonderful country. We pray that the Almighty will strengthen America's families. A caring family is the foundation of a hopeful society. We pray that every child in America can grow up in a loving and stable home. We pray for the day when every child in America is welcomed in life and protected in law. And we pray that in every community across this great land, the Almighty will strengthen *los valores de la familia y de la fe.*

We pray that America will strengthen those who serve *nuestros hermanos y hermanas* in need. We pray for the continued success of faith-based and community groups like Esperanza, all aiming to transfer [transform]° our great country one heart, one soul, one conscience at a time. I was proud to hear of the work of Esperanza in Philadelphia. I've known Esperanza for *ochos años.* I was first impressed by the vision of making sure that every child gets a good education. It's Luis who started a charter school. It's a tremendous school. Less than 1 percent of students drop out, and more than 90 percent of the graduates are planning to go to college this fall. There's nothing more hopeful than to give a child a good education.

I'm impressed by the program called Esperanza Trabajando. This program helps at-risk youths and former prisoners move from lives of hopelessness to futures of accomplishment and self-sufficiency. "Esperanza Trabajando," for those of you who don't speak Spanish—and frankly, mine isn't all that good—[*laughter*]—means "Hope is Working," and that's exactly what you are demonstrating, Luis, and others in this room demonstrate *cada dia*—every day.

For the past 8 years, my administration has provided unprecedented support for the compassionate work performed by faith-based and community groups, because I understand this: Government can hand out money, but government cannot put hope in a person's heart. And oftentimes that is found in our faith community and our community organizations. And so we've lowered the barriers that kept government and faith-based groups needlessly divided and ensured that America's armies of compassion are at the center of our Nation's efforts to make our society more hopeful for every individual.

Organizations like yours have shown the ability to save and change lives. And in your mercies of love and mercy, you must always have a strong and reliable partner in government.

We pray that Almighty will strengthen and protect those who serve the cause of freedom. These brave men and women

---

° White House correction.

share our cherished belief that the desire for liberty is written by the Almighty in every human heart. We believe in the universality of freedom. And where we see people suffer from forms of government that create hopelessness or disease and hunger and mosquito bites, that deny people a hopeful life, the United States must act under the theory, under the principle that to whom much is given, much is required.

Audience member. Amen!

The President. I'm impressed—deeply impressed by those who wear our Nation's uniform. I appreciate—some have given their lives, others have suffered injuries in freedom's cause. And this morning I am honored to note that five brave servicemen who are being treated at Walter Reed Army Medical Center are with us today. We thank you for your sacrifice, we pray for your recovery, and we honor your service to the United States of America.

This, like, might not be on the schedule, but if you five guys would mind letting me have my picture taken with you, I'd be honored. So like, when the speech is about to end, which is soon—[*laughter*]—head to the exits, and I'll see you.

We also honor those who struggle for freedom against oppressive regimes. It's essential that the United States always remember—in our great comfort—that we always remember that there are those who want their freedom just like we have our freedom. One of those men is Juan Carlos Gonzalez Leiva. He's a lawyer and human rights activist on the island of Cuba. Juan Carlos was unjustly jailed for more than 2 years by the Cuban regime because he supported a dissident journalist. While he was imprisoned, his cane and his dark glasses were confiscated, which is especially cruel because Juan Carlos is blind. The guards took away his braille Bible, but they could not take away his spirit. Today, Juan Carlos is no longer in jail, but he remains under the surveillance of the Cuban Government.

Juan Carlos continues his important fight for human rights in Cuba, and the United States must always stand squarely with those who struggle for their human rights against tyranny. And today we're honored that his *hermano* is with us. Onel Ramon Gonzalez Leiva is here on his behalf. Onel, we want to thank you for coming. Our prayers go out to your brother and those who struggle with him. And we ask for the day, we pray for the day when the light of liberty shines on the people of Cuba and those who long for freedom. Onel, *bienvenidos.*

So as I mentioned, this is my last visit as your President to the Hispanic Prayer Breakfast. It's been a joy every time I have come. During the last 7½ years, I have been touched by how many Americans have come up and said, "I'm praying for you, Mr. President," people I've never seen before in my life, may never see again. It's amazing. You would think they would come up and say, you know, "I'd like a new highway," or "How about an additional bridge?"

[*Laughter*] But no, total strangers come and say, "I just want you to know, we lift you up in prayer." Somebody asked me what all that meant, and I said, well, you know, I'm finally beginning to understand the story of the calm in the rough seas. And I attribute it to the fact that millions of people have been so kind and generous to pray for me and Laura.

And so on my final trip here as your sitting President, I thank you for your prayers. I can't thank you enough for your spiritual support. And it's made a significant difference during these 7½ years. Being your President has been an unimaginable honor and a joyous experience.

Thank you, and God bless.

NOTE: The President spoke at 8:37 a.m. at the JW Marriott Hotel. In his remarks, he referred to Rev. Luis Cortes, Jr., president, Esperanza; and President Martin Torrijos Espino of Panama. The Office of the Press Secretary also released a Spanish language transcript of these remarks.

Remarks at the Office of Faith-Based and Community Initiatives' National Conference
June 26, 2008

Thank you very much. Please be seated. Now how beautiful was that; from being a homeless mother of two to introducing the President of the United States. There has to be a higher power. I love being with members of the armies of compassion, foot soldiers in helping make America a more hopeful place. Every day, you mend broken hearts with love. You mend broken lives with hope, and you mend broken communities with countless acts of extraordinary kindness.

Groups like yours have harnessed the power that no government bureaucracy can match. So when I came to Washington, my goal was to ensure that government made you a full partner in our efforts to serve those in need. And the results have been uplifting, and that's what we're here to talk about today. It's an opportunity to celebrate your achievements, to thank you for your life-changing work, and to look ahead to ways that you will extend your record of compassion in the years to come.

I really want to thank Jay Hein and those who worked hard to put on this conference. It looks like it's a successful one from here. I'm honored that members of the administration have come—the Attorney General, Judge Michael Mukasey. Mr. General, thanks for coming. Secretary Ed Schafer,

Department of Agriculture; Secretary Carlos Gutierrez, Department of Commerce; Director John Walters, Office of National Drug Control Policy—thank you all for taking time to be here.

Ambassador Mark Dybul, U.S. Global AIDS Coordinator—Mark, thanks for coming; appreciate you being here. I'm going to talk about PEPFAR in a minute. But when I talk about PEPFAR, think about his extraordinary leadership, as I do.

I want to thank the Ambassador from the Republic of Rwanda. Mr. Ambassador, I'm proud you're here. And I want to thank all of those who've come around the country who work in our Faith-Based and Community Initiative for your leadership and your compassion and your decency.

You know, when I ran for President, like a lot of others around our country, I was troubled to see so many of our citizens' greatest needs going unmet. Too many addicts walked the rough road of recovery alone. Too many prisoners had the desire for reform, but no one showed them a way. Across the country, the hungry and the homeless, the sick and the suffering begged for deliverance, and too many heard only silence.

And the tragedy that was—a lot of good folks in America—a lot of good men and women who had the desire to help, but didn't have the resources—they had the heart, but not the resources. And because many of them worked with small charities, they were overlooked by Washington as potential partners in service. And because many of them belonged to faith-based organizations, they were often barred from receiving support from the Federal Government.

So I set about to change that, at least from the Federal perspective, with an approach called compassionate conservatism. This approach was compassionate because it was rooted in a timeless truth: that we ought to love our neighbors as we'd like to be loved ourselves. And it was conservative because it recognized the limits of

government. Bureaucracies can put money in people's hands, but they cannot put hope in a person's heart.

Putting hope in people's hearts is the mission of our Nation's faith-based and community groups. And today we're going to herald some of the results of the collective work of compassionate Americans. To me, it does not matter if there's a crescent on your group's wall, a rabbi on your group's board, or Christ in your group's name. If your organization puts medicine in the people's hands, food in people's mouths, or a roof over people's heads, then you're succeeding. And for the sake of our country, the Government ought to support your work.

I was reviewing my first major policy speech as a candidate for President. It seems like a long time ago, July 22, 1999. Here's what I said, I said: "In every instance where my administration sees a responsibility to help people, we will look first to faith-based organizations, charities, and community groups that have shown their ability to save and change lives. We will make a determined attack on need by promoting the compassionate acts of others."

As my—President, my first Executive order was to establish the Office of Faith-Based and Community Initiatives at the White House. And my next one led to the creation of faith-based and community offices at 11 Federal agencies. These offices were tasked with the—this new mission: to lower the legal and institutional barriers that prevented government and faith-based groups from working as partners and to ensure that the armies of compassion played a central role in our campaign to make America more promising and more just.

We've carried out this mission in two ways. First, we have helped level the playing field for faith-based groups and other charities, especially small organizations that have struggled to compete for funds in the past. We've educated religious groups about their civil rights. We've made the Federal grant application process more accessible and transparent. We've trained thousands of Federal employees to ensure that government does not discriminate against faith-based organizations. We've ensured that these groups do not have to give up their religious character to receive taxpayer money.

With these steps, we followed a principle rooted both in our Constitution and the best traditions of our Nation. Government should never fund the teaching of faith, but it should support the good works of the faithful.

Second, my administration has advanced policies that yield greater support for faith-based and community groups. In other words, it's one thing to talk it, it's another thing to act. So we worked with Congress, and we've had a lot of help in the Congress.

By the way, this wasn't an easy idea for some to swallow in the Congress, and yet we did have good help. We amended the Tax Code to provide greater incentives for charitable donations, and we established what's called the Compassion Capital Fund to help faith-based and community groups operate more efficiently and secure additional funding from the private sector. This year, we launched what's called the Pro Bono Challenge, a 3-year campaign to encourage corporate professionals like accountants and lawyers to share their time and expertise with groups such as yours.

In all these ways, the administration has upheld its promise to treat community and faith-based organizations as trusted partners. We've held your organizations to high standard and insisted on clear results. And your organizations have delivered on those results. You've helped revolutionize the way government addresses the greatest challenges facing our society. I truly believe the faith-based initiative is one of the most important initiatives of this administration.

I would like to share with you some of your record. Faith-based and community groups have revolutionized the way our government shelters the homeless. Together, we've worked to reduce the number of Americans who go to sleep each night vulnerable and exposed, unsure of where they'll sleep tomorrow. For example, the Department of Housing and Urban Development has partnered with faith-based and community groups to find homeless Americans safe places to stay. And according to the most recent data, this program has helped reduce the number of chronically ill homeless by nearly 12 percent, getting more than 20,000 Americans off the street.

Faith-based and community groups have revolutionized the way we help Americans break the chains of addiction. Through our Access to Recovery program, we provide addicts with vouchers that they can redeem at treatment centers of their choice. So far, Access to Recovery has helped approximately 200,000 addicts along the path to clean lives. And many have been inspired to call upon a higher power to help them break the chains of addiction.

One person who's turned her life around through this program is Ramie Siler. You don't know Ramie yet, but you're about to. Ramie was once lost to substance abuse and depression. Even when she tried to get clean for her daughter's high school graduation, Ramie could not break free from her addiction. And then she found a faith-based group, a group of decent citizens reaching out to people like Ramie. It was called the Next Door.

At the Next Door, Ramie met people who stood by her during the difficult times of recovery. They gave Ramie a second chance to become a productive citizen and a good mother. Today, she's reunited with her daughter Dawn. She helps other women as a Next Door case manager. And I'd like to tell you what she said. She used the words of Saint Paul: "Old things have passed away; behold, all things are becoming new."

Ramie is with us today with a Vanderbilt sophomore, her daughter Dawn. Ramie, where are you? Oh, there they are. [*Applause*] So you applaud for Ramie, but you're also applauding for those compassionate souls at the Next Door. Faith-based community is—[*applause*]—our faith community is doing a fantastic job of saving lives.

Faith-based and community groups have revolutionized the way our government helps the children of prisoners. It's hard to imagine what it's like for a child to have to enter a prison gate just to get a hug from a mom or a dad. Government can't hug these kids, but it can support caring mentors who do. Through our Mentoring Children of Prisoners program, we've joined with faith-based and community groups to match nearly 90,000 children of prisoners with adults who offer love and guidance and a positive example.

Faith and community groups have revolutionized the way our government gives prisoners across America a second chance. In the past, government frequently ignored groups like yours in its efforts to help former prisoners become productive citizens. Like, it just didn't enter people's minds that the faith-based and community groups could actually help change lives. Yet through the prisoner reentry initiative that we created in 2004, we've enlisted faith-based and community groups to help provide services like job placement and mentoring programs for thousands of former inmates. Really, what we did is help them find love.

And the work has made a huge difference. Nationwide, 44 percent of prisoners are rearrested within a year of their release. Yet among prisoners that have been helped by people, like people in this room, the number is three times lower, just 15 percent.

Faith-based and community groups have helped a lot in America, and they've helped revolutionize the way our government alleviates suffering and disease around the world. I'm about to describe some of our programs. But oftentimes, I'm asked, why?

Why do you care what happens outside of America? I believe to whom much is given, much is required. And I believe we got plenty of capacity to help people at home and abroad. And I believe it is in the moral interests of the United States to help when it comes to defeating malaria, for example.

Malaria is a disease which kills one African child every 30 seconds. And it is something we can do something about. The U.S. Government launched a 5-year, $1.2 billion initiative in 2005 to cut the number of malaria-related deaths in 15 African nations by half. With strong support from groups like yours, our malaria initiative is producing results, tangible results. In just over 2 years, it's reached more than 25 million people.

The island of Zanzibar, which is affiliated with Tanzania, the infection rate has gone from 20 percent of babies born to less than 1 percent of babies born in 16 months.

The organizations about which I'm talking today are vital to the Emergency Plan for AIDS Relief, known as PEPFAR. We got to give everything initials in Washington. [*Laughter*] We launched this program in 2003—this is a program that Ambassador Dybul runs so effectively. We launched this program in 2003. When we launched it there was about 50,000 people in sub-Sahara Africa that were receiving antiretroviral treatment for HIV/AIDS. As a result of a focused campaign, I'm pleased to announced that today we support treatment for nearly 1.7 million people. Think about that.

And one of the beautiful things about this initiative is that we're saving babies. To date, PEPFAR has allowed nearly 200,000 African babies to be born HIV-free.

These new numbers show the program is a huge success. And it would not have been a—nearly the success it's been without the partners who carry out the work, without the faith-based community that is on the frontline of saving lives, not only here at home but in places like Africa.

You know, it's been amazing to watch this experience. People who report back to Mark and myself talk about what's called the Lazarus effect, where communities were once given up for dead have now found new life and new hope.

I traveled to—you know, we had a fantastic trip to Africa; Laura and I went. And the outpouring of love for the American citizens is great. I mean, this—it is such an honor to represent our country and to see the hard work of the American citizens and the generosity of the American citizens paying off in the smiling faces that line the road.

When we were in Tanzania, we went to visit a clinic where a 9-year-old girl was HIV-positive, and she'd lost both her parents to AIDS. And for the last year, Catholic Relief Services had been helping the girl. And her grandmother said this: "As a Muslim, I never imagined that a Catholic group would help me like that." And she went on to say, "I'm so grateful to the American people."

The United States Senate must follow the lead of the United States House and reauthorize this vital program.

I really am grateful for those who are here and those around the country who serve in the armies of compassion. It didn't require a government law to get you to sign up. You chose to do so out of the goodness of your heart. We've made great strides in fulfilling the goal, and I am confident that the progress that you have made over the last 8 years will continue.

I'm confident because the movement is bigger than politics or any political party. This is not a political convention. This is a compassion convention. This is, "we don't care about politic" convention. We care about saving lives.

You realize that 35 Governors have faith-based offices, 19 of them Democrats, 16 of them Republicans. Seventy mayors of both parties have similar programs at the municipal level.

I'm confident that this initiative has built a powerful grassroots network. We've trained over 100,000 social entrepreneurs. Isn't that amazing? In this brief period of time, 100,000 people have been trained. Last year, we provided more than 19,000 competitive grants to community and faith-based organizations. Why? Because we want to change America for the better. We want people to be able to be empowered to do their work of love and compassion and bringing dignity to every human life. We've laid the foundation for an effort that will continue transforming lives long after I've been back to Texas.

I am confident about the power of this program because the initiative has tapped into the compassionate spirit of America. Over the past 7 years, more of our fellow citizens have discovered that the pursuit of happiness leads by following the path of service. It's amazing what happens when you love somebody like you like to be loved yourself; your own soul is enriched. More citizens are understanding that by serving, you serve yourself. Americans have volunteered in record numbers. Sixty million people have volunteered in America this year, nearly a third of them through faith-based groups. It's an amazing statistic, isn't it? It really speaks to the great beauty of our country.

I'm confident because I know how easily the compassionate spirit can spread. There's an interesting story that I want to share with you about Ugandan women who help—have been helped by PEPFAR. These were good souls who worked in a mine. They crushed rocks into gravel by hand. And it is tough work, really hard work. Then they heard about Katrina, and somehow they scraped together $1,000, and they gave it to the U.S. Embassy for the storm's victim. And one woman said with pride, "We are now donors."

And I'm confident above all because I know the character of the men and women gathered in this hall. In your countless quiet acts of grace, you serve the highest ideals of our Nation. These are the ideals that preserve America as the beacon of hope, the great light of freedom.

A few years ago, I met a young guy named Elijah Anyieth. Elijah was a little boy, and his village was bombed during Sudan's civil war. He lost both his parents, and he spent years wandering from one refugee camp to another. Eventually, he resettled in Virginia, thanks to a partnership between a faith-based group and the State Department.

Once Elijah arrived, a local Catholic charity found him a place to call home. He came to a foreign soil after wandering in refugee camps, and he found some love. He enrolled in high school. Just last month, he graduated from college. He's landed his dream job. The boy who grew up without electricity or running water is now a mechanical engineer. Elijah, where are you? There he is, right there. [*Applause*] You applaud for a good man named Elijah, but also for those kind souls who share in the great story of this good man.

It's only in a place like America—think about it; think about our country for a second—could a life nearly extinguished by hate be restored by love and compassion.

So I've been proud to stand by you as you have worked these miracles across our country. You probably don't even realize some of the acts of kindness are miracles. I'm telling you, they are. And you can find it in the hopeful expressions on the people you've helped. And so I thank you for your efforts. I thank you for your life-changing work. And I thank you for your record of compassion that I'm confident you will build on in the years to come.

May God bless you, and may God continue to bless our country. Thank you all.

NOTE: The President spoke at 12:59 p.m. at the Omni Shoreham Hotel. In his remarks, he referred to Edith Espinoza, administrative assistant, Chicano Federation of San Diego County, Inc., who introduced the President; Jay F. Hein, Director, Office of Faith-Based and Community Initiatives; and Rwanda's Ambassador to the U.S. James Kimonyo.

Remarks on Congressional Action on the Legislative Agenda
June 26, 2008

Fourth of July is fast approaching, and Democratic leaders in Congress have scheduled another recess. Americans are concerned that Congress may leave town with a lot of important business that hasn't been completed.

Before they leave, the Congress needs to pass an emergency war funding bill so that our troops on the frontlines have the tools they need to protect themselves and us. The House passed a good bill, and now the Senate needs to act.

Before they leave, Congress needs to give our intelligence professionals the tools they need to act quickly and effectively to monitor foreign terrorist communications so

we can stop any new attack. The House passed a good—very good bipartisan bill, and the Senate needs to act.

Before they leave, the Senate needs to make progress on the enormous backlog of nominations that they've held up. Many of these nominations are for vital positions affecting our courts, our economy, our public safety, and our national security. Every day that these nominees are delayed makes it harder for the Government to meet its responsibilities, and the Senate needs to act right away.

Now, when they come back—when they get off their recess, the Democratic Congress needs to act on critical issues that they've failed to address. One such issue is housing legislation. The Congress needs to come together and pass responsible housing legislation to help more Americans keep their homes.

Another area of concern for the American citizens is the price of gasoline. And one way to relieve the price of gasoline is to expand domestic production of crude oil here at home. The Congress failed to act on this measure, and they got to when they come back.

And finally, the Congress needs to act when it comes to the Colombia free trade agreement. This is a good deal for our economy. It will help our economy grow, and it's strong—to support our friend and ally in the neighborhood, Colombia.

I'm—I asked the Democratic leaders to make the last 2 days before their recess productive. I will, of course, wish the Members—to have a great Fourth of July week. And I'm looking forward to working with them to address critical issues facing our Nation when they return.

Thank you.

NOTE: The President spoke at 1:45 p.m. in the Diplomatic Reception Room at the White House.

Statement on the United States Supreme Court Ruling on Individual Gun Rights
June 26, 2008

As a longstanding advocate of the rights of gun owners in America, I applaud the Supreme Court's historic decision today confirming what has always been clear in the Constitution: The Second Amendment protects an individual right to keep and bear firearms.

I also agree with the Supreme Court's conclusion that the DC firearm laws violate this fundamental constitutional right. The District of Columbia should now swiftly move to ensure that its residents' rights under the Second Amendment are fully protected.

The President's Radio Address
June 28, 2008

Good morning. This week, the White House Office of Faith-Based and Community Initiatives held a conference to highlight the work being done by our Nation's armies of compassion, with help from the Federal Government. This conference demonstrated the remarkable difference these groups have made over the past 8 years.

When I first came to office, I was troubled to see many of our citizens' greatest needs going unmet: Too many addicts walked the rough road to recovery alone, too many prisoners had the desire for reform, but no one to show them the way. Across our country, the hungry, homeless, and sick begged for deliverance, and too many heard only silence in reply.

The tragedy was that there were good men and women across America who had the desire to help but not the resources. Because many of them worked with small charities, they were overlooked by Washington as potential partners in service. And because many of them belonged to faith-based organizations, they were often barred from receiving support from the Federal Government.

So I set about to change this with a new approach called compassionate conservatism. This approach was compassionate, because it was rooted in a timeless truth: that we ought to love our neighbors as we'd like to be loved ourselves. And this approach was conservative, because it recognized the limits of government: that bureaucracies can put money in people's hands, but they cannot put hope in people's hearts.

Putting hope in people's hearts is the mission of our Nation's faith-based and community groups, so my administration decided to treat them as trusted partners. We held these groups to high standards and insisted on demonstrable results. And they have delivered on those expectations.

Through their partnerships with the Government, these organizations have helped reduce the number of chronically homeless by nearly 12 percent, getting more than 20,000 Americans off the streets. They have helped match nearly 90,000 children of prisoners with adult mentors. And they have helped provide services such as job placement for thousands of former inmates.

Faith-based and community groups have also had a powerful impact overseas. In Africa, they have participated in our malaria initiative. In just over 2 years, this effort has reached more than 25 million people. And according to new data, malaria rates are dropping dramatically in many parts of that continent.

These groups have also been a vital part of the Emergency Plan for AIDS Relief. When we launched this program in 2003, about 50,000 people in sub-Sahara Africa were receiving antiretroviral treatment for HIV/AIDS. Today, that number is nearly 1.7 million.

Behind each of these statistics, there are stories of people whose lives have been changed by the kindness of faith-based and community organizations. One such person is Ramie Siler.

Ramie was once lost to substance abuse, recidivism, and depression. Even when she tried to get clean for her daughter's high school graduation, Ramie couldn't break free from her addiction. Then she found a faith-based group called the Next Door. At the Next Door, Ramie met people who stood by her throughout her difficult recovery. They gave her a second chance to become a productive citizen and good mother.

Today, Ramie is reunited with her daughter. She now helps other women as the Next Door case manager. When Ramie describes her turnaround, she uses the words of Saint Paul: "Old things have passed away; behold, all things are becoming new."

I'm grateful to every American who works to create this spirit of hope. Because of you, our Nation has made great strides toward fulfilling the noble goals that gave rise to the Faith-Based and Community Initiative. And because of you, I'm confident that the progress we have made over the past 8 years will continue. Because of you, countless souls have been touched and lives have been healed.

Thank you for listening.

NOTE: The address was recorded at 7:50 a.m. on June 27 at Camp David, MD, for broadcast at 10:06 a.m. on June 28. The transcript was made available by the Office of the Press Secretary on June 27, but was embargoed for release until the broadcast. The Office of the Press Secretary also released a Spanish language transcript of this address.

Statement on the Situation in Zimbabwe
June 28, 2008

On Friday, the Mugabe regime held a sham election that ignored the will of the people of Zimbabwe. The international community has condemned the Mugabe regime's ruthless campaign of politically motivated violence and intimidation with a strong and unified voice that makes clear that yesterday's election was in no way free and fair. Any legitimate Government of Zimbabwe must represent the interests of all its citizens and the outcome of the March 29 elections.

Given the Mugabe regime's blatant disregard for the Zimbabwean people's democratic will and human rights, I am instructing the Secretaries of State and Treasury to develop sanctions against this illegitimate Government of Zimbabwe and those who support it. We will press for strong action by the United Nations, including an arms embargo on Zimbabwe and travel ban on regime officials. We will continue to work closely with the African Union, Southern African Development Community, and other world leaders to resolve this crisis.

The United States stands ready to support a legitimate government through a robust package of development assistance, debt relief, and normalization with international financial institutions. In the meantime, we will continue to support the people of Zimbabwe by providing food assistance to more than 1 million people and AIDS treatment to more than 40,000 people.

NOTE: The statement referred to President Robert Mugabe of Zimbabwe.

Remarks on Signing the Supplemental Appropriations Act, 2008
June 30, 2008

Good morning. A few moments ago, I signed legislation that funds our troops who are in harm's way. Our Nation has no greater responsibility than supporting our men and women in uniform, especially since we're at war. This is a responsibility all of us in Washington share, not as Republicans or Democrats, but as Americans. And I want to thank leaders of the House and Senate for getting this bill to my office.

America remains a nation at war. There are enemies who intend to harm us. Standing in their way are brave men and women who put on the uniform, who raised their right hand and took an oath to defend our freedom. They volunteered to deploy in distant lands, far from their families, far from their homes, and far from comfort of America. And every day, they risk their lives to defeat our adversaries and to keep our country safe.

We owe these brave Americans our gratitude; we owe them our unflinching support. And the best way to demonstrate that support is to give them the resources they need to do their jobs and to prevail. The bill I signed today does exactly that. It provides necessary funds to support our troops as they conduct military operations in Iraq, in Afghanistan, and in other theaters in the war on terror.

I appreciate that Republicans and Democrats in Congress agreed to provide these vital funds without tying the hands of our commanders and without an artificial timetable of withdrawal from Iraq. Our troops have driven the terrorists and extremists from many strongholds in Iraq. Today, violence is at the lowest level since March of 2004. As a result of this progress—some of our troops are coming home as result of our policy of—called return on success. We welcome them home. And with this legislation we send a clear message to all that are serving on the frontline that our Nation continues to support them.

We also owe a debt of gratitude to our Nation's military families. They endure sleepless nights and the daily struggle of caring for children while a loved one is serving far from home. We have a responsibility to provide for them. So I'm pleased that the bill I sign today includes an expansion of the GI bill. This legislation will make it easier for our troops to transfer unused education benefits to their spouses and children. It will help us to recruit and reward the best military on the face of the Earth. It will help us to meet our responsibilities to those who support our troops every day, America's great military families.

The bill also includes agreed-upon funding for other critical national priorities. This bill includes $465 million for the Merida Initiative, a partnership with Mexico and nations in Central America to crack down on violent drug-trafficking gangs. The bill includes nearly $2.7 billion to help ensure that any State facing a disaster, like the recent flooding and tornadoes in the Midwest, has access to needed resources. This bill includes a measured expansion of un-employment insurance benefits with a reasonable work requirement. And this bill holds overall discretionary spending within the sensible limits that I requested.

The bill is a result of close collaboration between my administration and members of both parties on Capitol Hill. I appreciate the hard work of my Cabinet, especially the leaders of Defense and State and Veterans Affairs, the Office of National Drug Control Policy, as well as OMB. I want to thank House and Senate leadership and leaders of the House and Senate Appropriations Committees. I am particularly grateful to Congressmen Boehner, Hoyer, Obey, and Lewis. And I want to thank Members who worked hard for the GI bill expansion, especially Senators Webb and Warner, Graham, Burr, and McCain.

This bill shows the American people that even in an election year, Republicans and Democrats can come together to stand behind our troops and their families.

Thank you for coming.

NOTE: The President spoke at 9:48 a.m. in the Oval Office at the White House. In his remarks, he referred to Secretary of Veterans Affairs James B. Peake; and James A. Nussle, Director, Office of Management and Budget. H.R. 2642, approved June 30, was assigned Public Law No. 110–252. The Office of the Press Secretary also released a Spanish language transcript of these remarks.

Remarks at Opening Day of 2008 White House Tee-Ball
June 30, 2008

The President. Menudo, thank you. Yes, we're glad you're here. Opening day 2008, tee-ball on the South Lawn. I'm proud to be joined by the commissioner for the day, Roberto Clemente, Jr. *Bienvenido.*

Roberto Clemente, Jr. Gracias, gracias.

The President. Si. Roberto, I don't know if you know this or not, but we've got a special right field porch this year. This is an addition—we might just call that Clemente porch. After all, we did retire your dad's number this year.

Mr. Clemente. Thank you.

The President. I'm so proud to welcome, from Manati, Puerto Rico, the Little Angels. We're glad you're here; and from Camden, New Jersey, the mighty Red Sox; first base coach, Jose Rijo—he could deliver that fast ball in the best of times—now with the Washington Nationals. Third base coach, Carlos Gutierrez, Secretary of Commerce; Carlos, glad you're here. Congressman Rob Andrews—Congressman, thanks for coming. We're sure proud you're here.

Today we're very lucky to have our game called by Natalie Morales.

Natalie Morales. Thank you.

The President. Natalie, *bienvenidos.* Thank you for coming.

Ms. Morales. Gracias.

The President. Natalie happens to work for NBC's "Today" show. We really appreciate you coming.

Ms. Morales. That's right. Thank you, sir, for having me.

The President. No problem.

Boy Scout Troop 457 from Rockville, Maryland, is with us today. Thanks for coming. Steve Keener, president of Little League America, we're glad you're here, Steve. Thanks for coming back. Appreciate you supporting baseball throughout America.

Laura and I are thrilled also to be joined today by our first pitch kind of semi-thrower-outers. [*Laughter*] Angel Macias is with us. For those of you who follow Little League baseball, you might remember, in 1957, *es verdad*?

Angel Macias. Right.

The President. Si. He threw a perfect game for Monterrey, Mexico, in the Little League World Series, and Mexico went on to win the world series. And we're so glad you're here. Welcome to the White House.

And standing with you is Jake T. Austin, who happens—who's going to be playing Angel in the movie——

Jake T. Austin. Yes, I play Angel Macias in the movie.

The President. And what's the movie?

Mr. Austin. The movie is called "The Perfect Game," and it's coming out in 2008, this year.

The President. ——2008, yes. You probably recommend we all go see it.

Mr. Austin. We'd greatly appreciate it. [*Laughter*]

The President. Yes. Well, Laura was suggesting, Jake T., that we actually have a showing here at the White House.

Mr. Austin. Great.

The President. Yes, see, he's for that.

Before we get started, I do want the players to join me in the Little League Pledge. Are you ready?

[*At this point, the pledge was recited.*]

Play ball!

NOTE: The President spoke at 3:23 p.m. on the South Lawn at the White House. In his remarks, he referred to entertainers Menudo, who sang the national anthem; sports broadcaster Roberto Clemente, Jr.; and Jose Rijo, special assistant to the general manager, Washington Nationals. The Office of the Press Secretary also released a Spanish language transcript of these remarks.

Letter to Congressional Leaders on Extending and Terminating Generalized System of Preferences Benefits
June 30, 2008

Dear Madam Speaker: *(Dear Mr. President:)*

In accordance with section 502(f) of the Trade Act of 1974, as amended (the "1974 Act"), I am notifying the Congress of my intent to (a) designate the Republic of Serbia (Serbia) and the Republic of Montenegro (Montenegro) as separate beneficiary developing countries under the Generalized System of Preferences (GSP); and (b) terminate the designation of Trinidad and Tobago as a beneficiary developing country under the GSP.

In Proclamation 7912 of June 29, 2005, I designated Serbia and Montenegro as a beneficiary developing country for purposes of the GSP. On June 3, 2006, Montenegro declared independence from Serbia and Montenegro and the country separated into two independent republics, the Republic of Serbia and the Republic of Montenegro. Pursuant to section 502 of the 1974 Act, and having considered the factors set forth in sections 501 and 502(c), I have determined that, in light of the separation of Serbia and Montenegro into two countries, the Republic of Serbia and the Republic of Montenegro should each be designated as beneficiary developing countries for purposes of the GSP.

Section 502(e) of the 1974 Act, provides that the President shall terminate the designation of a country as a beneficiary developing country for purposes of the GSP if the President determines that such country has become a "high income" country as defined by the official statistics of the International Bank for Reconstruction and Development. Termination is effective on January 1 of the second year following the year in which such determination is made. I have determined that Trinidad and Tobago has become a "high income" country, and I am terminating the designation of that country as a beneficiary developing country for purposes of the GSP, effective January 1, 2010.

Sincerely,

GEORGE W. BUSH

NOTE: Identical letters were sent to Nancy Pelosi, Speaker of the House of Representatives, and Richard B. Cheney, President of the Senate.

Letter to Congressional Leaders Reporting on the Issuance of Temporary Munitions Export Licenses for Exports to China
June 30, 2008

Dear Madam Speaker: *(Dear Mr. President:)*

Pursuant to the authority vested in me by section 902(b)(2) of the Foreign Relations Authorization Act, FY 1990 and 1991 (Public Law 101–246) (the "Act"), and as President of the United States, I hereby report to the Congress that it is in the national interest of the United States to terminate temporarily the suspensions under section 902(a)(3) of the Act with respect to the issuance of temporary munitions export licenses for exports to the People's Republic of China insofar as these restrictions pertain to firearms and related items for use by U.S. and non-U.S. athletes competing in shooting events, and military gyroscopes that are embedded in mobile high definition television camera systems for use by U.S. filming crews, at the Beijing Olympics. Licensing requirements remain in place for these exports and require review and approval on a case-by-case basis by the United States Government. The equipment will be returned to the United States following the end of the games.

Sincerely,

GEORGE W. BUSH

NOTE: Identical letters were sent to Nancy Pelosi, Speaker of the House of Representatives, and Richard B. Cheney, President of the Senate.

Appendix A—Digest of Other White House Announcements

The following list includes the President's public schedule and other items of general interest announced by the Office of the Press Secretary and not included elsewhere in this book.

January 1

In the morning, at the Bush Ranch in Crawford, TX, the President had an intelligence briefing. Later, he and Mrs. Bush returned to Washington, DC, arriving in the afternoon.

January 2

In the morning, the President had an intelligence briefing. Later, he had a video teleconference with President Hamid Karzai of Afghanistan. He then met with Secretary of State Condoleezza Rice.

The President announced his intention to nominate Jan Cellucci, William J. Hagenah, and Mark Y. Herring to be members of the National Museum and Library Services Board.

The President announced that he has nominated the following individuals to be members of the National Council on the Humanities:

Jamsheed K. Choksy;
Dawn Ho Delbanco;
Gary D. Glenn;
David Hertz;
Marvin Bailey Scott; and
Carol M. Swain.

January 3

In the morning, the President had an intelligence briefing. Later, he participated in an interview with Bret Baier of FOX News. Then, in the Oval Office, he participated in a roundtable interview with reporters from Reuters.

In the afternoon, the President participated in another interview with Bret Baier of FOX News.

The President announced his intention to designate Jeffrey L. Sedgwick as Acting Assistant Attorney General (Office of Justice Programs).

January 4

In the morning, the President had an intelligence briefing. Later, he had a telephone conversation with King Abdullah II of Jordan.

The President announced his intention to nominate Julia W. Bland to be a member of the National Museum and Library Services Board.

The President announced his intention to designate Richard Stickler as Acting Assistant Secretary of Labor for Mine Safety and Health.

The President announced that he has named Janet Weir Creighton as Deputy Assistant to the President and Director of Intergovernmental Affairs.

The President announced that he has named Christopher Frech as Deputy Assistant to the President for Legislative Affairs.

The President announced that he has named Daniel McCardell as Special Assistant to the President and Deputy Director of Public Liaison.

The President announced that he has named Emory Rounds as Associate Counsel to the President.

The President declared a major disaster in Iowa and ordered Federal aid to supplement State and local recovery efforts in the area struck by a severe winter storm on December 10 and 11.

January 5

In the morning, the President had an intelligence briefing.

January 7

In the morning, the President had an intelligence briefing. Later, he traveled to Chicago, IL, where he visited Horace Greeley Elementary School. Then, at the Union League Club of Chicago, he had lunch with business and community leaders.

In the afternoon, the President returned to Washington, DC.

January 8

In the morning, the President had an intelligence briefing.

In the afternoon, in the Old Family Dining Room, the President had lunch with President Abdullah Gul of Turkey.

In the evening, the President traveled to Tel Aviv, Israel, arriving the following morning.

The President declared a major disaster in Nevada and ordered Federal aid to supplement State and local recovery efforts in the area struck by severe winter storms and flooding beginning on January 5 and continuing.

January 9

In the morning, aboard Air Force One, the President had an intelligence briefing.

In the afternoon, the President traveled to the King David Hotel in Jerusalem, Israel. Later, he traveled to the President's residence, where he and President Shimon Peres of Israel attended cultural performances. He then traveled to the Prime Minister's residence, where he met with Prime Minister Ehud Olmert, Deputy Prime Minister and Minister of Foreign Affairs Tzipora "Tzipi" Livni, and Minister of Defense Ehud Barak of Israel.

In the evening, the President returned to the King David Hotel.

January 10

In the morning, the President had an intelligence briefing. Later, he met with Opposition Leader Benjamin Netanyahu of Israel. He then met with the family of former Prime Minister Ariel Sharon of Israel.

Later in the morning, the President traveled to Ramallah, Palestinian Territories, where, at the Muqata, he participated in a greeting with President Mahmoud Abbas of the Palestinian Authority. Then, in the President's small conference room of the Muqata, he met with Prime Minister Salam Fayyad of the Palestinian Authority.

In the afternoon, in the President's dining room of the Muqata, the President had a working lunch with President Abbas. Later, he met with former Prime Minister Tony Blair of the United Kingdom, Quartet Representative in the Middle East. He then traveled to Bethlehem, Palestinian Territories, where he visited the Church of St. Catherine of Alexandria at the Basilica of the Nativity.

Later in the afternoon, the President returned to the King David Hotel in Jerusalem, Israel, where he met with U.S. Embassy staff and their families.

In the evening, the President traveled to the Prime Minister's residence, where, in the Dining Room, he had a working dinner with Prime Minister Ehud Olmert of Israel. Later, he returned to the King David Hotel.

The President announced the designation of the following individuals as members of the Presidential delegation to Guatemala City, Guatemala, to attend the inauguration of Alvaro Colom Caballeros as President of Guatemala on January 14:

Michael O. Leavitt (head of delegation);
James M. Derham;
Robert A. Mosbacher, Jr.;
Sara Martinez Tucker; and
Christopher A. Padilla.

The President announced his intention to nominate William J. Brennan to be Assistant Secretary of Commerce for Oceans and Atmosphere.

The President announced his intention to nominate J. Gregory Copeland to be General Counsel of the Department of Energy.

The President announced his intention to nominate Dorla M. Salling to be a member of the U.S. Parole Commission.

The President announced his intention to nominate Kurt D. Volker to be U.S. Permanent Representative on the Council of the North Atlantic Treaty Organization, with the rank and status of Ambassador.

January 11

In the morning, the President had an intelligence briefing. Later, he met with former Prime Minister Tony Blair of the United Kingdom, Quartet Representative in the Middle East. He then visited the Yad Vashem, the Holocaust Martyrs' and Heroes' Remembrance Authority, where he rekindled the Eternal Flame and participated in a wreath-laying ceremony.

Later in the morning, the President traveled to Galilee, Israel, where he toured the Capernaum archaeological ruins. He then visited the Mount of the Beatitudes Chapel.

In the afternoon, the President traveled to Tel Aviv, Israel. He then traveled to Kuwait City, Kuwait, where, upon arrival at the Kuwait

International Airport, he participated in an arrival ceremony with Amir Sabah al-Ahmad al-Jabir al-Sabah of Kuwait. Later, he traveled to the Bayan Palace Guest House.

In the evening, the President traveled to Dar Salwa Palace, where he participated in a greeting with Amir Sabah. Then, in the dining room, he had dinner with Amir Sabah. Later, he returned to the Bayan Palace Guest House.

The President declared a major disaster in Nebraska and ordered Federal aid to supplement State and local recovery efforts in the area struck by a severe winter storm from December 10 to 12.

January 12

In the morning, the President had an intelligence briefing. He then traveled to Camp Arifjan, Kuwait, where, in a briefing room, he met with Gen. David H. Petraeus, USA, commanding general, Multi-National Force—Iraq, and U.S. Ambassador to Iraq Ryan C. Crocker. Later, he toured the Operations Center.

Later in the morning, the President traveled to the U.S. Embassy in Kuwait City, Kuwait.

In the afternoon, the President met with U.S. Embassy staff and their families. Later, he traveled to Kuwait International Airport, where, upon arrival, he participated in a greeting with Amir Sabah al-Ahmad al-Jabir al-Sabah of Kuwait. He then traveled to Manama, Bahrain, where, upon arrival at Bahrain International Airport, he participated in a greeting with King Hamad bin Isa al-Khalifa of Bahrain.

Later in the afternoon, the President traveled to Sakhir Palace. Later, he traveled to the Ritz-Carlton, Bahrain Hotel & Spa, where, in the Al Noor Ballroom, he met with U.S. Embassy staff and their families.

In the evening, the President had a telephone conversation with King Abdullah II of Jordan to discuss his Middle East trip. Later, he met and had dinner with King Hamad.

January 13

In the morning, the President traveled to Naval Support Activity Bahrain, where, in the multipurpose room, he had breakfast with U.S. military personnel. Later, he traveled to Abu Dhabi, United Arab Emirates, where, at Abu Dhabi International Airport, he participated in a greeting with President Khalifa bin Zayid Al Nuhayyan of the United Arab Emirates.

Later in the morning, the President traveled to Al Mushref Palace, where he participated in an arrival ceremony with President Khalifa.

In the afternoon, in the Al Etihad Majlis of Al Mushref Palace, the President met with President Khalifa. Then, in the dining room, they had lunch. Later, he traveled to the Emirates Palace Hotel.

Later in the afternoon, the President traveled to the Desert Encampment Falcon Farm, where he had dinner with Crown Prince Muhammad bin Zayid Al Nuhayyan of Abu Dhabi.

In the evening, the President returned to the Emirates Palace Hotel.

January 14

In the morning, the President had an intelligence briefing. He then participated in an interview with Greta Van Susteren of FOX News. Later, in the ballroom of the Emirates Palace Hotel, he met with U.S. Embassy staff and their families.

Later in the morning, the President traveled to Dubai, United Arab Emirates, where, upon arrival at Dubai International Airport, he participated in a greeting with Vice President and Prime Minister Muhammad bin Rashid Al Maktum of the United Arab Emirates. He then toured the Sheikh Saeed Al Maktoum House.

In the afternoon, the President traveled to the Sheikh Mohammed Centre for Cultural Understanding, where he had lunch with Dubai School of Government students. He then traveled to the Burj Al Arab Hotel. Later, he returned to Dubai International Airport, where, in the Royal Air Wing, he met with U.S. Embassy staff and their families.

Later in the afternoon, the President traveled to Riyadh, Saudi Arabia. While en route aboard Air Force One, he had a telephone conversation with President-elect Mikheil Saakashvili of Georgia to congratulate him on his election victory. Upon arrival at King Khaled International Airport, he participated in an arrival ceremony with King Abdallah bin Abd al-Aziz Al Saud of Saudi Arabia.

Later in the afternoon, the President traveled to Nasiriyah Guest Palace.

In the evening, the President traveled to Riyadh Palace, where he had dinner and met with King Abdallah. Later, he returned to Nasiriyah Guest Palace.

January 15

In the morning, the President had an intelligence briefing. Later, he traveled to the U.S. Embassy Riyadh, where, in the lobby, he met with Embassy staff and their families. He then visited Al Murabba Palace and National History Museum.

Later in the morning, the President returned to Nasiriyah Guest Palace.

In the afternoon, the President traveled to the Al Janadriyah Farm in Al Janadriyah, Saudi Arabia. Upon arrival, he participated in a photo opportunity with King Abdallah bin Abd al-Aziz Al Saud of Saudi Arabia. They then toured the farm.

In the evening, the President had dinner and met with King Abdallah.

January 16

In the morning, the President had an intelligence briefing. Later, he had breakfast with King Abdallah bin Abd al-Aziz Al Saud of Saudi Arabia. He then returned to Riyadh, Saudi Arabia.

Later in the morning, the President traveled to the Four Seasons Resort in Sharm el-Sheikh, Egypt.

In the afternoon, the President had lunch with President Mohamed Hosni Mubarak of Egypt. Later, he traveled to Sharm el-Sheikh International Airport, where he participated in a greeting with President Mubarak. He then returned to Washington, DC, arriving in the evening.

January 17

In the morning, the President had an intelligence briefing.

In the afternoon, the President and Secretary of the Treasury Henry M. Paulson, Jr., had a conference call with congressional leaders. Later, in the East Room, he met with Republican National Committee members.

The President announced his intention to nominate Nelson M. Ford to be Under Secretary of the Army.

The President announced his intention to nominate Joxel Garcia to be Medical Director in the Regular Corps of the Public Health Service and Assistant Secretary of Health and Human Services (Health).

The President announced his intention to nominate Jeffrey J. Grieco to be Assistant Administrator of the U.S. Agency for International Development (Legislative and Public Affairs).

The President announced his intention to nominate the following individuals to be members of the Board of Directors of the National Board of Education Sciences:

Jonathan Baron;
Frank Philip Handy;
Sally Epstein Shaywitz; and
Joanne Weiss.

The President announced his intention to appoint H.H. Barlow III, William B. DeLauder, and Keith W. Eckel as members of the Board for International Food and Agricultural Development.

The President announced his intention to appoint Robert A. Easter as Chairman of the Board for International Food and Agricultural Development.

The President announced his intention to appoint John M. Townsend as a member of the Panel of Arbitrators of the International Centre for Settlement of Investment Disputes.

January 18

In the morning, the President had an intelligence briefing.

In the afternoon, the President traveled to Frederick, MD. Later, he returned to Washington, DC.

During the day, in the Roosevelt Room, the President met with former Secretary of State Henry A. Kissinger, former Prime Minister Yevgeniy M. Primakov of Russia, and senior American and Russian statesmen and policy experts to discuss Russia-U.S. relations.

The President announced the designation of the following individuals as members of the Presidential delegation to Tbilisi, Georgia, to attend the inauguration of Mikheil Saakashvili as President of Georgia on January 20: Carlos M. Gutierrez (head of delegation); and John F. Tefft.

The President announced the designation of the following individuals as members of the Presidential delegation to Auckland, New Zealand, to attend the state funeral of Sir Edmund Hillary on January 22: Mary A. Bomar (head of delegation); William P. McCormick; and Jim Whittaker.

January 19

In the morning, the President had an intelligence briefing.

January 21

In the morning, the President had an intelligence briefing.

In the afternoon, the President had a telephone briefing with Secretary of the Treasury Henry M. Paulson, Jr., on the global financial markets situation.

January 22

In the morning, the President had an intelligence briefing. Later, he met with his economic advisers.

The President announced his intention to nominate Margaret Scobey to be Ambassador to Egypt.

The President announced his intention to nominate D. Kathleen Stephens to be Ambassador to South Korea.

The President announced his intention to appoint Nancy Hellman Bechtle, J. Michael Shepherd, and William Wilson III as members of the Board of Directors of the Presidio Trust.

The President announced that he has appointed Charles R. Schwab as a member of the President's Advisory Council on Financial Literacy and, upon appointment, designated him as Chair.

The President announced that he has appointed John Bryant as a member of the President's Advisory Council on Financial Literacy and, upon appointment, designated him as Vice Chair.

The President announced that he has appointed the following individuals as members of the President's Advisory Council on Financial Literacy:

Theodore Beck;
Theodore R. Daniels;
Cutler Dawson;
Robert F. Duvall;
Tahira K. Hira;
Jack E. Kosakowski;
Sharon L. Lechter;
Robert V. Lee III;
Laura Levine;
David D. Mancl;
Don J. McGrath;
Janet Parker;
Ignacio Salazar; and

Mary L. Schapiro.

January 23

In the morning, the President had an intelligence briefing.

In the afternoon, the President participated in an interview with Jimmy Roberts of NBC Sports for a U.S. Golf Association documentary. Later, in the Yellow Oval Room, he and Mrs. Bush hosted a social reception for Senate Republicans and their spouses.

January 24

In the morning, the President had an intelligence briefing. Later, he had a telephone conversation with King Abdullah II of Jordan.

In the afternoon, the President participated in an interview with Susan Page and Richard Wolf of USA Today.

The President announced that he has named Jonathan Horn as Special Assistant to the President for Speechwriting.

The President announced that he has named Jeffrey Lungren as Special Assistant to the President for Legislative Affairs.

The President announced that he has named Justin J. McCarthy as Special Assistant to the President for Legislative Affairs.

The President announced that he has named Richard Reed as Special Assistant to the President for Homeland Security and Senior Director for Continuity Policy.

The President announced that he has accorded the personal rank of Ambassador to Lincoln P. Bloomfield, Jr., during his tenure and service as Special Envoy for Man-Portable Air Defense Systems.

January 25

In the morning, the President had an intelligence briefing. Later, he traveled to White Sulphur Springs, WV.

In the afternoon, the President returned to Washington, DC. Later, he participated in a speech preparation session for his January 28 State of the Union Address.

The White House announced that the President and Mrs. Bush will travel to Africa and visit Benin, Tanzania, Rwanda, Ghana, and Liberia from February 15 to 21.

The President announced his intention to nominate Robert J. Battista to be a member of the National Labor Relations Board and, upon confirmation, to designate him as Chair.

901

The President announced his intention to nominate Gerard Morales and Dennis P. Walsh to be members of the National Labor Relations Board.

The President announced his intention to appoint Charles P. Garcia and Susan Ross as members of the Board of Visitors to the U.S. Air Force Academy.

The President announced his intention to designate Elisebeth C. Cook as Acting Assistant Attorney General (Legal Policy).

January 26

In the morning, the President had an intelligence briefing.

In the evening, at the Capital Hilton Hotel, the President and Mrs. Bush attended the Alfalfa Club dinner.

January 27

In the afternoon, the President participated in a speech preparation session for his January 28 State of the Union Address.

January 28

In the morning, the President had an intelligence briefing. Later, in the Family Theater, he participated in a speech preparation session for his State of the Union Address. Then, in the Oval Office, he participated in an interview with Ann Compton of ABC News Radio.

In the afternoon, in the Second Floor Family Dining Room, the President had a background lunch with television correspondents.

The White House announced that the President will welcome Prime Minister Mirek Topolanek of the Czech Republic to the White House on February 27.

January 29

In the morning, the President had an intelligence briefing. Later, he traveled to Baltimore, MD, where he met with Jericho Program graduates.

In the afternoon, the President returned to Washington, DC.

The President announced his intention to nominate Robert J. Callahan to be Ambassador to Nicaragua.

The President announced his intention to nominate Heather M. Hodges to be Ambassador to Ecuador.

The President announced his intention to nominate Barbara J. Stephenson to be Ambassador to Panama.

The President announced his intention to nominate William E. Todd to be Ambassador to Brunei.

January 30

In the morning, the President had an intelligence briefing. Later, he traveled to Torrance, CA.

In the afternoon, the President traveled to Los Angeles, CA, where, upon arrival, he met with USA Freedom Corps volunteers Marni and Berni Barta. Later, at a private residence, he attended a Republican National Committee luncheon.

Later in the afternoon, the President traveled to San Francisco, CA, where, upon arrival at San Francisco International Airport, he met with USA Freedom Corps volunteer Richard Berwick. He then met with Amador Valley High School student Kevin Laue and his parents, Jodi and Jim Jarnagin. Later, he traveled to Hillsborough, CA, where, at a private residence, he attended a Republican National Committee dinner.

During the day, the President had a telephone conversation with Prime Minister Stephen Harper of Canada to discuss the situation in Afghanistan.

In the evening, the President returned to San Francisco International Airport, where he met with the family of a marine killed in Iraq. He then traveled to Las Vegas, NV.

The President announced that he has asked Secretary of Health and Human Services Michael O. Leavitt to serve as his personal representative at the funeral of Gordon B. Hinckley on February 2, 2008, in Salt Lake City, UT.

The President announced his intention to nominate Marianne M. Myles to be Ambassador to Cape Verde.

The President announced that he has nominated Elisebeth C. Cook to be Assistant Attorney General (Legal Policy).

The President declared a major disaster in Indiana and ordered Federal aid to supplement State and local recovery efforts in the area struck by severe storms and flooding beginning on January 7 and continuing.

January 31

In the morning, the President had an intelligence briefing. Later, at a private residence, he attended a Nevada Victory luncheon.

In the afternoon, the President traveled to Denver, CO, where, upon arrival, he met with USA Freedom Corps volunteer Cherie Yager. He then met with Jeanne Assam, a security guard who stopped the December 9, 2007, fatal shooting at New Life Church in Colorado Springs, CO. Later, he traveled to Cherry Hills Village, CO, where, at a private residence, he attended a Colorado Victory and Bob Schaffer for Senate reception.

In the evening, the President traveled to Kansas City, MO, where, upon arrival, he met with USA Freedom Corps volunteer Samuel Turner, Sr.

The White House announced that the President will host the North American Leaders' Summit on April 21 and 22 in New Orleans, LA.

February 1

In the morning, the President had an intelligence briefing. Then, at eggtc. restaurant, he had breakfast with local business leaders. Later, he traveled to Parkville, MO.

In the afternoon, at a private residence, the President attended a Missouri Victory and Sam Graves for Congress reception. Later, he traveled to Camp David, MD.

The White House announced that the President will welcome President Amadou Toumani Toure of Mali to the White House on February 8.

The President declared a major disaster in Kansas and ordered Federal aid to supplement State and local recovery efforts in the area struck by severe winter storms from December 6 to 19.

February 2

In the morning, the President had an intelligence briefing.

February 3

In the afternoon, the President and Mrs. Bush returned to Washington, DC.

February 4

In the morning, the President had an intelligence briefing. Later, he had a telephone conversation with Prime Minister-elect Samak

Sundaravej of Thailand to congratulate him on his appointment. He then had separate telephone conversations with New York Giants president and chief executive officer John K. Mara, chairman and executive vice president Steve Tisch, head coach Tom Coughlin, and quarterback Eli Manning to congratulate them on their February 3 Super Bowl victory.

February 5

In the morning, the President had an intelligence briefing.

The President announced his intention to nominate Hugo Llorens to be Ambassador to Honduras.

The President announced his intention to designate John L. Morrison as a member of the Intelligence Oversight Board on the President's Foreign Intelligence Advisory Board.

The President declared a major disaster in Missouri and ordered Federal aid to supplement State and local recovery efforts in the area struck by severe storms, tornadoes, and flooding from January 7 to 10.

February 6

In the morning, the President had an intelligence briefing. Later, he had separate telephone conversations with Governor Robert R. Riley of Alabama, Governor Haley R. Barbour of Mississippi, Governor Michael D. Beebe of Arkansas, Governor Steven L. Beshear of Kentucky, and Governor Philip N. Bredesen, Jr., of Tennessee to discuss damage and recovery efforts in the areas struck by severe storms and tornadoes on February 5.

The White House announced that the President will host Secretary General Jakob Gijsbert "Jaap" de Hoop Scheffer of the North Atlantic Treaty Organization at the White House on February 29.

The President announced his intention to nominate Linda Thomas-Greenfield to be Ambassador to Liberia.

The President announced his intention to nominate Susan D. Peppler to be Assistant Secretary of Housing and Urban Development (Community Planning and Development).

The President announced his intention to nominate Ralph E. Martinez to be a member of the Foreign Claims Settlement Commission.

The President declared a major disaster in Hawaii and ordered Federal aid to supplement State and local recovery efforts in the area struck by severe storms, high surf, flooding, and mudslides from December 4 to 7.

February 7

In the morning, the President had an intelligence briefing.

The White House announced that due to the President's travel to Tennessee on February 8, he will now welcome President Amadou Toumani Toure of Mali to the White House on February 12.

The White House announced that the President will welcome Prime Minister Donald Tusk of Poland to the White House on March 10.

The President declared a major disaster in Arkansas and ordered Federal aid to supplement State and local recovery efforts in the area struck by severe storms, tornadoes, and flooding beginning on February 5 and continuing.

The President declared a major disaster in Tennessee and ordered Federal aid to supplement State and local recovery efforts in the area struck by severe storms, tornadoes, straight-line winds, and flooding on February 5 and 6.

February 8

In the morning, the President had an intelligence briefing. Later, he traveled to Nashville, TN, where, upon arrival, he met with Wilson County Emergency Management employee David Harmon, who rescued an 11-month-old baby after the February 5 tornadoes.

Later in the morning, the President traveled to Lafayette, TN. While en route aboard Marine One, he, Governor Philip N. Bredesen, Jr., of Tennessee, and Federal Emergency Management Agency Administrator R. David Paulison took an aerial tour of the areas damaged by the February 5 tornadoes.

In the afternoon, the President traveled to Camp David, MD.

The White House announced that the President and Mrs. Bush will host Prime Minister Anders Fogh Rasmussen of Denmark and his wife Anne-Mette Rasmussen at the Bush Ranch in Crawford, TX, on February 29 and March 1.

The White House announced that the President will welcome President Mikheil Saakashvili of Georgia to Washington on March 19.

February 9

In the morning, the President had an intelligence briefing.

February 10

In the afternoon, the President and Mrs. Bush returned to Washington, DC.

February 11

In the morning, the President had an intelligence briefing. Later, he had separate telephone conversations with Annette Lantos, wife of Representative Thomas P. Lantos, and Speaker of the House of Representatives Nancy Pelosi to express his condolences for the death of Representative Lantos. Then, in the National Security Adviser's office, he dropped by a meeting between National Security Adviser Stephen J. Hadley and Prime Minister Salam Fayyad of the Palestinian Authority.

The White House announced that the President will meet with United Nations Secretary-General Ban Ki-moon at the White House on February 15.

February 12

In the morning, the President had an intelligence briefing.

In the afternoon, at the historic Evermay House, the President attended a Republican National Committee luncheon.

During the day, in the Roosevelt Room, the President attended National Security Adviser Stephen J. Hadley's meeting with the Helping to Enhance the Livelihood of People (HELP) Around the Globe Commission.

The President announced his intention to nominate Peter E. Cianchette to be Ambassador to Costa Rica.

The President announced his intention to nominate Jeffrey R. Brown to be a member of the Board of Trustees of the Federal Old-Age and Survivors Insurance Trust Fund and Federal Disability Insurance Trust Fund as well as a member of the Board of Trustees of the Federal Hospital Insurance Trust Fund.

The President announced his intention to nominate the following individuals to be members of the National Institute for Literacy Advisory Board:

Perri Klass;
Katherine Mitchell;
Eduardo J. Padron;
Alexa E. Posny;
Timothy Shanahan; and
Richard K. Wagner.

The President announced his intention to nominate Hyepin Christine Im and Laysha Ward to be members of the Board of Directors of the Corporation for National and Community Service.

February 13

In the morning, the President had an intelligence briefing.

February 14

In the morning, the President had an intelligence briefing. Later, he had separate telephone conversations with Prime Minister Nuri al-Maliki of Iraq and Speaker Mahmud al-Mashhadani, First Deputy Speaker Khalid al-Attiya, and Second Deputy Speaker Arif Tayfur of the Iraqi House of Representatives.

In the evening, in the Blue Room, the President and Mrs. Bush hosted a Valentine's Day social dinner followed by a performance in the East Room by entertainer Denise Thimes.

The President announced his intention to nominate Stephen J. Nolan to be Ambassador to Botswana.

The President announced his intention to nominate Joseph E. LeBaron to be Ambassador to Qatar.

The President announced that he has named Christopher Michel as Deputy Assistant to the President and Deputy Director of Speechwriting.

The President announced that he has named Sara Armstrong as Special Assistant to the President.

The President announced that he has named Meghan Clyne as Special Assistant to the President for Speechwriting.

The President announced that he has named Matthew Latimer as Special Assistant to the President and Deputy Director of Speechwriting.

The President announced that he has named Mark J. Webber as Special Assistant to the President and Senior Director for South and Central Asian Affairs in the National Security Council.

February 15

In the morning, the President had an intelligence briefing. Later, he had a telephone conversation with Northern Illinois University President John G. Peters to express his condolences for the victims of the February 14 campus

shooting. Then, in the Oval Office, he met with Minister of Foreign Affairs Saud al-Faysal bin Abd al-Aziz Al Saud of Saudi Arabia.

In the afternoon, the President and Mrs. Bush traveled to Cotonou, Benin, arriving the following morning.

The White House announced that the President and Mrs. Bush will welcome His Holiness Pope Benedict XVI to the White House on April 16.

The President announced his designation of the following individuals as members of a Presidential delegation to Seoul, South Korea, to attend the inauguration of Lee Myung-bak as President of South Korea on February 25:

Condoleezza Rice (head of delegation);
Alexander R. Vershbow;
Wendy Cutler;
Gen. Burwell B. Bell III;
Andy Groseta;
William R. Rhodes; and
Hines Ward.

The President announced his intention to nominate Joseph A. Benkert to be Assistant Secretary of Defense (Global Security Affairs).

The President announced his intention to nominate Carol Dillon Kissal to be Inspector General of the Small Business Administration.

February 16

In the morning, while en route to Cotonou, Benin, aboard Air Force One, the President had an intelligence briefing. Upon arrival at Cadjehoun International Airport, he and Mrs. Bush participated in an arrival ceremony with President Thomas Yayi Boni of Benin and his wife Chantal de Souza Yayi. He then met with President Yayi.

Later in the morning, the President and Mrs. Bush met with U.S. Embassy staff and their families. They then traveled to Dar es Salaam, Tanzania, where, upon arrival in the evening at Julius Nyerere International Airport, they participated in an arrival ceremony with President Jakaya Mrisho Kikwete of Tanzania and his wife Mama Salma Kikwete.

Later in the evening, the President and Mrs. Bush traveled to the Kilimanjaro Hotel Kempinski Dar es Salaam.

February 17

In the morning, the President traveled to the State House, where he participated in a signing ceremony of the Millennium Challenge compact with President Jakaya Mrisho Kikwete of Tanzania. Later, he returned to the Kilimanjaro Hotel Kempinski Dar es Salaam.

In the afternoon, the President and Mrs. Bush traveled to the U.S. Embassy, where, in the memorial garden, they met with family members of victims of the 1998 Embassy bombing and participated in a wreath-laying ceremony for the victims. Later, in the atrium of the Embassy, they met with Embassy staff and their families. They then returned to the Kilimanjaro Hotel.

In the evening, the President and Mrs. Bush traveled to the State House, where they attended entertainment hosted by President Kikwete and his wife Mama Salma Kikwete. Later, they returned to the Kilimanjaro Hotel.

February 18

In the morning, the President had an intelligence briefing. Later, he and Mrs. Bush traveled to Arusha, Tanzania, where, upon arrival at Kilimanjaro International Airport, they attended a cultural performance.

In the afternoon, the President and Mrs. Bush toured A to Z Textile Mills. Later, they traveled to the Arusha Coffee Lodge. They then visited the Emusoi Center, a school for Maasai girls.

Later in the afternoon, the President and Mrs. Bush participated in an interview with Ann Curry of NBC's "Today" show. They then returned to the Kilimanjaro Hotel Kempinski Dar es Salaam in Dar es Salaam, Tanzania, arriving in the evening.

During the day, the President and Mrs. Bush met with their niece Ellie LeBlond, volunteer, India Howell, founder and executive director, and Nano Chatfield, chairman of the board of directors, Tanzanian Children's Fund.

February 19

In the morning, the President had an intelligence briefing. Later, he and Mrs. Bush traveled to Julius Nyerere International Airport, where they participated in a departure ceremony with President Jakaya Mrisho Kikwete of Tanzania and his wife Mama Salma Kikwete. They then traveled to Kigali, Rwanda, where, upon arrival at Kigali International Airport, they participated in an arrival ceremony and attended a cultural performance with President Paul Kagame and his wife Jeannette Nyiramongi.

Later in the morning, the President and Mrs. Bush traveled to the Kigali Memorial Centre,

where they participated in a wreath-laying ceremony at the genocide memorial. Later, they traveled to the Presidency—VIP Building.

In the afternoon, the President participated in a signing ceremony of the Rwanda-U.S. Bilateral Investment Treaty with President Kagame. Later, he and Mrs. Bush attended a social lunch hosted by President Kagame and his wife Jeannette.

Later in the afternoon, the President and Mrs. Bush visited the Lycee de Kigali and met with students involved in the Anti-AIDS Club. Later, they traveled to Accra, Ghana, arriving in the evening. While en route aboard Air Force One, he participated in an interview with Robert Geldof for Time magazine.

Later in the evening, the President and Mrs. Bush traveled to the La Palm Royal Beach Hotel.

February 20

In the morning, the President had an intelligence briefing. He then traveled to Osu Castle, where he participated in an arrival ceremony with President John Agyekum Kufuor of Ghana. Later, he traveled to the U.S. Embassy, where he was joined by Mrs. Bush.

In the afternoon, in the Ambassador's residence, the President and Mrs. Bush met with Embassy staff and their families. Later, they traveled to the International Trade Fair Center, where they visited with USAID West Africa Trade Hub beneficiaries. They then toured the center and met with 30 tribal chiefs.

Later in the afternoon, the President and Mrs. Bush traveled to the Ghana International School. They then returned to the La Palm Royal Beach Hotel.

In the evening, the President and Mrs. Bush traveled to the State Banquet Hall. Later, they returned to the La Palm Hotel.

February 21

In the morning, the President had an intelligence briefing. Later, he and Mrs. Bush traveled to Monrovia, Liberia. While en route aboard Air Force One, he had a telephone conversation with President Pervez Musharraf of Pakistan to discuss the results of Pakistan's February 18 parliamentary elections.

Later in the morning, upon arrival at Spriggs Payne Airport, the President and Mrs. Bush participated in an arrival ceremony with President

Ellen Johnson Sirleaf of Liberia. He then traveled to the Ministry of Foreign Affairs, where he met with President Johnson Sirleaf.

In the afternoon, the President traveled to the Executive Mansion, where he was joined by Mrs. Bush. They then participated in a gowning and investiture ceremony.

Later in the afternoon, the President and Mrs. Bush traveled to the University of Liberia. They then returned to Washington, DC, arriving in the evening.

The President announced his intention to nominate Stephen G. McFarland to be Ambassador to Guatemala.

The President announced his intention to nominate Donald E. Booth to be Ambassador to Zambia.

The President announced his intention to nominate Gillian Arlette Milovanovic to be Ambassador to Mali.

The President announced his intention to nominate Nancy E. McEldowney to be Ambassador to Bulgaria.

The President announced his intention to nominate Scot A. Marciel to be given the rank of Ambassador during his tenure of service as Ambassador for the Association of Southeast Asian Nations (ASEAN) Affairs.

The President announced his intention to appoint John J. Sullivan as a member of the Board of Directors of the Overseas Private Investment Corporation.

The President announced his intention to appoint the following individuals as members on the Board of Visitors to the U.S. Naval Academy:

Michael R. Hightower;
Nancy L. Johnson;
J. Patrick Michaels, Jr.; and
Anthony J. Principi.

The President declared a major disaster in Kentucky and ordered Federal aid to supplement Commonwealth and local recovery efforts in the area struck by severe storms, tornadoes, straight-line winds, and flooding on February 5 and 6.

February 22

In the morning, the President had an intelligence briefing.

February 23

In the morning, the President had an intelligence briefing.

February 24

In the evening, in the East Room, the President and Mrs. Bush hosted entertainment for the Nation's Governors.

February 25

In the morning, the President had an intelligence briefing. Later, in the Oval Office, he participated in a briefing on the Office of Faith-Based and Community Initiatives' "Quiet Revolution" report. Then, on the North Portico, he participated in a photo opportunity with the National Governors Association.

The White House announced that the President and Mrs. Bush will welcome King Abdullah II and Queen Rania of Jordan to the White House on March 4.

February 26

In the morning, the President had an intelligence briefing. Later, he participated in an interview with April Ryan of American Urban Radio Networks.

The President announced his intention to nominate Daniel W. Sutherland to be Chairman of the Privacy and Civil Liberties Oversight Board.

The President announced his intention to nominate Ronald D. Rotunda and Francis X. Taylor to be members of the Privacy and Civil Liberties Oversight Board.

The President announced his intention to nominate Nanci E. Langley to be Commissioner of the Postal Regulatory Commission.

The President announced his intention to nominate Paul A. Schneider to be Deputy Secretary of Homeland Security.

The President announced his intention to nominate Sheila McNamara Greenwood to be Assistant Secretary of Housing and Urban Development (Congressional and Intergovernmental Relations).

The President announced his intention to nominate Kenneth E. Carfine and E. Edwin Eck II to be members of the Internal Revenue Service Oversight Board.

The President announced his intention to appoint Joseph P. Torre as a member of the President's Cancer Panel.

February 27

In the morning, the President had an intelligence briefing. Later, in the Oval Office, he met with White House Press Secretary Dana Perino, who informed him of the death of William F. Buckley, Jr.

The President announced that he has named Sonya E. Medina as Deputy Assistant to the President for Domestic Policy and Director of Projects for the First Lady.

The President announced that he has named Cynthia Stowe as Special Assistant to the President for Homeland Security and Senior Director for Prevention Policy.

The President announced that he has named Alison Teal Young as Special Assistant to the President and Deputy Director of the USA Freedom Corps.

February 28

In the morning, the President had an intelligence briefing.

February 29

In the morning, the President had an intelligence briefing.

In the afternoon, in the Old Family Dining Room, the President had lunch with Secretary General Jakob Gijsbert "Jaap" de Hoop Scheffer of the North Atlantic Treaty Organization. He then traveled to the Bush Ranch in Crawford, TX, where he was joined by Mrs. Bush. Later, they welcomed Prime Minister Anders Fogh Rasmussen of Denmark and his wife Anne-Mette Rasmussen to the ranch.

In the evening, the President and Mrs. Bush had dinner with Prime Minister Rasmussen and Mrs. Rasmussen.

March 1

In the morning, the President had an intelligence briefing.

March 3

In the morning, the President had an intelligence briefing. Later, he returned to Washington, DC, arriving in the afternoon.

Later in the afternoon, on the North Portico, the President participated in a photo opportunity with the Veterans of Foreign Wars National Voice of Democracy Award recipients.

The President announced his intention to nominate the following individuals to be members of the Board of Directors of the U.S. Institute of Peace:

Kerry Kennedy;
Ikram U. Khan;
Stephen D. Krasner;
J. Robinson West; and
Nancy M. Zirkin.

The President announced his intention to appoint Nancy Davenport as a member of the National Historical Publications and Records Commission.

The President announced his intention to appoint Frances Fragos Townsend as a member of the President's Intelligence Advisory Board.

The President announced his intention to designate Jeffrey F. Kupfer as Acting Deputy Secretary of Energy.

March 4

In the morning, the President had an intelligence briefing. Later, in an Oval Office ceremony, he received the annual report of the Boy Scouts of America.

In the afternoon, in the second floor Family Dining Room, the President and Mrs. Bush hosted a social lunch for King Abdullah II and Queen Rania of Jordan. Later, at DAR Constitution Hall, he made remarks to political appointees and Federal Government employees.

During the day, the President had a telephone conversation with President-elect Dmitry A. Medvedev of Russia.

The White House announced that the President will welcome Prime Minister Kevin M. Rudd of Australia to the White House on March 28.

March 5

In the morning, the President had an intelligence briefing. He then had separate telephone conversations with former Republican Presidential candidates Michael D. Huckabee, W. Mitt Romney, Fred D. Thompson, Rudolph W. Giuliani, and Duncan L. Hunter to thank them for their campaigns. Later, at the Washington Convention Center, he toured the trade show floor of the Washington International Renewable Energy Conference.

In the afternoon, on the North Portico, the President greeted Senator John McCain of Arizona and his wife Cindy Hensley McCain. Later, in the Private Dining Room, he had lunch with

Senator McCain. He then met with Republican congressional leaders.

The President announced that he has nominated James B. Cunningham to be Ambassador to Israel.

The President announced that he has nominated Neil Suryakant Patel to be Assistant Secretary for Communications Information at the Department of Commerce.

The President announced that he has nominated Alexander Passantino to be Administrator of the Wage and Hour Division at the Department of Labor.

The President announced that he has nominated Donald G. Teitelbaum to be Ambassador to Ghana.

The President announced that he has nominated Frank C. Urbancic, Jr., to be Ambassador to Cyprus.

March 6

In the morning, the President had an intelligence briefing. Later, he met with Shi'a city councilmen from Sadr City, Iraq, and Sunni city councilmen from Adhamiyah, Iraq.

In the afternoon, in the Yellow Oval Room of the Residence, the President met with the Washington Post Editorial Board.

The President announced that he has named Tobi Merritt Edwards as Associate Counsel to the President.

The President announced that he has named Felipe Eduardo Sixto as Special Assistant to the President for Intergovernmental Affairs.

The President announced that he has named Nancy Theis as Special Assistant to the President and Director of Presidential Correspondence.

March 7

In the morning, the President had an intelligence briefing. Later, he participated in an interview with Major League Baseball Productions.

In the afternoon, in the Oval Office, the President met with Miguel Sigler Amaya and Josefa Lopez Pena, brother and sister-in-law of Cuban political prisoners Ariel and Guido Sigler Amaya. Later, he traveled to Arlington, VA, where, at the Pentagon, he participated in Defense Department briefings. He then returned to Washington, DC.

The President declared a major disaster in Illinois and ordered Federal aid to supplement State and local recovery efforts in the area struck by severe storms and flooding beginning on January 7 and continuing.

March 8

In the morning, the President had an intelligence briefing.

In the evening, the President and Mrs. Bush attended the Gridiron Club dinner at the Renaissance Washington, DC Hotel.

March 10

In the morning, the President had an intelligence briefing.

March 11

In the morning, the President had an intelligence briefing. Later, he traveled to Nashville, TN, where, upon arrival, he met with USA Freedom Corps volunteer Fred Pancoast. He then met with Karla G. Christian, associate chief of pediatric cardiac surgery and director of pediatric cardiac surgical education, Monroe Carell Jr. Children's Hospital at Vanderbilt.

In the afternoon, at a private residence, the President attended a Republican National Committee luncheon. Later, he returned to Washington, DC.

The President announced his intention to nominate Mimi Alemayehou to be U.S. Director of the African Development Bank.

The President announced his intention to nominate Rear Adm. Jonathan W. Bailey to be Commissioner of the Mississippi River Commission.

The President announced his intention to nominate William C. Smith to be a member of the Mississippi River Commission.

The President announced his intention to appoint Karen P. Hughes and Charles M. Younger as members of the Board of Visitors to the U.S. Military Academy.

March 12

In the morning, the President had an intelligence briefing.

In the afternoon, the President participated in an interview with Susie Gharib of PBS's "Nightly Business Report."

The White House announced that the President will welcome Prime Minister Hubert Ingraham of the Bahamas, Prime Minister David Thompson of Barbados, and Prime Minister

Dean Barrow of Belize to the White House on March 20.

The White House announced that the President will host President Lee Myung-bak of South Korea and his wife Kim Yoon-ok at Camp David on April 18 and 19.

The President declared a major disaster in Missouri and ordered Federal aid to supplement State and local recovery efforts in the area struck by severe winter storms and flooding from February 10 to 14.

March 13

In the morning, the President had an intelligence briefing.

In the afternoon, in the Oval Office, the President met with National Mathematics Advisory Panel Chairman Larry R. Faulkner, who presented him with the panel's final report.

The White House announced that to commemorate Saint Patrick's Day, the President will host Prime Minister Bertie Ahern of Ireland at the White House on March 17.

The White House announced that the President and Mrs. Bush will travel to Ukraine, Romania, and Croatia in April.

The President announced his intention to nominate Barbara McConnell Barrett to be Ambassador to Finland.

The President announced his intention to nominate David R. Hill to be Assistant Administrator (General Counsel) of the Environmental Protection Agency.

The President announced his intention to nominate T. Vance McMahan to be Representative of the U.S. on the Economic and Social Council of the United Nations, with the rank of Ambassador.

The President announced his intention to appoint the following individuals as members of the Community Development Advisory Board:

Darlene Bramon;
William Bynum;
J. French Hill;
Farah M. Jimenez;
Nancy J. Leake;
Terri Ludwig;
Neal A. McCaleb;
L. Raymond Moncrief; and
Edwin A. Rodriguez.

The President declared an emergency in Illinois and ordered Federal aid to supplement State and local response efforts in the area

struck by record snow and near record snow on February 5 and 6.

March 14

In the morning, the President had an intelligence briefing. He then traveled to New York City. Later, at the Hilton New York Hotel, he participated in separate interviews with the Wall Street Journal Editorial Board and Larry Kudlow of CNBC.

In the afternoon, at a private residence, the President attended a Republican National Committee luncheon. Later, he traveled to Camp David, MD.

The President announced his intention to nominate Lily Fu Claffee to be General Counsel of the Department of Commerce.

March 15

In the morning, the President had an intelligence briefing.

The President declared an emergency in Texas and ordered Federal aid to supplement State and local response efforts in the area struck by wildfires beginning on March 14 and continuing.

March 16

In the afternoon, the President and Mrs. Bush returned to Washington, DC. Later, he met with Secretary of the Treasury Henry M. Paulson, Jr., who briefed him on the Federal Reserve's latest actions to help the economy.

March 17

In the morning, the President had an intelligence briefing. Later, he had a telephone conversation with Governor David A. Paterson of New York to wish him well in his new position.

In the afternoon, at the U.S. Capitol, the President attended the Speaker of the House of Representatives annual St. Patrick's Day luncheon. Later, in the Roosevelt Room, he met with the President's Working Group on Financial Markets. Then, on the South Portico, he participated in a photo opportunity with Children's Miracle Network Champions Across America representatives.

In the evening, in the State Dining Room, the President and Mrs. Bush hosted a St. Patrick's Day social dinner.

March 18

In the morning, the President had an intelligence briefing. Later, he traveled to Jacksonville, FL, where, upon arrival, he met with USA Freedom Corps volunteer Holly Cleveland.

In the afternoon, at a private residence, the President attended a Republican National Committee luncheon. Later, at the Jacksonville Port Authority Blount Island Marine Terminal, he toured Coastal Maritime Stevedoring, LLC.

Later in the afternoon, the President traveled to Palm Beach, FL, where, upon arrival, he met with USA Freedom Corps volunteer Cheryl Crowley. Then, at a private residence, he attended a Republican National Committee reception.

In the evening, the President returned to Washington, DC.

The President announced his intention to nominate Philip T. Reeker to be Ambassador to Macedonia.

The President announced his intention to nominate Christopher R. Wall to be Assistant Secretary of Commerce (Export Administration).

The President announced his intention to nominate Miguel R. San Juan to be U.S. Executive Director of the Inter-American Development Bank.

The President announced his intention to appoint Peter Pace as a member of the President's Intelligence Advisory Board.

The President announced his intention to appoint James B. Peake as a member of the Advisory Council to the Board of Governors of the American Red Cross.

The President announced his intention to designate Peter C. Schaumber as Chairman of the National Labor Relations Board.

March 19

In the morning, the President had an intelligence briefing.

In the afternoon, in the Old Family Dining Room, the President had a working lunch with President Mikheil Saakashvili of Georgia.

The President announced his intention to nominate Michael E. Leiter to be Director of the National Counterterrorism Center in the Office of the Director of National Intelligence.

The President announced that he has named Heather Ann Hopkins as Special Assistant to the President and Senior Director for Legislative Affairs in the National Security Council.

The President announced that he has named La Rhonda M. Houston as Special Assistant to the President and Deputy Director for Appointments and Scheduling.

The President declared an emergency in Wisconsin and ordered Federal aid to supplement State and local response efforts in the area struck by record snow and near record snow on February 5 and 6.

The President declared a major disaster in Missouri and ordered Federal aid to supplement State and local recovery efforts in the area struck by severe storms and flooding beginning on March 17 and continuing.

March 20

In the morning, the President had breakfast with Secretary of State Condoleezza Rice, Secretary of Defense Robert M. Gates, and National Security Adviser Stephen J. Hadley. He then had an intelligence briefing. Later, in the Old Family Dining Room, he participated in an interview with Brian P. Lamb of C–SPAN.

In the afternoon, the President and Mrs. Bush traveled to Camp David, MD.

The White House announced that the President will welcome King Hamad bin Isa al-Khalifa of Bahrain to the White House on March 25.

The President announced his intention to nominate Constance S. Barker to be a member of the Equal Employment Opportunity Commission.

The President announced his intention to nominate Robert S. Beecroft to be Ambassador to Jordan.

The President announced his intention to nominate Tyler D. Duvall to be Under Secretary (Transportation Policy) at the Department of Transportation.

The President announced his intention to nominate John R. Vaughn to be a member of the National Council on Disability and, upon appointment, to redesignate him as Chairperson.

The President announced his intention to nominate the following individuals to be members of the National Council on Disability:

Victoria Ray Carlson;
Chad Colley;
Kristen Cox;
Marvin G. Fifield;
John H. Hager;
Lisa Mattheiss;
Katherine O. McCary;

Anne M. Rader;
Renee L. Tyree; and
Tony J. Williams.

The President announced his intention to appoint William D. James as Commissioner of the U.S. section of the Great Lakes Fishery Commission.

The President declared a major disaster in Georgia and ordered Federal aid to supplement State and local recovery efforts in the area struck by severe storms and tornadoes from March 14 to 16.

March 21

In the morning, the President had an intelligence briefing.

March 22

In the morning, the President had an intelligence briefing.

March 23

In the afternoon, the President and Mrs. Bush returned to Washington, DC.

In the evening, the President had a telephone conversation with Secretary of the Treasury Henry M. Paulson, Jr., who briefed him on the discussions between JPMorgan Chase & Co., Bear Stearns Companies Inc., and Federal Reserve representatives.

March 24

In the morning, the President had an intelligence briefing. Later, in the Situation Room, he participated in a National Security Council meeting, where he was briefed by U.S. Ambassador to Iraq Ryan C. Crocker and Gen. David H. Petraeus, USA, commanding general, Multi-National Force—Iraq, via secure video teleconference.

In the afternoon, in the Oval Office, the President met with Minister of External Affairs Pranab Mukherjee of India.

March 25

In the morning, the President had a telephone conversation with Prime Minister Syed Yousuf Raza Gilani of Pakistan to congratulate him on his recent nomination and discuss Pakistan-U.S. relations and the war on terror. Later, he had an intelligence briefing.

In the afternoon, in the Old Family Dining Room, the President had a working lunch with King Hamad bin Isa al-Khalifa of Bahrain.

Later, he traveled to McLean, VA, arriving in the evening.

Later in the evening, at a private residence, the President attended a National Republican Senatorial Committee reception. He then returned to Washington, DC.

March 26

In the morning, the President had a telephone conversation with President Hu Jintao of China. He then had an intelligence briefing. Later, he traveled to Arlington, VA, where, at the Pentagon, he participated in Defense Department briefings.

Later in the morning, the President traveled to Sterling, VA.

In the afternoon, the President returned to Washington, DC.

The President announced his intention to nominate Kameran L. Onley to be Assistant Secretary of the Interior (Water and Science).

The President announced his intention to nominate A. Ellen Terpstra to be Chief Agricultural Negotiator in the Office of the U.S. Trade Representative, with the rank of Ambassador.

The President announced his intention to designate William E. Kovacic as Chairman of the Federal Trade Commission.

The President declared a major disaster in Arkansas and ordered Federal aid to supplement State and local recovery efforts in the area struck by severe storms, tornadoes, and flooding beginning on March 18 and continuing.

March 27

In the morning, the President had a telephone conversation with President Mohamed Hosni Mubarak of Egypt to express his condolences for the accidental death of a citizen who was killed in the Suez Canal by U.S. naval gunfire. Later, he had an intelligence briefing. He then traveled to Dayton, OH.

Later in the morning, the President traveled to Bellbrook, OH.

In the afternoon, at a private residence, the President attended an Ohio Victory 2008 reception. Later, he returned to Dayton, OH, where, at Wright-Patterson Air Force Base, he met with families of military personnel killed in the war on terror.

Later in the afternoon, the President traveled to Pittsburgh, PA, where, upon arrival, he met with USA Freedom Corps volunteer Lydia Humenycky. He then traveled to Sewickley, PA, where, at a private residence, he attended a Pennsylvania Victory 2008 reception.

In the evening, the President returned to Washington, DC. While en route aboard Air Force One, he participated in an interview with the History Channel for the documentary "Air Force One: Behind the Scenes."

March 28

In the morning, the President had an intelligence briefing.

In the afternoon, the President traveled to Wrightstown, NJ, where, upon arrival, he met with USA Freedom Corps volunteer Andrell Reid. Later, he traveled to Freehold, NJ, where, at Novadebt, he participated in a roundtable on the HOPE NOW Alliance. He then toured Novadebt.

Later in the afternoon, the President returned to Washington, DC.

The White House announced that the President and Mrs. Bush will welcome Prime Minister Gordon Brown of the United Kingdom and his wife Sarah to the White House on April 17.

The President announced his intention to nominate Luis Aguilar and Elisse B. Walter to be Commissioners of the Securities and Exchange Commission.

The President announced his intention to nominate Marie L. Yovanovitch to be Ambassador to Armenia.

The President announced his intention to appoint Christopher A. Padilla as a member of the Congressional-Executive Commission on the People's Republic of China.

The President announced his intention to appoint Alexa E. Posny as a member of the National Institute for Literacy Advisory Board.

The President announced his intention to designate Stephanie Johnson Monroe as Acting Assistant Secretary for Legislation and Congressional Affairs at the Department of Education.

March 29

In the morning, the President had an intelligence briefing.

March 30

In the evening, at Nationals Park, the President and Mrs. Bush visited the clubhouses of Major League Baseball's Washington Nationals and Atlanta Braves. Later, he threw out the ceremonial first pitch to open the game, and he and Mrs. Bush watched the game.

March 31

In the morning, the President and Mrs. Bush traveled to Kiev, Ukraine, arriving in the evening. While en route aboard Air Force One, he had an intelligence briefing.

Later in the evening, the President and Mrs. Bush traveled to the Hyatt Regency Kiev hotel.

April 1

In the morning, the President had an intelligence briefing. Later, he and Mrs. Bush met with U.S. Embassy staff and their families. They then traveled to the Presidential Secretariat, where they participated in an arrival ceremony with President Viktor Yushchenko of Ukraine and his wife Kateryna Mykhailivna Yushchenko.

Later in the morning, the President and Mrs. Bush participated in a reception with President Yushchenko and Mrs. Yushchenko. During the reception, he met with Yatseniuk Arseniy Petrovych, Chairman of the Verkhovna Rada, and Viktor Yanukovych, Leader of the Party of Regions of Ukraine.

In the afternoon, the President traveled to the Club of Cabinet Ministers, where he met with Prime Minister Yuliya Tymoshenko of Ukraine. Later, he traveled to the Holodomor Memorial, where he was joined by Mrs. Bush, President Yushchenko, and Mrs. Yushchenko. They all then traveled to St. Sophia's Cathedral, where they toured the cathedral and attended a musical performance.

Later in the afternoon, the President and Mrs. Bush traveled to Bucharest, Romania, arriving in the evening.

Later in the evening, the President and Mrs. Bush traveled to the JW Marriott Bucharest Grand Hotel.

The President announced the designation of the following individuals as members of the Presidential delegation to Warsaw, Poland, to attend the ceremony commemorating the 65th anniversary of the Warsaw ghetto uprising on April 15:

Michael Chertoff (head of delegation);
Victor Ashe;
Phyllis Heideman;
David Mitzner; and
William J. Lowenberg.

April 2

In the morning, the President had an intelligence briefing. Later, he and Mrs. Bush traveled to Mihail Kogalniceanu, Romania, where, upon arrival at Mihail Kogalniceanu Airport, they participated in an arrival ceremony with President Traian Basescu of Romania and his wife Maria. They then traveled to the Protocol Villas Neptun-Olimp in Neptun, Romania, arriving in the afternoon.

Later in the afternoon, in the Protocol Villas Neptun-Olimp dining room, the President had a working lunch with President Basescu. Later, he and Mrs. Bush returned to the JW Marriott Bucharest Grand Hotel in Bucharest, Romania.

In the evening, the President and Mrs. Bush traveled to Cotroceni Palace, where, in the Union Hall, they participated in the North Atlantic Treaty Organization summit official greeting. He then participated in the North Atlantic Council summit working dinner. Later, he returned to the JW Marriott Bucharest Grand Hotel.

The President announced his intention to nominate Richard E. Hoagland to be Ambassador to Kazakhstan.

The President announced his intention to nominate Jeffrey F. Kupfer to be Deputy Secretary of Energy.

The President announced his intention to nominate Elaine C. Duke to be Under Secretary for Management at the Department of Homeland Security.

The President announced his intention to nominate Brandon C. Bungard to be General Counsel of the Federal Labor Relations Authority.

The President announced his intention to nominate John P. Hewko to be Assistant Secretary (Aviation and International Affairs) at the Department of Transportation.

The President announced his intention to nominate Janice L. Jacobs to be Assistant Secretary (Bureau of Consular Affairs) at the Department of State.

The President announced his intention to designate Patrick W. Dunne as Acting Under Secretary for Benefits of the Department of Veterans Affairs.

April 3

In the morning, the President had an intelligence briefing. Later, he traveled to the Palace of Parliament.

In the afternoon, in the Rustic Hall of the Palace of Parliament, the President attended the Euro-Atlantic Partnership Council summit working lunch. Later, in the Unirii Hall of the Palace of Parliament, he attended the NATO summit meeting on Afghanistan. He then participated in an official photograph with participants of the NATO summit meeting on Afghanistan.

In the evening, the President returned to the JW Marriott Bucharest Grand Hotel. Later, he and Mrs. Bush traveled to the Athenaeum, where, in the theater, they attended a NATO cultural event. They then traveled to the Athenee Palace Hilton Bucharest Hotel, where they attended the NATO gala dinner.

Later in the evening, the President and Mrs. Bush returned to the JW Marriott Bucharest Grand Hotel.

The President announced his intention to nominate Bartholomew H. Chilton and Scott O'Malia to be Commissioners of the Commodity Futures Trading Commission.

April 4

In the morning, the President had an intelligence briefing. Later, he traveled to the Palace of Parliament, where he attended the NATO-Ukraine Commission summit meeting. He then attended the NATO-Russia Council summit meeting.

In the afternoon, the President and Mrs. Bush traveled to Zagreb, Croatia. While en route aboard Air Force One, he had a telephone conversation with President Thabo Mvuyelwa Mbeki of South Africa to discuss the situation in Zimbabwe. They then traveled to the Westin Zagreb hotel.

In the evening, the President and Mrs. Bush traveled to the Office of the President, where they participated in an arrival ceremony with President Stjepan Mesic of Croatia and his wife Milka. He then met with President Mesic. Later they returned to the Westin Zagreb hotel.

The President announced that he has named Patrick S. Aylward as Special Assistant to the President and Director, Office of the Chief of Staff.

The President announced that he has named Amy L. Farrell as Special Assistant to the President for Economic Policy at the National Economic Council.

The President announced that he has named John S. Roberts as Special Assistant to the President for Intergovernmental Affairs.

April 5

In the morning, the President had an intelligence briefing. He and Mrs. Bush then met with U.S. Embassy staff and their families. Later, he traveled to the Banski Dvori.

Later in the morning, the President traveled to the Vila Prekrizje. He then participated in a working lunch and a photo opportunity with future NATO leaders.

In the afternoon, the President and Mrs. Bush traveled to Sochi, Russia, arriving in the evening.

Later in the evening, the President and Mrs. Bush traveled to the Bocharov Ruchei, where they participated in a briefing on the 2014 Winter Olympic Games with President Vladimir V. Putin of Russia. They then participated in a social dinner and entertainment with President Putin. Later, they traveled to the Radisson SAS Lazurnaya Hotel.

April 6

In the morning, the President traveled to the Bocharov Ruchei.

In the afternoon, the President participated in a working lunch with President Vladimir V. Putin and President-elect Dmitry A. Medvedev of Russia. Later, he and Mrs. Bush returned to Washington, DC.

April 7

In the morning, the President had an intelligence briefing. Later, he had a telephone conversation with Speaker of the House of Representatives Nancy Pelosi to discuss the Colombia free trade agreement.

The President announced his intention to nominate Peter W. Bodde to be Ambassador to Malawi.

The President announced his intention to appoint David S. Bohigian as a Commissioner-Observer of the Commission on Security and Cooperation in Europe.

The President announced his intention to appoint Richard F. Mangogna as Chief Information Officer for the Department of Homeland Security.

The President announced his intention to appoint Edward A. Mueller as a member of the President's National Security Telecommunications Advisory Committee and, upon appointment, designate him as Chairman.

The President announced his intention to appoint John T. Stankey as a member of the President's National Security Telecommunications Advisory Committee and, upon appointment, designate him as Vice Chairman.

The President announced his intention to appoint Michael W. Laphen, Thomas J. Lynch, and William A. Roper as members of the President's National Security Telecommunications Advisory Committee.

The President announced his intention to appoint the following individuals as members of the National Infrastructure Advisory Council:

David J. Bronczek;
Wesley Bush;
Philip G. Heasley;
D.M. Houston;
David Kepler;
James A. Reid;
Matthew K. Rose;
Michael J. Wallace;
Greg Wells;
John M. Williams, Jr.; and
Martha B. Wyrsch.

The President announced his intention to designate Alfred R. Berkeley III as Vice Chairman of the National Infrastructure Advisory Council.

April 8

In the morning, the President had an intelligence briefing. He then had a telephone conversation with head coach Bill Self of the University of Kansas men's basketball team to congratulate him on the team's April 7 NCAA championship. Later, in the Library, he participated in an interview with EWTN Global Catholic Network on the visit of Pope Benedict XVI to Washington, DC.

In the afternoon, in the Oval Office, the President participated in a photo opportunity with the 2008 White House News Photographers Association "Eyes of History" winners.

April 9

In the morning, the President had an intelligence briefing. Later, on the North Lawn, he and Mrs. Bush participated in a commemorative tree planting ceremony.

In the afternoon, in the Cabinet Room, the President met with bipartisan congressional leaders.

In the evening, in the Residence, the President met with Prime Minister Jean-Claude Juncker of Luxembourg.

The President announced that he has named William B. Wichterman as Special Assistant to the President and Deputy Director of Public Liaison.

April 10

In the morning, in the Private Dining Room, the President had breakfast with U.S. Ambassador to Iraq Ryan C. Crocker and Gen. David H. Petraeus, USA, commanding general, Multi-National Force—Iraq. He then had an intelligence briefing. Later, in the Oval Office, he met with U.S. Special Envoy to Sudan Richard S. Williamson.

In the afternoon, the President traveled to the Bush Ranch in Crawford, TX.

April 11

In the morning, the President had an intelligence briefing. Later, he participated in an interview with Martha Raddatz of ABC News.

In the evening, at the Broken Spoke Ranch, the President and Mrs. Bush attended a Republican National Committee reception.

The President announced his intention to appoint Robert Kelly as a member of the Committee for Purchase From People Who Are Blind or Severely Disabled.

The President announced his intention to appoint the following individuals as members of the J. William Fulbright Foreign Scholarship Board:

John W. Johnson;
James L. Oblinger;
Dina Habib Powell; and
Donald E. Vermeil.

The President announced his intention to appoint Mary Beth Long as a Commissioner-Observer of the Commission on Security and Co-operation in Europe.

The President announced his intention to appoint the following individuals as members of the U.S. Holocaust Memorial Council:

Norman R. Bobins;
Joseph M. Brodecki;
Michael D. Epstein;
Donald Etra
David M. Flaum;
Andrew Hochberg;
Ezra Katz;
Howard Konar;
Douglas R. Korn;
Hadassah F. Lieberman; and
Pierre-Richard Prosper.

The President announced his intention to designate Kameran L. Onley as Acting Assistant Secretary of the Interior (Water and Science).

April 12

In the morning, the President had an intelligence briefing.

April 13

In the afternoon, the President and Mrs. Bush returned to Washington, DC.

April 14

In the morning, the President had an intelligence briefing.

April 15

In the morning, the President had an intelligence briefing. Later, in the Oval Office, he presented the Lifetime President's Volunteer Service Award to S. Truett Cathy. Then, also in the Oval Office, he participated in a signing ceremony for the Education and Sharing Day, U.S.A., proclamation.

In the afternoon, the President and Mrs. Bush traveled to Andrews Air Force Base, MD, where they greeted Pope Benedict XVI upon his arrival. He then met with Pope Benedict XVI. Later, they returned to Washington, DC.

During the day, the President had a telephone conversation with Prime Minister Silvio Berlusconi of Italy to congratulate him on his election victory. He also had a telephone conversation with Secretary-General Ban Ki-moon of the United Nations.

The President announced his intention to nominate Michele M. Leonhart to be Administrator of the Drug Enforcement Administration.

April 16

In the morning, the President had an intelligence briefing. Later, in the Oval Office, he met with Pope Benedict XVI.

In the evening, in the East Room, the President and Mrs. Bush hosted a dinner for Pope Benedict XVI.

April 17

In the morning, the President had an intelligence briefing.

In the evening, on the North Portico, the President and Mrs. Bush participated in a welcoming ceremony for Prime Minister Gordon Brown of the United Kingdom and his wife Sarah. Later, in the Yellow Oval Room, they hosted a social dinner for Prime Minister Brown and Mrs. Brown.

April 18

In the morning, the President had an intelligence briefing.

In the afternoon, the President and Mrs. Bush traveled to Camp David, MD. Later, they participated in a welcoming ceremony for President Lee Myung-bak of South Korea and his wife Kim Yoon-ok.

In the evening, the President and Mrs. Bush hosted a social dinner for President Lee and Kim Yoon-ok.

The White House announced that the President will welcome President Alvaro Colom Caballeros of Guatemala to the White House on April 28.

The President announced his intention to nominate Steven C. Preston to be Secretary of Housing and Urban Development.

April 19

In the morning, the President had an intelligence briefing.

April 20

In the afternoon, the President and Mrs. Bush returned to Washington, DC.

April 21

In the morning, the President had an intelligence briefing. He then traveled to New Orleans, LA, where, upon arrival, he met with USA Freedom Corps volunteer Audrey Browder.

Later in the morning, the President traveled to the Windsor Court Hotel.

In the evening, the President traveled to Commander's Palace restaurant, where he attended a dinner and entertainment with President Felipe de Jesus Calderon Hinojosa of Mexico and Prime Minister Stephen Harper of Canada. Later, he returned to the Windsor Court Hotel.

The White House announced that the President will meet with King Abdullah II of Jordan at the White House on April 23.

April 22

In the morning, the President had an intelligence briefing. Later, he traveled to Dooky Chase's Restaurant, where he had breakfast with President Felipe de Jesus Calderon Hinojosa of Mexico and Prime Minister Stephen Harper of Canada. He then traveled to Gallier Hall, where

he met with the North American Competitiveness Council.

In the afternoon, the President traveled to Lafayette Square, where he, President Calderon, and Prime Minister Harper participated in a tree planting ceremony in honor of Earth Day. Later, he traveled to Baton Rouge, LA, where, upon arrival, he met with USA Freedom Corps volunteer Randle D. Raggio. Then, at a private residence, he attended a Kennedy Majority Committee reception.

Later in the afternoon, the President returned to Washington, DC, arriving in the evening.

The President announced the designation of the following individuals as members of the Presidential delegation to Belfast, Northern Ireland, to attend the U.S.-Northern Ireland Investment Conference from May 7 to 9:

Paula J. Dobriansky (head of delegation);
Robert H. Tuttle;
Thomas C. Foley;
Michael R. Bloomberg;
David Scott; and
Catherine Brune.

The President announced his intention to nominate C. Steven McGann to be Ambassador to Fiji, Kiribati, Nauru, Tonga, and Tuvalu.

The President announced his intention to nominate Christine O. Hill to be Assistant Secretary of Veterans Affairs (Congressional Affairs).

The President announced his intention to nominate Jeffrey L. Sedgwick to be Assistant Attorney General (Office of Justice Programs) at the Department of Justice.

The President announced his intention to nominate T. Vance McMahan to be an Alternate Representative of the U.S. to the Sessions of the United Nations General Assembly during his tenure of service as the U.S. Representative on the Economic and Social Council to the United Nations.

April 23

In the morning, in the Private Dining Room, the President had breakfast with King Abdullah II of Jordan. Later, he had an intelligence briefing.

In the afternoon, in the Oval Office, the President met with Johns Hopkins Hospital organ donors and recipients. Later, also in the

Oval Office, he participated in a photo opportunity with recipients of the Malcolm Baldrige National Quality Award.

April 24

In the morning, the President had a telephone conversation with President-elect Fernando Armindo Lugo Mendez of Paraguay to congratulate him on his April 21 election victory and discuss Paraguay-U.S. relations. He then had an intelligence briefing.

The President announced his intention to nominate Kristen Silverberg to be Representative of the U.S. to the European Union, with the rank and status of Ambassador.

The President announced his intention to nominate Lyndon L. Olson, Jr., to be a member of the U.S. Advisory Commission on Public Diplomacy.

The President announced his intention to appoint Victor D. Hanson as a member of the American Battle Monuments Commission.

The President declared an emergency in Ohio and ordered Federal aid to supplement State and local response efforts in the area struck by record snow and near record snow from March 7 to 9.

April 25

In the morning, the President had an intelligence briefing. Later, in the Oval Office, he participated in a signing ceremony for the Malaria Awareness Day proclamation. He then traveled to Hartford, CT, where, upon arrival, he met with USA Freedom Corps volunteers Kevin Eberly, Jr., and Joe Lapenta, Jr.

In the afternoon, the President traveled to South Kent, CT, where, at a private residence, he attended a David Cappiello for Congress and Connecticut Victory 2008 luncheon. Later, he returned to Washington, DC.

The President announced his intention to designate Clay Lowery as Acting U.S. Director of the European Bank for Reconstruction and Development and Acting U.S. Director of the African Development Bank.

The President announced his intention to designate David R. Murtaugh as Acting Deputy Director for State, Local and Tribal Affairs in the Office of National Drug Control Policy.

The President announced that he has named Robert R. Hood as Special Assistant to the President for Legislative Affairs.

The President announced that he has named Richard G.F. O'Donoghue as Associate Counsel to the President.

April 26

In the morning, the President had an intelligence briefing.

April 28

In the morning, the President had an intelligence briefing.

In the afternoon, in the Oval Office, the President met with American Legion national commander Martin F. Conatser.

The White House announced that the President and Mrs. Bush will travel to Israel, Saudi Arabia, and Egypt from May 13 to 18.

April 29

In the morning, the President had an intelligence briefing.

The President announced his intention to nominate Eric J. Boswell to be Assistant Secretary of State (Diplomatic Security) and Director of the Office of Foreign Missions, with the rank of Ambassador.

The President announced his intention to nominate Patricia McMahon Hawkins to be Ambassador to Togo.

The President announced his intention to designate William W. Park as a member of the Panel of Arbitrators of the International Centre for Settlement of Investment Disputes.

April 30

In the morning, the President had an intelligence briefing. Later, in the Oval Office, he participated in a photo opportunity with the 2008 National and State Teachers of the Year.

In the afternoon, in the Oval Office, the President met with Prime Minister Bertie Ahern of Ireland. Later, he traveled to Fairfax, VA, arriving in the evening.

Later in the evening, at a private residence, the President attended a National Republican Congressional Committee reception. Later, he returned to Washington, DC.

May 1

In the morning, the President had an intelligence briefing.

The White House announced that the President will welcome President Martin Torrijos Espino of Panama to the White House on May 6.

The President announced his intention to nominate Liliana Ayalde to be Ambassador to Paraguay.

The President announced his intention to nominate Tatiana C. Gfoeller-Volkoff to be Ambassador to Kyrgyzstan.

The President announced his intention to nominate Sean J. Stackley to be Assistant Secretary of the Navy for Research, Development and Acquisition.

The President announced his intention to appoint Martin J. Dannenfelser, Jr., as Staff Director of the U.S. Commission on Civil Rights.

The President announced his intention to designate Gregory G. Katsas as Acting Assistant Attorney General (Civil Division) at the Department of Justice.

May 2

In the morning, the President had an intelligence briefing. Later, he traveled to St. Louis, MO, where, upon arrival, he met with USA Freedom Corps volunteer Jerron Johnson. He then traveled to Maryland Heights, MO, where he toured World Wide Technology, Inc.

In the afternoon, the President traveled to the Bush Ranch in Crawford, TX.

May 3

In the morning, the President had an intelligence briefing.

May 4

In the afternoon, the President traveled to Wichita, KS, where, upon arrival, he met with USA Freedom Corps volunteer Buddy Shannon III. He then traveled to Greensburg, KS. Later, he returned to Washington, DC, arriving in the evening.

May 5

In the morning, on the South Lawn, the President and Mrs. Bush participated in an interview with Robin Roberts of ABC's "Good Morning America." Later, he had an intelligence briefing. Then, he participated in a photo opportunity with the Westminster Kennel Club's 2008 Best in Show award winner, Uno.

In the evening, in the Rose Garden, the President and Mrs. Bush hosted a social dinner and entertainment in honor of Cinco de Mayo.

The President announced his intention to appoint Michael R. Anderson and Gregg C. Lord

as members of the National Commission on Children and Disasters.

The President declared a major disaster in Oklahoma and ordered Federal aid to supplement State and local recovery efforts in the area struck by severe storms, tornadoes, and flooding from March 17 to 23.

May 6

In the morning, the President had an intelligence briefing.

In the afternoon, in the Situation Room, the President had a video teleconference with Cuban dissident Martha Beatriz Roque Cabello, former Cuban political prisoner Jorge Luis Garcia Perez, and Berta Soler Fernandez, wife of Cuban political prisoner Angel Moya Acosta.

The President announced his intention to nominate Cynthia L. Bauerly, Caroline C. Hunter, and Donald F. McGahn to be members of the Federal Election Commission.

The President announced his intention to nominate Troy A. Paredes to be a Commissioner of the Securities and Exchange Commission.

May 7

In the morning, the President had an intelligence briefing. Later, in the Oval Office, he participated in a bill signing ceremony for H.R. 5715, the Ensuring Continued Access to Student Loans Act of 2008. Then, also in the Oval Office, he participated in a briefing with Secretary of Agriculture Edward T. Schafer and Under Secretary of Agriculture for Food, Nutrition, and Consumer Services Nancy Montanez Johner on food aid programs.

May 8

In the morning, the President had an intelligence briefing. Later, he traveled to the Bush Ranch in Crawford, TX.

The President announced his intention to nominate Donetta Davidson and Rosemary E. Rodriguez to be members of the Election Assistance Commission.

The President announced his intention to appoint Thomas D. Cairns as Chief Human Capital Officer at the Department of Homeland Security.

The President announced his intention to appoint the following individuals as members of the President's Committee for People with Intellectual Disabilities:

James M. Boles;

Stephanie Preshong Brown;
Olegario D. Cantos VII;
Eric L. Cole;
Berthy De La Rosa-Aponte;
William J. Edwards;
MaryMargaret Sharp-Pucci;
Linda Hampton Starnes;
Dallas R. Sweezy;
William E. Tienken;
Eric T. Treat;
Charles J. Weis; and
Mary Ellen Zeppuhar.

The President announced his intention to appoint the following individuals as members of the Commission of Fine Arts:

Diana Balmori;
Elizabeth Plater-Zyberk;
Earl A. Powell III; and
Witold Rybczynski.

The President announced his intention to designate Thomas R. Barker as Acting General Counsel of the Department of Health and Human Services.

The President announced his intention to designate Steven C. Rhatigan as Chair of the President's Committee for People with Intellectual Disabilities.

The President declared a major disaster in Mississippi and ordered Federal aid to supplement State and local recovery efforts in the area struck by severe storms and flooding beginning on March 20 and continuing.

May 9

In the morning, the President had an intelligence briefing.

The President declared a major disaster in Oklahoma and ordered Federal aid to supplement State and local recovery efforts in the area struck by severe storms, tornadoes, and flooding from April 9 to 28.

The President declared a major disaster in Maine and ordered Federal aid to supplement State and local recovery efforts in the area struck by severe storms and flooding beginning on April 28 and continuing.

May 10

In the morning, the President had an intelligence briefing.

May 11

In the afternoon, the President and Mrs. Bush returned to Washington, DC. While en route aboard Air Force One, he had separate telephone conversations with Governors Matthew R. Blunt of Missouri and George E. "Sonny" Perdue of Georgia to discuss the recent storms and tornadoes in the States.

Later in the afternoon, the President had a telephone conversation with Governor C. Bradford Henry of Oklahoma to discuss the recent storms and tornadoes in the State.

May 12

In the morning, the President had an intelligence briefing. Later, he had separate telephone conversations with President Dmitry A. Medvedev and Prime Minister Vladimir V. Putin of Russia. Then, in the Oval Office, he participated in a roundtable interview with foreign print media.

In the afternoon, in the Roosevelt Room, the President participated in an interview with Mark Knoller and Peter Maer of CBS Radio.

The President announced the designation of a U.S. honorary delegation to Jerusalem, Israel, to attend celebrations in honor of the 60th anniversary of the State of Israel on May 14 and 15.

May 13

In the morning, the President had a telephone conversation with President Hu Jintao of China. He then had an intelligence briefing. Later, in the Roosevelt Room, he participated in an interview with Mike Allen of Politico for Yahoo! News.

In the afternoon, the President and Mrs. Bush traveled to Tel Aviv, Israel, arriving the following morning.

The President announced his intention to nominate John R. Beyrle to be Ambassador to Russia.

The President announced his intention to nominate Rosemary A. DiCarlo to be the Alternate Representative of the U.S. for Special Political Affairs to the United Nations, with the rank of Ambassador, and an Alternate Representative of the U.S. to the Sessions of the General Assembly of the United Nations.

The President announced his intention to nominate Carol A. Rodley to be Ambassador to Cambodia.

The President announced his intention to appoint Jan Donnelly O'Neill as a member of the J. William Fulbright Foreign Scholarship Board.

The President announced his intention to designate Leland A. Strom as Chairman of the Farm Credit Administration Board.

May 14

In the morning, aboard Air Force One, the President had an intelligence briefing. Later, after arriving in Tel Aviv, Israel, he and Mrs. Bush traveled to the King David Hotel in Jerusalem, Israel, arriving in the afternoon.

Later in the afternoon, the President traveled to the President's residence. Later, he traveled to the Prime Minister's residence. He then returned to the King David Hotel.

In the evening, the President and Mrs. Bush traveled to the ICC Jerusalem International Convention Center. Later, they returned to the King David Hotel.

The President declared a major disaster in Oklahoma and ordered Federal aid to supplement State and local recovery efforts in the area struck by severe storms, tornadoes, and flooding beginning on May 10 and continuing.

May 15

In the morning, the President had an intelligence briefing. Later, he and Mrs. Bush traveled to Masada, Israel, where they participated in a greeting with Prime Minister Ehud Olmert of Israel and his wife Aliza. They all then visited Masada National Park.

Later in the morning, the President and Mrs. Bush participated in a gift presentation with Prime Minister Olmert and Mrs. Olmert. They then returned to the King David Hotel in Jerusalem, Israel.

In the afternoon, the President and Mrs. Bush traveled to the Knesset, where they participated in an arrival ceremony and met with Israeli Government officials. Later, they returned to the King David Hotel.

Later in the afternoon, the President met with former Prime Minister Tony Blair of the United Kingdom, Quartet Representative in the Middle East.

In the evening, the President and Mrs. Bush traveled to the Israel Museum, where they participated in a greeting with President Peres and Prime Minister Olmert and Mrs. Olmert. They then toured the museum. Later, they attended

a reception in honor of the 60th anniversary of the State of Israel.

Later in the evening, the President and Mrs. Bush traveled to the Prime Minister's residence, where, in the dining room, they attended a social dinner with Prime Minister Olmert and Mrs. Olmert. Later, they returned to the King David Hotel.

The President announced the designation of the following individuals as members of the Presidential delegation to Bethlehem to attend the Palestine Investment Conference from May 21 to 23:

Robert M. Kimmitt (head of delegation);
John J. Sullivan;
Robert A. Mosbacher, Jr.;
Larry W. Walther;
Walter Isaacson; and
Ziad Asali.

May 16

In the morning, the President had an intelligence briefing. Later, he and Mrs. Bush toured the Bible Lands Museum Jerusalem. They then traveled to Ben Gurion International Airport, where they participated in a greeting with President Shimon Peres and Prime Minister Ehud Olmert of Israel and Prime Minister's wife Aliza.

Later in the morning, the President and Mrs. Bush traveled to Riyadh, Saudi Arabia, where, upon arrival in the afternoon at King Khaled International Airport, they participated in an arrival ceremony with King Abdallah bin Abd al-Aziz Al Saud of Saudi Arabia.

Later in the afternoon, the President and Mrs. Bush traveled to Al Janadriyah, Saudi Arabia, where, at Al Janadriyah Farm, they had lunch with King Abdallah. Later, he met with King Abdallah.

In the evening, the President had dinner with King Abdallah.

The White House announced that the President will welcome Prime Minister Sergei Stanishev of Bulgaria to the White House on June 18.

The White House announced that the President will welcome Prime Minister Jan Peter Balkenende of the Netherlands to the White House on June 5.

The President announced his intention to designate Michael O. Leavitt (chief delegate), William R. Steiger, and Warren W. Tichenor as

U.S. delegates to the 61st World Health Assembly of the World Health Organization.

The President announced his intention to designate the following individuals as alternate U.S. delegates to the 61st World Health Assembly of the World Health Organization:

Mark A. Abdoo;
Gerald C. Anderson;
Joxel Garcia;
David E. Hohman;
John E. Lange;
Michael W. Miller;
Penelope S. Royall; and
Mary Lou Valdez.

May 17

In the morning, the President had an intelligence briefing. He then had breakfast with King Abdallah bin Abd al-Aziz Al Saud of Saudi Arabia. Later, he and Mrs. Bush traveled to Sharm el-Sheikh, Egypt, where, upon arrival at Sharm el-Sheikh International Airport, they participated in a greeting with President Mohamed Hosni Mubarak of Egypt and his wife Suzanne Thabet.

In the afternoon, the President and Mrs. Bush traveled to the Four Seasons Resort, where he met with President Mubarak. They then had a working lunch. Later, he traveled to the Hyatt Regency Sharm El Sheikh hotel.

In the evening, the President had a working dinner with President Mahmoud Abbas of the Palestinian Authority.

May 18

In the morning, the President met with King Abdullah II of Jordan. He then met with Prime Minister Salam Fayyad of the Palestinian Authority.

In the afternoon, the President and Mrs. Bush traveled to the Maritim Sharm El Sheikh International Congress Center. Later, they returned to Washington, DC, arriving in the evening.

May 19

In the morning, the President had an intelligence briefing. Later, in the Situation Room, he had a video teleconference with Prime Minister Nuri al-Maliki of Iraq.

May 20

In the morning, the President had an intelligence briefing. Later, in the Oval Office, he and Mrs. Bush met with Japan's outgoing Am-

bassador to the U.S. Ryozo Kato and his wife Hanayo.

The White House announced that the President and Mrs. Bush will travel to Slovenia, Germany, Italy, the Holy See, France, and the United Kingdom from June 9 to 16.

The President announced his intention to nominate Asif J. Chaudhry to be Ambassador to Moldova.

The President announced his intention to nominate Husein A. Cumber to be a member of the Surface Transportation Board.

The President announced his intention to nominate Tina S. Kaidanow to be Ambassador to Kosovo.

The President announced his intention to appoint Grant S. Green and Dov S. Zakheim as members of the Commission on Wartime Contracting in Iraq and Afghanistan.

The President declared a major disaster in Kentucky and ordered Federal aid to supplement Commonwealth and local recovery efforts in the area struck by severe storms, tornadoes, flooding, mudslides, and landslides on April 3 and 4.

The President declared a major disaster in Arkansas and ordered Federal aid to supplement State and local recovery efforts in the area struck by severe storms, flooding, and tornadoes beginning on May 2 and continuing.

May 21

In the morning, the President had an intelligence briefing. Later, in the Oval Office, he met with George J. Lisicki, national commander-in-chief, Veterans of Foreign Wars.

In the afternoon, in the Oval Office, the President met with Nasrallah Boutros Cardinal Sfeir, the Maronite Patriarch of Antioch and All the East.

May 22

In the morning, the President had an intelligence briefing. Later, he traveled to Pope Air Force Base, NC, where, upon arrival, he met with USA Freedom Corps volunteer Amy Petrenko. He then traveled to Fort Bragg, NC, where he presented medals to soldiers and family members of soldiers killed in the war on terror.

In the afternoon, the President toured Barracks C–4122 and C–5624. Later, at the 82d Airborne Division War Memorial Museum, he attended the All American Memorial Ceremony and the unveiling of the Global War on Terror Memorial. He then returned to Washington, DC.

The President announced his intention to nominate David F. Girard-diCarlo to be Ambassador to Austria.

The President announced his intention to nominate Patrick J. Durkin to be a member of the Board of Directors of the Overseas Private Investment Corporation.

The President announced his intention to nominate Michael B. Bemis to be a member of the Board of Directors of the Tennessee Valley Authority.

The President announced his intention to nominate John J. Faso, Joseph Manchin III, and Harvey M. Tettlebaum to be members of the Board of Trustees of the James Madison Memorial Fellowship Foundation.

The President announced his intention to nominate Matthew S. Petersen to be a member of the Federal Election Commission.

The President announced his intention to appoint Joseph Cascio as Federal Environmental Executive of the Environmental Protection Agency.

The President announced his intention to appoint Gary S. Becker, Lucille Shapiro, and Robert J. Zimmer as members of the President's Committee on the National Medal of Science.

The President announced his intention to designate Matthew W. Friedrich as Acting Assistant Attorney General (Criminal Division).

The President announced his intention to designate Jason J. Fichtner as Acting Deputy Commissioner of Social Security.

The President announced his intention to designate Linda P.B. Katehi as Chairman of the President's Committee on the National Medal of Science.

The President declared a major disaster in South Dakota and ordered Federal aid to supplement State and local recovery efforts in the area struck by a severe winter storm and record and near-record snow on May 1 and 2.

May 23

In the morning, the President had an intelligence briefing. Later, in the Situation Room, he participated in a Homeland Security Council meeting, where he was briefed on the upcoming hurricane season. Then, on the South Lawn, he participated in an interview with Neil Cavuto of FOX News.

In the afternoon, the President traveled to Camp David, MD.

The President declared a major disaster in Missouri and ordered Federal aid to supplement State and local recovery efforts in the area struck by severe storms and tornadoes on May 10 and 11.

The President declared a major disaster in Georgia and ordered Federal aid to supplement State and local recovery efforts in the area struck by severe storms and tornadoes on May 11 and 12.

May 24

In the morning, the President had an intelligence briefing.

May 25

In the afternoon, the President and Mrs. Bush returned to Washington, DC.

May 26

In the morning, the President had an intelligence briefing. Later, he and Mrs. Bush traveled to Arlington, VA, where they participated in a Memorial Day wreath-laying ceremony at the Tomb of the Unknowns in Arlington National Cemetery.

In the afternoon, the President and Mrs. Bush returned to Washington, DC.

The President declared a major disaster in Colorado and ordered Federal aid to supplement State and local recovery efforts in the area struck by severe storms and tornadoes on May 22.

May 27

In the morning, the President had an intelligence briefing. Later, he traveled to Kirtland Air Force Base, NM, where, upon arrival, he met with USA Freedom Corps volunteer Fran Macintyre.

In the afternoon, the President traveled to Los Ranchos de Albuquerque, NM, where, at a private residence, he attended a White for Congress and New Mexico Victory 2008 luncheon. Later, he traveled to Phoenix, AZ, where, upon arrival, he met with four generations of Eagle Scouts: Thomas S. Boggess, Jr., Thomas S. Boggess III, Thomas S. Boggess IV, and Thomas S. Boggess V. He then met with USA Freedom Corps volunteer Tamara Skinner.

Later in the afternoon, the President traveled to Mesa, AZ. He then returned to Phoenix, AZ, where, at a private residence, he attended a McCain for President and Republican National Committee Victory reception.

In the evening, the President traveled to Colorado Springs, CO.

The President announced the designation of the following individuals as members of the Presidential delegation to Arusha, Tanzania, to attend the Leon H. Sullivan Summit VIII on June 2:

Dirk Kempthorne (head of delegation);
Mark A. Green;
Jendayi E. Frazer;
John A. Simon;
Michael S. Steele;
Edward W. "Ward" Brehm III; and
Melinda Doolittle.

The President announced his intention to nominate James Culbertson to be Ambassador to the Netherlands.

The President announced his intention to nominate W. Stuart Symington to be Ambassador to Rwanda.

The President declared a major disaster in Iowa and ordered Federal aid to supplement State and local recovery efforts in the area struck by severe storms, tornadoes, and flooding beginning on May 25 and continuing.

May 28

In the morning, the President had an intelligence briefing. Later, he traveled to the U.S. Air Force Academy, where he participated in a photo opportunity with members of the U.S. Air Force Thunderbirds.

In the afternoon, the President traveled to Salt Lake City, UT, where, upon arrival, he met with USA Freedom Corps volunteer Richard Pehrson. Then, at a private residence, he attended a McCain for President and Republican National Committee Victory reception. Later, he traveled to Park City, UT.

In the evening, at a private residence, the President attended a McCain for President and Republican National Committee Victory reception.

The President declared a major disaster in Mississippi and ordered Federal aid to supplement State and local recovery efforts in the area struck by severe storms and tornadoes on April 4.

May 29

In the morning, the President had an intelligence briefing. Later, he traveled to Salt Lake City, UT, where, at the Church of Jesus Christ of Latter-day Saints worldwide headquarters, he met with Thomas S. Monson, president, Henry B. Eyring, first counselor, and Dieter F. Uchtdorf, second counselor, Church of Jesus Christ of Latter-day Saints. He then traveled to Olathe, KS, where, upon arrival in the afternoon, he met with USA Freedom Corps volunteer Ashley Knight.

Later in the afternoon, the President traveled to Bucyrus, KS, where, at a private residence, he attended a Nick Jordan for Congress and Kansas Victory 2008 reception. He then returned to Washington, DC.

The White House announced that the President will welcome President Gloria Macapagal-Arroyo of the Philippines to the White House on June 24.

The President announced his intention to nominate Alan W. Eastham, Jr., to be Ambassador to the Republic of the Congo.

The President announced his intention to nominate the following individuals to be members of the Board of Directors of the Corporation for Public Broadcasting:

Lori Gilbert;
Cheryl Feldman Halpern;
David H. Pryor;
Bruce M. Ramer; and
Elizabeth Sembler.

The President announced his intention to appoint Don A. Christiansen as a member of the Utah Reclamation Mitigation and Conservation Commission.

The President announced his intention to appoint Arnold Fields as Special Inspector General for Afghanistan Reconstruction.

The President announced his intention to designate Clay Lowery as Acting U.S. Executive Director of the Inter-American Development Bank.

May 30

In the morning, the President had a telephone conversation with President Pervez Musharraf of Pakistan to discuss Pakistan-U.S. relations and the war on terror. He then had an intelligence briefing.

The President declared a major disaster in Nebraska and ordered Federal aid to supplement State and local recovery efforts in the area struck by severe storms, tornadoes, and flooding from April 23 to 26.

May 31

In the morning, the President had an intelligence briefing.

In the afternoon, the President traveled to Greenville, SC, where, upon arrival in the evening, he met with USA Freedom Corps volunteer Andrew Barnhill.

Later in the evening, the President returned to Washington, DC.

June 2

In the morning, the President had an intelligence briefing. Later, he chaired a National Security Council meeting on Iraq, in which he was briefed by Gen. David H. Petraeus, USA, commanding general, Multi-National Force—Iraq, via video teleconference.

The President announced his intention to nominate Kenneth L. Peel to be U.S. Director of the European Bank for Reconstruction and Development.

The President announced his intention to nominate Gregory G. Garre to be Solicitor General at the Department of Justice and designate him as Acting Solicitor General.

June 3

In the morning, the President had an intelligence briefing.

In the afternoon, in the Roosevelt Room, the President met with Iraqi Shi'a and Sunni tribal leaders.

June 4

In the morning, the President had an intelligence briefing.

During the day, the President met with Secretary of Defense Robert M. Gates to discuss personnel changes at the Department of the Air Force.

June 5

In the morning, the President had an intelligence briefing. Later, in the Rose Garden, he participated in a photo opportunity with the 2007 Major League Soccer Cup champion Houston Dynamo.

The President announced his intention to nominate James F. Jeffrey to be Ambassador to Turkey.

The President announced his intention to nominate the following individuals to be members of the National Council on Disability:

Marylyn Andrea Howe;
Heather McCallum;
Lonnie C. Moore; and
Christina Alvarado Shanahan.

The President announced his intention to nominate the following individuals to be members of the Board of Directors of the African Development Foundation:

John O. Agwunobi;
Julius E. Coles;
Morgan W. Davis; and
John W. Leslie, Jr.

The President announced his intention to appoint Wayne B. Paugh as Coordinator for International Intellectual Property Enforcement at the Department of Commerce.

The President announced that he has named Thomas P. Bossert as Deputy Assistant to the President for Homeland Security.

The President announced that he has named Pete Patterson as Associate Counsel to the President.

June 6

In the morning, the President had an intelligence briefing. He then had a telephone conversation with Prime Minister Fredrik Reinfeldt of Sweden to wish him a happy National Day of Sweden and thank him for hosting the first International Compact with Iraq Annual Review Conference in Stockholm.

In the afternoon, the President traveled to Camp David, MD.

June 7

In the morning, the President had an intelligence briefing.

June 8

In the afternoon, the President returned to Washington, DC.

June 9

In the morning, the President had an intelligence briefing. Later, he traveled to Ljubljana, Slovenia, arriving in the evening. While en route aboard Air Force One, he participated in an interview with Gerard Baker and Tom Baldwin of The Times newspaper.

Later in the evening, upon arrival at Ljubljana Joze Pucnik Airport, the President participated in a greeting with Prime Minister Janez Jansa of Slovenia. He then traveled to the Kokra Hotel in Kranj, Slovenia.

The President announced his intention to nominate Michael Bruce Donley to be Secretary of the Air Force and designate him as Acting Secretary.

The President declared a major disaster in Indiana and ordered Federal aid to supplement State and local recovery efforts in the area struck by severe storms and flooding beginning on June 6 and continuing.

June 10

In the morning, the President had an intelligence briefing. Later, he traveled to Brdo Castle, where he met separately with President Danilo Turk and Prime Minister Janez Jansa of Slovenia. He then returned to the Kokra Hotel, where he was joined by Mrs. Bush.

Later in the morning, the President and Mrs. Bush met with U.S. Embassy staff and their families. He then returned to Brdo Castle, where he participated in a photo opportunity and met with European Union leaders. Later, he traveled to the Brdo Congress Centre, where, in Splendens Hall, he participated in the EU-U.S. summit.

In the afternoon, in Glass Hall at the Brdo Congress Centre, the President participated in the EU-U.S. summit working lunch. Later, he returned to Brdo Castle, where he was joined by Mrs. Bush. Then, on the South Lawn of Brdo Castle, they viewed the Lipizzaner Horse Exhibition.

Later in the afternoon, the President and Mrs. Bush traveled to Ljubljana Joze Pucnik Airport, where they, Prime Minister Jansa, and his fiancee Urska Bacovnik participated in photo opportunities and met with Slovenian military personnel. They then traveled to Meseberg, Germany, arriving in the evening.

Later in the evening, the President and Mrs. Bush traveled to the Schloss Meseberg, where they had dinner with Chancellor Angela Merkel of Germany and her husband Joachim Sauer.

The President announced his intention to nominate Frederick S. Celec to be Assistant to the Secretary of Defense for Nuclear, Chemical, and Biological Defense Programs.

The President announced his intention to nominate John M. Jones to be Ambassador to Guyana.

The President announced his intention to appoint the following individuals as members of the President's Commission on White House Fellowships:

Dionel M. Aviles;
Ari Bousbib;
Amy Woods Brinkley;
Deirdre P. Connelly;
Louis DeJoy;
George M. Drysdale;
John H. Frey;
Trey Grayson;
Frederick D. Gregory;
Mark F. Hearne II;
Thomas C. Leppert;
Catherine J. Martin;
Roger B. Porter;
Amy Tuck; and
Dennis Zeleny.

The President announced his intention to appoint Brig. Gen. Errol R. Schwartz as Commanding General of the Militia of the District of Columbia.

June 11

In the morning, the President had an intelligence briefing. Later, in the Garden Salon of Schloss Meseberg, he and Mrs. Bush had breakfast with Chancellor Angela Merkel of Germany.

In the afternoon, in the Garden at Schloss Meseberg, the President had lunch with Chancellor Merkel. Later, he traveled to Rome, Italy. Upon arrival, he traveled to the Villa Taverna, the official residence of U.S. Ambassador to Italy Ronald P. Spogli.

June 12

In the morning, the President had an intelligence briefing. He then traveled to the Villa Aurelia at the American Academy.

In the afternoon, the President traveled to Quirinale Palace, where, in the President's Office, he met with President Giorgio Napolitano of Italy. Then, in the Mirror Room, they had lunch. Later, he returned to the Villa Taverna.

During the day, the President was briefed on the June 11 storms and flooding in the Midwest.

In the evening, the President traveled to the Villa Madama, where, in the Dining Room, he had a working dinner with Prime Minister Silvio Berlusconi of Italy. Later, he returned to the Villa Taverna.

The President announced his intention to nominate Michele J. Sison to be Ambassador to Lebanon.

The President announced his intention to nominate James C. Swan to be Ambassador to Djibouti.

The President announced his intention to appoint Carole Jean Jordan as Chairperson of the National Women's Business Council.

The President announced his intention to appoint Florence Shapiro as a member of the U.S. Holocaust Memorial Council.

The President announced his intention to appoint the following individuals as members of the National Cancer Advisory Board:

Victoria Lee Champion;
William H. Goodwin, Jr.;
Waun Ki Hong;
Judith Salmon Kaur;
Mary Vaughan Lester;
Herbert K. Lyerly; and
Jennifer A. Pietenpol.

The President announced his intention to designate Carolyn D. Runowicz as Chairman of the National Cancer Advisory Board.

June 13

In the morning, the President had an intelligence briefing. Later, he traveled to the Vatican, where he was joined by Mrs. Bush. They then participated in a greeting with Pope Benedict XVI.

Later in the morning, the President met with Pope Benedict XVI. They then toured the Vatican Gardens. Later, he, Mrs. Bush, and Pope Benedict XVI attended a cultural performance.

In the afternoon, the President and Mrs. Bush traveled to Paris, France. Later, he traveled to the Organisation for Economic Co-operation and Development headquarters. He then traveled to the U.S. Embassy residence, where he was joined by Mrs. Bush.

In the evening, the President and Mrs. Bush traveled to Elysee Palace, where he participated in an arrival ceremony with President Nicolas Sarkozy of France. They then had dinner with President Sarkozy and his wife Carla Bruni-Sarkozy. Later, they returned to the U.S. Embassy residence.

The President declared a major disaster in Montana and ordered Federal aid to supplement State and local recovery efforts in the area struck by a severe winter storm on May 1 and 2.

June 14

In the morning, at the U.S. Ambassador's residence in Paris, France, the President had an intelligence briefing. Later, he traveled to Elysee Palace.

In the afternoon, the President and President Nicolas Sarkozy of France returned to the U.S. Ambassador's residence, where they were joined by Mrs. Bush. They all then attended the unveiling of the Flamme de la Liberte statue. Later, he visited the Suresnes American Cemetery and Memorial, where he participated in a wreath-laying ceremony.

Later in the afternoon, the President visited Mont Valerien, where he participated in a wreath-laying ceremony. He then returned to the U.S. Ambassador's residence, where he met with U.S. Embassy staff and their families.

In the evening, the President had a telephone conversation with Secretary of Homeland Security Michael Chertoff and Federal Emergency Management Agency Administrator R. David Paulison, in which he was briefed on the flooding in the Midwest. Later, he and Mrs. Bush attended entertainment and a dinner hosted by U.S. Ambassador to France Craig R. Stapleton and his wife Dorothy.

The President declared a major disaster in Wisconsin and ordered Federal aid to supplement State and local recovery efforts in the area struck by severe storms, tornadoes, and flooding beginning on June 5 and continuing.

June 15

In the afternoon, the President and Mrs. Bush traveled to Windsor, England, where, at Windsor Castle, they met with Queen Elizabeth II and her husband Prince Philip, Duke of Edinburgh. Later, they traveled to Winfield House, the U.S. Ambassador's residence in London, England. Then, in the Yellow Room, they participated in an interview with Adam Boulton of Sky News.

Later in the afternoon, in the Green Room, the President and Mrs. Bush attended a reception with British military personnel.

In the evening, the President and Mrs. Bush traveled to 10 Downing Street, the Prime Minister's residence, where, in the State Dining Room, they had dinner with Prime Minister Gordon Brown of the United Kingdom and his wife Sarah. Later, they returned to Winfield House.

June 16

In the morning, the President had an intelligence briefing. Later, in the Family Dining Room, he had breakfast with former Prime Minister Tony Blair of the United Kingdom, Quartet Representative in the Middle East. He then traveled to 10 Downing Street, the Prime Minister's residence.

Later in the morning, the President traveled to the U.S. Embassy, where he was joined by Mrs. Bush. They then met with U.S. Embassy staff and their families.

In the afternoon, the President returned to Winfield House, where, in the Yellow Room, he met with Conservative Party Leader and Opposition Leader David Cameron of the United Kingdom. Later, he and Mrs. Bush traveled to Belfast, Northern Ireland.

Later in the afternoon, the President traveled to Stormont Castle. Later, he traveled to the Lough View Integrated Primary & Nursery School, where he was joined by Mrs. Bush. They then toured the school.

Later in the afternoon, the President and Mrs. Bush returned to Washington, DC, arriving in the evening.

June 17

In the morning, the President had an intelligence briefing.

In the afternoon, the President and Mrs. Bush traveled to St. Albans School, where they attended the wake for Tim Russert, moderator of NBC's "Meet the Press," who died on June 13.

The White House announced that the President will welcome Prime Minister Nguyen Tan Dung of Vietnam to the White House on June 24.

June 18

In the morning, the President had a telephone conversation with President Levy Patrick Mwanawasa of Zambia to discuss the situation in Zimbabwe. Later, he had an intelligence briefing.

In the afternoon, in Room 350 of the Dwight D. Eisenhower Executive Office Building, the President met with the Chinese delegation to the U.S.-China Strategic Economic Dialogue.

The President announced his intention to nominate J.V. Schwan to be Commissioner of the U.S. International Trade Commission.

The President announced his intention to designate Shara L. Aranoff as Chairman of the U.S. International Trade Commission.

The President announced his intention to designate Daniel Pearson as Vice Chairman of the U.S. International Trade Commission.

June 19

In the morning, the President had an intelligence briefing. Later, he traveled to Cedar Rapids, IA, where he participated in a briefing on the flooding in the Midwest.

In the afternoon, the President traveled to Iowa City, IA. While en route aboard Marine One, he took an aerial tour of the areas damaged by flooding. Later, he returned to Washington, DC, arriving in the evening.

The President announced his intention to nominate J. Patrick Rowan to be Assistant Attorney General (National Security Division) at the Department of Justice.

The President announced his intention to nominate Brent R. Orrell to be Assistant Secretary of Labor (Employment and Training).

The President announced his intention to nominate Richard G. Olson, Jr., to be Ambassador to the United Arab Emirates.

The President announced his intention to nominate Diane Barone and Mary E. Curtis to be members of the National Institute for Literacy Advisory Board.

The President declared a major disaster in West Virginia and ordered Federal aid to supplement State and local recovery efforts in the area struck by severe storms, tornadoes, flooding, mudslides, and landslides from June 3 to 7.

June 20

In the morning, the President had an intelligence briefing. Later, he traveled to Fort Myers, FL, where, upon arrival, he met with USA Freedom Corps volunteer Josh Kelchner. He then traveled to Naples, FL, arriving in the afternoon.

Later in the afternoon, at a private residence, the President attended a Lincoln and Mario

Diaz-Balart Florida Victory 2008 Committee luncheon. Later, he traveled to Raleigh, NC, where, upon arrival, he met with USA Freedom Corps volunteer Nick Marriam. Then, at a private residence, he attended a Pat McCrory for Governor reception.

In the evening, the President returned to Washington, DC.

The President declared a major disaster in Nebraska and ordered Federal aid to supplement State and local recovery efforts in the area struck by severe storms, tornadoes, and flooding beginning on May 22 and continuing.

June 21

In the morning, the President had an intelligence briefing.

June 23

In the morning, the President had an intelligence briefing.

In the afternoon, on the South Portico, the President participated in a photo opportunity with the 2008 Presidential Scholars.

June 24

In the morning, the President had a video teleconference with President Hamid Karzai of Afghanistan. Later, he had an intelligence briefing.

In the afternoon, the President traveled to McLean, VA.

In the evening, at a private residence, the President attended a Republican National Committee reception. He then returned to Washington, DC.

The President announced his intention to nominate Holly A. Kuzmich to be Assistant Secretary for Legislation and Congressional Affairs at the Department of Education.

The President announced his intention to nominate Christopher M. Marston to be Assistant Secretary for Management at the Department of Education.

The President announced his intention to nominate David D. Pearce to be Ambassador to Algeria.

The President announced his intention to nominate Lyndon L. Olson, Jr., to be a member of the U.S. Advisory Commission on Public Diplomacy.

The President announced his intention to appoint Sambhu N. Banik as a member of the President's Committee for People With Intellectual Disabilities.

The President announced his intention to appoint the following individuals as members of the President's Council on Bioethics:

Floyd E. Bloom;
Benjamin S. Carson, Sr.;
Rebecca Susan Dresser;
Nicholas Eberstadt;
Jean B. Elshtain;
Daniel W. Foster;
Michael S. Gazzaniga;
Robert P. George;
Alfonso Gomez-Lobo;
William B. Hurlbut;
Donald W. Landry;
Peter A. Lawler;
Paul R. McHugh;
Gilbert C. Meilaender, Jr.;
Edmund D. Pellegrino;
Janet Davison Rowley;
Diana J. Schaub; and
Carl E. Schneider.

The President declared a major disaster in Illinois and ordered Federal aid to supplement State and local recovery efforts in the area struck by severe storms and flooding beginning on June 1.

June 25

In the morning, the President had a telephone conversation with Prime Minister Yasuo Fukuda of Japan. He then had an intelligence briefing. Later, he met with Secretary of the Treasury Henry M. Paulson, Jr., to discuss the economic situation.

In the afternoon, the President traveled to Detroit, MI, where, upon arrival, he met with USA Freedom Corps volunteer Jean Peirce. He then traveled to Livonia, MI.

In the evening, the President returned to Washington, DC.

The President announced his intention to nominate Santanu K. "Sandy" Baruah to be Administrator of the Small Business Administration.

The President announced his intention to nominate Jason J. Fichtner to be Deputy Commissioner of Social Security.

The President announced his intention to nominate James A. Williams to be Administrator of the General Services Administration.

The President declared a major disaster in Missouri and ordered Federal aid to supplement

State and local recovery efforts in the area struck by severe storms and flooding beginning on June 1 and continuing.

The President declared a major disaster in Minnesota and ordered Federal aid to supplement State and local recovery efforts in the area struck by severe storms and flooding beginning on June 7 and continuing.

June 26

In the morning, the President had an intelligence briefing.

In the afternoon, the President traveled to Camp David, MD. Later, he participated in a welcoming ceremony with Crown Prince Muhammad bin Zayid Al Nuhayyan of Abu Dhabi.

The President announced that he has nominated Richard A. Anderson to be a member of the Internal Revenue Service Oversight Board.

The President announced that he has nominated Joseph F. Bader to be a member of the Defense Nuclear Facilities Safety Board.

The President announced that he has nominated Mark E. Keenum to be a member of the Farm Credit Administration Board.

The President announced that he has nominated Mary Lucille Jordan to be a member of the Federal Mine Safety and Health Review Commission.

The President announced that he has nominated Matthew A. Reynolds to be Assistant Secretary of State (Legislative Affairs).

The President announced that he has nominated Peter R. Kann and Michael Meehan to be members of the Broadcasting Board of Governors.

June 27

In the morning, the President had an intelligence briefing.

The President announced that he has nominated Thomas A. Betro to be Inspector General at the Department of State.

The President announced that he has nominated Brian H. Hook to be Assistant Secretary of State (International Organization Affairs) and his intention to designate him as Acting Assistant Secretary of State.

June 28

In the morning, the President had an intelligence briefing.

The President declared an emergency in California and ordered Federal aid to supplement State and local response efforts in the area struck by wildfires beginning June 20 and continuing.

June 29

In the afternoon, the President and Mrs. Bush returned to Washington, DC.

June 30

In the morning, the President had an intelligence briefing. Later, he participated in an interview with print journalists.

The President made additional disaster assistance available to Iowa by authorizing an increase in the level of Federal funding for emergency protective measures undertaken as a result of the severe storms, tornadoes, and flooding beginning on May 25 and continuing.

The President made additional disaster assistance available to Missouri by authorizing an increase in the level of Federal funding for emergency protective measures undertaken as a result of the severe storms and flooding beginning on June 1 and continuing.

The President made additional disaster assistance available to Illinois by authorizing an increase in the level of Federal funding for emergency protective measures undertaken as a result of the severe storms and flooding beginning on June 1 and continuing.

The President made additional disaster assistance available to Wisconsin by authorizing an increase in the level of Federal funding for emergency protective measures undertaken as a result of the severe storms, tornadoes, and flooding beginning on June 5 and continuing.

The President made additional disaster assistance available to Indiana by authorizing an increase in the level of Federal funding for emergency protective measures undertaken as a result of the severe storms and flooding beginning on June 6 and continuing.

Appendix B—Nominations Submitted to the Senate

The following list does not include promotions of members of the Uniformed Services, nominations to the Service Academies, or nominations of Foreign Service officers.

Submitted January 22

Jonathan Baron,
of Maryland, to be a member of the Board of Directors of the National Board for Education Sciences for a term expiring November 28, 2011 (reappointment).

Julia W. Bland,
of Louisiana, to be a member of the National Museum and Library Services Board for a term expiring December 6, 2012, vice Margaret Scarlett, term expired.

William J. Brennan,
of Maine, to be Assistant Secretary of Commerce for Oceans and Atmosphere, vice James R. Mahoney.

Jan Cellucci,
of Massachusetts, to be a member of the National Museum and Library Services Board for a term expiring December 6, 2012, vice Edwin Joseph Rigaud, term expired.

J. Gregory Copeland,
of Texas, to be General Counsel of the Department of Energy, vice David R. Hill.

Nelson M. Ford,
of Virginia, to be Under Secretary of the Army, vice Preston M. Geren.

Joxel Garcia,
of Connecticut, to be Medical Director in the Regular Corps of the Public Health Service, subject to the qualifications therefor as provided by law and regulations, and to be an Assistant Secretary of Health and Human Services, vice John O. Agwunobi, resigned.

Joxel Garcia,
of Connecticut, to be Representative of the U.S. on the Executive Board of the World Health Organization, vice James O. Mason.

Jeffrey J. Grieco,
of Virginia, to be an Assistant Administrator of the U.S. Agency for International Development, vice J. Edward Fox.

William J. Hagenah,
of Illinois, to be a member of the National Museum and Library Services Board for a term expiring December 6, 2012, vice Judith Ann Rapanos, term expired.

Frank Philip Handy,
of Florida, to be a member of the Board of Directors of the National Board for Education Sciences for a term expiring November 28, 2011 (reappointment).

Mark Y. Herring,
of South Carolina, to be a member of the National Museum and Library Services Board for a term expiring December 6, 2012, vice Renee Swartz, term expired.

Dorla M. Salling,
of Texas, to be a Commissioner of the U.S. Parole Commission for a term of 6 years, vice Deborah Ann Spagnoli, resigned.

Sally Epstein Shaywitz,
of Connecticut, to be a member of the Board of Directors of the National Board for Education Sciences for a term expiring November 28, 2011 (reappointment).

Kurt Douglas Volker,
of Pennsylvania, a career Foreign Service Officer of class One, to be U.S. Permanent Representative on the Council of the North Atlantic Treaty Organization, with the rank and status of Ambassador Extraordinary and Plenipotentiary.

Joanne Weiss,
of California, to be a member of the Board of Directors of the National Board for Education Sciences for a term expiring November 28, 2010, vice James R. Davis, term expired.

Submitted January 23

Anita K. Blair,
of Virginia, to be an Assistant Secretary of the Navy, vice William A. Navas, Jr., resigned.

Steven G. Bradbury,
of Maryland, to be an Assistant Attorney General, vice Jack Landman Goldsmith III, resigned.

Margaret Scobey,
of Tennessee, a career member of the Senior Foreign Service, class of Minister-Counselor, to be Ambassador Extraordinary and Plenipotentiary of the United States of America to the Arab Republic of Egypt.

D. Kathleen Stephens,
of Montana, a career member of the Senior Foreign Service, class of Minister-Counselor, to be Ambassador Extraordinary and Plenipotentiary of the United States of America to the Republic of Korea.

Withdrawn January 23

Andrew G. Biggs,
of New York, to be Deputy Commissioner of Social Security for the term expiring January 19, 2013, vice James B. Lockhart III, which was sent to the Senate on January 9, 2007.

Andrew G. Biggs,
of New York, to be Deputy Commissioner of Social Security for a term expiring January 19, 2013, vice James B. Lockhart III, which was sent to the Senate on May 16, 2007.

E. Duncan Getchell, Jr.,
of Virginia, to be U.S. Circuit Judge for the Fourth Circuit, vice H. Emory Widener, Jr., retired, which was sent to the Senate on September 6, 2007.

Submitted January 25

Robert J. Battista,
of Michigan, to be member of the National Labor Relations Board for the term of 5 years expiring December 16, 2009, vice Dennis P. Walsh.

Gerard Morales,
of Arizona, to be member of the National Labor Relations Board for the term of 5 years expiring December 16, 2012, vice Robert J. Battista, term expired.

Dennis P. Walsh,
of Maryland, to be member of the National Labor Relations Board for the term of 5 years expiring August 27, 2008, vice Peter N. Kirsanow.

Dennis P. Walsh,
of Maryland, to be member of the National Labor Relations Board for the term of 5 years expiring August 27, 2013 (reappointment).

Withdrawn January 25

Peter N. Kirsanow,
of Ohio, to be member of the National Labor Relations Board for the term of 5 years expiring August 27, 2008, vice Ronald E. Meisburg, which was sent to the Senate on January 9, 2007.

Dennis P. Walsh,
of Ohio, to be member of the National Labor Relations Board for the term of 5 years expiring December 16, 2009 (reappointment), which was sent to the Senate on January 9, 2007.

Submitted January 30

Robert J. Callahan,
of Virginia, a career member of the Senior Foreign Service, class of Minister-Counselor, to be Ambassador Extraordinary and Plenipotentiary of the United States of America to the Republic of Nicaragua.

Elisebeth C. Cook,
of Virginia, to be an Assistant Attorney General, vice Rachel Brand.

Heather M. Hodges,
of Ohio, a career member of the Senior Foreign Service, class of Minister-Counselor, to be Ambassador Extraordinary and Plenipotentiary of the United States of America to the Republic of Ecuador.

Barbara J. Stephenson,
of Florida, a career member of the Senior Foreign Service, class of Minister-Counselor, to be Ambassador Extraordinary and Plenipotentiary of the United States of America to the Republic of Panama.

William Edward Todd,
of Virginia, a career member of the Senior Executive Service, to be Ambassador Extraordinary

and Plenipotentiary of the United States of America to Brunei Darussalam.

Withdrawn January 30

Dennis W. Carlton,
of Illinois, to be a member of the Council of Economic Advisers, vice Katherine Baicker, resigned, which was sent to the Senate on August 2, 2007.

Andrew J. McKenna, Jr.,
of Illinois, to be a member of the National Security Education Board for a term of 4 years, vice Robert N. Shamansky, term expired, which was sent to the Senate on January 9, 2007.

Submitted February 5

Clyde R. Cook, Jr.,
of North Carolina, to be U.S. Marshal for the Eastern District of North Carolina for the term of 4 years, vice Charles R. Reavis.

Hugo Llorens,
of Florida, a career member of the Senior Foreign Service, class of Minister-Counselor, to be Ambassador Extraordinary and Plenipotentiary of the United States of America to the Republic of Honduras.

Marianne Matuzic Myles,
of New York, a career member of the Senior Foreign Service, class of Minister-Counselor, to be Ambassador Extraordinary and Plenipotentiary of the United States of America to the Republic of Cape Verde.

Submitted February 6

Ralph E. Martinez,
of Florida, to be a member of the Foreign Claims Settlement Commission of the U.S. for a term expiring September 30, 2010, vice Laramie Faith McNamara.

Susan D. Peppler,
of California, to be an Assistant Secretary of Housing and Urban Development, vice Pamela Hughes Patenaude.

Linda Thomas-Greenfield,
of Louisiana, a career member of the Senior Foreign Service, class of Minister-Counselor, to be Ambassador Extraordinary and Plenipotentiary of the United States of America to the Republic of Liberia.

Withdrawn February 7

Paul DeCamp,
of Virginia, to be Administrator of the Wage and Hour Division, Department of Labor, vice Tammy Dee McCutchen, resigned, which was sent to the Senate on January 9, 2007.

Submitted February 12

Jeffrey Robert Brown,
of Illinois, to be a member of the Board of Trustees of the Federal Hospital Insurance Trust Fund for a term of 4 years, vice Thomas R. Saving.

Jeffrey Robert Brown,
of Illinois, to be a member of the Board of Trustees of the Federal Old-Age and Survivors Insurance Trust Fund and the Federal Disability Insurance Trust Fund for a term of 4 years, vice Thomas R. Saving.

Hyepin Christine Im,
of California, to be a member of the Board of Directors of the Corporation for National and Community Service for the remainder of the term expiring October 6, 2008, vice Henry Lozano, resigned.

Hyepin Christine Im,
of California, to be a member of the Board of Directors of the Corporation for National and Community Service for a term expiring October 6, 2013 (reappointment).

Perri Klass,
of New York, to be a member of the National Institute for Literacy Advisory Board for a term expiring November 25, 2009, vice William T. Hiller, term expired.

Katherine Mitchell,
of Alabama, to be a member of the National Institute for Literacy Advisory Board for a term expiring November 25, 2010, vice Mark G. Yudof, resigned.

Eduardo J. Padron,
of Florida, to be a member of the National Institute for Literacy Advisory Board for a term expiring November 25, 2009, vice Juan R. Olivarez, term expired.

Alexa E. Posny,
of Kansas, to be a member of the National Institute for Literacy Advisory Board for a term expiring November 25, 2008, vice Carol C. Gambill, term expired.

Timothy Shanahan,
of Illinois, to be a member of the National Institute for Literacy Advisory Board for a term expiring November 25, 2010 (reappointment).

Richard Kenneth Wagner,
of Florida, to be a member of the National Institute for Literacy Advisory Board for a term expiring November 25, 2009 (reappointment).

Laysha Ward,
of Minnesota, to be a member of the Board of Directors of the Corporation for National and Community Service for a term expiring December 27, 2012, vice Mimi Mager, term expired.

Withdrawn February 12

Warren Bell,
of California, to be a member of the Board of Directors of the Corporation for Public Broadcasting for a term expiring January 31, 2012, vice Kenneth Y. Tomlinson, resigned, which was sent to the Senate on January 9, 2007.

Patricia Mathes,
of Texas, to be a member of the National Institute for Literacy Advisory Board for a term expiring November 25, 2007, vice Mark G. Yudof, resigned, which was sent to the Senate on January 9, 2007.

John L. Palmer,
of New York, to be a member of the Board of Trustees of the Federal Old-Age and Survivors Insurance Trust Fund and the Federal Disability Insurance Trust Fund for a term of 4 years (reappointment), which was sent to the Senate on January 9, 2007.

John L. Palmer,
of New York, to be a member of the Board of Trustees of the Federal Supplementary Medical Insurance Trust Fund for a term of 4 years (reappointment), which was sent to the Senate on January 9, 2007.

John L. Palmer,
of New York, to be a member of the Board of Trustees of the Federal Hospital Insurance Trust Fund for a term of 4 years (reappointment), which was sent to the Senate on January 9, 2007.

Thomas R. Saving,
of Texas, to be a member of the Board of Trustees of the Federal Supplementary Medical Insurance Trust Fund for a term of 4 years (reappointment), which was sent to the Senate on January 9, 2007.

Thomas R. Saving,
of Texas, to be a member of the Board of Trustees of the Federal Old-Age and Survivors Insurance Trust Fund and the Federal Disability Insurance Trust Fund for a term of 4 years (reappointment), which was sent to the Senate on January 9, 2007.

Thomas R. Saving,
of Texas, to be a member of the Board of Trustees of the Federal Hospital Insurance Trust Fund for a term of 4 years (reappointment), which was sent to the Senate on January 9, 2007.

Submitted February 14

Jeffrey Robert Brown,
of Illinois, to be a member of the Board of Trustees of the Federal Supplementary Medical Insurance Trust Fund for a term of 4 years, vice Thomas R. Saving.

David Gustafson,
of Virginia, to be a Judge of the U.S. Tax Court for a term of 15 years, vice Carolyn P. Chiechi, term expired.

William T. Lawrence,
of Indiana, to be U.S. District Judge for the Southern District of Indiana, vice John Daniel Tinder, elevated.

Joseph Evan LeBaron,
of Oregon, a career member of the Senior Foreign Service, class of Minister-Counselor, to be Ambassador Extraordinary and Plenipotentiary of the United States of America to the State of Qatar.

Stephen James Nolan,
of Virginia, a career member of the Senior Foreign Service, class of Minister-Counselor, to be Ambassador Extraordinary and Plenipotentiary of the United States of America to the Republic of Botswana.

Elizabeth Crewson Paris,
of the District of Columbia, to be a Judge of the U.S. Tax Court for a term of 15 years, vice Joel Gerber, retired.

Samuel W. Speck,
of Ohio, to be a Commissioner on the part of the U.S. on the International Joint Commission, United States and Canada, vice Dennis L. Schornack.

Submitted February 25

Joseph A. Benkert,
of Virginia, to be an Assistant Secretary of Defense, vice Peter Cyril Wyche Flory, resigned.

Donald E. Booth,
of Virginia, a career member of the Senior Foreign Service, class of Minister-Counselor, to be Ambassador Extraordinary and Plenipotentiary of the United States of America to the Republic of Zambia.

Carol Dillon Kissal,
of Maryland, to be Inspector General, Small Business Administration, vice Eric M. Thorson.

Scot A. Marciel,
of California, for the rank of Ambassador during his tenure of service as Deputy Assistant Secretary of State for East Asian and Association of Southeast Asian Nations (ASEAN) Affairs.

Nancy E. McEldowney,
of Florida, a career member of the Senior Foreign Service, class of Minister-Counselor, to be Ambassador Extraordinary and Plenipotentiary of the United States of America to the Republic of Bulgaria.

Stephen George McFarland,
of Texas, a career member of the Senior Foreign Service, class of Minister-Counselor, to be Ambassador Extraordinary and Plenipotentiary of the United States of America to the Republic of Guatemala.

Gillian Arlette Milovanovic,
of Pennsylvania, a career member of the Senior Foreign Service, class of Minister-Counselor, to be Ambassador Extraordinary and Plenipotentiary of the United States of America to the Republic of Mali.

Submitted February 26

Kenneth E. Carfine,
of Maryland, to be a member of the Internal Revenue Service Oversight Board for a term expiring September 21, 2010, vice Robert M. Tobias, term expired.

Peter E. Cianchette,
of Maine, to be Ambassador Extraordinary and Plenipotentiary of the United States of America to the Republic of Costa Rica.

Colm F. Connolly,
of Delaware, to be U.S. District Judge for the District of Delaware, vice Kent A. Jordan, elevated.

E. Edwin Eck,
of Montana, to be a member of the Internal Revenue Service Oversight Board for a term expiring September 14, 2008, vice Karen Hastie Williams, term expired.

Sheila McNamara Greenwood,
of Louisiana, to be an Assistant Secretary of Housing and Urban Development, vice Steven B. Nesmith, resigned.

Paul A. Schneider,
of Maryland, to be Deputy Secretary of Homeland Security, vice Michael Jackson, resigned.

Withdrawn February 26

Peter E. Cianchette,
of Maine, to be a member of the Internal Revenue Service Oversight Board for a term expiring September 14, 2010, vice Nancy Killefer, term expired, which was sent to the Senate on January 9, 2007.

Stanley C. Suboleski,
of Virginia, to be an Assistant Secretary of Energy (Fossil Energy), vice Jeffrey D. Jarrett, resigned, which was sent to the Senate on December 11, 2007.

Catherine G. West,
of the District of Columbia, to be a member of the Internal Revenue Service Oversight Board for a term expiring September 14, 2008, vice Karen Hastie Williams, term expired, which was sent to the Senate on January 9, 2007.

Submitted February 27

Nanci E. Langley,
of Virginia, to be a Commissioner of the Postal Regulatory Commission for a term expiring November 22, 2012, vice Dawn A. Tisdale, term expired.

Ronald D. Rotunda,
of Virginia, to be a member of the Privacy and Civil Liberties Oversight Board for a term of 4 years expiring January 29, 2012 (new position).

Daniel W. Sutherland,
of Virginia, to be Chairman of the Privacy and Civil Liberties Oversight Board for a term of 6 years expiring January 29, 2014 (new position).

Francis X. Taylor,
of Maryland, to be a member of the Privacy and Civil Liberties Oversight Board for a term of 2 years expiring January 29, 2010 (new position).

Submitted March 5

James B. Cunningham,
of New York, a career member of the Senior Foreign Service, class of Career Minister, to be Ambassador Extraordinary and Plenipotentiary of the United States of America to Israel.

Kerry Kennedy,
of New York, to be a member of the Board of Directors of the U.S. Institute of Peace for a term expiring January 19, 2011, vice Laurie Susan Fulton, term expired.

Ikram U. Khan,
of Nevada, to be a member of the Board of Directors of the U.S. Institute of Peace for a term expiring January 19, 2009, vice Holly J. Burkhalter, term expired.

Stephen D. Krasner,
of California, to be a member of the Board of Directors of the U.S. Institute of Peace for a term expiring January 19, 2011, vice Charles Edward Horner, term expired.

Alexander Passantino,
of Virginia, to be Administrator of the Wage and Hour Division, Department of Labor, vice Paul DeCamp.

Neil Suryakant Patel,
of the District of Columbia, to be Assistant Secretary of Commerce for Communications and Information, vice John M.R. Kneuer.

Donald Gene Teitelbaum,
of Texas, a career member of the Senior Foreign Service, class of Minister-Counselor, to be Ambassador Extraordinary and Plenipotentiary of the United States of America to the Republic of Ghana.

Frank Charles Urbancic, Jr.,
of Indiana, a career member of the Senior Foreign Service, class of Minister-Counselor, to be Ambassador Extraordinary and Plenipotentiary of the United States of America to the Republic of Cyprus.

J. Robinson West,
of the District of Columbia, to be a member of the Board of Directors of the U.S. Institute of Peace for a term expiring January 19, 2011 (reappointment).

Submitted March 11

Mimi Alemayehou,
of the District of Columbia, to be U.S. Director of the African Development Bank for a term of 5 years, vice Cynthia Shepard Perry, term expired.

Rear Admiral Jonathan W. Bailey,
NOAA, to be a member of the Mississippi River Commission.

Kiyo A. Matsumoto,
of New York, to be U.S. District Judge for the Eastern District of New York, vice Edward R. Korman, retired.

Cathy Seibel,
of New York, to be U.S. District Judge for the Southern District of New York, vice Richard Conway Casey, deceased.

William Clifford Smith,
of Louisiana, to be a member of the Mississippi River Commission for a term of 9 years (reappointment).

Submitted March 13

G. Steven Agee,
of Virginia, to be U.S. Circuit Judge for the Fourth Circuit, vice J. Michael Luttig, resigned.

Barbara McConnell Barrett,
of Arizona, to be Ambassador Extraordinary and Plenipotentiary of the United States of America to the Republic of Finland.

David R. Hill,
of Missouri, to be an Assistant Administrator of the Environmental Protection Agency, vice Roger Romulus Martella, Jr.

T. Vance McMahan,
of Texas, to be Representative of the United States of America on the Economic and Social Council of the United Nations, with the rank of Ambassador.

Withdrawn March 13

Charles A. Gargano,
of New York, to be Ambassador Extraordinary and Plenipotentiary of the United States of America to the Republic of Austria, which was sent to the Senate on November 7, 2007.

David R. Hill,
of Missouri, to be an Assistant Administrator of the Environmental Protection Agency, vice Jeffrey R. Holmstead, resigned, which was sent to the Senate on December 3, 2007.

Submitted March 31

Luis Aguilar,
of Georgia, to be a member of the Securities and Exchange Commission for the remainder of the term expiring June 5, 2010, vice Roel C. Campos, resigned.

Constance S. Barker,
of Alabama, to be a member of the Equal Employment Opportunity Commission for a term expiring July 1, 2011, vice Cari M. Dominguez, resigned.

Robert Stephen Beecroft,
of California, a career member of the Senior Foreign Service, class of Counselor, to be Ambassador Extraordinary and Plenipotentiary of the United States of America to the Hashemite Kingdom of Jordan.

Victoria Ray Carlson,
of Iowa, to be a member of the National Council on Disability for a term expiring September 17, 2010 (reappointment).

Lily Fu Claffee,
of Illinois, to be General Counsel of the Department of Commerce, vice John J. Sullivan.

Chad Colley,
of Florida, to be a member of the National Council on Disability for a term expiring September 17, 2010 (reappointment).

Kristen Cox,
of Utah, to be a member of the National Council on Disability for a term expiring September 17, 2009, vice Linda Wetters, term expired.

Tyler D. Duvall,
of Virginia, to be Under Secretary of Transportation for Policy, vice Jeffrey Shane, resigned.

Marvin G. Fifield,
of Utah, to be a member of the National Council on Disability for a term expiring September 17, 2008, vice Graham Hill, term expired.

Marvin G. Fifield,
of Utah, to be a member of the National Council on Disability for a term expiring September 17, 2011 (reappointment).

John H. Hager,
of Virginia, to be a member of the National Council on Disability for a term expiring September 17, 2009, vice Robert Davila, term expired.

Michael E. Leiter,
of the District of Columbia, to be Director of the National Counterterrorism Center, Office of the Director of National Intelligence, vice John S. Redd, resigned.

Lisa Mattheiss,
of Tennessee, to be a member of the National Council on Disability for a term expiring September 17, 2010 (reappointment).

Katherine O. McCary,
of Virginia, to be a member of the National Council on Disability for a term expiring September 17, 2009, vice Milton Aponte, term expired.

Kameran L. Onley,
of Washington, to be an Assistant Secretary of the Interior, vice Mark A. Limbaugh.

Anne Rader,
of Virginia, to be a member of the National Council on Disability for a term expiring September 17, 2010 (reappointment).

Philip Thomas Reeker,
of the District of Columbia, a career member of the Senior Foreign Service, class of Counselor, to be Ambassador Extraordinary and Plenipotentiary of the United States of America to the Republic of Macedonia.

Miguel R. San Juan,
of Texas, to be U.S. Executive Director of the Inter-American Development Bank for a term of 3 years, vice Hector E. Morales, term expired.

A. Ellen Terpstra,
of New York, to be Chief Agricultural Negotiator, Office of the U.S. Trade Representative, with the rank of Ambassador, vice Richard T. Crowder.

Renee L. Tyree,
of Arizona, to be a member of the National Council on Disability for a term expiring September 17, 2009, vice Kathleen Martinez, term expired.

John R. Vaughn,
of Florida, to be a member of the National Council on Disability for a term expiring September 17, 2010 (reappointment).

Christopher R. Wall,
of Virginia, to be an Assistant Secretary of Commerce, vice Christopher A. Padilla.

Elisse Walter,
of Maryland, to be a member of the Securities and Exchange Commission for a term expiring June 5, 2012, vice Annette L. Nazareth, term expired.

Tony J. Williams,
of Washington, to be a member of the National Council on Disability for a term expiring September 17, 2009, vice Young Woo Kang, term expired.

Submitted April 2

Brandon Chad Bungard,
of Virginia, to be General Counsel of the Federal Labor Relations Authority for a term of 5 years, vice Colleen Duffy Kiko, resigned.

William J. Burns,
of the District of Columbia, a career member of the Senior Foreign Service, class of Career Minister, to be an Under Secretary of State (Political Affairs), vice R. Nicholas Burns, resigned.

Elaine C. Duke,
of Virginia, to be Under Secretary for Management, Department of Homeland Security, vice Paul A. Schneider.

John P. Hewko,
of Michigan, to be an Assistant Secretary of Transportation, vice Andrew B. Steinberg.

Richard E. Hoagland,
of the District of Columbia, a career member of the Senior Foreign Service, class of Minister-Counselor, to be Ambassador Extraordinary and Plenipotentiary of the United States of America to the Republic of Kazakhstan.

Janice L. Jacobs,
of Virginia, a career member of the Senior Foreign Service, class of Minister-Counselor, to be an Assistant Secretary of State (Bureau of Consular Affairs), vice Maura Ann Harty, resigned.

Jeffrey F. Kupfer,
of Maryland, to be Deputy Secretary of Energy, vice Jeffrey Clay Sell, resigned.

Alexa E. Posny,
of Kansas, to be a member of the National Institute for Literacy Advisory Board for a term expiring November 25, 2011 (reappointment).

Marie L. Yovanovitch,
of Connecticut, a career member of the Senior Foreign Service, class of Minister-Counselor, to be Ambassador Extraordinary and Plenipotentiary of the United States of America to the Republic of Armenia.

Submitted April 3

Bartholomew H. Chilton,
of Delaware, to be a Commissioner of the Commodity Futures Trading Commission for a term expiring April 13, 2013 (reappointment).

Scott O'Malia,
of Michigan, to be a Commissioner of the Commodity Futures Trading Commission for a term expiring April 13, 2012, vice Reuben Jeffery III, resigned.

Submitted April 7

Peter William Bodde,
of Maryland, a career member of the Senior Foreign Service, class of Minister-Counselor, to be Ambassador Extraordinary and Plenipotentiary of the United States of America to the Republic of Malawi.

Submitted April 15

Michele M. Leonhart,
of California, to be Administrator of Drug Enforcement, vice Karen P. Tandy, resigned.

Stephen Joseph Murphy III,
of Michigan, to be U.S. District Judge for the Eastern District of Michigan, vice Patrick J. Duggan, retired.

Helene N. White,
of Michigan, to be U.S. Circuit Judge for the Sixth Circuit, vice Susan Bieke Neilson, deceased.

Withdrawn April 15

Stephen Joseph Murphy III,
of Michigan, to be U.S. Circuit Judge for the Sixth Circuit, vice Susan Bieke Neilson, deceased, which was sent to the Senate on March 19, 2007.

Submitted April 17

Kelly Harrison Rankin,
of Wyoming, to be U.S. Attorney for the District of Wyoming for the term of 4 years, vice Matthew Hansen Mead, resigned.

Submitted April 23

Christine O. Hill,
of Georgia, to be an Assistant Secretary of Veterans Affairs (Congressional Affairs), vice Thomas E. Harvey, resigned.

C. Steven McGann,
of New York, a career member of the Senior Foreign Service, class of Counselor, to be Ambassador Extraordinary and Plenipotentiary of the United States of America to the Republic of the Fiji Islands, and to serve concurrently and without additional compensation as Ambassador Extraordinary and Plenipotentiary of the United States of America to the Republic of Nauru, the Kingdom of Tonga, Tuvalu, and the Republic of Kiribati.

T. Vance McMahan,
of Texas, to be an Alternate Representative of the United States of America to the Sessions of the General Assembly of the United Nations, during his tenure of service as Representative of the United States of America on the Economic and Social Council of the United Nations.

Jeffrey Leigh Sedgwick,
of Massachusetts, to be an Assistant Attorney General, vice Regina B. Schofield, resigned.

Submitted April 24

Kristen Silverberg,
of Texas, to be Representative of the United States of America to the European Union, with the rank and status of Ambassador Extraordinary and Plenipotentiary.

Lyndon L. Olson, Jr.,
of Texas, to be a member of the U.S. Advisory Commission on Public Diplomacy for a term expiring July 1, 2008, vice Harold C. Pachios, term expired.

Withdrawn April 24

C. Boyden Gray,
of the District of Columbia, to be Representative of the United States of America to the European Union, with the rank and status of Ambassador Extraordinary and Plenipotentiary, which was sent to the Senate on January 9, 2007.

Withdrawn April 28

George A. Krol,
of New Jersey, a career member of the Senior Foreign Service, class of Minister-Counselor, to be Ambassador Extraordinary and Plenipotentiary of the United States of America to Turkmenistan, which was sent to the Senate on June 27, 2007.

Submitted April 29

Eric J. Boswell,
of the District of Columbia, to be an Assistant Secretary of State (Diplomatic Security), vice Richard J. Griffin, resigned.

Eric J. Boswell,
of the District of Columbia, to be Director of the Office of Foreign Missions, and to have the rank of Ambassador during his tenure of service, vice Richard J. Griffin, resigned.

Paul G. Gardephe,
of New York, to be U.S. District Judge for the Southern District of New York, vice Charles L. Brieant, retired.

Patricia McMahon Hawkins,
of Virginia, a career member of the Senior Foreign Service, class of Counselor, to be Ambassador Extraordinary and Plenipotentiary of the United States of America to the Togolese Republic.

Clark Waddoups,
of Utah, to be U.S. District Judge for the District of Utah, vice Paul G. Cassell, resigned.

Submitted April 30

Michael M. Anello,
of California, to be U.S. District Judge for the Southern District of California, vice Napoleon A. Jones, retired.

Submitted May 1

Liliana Ayalde,
of Maryland, a career member of the Senior Foreign Service, class of Minister-Counselor, to be Ambassador Extraordinary and Plenipotentiary of the United States of America to the Republic of Paraguay.

Tatiana C. Gfoeller-Volkoff,
of the District of Columbia, a career member of the Senior Foreign Service, class of Counselor, to be Ambassador Extraordinary and Plenipotentiary of the United States of America to the Kyrgyz Republic.

Steven C. Preston,
of Illinois, to be Secretary of Housing and Urban Development, vice Alphonso R. Jackson, resigned.

Sean Joseph Stackley,
of Virginia, to be an Assistant Secretary of the Navy, vice Delores M. Etter, resigned.

Submitted May 6

Cynthia L. Bauerly,
of Minnesota, to be a member of the Federal Election Commission for a term expiring April 30, 2011, vice Robert D. Lenhard.

Caroline C. Hunter,
of Florida, to be a member of the Federal Election Commission for a term expiring April 30, 2013, vice Michael E. Toner, resigned.

Donald F. McGahn,
of the District of Columbia, to be a member of the Federal Election Commission for a term expiring April 30, 2009, vice David M. Mason, term expired.

Troy A. Paredes,
of Missouri, to be a member of the Securities and Exchange Commission for a term expiring June 5, 2013, vice Paul S. Atkins, resigned.

Withdrawn May 6

Robert J. Battista,
of Michigan, to be a member of the National Labor Relations Board for the term of 5 years expiring December 16, 2009, vice Dennis P. Walsh, which was sent to the Senate on January 25, 2008.

Robert D. Lenhard,
of Maryland, to be a member of the Federal Election Commission for a term expiring April 30, 2011, vice Danny Lee McDonald, term expired, which was sent to the Senate on January 9, 2007.

David M. Mason,
of Virginia, to be a member of the Federal Election Commission for a term expiring April 30, 2009 (reappointment), which was sent to the Senate on January 9, 2007.

Submitted May 7

William Walter Wilkins III,
of South Carolina, to be U.S. Attorney for the District of South Carolina for the term of 4 years, vice Reginald I. Lloyd, resigned.

Submitted May 8

Glen E. Conrad,
of Virginia, to be U.S. Circuit Judge for the Fourth Circuit, vice H. Emory Widener, retired.

Donetta Davidson,
of Colorado, to be a member of the Election Assistance Commission for a term expiring December 12, 2011 (reappointment).

Rosemary E. Rodriguez,
of Colorado, to be a member of the Election Assistance Commission for a term expiring December 12, 2011 (reappointment).

Submitted May 13

John R. Beyrle,
of Michigan, a career member of the Senior Foreign Service, class of Minister-Counselor, to be Ambassador Extraordinary and Plenipotentiary of the United States of America to the Russian Federation.

Rosemary Anne DiCarlo,
of the District of Columbia, a career member of the Senior Foreign Service, class of Minister-Counselor, to be Alternate Representative of the United States of America for Special Political Affairs in the United Nations, with the rank of Ambassador.

Rosemary Anne DiCarlo,
of the District of Columbia, a career member of the Senior Foreign Service, class of Minister-Counselor, to be an Alternate Representative of the United States of America to the Sessions of the General Assembly of the United Nations during her tenure of service as Alternate Representative of the United States of America for Special Political Affairs in the United Nations.

Carol Ann Rodley,
of Virginia, a career member of the Senior Foreign Service, class of Minister-Counselor, to be Ambassador Extraordinary and Plenipotentiary of the United States of America to the Kingdom of Cambodia.

Submitted May 20

Asif J. Chaudhry,
of Washington, a career member of the Senior Foreign Service, class of Minister-Counselor, to be Ambassador Extraordinary and Plenipotentiary of the United States of America to the Republic of Moldova.

Husein A. Cumber,
of Florida, to be a member of the Surface Transportation Board for a term expiring December 31, 2013, vice W. Douglas Buttrey, term expiring.

Tina S. Kaidanow,
of the District of Columbia, a career member of the Senior Foreign Service, class of Counselor, to be Ambassador Extraordinary and Plenipotentiary of the United States of America to the Republic of Kosovo.

Withdrawn May 20

A. Paul Anderson,
of Florida, to be a Federal Maritime Commissioner for the term expiring June 30, 2012 (reappointment), which was sent to the Senate on August 2, 2007.

Arlene Holen,
of the District of Columbia, to be a member of the Federal Mine Safety and Health Review Commission for a term of 6 years, expiring August 30, 2010, vice Robert H. Beatty, Jr., term expired, which was sent to the Senate on January 9, 2007.

Hans von Spakovsky,
of Georgia, to be a member of the Federal Election Commission for a term expiring April 30, 2011, vice Bradley A. Smith, resigned, which was sent to the Senate on January 9, 2007.

Submitted May 22

Michael B. Bemis,
of Mississippi, to be a member of the Board of Directors of the Tennessee Valley Authority

for a term expiring May 18, 2013, vice Skila Harris, resigned.

Patrick J. Durkin,
of Connecticut, to be a member of the Board of Directors of the Overseas Private Investment Corporation for a term expiring December 17, 2009, vice Ned L. Siegel, term expired.

John J. Faso,
of New York, to be a member of the Board of Trustees of the James Madison Memorial Fellowship Foundation for a term expiring May 29, 2013, vice David Wesley Fleming, term expired.

David F. Girard-diCarlo,
of Pennsylvania, to be Ambassador Extraordinary and Plenipotentiary of the United States of America to the Republic of Austria.

Joe Manchin III,
of West Virginia, to be a member of the Board of Trustees of the James Madison Memorial Fellowship Foundation for a term expiring November 5, 2012, vice George Perdue, term expired.

Harvey M. Tettlebaum,
of Missouri, to be a member of the Board of Trustees of the James Madison Memorial Fellowship Foundation for a term expiring October 3, 2012, vice Marc R. Pacheco, term expired.

Submitted June 3

James Culbertson,
of North Carolina, to be Ambassador Extraordinary and Plenipotentiary of the United States of America to the Kingdom of the Netherlands.

Alan W. Eastham, Jr.,
of Arkansas, a career member of the Senior Foreign Service, class of Minister-Counselor, to be Ambassador Extraordinary and Plenipotentiary of the United States of America to the Republic of the Congo.

Cheryl Feldman Halpern,
of New Jersey, to be a member of the Board of Directors of the Corporation for Public Broadcasting for a term expiring January 31, 2014 (reappointment).

Dennis Michael Klein,
of Kentucky, to be U.S. Marshal for the Eastern District of Kentucky for the term of 4 years, vice John Schickel, resigned.

Kenneth L. Peel,
of Maryland, to be U.S. Director of the European Bank for Reconstruction and Development, vice Mark Sullivan, resigned.

David H. Pryor,
of Arkansas, to be a member of the Board of Directors of the Corporation for Public Broadcasting for a term expiring January 31, 2014 (reappointment).

Bruce M. Ramer,
of California, to be a member of the Board of Directors of the Corporation for Public Broadcasting for a term expiring January 31, 2012, vice Warren Bell.

Elizabeth Sembler,
of Florida, to be a member of the Board of Directors of the Corporation for Public Broadcasting for a term expiring January 31, 2014, vice Claudia Puig, term expired.

Loretta Cheryl Sutliff,
of Nevada, to be a member of the Board of Directors of the Corporation for Public Broadcasting for a term expiring January 31, 2012, vice Frank Henry Cruz, term expired.

W. Stuart Symington,
of Missouri, a career member of the Senior Foreign Service, class of Counselor, to be Ambassador Extraordinary and Plenipotentiary of the United States of America to the Republic of Rwanda.

Submitted June 4

William B. Carr, Jr.,
of Pennsylvania, to be a member of the U.S. Sentencing Commission for a term expiring October 31, 2011, vice John R. Steer.

Withdrawn June 4

John R. Steer,
of Virginia, to be a member of the U.S. Sentencing Commission for a term expiring October 31, 2011 (reappointment), which was sent to the Senate on January 9, 2007.

Submitted June 10

John O. Agwunobi,
of Florida, to be a member of the Board of
Directors of the African Development Foundation for a term expiring February 9, 2014, vice
Ephraim Batambuze, term expired.

Frederick S. Celec,
of Virginia, to be Assistant to the Secretary of
Defense for Nuclear and Chemical and Biological Defense Programs, vice Dale Klein, resigned.

Julius E. Coles,
of Georgia, to be a member of the Board of
Directors of the African Development Foundation for a term expiring September 22, 2011,
vice Willie Grace Campbell, term expired.

Morgan W. Davis,
of California, to be a member of the Board
of Directors of the African Development Foundation for a term expiring November 13, 2013,
vice Edward Brehm, term expired.

Marylyn Andrea Howe,
of Massachusetts, to be a member of the National Council on Disability for a term expiring
September 17, 2011 (reappointment).

John Melvin Jones,
of Virginia, a career member of the Senior Foreign Service, class of Counselor, to be Ambassador Extraordinary and Plenipotentiary of the
United States of America to the Cooperative
Republic of Guyana.

John W. Leslie, Jr.,
of Connecticut, to be a member of the Board
of Directors of the African Development Foundation for a term expiring September 22, 2013
(reappointment).

Heather McCallum,
of Georgia, to be a member of the National
Council on Disability for a term expiring September 17, 2011, vice Cynthia Allen Wainscott,
term expiring.

Lonnie C. Moore,
of Kansas, to be a member of the National
Council on Disability for a term expiring September 17, 2011 (reappointment).

Christina Alvarado Shanahan,
of North Carolina, to be a member of the National Council on Disability for a term expiring
September 17, 2011, vice Patricia Pound, term
expired.

Submitted June 12

Matthew S. Petersen,
of Utah, to be a member of the Federal Election Commission for a term expiring April 30,
2011, vice Hans von Spakovsky.

Submitted June 16

Michele Jeanne Sison,
of Maryland, a career member of the Senior
Foreign Service, class of Minister-Counselor, to
be Ambassador Extraordinary and Plenipotentiary of the United States of America to
the Republic of Lebanon.

James Christopher Swan,
of California, a career member of the Senior
Foreign Service, class of Counselor, to be Ambassador Extraordinary and Plenipotentiary of
the United States of America to the Republic
of Djibouti.

Submitted June 18

J.V. Schwan,
of Virginia, to be a member of the U.S. International Trade Commission for a term expiring
June 16, 2017, vice Deanna Tanner Okur, term
expired.

Submitted June 19

Diane Barone,
of Nevada, to be a member of the National
Institute for Literacy Advisory Board for a term
expiring January 30, 2011, vice Donald D.
Deshler, term expired.

Mary E. Curtis,
of Massachusetts, to be a member of the National Institute for Literacy Advisory Board for
a term expiring November 25, 2011, vice Carmel
Borders, term expiring.

Gregory G. Garre,
of Maryland, to be Solicitor General of the
United States, vice Paul D. Clement, resigned.

Richard G. Olson, Jr.,
of New Mexico, a career member of the Senior Foreign Service, class of Counselor, to be Ambassador Extraordinary and Plenipotentiary of the United States of America to the United Arab Emirates.

Michael O'Neill,
of Maryland, to be U.S. District Judge for the District of Columbia, vice Gladys Kessler, retired.

Brent R. Orrell,
of Virginia, to be an Assistant Secretary of Labor, vice Emily Stover DeRocco.

Jeffrey Adam Rosen,
of Virginia, to be U.S. District Judge for the District of Columbia, vice Thomas F. Hogan, retired.

J. Patrick Rowan,
of Maryland, to be an Assistant Attorney General, vice Kenneth L. Wainstein.

Submitted June 24

Holly A. Kuzmich,
of Indiana, to be Assistant Secretary for Legislation and Congressional Affairs, Department of Education, vice Terrell Halaska, resigned.

Christopher M. Marston,
of Virginia, to be Assistant Secretary for Management, Department of Education, vice Michell C. Clark, resigned.

Lyndon L. Olson, Jr.,
of Texas, to be a member of the U.S. Advisory Commission on Public Diplomacy for a term expiring July 1, 2011 (reappointment).

David D. Pearce,
of Virginia, a career member of the Senior Foreign Service, class of Minister-Counselor, to be Ambassador Extraordinary and Plenipotentiary of the United States of America to the People's Democratic Republic of Algeria.

Withdrawn June 24

J. Gregory Copeland,
of Texas, to be General Counsel of the Department of Energy, vice David R. Hill, which was sent to the Senate on January 22, 2008.

Submitted June 25

Santanu K. Baruah,
of Oregon, to be Administrator of the Small Business Administration, vice Steven C. Preston, resigned.

Michael Bruce Donley,
of Virginia, to be Secretary of the Air Force, vice Michael W. Wynne, resigned.

Jason J. Fichtner,
of Virginia, to be Deputy Commissioner of Social Security for the term expiring January 19, 2013, vice Andrew G. Biggs, resigned.

James A. Williams,
of Virginia, to be Administrator of General Services, vice Lurita Alexis Doan, resigned.

Submitted June 26

Richard A. Anderson,
of Georgia, to be a member of the Internal Revenue Service Oversight Board for a term expiring September 14, 2013, vice Paul Jones, term expiring.

Joseph F. Bader,
of the District of Columbia, to be a member of the Defense Nuclear Facilities Safety Board for a term expiring October 18, 2012 (reappointment).

Mary Lucille Jordan,
of Maryland, to be a member of the Federal Mine Safety and Health Review Commission for a term of 6 years expiring August 30, 2014 (reappointment).

Peter Robert Kann,
of New Jersey, to be a member of the Broadcasting Board of Governors for a term expiring August 13, 2010, vice James K. Glassman, resigned.

Mark Everett Keenum,
of Mississippi, to be a member of the Farm Credit Administration Board, Farm Credit Administration for a term expiring May 21, 2014, vice Nancy C. Pellett, term expired.

Michael Meehan,
of Virginia, to be a member of the Broadcasting Board of Governors for a term expiring August 13, 2010, vice D. Jeffrey Hirschberg, term expired.

Matthew A. Reynolds,
of Massachusetts, to be an Assistant Secretary of State (Legislative Affairs), vice Jeffrey Thomas Bergner, resigned.

Withdrawn June 26

D. Jeffrey Hirschberg,
of Wisconsin, to be a member of the Broadcasting Board of Governors for a term expiring August 13, 2007 (reappointment), which was sent to the Senate on January 9, 2007.

Submitted June 27

Thomas A. Betro,
of Virginia, to be Inspector General, Department of State, vice Howard J. Krongard, resigned.

Brian H. Hook,
of Iowa, to be an Assistant Secretary of State (International Organization Affairs), vice Kristen Silverberg.

Appendix C—Checklist of White House Press Releases

The following list contains releases of the Office of the Press Secretary which are not included in this book.

Released January 2

Transcript of a press briefing by Press Secretary Dana Perino

Released January 3

Transcript of a briefing by National Security Adviser Stephen J. Hadley on the President's upcoming trip to the Middle East

Statement by National Security Adviser Stephen J. Hadley announcing the appointment of John I. Pray, Jr., as Executive Secretary of the National Security Council

Statement by the Press Secretary announcing that the President received the report and recommendations of Presidential Emergency Board No. 242

Released January 4

Transcript of a press briefing by Deputy Press Secretary Tony Fratto

Statement by the Press Secretary announcing that the President signed S. 2436

Statement by the Press Secretary on disaster assistance to Iowa

Fact sheet: December 2007 Marks Record 52d Consecutive Month of Job Growth

Released January 7

Transcript of a press gaggle by Deputy Press Secretary Tony Fratto and Secretary of Education Margaret Spellings

Fact sheet: Six Years of Student Achievement Under No Child Left Behind

Released January 8

Transcript of a press gaggle by Press Secretary Dana Perino

Transcript of a background briefing by a senior administration official on the President's meeting with President Gul of Turkey

Statement by the Press Secretary announcing that on January 7 the President signed H.R. 660, H.R. 3690, and S. 863 and on January 8 he signed H.R. 2640

Statement by the Press Secretary on disaster assistance to Nevada

Fact sheet: Helping Iraq Achieve Economic and Political Stabilization

Released January 9

Transcript of a press briefing by National Security Adviser Stephen J. Hadley and Press Secretary Dana Perino

Transcript of a press briefing by National Security Adviser Stephen J. Hadley

Released January 10

Transcript of a press briefing by National Security Adviser Stephen J. Hadley on the Middle East peace process

Released January 11

Transcript of a press gaggle by Secretary of State Condoleezza Rice

Statement by the Press Secretary on the selection of C. Boyden Gray as U.S. Special Envoy for European Union Affairs

Statement by the Press Secretary on disaster assistance to Nebraska

Released January 12

Transcript of a press briefing by Gen. David H. Petraeus, USA, commanding general, Multi-National Force—Iraq, and U.S. Ambassador to Iraq Ryan C. Crocker

Transcript of a press gaggle by Press Secretary Dana Perino

Statement by the Press Secretary on the death of Sir Edmund Hillary of New Zealand

Released January 13

Transcript of a background briefing by a senior administration official on the President's trip to Saudi Arabia

Fact sheet: Fostering Freedom and Justice in the Middle East

Released January 14

Transcript of a press briefing by Counselor to the President Edward W. Gillespie and Press Secretary Dana Perino

Transcript of a press gaggle by National Security Adviser Stephen J. Hadley

Released January 16

Transcript of a press gaggle by Press Secretary Dana Perino

Released January 17

Transcript of a press briefing by Deputy Press Secretary Tony Fratto

Released January 18

Transcript of a press briefing by Secretary of the Treasury Henry M. Paulson, Jr., and Council of Economic Advisers Chairman Edward P. Lazear

Statement by the Press Secretary on the resignation of Under Secretary of State for Political Affairs Nicholas R. Burns

Fact sheet: Taking Action To Keep Our Economy Healthy

Released January 22

Transcript of a press briefing by Press Secretary Dana Perino

Statement by the Press Secretary: U.S. Export Control Reform Directives

Fact sheet: Protect America Alert: Congress Must Act Now To Keep a Critical Intelligence Gap Closed

Released January 23

Transcript of a press briefing by Press Secretary Dana Perino

Statement by the Press Secretary on the reauthorization of State Children's Health Insurance Program (SCHIP) legislation

Statement by the Press Secretary on the signing of a peace agreement in the Democratic Republic of the Congo

Released January 24

Transcript of a press briefing by Secretary of the Treasury Henry M. Paulson, Jr., on the bipartisan economic growth agreement

Fact sheet: New Growth Package Meets Criteria to Keep Our Economy Healthy

Released January 25

Transcript of a press briefing by Press Secretary Dana Perino

Transcript of a press briefing by Council on Environmental Quality Chairman James L. Connaughton and Under Secretary of State for Democracy and Global Affairs Paula J. Dobriansky on the second major economies meeting

Statement by the Press Secretary on the President and Mrs. Bush's upcoming visit to Africa

Released January 28

Transcript of a press gaggle by Press Secretary Dana Perino

Transcript of a press briefing by Counselor to the President Edward W. Gillespie on the President's State of the Union Address

Statement by the Press Secretary: Visit of Prime Minister Mirek Topolanek of the Czech Republic

Fact sheet: President Bush Takes Action To Prevent Wasteful Earmarks

Excerpts: State of the Union Address

Text: Guest List for the First Lady's Box at the 2008 State of the Union

Text: Memorandum of Justification for Waiver of Section 1083 of the National Defense Authorization Act for Fiscal Year 2008 With Respect to Iraq

Released January 29

Fact sheet: President Bush Takes Unprecedented Steps To Advance Earmark Reform

Fact sheet: The Faith-Based and Community Initiative: A Quiet Revolution in the Way Government Addresses Human Need

Released January 30

Transcript of a press gaggle by Deputy Press Secretary Tony Fratto

Statement by the Deputy Press Secretary on the arrest of Riad Seif of Syria

Statement by the Deputy Press Secretary on the President's telephone conversation with Prime Minister Stephen Harper of Canada on Afghanistan

Statement by the Deputy Press Secretary on disaster assistance to Indiana

Released January 31

Statement by the Deputy Press Secretary: North American Leaders' Summit, April 21 and 22, 2008

Statement by the Deputy Press Secretary announcing that the President signed H.R. 5104

Released February 1

Transcript of a press gaggle by Deputy Press Secretary Tony Fratto

Statement by the Press Secretary: Visit by President Amadou Toumani Toure of the Republic of Mali

Statement by the Deputy Press Secretary on disaster assistance to Kansas

Fact sheet: Addressing Uncertainties To Help Keep Our Economy Growing

Transcript: Radio Address by the First Lady to the Nation

Released February 4

Transcript of a press briefing by Office of Management and Budget Director James A. Nussle

Transcript of remarks by National Security Adviser Stephen J. Hadley at the Carnegie Endowment for International Peace °

Statement by the Press Secretary on the terrorist attack in Dimona, Israel

Fact sheet: The President's FY09 Budget

Released February 5

Transcript of a press briefing by Press Secretary Dana Perino

Statement by the Press Secretary on the situation in Burma

° This transcript was released by the Office of the Press Secretary on February 5.

Statement by the Press Secretary announcing that the President signed H.R. 3432

Statement by the Press Secretary on disaster assistance to Missouri

Released February 6

Transcript of a press briefing by Deputy Press Secretary Tony Fratto

Statement by the Press Secretary: Visit of NATO Secretary General Jakob Gijsbert "Jaap" de Hoop Scheffer

Statement by the Press Secretary on Senate action on the economic growth legislation

Statement by the Press Secretary announcing that the President signed S. 2110

Statement by the Press Secretary on disaster assistance to Hawaii

Released February 7

Transcript of a press briefing by Deputy Press Secretary Tony Fratto

Statement by the Press Secretary: Visit of Prime Minister Donald Tusk of Poland

Statement by the Press Secretary: Visit by President Amadou Toumani Toure of the Republic of Mali

Statement by the Press Secretary on the International Convention Against Doping in Sport

Statement by the Press Secretary on disaster assistance to Arkansas

Statement by the Press Secretary on disaster assistance to Tennessee

Fact sheet: Senate Must Act on Nominations to Federal Courts and Agencies

Fact sheet: Continuing the Work of Helping Our Nation's Youth

Excerpts of the President's remarks to the Conservative Political Action Conference

Released February 8

Transcript of a press gaggle by Deputy Press Secretary Scott M. Stanzel

Statement by the Press Secretary: Visit of Prime Minister Anders Fogh Rasmussen of Denmark

Statement by the Press Secretary: Visit of President Mikheil Saakashvili of Georgia

Transcript of remarks by National Security Adviser Stephen J. Hadley to the Center for International Security and Cooperation °

Released February 11

Transcript of a press briefing by Press Secretary Dana Perino

Transcript of a press briefing by Chairman of the Council of Economic Advisers Edward P. Lazear on the Economic Report of the President

Statement by the Press Secretary: Visit by United Nations Secretary-General Ban Ki-moon

Fact sheet: The Economic Report of the President

Fact sheet: The Heart Truth: Helping Prevent Heart Disease in Women

Released February 12

Transcript of a press briefing by Press Secretary Dana Perino

Advance text of the President's remarks on African American History Month

Released February 13

Transcript of a press briefing by National Security Adviser Stephen J. Hadley on the President's trip to Africa

Transcript of remarks by Senator A. Mitchell McConnell of Kentucky and Representative John A. Boehner of Ohio following a meeting with the President

Statement by the Press Secretary on the Executive order blocking property of persons in connection with the national emergency with respect to Syria

Statement by the Press Secretary on House of Representatives action on intelligence reform legislation

Fact sheet: The House Must Act Quickly To Pass Bipartisan Senate FISA Modernization Bill

Fact sheet: Bipartisan Growth Package Will Help Protect Our Nation's Economic Health

Released February 14

Transcript of a press gaggle by Press Secretary Dana Perino

Statement by the Press Secretary on intelligence reform legislation

Statement by the Press Secretary on the House of Representatives vote to hold two top White House officials in contempt

Statement by the Press Secretary announcing that the President signed H.R. 4253

Fact sheet: Congress Must Act Now To Ensure That We Have the Tools To Keep America Safe

Fact sheet: U.S. Africa Policy: An Unparalleled Partnership Strengthening Democracy, Overcoming Poverty, and Saving Lives

Released February 15

Transcript of a press gaggle by Deputy Press Secretary Scott M. Stanzel

Statement by the Press Secretary: Visit of His Holiness Pope Benedict XVI to the White House

Statement by the Press Secretary announcing that the President signed H.R. 3541 and S. 781

Released February 16

Transcript of a press gaggle by National Security Adviser Stephen J. Hadley

Transcript of a press briefing by Assistant Secretary of State for African Affairs Jendayi E. Frazer

Released February 17

Transcript of a press briefing by White House Press Secretary Dana Perino and Global AIDS Coordinator Mark R. Dybul

Released February 18

Transcript of a press gaggle by Press Secretary Dana Perino and Special Assistant to the President for African Affairs Bobby J. Pittman, Jr.

Released February 19

Transcripts of press gaggles by Press Secretary Dana Perino

Fact sheet: United States Leading the Global Response to Crisis in Darfur

Fact sheet: United States-Rwanda Bilateral Investment Treaty

° This transcript was released by the Office of the Press Secretary on February 11.

° This briefing began on April 2 at 11:50 p.m. and concluded April 3 at 12:17 a.m., when it was released by the Office of the Press Secretary.

Released April 7

Transcript of a press briefing by Deputy Press Secretary Tony Fratto and U.S. Trade Representative Susan C. Schwab

Transcript of remarks by First Lady Laura Bush at a performance of "One Destiny"

Fact sheet: Encouraging American Businesses To Invest and Expand

Fact sheet: President Bush Signs Letter To Send the United States-Colombia Free Trade Agreement Implementing Legislation to Congress

Released April 8

Transcript of a press briefing by Press Secretary Dana Perino

Released April 9

Transcript of a press briefing by Press Secretary Dana Perino

Transcript of a press briefing by Secretary of State Condoleezza Rice, Secretary of the Treasury Henry M. Paulson, Jr., U.S. Trade Representative Susan C. Schwab, Secretary of Commerce Carlos M. Gutierrez, Secretary of Labor Elaine L. Chao, Secretary of Agriculture Edward T. Schafer, and Small Business Administration Administrator Steven C. Preston on the Colombia free trade agreement

Transcript of remarks by the President and First Lady Laura Bush at a commemorative tree planting ceremony

Statement by the Press Secretary on Egypt's April 8 local council elections

Fact sheet: President Bush Signs Second Chance Act of 2007

Released April 10

Transcript of a press gaggle by Press Secretary Dana Perino

Fact sheet: The Way Forward in Iraq

Released April 11

Transcript of a press briefing by Deputy Press Secretary Scott M. Stanzel

Announcement: President and Mrs. Bush Release 2007 Tax Return

Released April 14

Transcript of a press briefing by Press Secretary Dana Perino

Statement by the Press Secretary on the Bill Emerson Humanitarian Trust to meet emergency food aid needs abroad

Released April 15

Transcript of a press briefing by Press Secretary Dana Perino

Released April 16

Transcript of a press briefing by Press Secretary Dana Perino and White House Council on Environmental Quality Chairman James L. Connaughton

Excerpts from the President's remarks on energy and climate change

Fact sheet: Taking Additional Action To Confront Climate Change

Released April 17

Transcript of a press gaggle by Deputy Press Secretary Tony Fratto and National Security Council Senior Director for East Asian Affairs Dennis C. Wilder

Text of U.S.-U.K. announcement on health and health workers

Released April 18

Transcript of a press briefing by Deputy Press Secretary Tony Fratto

Transcript of a press briefing by White House Council on Environmental Quality Chairman James L. Connaughton and Under Secretary of State for Democracy and Global Affairs Paula J. Dobriansky on the major economies meeting in Paris, France

Excerpts from a press gaggle by Deputy Press Secretary Tony Fratto and National Security Council Senior Director for Western Hemisphere Affairs Daniel W. Fisk on the North American Leaders' Summit

Statement by the Deputy Press Secretary: Visit by the President of the Republic of Guatemala

Statement by the Deputy Press Secretary announcing that the President signed H.R. 5813 and S. 550

Released May 4

Advance text of the President's commencement address at Greensburg High School in Greensburg, KS

Released May 5

Transcript of a press briefing by Deputy Press Secretary Scott M. Stanzel

Statement by the Press Secretary on disaster assistance to Oklahoma

Released May 6

Transcript of a press briefing by Press Secretary Dana Perino

Statement by the Press Secretary on the Russia-U.S. agreement for peaceful nuclear cooperation

Statement by the Press Secretary announcing that the President signed H.R. 4286

Released May 7

Transcript of a press briefing by National Security Adviser Stephen J. Hadley on the President's upcoming visit to the Middle East

Statement by the Press Secretary announcing that the President signed H.R. 5715

Statement by the Press Secretary announcing that the President signed H.R. 3196, H.R. 3468, H.R. 3532, H.R. 3720, H.R. 3803, H.R. 3936, H.R. 3988, H.R. 4166, H.R. 4203, H.R. 4211, H.R. 4240, H.R. 4454, H.R. 5135, H.R. 5220, H.R. 5400, H.R. 5472, and H.R. 5489

Released May 8

Transcript of a press gaggle by National Security Council Press Secretary Gordon Johndroe

Statement by the Press Secretary announcing that the President signed S. 2457 and S. 2739

Statement by the Deputy Press Secretary on disaster assistance to Mississippi

Released May 9

Transcript of a press briefing by National Security Council Press Secretary Gordon Johndroe

Statement by the Deputy Press Secretary on the situation in Lebanon

Statement by the Deputy Press Secretary on disaster assistance to Oklahoma

Statement by the Deputy Press Secretary on disaster assistance to Maine

Fact sheet: Congress's Farm Bill is Bad for American Taxpayers

Released May 12

Transcript of a press briefing by Press Secretary Dana Perino

Statement by the Press Secretary on the President's honorary delegation attending celebrations in honor of the 60th anniversary of the State of Israel on May 14 and 15 in Jerusalem, Israel

Released May 13

Transcript of a press gaggle by Press Secretary Dana Perino

Statement by the Press Secretary announcing that the President signed S. 2929

Released May 14

Transcript of a press gaggle by Press Secretary Dana Perino, National Security Adviser Stephen J. Hadley, and Deputy Assistant to the President for National Security Elliott Abrams

Released May 15

Transcript of a press gaggle by Press Secretary Dana Perino

Statement by the Press Secretary on disaster assistance to Oklahoma

Advance text of the President's remarks to members of the Knesset in Jerusalem

Released May 16

Transcript of a press gaggle by Press Secretary Dana Perino and Counselor to the President Edward W. Gillespie

Transcript of a press briefing by National Security Adviser Stephen J. Hadley

Statement by the Press Secretary: President Bush To Welcome Prime Minister Jan Peter Balkenende of the Netherlands

Statement by the Press Secretary: Visit of Prime Minister Sergei Stanishev of Bulgaria

Statement by the Press Secretary on the announcement by Secretary of Transportation Mary E. Peters on action to reduce flight backups, add competition, lower fares, and give airlines incentives to offer better service

Fact sheet: Strengthening Diplomatic Ties With Saudi Arabia

Released May 18

Transcript of a press briefing by Secretary of State Condoleezza Rice

Transcript of a press briefing by National Security Adviser Stephen J. Hadley

Statement by the Press Secretary announcing that the President signed H.R. 6051

Advance text of the President's remarks to the World Economic Forum in Sharm el-Sheikh, Egypt

Released May 19

Transcript of a press briefing by Deputy Press Secretary Scott M. Stanzel

Statement by Counselor to the President Edward W. Gillespie on the President's interview with Richard Engel of NBC News in Sharm el-Sheikh, Egypt

Statement by the Press Secretary announcing that the President signed H.R. 6022

Statement by the Press Secretary on disaster assistance to Kentucky

Released May 20

Transcript of a press briefing by Press Secretary Dana Perino

Statement by the Press Secretary on the President and Mrs. Bush's upcoming visit to Europe

Statement by the Press Secretary on Iran

Statement by the Press Secretary on disaster assistance to Arkansas

Released May 21

Transcript of a press briefing by Press Secretary Dana Perino and Office of Management and Budget Director James A. Nussle

Transcript of a press gaggle by Press Secretary Dana Perino and National Security Council Senior Director for Western Hemisphere Affairs Daniel W. Fisk

Fact sheet: Promoting Democracy in Cuba

Released May 22

Transcript of a press gaggle by Press Secretary Dana Perino

Statement by the Press Secretary on disaster assistance to South Dakota

Fact sheet: An Opportunity To Reconsider a Wasteful Farm Bill

Released May 23

Transcript of a press briefing by Press Secretary Dana Perino

Statement by the Press Secretary announcing that the President signed S. 3029

Statement by the Press Secretary on disaster assistance to Georgia

Statement by the Press Secretary on disaster assistance to Missouri

Fact sheet: Expanding Economic Opportunities Through Free and Fair Trade

Released May 26

Statement by the Press Secretary on military personnel and family benefits legislation

Statement by the Press Secretary on disaster assistance to Colorado

Released May 27

Transcript of a press gaggle by Press Secretary Dana Perino

Statement by the Press Secretary announcing that the President signed H.R. 3522 and H.R. 5919

Statement by the Press Secretary on disaster assistance to Iowa

Released May 28

Transcript of a press gaggle by Press Secretary Dana Perino

Transcript of remarks by National Security Adviser Stephen J. Hadley at the Proliferation Security Initiative's fifth anniversary senior-level meeting

Statement by the Press Secretary on disaster assistance to Mississippi

Fact sheet: The Largest Tax Increase in History is Looming

Released May 29

Transcript of a press gaggle by Press Secretary Dana Perino

Statement by the Press Secretary: Visit of President Gloria Macapagal-Arroyo of the Republic of the Philippines

Released May 30

Transcript of a press briefing by Press Secretary Dana Perino

Statement by the Press Secretary: Presidential Designation of Foreign Narcotics Kingpins

Statement by the Press Secretary announcing that the President signed S. 3035

Statement by the Press Secretary on disaster assistance to Nebraska

Released June 2

Transcript of a press briefing by Press Secretary Dana Perino

Released June 3

Transcript of a press briefing by Press Secretary Dana Perino

Statement by the Press Secretary announcing that the President signed H.R. 2356, H.R. 2517, H.R. 4008, S. 2829, and S.J. Res. 17

Released June 4

Transcript of a press briefing by National Security Adviser Stephen J. Hadley on the President's trip to Europe

Statement by the Press Secretary on U.S. aid following Cyclone Nargis in Burma

Released June 5

Transcript of a press briefing by Press Secretary Dana Perino

Transcript of remarks by National Security Adviser Stephen J. Hadley at a luncheon in honor of the U.S. Institute of Peace

Released June 6

Transcript of a press briefing by Press Secretary Dana Perino

Statement by the Press Secretary announcing that the President signed H.R. 1195

Fact sheet: A Clear Agenda for Overcoming Economic Challenges

Released June 9

Transcript of a press gaggle by Press Secretary Dana Perino, Deputy National Security Adviser for Regional Affairs Judith Ansley, and Assistant to the President for International Economic Affairs Daniel M. Price

Statement by the Press Secretary on disaster assistance to Indiana

Released June 10

Transcript of a press gaggle by Press Secretary Dana Perino and National Security Adviser Stephen J. Hadley

Fact sheet: The United States and the European Union: Working Together To Advance Freedom and Prosperity Around the World

Text of U.S.-EU Summit Declaration

Text of Transatlantic Economic Council report to the EU-U.S. Summit 2008

Released June 11

Transcript of a press gaggle by Press Secretary Dana Perino, Deputy National Security Adviser for Regional Affairs Judith Ansley, and Assistant to the President for International Economic Affairs Daniel M. Price

Announcement of Presidential Medal of Freedom recipients

Released June 12

Transcript of a press briefing by Press Secretary Dana Perino and National Security Adviser Stephen J. Hadley

Statement by the Press Secretary on reports on the arrest in Zimbabwe of Secretary General Tendai Biti of the Movement for Democratic Change

Excerpts from the President's remarks in Paris, France

Fact sheet: The Afghanistan Support Conference: Renewed U.S. and International Commitment

Released June 13

Transcript of a press gaggle by Press Secretary Dana Perino and the First Lady

Statement by the Press Secretary on disaster assistance to Montana

Released June 14

Statement by the Press Secretary on disaster assistance to Wisconsin

Released June 28

Statement by the Press Secretary on disaster assistance to California

Released June 30

Transcript of a press briefing by Press Secretary Dana Perino

Statement by the Press Secretary announcing that the President signed H.R. 6327, S. 1692, S. 2146, and S. 3180

Statement by the Press Secretary on disaster assistance to Iowa

Statement by the Press Secretary on disaster assistance to Indiana

Statement by the Press Secretary on disaster assistance to Illinois

Statement by the Press Secretary on disaster assistance to Wisconsin

Statement by the Press Secretary on disaster assistance to Missouri

Appendix D—Presidential Documents Published in the Federal Register

This appendix lists Presidential documents released by the Office of the Press Secretary and published in the Federal Register. The texts of the documents are printed in the Federal Register (F.R.) at the citations listed below. The documents are also printed in title 3 of the Code of Federal Regulations and in the Weekly Compilation of Presidential Documents.

PROCLAMATIONS

PROCLAMATIONS—Continued

EXECUTIVE ORDERS

EXECUTIVE ORDERS—Continued

OTHER PRESIDENTIAL DOCUMENTS

OTHER PRESIDENTIAL DOCUMENTS—Continued

OTHER PRESIDENTIAL DOCUMENTS—Continued

Subject Index

Name Index

Document Categories List